W9-CRK-181

American

Government 2e

Senior Contributing Authors

Glen Krutz, University of Oklahoma

Table of Contents

Preface

Welcome to *American Government 2e*, an OpenStax resource. This textbook was written to increase student access to high-quality learning materials, maintaining highest standards of academic rigor at little to no cost.

ABOUT OPENSTAX

OpenStax is a nonprofit based at Rice University, and it's our mission to improve student access to education. Our first openly licensed college textbook was published in 2012, and our library has since scaled to over 30 books for college and AP® courses used by hundreds of thousands of students. OpenStax Tutor, our low-cost personalized learning tool, is being used in college courses throughout the country. Through our partnerships with philanthropic foundations and our alliance with other educational resource organizations, OpenStax is breaking down the most common barriers to learning and empowering students and instructors to succeed.

ABOUT OPENSTAX'S RESOURCES

Customization

American Government 2e is licensed under a Creative Commons Attribution 4.0 International (CC BY) license, which means that you can distribute, remix, and build upon the content, as long as you provide attribution to OpenStax and its content contributors.

Because our books are openly licensed, you are free to use the entire book or pick and choose the sections that are most relevant to the needs of your course. Feel free to remix the content by assigning your students certain chapters and sections in your syllabus, in the order that you prefer. You can even provide a direct link in your syllabus to the sections in the web view of your book.

Instructors also have the option of creating a customized version of their OpenStax book. The custom version can be made available to students in low-cost print or digital form through their campus bookstore. Visit the Instructor Resources section of your book page on openstax.org for more information.

Errata

All OpenStax textbooks undergo a rigorous review process. However, like any professional-grade textbook, errors sometimes occur. Since our books are web-based, we can make updates periodically when deemed pedagogically necessary. If you have a correction to suggest, submit it through the link on your book page on OpenStax.org. Subject matter experts review all errata suggestions. OpenStax is committed to remaining transparent about all updates, so you will also find a list of past errata changes on your book page on OpenStax.org.

Format

You can access this textbook for free in web view or PDF through OpenStax.org, and in low-cost print and iBooks editions.

ABOUT *AMERICAN GOVERNMENT 2E*

American Government 2e is designed to meet the scope and sequence requirements of the single-semester American Government course. This title includes innovative features designed to enhance student learning, including Insider Perspective features and a Get Connected module that shows students how they can get engaged in the political process. The book provides an important opportunity for students to learn the core concepts of American Government and understand how those concepts apply to their lives and the world around them.

Coverage and scope

Our *American Government 2e* textbook adheres to the scope and sequence of introductory American government courses nationwide. We have endeavored to make the workings of American Government interesting and accessible to students while maintaining the conceptual coverage and rigor inherent in the subject at the college level. With this objective in mind, the content of this textbook has been developed and arranged to provide a logical progression from the fundamental principles of institutional design at the founding, to avenues of political participation, to thorough coverage of the political structures that constitute American government. The book builds upon what students have already learned and emphasizes connections between topics as well as between theory and applications. The goal of each section is to enable students not just to recognize concepts, but to work with them in ways that will be useful in later courses, future careers, and as engaged citizens. The organization and pedagogical features were developed and vetted with feedback from American government instructors dedicated to the project.

Unit I: Students and the System

Unit II: Individual Agency and Action

Unit III: Toward Collective Action: Mediating Institutions

Unit IV: Delivering Collective Action: Formal Institutions

Unit V: Outputs of Government

Appendixes

Changes to the second edition

OpenStax only undertakes second editions when significant modifications to the text are necessary. After publishing the first edition of American Government soon after the 2016 election, adopter feedback indicated that the 2018 midterm elections were a logical timeline for an update. Faculty indicated that waiting until this point would allow more time for analysis of the 2016 election and its outcomes, and that the results of the 2018 elections would be significant enough to drive discussion in courses. Nearly all of the revisions are focused on careful and balanced treatment of the events and developments of the past two years, and the manner in which those developments connect to core concepts.

As always with OpenStax textbooks, we will undertake efforts to keep the book as current as possible through our errata and updating process. However, in order to minimize disruption, we will not adjust to every new development in the political or government arena. We welcome feedback on the content and approach on our errata page and invite adopters to send other inquiries or suggestions to info@openstax.org.

Engaging feature boxes

Throughout *American Government 2e*, you will find features that engage students by taking selected topics a step further. Our features include:

Get Connected! This feature shows students ways they can become engaged in the U.S. political system. Follow-up may include an activity prompt or a discussion question on how students might address a particular problem.

Finding a Middle Ground. This feature highlights a tradeoff or compromise related to the chapter's content area. Follow-up questions guide students to examine multiple perspectives on an issue, think critically about the complexities of the topic, and share their opinions.

Insider Perspective. This feature takes students behind the scenes of the governmental system to see how things actually work. Follow-up questions ask students for their reaction to this peek inside the "black box" of politics.

Link to Learning. This feature provides a very brief introduction to a website that is pertinent to students' exploration of the topic at hand. Included in every module, Link to Learning boxes allow students to connect easily to the most current data on ever-changing content such as poll research, budget statistics, and election coverage.

Milestone. This feature looks at a key historical moment or series of events in the topic area. Follow-up questions link the milestone to the larger chapter theme and probe students' knowledge and opinions about the events under discussion.

Effective art program

Our art program is designed to enhance students' understanding of concepts through clear and effective statistical graphs, tables, and photographs.

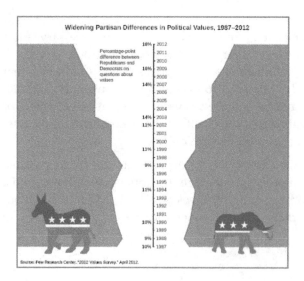

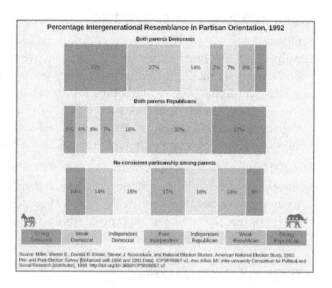

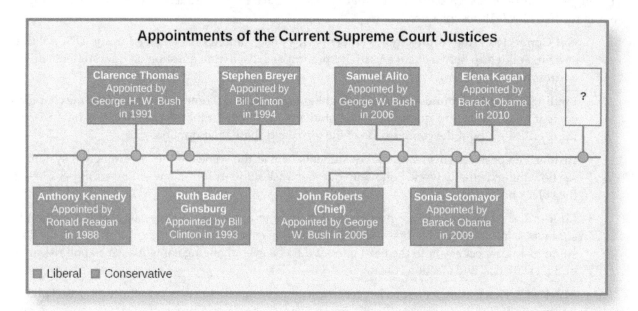

Module materials that reinforce key concepts

Learning Objectives. Every module begins with a set of clear and concise learning objectives. These objectives are designed to help the instructor decide what content to include or assign, and to guide students with respect to what they can expect to learn. After completing the module and end-of-module exercises, students should be able to demonstrate mastery of the learning objectives.

Summaries. Section summaries distill the information in each module for both students and instructors down to key, concise points addressed in the section.

Key Terms. Key terms are in bold and are followed by a definition in context. Definitions of key terms are also listed in the Glossary, which appears at the end of the chapter.

Assessments. Multiple-choice and short-answer Review Questions provide opportunities to recall and test the information students learn throughout each module. End-of-chapter Critical Thinking Questions encourage deeper reflection on the chapter concepts and themes.

Suggestions for Further Study. This curated list of books, films, and online resources helps students further explore the chapter topic.

ADDITIONAL RESOURCES

Student and instructor resources

We've compiled additional resources for both students and instructors, including Getting Started Guides, PowerPoint slides, and an instructor answer guide. Instructor resources require a verified instructor account, which you can apply for when you log in or create your account on OpenStax.org. Take advantage of these resources to supplement your OpenStax book.

Community hubs

OpenStax partners with the Institute for the Study of Knowledge Management in Education (ISKME) to offer Community Hubs on OER Commons—a platform for instructors to share community-created resources that support OpenStax books, free of charge. Through our Community Hubs, instructors can upload their own materials or download resources to use in their own courses, including additional ancillaries, teaching material, multimedia, and relevant course content. We encourage instructors to join the hubs for the subjects most relevant to your teaching and research as an opportunity both to enrich your courses and to engage with other faculty.

To reach the Community Hubs, visit OER Commons (https://www.oercommons.org/hubs/OpenStax) .

Technology partners

As allies in making high-quality learning materials accessible, our technology partners offer optional low-cost tools that are integrated with OpenStax books. To access the technology options for your text, visit your book page on openstax.org.

ABOUT THE AUTHORS

Senior contributing authors

Glen Krutz (Content Lead), University of Oklahoma
Dr. Glen Krutz received his BA and MPA from the University of Nevada–Reno, and his PhD from Texas A&M University. He joined the University of Oklahoma's Department of Political Science in 2002 and serves as Professor of Political Science, teaching the American Government course to hundreds of students each semester. Prior to his academic career, Dr. Krutz worked in politics and policy, as a campaign assistant and then Capitol Hill aide to a U.S. senator, and as a research analyst for what would become the Nevada System of Higher Education. He has authored and co-authored several books, and his work has appeared in numerous leading journals. Dr. Krutz's current research probes questions of public policy agenda-setting in democratic political institutions, especially Congress.

Sylvie Waskiewicz (Lead Editor), PhD
Dr. Waskiewicz received her BSBA from Georgetown University and her MA and PhD from the Institute of French Studies at New York University. With a specialization in Franco-American relations and over ten years of teaching experience at the university level, Sylvie left academia to join the ranks of higher education publishing. She has spent the last nine years editing college textbooks and academic journals in the humanities, social sciences, and world languages.

Contributing authors

Prosper Bernard, Jr., City University of New York
Jennifer Danley-Scott, Texas Woman's University
Ann Kordas, Johnson & Wales University
Christopher Lawrence, Middle Georgia State College

Tonya Neaves, George Mason University
Adam Newmark, Appalachian State University
Brooks D. Simpson, Arizona State University
Joel Webb, Tulane University
Shawn Williams, Campbellsville University
Rhonda Wrzenski, Indiana University Southeast

Reviewers

Brad Allard, Hill College
Milan Andrejevich, Ivy Tech Community College
Thomas Arndt, Rowan University
Sue Atkinson, University of Maryland–University College
Edward Bond, Alabama A&M University
Joseph Campbell, Rose State College
James Davenport, Rose State College
Sharon Deubreau, Rhodes State College
Henry Esparza, University of Texas–San Antonio
Terri Fine, University of Central Florida
Mark Francisco, Volunteer State Community College
Sarah Gershon, Georgia State University
Rick Gianni, Indiana University Northwest
Travis Grasser, Commerce High School
Eric Herzik, University of Nevada–Reno
Matthew Hipps, Dalton State College
Alexander Hogan, Lone Star College–CyFair
Cynthia Hunter-Summerlin, Tarrant County College
Tseggai Isaac, University of Missouri-Rolla
Walter Jatkowski, III, Northwest College
Kevin Jeffries, Alvin Community College
J. Aaron Knight, Houston Community College
Robert Lancaster, Kentucky State University
John Lund, Keene State College
Shari MacLachlan, Palm Beach State College
Carol Marmaduke-Sands, North Central Texas College
James McCormick, Iowa State University
Eric Miller, Blinn College
Sara Moats, Florida International University
Marie Natoli, Emmanuel College
Caryn Neumann, Miami University of Ohio
James Newman, Southeast Missouri State University
Cynthia Newton, Wesley College
Jeffrey S. Peake, Clemson University
G. David Price, Santa Fe College
James Ronan, Rowan University
David Smith, Texas A&M University-Corpus Christi
Leniece Smith, Jackson State University
Kai Sorensen, Central Michigan University
James Starkey, Pasadena City College
Karen Stewart, Collin College
Abram Trosky, United States Coast Guard Academy
Adam Warber, Clemson University

Alexander Wathen, University of Houston–Downtown
Reed Welch, West Texas A&M University
Yvonne Wollenberg, Rutgers University
John Wood, University of Central Oklahoma
Laura Wood, Tarrant County College
Michael Zarkin, Westminster College

Chapter 1

American Government and Civic Engagement

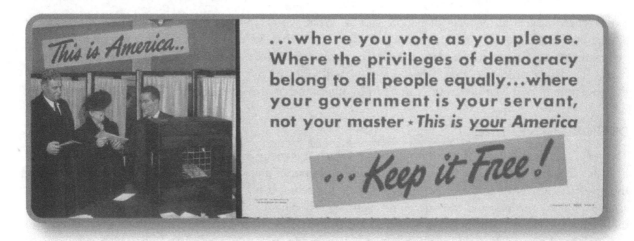

Figure 1.1 In the United States, the right to vote is an important feature of the nation's system of government, and over the years many people have fought and sacrificed to obtain it. Yet, today, many people ignore this important means of civic engagement. (credit: modification of work by the National Archives and Records Administration)

Chapter Outline

1.1 What is Government?
1.2 Who Governs? Elitism, Pluralism, and Tradeoffs
1.3 Engagement in a Democracy

Introduction

Since its founding, the United States has relied on citizen participation to govern at the local, state, and national levels. This civic engagement ensures that representative democracy will continue to flourish and that people will continue to influence government. The right of citizens to participate in government is an important feature of democracy, and over the centuries many have fought to acquire and defend this right. During the American Revolution (1775–1783), British colonists fought for the right to govern themselves. In the early nineteenth century, agitated citizens called for the removal of property requirements for voting so poor white men could participate in government just as wealthy men could. Throughout the late nineteenth and twentieth centuries, women, African Americans, Native Americans, and many other groups fought for the right to vote and hold office.

The poster shown above (Figure 1.1), created during World War II, depicts voting as an important part of the fight to keep the United States free. The purpose of voting and other forms of political engagement is to ensure that government serves the people, and not the other way around. But what does government do to serve the people? What different forms of government exist? How do they differ? How can citizens best engage with and participate in the crucial process of governing the nation? This chapter seeks to answer these questions.

1.1 What is Government?

Learning Objectives

By the end of this section, you will be able to:
- Explain what government is and what it does
- Identify the type of government in the United States and compare it to other forms of government

Government affects all aspects of people's lives. What we eat, where we go to school, what kind of education we receive, how our tax money is spent, and what we do in our free time are all affected by government. Americans are often unaware of the pervasiveness of government in their everyday lives, and many are unsure precisely what it does. Here we will look at what government is, what it does, and how the government of the United States differs from other kinds of governments.

DEFINING GOVERNMENT

The term **government** describes the means by which a society organizes itself and allocates authority in order to accomplish collective goals and provide benefits that the society as a whole needs. Among the goals that governments around the world seek to accomplish are economic prosperity for the nation, secure national borders, and the safety and well-being of citizens. Governments also provide benefits for their citizens. The type of benefits provided differ according to the country and their specific type of governmental system, but governments commonly provide such things as education, health care, and an infrastructure for transportation. The term **politics** refers to the process of gaining and exercising control within a government for the purpose of setting and achieving particular goals, especially those related to the division of resources within a nation.

Sometimes governmental systems are confused with economic systems. This is because certain types of political thought or governmental organization are closely related to or develop with certain types of economic systems. For example, the economic system of capitalism in Western Europe and North America developed at roughly the same time as ideas about democratic republics, self-government, and natural rights. At this time, the idea of liberty became an important concept. According to John Locke, an English political philosopher of the seventeenth century, all people have natural rights to life, liberty, and property. From this came the idea that people should be free to consent to being governed. In the eighteenth century, in Great Britain's North American colonies, and later in France, this developed into the idea that people should govern themselves through elected representatives and not a king; only those representatives chosen by the people had the right to make laws to govern them.

Similarly, Adam Smith, a Scottish philosopher who was born nineteen years after Locke's death, believed that all people should be free to acquire property in any way that they wished. Instead of being controlled by government, business, and industry, Smith argued, people should be allowed to operate as they wish and keep the proceeds of their work. Competition would ensure that prices remained low and faulty goods disappeared from the market. In this way, businesses would reap profits, consumers would have their needs satisfied, and society as a whole would prosper. Smith discussed these ideas, which formed the basis for industrial capitalism, in his book *The Wealth of Nations*, which was published in 1776, the same year that the Declaration of Independence was written.

Representative government and capitalism developed together in the United States, and many Americans tend to equate **democracy**, a political system in which people govern themselves, with capitalism. In theory, a democratic government promotes individualism and the freedom to act as one chooses instead of being controlled, for good or bad, by government. Capitalism, in turn, relies on individualism. At the same time, successful capitalists prefer political systems over which they can exert at least some influence in order to maintain their liberty.

Democracy and capitalism do not have to go hand in hand, however. Indeed, one might argue that a capitalist economic system might be bad for democracy in some respects. Although Smith theorized that capitalism would lead to prosperity for all, this has not necessarily been the case. Great gaps in wealth between the owners of major businesses, industries, and financial institutions and those who work for others in exchange for wages exist in many capitalist nations. In turn, great wealth may give a very small minority great influence over the government—a greater influence than that held by the majority of the population, which will be discussed later.

Socialism is an alternative economic system. In socialist societies, the means of generating wealth, such as factories, large farms, and banks, are owned by the government and not by private individuals. The government accumulates wealth and then redistributes it to citizens, primarily in the form of social programs that provide such things as free or inexpensive health care, education, and childcare. In socialist countries, the government also usually owns and controls utilities such as electricity, transportation systems like airlines and railroads, and telecommunications systems. In many socialist countries the government is an **oligarchy**: only members of a certain political party or ruling elite can participate in government. For example, in China, the government is run by members of the Chinese Communist Party. However, socialist countries can have democratic forms of government as well, such as Sweden. Although many Americans associate socialism with tyranny and a loss of individual liberties, this does not have to be the case, as we see in Sweden.

In the United States, the democratic government works closely together with its capitalist economic system. The interconnectedness of the two affects the way in which goods and services are distributed. The market provides many goods and services needed by Americans. For example, food, clothing, and housing are provided in ample supply by private businesses that earn a profit in return. These goods and services are known as **private goods**.[1] People can purchase what they need in the quantity in which they need it. This, of course, is the ideal. In reality, those who live in poverty cannot always afford to buy ample food and clothing to meet their needs, or the food and clothing that they can afford to buy in abundance is of inferior quality. Also, it is often difficult to find adequate housing; housing in the most desirable neighborhoods—those that have low crime rates and good schools—is often too expensive for poor or working-class (and sometimes middle-class) people to buy or rent.

Thus, the market cannot provide everything (in enough quantity or at low enough costs) in order to meet everyone's needs. Therefore, some goods are provided by the government. Such goods or services that are available to all without charge are called **public goods**. Two such public goods are national security and education. It is difficult to see how a private business could protect the United States from attack. How could it build its own armies and create plans for defense and attack? Who would pay the men and women who served? Where would the intelligence come from? Due to its ability to tax, draw upon the resources of an entire nation, and compel citizen compliance, only government is capable of protecting the nation.

Similarly, public schools provide education for all children in the United States. Children of all religions, races and ethnicities, socioeconomic classes, and levels of academic ability can attend public schools free of charge from kindergarten through the twelfth grade. It would be impossible for private schools to provide an education for all of the nation's children. Private schools do provide some education in the United States; however, they charge tuition, and only those parents who can afford to pay their fees (or whose children gain a scholarship) can attend these institutions. Some schools charge very high tuition, the equivalent to the tuition at a private college. If private schools were the only educational institutions, most poor and working-class children and many middle-class children would be uneducated. Private schooling is a type of good called a **toll good**. Toll goods are available to many people, and many people can make use of them, but only if they can pay the price. They occupy a middle ground between public and private goods. All parents may send their children to public schools in the United States. They can choose to send their children to a private school, but the private school will charge them. On the other hand, public schools, which are operated by the government, provide free education so all children can attend school. Therefore, everyone in the nation benefits from the educated voters and workers produced by the public school system. Another distinction between public and private goods is that public goods are available to all, typically without additional charge.

What other public goods does government provide in the United States? At the federal, state, and local level, government provides stability and security, not only in the form of a military but also in the form of police and fire departments. Government provides other valuable goods and services such as public education, public transportation, mail service, and food, housing, and health care for the poor (Figure 1.2). If a house catches on fire, the fire department does not demand payment before they put the fire out. If someone breaks into a house and tries to harm the occupants, the police will try to protect them and arrest the intruder, but the police department will not request payment for services rendered. The provision of these goods and services is funded by citizens paying into the general tax base.

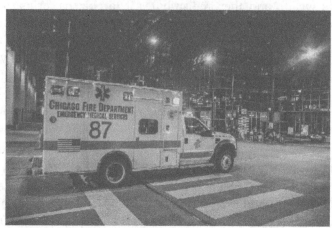

Figure 1.2   A fire department ambulance rushes to the rescue in Chicago. Emergency medical services, fire departments, and police departments are all paid for by government through the tax base, and they provide their services without an additional charge. (credit: Tony Webster)

Government also performs the important job of protecting **common goods**: goods that all people may use free of charge but that are of limited supply, such as fish in the sea or clean drinking water. Because everyone can use these goods, they must be protected so a few people do not take everything that is available and leave others with nothing. Some examples of common goods, private goods, public goods, and toll goods are listed below (Figure 1.3).

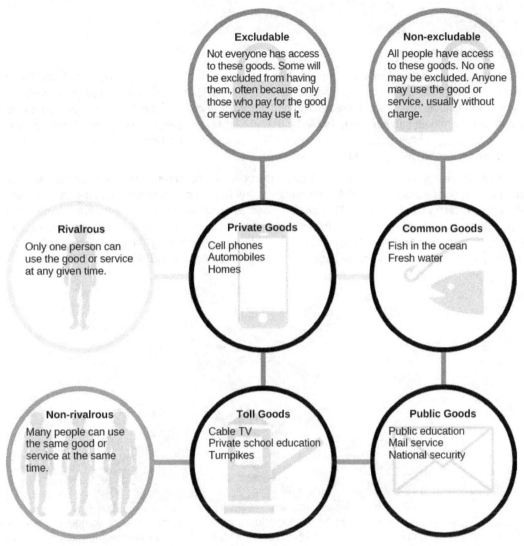

Source: John L. Mikesell. 2014. *Fiscal Administration: Analysis and Applications for the Public Sector*, 9th ed. Boston: Wadsworth.

Figure 1.3 One can distinguish between different types of goods by considering who has access to the goods (excludable/non-excludable) and how many people can access the good at the same time (rivalrous/non-rivalrous).[2]

Link to Learning

This **federal website (https://openstax.org/l/29usagovtopics)** shares information about the many services the government provides.

Finding a Middle Ground

Fishing Regulations

One of the many important things government does is regulate public access to common goods like natural resources. Unlike public goods, which all people may use without charge, common goods are in limited supply. If more public schools are needed, the government can build more. If more firefighters or mail carriers are needed, the government can hire them. Public lands and wildlife, however, are not goods the government can simply multiply if supply falls due to demand. Indeed, if some people take too freely from the supply of common goods, there will not be enough left for others to use.

Fish are one of the many common goods in which the government currently regulates access. It does so to ensure that certain species are not fished into extinction, thus depriving future generations of an important food source and a means to make a living. This idea is known as sustainability. Environmentalists want to set strict fishing limits on a variety of species. Commercial fishers resist these limits, claiming they are unnecessary and, if enforced, would drive them out of business (Figure 1.4). Currently, fishing limits are set by a combination of scientists, politicians, local resource managers, and groups representing the interests of fishers.[3]

Figure 1.4 Fishing provides income, as well as food, for many Americans. However, without government restrictions on the kinds and number of fish that can be caught, the fish population would decline and certain species could become extinct. This would ultimately lead to the loss of jobs and income as well as a valuable source of nourishment. (credit: Michael L. Baird)

Should the government regulate fishing? Is it right to interfere with people's ability to earn money today in order to protect the access of future generations to the nation's common goods?

Besides providing stability and goods and services for all, government also creates a structure by which goods and services can be made available to the people. In the United States, people elect representatives to city councils, state legislatures, and Congress. These bodies make laws to govern their respective jurisdictions. They also pass measures to raise money, through the imposition of taxes on such things as income, property, and sales. Local, state, and national governments also draft budgets to determine how the revenue taken in will be spent for services. On the local level, funds are allotted for education, police and fire departments, and maintenance of public parks. State governments allocate money for state colleges and universities, maintenance of state roads and bridges, and wildlife management, among other priorities. On the national level, money goes to such things as defense, Social Security, pensions for veterans, maintenance of federal courts and prisons, and management of national parks. At each level, representatives elected by the people try to secure funding for things that will benefit those who live in the areas they represent. Once money has been allocated, government agencies at each level then receive funds for the purposes mentioned above and use them to provide services to the public.

Local, state, and national governments also make laws to maintain order and to ensure the efficient functioning of society, including the fair operation of the business marketplace. In the United States, for example, Congress passes laws regulating banking, and government agencies regulate such things as the amount of toxic gases that can be emitted by factories, the purity of food offered for sale, and the safety of toys and automobiles. In this way, government checks the actions of business, something that it would not do if capitalism in the United States functioned strictly in the manner that Adam Smith believed it should…almost entirely unregulated.

Besides providing goods to citizens and maintaining public safety, most governments also provide a means for citizens to participate in government and to make their opinions known to those in power. Western democracies like the United States, Britain, France, and others protect citizens' freedom of speech and the press. These nations, and others in the world, also allow citizens to vote.

As noted earlier, politics is the process by which choices are made regarding how resources will be allocated and which economic and social policies government will pursue. Put more simply, politics is the process of who gets what and how. Politics involves choosing which values government will support and which it will not. If government chooses to support an ideal such as individualism, it may choose to loosen regulations on business and industry or to cut taxes so that people have more money to invest in business. If it chooses to support an ideal such as egalitarianism, which calls for equal treatment for all and the destruction of socioeconomic inequalities, it may raise taxes in order to be able to spend more on public education, public transportation, housing for the poor, and care for the elderly. If, for example, the government is more concerned with national security than with individual liberty, it may authorize the tapping of people's phones and restrict what newspapers may publish. If liberty is more important, then government will place greater restrictions on the extent that law enforcement agencies can intrude upon citizens' private communications. The political process and the input of citizens help determine the answer.

Civic engagement, or the participation that connects citizens to government, is a vital ingredient of politics. In the United States, citizens play an important role in influencing what policies are pursued, what values the government chooses to support, what initiatives are granted funding, and who gets to make the final decisions. Political engagement can take many forms: reading about politics, listening to news reports, discussing politics, attending (or watching televised) political debates, donating money to political campaigns, handing out flyers promoting a candidate, voting, joining protest marches, and writing letters to their elected representatives.

DIFFERENT TYPES OF GOVERNMENT

The government of the United States can best be described as a republic, or representative democracy. A democracy is a government in which **political power**—influence over institutions, leaders, and policies—rests in the hands of the people. In a **representative democracy**, however, the citizens do not govern directly. Instead, they elect representatives to make decisions and pass laws on behalf of all the people. Thus, U.S. citizens vote for members of Congress, the president and vice president, members of state legislatures, governors, mayors, and members of town councils and school boards to act on their behalf. Most representative governments favor **majority rule**: the opinions of the majority of the people have more influence with government than those of the minority. If the number of elected representatives who favor a proposed law is greater than those who oppose it, the law will be enacted.

However, in representative governments like the United States, **minority rights** are protected: people cannot be deprived of certain rights even if an overwhelming number of people think that they should be. For example, let's say American society decided that atheists, people who do not believe that God exists, were evil and should be imprisoned or expelled from the country. Even though atheists only account for about 7 percent of the population, they would be protected due to minority rights.[4] Even though the number of Americans who believe in God far outweighs the number who do not, the minority is still protected. Because decisions are made through majority rule, making your opinions known and voting for those men and women who make decisions that affect all of us are critical and influential forms of civic engagement in a representative democracy such as the United States.

In a **direct democracy**, unlike representative democracy, people participate directly in making government decisions. For example, in ancient Athens, the most famous example of a direct democracy, all male citizens were allowed to attend meetings of the Assembly. Here they debated and voted for or against all proposed laws. Although neither the federal government nor any of the state governments function as a direct democracy—the Constitution requires the national and state governments to be representative forms of government—some elements of direct democracy do exist in the United States. While residents of the different states vote for people to represent them and to make laws in their behalf in the state legislatures and in Congress, people may still directly vote on certain issues. For example, a referendum or proposed law might be placed on the ballot for citizens to vote on directly during state or local elections instead of leaving the matter in the hands of the state legislature. At New England town meetings, all residents are allowed to debate decisions affecting the town (Figure 1.5). Such occasions provide additional opportunities for civic engagement.

Figure 1.5   Residents of Boxborough, Massachusetts, gather in a local hotel to discuss issues affecting their town. New England town meetings provide an opportunity for people to experience direct democracy. This tradition has lasted for hundreds of years. (credit: modification of work by Liz West)

Most countries now have some form of representative government (Figure 1.6).[5] At the other end of the political spectrum are elite-driven forms of government. In a **monarchy**, one ruler, usually a hereditary ruler, holds political power. Although the power of some monarchs is limited by law, and such kings and queens often rule along with an elected legislature that makes laws for the country, this is not always the case. Many southwest Asian kingdoms, such as Saudi Arabia, Qatar, and the United Arab Emirates, have absolute monarchs whose power is unrestricted. As discussed earlier, another nondemocratic form of government is oligarchy, in which a handful of elite members of society, often those who belong to a particular political party, hold all political power. For example, in Cuba, as in China, only members of the Communist Party are allowed to vote or hold public office, and the party's most important members make all government decisions. Some nondemocratic societies are totalitarian in nature. Under **totalitarianism**, the government is more important than the citizens, and it controls all aspects of citizens' lives. Citizens' rights are limited, and the government does not allow political criticism or opposition. These forms of government are fairly rare. North Korea is an example of a totalitarian government.

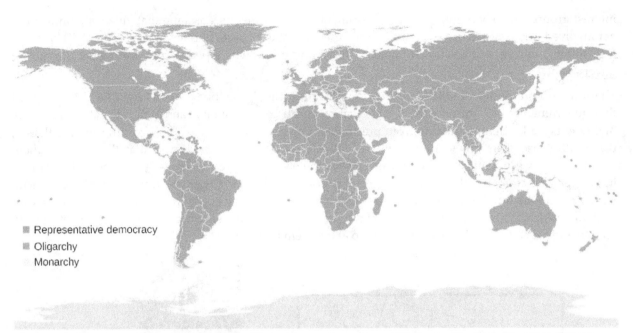

Figure 1.6 The map of the world shows the different forms of government that currently exist. Countries that are colored blue have some form of representative democracy, although the people may not have as much political power as they do in the United States. Countries that are colored red, like China, Vietnam, and Cuba, have an oligarchic form of government. Countries that are colored yellow are monarchies where the people play little part in governing.

Link to Learning

The CIA website (https://openstax.org/l/29ciaworgovtyp) provides information about the types of government across the world.

1.2 Who Governs? Elitism, Pluralism, and Tradeoffs

Learning Objectives

By the end of this section, you will be able to:
- Describe the pluralism-elitism debate
- Explain the tradeoffs perspective on government

The United States allows its citizens to participate in government in many ways. The United States also has many different levels and branches of government that any citizen or group might approach. Many people take this as evidence that U.S. citizens, especially as represented by competing groups, are able to influence government actions. Some political theorists, however, argue that this is not the case. They claim that only a handful of economic and political elites have any influence over government.

ELITISM VS. PLURALISM

Many Americans fear that a set of elite citizens is really in charge of government in the United States and that others have no influence. This belief is called the **elite theory** of government. In contrast to that perspective is the **pluralist theory** of government, which says that political power rests with competing interest groups who share influence in government. Pluralist theorists assume that citizens who want to get involved in the system do so because of the great number of access points to government. That is, the U.S. system, with several levels and branches, has many places where people and groups can engage the government.

The foremost supporter of elite theory was C. Wright Mills. In his book, *The Power Elite*, Mills argued that government was controlled by a combination of business, military, and political elites.[6] Most are highly educated, often graduating from prestigious universities (Figure 1.7). According to elite theory, the wealthy use their power to control the nation's economy in such a way that those below them cannot advance economically. Their wealth allows the elite to secure for themselves important positions in politics. They then use this power to make decisions and allocate resources in ways that benefit them. Politicians do the bidding of the wealthy instead of attending to the needs of ordinary people, and order is maintained by force. Indeed, those who favor government by the elite believe the elite are better fit to govern and that average citizens are content to allow them to do so.[7]

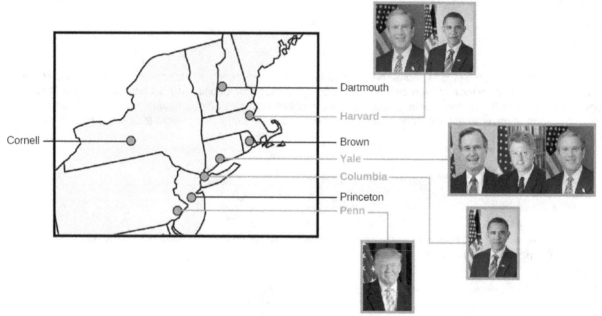

Figure 1.7   The five most recent U.S. presidents have all graduated from an Ivy League university.

In apparent support of the elite perspective, one-third of U.S. presidents have attended Ivy League schools, a much higher percentage than the rest of the U.S. population.[8] All five of the most recent U.S. presidents attended Ivy League schools such as Harvard, Yale, or Columbia. Among members of the House of Representatives, 95 percent have a bachelor's degree, as do 100 percent of members of the Senate.[9] Fewer than 40 percent of U.S. adults have even an associate's degree.[10] The majority of the men and women in Congress also engaged in either state or local politics, were business people, or practiced law before being elected to Congress.[11] Approximately 75 percent of both the Senate and the House of Representatives are male, and about 21 percent of members of Congress are people of color.[12] The nation's laws are made primarily by well-educated white male professionals and businessmen.

The makeup of Congress is important because race, sex, profession, education, and socioeconomic class have an important effect on people's political interests. For example, changes in the way taxes are levied and spent do not affect all citizens equally. A flat tax, which generally requires that everyone pay the same percentage rate, hurts the poor more than it does the rich. If the income tax rate was flat at 10 percent, all Americans would have to pay 10 percent of their income to the federal government. Someone who made $40,000 a year would have to pay $4,000 and be left with only $36,000 to live on. Someone who made $1,000,000 would have to pay $100,000, a greater sum, but he or she would still be left with $900,000. People who were not wealthy would probably pay more than they could comfortably afford, while the wealthy, who could afford to pay more and still live well, would not see a real impact on their daily lives. Similarly, the allocation of revenue affects the rich and the poor differently. Giving more money to public education does not benefit the wealthy as much as it does the poor, because the wealthy are more likely than the poor to send their children to private schools or to at least have the option of doing so. However, better funded public schools have the potential to greatly improve the upward mobility of members of other socioeconomic classes who have no other option than to send their children to public schools.

Currently, about 40 percent of the members of Congress are millionaires; twelve members hold over half of the Congress's collective net worth.[13] As of 2009, approximately 38 percent of Congress sent their children to private schools. Overall, only 11 percent of the American population did so.[14] Therefore, a Congress dominated by millionaires who send their children to private schools is more likely to believe that flat taxes are fair and that increased funding for public education is not a necessity. Their experience, however, does not reflect the experience of average Americans.

Pluralist theory rejects this approach, arguing that although there are elite members of society they do not control government. Instead, pluralists argue, political power is distributed throughout society. Rather than resting in the hands of individuals, a variety of organized groups hold power, with some groups having more influence on certain issues than others. Thousands of interest groups exist in the United States.[15] Approximately 70–90 percent of Americans report belonging to at least one group.[16]

According to pluralist theory, people with shared interests will form groups in order to make their desires known to politicians. These groups include such entities as environmental advocates, unions, and organizations that represent the interests of various businesses. Because most people lack the inclination, time, or expertise necessary to decide political issues, these groups will speak for them. As groups compete with one another and find themselves in conflict regarding important issues, government policy begins to take shape. In this way, government policy is shaped from the bottom up and not from the top down, as we see in elitist theory. Robert Dahl, author of *Who Governs?*, was one of the first to advance the pluralist theory, and argued that politicians seeking an "electoral payoff" are attentive to the concerns of politically active citizens and, through them, become acquainted with the needs of ordinary people. They will attempt to give people what they want in exchange for their votes.[17]

Link to Learning

The Center for Responsive Politics is a non-partisan research group that provides data on who gives to whom in elections. Visit OpenSecrets.org: Center for Responsive Politics (https://openstax.org/l/29opensecrets) to track campaign contributions, congressional bills and committees, and interest groups and lobbyists.

THE TRADEOFFS PERSPECTIVE

Although elitists and pluralists present political influence as a tug-of-war with people at opposite ends of a rope trying to gain control of government, in reality government action and public policy are influenced by an ongoing series of tradeoffs or compromises. For instance, an action that will meet the needs of large numbers of people may not be favored by the elite members of society. Giving the elite what they want may interfere with plans to help the poor. As pluralists argue, public policy is created as a result of competition among groups. In the end, the interests of both the elite and the people likely influence government action, and compromises will often attempt to please them both.

Since the framing of the U.S. Constitution, tradeoffs have been made between those who favor the supremacy of the central government and those who believe that state governments should be more powerful. Should state governments be able to respond to the desires of citizen groups by legalizing the use of marijuana? Should the national government be able to close businesses that sell marijuana even in states where it is legal? Should those who control the Federal Bureau of Investigation (FBI) and the National Security Agency (NSA) be allowed to eavesdrop on phone conversations of Americans and read their email? Should groups like the American Civil Liberties Union (ACLU), which protect all citizens' rights to freedom of speech, be able to prevent this?

Many of the tradeoffs made by government are about freedom of speech. The First Amendment of the Constitution gives Americans the right to express their opinions on matters of concern to them; the federal government cannot interfere with this right. Because of the Fourteenth Amendment, state governments must protect this right also. At the same time, neither the federal government nor state governments can allow someone's right to free expression to interfere with someone else's ability to exercise his or her own rights. For example, in the United States, it is legal for women to have abortions. Many people oppose this right, primarily for religious reasons, and often protest outside facilities that provide abortions. In 2007, the state of Massachusetts enacted a law that required protestors to stand thirty-five feet away from clinic entrances. The intention was to prevent women seeking abortions from being harassed or threatened with violence. Groups favoring the protection of women's reproductive rights supported the law. Groups opposed to abortion argued that the buffer zone prevented them from speaking to women to try to persuade them not to have the procedure done. In 2014, in the case of *McCullen v. Coakley*, the U.S. Supreme Court struck down the law that created a buffer zone between protestors and clinic entrances.[18] The federal government does not always side with those who oppose abortion, however. Several states have attempted to pass laws requiring women to notify their husbands, and often obtain their consent, before having an abortion. All such laws have been found unconstitutional by the courts.

Tradeoffs also occur as a result of conflict between groups representing the competing interests of citizens. Many Americans believe that the U.S. must become less dependent on foreign sources of energy. Many also would like people to have access to inexpensive sources of energy. Such people are likely to support fracking: the process of hydraulic fracturing that gives drilling companies access to natural gas trapped between layers of shale underground. Fracking produces abundant, inexpensive natural gas, a great benefit to people who live in parts of the country where it is expensive to heat homes during the winter. Fracking also creates jobs. At the same time, many scholars argue that fracking can result in the contamination of drinking water, air pollution, and increased risk of earthquakes. One study has even linked fracking to cancer. Thus, those who want to provide jobs and inexpensive natural gas are in conflict with those who wish to protect the natural environment and human health (Figure 1.8). Both sides are well intentioned, but they disagree over what is best for people.[19]

(a)   (b)

Figure 1.8   A person in Ohio protests fracking (a). An announcement of a public meeting regarding fracking illustrates what some of the tradeoffs involved with the practice might be (b). (credit a: modification of work by "ProgressOhio/Flickr"; credit b: modification of work by Martin Thomas)

Tradeoffs are especially common in the United States Congress. Members of the Senate and the House of Representatives usually vote according to the concerns of people who live in their districts. Not only does this often pit the interests of people in different parts of the country against one another, but it also frequently favors the interests of certain groups of people over the interests of others within the same state. For example, allowing oil companies to drill off the state's coast may please those who need the jobs that will be created, but it will anger those who wish to preserve coastal lands as a refuge for wildlife and, in the event of an accident, may harm the interests of people who depend on fishing and tourism for their living. At times, House members and senators in Congress may ignore the voters in their home states and the groups that represent them in order to follow the dictates of the leaders of the political party to which they belong. For example, a member of Congress from a state with a large elderly population may be inclined to vote in favor of legislation to increase benefits for retired people; however, his or her political party leaders, who disapprove of government spending on social programs, may ask for a vote against it. The opposite can occur as well, especially in the case of a legislator soon facing re-election. With two-year terms of office, we are more likely to see House members buck their party in favor of their constituents.

Finally, the government may attempt to resolve conflicting concerns within the nation as a whole through tradeoffs. After repeated incidents of mass shootings at schools, theaters, churches, concerts, night clubs, and shopping malls, many are concerned with protecting themselves and their families from firearm violence. Some groups would like to ban the sale of automatic weapons completely. Some do not want to ban gun ownership; they merely want greater restrictions to be put in place on who can buy guns or how long people must wait between the time they enter the store to make a purchase and the time when they are actually given possession of the weapon. Others represent the interests of those who oppose any restrictions on the number or type of weapons Americans may own. So far, state governments have attempted to balance the interests of both groups by placing restrictions on such things as who can sell guns, where gun sales may take place, or requirements for background checks, but they have not attempted to ban gun sales altogether. For example, although federal law does not require private gun dealers (people who sell guns but do not derive most of their income from doing so) to conduct background checks before selling firearms to people at gun shows, some states have passed laws requiring this.[20]

At the federal level, there has been widespread support in Congress to improve the background checking process. Indeed, despite objections from the National Rifle Association, the Fix-NICS Act passed the House and Senate and was signed into law by President Trump as part of an omnibus spending bill in March 2018.[21]

1.3 Engagement in a Democracy

Learning Objectives

By the end of this section, you will be able to:
- Explain the importance of citizen engagement in a democracy
- Describe the main ways Americans can influence and become engaged in government
- Discuss factors that may affect people's willingness to become engaged in government

Participation in government matters. Although people may not get all that they want, they can achieve many goals and improve their lives through civic engagement. According to the pluralist theory, government cannot function without active participation by at least some citizens. Even if we believe the elite make political decisions, participation in government through the act of voting can change who the members of the elite are.

WHY GET INVOLVED?

Are fewer people today active in politics than in the past? Political scientist Robert Putnam has argued that civic engagement is declining; although many Americans may report belonging to groups, these groups are usually large, impersonal ones with thousands of members. People who join groups such as Amnesty International or Greenpeace may share certain values and ideals with other members of the group, but they do not actually interact with these other members. These organizations are different from the types of groups Americans used to belong to, like church groups or bowling leagues. Although people are still interested in volunteering and working for the public good, they are more interested in either working individually or joining large organizations where they have little opportunity to interact with others. Putnam considers a number of explanations for this decline in small group membership, including increased participation by women in the workforce, a decrease in the number of marriages and an increase in divorces, and the effect of technological developments, such as the internet, that separate people by allowing them to feel connected to others without having to spend time in their presence.[22]

Putnam argues that a decline in **social capital**—"the collective value of all 'social networks' [those whom people know] and the inclinations that arise from these networks to do things for each other"—accompanies this decline in membership in small, interactive groups.[23] Included in social capital are such things as networks of individuals, a sense that one is part of an entity larger than oneself, concern for the collective good and a willingness to help others, and the ability to trust others and to work with them to find solutions to problems. This, in turn, has hurt people's willingness and ability to engage in representative government. If Putnam is correct, this trend is unfortunate, because becoming active in government and community organizations is important for many reasons.

Some have countered Putnam's thesis and argue that participation is in better shape than what he portrays. Everett Ladd shows many positive trends in social involvement in American communities that serve to soften some of the declines identified by Putnam. For example, while bowling league participation is down, soccer league participation has proliferated.[24] April Clark examines and analyzes a wide variety of social capital data trends and disputes the original thesis of erosion.[25] Others have suggested that technology has increased connectedness, an idea that Putnam himself has critiqued as not as deep as in-person connections.[26]

Link to Learning

To learn more about political engagement in the United States, read "The Current State of Civic Engagement in America" (https://openstax.org/l/29pewrescenrep) by the Pew Research Center.

Civic engagement can increase the power of ordinary people to influence government actions. Even those without money or connections to important people can influence the policies that affect their lives and change the direction taken by government. U.S. history is filled with examples of people actively challenging the power of elites, gaining rights for themselves, and protecting their interests. For example, slavery was once legal in the United States and large sectors of the U.S. economy were dependent on this forced labor. Slavery was outlawed and blacks were granted citizenship because of the actions of abolitionists. Although some abolitionists were wealthy white men, most were ordinary people, including men and women of both races. White women and blacks were able to actively assist in the campaign to end slavery despite the fact that, with few exceptions, they were unable to vote. Similarly, the right to vote once belonged solely to white men until the Fifteenth Amendment gave the vote to African American men. The Nineteenth Amendment extended the vote to include women, and the Voting Rights Act of 1965 made exercising the right to vote a reality for African American men and women in the South. None of this would have happened, however, without the efforts of people who marched in protest, participated in boycotts, delivered speeches, wrote letters to politicians, and sometimes risked arrest in order to be heard (Figure 1.9). The tactics used to influence the government and effect change by abolitionists and members of the women's rights and African American civil rights movements are still used by many activists today.

Figure 1.9 The print above, published in 1870, celebrates the extension of the right to vote to African American men. The various scenes show legal rights black slaves did not have.

The rights gained by these activists and others have dramatically improved the quality of life for many in the United States. Civil rights legislation did not focus solely on the right to vote or to hold public office; it also integrated schools and public accommodations, prohibited discrimination in housing and employment, and increased access to higher education. Activists for women's rights fought for, and won, greater reproductive freedom for women, better wages, and access to credit. Only a few decades ago, homosexuality was considered a mental disorder, and intercourse between consenting adults of the same sex was illegal in many states. Although legal discrimination against gays and lesbians still remains, consensual intercourse between homosexual adults is no longer illegal anywhere in the United States, and same-sex couples have the right to legally marry.

Activism can improve people's lives in less dramatic ways as well. Working to make cities clean up vacant lots, destroy or rehabilitate abandoned buildings, build more parks and playgrounds, pass ordinances requiring people to curb their dogs, and ban late-night noise greatly affects people's quality of life. The actions of individual Americans can make their own lives better and improve their neighbors' lives as well.

Representative democracy cannot work effectively without the participation of informed citizens, however. Engaged citizens familiarize themselves with the most important issues confronting the country and with the plans different candidates have for dealing with those issues. Then they vote for the candidates they believe will be best suited to the job, and they may join others to raise funds or campaign for those they support. They inform their representatives how they feel about important issues. Through these efforts and others, engaged citizens let their representatives know what they want and thus influence policy. Only then can government actions accurately reflect the interests and concerns of the majority. Even people who believe the elite rule government should recognize that it is easier for them to do so if ordinary people make no effort to participate in public life.

PATHWAYS TO ENGAGEMENT

People can become civically engaged in many ways, either as individuals or as members of groups. Some forms of individual engagement require very little effort. One of the simplest ways is to stay informed about debates and events in the community, in the state, and in the nation. Awareness is the first step toward engagement. News is available from a variety of reputable sources, such as newspapers like the *New York Times*; national news shows, including those offered by the Public Broadcasting Service and National Public Radio; and reputable internet sites.

Link to Learning

Visit Avaaz (https://openstax.org/l/29avaazorg) and Change.org (https://openstax.org/l/29changeorg) for more information on current political issues.

Another form of individual engagement is to write or email political representatives. Filing a complaint with the city council is another avenue of engagement. City officials cannot fix problems if they do not know anything is wrong to begin with. Responding to public opinion polls, actively contributing to a political blog, or starting a new blog are all examples of different ways to be involved.

One of the most basic ways to engage with government as an individual is to vote (Figure 1.10). Individual votes do matter. City council members, mayors, state legislators, governors, and members of Congress are all chosen by popular vote. Although the president of the United States is not chosen directly by popular vote but by a group called the Electoral College, the votes of individuals in their home states determine how the Electoral College ultimately votes. Registering to vote beforehand is necessary in most states, but it is usually a simple process, and many states allow registration online. (We discuss voter registration and voter turnout in more depth in a later chapter.)

Figure 1.10 Voters line up to vote early outside an Ohio polling station in 2008. Many who had never voted before did so because of the presidential candidacy of then-senator Barack Obama. (credit: Dean Beeler)

Voting, however, is not the only form of political engagement in which people may participate. Individuals can engage by attending political rallies, donating money to campaigns, and signing petitions. Starting a petition of one's own is relatively easy, and some websites that encourage people to become involved in political activism provide petitions that can be circulated through email. Taking part in a poll or survey is another simple way to make your voice heard.

Milestone

Votes for Eighteen-Year-Olds

Young Americans are often reluctant to become involved in traditional forms of political activity. They may believe politicians are not interested in what they have to say, or they may feel their votes do not matter. However, this attitude has not always prevailed. Indeed, today's college students can vote because of the activism of college students in the 1960s. Most states at that time required citizens to be twenty-one years of age before they could vote in national elections. This angered many young people, especially young men who could be drafted to fight the war in Vietnam. They argued that it was unfair to deny eighteen-year-olds the right to vote for the people who had the power to send them to war. As a result, the Twenty-Sixth Amendment, which lowered the voting age in national elections to eighteen, was ratified by the states and went into effect in 1971.

Are you engaged in or at least informed about actions of the federal or local government? Are you registered to vote? How would you feel if you were not allowed to vote until age twenty-one?

Some people prefer to work with groups when participating in political activities or performing service to the community. Group activities can be as simple as hosting a book club or discussion group to talk about politics. Coffee Party USA provides an online forum for people from a variety of political perspectives to discuss issues that are of concern to them. People who wish to be more active often work for political campaigns. Engaging in fundraising efforts, handing out bumper stickers and campaign buttons, helping people register to vote, and driving voters to the polls on Election Day are all important activities that anyone can engage in. Individual citizens can also join interest groups that promote the causes they favor.

Get Connected!

Getting Involved

In many ways, the pluralists were right. There is plenty of room for average citizens to become active in government, whether it is through a city council subcommittee or another type of local organization. Civic organizations always need volunteers, sometimes for only a short while and sometimes for much longer.

For example, Common Cause (https://openstax.org/l/29comcause) is a non-partisan organization that seeks to hold government accountable for its actions. It calls for campaign finance reform and paper verification of votes registered on electronic voting machines. Voters would then receive proof that the machine recorded their actual vote. This would help to detect faulty machines that were inaccurately tabulating votes or election fraud. Therefore, one could be sure that election results were reliable and that the winning candidate had in fact received the votes counted in their favor. Common Cause has also advocated that the Electoral College be done away with and that presidential elections be decided solely on the basis of the popular vote.

Follow-up activity: Choose one of the following websites to connect with organizations and interest groups in need of help:

- Common Cause (https://openstax.org/l/29comcause) ;

- Friends of the Earth (https://openstax.org/l/29takeactcen) which mobilizes people to protect the natural environment;

- Grassroots International (https://openstax.org/l/29grassrootsint) which works for global justice;

- The Committee for a Responsible Federal Budget (https://openstaxcollege.org/l/29ComResponBudg) which seeks to inform the public on issues with fiscal impact and favors smaller budget deficits; or

- Eagle Forum (https://openstax.org/l/29eagleforum) which supports greater restrictions on immigration and fewer restrictions on home schooling.

Political activity is not the only form of engagement, and many people today seek other opportunities to become involved. This is particularly true of young Americans. Although young people today often shy away from participating in traditional political activities, they do express deep concern for their communities and seek out volunteer opportunities.[27] Although they may not realize it, becoming active in the community and engaging in a wide variety of community-based volunteer efforts are important forms of civic engagement and help government do its job. The demands on government are great, and funds do not always exist to enable it to undertake all the projects it may deem necessary. Even when there are sufficient funds, politicians have differing ideas regarding how much government should do and what areas it should be active in. Volunteers and community organizations help fill the gaps. Examples of community action include tending a community garden, building a house for Habitat for Humanity, cleaning up trash in a vacant lot, volunteering to deliver meals to the elderly, and tutoring children in after-school programs (Figure 1.11).

Figure 1.11   After the Southern California wildfires in 2003, sailors from the USS *Ronald Reagan* helped volunteers rebuild houses in San Pasqual as part of Habitat for Humanity. Habitat for Humanity builds homes for low-income people. (credit: Johansen Laurel, U. S. Navy)

Some people prefer even more active and direct forms of engagement such as protest marches and demonstrations, including civil disobedience. Such tactics were used successfully in the African American civil rights movement of the 1950s and 1960s and remain effective today. Likewise, the sit-ins (and sleep-ins and pray-ins) staged by African American civil rights activists, which they employed successfully to desegregate lunch counters, motels, and churches, have been adopted today by movements such as Black Lives Matter and Occupy Wall Street (Figure 1.12). Other tactics, such as boycotting businesses of whose policies the activists disapproved, are also still common. Along with boycotts, there are now "buycotts," in which consumers purchase goods and services from companies that give extensively to charity, help the communities in which they are located, or take steps to protect the environment.

Figure 1.12   Volunteers fed people at New York's Zuccotti Park during the Occupy Wall Street protest in September 2011. (credit: David Shankbone)

Link to Learning

Many ordinary people have become political activists. Read "19 Young Activists Changing America" (https://openstax.org/l/29billmoyersact) to learn about people who are working to make people's lives better.

Insider Perspective

Ritchie Torres

In 2013, at the age of twenty-five, Ritchie Torres became the youngest member of the New York City Council and the first gay council member to represent the Bronx (Figure 1.13). Torres became interested in social justice early in his life. He was raised in poverty in the Bronx by his mother and a stepfather who left the family when Torres was twelve. The mold in his family's public housing apartment caused him to suffer from asthma as a child, and he spent time in the hospital on more than one occasion because of it. His mother's complaints to the New York City Housing Authority were largely ignored. In high school, Torres decided to become a lawyer, participated in mock trials, and met a young and aspiring local politician named James Vacca. After graduation, he volunteered to campaign for Vacca in his run for a seat on the City Council. After Vacca was elected, he hired Torres to serve as his housing director to reach out to the community on Vacca's behalf. While doing so, Torres took pictures of the poor conditions in public housing and collected complaints from residents. In 2013, Torres ran for a seat on the City Council himself and won. He remains committed to improving housing for the poor.[28]

(a)   (b)

Figure 1.13   Ritchie Torres (a) served alongside his mentor, James Vacca (b), on the New York City Council from 2014 to 2017, both representing the Bronx.

Why don't more young people run for local office as Torres did? What changes might they effect in their communities if they were elected to a government position?

FACTORS OF ENGAGEMENT

Many Americans engage in political activity on a regular basis. A survey conducted in 2018 revealed that almost 70 percent of American adults had participated in some type of political action in the past five years. These activities included largely non-personal activities that did not require a great deal of interaction with others, such as signing petitions, expressing opinions on social media, contacting elected representatives, or contributing money to campaigns. During the same period, approximately 30 percent of people attended a local government meeting or a political rally or event, while 16 percent worked or volunteered for a campaign.[29]

Americans aged 18–29 were less likely to become involved in traditional forms of political activity than older Americans. A 2018 poll of more than two thousand young adults by Harvard University's Institute of Politics revealed that only 24 percent claimed to be politically engaged, and fewer than 35 percent said that they had voted in a primary. Only 9 percent said that they had gone to a political demonstration, rally, or march.[30] However, in the 2018 midterm elections, an estimated 31 percent of Americans under thirty turned out to vote, the highest level of young adult engagement in decades.[31]

Why are younger Americans less likely to become involved in traditional political organizations? One answer may be that as American politics become more partisan in nature, young people turn away. Committed **partisanship**, which is the tendency to identify with and to support (often blindly) a particular political party, alienates some Americans who feel that elected representatives should vote in support of the nation's best interests instead of voting in the way their party wishes them to. When elected officials ignore all factors other than their party's position on a particular issue, some voters become disheartened while others may become polarized. However, a recent study reveals that it is a distrust of the opposing party and not an ideological commitment to their own party that is at the heart of most partisanship among voters.[32]

Young Americans are particularly likely to be put off by partisan politics. More Americans under the age of thirty now identify themselves as Independents instead of Democrats or Republicans (Figure 1.14). Instead of identifying with a particular political party, young Americans are increasingly concerned about specific issues, such as same-sex marriage.[33] People whose votes are determined based on single issues are unlikely to vote according to party affiliation.

The other factor involved in low youth voter turnout in the past was that younger Americans did not feel that candidates generally tackle issues relevant to their lives. When younger voters cannot relate to the issues put forth in a campaign, such as entitlements for seniors, they lose interest. This dynamic changed somewhat in 2016 as Democratic candidate Bernie Sanders made college costs an issue, even promising free college tuition for undergraduates at public institutions. Senator Sanders enjoyed intense support on college campuses across the United States. After his nomination campaign failed, this young voter enthusiasm faded. Despite the fact that Democratic nominee Hillary Clinton eventually took up the free tuition issue, young people did not flock to her as well as they had to Sanders. In the general election, won by Republican nominee Donald Trump, turnout was down and Clinton received a smaller proportion of the youth vote than President Obama had in 2012.[34]

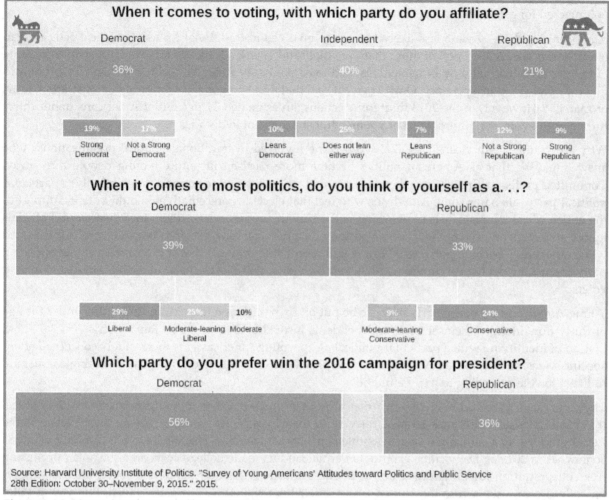

Figure 1.14 Young Americans are likely to identify as an Independent rather than a Democrat or a Republican. However, younger voters are more likely to lean in a liberal direction on issues and therefore favor the Democratic Party at the ballot box.

While some Americans disapprove of partisanship in general, others are put off by the **ideology**—established beliefs and ideals that help shape political policy—of one of the major parties. This is especially true among the young. As some members of the Republican Party have become more ideologically conservative (e.g., opposing same-sex marriage, legalization of certain drugs, immigration reform, gun control, separation of church and state, and access to abortion), those young people who do identify with one of the major parties have in recent years tended to favor the Democratic Party.[35] Of the Americans under age thirty who were surveyed by Harvard in 2015, more tended to hold a favorable opinion of Democrats in Congress than of Republicans, and 56 percent reported that they wanted the Democrats to win the presidency in 2016 (Figure 1.14). Even those young Americans who identify themselves as Republicans are more liberal on certain issues, such as being supportive of same-sex marriage and immigration reform, than are older Republicans. The young Republicans also may be more willing to see similarities between themselves and Democrats.[36] Once again, support for the views of a particular party does not necessarily mean that someone will vote for members of that party.

Other factors may keep even those college students who do wish to vote away from the polls. Because many young Americans attend colleges and universities outside of their home states, they may find it difficult to register to vote. In places where a state-issued ID is required, students may not have one or may be denied one if they cannot prove that they paid in-state tuition rates.[37]

The likelihood that people will become active in politics also depends not only on age but on such factors as wealth and education. In a 2006 poll, the percentage of people who reported that they were regular voters grew as levels of income and education increased.[38] Political involvement also depends on how strongly people feel about current political issues. Unfortunately, public opinion polls, which politicians may rely on when formulating policy or deciding how to vote on issues, capture only people's **latent preferences** or beliefs. Latent preferences are not deeply held and do not remain the same over time. They may not even represent a person's true feelings, since they may be formed on the spot when someone is asked a question about which he or she has no real opinion. Indeed, voting itself may reflect merely a latent preference because even people who do not feel strongly about a particular political candidate or issue vote. On the other hand, **intense preferences** are based on strong feelings regarding an issue that someone adheres to over time. People with intense preferences tend to become more engaged in politics; they are more likely to donate time and money to campaigns or to attend political rallies. The more money that one has and the more highly educated one is, the more likely that he or she will form intense preferences and take political action.[39]

Key Terms

common goods goods that all people may use but that are of limited supply

democracy a form of government where political power rests in the hands of the people

direct democracy a form of government where people participate directly in making government decisions instead of choosing representatives to do this for them

elite theory claims political power rests in the hands of a small, elite group of people

government the means by which a society organizes itself and allocates authority in order to accomplish collective goals

ideology the beliefs and ideals that help to shape political opinion and eventually policy

intense preferences beliefs and preferences based on strong feelings regarding an issue that someone adheres to over time

latent preferences beliefs and preferences people are not deeply committed to and that change over time

majority rule a fundamental principle of democracy; the majority should have the power to make decisions binding upon the whole

minority rights protections for those who are not part of the majority

monarchy a form of government where one ruler, usually a hereditary one, holds political power

oligarchy a form of government where a handful of elite society members hold political power

partisanship strong support, or even blind allegiance, for a particular political party

pluralist theory claims political power rests in the hands of groups of people

political power influence over a government's institutions, leadership, or policies

politics the process by which we decide how resources will be allocated and which policies government will pursue

private goods goods provided by private businesses that can be used only by those who pay for them

public goods goods provided by government that anyone can use and that are available to all without charge

representative democracy a form of government where voters elect representatives to make decisions and pass laws on behalf of all the people instead of allowing people to vote directly on laws

social capital connections with others and the willingness to interact and aid them

toll good a good that is available to many people but is used only by those who can pay the price to do so

totalitarianism a form of government where government is all-powerful and citizens have no rights

Summary

1.1 What is Government?

Government provides stability to society, as well as many crucial services such as free public education, police and fire services, and mail delivery. It also regulates access to common goods, such as public land, for the benefit of all. Government creates a structure whereby people can make their needs and opinions known to public officials. This is one of the key factors that makes the United States a representative democracy. A country where people elect representatives to make political decisions for them depends on the ability and willingness of ordinary people to make their voices known, unlike an oligarchy dominated by only a small group of people.

1.2 Who Governs? Elitism, Pluralism, and Tradeoffs

Many question whether politicians are actually interested in the needs of average citizens and debate how much influence ordinary people have over what government does. Those who support the elite theory of government argue that a small, wealthy, powerful elite controls government and makes policy to benefit its members and perpetuate their power. Others favor the pluralist theory, which maintains that groups representing the people's interests do attract the attention of politicians and can influence government policy. In reality, government policy usually is the result of a series of tradeoffs as groups and elites fight with one another for influence and politicians attempt to balance the demands of competing interests, including the interests of the constituents who elected them to office.

1.3 Engagement in a Democracy

Civic and political engagement allows politicians to know how the people feel. It also improves people's lives and helps them to build connections with others. Individuals can educate themselves on important issues and events, write to their senator or representative, file a complaint at city hall, attend a political rally, or vote. People can also work in groups to campaign or raise funds for a candidate, volunteer in the community, or protest a social injustice or an unpopular government policy. Although wealthier, older, more highly educated citizens are the most likely to be engaged with their government, especially if they have intense preferences about an issue, younger, less wealthy people can do much to change their communities and their country.

Review Questions

1. What goods are available to all without direct payment?

    a. private goods
    b. public goods
    c. common goods
    d. toll goods

2. In which form of government does a small group of elite people hold political power?

    a. direct democracy
    b. monarchy
    c. oligarchy
    d. totalitarian

3. What is the difference between a representative democracy and a direct democracy?

4. What does government do for people?

5. The elite theory of government maintains that _____.

    a. special interest groups make government policy
    b. politicians who have held office for a long time are favored by voters
    c. poor people and people of color should not be allowed to vote
    d. wealthy, politically powerful people control government, and government has no interest in meeting the needs of ordinary people

6. According to the pluralist theory of government, _____.

    a. government does what the majority of voters want it to do

    b. government policy is formed as a result of the competition between groups with different goals and interests

    c. ordinary people acting on their own have a significant influence on government

    d. wealthy people decide what government policy will be, and politicians have no interest in pleasing anyone else

7. Which of the following is a good example of a tradeoff?

    a. The government pleases environmental activists by preserving public lands but also pleases ranchers by allowing them to rent public lands for grazing purposes.

    b. The government pleases environmental activists by reintroducing wolves to Yellowstone National Park but angers ranchers by placing their cattle in danger.

    c. The government pleases oil companies by allowing them to drill on lands set aside for conservation but allows environmental activist groups to protest the drilling operations.

    d. Groups that represent a variety of conflicting interests are all allowed to protest outside Congress and the White House.

8. Supporting the actions of the Democratic Party simply because one identifies oneself as a member of that party is an example of _____.

    a. partisanship

    b. ideology

    c. latent preference

    d. social capital

9. When a person is asked a question about a political issue that he or she has little interest in and has not thought much about, that person's answer will likely reflect _____.

    a. ideology

    b. partisanship

    c. intense preferences

    d. latent preferences

10. What kinds of people are most likely to become active in politics or community service?

11. What political activities can people engage in other than running for office?

Critical Thinking Questions

12. Is citizen engagement necessary for a democracy to function? Explain.

13. Which is the more important reason for being engaged: to gain power or improve the quality of life? Why?

14. Are all Americans equally able to become engaged in government? What factors make it more possible for some people to become engaged than others? What could be done to change this?

15. Which pathways of engagement in U.S. government do you plan to follow? Why do you prefer these approaches?

16. Are there any redeeming qualities to elitism and any downsides to pluralism? Are there benefits to having elites rule? Are there problems with allowing interest groups to exercise influence over government? Explain.

Suggestions for Further Study

Books:

Dahl, Robert A. 1991. *Democracy and Its Critics*. New Haven, CT: Yale University Press.

———. 1961. *Who Governs? Democracy and Power in an American City*. New Haven, CT: Yale University Press.

Dolan, Julie, Melissa M. Deckman, and Michele L. Swers. 2015. *Women and Politics: Paths to Power and Political Influence*. Lanham, MD: Rowman & Littlefield.

Mills, C. Wright. 1956. *The Power Elite*. New York: Oxford University Press.

Olson, Mancur. 1971. *The Logic of Collective Action: Public Goods and the Theory of Groups*. Cambridge: Harvard University Press.

Putnam, Robert D. 2001. *Bowling Alone: The Collapse and Revival of American Community*. New York: Simon & Schuster.

Films:

1949. *All the King's Men*.

1976. *All the President's Men*.

1972. *The Candidate*.

2007. *Charlie Wilson's War*.

2008. *Frost/Nixon*.

1933. *Gabriel over the White House*.

2008. *Milk*.

1939. *Mr. Smith Goes to Washington*.

Chapter 2

The Constitution and Its Origins

Figure 2.1 Written in 1787 and amended twenty-seven times, the U.S. Constitution is a living document that has served as the basis for U.S. government for more than two hundred years. (credit: modification of work by National Archives and Records Administration)

Chapter Outline

2.1 The Pre-Revolutionary Period and the Roots of the American Political Tradition
2.2 The Articles of Confederation
2.3 The Development of the Constitution
2.4 The Ratification of the Constitution
2.5 Constitutional Change

Introduction

The **U.S. Constitution**, see **Figure 2.1**, is one of the world's most enduring symbols of democracy. It is also the oldest, and shortest, written constitutions of the modern era still in existence. Its writing was by no means inevitable, however. Indeed, in many ways the Constitution was not the beginning but rather the culmination of American (and British) political thought about government power as well as a blueprint for the future.

It is tempting to think of the framers of the Constitution as a group of like-minded men aligned in their lofty thinking regarding rights and freedoms. This assumption makes it hard to oppose constitutional principles in modern-day politics because people admire the longevity of the Constitution and like to consider its ideals above petty partisan politics. However, the Constitution was designed largely out of necessity following the failure of the first revolutionary government, and it featured a series of pragmatic compromises among its disparate stakeholders. It is therefore quite appropriate that more than 225 years later the U.S. government still requires compromise to function properly.

How did the Constitution come to be written? What compromises were needed to ensure the ratification that made it into law? This chapter addresses these questions and also describes why the Constitution remains a living, changing document.

2.1 The Pre-Revolutionary Period and the Roots of the American Political Tradition

Learning Objectives

By the end of this section, you will be able to:
- Identify the origins of the core values in American political thought, including ideas regarding representational government
- Summarize Great Britain's actions leading to the American Revolution

American political ideas regarding liberty and self-government did not suddenly emerge full-blown at the moment the colonists declared their independence from Britain. The varied strands of what became the American republic had many roots, reaching far back in time and across the Atlantic Ocean to Europe. Indeed, it was not new ideas but old ones that led the colonists to revolt and form a new nation.

POLITICAL THOUGHT IN THE AMERICAN COLONIES

The beliefs and attitudes that led to the call for independence had long been an important part of colonial life. Of all the political thinkers who influenced American beliefs about government, the most important is surely John Locke (**Figure 2.2**). The most significant contributions of Locke, a seventeenth-century English philosopher, were his ideas regarding the relationship between government and **natural rights**, which were believed to be God-given rights to life, liberty, and property.

Figure 2.2 John Locke was one of the most influential thinkers of the Enlightenment. His writings form the basis for many modern political ideas.

Locke was not the first Englishman to suggest that people had rights. The British government had recognized its duty to protect the lives, liberties, and property of English citizens long before the settling of its North American colonies. In 1215, King John signed Magna Carta—a promise to his subjects that he and future monarchs would refrain from certain actions that harmed, or had the potential to harm, the people of England. Prominent in Magna Carta's many provisions are protections for life, liberty, and property. For example, one of the document's most famous clauses promises, "No freemen shall be taken, imprisoned . . . or in any way destroyed . . . except by the lawful judgment of his peers or by the law of the land." Although it took a long time for modern ideas regarding due process to form, this clause lays the foundation for the Fifth and Sixth Amendments to the U.S. Constitution. While Magna Carta was intended to grant protections only to the English barons who were in revolt against King John in 1215, by the time of the American Revolution, English subjects, both in England and in North America, had come to regard the document as a cornerstone of liberty for men of all stations—a right that had been recognized by King John I in 1215, but the people had actually possessed long before then.

The rights protected by Magna Carta had been granted by the king, and, in theory, a future king or queen could take them away. The natural rights Locke described, however, had been granted by God and thus could never be abolished by human beings, even royal ones, or by the institutions they created.

So committed were the British to the protection of these natural rights that when the royal Stuart dynasty began to intrude upon them in the seventeenth century, Parliament removed King James II, already disliked because he was Roman Catholic, in the Glorious Revolution and invited his Protestant daughter and her husband to rule the nation. Before offering the throne to William and Mary, however, Parliament passed the English Bill of Rights in 1689. A bill of rights is a list of the liberties and protections possessed by a nation's citizens. The English Bill of Rights, heavily influenced by Locke's ideas, enumerated the rights of English citizens and explicitly guaranteed rights to life, liberty, and property. This document would profoundly influence the U.S. Constitution and Bill of Rights.

American colonists also shared Locke's concept of property rights. According to Locke, anyone who invested labor in the *commons*—the land, forests, water, animals, and other parts of nature that were free for the taking—might take as much of these as needed, by cutting trees, for example, or building a fence around a field. The only restriction was that no one could take so much that others were deprived of their right to take from the commons as well. In the colonists' eyes, all free white males should have the right to acquire property, and once it had been acquired, government had the duty to protect it. (The rights of women remained greatly limited for many more years.)

Perhaps the most important of Locke's ideas that influenced the British settlers of North America were those regarding the origins and purpose of government. Most Europeans of the time believed the institution of monarchy had been created by God, and kings and queens had been divinely appointed to rule. Locke, however, theorized that human beings, not God, had created government. People sacrificed a small portion of their freedom and consented to be ruled in exchange for the government's protection of their lives, liberty, and property. Locke called this implicit agreement between a people and their government the **social contract**. Should government deprive people of their rights by abusing the power given to it, the contract was broken and the people were no longer bound by its terms. The people could thus withdraw their consent to obey and form another government for their protection.

The belief that government should not deprive people of their liberties and should be restricted in its power over citizens' lives was an important factor in the controversial decision by the American colonies to declare independence from England in 1776. For Locke, withdrawing consent to be ruled by an established government and forming a new one meant replacing one monarch with another. For those colonists intent on rebelling, however, it meant establishing a new nation and creating a new government, one that would be greatly limited in the power it could exercise over the people.

The desire to limit the power of government is closely related to the belief that people should govern themselves. This core tenet of American political thought was rooted in a variety of traditions. First, the British government did allow for a degree of self-government. Laws were made by Parliament, and property-owning males were allowed to vote for representatives to Parliament. Thus, Americans were accustomed to the idea of representative government from the beginning. For instance, Virginia established its House of Burgesses in 1619. Upon their arrival in North America a year later, the English Separatists who settled the Plymouth Colony, commonly known as the Pilgrims, promptly authored the Mayflower Compact, an agreement to govern themselves according to the laws created by the male voters of the colony.[1] By the eighteenth century, all the colonies had established legislatures to which men were elected to make the laws for their fellow colonists. When American colonists felt that this longstanding tradition of representative self-government was threatened by the actions of Parliament and the King, the American Revolution began.

THE AMERICAN REVOLUTION

The American Revolution began when a small and vocal group of colonists became convinced the king and Parliament were abusing them and depriving them of their rights. By 1776, they had been living under the rule of the British government for more than a century, and England had long treated the thirteen colonies with a degree of benign neglect. Each colony had established its own legislature. Taxes imposed by England were low, and property ownership was more widespread than in England. People readily proclaimed their loyalty to the king. For the most part, American colonists were proud to be British citizens and had no desire to form an independent nation.

All this began to change in 1763 when the Seven Years War between Great Britain and France came to an end, and Great Britain gained control of most of the French territory in North America. The colonists had fought on behalf of Britain, and many colonists expected that after the war they would be allowed to settle on land west of the Appalachian Mountains that had been taken from France. However, their hopes were not realized. Hoping to prevent conflict with Indian tribes in the Ohio Valley, Parliament passed the Proclamation of 1763, which forbade the colonists to purchase land or settle west of the Appalachian Mountains.[2]

To pay its debts from the war and maintain the troops it left behind to protect the colonies, the British government had to take new measures to raise revenue. Among the acts passed by Parliament were laws requiring American colonists to pay British merchants with gold and silver instead of paper currency and a mandate that suspected smugglers be tried in vice-admiralty courts, without jury trials. What angered the colonists most of all, however, was the imposition of direct taxes: taxes imposed on individuals instead of on transactions.

Because the colonists had not consented to direct taxation, their primary objection was that it reduced their status as free men. The right of the people or their representatives to consent to taxation was enshrined in both Magna Carta and the English Bill of Rights. Taxes were imposed by the House of Commons, one of the two houses of the British Parliament. The North American colonists, however, were not allowed to elect representatives to that body. In their eyes, taxation by representatives they had not voted for was a denial of their rights. Members of the House of Commons and people living in England had difficulty understanding this argument. All British subjects had to obey the laws passed by Parliament, including the requirement to pay taxes. Those who were not allowed to vote, such as women and blacks, were considered to have virtual representation in the British legislature; representatives elected by those who could vote made laws on behalf of those who could not. Many colonists, however, maintained that anything except direct representation was a violation of their rights as English subjects.

The first such tax to draw the ire of colonists was the Stamp Act, passed in 1765, which required that almost all paper goods, such as diplomas, land deeds, contracts, and newspapers, have revenue stamps placed on them. The outcry was so great that the new tax was quickly withdrawn, but its repeal was soon followed by a series of other tax acts, such as the Townshend Acts (1767), which imposed taxes on many everyday objects such as glass, tea, and paint.

The taxes imposed by the Townshend Acts were as poorly received by the colonists as the Stamp Act had been. The Massachusetts legislature sent a petition to the king asking for relief from the taxes and requested that other colonies join in a boycott of British manufactured goods. British officials threatened to suspend the legislatures of colonies that engaged in a boycott and, in response to a request for help from Boston's customs collector, sent a warship to the city in 1768. A few months later, British troops arrived, and on the evening of March 5, 1770, an altercation erupted outside the customs house. Shots rang out as the soldiers fired into the crowd (Figure 2.3). Several people were hit; three died immediately. Britain had taxed the colonists without their consent. Now, British soldiers had taken colonists' lives.

Figure 2.3 The Sons of Liberty circulated this sensationalized version of the events of March 5, 1770, in order to promote the rightness of their cause; it depicts British soldiers firing on unarmed civilians in the event that became known as the Boston Massacre. Later portrayals would more prominently feature Crispus Attucks, an African American who was one of the first to die. Eight British soldiers were tried for murder as a result of the confrontation.

Following this event, later known as the Boston Massacre, resistance to British rule grew, especially in the colony of Massachusetts. In December 1773, a group of Boston men boarded a ship in Boston harbor and threw its cargo of tea, owned by the British East India Company, into the water to protest British policies, including the granting of a monopoly on tea to the British East India Company, which many colonial merchants resented.[3] This act of defiance became known as the Boston Tea Party. Today, many who do not agree with the positions of the Democratic or the Republican Party have organized themselves into an oppositional group dubbed the Tea Party (Figure 2.4).

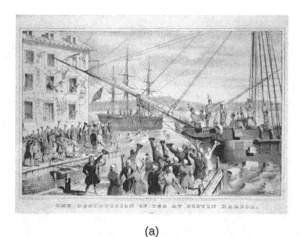

(a)

(b)

Figure 2.4 Members of the modern Tea Party movement claim to represent the same spirit as their colonial forebears in the iconic lithograph *The Destruction of Tea at Boston Harbor* (a) and protest against what they perceive as government's interference with people's rights. In April 2010, members of a Tea Party Express rally on the Boston Common signed a signature wall to record their protest (b). (credit b: modification of work by Tim Pierce)

In the early months of 1774, Parliament responded to this latest act of colonial defiance by passing a series of laws called the Coercive Acts, intended to punish Boston for leading resistance to British rule and to restore order in the colonies. These acts virtually abolished town meetings in Massachusetts and otherwise interfered with the colony's ability to govern itself. This assault on Massachusetts and its economy enraged people throughout the colonies, and delegates from all the colonies except Georgia formed the First Continental Congress to create a unified opposition to Great Britain. Among other things, members of the institution developed a declaration of rights and grievances.

In May 1775, delegates met again in the Second Continental Congress. By this time, war with Great Britain had already begun, following skirmishes between colonial militiamen and British troops at Lexington and Concord, Massachusetts. Congress drafted a Declaration of Causes explaining the colonies' reasons for rebellion. On July 2, 1776, Congress declared American independence from Britain and two days later signed the **Declaration of Independence**.

Drafted by Thomas Jefferson, the Declaration of Independence officially proclaimed the colonies' separation from Britain. In it, Jefferson eloquently laid out the reasons for rebellion. God, he wrote, had given everyone the rights of life, liberty, and the pursuit of happiness. People had created governments to protect these rights and consented to be governed by them so long as government functioned as intended. However, "whenever any Form of Government becomes destructive of these ends, it is the Right of the People to alter or to abolish it, and to institute new Government." Britain had deprived the colonists of their rights. The king had "establish[ed] . . . an absolute Tyranny over these States." Just as their English forebears had removed King James II from the throne in 1689, the colonists now wished to establish a new rule.

Jefferson then proceeded to list the many ways in which the British monarch had abused his power and failed in his duties to his subjects. The king, Jefferson charged, had taxed the colonists without the consent of their elected representatives, interfered with their trade, denied them the right to trial by jury, and deprived them of their right to self-government. Such intrusions on their rights could not be tolerated. With their signing of the Declaration of Independence (Figure 2.5), the founders of the United States committed themselves to the creation of a new kind of government.

Figure 2.5 The presentation of the Declaration of Independence is commemorated in a painting by John Trumbull in 1817. It was commissioned to hang in the Capitol in Washington, DC.

Link to Learning

Thomas Jefferson explains in the Declaration of Independence (http://www.openstax.org/l/29DeclarationIn) why many colonists felt the need to form a new nation. His evocation of the natural rights of man and his list of grievances against the king also served as the model for the Declaration of Sentiments (http://www.openstax.org/l/29DeclarationSe) that was written in 1848 in favor of giving women in the United States rights equal to those of men. View both documents and compare.

2.2 The Articles of Confederation

Learning Objectives

By the end of this section, you will be able to:
- Describe the steps taken during and after the American Revolution to create a government
- Identify the main features of the Articles of Confederation
- Describe the crises resulting from key features of the Articles of Confederation

Waging a successful war against Great Britain required that the individual colonies, now sovereign states that often distrusted one another, form a unified nation with a central government capable of directing the country's defense. Gaining recognition and aid from foreign nations would also be easier if the new United States had a national government able to borrow money and negotiate treaties. Accordingly, the Second Continental Congress called upon its delegates to create a new government strong enough to win the country's independence but not so powerful that it would deprive people of the very liberties for which they were fighting.

PUTTING A NEW GOVERNMENT IN PLACE

The final draft of the **Articles of Confederation**, which formed the basis of the new nation's government, was accepted by Congress in November 1777 and submitted to the states for ratification. It would not become the law of the land until all thirteen states had approved it. Within two years, all except Maryland had done so. Maryland argued that all territory west of the Appalachians, to which some states had laid claim, should instead be held by the national government as public land for the benefit of all the states. When the last of these states, Virginia, relinquished its land claims in early 1781, Maryland approved the Articles.[4] A few months later, the British surrendered.

Americans wished their new government to be a **republic**, a regime in which the people, not a monarch, held power and elected representatives to govern according to the rule of law. Many, however, feared that a nation as large as the United States could not be ruled effectively as a republic. Many also worried that even a government of representatives elected by the people might become too powerful and overbearing. Thus, a **confederation** was created—an entity in which independent, self-governing states form a union for the purpose of acting together in areas such as defense. Fearful of replacing one oppressive national government with another, however, the framers of the Articles of Confederation created an alliance of sovereign states held together by a weak central government.

Link to Learning

View the Articles of Confederation (http://www.openstax.org/l/29ArticlesConf) at the National Archives. The timeline for drafting and ratifying the Articles of Confederation (http://www.openstax.org/l/29Arttimeline) is available at the Library of Congress.

Following the Declaration of Independence, each of the thirteen states had drafted and ratified a constitution providing for a republican form of government in which political power rested in the hands of the people, although the right to vote was limited to free (white) men, and the property requirements for voting differed among the states. Each state had a governor and an elected legislature. In the new nation, the states remained free to govern their residents as they wished. The central government had authority to act in only a few areas, such as national defense, in which the states were assumed to have a common interest (and would, indeed, have to supply militias). This arrangement was meant to prevent the national government from becoming too powerful or abusing the rights of individual citizens. In the careful balance between power for the national government and liberty for the states, the Articles of Confederation favored the states.

Thus, powers given to the central government were severely limited. The Confederation Congress, formerly the Continental Congress, had the authority to exchange ambassadors and make treaties with foreign governments and Indian tribes, declare war, coin currency and borrow money, and settle disputes between states. Each state legislature appointed delegates to the Congress; these men could be recalled at any time. Regardless of its size or the number of delegates it chose to send, each state would have only one vote. Delegates could serve for no more than three consecutive years, lest a class of elite professional politicians develop. The nation would have no independent chief executive or judiciary. Nine votes were required before the central government could act, and the Articles of Confederation could be changed only by unanimous approval of all thirteen states.

WHAT WENT WRONG WITH THE ARTICLES?

The Articles of Confederation satisfied the desire of those in the new nation who wanted a weak central government with limited power. Ironically, however, their very success led to their undoing. It soon became apparent that, while they protected the sovereignty of the states, the Articles had created a central government too weak to function effectively.

One of the biggest problems was that the national government had no power to impose taxes. To avoid any perception of "taxation without representation," the Articles of Confederation allowed only state governments to levy taxes. To pay for its expenses, the national government had to request money from the states, which were required to provide funds in proportion to the value of the land within their borders.

The states, however, were often negligent in this duty, and the national government was underfunded. Without money, it could not pay debts owed from the Revolution and had trouble conducting foreign affairs. For example, the inability of the U.S. government to raise sufficient funds to compensate colonists who had remained loyal to Great Britain for their property losses during and after the American Revolution was one of the reasons the British refused to evacuate the land west of the Appalachians. The new nation was also unable to protect American ships from attacks by the Barbary pirates.[5] Foreign governments were also, understandably, reluctant to loan money to a nation that might never repay it because it lacked the ability to tax its citizens.

The fiscal problems of the central government meant that the currency it issued, called the Continental, was largely worthless and people were reluctant to use it. Furthermore, while the Articles of Confederation had given the national government the power to coin money, they had not prohibited the states from doing so as well. As a result, numerous state banks issued their own banknotes, which had the same problems as the Continental. People who were unfamiliar with the reputation of the banks that had issued the banknotes often refused to accept them as currency. This reluctance, together with the overwhelming debts of the states, crippled the young nation's economy.

The country's economic woes were made worse by the fact that the central government also lacked the power to impose tariffs on foreign imports or regulate interstate commerce. Thus, it was unable to prevent British merchants from flooding the U.S. market with low-priced goods after the Revolution, and American producers suffered from the competition. Compounding the problem, states often imposed tariffs on items produced by other states and otherwise interfered with their neighbors' trade.

The national government also lacked the power to raise an army or navy. Fears of a standing army in the employ of a tyrannical government had led the writers of the Articles of Confederation to leave defense largely to the states. Although the central government could declare war and agree to peace, it had to depend upon the states to provide soldiers. If state governors chose not to honor the national government's request, the country would lack an adequate defense. This was quite dangerous at a time when England and Spain still controlled large portions of North America (Table 2.1).

Problems with the Articles of Confederation

Weakness of the Articles of Confederation	Why Was This a Problem?
The national government could not impose taxes on citizens. It could only request money from the states.	Requests for money were usually not honored. As a result, the national government did not have money to pay for national defense or fulfill its other responsibilities.
The national government could not regulate foreign trade or interstate commerce.	The government could not prevent foreign countries from hurting American competitors by shipping inexpensive products to the United States. It could not prevent states from passing laws that interfered with domestic trade.
The national government could not raise an army. It had to request the states to send men.	State governments could choose not to honor Congress's request for troops. This would make it hard to defend the nation.
Each state had only one vote in Congress regardless of its size.	Populous states were less well represented.
The Articles could not be changed without a unanimous vote to do so.	Problems with the Articles could not be easily fixed.

Table 2.1 The Articles of Confederation suffered from many problems that could not be easily repaired. The biggest problem was the lack of power given to the national government.

Problems with the Articles of Confederation

Weakness of the Articles of Confederation	Why Was This a Problem?
There was no national judicial system.	Judiciaries are important enforcers of national government power.

Table 2.1 The Articles of Confederation suffered from many problems that could not be easily repaired. The biggest problem was the lack of power given to the national government.

The weaknesses of the Articles of Confederation, already recognized by many, became apparent to all as a result of an uprising of Massachusetts farmers, led by Daniel Shays. Known as Shays' Rebellion, the incident panicked the governor of Massachusetts, who called upon the national government for assistance. However, with no power to raise an army, the government had no troops at its disposal. After several months, Massachusetts crushed the uprising with the help of local militias and privately funded armies, but wealthy people were frightened by this display of unrest on the part of poor men and by similar incidents taking place in other states.[6] To find a solution and resolve problems related to commerce, members of Congress called for a revision of the Articles of Confederation.

Shays' Rebellion: Symbol of Disorder and Impetus to Act

In the summer of 1786, farmers in western Massachusetts were heavily in debt, facing imprisonment and the loss of their lands. They owed taxes that had gone unpaid while they were away fighting the British during the Revolution. The Continental Congress had promised to pay them for their service, but the national government did not have sufficient money. Moreover, the farmers were unable to meet the onerous new tax burden Massachusetts imposed in order to pay its own debts from the Revolution.

Led by Daniel Shays (Figure 2.6), the heavily indebted farmers marched to a local courthouse demanding relief. Faced with the refusal of many Massachusetts militiamen to arrest the rebels, with whom they sympathized, Governor James Bowdoin called upon the national government for aid, but none was available. The uprising was finally brought to an end the following year by a privately funded militia after the protestors' unsuccessful attempt to raid the Springfield Armory.

Figure 2.6   This contemporary depiction of Continental Army veteran Daniel Shays (left) and Job Shattuck (right), who led an uprising of Massachusetts farmers in 1786–1787 that prompted calls for a stronger national government, appeared on the cover of *Bickerstaff's Genuine Boston Almanack for 1787*.

Were Shays and his followers justified in their attacks on the government of Massachusetts? What rights might they have sought to protect?

2.3 The Development of the Constitution

Learning Objectives

By the end of this section, you will be able to:
- Identify the conflicts present and the compromises reached in drafting the Constitution
- Summarize the core features of the structure of U.S. government under the Constitution

In 1786, Virginia and Maryland invited delegates from the other eleven states to meet in Annapolis, Maryland, for the purpose of revising the Articles of Confederation. However, only five states sent representatives. Because all thirteen states had to agree to any alteration of the Articles, the convention in Annapolis could not accomplish its goal. Two of the delegates, Alexander Hamilton and James Madison, requested that all states send delegates to a convention in Philadelphia the following year to attempt once again to revise the Articles of Confederation. All the states except Rhode Island chose delegates to send to the meeting, a total of seventy men in all, but many did not attend. Among those not in attendance were John Adams and Thomas Jefferson, both of whom were overseas representing the country as diplomats. Because the shortcomings of the Articles of Confederation proved impossible to overcome, the convention that met in Philadelphia in 1787 decided to create an entirely new government.

POINTS OF CONTENTION

Fifty-five delegates arrived in Philadelphia in May 1787 for the meeting that became known as the Constitutional Convention. Many wanted to strengthen the role and authority of the national government but feared creating a central government that was too powerful. They wished to preserve state autonomy, although not to a degree that prevented the states from working together collectively or made them entirely independent of the will of the national government. While seeking to protect the rights of individuals from government abuse, they nevertheless wished to create a society in which concerns for law and order did not give way in the face of demands for individual liberty. They wished to give political rights to all free men but also feared mob rule, which many felt would have been the result of Shays' Rebellion had it succeeded. Delegates from small states did not want their interests pushed aside by delegations from more populous states like Virginia. And everyone was concerned about slavery. Representatives from southern states worried that delegates from states where it had been or was being abolished might try to outlaw the institution. Those who favored a nation free of the influence of slavery feared that southerners might attempt to make it a permanent part of American society. The only decision that all could agree on was the election of George Washington, the former commander of the Continental Army and hero of the American Revolution, as the president of the convention.

The Question of Representation: Small States vs. Large States

One of the first differences among the delegates to become clear was between those from large states, such as New York and Virginia, and those who represented small states, like Delaware. When discussing the structure of the government under the new constitution, the delegates from Virginia called for a **bicameral legislature** consisting of two houses. The number of a state's representatives in each house was to be based on the state's population. In each state, representatives in the lower house would be elected by popular vote. These representatives would then select their state's representatives in the upper house from among candidates proposed by the state's legislature. Once a representative's term in the legislature had ended, the representative could not be reelected until an unspecified amount of time had passed.

Delegates from small states objected to this **Virginia Plan**. Another proposal, the **New Jersey Plan**, called for a **unicameral legislature** with one house, in which each state would have one vote. Thus, smaller states would have the same power in the national legislature as larger states. However, the larger states argued that because they had more residents, they should be allotted more legislators to represent their interests (Figure 2.7).

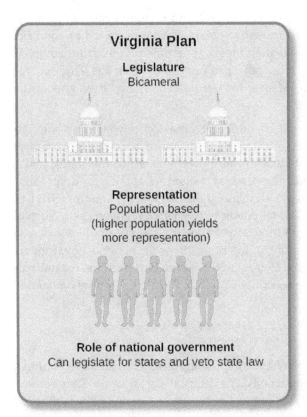
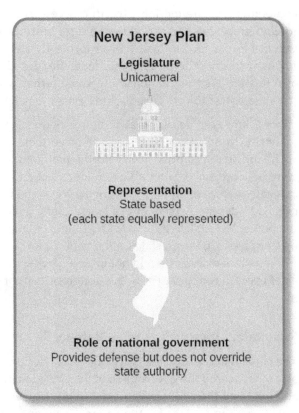

Figure 2.7 The Virginia Plan called for a two-house legislature. Representation in both houses would be based on population. A state's representatives in one house would be elected by the state's voters. These representatives would then appoint representatives to the second house from among candidates chosen by the state's legislature. The New Jersey Plan favored maintaining a one-house Congress with each state being equally represented.

Slavery and Freedom

Another fundamental division separated the states. Following the Revolution, some of the northern states had either abolished slavery or instituted plans by which slaves would gradually be emancipated. Pennsylvania, for example, had passed the Act for the Gradual Abolition of Slavery in 1780. All people born in the state to enslaved mothers after the law's passage would become indentured servants to be set free at age twenty-eight. In 1783, Massachusetts had freed all enslaved people within the state. Many Americans believed slavery was opposed to the ideals stated in the Declaration of Independence. Others felt it was inconsistent with the teachings of Christianity. Some feared for the safety of the country's white population if the number of slaves and white Americans' reliance on them increased. Although some southerners shared similar sentiments, none of the southern states had abolished slavery and none wanted the Constitution to interfere with the institution. In addition to supporting the agriculture of the South, slaves could be taxed as property and counted as population for purposes of a state's representation in the government.

Federal Supremacy vs. State Sovereignty

Perhaps the greatest division among the states split those who favored a strong national government and those who favored limiting its powers and allowing states to govern themselves in most matters. Supporters of a strong central government argued that it was necessary for the survival and efficient functioning of the new nation. Without the authority to maintain and command an army and navy, the nation could not defend itself at a time when European powers still maintained formidable empires in North America. Without the power to tax and regulate trade, the government would not have enough money to maintain the nation's defense, protect American farmers and manufacturers from foreign competition, create the infrastructure necessary for interstate commerce and communications, maintain foreign embassies, or pay federal judges and other government officials. Furthermore, other countries would be reluctant to loan money to the United States if the federal government lacked the ability to impose taxes in order to repay its debts. Besides giving more power to populous states, the Virginia Plan also favored a strong national government that would legislate for the states in many areas and would have the power to veto laws passed by state legislatures.

Others, however, feared that a strong national government might become too powerful and use its authority to oppress citizens and deprive them of their rights. They advocated a central government with sufficient authority to defend the nation but insisted that other powers be left to the states, which were believed to be better able to understand and protect the needs and interests of their residents. Such delegates approved the approach of the New Jersey Plan, which retained the unicameral Congress that had existed under the Articles of Confederation. It gave additional power to the national government, such as the power to regulate interstate and foreign commerce and to compel states to comply with laws passed by Congress. However, states still retained a lot of power, including power over the national government. Congress, for example, could not impose taxes without the consent of the states. Furthermore, the nation's chief executive, appointed by the Congress, could be removed by Congress if state governors demanded it.

Individual Liberty vs. Social Stability

The belief that the king and Parliament had deprived colonists of their liberties had led to the Revolution, and many feared the government of the United States might one day attempt to do the same. They wanted and expected their new government to guarantee the rights of life, liberty, and property. Others believed it was more important for the national government to maintain order, and this might require it to limit personal liberty at times. All Americans, however, desired that the government not intrude upon people's rights to life, liberty, and property without reason.

COMPROMISE AND THE CONSTITUTIONAL DESIGN OF AMERICAN GOVERNMENT

Beginning in May 1787 and throughout the long, hot Philadelphia summer, the delegations from twelve states discussed, debated, and finally—after compromising many times—by September had worked out a new blueprint for the nation. The document they created, the U.S. Constitution, was an ingenious instrument that allayed fears of a too-powerful central government and solved the problems that had beleaguered the national government under the Articles of Confederation. For the most part, it also resolved the conflicts between small and large states, northern and southern states, and those who favored a strong federal government and those who argued for state sovereignty.

Link to Learning

The closest thing to minutes of the Constitutional Convention is the collection of James Madison's letters and notes (http://www.openstax.org/l/29MadisonPapers) about the proceedings in Philadelphia. Several such letters and notes may be found at the Library of Congress's American Memory project.

The Great Compromise

The Constitution consists of a preamble and seven articles. The first three articles divide the national government into three branches—Congress, the executive branch, and the federal judiciary—and describe the powers and responsibilities of each. In Article I, ten sections describe the structure of Congress, the basis for representation and the requirements for serving in Congress, the length of Congressional terms, and the powers of Congress. The national legislature created by the article reflects the compromises reached by the delegates regarding such issues as representation, slavery, and national power.

After debating at length over whether the Virginia Plan or the New Jersey Plan provided the best model for the nation's legislature, the framers of the Constitution had ultimately arrived at what is called the **Great Compromise**, suggested by Roger Sherman of Connecticut. Congress, it was decided, would consist of two chambers: the Senate and the House of Representatives. Each state, regardless of size, would have two senators, making for equal representation as in the New Jersey Plan. Representation in the House would be based on population. Senators were to be appointed by state legislatures, a variation on the Virginia Plan. Members of the House of Representatives would be popularly elected by the voters in each state. Elected members of the House would be limited to two years in office before having to seek reelection, and those appointed to the Senate by each state's political elite would serve a term of six years.

Congress was given great power, including the power to tax, maintain an army and a navy, and regulate trade and commerce. Congress had authority that the national government lacked under the Articles of Confederation. It could also coin and borrow money, grant patents and copyrights, declare war, and establish laws regulating naturalization and bankruptcy. While legislation could be proposed by either chamber of Congress, it had to pass both chambers by a majority vote before being sent to the president to be signed into law, and all bills to raise revenue had to begin in the House of Representatives. Only those men elected by the voters to represent them could impose taxes upon them. There would be no more taxation without representation.

The Three-Fifths Compromise and the Debates over Slavery

The Great Compromise that determined the structure of Congress soon led to another debate, however. When states took a census of their population for the purpose of allotting House representatives, should slaves be counted? Southern states were adamant that they should be, while delegates from northern states were vehemently opposed, arguing that representatives from southern states could not represent the interests of enslaved people. If slaves were not counted, however, southern states would have far fewer representatives in the House than northern states did. For example, if South Carolina were allotted representatives based solely on its free population, it would receive only half the number it would have received if slaves, who made up approximately 43 percent of the population, were included.[7]

The **Three-Fifths Compromise**, illustrated in Figure 2.8, resolved the impasse, although not in a manner that truly satisfied anyone. For purposes of Congressional apportionment, slaveholding states were allowed to count all their free population, including free African Americans and 60 percent (three-fifths) of their enslaved population. To mollify the north, the compromise also allowed counting 60 percent of a state's slave population for federal taxation, although no such taxes were ever collected. Another compromise regarding the institution of slavery granted Congress the right to impose taxes on imports in exchange for a twenty-year prohibition on laws attempting to ban the importation of slaves to the United States, which would hurt the economy of southern states more than that of northern states. Because the southern states, especially South Carolina, had made it clear they would leave the convention if abolition were attempted, no serious effort was made by the framers to abolish slavery in the new nation, even though many delegates disapproved of the institution.

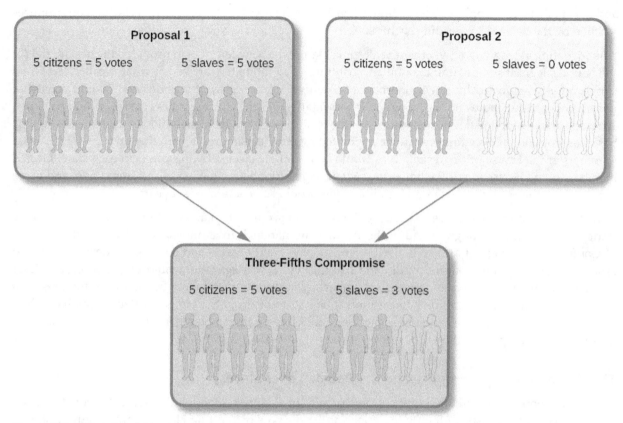

Figure 2.8 This infographic shows the methods proposed for counting slave populations and the resulting Three-Fifths Compromise.

Indeed, the Constitution contained two protections for slavery. Article I postponed the abolition of the foreign slave trade until 1808, and in the interim, those in slaveholding states were allowed to import as many slaves as they wished.[8] Furthermore, the Constitution placed no restrictions on the domestic slave trade, so residents of one state could still sell enslaved people to other states. Article IV of the Constitution—which, among other things, required states to return fugitives to the states where they had been charged with crimes—also prevented slaves from gaining their freedom by escaping to states where slavery had been abolished. Clause 3 of Article IV (known as the fugitive slave clause) allowed slave owners to reclaim their human property in the states where slaves had fled.[9]

Separation of Powers and Checks and Balances

Although debates over slavery and representation in Congress occupied many at the convention, the chief concern was the challenge of increasing the authority of the national government while ensuring that it did not become too powerful. The framers resolved this problem through a **separation of powers**, dividing the national government into three separate branches and assigning different responsibilities to each one, as shown in Figure 2.9. They also created a system of **checks and balances** by giving each of three branches of government the power to restrict the actions of the others, thus requiring them to work together.

Executive	Judicial	Legislative
	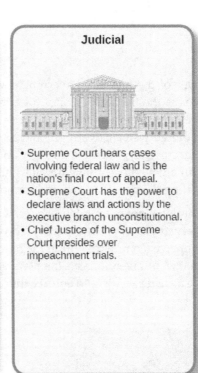	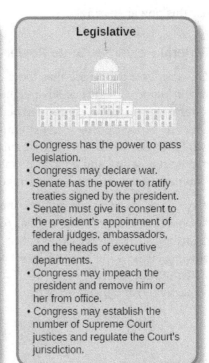
• President is commander-in-chief of the nation's armed forces. • President is responsible for conducting foreign affairs. • President appoints federal judges, ambassadors, and the heads of executive departments. • President may grant pardons to those who have broken federal laws. • President has the power to veto legislation passed by Congress.	• Supreme Court hears cases involving federal law and is the nation's final court of appeal. • Supreme Court has the power to declare laws and actions by the executive branch unconstitutional. • Chief Justice of the Supreme Court presides over impeachment trials.	• Congress has the power to pass legislation. • Congress may declare war. • Senate has the power to ratify treaties signed by the president. • Senate must give its consent to the president's appointment of federal judges, ambassadors, and the heads of executive departments. • Congress may impeach the president and remove him or her from office. • Congress may establish the number of Supreme Court justices and regulate the Court's jurisdiction.

Figure 2.9 To prevent the national government, or any one group within it, from becoming too powerful, the Constitution divided the government into three branches with different powers. No branch could function without the cooperation of the others, and each branch could restrict the powers of the others.

Congress was given the power to make laws, but the executive branch, consisting of the president and the vice president, and the federal judiciary, notably the Supreme Court, were created to, respectively, enforce laws and try cases arising under federal law. Neither of these branches had existed under the Articles of Confederation. Thus, Congress can pass laws, but its power to do so can be checked by the president, who can **veto** potential legislation so that it cannot become a law. Later, in the 1803 case of *Marbury* v. *Madison*, the U.S. Supreme Court established its own authority to rule on the constitutionality of laws, a process called judicial review.

Other examples of checks and balances include the ability of Congress to limit the president's veto. Should the president veto a bill passed by both houses of Congress, the bill is returned to Congress to be voted on again. If the bill passes both the House of Representatives and the Senate with a two-thirds vote in its favor, it becomes law even though the president has refused to sign it.

Congress is also able to limit the president's power as commander-in-chief of the armed forces by refusing to declare war or provide funds for the military. To date, the Congress has never refused a president's request for a declaration of war. The president must also seek the advice and consent of the Senate before appointing members of the Supreme Court and ambassadors, and the Senate must approve the ratification of all treaties signed by the president. Congress may even remove the president from office. To do this, both chambers of Congress must work together. The House of Representatives impeaches the president by bringing formal charges against him or her, and the Senate tries the case in a proceeding overseen by the Chief Justice of the Supreme Court. The president is removed from office if found guilty.

According to political scientist Richard Neustadt, the system of separation of powers and checks and balances does not so much allow one part of government to control another as it encourages the branches to cooperate. Instead of a true separation of powers, the Constitutional Convention "created a government of separated institutions *sharing* powers."[10] For example, knowing the president can veto a law he or she disapproves, Congress will attempt to draft a bill that addresses the president's concerns before sending it to the White House for signing. Similarly, knowing that Congress can override a veto, the president will use this power sparingly.

Federal Power vs. State Power

The strongest guarantee that the power of the national government would be restricted and the states would retain a degree of sovereignty was the framers' creation of a federal system of government. In a **federal system**, power is divided between the federal (or national) government and the state governments. Great or explicit powers, called **enumerated powers**, were granted to the federal government to declare war, impose taxes, coin and regulate currency, regulate foreign and interstate commerce, raise and maintain an army and a navy, maintain a post office, make treaties with foreign nations and with Native American tribes, and make laws regulating the naturalization of immigrants.

All powers not expressly given to the national government, however, were intended to be exercised by the states. These powers are known as **reserved powers** (Figure 2.10). Thus, states remained free to pass laws regarding such things as intrastate commerce (commerce within the borders of a state) and marriage. Some powers, such as the right to levy taxes, were given to both the state and federal governments. Both the states and the federal government have a chief executive to enforce the laws (a governor and the president, respectively) and a system of courts.

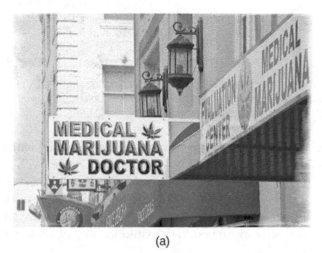

(a)   (b)

Figure 2.10   Reserve powers allow the states to pass intrastate legislation, such as laws on commerce, drug use, and marriage (a). However, sometimes judicial rulings at the federal level may supersede such legislation, as happened in *Obergefell* v. *Hodges* (2015), the recent Supreme Court case regarding marriage equality (b). (credit a: modification of work by Damian Gadal; credit b: modification of work by Ludovic Bertron)

Although the states retained a considerable degree of sovereignty, the **supremacy clause** in Article VI of the Constitution proclaimed that the Constitution, laws passed by Congress, and treaties made by the federal government were "the supreme Law of the Land." In the event of a conflict between the states and the national government, the national government would triumph. Furthermore, although the federal government was to be limited to those powers enumerated in the Constitution, Article I provided for the expansion of Congressional powers if needed. The "necessary and proper" clause of Article I provides that Congress may "make all Laws which shall be necessary and proper for carrying into Execution the foregoing [enumerated] Powers, and all other Powers vested by this Constitution in the Government of the United States, or in any Department or Officer thereof."

The Constitution also gave the federal government control over all "Territory or other Property belonging to the United States." This would prove problematic when, as the United States expanded westward and population growth led to an increase in the power of the northern states in Congress, the federal government sought to restrict the expansion of slavery into newly acquired territories.

2.4 The Ratification of the Constitution

Learning Objectives

By the end of this section, you will be able to:
- Identify the steps required to ratify the Constitution
- Describe arguments the framers raised in support of a strong national government and counterpoints raised by the Anti-Federalists

On September 17, 1787, the delegates to the Constitutional Convention in Philadelphia voted to approve the document they had drafted over the course of many months. Some did not support it, but the majority did. Before it could become the law of the land, however, the Constitution faced another hurdle. It had to be ratified by the states.

THE RATIFICATION PROCESS

Article VII, the final article of the Constitution, required that before the Constitution could become law and a new government could form, the document had to be ratified by nine of the thirteen states. Eleven days after the delegates at the Philadelphia convention approved it, copies of the Constitution were sent to each of the states, which were to hold ratifying conventions to either accept or reject it.

This approach to ratification was an unusual one. Since the authority inherent in the Articles of Confederation and the Confederation Congress had rested on the consent of the states, changes to the nation's government should also have been ratified by the state legislatures. Instead, by calling upon state legislatures to hold ratification conventions to approve the Constitution, the framers avoided asking the legislators to approve a document that would require them to give up a degree of their own power. The men attending the ratification conventions would be delegates elected by their neighbors to represent their interests. They were not being asked to relinquish their power; in fact, they were being asked to place limits upon the power of their state legislators, whom they may not have elected in the first place. Finally, because the new nation was to be a republic in which power was held by the people through their elected representatives, it was considered appropriate to leave the ultimate acceptance or rejection of the Constitution to the nation's citizens. If convention delegates, who were chosen by popular vote, approved it, then the new government could rightly claim that it ruled with the consent of the people.

The greatest sticking point when it came to ratification, as it had been at the Constitutional Convention itself, was the relative power of the state and federal governments. The framers of the Constitution believed that without the ability to maintain and command an army and navy, impose taxes, and force the states to comply with laws passed by Congress, the young nation would not survive for very long. But many people resisted increasing the powers of the national government at the expense of the states. Virginia's Patrick Henry, for example, feared that the newly created office of president would place excessive power in the hands of one man. He also disapproved of the federal government's new ability to tax its citizens. This right, Henry believed, should remain with the states.

Other delegates, such as Edmund Randolph of Virginia, disapproved of the Constitution because it created a new federal judicial system. Their fear was that the federal courts would be too far away from where those who were tried lived. State courts were located closer to the homes of both plaintiffs and defendants, and it was believed that judges and juries in state courts could better understand the actions of those who appeared before them. In response to these fears, the federal government created federal courts in each of the states as well as in Maine, which was then part of Massachusetts, and Kentucky, which was part of Virginia.[11]

Perhaps the greatest source of dissatisfaction with the Constitution was that it did not guarantee protection of individual liberties. State governments had given jury trials to residents charged with violating the law and allowed their residents to possess weapons for their protection. Some had practiced religious tolerance as well. The Constitution, however, did not contain reassurances that the federal government would do so. Although it provided for habeas corpus and prohibited both a religious test for holding office and granting noble titles, some citizens feared the loss of their traditional rights and the violation of their liberties. This led many of the Constitution's opponents to call for a bill of rights and the refusal to ratify the document without one. The lack of a bill of rights was especially problematic in Virginia, as the Virginia Declaration of Rights was the most extensive rights-granting document among the states. The promise that a bill of rights would be drafted for the Constitution persuaded delegates in many states to support ratification.[12]

Insider Perspective

Thomas Jefferson on the Bill of Rights

John Adams and Thomas Jefferson carried on a lively correspondence regarding the ratification of the Constitution. In the following excerpt (reproduced as written) from a letter dated March 15, 1789, after the Constitution had been ratified by nine states but before it had been approved by all thirteen, Jefferson reiterates his previously expressed concerns that a bill of rights to protect citizens' freedoms was necessary and should be added to the Constitution:

> "In the arguments in favor of a declaration of rights, . . . I am happy to find that on the whole you are a friend to this amendment. The Declaration of rights is like all other human blessings alloyed with some inconveniences, and not accomplishing fully it's object. But the good in this instance vastly overweighs the evil. . . . This instrument [the Constitution] forms us into one state as to certain objects, and gives us a legislative & executive body for these objects. It should therefore guard us against their abuses of power. . . . Experience proves the inefficacy of a bill of rights. True. But tho it is not absolutely efficacious under all circumstances, it is of great potency always, and rarely inefficacious. . . . There is a remarkable difference between the . . . Inconveniences which attend a Declaration of rights, & those which attend the want of it. . . . The inconveniences of the want of a Declaration are permanent, afflicting & irreparable: they are in constant progression from bad to worse."[13]

What were some of the inconveniences of not having a bill of rights that Jefferson mentioned? Why did he decide in favor of having one?

It was clear how some states would vote. Smaller states, like Delaware, favored the Constitution. Equal representation in the Senate would give them a degree of equality with the larger states, and a strong national government with an army at its command would be better able to defend them than their state militias could. Larger states, however, had significant power to lose. They did not believe they needed the federal government to defend them and disliked the prospect of having to provide tax money to support the new government. Thus, from the very beginning, the supporters of the Constitution feared that New York, Massachusetts, Pennsylvania, and Virginia would refuse to ratify it. That would mean all nine of the remaining states would have to, and Rhode Island, the smallest state, was unlikely to do so. It had not even sent delegates to the convention in Philadelphia. And even if it joined the other states in ratifying the document and the requisite nine votes were cast, the new nation would not be secure without its largest, wealthiest, and most populous states as members of the union.

THE RATIFICATION CAMPAIGN

On the question of ratification, citizens quickly separated into two groups: Federalists and Anti-Federalists. The **Federalists** supported it. They tended to be among the elite members of society—wealthy and well-educated landowners, businessmen, and former military commanders who believed a strong government would be better for both national defense and economic growth. A national currency, which the federal government had the power to create, would ease business transactions. The ability of the federal government to regulate trade and place tariffs on imports would protect merchants from foreign competition. Furthermore, the power to collect taxes would allow the national government to fund internal improvements like roads, which would also help businessmen. Support for the Federalists was especially strong in New England.

Opponents of ratification were called **Anti-Federalists**. Anti-Federalists feared the power of the national government and believed state legislatures, with which they had more contact, could better protect their freedoms. Although some Anti-Federalists, like Patrick Henry, were wealthy, most distrusted the elite and believed a strong federal government would favor the rich over those of "the middling sort." This was certainly the fear of Melancton Smith, a New York merchant and landowner, who believed that power should rest in the hands of small, landowning farmers of average wealth who "are more temperate, of better morals and less ambitious than the great."[14] Even members of the social elite, like Henry, feared that the centralization of power would lead to the creation of a political aristocracy, to the detriment of state sovereignty and individual liberty.

Related to these concerns were fears that the strong central government Federalists advocated for would levy taxes on farmers and planters, who lacked the hard currency needed to pay them. Many also believed Congress would impose tariffs on foreign imports that would make American agricultural products less welcome in Europe and in European colonies in the western hemisphere. For these reasons, Anti-Federalist sentiment was especially strong in the South.

Some Anti-Federalists also believed that the large federal republic that the Constitution would create could not work as intended. Americans had long believed that virtue was necessary in a nation where people governed themselves (i.e., the ability to put self-interest and petty concerns aside for the good of the larger community). In small republics, similarities among members of the community would naturally lead them to the same positions and make it easier for those in power to understand the needs of their neighbors. In a larger republic, one that encompassed nearly the entire Eastern Seaboard and ran west to the Appalachian Mountains, people would lack such a strong commonality of interests.[15]

Likewise, Anti-Federalists argued, the diversity of religion tolerated by the Constitution would prevent the formation of a political community with shared values and interests. The Constitution contained no provisions for government support of churches or of religious education, and Article VI explicitly forbade the use of religious tests to determine eligibility for public office. This caused many, like Henry Abbot of North Carolina, to fear that government would be placed in the hands of "pagans . . . and Mahometans [Muslims]."[16]

It is difficult to determine how many people were Federalists and how many were Anti-Federalists in 1787. The Federalists won the day, but they may not have been in the majority. First, the Federalist position tended to win support among businessmen, large farmers, and, in the South, plantation owners. These people tended to live along the Eastern Seaboard. In 1787, most of the states were divided into voting districts in a manner that gave more votes to the eastern part of the state than to the western part.[17] Thus, in some states, like Virginia and South Carolina, small farmers who may have favored the Anti-Federalist position were unable to elect as many delegates to state ratification conventions as those who lived in the east. Small settlements may also have lacked the funds to send delegates to the convention.[18]

In all the states, educated men authored pamphlets and published essays and cartoons arguing either for or against ratification (Figure 2.11). Although many writers supported each position, it is the Federalist essays that are now best known. The arguments these authors put forth, along with explicit guarantees that amendments would be added to protect individual liberties, helped to sway delegates to ratification conventions in many states.

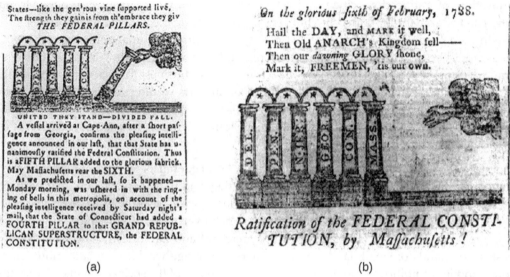

(a)   (b)

Figure 2.11 This *Massachusetts Sentinel* cartoon (a) encourages the state's voters to join Georgia and neighboring Connecticut in ratifying the Constitution. Less than a month later, on February 6, 1788, Massachusetts became the sixth member of the newly formed federal union (b).

For obvious reasons, smaller, less populous states favored the Constitution and the protection of a strong federal government. As shown in Figure 2.12, Delaware and New Jersey ratified the document within a few months after it was sent to them for approval in 1787. Connecticut ratified it early in 1788. Some of the larger states, such as Pennsylvania and Massachusetts, also voted in favor of the new government. New Hampshire became the ninth state to ratify the Constitution in the summer of 1788.

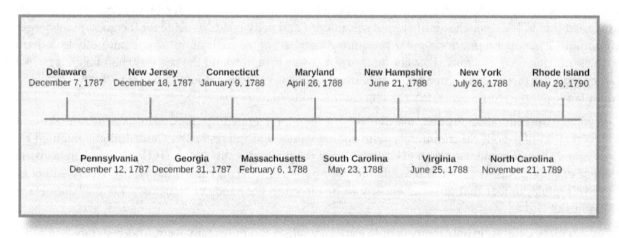

Figure 2.12 This timeline shows the order in which states ratified the new Constitution. Small states that would benefit from the protection of a larger union ratified the Constitution fairly quickly, such as Delaware and Connecticut. Larger, more populous states like Virginia and New York took longer. The last state to ratify was Rhode Island, a state that had always proven reluctant to act alongside the others.

Although the Constitution went into effect following ratification by New Hampshire, four states still remained outside the newly formed union. Two were the wealthy, populous states of Virginia and New

York. In Virginia, James Madison's active support and the intercession of George Washington, who wrote letters to the convention, changed the minds of many. Some who had initially opposed the Constitution, such as Edmund Randolph, were persuaded that the creation of a strong union was necessary for the country's survival and changed their position. Other Virginia delegates were swayed by the promise that a bill of rights similar to the Virginia Declaration of Rights would be added after the Constitution was ratified. On June 25, 1788, Virginia became the tenth state to grant its approval.

The approval of New York was the last major hurdle. Facing considerable opposition to the Constitution in that state, Alexander Hamilton, James Madison, and John Jay wrote a series of essays, beginning in 1787, arguing for a strong federal government and support of the Constitution (Figure 2.13). Later compiled as *The Federalist* and now known as ***The Federalist Papers***, these eighty-five essays were originally published in newspapers in New York and other states under the name of Publius, a supporter of the Roman Republic.

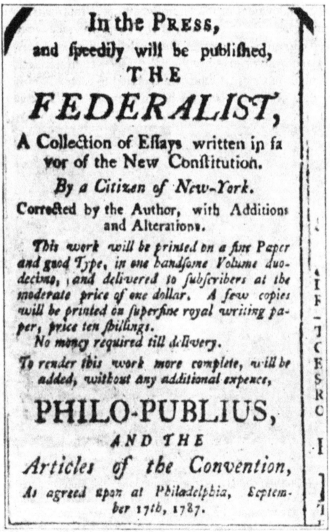

Figure 2.13 From 1787 to 1788, Alexander Hamilton, James Madison, and John Jay authored a series of essays intended to convince Americans, especially New Yorkers, to support the new Constitution. These essays, which originally appeared in newspapers, were collected and published together under the title *The Federalist* in 1788. They are now known as *The Federalist Papers*.

The essays addressed a variety of issues that troubled citizens. For example, in *Federalist* No. 51, attributed to James Madison (Figure 2.14), the author assured readers they did not need to fear that the national government would grow too powerful. The federal system, in which power was divided between the national and state governments, and the division of authority within the federal government into separate branches would prevent any one part of the government from becoming too strong. Furthermore, tyranny could not arise in a government in which "the legislature necessarily predominates." Finally, the desire of office holders in each branch of government to exercise the powers given to them, described as "personal motives," would encourage them to limit any attempt by the other branches to overstep their authority. According to Madison, "Ambition must be made to counteract ambition."

Other essays countered different criticisms made of the Constitution and echoed the argument in favor of a strong national government. In *Federalist* No. 35, for example, Hamilton (Figure 2.14) argued that people's interests could in fact be represented by men who were not their neighbors. Indeed, Hamilton asked rhetorically, would American citizens best be served by a representative "whose observation does not travel beyond the circle of his neighbors and his acquaintances" or by someone with more extensive knowledge of the world? To those who argued that a merchant and land-owning elite would come to dominate Congress, Hamilton countered that the majority of men currently sitting in New York's state senate and assembly were landowners of moderate wealth and that artisans usually chose merchants, "their natural patron[s] and friend[s]," to represent them. An aristocracy would not arise, and if it did, its members would have been chosen by lesser men. Similarly, Jay reminded New Yorkers in *Federalist* No. 2 that union had been the goal of Americans since the time of the Revolution. A desire for union was natural among people of such "similar sentiments" who "were united to each other by the strongest ties," and the government proposed by the Constitution was the best means of achieving that union.

(a)   (b)

Figure 2.14   James Madison (a) played a vital role in the formation of the Constitution. He was an important participant in the Constitutional Convention and authored many of *The Federalist Papers*. Despite the fact that he did not believe that a Bill of Rights was necessary, he wrote one in order to allay the fears of those who believed the federal government was too powerful. He also served as Thomas Jefferson's vice president and was elected president himself in 1808. Alexander Hamilton (b) was one of the greatest political minds of the early United States. He authored the majority of *The Federalist Papers* and served as Secretary of the Treasury in George Washington's administration.

Objections that an elite group of wealthy and educated bankers, businessmen, and large landowners would come to dominate the nation's politics were also addressed by Madison in *Federalist* No. 10. Americans need not fear the power of factions or special interests, he argued, for the republic was too big and the interests of its people too diverse to allow the development of large, powerful political parties.

Likewise, elected representatives, who were expected to "possess the most attractive merit," would protect the government from being controlled by "an unjust and interested [biased in favor of their own interests] majority."

For those who worried that the president might indeed grow too ambitious or king-like, Hamilton, in *Federalist* No. 68, provided assurance that placing the leadership of the country in the hands of one person was not dangerous. Electors from each state would select the president. Because these men would be members of a "transient" body called together only for the purpose of choosing the president and would meet in separate deliberations in each state, they would be free of corruption and beyond the influence of the "heats and ferments" of the voters. Indeed, Hamilton argued in *Federalist* No. 70, instead of being afraid that the president would become a tyrant, Americans should realize that it was easier to control one person than it was to control many. Furthermore, one person could also act with an "energy" that Congress did not possess. Making decisions alone, the president could decide what actions should be taken faster than could Congress, whose deliberations, because of its size, were necessarily slow. At times, the "decision, activity, secrecy, and dispatch" of the chief executive might be necessary.

Link to Learning

The Library of Congress has *The Federalist Papers (http://www.openstax.org/l/29FedPapers)* on their website. The Anti-Federalists also produced a body of writings, less extensive than *The Federalists Papers*, which argued against the ratification of the Constitution. However, these were not written by one small group of men as *The Federalist Papers* had been. A collection of the writings that are unofficially called *The Anti-Federalist Papers (http://www.openstax.org/l/29AntiFedPapers)* is also available online.

The arguments of the Federalists were persuasive, but whether they actually succeeded in changing the minds of New Yorkers is unclear. Once Virginia ratified the Constitution on June 25, 1788, New York realized that it had little choice but to do so as well. If it did not ratify the Constitution, it would be the last large state that had not joined the union. Thus, on July 26, 1788, the majority of delegates to New York's ratification convention voted to accept the Constitution. A year later, North Carolina became the twelfth state to approve. Alone and realizing it could not hope to survive on its own, Rhode Island became the last state to ratify, nearly two years after New York had done so.

Finding a Middle Ground

Term Limits

One of the objections raised to the Constitution's new government was that it did not set term limits for members of Congress or the president. Those who opposed a strong central government argued that this failure could allow a handful of powerful men to gain control of the nation and rule it for as long as they wished. Although the framers did not anticipate the idea of career politicians, those who supported the Constitution argued that reelecting the president and reappointing senators by state legislatures would create a body of experienced men who could better guide the country through crises. A president who did not prove to be a good leader would be voted out of office instead of being reelected. In fact, presidents long followed George Washington's example and limited themselves to two terms. Only in 1951, after Franklin Roosevelt had been elected four times, was the Twenty-Second Amendment passed to restrict the presidency to two terms.

Are term limits a good idea? Should they have originally been included in the Constitution? Why or why not? Are there times when term limits might not be good?

2.5 Constitutional Change

Learning Objectives

By the end of this section, you will be able to:
* Describe how the Constitution can be formally amended
* Explain the contents and significance of the Bill of Rights
* Discuss the importance of the Thirteenth, Fourteenth, Fifteenth, and Nineteenth Amendments

A major problem with the Articles of Confederation had been the nation's inability to change them without the unanimous consent of all the states. The framers learned this lesson well. One of the strengths they built into the Constitution was the ability to amend it to meet the nation's needs, reflect the changing times, and address concerns or structural elements they had not anticipated.

THE AMENDMENT PROCESS

Since ratification in 1789, the Constitution has been amended only twenty-seven times. The first ten amendments were added in 1791. Responding to charges by Anti-Federalists that the Constitution made the national government too powerful and provided no protections for the rights of individuals, the newly elected federal government tackled the issue of guaranteeing liberties for American citizens. James Madison, a member of Congress from Virginia, took the lead in drafting nineteen potential changes to the Constitution.

Madison followed the procedure outlined in Article V that says amendments can originate from one of two sources. First, they can be proposed by Congress. Then, they must be approved by a two-thirds majority in both the House and the Senate before being sent to the states for potential ratification. States have two ways to ratify or defeat a proposed amendment. First, if three-quarters of state legislatures vote to approve an amendment, it becomes part of the Constitution. Second, if three-quarters of state-ratifying conventions support the amendment, it is ratified. A second method of proposal of an amendment allows for the petitioning of Congress by the states: Upon receiving such petitions from two-thirds of the states, Congress must call a convention for the purpose of proposing amendments, which would then be forwarded to the states for ratification by the required three-quarters. All the current constitutional amendments were created using the first method of proposal (via Congress).

Having drafted nineteen proposed amendments, Madison submitted them to Congress. Only twelve were approved by two-thirds of both the Senate and the House of Representatives and sent to the states for ratification. Of these, only ten were accepted by three-quarters of the state legislatures. In 1791, these first ten amendments were added to the Constitution and became known as the **Bill of Rights**.

The ability to change the Constitution has made it a flexible, living document that can respond to the nation's changing needs and has helped it remain in effect for more than 225 years. At the same time, the framers made amending the document sufficiently difficult that it has not been changed repeatedly; only seventeen amendments have been added since the ratification of the first ten (one of these, the Twenty-Seventh Amendment, was among Madison's rejected nine proposals).

KEY CONSTITUTIONAL CHANGES

The Bill of Rights was intended to quiet the fears of Anti-Federalists that the Constitution did not adequately protect individual liberties and thus encourage their support of the new national government. Many of these first ten amendments were based on provisions of the English Bill of Rights and the Virginia Declaration of Rights. For example, the right to bear arms for protection (Second Amendment), the right not to have to provide shelter and provision for soldiers in peacetime (Third Amendment), the right to a trial by jury (Sixth and Seventh Amendments), and protection from excessive fines and from cruel and unusual punishment (Eighth Amendment) are taken from the English Bill of Rights. The Fifth Amendment, which requires among other things that people cannot be deprived of their life, liberty, or property except by a legal proceeding, was also greatly influenced by English law as well as the protections granted to Virginians in the Virginia Declaration of Rights.

Link to Learning

Learn more about the formal **process of amending the Constitution (http://www.openstax.org/l/ 29AmendProcess)** and view exhibits related to the passage of specific amendments at the National Archives website.

Other liberties, however, do not derive from British precedents. The protections for religion, speech, the press, and assembly that are granted by the First Amendment did not exist under English law. (The right to petition the government did, however.) The prohibition in the First Amendment against the establishment of an official church by the federal government differed significantly from both English precedent and the practice of several states that had official churches. The Fourth Amendment, which protects Americans from unwarranted search and seizure of their property, was also new.

The Ninth and Tenth Amendments were intended to provide yet another assurance that people's rights would be protected and that the federal government would not become too powerful. The Ninth Amendment guarantees that liberties extend beyond those described in the preceding documents. This was an important acknowledgment that the protected rights were extensive, and the government should not attempt to interfere with them. The Supreme Court, for example, has held that the Ninth Amendment protects the right to privacy even though none of the preceding amendments explicitly mentions this right. The Tenth Amendment, one of the first submitted to the states for ratification, ensures that states possess all powers not explicitly assigned to the federal government by the Constitution. This guarantee protects states' reserved powers to regulate such things as marriage, divorce, and intrastate transportation and commerce, and to pass laws affecting education and public health and safety.

Of the later amendments only one, the Twenty-First, repealed another amendment, the Eighteenth, which had prohibited the manufacture, import, export, distribution, transportation, and sale of alcoholic beverages. Other amendments rectify problems that have arisen over the years or that reflect changing times. For example, the Seventeenth Amendment, ratified in 1913, gave voters the right to directly elect U.S. senators. The Twentieth Amendment, which was ratified in 1933 during the Great Depression, moved the date of the presidential inauguration from March to January. In a time of crisis, like a severe economic depression, the president needed to take office almost immediately after being elected, and modern transportation allowed the new president to travel to the nation's capital quicker than before. The Twenty-Second Amendment, added in 1955, limits the president to two terms in office, and the Twenty-Seventh Amendment, first submitted for ratification in 1789, regulates the implementation of laws regarding salary increases or decreases for members of Congress.

Of the remaining amendments, four are of especially great significance. The Thirteenth, Fourteenth, and Fifteenth Amendments, ratified at the end of the Civil War, changed the lives of African Americans who had been held in slavery. The Thirteenth Amendment abolished slavery in the United States. The Fourteenth Amendment granted citizenship to African Americans and equal protection under the law regardless of race or color. It also prohibited states from depriving their residents of life, liberty, or property without a legal proceeding. Over the years, the Fourteenth Amendment has been used to require states to protect most of the same federal freedoms granted by the Bill of Rights.

The Fifteenth and Nineteenth Amendments extended the right to vote. The Constitution had given states the power to set voting requirements, but the states had used this authority to deny women the right to vote. Most states before the 1830s had also used this authority to deny suffrage to property-less men and often to African American men as well. When states began to change property requirements for voters in the 1830s, many that had allowed free, property-owning African American men to vote restricted the suffrage to white men. The Fifteenth Amendment gave men the right to vote regardless of race or color, but women were still prohibited from voting in most states. After many years of campaigns for suffrage, as shown in Figure 2.15, the Nineteenth Amendment finally gave women the right to vote in 1920.

Subsequent amendments further extended the suffrage. The Twenty-Third Amendment (1961) allowed residents of Washington, DC to vote for the president. The Twenty-Fourth Amendment (1964) abolished the use of poll taxes. Many southern states had used a poll tax, a tax placed on voting, to prevent poor African Americans from voting. Thus, the states could circumvent the Fifteenth Amendment; they argued that they were denying African American men and women the right to vote not because of their race but because of their inability to pay the tax. The last great extension of the suffrage occurred in 1971 in the midst of the Vietnam War. The Twenty-Sixth Amendment reduced the voting age from twenty-one to eighteen. Many people had complained that the young men who were fighting in Vietnam should have the right to vote for or against those making decisions that might literally mean life or death for them. Many other amendments have been proposed over the years, including an amendment to guarantee equal rights to women, but all have failed.

Figure 2.15 Suffragists encourage Ohio men to support votes for women. Before the Nineteenth Amendment was added to the Constitution in 1920, only a few western states such as Wyoming gave women the right to vote. These women seem to be attracting a primarily female audience to hear their cause.

Get Connected!

Guaranteeing Your First Amendment Rights

The liberties of U.S. citizens are protected by the Bill of Rights, but potential or perceived threats to these freedoms arise constantly. This is especially true regarding First Amendment rights. Read about some of these threats at the American Civil Liberties Union (ACLU) (https://openstax.org/l/29AmCivLU) website and let people know how you feel about these issues.

What issue regarding First Amendment protections causes you the most concern?

Key Terms

Anti-Federalists those who did not support ratification of the Constitution

Articles of Confederation the first basis for the new nation's government; adopted in 1781; created an alliance of sovereign states held together by a weak central government

bicameral legislature a legislature with two houses, such as the U.S. Congress

Bill of Rights the first ten amendments to the U.S. Constitution; most were designed to protect fundamental rights and liberties

checks and balances a system that allows one branch of government to limit the exercise of power by another branch; requires the different parts of government to work together

confederation a highly decentralized form of government; sovereign states form a union for purposes such as mutual defense

Declaration of Independence a document written in 1776 in which the American colonists proclaimed their independence from Great Britain and listed their grievances against the British king

enumerated powers the powers given explicitly to the federal government by the Constitution (Article I, Section 8); power to regulate interstate and foreign commerce, raise and support armies, declare war, coin money, and conduct foreign affairs

federal system a form of government in which power is divided between state governments and a national government

Federalists those who supported ratification of the Constitution

Great Compromise a compromise between the Virginia Plan and the New Jersey Plan that created a two-house Congress; representation based on population in the House of Representatives and equal representation of states in the Senate

natural rights the right to life, liberty, and property; believed to be given by God; no government may take away

New Jersey Plan a plan that called for a one-house national legislature; each state would receive one vote

republic a form of government in which political power rests in the hands of the people, not a monarch, and is exercised by elected representatives

reserved powers any powers not prohibited by the Constitution or delegated to the national government; powers reserved to the states and denied to the federal government

separation of powers the sharing of powers among three separate branches of government

social contract an agreement between people and government in which citizens consent to be governed so long as the government protects their natural rights

supremacy clause the statement in Article VI of the Constitution that federal law is superior to laws passed by state legislatures

The Federalist Papers a collection of eighty-five essays written by Alexander Hamilton, James Madison, and John Jay in support of ratification of the Constitution

Three-Fifths Compromise a compromise between northern and southern states that called for counting of all a state's free population and 60 percent of its slave population for both federal taxation and representation in Congress

unicameral legislature a legislature with only one house, like the Confederation Congress or the legislature proposed by the New Jersey Plan

veto the power of the president to reject a law proposed by Congress

Virginia Plan a plan for a two-house legislature; representatives would be elected to the lower house based on each state's population; representatives for the upper house would be chosen by the lower house

Summary

2.1 The Pre-Revolutionary Period and the Roots of the American Political Tradition

For many years the British colonists in North America had peacefully accepted rule by the king and Parliament. They were proud to be Englishmen. Much of their pride, however, stemmed from their belief that they were heirs to a tradition of limited government and royal acknowledgement of the rights of their subjects.

Colonists' pride in their English liberties gave way to dismay when they perceived that these liberties were being abused. People had come to regard life, liberty, and property not as gifts from the monarch but as natural rights no government could take away. A chain of incidents—the Proclamation of 1763, the trial of smugglers in courts without juries, the imposition of taxes without the colonists' consent, and the attempted interference with self-government in the colonies—convinced many colonists that the social contract between the British government and its citizens had been broken. In 1776, the Second Continental Congress declared American independence from Great Britain.

2.2 The Articles of Confederation

Fearful of creating a system so powerful that it might abuse its citizens, the men who drafted the Articles of Confederation deliberately sought to limit the powers of the national government. The states maintained the right to govern their residents, while the national government could declare war, coin money, and conduct foreign affairs but little else. Its inability to impose taxes, regulate commerce, or raise an army hindered its ability to defend the nation or pay its debts. A solution had to be found.

2.3 The Development of the Constitution

Realizing that flaws in the Articles of Confederation could harm the new country and recognizing that the Articles could not easily be revised as originally intended, delegates from the states who met in Philadelphia from May through September 1787 set about drafting a new governing document. The United States that emerged from the Constitutional Convention in September was not a confederation, but it was a republic whose national government had been strengthened greatly. Congress had been transformed into a bicameral legislature with additional powers, and a national judicial system had been created. Most importantly, a federal system had been established with the power to govern the new country.

To satisfy the concerns of those who feared an overly strong central government, the framers of the Constitution created a system with separation of powers and checks and balances. Although such measures satisfied many, concerns still lingered that the federal government remained too powerful.

2.4 The Ratification of the Constitution

Anti-Federalists objected to the power the Constitution gave the federal government and the absence of a bill of rights to protect individual liberties. The Federalists countered that a strong government was necessary to lead the new nation and promised to add a bill of rights to the Constitution. *The Federalist Papers*, in particular, argued in favor of ratification and sought to convince people that the new government would not become tyrannical. Finally, in June 1788, New Hampshire became the ninth state to approve the Constitution, making it the law of the land. The large and prosperous states of Virginia and New York followed shortly thereafter, and the remaining states joined as well.

2.5 Constitutional Change

One of the problems with the Articles of Confederation was the difficulty of changing it. To prevent this difficulty from recurring, the framers provided a method for amending the Constitution that required a two-thirds majority in both houses of Congress and in three-quarters of state legislatures to approve a change.

The possibility of amending the Constitution helped ensure its ratification, although many feared the powerful federal government it created would deprive them of their rights. To allay their anxieties, the framers promised that a Bill of Rights safeguarding individual liberties would be added following ratification. These ten amendments were formally added to the document in 1791 and other amendments followed over the years. Among the most important were those ending slavery, granting citizenship to African Americans, and giving the right to vote to Americans regardless of race, color, or sex.

Review Questions

1. British colonists in North America in the late seventeenth century were greatly influenced by the political thought of _____.
    a. King James II
    b. Thomas Jefferson
    c. John Locke
    d. James Madison

2. The agreement that citizens will consent to be governed so long as government protects their natural rights is called _____.
    a. the divine right of kings
    b. the social contract
    c. a bill of rights
    d. due process

3. What key tenets of American political thought were influential in the decision to declare independence from Britain?

4. What actions by the British government convinced the colonists that they needed to declare their independence?

5. What important power did the national government lack under the Articles of Confederation?
    a. It could not coin money.
    b. It could not declare war.
    c. It could not impose taxes.
    d. It could not conduct foreign affairs.

6. In what ways did Shays' Rebellion reveal the weaknesses of the Articles of Confederation?

7. According to the Great Compromise, how would representation in Congress be apportioned?

    a. Each state would have equal representation in both the House of Representatives and the Senate.
    b. Congress would be a unicameral legislature with each state receiving equal representation.
    c. Representation in the House of Representatives would be based on each state's population and every state would have two senators.
    d. Representation in both the House of Representatives and the Senate would be based on a state's population.

8. How did the delegates to the Constitutional Convention resolve their disagreement regarding slavery?

    a. It was agreed that Congress would abolish slavery in 1850.

    b. It was agreed that a state's slave population would be counted for purposes of representation but not for purposes of taxation.

    c. It was agreed that a state's slave population would be counted for purposes of taxation but not for purposes of representation.

    d. It was agreed that 60 percent of a state's slave population would be counted for purposes of both representation and taxation.

9. What does separation of powers mean?

10. Why were *The Federalist Papers* written?

    a. To encourage states to oppose the Constitution.

    b. To encourage New York to ratify the Constitution.

    c. To oppose the admission of slaveholding states to the federal union.

    d. To encourage people to vote for George Washington as the nation's first president.

11. What argument did Alexander Hamilton use to convince people that it was not dangerous to place power in the hands of one man?

    a. That man would have to pass a religious test before he could become president; thus, citizens could be sure that he was of good character.

    b. One man could respond to crises more quickly than a group of men like Congress.

    c. It was easier to control the actions of one man than the actions of a group.

    d. both B and C

12. Why did so many people oppose ratification of the Constitution, and how was their opposition partly overcome?

13. How many states must ratify an amendment before it becomes law?

    a. all

    b. three-fourths

    c. two-thirds

    d. one-half

14. What is the Bill of Rights?

    a. first ten amendments to the Constitution that protect individual freedoms

    b. powers given to Congress in Article I of the Constitution

    c. twenty-seven amendments added to the Constitution over the years

    d. document authored by Thomas Jefferson that details the rights of the citizens

15. What did the Fourteenth Amendment achieve?

Critical Thinking Questions

16. What core values and beliefs led to the American Revolution and the writing of the Articles of Confederation? How do these values and beliefs affect American politics today?

17. Was Britain truly depriving colonists of their natural rights? Explain your reasoning.

18. Do the Constitution and the Bill of Rights protect the life, liberty, and property of all Americans? Why or why not?

19. Was the Bill of Rights a necessary addition to the Constitution? Defend your answer.

20. One of the chief areas of compromise at the Constitutional Convention was the issue of slavery. Should delegates who opposed slavery have been willing to compromise? Why or why not?

21. Is the federal government too powerful? Should states have more power? If so, what specific power(s) should states have?

22. What new amendments should be added to the Constitution? Why?

Suggestions for Further Study

Appleby, Joyce. 1976. "Liberalism and the American Revolution." *The New England Quarterly* 49 (March): 3–26.

Bailyn, Bernard. 1967. *The Ideological Origins of the American Revolution*. Massachusetts: Belknap Press.

Beeman, Richard. 2010. *Plain, Honest Men: The Making of the American Constitution*. New York: Random House.

Cook, Don. 1995. *The Long Fuse: How England Lost the American Colonies, 1760–1785*. New York: Atlantic Monthly Press.

Drinker Bowen, Catherine. 1967. *Miracle at Philadelphia: The Story of the Constitutional Convention, May to September 1787*. Boston: Little, Brown.

Ellis, Joseph. 2015. *The Quartet: Orchestrating the Second American Revolution, 1783–1789*. New York: Knopf.

Grant, Ruth W. 1991. *John Locke's Liberalism*. Chicago: University of Chicago Press.

Knollenberg, Bernard. 1975. *Growth of the American Revolution: 1766–1775*. New York: Free Press.

Lipsky, Seth. 2011. *The Citizen's Constitution: An Annotated Guide*. New York: Basic Books.

Locke, John. 1689. *A Letter Concerning Toleration*. Translated by William Popple. http://socserv2.socsci.mcmaster.ca/econ/ugcm/3ll3/locke/toleration.pdf

———. 1690. *Two Treatises of Government*. http://socserv2.socsci.mcmaster.ca/econ/ugcm/3ll3/locke/government.pdf

Maier, Pauline. 2010. *Ratification: The People Debate the Constitution, 1787–1788*. New York: Simon & Schuster.

Morgan, Edward S. 1975. *American Slavery, American Freedom*. New York: W. Norton and Company.

Szatmary, David P. 1980. *Shays' Rebellion: The Making of an Agrarian Insurrection*. Amherst, MA: University of Massachusetts Press.

Urofsky, Melvin I., and Paul Finkelman. 2011. *A March of Liberty: A Constitutional History of the United States. Volume I: From the Founding to 1890*. New York: Oxford University Press.

Wood, Gordon. 1998. *The Creation of the American Republic, 1776–1787*. Chapel Hill, NC: University of North Carolina Press.

Chapter 3

American Federalism

Figure 3.1 Your first encounter with differences across states may have come from visiting relatives or going on a cross-country trip with your parents during vacation. The distinct postcard images of different states that come to your mind are symbolic of American federalism. (credit: modification of work by Boston Public Library)

Chapter Outline

3.1 The Division of Powers
3.2 The Evolution of American Federalism
3.3 Intergovernmental Relationships
3.4 Competitive Federalism Today
3.5 Advantages and Disadvantages of Federalism

Introduction

Federalism figures prominently in the U.S. political system. Specifically, the federal design spelled out in the Constitution divides powers between two levels of government—the states and the federal government—and creates a mechanism for them to check and balance one another. As an institutional design, federalism both safeguards state interests and creates a strong union led by a capable central government. American federalism also seeks to balance the forces of decentralization and centralization. We see decentralization when we cross state lines and encounter different taxation levels, welfare eligibility requirements, and voting regulations. Centralization is apparent in the fact that the federal government is the only entity permitted to print money, to challenge the legality of state laws, or to employ money grants and mandates to shape state actions. Colorful billboards with simple messages may greet us at state borders (Figure 3.1), but behind them lies a complex and evolving federal design that has structured relationships between states and the federal government since the late 1700s.

What specific powers and responsibilities are granted to the federal and state governments? How does our process of government keep these separate governing entities in balance? To answer these questions and more, this chapter traces the origins, evolution, and functioning of the American system of federalism, as well as its advantages and disadvantages for citizens.

3.1 The Division of Powers

Learning Objectives

By the end of this section, you will be able to:
- Explain the concept of federalism
- Discuss the constitutional logic of federalism
- Identify the powers and responsibilities of federal, state, and local governments

Modern democracies divide governmental power in two general ways; some, like the United States, use a combination of both structures. The first and more common mechanism shares power among three branches of government—the legislature, the executive, and the judiciary. The second, federalism, apportions power between two levels of government: national and subnational. In the United States, the term *federal government* refers to the government at the national level, while the term *states* means governments at the subnational level.

FEDERALISM DEFINED AND CONTRASTED

Federalism is an institutional arrangement that creates two relatively autonomous levels of government, each possessing the capacity to act directly on behalf of the people with the authority granted to it by the national constitution.[1] Although today's federal systems vary in design, five structural characteristics are common to the United States and other federal systems around the world, including Germany and Mexico.

First, all federal systems establish two levels of government, with both levels being elected by the people and each level assigned different functions. The national government is responsible for handling matters that affect the country as a whole, for example, defending the nation against foreign threats and promoting national economic prosperity. Subnational, or state governments, are responsible for matters that lie within their regions, which include ensuring the well-being of their people by administering education, health care, public safety, and other public services. By definition, a system like this requires that different levels of government cooperate, because the institutions at each level form an interacting network. In the U.S. federal system, all national matters are handled by the federal government, which is led by the president and members of Congress, all of whom are elected by voters across the country. All matters at the subnational level are the responsibility of the fifty states, each headed by an elected governor and legislature. Thus, there is a separation of functions between the federal and state governments, and voters choose the leader at each level.[2]

The second characteristic common to all federal systems is a written national constitution that cannot be changed without the substantial consent of subnational governments. In the American federal system, the twenty-seven amendments added to the Constitution since its adoption were the result of an arduous process that required approval by two-thirds of both houses of Congress and three-fourths of the states. The main advantage of this supermajority requirement is that no changes to the Constitution can occur unless there is broad support within Congress and among states. The potential drawback is that numerous national amendment initiatives—such as the Equal Rights Amendment (ERA), which aims to guarantee equal rights regardless of sex—have failed because they cannot garner sufficient consent among members of Congress or, in the case of the ERA, the states.

Third, the constitutions of countries with federal systems formally allocate legislative, judicial, and executive authority to the two levels of government in such a way as to ensure each level some degree of autonomy from the other. Under the U.S. Constitution, the president assumes executive power, Congress exercises legislative powers, and the federal courts (e.g., U.S. district courts, appellate courts, and the Supreme Court) assume judicial powers. In each of the fifty states, a governor assumes executive authority, a state legislature makes laws, and state-level courts (e.g., trial courts, intermediate appellate courts, and supreme courts) possess judicial authority.

While each level of government is somewhat independent of the others, a great deal of interaction occurs among them. In fact, the ability of the federal and state governments to achieve their objectives often depends on the cooperation of the other level of government. For example, the federal government's efforts to ensure homeland security are bolstered by the involvement of law enforcement agents working at local and state levels. On the other hand, the ability of states to provide their residents with public education and health care is enhanced by the federal government's financial assistance.

Another common characteristic of federalism around the world is that national courts commonly resolve disputes between levels and departments of government. In the United States, conflicts between states and the federal government are adjudicated by federal courts, with the U.S. Supreme Court being the final arbiter. The resolution of such disputes can preserve the autonomy of one level of government, as illustrated recently when the Supreme Court ruled that states cannot interfere with the federal government's actions relating to immigration.[3] In other instances, a Supreme Court ruling can erode that autonomy, as demonstrated in the 1940s when, in *United States v. Wrightwood Dairy Co.*, the Court enabled the federal government to regulate commercial activities that occurred within states, a function previously handled exclusively by the states.[4]

Finally, subnational governments are always represented in the upper house of the national legislature, enabling regional interests to influence national lawmaking.[5] In the American federal system, the U.S. Senate functions as a territorial body by representing the fifty states: Each state elects two senators to ensure equal representation regardless of state population differences. Thus, federal laws are shaped in part by state interests, which senators convey to the federal policymaking process.

Link to Learning

The governmental design of the United States is unusual; most countries do not have a federal structure. Aside from the United States, how many other countries (https://openstax.org/l/29fedsystems) have a federal system?

Division of power can also occur via a unitary structure or confederation (Figure 3.2). In contrast to federalism, a **unitary system** makes subnational governments dependent on the national government, where significant authority is concentrated. Before the late 1990s, the United Kingdom's unitary system was centralized to the extent that the national government held the most important levers of power. Since then, power has been gradually decentralized through a process of **devolution**, leading to the creation of regional governments in Scotland, Wales, and Northern Ireland as well as the delegation of specific responsibilities to them. Other democratic countries with unitary systems, such as France, Japan, and Sweden, have followed a similar path of decentralization.

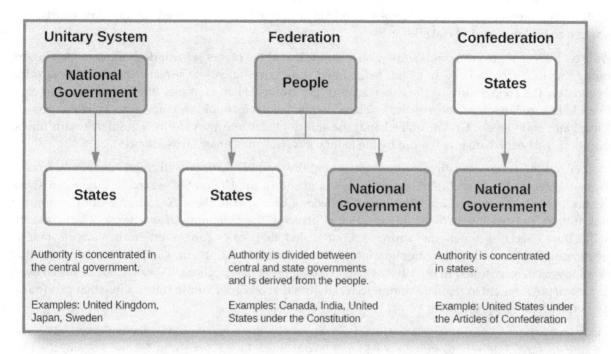

Figure 3.2 There are three general systems of government—unitary systems, federations, and confederations—each of which allocates power differently.

In a confederation, authority is decentralized, and the central government's ability to act depends on the consent of the subnational governments. Under the Articles of Confederation (the first constitution of the United States), states were sovereign and powerful while the national government was subordinate and weak. Because states were reluctant to give up any of their power, the national government lacked authority in the face of challenges such as servicing the war debt, ending commercial disputes among states, negotiating trade agreements with other countries, and addressing popular uprisings that were sweeping the country. As the brief American experience with confederation clearly shows, the main drawback with this system of government is that it maximizes regional self-rule at the expense of effective national governance.

FEDERALISM AND THE CONSTITUTION

The Constitution contains several provisions that direct the functioning of U.S. federalism. Some delineate the scope of national and state power, while others restrict it. The remaining provisions shape relationships among the states and between the states and the federal government.

The enumerated powers of the national legislature are found in Article I, Section 8. These powers define the jurisdictional boundaries within which the federal government has authority. In seeking not to replay the problems that plagued the young country under the Articles of Confederation, the Constitution's framers granted Congress specific powers that ensured its authority over national and foreign affairs. To provide for the general welfare of the populace, it can tax, borrow money, regulate interstate and foreign commerce, and protect property rights, for example. To provide for the common defense of the people, the federal government can raise and support armies and declare war. Furthermore, national integration and unity are fostered with the government's powers over the coining of money, naturalization, postal services, and other responsibilities.

The last clause of Article I, Section 8, commonly referred to as the **elastic clause** or the *necessary and proper cause*, enables Congress "to make all Laws which shall be necessary and proper for carrying" out its constitutional responsibilities. While the enumerated powers define the policy areas in which the national government has authority, the elastic clause allows it to create the legal means to fulfill those responsibilities. However, the open-ended construction of this clause has enabled the national government to expand its authority beyond what is specified in the Constitution, a development also motivated by the expansive interpretation of the *commerce clause,* which empowers the federal government to regulate interstate economic transactions.

The powers of the state governments were never listed in the original Constitution. The consensus among the framers was that states would retain any powers not prohibited by the Constitution or delegated to the national government.[6] However, when it came time to ratify the Constitution, a number of states requested that an amendment be added explicitly identifying the reserved powers of the states. What these Anti-Federalists sought was further assurance that the national government's capacity to act directly on behalf of the people would be restricted, which the first ten amendments (Bill of Rights) provided. The Tenth Amendment affirms the states' reserved powers: "The powers not delegated to the United States by the Constitution, nor prohibited by it to the States, are reserved to the States respectively, or to the people." Indeed, state constitutions had bills of rights, which the first Congress used as the source for the first ten amendments to the Constitution.

Some of the states' reserved powers are no longer exclusively within state domain, however. For example, since the 1940s, the federal government has also engaged in administering health, safety, income security, education, and welfare to state residents. The boundary between intrastate and interstate commerce has become indefinable as a result of broad interpretation of the commerce clause. Shared and overlapping powers have become an integral part of contemporary U.S. federalism. These **concurrent powers** range from taxing, borrowing, and making and enforcing laws to establishing court systems (**Figure 3.3**).[7]

Federal Government		State Government
Enumerated Powers	**Concurrent Powers**	**Reserved Powers**
• Coin money	• Levy and collect taxes	• Regulate intrastate commerce
• Regulate interstate and foreign commerce	• Borrow money	• Conduct elections
• Conduct foreign affairs	• Make and enforce laws	• Provide for public health, safety, welfare, and morals
• Establish rules of naturalization	• Establish courts	• Establish local governments
• Punish counterfeiting	• Charter banks and corporations	• Maintain militia (National Guard)
• Establish copyright/patent laws	• Take property for public purpose with just compensation (eminent domain)	• Ratify amendments to the Constitution
• Regulate postal system		
• Establish courts inferior to Supreme Court		**Powers Denied**
• Declare war		• Tax imports and exports
• Raise and support armies		• Coin money
• Make all laws "necessary and proper" to carry out responsibilities		• Enter into treaties
		• Impair obligation of contracts
Powers Denied		• Abridge the privileges or immunities of citizens or deny due process and equal protection of the laws
• Tax state exports		
• Change state boundaries		
• Violate the Bill of Rights		

Figure 3.3 Constitutional powers and responsibilities are divided between the U.S. federal and state governments. The two levels of government also share concurrent powers.

Article I, Sections 9 and 10, along with several constitutional amendments, lay out the restrictions on federal and state authority. The most important restriction Section 9 places on the national government prevents measures that cause the deprivation of personal liberty. Specifically, the government cannot suspend the **writ of habeas corpus**, which enables someone in custody to petition a judge to determine whether that person's detention is legal; pass a **bill of attainder**, a legislative action declaring someone guilty without a trial; or enact an **ex post facto law**, which criminalizes an act retroactively. The Bill of Rights affirms and expands these constitutional restrictions, ensuring that the government cannot encroach on personal freedoms.

The states are also constrained by the Constitution. Article I, Section 10, prohibits the states from entering into treaties with other countries, coining money, and levying taxes on imports and exports. Like the federal government, the states cannot violate personal freedoms by suspending the writ of habeas corpus, passing bills of attainder, or enacting ex post facto laws. Furthermore, the Fourteenth Amendment, ratified in 1868, prohibits the states from denying citizens the rights to which they are entitled by the Constitution, due process of law, or the equal protection of the laws. Lastly, three civil rights amendments—the Fifteenth, Nineteenth, and Twenty-Sixth—prevent both the states and the federal government from abridging citizens' right to vote based on race, sex, and age. This topic remains controversial because states have not always ensured equal protection.

The supremacy clause in Article VI of the Constitution regulates relationships between the federal and state governments by declaring that the Constitution and federal law are the supreme law of the land. This means that if a state law clashes with a federal law found to be within the national government's constitutional authority, the federal law prevails. The intent of the supremacy clause is not to subordinate the states to the federal government; rather, it affirms that one body of laws binds the country. In fact, all national and state government officials are bound by oath to uphold the Constitution regardless of the offices they hold. Yet enforcement is not always that simple. In the case of marijuana use, which the federal government defines to be illegal, twenty-three states and the District of Columbia have nevertheless established medical marijuana laws, others have decriminalized its recreational use, and four states have completely legalized it. The federal government could act in this area if it wanted to. For example, in addition to the legalization issue, there is the question of how to treat the money from marijuana sales, which the national government designates as drug money and regulates under laws regarding its deposit in banks.

Various constitutional provisions govern state-to-state relations. Article IV, Section 1, referred to as the **full faith and credit clause** or the *comity clause*, requires the states to accept court decisions, public acts, and contracts of other states. Thus, an adoption certificate or driver's license issued in one state is valid in any other state. The movement for marriage equality has put the full faith and credit clause to the test in recent decades. In light of *Baehr v. Lewin*, a 1993 ruling in which the Hawaii Supreme Court asserted that the state's ban on same-sex marriage was unconstitutional, a number of states became worried that they would be required to recognize those marriage certificates.[8] To address this concern, Congress passed and President Clinton signed the Defense of Marriage Act (DOMA) in 1996. The law declared that "No state (or other political subdivision within the United States) need recognize a marriage between persons of the same sex, even if the marriage was concluded or recognized in another state." The law also barred federal benefits for same-sex partners.

DOMA clearly made the topic a state matter. It denoted a choice for states, which led many states to take up the policy issue of marriage equality. Scores of states considered legislation and ballot initiatives on the question. The federal courts took up the issue with zeal after the U.S. Supreme Court in *United States v. Windsor* struck down the part of DOMA that outlawed federal benefits.[9] That move was followed by upwards of forty federal court decisions that upheld marriage equality in particular states. In 2014, the Supreme Court decided not to hear several key case appeals from a variety of states, all of which were brought by opponents of marriage equality who had lost in the federal courts. The outcome of not hearing these cases was that federal court decisions in four states were affirmed, which, when added to other states in the same federal circuit districts, brought the total number of states permitting same-sex marriage to thirty.[10] Then, in 2015, the *Obergefell v. Hodges* case had a sweeping effect when the Supreme Court clearly identified a constitutional right to marriage based on the Fourteenth Amendment.[11]

The **privileges and immunities clause** of Article IV asserts that states are prohibited from discriminating against out-of-staters by denying them such guarantees as access to courts, legal protection, property rights, and travel rights. The clause has not been interpreted to mean there cannot be *any* difference in the way a state treats residents and non-residents. For example, individuals cannot vote in a state in which they do not reside, tuition at state universities is higher for out-of-state residents, and in some cases individuals who have recently become residents of a state must wait a certain amount of time to be eligible for social welfare benefits. Another constitutional provision prohibits states from establishing trade restrictions on goods produced in other states. However, a state can tax out-of-state goods sold within its borders as long as state-made goods are taxed at the same level.

THE DISTRIBUTION OF FINANCES

Federal, state, and local governments depend on different sources of revenue to finance their annual expenditures. In 2014, total revenue (or receipts) reached $3.2 trillion for the federal government, $1.7 trillion for the states, and $1.2 trillion for local governments.[12] Two important developments have fundamentally changed the allocation of revenue since the early 1900s. First, the ratification of the Sixteenth Amendment in 1913 authorized Congress to impose income taxes without apportioning it among the states on the basis of population, a burdensome provision that Article I, Section 9, had imposed on the national government.[13] With this change, the federal government's ability to raise revenue significantly increased and so did its ability to spend.

The second development regulates federal grants, that is, transfers of federal money to state and local governments. These transfers, which do not have to be repaid, are designed to support the activities of the recipient governments, but also to encourage them to pursue federal policy objectives they might not otherwise adopt. The expansion of the federal government's spending power has enabled it to transfer more grant money to lower government levels, which has accounted for an increasing share of their total revenue.[14]

The sources of revenue for federal, state, and local governments are detailed in Figure 3.4. Although the data reflect 2013 results, the patterns we see in the figure give us a good idea of how governments have funded their activities in recent years. For the federal government, 47 percent of 2013 revenue came from individual income taxes and 34 percent from payroll taxes, which combine Social Security tax and Medicare tax.

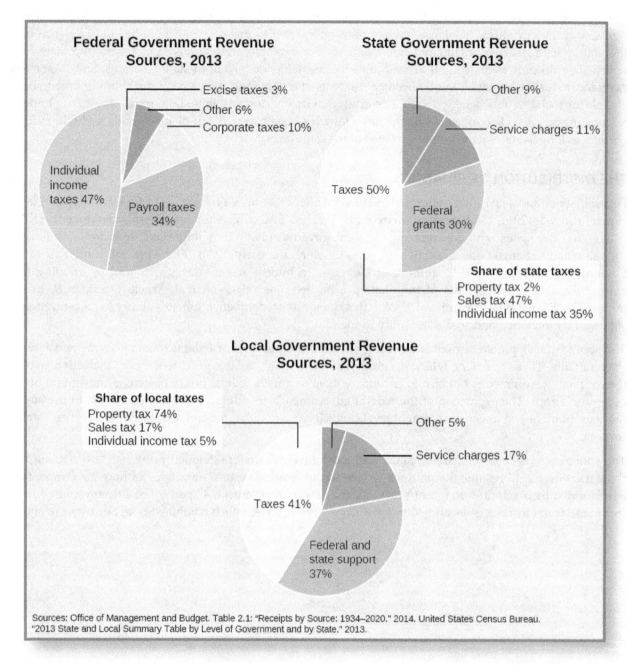

Figure 3.4 As these charts indicate, federal, state, and local governments raise revenue from different sources.

For state governments, 50 percent of revenue came from taxes, while 30 percent consisted of federal grants. Sales tax—which includes taxes on purchased food, clothing, alcohol, amusements, insurance, motor fuels, tobacco products, and public utilities, for example—accounted for about 47 percent of total tax revenue, and individual income taxes represented roughly 35 percent. Revenue from service charges (e.g., tuition revenue from public universities and fees for hospital-related services) accounted for 11 percent.

The tax structure of states varies. Alaska, Florida, Nevada, South Dakota, Texas, Washington, and Wyoming do not have individual income taxes. Figure 3.5 illustrates yet another difference: Fuel tax as a percentage of total tax revenue is much higher in South Dakota and West Virginia than in Alaska and Hawaii. However, most states have done little to prevent the erosion of the fuel tax's share of their total tax revenue between 2007 and 2014 (notice that for many states the dark blue dots for 2014 are to the *left* of the light blue numbers for 2007). Fuel tax revenue is typically used to finance state highway transportation projects, although some states do use it to fund non-transportation projects.

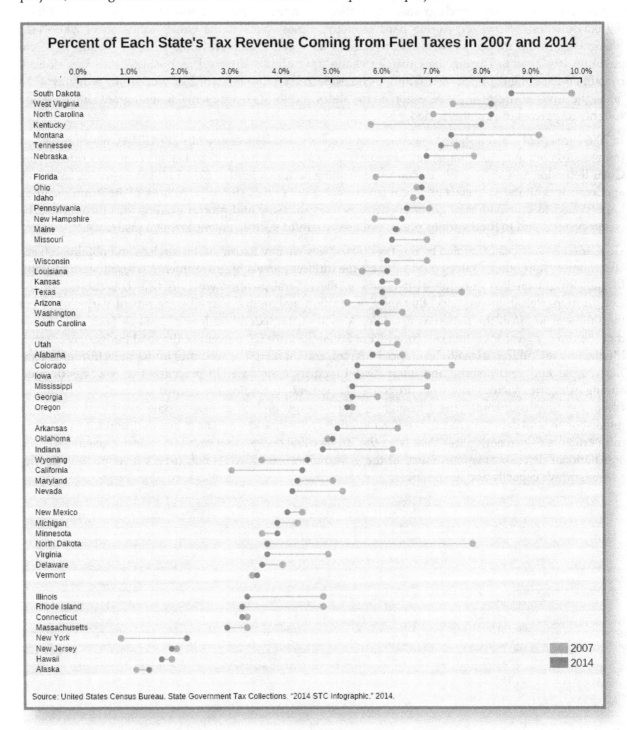

Figure 3.5 The fuel tax as a percentage of tax revenue varies greatly across states.

The most important sources of revenue for local governments in 2013 were taxes, federal and state grants, and service charges. For local governments the property tax, a levy on residential and commercial real estate, was the most important source of tax revenue, accounting for about 74 percent of the total. Federal and state grants accounted for 37 percent of local government revenue. State grants made up 87 percent of total local grants. Charges for hospital-related services, sewage and solid-waste management, public city university tuition, and airport services are important sources of general revenue for local governments.

Intergovernmental grants are important sources of revenue for both state and local governments. When economic times are good, such grants help states, cities, municipalities, and townships carry out their regular functions. However, during hard economic times, such as the Great Recession of 2007–2009, intergovernmental transfers provide much-needed fiscal relief as the revenue streams of state and local governments dry up. During the Great Recession, tax receipts dropped as business activities slowed, consumer spending dropped, and family incomes decreased due to layoffs or work-hour reductions. To offset the adverse effects of the recession on the states and local governments, federal grants increased by roughly 33 percent during this period.[15]

In 2009, President Obama signed the American Recovery and Reinvestment Act (ARRA), which provided immediate economic-crisis management assistance such as helping local and state economies ride out the Great Recession and shoring up the country's banking sector. A total of $274.7 billion in grants, contracts, and loans was allocated to state and local governments under the ARRA.[16] The bulk of the stimulus funds apportioned to state and local governments was used to create and protect existing jobs through public works projects and to fund various public welfare programs such as unemployment insurance.[17]

How are the revenues generated by our tax dollars, fees we pay to use public services and obtain licenses, and monies from other sources put to use by the different levels of government? A good starting point to gain insight on this question as it relates to the federal government is Article I, Section 8, of the Constitution. Recall, for instance, that the Constitution assigns the federal government various powers that allow it to affect the nation as a whole. A look at the federal budget in 2014 (Figure 3.6) shows that the three largest spending categories were Social Security (24 percent of the total budget); Medicare, Medicaid, the Children's Health Insurance Program, and marketplace subsidies under the Affordable Care Act (24 percent); and defense and international security assistance (18 percent). The rest was divided among categories such as safety net programs (11 percent), including the Earned Income Tax Credit and Child Tax Credit, unemployment insurance, food stamps, and other low-income assistance programs; interest on federal debt (7 percent); benefits for federal retirees and veterans (8 percent); and transportation infrastructure (3 percent).[18] It is clear from the 2014 federal budget that providing for the general welfare and national defense consumes much of the government's resources—not just its revenue, but also its administrative capacity and labor power.

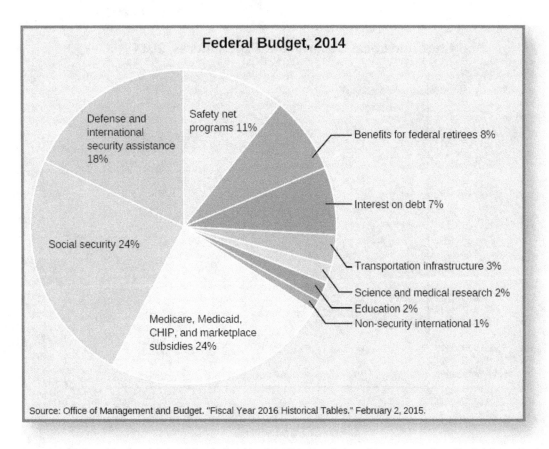

Federal Budget, 2014

- Defense and international security assistance 18%
- Safety net programs 11%
- Benefits for federal retirees 8%
- Interest on debt 7%
- Transportation infrastructure 3%
- Science and medical research 2%
- Education 2%
- Non-security international 1%
- Medicare, Medicaid, CHIP, and marketplace subsidies 24%
- Social security 24%

Source: Office of Management and Budget. "Fiscal Year 2016 Historical Tables." February 2, 2015.

Figure 3.6 Approximately two-thirds of the federal budget is spent in just three categories: Social Security, health care and health insurance programs, and defense.

Figure 3.7 compares recent spending activities of local and state governments. Educational expenditures constitute a major category for both. However, whereas the states spend comparatively more than local governments on university education, local governments spend even more on elementary and secondary education. That said, nationwide, state funding for public higher education has declined as a percentage of university revenues; this is primarily because states have taken in lower amounts of sales taxes as internet commerce has increased. Local governments allocate more funds to police protection, fire protection, housing and community development, and public utilities such as water, sewage, and electricity. And while state governments allocate comparatively more funds to public welfare programs, such as health care, income support, and highways, both local and state governments spend roughly similar amounts on judicial and legal services and correctional services.

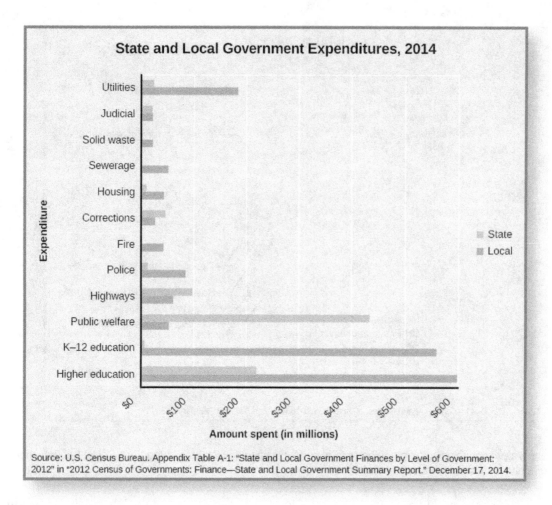

Figure 3.7   This list includes some of the largest expenditure items for state and local governments.

3.2 The Evolution of American Federalism

Learning Objectives

By the end of this section, you will be able to:

* Describe how federalism has evolved in the United States
* Compare different conceptions of federalism

The Constitution sketches a federal framework that aims to balance the forces of decentralized and centralized governance in general terms; it does not flesh out standard operating procedures that say precisely how the states and federal governments are to handle all policy contingencies imaginable. Therefore, officials at the state and national levels have had some room to maneuver as they operate within the Constitution's federal design. This has led to changes in the configuration of federalism over time, changes corresponding to different historical phases that capture distinct balances between state and federal authority.

THE STRUGGLE BETWEEN NATIONAL POWER AND STATE POWER

As George Washington's secretary of the treasury from 1789 to 1795, Alexander Hamilton championed legislative efforts to create a publicly chartered bank. For Hamilton, the establishment of the Bank of the United States was fully within Congress's authority, and he hoped the bank would foster economic development, print and circulate paper money, and provide loans to the government. Although Thomas Jefferson, Washington's secretary of state, staunchly opposed Hamilton's plan on the constitutional grounds that the national government had no authority to create such an instrument, Hamilton managed to convince the reluctant president to sign the legislation.[19]

When the bank's charter expired in 1811, Jeffersonian Democratic-Republicans prevailed in blocking its renewal. However, the fiscal hardships that plagued the government during the War of 1812, coupled with the fragility of the country's financial system, convinced Congress and then-president James Madison to create the Second Bank of the United States in 1816. Many states rejected the Second Bank, arguing that the national government was infringing upon the states' constitutional jurisdiction.

A political showdown between Maryland and the national government emerged when James McCulloch, an agent for the Baltimore branch of the Second Bank, refused to pay a tax that Maryland had imposed on all out-of-state chartered banks. The standoff raised two constitutional questions: Did Congress have the authority to charter a national bank? Were states allowed to tax federal property? In *McCulloch v. Maryland*, Chief Justice John Marshall (**Figure 3.8**) argued that Congress could create a national bank even though the Constitution did not expressly authorize it.[20] Under the necessary and proper clause of Article I, Section 8, the Supreme Court asserted that Congress could establish "all means which are appropriate" to fulfill "the legitimate ends" of the Constitution. In other words, the bank was an appropriate instrument that enabled the national government to carry out several of its enumerated powers, such as regulating interstate commerce, collecting taxes, and borrowing money.

Figure 3.8 Chief Justice John Marshall, shown here in a portrait by Henry Inman, was best known for the principle of judicial review established in *Marbury v. Madison* (1803), which reinforced the influence and independence of the judiciary branch of the U.S. government.

This ruling established the doctrine of implied powers, granting Congress a vast source of discretionary power to achieve its constitutional responsibilities. The Supreme Court also sided with the federal government on the issue of whether states could tax federal property. Under the supremacy clause of Article VI, legitimate national laws trump conflicting state laws. As the court observed, "the government of the Union, though limited in its powers, is supreme within its sphere of action and its laws, when made in pursuance of the constitution, form the supreme law of the land." Maryland's action violated national supremacy because "the power to tax is the power to destroy." This second ruling established the principle of national supremacy, which prohibits states from meddling in the lawful activities of the national government.

Defining the scope of national power was the subject of another landmark Supreme Court decision in 1824. In *Gibbons v. Ogden*, the court had to interpret the commerce clause of Article I, Section 8; specifically, it had to determine whether the federal government had the sole authority to regulate the licensing of steamboats operating between New York and New Jersey.[21] Aaron Ogden, who had obtained an exclusive license from New York State to operate steamboat ferries between New York City and New Jersey, sued Thomas Gibbons, who was operating ferries along the same route under a coasting license issued by the federal government. Gibbons lost in New York state courts and appealed. Chief Justice Marshall delivered a two-part ruling in favor of Gibbons that strengthened the power of the national government. First, interstate commerce was interpreted broadly to mean "commercial intercourse" among states, thus allowing Congress to regulate navigation. Second, because the federal Licensing Act of 1793, which regulated coastal commerce, was a constitutional exercise of Congress's authority under the commerce clause, federal law trumped the New York State license-monopoly law that had granted Ogden an exclusive steamboat operating license. As Marshall pointed out, "the acts of New York must yield to the law of Congress."[22]

Various states railed against the nationalization of power that had been going on since the late 1700s. When President John Adams signed the Sedition Act in 1798, which made it a crime to speak openly against the government, the Kentucky and Virginia legislatures passed resolutions declaring the act null on the grounds that they retained the discretion to follow national laws. In effect, these resolutions articulated the legal reasoning underpinning the doctrine of **nullification**—that states had the right to reject national laws they deemed unconstitutional.[23]

A nullification crisis emerged in the 1830s over President Andrew Jackson's tariff acts of 1828 and 1832. Led by John Calhoun, President Jackson's vice president, nullifiers argued that high tariffs on imported goods benefited northern manufacturing interests while disadvantaging economies in the South. South Carolina passed an Ordinance of Nullification declaring both tariff acts null and void and threatened to leave the Union. The federal government responded by enacting the Force Bill in 1833, authorizing President Jackson to use military force against states that challenged federal tariff laws. The prospect of military action coupled with the passage of the Compromise Tariff Act of 1833 (which lowered tariffs over time) led South Carolina to back off, ending the nullification crisis.

The ultimate showdown between national and state authority came during the Civil War. Prior to the conflict, in *Dred Scott v. Sandford*, the Supreme Court ruled that the national government lacked the authority to ban slavery in the territories.[24] But the election of President Abraham Lincoln in 1860 led eleven southern states to secede from the United States because they believed the new president would challenge the institution of slavery. What was initially a conflict to preserve the Union became a conflict to end slavery when Lincoln issued the Emancipation Proclamation in 1863, freeing all slaves in the rebellious states. The defeat of the South had a huge impact on the balance of power between the states and the national government in two important ways. First, the Union victory put an end to the right of states to secede and to challenge legitimate national laws. Second, Congress imposed several conditions for readmitting former Confederate states into the Union; among them was ratification of the Fourteenth and Fifteenth Amendments. In sum, after the Civil War the power balance shifted toward the national government, a movement that had begun several decades before with *McCulloch v. Maryland* (1819) and *Gibbons v. Odgen* (1824).

The period between 1819 and the 1860s demonstrated that the national government sought to establish its role within the newly created federal design, which in turn often provoked the states to resist as they sought to protect their interests. With the exception of the Civil War, the Supreme Court settled the power struggles between the states and national government. From a historical perspective, the national supremacy principle introduced during this period did not so much narrow the states' scope of constitutional authority as restrict their encroachment on national powers.[25]

DUAL FEDERALISM

The late 1870s ushered in a new phase in the evolution of U.S. federalism. Under **dual federalism**, the states and national government exercise exclusive authority in distinctly delineated spheres of jurisdiction. Like the layers of a cake, the levels of government do not blend with one another but rather are clearly defined. Two factors contributed to the emergence of this conception of federalism. First, several Supreme Court rulings blocked attempts by both state and federal governments to step outside their jurisdictional boundaries. Second, the prevailing economic philosophy at the time loathed government interference in the process of industrial development.

Industrialization changed the socioeconomic landscape of the United States. One of its adverse effects was the concentration of market power. Because there was no national regulatory supervision to ensure fairness in market practices, collusive behavior among powerful firms emerged in several industries.[26] To curtail widespread anticompetitive practices in the railroad industry, Congress passed the Interstate Commerce Act in 1887, which created the Interstate Commerce Commission. Three years later, national regulatory capacity was broadened by the Sherman Antitrust Act of 1890, which made it illegal to monopolize or attempt to monopolize and conspire in restraining commerce (Figure 03_02_Commerce). In the early stages of industrial capitalism, federal regulations were focused for the most part on promoting market competition rather than on addressing the social dislocations resulting from market operations, something the government began to tackle in the 1930s.[27]

(a)

(b)

Figure 3.9 *Puck*, a humor magazine published from 1871 to 1918, satirized political issues of the day such as federal attempts to regulate commerce and prevent monopolies. "'Will you walk into my parlor?' said the spider to the fly" (a) by Udo Keppler depicts a spider labeled "Interstate Commerce Commission" capturing a large fly in a web labeled "The Law" while "Plague take it! Why doesn't it stay down when I hit it?" (b), also drawn by Keppler, shows President William Howard Taft and his attorney general, George W. Wickersham, trying to beat a "Monopoly" into submission with a stick labeled "Sherman Law."

The new federal regulatory regime was dealt a legal blow early in its existence. In 1895, in *United States v. E. C. Knight*, the Supreme Court ruled that the national government lacked the authority to regulate manufacturing.[28] The case came about when the government, using its regulatory power under the Sherman Act, attempted to override American Sugar's purchase of four sugar refineries, which would give the company a commanding share of the industry. Distinguishing between commerce among states and the production of goods, the court argued that the national government's regulatory authority applied only to commercial activities. If manufacturing activities fell within the purview of the commerce clause of the Constitution, then "comparatively little of business operations would be left for state control," the court argued.

In the late 1800s, some states attempted to regulate working conditions. For example, New York State passed the Bakeshop Act in 1897, which prohibited bakery employees from working more than sixty hours in a week. In *Lochner v. New York*, the Supreme Court ruled this state regulation that capped work hours unconstitutional, on the grounds that it violated the due process clause of the Fourteenth Amendment.[29] In other words, the right to sell and buy labor is a "liberty of the individual" safeguarded by the Constitution, the court asserted. The federal government also took up the issue of working conditions, but that case resulted in the same outcome as in the *Lochner* case.[30]

COOPERATIVE FEDERALISM

The Great Depression of the 1930s brought economic hardships the nation had never witnessed before (Figure 3.10). Between 1929 and 1933, the national unemployment rate reached 25 percent, industrial output dropped by half, stock market assets lost more than half their value, thousands of banks went out of business, and the gross domestic product shrunk by one-quarter.[31] Given the magnitude of the economic depression, there was pressure on the national government to coordinate a robust national response along with the states.

Figure 3.10 A line outside a Chicago soup kitchen in 1931, in the midst of the Great Depression. The sign above reads "Free Soup, Coffee, and Doughnuts for the Unemployed."

Cooperative federalism was born of necessity and lasted well into the twentieth century as the national and state governments each found it beneficial. Under this model, both levels of government coordinated their actions to solve national problems, such as the Great Depression and the civil rights struggle of the following decades. In contrast to dual federalism, it erodes the jurisdictional boundaries between the states and national government, leading to a blending of layers as in a marble cake. The era of cooperative federalism contributed to the gradual incursion of national authority into the jurisdictional domain of the states, as well as the expansion of the national government's power in concurrent policy areas.[32]

The New Deal programs President Franklin D. Roosevelt proposed as a means to tackle the Great Depression ran afoul of the dual-federalism mindset of the justices on the Supreme Court in the 1930s. The court struck down key pillars of the New Deal—the National Industrial Recovery Act and the Agricultural Adjustment Act, for example—on the grounds that the federal government was operating in matters that were within the purview of the states. The court's obstructionist position infuriated Roosevelt, leading him in 1937 to propose a court-packing plan that would add one new justice for each one over the age of seventy, thus allowing the president to make a maximum of six new appointments. Before Congress took action on the proposal, the Supreme Court began leaning in support of the New Deal as Chief Justice Charles Evans Hughes and Justice Owen Roberts changed their view on federalism.[33]

In *National Labor Relations Board (NLRB) v. Jones and Laughlin Steel*,[34] for instance, the Supreme Court ruled the National Labor Relations Act of 1935 constitutional, asserting that Congress can use its authority under the commerce clause to regulate both manufacturing activities and labor-management relations. The New Deal changed the relationship Americans had with the national government. Before the Great Depression, the government offered little in terms of financial aid, social benefits, and economic rights. After the New Deal, it provided old-age pensions (Social Security), unemployment insurance, agricultural subsidies, protections for organizing in the workplace, and a variety of other public services created during Roosevelt's administration.

In the 1960s, President Lyndon Johnson's administration expanded the national government's role in society even more. Medicaid (which provides medical assistance to the indigent), Medicare (which provides health insurance to the elderly and disabled), and school nutrition programs were created. The Elementary and Secondary Education Act (1965), the Higher Education Act (1965), and the Head Start preschool program (1965) were established to expand educational opportunities and equality (Figure 3.11). The Clean Air Act (1965), the Highway Safety Act (1966), and the Fair Packaging and Labeling Act (1966) promoted environmental and consumer protection. Finally, laws were passed to promote urban renewal, public housing development, and affordable housing. In addition to these Great Society programs, the Civil Rights Act (1964) and the Voting Rights Act (1965) gave the federal government effective tools to promote civil rights equality across the country.

(a)

(b)

Figure 3.11 Lady Bird Johnson, the First Lady, reads to students enrolled in Head Start (a) at the Kemper School in Washington, DC, on March 19, 1966. President Obama visits a Head Start classroom (b) in Lawrence, Kansas, on January 22, 2015.

While the era of cooperative federalism witnessed a broadening of federal powers in concurrent and state policy domains, it is also the era of a deepening coordination between the states and the federal government in Washington. Nowhere is this clearer than with respect to the social welfare and social insurance programs created during the New Deal and Great Society eras, most of which are administered by both state and federal authorities and are jointly funded. The Social Security Act of 1935, which created federal subsidies for state-administered programs for the elderly; people with handicaps; dependent mothers; and children, gave state and local officials wide discretion over eligibility and benefit levels. The unemployment insurance program, also created by the Social Security Act, requires states to provide jobless benefits, but it allows them significant latitude to decide the level of tax to impose on businesses in order to fund the program as well as the duration and replacement rate of unemployment benefits. A similar multilevel division of labor governs Medicaid and Children's Health Insurance.[35]

Thus, the era of cooperative federalism left two lasting attributes on federalism in the United States.

First, a nationalization of politics emerged as a result of federal legislative activism aimed at addressing national problems such as marketplace inefficiencies, social and political inequality, and poverty. The nationalization process expanded the size of the federal administrative apparatus and increased the flow of federal grants to state and local authorities, which have helped offset the financial costs of maintaining a host of New Deal- and Great Society–era programs. The second lasting attribute is the flexibility that states and local authorities were given in the implementation of federal social welfare programs. One consequence of administrative flexibility, however, is that it has led to cross-state differences in the levels of benefits and coverage.[36]

NEW FEDERALISM

During the administrations of Presidents Richard Nixon (1969–1974) and Ronald Reagan (1981–1989), attempts were made to reverse the process of nationalization—that is, to restore states' prominence in policy areas into which the federal government had moved in the past. **New federalism** is premised on the idea that the decentralization of policies enhances administrative efficiency, reduces overall public spending, and improves policy outcomes. During Nixon's administration, **general revenue sharing** programs were created that distributed funds to the state and local governments with minimal restrictions on how the money was spent. The election of Ronald Reagan heralded the advent of a "devolution revolution" in U.S. federalism, in which the president pledged to return authority to the states according to the Constitution. In the Omnibus Budget Reconciliation Act of 1981, congressional leaders together with President Reagan consolidated numerous federal grant programs related to social welfare and reformulated them in order to give state and local administrators greater discretion in using federal funds.[37]

However, Reagan's track record in promoting new federalism was inconsistent. This was partly due to the fact that the president's devolution agenda met some opposition from Democrats in Congress, moderate Republicans, and interest groups, preventing him from making further advances on that front. For example, his efforts to completely devolve Aid to Families With Dependent Children (a New Deal-era program) and food stamps (a Great Society-era program) to the states were rejected by members of Congress, who feared states would underfund both programs, and by members of the National Governors' Association, who believed the proposal would be too costly for states. Reagan terminated general revenue sharing in 1986.[38]

Several Supreme Court rulings also promoted new federalism by hemming in the scope of the national government's power, especially under the commerce clause. For example, in *United States v. Lopez*, the court struck down the Gun-Free School Zones Act of 1990, which banned gun possession in school zones.[39] It argued that the regulation in question did not "substantively affect interstate commerce." The ruling ended a nearly sixty-year period in which the court had used a broad interpretation of the commerce clause that by the 1960s allowed it to regulate numerous local commercial activities.[40]

However, many would say that the years since the 9/11 attacks have swung the pendulum back in the direction of central federal power. The creation of the Department of Homeland Security federalized disaster response power in Washington, and the Transportation Security Administration was created to federalize airport security. Broad new federal policies and mandates have also been carried out in the form of the Faith-Based Initiative and No Child Left Behind (during the George W. Bush administration) and the Affordable Care Act (during Barack Obama's administration).

Finding a Middle Ground

Cooperative Federalism versus New Federalism

Morton Grodzins coined the cake analogy of federalism in the 1950s while conducting research on the evolution of American federalism. Until then most scholars had thought of federalism as a layer cake, but according to Grodzins the 1930s ushered in "marble-cake federalism" (Figure 3.12): "The American form of government is often, but erroneously, symbolized by a three-layer cake. A far more accurate image is the rainbow or marble cake, characterized by an inseparable mingling of differently colored ingredients, the colors appearing in vertical and diagonal strands and unexpected whirls. As colors are mixed in the marble cake, so functions are mixed in the American federal system."[41]

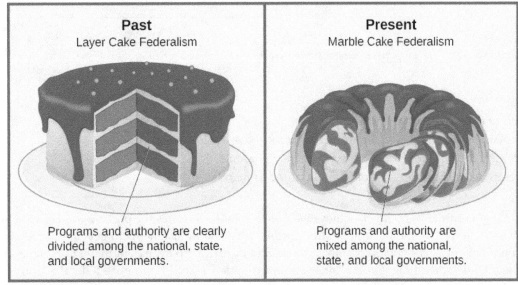

Figure 3.12 Morton Grodzins, a professor of political science at the University of Chicago, coined the expression "marble-cake federalism" in the 1950s to explain the evolution of federalism in the United States.

Cooperative federalism has several merits:

- Because state and local governments have varying fiscal capacities, the national government's involvement in state activities such as education, health, and social welfare is necessary to ensure some degree of uniformity in the provision of public services to citizens in richer and poorer states.

- The problem of collective action, which dissuades state and local authorities from raising regulatory standards for fear they will be disadvantaged as others lower theirs, is resolved by requiring state and local authorities to meet minimum federal standards (e.g., minimum wage and air quality).

- Federal assistance is necessary to ensure state and local programs that generate positive externalities are maintained. For example, one state's environmental regulations impose higher fuel prices on its residents, but the externality of the cleaner air they produce benefits neighboring states. Without the federal government's support, this state and others like it would underfund such programs.

New federalism has advantages as well:

- Because of differences among states, one-size-fits-all features of federal laws are suboptimal. Decentralization accommodates the diversity that exists across states.

- By virtue of being closer to citizens, state and local authorities are better than federal agencies at discerning the public's needs.

- Decentralized federalism fosters a marketplace of innovative policy ideas as states compete against each other to minimize administrative costs and maximize policy output.

Which model of federalism do you think works best for the United States? Why?

Link to Learning

The leading international journal devoted to the practical and theoretical study of federalism is called *Publius: The Journal of Federalism (https://www.openstax.org/l/29publius)* . Find out where its name comes from.

3.3 Intergovernmental Relationships

Learning Objectives

By the end of this section, you will be able to:
- Explain how federal intergovernmental grants have evolved over time
- Identify the types of federal intergovernmental grants
- Describe the characteristics of federal unfunded mandates

The national government's ability to achieve its objectives often requires the participation of state and local governments. Intergovernmental grants offer positive financial inducements to get states to work toward selected national goals. A grant is commonly likened to a "carrot" to the extent that it is designed to entice the recipient to do something. On the other hand, unfunded mandates impose federal requirements on state and local authorities. Mandates are typically backed by the threat of penalties for non-compliance and provide little to no compensation for the costs of implementation. Thus, given its coercive nature, a mandate is commonly likened to a "stick."

GRANTS

The national government has used grants to influence state actions as far back as the Articles of Confederation when it provided states with land grants. In the first half of the 1800s, land grants were the primary means by which the federal government supported the states. Millions of acres of federal land were donated to support road, railroad, bridge, and canal construction projects, all of which were instrumental in piecing together a national transportation system to facilitate migration, interstate commerce, postal mail service, and movement of military people and equipment. Numerous universities and colleges across the country, such as Ohio State University and the University of Maine, are land-grant institutions because their campuses were built on land donated by the federal government. At the turn of the twentieth century, cash grants replaced land grants as the main form of federal intergovernmental transfers and have become a central part of modern federalism.[42]

Federal cash grants do come with strings attached; the national government has an interest in seeing that public monies are used for policy activities that advance national objectives. **Categorical grants** are federal transfers formulated to limit recipients' discretion in the use of funds and subject them to strict administrative criteria that guide project selection, performance, and financial oversight, among other things. These grants also often require some commitment of matching funds. Medicaid and the food stamp program are examples of categorical grants. **Block grants** come with less stringent federal administrative conditions and provide recipients more flexibility over how to spend grant funds. Examples of block grants include the Workforce Investment Act program, which provides state and local agencies money to help youths and adults obtain skill sets that will lead to better-paying jobs, and the Surface Transportation Program, which helps state and local governments maintain and improve highways, bridges, tunnels, sidewalks, and bicycle paths. Finally, recipients of general revenue sharing faced the least restrictions on the use of federal grants. From 1972 to 1986, when revenue sharing was abolished, upwards of $85 billion of federal money was distributed to states, cities, counties, towns, and villages.[43]

During the 1960s and 1970s, funding for federal grants grew significantly, as the trend line shows in Figure 3.13. Growth picked up again in the 1990s and 2000s. The upward slope since the 1990s is primarily due to the increase in federal grant money going to Medicaid. Federally funded health-care programs jumped from $43.8 billion in 1990 to $320 billion in 2014.[44] Health-related grant programs such as Medicaid and the Children's Health Insurance Program (CHIP) represented more than half of total federal grant expenses.

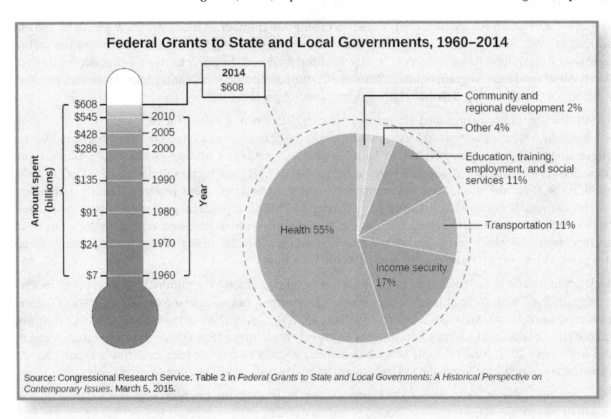

Source: Congressional Research Service. Table 2 in *Federal Grants to State and Local Governments: A Historical Perspective on Contemporary Issues*. March 5, 2015.

Figure 3.13 As the thermometer shows, federal grants to state and local governments have steadily increased since the 1960s. The pie chart shows how federal grants are allocated among different functional categories today.

Link to Learning

The federal government uses grants and other tools to achieve its national policy priorities. Take a look at the National Priorities Project (https://www.openstax.org/l/29natpriproj) to find out more.

The national government has greatly preferred using categorical grants to transfer funds to state and local authorities because this type of grant gives them more control and discretion in how the money is spent. In 2014, the federal government distributed 1,099 grants, 1,078 of which were categorical, while only 21 were block grants.[45] In response to the terrorist attack on the United States on September 11, 2001, more than a dozen new federal grant programs relating to homeland security were created, but as of 2011, only three were block grants.

There are a couple of reasons that categorical grants are more popular than block grants despite calls to decentralize public policy. One reason is that elected officials who sponsor these grants can take credit for their positive outcomes (e.g., clean rivers, better-performing schools, healthier children, a secure homeland) since elected officials, not state officials, formulate the administrative standards that lead to the results. Another reason is that categorical grants afford federal officials greater command over grant program performance. A common criticism leveled against block grants is that they lack mechanisms to hold state and local administrators accountable for outcomes, a reproach the Obama administration made about the Community Services Block Grant program. Finally, once categorical grants have been established, vested interests in Congress and the federal bureaucracy seek to preserve them. The legislators who enact them and the federal agencies that implement them invest heavily in defending them, ensuring their continuation.[46]

Reagan's "devolution revolution" contributed to raising the number of block grants from six in 1981 to fourteen in 1989. Block grants increased to twenty-four in 1999 during the Clinton administration and to twenty-six during Obama's presidency, but by 2014 the total had dropped to twenty-one, accounting for 10 percent of total federal grant outlay.[47] President Trump proposed eliminating four discretionary block grants in his "skinny" budget, although the budget was not passed.

In 1994, the Republican-controlled Congress passed legislation that called for block-granting Medicaid, which would have capped federal Medicaid spending. President Clinton vetoed the legislation. However, congressional efforts to convert Aid to Families with Dependent Children (AFDC) to a block grant succeeded. The Temporary Assistance for Needy Families (TANF) block grant replaced the AFDC in 1996, marking the first time the federal government transformed an entitlement program (which guarantees individual rights to benefits) into a block grant. Under the AFDC, the federal government had reimbursed states a portion of the costs they bore for running the program without placing a ceiling on the amount. In contrast, the TANF block grant caps annual federal funding at $16.489 billion and provides a yearly lump sum to each state, which it can use to manage its own program.

Block grants have been championed for their cost-cutting effects. By eliminating uncapped federal funding, as the TANF issue illustrates, the national government can reverse the escalating costs of federal grant programs. This point was not lost on Paul Ryan (R-WI), former chair of the House Budget Committee and the House Ways and Means Committee, who, during his tenure as Speaker of the House from October 2015 to January 2019, tried multiple times but without success to convert Medicaid into a block grant, a reform he estimated could save the federal government upwards of $732 billion over ten years.[48]

Another noteworthy characteristic of block grants is that their flexibility has been undermined over time as a result of **creeping categorization**, a process in which the national government places new administrative requirements on state and local governments or supplants block grants with new categorical grants.[49] Among the more common measures used to restrict block grants' programmatic flexibility are set-asides (i.e., requiring a certain share of grant funds to be designated for a specific purpose) and cost ceilings (i.e., placing a cap on funding other purposes).

UNFUNDED MANDATES

Unfunded mandates are federal laws and regulations that impose obligations on state and local governments without fully compensating them for the administrative costs they incur. The federal government has used mandates increasingly since the 1960s to promote national objectives in policy areas such as the environment, civil rights, education, and homeland security. One type of mandate threatens civil and criminal penalties for state and local authorities that fail to comply with them across the board in all programs, while another provides for the suspension of federal grant money if the mandate is not followed. These types of mandates are commonly referred to as *crosscutting* mandates. Failure to fully comply with crosscutting mandates can result in punishments that normally include reduction of or suspension of federal grants, prosecution of officials, fines, or some combination of these penalties. If only one requirement is not met, state or local governments may not get any money at all.

For example, Title VI of the Civil Rights Act of 1964 authorizes the federal government to withhold federal grants as well as file lawsuits against state and local officials for practicing racial discrimination. Finally, some mandates come in the form of partial preemption regulations, whereby the federal government sets national regulatory standards but delegates the enforcement to state and local governments. For example, the Clean Air Act sets air quality regulations but instructs states to design implementation plans to achieve such standards (Figure 3.14).[50]

Figure 3.14 The Clean Air Act is an example of an unfunded mandate. The Environmental Protection Agency sets federal standards regarding air and water quality, but it is up to each state to implement plans to achieve these standards.

The widespread use of federal mandates in the 1970s and 1980s provoked a backlash among state and local authorities, which culminated in the Unfunded Mandates Reform Act (UMRA) in 1995. The UMRA's main objective has been to restrain the national government's use of mandates by subjecting rules that impose unfunded requirements on state and local governments to greater procedural scrutiny. However, since the act's implementation, states and local authorities have obtained limited relief. A new piece of legislation aims to take this approach further. The 2017 Unfunded Mandates and Information Transparency Act, HR 50, passed the House in July 2018 before being referred to the Senate, where in December it was placed on the legislative calendar.[51]

The number of mandates has continued to rise, and some have been especially costly to states and local authorities. Consider the Real ID Act of 2005, a federal law designed to beef up homeland security. The law requires driver's licenses and state-issued identification cards (DL/IDs) to contain standardized anti-fraud security features, specific data, and machine-readable technology. It also requires states to verify the identity of everyone being reissued DL/IDs. The Department of Homeland Security announced a phased enforcement of the law in 2013, which required individuals to present compliant DL/IDs to board commercial airlines starting in 2016. The cost to states of re-issuing DL/IDs, implementing new identity verification procedures, and redesigning DL/IDs is estimated to be $11 billion, and the federal government stands to reimburse only a small fraction.[52] Compliance with the federal law has been onerous for many states; numerous extensions to states have been granted since 2016 and only thirty-eight were in full compliance with Real ID as of December 2018.[53]

The continued use of unfunded mandates clearly contradicts new federalism's call for giving states and local governments more flexibility in carrying out national goals. The temptation to use them appears to be difficult for the federal government to resist, however, as the UMRA's poor track record illustrates. This is because mandates allow the federal government to fulfill its national priorities while passing most of the cost to the states, an especially attractive strategy for national lawmakers trying to cut federal spending.[54] Some leading federalism scholars have used the term *coercive federalism* to capture this aspect of contemporary U.S. federalism.[55] In other words, Washington has been as likely to use the stick of mandates as the carrot of grants to accomplish its national objectives. As a result, there have been more instances of confrontational interactions between the states and the federal government.

Milestone

The Clery Act

The Clery Act of 1990, formally the Jeanne Clery Disclosure of Campus Security Policy and Campus Crime Statistics Act, requires public and private colleges and universities that participate in federal student aid programs to disclose information about campus crime. The Act is named after Jeanne Clery, who in 1986 was raped and murdered by a fellow student in her Lehigh University dorm room.

The U.S. Department of Education's Clery Act Compliance Division is responsible for enforcing the 1990 Act. Specifically, to remain eligible for federal financial aid funds and avoid penalties, colleges and universities must comply with the following provisions:

- Publish an annual security report and make it available to current and prospective students and employees;
- Keep a public crime log that documents each crime on campus and is accessible to the public;
- Disclose information about incidents of criminal homicide, sex offenses, robbery, aggravated assault, burglary, motor vehicle theft, arson, and hate crimes that occurred on or near campus;
- Issue warnings about Clery Act crimes that pose a threat to students and employees;
- Develop a campus community emergency response and notification strategy that is subject to annual testing;
- Gather and report fire data to the federal government and publish an annual fire safety report;
- Devise procedures to address reports of missing students living in on-campus housing.

For more about the Clery Act, see Clery Center for Security on Campus, http://clerycenter.org.

Were you made aware of your campus's annual security report before you enrolled? Do you think reporting about campus security is appropriately regulated at the federal level under the Clery Act? Why or why not?

3.4 Competitive Federalism Today

Learning Objectives

By the end of this section, you will be able to:
- Explain the dynamic of competitive federalism
- Analyze some issues over which the states and federal government have contended

Certain functions clearly belong to the federal government, the state governments, and local governments. National security is a federal matter, the issuance of licenses is a state matter, and garbage collection is a local matter. One aspect of competitive federalism today is that some policy issues, such as immigration and the marital rights of gays and lesbians, have been redefined as the roles that states and the federal government play in them have changed. Another aspect of competitive federalism is that interest groups seeking to change the status quo can take a policy issue up to the federal government or down to the states if they feel it is to their advantage. Interest groups have used this strategy to promote their views on such issues as abortion, gun control, and the legal drinking age.

CONTENDING ISSUES

Immigration and marriage equality have not been the subject of much contention between states and the federal government until recent decades. Before that, it was understood that the federal government handled immigration and states determined the legality of same-sex marriage. This understanding of exclusive responsibilities has changed; today both levels of government play roles in these two policy areas.

Immigration federalism describes the gradual movement of states into the immigration policy domain.[56] Since the late 1990s, states have asserted a right to make immigration policy on the grounds that they are enforcing, not supplanting, the nation's immigration laws, and they are exercising their jurisdictional authority by restricting illegal immigrants' access to education, health care, and welfare benefits, areas that fall under the states' responsibilities. In 2005, twenty-five states had enacted a total of thirty-nine laws related to immigration; by 2014, forty-three states and Washington, DC, had passed a total of 288 immigration-related laws and resolutions.[57]

Arizona has been one of the states at the forefront of immigration federalism. In 2010, it passed Senate Bill 1070, which sought to make it so difficult for illegal immigrants to live in the state that they would return to their native country, a strategy referred to as "attrition by enforcement."[58] The federal government filed suit to block the Arizona law, contending that it conflicted with federal immigration laws. Arizona's law has also divided society, because some groups, like the Tea Party movement, have supported its tough stance against illegal immigrants, while other groups have opposed it for humanitarian and human-rights reasons (Figure 3.15). According to a poll of Latino voters in the state by Arizona State University researchers, 81 percent opposed this bill.[59]

(a)   (b)

Figure 3.15 Tea Party members in St. Paul, Minnesota, protest amnesty and illegal immigration on November 14, 2009 (a). Following the adoption of Senate Bill 1070 in Arizona, which took a tough stance on illegal immigration, supporters of immigration reform demonstrated across the country in opposition to the bill, including in Lafayette Park (b), located across the street from the White House in Washington, DC. (credit a: modification of work by "Fibonacci Blue"/Flickr; credit b: modification of work by Nevele Otseog)

In 2012, in *Arizona v. United States*, the Supreme Court affirmed federal supremacy on immigration.[60] The court struck down three of the four central provisions of the Arizona law—namely, those allowing police officers to arrest an undocumented immigrant without a warrant if they had probable cause to think he or she had committed a crime that could lead to deportation, making it a crime to seek a job without proper immigration papers, and making it a crime to be in Arizona without valid immigration papers. The court upheld the "show me your papers" provision, which authorizes police officers to check the immigration status of anyone they stop or arrest who they suspect is an illegal immigrant.[61] However, in letting this provision stand, the court warned Arizona and other states with similar laws that they could face civil rights lawsuits if police officers applied it based on racial profiling.[62] All in all, Justice Anthony Kennedy's opinion embraced an expansive view of the U.S. government's authority to regulate immigration and aliens, describing it as broad and undoubted. That authority derived from the legislative power of Congress to "establish a uniform Rule of Naturalization," enumerated in the Constitution.

Link to Learning

Arizona's Senate Bill 1070 has been the subject of heated debate. Read the **views of proponents and opponents (https://www.openstax.org/l/29azimmigbill)** of the law.

Marital rights for gays and lesbians have also significantly changed in recent years. By passing the Defense of Marriage Act (DOMA) in 1996, the federal government stepped into this policy issue. Not only did DOMA allow states to choose whether to recognize same-sex marriages, it also defined marriage as a union between a man and a woman, which meant that same-sex couples were denied various federal provisions and benefits—such as the right to file joint tax returns and receive Social Security survivor benefits. In 1997, more than half the states in the union had passed some form of legislation banning same-sex marriage. By 2006, two years after Massachusetts became the first state to recognize marriage equality, twenty-seven states had passed constitutional bans on same-sex marriage. In *United States v. Windsor*, the Supreme Court changed the dynamic established by DOMA by ruling that the federal government had no authority to define marriage. The Court held that states possess the "historic and essential authority to define the marital relation," and that the federal government's involvement in this area "departs from this history and tradition of reliance on state law to define marriage."[63]

Insider Perspective

Edith Windsor: Icon of the Marriage Equality Movement

Edith Windsor, the plaintiff in the landmark Supreme Court case *United States v. Windsor*, has become an icon of the marriage equality movement for her successful effort to force repeal the DOMA provision that denied married same-sex couples a host of federal provisions and protections. In 2007, after having lived together since the late 1960s, Windsor and her partner Thea Spyer were married in Canada, where same-sex marriage was legal. After Spyer died in 2009, Windsor received a $363,053 federal tax bill on the estate Spyer had left her. Because her marriage was not valid under federal law, her request for the estate-tax exemption that applies to surviving spouses was denied. With the counsel of her lawyer, Roberta Kaplan, Windsor sued the federal government and won (Figure 3.16).

Figure 3.16   With her client Edith Windsor looking on, attorney Roberta Kaplan speaks to the crowd at the site of the 1969 Stonewall Riots, a historic landmark in the movement for LGBT rights. (credit: "Boss Tweed" /Flickr)

Because of the *Windsor* decision, federal laws could no longer discriminate against same-sex married couples. What is more, marriage equality became a reality in a growing number of states as federal court after federal court overturned state constitutional bans on same-sex marriage. The *Windsor* case gave federal judges the moment of clarity from the U.S. Supreme Court that they needed. James Esseks, director of the American Civil Liberties Union's (ACLU) Lesbian Gay Bisexual Transgender & AIDS Project, summarizes the significance of the case as follows: "Part of what's gotten us to this exciting moment in American culture is not just Edie's lawsuit but the story of her life. The love at the core of that story, as well as the injustice at its end, is part of what has moved America on this issue so profoundly."[64] In the final analysis, same-sex marriage is a protected constitutional right as decided by the U.S. Supreme Court, which took up the issue again when it heard *Obergefell v. Hodges* in 2015.

What role do you feel the story of Edith Windsor played in reframing the debate over same-sex marriage? How do you think it changed the federal government's view of its role in legislation regarding same-sex marriage relative to the role of the states?

Following the *Windsor* decision, the number of states that recognized same-sex marriages increased rapidly, as illustrated in Figure 3.17. In 2015, marriage equality was recognized in thirty-six states plus Washington, DC, up from seventeen in 2013. The diffusion of marriage equality across states was driven in large part by federal district and appeals courts, which have used the rationale underpinning the *Windsor* case (i.e., laws cannot discriminate between same-sex and opposite-sex couples based on the equal protection clause of the Fourteenth Amendment) to invalidate state bans on same-sex marriage. The 2014 court decision not to hear a collection of cases from four different states essentially affirmed same-sex marriage in thirty states. And in 2015 the Supreme Court gave same-sex marriage a constitutional basis of right nationwide in *Obergefell v. Hodges*. In sum, as the immigration and marriage equality examples illustrate, constitutional disputes have arisen as states and the federal government have sought to reposition themselves on certain policy issues, disputes that the federal courts have had to sort out.

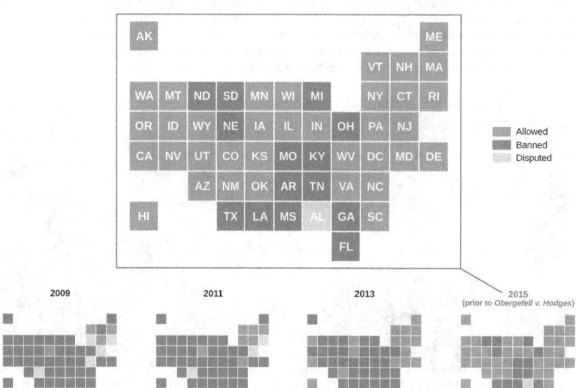

Figure 3.17 The number of states that practiced marriage equality gradually increased between 2008 and 2015, with the fastest increase occurring between *United States v. Windsor* in 2013 and *Obergefell v. Hodges* in 2015.

STRATEGIZING ABOUT NEW ISSUES

Mothers Against Drunk Driving (MADD) was established in 1980 by a woman whose thirteen-year-old daughter had been killed by a drunk driver. The organization lobbied state legislators to raise the drinking age and impose tougher penalties, but without success. States with lower drinking ages had an economic interest in maintaining them because they lured youths from neighboring states with restricted consumption laws. So MADD decided to redirect its lobbying efforts at Congress, hoping to find sympathetic representatives willing to take action. In 1984, the federal government passed the National Minimum Drinking Age Act (NMDAA), a crosscutting mandate that gradually reduced federal highway grant money to any state that failed to increase the legal age for alcohol purchase and possession to twenty-one. After losing a legal battle against the NMDAA, all states were in compliance by 1988.[65]

By creating two institutional access points—the federal and state governments—the U.S. federal system enables interest groups such as MADD to strategize about how best to achieve their policy objectives. The term **venue shopping** refers to a strategy in which interest groups select the level and branch of government (legislature, judiciary, or executive) they calculate will be most advantageous for them.[66] If one institutional venue proves unreceptive to an advocacy group's policy goal, as state legislators were to MADD, the group will attempt to steer its issue to a more responsive venue.

The strategy anti-abortion advocates have used in recent years is another example of venue shopping. In their attempts to limit abortion rights in the wake of the 1973 *Roe v. Wade* Supreme Court decision making abortion legal nationwide, anti-abortion advocates initially targeted Congress in hopes of obtaining restrictive legislation.[67] Lack of progress at the national level prompted them to shift their focus to state legislators, where their advocacy efforts have been more successful. By 2015, for example, thirty-eight states required some form of parental involvement in a minor's decision to have an abortion, forty-six states allowed individual health-care providers to refuse to participate in abortions, and thirty-two states prohibited the use of public funds to carry out an abortion except when the woman's life is in danger or the pregnancy is the result of rape or incest. While 31 percent of U.S. women of childbearing age resided in one of the thirteen states that had passed restrictive abortion laws in 2000, by 2013, about 56 percent of such women resided in one of the twenty-seven states where abortion is restricted.[68]

3.5 Advantages and Disadvantages of Federalism

Learning Objectives

By the end of this section, you will be able to:
- Discuss the advantages of federalism
- Explain the disadvantages of federalism

The federal design of our Constitution has had a profound effect on U.S. politics. Several positive and negative attributes of federalism have manifested themselves in the U.S. political system.

THE BENEFITS OF FEDERALISM

Among the merits of federalism are that it promotes policy innovation and political participation and accommodates diversity of opinion. On the subject of policy innovation, Supreme Court Justice Louis Brandeis observed in 1932 that "a single courageous state may, if its citizens choose, serve as a laboratory; and try novel social and economic experiments without risk to the rest of the country."[69] What Brandeis meant was that states could harness their constitutional authority to engage in policy innovations that might eventually be diffused to other states and at the national level. For example, a number of New Deal breakthroughs, such as child labor laws, were inspired by state policies. Prior to the passage of the Nineteenth Amendment, several states had already granted women the right to vote. California has led the way in establishing standards for fuel emissions and other environmental policies (Figure 3.18). Recently, the health insurance exchanges run by Connecticut, Kentucky, Rhode Island, and Washington have served as models for other states seeking to improve the performance of their exchanges.[70]

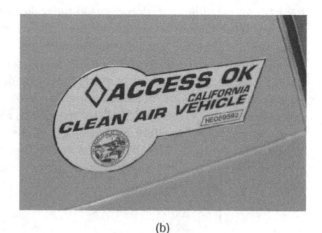

(a)   (b)

Figure 3.18 The California Air Resources Board was established in 1967, before passage of the federal Clean Air Act. The federal Environmental Protection Agency has adopted California emissions standards nationally, starting with the 2016 model year, and is working with California regulators to establish stricter national emissions standards going forward.(credit a: modification of work by Antti T. Nissinen; credit b: modification of work by Marcin Wichary)

Another advantage of federalism is that because our federal system creates two levels of government with the capacity to take action, failure to attain a desired policy goal at one level can be offset by successfully securing the support of elected representatives at another level. Thus, individuals, groups, and social movements are encouraged to actively participate and help shape public policy.

Get Connected!

Federalism and Political Office

Thinking of running for elected office? Well, you have several options. As Table 3.1 shows, there are a total of 510,682 elected offices at the federal, state, and local levels. Elected representatives in municipal and township governments account for a little more than half the total number of elected officials in the United States. Political careers rarely start at the national level. In fact, a very small share of politicians at the subnational level transition to the national stage as representatives, senators, vice presidents, or presidents.

Elected Officials at the Federal, State, and Local Levels

	Number of Elective Bodies	Number of Elected Officials
Federal Government	1	
Executive branch		2
U.S. Senate		100
U.S. House of Representatives		435
State Government	50	
State legislatures		7,382
Statewide offices		1,036
State boards		1,331
Local Government		
County governments	3,034	58,818
Municipal governments	19,429	135,531
Town governments	16,504	126,958
School districts	13,506	95,000
Special districts	35,052	84,089
Total	**87,576**	**510,682**

Table 3.1 This table lists the number of elected bodies and elected officials at the federal, state, and local levels.[71]

If you are interested in serving the public as an elected official, there are more opportunities to do so at the local and state levels than at the national level. As an added incentive for setting your sights at the subnational stage, consider the following. Whereas only 28 percent of U.S. adults trusted Congress in 2014, about 62 percent trusted their state governments and 72 percent had confidence in their local governments.[72]

If you ran for public office, what problems would you most want to solve? What level of government would best enable you to solve them, and why?

The system of checks and balances in our political system often prevents the federal government from imposing uniform policies across the country. As a result, states and local communities have the latitude to address policy issues based on the specific needs and interests of their citizens. The diversity of public viewpoints across states is manifested by differences in the way states handle access to abortion, distribution of alcohol, gun control, and social welfare benefits, for example.

THE DRAWBACKS OF FEDERALISM

Federalism also comes with drawbacks. Chief among them are economic disparities across states, **race-to-the-bottom** dynamics (i.e., states compete to attract business by lowering taxes and regulations), and the difficulty of taking action on issues of national importance.

Stark economic differences across states have a profound effect on the well-being of citizens. For example, in 2017, Maryland had the highest median household income ($80,776), while West Virginia had the lowest ($43,469).[73] There are also huge disparities in school funding across states. In 2016, New York spent $22,366 per student for elementary and secondary education, while Utah spent $6,953.[74] Furthermore, health-care access, costs, and quality vary greatly across states.[75] Proponents of social justice contend that federalism has tended to obstruct national efforts to effectively even out these disparities.

Link to Learning

The National Education Association discusses the problem of inequality in the educational system of the United States. Read its proposed solution (https://www.openstax.org/l/29equalityedu) and decide whether you agree.

The economic strategy of using race-to-the-bottom tactics in order to compete with other states in attracting new business growth also carries a social cost. For example, workers' safety and pay can suffer as workplace regulations are lifted, and the reduction in payroll taxes for employers has led a number of states to end up with underfunded unemployment insurance programs.[76] As of January 2019, fourteen states have also opted not to expand Medicaid, as encouraged by the Patient Protection and Affordable Care Act in 2010, for fear it will raise state public spending and increase employers' cost of employee benefits, despite provisions that the federal government will pick up nearly all cost of the expansion.[77] More than half of these states are in the South.

The federal design of our Constitution and the system of checks and balances has jeopardized or outright blocked federal responses to important national issues. President Roosevelt's efforts to combat the scourge of the Great Depression were initially struck down by the Supreme Court. More recently, President Obama's effort to make health insurance accessible to more Americans under the Affordable Care Act immediately ran into legal challenges[78] from some states, but it has been supported by the Supreme Court so far. However, the federal government's ability to defend the voting rights of citizens suffered a major setback when the Supreme Court in 2013 struck down a key provision of the Voting Rights Act of 1965.[79] No longer are the nine states with histories of racial discrimination in their voting processes required to submit plans for changes to the federal government for approval.

Key Terms

bill of attainder a legislative action declaring someone guilty without a trial; prohibited under the Constitution

block grant a type of grant that comes with less stringent federal administrative conditions and provide recipients more latitude over how to spend grant funds

categorical grant a federal transfer formulated to limit recipients' discretion in the use of funds and subject them to strict administrative criteria

concurrent powers shared state and federal powers that range from taxing, borrowing, and making and enforcing laws to establishing court systems

cooperative federalism a style of federalism in which both levels of government coordinate their actions to solve national problems, leading to the blending of layers as in a marble cake

creeping categorization a process in which the national government attaches new administrative requirements to block grants or supplants them with new categorical grants

devolution a process in which powers from the central government in a unitary system are delegated to subnational units

dual federalism a style of federalism in which the states and national government exercise exclusive authority in distinctly delineated spheres of jurisdiction, creating a layer-cake view of federalism

elastic clause the last clause of Article I, Section 8, which enables the national government "to make all Laws which shall be necessary and proper for carrying" out all its constitutional responsibilities

ex post facto law a law that criminalizes an act retroactively; prohibited under the Constitution

federalism an institutional arrangement that creates two relatively autonomous levels of government, each possessing the capacity to act directly on the people with authority granted by the national constitution

full faith and credit clause found in Article IV, Section 1, of the Constitution, this clause requires states to accept court decisions, public acts, and contracts of other states; also referred to as the comity provision

general revenue sharing a type of federal grant that places minimal restrictions on how state and local governments spend the money

immigration federalism the gradual movement of states into the immigration policy domain traditionally handled by the federal government

new federalism a style of federalism premised on the idea that the decentralization of policies enhances administrative efficiency, reduces overall public spending, and improves outcomes

nullification a doctrine promoted by John Calhoun of South Carolina in the 1830s, asserting that if a state deems a federal law unconstitutional, it can nullify it within its borders

privileges and immunities clause found in Article IV, Section 2, of the Constitution, this clause prohibits states from discriminating against out-of-staters by denying such guarantees as access to courts, legal protection, and property and travel rights

race-to-the-bottom a dynamic in which states compete to attract business by lowering taxes and regulations, often to workers' detriment

unfunded mandates federal laws and regulations that impose obligations on state and local governments without fully compensating them for the costs of implementation

unitary system a centralized system of government in which the subnational government is dependent on the central government, where substantial authority is concentrated

venue shopping a strategy in which interest groups select the level and branch of government they calculate will be most receptive to their policy goals

writ of habeas corpus a petition that enables someone in custody to petition a judge to determine whether that person's detention is legal

Summary

3.1 The Division of Powers
Federalism is a system of government that creates two relatively autonomous levels of government, each possessing authority granted to them by the national constitution. Federal systems like the one in the United States are different from unitary systems, which concentrate authority in the national government, and from confederations, which concentrate authority in subnational governments.

The U.S. Constitution allocates powers to the states and federal government, structures the relationship between these two levels of government, and guides state-to-state relationships. Federal, state, and local governments rely on different sources of revenue to enable them to fulfill their public responsibilities.

3.2 The Evolution of American Federalism
Federalism in the United States has gone through several phases of evolution during which the relationship between the federal and state governments has varied. In the era of dual federalism, both levels of government stayed within their own jurisdictional spheres. During the era of cooperative federalism, the federal government became active in policy areas previously handled by the states. The 1970s ushered in an era of new federalism and attempts to decentralize policy management.

3.3 Intergovernmental Relationships
To accomplish its policy priorities, the federal government often needs to elicit the cooperation of states and local governments, using various strategies. Block and categorical grants provide money to lower government levels to subsidize the cost of implementing policy programs fashioned in part by the federal government. This strategy gives state and local authorities some degree of flexibility and discretion as they coordinate with the federal government. On the other hand, mandate compels state and local governments to abide by federal laws and regulations or face penalties.

3.4 Competitive Federalism Today
Some policy areas have been redefined as a result of changes in the roles that states and the federal government play in them. The constitutional disputes these changes often trigger have had to be sorted out by the Supreme Court. Contemporary federalism has also witnessed interest groups engaging in venue shopping. Aware of the multiple access points to our political system, such groups seek to access the level of government they deem will be most receptive to their policy views.

3.5 Advantages and Disadvantages of Federalism
The benefits of federalism are that it can encourage political participation, give states an incentive to engage in policy innovation, and accommodate diverse viewpoints across the country. The disadvantages are that it can set off a race to the bottom among states, cause cross-state economic and social disparities, and obstruct federal efforts to address national problems.

Review Questions

1. Which statement about federal and unitary systems is most accurate?

   a. In a federal system, power is concentrated in the states; in a unitary system, it is concentrated in the national government.

   b. In a federal system, the constitution allocates powers between states and federal government; in a unitary system, powers are lodged in the national government.

   c. Today there are more countries with federal systems than with unitary systems.

   d. The United States and Japan have federal systems, while Great Britain and Canada have unitary systems.

2. Which statement is most accurate about the sources of revenue for local and state governments?

   a. Taxes generate well over one-half the total revenue of local and state governments.

   b. Property taxes generate the most tax revenue for both local and state governments.

   c. Between 30 and 40 percent of the revenue for local and state governments comes from grant money.

   d. Local and state governments generate an equal amount of revenue from issuing licenses and certificates.

3. What key constitutional provisions define the scope of authority of the federal and state governments?

4. What are the main functions of federal and state governments?

5. In *McCulloch v. Maryland*, the Supreme Court invoked which provisions of the constitution?

   a. Tenth Amendment and spending clause

   b. commerce clause and supremacy clause

   c. necessary and proper clause and supremacy clause

   d. taxing power and necessary and proper clause

6. Which statement about new federalism is *not* true?

   a. New federalism was launched by President Nixon and continued by President Reagan.

   b. New federalism is based on the idea that decentralization of responsibility enhances administrative efficiency.

   c. *United States v. Lopez* is a Supreme Court ruling that advanced the logic of new federalism.

   d. President Reagan was able to promote new federalism consistently throughout his administration.

7. Which is *not* a merit of cooperative federalism?

   a. Federal cooperation helps mitigate the problem of collective action among states.

   b. Federal assistance encourages state and local governments to generate positive externalities.

   c. Cooperative federalism respects the traditional jurisdictional boundaries between states and federal government.

   d. Federal assistance ensures some degree of uniformity of public services across states.

8. What are the main differences between cooperative federalism and dual federalism?

9. What were the implications of *McCulloch v. Maryland* for federalism?

10. Which statement about federal grants in recent decades is most accurate?

   a. The federal government allocates the most grant money to income security.

   b. The amount of federal grant money going to states has steadily increased since the 1960s.

   c. The majority of federal grants are block grants.

   d. Block grants tend to gain more flexibility over time.

11. Which statement about unfunded mandates is *false?*
   a. The Unfunded Mandates Reform Act has prevented Congress from using unfunded mandates.
   b. The Clean Air Act is a type of federal partial preemptive regulation.
   c. Title VI of the Civil Rights Act establishes crosscutting requirements.
   d. New federalism does not promote the use of unfunded mandates.

12. What does it mean to refer to the carrot of grants and the stick of mandates?

13. Which statement about immigration federalism is *false?*
   a. The *Arizona v. United States* decision struck down all Arizona's most restrictive provisions on illegal immigration.
   b. Since the 1990s, states have increasingly moved into the policy domain of immigration.
   c. Federal immigration laws trump state laws.
   d. States' involvement in immigration is partly due to their interest in preventing illegal immigrants from accessing public services such as education and welfare benefits.

14. Which statement about the evolution of same-sex marriage is *false?*
   a. The federal government became involved in this issue when it passed DOMA.
   b. In the 1990s and 2000s, the number of state restrictions on same-sex marriage increased.
   c. *United States v. Windsor* legalized same-sex marriage in the United States.
   d. More than half the states had legalized same-sex marriage by the time the Supreme Court made same-sex marriage legal nationwide in 2015.

15. Which statement about venue shopping is true?
   a. MADD steered the drinking age issue from the federal government down to the states.
   b. Anti-abortion advocates have steered the abortion issue from the states up to the federal government.
   c. Both MADD and anti-abortion proponents redirected their advocacy from the states to the federal government.
   d. None of the statements are correct.

16. What does venue shopping mean?

17. Which of the following is *not* a benefit of federalism?
   a. Federalism promotes political participation.
   b. Federalism encourages economic equality across the country.
   c. Federalism provides for multiple levels of government action.
   d. Federalism accommodates a diversity of opinion.

18. Describe the advantages of federalism.

19. Describe the disadvantages of federalism.

Critical Thinking Questions

20. Describe the primary differences in the role of citizens in government among the federal, confederation, and unitary systems.

21. How have the political and economic relationships between the states and federal government evolved since the early 1800s?

22. Discuss how the federal government shapes the actions of state and local governments.

23. What are the merits and drawbacks of American federalism?

24. What do you see as the upcoming challenges to federalism in the next decade? Choose an issue and outline how the states and the federal government could respond.

Suggestions for Further Study

Beer, Samuel H. 1998. *To Make a Nation: The Rediscovery of American Federalism*. Cambridge, MA: Harvard University Press.

Berry, Christopher R. 2009. *Imperfect Union: Representation and Taxation in Multilevel Governments*. New York: Cambridge University Press.

Derthick, Martha, ed. 1999. *Dilemmas of Scale in America's Federal Democracy*. New York: Cambridge University Press.

Diamond, Martin. 1981. *The Founding of the American Democratic Republic*. Belmont, CA: Wadsworth Cengage Learning.

Elazar, Daniel J. 1992. *Federal Systems of the World: A Handbook of Federal, Confederal and Autonomy Arrangements*. Harlow, Essex: Longman Current Affairs.

Grodzins, Morton. 2004. "The Federal System." In *American Government Readings and Cases*, ed. P. Woll. New York: Pearson Longman, 74–78.

LaCroix, Alison. 2011. *The Ideological Origins of American Federalism*. Cambridge, MA: Harvard University Press.

Orren, Karen, and Stephen Skowronek. 2004. *The Search for American Political Development*. New York: Cambridge University Press.

O'Toole, Laurence J., Jr., and Robert K. Christensen, eds. 2012. *American Intergovernmental Relations: Foundations, Perspectives, and Issues*. Thousand Oaks, CA: CQ Press.

Peterson, Paul E. 1995. *The Price of Federalism*. Washington, DC: Brookings Institution Press.

Watts, Ronald L. 1999. *Comparing Federal Systems*. 2nd ed. Kingston, Ontario: McGill-Queen's University Press.

Chapter 4

Civil Liberties

Figure 4.1 Those concerned about government surveillance have found a champion in Edward Snowden, a former contractor for the U.S. government who leaked thousands of classified documents to journalists in June 2013. These documents revealed the existence of multiple global surveillance programs run by the National Security Agency. (credit: modification of work by Bruno Sanchez-Andrade Nuño)

Chapter Outline

4.1 What Are Civil Liberties?
4.2 Securing Basic Freedoms
4.3 The Rights of Suspects
4.4 Interpreting the Bill of Rights

Introduction

Americans have recently confronted situations in which government officials appeared not to provide citizens their basic freedoms and rights. Protests have erupted nationwide in response to the deaths of African Americans during interactions with police. Many people were deeply troubled by the revelations of Edward Snowden (Figure 4.1) that U.S. government agencies are conducting widespread surveillance, capturing not only the conversations of foreign leaders and suspected terrorists but also the private communications of U.S. citizens, even those not suspected of criminal activity.

These situations are hardly unique in U.S. history. The framers of the Constitution wanted a government that would not repeat the abuses of individual liberties and rights that caused them to declare independence from Britain. However, laws and other "parchment barriers" (or written documents) alone have not protected freedoms over the years; instead, citizens have learned the truth of the old saying (often attributed to Thomas Jefferson but actually said by Irish politician John Philpot Curran), "Eternal vigilance is the price of liberty." The actions of ordinary citizens, lawyers, and politicians have been at the core of a vigilant effort to protect constitutional liberties.

But what are those freedoms? And how should we balance them against the interests of society and other individuals? These are the key questions we will tackle in this chapter.

4.1 What Are Civil Liberties?

Learning Objectives

By the end of this section, you will be able to:
- Define civil liberties and civil rights
- Describe the origin of civil liberties in the U.S. context
- Identify the key positions on civil liberties taken at the Constitutional Convention
- Explain the Civil War origin of concern that the states should respect civil liberties

The U.S. Constitution—in particular, the first ten amendments that form the Bill of Rights—protects the freedoms and rights of individuals. It does not limit this protection just to citizens or adults; instead, in most cases, the Constitution simply refers to "persons," which over time has grown to mean that even children, visitors from other countries, and immigrants—permanent or temporary, legal or undocumented—enjoy the same freedoms when they are in the United States or its territories as adult citizens do. So, whether you are a Japanese tourist visiting Disney World or someone who has stayed beyond the limit of days allowed on your visa, you do not sacrifice your liberties. In everyday conversation, we tend to treat freedoms, liberties, and rights as being effectively the same thing—similar to how separation of powers and checks and balances are often used as if they are interchangeable, when in fact they are distinct concepts.

DEFINING CIVIL LIBERTIES

To be more precise in their language, political scientists and legal experts make a distinction between civil liberties and civil rights, even though the Constitution has been interpreted to protect both. We typically envision **civil liberties** as being limitations on government power, intended to protect freedoms that governments may not legally intrude on. For example, the First Amendment denies the government the power to prohibit "the free exercise" of religion; the states and the national government cannot forbid people to follow a religion of their choice, even if politicians and judges think the religion is misguided, blasphemous, or otherwise inappropriate. You are free to create your own religion and recruit followers to it (subject to the U.S. Supreme Court deeming it a religion), even if both society and government disapprove of its tenets. That said, the way you practice your religion may be regulated if it impinges on the rights of others. Similarly, the Eighth Amendment says the government cannot impose "cruel and unusual punishments" on individuals for their criminal acts. Although the definitions of *cruel* and *unusual* have expanded over the years, as we will see later in this chapter, the courts have generally and consistently interpreted this provision as making it unconstitutional for government officials to torture suspects.

Civil rights, on the other hand, are guarantees that government officials will treat people equally and that decisions will be made on the basis of merit rather than race, gender, or other personal characteristics. Because of the Constitution's civil rights guarantee, it is unlawful for a school or university run by a state government to treat students differently based on their race, ethnicity, age, sex, or national origin. In the 1960s and 1970s, many states had separate schools where only students of a certain race or gender were able to study. However, the courts decided that these policies violated the civil rights of students who could not be admitted because of those rules.[1]

The idea that Americans—indeed, people in general—have fundamental rights and liberties was at the core of the arguments in favor of their independence. In writing the Declaration of Independence in 1776, Thomas Jefferson drew on the ideas of John Locke to express the colonists' belief that they had certain inalienable or natural rights that no ruler had the power or authority to deny to his or her subjects. It was a scathing legal indictment of King George III for violating the colonists' liberties. Although the Declaration of Independence does not guarantee specific freedoms, its language was instrumental in inspiring many of the states to adopt protections for civil liberties and rights in their own constitutions, and in expressing principles of the founding era that have resonated in the United States since its independence. In particular, Jefferson's words "all men are created equal" became the centerpiece of struggles for the rights of women and minorities (**Figure 4.2**).

Figure 4.2 Actors and civil rights activists Sidney Poitier (left), Harry Belafonte (center), and Charlton Heston (right) on the steps of the Lincoln Memorial on August 28, 1963, during the March on Washington.

Link to Learning

Founded in 1920, the American Civil Liberties Union (ACLU) (https://www.openstax.org/l/29aclu) is one of the oldest interest groups in the United States. The mission of this non-partisan, not-for-profit organization is "to defend and preserve the individual rights and liberties guaranteed to every person in this country by the Constitution and laws of the United States." Many of the Supreme Court cases in this chapter were litigated by, or with the support of, the ACLU. The ACLU offers a listing of state and local chapters (https://www.openstax.org/l/29acluaffiliate) on their website.

CIVIL LIBERTIES AND THE CONSTITUTION

The Constitution as written in 1787 did not include a Bill of Rights, although the idea of including one was proposed and, after brief discussion, dismissed in the final week of the Constitutional Convention. The framers of the Constitution believed they faced much more pressing concerns than the protection of civil rights and liberties, most notably keeping the fragile union together in the light of internal unrest and external threats.

Moreover, the framers thought that they had adequately covered rights issues in the main body of the document. Indeed, the Federalists did include in the Constitution some protections against legislative acts that might restrict the liberties of citizens, based on the history of real and perceived abuses by both British kings and parliaments as well as royal governors. In Article I, Section 9, the Constitution limits the power of Congress in three ways: prohibiting the passage of bills of attainder, prohibiting ex post facto laws, and limiting the ability of Congress to suspend the writ of habeas corpus.

A bill of attainder is a law that convicts or punishes someone for a crime without a trial, a tactic used fairly frequently in England against the king's enemies. Prohibition of such laws means that the U.S. Congress cannot simply punish people who are unpopular or seem to be guilty of crimes. An ex post facto law has a retroactive effect: it can be used to punish crimes that were not crimes at the time they were committed, or it can be used to increase the severity of punishment after the fact.

Finally, the writ of habeas corpus is used in our common-law legal system to demand that a neutral judge decide whether someone has been lawfully detained. Particularly in times of war, or even in response to threats against national security, the government has held suspected enemy agents without access to civilian courts, often without access to lawyers or a defense, seeking instead to try them before military tribunals or detain them indefinitely without trial. For example, during the Civil War, President Abraham Lincoln detained suspected Confederate saboteurs and sympathizers in Union-controlled states and attempted to have them tried in military courts, leading the Supreme Court to rule in *Ex parte Milligan* that the government could not bypass the civilian court system in states where it was operating.[2]

During World War II, the Roosevelt administration interned Japanese Americans and had other suspected enemy agents—including U.S. citizens—tried by military courts rather than by the civilian justice system, a choice the Supreme Court upheld in *Ex parte Quirin* (**Figure 4.3**).[3] More recently, in the wake of the 9/11 attacks on the World Trade Center and the Pentagon, the Bush and Obama administrations detained suspected terrorists captured both within and outside the United States and sought, with mixed results, to avoid trials in civilian courts. Hence, there have been times in our history when national security issues trumped individual liberties.

Figure 4.3 Richard Quirin and seven other trained German saboteurs had once lived in the United States and had secretly returned in June 1942. Upon their capture, a military commission (shown here) convicted the men—six of them received death sentences. *Ex parte Quirin* set a precedent for the trial by military commission of any unlawful combatant against the United States. (credit: Library of Congress)

Debate has always swirled over these issues. The Federalists reasoned that the limited set of enumerated powers of Congress, along with the limitations on those powers in Article I, Section 9, would suffice, and no separate bill of rights was needed. Alexander Hamilton, writing as Publius in *Federalist* No. 84, argued that the Constitution was "merely intended to regulate the general political interests of the nation," rather than to concern itself with "the regulation of every species of personal and private concerns." Hamilton went on to argue that listing some rights might actually be dangerous, because it would provide a pretext for people to claim that rights *not* included in such a list were not protected. Later, James Madison, in his speech introducing the proposed amendments that would become the Bill of Rights, acknowledged another Federalist argument: "It has been said, that a bill of rights is not necessary, because the establishment of this government has not repealed those declarations of rights which are added to the several state constitutions."[4] For that matter, the Articles of Confederation had not included a specific listing of rights either.

However, the Anti-Federalists argued that the Federalists' position was incorrect and perhaps even insincere. The Anti-Federalists believed provisions such as the elastic clause in Article I, Section 8, of the Constitution would allow Congress to legislate on matters well beyond the limited ones foreseen by the Constitution's authors; thus, they held that a bill of rights was necessary. One of the Anti-Federalists, Brutus, whom most scholars believe to be Robert Yates, wrote: "The powers, rights, and authority, granted to the general government by this Constitution, are as complete, with respect to every object to which they extend, as that of any state government—It reaches to every thing which concerns human happiness—Life, liberty, and property, are under its controul [sic]. There is the same reason, therefore, that the exercise of power, in this case, should be restrained within proper limits, as in that of the state governments."[5] The experience of the past two centuries has suggested that the Anti-Federalists may have been correct in this regard; while the states retain a great deal of importance, the scope and powers of the national government are much broader today than in 1787—likely beyond even the imaginings of the Federalists themselves.

The struggle to have rights clearly delineated and the decision of the framers to omit a bill of rights nearly derailed the ratification process. While some of the states were willing to ratify without any further guarantees, in some of the larger states—New York and Virginia in particular—the Constitution's lack of specified rights became a serious point of contention. The Constitution could go into effect with the support of only nine states, but the Federalists knew it could not be effective without the participation of the largest states. To secure majorities in favor of ratification in New York and Virginia, as well as Massachusetts, they agreed to consider incorporating provisions suggested by the ratifying states as amendments to the Constitution.

Ultimately, James Madison delivered on this promise by proposing a package of amendments in the First Congress, drawing from the Declaration of Rights in the Virginia state constitution, suggestions from the ratification conventions, and other sources, which were extensively debated in both houses of Congress and ultimately proposed as twelve separate amendments for ratification by the states. Ten of the amendments were successfully ratified by the requisite 75 percent of the states and became known as the Bill of Rights (Table 4.1).

Rights and Liberties Protected by the First Ten Amendments

First Amendment	Right to freedoms of religion and speech; right to assemble and to petition the government for redress of grievances
Second Amendment	Right to keep and bear arms to maintain a well-regulated militia
Third Amendment	Right to not house soldiers during time of war
Fourth Amendment	Right to be secure from unreasonable search and seizure
Fifth Amendment	Rights in criminal cases, including due process and indictment by grand jury for capital crimes, as well as the right not to testify against oneself
Sixth Amendment	Right to a speedy trial by an impartial jury

Table 4.1

Rights and Liberties Protected by the First Ten Amendments

Seventh Amendment	Right to a jury trial in civil cases
Eighth Amendment	Right to not face excessive bail, excessive fines, or cruel and unusual punishment
Ninth Amendment	Rights retained by the people, even if they are not specifically enumerated by the Constitution
Tenth Amendment	States' rights to powers not specifically delegated to the federal government

Table 4.1

Finding a Middle Ground

Debating the Need for a Bill of Rights

One of the most serious debates between the Federalists and the Anti-Federalists was over the necessity of limiting the power of the new federal government with a Bill of Rights. As we saw in this section, the Federalists believed a Bill of Rights was unnecessary—and perhaps even dangerous to liberty, because it might invite violations of rights that weren't included in it—while the Anti-Federalists thought the national government would prove adept at expanding its powers and influence and that citizens couldn't depend on the good judgment of Congress alone to protect their rights.

As George Washington's call for a bill of rights in his first inaugural address suggested, while the Federalists ultimately had to add the Bill of Rights to the Constitution in order to win ratification, and the Anti-Federalists would soon be proved right that the national government might intrude on civil liberties. In 1798, at the behest of President John Adams during the Quasi-War with France, Congress passed a series of four laws collectively known as the Alien and Sedition Acts. These were drafted to allow the president to imprison or deport foreign citizens he believed were "dangerous to the peace and safety of the United States" and to restrict speech and newspaper articles that were critical of the federal government or its officials; the laws were primarily used against members and supporters of the opposition Democratic-Republican Party.

State laws and constitutions protecting free speech and freedom of the press proved ineffective in limiting this new federal power. Although the courts did not decide on the constitutionality of these laws at the time, most scholars believe the Sedition Act, in particular, would be unconstitutional if it had remained in effect. Three of the four laws were repealed in the Jefferson administration, but one—the Alien Enemies Act—remains on the books today. Two centuries later, the issue of free speech and freedom of the press during times of international conflict remains a subject of public debate.

Should the government be able to restrict or censor unpatriotic, disloyal, or critical speech in times of international conflict? How much freedom should journalists have to report on stories from the perspective of enemies or to repeat propaganda from opposing forces?

EXTENDING THE BILL OF RIGHTS TO THE STATES

In the decades following the Constitution's ratification, the Supreme Court declined to expand the Bill of Rights to curb the power of the states, most notably in the 1833 case of *Barron v. Baltimore*.[6] In this case, which dealt with property rights under the Fifth Amendment, the Supreme Court unanimously decided that the Bill of Rights applied only to actions by the federal government. Explaining the court's ruling, Chief Justice John Marshall wrote that it was incorrect to argue that "the Constitution was intended to secure the people of the several states against the undue exercise of power by their respective state governments; as well as against that which might be attempted by their [Federal] government."

In the wake of the Civil War, however, the prevailing thinking about the application of the Bill of Rights to the states changed. Soon after slavery was abolished by the Thirteenth Amendment, state governments—particularly those in the former Confederacy—began to pass "black codes" that restricted the rights of former slaves and effectively relegated them to second-class citizenship under their state laws and constitutions. Angered by these actions, members of the Radical Republican faction in Congress demanded that the laws be overturned. In the short term, they advocated suspending civilian government in most of the southern states and replacing politicians who had enacted the black codes. Their long-term solution was to propose two amendments to the Constitution to guarantee the rights of freed slaves on an equal standing with whites; these rights became the Fourteenth Amendment, which dealt with civil liberties and rights in general, and the Fifteenth Amendment, which protected the right to vote in particular (Figure 4.4). But, the right to vote did not yet apply to women or to Native Americans.

(a)   (b)

Figure 4.4 Representative John Bingham (R-OH) (a) is considered the author of the Fourteenth Amendment, adopted on July 9, 1868. Influenced by his mentor, Salmon P. Chase, Bingham was a strong supporter of the antislavery cause; after Chase lost the Republican presidential nomination to Abraham Lincoln (b), Bingham became one of the president's most ardent supporters.

With the ratification of the Fourteenth Amendment in 1868, civil liberties gained more clarification. First, the amendment says, "no State shall make or enforce any law which shall abridge the privileges or immunities of citizens of the United States," which is a provision that echoes the privileges and immunities clause in Article IV, Section 2, of the original Constitution ensuring that states treat citizens of other states the same as their own citizens. (To use an example from today, the punishment for speeding by an out-of-state driver cannot be more severe than the punishment for an in-state driver). Legal scholars and the courts have extensively debated the meaning of this privileges or immunities clause over the years; some have argued that it was supposed to extend the entire Bill of Rights (or at least the first eight amendments) to the states, while others have argued that only some rights are extended. In 1999, Justice John Paul Stevens, writing for a majority of the Supreme Court, argued in *Saenz v. Roe* that the clause protects the right to travel from one state to another.[7] More recently, Justice Clarence Thomas argued in the 2010 *McDonald v. Chicago* ruling that the individual right to bear arms applied to the states because of this clause.[8]

The second provision of the Fourteenth Amendment that pertains to applying the Bill of Rights to the states is the **due process clause**, which says, "nor shall any State deprive any person of life, liberty, or property, without due process of law." This provision is similar to the Fifth Amendment in that it also refers to "due process," a term that generally means people must be treated fairly and impartially by government officials (or with what is commonly referred to as substantive due process). Although the text of the provision does not mention rights specifically, the courts have held in a series of cases that it indicates there are certain fundamental liberties that cannot be denied by the states. For example, in *Sherbert v. Verner* (1963), the Supreme Court ruled that states could not deny unemployment benefits to an individual who turned down a job because it required working on the Sabbath.[9]

Beginning in 1897, the Supreme Court has found that various provisions of the Bill of Rights protecting these fundamental liberties must be upheld by the states, even if their state constitutions and laws do not protect them as fully as the Bill of Rights does—or at all. This means there has been a process of **selective incorporation** of the Bill of Rights into the practices of the states; in other words, the Constitution effectively inserts parts of the Bill of Rights into state laws and constitutions, even though it doesn't do so explicitly. When cases arise to clarify particular issues and procedures, the Supreme Court decides whether state laws violate the Bill of Rights and are therefore unconstitutional.

For example, under the Fifth Amendment a person can be tried in federal court for a felony—a serious crime—only after a grand jury issues an indictment indicating that it is reasonable to try the person for the crime in question. (A grand jury is a group of citizens charged with deciding whether there is enough evidence of a crime to prosecute someone.) But the Supreme Court has ruled that states don't have to use grand juries as long as they ensure people accused of crimes are indicted using an equally fair process.

Selective incorporation is an ongoing process. When the Supreme Court initially decided in 2008 that the Second Amendment protects an individual's right to keep and bear arms, it did not decide then that it was a fundamental liberty the states must uphold as well. It was only in the *McDonald v. Chicago* case two years later that the Supreme Court incorporated the Second Amendment into state law. Another area in which the Supreme Court gradually moved to incorporate the Bill of Rights regards censorship and the Fourteenth Amendment. In *Near v. Minnesota* (1931), the Court disagreed with state courts regarding censorship and ruled it unconstitutional except in rare cases.[10]

4.2 Securing Basic Freedoms

Learning Objectives

By the end of this section, you will be able to:
- Identify the liberties and rights guaranteed by the first four amendments to the Constitution
- Explain why in practice these rights and liberties are limited
- Explain why interpreting some amendments has been controversial

We can broadly divide the provisions of the Bill of Rights into three categories. The First, Second, Third, and Fourth Amendments protect basic individual freedoms; the Fourth (partly), Fifth, Sixth, Seventh, and Eighth protect people suspected or accused of criminal activity or facing civil litigation; and the Ninth and Tenth, are consistent with the framers' view that the Bill of Rights is not necessarily an exhaustive list of all the rights people have and guarantees a role for state as well as federal government (Figure 4.5).

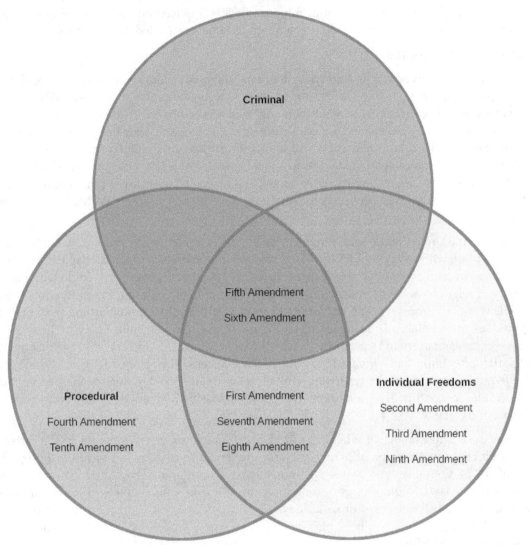

Categories of Rights and Protections

Criminal

Fifth Amendment

Sixth Amendment

Procedural

Fourth Amendment

Tenth Amendment

First Amendment

Seventh Amendment

Eighth Amendment

Individual Freedoms

Second Amendment

Third Amendment

Ninth Amendment

Figure 4.5

The First Amendment protects the right to freedom of religious conscience and practice and the right to free expression, particularly of political and social beliefs. The Second Amendment—perhaps the most controversial today—protects the right to defend yourself in your home or other property, as well as the collective right to protect the community as part of the militia. The Third Amendment prohibits the government from commandeering people's homes to house soldiers, particularly in peacetime. Finally, the Fourth Amendment prevents the government from searching our persons or property or taking evidence without a warrant issued by a judge, with certain exceptions.

THE FIRST AMENDMENT

The First Amendment is perhaps the most famous provision of the Bill of Rights; it is arguably also the most extensive, because it guarantees both religious freedoms and the right to express your views in public. Specifically, the First Amendment says:

> "Congress shall make no law respecting an establishment of religion, or prohibiting the free exercise thereof; or abridging the freedom of speech, or of the press; or the right of the people peaceably to assemble, and to petition the Government for a redress of grievances."

Given the broad scope of this amendment, it is helpful to break it into its two major parts.

The first portion deals with religious freedom. However, it actually protects two related sorts of freedom: first, it protects people from having a set of religious beliefs imposed on them by the government, and second, it protects people from having their own religious beliefs restricted by government authorities.

The Establishment Clause

The first of these two freedoms is known as the **establishment clause**. Congress is prohibited from creating or promoting a state-sponsored religion (this now includes the states too). When the United States was founded, most countries around the world had an established church or religion, an officially sponsored set of religious beliefs and values. In Europe, bitter wars were fought between and within states, often because the established church of one territory was in conflict with that of another; wars and civil strife were common, particularly between states with Protestant and Catholic churches that had differing interpretations of Christianity. Even today, the legacy of these wars remains, most notably in Ireland, which has been divided between a mostly Catholic south and a largely Protestant north for nearly a century.

Many settlers in the United States found themselves on this continent as refugees from such wars; others came to find a place where they could follow their own religion with like-minded people in relative peace. So as a practical matter, even if the early United States had wanted to establish a single national religion, the diversity of religious beliefs would already have prevented it. Nonetheless the differences were small; most people were of European origin and professed some form of Christianity (although in private some of the founders, most notably Thomas Jefferson, Thomas Paine, and Benjamin Franklin, held what today would be seen as Unitarian and/or deistic views). So for much of U.S. history, the establishment clause was not particularly important—the vast majority of citizens were Protestant Christians of some form, and since the federal government was relatively uninvolved in the day-to-day lives of the people, there was little opportunity for conflict. That said, there were some citizenship and office-holding restrictions on Jews within some of the states.

Worry about state sponsorship of religion in the United States began to reemerge in the latter part of the nineteenth century. An influx of immigrants from Ireland and eastern and southern Europe brought large numbers of Catholics, and states—fearing the new immigrants and their children would not assimilate—passed laws forbidding government aid to religious schools. New religious organizations, such as The Church of Jesus Christ of Latter-day Saints (the Mormon Church), Seventh-day Adventists, Jehovah's Witnesses, and many others, also emerged, blending aspects of Protestant beliefs with other ideas and teachings at odds with the more traditional Protestant churches of the era. At the same time, public schooling was beginning to take root on a wide scale. Since most states had traditional Protestant majorities and most state officials were Protestants themselves, the public school curriculum incorporated many Protestant features; at times, these features would come into conflict with the beliefs of children from other Christian sects or from other religious traditions.

The establishment clause today tends to be interpreted a bit more broadly than in the past; it not only forbids the creation of a "Church of the United States" or "Church of Ohio" it also forbids the government from favoring one set of religious beliefs over others or favoring religion (of any variety) over non-religion. Thus, the government cannot promote, say, Islamic beliefs over Sikh beliefs or belief in God over atheism or agnosticism (Figure 4.6).

Figure 4.6 In this illustration from a contemporary manuscript, Henry Bolingbroke (i.e., Henry IV) claims the throne in 1399 surrounded by the Lords Spiritual and Temporal (secular). While the Lords Spiritual have been a minority in the House of Lords since the time of Henry VIII, and religion does not generally play a large role in British politics today, the Church of England nevertheless remains represented in Parliament by twenty-six bishops.

The key question that faces the courts is whether the establishment clause should be understood as imposing, in Thomas Jefferson's words, "a wall of separation between church and state." In a 1971 case known as *Lemon v. Kurtzman*, the Supreme Court established the Lemon test for deciding whether a law or other government action that might promote a particular religious practice should be allowed to stand.[11] The Lemon test has three criteria that must be satisfied for such a law or action to be found constitutional and remain in effect:

1. The action or law must not lead to *excessive government entanglement* with religion; in other words, policing the boundary between government and religion should be relatively straightforward and not require extensive effort by the government.

2. The action or law cannot either *inhibit* or *advance* religious practice; it should be neutral in its effects on religion.

3. The action or law must have some *secular purpose*; there must be some non-religious justification for the law.

For example, imagine your state decides to fund a school voucher program that allows children to attend private and parochial schools at public expense; the vouchers can be used to pay for school books and transportation to and from school. Would this voucher program be constitutional?

Let's start with the secular-purpose prong of the test. Educating children is a clear, non-religious purpose, so the law has a secular purpose. The law would neither inhibit nor advance religious practice, so that prong would be satisfied. The remaining question—and usually the one on which court decisions turn—is whether the law leads to excessive government entanglement with religious practice. Given that transportation and school books generally have no religious purpose, there is little risk that paying for them would lead the state to much entanglement with religion. The decision would become more difficult if the funding were unrestricted in use or helped to pay for facilities or teacher salaries; if that were the case, it might indeed be used for a religious purpose, and it would be harder for the government to ensure that it wasn't without audits or other investigations that could lead to too much government entanglement with religion.

The use of education as an example is not an accident; in fact, many of the court's cases dealing with the establishment clause have involved education, particularly public education, because school-age children are considered a special and vulnerable population. Perhaps no subject affected by the First Amendment has been more controversial than the issue of prayer in public schools. Discussion about school prayer has been particularly fraught because in many ways it appears to bring the two religious liberty clauses into conflict with each other. The free exercise clause, discussed below, guarantees the right of individuals to practice their religion without government interference—and while the rights of children are not as extensive in all areas as those of adults, the courts have consistently ruled that the free exercise clause's guarantee of religious freedom applies to children as well.

At the same time, however, government actions that require or encourage particular religious practices might infringe upon children's rights to follow their own religious beliefs and thus, in effect, be unconstitutional establishments of religion. For example, a teacher, an athletic coach, or even a student reciting a prayer in front of a class or leading students in prayer as part of the organized school activities constitutes an illegal establishment of religion.[12] Yet a school cannot prohibit voluntary, non-disruptive prayer by its students, because that would impair the free exercise of religion. So although the blanket statement that "prayer in schools is illegal" or unconstitutional is incorrect, the establishment clause does limit official endorsement of religion, including prayers organized or otherwise facilitated by school authorities, even as part of off-campus or extracurricular activities.[13]

But some laws that may appear to establish certain religious practices are allowed. For example, the courts have permitted religiously inspired **blue laws** that limit working hours or even shutter businesses on Sunday, the Christian day of rest, because by allowing people to practice their (Christian) faith, such rules may help ensure the "health, safety, recreation, and general well-being" of citizens. They have allowed restrictions on the sale of alcohol and sometimes other goods on Sunday for similar reasons.

The meaning of the establishment clause has been controversial at times because, as a matter of course, government officials acknowledge that we live in a society with vigorous religious practice where most people believe in God—even if we disagree on what God is. Disputes often arise over how much the government can acknowledge this widespread religious belief. The courts have generally allowed for a certain tolerance of what is described as ceremonial deism, an acknowledgement of God or a creator that generally lacks any substantive religious content. For example, the national motto "In God We Trust," which appears on our coins and paper money (Figure 4.7), is seen as more an acknowledgment that most citizens believe in God than any serious effort by government officials to promote religious belief and practice. This reasoning has also been used to permit the inclusion of the phrase "under God" in the Pledge of Allegiance—a change that came about during the early years of the Cold War as a means of contrasting the United States with the "godless" Soviet Union.

In addition, the courts have allowed some religiously motivated actions by government agencies, such as clergy delivering prayers to open city council meetings and legislative sessions, on the presumption that—unlike school children—adult participants can distinguish between the government's allowing someone to speak and endorsing that person's speech. Yet, while some displays of religious codes (e.g., Ten Commandments) are permitted in the context of showing the evolution of law over the centuries (Figure 4.7), in other cases, these displays have been removed after state supreme court rulings. In Oklahoma, the courts ordered the removal of a Ten Commandments sculpture at the state capitol when other groups, including Satanists and the Church of the Flying Spaghetti Monster, attempted to get their own sculptures allowed there.

(a)   (b)

Figure 4.7   The motto "In God We Trust" has appeared intermittently on U.S. coins since the 1860s (a), yet it was not mandated on paper currency until 1957. The Ten Commandments are prominently displayed on the grounds of the Texas State Capitol in Austin (b), though a similar sculpture was ordered to be removed in Oklahoma. (credit a: modification of work by Kevin Dooley)

The Free Exercise Clause

The **free exercise clause**, on the other hand, limits the ability of the government to control or restrict religious practices. This portion of the First Amendment regulates not the government's promotion of religion, but rather government *suppression* of religious beliefs and practices. Much of the controversy surrounding the free exercise clause reflects the way laws or rules that apply to everyone might apply to people with particular religious beliefs. For example, can a Jewish police officer whose religious belief, if followed strictly, requires her to observe Shabbat be compelled to work on a Friday night or during the day on Saturday? Or must the government accommodate this religious practice, even if it means the general law or rule in question is not applied equally to everyone?

In the 1930s and 1940s, cases involving Jehovah's Witnesses demonstrated the difficulty of striking the right balance. In addition to following their church's teaching that they should not participate in military combat, members refuse to participate in displays of patriotism, including saluting the flag and reciting the Pledge of Allegiance, and they regularly engage in door-to-door evangelism to recruit converts. These activities have led to frequent conflict with local authorities. Jehovah's Witness children were punished in public schools for failing to salute the flag or recite the Pledge of Allegiance, and members attempting to evangelize were arrested for violating laws against door-to-door solicitation of customers. In early legal challenges brought by Jehovah's Witnesses, the Supreme Court was reluctant to overturn state and local laws that burdened their religious beliefs.[14] However, in later cases, the court was willing to uphold the rights of Jehovah's Witnesses to proselytize and refuse to salute the flag or recite the Pledge.[15]

The rights of **conscientious objectors**—individuals who claim the right to refuse to perform military service on the grounds of freedom of thought, conscience, or religion—have also been controversial, although many conscientious objectors have contributed service as non-combatant medics during wartime. To avoid serving in the Vietnam War, many people claimed to have a conscientious objection to military service on the basis that they believed this particular war was unwise or unjust. However, the Supreme Court ruled in *Gillette v. United States* that to claim to be a conscientious objector, a person must be opposed to serving in *any* war, not just some wars.[16]

Establishing a general framework for deciding whether a religious belief can trump general laws and policies has been a challenge for the Supreme Court. In the 1960s and 1970s, the court decided two cases in which it laid out a general test for deciding similar cases in the future. In both *Sherbert v. Verner*, a case dealing with unemployment compensation, and *Wisconsin v. Yoder*, which dealt with the right of Amish parents to homeschool their children, the court said that for a law to be allowed to limit or burden a religious practice, the government must meet two criteria.[17] It must demonstrate both that it had a "compelling governmental interest" in limiting that practice and that the restriction was "narrowly tailored." In other words, it must show there was a very good reason for the law in question and that the law was the only feasible way of achieving that goal. This standard became known as the **Sherbert test**. Since the burden of proof in these cases was on the government, the Supreme Court made it very difficult for the federal and state governments to enforce laws against individuals that would infringe upon their religious beliefs.

In 1990, the Supreme Court made a controversial decision substantially narrowing the Sherbert test in *Employment Division v. Smith*, more popularly known as "the peyote case."[18] This case involved two men who were members of the Native American Church, a religious organization that uses the hallucinogenic peyote plant as part of its sacraments. After being arrested for possession of peyote, the two men were fired from their jobs as counselors at a private drug rehabilitation clinic. When they applied for unemployment benefits, the state refused to pay on the basis that they had been dismissed for work-related reasons. The men appealed the denial of benefits and were initially successful, since the state courts applied the Sherbert test and found that the denial of unemployment benefits burdened their religious beliefs. However, the Supreme Court ruled in a 6–3 decision that the "compelling governmental interest" standard should not apply; instead, so long as the law was not designed to target a person's religious beliefs in particular, it was not up to the courts to decide that those beliefs were more important than the law in question.

On the surface, a case involving the Native American Church seems unlikely to arouse much controversy. But because it replaced the Sherbert test with one that allowed more government regulation of religious practices, followers of other religious traditions grew concerned that state and local laws, even ones neutral on their face, might be used to curtail their religious practices. In 1993, in response to this decision, Congress passed a law known as the Religious Freedom Restoration Act (RFRA), which was followed in 2000 by the Religious Land Use and Institutionalized Persons Act after part of the RFRA was struck down by the Supreme Court. In addition, since 1990, twenty-one states have passed state RFRAs that include the Sherbert test in state law, and state court decisions in eleven states have enshrined the Sherbert test's compelling governmental interest interpretation of the free exercise clause into state law.[19]

However, the RFRA itself has not been without its critics. While it has been relatively uncontroversial as applied to the rights of individuals, debate has emerged about whether businesses and other groups can be said to have religious liberty. In explicitly religious organizations, such as a fundamentalist congregation (fundamentalists adhere very strictly to biblical absolutes) or the Roman Catholic Church, it is fairly obvious members have a meaningful, shared religious belief. But the application of the RFRA has become more problematic in businesses and non-profit organizations whose owners or organizers may share a religious belief while the organization has some secular, non-religious purpose.

Such a conflict emerged in the 2014 Supreme Court case known as *Burwell v. Hobby Lobby*.[20] The Hobby Lobby chain of stores sells arts and crafts merchandise at hundreds of stores; its founder, David Green, is a devout fundamentalist Christian whose beliefs include opposition to abortion and contraception. Consistent with these beliefs, he used his business to object to a provision of the Patient Protection and Affordable Care Act (ACA or Obamacare) requiring employer-backed insurance plans to include no-charge access to the morning-after pill, a form of emergency contraception, arguing that this requirement infringed on his conscience. Based in part on the federal RFRA, the Supreme Court agreed 5–4 with Green and Hobby Lobby's position and said that Hobby Lobby and other closely held businesses did not have to provide employees free access to emergency contraception or other birth control if doing so would violate the religious beliefs of the business' owners, because there were other less restrictive ways the government could ensure access to these services for Hobby Lobby's employees (e.g., paying for them directly).

In 2015, state RFRAs became controversial when individuals and businesses that provided wedding services (e.g., catering and photography) were compelled to provide these for same-sex weddings in states where the practice had been newly legalized (Figure 4.8). Proponents of state RFRA laws argued that people and businesses ought not be compelled to endorse practices their religious beliefs held to be immoral or indecent and feared clergy might be compelled to officiate same-sex marriages against their religion's teachings. Opponents of RFRA laws argued that individuals and businesses should be required, per *Obergefell v. Hodges*, to serve same-sex marriages on an equal basis as a matter of ensuring the civil rights of gays and lesbians, just as they would be obliged to cater or photograph an interracial marriage.[21]

Figure 4.8 One of the most recent notorious cases related to the free exercise clause involved an Oregon bakery whose owners refused to bake a wedding cake for a lesbian couple in January 2013, citing the owners' religious beliefs. The couple was eventually awarded $135,000 in damages as a result of the ongoing dispute. However, in a similar case, *Masterpiece Cakeshop v. Colorado Civil Rights Commission*, the U.S. Supreme Court ruled in favor of the baker's rights.(credit: modification of work by Bev Sykes)

Despite ongoing controversy, however, the courts have consistently found some public interests sufficiently compelling to override the free exercise clause. For example, since the late nineteenth century, the courts have consistently held that people's religious beliefs do not exempt them from the general laws against polygamy. Other potential acts in the name of religion that are also out of the question are drug use and human sacrifice.

Freedom of Expression

Although the remainder of the First Amendment protects four distinct rights—free speech, press, assembly, and petition—we generally think of these rights today as encompassing a right to freedom of expression, particularly since the world's technological evolution has blurred the lines between oral and written communication (i.e., speech and press) in the centuries since the First Amendment was written and adopted.

Controversies over freedom of expression were rare until the 1900s, even though government censorship was quite common. For example, during the Civil War, the Union post office refused to deliver newspapers that opposed the war or sympathized with the Confederacy, while allowing pro-war newspapers to be mailed. The emergence of photography and movies, in particular, led to new public concerns about morality, causing both state and federal politicians to censor lewd and otherwise improper content. At the same time, writers became more ambitious in their subject matter by including explicit references to sex and using obscene language, leading to government censorship of books and magazines.

Censorship reached its height during World War I. The United States was swept up in two waves of hysteria. Anti-German feeling was provoked by the actions of Germany and its allies leading up to the war, including the sinking of the RMS *Lusitania* and the Zimmerman Telegram, an effort by the Germans to conclude an alliance with Mexico against the United States. This concern was compounded in 1917 by the Bolshevik revolution against the more moderate interim government of Russia; the leaders of the Bolsheviks, most notably Vladimir Lenin, Leon Trotsky, and Joseph Stalin, withdrew from the war against Germany and called for communist revolutionaries to overthrow the capitalist, democratic governments in western Europe and North America.

Americans who vocally supported the communist cause or opposed the war often found themselves in jail. In *Schenck v. United States*, the Supreme Court ruled that people encouraging young men to dodge the draft could be imprisoned for doing so, arguing that recommending that people disobey the law was tantamount to "falsely shouting fire in a theatre and causing a panic" and thus presented a "clear and present danger" to public order.[22] Similarly, communists and other revolutionary anarchists and socialists during the Red Scare after the war were prosecuted under various state and federal laws for supporting the forceful or violent overthrow of government. This general approach to political speech remained in place for the next fifty years.

In the 1960s, however, the Supreme Court's rulings on free expression became more liberal, in response to the Vietnam War and the growing antiwar movement. In a 1969 case involving the Ku Klux Klan, *Brandenburg v. Ohio*, the Supreme Court found that only speech or writing that constituted a direct call or plan to imminent lawless action, an illegal act in the immediate future, could be suppressed; the mere advocacy of a hypothetical revolution was not enough.[23] The Supreme Court also found that various forms of **symbolic speech**—wearing clothing like an armband that carried a political symbol or raising a fist in the air, for example—were subject to the same protections as written and spoken communication.

Milestone

Burning the U.S. Flag

Perhaps no act of symbolic speech has been as controversial in U.S. history as the burning of the flag (Figure 4.9). Citizens tend to revere the flag as a unifying symbol of the country in much the same way most people in Britain would treat the reigning queen (or king). States and the federal government have long had laws protecting the flag from being desecrated—defaced, damaged, or otherwise treated with disrespect. Perhaps in part because of these laws, people who have wanted to drive home a point in opposition to U.S. government policies have found desecrating the flag a useful way to gain public and press attention to their cause.

Figure 4.9 On the eve of the 2008 election, a U.S. flag was burned in protest in New Hampshire. (credit: modification of work by Jennifer Parr)

One such person was Gregory Lee Johnson, a member of various pro-communist and antiwar groups. In 1984, as part of a protest near the Republican National Convention in Dallas, Texas, Johnson set fire to a U.S. flag that another protestor had torn from a flagpole. He was arrested, charged with "desecration of a venerated object" (among other offenses), and eventually convicted of that offense. However, in 1989, the Supreme Court decided in *Texas v. Johnson* that burning the flag was a form of symbolic speech protected by the First Amendment and found the law, as applied to flag desecration, to be unconstitutional.[24]

This court decision was strongly criticized, and Congress responded by passing a federal law, the Flag Protection Act, intended to overrule it; the act, too, was struck down as unconstitutional in 1990.[25] Since then, Congress has attempted on several occasions to propose constitutional amendments allowing the states and federal government to re-criminalize flag desecration—to no avail.

Should we amend the Constitution to allow Congress or the states to pass laws protecting the U.S. flag from desecration? Should we protect other symbols as well? Why or why not?

Freedom of the press is an important component of the right to free expression as well. In *Near v. Minnesota*, an early case regarding press freedoms, the Supreme Court ruled that the government generally could not engage in **prior restraint**; that is, states and the federal government could not in advance prohibit someone from publishing something without a very compelling reason.[26] This standard was reinforced in 1971 in the Pentagon Papers case, in which the Supreme Court found that the government could not prohibit the *New York Times* and *Washington Post* newspapers from publishing the Pentagon Papers.[27] These papers included materials from a secret history of the Vietnam War that had been compiled by the military. More specifically, the papers were compiled at the request of Secretary of Defense Robert McNamara and provided a study of U.S. political and military involvement in Vietnam from 1945 to 1967. Daniel Ellsberg famously released passages of the Papers to the press to show that the United States had secretly enlarged the scope of the war by bombing Cambodia and Laos among other deeds while lying to the American public about doing so.

Although people who leak secret information to the media can still be prosecuted and punished, this does not generally extend to reporters and news outlets that pass that information on to the public. The Edward Snowden case is another good case in point. Snowden himself, rather than those involved in promoting the information that he shared, is the object of criminal prosecution.

Furthermore, the courts have recognized that government officials and other public figures might try to silence press criticism and avoid unfavorable news coverage by threatening a lawsuit for defamation of character. In the 1964 *New York Times v. Sullivan* case, the Supreme Court decided that public figures needed to demonstrate not only that a negative press statement about them was untrue but also that the statement was published or made with either malicious intent or "reckless disregard" for the truth.[28] This ruling made it much harder for politicians to silence potential critics or to bankrupt their political opponents through the courts.

The right to freedom of expression is not absolute; several key restrictions limit our ability to speak or publish opinions under certain circumstances. We have seen that the Constitution protects most forms of offensive and unpopular expression, particularly political speech; however, *incitement* of a criminal act, "fighting words," and genuine threats are not protected. So, for example, you can't point at someone in front of an angry crowd and shout, "Let's beat up that guy!" And the Supreme Court has allowed laws that ban threatening symbolic speech, such as burning a cross on the lawn of an African American family's home (**Figure 4.10**).[29] Finally, as we've just seen, defamation of character—whether in written form (libel) or spoken form (slander)—is not protected by the First Amendment, so people who are subject to false accusations can sue to recover damages, although criminal prosecutions of libel and slander are uncommon.

Figure 4.10 The Supreme Court has allowed laws that ban threatening symbolic speech, such as burning crosses on the lawns of African American families, an intimidation tactic used by the Ku Klux Klan, pictured here at a meeting in Gainesville, Florida, on December 31, 1922.

Another key exception to the right to freedom of expression is **obscenity**, acts or statements that are extremely offensive under current societal standards. Defining obscenity has been something of a challenge for the courts; Supreme Court Justice Potter Stewart famously said of obscenity, having watched pornography in the Supreme Court building, "I know it when I see it." Into the early twentieth century, written work was frequently banned as being obscene, including works by noted authors such as James Joyce and Henry Miller, although today it is rare for the courts to uphold obscenity charges for written material alone. In 1973, the Supreme Court established the Miller test for deciding whether something is obscene: "(a) whether the average person, applying contemporary community standards, would find that the work, taken as a whole, appeals to the prurient interest, (b) whether the work depicts or describes, in a patently offensive way, sexual conduct specifically defined by the applicable state law; and (c) whether the work, taken as a whole, lacks serious literary, artistic, political, or scientific value."[30] However, the application of this standard has at times been problematic. In particular, the concept of "contemporary community standards" raises the possibility that obscenity varies from place to place; many people in New York or San Francisco might not bat an eye at something people in Memphis or Salt Lake City would consider offensive. The one form of obscenity that has been banned almost without challenge is child pornography, although even in this area the courts have found exceptions.

The courts have allowed censorship of less-than-obscene content when it is broadcast over the airwaves, particularly when it is available for anyone to receive. In general, these restrictions on indecency—a quality of acts or statements that offend societal norms or may be harmful to minors—apply only to radio and television programming broadcast when children might be in the audience, although most cable and satellite channels follow similar standards for commercial reasons. An infamous case of televised indecency occurred during the halftime show of the 2004 Super Bowl, during a performance by singer Janet Jackson in which a part of her clothing was removed by fellow performer Justin Timberlake, revealing her right breast. The network responsible for the broadcast, CBS, was ultimately presented with a fine of $550,000 by the Federal Communications Commission, the government agency that regulates television broadcasting. However, CBS was not ultimately required to pay.

On the other hand, in 1997, the NBC network showed a broadcast of *Schindler's List*, a film depicting events during the Holocaust in Nazi Germany, without any editing, so it included graphic nudity and depictions of violence. NBC was not fined or otherwise punished, suggesting there is no uniform standard for indecency. Similarly, in the 1990s Congress compelled television broadcasters to implement a television ratings system, enforced by a "V-Chip" in televisions and cable boxes, so parents could better control the television programming their children might watch. However, similar efforts to regulate indecent content on the Internet to protect children from pornography have largely been struck down as unconstitutional. This outcome suggests that technology has created new avenues for obscene material to be disseminated. The Children's Internet Protection Act, however, requires K–12 schools and public libraries receiving Internet access using special E-rate discounts to filter or block access to obscene material and other material deemed harmful to minors, with certain exceptions.

The courts have also allowed laws that forbid or compel certain forms of expression by businesses, such as laws that require the disclosure of nutritional information on food and beverage containers and warning labels on tobacco products (Figure 4.11). The federal government requires the prices advertised for airline tickets to include all taxes and fees. Many states regulate advertising by lawyers. And, in general, false or misleading statements made in connection with a commercial transaction can be illegal if they constitute fraud.

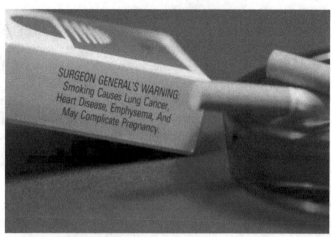

Figure 4.11 The surgeon general's warning label on a box of cigarettes is mandated by the Food and Drug Administration. The United States was the first nation to require a health warning on cigarette packages. (credit: Debora Cartagena, Centers for Disease Control and Prevention)

Furthermore, the courts have ruled that, although public school officials are government actors, the First Amendment freedom of expression rights of children attending public schools are somewhat limited. In particular, in *Tinker v. Des Moines* (1969) and *Hazelwood v. Kuhlmeier* (1988), the Supreme Court has upheld restrictions on speech that creates "substantial interference with school discipline or the rights of others"[31] or is "reasonably related to legitimate pedagogical concerns."[32] For example, the content of school-sponsored activities like school newspapers and speeches delivered by students can be controlled, either for the purposes of instructing students in proper adult behavior or to deter conflict between students.

Free expression includes the right to assemble peaceably and the right to petition government officials. This right even extends to members of groups whose views most people find abhorrent, such as American Nazis and the vehemently anti-gay Westboro Baptist Church, whose members have become known for their protests at the funerals of U.S. soldiers who have died fighting in the war on terror (Figure 4.12).[33] Free expression—although a broad right—is subject to certain constraints to balance it against the interests of public order. In particular, the nature, place, and timing of protests—but not their substantive content—are subject to reasonable limits. The courts have ruled that while people may peaceably assemble in a place that is a public forum, not all public property is a public forum. For example, the inside of a government office building or a college classroom—particularly while someone is teaching—is not generally considered a public forum.

Figure 4.12 Protesters from Westboro Baptist Church picket outside the U.S. Supreme Court in July 2014 prior to the decision ruling that Section 3 of the Defense of Marriage Act (DOMA) is unconstitutional. (credit: Jordan Uhl)

Rallies and protests on land that has other dedicated uses, such as roads and highways, can be limited to groups that have secured a permit in advance, and those organizing large gatherings may be required to give sufficient notice so government authorities can ensure there is enough security available. However, any such regulation must be viewpoint-neutral; the government may not treat one group differently than another because of its opinions or beliefs. For example, the government can't permit a rally by a group that favors a government policy but forbid opponents from staging a similar rally. Finally, there have been controversial situations in which government agencies have established free-speech zones for protesters during political conventions, presidential visits, and international meetings in areas that are arguably selected to minimize their public audience or to ensure that the subjects of the protests do not have to encounter the protesters.

THE SECOND AMENDMENT

There has been increased conflict over the Second Amendment in recent years due to school shootings and gun violence. As a result, gun rights have become a highly charged political issue. The text of the Second Amendment is among the shortest of those included in the Constitution:

> "A well regulated Militia, being necessary to the security of a free State, the right of the people to keep and bear Arms, shall not be infringed."

But the relative simplicity of its text has not kept it from controversy; arguably, the Second Amendment has become controversial in large part because of its text. Is this amendment merely a protection of the right of the states to organize and arm a "well regulated militia" for civil defense, or is it a protection of a "right of the people" as a whole to individually bear arms?

Before the Civil War, this would have been a nearly meaningless distinction. In most states at that time, white males of military age were considered part of the militia, liable to be called for service to put down rebellions or invasions, and the right "to keep and bear Arms" was considered a **common-law right** inherited from English law that predated the federal and state constitutions. The Constitution was not seen as a limitation on state power, and since the states expected all able-bodied free men to keep arms as a matter of course, what gun control there was mostly revolved around ensuring slaves (and their abolitionist allies) didn't have guns.

With the beginning of selective incorporation after the Civil War, debates over the Second Amendment were reinvigorated. In the meantime, as part of their black codes designed to reintroduce most of the trappings of slavery, several southern states adopted laws that restricted the carrying and ownership of weapons by former slaves. Despite acknowledging a common-law individual right to keep and bear arms, in 1876 the Supreme Court declined, in *United States v. Cruickshank*, to intervene to ensure the states would respect it.[34]

In the following decades, states gradually began to introduce laws to regulate gun ownership. Federal gun control laws began to be introduced in the 1930s in response to organized crime, with stricter laws that regulated most commerce and trade in guns coming into force in the wake of the street protests of the 1960s. In the early 1980s, following an assassination attempt on President Ronald Reagan, laws requiring background checks for prospective gun buyers were passed. During this period, the Supreme Court's decisions regarding the meaning of the Second Amendment were ambiguous at best. In *United States v. Miller*, the Supreme Court upheld the 1934 National Firearms Act's prohibition of sawed-off shotguns, largely on the basis that possession of such a gun was not related to the goal of promoting a "well regulated militia."[35] This finding was generally interpreted as meaning that the Second Amendment protected the right of the states to organize a militia, rather than an individual right, and thus lower courts generally found most firearm regulations—including some city and state laws that virtually outlawed the private ownership of firearms—to be constitutional.

However, in 2008, in a narrow 5–4 decision on *District of Columbia v. Heller*, the Supreme Court found that at least some gun control laws *did* violate the Second Amendment and that this amendment does protect an individual's right to keep and bear arms, at least in some circumstances—in particular, "for traditionally lawful purposes, such as self-defense within the home."[36] Because the District of Columbia is not a state, this decision immediately applied the right only to the federal government and territorial governments. Two years later, in *McDonald v. Chicago*, the Supreme Court overturned the *Cruickshank* decision (5–4) and again found that the right to bear arms was a fundamental right incorporated against the states, meaning that state regulation of firearms might, in some circumstances, be unconstitutional. In 2015, however, the Supreme Court allowed several of San Francisco's strict gun control laws to remain in place, suggesting that—as in the case of rights protected by the First Amendment—the courts will not treat gun rights as absolute (Figure 4.13).[37] Elsewhere in the political system, the gun issue remains similarly unsettled. However, in the wake of especially traumatic shootings at a Las Vegas outdoor concert and at a school in Parkland, Florida, there has been increased activism around gun control and community safety, especially among the young.[38]

Figure 4.13 A "No Firearms" sign is posted at Binghamton Park in Memphis, Tennessee, demonstrating that the right to possess a gun is not absolute. (credit: modification of work by Thomas R Machnitzki)

THE THIRD AMENDMENT

The Third Amendment says in full:

> "No Soldier shall, in time of peace be quartered in any house, without the consent of the Owner, nor in time of war, but in a manner to be prescribed by law."

Most people consider this provision of the Constitution obsolete and unimportant. However, it is worthwhile to note its relevance in the context of the time: citizens remembered having their cities and towns occupied by British soldiers and mercenaries during the Revolutionary War, and they viewed the British laws that required the colonists to house soldiers particularly offensive, to the point that it had been among the grievances listed in the Declaration of Independence.

Today it seems unlikely the federal government would need to house military forces in civilian lodgings against the will of property owners or tenants; however, perhaps in the same way we consider the Second and Fourth amendments, we can think of the Third Amendment as reflecting a broader idea that our homes lie within a "zone of privacy" that government officials should not violate unless absolutely necessary.

THE FOURTH AMENDMENT

The Fourth Amendment sits at the boundary between general individual freedoms and the rights of those suspected of crimes. We saw earlier that perhaps it reflects James Madison's broader concern about establishing an expectation of privacy from government intrusion at home. Another way to think of the Fourth Amendment is that it protects us from overzealous efforts by law enforcement to root out crime by ensuring that police have good reason before they intrude on people's lives with criminal investigations.

The text of the Fourth Amendment is as follows:

> "The right of the people to be secure in their persons, houses, papers, and effects, against unreasonable searches and seizures, shall not be violated, and no Warrants shall issue, but upon probable cause, supported by Oath or affirmation, and particularly describing the place to be searched, and the persons or things to be seized."

The amendment places limits on both *searches* and *seizures*: Searches are efforts to locate documents and contraband. Seizures are the taking of these items by the government for use as evidence in a criminal prosecution (or, in the case of a person, the detention or taking of the person into custody).

In either case, the amendment indicates that government officials are required to apply for and receive a **search warrant** prior to a search or seizure; this warrant is a legal document, signed by a judge, allowing police to search and/or seize persons or property. Since the 1960s, however, the Supreme Court has issued a series of rulings limiting the warrant requirement in situations where a person can be said to lack a "reasonable expectation of privacy" outside the home. Police can also search and/or seize people or property without a warrant if the owner or renter consents to the search, if there is a reasonable expectation that evidence may be destroyed or tampered with before a warrant can be issued (i.e., exigent circumstances), or if the items in question are in plain view of government officials.

Furthermore, the courts have found that police do not generally need a warrant to search the passenger compartment of a car (Figure 4.14), or to search people entering the United States from another country.[39] When a warrant is needed, law enforcement officers do not need enough evidence to secure a conviction, but they must demonstrate to a judge that there is probable cause to believe a crime has been committed or evidence will be found. **Probable cause** is the legal standard for determining whether a search or seizure is constitutional or a crime has been committed; it is a lower threshold than the standard of proof at a criminal trial.

Critics have argued that this requirement is not very meaningful because law enforcement officers are almost always able to get a search warrant when they request one; on the other hand, since we wouldn't expect the police to waste their time or a judge's time trying to get search warrants that are unlikely to be granted, perhaps the high rate at which they get them should not be so surprising.

Figure 4.14 A state police officer conducting a traffic stop near Walla Walla, Washington. (credit: modification of work by Richard Bauer)

What happens if the police conduct an illegal search or seizure without a warrant and find evidence of a crime? In the 1961 Supreme Court case *Mapp v. Ohio*, the court decided that evidence obtained without a warrant that didn't fall under one of the exceptions mentioned above could not be used as evidence in a state criminal trial, giving rise to the broad application of what is known as the **exclusionary rule**, which was first established in 1914 on a federal level in *Weeks v. United States*.[40] The exclusionary rule doesn't just apply to evidence found or to items or people seized without a warrant (or falling under an exception noted above); it also applies to any evidence developed or discovered as a result of the illegal search or seizure.

For example, if police search your home without a warrant, find bank statements showing large cash deposits on a regular basis, and discover you are engaged in some other crime in which they were previously unaware (e.g., blackmail, drugs, or prostitution), not only can they not use the bank statements as evidence of criminal activity—they also can't prosecute you for the crimes they discovered during the illegal search. This extension of the exclusionary rule is sometimes called the "fruit of the poisonous tree," because just as the metaphorical tree (i.e., the original search or seizure) is poisoned, so is anything that grows out of it.[41]

However, like the requirement for a search warrant, the exclusionary rule does have exceptions. The courts have allowed evidence to be used that was obtained without the necessary legal procedures in circumstances where police executed warrants they believed were correctly granted but in fact were not ("good faith" exception), and when the evidence would have been found anyway had they followed the law ("inevitable discovery").

The requirement of probable cause also applies to arrest warrants. A person cannot generally be detained by police or taken into custody without a warrant, although most states allow police to arrest someone suspected of a felony crime without a warrant so long as probable cause exists, and police can arrest people for minor crimes or misdemeanors they have witnessed themselves.

4.3 The Rights of Suspects

Learning Objectives

By the end of this section, you will be able to:
- Identify the rights of those suspected or accused of criminal activity
- Explain how Supreme Court decisions transformed the rights of the accused
- Explain why the Eighth Amendment is controversial regarding capital punishment

In addition to protecting the personal freedoms of individuals, the Bill of Rights protects those suspected or accused of crimes from various forms of unfair or unjust treatment. The prominence of these protections in the Bill of Rights may seem surprising. Given the colonists' experience of what they believed to be unjust rule by British authorities, however, and the use of the legal system to punish rebels and their sympathizers for political offenses, the impetus to ensure fair, just, and impartial treatment to everyone accused of a crime—no matter how unpopular—is perhaps more understandable. What is more, the revolutionaries, and the eventual framers of the Constitution, wanted to keep the best features of English law as well.

In addition to the protections outlined in the Fourth Amendment, which largely pertain to investigations conducted before someone has been charged with a crime, the next four amendments pertain to those suspected, accused, or convicted of crimes, as well as people engaged in other legal disputes. At every stage of the legal process, the Bill of Rights incorporates protections for these people.

THE FIFTH AMENDMENT

Many of the provisions dealing with the rights of the accused are included in the Fifth Amendment; accordingly, it is one of the longest in the Bill of Rights. The Fifth Amendment states in full:

> "No person shall be held to answer for a capital, or otherwise infamous crime, unless on a presentment or indictment of a Grand Jury, except in cases arising in the land or naval forces, or in the Militia, when in actual service in time of War or public danger; nor shall any person be subject for the same offence to be twice put in jeopardy of life or limb; nor shall be compelled in any criminal case to be a witness against himself, nor be deprived of life, liberty, or property, without due process of law; nor shall private property be taken for public use, without just compensation."

The first clause requires that serious crimes be prosecuted only after an indictment has been issued by a grand jury. However, several exceptions are permitted as a result of the evolving interpretation and understanding of this amendment by the courts, given the Constitution is a living document. First, the courts have generally found this requirement to apply only to felonies; less serious crimes can be tried without a grand jury proceeding. Second, this provision of the Bill of Rights does *not* apply to the states because it has not been incorporated; many states instead require a judge to hold a preliminary hearing to decide whether there is enough evidence to hold a full trial. Finally, members of the armed forces who are accused of crimes are not entitled to a grand jury proceeding.

The Fifth Amendment also protects individuals against **double jeopardy**, a process that subjects a suspect to prosecution twice for the same criminal act. No one who has been acquitted (found not guilty) of a crime can be prosecuted again for that crime. But the prohibition against double jeopardy has its own exceptions. The most notable is that it prohibits a second prosecution only at the same level of government (federal or state) as the first; the federal government can try you for violating federal law, even if a state or local court finds you not guilty of the same action. For example, in the early 1990s, several Los Angeles police officers accused of brutally beating motorist Rodney King during his arrest were acquitted of various charges in a state court, but some were later convicted in a federal court of violating King's civil rights.

The double jeopardy rule does not prevent someone from recovering damages in a civil case—a legal dispute between individuals over a contract or compensation for an injury—that results from a criminal act, even if the person accused of that act is found not guilty. One famous case from the 1990s involved former football star and television personality O. J. Simpson. Simpson, although acquitted of the murders of his ex-wife Nicole Brown and her friend Ron Goldman in a criminal court, was later found to be responsible for their deaths in a subsequent civil case and as a result was forced to forfeit most of his wealth to pay damages to their families.

Perhaps the most famous provision of the Fifth Amendment is its protection against **self-incrimination**, or the right to remain silent. This provision is so well known that we have a phrase for it: "taking the Fifth." People have the right not to give evidence in court or to law enforcement officers that might constitute an admission of guilt or responsibility for a crime. Moreover, in a criminal trial, if someone does not testify in his or her own defense, the prosecution cannot use that failure to testify as evidence of guilt or imply that an innocent person would testify. This provision became embedded in the public consciousness following the Supreme Court's 1966 ruling in *Miranda v. Arizona*, whereby suspects were required to be informed of their most important rights, including the right against self-incrimination, before being interrogated in police custody.[42] However, contrary to some media depictions of the **Miranda warning**, law enforcement officials do not necessarily have to inform suspects of their rights before they are questioned in situations where they are free to leave.

Like the Fourteenth Amendment's due process clause, the Fifth Amendment prohibits the federal government from depriving people of their "life, liberty, or property, without due process of law." Recall that due process is a guarantee that people will be treated fairly and impartially by government officials when the government seeks to fine or imprison them or take their personal property away from them. The courts have interpreted this provision to mean that government officials must establish consistent, fair procedures to decide when people's freedoms are limited; in other words, citizens cannot be detained, their freedom limited, or their property taken arbitrarily or on a whim by police or other government officials. As a result, an entire body of procedural safeguards comes into play for the legal prosecution of crimes. However, the Patriot Act, passed into law after the 9/11 terrorist attacks, somewhat altered this notion.

The final provision of the Fifth Amendment has little to do with crime at all. The *takings clause* says that "private property [cannot] be taken for public use, without just compensation." This provision, along with the due process clause's provisions limiting the taking of property, can be viewed as a protection of individuals' **economic liberty**: their right to obtain, use, and trade tangible and intangible property for their own benefit. For example, you have the right to trade your knowledge, skills, and labor for money through work or the use of your property, or trade money or goods for other things of value, such as clothing, housing, education, or food.

The greatest recent controversy over economic liberty has been sparked by cities' and states' use of the power of **eminent domain** to take property for redevelopment. Traditionally, the main use of eminent domain was to obtain property for transportation corridors like railroads, highways, canals and reservoirs, and pipelines, which require fairly straight routes to be efficient. Because any single property owner could effectively block a particular route or extract an unfair price for land if it was the last piece needed to assemble a route, there are reasonable arguments for using eminent domain as a last resort in these circumstances, particularly for projects that convey substantial benefits to the public at large.

However, increasingly eminent domain has been used to allow economic development, with beneficiaries ranging from politically connected big businesses such as car manufacturers building new factories to highly profitable sports teams seeking ever-more-luxurious stadiums (Figure 4.15). And, while we traditionally think of property owners as relatively well-off people whose rights don't necessarily need protecting since they can fend for themselves in the political system, frequently these cases pit lower- and middle-class homeowners against multinational corporations or multimillionaires with the ear of city and state officials. In a notorious 2005 case, *Kelo v. City of New London*, the Supreme Court sided with municipal officials taking homes in a middle-class neighborhood to obtain land for a large pharmaceutical company's corporate campus.[43] The case led to a public backlash against the use of eminent domain and legal changes in many states, making it harder for cities to take property from one private party and give it to another for economic redevelopment purposes. Eminent domain has once again become a salient issue in the context of President Trump's proposed border wall. To build the wall, the federal government is attempting to use the doctrine to seize a wide swath of property, including religious grounds.[44]

Figure 4.15   AT&T Stadium in Arlington, Texas, sits on land taken by eminent domain. (credit: John Purget)

Some disputes over economic liberty have gone beyond the idea of eminent domain. In the past few years, the emergence of on-demand ride-sharing services like Lyft and Uber, direct sales by electric car manufacturer Tesla Motors, and short-term property rentals through companies like Airbnb have led to conflicts between people seeking to offer profitable services online, states and cities trying to regulate these businesses, and the incumbent service providers that compete with these new business models. In the absence of new public policies to clarify rights, the path forward is often determined through norms established in practice, by governments, or by court cases.

THE SIXTH AMENDMENT

Once someone has been charged with a crime and indicted, the next stage in a criminal case is typically the trial itself, unless a plea bargain is reached. The Sixth Amendment contains the provisions that govern criminal trials; in full, it states:

> "In all criminal prosecutions, the accused shall enjoy the right to a speedy and public trial, by an impartial jury of the State and district wherein the crime shall have been committed, which district shall have been previously ascertained by law, and to be informed of the nature and cause of the accusation; to be confronted with the witnesses against him; to have compulsory process for obtaining witnesses in his favor, and to have the Assistance of Counsel for his defence [sic]."

The first of these guarantees is the right to have a speedy, public trial by an impartial jury. Although there is no absolute limit on the length of time that may pass between an indictment and a trial, the Supreme Court has said that excessively lengthy delays must be justified and balanced against the potential harm to the defendant.[45] In effect, the speedy trial requirement protects people from being detained indefinitely by the government. Yet the courts have ruled that there are exceptions to the public trial requirement; if a public trial would undermine the defendant's right to a fair trial, it can be held behind closed doors, while prosecutors can request closed proceedings only in certain, narrow circumstances (generally, to protect witnesses from retaliation or to guard classified information). In general, a prosecution must also be made in the "state and district" where the crime was committed; however, people accused of crimes may ask for a change of venue for their trial if they believe pre-trial publicity or other factors make it difficult or impossible for them to receive a fair trial where the crime occurred.

Link to Learning

Although the Supreme Court's proceedings are not televised and there is no video of the courtroom, audio recordings of the oral arguments and decisions announced in cases have been made since 1955. A complete collection of these recordings can be found at the Oyez Project (https://www.openstax.org/l/29oyezproject) website along with full information about each case.

Most people accused of crimes decline their right to a jury trial. This choice is typically the result of a **plea bargain**, an agreement between the defendant and the prosecutor in which the defendant pleads guilty to the charge(s) in question, or perhaps to less serious charges, in exchange for more lenient punishment than he or she might receive if convicted after a full trial. There are a number of reasons why this might happen. The evidence against the accused may be so overwhelming that conviction is a near-certainty, so he or she might decide that avoiding the more serious penalty (perhaps even the death penalty) is better than taking the small chance of being acquitted after a trial. Someone accused of being part of a larger crime or criminal organization might agree to testify against others in exchange for lighter punishment. At the same time, prosecutors might want to ensure a win in a case that might not hold up in court by securing convictions for offenses they know they can prove, while avoiding a lengthy trial on other charges they might lose.

The requirement that a jury be impartial is a critical requirement of the Sixth Amendment. Both the prosecution and the defense are permitted to reject potential jurors who they believe are unable to fairly decide the case without prejudice. However, the courts have also said that the composition of the jury as a whole may in itself be prejudicial; potential jurors may not be excluded simply because of their race or sex, for example.[46]

The Sixth Amendment guarantees the right of those accused of crimes to present witnesses in their own defense (if necessary, compelling them to testify) and to confront and cross-examine witnesses presented by the prosecution. In general, the only testimony acceptable in a criminal trial must be given in a courtroom and be subject to cross-examination; hearsay, or testimony by one person about what another person has said, is generally inadmissible, although hearsay may be presented as evidence when it is an admission of guilt by the defendant or a "dying declaration" by a person who has passed away. Although both sides in a trial have the opportunity to examine and cross-examine witnesses, the judge may exclude testimony deemed irrelevant or prejudicial.

Finally, the Sixth Amendment guarantees the right of those accused of crimes to have the assistance of an attorney in their defense. Historically, many states did not provide attorneys to those accused of most crimes who could not afford one themselves; even when an attorney was provided, his or her assistance was often inadequate at best. This situation changed as a result of the Supreme Court's decision in *Gideon v. Wainwright* (1963).[47] Clarence Gideon, a poor drifter, was accused of breaking into and stealing money and other items from a pool hall in Panama City, Florida. Denied a lawyer, Gideon was tried and convicted and sentenced to a five-year prison term. While in prison—still without assistance of a lawyer—he drafted a handwritten appeal and sent it to the Supreme Court, which agreed to hear his case (Figure 4.16). The justices unanimously ruled that Gideon, and anyone else accused of a serious crime, was entitled to the assistance of a lawyer, even if they could not afford one, as part of the general due process right to a fair trial.

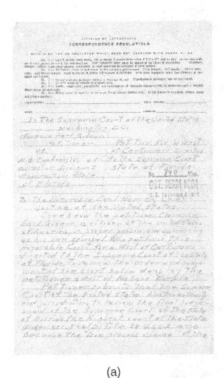

(a)   (b)

Figure 4.16 The handwritten petition for appeal (a) sent to the Supreme Court by Clarence Gideon, shown here circa 1961 (b), the year of his Florida arrest for breaking and entering.

The Supreme Court later extended the *Gideon v. Wainwright* ruling to apply to any case in which an accused person faced the possibility of "loss of liberty," even for one day. The courts have also overturned convictions in which people had incompetent or ineffective lawyers through no fault of their own. The *Gideon* ruling has led to an increased need for professional public defenders, lawyers who are paid by the government to represent those who cannot afford an attorney themselves, although some states instead require practicing lawyers to represent poor defendants on a pro bono basis (essentially, donating their time and energy to the case).

Link to Learning

The **National Association for Public Defense (https://www.openstax.org/l/29publicdefend)** represents public defenders, lobbying for better funding for public defense and improvements in the justice system in general.

Criminal Justice: Theory Meets Practice

Typically a person charged with a serious crime will have a brief hearing before a judge to be informed of the charges against him or her, to be made aware of the right to counsel, and to enter a plea. Other hearings may be held to decide on the admissibility of evidence seized or otherwise obtained by prosecutors.

If the two sides cannot agree on a plea bargain during this period, the next stage is the selection of a jury. A pool of potential jurors is summoned to the court and screened for impartiality, with the goal of seating twelve (in most states) and one or two alternates. All hear the evidence in the trial; unless an alternate must serve, the original twelve decide whether the evidence overwhelmingly points toward guilt or innocence beyond a reasonable doubt.

In the trial itself, the lawyers for the prosecution and defense make opening arguments, followed by testimony by witnesses for the prosecution (and any cross-examination), and then testimony by witnesses for the defense, including the defendant if he or she chooses. Additional prosecution witnesses may be called to rebut testimony by the defense. Finally, both sides make closing arguments. The judge then issues instructions to the jury, including an admonition not to discuss the case with anyone outside the jury room. The jury members leave the courtroom to enter the jury room and begin their deliberations (Figure 4.17).

Figure 4.17   A typical courtroom in the United States. The jury sits along one side, between the judge/witness stand and the tables for the defense and prosecution.

The jurors pick a foreman or forewoman to coordinate their deliberations. They may ask to review evidence or to hear transcripts of testimony. They deliberate in secret and their decision must be unanimous; if they are unable to agree on a verdict after extensive deliberation, a mistrial may be declared, which in effect requires the prosecution to try the case all over again.

A defendant found not guilty of all charges will be immediately released unless other charges are pending (e.g., the defendant is wanted for a crime in another jurisdiction). If the defendant is found guilty of one or more offenses, the judge will choose an appropriate sentence based on the law and the circumstances; in the federal system, this sentence will typically be based on guidelines that assign point values to various offenses and facts in the case. If the prosecution is pursuing the death penalty, the jury will decide whether the defendant should be subject to capital punishment or life imprisonment.

The reality of court procedure is much less dramatic and exciting than what is typically portrayed in television shows and movies. Nonetheless, most Americans will participate in the legal system at least once in their lives as a witness, juror, or defendant.

Have you or any member of your family served on a jury? If so, was the experience a positive one? Did the trial proceed as expected? If you haven't served on a jury, is it something you look forward to? Why or why not?

THE SEVENTH AMENDMENT

The Seventh Amendment deals with the rights of those engaged in civil disputes; as noted earlier, these are disagreements between individuals or businesses in which people are typically seeking compensation for some harm caused. For example, in an automobile accident, the person responsible is compelled to compensate any others (either directly or through his or her insurance company). Much of the work of the legal system consists of efforts to resolve civil disputes. The Seventh Amendment, in full, reads:

> "In Suits at common law, where the value in controversy shall exceed twenty dollars, the right of trial by jury shall be preserved, and no fact tried by a jury, shall be otherwise re-examined in any Court of the United States, than according to the rules of the common law."

Because of this provision, all trials in civil cases must take place before a jury unless both sides waive their right to a jury trial. However, this right is not always incorporated; in many states, civil disputes—particularly those involving small sums of money, which may be heard by a dedicated small claims court—need not be tried in front of a jury and may instead be decided by a judge working alone.

The Seventh Amendment limits the ability of judges to reconsider questions of fact, rather than of law, that were originally decided by a jury. For example, if a jury decides a person was responsible for an action and the case is appealed, the appeals judge cannot decide someone else was responsible. This preserves the traditional common-law distinction that judges are responsible for deciding questions of law while jurors are responsible for determining the facts of a particular case.

THE EIGHTH AMENDMENT

The Eighth Amendment says, in full:

> "Excessive bail shall not be required, nor excessive fines imposed, nor cruel and unusual punishments inflicted."

Bail is a payment of money that allows a person accused of a crime to be freed pending trial; if you "make bail" in a case and do not show up for your trial, you will forfeit the money you paid. Since many people cannot afford to pay bail directly, they may instead get a *bail bond*, which allows them to pay a fraction of the money (typically 10 percent) to a person who sells bonds and who pays the full bail amount. (In most states, the bond seller makes money because the defendant does not get back the money for the bond, and most people show up for their trials.) However, people believed likely to flee or who represent a risk to the community while free may be denied bail and held in jail until their trial takes place.

It is rare for bail to be successfully challenged for being excessive. The Supreme Court has defined an excessive fine as one "so grossly excessive as to amount to deprivation of property without due process of law" or "grossly disproportional to the gravity of a defendant's offense."[48] In practice the courts have rarely struck down fines as excessive either.

The most controversial provision of the Eighth Amendment is the ban on "cruel and unusual punishments." Various torturous forms of execution common in the past—drawing and quartering, burning people alive, and the like—are prohibited by this provision.[49] Recent controversies over lethal injections and firing squads to administer the death penalty suggest the topic is still salient. While the Supreme Court has never established a definitive test for what constitutes a cruel and unusual punishment, it has generally allowed most penalties short of death for adults, even when to outside observers the punishment might be reasonably seen as disproportionate or excessive.[50]

In recent years the Supreme Court has issued a series of rulings substantially narrowing the application of the death penalty. As a result, defendants who have mental disabilities may not be executed.[51] Also, defendants who were under eighteen when they committed an offense that is otherwise subject to the death penalty may not be executed.[52] The court has generally rejected the application of the death penalty to crimes that did not result in the death of another human being, most notably in the case of rape.[53] And, while permitting the death penalty to be applied to murder in some cases, the Supreme Court has generally struck down laws that require the application of the death penalty in certain circumstances. Still, the United States is among ten countries with the most executions worldwide (Figure 4.18).

Rate of Execution in the 10 Countries with the Most Executions, 2007–2012

Country	Number of annual executions, on average	Number of annual executions, per capita
Iran	277.2	0.000381%
Saudi Arabia	70.5	0.000257%
Iraq	42.7	0.000157%
China	1720–2400	0.000129–0.000180% (estimate)
Libya	6.5	0.000116%
Yemen	25.3	0.000109%
North Korea	17.5	0.000073%
Pakistan	28.5	0.000016%
United States	36.7	0.000012%
Vietnam	9.7	0.000001%

Source: Amnesty International. "Death Penalty Statistics, Country by Country." 2012.

Figure 4.18 The United States has the ninth highest per capita rate of execution in the world.

At the same time, however, it appears that the public mood may have shifted somewhat against the death penalty, perhaps due in part to an overall decline in violent crime. The reexamination of past cases through DNA evidence has revealed dozens in which people were wrongfully executed.[54] For example, Claude Jones was executed for murder based on 1990-era DNA testing of a single hair that was determined at that time to be his; however, with better DNA testing technology, it was later found to be that of the victim.[55] Perhaps as a result of this and other cases, seven additional states have abolished capital punishment since 2007. As of 2015, nineteen states and the District of Columbia no longer apply the death penalty in new cases, and several other states do not carry out executions despite sentencing people to death.[56] It remains to be seen whether this gradual trend toward the elimination of the death penalty by the states will continue, or whether the Supreme Court will eventually decide to follow former Justice Harry Blackmun's decision to "no longer... tinker with the machinery of death" and abolish it completely.

4.4 Interpreting the Bill of Rights

Learning Objectives

By the end of this section, you will be able to:
- Describe how the Ninth and Tenth Amendments reflect on our other rights
- Identify the two senses of "right to privacy" embodied in the Constitution
- Explain the controversy over privacy when applied to abortion and same-sex relationships

As this chapter has suggested, the provisions of the Bill of Rights have been interpreted and reinterpreted repeatedly over the past two centuries. However, the first eight amendments are largely silent on the status of traditional common law, which was the legal basis for many of the natural rights claimed by the framers in the Declaration of Independence. These amendments largely reflect the worldview of the time in which they were written; new technology and an evolving society and economy have presented us with novel situations that do not fit neatly into the framework established in the late eighteenth century.

In this section, we consider the final two amendments of the Bill of Rights and the way they affect our understanding of the Constitution as a whole. Rather than protecting specific rights and liberties, the Ninth and Tenth Amendments indicate how the Constitution and the Bill of Rights should be interpreted, and they lay out the residual powers of the state governments. We will also examine privacy rights, an area the Bill of Rights does not address directly; instead, the emergence of defined privacy rights demonstrates how the Ninth and Tenth Amendments have been applied to expand the scope of rights protected by the Constitution.

THE NINTH AMENDMENT

We saw above that James Madison and the other framers were aware they might endanger some rights if they listed a few in the Constitution and omitted others. To ensure that those interpreting the Constitution would recognize that the listing of freedoms and rights in the Bill of Rights was not exhaustive, the Ninth Amendment states:

> "The enumeration in the Constitution, of certain rights, shall not be construed to deny or disparage others retained by the people."

These rights "retained by the people" include the common-law and natural rights inherited from the laws, traditions, and past court decisions of England. To this day, we regularly exercise and take for granted rights that aren't written down in the federal constitution, like the right to marry, the right to seek opportunities for employment and education, and the right to have children and raise a family. Supreme Court justices over the years have interpreted the Ninth Amendment in different ways; some have argued that it was intended to extend the rights protected by the Constitution to those natural and common-law rights, while others have argued that it does not prohibit states from changing their constitutions and laws to modify or limit those rights as they see fit.

Critics of a broad interpretation of the Ninth Amendment point out that the Constitution provides ways to protect newly formalized rights through the amendment process. For example, in the nineteenth and twentieth centuries, the right to vote was gradually expanded by a series of constitutional amendments (the Fifteenth and Nineteenth), even though at times this expansion was the subject of great public controversy. However, supporters of a broad interpretation of the Ninth Amendment point out that the rights of the people—particularly people belonging to political or demographic minorities—should not be subject to the whims of popular majorities. One right the courts have said may be at least partially based on the Ninth Amendment is a general right to privacy, discussed later in the chapter.

THE TENTH AMENDMENT

The Tenth Amendment is as follows:

> "The powers not delegated to the United States by the Constitution, nor prohibited by it to the States, are reserved to the States respectively, or to the people."

Unlike the other provisions of the Bill of Rights, this amendment focuses on *power* rather than rights. The courts have generally read the Tenth Amendment as merely stating, as Chief Justice Harlan Stone put it, a "truism that all is retained which has not been surrendered."[57] In other words, rather than limiting the power of the federal government in any meaningful way, it simply restates what is made obvious elsewhere in the Constitution: the federal government has both enumerated and implied powers, but where the federal government does not (or chooses not to) exercise power, the states may do so.

At times, politicians and state governments have argued that the Tenth Amendment means states can engage in *interposition* or *nullification* by blocking federal government laws and actions they deem to exceed the constitutional powers of the national government. But the courts have rarely been sympathetic to these arguments, except when the federal government appears to be directly requiring state and local officials to do something. For example, in 1997 the Supreme Court struck down part of a federal law that required state and local law enforcement to participate in conducting background checks for prospective gun purchasers, while in 2012 the court ruled that the government could not compel states to participate in expanding the joint state-federal Medicaid program by taking away all their existing Medicaid funding if they refused to do so.[58]

However, the Tenth Amendment also allows states to guarantee rights and liberties more fully or extensively than the federal government does, or to include additional rights. For example, many state constitutions guarantee the right to a free public education, several states give victims of crimes certain rights, and eighteen states include the right to hunt game and/or fish.[59] A number of state constitutions explicitly guarantee equal rights for men and women. Some permitted women to vote before that right was expanded to all women with the Nineteenth Amendment in 1920, and people aged 18–20 could vote in a few states before the Twenty-Sixth Amendment came into force in 1971. As we will see below, several states also explicitly recognize a right to privacy. State courts at times have interpreted state constitutional provisions to include broader protections for basic liberties than their federal counterparts. For example, although in general people do not have the right to free speech and assembly on private property owned by others without their permission, California's constitutional protection of freedom of expression was extended to portions of some privately owned shopping centers by the state's supreme court (Figure 4.19).[60]

Figure 4.19 This sign outside a California branch of the Trader Joe's supermarket chain is one of many anti-solicitation signs that sprang up in the wake of a court case involving the Pruneyard Shopping Center, which resulted in the protection of free expression in some privately owned shopping centers. (credit: modification of work by "IvyMike"/Flickr)

These state protections do not extend the other way, however. If the federal government passes a law or adopts a constitutional amendment that restricts rights or liberties, or a Supreme Court decision interprets the Constitution in a way that narrows these rights, the state's protection no longer applies. For example, if Congress decided to outlaw hunting and fishing and the Supreme Court decided this law was a valid exercise of federal power, the state constitutional provisions that protect the right to hunt and fish would effectively be meaningless. More concretely, federal laws that control weapons and drugs override state laws and constitutional provisions that otherwise permit them. While federal marijuana policies are not strictly enforced, state-level marijuana policies in Colorado and Washington provide a prominent exception to that clarity.

Get Connected!

Student-Led Constitutional Change

Although the United States has not had a national constitutional convention since 1787, the states have generally been much more willing to revise their constitutions. In 1998, two politicians in Texas decided to do something a little bit different: they enlisted the help of college students at Angelo State University to draft a completely new constitution for the state of Texas, which was then formally proposed to the state legislature.[61] Although the proposal failed, it was certainly a valuable learning experience for the students who took part.

Each state has a different process for changing its constitution. In some, like California and Mississippi, voters can propose amendments to their state constitution directly, bypassing the state legislature. In others, such as Tennessee and Texas, the state legislature controls the process of initiation. The process can affect the sorts of amendments likely to be considered; it shouldn't be surprising, for example, that amendments limiting the number of terms legislators can serve in office have been much more common in states where the legislators themselves have no say in whether such provisions are adopted.

What rights or liberties do you think ought to be protected by your state constitution that aren't already? Or would you get rid of some of these protections instead? Find a copy of your current state constitution, read through it, and decide. Then find out what steps would be needed to amend your state's constitution to make the changes you would like to see.

THE RIGHT TO PRIVACY

Although the term *privacy* does not appear in the Constitution or Bill of Rights, scholars have interpreted several Bill of Rights provisions as an indication that James Madison and Congress sought to protect a common-law **right to privacy** as it would have been understood in the late eighteenth century: a right to be free of government intrusion into our personal life, particularly within the bounds of the home. For example, we could perhaps see the Second Amendment as standing for the common-law right to self-defense in the home; the Third Amendment as a statement that government soldiers should not be housed in anyone's home; the Fourth Amendment as setting a high legal standard for allowing agents of the state to intrude on someone's home; and the due process and takings clauses of the Fifth Amendment as applying an equally high legal standard to the government's taking a home or property (reinforced after the Civil War by the Fourteenth Amendment). Alternatively, we could argue that the Ninth Amendment anticipated the existence of a common-law right to privacy, among other rights, when it acknowledged the existence of basic, natural rights not listed in the Bill of Rights or the body of the Constitution itself.[62] Lawyers Samuel D. Warren and Louis Brandeis (the latter a future Supreme Court justice) famously developed the concept of privacy rights in a law review article published in 1890.[63]

Although several state constitutions do list the right to privacy as a protected right, the explicit recognition by the Supreme Court of a right to privacy in the U.S. Constitution emerged only in the middle of the twentieth century. In 1965, the court spelled out the right to privacy for the first time in *Griswold v. Connecticut*, a case that struck down a state law forbidding even married individuals to use any form of contraception.[64] Although many subsequent cases before the Supreme Court also dealt with privacy in the course of intimate, sexual conduct, the issue of privacy matters as well in the context of surveillance and monitoring by government and private parties of our activities, movements, and communications. Both these senses of privacy are examined below.

Sexual Privacy

Although the *Griswold* case originally pertained only to married couples, in 1972 it was extended to apply the right to obtain contraception to unmarried people as well.[65] Although neither decision was entirely without controversy, the "sexual revolution" taking place at the time may well have contributed to a sense that anti-contraception laws were at the very least dated, if not in violation of people's rights. The contraceptive coverage controversy surrounding the Hobby Lobby case shows that this topic remains relevant.

The Supreme Court's application of the right to privacy doctrine to abortion rights proved far more problematic, legally and politically. In 1972, four states permitted abortions without restrictions, while thirteen allowed abortions "if the pregnant woman's life or physical or mental health were endangered, if the fetus would be born with a severe physical or mental defect, or if the pregnancy had resulted from rape or incest"; abortions were completely illegal in Pennsylvania and heavily restricted in the remaining states.[66] On average, several hundred American women a year died as a result of "back alley abortions" in the 1960s.

The legal landscape changed dramatically as a result of the 1973 ruling in *Roe v. Wade*,[67] in which the Supreme Court decided the right to privacy encompassed a right for women to terminate a pregnancy, at least under certain scenarios. The justices ruled that while the government did have an interest in protecting the "potentiality of human life," nonetheless this had to be balanced against the interests of both women's health and women's right to decide whether to have an abortion. Accordingly, the court established a framework for deciding whether abortions could be regulated based on the fetus's viability (i.e., potential to survive outside the womb) and the stage of pregnancy, with no restrictions permissible during the first three months of pregnancy (i.e., the first trimester), during which abortions were deemed safer for women than childbirth itself.

Starting in the 1980s, Supreme Court justices appointed by Republican presidents began to roll back the *Roe* decision. A key turning point was the court's ruling in *Planned Parenthood v. Casey* in 1992, in which a plurality of the court rejected *Roe's* framework based on trimesters of pregnancy and replaced it with the **undue burden test**, which allows restrictions prior to viability that are not "substantial obstacle[s]" (undue burdens) to women seeking an abortion.[68] Thus, the court upheld some state restrictions, including a required waiting period between arranging and having an abortion, parental consent (or, if not possible for some reason such as incest, authorization of a judge) for minors, and the requirement that women be informed of the health consequences of having an abortion. Other restrictions such as a requirement that a married woman notify her spouse prior to an abortion were struck down as an undue burden. Since the *Casey* decision, many states have passed other restrictions on abortions, such as banning certain procedures, requiring women to have and view an ultrasound before having an abortion, and implementing more stringent licensing and inspection requirements for facilities where abortions are performed. Although no majority of Supreme Court justices has ever moved to overrule *Roe*, the restrictions on abortion the Court has upheld in the last few decades have made access to abortions more difficult in many areas of the country, particularly in rural states and communities along the U.S.–Mexico border (Figure 4.20). However, in *Whole Woman's Health v. Hellerstedt* (2016), the Court reinforced Roe 5–3 by disallowing two Texas state regulations regarding the delivery of abortion services.[69]

(a)   (b)

Figure 4.20   A "March for Life" in Knoxville, Tennessee, on January 20, 2013 (a), marks the anniversary of the *Roe v. Wade* decision. On November 15, 2014, protestors in Chicago demonstrate against a crisis pregnancy center (b), a type of organization that counsels against abortion. (credit a: modification of work by Brian Stansberry; credit b: modification of work by Samuel Henderson)

Beyond the issues of contraception and abortion, the right to privacy has been interpreted to encompass a more general right for adults to have noncommercial, consensual sexual relationships in private. However, this legal development is relatively new; as recently as 1986, the Supreme Court ruled that states could still criminalize sex acts between two people of the same sex.[70] That decision was overturned in 2003 in *Lawrence v. Texas*, which invalidated state laws that criminalized sodomy.[71]

The state and national governments still have leeway to regulate sexual morality to some degree; "anything goes" is not the law of the land, even for actions that are consensual. The Supreme Court has declined to strike down laws in a few states that outlaw the sale of vibrators and other sex toys. Prostitution remains illegal in every state except in certain rural counties in Nevada; both polygamy (marriage to more than one other person) and bestiality (sex with animals) are illegal everywhere. And, as we saw earlier, the states may regulate obscene materials and, in certain situations, material that may be harmful to minors or otherwise indecent; to this end, states and localities have sought to ban or regulate the production, distribution, and sale of pornography.

Privacy of Communications and Property

Another example of heightened concerns about privacy in the modern era is the reality that society is under pervasive surveillance. In the past, monitoring the public was difficult at best. During the Cold War, regimes in the Soviet bloc employed millions of people as domestic spies and informants in an effort to suppress internal dissent through constant monitoring of the general public. Not only was this effort extremely expensive in terms of the human and monetary capital it required, but it also proved remarkably ineffective. Groups like the East German Stasi and the Romanian Securitate were unable to suppress the popular uprisings that undermined communist one-party rule in most of those countries in the late 1980s.

Technology has now made it much easier to track and monitor people. Police cars and roadways are equipped with cameras that can photograph the license plate of every passing car or truck and record it in a database; while allowing police to recover stolen vehicles and catch fleeing suspects, this data can also be used to track the movements of law-abiding citizens. But law enforcement officials don't even have to go to this much work; millions of car and truck drivers pay tolls electronically without stopping at toll booths thanks to transponders attached to their vehicles, which can be read by scanners well away from any toll road or bridge to monitor traffic flow or any other purpose (Figure 4.21). The pervasive use of GPS (Global Positioning System) raises similar issues.

Figure 4.21 One form of technology that has made it easier to potentially monitor people's movements is electronic toll collection, such as the E-ZPass system in the Midwest and Northeast, FasTrak in California, and I-Pass in Illinois. (credit: modification of work by Kerry Ceszyk)

Even pedestrians and cyclists are relatively easy to track today. Cameras pointed at sidewalks and roadways can employ facial recognition software to identify people as they walk or bike around a city. Many people carry smartphones that constantly report their location to the nearest cell phone tower and broadcast a beacon signal to nearby wireless hotspots and Bluetooth devices. Police can set up a small device called a Stingray that identifies and tracks all cell phones that attempt to connect to it within a radius of several thousand feet. With the right software, law enforcement and criminals can remotely activate a phone's microphone and camera, effectively planting a bug in someone's pocket without the person even knowing it.

These aren't just gimmicks in a bad science fiction movie; businesses and governments have openly admitted they are using these methods. Research shows that even metadata—information about the messages we send and the calls we make and receive, such as time, location, sender, and recipient but excluding their content—can tell governments and businesses a lot about what someone is doing. Even when this information is collected in an anonymous way, it is often still possible to trace it back to specific individuals, since people travel and communicate in largely predictable patterns.

The next frontier of privacy issues may well be the increased use of drones, small preprogrammed or remotely piloted aircraft. Drones can fly virtually undetected and monitor events from overhead. They can peek into backyards surrounded by fences, and using infrared cameras they can monitor activity inside houses and other buildings. The Fourth Amendment was written in an era when finding out what was going on in someone's home meant either going inside or peeking through a window; applying its protections today, when seeing into someone's house can be as easy as looking at a computer screen miles away, is no longer simple.

In the United States, many advocates of civil liberties are concerned that laws such as the USA **PATRIOT Act** (i.e., Uniting and Strengthening America by Providing Appropriate Tools Required to Intercept and Obstruct Terrorism Act), passed weeks after the 9/11 attacks in 2001, have given the federal government too much power by making it easy for officials to seek and obtain search warrants or, in some cases, to bypass warrant requirements altogether. Critics have argued that the Patriot Act has largely been used to prosecute ordinary criminals, in particular drug dealers, rather than terrorists as intended. Most European countries, at least on paper, have opted for laws that protect against such government surveillance, perhaps mindful of past experience with communist and fascist regimes. European countries also tend to have stricter laws limiting the collection, retention, and use of private data by companies, which makes it harder for governments to obtain and use that data. Most recently, the battle between Apple Inc. and the National Security Agency (NSA) over whether Apple should allow the government access to key information that is encrypted has made the discussion of this tradeoff salient once again. A recent court outcome in the United States suggests that America may follow Europe's lead. In *Carpenter v. United States* (2018), the first case of its kind, the U.S. Supreme Court ruled that, under the Fourth Amendment, police need a search warrant to gather phone location data as evidence to be used in trials.[72]

Link to Learning

Several groups lobby the government, such as The Electronic Frontier Foundation (https://www.openstax.org/l/29elecfronfoun) and The Electronic Privacy Information Center (https://www.openstax.org/l/29elecprivinf) , on issues related to privacy in the information age, particularly on the Internet.

All this is not to say that technological surveillance tools do not have value or are inherently bad. They can be used for many purposes that would benefit society and, perhaps, even enhance our freedoms. Spending less time stuck in traffic because we know there's been an accident—detected automatically because the cell phones that normally whiz by at the speed limit are now crawling along—gives us time to spend on more valuable activities. Capturing criminals and terrorists by recognizing them or their vehicles before they can continue their agendas will protect the life, liberty, and property of the public at large. At the same time, however, the emergence of these technologies means calls for vigilance and limits on what businesses and governments can do with the information they collect and the length of time they may retain it. We might also be concerned about how this technology could be used by more oppressive regimes. If the technological resources that are at the disposal of today's governments had been available to the East Germany Stasi and the Romanian Securitate, would those repressive regimes have fallen? How much privacy and freedom should citizens sacrifice in order to feel safe?

Key Terms

blue law a law originally created to uphold a religious or moral standard, such as a prohibition against selling alcohol on Sundays

civil liberties limitations on the power of government, designed to ensure personal freedoms

civil rights guarantees of equal treatment by government authorities

common-law right a right of the people rooted in legal tradition and past court rulings, rather than the Constitution

conscientious objector a person who claims the right to refuse to perform military service on the grounds of freedom of thought, conscience, or religion

double jeopardy a prosecution pursued twice at the same level of government for the same criminal action

due process clause provisions of the Fifth and Fourteenth Amendments that limit government power to deny people "life, liberty, or property" on an unfair basis

economic liberty the right of individuals to obtain, use, and trade things of value for their own benefit

eminent domain the power of government to take or use property for a public purpose after compensating its owner; also known as the takings clause of the Fifth Amendment

establishment clause the provision of the First Amendment that prohibits the government from endorsing a state-sponsored religion; interpreted as preventing government from favoring some religious beliefs over others or religion over non-religion

exclusionary rule a requirement, from Supreme Court case *Mapp v. Ohio*, that evidence obtained as a result of an illegal search or seizure cannot be used to try someone for a crime

free exercise clause the provision of the First Amendment that prohibits the government from regulating religious beliefs and practices

Miranda warning a statement by law enforcement officers informing a person arrested or subject to interrogation of his or her rights

obscenity acts or statements that are extremely offensive by contemporary standards

Patriot Act a law passed by Congress in the wake of the 9/11 attacks that broadened federal powers to monitor electronic communications; the full name is the USA PATRIOT Act (Uniting and Strengthening America by Providing Appropriate Tools Required to Intercept and Obstruct Terrorism Act)

plea bargain an agreement between the defendant and the prosecutor in which the defendant pleads guilty to the charge(s) in question or perhaps to less serious charges, in exchange for more lenient punishment than if convicted after a full trial

prior restraint a government action that stops someone from doing something before they are able to do it (e.g., forbidding someone to publish a book he or she plans to release)

probable cause legal standard for determining whether a search or seizure is constitutional or a crime has been committed; a lower threshold than the standard of proof needed at a criminal trial

right to privacy the right to be free of government intrusion

search warrant a legal document, signed by a judge, allowing police to search and/or seize persons or property

selective incorporation the gradual process of making some guarantees of the Bill of Rights (so far) apply to state governments and the national government

self-incrimination an action or statement that admits guilt or responsibility for a crime

Sherbert test a standard for deciding whether a law violates the free exercise clause; a law will be struck down unless there is a "compelling governmental interest" at stake and it accomplishes its goal by the "least restrictive means" possible

symbolic speech a form of expression that does not use writing or speech but nonetheless communicates an idea (e.g., wearing an article of clothing to show solidarity with a group)

undue burden test a means of deciding whether a law that makes it harder for women to seek abortions is constitutional

Summary

4.1 What Are Civil Liberties?
The Bill of Rights is designed to protect the freedoms of individuals from interference by government officials. Originally these protections were applied only to actions by the national government; different sets of rights and liberties were protected by state constitutions and laws, and even when the rights themselves were the same, the level of protection for them often differed by definition across the states. Since the Civil War, as a result of the passage and ratification of the Fourteenth Amendment and a series of Supreme Court decisions, most of the Bill of Rights' protections of civil liberties have been expanded to cover actions by state governments as well through a process of selective incorporation. Nonetheless there is still vigorous debate about what these rights entail and how they should be balanced against the interests of others and of society as a whole.

4.2 Securing Basic Freedoms
The first four amendments of the Bill of Rights protect citizens' key freedoms from governmental intrusion. The First Amendment limits the government's ability to impose certain religious beliefs on the people, or to limit the practice of one's own religion. The First Amendment also protects freedom of expression by the public, the media, and organized groups via rallies, protests, and the petition of grievances. The Second Amendment today protects an individual's right to keep and bear arms for personal defense in the home, while the Third Amendment limits the ability of the government to allow the military to occupy civilians' homes except under extraordinary circumstances. Finally, the Fourth Amendment protects our persons, homes, and property from unreasonable searches and seizures, and it protects the people from unlawful arrests. However, all these provisions are subject to limitations, often to protect the interests of public order, the good of society as a whole, or to balance the rights of some citizens against those of others.

4.3 The Rights of Suspects
The rights of those suspected, accused, and convicted of crimes, along with rights in civil cases and economic liberties, are protected by the second major grouping of amendments within the Bill of Rights. The Fifth Amendment secures various procedural safeguards, protects suspects' right to remain silent, forbids trying someone twice at the same level of government for the same criminal act, and limits the taking of property for public uses. The Sixth Amendment ensures fairness in criminal trials, including through a fair and speedy trial by an impartial jury, the right to assistance of counsel, and the right to examine and compel testimony from witnesses. The Seventh Amendment ensures the right to jury trials in most civil cases (but only at the federal level). Finally, the Eighth Amendment prohibits excessive fines and bails, as well as "cruel and unusual punishments," although the scope of what is cruel and unusual is

subject to debate.

4.4 Interpreting the Bill of Rights

The interrelationship of constitutional amendments continues to be settled through key court cases over time. Because it was not explicitly laid out in the Constitution, privacy rights required clarification through public laws and court precedents. Important cases addressing the right to privacy relate to abortion, sexual behavior, internet activity, and the privacy of personal texts and cell phone calls. The place where we draw the line between privacy and public safety is an ongoing discussion in which the courts are a significant player.

Review Questions

1. The Bill of Rights was added to the Constitution because _____.
   a. key states refused to ratify the Constitution unless it was added
   b. Alexander Hamilton believed it was necessary
   c. it was part of the Articles of Confederation
   d. it was originally part of the Declaration of Independence

2. An example of a right explicitly protected by the Constitution as drafted at the Constitutional Convention is the _____.
   a. right to free speech
   b. right to keep and bear arms
   c. right to a writ of habeas corpus
   d. right not to be subjected to cruel and unusual punishment

3. The Fourteenth Amendment was critically important for civil liberties because it _____.
   a. guaranteed freed slaves the right to vote
   b. outlawed slavery
   c. helped start the process of selective incorporation of the Bill of Rights
   d. allowed the states to continue to enact black codes

4. Briefly explain the difference between civil liberties and civil rights.

5. Briefly explain the concept of selective incorporation, and why it became necessary.

6. Which of the following provisions is *not* part of the First Amendment?
   a. the right to keep and bear arms
   b. the right to peaceably assemble
   c. the right to free speech
   d. the protection of freedom of religion

7. The Third Amendment can be thought of as _____.
   a. reinforcing the right to keep and bear arms guaranteed by the Second Amendment
   b. ensuring the right to freedom of the press
   c. forming part of a broader conception of privacy in the home that is also protected by the Second and Fourth Amendments
   d. strengthening the right to a jury trial in criminal cases

8. The Fourth Amendment's requirement for a warrant _____.
   a. applies only to searches of the home
   b. applies only to the seizure of property as evidence
   c. does not protect people who rent or lease property
   d. does not apply when there is a serious risk that evidence will be destroyed before a warrant can be issued

9. Explain the difference between the *establishment clause* and the *free exercise clause*, and explain how these two clauses work together to guarantee religious freedoms.

10. Explain the difference between the *collective rights* and *individual rights* views of the Second Amendment. Which of these views did the Supreme Court's decision in *District of Columbia v. Heller* reflect?

11. The Supreme Court case known as *Kelo v. City of New London* was controversial because it _____.

   a. allowed greater use of the power of eminent domain
   b. regulated popular ride-sharing services like Lyft and Uber
   c. limited the application of the death penalty
   d. made it harder for police to use evidence obtained without a warrant

12. Which of the following rights is not protected by the Sixth Amendment?

   a. the right to trial by an impartial jury
   b. the right to cross-examine witnesses in a trial
   c. the right to remain silent
   d. the right to a speedy trial

13. The double jeopardy rule in the Bill of Rights forbids which of the following?

   a. prosecuting someone in a state court for a criminal act he or she had been acquitted of in federal court
   b. prosecuting someone in federal court for a criminal act he or she had been acquitted of in a state court
   c. suing someone for damages for an act the person was found not guilty of
   d. none of these options

14. The Supreme Court has decided that the death penalty _____.

   a. is always cruel and unusual punishment
   b. is never cruel and unusual punishment
   c. may be applied only to acts of terrorism
   d. may not be applied to those who were under 18 when they committed a crime

15. Explain why someone accused of a crime might negotiate a plea bargain rather than exercising the right to a trial by jury.

16. Explain the difference between a criminal case and a civil case.

17. Which of the following rights is not explicitly protected by some state constitutions?

   a. the right to hunt
   b. the right to privacy
   c. the right to polygamous marriage
   d. the right to a free public education

18. The right to privacy has been controversial for all the following reasons *except* _____.

   a. it is not explicitly included in the Constitution or Bill of Rights
   b. it has been interpreted to protect women's right to have an abortion
   c. it has been used to overturn laws that have substantial public support
   d. most U.S. citizens today believe the government should be allowed to outlaw birth control

19. Which of the following rules has the Supreme Court said is an *undue burden* on the right to have an abortion?

   a. Women must make more than one visit to an abortion clinic before the procedure can be performed.
   b. Minors must gain the consent of a parent or judge before seeking an abortion.
   c. Women must notify their spouses before having an abortion.
   d. Women must be informed of the health consequences of having an abortion.

20. A major difference between most European countries and the United States today is _____.

   a. most Europeans don't use technologies that can easily be tracked
   b. laws in Europe more strictly regulate how government officials can use tracking technology
   c. there are more legal restrictions on how the U.S. government uses tracking technology than in Europe
   d. companies based in Europe don't have to comply with U.S. privacy laws

21. Explain the difference between a right listed in the Bill of Rights and a common-law right.

22. Describe two ways in which new technological developments challenge traditional notions of privacy.

Critical Thinking Questions

23. The framers of the Constitution were originally reluctant to include protections of civil liberties and rights in the Constitution. Do you think this would be the case if the Constitution were written today? Why or why not?

24. Which rights and freedoms for citizens do you think our government does a good job of protecting? Why? Which rights and freedoms could it better protect, and how?

25. In which areas do you think people's rights and liberties are at risk of government intrusion? Why? Which solutions would you propose?

26. What are the implications of the Supreme Court decision in *Burwell v. Hobby*?

27. How does the provision for and the protection of individual rights and freedoms consume government resources of time and money? Since these are in effect the people's resources, do you think they are being well spent? Why or why not?

28. There is an old saying that it's better for 100 guilty people to go free than for an innocent person to be unjustly punished. Do you agree? Why or why? What do you think is the right balance for our society to strike?

Suggestions for Further Study

Abraham, Henry J. 2003. *Freedom and the Court*. New York: Oxford University Press.

Ackerman, Bruce. 2007. *Before the Next Attack: Preserving Civil Liberties in an Age of Terrorism*. New Haven, CT: Yale University Press.

Bilder, Mary Sarah. 2008. *The Transatlantic Constitution: Colonial Legal Culture and the Empire*. Cambridge, MA: Harvard University Press.

Carter, Barton T., Marc A. Franklin, and Jay B. Wright. 1993. *The First Amendment and the Fifth Estate: Regulation of Electronic Mass Media*. Westbury, NY: Foundation Press.

Domino, John C. 2002. *Civil Rights and Liberties in the 21st Century*, 2nd ed. New York: Longman.

Garrow, David J. 1998. *Liberty and Sexuality: The Right to Privacy and the Making of Roe v. Wade*. Berkeley: University of California Press.

Levy, Leonard. 1968. *Origins of the Fifth Amendment: The Right Against Self-Incrimination*. New York: Oxford University Press.

Lewis, Anthony. 2007. *Freedom for the Thought That We Hate: A Biography of the First Amendment*. New York: Basic Books.

Lukianoff, Greg. 2002. *Unlearning Liberty: Campus Censorship and the End of American Debate*. New York: Encounter Books.

Schwarz, John E. 2005. *Freedom Reclaimed: Rediscovering the American Vision*. Baltimore: John Hopkins University Press.

Waldman, Michael. 2015. *The Second Amendment: A Biography*. New York: Simon & Schuster.

Chapter 5

Civil Rights

Figure 5.1 Supporters rally in defense of Park51, a planned Islamic community center in Lower Manhattan. Due to the development's proximity to the World Trade Center site, it was controversially referred to as the Ground Zero mosque. While a temporary Islamic center opened there in September 2011, the owner now plans to build luxury condominiums on the site.[1] (credit: modification of work by David Shankbone)

Chapter Outline

5.1 What Are Civil Rights and How Do We Identify Them?

5.2 The African American Struggle for Equality

5.3 The Fight for Women's Rights

5.4 Civil Rights for Indigenous Groups: Native Americans, Alaskans, and Hawaiians

5.5 Equal Protection for Other Groups

Introduction

The United States' founding principles are liberty, equality, and justice. However, not all its citizens have always enjoyed equal opportunities, the same treatment under the law, or all the liberties extended to others. Well into the twentieth century, many were routinely discriminated against because of sex, race, ethnicity or country of origin, religion, sexual orientation, or physical or mental abilities. When we consider the experiences of white women and ethnic minorities, for much of U.S. history the majority of its people have been deprived of basic rights and opportunities, and sometimes of citizenship itself.

The fight to secure equal rights for all continues today. While many changes must still be made, the past one hundred years, especially the past few decades, have brought significant gains for people long discriminated against. Yet, as the protest over the building of an Islamic community center in Lower Manhattan demonstrates (Figure 5.1), people still encounter prejudice, injustice, and negative stereotypes that lead to discrimination, marginalization, and even exclusion from civic life.

What is the difference between civil liberties and civil rights? How did the African American struggle for civil rights evolve? What challenges did women overcome in securing the right to vote, and what obstacles do they and other U.S. groups still face? This chapter addresses these and other questions in exploring the essential concepts of civil rights.

5.1 What Are Civil Rights and How Do We Identify Them?

Learning Objectives

By the end of this section, you will be able to:
- Define the concept of civil rights
- Describe the standards that courts use when deciding whether a discriminatory law or regulation is unconstitutional
- Identify three core questions for recognizing a civil rights problem

The belief that people should be treated equally under the law is one of the cornerstones of political thought in the United States. Yet not all citizens have been treated equally throughout the nation's history, and some are treated differently even today. For example, until 1920, nearly all women in the United States lacked the right to vote. Black men received the right to vote in 1870, but as late as 1940 only 3 percent of African American adults living in the South were registered to vote, largely due to laws designed to keep them from the polls.[2] Americans were not allowed to enter into legal marriage with a member of the same sex in many U.S. states until 2015. Some types of unequal treatment are considered acceptable, while others are not. No one would consider it acceptable to allow a ten-year-old to vote, because a child lacks the ability to understand important political issues, but all reasonable people would agree that it is wrong to mandate racial segregation or to deny someone the right to vote on the basis of race. It is important to understand which types of inequality are unacceptable and why.

DEFINING CIVIL RIGHTS

Civil rights are, at the most fundamental level, guarantees by the government that it will treat people equally, particularly people belonging to groups that have historically been denied the same rights and opportunities as others. The proclamation that "all men are created equal" appears in the Declaration of Independence, and the due process clause of the Fifth Amendment to the U.S. Constitution requires that the federal government treat people equally. According to Chief Justice Earl Warren in the Supreme Court case of *Bolling v. Sharpe* (1954), "discrimination may be so unjustifiable as to be violative of due process."[3] Additional guarantees of equality are provided by the **equal protection clause** of the Fourteenth Amendment, ratified in 1868, which states in part that "No State shall . . . deny to any person within its jurisdiction the equal protection of the laws." Thus, between the Fifth and Fourteenth Amendments, neither state governments nor the federal government may treat people unequally unless unequal treatment is necessary to maintain important governmental interests, like public safety.

We can contrast civil rights with *civil liberties*, which are limitations on government power designed to protect our fundamental freedoms. For example, the Eighth Amendment prohibits the application of "cruel and unusual punishments" to those convicted of crimes, a limitation on government power. As another example, the guarantee of equal protection means the laws and the Constitution must be applied on an equal basis, limiting the government's ability to discriminate or treat some people differently, unless the unequal treatment is based on a valid reason, such as age. A law that imprisons Asian Americans twice as long as Latinos for the same offense, or a law that says people with disabilities don't have the right to contact members of Congress while other people do, would treat some people differently from others for no valid reason and might well be unconstitutional. According to the Supreme Court's interpretation of the Equal Protection Clause, "all persons similarly circumstanced shall be treated alike."[4] If people are not similarly circumstanced, however, they may be treated differently. Asian Americans and Latinos who have broken the same law are similarly circumstanced; however, a blind driver or a ten-year-old driver is differently circumstanced than a sighted, adult driver.

IDENTIFYING DISCRIMINATION

Laws that treat one group of people differently from others are not always unconstitutional. In fact, the government engages in legal discrimination quite often. In most states, you must be eighteen years old to smoke cigarettes and twenty-one to drink alcohol; these laws discriminate against the young. To get a driver's license so you can legally drive a car on public roads, you have to be a minimum age and pass tests showing your knowledge, practical skills, and vision. Perhaps you are attending a public college or university run by the government; the school you attend has an open admission policy, which means the school admits all who apply. Not all public colleges and universities have an open admissions policy, however. These schools may require that students have a high school diploma or a particular score on the SAT or ACT or a GPA above a certain number. In a sense, this is discrimination, because these requirements treat people unequally; people who do not have a high school diploma or a high enough GPA or SAT score are not admitted. How can the federal, state, and local governments discriminate in all these ways even though the equal protection clause seems to suggest that everyone be treated the same?

The answer to this question lies in the *purpose* of the discriminatory practice. In most cases when the courts are deciding whether discrimination is unlawful, the government has to demonstrate only that it has a good reason for engaging in it. Unless the person or group challenging the law can prove otherwise, the courts will generally decide the discriminatory practice is allowed. In these cases, the courts are applying the **rational basis test**. That is, as long as there's a reason for treating some people differently that is "rationally related to a legitimate government interest," the discriminatory act or law or policy is acceptable.[5] For example, since letting blind people operate cars would be dangerous to others on the road, the law forbidding them to drive is reasonably justified on the grounds of safety; thus, it is allowed even though it discriminates against the blind. Similarly, when universities and colleges refuse to admit students who fail to meet a certain test score or GPA, they can discriminate against students with weaker grades and test scores because these students most likely do not possess the knowledge or skills needed to do well in their classes and graduate from the institution. The universities and colleges have a legitimate reason for denying these students entrance.

The courts, however, are much more skeptical when it comes to certain other forms of discrimination. Because of the United States' history of discrimination against people of non-white ancestry, women, and members of ethnic and religious minorities, the courts apply more stringent rules to policies, laws, and actions that discriminate on the basis of race, ethnicity, gender, religion, or national origin.[6]

Discrimination based on gender or sex is generally examined with **intermediate scrutiny**. The standard of intermediate scrutiny was first applied by the Supreme Court in *Craig v. Boren* (1976) and again in *Clark v. Jeter* (1988).[7] It requires the government to demonstrate that treating men and women differently is "substantially related to an important governmental objective." This puts the burden of proof on the *government* to demonstrate why the unequal treatment is justifiable, not on the individual who alleges unfair discrimination has taken place. In practice, this means laws that treat men and women differently are sometimes upheld, although usually they are not. For example, in the 1980s and 1990s, the courts ruled that states could not operate single-sex institutions of higher education and that such schools, like South Carolina's military college The Citadel, shown in Figure 5.2, must admit both male and female students.[8] Women in the military are now also allowed to serve in all combat roles, although the courts have continued to allow the Selective Service System (the draft) to register only men and not women.[9]

(a)   (b)

Figure 5.2   While the first female cadets graduated from the U.S. Military Academy at West Point in 1980 (a), The Citadel, a military college in South Carolina (b), was an all-male institution until 1995 when a young woman named Shannon Faulkner enrolled in the school.

Discrimination against members of racial, ethnic, or religious groups or those of various national origins is reviewed to the greatest degree by the courts, which apply the **strict scrutiny** standard in these cases. Under strict scrutiny, the burden of proof is on the government to demonstrate that there is a compelling governmental interest in treating people from one group differently from those who are not part of that group—the law or action can be "narrowly tailored" to achieve the goal in question, and that it is the "least restrictive means" available to achieve that goal.[10] In other words, if there is a non-discriminatory way to accomplish the goal in question, discrimination should not take place. In the modern era, laws and actions that are challenged under strict scrutiny have rarely been upheld. Strict scrutiny, however, was the legal basis for the Supreme Court's 1944 upholding of the legality of the internment of Japanese Americans during World War II, discussed later in this chapter.[11] Finally, **affirmative action** consists of government programs and policies designed to benefit members of groups historically subject to discrimination. Much of the controversy surrounding affirmative action is about whether strict scrutiny should be applied to these cases.

PUTTING CIVIL RIGHTS IN THE CONSTITUTION

At the time of the nation's founding, of course, the treatment of many groups was unequal: hundreds of thousands of people of African descent were not free, the rights of women were decidedly fewer than those of men, and the native peoples of North America were generally not considered U.S. citizens at all. While the early United States was perhaps a more inclusive society than most of the world at that time, equal treatment of all was at best still a radical idea.

The aftermath of the Civil War marked a turning point for civil rights. The Republican majority in Congress was enraged by the actions of the reconstituted governments of the southern states. In these states, many former Confederate politicians and their sympathizers returned to power and attempted to circumvent the Thirteenth Amendment's freeing of slaves by passing laws known as the **black codes**. These laws were designed to reduce former slaves to the status of serfs or indentured servants; blacks were not just denied the right to vote but also could be arrested and jailed for vagrancy or idleness if they lacked jobs. Blacks were excluded from public schools and state colleges and were subject to violence at the hands of whites (**Figure 5.3**).[12]

SCENES IN MEMPHIS, TENNESSEE, DURING THE RIOT—BURNING A FREEDMEN'S SCHOOL-HOUSE.
[SKETCHED BY A. R. W.]

Figure 5.3 A school built by the federal government for former slaves burned after being set on fire during a race riot in Memphis, Tennessee, in 1866. White southerners, angered by their defeat in the Civil War and the loss of their slave property, attacked and killed former slaves, destroyed their property, and terrorized white northerners who attempted to improve the freed slaves' lives.

To override the southern states' actions, lawmakers in Congress proposed two amendments to the Constitution designed to give political equality and power to former slaves; once passed by Congress and ratified by the necessary number of states, these became the Fourteenth and Fifteenth Amendments. The Fourteenth Amendment, in addition to including the equal protection clause as noted above, also was designed to ensure that the states would respect the civil liberties of freed slaves. The Fifteenth Amendment was proposed to ensure the right to vote for black men, which will be discussed in more detail later in this chapter.

IDENTIFYING CIVIL RIGHTS ISSUES

When we look back at the past, it's relatively easy to identify civil rights issues that arose. But looking into the future is much harder. For example, few people fifty years ago would have identified the rights of the LGBT community as an important civil rights issue or predicted it would become one, yet in the intervening decades it has certainly done so. Similarly, in past decades the rights of those with disabilities, particularly mental disabilities, were often ignored by the public at large. Many people with disabilities were institutionalized and given little further thought, and within the past century, it was common for those with mental disabilities to be subject to forced sterilization.[13] Today, most of us view this treatment as barbaric.

Clearly, then, new civil rights issues can emerge over time. How can we, as citizens, identify them as they emerge and distinguish genuine claims of discrimination from claims by those who have merely been unable to convince a majority to agree with their viewpoints? For example, how do we decide if twelve-year-olds are discriminated against because they are not allowed to vote? We can identify true discrimination by applying the following analytical process:

1. *Which groups?* First, identify the group of people who are facing discrimination.

2. *Which right(s) are threatened?* Second, what right or rights are being denied to members of this group?

3. *What do we do?* Third, what can the government do to bring about a fair situation for the affected group? Is proposing and enacting such a remedy realistic?

Get Connected!

Join the Fight for Civil Rights

One way to get involved in the fight for civil rights is to stay informed. The Southern Poverty Law Center (SPLC) is a not-for-profit advocacy group based in Montgomery, Alabama. Lawyers for the SPLC specialize in civil rights litigation and represent many people whose rights have been violated, from victims of hate crimes to undocumented immigrants. They provide summaries of important civil rights cases (https://openstax.org/l/29SPLCcivri) under their Docket section.

Activity: Visit the SPLC website (https://www.openstax.org/l/29splcwebsite) to find current information about a variety of different hate groups. In what part of the country do hate groups seem to be concentrated? Where are hate incidents most likely to occur? What might be some reasons for this?

Link to Learning

Civil rights institutes are found throughout the United States and especially in the south. One of the most prominent civil rights institutes is the Birmingham Civil Rights Institute, (https://www.openstax.org/l/29birmingcilrig) which is located in Alabama.

5.2 The African American Struggle for Equality

Learning Objectives

By the end of this section, you will be able to:
- Identify key events in the history of African American civil rights
- Explain how the courts, Congress, and the executive branch supported the civil rights movement
- Describe the role of grassroots efforts in the civil rights movement

Many groups in U.S. history have sought recognition as equal citizens. Although each group's efforts have been notable and important, arguably the greatest, longest, and most violent struggle was that of African Americans, whose once-inferior legal status was even written into the text of the Constitution. Their fight for freedom and equality provided the legal and moral foundation for others who sought recognition of their equality later on.

SLAVERY AND THE CIVIL WAR

In the Declaration of Independence, Thomas Jefferson made the radical statement that "all men are created equal" and "are endowed by their Creator with certain unalienable Rights, that among these are Life, Liberty and the pursuit of Happiness." Yet like other wealthy landowners of his time, Jefferson also owned dozens of other human beings as his personal property. He recognized this contradiction and personally considered the institution of slavery to be a "hideous blot" on the nation.[14] However, in order to forge a political union that would stand the test of time, he and the other founders—and later the framers of the Constitution—chose not to address the issue in any definitive way. Political support for abolition was very much a minority stance at the time, although after the Revolution many of the northern states did abolish slavery for a variety of reasons.[15]

As the new United States expanded westward, however, the issue of slavery became harder to ignore and ignited much controversy. Many opponents of slavery were willing to accept the institution if it remained largely confined to the South but did not want it to spread westward. They feared the expansion of slavery would lead to the political dominance of the South over the North and would deprive small farmers in the newly acquired western territories who could not afford slaves.[16] Abolitionists, primarily in the North, also argued that slavery was both immoral and opposed basic U.S. values; they demanded an end to it.

The spread of slavery into the West seemed inevitable, however, following the Supreme Court's ruling in the case *Dred Scott v. Sandford*,[17] decided in 1857. Scott, who had been born into slavery but had spent time in free states and territories, argued that his temporary residence in a territory where slavery had been banned by the federal government had made him a free man. The Supreme Court rejected his argument. In fact, the Court's majority stated that Scott had no legal right to sue for his freedom at all because blacks (whether free or slave) were not and could not become U.S. citizens. Thus, Scott lacked the standing to even appear before the court. The Court also held that Congress lacked the power to decide whether slavery would be permitted in a territory that had been acquired after the Constitution was ratified, in effect prohibiting the federal government from passing any laws that would limit the expansion of slavery into any part of the West.

Ultimately, of course, the issue was decided by the Civil War (1861–1865), with the southern states seceding to defend their "states' rights" to determine their own destinies without interference by the federal government. Foremost among the rights claimed by the southern states was the right to decide whether their residents would be allowed to own slaves.[18] Although at the beginning of the war President Abraham Lincoln had been willing to allow slavery to continue in the South to preserve the Union, he changed his policies regarding abolition over the course of the war. The first step was the issuance of the Emancipation Proclamation on January 1, 1863 (**Figure 5.4**). Although it stated "all persons held as slaves . . . henceforward shall be free," the proclamation was limited in effect to the states that had rebelled. Slaves in states that had remained within the Union, such as Maryland and Delaware, and in parts of the Confederacy that were already occupied by the Union army, were not set free. Although slaves in states in rebellion were technically freed, because Union troops controlled relatively small portions of these states at the time, it was impossible to ensure that enslaved people were freed in reality and not simply on paper.[19]

(a)

(b)

Figure 5.4   In this memorial engraving from 1865 (the year he was assassinated), President Abraham Lincoln is shown with his hand resting on a copy of the Emancipation Proclamation (a). Despite popular belief, the Emancipation Proclamation (b) actually freed very few slaves, though it did change the meaning of the war.

RECONSTRUCTION

At the end of the Civil War, the South entered a period called **Reconstruction** (1865–1877) during which state governments were reorganized before the rebellious states were allowed to be readmitted to the Union. As part of this process, the Republican Party pushed for a permanent end to slavery. A constitutional amendment to this effect was passed by the House of Representatives in January 1865, after having already been approved by the Senate in April 1864, and it was ratified in December 1865 as the Thirteenth Amendment. The amendment's first section states, "Neither slavery nor involuntary servitude, except as a punishment for crime whereof the party shall have been duly convicted, shall exist within the United States, or any place subject to their jurisdiction." In effect, this amendment outlawed slavery in the United States.

The changes wrought by the Fourteenth Amendment were more extensive. In addition to introducing the equal protection clause to the Constitution, this amendment also extended the due process clause of the Fifth Amendment to the states, required the states to respect the privileges or immunities of all citizens, and, for the first time, defined citizenship at the national and state levels. People could no longer be excluded from citizenship based solely on their race. Although some of these provisions were rendered mostly toothless by the courts or the lack of political action to enforce them, others were pivotal in the expansion of civil rights.

The Fifteenth Amendment stated that people could not be denied the right to vote based on "race, color, or previous condition of servitude." This construction allowed states to continue to decide the qualifications of voters as long as those qualifications were ostensibly race-neutral. Thus, while states could not deny

African American men the right to vote on the basis of race, they could deny it to women on the basis of sex or to people who could not prove they were literate.

Although the immediate effect of these provisions was quite profound, over time the Republicans in Congress gradually lost interest in pursuing Reconstruction policies, and the Reconstruction ended with the end of military rule in the South and the withdrawal of the Union army in 1877.[20] Following the army's removal, political control of the South fell once again into the hands of white men, and violence was used to discourage blacks from exercising the rights they had been granted.[21] The revocation of voting rights, or **disenfranchisement**, took a number of forms; not every southern state used the same methods, and some states used more than one, but they all disproportionately affected black voter registration and turnout.[22]

Perhaps the most famous of the tools of disenfranchisement were **literacy tests** and **understanding tests**. Literacy tests, which had been used in the North since the 1850s to disqualify naturalized European immigrants from voting, called on the prospective voter to demonstrate his (and later her) ability to read a particular passage of text. However, since voter registration officials had discretion to decide what text the voter was to read, they could give easy passages to voters they wanted to register (typically whites) and more difficult passages to those whose registration they wanted to deny (typically blacks). Understanding tests required the prospective voter to explain the *meaning* of a particular passage of text, often a provision of the U.S. Constitution, or answer a series of questions related to citizenship. Again, since the official examining the prospective voter could decide which passage or questions to choose, the difficulty of the test might vary dramatically between white and black applicants.[23] Even had these tests been administered fairly and equitably, however, most blacks would have been at a huge disadvantage, because few could read. Although schools for blacks had existed in some places, southern states had made it largely illegal to teach slaves to read and write. At the beginning of the Civil War, only 5 percent of blacks could read and write, and most of them lived in the North.[24] Some were able to take advantage of educational opportunities after they were freed, but many were not able to gain effective literacy.

In some states, poorer, less literate white voters feared being disenfranchised by the literacy and understanding tests. Some states introduced a loophole, known as the **grandfather clause**, to allow less literate whites to vote. The grandfather clause exempted those who had been allowed to vote in that state prior to the Civil War and their descendants from literacy and understanding tests.[25] Because blacks were not allowed to vote prior to the Civil War, but most white men had been voting at a time when there were no literacy tests, this loophole allowed most illiterate whites to vote (Figure 5.5) while leaving obstacles in place for blacks who wanted to vote as well. Time limits were often placed on these provisions because state legislators realized that they might quickly be declared unconstitutional, but they lasted long enough to allow illiterate white men to register to vote.[26]

Figure 5.5 A magazine cartoon from 1879 ridicules the practice of illiterate, southern whites requiring that a "blakman" be "eddikated" before he could vote. The grandfather clause made such a situation possible.

In states where the voting rights of poor whites were less of a concern, another tool for disenfranchisement was the **poll tax** (Figure 5.6). This was an annual per-person tax, typically one or two dollars (on the order of $20 to $50 today), that a person had to pay to register to vote. People who didn't want to vote didn't have to pay, but in several states the poll tax was cumulative, so if you decided to vote you would have to pay not only the tax due for that year but any poll tax from previous years as well. Because former slaves were usually quite poor, they were less likely than white men to be able to pay poll taxes.[27]

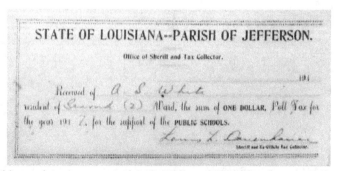

Figure 5.6 According to this receipt, a man named A. S. White paid his $1 poll tax in Jefferson Parish, Louisiana, in 1917.

Although these methods were usually sufficient to ensure that blacks were kept away from the polls, some dedicated African Americans did manage to register to vote despite the obstacles placed in their way. To ensure their vote was largely meaningless, the white elites used their control of the Democratic Party to create the **white primary**: primary elections in which only whites were allowed to vote. The state party organizations argued that as private groups, rather than part of the state government, they had no obligation to follow the Fifteenth Amendment's requirement not to deny the right to vote on the basis of race. Furthermore, they contended, voting for nominees to run for office was not the same as electing those who would actually hold office. So they held primary elections to choose the Democratic nominee in which only white citizens were allowed to vote.[28] Once the nominee had been chosen, he or she might face token opposition from a Republican or minor-party candidate in the general election, but since white voters had agreed beforehand to support whoever won the Democrats' primary, the outcome of the general election was a foregone conclusion.

With blacks effectively disenfranchised, the restored southern state governments undermined guarantees of equal treatment in the Fourteenth Amendment. They passed laws that excluded African Americans from juries and allowed the imprisonment and forced labor of "idle" black citizens. The laws also called for segregation of whites and blacks in public places under the doctrine known as "separate but equal." As long as nominally equal facilities were provided for both whites and blacks, it was legal to require members of each race to use the facilities designated for them. Similarly, state and local governments passed laws limiting what neighborhoods blacks and whites could live in. Collectively, these discriminatory laws came to be known as **Jim Crow laws**. The Supreme Court upheld the separate but equal doctrine in 1896 in *Plessy v. Ferguson*, consistent with the Fourteenth Amendment's equal protection clause, and allowed segregation to continue.[29]

CIVIL RIGHTS IN THE COURTS

By the turn of the twentieth century, the position of African Americans was quite bleak. Even outside the South, racial inequality was a fact of everyday life. African American leaders and thinkers themselves disagreed on the right path forward. Some, like Booker T. Washington, argued that acceptance of inequality and segregation over the short term would allow African Americans to focus their efforts on improving their educational and social status until whites were forced to acknowledge them as equals. W. E. B. Du Bois, however, argued for a more confrontational approach and in 1909 founded the National Association for the Advancement of Colored People (NAACP) as a rallying point for securing equality. Liberal whites dominated the organization in its early years, but African Americans assumed control over its operations in the 1920s.[30]

The NAACP soon focused on a strategy of overturning Jim Crow laws through the courts. Perhaps its greatest series of legal successes consisted of its efforts to challenge segregation in education. Early cases brought by the NAACP dealt with racial discrimination in higher education. In 1938, the Supreme Court essentially gave states a choice: they could either integrate institutions of higher education, or they could establish an equivalent university or college for African Americans.[31] Southern states chose to establish colleges for blacks rather than allow them into all-white state institutions. Although this ruling expanded opportunities for professional and graduate education in areas such as law and medicine for African Americans by requiring states to provide institutions for them to attend, it nevertheless allowed segregated colleges and universities to continue to exist.

Link to Learning

The **NAACP (https://www.openstax.org/l/29naacporg)** was pivotal in securing African American civil rights and today continues to address civil rights violations, such as police brutality and the disproportionate percentage of African American convicts that are given the death penalty.

The landmark court decision of the judicial phase of the civil rights movement settled the **Brown v. Board of Education** case in 1954.[32] In this case, the Supreme Court unanimously overturned its decision in *Plessy v. Ferguson* as it pertained to public education, stating that a separate but equal education was a logical impossibility. Even with the same funding and equivalent facilities, a segregated school could not have the same teachers or environment as the equivalent school for another race. The court also rested its decision in part on social science studies suggesting that racial discrimination led to feelings of inferiority among African American children. The only way to dispel this sense of inferiority was to end segregation and integrate public schools.

It is safe to say this ruling was controversial. While integration of public schools took place without much incident in some areas of the South, particularly where there were few black students, elsewhere it was often confrontational—or nonexistent. In recognition of the fact that southern states would delay school integration for as long as possible, civil rights activists urged the federal government to enforce the Supreme Court's decision. Organized by A. Philip Randolph and Bayard Rustin, approximately twenty-five thousand African Americans gathered in Washington, DC, on May 17, 1957, to participate in a Prayer Pilgrimage for Freedom.[33]

A few months later, in Little Rock, Arkansas, governor Orval Faubus resisted court-ordered integration and mobilized National Guard troops to keep black students out of Central High School. President Eisenhower then called up the Arkansas National Guard for federal duty (essentially taking the troops out of Faubus's hands) and sent soldiers of the 101st Airborne Division to escort students to and from classes, as shown in Figure 5.7. To avoid integration, Faubus closed four high schools in Little Rock the following school year.[34]

Figure 5.7 Opposition to the 1957 integration of Little Rock's all-white Central High School led President Eisenhower to call in soldiers of the 101st Airborne Division. For a year, they escorted nine African American students to and from school and to and from classes within the school. (credit: The U.S. Army)

In Virginia, state leaders employed a strategy of "massive resistance" to school integration, which led to the closure of a large number of public schools across the state, some for years.[35] Although *de jure* **segregation**, segregation mandated by law, had ended on paper, in practice, few efforts were made to integrate schools in most school districts with substantial black student populations until the late 1960s. Many white southerners who objected to sending their children to school with blacks then established private academies that admitted only white students.[36]

Advances were made in the courts in areas other than public education. In many neighborhoods in northern cities, which technically were not segregated, residents were required to sign restrictive real estate covenants promising that if they moved, they would not sell their houses to African Americans and sometimes not to Chinese, Japanese, Mexicans, Filipinos, Jews, and other ethnic minorities as well.[37] In the case of *Shelley v. Kraemer* (1948), the Supreme Court held that while such covenants did not violate the Fourteenth Amendment because they consisted of agreements between private citizens, their provisions could not be enforced by courts.[38] Because state courts are government institutions and the Fourteenth Amendment prohibits the government from denying people equal protection of the law, the courts' enforcement of such covenants would be a violation of the amendment. Thus, if a white family chose to sell its house to a black family and the other homeowners in the neighborhood tried to sue the seller, the court would not hear the case. In 1967, the Supreme Court struck down a Virginia law that prohibited interracial marriage in *Loving v. Virginia*.[39]

LEGISLATING CIVIL RIGHTS

Beyond these favorable court rulings, however, progress toward equality for African Americans remained slow in the 1950s. In 1962, Congress proposed what later became the Twenty-Fourth Amendment, which banned the poll tax in elections to federal (but not state or local) office; the amendment went into effect after being ratified in early 1964. Several southern states continued to require residents to pay poll taxes in order to vote in state elections until 1966 when, in the case of *Harper v. Virginia Board of Elections*, the Supreme Court declared that requiring payment of a poll tax in order to vote in an election at any level was unconstitutional.[40]

The slow rate of progress led to frustration within the African American community. Newer, grassroots organizations such as the Southern Christian Leadership Conference (SCLC), Congress of Racial Equality (CORE), and Student Non-Violent Coordinating Committee (SNCC) challenged the NAACP's position as the leading civil rights organization and questioned its legal-focused strategy. These newer groups tended to prefer more confrontational approaches, including the use of **direct action** campaigns relying on marches and demonstrations. The strategies of nonviolent resistance and **civil disobedience**, or the refusal to obey an unjust law, had been effective in the campaign led by Mahatma Gandhi to liberate colonial India from British rule in the 1930s and 1940s. Civil rights pioneers adopted these measures in the 1955–1956 Montgomery bus boycott. After Rosa Parks refused to give up her bus seat to a white person and was arrested, a group of black women carried out a day-long boycott of Montgomery's public transit system. This boycott was then extended for over a year and overseen by union organizer E. D. Nixon. The effort desegregated public transportation in that city.[41]

Direct action also took such forms as the sit-in campaigns to desegregate lunch counters that began in Greensboro, North Carolina, in 1960, and the 1961 Freedom Rides in which black and white volunteers rode buses and trains through the South to enforce a 1946 Supreme Court decision that desegregated interstate transportation (*Morgan v. Virginia*).[42] While such focused campaigns could be effective, they often had little impact in places where they were not replicated. In addition, some of the campaigns led to violence against both the campaigns' leaders and ordinary people; Rosa Parks, a longtime NAACP member and graduate of the Highlander Folk School for civil rights activists, whose actions had begun the Montgomery boycott, received death threats, E. D. Nixon's home was bombed, and the Freedom Riders were attacked in Alabama.[43]

As the campaign for civil rights continued and gained momentum, President John F. Kennedy called for Congress to pass new civil rights legislation, which began to work its way through Congress in 1963.

The resulting law (pushed heavily and then signed by President Lyndon B. Johnson after Kennedy's assassination) was the Civil Rights Act of 1964, which had wide-ranging effects on U.S. society. Not only did the act outlaw government discrimination and the unequal application of voting qualifications by race, but it also, for the first time, outlawed segregation and other forms of discrimination by most businesses that were open to the public, including hotels, theaters, and restaurants that were not private clubs. It outlawed discrimination on the basis of race, ethnicity, religion, sex, or national origin by most employers, and it created the Equal Employment Opportunity Commission (EEOC) to monitor employment discrimination claims and help enforce this provision of the law. The provisions that affected private businesses and employers were legally justified not by the Fourteenth Amendment's guarantee of equal protection of the laws but instead by Congress's power to regulate interstate commerce.[44]

Even though the Civil Rights Act of 1964 had a monumental impact over the long term, it did not end efforts by many southern whites to maintain the white-dominated political power structure in the region. Progress in registering African American voters remained slow in many states despite increased federal activity supporting it, so civil rights leaders including Martin Luther King, Jr. decided to draw the public eye to the area where the greatest resistance to voter registration drives were taking place. The SCLC and SNCC particularly focused their attention on the city of Selma, Alabama, which had been the site of violent reactions against civil rights activities.

The organizations' leaders planned a march from Selma to Montgomery in March 1965. Their first attempt to march was violently broken up by state police and sheriff's deputies (Figure 5.8). The second attempt was aborted because King feared it would lead to a brutal confrontation with police and violate a court order from a federal judge who had been sympathetic to the movement in the past. That night, three of the marchers, white ministers from the north, were attacked and beaten with clubs by members of the Ku Klux Klan; one of the victims died from his injuries. Televised images of the brutality against protesters and the death of a minister led to greater public sympathy for the cause. Eventually, a third march was successful in reaching the state capital of Montgomery.[45]

Figure 5.8   The police attack on civil rights demonstrators as they crossed the Edmund Pettus Bridge on their way from Selma to Montgomery on March 7, 1965, is remembered as "Bloody Sunday."

Link to Learning

The 1987 PBS documentary *Eyes on the Prize (https://www.openstaxcollege.org/l/29eyesonthepriz)* won several Emmys and other awards for its coverage of major events in the civil rights movement, including the Montgomery bus boycott, the battle for school integration in Little Rock, the march from Selma to Montgomery, and Martin Luther King, Jr.'s leadership of the march on Washington, DC.

The events at Selma galvanized support in Congress for a follow-up bill solely dealing with the right to vote. The Voting Rights Act of 1965 went beyond previous laws by requiring greater oversight of elections by federal officials. Literacy and understanding tests, and other devices used to discriminate against voters on the basis of race, were banned. The Voting Rights Act proved to have much more immediate and dramatic effect than the laws that preceded it; what had been a fairly slow process of improving voter registration and participation was replaced by a rapid increase of black voter registration rates—although white registration rates increased over this period as well.[46] To many people's way of thinking, however, the Supreme Court turned back the clocks when it gutted a core aspect of the Voting Rights Act in *Shelby County v. Holder* (2013).[47] No longer would states need federal approval to change laws and policies related to voting. Indeed, many states with a history of voter discrimination quickly resumed restrictive practices with laws requiring photo ID and limiting early voting. Some of the new restrictions are already being challenged in the courts.[48]

Not all African Americans in the civil rights movement were comfortable with gradual change. Instead of using marches and demonstrations to change people's attitudes, calling for tougher civil rights laws, or suing for their rights in court, they favored more immediate action that forced whites to give in to their demands. Men like Malcolm X, the leader of the Nation of Islam, and groups like the Black Panthers were willing to use violence to achieve their goals (Figure 5.9).[49] These activists called for Black Power and Black Pride, not assimilation into white society. Their position was attractive to many young African Americans, especially after Martin Luther King, Jr. was assassinated in 1968.

Figure 5.9   Martin Luther King, Jr. (left) and Malcolm X (right) adopted different approaches to securing civil rights for African Americans. This occasion, a Senate debate of the Civil Rights Act of 1964, was the only time the two men ever met.

CONTINUING CHALLENGES FOR AFRICAN AMERICANS

The civil rights movement for African Americans did not end with the passage of the Voting Rights Act in 1965. For the last fifty years, the African American community has faced challenges related to both past and current discrimination; progress on both fronts remains slow, uneven, and often frustrating.

Legacies of the *de jure* segregation of the past remain in much of the United States. Many African Americans still live in predominantly black neighborhoods where their ancestors were forced by laws and housing covenants to live.[50] Even those who live in the suburbs, once largely white, tend to live in suburbs that are mostly black.[51] Some two million African American young people attend schools whose student body is composed almost entirely of students of color.[52] During the late 1960s and early 1970s, efforts to tackle these problems were stymied by large-scale public opposition, not just in the South but across the nation. Attempts to integrate public schools through the use of busing—transporting students from one segregated neighborhood to another to achieve more racially balanced schools—were particularly unpopular and helped contribute to "white flight" from cities to the suburbs.[53] This white flight has created *de facto* **segregation**, a form of segregation that results from the choices of individuals to live in segregated communities without government action or support.

Today, a lack of high-paying jobs in many urban areas, combined with the poverty resulting from the legacies of slavery and Jim Crow and persistent racism, has trapped many African Americans in poor neighborhoods. While the Civil Rights Act of 1964 created opportunities for members of the black middle class to advance economically and socially, and to live in the same neighborhoods as the white middle class did, their departure left many black neighborhoods mired in poverty and without the strong community ties that existed during the era of legal segregation. Many of these neighborhoods also suffered from high rates of crime and violence.[54] Police also appear, consciously or subconsciously, to engage in racial profiling: singling out blacks (and Latinos) for greater attention than members of other racial and ethnic groups, as former FBI director James B. Comey has admitted.[55] When incidents of real or perceived injustice arise, as recently occurred after a series of deaths of young black men at the hands of police in Ferguson, Missouri; Staten Island, New York; and Baltimore, Maryland, many African Americans turn to the streets to protest because they believe that politicians—white and black alike—fail to pay sufficient attention to these problems.

While the public mood may have shifted toward greater concern about economic inequality in the United States, substantial policy changes to immediately improve the economic standing of African Americans in general have not followed, that is, if government-based policies and solutions are the answer. The Obama administration proposed new rules under the Fair Housing Act that were intended to lead to more integrated communities in the future; however, the Trump administration has repeatedly sought to weaken the Fair Housing Act, primarily through lack of enforcement of existing regulations.[56] Meanwhile, grassroots movements to improve neighborhoods and local schools have taken root in many black communities across America, and perhaps in those movements is the hope for greater future progress.

Figure 5.10   As part of the "Unite the Right" rally on August 12, 2017, white supremacists and other alt-right groups prepare to enter Emancipation Park in Charlottesville, Virginia, carrying Nazi and Confederate flags. The rally was planned in part as a response to the removal of a statue of Robert E. Lee from the park earlier that year. (credit: Anthony Crider)

Other recent movements are more troubling, notably the increased presence and influence of white nationalism throughout the country. This movement espouses white supremacy and does not shrink from the threat or use of violence to achieve it. Such violence occurred in Charlottesville, Virginia, in August 2017, when various white supremacist groups and alt-right forces joined together in a "Unite the Right" rally (**Figure 5.10**). This rally included chants and racial slurs against African Americans and Jews. Those rallying clashed with counter-protestors, one of whom died when an avowed Neo-Nazi deliberately drove his car into a group of peaceful protestors. He has since been convicted and sentenced to life in prison for his actions. This event sent troubling shockwaves through U.S. politics, as leaders tried to grapple with the significance of the event. President Trump took some heat for suggesting that "good people existed on both sides of the clash."[57]

Finding a Middle Ground

Affirmative Action

One of the major controversies regarding race in the United States today is related to affirmative action, the practice of ensuring that members of historically disadvantaged or underrepresented groups have equal access to opportunities in education, the workplace, and government contracting. The phrase *affirmative action* originated in the Civil Rights Act of 1964 and Executive Order 11246, and it has drawn controversy ever since. The Civil Rights Act of 1964 prohibited discrimination in employment, and Executive Order 11246, issued in 1965, forbade employment discrimination not only within the federal government but by federal contractors and contractors and subcontractors who received government funds.

Clearly, African Americans, as well as other groups, have been subject to discrimination in the past and present, limiting their opportunity to compete on a level playing field with those who face no such challenge. Opponents of affirmative action, however, point out that many of its beneficiaries are ethnic minorities from relatively affluent backgrounds, while whites and Asian Americans who grew up in poverty are expected to succeed despite facing many of the same handicaps.

Because affirmative action attempts to redress discrimination on the basis of race or ethnicity, it is generally subject to the strict scrutiny standard, which means the burden of proof is on the government to demonstrate the necessity of racial discrimination to achieve a compelling governmental interest. In 1978, in *Bakke v. California*, the Supreme Court upheld affirmative action and said that colleges and universities could consider race when deciding whom to admit but could not establish racial quotas.[58] In 2003, the Supreme Court reaffirmed the Bakke decision in *Grutter v. Bollinger*, which said that taking race or ethnicity into account as one of several factors in admitting a student to a college or university was acceptable, but a system setting aside seats for a specific quota of minority students was not.[59] All these issues are back under discussion in the Supreme Court with the re-arguing of *Fisher v. University of Texas*.[60] In *Fisher v. University of Texas* (2013, known as *Fisher I*), University of Texas student Abigail Fisher brought suit to declare UT's race-based admissions policy as inconsistent with *Grutter*. The court did not see the UT policy that way and allowed it, so long as it remained narrowly tailored and not quota-based. *Fisher II* (2016) was decided by a 4–3 majority. It allowed race-based admissions, but required that the utility of such an approach had to be re-established on a regular basis.

Should race be a factor in deciding who will be admitted to a particular college? Why or why not?

5.3 The Fight for Women's Rights

Learning Objectives

By the end of this section, you will be able to:

- Describe early efforts to achieve rights for women
- Explain why the Equal Rights Amendment failed to be ratified
- Describe the ways in which women acquired greater rights in the twentieth century
- Analyze why women continue to experience unequal treatment

Along with African Americans, women of all races and ethnicities have long been discriminated against in the United States, and the women's rights movement began at the same time as the movement to abolish slavery in the United States. Indeed, the women's movement came about largely as a result of the difficulties women encountered while trying to abolish slavery. The trailblazing Seneca Falls Convention for women's rights was held in 1848, a few years before the Civil War. But the abolition and African American civil rights movements largely eclipsed the women's movement throughout most of the nineteenth century. Women began to campaign actively again in the late nineteenth and early twentieth centuries, and another movement for women's rights began in the 1960s.

THE EARLY WOMEN'S RIGHTS MOVEMENT AND WOMEN'S SUFFRAGE

At the time of the American Revolution, women had few rights. Although single women were allowed to own property, married women were not. When women married, their separate legal identities were erased under the legal principle of **coverture**. Not only did women adopt their husbands' names, but all personal property they owned legally became their husbands' property. Husbands could not sell their wives' real property—such as land or in some states slaves—without their permission, but they were allowed to manage it and retain the profits. If women worked outside the home, their husbands were entitled to their wages.[61] So long as a man provided food, clothing, and shelter for his wife, she was not legally allowed to leave him. Divorce was difficult and in some places impossible to obtain.[62] Higher education for women was not available, and women were barred from professional positions in medicine, law, and ministry.

Following the Revolution, women's conditions did not improve. Women were not granted the right to vote by any of the states except New Jersey, which at first allowed all taxpaying property owners to vote. However, in 1807, the law changed to limit the vote to men.[63] Changes in property laws actually hurt women by making it easier for their husbands to sell their real property without their consent.

Although women had few rights, they nevertheless played an important role in transforming American society. This was especially true in the 1830s and 1840s, a time when numerous social reform movements swept across the United States. Many women were active in these causes, especially the abolition movement and the temperance movement, which tried to end the excessive consumption of liquor. They often found they were hindered in their efforts, however, either by the law or by widely held beliefs that they were weak, silly creatures who should leave important issues to men.[64] One of the leaders of the early women's movement, Elizabeth Cady Stanton (Figure 5.11), was shocked and angered when she sought to attend an 1840 antislavery meeting in London, only to learn that women would not be allowed to participate and had to sit apart from the men. At this convention, she made the acquaintance of another American female abolitionist, Lucretia Mott (Figure 5.11), who was also appalled by the male reformers' treatment of women.[65]

(a)   (b)

Figure 5.11 Elizabeth Cady Stanton (a) and Lucretia Mott (b) both emerged from the abolitionist movement as strong advocates of women's rights.

In 1848, Stanton and Mott called for a women's rights convention, the first ever held specifically to address the subject, at Seneca Falls, New York. At the Seneca Falls Convention, Stanton wrote the Declaration of Sentiments, which was modeled after the Declaration of Independence and proclaimed women were equal to men and deserved the same rights. Among the rights Stanton wished to see granted to women was suffrage, the right to vote. When called upon to sign the Declaration, many of the delegates feared that if women demanded the right to vote, the movement would be considered too radical and its members would become a laughingstock. The Declaration passed, but the resolution demanding suffrage was the only one that did not pass unanimously.[66]

Along with other feminists (advocates of women's equality), such as her friend and colleague Susan B. Anthony, Stanton fought for rights for women besides suffrage, including the right to seek higher education. As a result of their efforts, several states passed laws that allowed married women to retain control of their property and let divorced women keep custody of their children.[67] Amelia Bloomer, another activist, also campaigned for dress reform, believing women could lead better lives and be more useful to society if they were not restricted by voluminous heavy skirts and tight corsets.

The women's rights movement attracted many women who, like Stanton and Anthony, were active in either the temperance movement, the abolition movement, or both movements. Sarah and Angelina Grimke, the daughters of a wealthy slaveholding family in South Carolina, became first abolitionists and then women's rights activists.[68] Many of these women realized that their effectiveness as reformers was limited by laws that prohibited married women from signing contracts and by social proscriptions against women addressing male audiences. Without such rights, women found it difficult to rent halls in which to deliver lectures or to hire printers to produce antislavery literature.

Following the Civil War and the abolition of slavery, the women's rights movement fragmented. Stanton and Anthony denounced the Fifteenth Amendment because it granted voting rights only to black men and not to women of any race.[69] The fight for women's rights did not die, however. In 1869, Stanton and Anthony formed the National Woman Suffrage Association (NWSA), which demanded that the Constitution be amended to grant the right to vote to all women. It also called for more lenient divorce laws and an end to sex discrimination in employment. The less radical Lucy Stone formed the American Woman Suffrage Association (AWSA) in the same year; AWSA hoped to win the suffrage for women by working on a state-by-state basis instead of seeking to amend the Constitution.[70] Four western states—Utah, Colorado, Wyoming, and Idaho—did extend the right to vote to women in the late nineteenth century, but no other states did.

Women were also granted the right to vote on matters involving liquor licenses, in school board elections, and in municipal elections in several states. However, this was often done because of stereotyped beliefs that associated women with moral reform and concern for children, not as a result of a belief in women's equality. Furthermore, voting in municipal elections was restricted to women who owned property.[71] In 1890, the two suffragist groups united to form the National American Woman Suffrage Association (NAWSA). To call attention to their cause, members circulated petitions, lobbied politicians, and held parades in which hundreds of women and girls marched through the streets (Figure 5.12).

Figure 5.12   In October 1917, suffragists marched down Fifth Avenue in New York demanding the right to vote. They carried a petition that had been signed by one million women.

The more radical National Woman's Party (NWP), led by Alice Paul, advocated the use of stronger tactics. The NWP held public protests and picketed outside the White House (Figure 5.13).[72] Demonstrators were often beaten and arrested, and suffragists were subjected to cruel treatment in jail. When some, like Paul, began hunger strikes to call attention to their cause, their jailers force-fed them, an incredibly painful and invasive experience for the women.[73] Finally, in 1920, the triumphant passage of the Nineteenth Amendment granted all women the right to vote.

Figure 5.13   Members of the National Woman's Party picketed outside the White House six days a week from January 10, 1917, when President Woodrow Wilson took office, until June 4, 1919, when the Nineteenth Amendment was passed by Congress. The protesters wore banners proclaiming the name of the institution of higher learning they attended.

CIVIL RIGHTS AND THE EQUAL RIGHTS AMENDMENT

Just as the passage of the Thirteenth, Fourteenth, and Fifteenth Amendments did not result in equality for African Americans, the Nineteenth Amendment did not end discrimination against women in education, employment, or other areas of life, which continued to be legal. Although women could vote, they very rarely ran for or held public office. Women continued to be underrepresented in the professions, and relatively few sought advanced degrees. Until the mid-twentieth century, the ideal in U.S. society was typically for women to marry, have children, and become housewives. Those who sought work for pay outside the home were routinely denied jobs because of their sex and, when they did find employment, were paid less than men. Women who wished to remain childless or limit the number of children they had in order to work or attend college found it difficult to do so. In some states it was illegal to sell contraceptive devices, and abortions were largely illegal and difficult for women to obtain.

A second women's rights movement emerged in the 1960s to address these problems. Title VII of the Civil Rights Act of 1964 prohibited discrimination in employment on the basis of sex as well as race, color, national origin, and religion. Nevertheless, women continued to be denied jobs because of their sex and were often sexually harassed at the workplace. In 1966, feminists who were angered by the lack of progress made by women and by the government's lackluster enforcement of Title VII organized the National Organization for Women (NOW). NOW promoted workplace equality, including equal pay for women, and also called for the greater presence of women in public office, the professions, and graduate and professional degree programs.

NOW also declared its support for the **Equal Rights Amendment (ERA)**, which mandated equal treatment for all regardless of sex. The ERA, written by Alice Paul and Crystal Eastman, was first proposed to Congress, unsuccessfully, in 1923. It was introduced in every Congress thereafter but did not pass both the House and the Senate until 1972. The amendment was then sent to the states for ratification with a deadline of March 22, 1979. Although many states ratified the amendment in 1972 and 1973, the ERA still lacked sufficient support as the deadline drew near. Opponents, including both women and men, argued that passage would subject women to military conscription and deny them alimony and custody of their children should they divorce.[74] In 1978, Congress voted to extend the deadline for ratification to June 30, 1982. Even with the extension, however, the amendment failed to receive the support of the required thirty-eight states; by the time the deadline arrived, it had been ratified by only thirty-five, some of those had rescinded their ratifications, and no new state had ratified the ERA during the extension period (Figure 5.14).

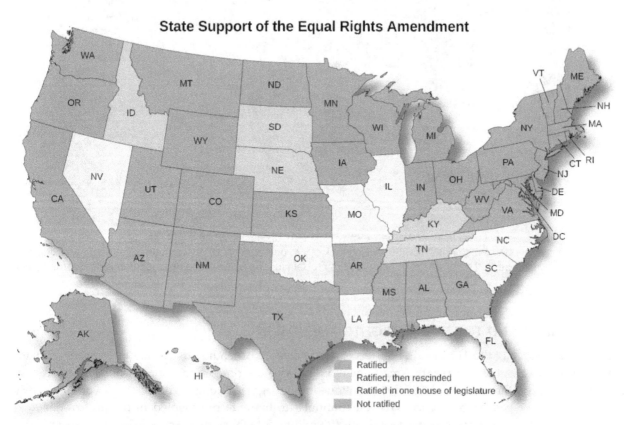

State Support of the Equal Rights Amendment

Ratified
Ratified, then rescinded
Ratified in one house of legislature
Not ratified

Figure 5.14 The map shows which states supported the ERA and which did not. The dark blue states ratified the amendment. The amendment was ratified but later rescinded in the light blue states and was ratified in only one branch of the legislature in the yellow states. The ERA was never ratified by the purple states.

Although the ERA failed to be ratified, **Title IX** of the United States Education Amendments of 1972 passed into law as a federal statute (not as an amendment, as the ERA was meant to be). Title IX applies to all educational institutions that receive federal aid and prohibits discrimination on the basis of sex in academic programs, dormitory space, health-care access, and school activities including sports. Thus, if a school receives federal aid, it cannot spend more funds on programs for men than on programs for women.

CONTINUING CHALLENGES FOR WOMEN

There is no doubt that women have made great progress since the Seneca Falls Convention. Today, more women than men attend college, and they are more likely than men to graduate.[75] Women are represented in all the professions, and approximately half of all law and medical school students are women.[76] Women have held Cabinet positions and have been elected to Congress. They have run for president and vice president, and three female justices currently serve on the Supreme Court. Women are also represented in all branches of the military and can serve in combat. As a result of the 1973 Supreme Court decision in *Roe v. Wade*, women now have legal access to abortion.[77]

Nevertheless, women are still underrepresented in some jobs and are less likely to hold executive positions than are men. Many believe the **glass ceiling**, an invisible barrier caused by discrimination, prevents women from rising to the highest levels of American organizations, including corporations, governments, academic institutions, and religious groups. Women earn less money than men for the same work. As of 2014, fully employed women earned seventy-nine cents for every dollar earned by a fully employed man.[78] Women are also more likely to be single parents than are men.[79] As a result, more women live below the poverty line than do men, and, as of 2012, households headed by single women are twice as likely to live below the poverty line than those headed by single men.[80] Women remain underrepresented in elective offices. As of January 2019, women held only about 24 percent of seats in Congress and only about 29 percent of seats in state legislatures.[81]

Women remain subject to sexual harassment in the workplace and are more likely than men to be the victims of domestic violence. Approximately one-third of all women have experienced domestic violence; one in five women is assaulted during her college years.[82]

Many in the United States continue to call for a ban on abortion, and states have attempted to restrict women's access to the procedure. For example, many states have required abortion clinics to meet the same standards set for hospitals, such as corridor size and parking lot capacity, despite lack of evidence regarding the benefits of such standards. Abortion clinics, which are smaller than hospitals, often cannot meet such standards. Other restrictions include mandated counseling before the procedure and the need for minors to secure parental permission before obtaining abortion services.[83] *Whole Woman's Health v. Hellerstedt* (2016) cited the lack of evidence for the benefit of larger clinics and further disallowed two Texas laws that imposed special requirements on doctors in order to perform abortions.[84] Furthermore, the federal government will not pay for abortions for low-income women except in cases of rape or incest or in situations in which carrying the fetus to term would endanger the life of the mother.[85]

To address these issues, many have called for additional protections for women. These include laws mandating equal pay for equal work. According to the doctrine of **comparable worth**, people should be compensated equally for work requiring comparable skills, responsibilities, and effort. Thus, even though women are underrepresented in certain fields, they should receive the same wages as men if performing jobs requiring the same level of accountability, knowledge, skills, and/or working conditions, even though the specific job may be different.

For example, garbage collectors are largely male. The chief job requirements are the ability to drive a sanitation truck and to lift heavy bins and toss their contents into the back of truck. The average wage for a garbage collector is $15.34 an hour.[86] Daycare workers are largely female, and the average pay is $9.12 an hour.[87] However, the work arguably requires more skills and is a more responsible position. Daycare workers must be able to feed, clean, and dress small children; prepare meals for them; entertain them; give them medicine if required; and teach them basic skills. They must be educated in first aid and assume responsibility for the children's safety. In terms of the skills and physical activity required and the associated level of responsibility of the job, daycare workers should be paid at least as much as garbage collectors and perhaps more. Women's rights advocates also call for stricter enforcement of laws prohibiting sexual harassment, and for harsher punishment, such as mandatory arrest, for perpetrators of domestic violence.

Insider Perspective

Harry Burn and the Tennessee General Assembly

In 1918, the proposed Nineteenth Amendment to the Constitution, extending the right to vote to all adult female citizens of the United States, was passed by both houses of Congress and sent to the states for ratification. Thirty-six votes were needed. Throughout 1918 and 1919, the Amendment dragged through legislature after legislature as pro- and anti-suffrage advocates made their arguments. By the summer of 1920, only one more state had to ratify it before it became law. The Amendment passed through Tennessee's state Senate and went to its House of Representatives. Arguments were bitter and intense. Pro-suffrage advocates argued that the amendment would reward women for their service to the nation during World War I and that women's supposedly greater morality would help to clean up politics. Those opposed claimed women would be degraded by entrance into the political arena and that their interests were already represented by their male relatives. On August 18, the amendment was brought for a vote before the House. The vote was closely divided, and it seemed unlikely it would pass. But as a young anti-suffrage representative waited for his vote to be counted, he remembered a note he had received from his mother that day. In it, she urged him, "Hurrah and vote for suffrage!" At the last minute, Harry Burn abruptly changed his ballot. The amendment passed the House by one vote, and eight days later, the Nineteenth Amendment was added to the Constitution.

How are women perceived in politics today compared to the 1910s? What were the competing arguments for Harry Burn's vote?

Link to Learning

The website for the Women's National History Project (https://www.openstax.org/l/29womnathispro) contains a variety of resources for learning more about the women's rights movement and women's history. It features a history of the women's movement, a "This Day in Women's History" page, and quizzes to test your knowledge.

5.4 Civil Rights for Indigenous Groups: Native Americans, Alaskans, and Hawaiians

Learning Objectives

By the end of this section, you will be able to:
* Outline the history of discrimination against Native Americans
* Describe the expansion of Native American civil rights from 1960 to 1990
* Discuss the persistence of problems Native Americans face today

Native Americans have long suffered the effects of segregation and discrimination imposed by the U.S. government and the larger white society. Ironically, Native Americans were not granted the full rights and protections of U.S. citizenship until long after African Americans and women were, with many having to wait until the Nationality Act of 1940 to become citizens.[88] This was long after the passage of the Fourteenth Amendment in 1868, which granted citizenship to African Americans but not, the Supreme Court decided in *Elk v. Wilkins* (1884), to Native Americans.[89] White women had been citizens of the United States since its very beginning even though they were not granted the full rights of citizenship. Furthermore, Native Americans are the only group of Americans who were forcibly removed en masse from the lands on which they and their ancestors had lived so that others could claim this land and its resources. This issue remains relevant today as can be seen in the recent protests of the Dakota Access Pipeline, which have led to intense confrontations between those in charge of the pipeline and Native Americans.

NATIVE AMERICANS LOSE THEIR LAND AND THEIR RIGHTS

From the very beginning of European settlement in North America, Native Americans were abused and exploited. Early British settlers attempted to enslave the members of various tribes, especially in the southern colonies and states.[90] Following the American Revolution, the U.S. government assumed responsibility for conducting negotiations with Indian tribes, all of which were designated as sovereign nations, and regulating commerce with them. Because Indians were officially regarded as citizens of other nations, they were denied U.S. citizenship.[91]

As white settlement spread westward over the course of the nineteenth century, Indian tribes were forced to move from their homelands. Although the federal government signed numerous treaties guaranteeing Indians the right to live in the places where they had traditionally farmed, hunted, or fished, land-hungry white settlers routinely violated these agreements and the federal government did little to enforce them.[92]

In 1830, Congress passed the Indian Removal Act, which forced Native Americans to move west of the Mississippi River.[93] Not all tribes were willing to leave their land, however. The Cherokee in particular resisted, and in the 1820s, the state of Georgia tried numerous tactics to force them from their territory. Efforts intensified in 1829 after gold was discovered there. Wishing to remain where they were, the tribe sued the state of Georgia.[94] In 1831, the Supreme Court decided in *Cherokee Nation v. Georgia* that Indian tribes were not sovereign nations, but also that tribes were entitled to their ancestral lands and could not be forced to move from them.[95]

The next year, in *Worcester v. Georgia*, the Court ruled that whites could not enter tribal lands without the tribe's permission. White Georgians, however, refused to abide by the Court's decision, and President Andrew Jackson, a former Indian fighter, refused to enforce it.[96] Between 1831 and 1838, members of several southern tribes, including the Cherokees, were forced by the U.S. Army to move west along routes shown in Figure 5.15. The forced removal of the Cherokees to Oklahoma Territory, which had been set aside for settlement by displaced tribes and designated Indian Territory, resulted in the death of one-quarter of the tribe's population.[97] The Cherokees remember this journey as the **Trail of Tears**.

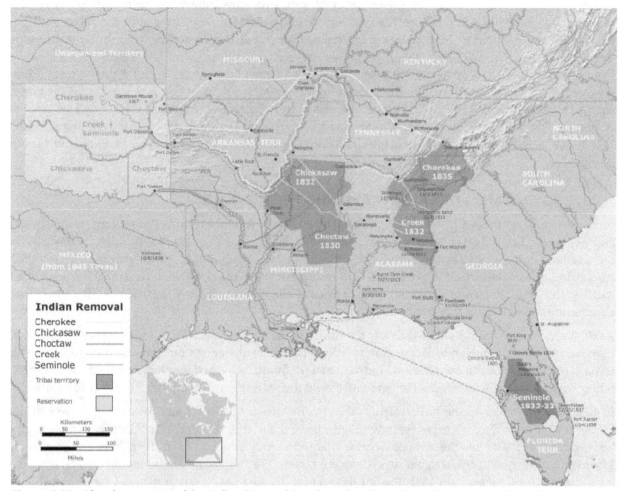

Figure 5.15 After the passage of the Indian Removal Act, the U.S. military forced the removal of the Cherokee, Chickasaw, Choctaw, Creek, and Seminole from the Southeast to the western territory (present-day Oklahoma), marching them along the routes shown here. The lines in yellow mark the routes taken by the Cherokee on the Trail of Tears.

By the time of the Civil War, most Indian tribes had been relocated west of the Mississippi. However, once large numbers of white Americans and European immigrants had also moved west after the Civil War, Native Americans once again found themselves displaced. They were confined to reservations, which are federal lands set aside for their use where non-Indians could not settle. Reservation land was usually poor, however, and attempts to farm or raise livestock, not traditional occupations for most western tribes anyway, often ended in failure. Unable to feed themselves, the tribes became dependent on the Bureau of Indian Affairs (BIA) in Washington, DC, for support. Protestant missionaries were allowed to "adopt" various tribes, to convert them to Christianity and thus speed their assimilation. In an effort to hasten this process, Indian children were taken from their parents and sent to boarding schools, many of them run by churches, where they were forced to speak English and abandon their traditional cultures.[98]

In 1887, the Dawes Severalty Act, another effort to assimilate Indians to white society, divided reservation lands into individual allotments. Native Americans who accepted these allotments and agreed to sever tribal ties were also given U.S. citizenship. All lands remaining after the division of reservations into allotments were offered for sale by the federal government to white farmers and ranchers. As a result, Indians swiftly lost control of reservation land.[99] In 1898, the Curtis Act dealt the final blow to Indian sovereignty by abolishing all tribal governments.[100]

THE FIGHT FOR NATIVE AMERICAN RIGHTS

As Indians were removed from their tribal lands and increasingly saw their traditional cultures being destroyed over the course of the nineteenth century, a movement to protect their rights began to grow. Sarah Winnemucca (Figure 5.16), member of the Paiute tribe, lectured throughout the east in the 1880s in order to acquaint white audiences with the injustices suffered by the western tribes.[101] Lakota physician Charles Eastman (Figure 5.16) also worked for Native American rights. In 1924, the Indian Citizenship Act granted citizenship to all Native Americans born after its passage. Native Americans born before the act took effect, who had not already become citizens as a result of the Dawes Severalty Act or service in the army in World War I, had to wait until the Nationality Act of 1940 to become citizens. In 1934, Congress passed the Indian Reorganization Act, which ended the division of reservation land into allotments. It returned to Native American tribes the right to institute self-government on their reservations, write constitutions, and manage their remaining lands and resources. It also provided funds for Native Americans to start their own businesses and attain a college education.[102]

(a)   (b)

Figure 5.16 Sarah Winnemucca (a), called the "Paiute Princess" by the press, and Dr. Charles Eastman (b), of the Lakota tribe, campaigned for Native American rights in the late nineteenth and early twentieth centuries. Winnemucca wears traditional dress for a publicity photograph.

Despite the Indian Reorganization Act, conditions on the reservations did not improve dramatically. Most tribes remained impoverished, and many Native Americans, despite the fact that they were now U.S. citizens, were denied the right to vote by the states in which they lived. States justified this violation of the Fifteenth Amendment by claiming that Native Americans might be U.S. citizens but were not state residents because they lived on reservations. Other states denied Native Americans voting rights if they did not pay taxes.[103] Despite states' actions, the federal government continued to uphold the rights of tribes to govern themselves. Federal concern for tribal sovereignty was part of an effort on the government's part to end its control of, and obligations to, Indian tribes.[104]

In the 1960s, a modern Native American civil rights movement, inspired by the African American civil rights movement, began to grow. In 1969, a group of Native American activists from various tribes, part of a new Pan-Indian movement, took control of Alcatraz Island in San Francisco Bay, which had once been the site of a federal prison. Attempting to strike a blow for Red Power, the power of Native Americans united by a Pan-Indian identity and demanding federal recognition of their rights, they maintained control of the island for more than a year and a half. They claimed the land as compensation for the federal government's violation of numerous treaties and offered to pay for it with beads and trinkets. In January 1970, some of the occupiers began to leave the island. Some may have been disheartened by the accidental death of the daughter of one of the activists. In May 1970, all electricity and telephone service to the island was cut off by the federal government, and more of the occupiers began to leave. In June, the few people remaining on the island were removed by the government. Though the goals of the activists were not achieved, the occupation of Alcatraz had brought national attention to the concerns of Native American activists.[105]

In 1973, members of the **American Indian Movement (AIM)**, a more radical group than the occupiers of Alcatraz, temporarily took over the offices of the Bureau of Indian Affairs in Washington, DC. The following year, members of AIM and some two hundred Oglala Lakota supporters occupied the town of Wounded Knee on the Lakota tribe's Pine Ridge Reservation in South Dakota, the site of an 1890 massacre of Lakota men, women, and children by the U.S. Army (Figure 5.17). Many of the Oglala were protesting the actions of their half-white tribal chieftain, who they claimed had worked too closely with the BIA. The occupiers also wished to protest the failure of the Justice Department to investigate acts of white violence against Lakota tribal members outside the bounds of the reservation.

The occupation led to a confrontation between the Native American protestors and the FBI and U.S. Marshals. Violence erupted; two Native American activists were killed, and a marshal was shot (Figure 5.17). After the second death, the Lakota called for an end to the occupation and negotiations began with the federal government. Two of AIM's leaders, Russell Means and Dennis Banks, were arrested, but the case against them was later dismissed.[106] Violence continued on the Pine Ridge Reservation for several years after the siege; the reservation had the highest per capita murder rate in the United States. Two FBI agents were among those who were killed. The Oglala blamed the continuing violence on the federal government.[107]

(a)

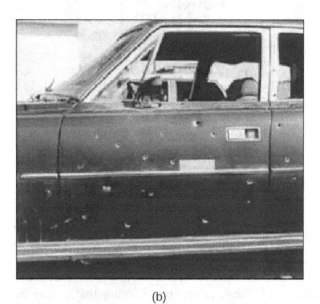
(b)

Figure 5.17   A memorial stone (a) marks the spot of the mass grave of the Lakotas killed in the 1890 massacre at Wounded Knee. The bullet-riddled car (b) of FBI agent Ronald Williams reveals the level of violence reached during—and for years after—the 1973 occupation of the town.

The official website of the American Indian Movement (https://www.openstax.org/l/29aimovement) provides information about ongoing issues in Native American communities in both North and South America.

The current relationship between the U.S. government and Native American tribes was established by the Indian Self-Determination and Education Assistance Act of 1975. Under the act, tribes assumed control of programs that had formerly been controlled by the BIA, such as education and resource management, and the federal government provided the funding.[108] Many tribes have also used their new freedom from government control to legalize gambling and to open casinos on their reservations. Although the states in which these casinos are located have attempted to control gaming on Native American lands, the Supreme Court and the Indian Gaming Regulatory Act of 1988 have limited their ability to do so.[109] The 1978 American Indian Religious Freedom Act granted tribes the right to conduct traditional ceremonies and rituals, including those that use otherwise prohibited substances like peyote cactus and eagle bones, which can be procured only from vulnerable or protected species.[110]

In an important recent development, several federal court cases have raised standing for Native American tribes to sue to regain former reservation lands lost to the U.S. government. If Native Americans were to gain a positive outcome in such a case, especially at the U.S. Supreme Court, it would be the most important advancement since the reapplication of the Winters Doctrine (which led to a stronger footing for tribes in water negotiations).[111] Among the reservation land cases making their way through the system, *Carpenter v. Murphy*, which revolves around a murder case in Oklahoma, would perhaps be the most profound, given the history of the Trail of Tears. At issue is whether Mr. Murphy committed murder on private land in the state of Oklahoma or on the Muscogee (Creek) reservation and who should have jurisdiction over his case. If the court decides to proclaim the land as a reservation, that potentially leads to half the State of Oklahoma being designated as such. The Court heard arguments in late 2018 and will make a decision in 2019.[112]

ALASKA NATIVES AND NATIVE HAWAIIANS REGAIN SOME RIGHTS

Alaska Natives and Native Hawaiians suffered many of the same abuses as Native Americans, including loss of land and forced assimilation. Following the discovery of oil in Alaska, however, the state, in an effort to gain undisputed title to oil rich land, settled the issue of Alaska Natives' land claims with the passage of the Alaska Native Claims Settlement Act in 1971. According to the terms of the act, Alaska Natives received 44 million acres of resource-rich land and more than $900 million in cash in exchange for relinquishing claims to ancestral lands to which the state wanted title.[113]

Native Hawaiians also lost control of their land—nearly two million acres—through the overthrow of the Hawaiian monarchy in 1893 and the subsequent formal annexation of the Hawaiian Islands by the United States in 1898. The indigenous population rapidly decreased in number, and white settlers tried to erase all trace of traditional Hawaiian culture. Two acts passed by Congress in 1900 and 1959, when the territory was granted statehood, returned slightly more than one million acres of federally owned land to the state of Hawaii. The state was to hold it in trust and use profits from the land to improve the condition of Native Hawaiians.[114]

In September 2015, the U.S. Department of Interior, the same department that contains the Bureau of Indian Affairs, created guidelines for Native Hawaiians who wish to govern themselves in a relationship with the federal government similar to that established with Native American and Alaska Native tribes. Such a relationship would grant Native Hawaiians power to govern themselves while remaining U.S. citizens. Voting began in fall 2015 for delegates to a constitutional convention that would determine whether or not such a relationship should exist between Native Hawaiians and the federal government.[115] When non-Native Hawaiians and some Native Hawaiians brought suit on the grounds that, by allowing only Native Hawaiians to vote, the process discriminated against members of other ethnic groups, a federal district court found the election to be legal. While the Supreme Court stopped the election, in September 2016 a separate ruling by the Interior Department allowed for a referendum to be held. Native Hawaiians in favor are working to create their own nation.[116]

Despite significant advances, American Indians, Alaska Natives, and Native Hawaiians still trail behind U.S. citizens of other ethnic backgrounds in many important areas. These groups continue to suffer widespread poverty and high unemployment. Some of the poorest counties in the United States are those in which Native American reservations are located. These minorities are also less likely than white Americans, African Americans, or Asian Americans to complete high school or college.[117] Many American Indian and Alaskan tribes endure high rates of infant mortality, alcoholism, and suicide.[118] Native Hawaiians are also more likely to live in poverty than whites in Hawaii, and they are more likely than white Hawaiians to be homeless or unemployed.[119]

5.5 Equal Protection for Other Groups

Learning Objectives

By the end of this section, you will be able to:
- Discuss the discrimination faced by Hispanic/Latino Americans and Asian Americans
- Describe the influence of the African American civil rights movement on Hispanic/Latino, Asian American, and LGBT civil rights movements
- Describe federal actions to improve opportunities for people with disabilities
- Describe discrimination faced by religious minorities

Many groups in American society have faced and continue to face challenges in achieving equality, fairness, and equal protection under the laws and policies of the federal government and/or the states. Some of these groups are often overlooked because they are not as large of a percentage of the U.S. population as women or African Americans, and because organized movements to achieve equality for them are relatively young. This does not mean, however, that the discrimination they face has not been as longstanding or as severe.

HISPANIC/LATINO CIVIL RIGHTS

Hispanics and Latinos in the United States have faced many of the same problems as African Americans and Native Americans. Although the terms Hispanic and Latino are often used interchangeably, they are not the same. *Hispanic* usually refers to native speakers of Spanish. *Latino* refers to people who come from, or whose ancestors came from, Latin America. Not all Hispanics are Latinos. Latinos may be of any race or ethnicity; they may be of European, African, Native American descent, or they may be of mixed ethnic background. Thus, people from Spain are Hispanic but are not Latino.[120]

Many Latinos became part of the U.S. population following the annexation of Texas by the United States in 1845 and of California, Arizona, New Mexico, Nevada, Utah, and Colorado following the War with Mexico in 1848. Most were subject to discrimination and could find employment only as poorly paid migrant farm workers, railroad workers, and unskilled laborers.[121] The Spanish-speaking population of the United States increased following the Spanish-American War in 1898 with the incorporation of Puerto Rico as a U.S. territory. In 1917, during World War I, the Jones Act granted U.S. citizenship to Puerto Ricans.

In the early twentieth century, waves of violence aimed at Mexicans and Mexican Americans swept the Southwest. Mexican Americans in Arizona and in parts of Texas were denied the right to vote, which they had previously possessed, and Mexican American children were barred from attending Anglo-American schools. During the Great Depression of the 1930s, Mexican immigrants and many Mexican Americans, both U.S.-born and naturalized citizens, living in the Southwest and Midwest were deported by the government so that Anglo-Americans could take the jobs that they had once held.[122] When the United States entered World War II, however, Mexicans were invited to immigrate to the United States as farmworkers under the Bracero (*bracero* meaning "manual laborer" in Spanish) Program to make it possible for these American men to enlist in the armed services.[123]

Mexican Americans and Puerto Ricans did not passively accept discriminatory treatment, however. In 1903, Mexican farmworkers joined with Japanese farmworkers, who were also poorly paid, to form the first union to represent agricultural laborers. In 1929, Latino civil rights activists formed the League of United Latin American Citizens (LULAC) to protest against discrimination and to fight for greater rights for Latinos.[124]

Just as in the case of African Americans, however, true civil rights advances for Hispanics and Latinos did not take place until the end of World War II. Hispanic and Latino activists targeted the same racist practices as did African Americans and used many of the same tactics to end them. In 1946, Mexican American parents in California, with the assistance of the NAACP, sued several California school districts that forced Mexican and Mexican American children to attend segregated schools. In the case of *Mendez v. Westminster* (1947), the Court of Appeals for the Ninth Circuit Court held that the segregation of Mexican and Mexican American students into separate schools was unconstitutional.[125]

Although Latinos made some civil rights advances in the decades following World War II, discrimination continued. Alarmed by the large number of undocumented Mexicans crossing the border into the United States in the 1950s, the United States government began Operation Wetback (*wetback* is a derogatory term for Mexicans living unofficially in the United States). From 1953 to 1958, more than three million Mexican immigrants, and some Mexican Americans as well, were deported from California, Texas, and Arizona.[126] To limit the entry of Hispanic and Latino immigrants to the United States, in 1965 Congress imposed an immigration quota of 120,000 newcomers from the Western Hemisphere.

At the same time that the federal government sought to restrict Hispanic and Latino immigration to the United States, the Mexican American civil rights movement grew stronger and more radical, just as the African American civil rights movement had done. While African Americans demanded Black Power and called for Black Pride, young Mexican American civil rights activists called for Brown Power and began to refer to themselves as **Chicanos**, a term disliked by many older, conservative Mexican Americans, in order to stress their pride in their hybrid Spanish-Native American cultural identity.[127] Demands by Mexican American activists often focused on improving education for their children, and they called upon school districts to hire teachers and principals who were bilingual in English and Spanish, to teach Mexican and Mexican American history, and to offer instruction in both English and Spanish for children with limited ability to communicate in English.[128]

Milestone

East L.A. Student Walkouts

In March 1968, Chicano students at five high schools in East Los Angeles went on strike to demand better education for students of Mexican ancestry. Los Angeles schools did not allow Latino students to speak Spanish in class and gave no place to study Mexican history in the curriculum. Guidance counselors also encouraged students, regardless of their interests or ability, to pursue vocational careers instead of setting their sights on college. Some students were placed in classes for the mentally challenged even though they were of normal intelligence. As a result, the dropout rate among Mexican American students was very high.

School administrators refused to meet with the student protestors to discuss their grievances. After a week, police were sent in to end the strike. Thirteen of the organizers of the walkout were arrested and charged with conspiracy to disturb the peace. After Sal Castro, a teacher who had led the striking students, was dismissed from his job, activists held a sit-in at school district headquarters until Castro was reinstated. Student protests spread across the Southwest, and in response many schools did change. That same year, Congress passed the Bilingual Education Act, which required school districts with large numbers of Hispanic or Latino students to provide instruction in Spanish.[129]

Bilingual education remains controversial, even among Hispanics and Latinos. What are some arguments they might raise both for and against it? Are these different from arguments coming from whites?

Mexican American civil rights leaders were active in other areas as well. Throughout the 1960s, Cesar Chavez and Dolores Huerta fought for the rights of Mexican American agricultural laborers through their organization, the United Farm Workers (UFW), a union for migrant workers they founded in 1962. Chavez, Huerta, and the UFW proclaimed their solidarity with Filipino farm workers by joining them in a strike against grape growers in Delano, California, in 1965. Chavez consciously adopted the tactics of the African American civil rights movement. In 1965, he called upon all U.S. consumers to boycott California grapes (Figure 5.18), and in 1966, he led the UFW on a 300-mile march to Sacramento, the state capital, to bring the state farm workers' problems to the attention of the entire country. The strike finally ended in 1970 when the grape growers agreed to give the pickers better pay and benefits.[130]

(a)   (b)

Figure 5.18   Protestors picket a grocery store in 1973, urging consumers not to buy grapes or lettuce picked by underpaid farm workers (a). The boycott, organized by Cesar Chavez and the United Farm Workers using the slogan "Sí se puede" or "Yes, it can be done!" (b), ultimately forced California growers to improve conditions for migrant laborers.

As Latino immigration to the United States increased in the late twentieth and early twenty-first centuries, discrimination also increased in many places. In 1994, California voters passed Proposition 187. The proposition sought to deny non-emergency health services, food stamps, welfare, and Medicaid to undocumented immigrants. It also banned children from attending public school unless they could present proof that they and their parents were legal residents of the United States. A federal court found it unconstitutional in 1997 on the grounds that the law's intention was to regulate immigration, a power held only by the federal government.[131]

In 2005, discussion began in Congress on proposed legislation that would make it a felony to enter the United States illegally or to give assistance to anyone who had done so. Although the bill quickly died, on May 1, 2006, hundreds of thousands of people, primarily Latinos, staged public demonstrations in major U.S. cities, refusing to work or attend school for one day.[132] The protestors claimed that people seeking a better life should not be treated as criminals and that undocumented immigrants already living in the United States should have the opportunity to become citizens.

Following the failure to make undocumented immigration a felony under federal law, several states attempted to impose their own sanctions on illegal immigration. In April 2010, Arizona passed a law that made illegal immigration a state crime. The law also forbade undocumented immigrants from seeking work and allowed law enforcement officers to arrest people suspected of being in the U.S. illegally. Thousands protested the law, claiming that it encouraged racial profiling. In 2012, in *Arizona v. United States*, the U.S. Supreme Court struck down those provisions of the law that made it a state crime to reside in the United States illegally, forbade undocumented immigrants to take jobs, and allowed the police to arrest those suspected of being illegal immigrants.[133] The court, however, upheld the authority of the police to ascertain the immigration status of someone suspected of being an undocumented alien if the person had been stopped or arrested by the police for other reasons.[134]

Today, Latinos constitute the largest minority group in the United States. They also have one of the highest birth rates of any ethnic group.[135] Although Hispanics lag behind whites in terms of income and high school graduation rates, they are enrolling in college at higher rates than whites.[136] Topics that remain at the forefront of public debate today include immigration reform, the DREAM Act (a proposal for granting undocumented immigrants permanent residency in stages), and court action on executive orders on immigration. President Trump and his administration have been quite active on issues of immigration and border security. Aside from the proposal to build a border wall, other areas of action have included various travel bans and the policy of separating families at the border as they attempt to enter the country.[137]

ASIAN AMERICAN CIVIL RIGHTS

Because Asian Americans are often stereotypically regarded as "the model minority" (because it is assumed they are generally financially successful and do well academically), it is easy to forget that they have also often been discriminated against and denied their civil rights. Indeed, in the nineteenth century, Asians were among the most despised of all immigrant groups and were often subjected to the same laws enforcing segregation and forbidding interracial marriage as were African Americans and American Indians.

The Chinese were the first large group of Asians to immigrate to the United States. They arrived in large numbers in the mid-nineteenth century to work in the mining industry and on the Central Pacific Railroad. Others worked as servants or cooks or operated laundries. Their willingness to work for less money than whites led white workers in California to call for a ban on Chinese immigration. In 1882, Congress passed the Chinese Exclusion Act, which prevented Chinese from immigrating to the United States for ten years and prevented Chinese already in the country from becoming citizens (Figure 5.19). In 1892, the Geary Act extended the ban on Chinese immigration for another ten years. In 1913, California passed a law preventing all Asians, not just the Chinese, from owning land. With the passage of the Immigration Act of 1924, all Asians, with the exception of Filipinos, were prevented from immigrating to the United States or becoming naturalized citizens. Laws in several states barred marriage between Chinese and white Americans, and some cities with large Asian populations required Asian children to attend segregated schools.[138]

Figure 5.19 The cartoon shows a Chinese laborer, the personification of industry and sobriety, outside the "Golden Gate of Liberty." The Chinese Exclusion Act of 1882 has barred him from entering the country, while communists and "hoodlums" are allowed in.

During World War II, citizens of Japanese descent living on the West Coast, whether naturalized immigrants or Japanese Americans born in the United States, were subjected to the indignity of being removed from their communities and interned under Executive Order 9066 (**Figure 5.20**). The reason was fear that they might prove disloyal to the United States and give assistance to Japan. Although Italians and Germans suspected of disloyalty were also interned by the U.S. government, only the Japanese were imprisoned solely on the basis of their ethnicity. None of the more than 110,000 Japanese and Japanese Americans internees was ever found to have committed a disloyal act against the United States, and many young Japanese American men served in the U.S. army during the war.[139] Although Japanese American Fred Korematsu challenged the right of the government to imprison law-abiding citizens, the Supreme Court decision in the 1944 case of *Korematsu v. United States* upheld the actions of the government as a necessary precaution in a time of war.[140] When internees returned from the camps after the war was over, many of them discovered that the houses, cars, and businesses they had left behind, often in the care of white neighbors, had been sold or destroyed.[141]

Figure 5.20 Japanese Americans displaced from their homes by the U.S. government during World War II stand in line outside the mess hall at a relocation center in San Bruno, California, on April 29, 1942.

Link to Learning

Explore the resources at Japanese American Internment (https://www.openstax.org/l/ 29japanamerint) and Digital History (https://www.openstax.org/l/29digitalhist) to learn more about experiences of Japanese Americans during World War II.

The growth of the African American, Chicano, and Native American civil rights movements in the 1960s inspired many Asian Americans to demand their own rights. Discrimination against Asian Americans, regardless of national origin, increased during the Vietnam War. Ironically, violence directed indiscriminately against Chinese, Japanese, Koreans, and Vietnamese caused members of these groups to unite around a shared pan-Asian identity, much as Native Americans had in the Pan-Indian movement. In 1968, students of Asian ancestry at the University of California at Berkeley formed the Asian American Political Alliance. Asian American students also joined Chicano, Native American, and African American students to demand that colleges offer ethnic studies courses.[142] In 1974, in the case of *Lau v. Nichols*, Chinese American students in San Francisco sued the school district, claiming its failure to provide them with assistance in learning English denied them equal educational opportunities.[143] The Supreme Court found in favor of the students.

The Asian American movement is no longer as active as other civil rights movements are. Although discrimination persists, Americans of Asian ancestry are generally more successful than members of other ethnic groups. They have higher rates of high school and college graduation and higher average income than other groups.[144] Although educational achievement and economic success do not protect them from discrimination, it does place them in a much better position to defend their rights.

THE FIGHT FOR CIVIL RIGHTS IN THE LGBT COMMUNITY

Laws against homosexuality, which was regarded as a sin and a moral failing, existed in most states throughout the nineteenth and twentieth centuries. By the late nineteenth century, homosexuality had come to be regarded as a form of mental illness as well as a sin, and gay men were often erroneously believed to be pedophiles.[145] As a result, lesbians, gay men, bisexuals, and transgender people, collectively known as the LGBT community, had to keep their sexual orientation hidden or "closeted." Secrecy became even more important in the 1950s, when fear of gay men increased and the federal government believed they could be led into disloyal acts either as a result of their "moral weakness" or through blackmail by Soviet agents. As a result, many men lost or were denied government jobs. Fears of lesbians also increased after World War II as U.S. society stressed conformity to traditional gender roles and the importance of marriage and childrearing.[146]

The very secrecy in which lesbian, gay, bisexual, and transgender people had to live made it difficult for them to organize to fight for their rights as other, more visible groups had done. Some organizations did exist, however. The Mattachine Society, established in 1950, was one of the first groups to champion the rights of gay men. Its goal was to unite gay men who otherwise lived in secrecy and to fight against abuse. The Mattachine Society often worked with the Daughters of Bilitis, a lesbian rights organization. Among the early issues targeted by the Mattachine Society was police entrapment of male homosexuals.[147]

In the 1960s, the gay and lesbian rights movements began to grow more radical, in a manner similar to other civil rights movements. In 1962, gay Philadelphians demonstrated in front of Independence Hall. In 1966, transgender prostitutes who were tired of police harassment rioted in San Francisco. In June 1969, gay men, lesbians, and transgender people erupted in violence when New York City police attempted to arrest customers at a gay bar in Greenwich Village called the **Stonewall Inn**. The patrons' ability to resist arrest and fend off the police inspired many members of New York's LGBT community, and the riots persisted over several nights. New organizations promoting LGBT rights that emerged after Stonewall were more radical and confrontational than the Mattachine Society and the Daughters of Bilitis had been. These groups, like the Gay Activists Alliance and the Gay Liberation Front, called not just for equality before the law and protection against abuse but also for "liberation," Gay Power, and Gay Pride.[148]

Although LGBT people gained their civil rights later than many other groups, changes did occur beginning in the 1970s, remarkably quickly when we consider how long other minority groups had fought for their rights. In 1973, the American Psychological Association ended its classification of homosexuality as a mental disorder. In 1994, the U.S. military adopted the policy of "Don't ask, don't tell." This act, Department of Defense Directive 1304.26, officially prohibited discrimination against suspected gays, lesbians, and bisexuals by the U.S. military. It also prohibited superior officers from asking about or investigating the sexual orientation of those below them in rank.[149] However, those gays, lesbians, and bisexuals who spoke openly about their sexual orientation were still subject to dismissal because it remained illegal for anyone except heterosexuals to serve in the armed forces. The policy ended in 2011, and now gays, lesbians, and bisexuals may serve openly in the military.[150] In 2006, in the case of *Lawrence v. Texas*, the Supreme Court ruled unconstitutional state laws that criminalized sexual intercourse between consenting adults of the same sex.[151]

Beginning in 2000, several states made it possible for same-sex couples to enter into legal relationships known as civil unions or domestic partnerships. These arrangements extended many of the same protections enjoyed by heterosexual married couples to same-sex couples. LGBT activists, however, continued to fight for the right to marry. Same-sex marriages would allow partners to enjoy exactly the same rights as married heterosexual couples and accord their relationships the same dignity and importance. In 2004, Massachusetts became the first state to grant legal status to same-sex marriage. Other states quickly followed. This development prompted a backlash among many religious conservatives, who considered homosexuality a sin and argued that allowing same-sex couples to marry would lessen the value and sanctity of heterosexual marriage. Many states passed laws banning same-sex marriage, and many gay and lesbian couples challenged these laws, successfully, in the courts. Finally, in *Obergefell v. Hodges*, the Supreme Court overturned state bans and made same-sex marriage legal throughout the United States on June 26, 2015 (**Figure 5.21**).[152]

Figure 5.21 Supporters of marriage equality celebrate outside the Supreme Court on June 26, 2015, following the announcement of the Court's decision in *Obergefell v. Hodges* declaring same-sex marriage a constitutional right under the Fourteenth Amendment. (credit: Matt Popovich)

The legalization of same-sex marriage throughout the United States led some people to feel their religious beliefs were under attack, and many religiously conservative business owners have refused to acknowledge LBGT rights or the legitimacy of same-sex marriages. Following swiftly upon the heels of the *Obergefell* ruling, the Indiana legislature passed a Religious Freedom Restoration Act (RFRA). Congress had already passed such a law in 1993; it was intended to extend protection to minority religions, such as by allowing rituals of the Native American Church. However, the Supreme Court in *City of Boerne v. Flores* (1997) ruled that the 1993 law applied only to the federal government and not to state governments.[153] Thus several state legislatures later passed their own Religious Freedom Restoration Acts. These laws state that the government cannot "substantially burden an individual's exercise of religion" unless it would serve a "compelling governmental interest" to do so. They allow individuals, which also include businesses and other organizations, to discriminate against others, primarily same-sex couples and LGBT people, if the individual's religious beliefs are opposed to homosexuality.

LGBT Americans still encounter difficulties in other areas as well. Discrimination continues in housing and employment, although federal courts are increasingly treating employment discrimination against transgender people as a form of sex discrimination prohibited by the Civil Rights Act of 1964. The federal Department of Housing and Urban Development has also indicated that refusing to rent or sell homes to transgendered people may be considered sex discrimination.[154] Violence against members of the LGBT community remains a serious problem; this violence occurs on the streets and in their homes.[155] The enactment of the Matthew Shepard and James Byrd Jr. Hate Crimes Prevention Act, also known as the Matthew Shepard Act, in 2009 made it a federal **hate crime** to attack someone based on his or her gender, gender identity, sexual orientation, or disability and made it easier for federal, state, and local authorities to investigate hate crimes, but it has not necessarily made the world safer for LGBT Americans.

CIVIL RIGHTS AND THE AMERICANS WITH DISABILITIES ACT

People with disabilities make up one of the last groups whose civil rights have been recognized. For a long time, they were denied employment and access to public education, especially if they were mentally or developmentally challenged. Many were merely institutionalized. A *eugenics* movement in the United States in the late nineteenth and early to mid-twentieth centuries sought to encourage childbearing among physically and mentally fit whites and discourage it among those with physical or mental disabilities. Many states passed laws prohibiting marriage among people who had what were believed to be hereditary "defects." Among those affected were people who were blind or deaf, those with epilepsy, people with mental or developmental disabilities, and those suffering mental illnesses. In some states, programs existed to sterilize people considered "feeble minded" by the standards of the time, without their will or consent.[156] When this practice was challenged by a "feeble-minded" woman in a state institution in Virginia, the Supreme Court, in the 1927 case of *Buck v. Bell*, upheld the right of state governments to sterilize those people believed likely to have children who would become dependent upon public welfare.[157] Some of these programs persisted into the 1970s, as Figure 5.22 shows.[158]

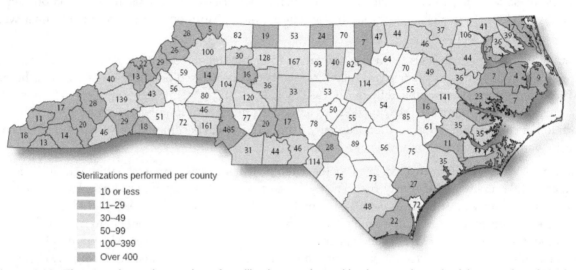

Peak of Eugenic Program in North Carolina, July 1946–June 1968

Sterilizations performed per county

- 10 or less
- 11–29
- 30–49
- 50–99
- 100–399
- Over 400

Figure 5.22   The map shows the number of sterilizations performed by the state in each of the counties of North Carolina between July 1946 and June 1968. Nearly five hundred sterilizations took place during this time period in the purple county.

By the 1970s, however, concern for extending equal opportunities to all led to the passage of two important acts by Congress. In 1973, the Rehabilitation Act made it illegal to discriminate against people with disabilities in federal employment or in programs run by federal agencies or receiving federal funding. This was followed by the Education for all Handicapped Children Act of 1975, which required public schools to educate children with disabilities. The act specified that schools consult with parents to create a plan tailored for each child's needs that would provide an educational experience as close as possible to that received by other children.

In 1990, the Americans with Disabilities Act (ADA) greatly expanded opportunities and protections for people of all ages with disabilities. It also significantly expanded the categories and definition of disability. The ADA prohibits discrimination in employment based on disability. It also requires employers to make reasonable accommodations available to workers who need them. Finally, the ADA mandates that public transportation and public accommodations be made accessible to those with disabilities. The Act was passed despite the objections of some who argued that the cost of providing accommodations would be prohibitive for small businesses.

Link to Learning

The community of people with disabilities is well organized in the twenty-first century, as evidenced by the considerable network of **disability rights organizations (https://www.openstax.org/l/29natdisrightor)** in the United States.

THE RIGHTS OF RELIGIOUS MINORITIES

The right to worship as a person chooses was one of the reasons for the initial settlement of the United States. Thus, it is ironic that many people throughout U.S. history have been denied their civil rights because of their status as members of a religious minority. Beginning in the early nineteenth century with the immigration of large numbers of Irish Catholics to the United States, anti-Catholicism became a common feature of American life and remained so until the mid-twentieth century. Catholic immigrants were denied jobs, and in the 1830s and 1840s anti-Catholic literature accused Catholic priests and nuns of committing horrific acts. Anti-Mormon sentiment was also quite common, and Mormons were accused of kidnapping women and building armies for the purpose of dominating their non-Mormon neighbors. At times, these fears led to acts of violence. A convent in Charlestown, Massachusetts, was burned to the ground in 1834.[159] In 1844, Joseph Smith, the founder of the Mormon religion, and his brother were murdered by a mob in Illinois.[160]

For many years, American Jews faced discrimination in employment, education, and housing based on their religion. Many of the restrictive real estate covenants that prohibited people from selling their homes to African Americans also prohibited them from selling to Jews, and a "gentlemen's agreement" among the most prestigious universities in the United States limited the number of Jewish students accepted. Indeed, a tradition of confronting discrimination led many American Jews to become actively involved in the civil rights movements for women and African Americans.[161]

Today, open discrimination against Jews in the United States is less common, although anti-Semitic sentiments still remain. In the twenty-first century, especially after the September 11 attacks, Muslims are the religious minority most likely to face discrimination. Although Title VII of the Civil Rights Act of 1964 prevents employment discrimination on the basis of religion and requires employers to make reasonable accommodations so that employees can engage in religious rituals and practices, Muslim employees are often discriminated against. Often the source of controversy is the wearing of head coverings by observant Muslims, which some employers claim violates uniform policies or dress codes, even when non-Muslim coworkers are allowed to wear head coverings that are not part of work uniforms.[162] Hate crimes against Muslims have also increased since 9/11, and many Muslims believe they are subject to racial profiling by law enforcement officers who suspect them of being terrorists.[163]

In another irony, many Christians have recently argued that they are being deprived of their rights because of their religious beliefs and have used this claim to justify their refusal to acknowledge the rights of others. The owner of Hobby Lobby Stores, for example, a conservative Christian, argued that his company's health-care plan should not have to pay for contraception because his religious beliefs are opposed to the practice. In 2014, in the case of *Burwell v. Hobby Lobby Stores, Inc.*, the Supreme Court ruled in his favor.[164] As discussed earlier, many conservative Christians have also argued that they should not have to recognize same-sex marriages because they consider homosexuality to be a sin.

Key Terms

affirmative action the use of programs and policies designed to assist groups that have historically been subject to discrimination

American Indian Movement (AIM) the Native American civil rights group responsible for the occupation of Wounded Knee, South Dakota, in 1973

black codes laws passed immediately after the Civil War that discriminated against freed slaves and other blacks and deprived them of their rights

Brown v. Board of Education the 1954 Supreme Court ruling that struck down *Plessy v. Ferguson* and declared segregation and "separate but equal" to be unconstitutional in public education

Chicano a term adopted by some Mexican American civil rights activists to describe themselves and those like them

civil disobedience an action taken in violation of the letter of the law to demonstrate that the law is unjust

comparable worth a doctrine calling for the same pay for workers whose jobs require the same level of education, responsibility, training, or working conditions

coverture a legal status of married women in which their separate legal identities were erased

***de facto* segregation** segregation that results from the private choices of individuals

***de jure* segregation** segregation that results from government discrimination

direct action civil rights campaigns that directly confronted segregationist practices through public demonstrations

disenfranchisement the revocation of someone's right to vote

equal protection clause a provision of the Fourteenth Amendment that requires the states to treat all residents equally under the law

Equal Rights Amendment (ERA) the proposed amendment to the Constitution that would have prohibited all discrimination based on sex

glass ceiling an invisible barrier caused by discrimination that prevents women from rising to the highest levels of an organization—including corporations, governments, academic institutions, and religious organizations

grandfather clause the provision in some southern states that allowed illiterate whites to vote because their ancestors had been able to vote before the Fifteenth Amendment was ratified

hate crime harassment, bullying, or other criminal acts directed against someone because of bias against that person's sex, gender, sexual orientation, religion, race, ethnicity, or disability

intermediate scrutiny the standard used by the courts to decide cases of discrimination based on gender and sex; burden of proof is on the government to demonstrate an important governmental interest is at stake in treating men differently from women

Jim Crow laws state and local laws that promoted racial segregation and undermined black voting rights in the south after Reconstruction

literacy tests tests that required the prospective voter in some states to be able to read a passage of text and answer questions about it; often used as a way to disenfranchise racial or ethnic minorities

Plessy v. Ferguson the 1896 Supreme Court ruling that allowed "separate but equal" racial segregation under the equal protection clause of the Fourteenth Amendment

poll tax annual tax imposed by some states before a person was allowed to vote

rational basis test the standard used by the courts to decide most forms of discrimination; the burden of proof is on those challenging the law or action to demonstrate there is no good reason for treating them differently from other citizens

Reconstruction the period from 1865 to 1877 during which the governments of Confederate states were reorganized prior to being readmitted to the Union

Stonewall Inn a bar in Greenwich Village, New York, where the modern Gay Pride movement began after rioters protested the police treatment of the LGBT community there

strict scrutiny the standard used by the courts to decide cases of discrimination based on race, ethnicity, national origin, or religion; burden of proof is on the government to demonstrate a compelling governmental interest is at stake and no alternative means are available to accomplish its goals

Title IX the section of the U.S. Education Amendments of 1972 that prohibits discrimination in education on the basis of sex

Trail of Tears the name given to the forced migration of the Cherokees from Georgia to Oklahoma in 1838–1839

understanding tests tests requiring prospective voters in some states to be able to explain the meaning of a passage of text or to answer questions related to citizenship; often used as a way to disenfranchise black voters

white primary a primary election in which only whites are allowed to vote

Summary

5.1 What Are Civil Rights and How Do We Identify Them?
The equal protection clause of the Fourteenth Amendment gives all people and groups in the United States the right to be treated equally regardless of individual attributes. That logic has been expanded in the twenty-first century to cover attributes such as race, color, ethnicity, sex, gender, sexual orientation, religion, and disability. People may still be treated unequally by the government, but only if there is at least a rational basis for it, such as a disability that makes a person unable to perform the essential functions required by a job, or if a person is too young to be trusted with an important responsibility, like driving safely. If the characteristic on which discrimination is based is related to sex, race, or ethnicity, the reason for it must serve, respectively, an important government interest or a compelling government interest.

5.2 The African American Struggle for Equality
Following the Civil War and the freeing of all slaves by the Thirteenth Amendment, a Republican Congress hoped to protect the freedmen from vengeful southern whites by passing the Fourteenth and Fifteenth Amendments, granting them citizenship and guaranteeing equal protection under the law and the right to vote (for black men). The end of Reconstruction, however, allowed white Southerners to regain control of the South's political and legal system and institute openly discriminatory Jim Crow laws. While some early efforts to secure civil rights were successful, the greatest gains came after World War II. Through a combination of lawsuits, Congressional acts, and direct action (such as President Truman's executive order

to desegregate the U.S. military), African Americans regained their voting rights and were guaranteed protection against discrimination in employment. Schools and public accommodations were desegregated. While much has been achieved, the struggle for equal treatment continues.

5.3 The Fight for Women's Rights

At the time of the Revolution and for many decades following it, married women had no right to control their own property, vote, or run for public office. Beginning in the 1840s, a women's movement began among women who were active in the abolition and temperance movements. Although some of their goals, such as achieving property rights for married women, were reached early on, their biggest goal—winning the right to vote—required the 1920 passage of the Nineteenth Amendment. Women secured more rights in the 1960s and 1970s, such as reproductive rights and the right not to be discriminated against in employment or education. Women continue to face many challenges: they are still paid less than men and are underrepresented in executive positions and elected office.

5.4 Civil Rights for Indigenous Groups: Native Americans, Alaskans, and Hawaiians

At the beginning of U.S. history, Indians were considered citizens of sovereign nations and thus ineligible for citizenship, and they were forced off their ancestral lands and onto reservations. Interest in Indian rights arose in the late nineteenth century, and in the 1930s, Native Americans were granted a degree of control over reservation lands and the right to govern themselves. Following World War II, they won greater rights to govern themselves, educate their children, decide how tribal lands should be used—to build casinos, for example—and practice traditional religious rituals without federal interference. Alaska Natives and Native Hawaiians have faced similar difficulties, but since the 1960s, they have been somewhat successful in having lands restored to them or obtaining compensation for their loss. Despite these achievements, members of these groups still tend to be poorer, less educated, less likely to be employed, and more likely to suffer addictions or to be incarcerated than other racial and ethnic groups in the United States.

5.5 Equal Protection for Other Groups

Many Hispanics and Latinos were deprived of their right to vote and forced to attend segregated schools. Asian Americans were also segregated and sometimes banned from immigrating to the United States. The achievements of the African American civil rights movement, such as the Civil Rights Act of 1964, benefited these groups, however, and Latinos and Asians also brought lawsuits on their own behalf. Many, like the Chicano youth of the Southwest, also engaged in direct action. This brought important gains, especially in education. Recent concerns over illegal immigration have resulted in renewed attempts to discriminate against Latinos, however.

For a long time, fear of discovery kept many LGBT people closeted and thus hindered their efforts to form a united response to discrimination. Since World War II, however, the LGBT community has achieved the right to same-sex marriage and protection from discrimination in other areas of life as well. The Americans with Disabilities Act, enacted in 1990, has recognized the equal rights of people with disabilities to employment, transportation, and access to public education. People with disabilities still face much discrimination, however, and LGBT people are frequently victims of hate crimes.

Some of the most serious forms of discrimination today are directed at religious minorities like Muslims, and many conservative Christians believe the recognition of LGBT rights threatens their religious freedoms.

Review Questions

1. A group of African American students believes a college admissions test that is used by a public university discriminates against them. What legal standard would the courts use in deciding their case?

    a. rational basis test

    b. intermediate scrutiny

    c. strict scrutiny

    d. equal protection

2. The equal protection clause became part of the Constitution as a result of _____.

    a. affirmative action

    b. the Fourteenth Amendment

    c. intermediate scrutiny

    d. strict scrutiny

3. Which of the following types of discrimination would be subject to the rational basis test?

    a. A law that treats men differently from women

    b. An action by a state governor that treats Asian Americans differently from other citizens

    c. A law that treats whites differently from other citizens

    d. A law that treats 10-year-olds differently from 28-year-olds

4. What is the difference between civil rights and civil liberties?

5. The Supreme Court decision ruling that "separate but equal" was constitutional and allowed racial segregation to take place was _____.

    a. *Brown v. Board of Education*

    b. *Plessy v. Ferguson*

    c. *Loving v. Virginia*

    d. *Shelley v. Kraemer*

6. The 1965 Selma-to-Montgomery march was an important milestone in the civil rights movement because it _____.

    a. vividly illustrated the continued resistance to black civil rights in the Deep South

    b. did not encounter any violent resistance

    c. led to the passage of the Civil Rights Act of 1964

    d. was the first major protest after the death of Martin Luther King, Jr.

7. What were the key provisions of the Civil Rights Act of 1964?

8. At the world's first women's rights convention in 1848, the most contentious issue proved to be _____.

    a. A. the right to education for women

    b. B. suffrage for women

    c. C. access to the professions for women

    d. D. greater property rights for women

9. How did NAWSA differ from the NWP?

    a. NAWSA worked to win votes for women on a state-by-state basis while the NWP wanted an amendment added to the Constitution.

    b. NAWSA attracted mostly middle-class women while NWP appealed to the working class.

    c. The NWP favored more confrontational tactics like protests and picketing while NAWSA circulated petitions and lobbied politicians.

    d. The NWP sought to deny African Americans the vote, but NAWSA wanted to enfranchise all women.

10. The doctrine that people who do jobs that require the same level of skill, training, or education are thus entitled to equal pay is known as _____.

    a. the glass ceiling

    b. substantial compensation

    c. comparable worth

    d. affirmative action

11. The Trail of Tears is the name given to the forced removal of this tribe from Georgia to Oklahoma.

    a. Lakota

    b. Paiute

    c. Navajo

    d. Cherokee

12. AIM was _____.

    a. a federal program that returned control of Native American education to tribal governments

    b. a radical group of Native American activists who occupied the settlement of Wounded Knee on the Pine Ridge Reservation

    c. an attempt to reduce the size of reservations

    d. a federal program to give funds to Native American tribes to help their members open small businesses that would employ tribal members

13. Briefly describe the similarities and differences between the experiences of Native Americans and Native Hawaiians.

14. Mexican American farm workers in California organized _____ to demand higher pay from their employers.

    a. the *bracero* program

    b. Operation Wetback

    c. the United Farm Workers union

    d. the Mattachine Society

15. Which of the following best describes attitudes toward Asian immigrants in the late nineteenth and early twentieth centuries?

    a. Asian immigrants were welcomed to the United States and swiftly became financially successful.

    b. Asian immigrants were disliked by whites who feared competition for jobs, and several acts of Congress sought to restrict immigration and naturalization of Asians.

    c. Whites feared Asian immigrants because Japanese and Chinese Americans were often disloyal to the U.S. government.

    d. Asian immigrants got along well with whites but not with Mexican Americans or African Americans.

16. Why did it take so long for an active civil rights movement to begin in the LGBT community?

Critical Thinking Questions

17. What is the better approach to civil rights—a peaceful, gradual one that focuses on passing laws and winning cases in court, or a radical one that includes direct action and acts of civil disobedience? Why do you consider this to be the better solution?

18. Should public funds be used to provide programs for Native Americans, Alaska Natives, and Native Hawaiians even though no one living today was responsible for depriving them of their lands? Why or why not?

19. Although some Native Hawaiians want the right to govern themselves, others want to secede from Hawaii and become an independent nation. If this is what the majority of Native Hawaiians want, should they be allowed to do so? Why or why not?

20. If a person's religious beliefs conflict with the law or lead to bias against other groups, should the government protect the exercise of those beliefs? Why or why not?

21. In 1944, the Supreme Court upheld the authority of the U.S. government to order the internment of a minority group in the interest of national security, even though there was no evidence that any members of this group were disloyal to the United States. Should the same policy be applied today against U.S. Muslims or Muslim immigrants? Why or why not?

Suggestions for Further Study

Anderson, Terry H. 2004. *The Pursuit of Fairness: A History of Affirmative Action*. New York: Oxford University Press.

Baker, Jean H., ed. 2002. *Votes for Women: The Struggle for Suffrage Revisited*. New York: Oxford University Press.

Blackmon, Douglas A. 2008. *Slavery by Another Name: The Re-Enslavement of Black Americans from the Civil War to World War II*. New York: Doubleday.

Catsam, Derek Charles. 2011. *Freedom's Main Line: The Journey of Reconciliation and the Freedom Rides*. Lexington: University Press of Kentucky.

Chappell, David L. 2014. *Waking from the Dream: The Struggle for Civil Rights in the Shadow of Martin Luther King, Jr.* New York: Random House.

Faderman, Lillian. 2015. *The Gay Revolution: The Story of the Struggle*. New York: Simon & Schuster.

Fairclough, Adam. 2002. *Better Day Coming: Blacks and Equality, 1890–2000*. New York: Penguin Books.

Flexner, Eleanor, and Ellen Fitzpatrick. 1996. *Century of Struggle: The Woman's Rights Movement in the United States*, 3rd ed. Cambridge, MA: Belknap Press.

Magnuson, Stewart. 2013. *Wounded Knee 1973: Still Bleeding: The American Indian Movement, the FBI, and their Fight to Bury the Sins of the Past*. Arlington, VA: Courtbridge Publishing.

Rosales, Arturo F., and Francisco A. Rosales. 1997. *Chicano! The History of the Mexican American Civil Rights Movement*, 2nd ed. Houston, TX: Arte Público Press.

Soennichsen, John. 2011. *The Chinese Exclusion Act of 1882*. Santa Barbara, CA: Greenwood.

Wilkins, David E., and K. Tsianina Lomawaima. 2002. *Uneven Ground: American Indian Sovereignty and Fede*

Chapter 6

The Politics of Public Opinion

Figure 6.1 Governor and presidential candidate Mitt Romney takes the stage in Boston, Massachusetts, to give his "Super Tuesday" victory speech (credit: modification of work by BU Interactive News/Flickr).

Chapter Outline

Introduction

On November 7, 2012, the day after the presidential election, journalists found Mitt Romney's transition website, detailing the Republican candidate's plans for the upcoming inauguration celebration and criteria for Cabinet and White House appointees and leaving space for video of his acceptance speech.[1] Yet, Romney had lost his bid for the White House. In fact, Romney's campaign staff had been so sure he would win that he had not written a concession speech. How could they have been wrong? Romney's staff blamed the campaign's own polls. Believing Republican voters to be highly motivated, Romney pollsters had overestimated how many would turn out (Figure 6.1).[2] The campaign's polls showed Romney close to President Barack Obama, although non-campaign polls showed Obama ahead.[3] On election night, Romney gave his hastily drafted concession speech, still unsure how he had lost.

In the 2016 election, most polls showed Democratic nominee Hillary Clinton with an advantage nationwide and in the battleground states in the days leading up to the election. However, Republican nominee Donald Trump was elected president as many new voters joined the process, voters who were not studied in the polls as likely voters. As many a disappointed candidate knows, public opinion matters. The way opinions are formed and the way we measure public opinion also matter. But how much, and why? These are some of the questions we'll explore in this chapter.

6.1 The Nature of Public Opinion

Learning Objectives

By the end of this section, you will be able to:
- Define public opinion and political socialization
- Explain the process and role of political socialization in the U.S. political system
- Compare the ways in which citizens learn political information
- Explain how beliefs and ideology affect the formation of public opinion

The collection of public opinion through polling and interviews is a part of American political culture. Politicians want to know what the public thinks. Campaign managers want to know how citizens will vote. Media members seek to write stories about what Americans want. Every day, polls take the pulse of the people and report the results. And yet we have to wonder: Why do we care what people think?

WHAT IS PUBLIC OPINION?

Public opinion is a collection of popular views about something, perhaps a person, a local or national event, or a new idea. For example, each day, a number of polling companies call Americans at random to ask whether they approve or disapprove of the way the president is guiding the economy.[4] When situations arise internationally, polling companies survey whether citizens support U.S. intervention in places like Syria or Ukraine. These individual opinions are collected together to be analyzed and interpreted for politicians and the media. The analysis examines how the public feels or thinks, so politicians can use the information to make decisions about their future legislative votes, campaign messages, or propaganda.

But where do people's opinions come from? Most citizens base their political opinions on their beliefs[5] and their attitudes, both of which begin to form in childhood. *Beliefs* are closely held ideas that support our values and expectations about life and politics. For example, the idea that we are all entitled to equality, liberty, freedom, and privacy is a belief most people in the United States share. We may acquire this belief by growing up in the United States or by having come from a country that did not afford these valued principles to its citizens.

Our *attitudes* are also affected by our personal beliefs and represent the preferences we form based on our life experiences and values. A person who has suffered racism or bigotry may have a skeptical attitude toward the actions of authority figures, for example.

Over time, our beliefs and our attitudes about people, events, and ideas will become a set of norms, or accepted ideas, about what we may feel should happen in our society or what is right for the government to do in a situation. In this way, attitudes and beliefs form the foundation for opinions.

POLITICAL SOCIALIZATION

At the same time that our beliefs and attitudes are forming during childhood, we are also being *socialized*; that is, we are learning from many information sources about the society and community in which we live and how we are to behave in it. **Political socialization** is the process by which we are trained to understand and join a country's political world, and, like most forms of socialization, it starts when we are very young. We may first become aware of politics by watching a parent or guardian vote, for instance, or by hearing presidents and candidates speak on television or the Internet, or seeing adults honor the American flag at an event (Figure 6.2). As socialization continues, we are introduced to basic political information in school. We recite the Pledge of Allegiance and learn about the Founding Fathers, the Constitution, the two major political parties, the three branches of government, and the economic system.

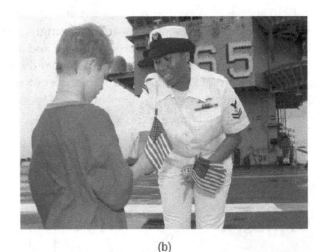

(a)   (b)

Figure 6.2 Political socialization begins early. Hans Enoksen, former prime minister of Greenland, receives a helping hand at the polls from five-year-old Pipaluk Petersen (a). Intelligence Specialist Second Class Tashawbaba McHerrin (b) hands a U.S. flag to a child visiting the USS *Enterprise* during Fleet Week in Port Everglades, Florida. (credit a: modification of work by Leiff Josefsen; credit b: modification of work by Matthew Keane, U.S. Navy)

By the time we complete school, we have usually acquired the information necessary to form political views and be contributing members of the political system. A young man may realize he prefers the Democratic Party because it supports his views on social programs and education, whereas a young woman may decide she wants to vote for the Republican Party because its platform echoes her beliefs about economic growth and family values.

Accounting for the process of socialization is central to our understanding of public opinion, because the beliefs we acquire early in life are unlikely to change dramatically as we grow older.[6] Our political ideology, made up of the attitudes and beliefs that help shape our opinions on political theory and policy, is rooted in who we are as individuals. Our ideology may change subtly as we grow older and are introduced to new circumstances or new information, but our underlying beliefs and attitudes are unlikely to change very much, unless we experience events that profoundly affect us. For example, family members of 9/11 victims became more Republican and more political following the terrorist attacks.[7] Similarly, young adults who attended political protest rallies in the 1960s and 1970s were more likely to participate in politics in general than their peers who had not protested.[8]

If enough beliefs or attitudes are shattered by an event, such as an economic catastrophe or a threat to personal safety, ideology shifts may affect the way we vote. During the 1920s, the Republican Party controlled the House of Representatives and the Senate, sometimes by wide margins.[9] After the stock market collapsed and the nation slid into the Great Depression, many citizens abandoned the Republican Party. In 1932, voters overwhelmingly chose Democratic candidates, for both the presidency and Congress. The Democratic Party gained registered members and the Republican Party lost them.[10] Citizens' beliefs had shifted enough to cause the control of Congress to change from one party to the other, and Democrats continued to hold Congress for several decades. Another sea change occurred in Congress in the 1994 elections when the Republican Party took control of both the House and the Senate for the first time in over forty years.

Today, polling agencies have noticed that citizens' beliefs have become far more polarized, or widely opposed, over the last decade.[11] To track this polarization, Pew Research conducted a study of Republican and Democratic respondents over a twenty-five-year span. Every few years, Pew would poll respondents, asking them whether they agreed or disagreed with statements. These statements are referred to as "value questions" or "value statements," because they measure what the respondent values. Examples of statements include "Government regulation of business usually does more harm than good," "Labor unions are necessary to protect the working person," and "Society should ensure all have equal opportunity to succeed." After comparing such answers for twenty-five years, Pew Research found that Republican and Democratic respondents are increasingly answering these questions very differently. This is especially true for questions about the government and politics. In 1987, 58 percent of Democrats and 60 percent of Republicans agreed with the statement that the government controlled too much of our daily lives. In 2012, 47 percent of Democrats and 77 percent of Republicans agreed with the statement. This is an example of polarization, in which members of one party see government from a very different perspective than the members of the other party (Figure 6.3).[12]

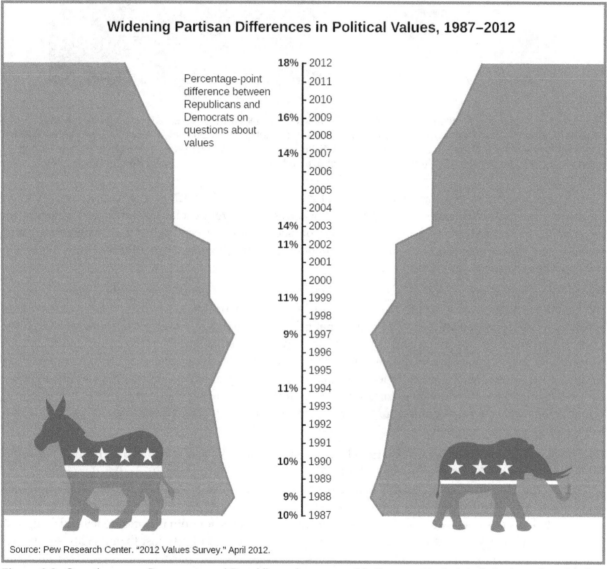

Figure 6.3 Over the years, Democrats and Republicans have moved further apart in their beliefs about the role of government. In 1987, Republican and Democratic answers to forty-eight values questions differed by an average of only 10 percent, but that difference has grown to 18 percent over the last twenty-five years.

Political scientists noted this and other changes in beliefs following the 9/11 terrorist attacks on the United States, including an increase in the level of trust in government[13] and a new willingness to limit liberties for groups or citizens who "[did] not fit into the dominant cultural type."[14] According to some scholars, these shifts led partisanship to become more polarized than in previous decades, as more citizens began thinking of themselves as conservative or liberal rather than moderate.[15] Some believe 9/11 caused a number of citizens to become more conservative overall, although it is hard to judge whether such a shift will be permanent.[16]

SOCIALIZATION AGENTS

An **agent of political socialization** is a source of political information intended to help citizens understand how to act in their political system and how to make decisions on political matters. The information may help a citizen decide how to vote, where to donate money, or how to protest decisions made by the government.

The most prominent agents of socialization are family and school. Other influential agents are social groups, such as religious institutions and friends, and the media. Political socialization is not unique to the United States. Many nations have realized the benefits of socializing their populations. China, for example, stresses nationalism in schools as a way to increase national unity.[17] In the United States, one benefit of socialization is that our political system enjoys **diffuse support**, which is support characterized by a high level of stability in politics, acceptance of the government as legitimate, and a common goal of preserving the system.[18] These traits keep a country steady, even during times of political or social upheaval. But diffuse support does not happen quickly, nor does it occur without the help of agents of political socialization.

For many children, family is the first introduction to politics. Children may hear adult conversations at home and piece together the political messages their parents support. They often know how their parents or grandparents plan to vote, which in turn can socialize them into political behavior such as political party membership.[19] Children who accompany their parents on Election Day in November are exposed to the act of voting and the concept of civic duty, which is the performance of actions that benefit the country or community. Families active in community projects or politics make children aware of community needs and politics.

Introducing children to these activities has an impact on their future behavior. Both early and recent findings suggest that children adopt some of the political beliefs and attitudes of their parents (Figure 6.4).[20] Children of Democratic parents often become registered Democrats, whereas children in Republican households often become Republicans. Children living in households where parents do not display a consistent political party loyalty are less likely to be strong Democrats or strong Republicans, and instead are often independents.[21]

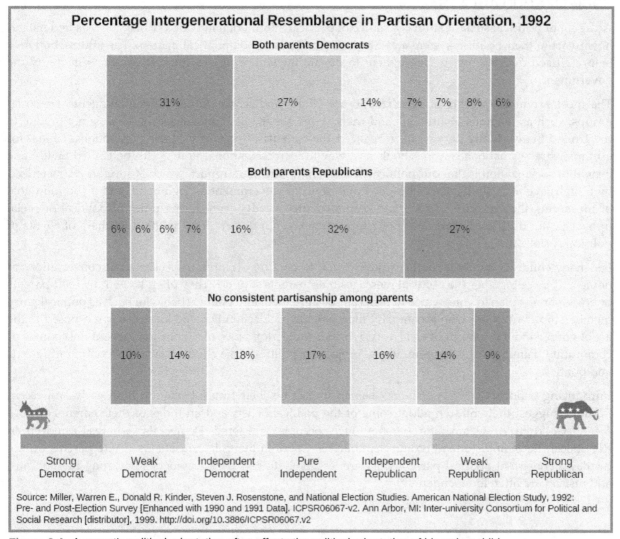

Figure 6.4 A parent's political orientation often affects the political orientation of his or her child.

While family provides an informal political education, schools offer a more formal and increasingly important one. The early introduction is often broad and thematic, covering explorers, presidents, victories, and symbols, but generally the lessons are idealized and do not discuss many of the specific problems or controversies connected with historical figures and moments. George Washington's contributions as our first president are highlighted, for instance, but teachers are unlikely to mention that he owned slaves. Lessons will also try to personalize government and make leaders relatable to children. A teacher might discuss Abraham Lincoln's childhood struggle to get an education despite the death of his mother and his family's poverty. Children learn to respect government, follow laws, and obey the requests of police, firefighters, and other first responders. The Pledge of Allegiance becomes a regular part of the school day, as students learn to show respect to our country's symbols such as the flag and to abstractions such as liberty and equality.

As students progress to higher grades, lessons will cover more detailed information about the history of the United States, its economic system, and the workings of the government. Complex topics such as the legislative process, checks and balances, and domestic policymaking are covered. Introductory economics classes teach about the various ways to build an economy, explaining how the capitalist system works. Many high schools have implemented civic volunteerism requirements as a way to encourage students to participate in their communities. Many offer Advanced Placement classes in U.S. government and history, or other honors-level courses, such as International Baccalaureate or dual-credit courses. These courses can introduce detail and realism, raise controversial topics, and encourage students to make comparisons and think critically about the United States in a global and historical context. College students may choose to pursue their academic study of the U.S. political system further, become active in campus advocacy or rights groups, or run for any of a number of elected positions on campus or even in the local community. Each step of the educational system's socialization process will ready students to make decisions and be participating members of political society.

We are also socialized outside our homes and schools. When citizens attend religious ceremonies, as 70 percent of Americans in a recent survey claimed,[22] they are socialized to adopt beliefs that affect their politics. Religion leaders often teach on matters of life, death, punishment, and obligation, which translate into views on political issues such as abortion, euthanasia, the death penalty, and military involvement abroad. Political candidates speak at religious centers and institutions in an effort to meet like-minded voters. For example, Senator Ted Cruz (R-TX) announced his 2016 presidential bid at Liberty University, a fundamentalist Christian institution. This university matched Cruz's conservative and religious ideological leanings and was intended to give him a boost from the faith-based community.

Friends and peers too have a socializing effect on citizens. Communication networks are based on trust and common interests, so when we receive information from friends and neighbors, we often readily accept it because we trust them.[23] Information transmitted through social media like Facebook is also likely to have a socializing effect. Friends "like" articles and information, sharing their political beliefs and information with one another.

Media—newspapers, television, radio, and the Internet—also socialize citizens through the information they provide. For a long time, the media served as gatekeepers of our information, creating reality by choosing what to present. If the media did not cover an issue or event, it was as if it did not exist. With the rise of the Internet and social media, however, traditional media have become less powerful agents of this kind of socialization.

Another way the media socializes audiences is through framing, or choosing the way information is presented. Framing can affect the way an event or story is perceived. Candidates described with negative adjectives, for instance, may do poorly on Election Day. Consider the recent demonstrations over the deaths of Michael Brown in Ferguson, Missouri, and of Freddie Gray in Baltimore, Maryland. Both deaths were caused by police actions against unarmed African American men. Brown was shot to death by an officer on August 9, 2014. Gray died from spinal injuries sustained in transport to jail in April 2015. Following each death, family, friends, and sympathizers protested the police actions as excessive and unfair. While some television stations framed the demonstrations as riots and looting, other stations framed them as protests and fights against corruption. The demonstrations contained both riot and protest, but individuals' perceptions were affected by the framing chosen by their preferred information sources (Figure 6.5).[24]

(a)   (b)

Figure 6.5 Images of protestors from the Baltimore "uprising" (a) and from the Baltimore "riots" (b) of April 25, 2015. (credit a: modification of work by Pete Santilli Live Stream/YouTube; credit b: modification of work by "Newzulu"/YouTube)

Finally, media information presented as fact can contain covert or overt political material. **Covert content** is political information provided under the pretense that it is neutral. A magazine might run a story on climate change by interviewing representatives of only one side of the policy debate and downplaying the opposing view, all without acknowledging the one-sided nature of its coverage. In contrast, when the writer or publication makes clear to the reader or viewer that the information offers only one side of the political debate, the political message is **overt content**. Political commentators like Rush Limbaugh and publications like *Mother Jones* openly state their ideological viewpoints. While such overt political content may be offensive or annoying to a reader or viewer, all are offered the choice whether to be exposed to the material.

SOCIALIZATION AND IDEOLOGY

The socialization process leaves citizens with attitudes and beliefs that create a personal ideology. Ideologies depend on attitudes and beliefs, and on the way we prioritize each belief over the others. Most citizens hold a great number of beliefs and attitudes about government action. Many think government should provide for the common defense, in the form of a national military. They also argue that government should provide services to its citizens in the form of free education, unemployment benefits, and assistance for the poor.

When asked how to divide the national budget, Americans reveal priorities that divide public opinion. Should we have a smaller military and larger social benefits, or a larger military budget and limited social benefits? This is the *guns versus butter* debate, which assumes that governments have a finite amount of money and must choose whether to spend a larger part on the military or on social programs. The choice forces citizens into two opposing groups.

Divisions like these appear throughout public opinion. Assume we have four different people named Garcia, Chin, Smith, and Dupree. Garcia may believe that the United States should provide a free education for every citizen all the way through college, whereas Chin may believe education should be free only through high school. Smith might believe children should be covered by health insurance at the government's expense, whereas Dupree believes all citizens should be covered. In the end, the way we prioritize our beliefs and what we decide is most important to us determines whether we are on the liberal or conservative end of the political spectrum, or somewhere in between.

Get Connected!

Express Yourself

You can volunteer to participate in public opinion surveys. Diverse respondents are needed across a variety of topics to give a reliable picture of what Americans think about politics, entertainment, marketing, and more. One polling group, Harris Interactive, maintains an Internet pool of potential respondents of varied ages, education levels, backgrounds, cultures, and more. When a survey is designed and put out into the field, Harris emails an invitation to the pool to find respondents. Respondents choose which surveys to complete based on the topics, time required, and compensation offered (usually small).

Harris Interactive is a subsidiary of Nielsen, a company with a long history of measuring television and media viewership in the United States and abroad. Nielsen ratings help television stations identify shows and newscasts with enough viewers to warrant being kept in production, and also to set advertising rates (based on audience size) for commercials on popular shows. Harris Interactive has expanded Nielsen's survey methods by using polling data and interviews to better predict future political and market trends.

Harris polls cover the economy, lifestyles, sports, international affairs, and more. Which topic has the most surveys? Politics, of course.

Wondering what types of surveys you might get? The results of some of the surveys will give you an idea. They are available to the public on the Harris website. For more information, log in to Harris Poll Online (https://www.openstax.org/l/29harrispole) .

IDEOLOGIES AND THE IDEOLOGICAL SPECTRUM

One useful way to look at ideologies is to place them on a spectrum that visually compares them based on what they prioritize. Liberal ideologies are traditionally put on the left and conservative ideologies on the right. (This placement dates from the French Revolution and is why liberals are called left-wing and conservatives are called right-wing.) The ideologies at the ends of the spectrum are the most extreme; those in the middle are moderate. Thus, people who identify with left- and right-wing ideologies identify with beliefs to the left and right ends of the spectrum, while moderates balance the beliefs at the extremes of the spectrum.

In the United States, ideologies at the right side of the spectrum prioritize government control over personal freedoms. They range from fascism to authoritarianism to conservatism. Ideologies on the left side of the spectrum prioritize equality and range from communism to socialism to liberalism (Figure 6.6). Moderate ideologies fall in the middle and try to balance the two extremes.

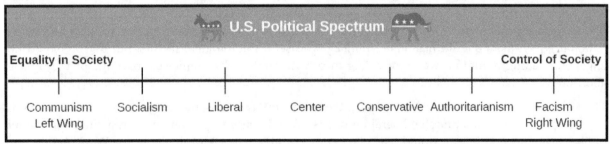

Figure 6.6 People who espouse left-wing ideologies in the United States identify with beliefs on the left side of the spectrum that prioritize equality, whereas those on the right side of the spectrum emphasize control.

Fascism promotes total control of the country by the ruling party or political leader. This form of government will run the economy, the military, society, and culture, and often tries to control the private lives of its citizens. Authoritarian leaders control the politics, military, and government of a country, and often the economy as well.

Conservative governments attempt to hold tight to the traditions of a nation by balancing individual rights with the good of the community. **Traditional conservatism** supports the authority of the monarchy and the church, believing government provides the rule of law and maintains a society that is safe and organized. **Modern conservatism** differs from traditional conservatism in assuming elected government will guard individual liberties and provide laws. Modern conservatives also prefer a smaller government that stays out of the economy, allowing the market and business to determine prices, wages, and supply.

Classical liberalism believes in individual liberties and rights. It is based on the idea of free will, that people are born equal with the right to make decisions without government intervention. It views government with suspicion, since history includes many examples of monarchs and leaders who limited citizens' rights. Today, **modern liberalism** focuses on equality and supports government intervention in society and the economy if it promotes equality. Liberals expect government to provide basic social and educational programs to help everyone have a chance to succeed.

Under **socialism**, the government uses its authority to promote social and economic equality within the country. Socialists believe government should provide everyone with expanded services and public programs, such as health care, subsidized housing and groceries, childhood education, and inexpensive college tuition. Socialism sees the government as a way to ensure all citizens receive both equal opportunities and equal outcomes. Citizens with more wealth are expected to contribute more to the state's revenue through higher taxes that pay for services provided to all. Socialist countries are also likely to have higher minimum wages than non-socialist countries.

In theory, **communism** promotes common ownership of all property, means of production, and materials. This means that the government, or states, should own the property, farms, manufacturing, and businesses. By controlling these aspects of the economy, Communist governments can prevent the exploitation of workers while creating an equal society. Extreme inequality of income, in which some citizens earn millions of dollars a year and other citizens merely hundreds, is prevented by instituting wage controls or by abandoning currency altogether. Communism presents a problem, however, because the practice differs from the theory. The theory assumes the move to communism is supported and led by the proletariat, or the workers and citizens of a country.[25] Human rights violations by governments of actual Communist countries make it appear the movement has been driven not by the people, but by leadership.

We can characterize economic variations on these ideologies by adding another dimension to the ideological spectrum above—whether we prefer that government control the state economy or stay out of it. The extremes are a command economy, such as existed in the former Soviet Russia, and a laissez-faire ("leave it alone") economy, such as in the United States prior to the 1929 market crash, when banks and corporations were largely unregulated. Communism prioritizes control of both politics and economy, while libertarianism is its near-opposite. Libertarians believe in individual rights and limited government intervention in private life and personal economic decisions. Government exists to maintain freedom and life, so its main function is to ensure domestic peace and national defense. Libertarians also believe the national government should maintain a military in case of international threats, but that it should not engage in setting minimum wages or ruling in private matters, like same-sex marriage or the right to abortion.[26]

The point where a person's ideology falls on the spectrum gives us some insight to his or her opinions. Though people can sometimes be liberal on one issue and conservative on another, a citizen to the left of liberalism, near socialism, would likely be happy with the passage of the Raise the Wage Act of 2015, which would eventually increase the minimum wage from $7.25 to $12 an hour. A citizen falling near conservatism would believe the Patriot Act is reasonable, because it allows the FBI and other government agencies to collect data on citizens' phone calls and social media communications to monitor potential terrorism (**Figure 6.7**). A citizen to the right of the spectrum is more likely to favor cutting social services like unemployment and Medicaid.

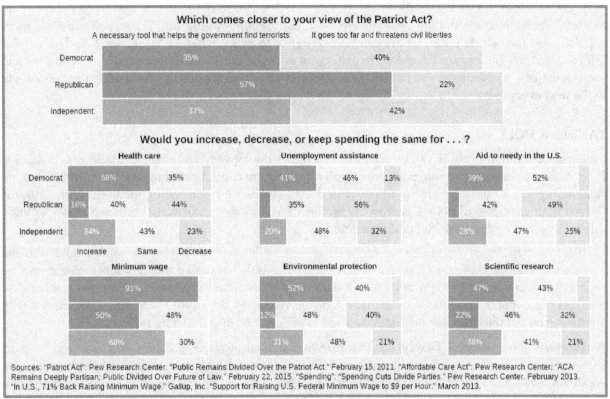

Figure 6.7 Public opinion on a given issue may differ dramatically depending on the political ideology or party of those polled.

Link to Learning

Where do your beliefs come from? The Pew Research Center offers a typology quiz (https://www.openstax.org/l/29typologyquiz) to help you find out. Ask a friend or family member to answer a few questions with you and compare results. What do you think about government regulation? The military? The economy? Now compare your results. Are you both liberal? Conservative? Moderate?

6.2 How Is Public Opinion Measured?

Learning Objectives

By the end of this section, you will be able to:
- Explain how information about public opinion is gathered
- Identify common ways to measure and quantify public opinion
- Analyze polls to determine whether they accurately measure a population's opinions

Polling has changed over the years. The first opinion poll was taken in 1824; it asked voters how they voted as they left their polling places. Informal polls are called **straw polls**, and they informally collect opinions of a non-random population or group. Newspapers and social media continue the tradition of unofficial polls, mainly because interested readers want to know how elections will end. Facebook and online newspapers often offer informal, pop-up quizzes that ask a single question about politics or an event. The poll is not meant to be formal, but it provides a general idea of what the readership thinks.

Modern public opinion polling is relatively new, only eighty years old. These polls are far more sophisticated than straw polls and are carefully designed to probe what we think, want, and value. The information they gather may be relayed to politicians or newspapers, and is analyzed by statisticians and social scientists. As the media and politicians pay more attention to the polls, an increasing number are put in the field every week.

TAKING A POLL

Most public opinion polls aim to be accurate, but this is not an easy task. Political polling is a science. From design to implementation, polls are complex and require careful planning and care. Mitt Romney's campaign polls are only a recent example of problems stemming from polling methods. Our history is littered with examples of polling companies producing results that incorrectly predicted public opinion due to poor survey design or bad polling methods.

In 1936, *Literary Digest* continued its tradition of polling citizens to determine who would win the presidential election. The magazine sent opinion cards to people who had a subscription, a phone, or a car registration. Only some of the recipients sent back their cards. The result? Alf Landon was predicted to win 55.4 percent of the popular vote; in the end, he received only 38 percent.[27] Franklin D. Roosevelt won another term, but the story demonstrates the need to be scientific in conducting polls.

A few years later, Thomas Dewey lost the 1948 presidential election to Harry Truman, despite polls showing Dewey far ahead and Truman destined to lose (**Figure 6.8**). More recently, John Zogby, of Zogby Analytics, went public with his prediction that John Kerry would win the presidency against incumbent president George W. Bush in 2004, only to be proven wrong on election night. These are just a few cases, but each offers a different lesson. In 1948, pollsters did not poll up to the day of the election, relying on old numbers that did not include a late shift in voter opinion. Zogby's polls did not represent likely voters and incorrectly predicted who would vote and for whom. These examples reinforce the need to use scientific methods when conducting polls, and to be cautious when reporting the results.

Figure 6.8 Polling process errors can lead to incorrect predictions. On November 3, the day after the 1948 presidential election, a jubilant Harry S. Truman triumphantly displays the inaccurate headline of the *Chicago Daily Tribune* announcing Thomas Dewey's supposed victory (credit: David Erickson/Flickr).

Most polling companies employ statisticians and methodologists trained in conducting polls and analyzing data. A number of criteria must be met if a poll is to be completed scientifically. First, the methodologists identify the desired population, or group, of respondents they want to interview. For example, if the goal is to project who will win the presidency, citizens from across the United States should be interviewed. If we wish to understand how voters in Colorado will vote on a proposition, the population of respondents should only be Colorado residents. When surveying on elections or policy matters, many polling houses will interview only respondents who have a history of voting in previous elections, because these voters are more likely to go to the polls on Election Day. Politicians are more likely to be influenced by the opinions of proven voters than of everyday citizens. Once the desired population has been identified, the researchers will begin to build a sample that is both random and representative.

A **random sample** consists of a limited number of people from the overall population, selected in such a way that each has an equal chance of being chosen. In the early years of polling, telephone numbers of potential respondents were arbitrarily selected from various areas to avoid regional bias. While landline phones allow polls to try to ensure randomness, the increasing use of cell phones makes this process difficult. Cell phones, and their numbers, are portable and move with the owner. To prevent errors, polls that include known cellular numbers may screen for zip codes and other geographic indicators to prevent regional bias. A **representative sample** consists of a group whose demographic distribution is similar to that of the overall population. For example, nearly 51 percent of the U.S. population is female.[28] To match this demographic distribution of women, any poll intended to measure what most Americans think about an issue should survey a sample containing slightly more women than men.

Pollsters try to interview a set number of citizens to create a reasonable sample of the population. This sample size will vary based on the size of the population being interviewed and the level of accuracy the pollster wishes to reach. If the poll is trying to reveal the opinion of a state or group, such as the opinion of Wisconsin voters about changes to the education system, the sample size may vary from five hundred to one thousand respondents and produce results with relatively low error. For a poll to predict what Americans think nationally, such as about the White House's policy on greenhouse gases, the sample size should be larger.

The sample size varies with each organization and institution due to the way the data are processed. Gallup often interviews only five hundred respondents, while Rasmussen Reports and Pew Research often interview one thousand to fifteen hundred respondents.[29] Academic organizations, like the American National Election Studies, have interviews with over twenty-five-hundred respondents.[30] A larger sample makes a poll more accurate, because it will have relatively fewer unusual responses and be more representative of the actual population. Pollsters do not interview more respondents than necessary, however. Increasing the number of respondents will increase the accuracy of the poll, but once the poll has enough respondents to be representative, increases in accuracy become minor and are not cost-effective.[31]

When the sample represents the actual population, the poll's accuracy will be reflected in a lower margin of error. The **margin of error** is a number that states how far the poll results may be from the actual opinion of the total population of citizens. The lower the margin of error, the more predictive the poll. Large margins of error are problematic. For example, if a poll that claims Hillary Clinton is likely to win 30 percent of the vote in the 2016 New York Democratic primary has a margin of error of +/-6, it tells us that Clinton may receive as little as 24 percent of the vote (30 − 6) or as much as 36 percent (30 + 6). A lower of margin of error is clearly desirable because it gives us the most precise picture of what people actually think or will do.

With many polls out there, how do you know whether a poll is a good poll and accurately predicts what a group believes? First, look for the numbers. Polling companies include the margin of error, polling dates, number of respondents, and population sampled to show their scientific reliability. Was the poll recently taken? Is the question clear and unbiased? Was the number of respondents high enough to predict the population? Is the margin of error small? It is worth looking for this valuable information when you interpret poll results. While most polling agencies strive to create quality polls, other organizations want fast results and may prioritize immediate numbers over random and representative samples. For example, instant polling is often used by news networks to quickly assess how well candidates are performing in a debate.

Insider Perspective

The Ins and Outs of Polls

Ever wonder what happens behind the polls? To find out, we posed a few questions to Scott Keeter, Director of Survey Research at Pew Research Center.

Q: What are some of the most common misconceptions about polling?

A: A couple of them recur frequently. The first is that it is just impossible for one thousand or fifteen hundred people in a survey sample to adequately represent a population of 250 million adults. But of course it is possible. Random sampling, which has been well understood for the past several decades, makes it possible. If you don't trust small random samples, then ask your doctor to take all of your blood the next time you need a diagnostic test.

The second misconception is that it is possible to get any result we want from a poll if we are willing to manipulate the wording sufficiently. While it is true that question wording can influence responses, it is not true that a poll can get any result it sets out to get. People aren't stupid. They can tell if a question is highly biased and they won't react well to it. Perhaps more important, the public can read the questions and know whether they are being loaded with words and phrases intended to push a respondent in a particular direction. That's why it's important to always look at the wording and the sequencing of questions in any poll.

Q: How does your organization choose polling topics?

A: We choose our topics in several ways. Most importantly, we keep up with developments in politics and public policy, and try to make our polls reflect relevant issues. Much of our research is driven by the news cycle and topics that we see arising in the near future. We also have a number of projects that we do regularly to provide a look at long-term trends in public opinion. For example, we've been asking a series of questions about political values since 1987, which has helped to document the rise of political polarization in the public. Another is a large (thirty-five thousand interviews) study of religious beliefs, behaviors, and affiliations among Americans. We released the first of these in 2007, and a second in 2015. Finally, we try to seize opportunities to make larger contributions on weighty issues when they arise. When the United States was on the verge of a big debate on immigration reform in 2006, we undertook a major survey of Americans' attitudes about immigration and immigrants. In 2007, we conducted the first-ever nationally representative survey of Muslim Americans.

Q: What is the average number of polls you oversee in a week?

A: It depends a lot on the news cycle and the needs of our research groups. We almost always have a survey in progress, but sometimes there are two or three going on at once. At other times, we are more focused on analyzing data already collected or planning for future surveys.

Q: Have you placed a poll in the field and had results that really surprised you?

A: It's rare to be surprised because we've learned a lot over the years about how people respond to questions. But here are some findings that jumped out to some of us in the past:

1) In 2012, we conducted a survey of people who said their religion is "nothing in particular." We asked them if they are "looking for a religion that would be right" for them, based on the expectation that many people without an affiliation—but who had not said they were atheists or agnostic—might be trying to find a religion that fit. Only 10 percent said that they were looking for the right religion.

2) We—and many others—were surprised that public opinion about Muslims became more favorable after the 9/11 terrorist attacks. It's possible that President Bush's strong appeal to people not to blame Muslims in general for the attack had an effect on opinions.

3) It's also surprising that basic public attitudes about gun control (whether pro or anti) barely move after highly publicized mass shootings.

Were you surprised by the results Scott Keeter reported in response to the interviewer's final question? Why or why not? Conduct some research online to discover what degree plans or work experience would help a student find a job in a polling organization.

TECHNOLOGY AND POLLING

The days of randomly walking neighborhoods and phone book cold-calling to interview random citizens are gone. Scientific polling has made interviewing more deliberate. Historically, many polls were conducted in person, yet this was expensive and yielded problematic results.

In some situations and countries, face-to-face interviewing still exists. Exit polls, focus groups, and some public opinion polls occur in which the interviewer and respondents communicate in person (Figure 6.9). Exit polls are conducted in person, with an interviewer standing near a polling location and requesting information as voters leave the polls. Focus groups often select random respondents from local shopping places or pre-select respondents from Internet or phone surveys. The respondents show up to observe or discuss topics and are then surveyed.

Figure 6.9   On November 6, 2012, the Connect2Mason.com team conducts exit surveys at the polls on the George Mason University campus. (credit: Mason Votes/Flickr).

When organizations like Gallup or Roper decide to conduct face-to-face public opinion polls, however, it is a time-consuming and expensive process. The organization must randomly select households or polling locations within neighborhoods, making sure there is a representative household or location in each neighborhood.[32] Then it must survey a representative number of neighborhoods from within a city. At a polling location, interviewers may have directions on how to randomly select voters of varied demographics. If the interviewer is looking to interview a person in a home, multiple attempts are made to reach a respondent if he or she does not answer. Gallup conducts face-to-face interviews in areas where less than 80 percent of the households in an area have phones, because it gives a more representative sample.[33] News networks use face-to-face techniques to conduct exit polls on Election Day.

Most polling now occurs over the phone or through the Internet. Some companies, like Harris Interactive, maintain directories that include registered voters, consumers, or previously interviewed respondents. If pollsters need to interview a particular population, such as political party members or retirees of a specific pension fund, the company may purchase or access a list of phone numbers for that group. Other organizations, like Gallup, use random-digit-dialing (RDD), in which a computer randomly generates phone numbers with desired area codes. Using RDD allows the pollsters to include respondents who may have unlisted and cellular numbers.[34] Questions about ZIP code or demographics may be asked early in the poll to allow the pollsters to determine which interviews to continue and which to end early.

The interviewing process is also partly computerized. Many polls are now administered through computer-assisted telephone interviewing (CATI) or through robo-polls. A CATI system calls random telephone numbers until it reaches a live person and then connects the potential respondent with a trained interviewer. As the respondent provides answers, the interviewer enters them directly into the computer program. These polls may have some errors if the interviewer enters an incorrect answer. The polls may also have reliability issues if the interviewer goes off the script or answers respondents' questions.

Robo-polls are entirely computerized. A computer dials random or pre-programmed numbers and a prerecorded electronic voice administers the survey. The respondent listens to the question and possible answers and then presses numbers on the phone to enter responses. Proponents argue that respondents are more honest without an interviewer. However, these polls can suffer from error if the respondent does not use the correct keypad number to answer a question or misunderstands the question. Robo-polls may also have lower response rates, because there is no live person to persuade the respondent to answer. There is also no way to prevent children from answering the survey. Lastly, the Telephone Consumer Protection Act (1991) made automated calls to cell phones illegal, which leaves a large population of potential respondents inaccessible to robo-polls.[35]

The latest challenges in telephone polling come from the shift in phone usage. A growing number of citizens, especially younger citizens, use only cell phones, and their phone numbers are no longer based on geographic areas. The Millennial generation (currently aged 21–37) is also more likely to text than to answer an unknown call, so it is harder to interview this demographic group. Polling companies now must reach out to potential respondents using email and social media to ensure they have a representative group of respondents.

Yet, the technology required to move to the Internet and handheld devices presents further problems. Web surveys must be designed to run on a varied number of browsers and handheld devices. Online polls cannot detect whether a person with multiple email accounts or social media profiles answers the same poll multiple times, nor can they tell when a respondent misrepresents demographics in the poll or on a social media profile used in a poll. These factors also make it more difficult to calculate response rates or achieve a representative sample. Yet, many companies are working with these difficulties, because it is necessary to reach younger demographics in order to provide accurate data.[36]

PROBLEMS IN POLLING

For a number of reasons, polls may not produce accurate results. Two important factors a polling company faces are timing and human nature. Unless you conduct an **exit poll** during an election and interviewers stand at the polling places on Election Day to ask voters how they voted, there is always the possibility the poll results will be wrong. The simplest reason is that if there is time between the poll and Election Day, a citizen might change his or her mind, lie, or choose not to vote at all. Timing is very important during elections, because surprise events can shift enough opinions to change an election result. Of course, there are many other reasons why polls, even those not time-bound by elections or events, may be inaccurate.

> ### Link to Learning
>
> Created in 2003 to survey the American public on all topics, Rasmussen Reports is a new entry (https://www.openstax.org/l/29rasmussenrep) in the polling business. Rasmussen also conducts exit polls for each national election.

Polls begin with a list of carefully written questions. The questions need to be free of framing, meaning they should not be worded to lead respondents to a particular answer. For example, take two questions about presidential approval. Question 1 might ask, "Given the high unemployment rate, do you approve of the job President Trump is doing?" Question 2 might ask, "Do you approve of the job President Trump is doing?" Both questions want to know how respondents perceive the president's success, but the first question sets up a frame for the respondent to believe the economy is doing poorly before answering. This is likely to make the respondent's answer more negative. Similarly, the way we refer to an issue or concept can affect the way listeners perceive it. The phrase "estate tax" did not rally voters to protest the inheritance tax, but the phrase "death tax" sparked debate about whether taxing estates imposed a double tax on income.[37]

Many polling companies try to avoid **leading questions**, which lead respondents to select a predetermined answer, because they want to know what people really think. Some polls, however, have a different goal. Their questions are written to guarantee a specific outcome, perhaps to help a candidate get press coverage or gain momentum. These are called push polls. In the 2016 presidential primary race, MoveOn tried to encourage Senator Elizabeth Warren (D-MA) to enter the race for the Democratic nomination (Figure 6.10). Its poll used leading questions for what it termed an "informed ballot," and, to show that Warren would do better than Hillary Clinton, it included ten positive statements about Warren before asking whether the respondent would vote for Clinton or Warren.[38] The poll results were blasted by some in the media for being fake.

(a)   (b)

Figure 6.10   Senator Elizabeth Warren (a) poses with Massachusetts representatives Joseph P. Kennedy III (left) and Barney Frank (right) at the 2012 Boston Pride Parade. Senator Hillary Clinton (b) during her 2008 presidential campaign in Concord, New Hampshire (credit a: modification of work by "ElizabethForMA"/Flickr; credit b: modification of work by Marc Nozell)

Sometimes lack of knowledge affects the results of a poll. Respondents may not know that much about the polling topic but are unwilling to say, "I don't know." For this reason, surveys may contain a quiz with questions that determine whether the respondent knows enough about the situation to answer survey questions accurately. A poll to discover whether citizens support changes to the Affordable Care Act or Medicaid might first ask who these programs serve and how they are funded. Polls about territory seizure by the Islamic State (or ISIS) or Russia's aid to rebels in Ukraine may include a set of questions to determine whether the respondent reads or hears any international news. Respondents who cannot answer correctly may be excluded from the poll, or their answers may be separated from the others.

People may also feel social pressure to answer questions in accordance with the norms of their area or peers.[39] If they are embarrassed to admit how they would vote, they may lie to the interviewer. In the 1982 governor's race in California, Tom Bradley was far ahead in the polls, yet on Election Day he lost. This result was nicknamed the **Bradley effect**, on the theory that voters who answered the poll were afraid to admit they would not vote for a black man because it would appear politically incorrect and racist. In the 2016 presidential election, the level of support for Republican nominee Donald Trump may have been artificially low in the polls due to the fact that some respondents did not want to admit they were voting for Trump.

In 2010, Proposition 19, which would have legalized and taxed marijuana in California, met with a new version of the Bradley effect. Nate Silver, a political blogger, noticed that polls on the marijuana proposition were inconsistent, sometimes showing the proposition would pass and other times showing it would fail. Silver compared the polls and the way they were administered, because some polling companies used an interviewer and some used robo-calling. He then proposed that voters speaking with a live interviewer gave the socially acceptable answer that they would vote against Proposition 19, while voters interviewed by a computer felt free to be honest (Figure 6.11).[40] While this theory has not been proven, it is consistent with other findings that interviewer demographics can affect respondents' answers. African Americans, for example, may give different responses to interviewers who are white than to interviewers who are black.[41]

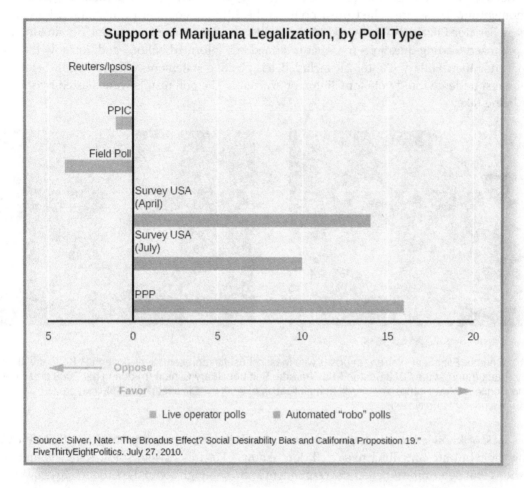

Source: Silver, Nate. "The Broadus Effect? Social Desirability Bias and California Proposition 19." FiveThirtyEightPolitics. July 27, 2010.

Figure 6.11 In 2010, polls about California's Proposition 19 were inconsistent, depending on how they were administered, with voters who spoke with a live interviewer declaring they would vote against Proposition 19 and voters who were interviewed via a computer declaring support for the legislation. The measure was defeated on Election Day.

PUSH POLLS

One of the newer byproducts of polling is the creation of **push polls**, which consist of political campaign information presented as polls. A respondent is called and asked a series of questions about his or her position or candidate selections. If the respondent's answers are for the wrong candidate, the next questions will give negative information about the candidate in an effort to change the voter's mind.

In 2014, a fracking ban was placed on the ballot in a town in Texas. Fracking, which includes injecting pressurized water into drilled wells, helps energy companies collect additional gas from the earth. It is controversial, with opponents arguing it causes water pollution, sound pollution, and earthquakes. During the campaign, a number of local voters received a call that polled them on how they planned to vote on the proposed fracking ban.[42] If the respondent was unsure about or planned to vote for the ban, the questions shifted to provide negative information about the organizations proposing the ban. One question asked, "If you knew the following, would it change your vote . . . two Texas railroad commissioners, the state agency that oversees oil and gas in Texas, have raised concerns about Russia's involvement in the anti-fracking efforts in the U.S.?" The question played upon voter fears about Russia and international instability in order to convince them to vote against the fracking ban.

These techniques are not limited to issue votes; candidates have used them to attack their opponents. The hope is that voters will think the poll is legitimate and believe the negative information provided by a "neutral" source.

6.3 What Does the Public Think?

Learning Objectives

By the end of this section, you will be able to:
- Explain why Americans hold a variety of views about politics, policy issues, and political institutions
- Identify factors that change public opinion
- Compare levels of public support for the branches of government

While attitudes and beliefs are slow to change, ideology can be influenced by events. A student might leave college with a liberal ideology but become more conservative as she ages. A first-year teacher may view unions with suspicion based on second-hand information but change his mind after reading newsletters and attending union meetings. These shifts may change the way citizens vote and the answers they give in polls. For this reason, political scientists often study when and why such changes in ideology happen, and how they influence our opinions about government and politicians.

EXPERIENCES THAT AFFECT PUBLIC OPINION

Ideological shifts are more likely to occur if a voter's ideology is only weakly supported by his or her beliefs. Citizens can also hold beliefs or opinions that are contrary or conflicting, especially if their knowledge of an issue or candidate is limited. And having limited information makes it easier for them to abandon an opinion. Finally, citizens' opinions will change as they grow older and separate from family.[43]

Citizens use two methods to form an opinion about an issue or candidate. The first is to rely on **heuristics**, shortcuts or rules of thumb (cues) for decision making. Political party membership is one of the most common heuristics in voting. Many voters join a political party whose platform aligns most closely with their political beliefs, and voting for a candidate from that party simply makes sense. A Republican candidate will likely espouse conservative beliefs, such as smaller government and lower taxes, that are often more appealing to a Republican voter. Studies have shown that up to half of voters make decisions using their political party identification, or party ID, especially in races where information about candidates is scarce.[44]

In non-partisan and some local elections, where candidates are not permitted to list their party identifications, voters may have to rely on a candidate's background or job description to form a quick opinion of a candidate's suitability. A candidate for judge may list "criminal prosecutor" as current employment, leaving the voter to determine whether a prosecutor would make a good judge.

The second method is to do research, learning background information before making a decision. Candidates, parties, and campaigns put out a large array of information to sway potential voters, and the media provide wide coverage, all of which is readily available online and elsewhere. But many voters are unwilling to spend the necessary time to research and instead vote with incomplete information.[45]

Gender, race, socio-economic status, and interest-group affiliation also serve as heuristics for decision making. Voters may assume female candidates have a stronger understanding about social issues relevant to women. Business owners may prefer to vote for a candidate with a college degree who has worked in business rather than a career politician. Other voters may look to see which candidate is endorsed by the National Organization of Women (NOW), because NOW's endorsement will ensure the candidate supports abortion rights.

Opinions based on heuristics rather than research are more likely to change when the cue changes. If a voter begins listening to a new source of information or moves to a new town, the influences and cues he or she meets will change. Even if the voter is diligently looking for information to make an informed decision, demographic cues matter. Age, gender, race, and socio-economic status will shape our opinions because they are a part of our everyday reality, and they become part of our barometer on whether a leader or government is performing well.

A look at the 2012 presidential election shows how the opinions of different demographic groups vary (**Figure 6.12**). For instance, 55 percent of women voted for Barack Obama and 52 percent of men voted for Mitt Romney. Age mattered as well—60 percent of voters under thirty voted for Obama, whereas 56 percent of those over sixty-five voted for Romney. Racial groups also varied in their support of the candidates. Ninety-three percent of African Americans and 71 percent of Hispanics voted for Obama instead of Romney.[46] These demographic effects are likely to be strong because of shared experiences, concerns, and ideas. Citizens who are comfortable with one another will talk more and share opinions, leading to more opportunities to influence or reinforce one another.

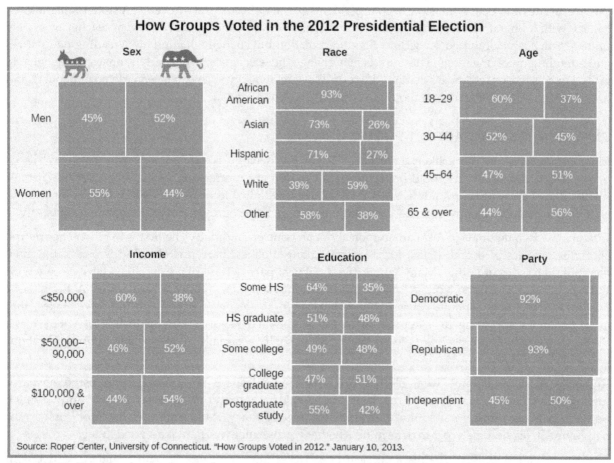

Figure 6.12 Breaking down voters by demographic groups may reveal very different levels of support for particular candidates or policies among the groups.

Similar demographic effects were seen in the 2016 presidential election. For instance, 54 percent of women voted for the Democratic candidate, Hillary Clinton, and 52 percent of men voted for the Republican candidate, Donald Trump. If considering age and race, Trump garnered percentages similar to Mitt

Romney in these categories as well. And, as in 2012, households with incomes below $50,000 heavily favored the Democratic candidate, while those households in the $50,000–90,000 bracket slightly favored the Republican.[47]

The political culture of a state can also have an effect on ideology and opinion. In the 1960s, Daniel Elazar researched interviews, voting data, newspapers, and politicians' speeches. He determined that states had unique cultures and that different state governments instilled different attitudes and beliefs in their citizens, creating **political cultures**. Some states value tradition, and their laws try to maintain longstanding beliefs. Other states believe government should help people and therefore create large bureaucracies that provide benefits to assist citizens. Some political cultures stress citizen involvement whereas others try to exclude participation by the masses.

State political cultures can affect the ideology and opinions of those who live in or move to them. For example, opinions about gun ownership and rights vary from state to state. Polls show that 61 percent of all Californians, regardless of ideology or political party, stated there should be more controls on who owns guns.[48] In contrast, in Texas, support for the right to carry a weapon is high. Fifty percent of self-identified Democrats—who typically prefer more controls on guns rather than fewer—said Texans should be allowed to carry a concealed weapon if they have a permit.[49] In this case, state culture may have affected citizens' feelings about the Second Amendment and moved them away from the expected ideological beliefs.

The workplace can directly or indirectly affect opinions about policies, social issues, and political leaders by socializing employees through shared experiences. People who work in education, for example, are often surrounded by others with high levels of education. Their concerns will be specific to the education sector and different from those in other workplaces. Frequent association with colleagues can align a person's thinking with theirs.

Workplace groups such as professional organizations or unions can also influence opinions. These organizations provide members with specific information about issues important to them and lobby on their behalf in an effort to better work environments, increase pay, or enhance shared governance. They may also pressure members to vote for particular candidates or initiatives they believe will help promote the organization's goals. For example, teachers' unions often support the Democratic Party because it has historically supported increased funding to public schools and universities.

Important political opinion leaders, or **political elites**, also shape public opinion, usually by serving as short-term cues that help voters pay closer attention to a political debate and make decisions about it. Through a talk program or opinion column, the elite commentator tells people when and how to react to a current problem or issue. Millennials and members of Generation X (currently ages 38–53) long used Jon Stewart of *The Daily Show* and later Stephen Colbert of *The Colbert Report* as shortcuts to becoming informed about current events. In the same way, older generations trusted Tom Brokaw and *60 Minutes*.

Because an elite source can pick and choose the information and advice to provide, the door is open to covert influence if this source is not credible or honest. Voters must be able to trust the quality of the information. When elites lose credibility, they lose their audience. News agencies are aware of the relationship between citizens and elites, which is why news anchors for major networks are carefully chosen. When Brian Williams of NBC was accused of lying about his experiences in Iraq and New Orleans, he was suspended pending an investigation. Williams later admitted to several misstatements and apologized to the public, and he was removed from *The Nightly News*.[50]

OPINIONS ABOUT POLITICS AND POLICIES

What *do* Americans think about their political system, policies, and institutions? Public opinion has not been consistent over the years. It fluctuates based on the times and events, and on the people holding major office (Figure 6.13). Sometimes a majority of the public express similar ideas, but many times not. Where, then, does the public agree and disagree? Let's look at the two-party system, and then at opinions about public policy, economic policy, and social policy.

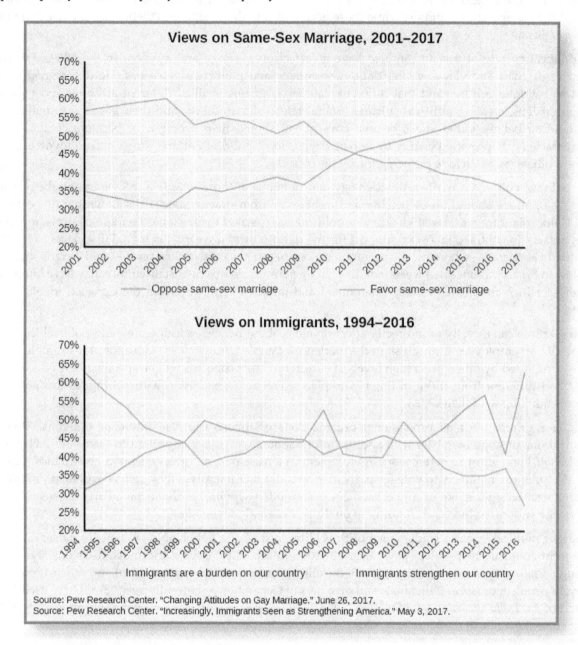

Figure 6.13 Public opinion may change significantly over time. Two issues that have undergone dramatic shifts in public opinion during the last twenty years are same-sex marriage and immigration.

The United States is traditionally a two-party system. Only Democrats and Republicans regularly win the presidency and, with few exceptions, seats in Congress. The majority of voters cast ballots only for Republicans and Democrats, even when third parties are represented on the ballot. Yet, citizens say they are frustrated with the current party system. Only 32 percent identify themselves as Democrats and only 23 percent as Republicans. Democratic membership has stayed relatively the same, but the Republican Party has lost about 6 percent of its membership over the last ten years, whereas the number of self-identified independents has grown from 30 percent in 2004 to 39 percent in 2014.[51] Given these numbers, it is not surprising that 58 percent of Americans say a third party is needed in U.S. politics today.[52]

Some of these changes in party allegiance may be due to generational and cultural shifts. Millennials and Generation Xers are more likely to support the Democratic Party than the Republican Party. In recent polling, 51 percent of Millennials and 49 percent of Generation Xers stated they did, whereas only 35 percent and 38 percent, respectively, supported the Republican Party. Baby Boomers (currently aged 54–72) are slightly less likely than the other groups to support the Democratic Party; only 47 percent reported doing so. The Silent Generation (born in the 1920s to early 1940s) is the only cohort whose members state they support the Republican Party as a majority.[53]

Another shift in politics may be coming from the increasing number of multiracial citizens with strong cultural roots. Almost 7 percent of the population now identifies as biracial or multiracial, and that percentage is likely to grow. The number of citizens identifying as both African American and white doubled between 2000 and 2010, whereas the number of citizens identifying as both Asian American and white grew by 87 percent. The Pew study found that only 37 percent of multiracial adults favored the Republican Party, while 57 percent favored the Democratic Party.[54] As the demographic composition of the United States changes and new generations become part of the voting population, public concerns and expectations will change as well.

At its heart, politics is about dividing scarce resources fairly and balancing liberties and rights. Public policy often becomes messy as politicians struggle to fix problems with the nation's limited budget while catering to numerous opinions about how best to do so. While the public often remains quiet, simply answering public opinion polls or dutifully casting their votes on Election Day, occasionally citizens weigh in more audibly by protesting or lobbying.

Some policy decisions are made without public input if they preserve the way money is allocated or defer to policies already in place. But policies that directly affect personal economics, such as tax policy, may cause a public backlash, and those that affect civil liberties or closely held beliefs may cause even more public upheaval. Policies that break new ground similarly stir public opinion and introduce change that some find difficult. The acceptance of same-sex marriage, for example, pitted those who sought to preserve their religious beliefs against those who sought to be treated equally under the law.

Where does the public stand on economic policy? Only 26 percent of citizens surveyed in 2015 thought the U.S. economy was in excellent or good condition,[55] yet 42 percent believed their personal financial situation was excellent to good.[56] While this seems inconsistent, it reflects the fact that we notice what is happening outside our own home. Even if a family's personal finances are stable, members will be aware of friends and relatives who are suffering job losses or foreclosures. This information will give them a broader, more negative view of the economy beyond their own pocketbook.

When asked about government spending, the public was more united in wanting policy to be fiscally responsible without raising taxes. In 2011, nearly 73 percent of interviewed citizens believed the government was creating a deficit by spending too much money on social programs like welfare and food stamps, and only 22 percent wanted to raise taxes to pay for them.[57] When polled on which programs to cut in order to balance the nation's budget, however, respondents were less united (Figure 6.14). Nearly 21 percent said to cut education spending, whereas 22 percent wanted to cut spending on health care. Only 12 percent said to cut spending on Social Security. All these programs are used by nearly everyone at some time, which makes them less controversial and less likely to actually be cut.

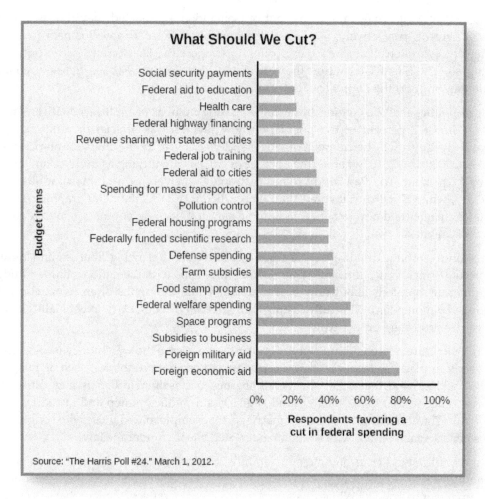

Figure 6.14 When asked about budget cuts, poll respondents seldom favor cutting programs that directly affect them, such as Social Security or health care.

In general, programs that benefit only some Americans or have unclear benefits cause more controversy and discussion when the economy slows. Few citizens directly benefit from welfare and business subsidies, so it is not surprising that 52 percent of respondents wanted to cut back on welfare and 57 percent wanted to cut back business subsidies. While some farm subsidies decrease the price of food items, like milk and corn, citizens may not be aware of how these subsidies affect the price of goods at the grocery store, perhaps explaining why 44 percent of respondents stated they would prefer to cut back on agricultural subsidies.[58]

Social policy consists of government's attempts to regulate public behavior in the service of a better society. To accomplish this, government must achieve the difficult task of balancing the rights and liberties of citizens. A person's right to privacy, for example, might need to be limited if another person is in danger. But to what extent should the government intrude in the private lives of its citizens? In a recent survey, 54 percent of respondents believed the U.S. government was too involved in trying to deal with issues of morality.[59]

Abortion is a social policy issue that has caused controversy for nearly a century. One segment of the population wants to protect the rights of the unborn child. Another wants to protect the bodily autonomy of women and the right to privacy between a patient and her doctor. The divide is visible in public opinion polls, where 51 percent of respondents said abortion should be legal in most cases and 43 percent said it should be illegal in most cases. The Affordable Care Act, which increased government involvement in health care, has drawn similar controversy. In a 2015 poll, 53 percent of respondents disapproved of the act, a 9-percent increase from five years before. Much of the public's frustration comes from the act's mandate that individuals purchase health insurance or pay a fine (in order to create a large enough pool of insured people to reduce the overall cost of coverage), which some see as an intrusion into individual decision making.[60]

Laws allowing same-sex marriage raise the question whether the government should be defining marriage and regulating private relationships in defense of personal and spousal rights. Public opinion has shifted dramatically over the last twenty years. In 1996, only 27 percent of Americans felt same-sex marriage should be legal, but recent polls show support has increased to 54 percent.[61] Despite this sharp increase, a number of states had banned same-sex marriage until the Supreme Court decided, in *Obergefell v. Hodges* (2015), that states were obliged to give marriage licenses to couples of the same sex and to recognize out-of-state, same-sex marriages.[62] Some churches and businesses continue to argue that no one should be compelled by the government to recognize or support a marriage between members of the same sex if it conflicts with their religious beliefs.[63] Undoubtedly, the issue will continue to cause a divide in public opinion.

Another area where social policy must balance rights and liberties is public safety. Regulation of gun ownership incites strong emotions, because it invokes the Second Amendment and state culture. Of those polled nationwide, 52 percent believed government should protect the right of citizens to own guns, while 46 percent felt there should be stronger controls over gun ownership.[64] These numbers change from state to state, however, because of political culture. Immigration similarly causes strife, with citizens fearing increases in crime and social spending due to large numbers of people entering the United States illegally. Yet, 72 percent of respondents did believe there should be a path to citizenship for non-documented aliens already in the country. And while the national government's drug policy still lists marijuana as an illegal substance, 45 percent of respondents stated they would agree if the government legalized marijuana.[65]

PUBLIC OPINION AND POLITICAL INSTITUTIONS

Public opinion about American institutions is measured in public approval ratings rather than in questions of choice between positions or candidates. The congressional and executive branches of government are the subject of much scrutiny and discussed daily in the media. Polling companies take daily approval polls of these two branches. The Supreme Court makes the news less frequently, and approval polls are more likely after the court has released major opinions. All three branches, however, are susceptible to swings in public approval in response to their actions and to national events. Approval ratings are generally not stable for any of the three. We next look at each in turn.

The president is the most visible member of the U.S. government and a lightning rod for disagreement. Presidents are often blamed for the decisions of their administrations and political parties, and are held accountable for economic and foreign policy downturns. For these reasons, they can expect their approval ratings to slowly decline over time, increasing or decreasing slightly with specific events. On average, presidents enjoy a 66 percent approval rating when starting office, but it drops to 53 percent by the end of the first term. Presidents serving a second term average a beginning approval rating of 55.5 percent, which falls to 47 percent by the end of office. For most of his term, President Obama's presidency followed the same trend. He entered office with a public approval rating of 67 percent, which fell to 54 percent by the third quarter, dropped to 52 percent after his reelection, and, as of October 2015, was at 46 percent. However, after January 2016, his approval rating began to climb, and he left office with an approval rating of 59 percent (Figure 6.15). President Trump has experienced significantly lower approval ratings than average, taking the oath of office with an approval rating of 45 percent, which declined to a low of 35 percent after a year in office, and stood at 40 percent in January 2019.[66]

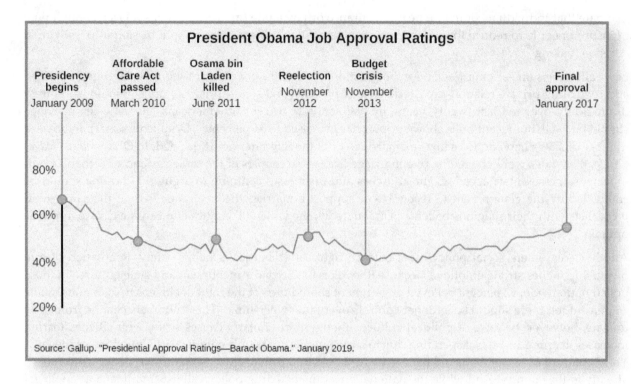

Figure 6.15 As President Obama's ratings demonstrate, presidential approval ratings generally decline over time but may fluctuate based on specific events or policies.

Events during a president's term may spike his or her public approval ratings. George W. Bush's public approval rating jumped from 51 percent on September 10, 2001, to 86 percent by September 15 following the 9/11 attacks. His father, George H. W. Bush, had received a similar spike in approval ratings (from 58 to 89 percent) following the end of the first Persian Gulf War in 1991.[67] These spikes rarely last more than a few weeks, so presidents try to quickly use the political capital they bring. For example, the 9/11 rally effect helped speed a congressional joint resolution authorizing the president to use troops, and the "global war on terror" became a reality.[68] The rally was short-lived, and support for the wars in Iraq and Afghanistan quickly deteriorated post-2003.[69]

Some presidents have had higher or lower public approval than others, though ratings are difficult to compare, because national and world events that affect presidential ratings are outside a president's control. Several chief executives presided over failing economies or wars, whereas others had the benefit of strong economies and peace. Gallup, however, gives an average approval rating for each president across the entire period served in office. George W. Bush's average approval rating from 2001 to 2008 was 49.4 percent. Ronald Reagan's from 1981 to 1988 was 52.8 percent, despite his winning all but thirteen electoral votes in his reelection bid. Bill Clinton's average approval from 1993 to 2000 was 55.1 percent, including the months surrounding the Monica Lewinsky scandal and his subsequent impeachment. To compare other notable presidents, John F. Kennedy averaged 70.1 percent and Richard Nixon 49 percent.[70] Kennedy's average was unusually high because his time in office was short; he was assassinated before he could run for reelection, leaving less time for his ratings to decline. Nixon's unusually low approval ratings reflect several months of media and congressional investigations into his involvement in the Watergate affair, as well as his resignation in the face of likely impeachment.

Link to Learning

Gallup polling has tracked approval ratings for all presidents since Harry Truman. The Presidential Job Approval Center (https://www.openstax.org/l/29presapproval) allows you to compare weekly approval ratings for all tracked presidents, as well as their average approval ratings.

Milestone

Public Mood and Watershed Moments

Polling is one area of U.S. politics in which political practitioners and political science scholars interact. Each election cycle, political scientists help media outlets interpret polling, statistical data, and election forecasts. One particular watershed moment in this regard occurred when Professor James Stimson, of the University of North Carolina at Chapel Hill, developed his aggregated measure of public mood. This measure takes a variety of issue positions and combines them to form a general ideology about the government. According to Professor Stimson, the American electorate became more conservative in the 1970s and again in the 1990s, as demonstrated by Republican gains in Congress. With this public mood measure in mind, political scientists can explain why and when Americans allowed major policy shifts. For example, the Great Society's expansion of welfare and social benefits occurred during the height of liberalism in the mid-1960s, while the welfare cuts and reforms of the 1990s occurred during the nation's move toward conservatism. Tracking conservative and liberal shifts in the public's ideology allows policy analysts to predict whether voters are likely to accept or reject major policies.

What other means of measuring the public mood do you think might be effective and reliable? How would you implement them? Do you agree that watershed moments in history signal public mood changes? If so, give some examples. If not, why not?

Congress as an institution has historically received lower approval ratings than presidents, a striking result because individual senators and representatives are generally viewed favorably by their constituents. While congressional representatives almost always win reelection and are liked by their constituents back home, the institution itself is often vilified as representing everything that is wrong with politics and partisanship.

As of August 2015, public approval of Congress sat at around 20 percent.[71] For most of the last forty years, congressional approval levels have bounced between 20 percent and 60 percent, but in the last fifteen years they have regularly fallen below 40 percent. Like President George W. Bush, Congress experienced a short-term jump in approval ratings immediately following 9/11, likely because of the rallying effect of the terrorist attacks. Congressional approval had dropped back below 50 percent by early 2003 (Figure 6.16).

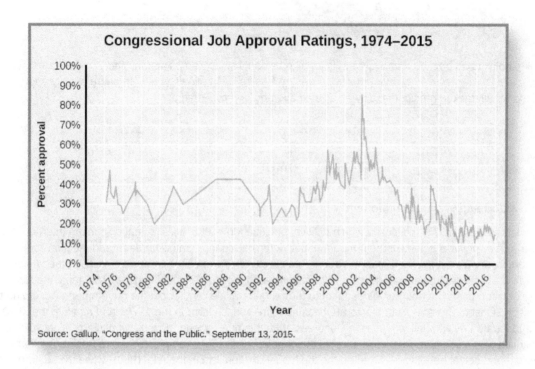

Figure 6.16 Congressional approval ratings over the past forty years have generally fallen between 20 and 50 percent; however, these ratings spiked to over 80 percent in the wake of the terrorist attacks on September 11, 2001.

While presidents are affected by foreign and domestic events, congressional approval is mainly affected by domestic events. When the economy rebounds or gas prices drop, public approval of Congress tends to go up. But when party politics within Congress becomes a domestic event, public approval falls. The passage of revenue bills has become an example of such an event, because deficits require Congress to make policy decisions before changing the budget. Deficit and debt are not new to the United States. Congress and presidents have attempted various methods of controlling debt, sometimes successfully and sometimes not. In the past three decades alone, however, several prominent examples have shown how party politics make it difficult for Congress to agree on a budget without a fight, and how these fights affect public approval.

In 1995, Democratic president Bill Clinton and the Republican Congress hit a notable stalemate on the national budget. In this case, the Republicans had recently gained control of the House of Representatives and disagreed with Democrats and the president on how to cut spending and reduce the deficit. The government shut down twice, sending non-essential employees home for a few days in November, and then again in December and January.[72] Congressional approval fell during the event, from 35 to 30 percent.[73]

Divisions between the political parties, inside the Republican Party, and between Congress and the president became more pronounced over the next fifteen years, with the media closely covering the political strife.[74] In 2011, the United States reached its debt ceiling, or maximum allowed debt amount. After much debate, the Budget Control Act was passed by Congress and signed by President Obama. The act increased the debt ceiling, but it also reduced spending and created automatic cuts, called sequestrations, if further legislation did not deal with the debt by 2013. When the country reached its new debt ceiling of $16.4 trillion in 2013, short-term solutions led to Congress negotiating both the debt ceiling and the national budget at the same time. The timing raised the stakes of the budget, and Democrats and Republicans fought bitterly over the debt ceiling, budget cuts, and taxes. Inaction triggered the automatic cuts to the budget in areas like defense, the courts, and public aid. By October, approximately 800,000 federal employees had been sent home, and the government went into partial shut-down for sixteen days before Congress passed a bill to raise the debt ceiling.[75] The handling of these events angered Americans, who felt the political parties needed to work together to solve problems rather than play political games. During the 2011 ceiling debate, congressional approval fell from 18 to 13 percent, while in 2013, congressional approval fell to a new low of 9 percent in November.[76]

The Supreme Court generally enjoys less visibility than the other two branches of government, which leads to more stable but also less frequent polling results. Indeed, 22 percent of citizens surveyed in 2014 had never heard of Chief Justice John Roberts, the head of the Supreme Court.[77] The court is protected by the justices' non-elected, non-political positions, which gives them the appearance of integrity and helps the Supreme Court earn higher public approval ratings than presidents and Congress. To compare, between 2000 and 2010, the court's approval rating bounced between 50 and 60 percent. During this same period, Congress had a 20 to 40 percent approval rating.

The Supreme Court's approval rating is also less susceptible to the influence of events. Support of and opinions about the court are affected when the justices rule on highly visible cases that are of public interest or other events occur that cause citizens to become aware of the court.[78] For example, following the *Bush v. Gore* case (2000), in which the court instructed Florida to stop recounting ballots and George W. Bush won the Electoral College, 80 percent of Republicans approved of the court, versus only 42 percent of Democrats.[79] Twelve years later, when the Supreme Court's ruling in *National Federation of Independent Business v. Sebelius* (2012) let stand the Affordable Care Act's requirement of individual coverage, approval by Democrats increased to 68 percent, while Republican support dropped to 29 percent.[80] Currently, following the handing down of decisions in *King v. Burwell* (2015) and *Obergefell v. Hodges* (2015), which allowed the Affordable Care Act's subsidies and prohibited states from denying same-sex marriage, respectively, 45 percent of people said they approved of the way the Supreme Court handled its job, down 4 percent from before the decisions.[81]

6.4 The Effects of Public Opinion

Learning Objectives

By the end of this section, you will be able to:
- Explain the circumstances that lead to public opinion affecting policy
- Compare the effects of public opinion on government branches and figures
- Identify situations that cause conflicts in public opinion

Public opinion polling is prevalent even outside election season. Are politicians and leaders listening to these polls, or is there some other reason for them? Some believe the increased collection of public opinion is due to growing support of delegate representation. The **theory of delegate representation** assumes the politician is in office to be the voice of the people.[82] If voters want the legislator to vote for legalizing marijuana, for example, the legislator should vote to legalize marijuana. Legislators or candidates who believe in delegate representation may poll the public before an important vote comes up for debate in order to learn what the public desires them to do.

Others believe polling has increased because politicians, like the president, operate in permanent campaign mode. To continue contributing money, supporters must remain happy and convinced the politician is listening to them. Even if the elected official does not act in a manner consistent with the polls, he or she can mollify everyone by explaining the reasons behind the vote.[83]

Regardless of why the polls are taken, studies have not clearly shown whether the branches of government consistently act on them. Some branches appear to pay closer attention to public opinion than other branches, but events, time periods, and politics may change the way an individual or a branch of government ultimately reacts.

PUBLIC OPINION AND ELECTIONS

Elections are the events on which opinion polls have the greatest measured effect. Public opinion polls do more than show how we feel on issues or project who might win an election. The media use public opinion polls to decide which candidates are ahead of the others and therefore of interest to voters and worthy of interview. From the moment President Obama was inaugurated for his second term, speculation began about who would run in the 2016 presidential election. Within a year, potential candidates were being ranked and compared by a number of newspapers.[84] The speculation included **favorability polls** on Hillary Clinton, which measured how positively voters felt about her as a candidate. The media deemed these polls important because they showed Clinton as the frontrunner for the Democrats in the next election.[85]

During presidential primary season, we see examples of the **bandwagon effect**, in which the media pays more attention to candidates who poll well during the fall and the first few primaries. Bill Clinton was nicknamed the "Comeback Kid" in 1992, after he placed second in the New Hampshire primary despite accusations of adultery with Gennifer Flowers. The media's attention on Clinton gave him the momentum to make it through the rest of the primary season, ultimately winning the Democratic nomination and the presidency.

Link to Learning

Wondering how your favorite candidate is doing in the polls? The site RealClearPolitics (https://www.openstax.org/l/29realclearpol) tracks a number of major polling sources on the major elections, including the presidential and Senate elections.

Polling is also at the heart of **horserace coverage**, in which, just like an announcer at the racetrack, the media calls out every candidate's move throughout the presidential campaign. Horserace coverage can be neutral, positive, or negative, depending upon what polls or facts are covered (Figure 6.17). During the 2012 presidential election, the Pew Research Center found that both Mitt Romney and President Obama received more negative than positive horserace coverage, with Romney's growing more negative as he fell in the polls.[86] Horserace coverage is often criticized for its lack of depth; the stories skip over the candidates' issue positions, voting histories, and other facts that would help voters make an informed decision. Yet, horserace coverage is popular because the public is always interested in who will win, and it often makes up a third or more of news stories about the election.[87] Exit polls, taken the day of the election, are the last election polls conducted by the media. Announced results of these surveys can deter voters from going to the polls if they believe the election has already been decided.

Figure 6.17 In 2016, Republican presidential candidate Donald Trump became the center of the media's horserace coverage. As the field winnowed from over twenty candidates down to three, the media incessantly compared everyone else in the field to Trump. (credit: Max Goldberg)

Finding a Middle Ground

Should Exit Polls Be Banned?

Exit polling seems simple. An interviewer stands at a polling place on Election Day and asks people how they voted. But the reality is different. Pollsters must select sites and voters carefully to ensure a representative and random poll. Some people refuse to talk and others may lie. The demographics of the polled population may lean more towards one party than another. Absentee and early voters cannot be polled. Despite these setbacks, exit polls are extremely interesting and controversial, because they provide early information about which candidate is ahead.

In 1985, a so-called gentleman's agreement between the major networks and Congress kept exit poll results from being announced before a state's polls closed.[88] This tradition has largely been upheld, with most media outlets waiting until 7 p.m. or later to disclose a state's returns. Internet and cable media, however, have not always kept to the agreement. Sources like Matt Drudge have been accused of reporting early, and sometimes incorrect, exit poll results.

On one hand, delaying results may be the right decision. Studies suggest that exit polls *can* affect voter turnout. Reports of close races may bring additional voters to the polls, whereas apparent landslides may prompt people to stay home. Other studies note that almost anything, including bad weather and lines at polling places, dissuades voters. Ultimately, it appears exit poll reporting affects turnout by up to 5 percent.[89]

On the other hand, limiting exit poll results means major media outlets lose out on the chance to share their carefully collected data, leaving small media outlets able to provide less accurate, more impressionistic results. And few states are affected anyway, since the media invest only in those where the election is close. Finally, an increasing number of voters are now voting up to two weeks early, and these numbers are updated daily without controversy.

What do you think? Should exit polls be banned? Why or why not?

Public opinion polls also affect how much money candidates receive in campaign donations. Donors assume public opinion polls are accurate enough to determine who the top two to three primary candidates will be, and they give money to those who do well. Candidates who poll at the bottom will have a hard time collecting donations, increasing the odds that they will continue to do poorly. This was apparent in the run-up to the 2016 presidential election. Bernie Sanders, Hillary Clinton, and Martin O'Malley each campaigned in the hope of becoming the Democratic presidential nominee. In June 2015, 75 percent of Democrats likely to vote in their state primaries said they would vote for Clinton, while 15 percent of those polled said they would vote for Sanders. Only 2 percent said they would vote for O'Malley.[90] During this same period, Clinton raised $47 million in campaign donations, Sanders raised $15 million, and O'Malley raised $2 million.[91] By September 2015, 23 percent of likely Democratic voters said they would vote for Sanders,[92] and his summer fundraising total increased accordingly.[93]

Presidents running for reelection also must perform well in public opinion polls, and being in office may not provide an automatic advantage. Americans often think about both the future and the past when they decide which candidate to support.[94] They have three years of past information about the sitting president, so they can better predict what will happen if the incumbent is reelected. That makes it difficult for the president to mislead the electorate. Voters also want a future that is prosperous. Not only should the economy look good, but citizens want to know they will do well in that economy.[95] For this reason, daily public approval polls sometimes act as both a referendum of the president and a predictor of success.

PUBLIC OPINION AND GOVERNMENT

The relationship between public opinion polls and government action is murkier than that between polls and elections. Like the news media and campaign staffers, members of the three branches of government are aware of public opinion. But do politicians use public opinion polls to guide their decisions and actions?

The short answer is "sometimes." The public is not perfectly informed about politics, so politicians realize public opinion may not always be the right choice. Yet many political studies, from the *American Voter* in the 1920s to the *American Voter Revisited* in the 2000s, have found that voters behave rationally despite having limited information. Individual citizens do not take the time to become fully informed about all aspects of politics, yet their collective behavior and the opinions they hold as a group make sense. They appear to be informed just enough, using preferences like their political ideology and party membership, to make decisions and hold politicians accountable during an election year.

Overall, the collective public opinion of a country changes over time, even if party membership or ideology does not change dramatically. As James Stimson's prominent study found, the public's mood, or collective opinion, can become more or less liberal from decade to decade. While the initial study on public mood revealed that the economy has a profound effect on American opinion,[96] further studies have gone beyond to determine whether public opinion, and its relative liberalness, in turn affect politicians and institutions. This idea does not argue that opinion never affects policy directly, rather that collective opinion also affects the politician's decisions on policy.[97]

Individually, of course, politicians cannot predict what will happen in the future or who will oppose them in the next few elections. They can look to see where the public is in agreement as a body. If public mood changes, the politicians may change positions to match the public mood. The more savvy politicians look carefully to recognize when shifts occur. When the public is more or less liberal, the politicians may make slight adjustments to their behavior to match. Politicians who frequently seek to win office, like House members, will pay attention to the long- and short-term changes in opinion. By doing this, they will be less likely to lose on Election Day.[98] Presidents and justices, on the other hand, present a more complex picture.

Public opinion of the president is different from public opinion of Congress. Congress is an institution of 535 members, and opinion polls look at both the institution and its individual members. The president is both a person and the head of an institution. The media pays close attention to any president's actions, and the public is generally well informed and aware of the office and its current occupant. Perhaps this is why public opinion has an inconsistent effect on presidents' decisions. As early as Franklin D. Roosevelt's administration in the 1930s, presidents have regularly polled the public, and since Richard Nixon's term

(1969–1974), they have admitted to using polling as part of the decision-making process.

Presidential responsiveness to public opinion has been measured in a number of ways, each of which tells us something about the effect of opinion. One study examined whether presidents responded to public opinion by determining how often they wrote amicus briefs and asked the court to affirm or reverse cases. It found that the public's liberal (or non-liberal) mood had an effect, causing presidents to pursue and file briefs in different cases.[99] But another author found that the public's level of liberalness is ignored when conservative presidents, such as Ronald Reagan or George W. Bush, are elected and try to lead. In one example, our five most recent presidents' moods varied from liberal to non-liberal, while public sentiment stayed consistently liberal.[100] While the public supported liberal approaches to policy, presidential action varied from liberal to non-liberal.

Overall, it appears that presidents try to move public opinion towards personal positions rather than moving themselves towards the public's opinion.[101] If presidents have enough public support, they use their level of public approval indirectly as a way to get their agenda passed. Immediately following Inauguration Day, for example, the president enjoys the highest level of public support for implementing campaign promises. This is especially true if the president has a *mandate*, which is more than half the popular vote. Barack Obama's recent 2008 victory was a mandate with 52.9 percent of the popular vote and 67.8 percent of the Electoral College vote.[102] In contrast, President Donald Trump's victory over Democratic nominee Hillary Clinton was a closer contest. While Clinton outdistanced him by 2.9 million votes nationally, after narrowly winning several states, Trump won a comfortable majority in the Electoral College.

When presidents have high levels of public approval, they are likely to act quickly and try to accomplish personal policy goals. They can use their position and power to focus media attention on an issue. This is sometimes referred to as the bully pulpit approach. The term "bully pulpit" was coined by President Theodore Roosevelt, who believed the presidency commanded the attention of the media and could be used to appeal directly to the people. Roosevelt used his position to convince voters to pressure Congress to pass laws.

Increasing partisanship has made it more difficult for presidents to use their power to get their own preferred issues through Congress, however, especially when the president's party is in the minority in Congress.[103] For this reason, modern presidents may find more success in using their popularity to increase media and social media attention on an issue. Even if the president is not the reason for congressional action, he or she can cause the attention that leads to change.[104]

Presidents may also use their popularity to ask the people to act. In October 2015, following a shooting at Umpqua Community College in Oregon, President Obama gave a short speech from the West Wing of the White House (Figure 6.18). After offering his condolences and prayers to the community, he remarked that prayers and condolences were no longer enough, and he called on citizens to push Congress for a change in gun control laws. President Obama had proposed gun control reform following the 2012 shooting at Sandy Hook Elementary in Connecticut, but it did not pass Congress. This time, the president asked citizens to use gun control as a voting issue and push for reform via the ballot box.

Figure 6.18 In the wake of a shooting at Umpqua Community College in Oregon in October 2015, President Obama called for a change in gun control laws (credit: The White House).

In some instances, presidents may appear to directly consider public opinion before acting or making decisions. In 2013, President Obama announced that he was considering a military strike on Syria in reaction to the Syrian government's illegal use of sarin gas on its own citizens. Despite agreeing that this chemical attack on the Damascan suburbs was a war crime, the public was against U.S. involvement. Forty-eight percent of respondents said they opposed airstrikes, and only 29 percent were in favor. Democrats were especially opposed to military intervention.[105] President Obama changed his mind and ultimately allowed Russian president Vladimir Putin to negotiate Syria's surrender of its chemical weapons.

However, further examples show that presidents do not consistently listen to public opinion. After taking office in 2009, President Obama did not order the closing of Guantanamo Bay prison, even though his proposal to do so had garnered support during the 2008 election. President Bush, despite growing public disapproval for the war in Iraq, did not end military support in Iraq after 2006. And President Bill Clinton, whose White House pollsters were infamous for polling on everything, sometimes ignored the public if circumstances warranted.[106] In 1995, despite public opposition, Clinton guaranteed loans for the Mexican government to help the country out of financial insolvency. He followed this decision with many speeches to help the American public understand the importance of stabilizing Mexico's economy. Individual examples like these make it difficult to persuasively identify the direct effects of public opinion on the presidency.

While presidents have at most only two terms to serve and work, members of Congress can serve as long as the public returns them to office. We might think that for this reason public opinion is important to representatives and senators, and that their behavior, such as their votes on domestic programs or funding, will change to match the expectation of the public. In a more liberal time, the public may expect to see more social programs. In a non-liberal time, the public mood may favor austerity, or decreased government spending on programs. Failure to recognize shifts in public opinion may lead to a politician's losing the next election.[107]

House of Representatives members, with a two-year term, have a more difficult time recovering from decisions that anger local voters. And because most representatives continually fundraise, unpopular decisions can hurt their campaign donations. For these reasons, it seems representatives should be susceptible to polling pressure. Yet one study, by James Stimson, found that the public mood does not directly affect elections, and shifts in public opinion do not predict whether a House member will win or lose. These elections are affected by the president on the ticket, presidential popularity (or lack thereof) during a midterm election, and the perks of incumbency, such as name recognition and media coverage. In fact, a later study confirmed that the incumbency effect is highly predictive of a win, and public opinion is not.[108] In spite of this, we still see policy shifts in Congress, often matching the policy preferences of the public. When the shifts happen within the House, they are measured by the way members vote. The study's authors hypothesize that House members alter their votes to match the public mood, perhaps in an effort to strengthen their electoral chances.[109]

The Senate is quite different from the House. Senators do not enjoy the same benefits of incumbency, and they win reelection at lower rates than House members. Yet, they do have one advantage over their colleagues in the House: Senators hold six-year terms, which gives them time to engage in fence-mending to repair the damage from unpopular decisions. In the Senate, Stimson's study confirmed that opinion affects a senator's chances at reelection, even though it did not affect House members. Specifically, the study shows that when public opinion shifts, fewer senators win reelection. Thus, when the public as a whole becomes more or less liberal, new senators are elected. Rather than the senators shifting their policy preferences and voting differently, it is the new senators who change the policy direction of the Senate.[110]

Beyond voter polls, congressional representatives are also very interested in polls that reveal the wishes of interest groups and businesses. If AARP, one of the largest and most active groups of voters in the United States, is unhappy with a bill, members of the relevant congressional committees will take that response into consideration. If the pharmaceutical or oil industry is unhappy with a new patent or tax policy, its members' opinions will have some effect on representatives' decisions, since these industries contribute heavily to election campaigns.

Link to Learning

The website of the **Policy Agendas Project (https://www.openstax.org/l/29polagendasprj)** details a National Science Foundation-funded policy project to provide data on public opinion, presidential public approval, and a variety of governmental measures of activity. All data are coded by policy topic, so you can look for trends in a policy topic of interest to you to see whether government attention tracks with public opinion.

There is some disagreement about whether the Supreme Court follows public opinion or shapes it. The lifetime tenure the justices enjoy was designed to remove everyday politics from their decisions, protect them from swings in political partisanship, and allow them to choose whether and when to listen to public opinion. More often than not, the public is unaware of the Supreme Court's decisions and opinions. When the justices accept controversial cases, the media tune in and ask questions, raising public awareness and affecting opinion. But do the justices pay attention to the polls when they make decisions?

Studies that look at the connection between the Supreme Court and public opinion are contradictory. Early on, it was believed that justices were like other citizens: individuals with attitudes and beliefs who would be affected by political shifts.[111] Later studies argued that Supreme Court justices rule in ways that maintain support for the institution. Instead of looking at the short term and making decisions day to day, justices are strategic in their planning and make decisions for the long term.[112]

Other studies have revealed a more complex relationship between public opinion and judicial decisions, largely due to the difficulty of measuring where the effect can be seen. Some studies look at the number of reversals taken by the Supreme Court, which are decisions with which the Court overturns the decision of a lower court. In one study, the authors found that public opinion slightly affects cases accepted by the justices.[113] In a study looking at how often the justices voted liberally on a decision, a stronger effect of public opinion was revealed.[114]

Whether the case or court is currently in the news may also matter. A study found that if the majority of Americans agree on a policy or issue before the court, the court's decision is likely to agree with public opinion.[115] A second study determined that public opinion is more likely to affect ignored cases than heavily reported ones.[116] In these situations, the court was also more likely to rule with the majority opinion than against it. For example, in *Town of Greece v. Galloway* (2014), a majority of the justices decided that ceremonial prayer before a town meeting was not a violation of the Establishment Clause.[117] The fact that 78 percent of U.S. adults recently said religion is fairly to very important to their lives[118] and 61 percent supported prayer in school[119] may explain why public support for the Supreme Court did not fall after this decision.[120]

Overall, however, it is clear that public opinion has a less powerful effect on the courts than on the other branches and on politicians.[121] Perhaps this is due to the lack of elections or justices' lifetime tenure, or perhaps we have not determined the best way to measure the effects of public opinion on the Court.

Key Terms

agent of political socialization a person or entity that teaches and influences others about politics through use of information

bandwagon effect increased media coverage of candidates who poll high

Bradley effect the difference between a poll result and an election result in which voters gave a socially desirable poll response rather than a true response that might be perceived as racist

classical liberalism a political ideology based on belief in individual liberties and rights and the idea of free will, with little role for government

communism a political and economic system in which, in theory, government promotes common ownership of all property, means of production, and materials to prevent the exploitation of workers while creating an equal society; in practice, most communist governments have used force to maintain control

covert content ideologically slanted information presented as unbiased information in order to influence public opinion

diffuse support the widespread belief that a country and its legal system are legitimate

exit poll an election poll taken by interviewing voters as they leave a polling place

fascism a political system of total control by the ruling party or political leader over the economy, the military, society, and culture and often the private lives of citizens

favorability poll a public opinion poll that measures a public's positive feelings about a candidate or politician

heuristics shortcuts or rules of thumb for decision making

horserace coverage day-to-day media coverage of candidate performance in the election

leading question a question worded to lead a respondent to give a desired answer

margin of error a number that states how far the poll results may be from the actual preferences of the total population of citizens

modern conservatism a political ideology that prioritizes individual liberties, preferring a smaller government that stays out of the economy

modern liberalism a political ideology focused on equality and supporting government intervention in society and the economy if it promotes equality

overt content political information whose author makes clear that only one side is presented

political culture the prevailing political attitudes and beliefs within a society or region

political elite a political opinion leader who alerts the public to changes or problems

political socialization the process of learning the norms and practices of a political system through others and societal institutions

public opinion a collection of opinions of an individual or a group of individuals on a topic, person, or event

push poll politically biased campaign information presented as a poll in order to change minds

random sample a limited number of people from the overall population selected in such a way that each has an equal chance of being chosen

representative sample a group of respondents demographically similar to the population of interest

socialism a political and economic system in which government uses its authority to promote social and economic equality, providing everyone with basic services and equal opportunities and requiring citizens with more wealth to contribute more

straw poll an informal and unofficial election poll conducted with a non-random population

theory of delegate representation a theory that assumes the politician is in office to be the voice of the people and to vote only as the people want

traditional conservatism a political ideology supporting the authority of the monarchy and the church in the belief that government provides the rule of law

Summary

6.1 The Nature of Public Opinion

Public opinion is more than a collection of answers to a question on a poll; it represents a snapshot of how people's experiences and beliefs have led them to feel about a candidate, a law, or a social issue. Our attitudes are formed in childhood as part of our upbringing. They blend with our closely held beliefs about life and politics to form the basis for our opinions. Beginning early in life, we learn about politics from agents of socialization, which include family, schools, friends, religious organizations, and the media. Socialization gives us the information necessary to understand our political system and make decisions. We use this information to choose our ideology and decide what the proper role of government should be in our society.

6.2 How Is Public Opinion Measured?

The purpose of a poll is to identify how a population feels about an issue or candidate. Many polling companies and news outlets use statisticians and social scientists to design accurate and scientific polls and to reduce errors. A scientific poll will try to create a representative and random sample to ensure the responses are similar to what the actual population of an area believes. Scientific polls also have lower margins of error, which means they better predict what the overall public or population thinks. Most polls are administered through phones, online, or via social media. Even in scientific polls, issues like timing, social pressure, lack of knowledge, and human nature can create results that do not match true public opinion. Polls can also be used as campaign devices to try to change a voter's mind on an issue or candidate.

6.3 What Does the Public Think?

When citizens change their sources of information, their opinions may change. The influence of elites and workplaces, life experiences, and state political culture can all help change our opinions. Economic and social policies are likely to cause controversy if the government has to serve the needs of many different groups or balance rights and liberties, all with limited resources.

What Americans think about their government institutions shifts over time as well. Overall approval for presidents begins high and drops over time, with expected increases and decreases occurring due to domestic and international events. Approval for Congress changes more dramatically with domestic events and partisan behavior. The public has a lower opinion of Congress than of the president, and recent congressional approval levels have hovered between 10 and 20 percent. The Supreme Court has the most stable public approval ratings, possibly due to its less visible nature. But the court's ratings can be affected by controversial decisions, such as its 2015 decisions on the Affordable Care Act and same-sex marriage.

6.4 The Effects of Public Opinion

Public opinion polls have some effect on politics, most strongly during election season. Candidates who do well in polls receive more media coverage and campaign donations than candidates who fare poorly. The effect of polling on government institutions is less clear. Presidents sometimes consider polls when making decisions, especially if the polls reflect high approval. A president who has an electoral mandate can use that high public approval rating to push policies through Congress. Congress is likely to be aware of public opinion on issues. Representatives must continually raise campaign donations for bi-yearly elections. For this reason, they must keep their constituents and donors happy. Representatives are also likely to change their voting behavior if public opinion changes. Senators have a longer span between elections, which gives them time to make decisions independent of opinion and then make amends with their constituents. Changes in public opinion do not affect senators' votes, but they do cause senators to lose reelection. It is less clear whether Supreme Court justices rule in ways that maintain the integrity of the branch or that keep step with the majority opinion of the public, but public approval of the court can change after high-profile decisions.

Review Questions

1. Which of the following is *not* an agent of political socialization?
- a. a family member
- b. a religious leader
- c. a teacher
- d. a U.S. senator

2. How are most attitudes formed?
- a. in adulthood, based on life choices
- b. in childhood, based on early childhood experiences
- c. in college, based on classes and majors
- d. after college, based on finances

3. _____ political content is given by a media source that lets the reader or viewer know upfront there is a political bias or position.
- a. Overt
- b. Covert
- c. Explanatory
- d. Expository

4. Where do your beliefs originate?

5. Which agents of socialization will have the strongest impact on an individual?

6. The Bradley effect occurs when people _____.
- a. say they will vote for a candidate based on the candidate's name
- b. say they will vote against a candidate because of the candidate's race
- c. say they will vote for a candidate but then vote against him or her
- d. say they will vote in the next election but instead stay home

7. Which of the following is *not* part of a scientific poll design?
- a. a leading question
- b. a random sample
- c. a representative sample
- d. a low margin of error

8. A poll states that Hillary Clinton will receive 43 percent of the vote. There is an 8 percent margin of error. What do you think of the poll?
- a. It is a good poll and the margin of error is small.
- b. It is a good poll and the margin of error is acceptable.
- c. It is a non-representative poll and the margin of error is too high.
- d. The poll accurately predicts Clinton will receive 43 percent of the vote.

9. Why do pollsters interview random people throughout the country when trying to project which candidate will win a presidential election?

10. How have changes in technology made polling more difficult?

11. Why are social policies controversial?
    a. They require people to accept the authority of the government.
    b. They require government to balance the rights and liberties of different groups.
    c. They require the government to increase spending.
    d. They require a decrease in regulations and laws.

12. Which factor affects congressional approval ratings the most?
    a. presidential actions
    b. foreign events
    c. Supreme Court actions
    d. domestic events

13. Which institution has the highest average public approval ratings?
    a. the presidency
    b. the U.S. House of Representatives
    c. the U.S. Senate
    d. the Supreme Court

14. Why might one branch's approval ratings be higher than another's?

15. When are social and economic issues more likely to cause polarization in public opinion?

16. How do polls affect presidential elections?
    a. Polls help voters research information about each of the candidates.
    b. Polls tell voters the issues that candidates support.
    c. Polls identify the top candidates and the media interview those candidates.
    d. Polls explain which candidates should win the election.

17. Presidential approval ratings _____ over a president's term of office.
    a. increase
    b. decline
    c. stay relatively stable
    d. seesaw

18. Which body of government is least susceptible to public opinion polls?
    a. the president
    b. U.S. Senate
    c. U.S. House of Representatives
    d. U.S. Supreme Court

19. Why would House of Representative members be more likely than the president to follow public opinion?

20. How do the media use public opinion polls during election season?

Critical Thinking Questions

21. Why is diffuse support important to maintaining a stable democracy? What happens when a government does not have diffuse support?

22. What are the ways the media socialize a person?

23. Is public opinion generally clear, providing broad signals to elected leaders about what needs to be done? Why or why not?

24. When should political leaders *not* follow public opinion, and why?

25. Why should a poll be scientific rather than informal?

26. What heuristics, or cues, do voters use to pick a presidential candidate? Are these a good way to pick a president?

Suggestions for Further Study

Alvarez, Michael, and John Brehm. 2002. *Hard Choices, Easy Answers: Values, Information and American Public Opinion.* Princeton: Princeton University Press.

Campbell, Angus, Philip Converse, Warren Miller, and Donald Stokes. 1980. *The American Voter: Unabridged Edition.* Chicago: University of Chicago Press.

Canes-Wrone, Brandice. 2005. *Who Leads Whom? Presidents, Policy and the Public.* Chicago: University of Chicago Press.

Downs, Anthony. 1957. *An Economic Theory of Democracy.* New York: Harper.

Lewis-Beck, Michael S., Helmut Norpoth, William Jacoby, and Herbert Weisberg. 2008. *The American Voter Revisited.* Ann Arbor: University of Michigan Press.

Lippmann, Walter. 1922. *Public Opinion.* New York: Harcourt, Brace and Co.

Lupia, Arthur, and Mathew McCubbins. 1998. *The Democratic Dilemma.* Cambridge: Cambridge University Press.

Pew Research Center (http://www.pewresearch.org/).

Real Clear Politics' Polling Center (http://www.realclearpolitics.com/epolls/latest_polls/).

Zaller, John. 1992. *The Nature and Origins of Mass Opinion.* Cambridge: Cambridge University Press.

Chapter 7

Voting and Elections

Figure 7.1 Senator Ted Cruz (R-TX) hosts a Rally for Religious Liberty at Bob Jones University, a Christian university in Greenville, South Carolina, on November 14, 2015. Cruz announced his campaign for president on March 23, 2015, at Liberty University in Lynchburg, Virginia. (credit: modification of work by Jamelle Bouie)

Chapter Outline

7.1 Voter Registration

7.2 Voter Turnout

7.3 Elections

7.4 Campaigns and Voting

7.5 Direct Democracy

Introduction

The first Republican candidate to throw a hat into the ring for 2016, Ted Cruz had been preparing for his presidential run since 2013 when he went hunting in Iowa and vacationed in New Hampshire, both key states in the nomination process.[1] He had also strongly opposed the Affordable Care Act while showcasing his family side by reading *Green Eggs and Ham* aloud in a filibuster attack on the act.[2] If Cruz had been campaigning all along, why make a grand announcement at Liberty University in 2015?

First, by officially declaring his candidacy at Liberty University, whose stated mission is to provide "a world-class education with a solid Christian foundation," Cruz sought to demonstrate that his values were the same as those of the Christian students before him (**Figure 7.1**).[3] Second, the speech reminded Christians to vote. As Cruz told the students, "imagine millions of young people coming together and standing together, saying 'we will stand for liberty.'"[4] Like candidates for office at all levels of U.S. government, Cruz understood that campaigns must reach out to the voters and compel them to vote or the candidate will fail miserably. But what brings voters to the polls, and how do they make their voting decisions? Those are just two of the questions about voting and elections this chapter will explore.

7.1 Voter Registration

Learning Objectives

By the end of this section, you will be able to:

- Identify ways the U.S. government has promoted voter rights and registration
- Summarize similarities and differences in states' voter registration methods
- Analyze ways states increase voter registration and decrease fraud

Before most voters are allowed to cast a ballot, they must register to vote in their state. This process may be as simple as checking a box on a driver's license application or as difficult as filling out a long form with complicated questions. Registration allows governments to determine which citizens are allowed to vote and, in some cases, from which list of candidates they may select a party nominee. Ironically, while government wants to increase voter turnout, the registration process may prevent various groups of citizens and non-citizens from participating in the electoral process.

VOTER REGISTRATION ACROSS THE UNITED STATES

Elections are state-by-state contests. They include general elections for president and statewide offices (e.g., governor and U.S. senator), and they are often organized and paid for by the states. Because political cultures vary from state to state, the process of voter registration similarly varies. For example, suppose an 85-year-old retiree with an expired driver's license wants to register to vote. He or she might be able to register quickly in California or Florida, but a current government ID might be required prior to registration in Texas or Indiana.

The varied registration and voting laws across the United States have long caused controversy. In the aftermath of the Civil War, southern states enacted literacy tests, grandfather clauses, and other requirements intended to disenfranchise black voters in Alabama, Georgia, and Mississippi. Literacy tests were long and detailed exams on local and national politics, history, and more. They were often administered arbitrarily with more blacks required to take them than whites.[5] Poll taxes required voters to pay a fee to vote. Grandfather clauses exempted individuals from taking literacy tests or paying poll taxes if they or their fathers or grandfathers had been permitted to vote prior to a certain point in time. While the Supreme Court determined that grandfather clauses were unconstitutional in 1915, states continued to use poll taxes and literacy tests to deter potential voters from registering.[6] States also ignored instances of violence and intimidation against African Americans wanting to register or vote.[7]

The ratification of the Twenty-Fourth Amendment in 1964 ended poll taxes, but the passage of the Voting Rights Act (VRA) in 1965 had a more profound effect (Figure 7.2). The act protected the rights of minority voters by prohibiting state laws that denied voting rights based on race. The VRA gave the attorney general of the United States authority to order federal examiners to areas with a history of discrimination. These examiners had the power to oversee and monitor voter registration and elections. States found to violate provisions of the VRA were required to get any changes in their election laws approved by the U.S. attorney general or by going through the court system. However, in *Shelby County v. Holder* (2013), the Supreme Court, in a 5–4 decision, threw out the standards and process of the VRA, effectively gutting the landmark legislation.[8] This decision effectively pushed decision-making and discretion for election policy in VRA states to the state and local level. Several such states subsequently made changes to their voter ID laws and North Carolina changed its plans for how many polling places were available in certain areas. The extent to which such changes will violate equal protection is unknown in advance, but such changes often do not have a neutral effect.

(a)   (b)

Figure 7.2 The Voting Rights Act (a) was signed into law by President Lyndon B. Johnson (b, left) on August 6, 1965, in the presence of major figures of the civil rights movement, including Rosa Parks and Martin Luther King Jr. (b, center).

The effects of the VRA were visible almost immediately. In Mississippi, only 6.7 percent of blacks were registered to vote in 1965; however, by the fall of 1967, nearly 60 percent were registered. Alabama experienced similar effects, with African American registration increasing from 19.3 percent to 51.6 percent. Voter turnout across these two states similarly increased. Mississippi went from 33.9 percent turnout to 53.2 percent, while Alabama increased from 35.9 percent to 52.7 percent between the 1964 and 1968 presidential elections.[9]

Following the implementation of the VRA, many states have sought other methods of increasing voter registration. Several states make registering to vote relatively easy for citizens who have government documentation. Oregon has few requirements for registering and registers many of its voters automatically. North Dakota has no registration at all. In 2002, Arizona was the first state to offer online voter registration, which allowed citizens with a driver's license to register to vote without any paper application or signature. The system matches the information on the application to information stored at the Department of Motor Vehicles, to ensure each citizen is registering to vote in the right precinct. Citizens without a driver's license still need to file a paper application. More than eighteen states have moved to online registration or passed laws to begin doing so. The National Conference of State Legislatures estimates, however, that adopting an online voter registration system can initially cost a state between $250,000 and $750,000.[10]

Other states have decided against online registration due to concerns about voter fraud and security. Legislators also argue that online registration makes it difficult to ensure that only citizens are registering and that they are registering in the correct precincts. As technology continues to update other areas of state recordkeeping, online registration may become easier and safer. In some areas, citizens have pressured the states and pushed the process along. A bill to move registration online in Florida stalled for over a year in the legislature, based on security concerns. With strong citizen support, however, it was passed and signed in 2015, despite the governor's lingering concerns. In other states, such as Texas, both the government and citizens are concerned about identity fraud, so traditional paper registration is still preferred.

HOW DOES SOMEONE REGISTER TO VOTE?

The National Commission on Voting Rights completed a study in September 2015 that found state registration laws can either raise or reduce voter turnout rates, especially among citizens who are young or whose income falls below the poverty line. States with simple voter registration had more registered citizens.[11]

In all states except North Dakota, a citizen wishing to vote must complete an application. Whether the form is online or on paper, the prospective voter will list his or her name, residency address, and in many cases party identification (with Independent as an option) and affirm that he or she is competent to vote. States may also have a **residency requirement**, which establishes how long a citizen must live in a state before becoming eligible to register: it is often thirty days. Beyond these requirements, there may be an oath administered or more questions asked, such as felony convictions. If the application is completely online and the citizen has government documents (e.g., driver's license or state identification card), the system will compare the application to other state records and accept an online signature or affidavit if everything matches up correctly. Citizens who do not have these state documents are often required to complete paper applications. States without online registration often allow a citizen to fill out an application on a website, but the citizen will receive a paper copy in the mail to sign and mail back to the state.

Another aspect of registering to vote is the timeline. States may require registration to take place as much as thirty days before voting, or they may allow same-day registration. Maine first implemented same-day registration in 1973. Fourteen states and the District of Columbia now allow voters to register the day of the election if they have proof of residency, such as a driver's license or utility bill. Many of the more populous states (e.g., Michigan and Texas), require registration forms to be mailed thirty days before an election. Moving means citizens must re-register or update addresses (Figure 7.3). College students, for example, may have to re-register or update addresses each year as they move. States that use same-day registration had a 4 percent higher voter turnout in the 2012 presidential election than states that did not.[12] Yet another consideration is how far in advance of an election one must apply to change one's political party affiliation. In states with closed primaries, it is important for voters to be allowed to register into whichever party they prefer. This issue came up during the 2016 presidential primaries in New York, where there is a lengthy timeline for changing your party affiliation.

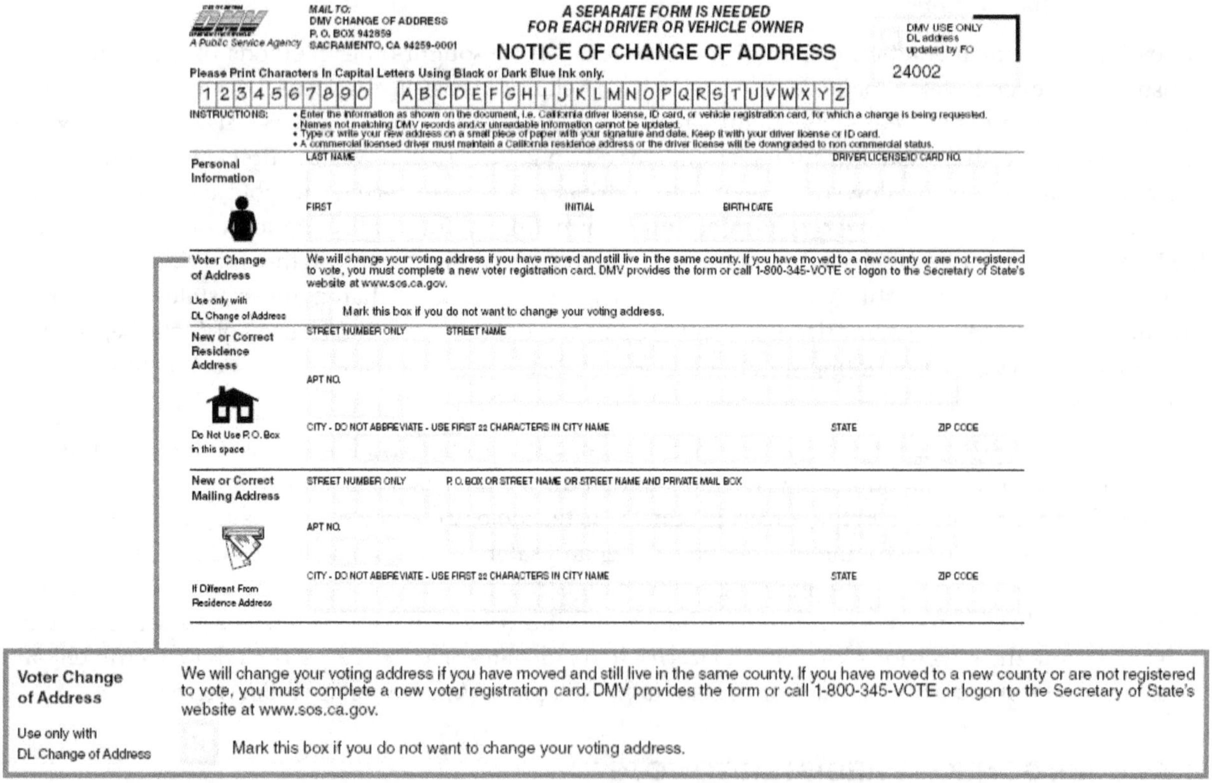
A Public Service Agency
MAIL TO:
DMV CHANGE OF ADDRESS
P. O. BOX 942859
SACRAMENTO, CA 94259-0001

A SEPARATE FORM IS NEEDED FOR EACH DRIVER OR VEHICLE OWNER

NOTICE OF CHANGE OF ADDRESS

DMV USE ONLY
DL address
updated by FO

24002

Please Print Characters In Capital Letters Using Black or Dark Blue Ink only.

1 2 3 4 5 6 7 8 9 0 A B C D E F G H I J K L M N O P Q R S T U V W X Y Z

INSTRUCTIONS:
- Enter the information as shown on the document, i.e. California driver license, ID card, or vehicle registration card, for which a change is being requested.
- Names not matching DMV records and/or unreadable information cannot be updated.
- Type or write your new address on a small piece of paper with your signature and date. Keep it with your driver license or ID card.
- A commercial licensed driver must maintain a California residence address or the driver license will be downgraded to non commercial status.

Personal Information — LAST NAME — DRIVER LICENSE/ID CARD NO. — FIRST — INITIAL — BIRTH DATE

Voter Change of Address — We will change your voting address if you have moved and still live in the same county. If you have moved to a new county or are not registered to vote, you must complete a new voter registration card. DMV provides the form or call 1-800-345-VOTE or logon to the Secretary of State's website at www.sos.ca.gov.

Use only with DL Change of Address — Mark this box if you do not want to change your voting address.

New or Correct Residence Address — STREET NUMBER ONLY — STREET NAME — APT NO. — CITY - DO NOT ABBREVIATE - USE FIRST 22 CHARACTERS IN CITY NAME — STATE — ZIP CODE

Do Not Use P.O. Box in this space

New or Correct Mailing Address — STREET NUMBER ONLY — P.O. BOX OR STREET NAME OR STREET NAME AND PRIVATE MAIL BOX — APT NO. — CITY - DO NOT ABBREVIATE - USE FIRST 22 CHARACTERS IN CITY NAME — STATE — ZIP CODE

If Different From Residence Address

Voter Change of Address — We will change your voting address if you have moved and still live in the same county. If you have moved to a new county or are not registered to vote, you must complete a new voter registration card. DMV provides the form or call 1-800-345-VOTE or logon to the Secretary of State's website at www.sos.ca.gov.

Use only with DL Change of Address — Mark this box if you do not want to change your voting address.

Figure 7.3 Moving requires a voter to re-register or update his or her address in the system. Depending on the state, this notification can sometimes be completed through the Department of Motor Vehicles, as in California.

Some attempts have been made to streamline voter registration. The National Voter Registration Act (1993), often referred to as Motor Voter, was enacted to expedite the registration process and make it as simple as possible for voters. The act required states to allow citizens to register to vote when they sign up for driver's licenses and Social Security benefits. On each government form, the citizen need only mark an additional box to also register to vote. Unfortunately, while increasing registrations by 7 percent between 1992 and 2012, Motor Voter did not dramatically increase voter turnout.[13] In fact, for two years following the passage of the act, voter turnout decreased slightly.[14] It appears that the main users of the expedited system were those already intending to vote. One study, however, found that preregistration may have a different effect on youth than on the overall voter pool; in Florida, it increased turnout of young voters by 13 percent.[15]

In 2015, Oregon made news when it took the concept of Motor Voter further. When citizens turn eighteen, the state now automatically registers most of them using driver's license and state identification information. When a citizen moves, the voter rolls are updated when the license is updated. While this policy has been controversial, with some arguing that private information may become public or that Oregon is moving toward mandatory voting, automatic registration is consistent with the state's efforts to increase registration and turnout.[16]

Oregon's example offers a possible solution to a recurring problem for states—maintaining accurate voter registration rolls. During the 2000 election, in which George W. Bush won Florida's electoral votes by a slim majority, attention turned to the state's election procedures and voter registration rolls. Journalists found that many states, including Florida, had large numbers of phantom voters on their rolls, voters had moved or died but remained on the states' voter registration rolls.[17] The Help America Vote Act of 2002 (HAVA) was passed in order to reform voting across the states and reduce these problems. As part of the Act, states were required to update voting equipment, make voting more accessible to the disabled, and maintain computerized voter rolls that could be updated regularly.[18]

Over a decade later, there has been some progress. In Louisiana, voters are placed on ineligible lists if a voting registrar is notified that they have moved or become ineligible to vote. If the voter remains on this list for two general elections, his or her registration is cancelled. In Oklahoma, the registrar receives a list of deceased residents from the Department of Health.[19] Twenty-nine states now participate in the Interstate Voter Registration Crosscheck Program, which allows states to check for duplicate registrations.[20] At the same time, Florida's use of the federal Systematic Alien Verification for Entitlements (SAVE) database has proven to be controversial, because county elections supervisors are allowed to remove voters deemed ineligible to vote.[21]

Despite these efforts, a study commissioned by the Pew Charitable Trust found twenty-four million voter registrations nationwide were no longer valid.[22] Pew is now working with eight states to update their voter registration rolls and encouraging more states to share their rolls in an effort to find duplicates.[23]

Link to Learning

The National Association of Secretaries of State maintains a website (https://openstax.org/l/29canivote) that directs users to their state's information regarding voter registration, identification policies, and polling locations.

WHO IS ALLOWED TO REGISTER?

In order to be eligible to vote in the United States, a person must be a citizen, resident, and eighteen years old. But states often place additional requirements on the right to vote. The most common requirement is that voters must be mentally competent and not currently serving time in jail. Some states enforce more stringent or unusual requirements on citizens who have committed crimes. Florida and Kentucky permanently bar felons and ex-felons from voting unless they obtain a pardon from the governor, while

Mississippi and Nevada allow former felons to apply to have their voting rights restored.[24] On the other end of the spectrum, Vermont does not limit voting based on incarceration unless the crime was election fraud.[25] Maine citizens serving in Maine prisons also may vote in elections.

Beyond those jailed, some citizens have additional expectations placed on them when they register to vote. Wisconsin requires that voters "not wager on an election," and Vermont citizens must recite the "Voter's Oath" before they register, swearing to cast votes with a conscience and "without fear or favor of any person."[26]

Get Connected!

Where to Register?

Across the United States, over twenty million college and university students begin classes each fall, many away from home. The simple act of moving away to college presents a voter registration problem. Elections are local. Each citizen lives in a district with state legislators, city council or other local elected representatives, a U.S. House of Representatives member, and more. State and national laws require voters to reside in their districts, but students are an unusual case. They often hold temporary residency while at school and return home for the summer. Therefore, they have to decide whether to register to vote near campus or vote back in their home district. What are the pros and cons of each option?

Maintaining voter registration back home is legal in most states, assuming a student holds only temporary residency at school. This may be the best plan, because students are likely more familiar with local politicians and issues. But it requires the student to either go home to vote or apply for an absentee ballot. With classes, clubs, work, and more, it may be difficult to remember this task. One study found that students living more than two hours from home were less likely to vote than students living within thirty minutes of campus, which is not surprising.[27]

Registering to vote near campus makes it easier to vote, but it requires an extra step that students may forget (Figure 7.4). And in many states, registration to vote in a November election takes place in October, just when students are acclimating to the semester. They must also become familiar with local candidates and issues, which takes time and effort they may not have. But they will not have to travel to vote, and their vote is more likely to affect their college and local town.

(a)   (b)

Figure 7.4   On National Voter Registration Day in 2012, Roshaunda McLean (a, left), campus director of the Associated Students of the University of Missouri, and David Vaughn (a, right), a Missouri Student Association senator, register voters on campus. Cassie Dorman (b, left) and Samantha Peterson (b, right), both eighteen years old, were just two of the University of Missouri students registering to vote for the first time. (credit a, b: modification of work by "KOMUnews"/Flickr)

Have you registered to vote in your college area, or will you vote back home? What factors influenced your decision about where to vote?

7.2 Voter Turnout

Learning Objectives

By the end of this section, you will be able to:
- Identify factors that motivate registered voters to vote
- Discuss circumstances that prevent citizens from voting
- Analyze reasons for low voter turnout in the United States

Campaign managers worry about who will show up at the polls on Election Day. Will more Republicans come? More Democrats? Will a surge in younger voters occur this year, or will an older population cast ballots? We can actually predict with strong accuracy who is likely to vote each year, based on identified influence factors such as age, education, and income. Campaigns will often target each group of voters in different ways, spending precious campaign dollars on the groups already most likely to show up at the polls rather than trying to persuade citizens who are highly unlikely to vote.

COUNTING VOTERS

Low voter turnout has long caused the media and others to express concern and frustration. A healthy democratic society is expected to be filled with citizens who vote regularly and participate in the electoral process. Organizations like Rock the Vote and Project Vote Smart (Figure 7.5) work alongside MTV to increase voter turnout in all age groups across the United States. But just how low is voter turnout? The answer depends on who is calculating it and how. There are several methods, each of which highlights a different problem with the electoral system in the United States.

(a)

(b)

Figure 7.5 Rock the Vote works with musicians and other celebrities across the country to encourage and register young people to vote (a). Sheryl Crow was one of Rock the Vote's strongest supporters in the 2008 election, subsequently performing at the Midwest Inaugural Ball in January 2009 (b). (credit a: modification of work by Jeff Kramer; credit b: modification of work by "cliff1066"/Flickr)

Link to Learning

Interested in mobilizing voters? Explore Rock the Vote (https://openstax.org/l/29rockthevote) and The Voter Participation Center (https://www.voterparticipation.org/our-mission/) for more information.

Calculating voter turnout begins by counting how many ballots were cast in a particular election. These votes must be cast on time, either by mail or in person. The next step is to count how many people *could* have voted in the same election. This is the number that causes different people to calculate different turnout rates. The complete population of the country includes all people, regardless of age, nationality, mental capacity, or freedom. We can count subsections of this population to calculate voter turnout. For instance, the next largest population in the country is the **voting-age population** (VAP), which consists of persons who are eighteen and older. Some of these persons may not be eligible to vote in their state, but they are included because they are of age to do so.[28]

An even smaller group is the **voting-eligible population** (VEP), citizens eighteen and older who, whether they have registered or not, are eligible to vote because they are citizens, mentally competent, and not imprisoned. If a state has more stringent requirements, such as not having a felony conviction, citizens counted in the VEP must meet those criteria as well. This population is much harder to measure, but statisticians who use the VEP will generally take the VAP and subtract the state's prison population and any other known group that cannot vote. This results in a number that is somewhat theoretical; however, in a way, it is more accurate when determining voter turnout.[29]

The last and smallest population is registered voters, who, as the name implies, are citizens currently registered to vote. Now we can appreciate how reports of voter turnout can vary. As Figure 7.6 shows, although 87 percent of registered voters voted in the 2012 presidential election, this represents only 42 percent of the total U.S. population. While 42 percent is indeed low and might cause alarm, some people included in it are under eighteen, not citizens, or unable to vote due to competency or prison status. The next number shows that just over 57 percent of the voting-age population voted, and 60 percent of the voting-eligible population. The best turnout ratio is calculated using the smallest population: 87 percent of registered voters voted. Those who argue that a healthy democracy needs high voter turnout will look at the voting-age population or voting-eligible population as proof that the United States has a problem. Those who believe only informed and active citizens should vote point to the registered voter turnout numbers instead.

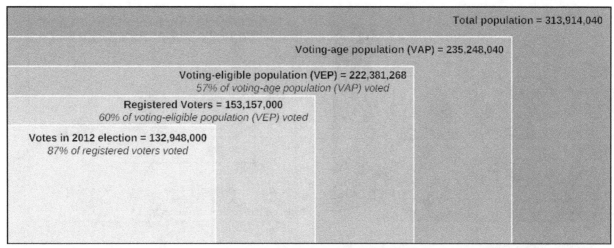

Figure 7.6   There are many ways to measure voter turnout depending on whether we calculate it using the total population, the voting-age population (VAP), the voting-eligible population (VEP), or the total number of registered voters.

WHAT FACTORS DRIVE VOTER TURNOUT?

Political parties and campaign managers approach every population of voters differently, based on what they know about factors that influence turnout. Everyone targets likely voters, which are the category of registered voters who vote regularly. Most campaigns also target registered voters in general, because they are more likely to vote than unregistered citizens. For this reason, many polling agencies ask respondents whether they are already registered and whether they voted in the last election. Those who are registered and did vote in the last election are likely to have a strong interest in politics and elections and will vote again, provided they are not angry with the political system or politicians.

Some campaigns and civic groups target members of the voting-eligible population who are not registered, especially in states that are highly contested during a particular election. The Association of Community Organizations for Reform Now (ACORN), which is now defunct, was both lauded and criticized for its efforts to get voters in low socio-economic areas registered during the 2008 election.[30] Similarly, interest groups in Los Angeles were criticized for registering homeless citizens as a part of an effort to gather signatures to place propositions on the ballot.[31] These potential voters may not think they can vote, but they might be persuaded to register and then vote if the process is simplified or the information they receive encourages them to do so.

Campaigns also target different age groups with different intensity, because age is a relatively consistent factor in predicting voting behavior. Those between eighteen and twenty-five are least likely to vote, while those sixty-five to seventy-four are most likely. One reason for lower voter turnout among younger citizens may be that they move frequently.[32] Another reason may be circular: Youth are less active in government and politics, leading the parties to neglect them. When people are neglected, they are in turn less likely to become engaged in government.[33] They may also be unaware of what a government provides. Younger people are often still in college, perhaps working part-time and earning low wages. They are unlikely to be receiving government benefits beyond Pell Grants or government-subsidized tuition and loans. They are also unlikely to be paying taxes at a high rate. Government is a distant concept rather than a daily concern, which may drive down turnout.

In 2012, for example, the Census Bureau reported that only 53.6 percent of eligible voters between the ages of eighteen and twenty-four registered and 41.2 percent voted, while 79.7 percent of sixty-five to seventy-four-year-olds registered and 73.5 percent voted.[34] Once a person has retired, reliance on the government will grow if he or she draws income from Social Security, receives health care from Medicare, and enjoys benefits such as transportation and social services from state and local governments (Figure 7.7).

(a)

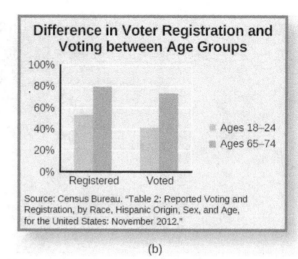
(b)

Figure 7.7 On January 7, 2008, John McCain campaigned in New Hampshire among voters holding AARP signs (a). AARP, formerly the American Association of Retired Persons, is one of the most influential interest groups because senior citizens are known to vote at nearly double the rate of young people (b), thanks in part to their increased reliance on government programs as they age. (credit a: modification of work by Ryan Glenn)

Due to consistently low turnout among the young, several organizations have made special efforts to demonstrate to younger citizens that voting is an important activity. Rock the Vote began in 1990, with the goal of bringing music, art, and pop culture together to encourage the youth to participate in government. The organization hosts rallies, festivals, and concerts that also register voters and promote voter awareness, bringing celebrities and musicians to set examples of civic involvement. Rock the Vote also maintains a website that helps young adults find out how to register in their state. Citizen Change, started by Sean "Diddy" Combs and other hip hop artists, pushed slogans such as "Vote or Die" during the 2004 presidential election in an effort to increase youth voting turnout. These efforts may have helped in 2004 and 2008, when the number of youth voting in the presidential elections increased (Figure 7.8).[35]

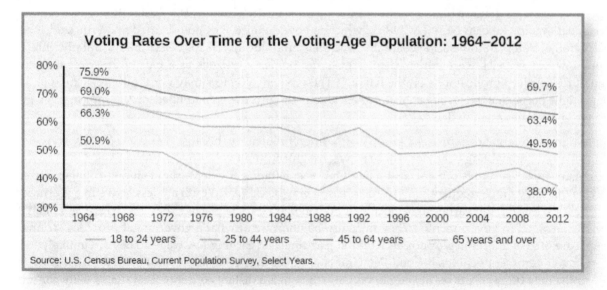

Figure 7.8

Milestone

Making a Difference

In 2008, for the first time since 1972, a presidential candidate intrigued America's youth and persuaded them to flock to the polls in record numbers. Barack Obama not only spoke to young people's concerns but his campaign also connected with them via technology, wielding texts and tweets to bring together a new generation of voters (Figure 7.9).

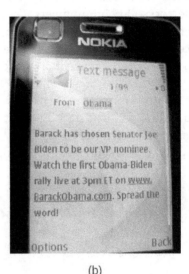

(a)   (b)

Figure 7.9 On November 5, 2008, union members get ready to hit the streets in Milwaukee, Wisconsin, to "get out the vote" (GOTV) for Barack Obama (a). On August 23, 2008, the Obama campaign texted supporters directly in order to announce that he had selected Senator Joe Biden (D-DE) as his running mate (b). (credit a: modification of work by Casie Yoder; credit b: modification of work by "brownpau"/Flickr)

The high level of interest Obama inspired among college-aged voters was a milestone in modern politics. Since the 1971 passage of the Twenty-Sixth Amendment, which lowered the voting age from 21 to 18, voter turnout in the under-25 range has been low. While opposition to the Vietnam War and the military draft sent 50.9 percent of 21- to 24-year-old voters to the polls in 1964, after 1972, turnout in that same age group dropped to below 40 percent as youth became disenchanted with politics. In 2008, however, it briefly increased to 45 percent from only 32 percent in 2000. Yet, despite high interest in Obama's candidacy in 2008, younger voters were less enchanted in 2012—only 38 percent showed up to vote that year.[36]

What qualities should a presidential or congressional candidate show in order to get college students excited and voting? Why?

A citizen's socioeconomic status—the combination of education, income, and social status—may also predict whether he or she will vote. Among those who have completed college, the 2012 voter turnout rate jumps to 75 percent of eligible voters, compared to about 52.6 percent for those who have completed only high school.[37] This is due in part to the powerful effect of education, one of the strongest predictors of voting turnout. Income also has a strong effect on the likelihood of voting. Citizens earning $100,000 to $149,999 a year are very likely to vote and 76.9 percent of them do, while only 50.4 percent of those who earn $15,000 to $19,999 vote.[38] Once high income and college education are combined, the resulting high socioeconomic status strongly predicts the likelihood that a citizen will vote.

Race is also a factor. Caucasians turn out to vote in the highest numbers, with 63 percent of white citizens voting in 2012. In comparison, 62 percent of African Americans, 31.3 percent of Asian Americans, and 31.8 percent of Hispanic citizens voted in 2012. Voting turnout can increase or decrease based upon the political culture of a state, however. Hispanics, for example, often vote in higher numbers in states where there has historically been higher Hispanic involvement and representation, such as New Mexico, where 49 percent of Hispanic voters turned out in 2012.[39] In 2016, while Donald Trump rode a wave of discontent among white voters to the presidency, the fact that Hillary Clinton nearly beat him may have had as much to do with the record turnout of Latinos in response to numerous remarks on immigration that Trump made throughout his campaign. Latinos made up 11 percent of the electorate in 2016, up from 10 percent in 2012 and 9 percent in 2008.[40]

While less of a factor today, gender has historically been a factor in voter turnout. After 1920, when the Nineteenth Amendment gave women the right to vote, women began slowly turning out to vote, and now they do so in high numbers. Today, more women vote than men. In 2012, 59.7 percent of men and 63.7 percent of women reported voting.[41] While women do not vote exclusively for one political party, 41 percent are likely to identify as Democrats and only 25 percent are likely to identify as Republicans.[42] In 2016, a record 73.7 percent of women reporting voting,[43] while a record 63.8 percent of men reported voting. In 2012, these numbers were 71.4 percent for women and 61.6 percent for men. The margin that Hillary Clinton won was more narrow in Florida than many presumed it would be and may have helped Donald Trump win that state. Even after allegations of sexual assault and revelations of several instances of sexism by Mr. Trump, Clinton only won 54 percent of the women's vote in Florida. In contrast, rural voters voted overwhelmingly for Trump, at much higher rates than they had for Mitt Romney in 2012.

Link to Learning

Check out this website (https://openstax.org/l/29fairvoteorg) to find out who is voting and who isn't.

WHAT FACTORS DECREASE VOTER TURNOUT?

Just as political scientists and campaign managers worry about who does vote, they also look at why people choose to stay home on Election Day. Over the years, studies have explored why a citizen might not vote. The reasons range from the obvious excuse of being too busy (19 percent) to more complex answers, such as transportation problems (3.3 percent) and restrictive registration laws (5.5 percent).[44] With only 57 percent of our voting-age population (VAP) voting in the presidential election of 2012,[45] however, we should examine why the rest do not participate.

One prominent reason for low national turnout is that participation is not mandated. Some countries, such as Belgium and Turkey, have compulsory voting laws, which require citizens to vote in elections or pay a fine. This helps the two countries attain VAP turnouts of 87 percent and 86 percent, respectively, compared to the U.S. turnout of 54 percent. Sweden and Germany automatically register their voters, and 83 percent and 66 percent vote, respectively. Chile's decision to move from compulsory voting to voluntary voting caused a drop in participation from 87 percent to 46 percent.[46]

Link to Learning

Do you wonder what voter turnout looks like in other developed countries? Visit the Pew Research Center report on international voting turnout (https://openstax.org/l/29pewrescenter) to find out.

Low turnout also occurs when some citizens are not allowed to vote. One method of limiting voter access is the requirement to show identification at polling places. The impetus for more stringent requirements for voter ID is to prevent voter fraud, such as someone voting multiple times or someone voting who does not meet the requirements to be a voter in that state; however, there is little evidence that such fraud is taking place. The downside of stricter voter ID laws is that they impact particular groups more so than others. Minority groups and the elderly, for example, see turnout numbers dampened when voter ID requirements become more rigorous.

In 2005, the Indiana legislature passed the first strict photo identification law. Voters must provide photo identification that shows their names match the voter registration records, clearly displays an expiration date, is current or has expired only since the last general election, and was issued by the state of Indiana or the U.S. government. Student identification cards that meet the standards and are from an Indiana state school are allowed.[47] Indiana's law allows voters without an acceptable identification to obtain a free state identification card.[48] The state also extended service hours for state offices that issue identification in the days leading up to elections.[49]

The photo identification law was quickly contested. The American Civil Liberties Union and other groups argued that it placed an unfair burden on people who were poor, older, or had limited finances, while the state argued that it would prevent fraud. In *Crawford v. Marion County Election Board* (2008), the Supreme Court decided that Indiana's voter identification requirement was constitutional, although the decision left open the possibility that another case might meet the burden of proof required to overturn the law.[50]

In 2011, Texas passed a strict photo identification law for voters, allowing concealed-handgun permits as identification but not student identification. The Texas law was blocked by the Obama administration before it could be implemented, because Texas was on the Voting Rights Act's preclearance list. Other states, such as Alabama, Alaska, Arizona, Georgia, and Virginia similarly had laws and districting changes blocked.[51] As a result, Shelby County, Alabama, and several other states sued the U.S. attorney general, arguing the Voting Rights Act's preclearance list was unconstitutional and that the formula that determined whether states had violated the VRA was outdated. In *Shelby County v. Holder* (2013), the Supreme Court agreed. In a 5–4 decision, the justices in the majority said the formula for placing states on the VRA preclearance list was outdated and reached into the states' authority to oversee elections.[52] States and counties on the preclearance list were released, and Congress was told to design new guidelines for placing states on the list.

Following the *Shelby* decision, Texas implemented its photo identification law, leading plaintiffs to bring cases against the state, charging that the law disproportionally affects minority voters.[53] Alabama, Georgia, and Virginia similarly implemented their photo identification laws, joining Kansas, South Carolina, Tennessee, and Wisconsin. Some of these states offer low-cost or free identification for the purposes of voting or will offer help with the completion of registration applications, but citizens must provide birth certificates or other forms of identification, which can be difficult and/or costly to obtain.

Opponents of photo identification laws argue that these restrictions are unfair because they have an unusually strong effect on some demographics. One study, done by Reuters, found that requiring a photo ID would disproportionally prevent citizens aged 18–24, Hispanics, and those without a college education from voting. These groups are unlikely to have the right paperwork or identification, unlike citizens who have graduated from college. The same study found that 4 percent of households with yearly incomes under $25,000 said they did not have an ID that would be considered valid for voting.[54] For this reason, some assert that such changes tend to favor Republicans over Democrats. In the 2018 elections, there were controversial results and allegations of voter suppression in Florida, Georgia, and North Carolina, three jurisdictions where elections were very close.[55]

Another reason for not voting is that polling places may be open only on Election Day. This makes it difficult for voters juggling school, work, and child care during polling hours (Figure 7.10). Many states have tried to address this problem with **early voting**, which opens polling places as much as two weeks early. Texas opened polling places on weekdays and weekends in 1988 and initially saw an increase in voting in gubernatorial and presidential elections, although the impact tapered off over time.[56] Other states with early voting, however, showed a decline in turnout, possibly because there is less social pressure to vote when voting is spread over several days.[57] Early voting was used in a widespread manner across most states in 2016, including Nevada, where 60 percent of votes were cast prior to Election Day.

Figure 7.10 On February 5, 2008, dubbed "Super Duper Tuesday" by the press, twenty-four states held caucuses or primary elections—the largest simultaneous number of state presidential primary elections in U.S. history. As a result, over half the Democratic delegates were allocated unusually early in the election season. This polling station, on the Stanford University campus in Palo Alto, California, had long lines, commonly seen only on Election Day, and nearly ran out of Democratic ballots. (credit: Josh Thompson)

In a similar effort, Oregon, Colorado, and Washington have moved to a mail-only voting system in which there are no polling locations, only mailed ballots. These states have seen a rise in turnout, with Colorado's numbers increasing from 1.8 million votes in the 2010 congressional elections to 2 million votes in the 2014 congressional elections.[58] One argument against early and mail-only voting is that those who vote early cannot change their minds during the final days of the campaign, such as in response to an "October surprise," a highly negative story about a candidate that leaks right before Election Day in November. (For example, a week before the 2000 election, a *Dallas Morning News* journalist reported that George W. Bush had lied about whether he had been arrested for driving under the influence.[59]) In 2016, two such stories, one for each nominee, broke just prior to Election Day. First, the Billy Bush Access Hollywood tape showed a braggadocian Donald Trump detailing his ability to do what he pleases with women, including grabbing at their genitals. This tape led some Republican officeholders, such as Senator Jeff Flake (R-AZ), to disavow Trump. However, perhaps eclipsing this episode was the release by former FBI director James Comey of a letter to Congress re-opening the Hillary Clinton email investigation a mere eleven days prior to the election. It is impossible to know the exact dynamics of how someone decides to vote, but one theory is that women jumped from Trump after the Access Hollywood tape emerged, only to go back to supporting him when the FBI seemed to reopen its investigation. Moreover, we later learned of significant Russian meddling in the 2016 election. Robert S. Mueller III, a well-respected former FBI director for presidents from both parties, was appointed as the independent special investigator to delve into matters related to the 2016 election and potential interaction between Russian actors and American election processes.[60] That investigation has led to a host of Trump campaign and Trump administration officials facing indictments and convictions, including his campaign manager Paul Manafort, personal attorney Michael Cohen, and long-time confidant Roger Stone. To date, the president has not faced charges.[61]

Apathy may also play a role. Some people avoid voting because their vote is unlikely to make a difference or the election is not competitive. If one party has a clear majority in a state or district, for instance, members of the minority party may see no reason to vote. Democrats in Utah and Republicans in California are so outnumbered that they are unlikely to affect the outcome of an election, and they may opt to stay home. Because the presidential candidate with the highest number of popular votes receives all of Utah's and California's electoral votes, there is little incentive for some citizens to vote: they will never change the outcome of the state-level election. These citizens, as well as those who vote for third parties like the Green Party or the Libertarian Party, are sometimes referred to as the **chronic minority**. While third-party candidates sometimes win local or state office or even dramatize an issue for national discussion, such as when Ross Perot discussed the national debt during his campaign as an independent presidential candidate in 1992, they never win national elections.

Finally, some voters may view non-voting as a means of social protest or may see volunteering as a better way to spend their time. Younger voters are more likely to volunteer their time rather than vote, believing that serving others is more important than voting.[62] Possibly related to this choice is **voter fatigue**. In many states, due to our federal structure with elections at many levels of government, voters may vote many times per year on ballots filled with candidates and issues to research. The less time there is between elections, the lower the turnout.[63]

7.3 Elections

Learning Objectives

By the end of this section, you will be able to:
- Describe the stages in the election process
- Compare the primary and caucus systems
- Summarize how primary election returns lead to the nomination of the party candidates

Elections offer American voters the opportunity to participate in their government with little investment of time or personal effort. Yet voters should make decisions carefully. The electoral system allows them the chance to pick party nominees as well as office-holders, although not every citizen will participate in every step. The presidential election is often criticized as a choice between two evils, yet citizens can play a prominent part in every stage of the race and influence who the final candidates actually are.

DECIDING TO RUN

Running for office can be as easy as collecting one hundred signatures on a city election form or paying a registration fee of several thousand dollars to run for governor of a state. However, a potential candidate still needs to meet state-specific requirements covering length of residency, voting status, and age. Potential candidates must also consider competitors, family obligations, and the likelihood of drawing financial backing. His or her spouse, children, work history, health, financial history, and business dealings also become part of the media's focus, along with many other personal details about the past. Candidates for office are slightly more diverse than the representatives serving in legislative and executive bodies, but the realities of elections drive many eligible and desirable candidates away from running.[64]

Despite these problems, most elections will have at least one candidate per party on the ballot. In states or districts where one party holds a supermajority, such as Georgia, candidates from the other party may be discouraged from running because they don't think they have a chance to win.[65] Candidates are likely to be moving up from prior elected office or are professionals, like lawyers, who can take time away from work to campaign and serve in office.[66]

When candidates run for office, they are most likely to choose local or state office first. For women, studies have shown that family obligations rather than desire or ambition account for this choice. Further, women are more likely than men to wait until their children are older before entering politics, and women say that they struggle to balance campaigning and their workload with parenthood.[67] Because higher office is often attained only after service in lower office, there are repercussions to women waiting so long. If they do decide to run for the U.S. House of Representatives or Senate, they are often older, and fewer in number, than their male colleagues (Figure 7.11). As of 2015, only 24.4 percent of state legislators and 20 percent of U.S. Congress members are women.[68] The number of women in executive office is often lower as well. However, in the 2018 midterm elections, a record number of women and younger members were elected to national office. Women will make up almost 25 percent of the 116th Congress, and the freshman class is the youngest incoming group of representatives since 2011.[69]

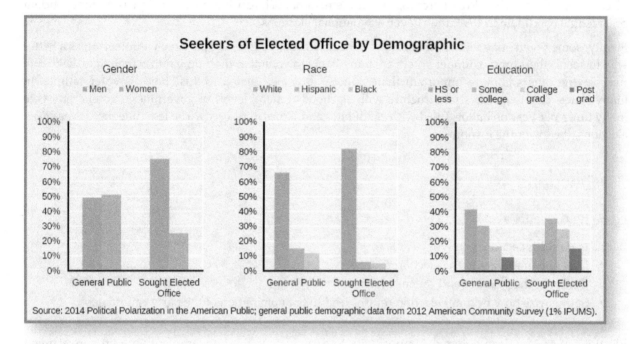

Figure 7.11   Those who seek elected office do not generally reflect the demographics of the general public: They are often disproportionately male, white, and more educated than the overall U.S. population.

Another factor for potential candidates is whether the seat they are considering is competitive or open. A *competitive seat* describes a race where a challenger runs against the **incumbent**—the current office holder. An *open seat* is one whose incumbent is not running for reelection. Incumbents who run for reelection are very likely to win for a number of reasons, which are discussed later in this chapter. In fact, in the U.S. Congress, 95 percent of representatives and 82 percent of senators were reelected in 2014.[70] But when an incumbent retires, the seat is open and more candidates will run for that seat.

Many potential candidates will also decline to run if their opponent has a lot of money in a campaign war chest. *War chests* are campaign accounts registered with the Federal Election Commission, and candidates are allowed to keep earlier donations if they intend to run for office again. Incumbents and candidates trying to move from one office to another very often have money in their war chests. Those with early money are hard to beat because they have an easier time showing they are a viable candidate (one likely to win). They can woo potential donors, which brings in more donations and strengthens the campaign. A challenger who does not have money, name recognition, or another way to appear viable will have fewer campaign donations and will be less competitive against the incumbent.

CAMPAIGN FINANCE LAWS

In the 2012 presidential election cycle, candidates for all parties raised a total of over $1.3 billion dollars for campaigns.[71] Congressional candidates running in the 2014 Senate elections raised $634 million, while candidates running for the House of Representatives raised $1.03 billion.[72] This, however, pales in comparison to the amounts raised by **political action committees (PACs)**, which are organizations created to raise and spend money to influence politics and contribute to candidates' campaigns. In the 2014 congressional elections, PACs raised over $1.7 billion to help candidates and political parties.[73] How does the government monitor the vast amounts of money that are now a part of the election process?

The history of campaign finance monitoring has its roots in a federal law written in 1867, which prohibited government employees from asking Naval Yard employees for donations.[74] In 1896, the Republican Party spent about $16 million overall, which includes William McKinley's $6–7 million campaign expenses.[75] This raised enough eyebrows that several key politicians, including Theodore Roosevelt, took note. After becoming president in 1901, Roosevelt pushed Congress to look for political corruption and influence in government and elections.[76] Shortly after, the Tillman Act (1907) was passed by Congress, which prohibited corporations from contributing money to candidates running in federal elections. Other congressional acts followed, limiting how much money individuals could contribute to candidates, how candidates could spend contributions, and what information would be disclosed to the public.[77]

While these laws intended to create transparency in campaign funding, government did not have the power to stop the high levels of money entering elections, and little was done to enforce the laws. In 1971, Congress again tried to fix the situation by passing the Federal Election Campaign Act (FECA), which outlined how candidates would report all contributions and expenditures related to their campaigns. The FECA also created rules governing the way organizations and companies could contribute to federal campaigns, which allowed for the creation of political action committees.[78] Finally, a 1974 amendment to the act created the Federal Election Commission (FEC), which operates independently of government and enforces the elections laws.

While some portions of the FECA were ruled unconstitutional by the courts in *Buckley v. Valeo* (1976), such as limits on personal spending on campaigns by candidates not using federal money, the FEC began enforcing campaign finance laws in 1976. [79] Even with the new laws and the FEC, money continued to flow into elections. By using loopholes in the laws, political parties and political action committees donated large sums of money to candidates, and new reforms were soon needed. Senators John McCain (R-AZ) and Russ Feingold (former D-WI) cosponsored the Bipartisan Campaign Reform Act of 2002 (BCRA), also referred to as the McCain–Feingold Act. McCain–Feingold restricts the amount of money given to political parties, which had become a way for companies and PACs to exert influence. It placed limits on total contributions to political parties, prohibited coordination between candidates and PAC campaigns, and required candidates to include personal endorsements on their political ads. It also limited advertisements run by unions and corporations thirty days before a primary election and sixty days before a general election.[80]

Soon after the passage of the McCain–Feingold Act, the FEC's enforcement of the law spurred court cases challenging it. The first, *McConnell v. Federal Election Commission* (2003), resulted in the Supreme Court's upholding the act's restrictions on how candidates and parties could spend campaign contributions. But later court challenges led to the removal of limits on personal spending and ended the ban on ads run by interest groups in the days leading up to an election.[81] In 2010, the Supreme Court's ruling on *Citizens United v. Federal Election Commission* led to the removal of spending limits on corporations. Justices in the majority argued that the BCRA violated a corporation's free speech rights.[82]

The court ruling also allowed corporations to place unlimited money into **super PACs**, or Independent Expenditure-Only Committees. These organizations cannot contribute directly to a candidate, nor can they strategize with a candidate's campaign. They can, however, raise and spend as much money as they please to support or attack a candidate, including running advertisements and hosting events.[83] In 2012, the super PAC "Restore Our Future" raised $153 million and spent $142 million supporting conservative candidates, including Mitt Romney. "Priorities USA Action" raised $79 million and spent $65 million supporting liberal candidates, including Barack Obama. The total expenditure by super PACs alone was $609 million in the 2012 election and $345 million in the 2014 congressional elections.[84]

Several limits on campaign contributions have been upheld by the courts and remain in place. Individuals may contribute up to $2,700 per candidate per election. This means a teacher living in Nebraska may contribute $2,700 to Bernie Sanders for his campaign to become to the Democratic presidential nominee, and if Sanders becomes the nominee, the teacher may contribute another $2,700 to his general election campaign. Individuals may also give $5,000 to political action committees and $33,400 to a national party committee. PACs that contribute to more than one candidate are permitted to contribute $5,000 per candidate per election, and up to $15,000 to a national party. PACs created to give money to only one candidate are limited to only $2,700 per candidate, however (Figure 7.12).[85] The amounts are adjusted every two years, based on inflation. These limits are intended to create a more equal playing field for the candidates, so that candidates must raise their campaign funds from a broad pool of contributors.

CONTRIBUTION LIMITS FOR 2015-2016 FEDERAL ELECTIONS					
	RECIPIENTS				
DONORS	Candidate Committee	PAC[1] (SSF and Nonconnected)	State/District/ Local Party Committee	National Party Committee	Additional National Party Committee Accounts[2]
Individual	$2,700* per election	$5,000 per year	$10,000 per year (combined)	$33,400* per year	$100,200* per account, per year
Candidate Committee	$2,000 per election	$5,000 per year	Unlimited Transfers	Unlimited Transfers	
PAC-Multicandidate	$5,000 per election	$5,000 per year	$5,000 per year (combined)	$15,000 per year	$45,000 per account, per year
PAC-Nonmulticandidate	$2,700 per election	$5,000 per year	$10,000 per year (combined)	$33,400* per year	$100,200* per account, per year
State/District/Local Party Committee	$5,000 per election	$5,000 per year	Unlimited Transfers		
National Party Committee	$5,000 per election[3]	$5,000 per year			

*- Indexed for inflation in odd-numbered years.

[1] "PAC" here refers to a committee that makes contributions to other federal political committees. Independent-expenditure-only political committees (sometimes called "super PACs") may accept unlimited contributions, including from corporations and labor organizations.

[2] The limits in this column apply to a national party committee's accounts for: (i) the presidential nominating convention; (ii) election recounts and contests and other legal proceedings; and (iii) national party headquarters buildings. A party's national committee, Senate campaign committee and House campaign committee are each considered separate national party committees with separate limits. Only a national party committee, not the parties' national congressional campaign committees, may have an account for the presidential nominating convention.

[3] Additionally, a national party committee and its Senatorial campaign committee may contribute up to $46,800 combined per campaign to each Senate candidate.

Source: Federal Election Commission. "Contribution Limits for 2015–2016 Federal Elections." June 25, 2015.

Figure 7.12

NOMINATION STAGE

Although the Constitution explains how candidates for national office are elected, it is silent on how those candidates are nominated. Political parties have taken on the role of promoting nominees for offices, such as the presidency and seats in the Senate and the House of Representatives. Because there are no national guidelines, there is much variation in the nomination process. States pass election laws and regulations, choose the selection method for party nominees, and schedule the election, but the process also greatly depends on the candidates and the political parties.

States, through their legislatures, often influence the nomination method by paying for an election to help parties identify the nominee the voters prefer. Many states fund elections because they can hold several nomination races at once. In 2012, many voters had to choose a presidential nominee, U.S. Senate nominee, House of Representatives nominee, and state-level legislature nominee for their parties.

The most common method of picking a party nominee for state, local, and presidential contests is the primary. Party members use a ballot to indicate which candidate they desire for the party nominee. Despite the ease of voting using a ballot, primary elections have a number of rules and variations that can still cause confusion for citizens. In a **closed primary**, only members of the political party selecting nominees may vote. A registered Green Party member, for example, is not allowed to vote in the Republican or Democratic primary. Parties prefer this method, because it ensures the nominee is picked by voters who legitimately support the party. An **open primary** allows all voters to vote. In this system, a Green Party member is allowed to pick either a Democratic or Republican ballot when voting.

For state-level office nominations, or the nomination of a U.S. Senator or House member, some states use the top-two primary method. A **top-two primary**, sometimes called a jungle primary, pits all candidates against each other, regardless of party affiliation. The two candidates with the most votes become the final candidates for the general election. Thus, two candidates from the same party could run against each other in the general election. In one California congressional district, for example, four Democrats and two Republicans all ran against one another in the June 2012 primary. The two Republicans received the most votes, so they ran against one another in the general election in November.[86] In 2016, thirty-four candidates filed to run to replace Senator Barbara Boxer (D-CA). In the end, two Democratic women of color emerged to compete head-to-head in the general election. California attorney general Kamala Harris eventually won the seat on Election Day, helping to quadruple the number of women of color in the U.S. Senate overnight. More often than not, however, the top-two system is used in state-level elections for non-partisan elections, in which none of the candidates are allowed to declare a political party.

In general, parties do not like nominating methods that allow non-party members to participate in the selection of party nominees. In 2000, the Supreme Court heard a case brought by the California Democratic Party, the California Republican Party, and the California Libertarian Party.[87] The parties argued that they had a right to determine who associated with the party and who participated in choosing the party nominee. The Supreme Court agreed, limiting the states' choices for nomination methods to closed and open primaries.

Despite the common use of the primary system, at least five states (Alaska, Hawaii, Idaho, Colorado, and Iowa) regularly use caucuses for presidential, state, and local-level nominations. A **caucus** is a meeting of party members in which nominees are selected informally. Caucuses are less expensive than primaries because they rely on voting methods such as dropping marbles in a jar, placing names in a hat, standing under a sign bearing the candidate's name, or taking a voice vote. Volunteers record the votes and no poll workers need to be trained or compensated. The party members at the caucus also help select **delegates**, who represent their choice at the party's state- or national-level nominating convention.

The Iowa Democratic Caucus is well-known for its spirited nature. The party's voters are asked to align themselves into preference groups, which often means standing in a room or part of a room that has been designated for the candidate of choice. The voters then get to argue and discuss the candidates, sometimes in a very animated and forceful manner. After a set time, party members are allowed to realign before the final count is taken. The caucus leader then determines how many members support each candidate, which determines how many delegates each candidate will receive.

The caucus has its proponents and opponents. Many argue that it is more interesting than the primary and brings out more sophisticated voters, who then benefit from the chance to debate the strengths and weaknesses of the candidates. The caucus system is also more transparent than ballots. The local party members get to see the election outcome and pick the delegates who will represent them at the national convention. There is less of a possibility for deception or dishonesty. Opponents point out that caucuses take two to three hours and are intimidating to less experienced voters. These factors, they argue, lead to lower voter turnout. And they have a point—voter turnout for a caucus is generally 20 percent lower than for a primary.[88]

Regardless of which nominating system the states and parties choose, states must also determine which day they wish to hold their nomination. When the nominations are for state-level office, such as governor, the state legislatures receive little to no input from the national political parties. In presidential election years, however, the national political parties pressure most states to hold their primaries or caucuses in March or later. Only Iowa, New Hampshire, and South Carolina are given express permission by the national parties to hold presidential primaries or caucuses in January or February (Figure 7.13). Both political parties protect the three states' status as the first states to host caucuses and primaries, due to tradition and the relative ease of campaigning in these smaller states.

(a)   (b)

Figure 7.13   Presidential candidates often spend a significant amount of time campaigning in states with early caucuses or primaries. In September 2015, Senator Bernie Sanders (a), a candidate for the Democratic nomination, speaks at the Amherst Democrats BBQ in Amherst, New Hampshire. In July 2015, John Ellis "Jeb" Bush (b), former Republican governor of Florida, greets the public at the Fourth of July parade in Merrimack, New Hampshire. (credit a, b: modification of work by Marc Nozell)

Other states, especially large states like California, Florida, Michigan, and Wisconsin, often are frustrated that they must wait to hold their presidential primary elections later in the season. Their frustration is reasonable: candidates who do poorly in the first few primaries often drop out entirely, leaving fewer candidates to run in caucuses and primaries held in February and later. In 2008, California, New York, and several other states disregarded the national party's guidelines and scheduled their primaries the first week of February. In response, Florida and Michigan moved their primaries to January and many other states moved forward to March. This was not the first time states participated in *frontloading* and scheduled the majority of the primaries and caucuses at the beginning of the primary season. It was, however, one of the worst occurrences. States have been frontloading since the 1976 presidential election, with the problem becoming more severe in the 1992 election and later.[89]

Political parties allot delegates to their national nominating conventions based on the number of registered party voters in each state. California, the state with the most Democrats, sent 548 delegates to the 2016 Democratic National Convention, while Wyoming, with far fewer Democrats, sent only 18 delegates. When the national political parties want to prevent states from frontloading, or doing anything else they deem detrimental, they can change the state's delegate count, which in essence increases or reduces the state's say in who becomes the presidential nominee. In 1996, the Republicans offered bonus delegates to states that held their primaries and caucuses later in the nominating season.[90] In 2008, the national parties ruled that only Iowa, South Carolina, and New Hampshire could hold primaries or caucuses in January. Both parties also reduced the number of delegates from Michigan and Florida as punishment for those states' holding early primaries.[91] Despite these efforts, candidates in 2008 had a very difficult time campaigning during the tight window caused by frontloading.

One of the criticisms of the modern nominating system is that parties today have less influence over who becomes their nominee. In the era of party "bosses," candidates who hoped to run for president needed the blessing and support of party leadership and a strong connection with the party's values. Now, anyone can run for a party's nomination. The candidates with enough money to campaign the longest, gaining media attention, momentum, and voter support are more likely to become the nominee than candidates without these attributes, regardless of what the party leadership wants.

This new reality has dramatically increased the number of politically inexperienced candidates running for national office. In 2012, for example, eleven candidates ran multistate campaigns for the Republican nomination. Dozens more had their names on one or two state ballots. With a long list of challengers, candidates must find more ways to stand out, leading them to espouse extreme positions or display high levels of charisma. Add to this that primary and caucus voters are often more extreme in their political beliefs, and it is easy to see why fewer moderates become party nominees. The 2016 primary campaign by President Donald Trump shows that grabbing the media's attention with fiery partisan rhetoric can get a campaign started strong. This does not guarantee a candidate will make it through the primaries, however.

Link to Learning

Take a look at Campaigns & Elections (https://openstax.org/l/29campaignsele) to see what hopeful candidates are reading.

CONVENTION SEASON

Once it is clear who the parties' nominees will be, presidential and gubernatorial campaigns enter a quiet period. Candidates run fewer ads and concentrate on raising funds for the fall. This is a crucial time because lack of money can harm their chances. The media spends much of the summer keeping track of the fundraising totals while the political parties plan their conventions. State parties host state-level conventions during gubernatorial elections, while national parties host national conventions during presidential election years.

Party conventions are typically held between June and September, with state-level conventions earlier in the summer and national conventions later. Conventions normally last four to five days, with days devoted to platform discussion and planning and nights reserved for speeches (Figure 7.14). Local media covers the speeches given at state-level conventions, showing speeches given by the party nominees for governor and lieutenant governor, and perhaps important guests or the state's U.S. senators. The national media covers the Democratic and Republican conventions during presidential election years, mainly showing the speeches. Some cable networks broadcast delegate voting and voting on party platforms. Members of the candidate's family and important party members generally speak during the first few days of a national convention, with the vice presidential nominee speaking on the next-to-last night and the presidential candidate on the final night. The two chosen candidates then hit the campaign trail for the general election. The party with the incumbent president holds the later convention, so in 2016, the Democrats held their convention after the Republicans.

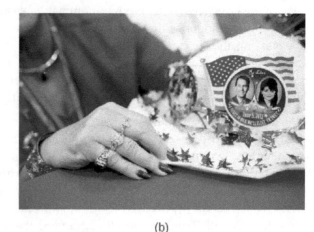

(a)   (b)

Figure 7.14 Reince Priebus, chairman of the Republican National Committee, opens the Republican National Convention in Tampa, Florida, on August 28, 2012 (a). Pageantry and symbolism, such as the flag motifs and political buttons shown on this Wisconsin attendee's hat (b), reign supreme during national conventions. (credit a, b: modification of work by Mallory Benedict/PBS NewsHour)

There are rarely surprises at the modern convention. Thanks to party rules, the nominee for each party is generally already clear. In 2008, John McCain had locked up the Republican nomination in March by having enough delegates, while in 2012, President Obama was an unchallenged incumbent and hence people knew he would be the nominee. In 2016, both apparent nominees (Democrat Hillary Clinton and Republican Donald Trump) faced primary opponents who stayed in the race even when the nominations were effectively sewn up—Democrat Bernie Sanders and Republican Ted Cruz—though no "convention surprise" took place. The naming of the vice president is generally not a surprise either. Even if a presidential nominee tries to keep it a secret, the news often leaks out before the party convention or official announcement. In 2004, the media announced John Edwards was John Kerry's running mate. The Kerry campaign had not made a formal announcement, but an amateur photographer had taken a picture of Edwards' name being added to the candidate's plane and posted it to an aviation message board.

Despite the lack of surprises, there are several reasons to host traditional conventions. First, the parties require that the delegates officially cast their ballots. Delegates from each state come to the national party convention to publicly state who their state's voters selected as the nominee.

Second, delegates will bring state-level concerns and issues to the national convention for discussion, while local-level delegates bring concerns and issues to state-level conventions. This list of issues that concern local party members, like limiting abortions in a state or removing restrictions on gun ownership, are called *planks*, and they will be discussed and voted upon by the delegates and party leadership at the convention. Just as wood planks make a platform, issues important to the party and party delegates make up the party **platform**. The parties take the cohesive list of issues and concerns and frame the election around the platform. Candidates will try to keep to the platform when campaigning, and outside groups that support them, such as super PACs, may also try to keep to these issues.

Third, conventions are covered by most news networks and cable programs. This helps the party nominee get positive attention while surrounded by loyal delegates, family members, friends, and colleagues. For presidential candidates, this positivity often leads to a bump in popularity, so the candidate gets a small increase in favorability. If a candidate does not get the bump, however, the campaign manager has to evaluate whether the candidate is connecting well with the voters or is out of step with the party faithful. In 2004, John Kerry spent the Democratic convention talking about getting U.S. troops out of the war in Iraq and increasing spending at home. Yet after his patriotic and positive convention, Gallup recorded no convention bump and the voters did not appear more likely to vote for him.

GENERAL ELECTIONS AND ELECTION DAY

The general election campaign period occurs between mid-August and early November. These elections are simpler than primaries and conventions, because there are only two major party candidates and a few minor party candidates. About 50 percent of voters will make their decisions based on party membership, so the candidates will focus on winning over independent voters and visiting states where the election is close.[92] In 2016, both candidates sensed shifts in the electorate that led them to visit states that were not recently battleground states. Clinton visited Republican stronghold Arizona as Latino voter interest surged. Defying conventional campaign movements, Trump spent many hours over the last days of the campaign in the Democratic Rust Belt states, namely Michigan and Wisconsin. President Trump ended up winning both states and industrial Pennsylvania by narrow margins, allowing him to achieve a comfortable majority in the Electoral College.

Debates are an important element of the general election season, allowing voters to see candidates answer questions on policy and prior decisions. While most voters think only of presidential debates, the general election season sees many debates. In a number of states, candidates for governor are expected to participate in televised debates, as are candidates running for the U.S. Senate. Debates not only give voters a chance to hear answers, but also to see how candidates hold up under stress. Because television and the Internet make it possible to stream footage to a wide audience, modern campaign managers understand the importance of a debate (Figure 7.15).

Figure 7.15 Sailors on the USS *McCampbell*, based out of Yokosuka, Japan, watch the first presidential debate between President Barack Obama and former Massachusetts governor Mitt Romney on October 4, 2012.

In 1960, the first televised presidential debate showed that answering questions well is not the only way to impress voters. Senator John F. Kennedy, the Democratic nominee, and Vice President Richard Nixon, the Republican nominee, prepared in slightly different ways for their first of four debates. Although both studied answers to possible questions, Kennedy also worked on the delivery of his answers, including accent, tone, facial displays, and body movements, as well as overall appearance. Nixon, however, was ill in the days before the debate and appeared sweaty and gaunt. He also chose not to wear makeup, a decision that left his pale, unshaven face vulnerable.[93] Interestingly, while people who watched the debate thought Kennedy won, those listening on radio saw the debate as more of a draw.

Insider Perspective

Inside the Debate

Debating an opponent in front of sixty million television voters is intimidating. Most presidential candidates spend days, if not weeks, preparing. Newspapers and cable news programs proclaim winners and losers, and debates can change the tide of a campaign. Yet, Paul Begala, a strategist with Bill Clinton's 1992 campaign, saw debates differently.

In one of his columns for CNN, Begala recommends that candidates relax and have a little fun. Debates are relatively easy, he says, more like a scripted program than an interview that puts candidates on the spot. They can memorize answers and deliver them convincingly, making sure they hit their mark. Second, a candidate needs a clear message explaining why the voters should pick him or her. Is he or she a needed change? Or the only experienced candidate? If the candidate's debate answers reinforce this message, the voters will remember. Third, candidates should be humorous, witty, and comfortable with their knowledge. Trying to be too formal or cramming information at the last minute will cause the candidate to be awkward or get overwhelmed. Finally, a candidate is always on camera. Making faces, sighing at an opponent, or simply making a mistake gives the media something to discuss and can cause a loss. In essence, Begala argues that if candidates wish to do well, preparation and confidence are key factors.[94]

Is Begala's advice good? Why or why not? What positives or negatives would make a candidate's debate performance stand out for you as a voter?

While debates are not just about a candidate's looks, most debate rules contain language that prevents candidates from artificially enhancing their physical qualities. For example, prior rules have prohibited shoes that increase a candidate's height, banned prosthetic devices that change a candidate's physical appearance, and limited camera angles to prevent unflattering side and back shots. Candidates and their campaign managers are aware that visuals matter.

Debates are generally over by the end of October, just in time for Election Day. Beginning with the election of 1792, presidential elections were to be held in the thirty-four days prior to the "first Wednesday in December."[95] In 1845, Congress passed legislation that moved the presidential Election Day to the first Tuesday after the first Monday in November, and in 1872, elections for the House of Representatives were also moved to that same Tuesday.[96] The United States was then an agricultural country, and because a number of states restricted voting to property-owning males over twenty-one, farmers made up nearly 74 percent of voters.[97] The tradition of Election Day to fall in November allowed time for the lucrative fall harvest to be brought in and the farming season to end. And, while not all members of government were of the same religion, many wanted to ensure that voters were not kept from the polls by a weekend religious observance. Finally, business and mercantile concerns often closed their books on the first of the month. Rather than let accounting get in the way of voting, the bill's language forces Election Day to fall between the second and eighth of the month.

THE ELECTORAL COLLEGE

Once the voters have cast ballots in November and all the election season madness comes to a close, races for governors and local representatives may be over, but the constitutional process of electing a president has only begun. The electors of the **Electoral College** travel to their respective state capitols and cast their votes in mid-December, often by signing a certificate recording their vote. In most cases, electors cast their ballots for the candidate who won the majority of votes in their state. The states then forward the certificates to the U.S. Senate.

The number of Electoral College votes granted to each state equals the total number of representatives and senators that state has in the U.S. Congress or, in the case of Washington, DC, as many electors as it would have if it were a state. The number of representatives may fluctuate based on state population, which is determined every ten years by the U.S. Census, mandated by Article I, Section 2, of the Constitution. For the 2016 and 2020 presidential elections, there are a total of 538 electors in the Electoral College, and a majority of 270 electoral votes is required to win the presidency.

Once the electoral votes have been read by the president of the Senate (i.e., the vice president of the United States) during a special joint session of Congress in January, the presidential candidate who received the majority of electoral votes is officially named president. Should a tie occur, the sitting House of Representatives elects the president, with each state receiving one vote. While this rarely occurs, both the 1800 and the 1824 elections were decided by the House of Representatives. As election night 2016 played out after the polls closed, one such scenario was in play for a tie. However, the states that Hillary Clinton needed to make that tie were lost narrowly to Trump. Had the tie occurred, the Republican House would have likely selected Trump as president anyway.

As political parties became stronger and the Progressive Era's influence shaped politics from the 1890s to the 1920s, states began to allow state parties rather than legislators to nominate a slate of electors. Electors cannot be elected officials nor can they work for the federal government. Since the Republican and Democratic parties choose faithful party members who have worked hard for their candidates, the modern system decreases the chance they will vote differently from the state's voters.

There is no guarantee of this, however. Occasionally there are examples of *faithless electors*. In 2000, the majority of the District of Columbia's voters cast ballots for Al Gore, and all three electoral votes should have been cast for him. Yet one of the electors cast a blank ballot, denying Gore a precious electoral vote, reportedly to contest the unequal representation of the District in the Electoral College. In 2004, one of the Minnesota electors voted for John Edwards, the vice presidential nominee, to be president (Figure 7.16) and misspelled the candidate's last name in the process. Some believe this was a result of confusion rather than a political statement. In the 2016 election, after a campaign to encourage faithless electors in the wake of what some viewed as controversial results, there were seven faithless electors: four in the state of Washington, two in Texas, and one in Hawaii. The electors' names and votes are publicly available on the electoral certificates, which are scanned and documented by the National Archives and easily available for viewing online.

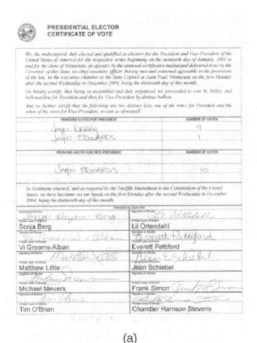

(a)   (b)

Figure 7.16 In 2004, Minnesota had an error or faithless voter when one elector cast a vote for John Edwards for president (a). On July 8, 2004, presidential candidate John Kerry and his running mate John Edwards arrive for a campaign rally in Fort Lauderdale, Florida (b). (credit b: modification of work by Richard Block)

In forty-eight states and the District of Columbia, the candidate who wins the most votes in November receives all the state's electoral votes, and only the electors from that party will vote. This is often called the **winner-take-all system**. In two states, Nebraska and Maine, the electoral votes are divided. The candidate who wins the state gets two electoral votes, but the winner of each congressional district also receives an electoral vote. In 2008, for example, Republican John McCain won two congressional districts and the majority of the voters across the state of Nebraska, earning him four electoral votes from Nebraska. Obama won in one congressional district and earned one electoral vote from Nebraska.[98] In 2016, Republican Donald Trump won one congressional district in Maine, even though Hillary Clinton won the state overall. This Electoral College voting method is referred to as the **district system**.

MIDTERM ELECTIONS

Presidential elections garner the most attention from the media and political elites. Yet they are not the only important elections. The even-numbered years between presidential years, like 2014 and 2018, are reserved for congressional elections—sometimes referred to as **midterm elections** because they are in the middle of the president's term. Midterm elections are held because all members of the House of Representatives and one-third of the senators come up for reelection every two years.

During a presidential election year, members of Congress often experience the **coattail effect**, which gives members of a popular presidential candidate's party an increase in popularity and raises their odds of retaining office. During a midterm election year, however, the president's party often is blamed for the president's actions or inaction. Representatives and senators from the sitting president's party are more likely to lose their seats during a midterm election year. Many recent congressional realignments, in which the House or Senate changed from Democratic to Republican control, occurred because of this reverse-coattail effect during midterm elections. The most recent example is the 2010 election, in which control of the House returned to the Republican Party after two years of a Democratic presidency.

7.4 Campaigns and Voting

Learning Objectives

By the end of this section, you will be able to:
- Compare campaign methods for elections
- Identify strategies campaign managers use to reach voters
- Analyze the factors that typically affect a voter's decision

Campaign managers know that to win an election, they must do two things: reach voters with their candidate's information and get voters to show up at the polls. To accomplish these goals, candidates and their campaigns will often try to target those most likely to vote. Unfortunately, these voters change from election to election and sometimes from year to year. Primary and caucus voters are different from voters who vote only during presidential general elections. Some years see an increase in younger voters turning out to vote. Elections are unpredictable, and campaigns must adapt to be effective.

FUNDRAISING

Even with a carefully planned and orchestrated presidential run, early fundraising is vital for candidates. Money helps them win, and the ability to raise money identifies those who are viable. In fact, the more money a candidate raises, the more he or she will continue to raise. EMILY's List, a political action group, was founded on this principle; its name is an acronym for "Early Money Is Like Yeast" (it makes the dough rise). This group helps progressive women candidates gain early campaign contributions, which in turn helps them get further donations (Figure 7.17).

(a)   (b)

Figure 7.17 EMILY's List candidates include members of Congress, such as Tammy Duckworth (D-IL) (a), and governors, such as Maggie Hassan (b) of New Hampshire, who both ran for U.S. Senate, and won, in 2016. (credit b: modification of work by Roger H. Goun)

Early in the 2016 election season, several candidates had fundraised well ahead of their opponents. Hillary Clinton, Jeb Bush, and Ted Cruz were the top fundraisers by July 2015. Clinton reported $47 million, Cruz with $14 million, and Bush with $11 million in contributions. In comparison, Bobby Jindal and George Pataki (who both dropped out relatively early) each reported less than $1 million in contributions during the same period. Bush later reported over $100 million in contributions, while the other Republican candidates continued to report lower contributions. Media stories about Bush's fundraising discussed his powerful financial networking, while coverage of the other candidates focused on their lack of money. Donald Trump, the eventual Republican nominee and president, showed a comparatively low fundraising amount in the primary phase as he enjoyed much free press coverage because of his notoriety. He also flirted with the idea of being an entirely self-funded candidate.

COMPARING PRIMARY AND GENERAL CAMPAIGNS

Although candidates have the same goal for primary and general elections, which is to win, these elections are very different from each other and require a very different set of strategies. Primary elections are more difficult for the voter. There are more candidates vying to become their party's nominee, and party identification is not a useful cue because each party has many candidates rather than just one. In the 2016 presidential election, Republican voters in the early primaries were presented with a number of options, including Mike Huckabee, Donald Trump, Jeb Bush, Ted Cruz, Marco Rubio, John Kasich, Chris Christie, Carly Fiorina, Ben Carson, and more. (Huckabee, Christie, and Fiorina dropped out relatively early.) Democrats had to decide between Hillary Clinton, Bernie Sanders, and Martin O'Malley (who soon dropped out). Voters must find more information about each candidate to decide which is closest to their preferred issue positions. Due to time limitations, voters may not research all the candidates. Nor will all the candidates get enough media or debate time to reach the voters. These issues make campaigning in a primary election difficult, so campaign managers tailor their strategy.

First, name recognition is extremely important. Voters are unlikely to cast a vote for an unknown. Some candidates, like Hillary Clinton and Jeb Bush, have held or are related to someone who held national office, but most candidates will be governors, senators, or local politicians who are less well-known nationally. Barack Obama was a junior senator from Illinois and Bill Clinton was a governor from Arkansas prior to running for president. Voters across the country had little information about them, and both candidates needed media time to become known. While well-known candidates have longer records that can be attacked by the opposition, they also have an easier time raising campaign funds because their odds of winning are better. Newer candidates face the challenge of proving themselves during the short primary season and are more likely to lose. In 2016, both eventual party nominees had massive name recognition. Hillary Clinton enjoyed notoriety from having been First Lady, a U.S. senator from New York, and secretary of state. Donald Trump had name recognition from being an iconic real estate tycoon with Trump buildings all over the world plus a reality TV star via shows like *The Apprentice*. With Arnold Schwarzenegger having successfully campaigned for California governor, perhaps it should not have surprised the country when Trump was elected president.

Second, visibility is crucial when a candidate is one in a long parade of faces. Given that voters will want to find quick, useful information about each, candidates will try to get the media's attention and pick up momentum. Media attention is especially important for newer candidates. Most voters assume a candidate's website and other campaign material will be skewed, showing only the most positive information. The media, on the other hand, are generally considered more reliable and unbiased than a candidate's campaign materials, so voters turn to news networks and journalists to pick up information about the candidates' histories and issue positions. Candidates are aware of voters' preference for quick information and news and try to get interviews or news coverage for themselves. Candidates also benefit from news coverage that is longer and cheaper than campaign ads.

For all these reasons, campaign ads in primary elections rarely mention political parties and instead focus on issue positions or name recognition. Many of the best primary ads help the voters identify issue positions they have in common with the candidate. In 2008, for example, Hillary Clinton ran a holiday ad in which she was seen wrapping presents. Each present had a card with an issue position listed, such as "bring back the troops" or "universal pre-kindergarten." In a similar, more humorous vein, Mike Huckabee gained name recognition and issue placement with his 2008 primary ad. The "HuckChuck" spot had Chuck Norris repeat Huckabee's name several times while listing the candidate's issue positions. Norris's line, "Mike Huckabee wants to put the IRS out of business," was one of many statements that repeatedly used Huckabee's name, increasing voters' recognition of it (Figure 7.18). While neither of these candidates won the nomination, the ads were viewed by millions and were successful as primary ads.

Figure 7.18   In February 2008, Chuck Norris speaks at a rally for Mike Huckabee in College Station, Texas. (credit: modification of work by "ensign_beedrill"/Flickr)

By the general election, each party has only one candidate, and campaign ads must accomplish a different goal with different voters. Because most party-affiliated voters will cast a ballot for their party's candidate, the campaigns must try to reach the independent and undecided, as well as try to convince their party members to get out and vote. Some ads will focus on issue and policy positions, comparing the two main party candidates. Other ads will remind party loyalists why it is important to vote. President Lyndon B. Johnson used the infamous "Daisy Girl" ad, which cut from a little girl counting daisy petals to an atomic bomb being dropped, to explain why voters needed to turn out and vote for him. If the voters stayed home, Johnson implied, his opponent, Republican Barry Goldwater, might start an atomic war. The ad aired once as a paid ad on NBC before it was pulled, but the footage appeared on other news stations as newscasters discussed the controversy over it.[99] More recently, Mitt Romney used the economy to remind moderates and independents in 2012 that household incomes had dropped and the national debt increased. The ad's goal was to reach voters who had not already decided on a candidate and would use the economy as a primary deciding factor.

Part of the reason Johnson's campaign ad worked is that more voters turn out for a general election than for other elections. These additional voters are often less ideological and more independent, making them harder to target but possible to win over. They are also less likely to complete a lot of research on the candidates, so campaigns often try to create emotion-based negative ads. While negative ads may decrease voter turnout by making voters more cynical about politics and the election, voters watch and remember them.[100]

Another source of negative ads is from groups outside the campaigns. Sometimes, **shadow campaigns**, run by political action committees and other organizations without the coordination or guidance of candidates, also use negative ads to reach voters. Even before the *Citizens United* decision allowed corporations and interest groups to run ads supporting candidates, shadow campaigns existed. In 2004, the Swift Boat Veterans for Truth organization ran ads attacking John Kerry's military service record, and MoveOn attacked George W. Bush's decision to commit to the wars in Afghanistan and Iraq. In 2014, super PACs poured more than $300 million into supporting candidates.[101]

Link to Learning

Want to know how much money federal candidates and PACs are raising? Visit the Campaign Finance Disclosure Portal at the Federal Election Commission (https://openstax.org/l/29fedelecomm) website.

General campaigns also try to get voters to the polls in closely contested states. In 2004, realizing that it would be difficult to convince Ohio Democrats to vote Republican, George W. Bush's campaign focused on getting the state's Republican voters to the polls. The volunteers walked through precincts and knocked on Republican doors to raise interest in Bush and the election. Volunteers also called Republican and former Republican households to remind them when and where to vote.[102] The strategy worked, and it reminded future campaigns that an organized effort to get out the vote is still a viable way to win an election.

TECHNOLOGY

Campaigns have always been expensive. Also, they have sometimes been negative and nasty. The 1828 "Coffin Handbill" that John Quincy Adams ran, for instance, listed the names and circumstances of the executions his opponent Andrew Jackson had ordered (Figure 7.19). This was in addition to gossip and verbal attacks against Jackson's wife, who had accidentally committed bigamy when she married him without a proper divorce. Campaigns and candidates have not become more amicable in the years since then.

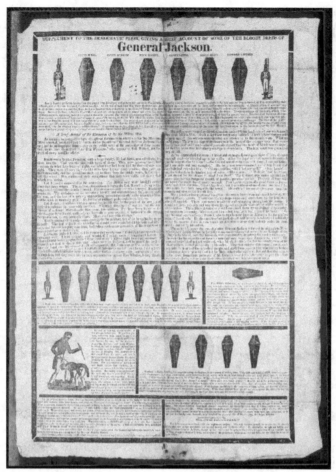

Figure 7.19   The infamous "Coffin Handbill" used by John Quincy Adams against Andrew Jackson in the 1828 presidential election.

Once television became a fixture in homes, campaign advertising moved to the airwaves. Television allowed candidates to connect with the voters through video, allowing them to appeal directly to and connect emotionally with voters. While Adlai Stevenson and Dwight D. Eisenhower were the first to use television in their 1952 and 1956 campaigns, the ads were more like jingles with images. Stevenson's "Let's Not Forget the Farmer" ad had a catchy tune, but its animated images were not serious and contributed little to the message. The "Eisenhower Answers America" spots allowed Eisenhower to answer policy questions, but his answers were glib rather than helpful.

John Kennedy's campaign was the first to use images to show voters that the candidate was the choice for everyone. His ad, "Kennedy," combined the jingle "Kennedy for me" and photographs of a diverse population dealing with life in the United States.

Link to Learning

The Museum of the Moving Image (https://openstax.org/l/29livinroomcan) has collected presidential campaign ads from 1952 through today, including the "Kennedy for Me" spot mentioned above. Take a look and see how candidates have created ads to get the voters' attention and votes over time.

Over time, however, ads became more negative and manipulative. In reaction, the Bipartisan Campaign

Reform Act of 2002, or McCain–Feingold, included a requirement that candidates stand by their ad and include a recorded statement within the ad stating that they approved the message. Although ads, especially those run by super PACs, continue to be negative, candidates can no longer dodge responsibility for them.

Candidates are also frequently using interviews on late night television to get messages out. Soft news, or infotainment, is a new type of news that combines entertainment and information. Shows like *The Daily Show* and *Last Week Tonight* make the news humorous or satirical while helping viewers become more educated about the events around the nation and the world.[103] In 2008, Huckabee, Obama, and McCain visited popular programs like *The Daily Show*, *The Colbert Report*, and *Late Night with Conan O'Brien* to target informed voters in the under-45 age bracket. The candidates were able to show their funny sides and appear like average Americans, while talking a bit about their policy preferences. By fall of 2015, *The Late Show with Stephen Colbert* had already interviewed most of the potential presidential candidates, including Hillary Clinton, Bernie Sanders, Jeb Bush, Ted Cruz, and Donald Trump.

The Internet has given candidates a new platform and a new way to target voters. In the 2000 election, campaigns moved online and created websites to distribute information. They also began using search engine results to target voters with ads. In 2004, Democratic candidate Howard Dean used the Internet to reach out to potential donors. Rather than host expensive dinners to raise funds, his campaign posted footage on his website of the candidate eating a turkey sandwich. The gimmick brought over $200,000 in campaign donations and reiterated Dean's commitment to be a down-to-earth candidate. Candidates also use social media, such as Facebook, Twitter, and YouTube, to interact with supporters and get the attention of younger voters.

VOTER DECISION MAKING

When citizens do vote, how do they make their decisions? The election environment is complex and most voters don't have time to research everything about the candidates and issues. Yet they will need to make a fully rational assessment of the choices for an elected office. To meet this goal, they tend to take shortcuts.

One popular shortcut is simply to vote using party affiliation. Many political scientists consider party-line voting to be rational behavior because citizens register for parties based upon either position preference or socialization. Similarly, candidates align with parties based upon their issue positions. A Democrat who votes for a Democrat is very likely selecting the candidate closest to his or her personal ideology. While party identification is a voting cue, it also makes for a logical decision.

Citizens also use party identification to make decisions via **straight-ticket voting**—choosing every Republican or Democratic Party member on the ballot. In some states, such as Texas or Michigan, selecting one box at the top of the ballot gives a single party all the votes on the ballot (Figure 7.20). Straight-ticket voting does cause problems in states that include non-partisan positions on the ballot. In Michigan, for example, the top of the ballot (presidential, gubernatorial, senatorial and representative seats) will be partisan, and a straight-ticket vote will give a vote to all the candidates in the selected party. But the middle or bottom of the ballot includes seats for local offices or judicial seats, which are non-partisan. These offices would receive no vote, because the straight-ticket votes go only to partisan seats. In 2010, actors from the former political drama *The West Wing* came together to create an advertisement for Mary McCormack's sister Bridget, who was running for a non-partisan seat on the Michigan Supreme Court. The ad reminded straight-ticket voters to cast a ballot for the court seats as well; otherwise, they would miss an important election. McCormack won the seat.

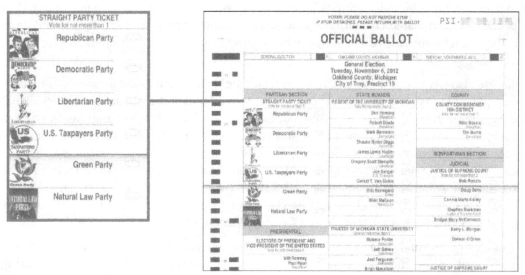

Figure 7.20 Voters in Michigan can use straight-ticket voting. To fill out their ballot, they select one box at the top to give a single party all the votes on the ballot.

Straight-ticket voting does have the advantage of reducing **ballot fatigue**. Ballot fatigue occurs when someone votes only for the top or important ballot positions, such as president or governor, and stops voting rather than continue to the bottom of a long ballot. In 2012, for example, 70 percent of registered voters in Colorado cast a ballot for the presidential seat, yet only 54 percent voted yes or no on retaining Nathan B. Coats for the state supreme court.[104]

Voters make decisions based upon candidates' physical characteristics, such as attractiveness or facial features.[105] They may also vote based on gender or race, because they assume the elected official will make policy decisions based on a demographic shared with the voters. Candidates are very aware of voters' focus on these non-political traits. In 2008, a sizable portion of the electorate wanted to vote for either Hillary Clinton or Barack Obama because they offered new demographics—either the first woman or the first black president. Demographics hurt John McCain that year, because many people believed that at 71 he was too old to be president.[106] Hillary Clinton faced this situation again in 2016 as she became the first female nominee from a major party. In essence, attractiveness can make a candidate appear more competent, which in turn can help him or her ultimately win.[107]

Aside from party identification and demographics, voters will also look at issues or the economy when making a decision. For some single-issue voters, a candidate's stance on abortion rights will be a major factor, while other voters may look at the candidates' beliefs on the Second Amendment and gun control. Single-issue voting may not require much more effort by the voter than simply using party identification; however, many voters are likely to seek out a candidate's position on a multitude of issues before making a decision. They will use the information they find in several ways.

Retrospective voting occurs when the voter looks at the candidate's past actions and the past economic climate and makes a decision only using these factors. This behavior may occur during economic downturns or after political scandals, when voters hold politicians accountable and do not wish to give the representative a second chance. *Pocketbook voting* occurs when the voter looks at his or her personal finances and circumstances to decide how to vote. Someone having a harder time finding employment or seeing investments suffer during a particular candidate or party's control of government will vote for a different candidate or party than the incumbent. *Prospective voting* occurs when the voter applies information about a candidate's past behavior to decide how the candidate will act in the future. For example, will the candidate's voting record or actions help the economy and better prepare him or her to be president during an economic downturn? The challenge of this voting method is that the voters must use a lot of information, which might be conflicting or unrelated, to make an educated guess about how the candidate will perform in the future. Voters do appear to rely on prospective and retrospective voting more often than on pocketbook voting.

In some cases, a voter may cast a ballot strategically. In these cases, a person may vote for a second- or third-choice candidate, either because his or her preferred candidate cannot win or in the hope of preventing another candidate from winning. This type of voting is likely to happen when there are multiple candidates for one position or multiple parties running for one seat.[108] In Florida and Oregon, for example, Green Party voters (who tend to be liberal) may choose to vote for a Democrat if the Democrat might otherwise lose to a Republican. Similarly, in Georgia, while a Libertarian may be the preferred candidate, the voter would rather have the Republican candidate win over the Democrat and will vote accordingly.[109]

One other way voters make decisions is through incumbency. In essence, this is retrospective voting, but it requires little of the voter. In congressional and local elections, incumbents win reelection up to 90 percent of the time, a result called the **incumbency advantage**. What contributes to this advantage and often persuades competent challengers not to run? First, incumbents have name recognition and voting records. The media is more likely to interview them because they have advertised their name over several elections and have voted on legislation affecting the state or district. Incumbents also have won election before, which increases the odds that political action committees and interest groups will give them money; most interest groups will not give money to a candidate destined to lose.

Incumbents also have franking privileges, which allows them a limited amount of free mail to communicate with the voters in their district. While these mailings may not be sent in the days leading up to an election—sixty days for a senator and ninety days for a House member—congressional representatives are able to build a free relationship with voters through them.[110] Moreover, incumbents have exiting campaign organizations, while challengers must build new organizations from the ground up. Lastly, incumbents have more money in their war chests than most challengers.

Another incumbent advantage is gerrymandering, the drawing of district lines to guarantee a desired electoral outcome. Every ten years, following the U.S. Census, the number of House of Representatives members allotted to each state is determined based on a state's population. If a state gains or loses seats in the House, the state must redraw districts to ensure each district has an equal number of citizens. States may also choose to redraw these districts at other times and for other reasons.[111] If the district is drawn to ensure that it includes a majority of Democratic or Republican Party members within its boundaries, for instance, then candidates from those parties will have an advantage.

Gerrymandering helps local legislative candidates and members of the House of Representatives, who win reelection over 90 percent of the time. Senators and presidents do not benefit from gerrymandering because they are not running in a district. Presidents and senators win states, so they benefit only from war chests and name recognition. This is one reason why senators running in 2014, for example, won reelection only 82 percent of the time.[112]

Link to Learning

Since 1960, the American National Election Studies (https://openstax.org/l/29amnatelestu) has been asking a random sample of voters a battery of questions about how they voted. The data are available at the Inter-university Consortium for Political and Social Research at the University of Michigan.

7.5 Direct Democracy

By the end of this section, you will be able to:

- Identify the different forms of and reasons for direct democracy
- Summarize the steps needed to place initiatives on a ballot
- Explain why some policies are made by elected representatives and others by voters

The majority of elections in the United States are held to facilitate indirect democracy. Elections allow the people to pick representatives to serve in government and make decisions on the citizens' behalf. Representatives pass laws, implement taxes, and carry out decisions. Although direct democracy had been used in some of the colonies, the framers of the Constitution granted voters no legislative or executive powers, because they feared the masses would make poor decisions and be susceptible to whims. During the Progressive Era, however, governments began granting citizens more direct political power. States that formed and joined the United States after the Civil War often assigned their citizens some methods of directly implementing laws or removing corrupt politicians. Citizens now use these powers at the ballot to change laws and direct public policy in their states.

DIRECT DEMOCRACY DEFINED

Direct democracy occurs when policy questions go directly to the voters for a decision. These decisions include funding, budgets, candidate removal, candidate approval, policy changes, and constitutional amendments. Not all states allow direct democracy, nor does the United States government.

Direct democracy takes many forms. It may occur locally or statewide. Local direct democracy allows citizens to propose and pass laws that affect local towns or counties. Towns in Massachusetts, for example, may choose to use town meetings, which is a meeting comprised of the town's eligible voters, to make decisions on budgets, salaries, and local laws.[113]

> ### Link to Learning
>
> To learn more about what type of direct democracy is practiced in your state, visit the University of Southern California's Initiative & Referendum Institute (https://openstax.org/l/29inirefinst) . This site also allows you to look up initiatives and measures that have appeared on state ballots.

Statewide direct democracy allows citizens to propose and pass laws that affect state constitutions, state budgets, and more. Most states in the western half of the country allow citizens all forms of direct democracy, while most states on the eastern and southern regions allow few or none of these forms (Figure 7.21). States that joined the United States after the Civil War are more likely to have direct democracy, possibly due to the influence of Progressives during the late 1800s and early 1900s. Progressives believed citizens should be more active in government and democracy, a hallmark of direct democracy.

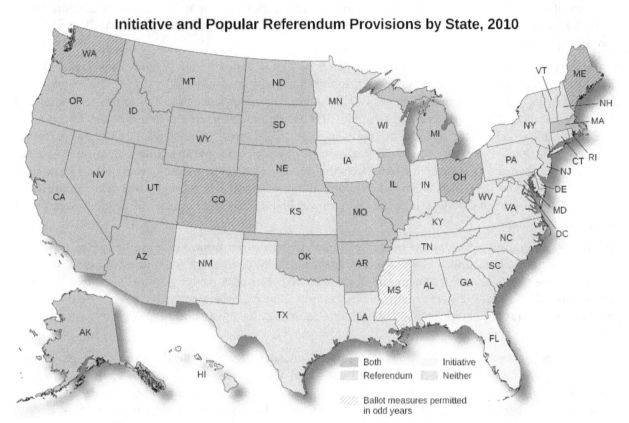

Figure 7.21 This map shows which states allow citizens to place laws and amendments on the ballot for voter approval or repeal.

There are three forms of direct democracy used in the United States. A **referendum** asks citizens to confirm or repeal a decision made by the government. A legislative referendum occurs when a legislature passes a law or a series of constitutional amendments and presents them to the voters to ratify with a yes or no vote. A judicial appointment to a state supreme court may require voters to confirm whether the judge should remain on the bench. Popular referendums occur when citizens petition to place a referendum on a ballot to repeal legislation enacted by their state government. This form of direct democracy gives citizens a limited amount of power, but it does not allow them to overhaul policy or circumvent the government.

The most common form of direct democracy is the **initiative**, or proposition. An initiative is normally a law or constitutional amendment proposed and passed by the citizens of a state. Initiatives completely bypass the legislatures and governor, but they are subject to review by the state courts if they are not consistent with the state or national constitution. The process to pass an initiative is not easy and varies from state to state. Most states require that a petitioner or the organizers supporting an initiative file paperwork with the state and include the proposed text of the initiative. This allows the state or local office to determine whether the measure is legal, as well as estimate the cost of implementing it. This approval may come at the beginning of the process or after organizers have collected signatures. The initiative may be reviewed by the state attorney general, as in Oregon's procedures, or by another state official or office. In Utah, the lieutenant governor reviews measures to ensure they are constitutional.

Next, organizers gather registered voters' signatures on a petition. The number of signatures required is often a percentage of the number of votes from a past election. In California, for example, the required numbers are 5 percent (law) and 8 percent (amendment) of the votes in the last gubernatorial election. This means through 2018, it will take 365,880 signatures to place a law on the ballot and 585,407 to place a constitutional amendment on the ballot.[114]

Once the petition has enough signatures from registered voters, it is approved by a state agency or the secretary of state for placement on the ballot. Signatures are verified by the state or a county elections office to ensure the signatures are valid. If the petition is approved, the initiative is then placed on the next ballot, and the organization campaigns to voters.

While the process is relatively clear, each step can take a lot of time and effort. First, most states place a time limit on the signature collection period. Organizations may have only 150 days to collect signatures, as in California, or as long as two years, as in Arizona. For larger states, the time limit may pose a dilemma if the organization is trying to collect more than 500,000 signatures from registered voters. Second, the state may limit who may circulate the petition and collect signatures. Some states, like Colorado, restrict what a signature collector may earn, while Oregon bans payments to signature-collecting groups. And the minimum number of signatures required affects the number of ballot measures. Arizona had more than sixty ballot measures on the 2000 general election ballot, because the state requires so few signatures to get an initiative on the ballot. Oklahomans see far fewer ballot measures because the number of required signatures is higher.

Another consideration is that, as we've seen, voters in primaries are more ideological and more likely to research the issues. Measures that are complex or require a lot of research, such as a lend-lease bond or changes in the state's eminent-domain language, may do better on a primary ballot. Measures that deal with social policy, such as laws preventing animal cruelty, may do better on a general election ballot, when more of the general population comes out to vote. Proponents for the amendments or laws will take this into consideration as they plan.

Finally, the **recall** is one of the more unusual forms of direct democracy; it allows voters to decide whether to remove a government official from office. All states have ways to remove officials, but removal by voters is less common. The recall of California Governor Gray Davis in 2003 and his replacement by Arnold Schwarzenegger is perhaps one of the more famous such recalls. The recent attempt by voters in Wisconsin to recall Governor Scott Walker show how contentious and expensive a recall can be. Walker spent over $60 million in the election to retain his seat.[115]

POLICYMAKING THROUGH DIRECT DEMOCRACY

Politicians are often unwilling to wade into highly political waters if they fear it will harm their chances for reelection. When a legislature refuses to act or change current policy, initiatives allow citizens to take part in the policy process and end the impasse. In Colorado, Amendment 64 allowed the recreational use of marijuana by adults, despite concerns that state law would then conflict with national law. Colorado and Washington's legalization of recreational marijuana use started a trend, leading to more states adopting similar laws.

Finding a Middle Ground

Too Much Democracy?

How much direct democracy is too much? When citizens want one policy direction and government prefers another, who should prevail?

Consider recent laws and decisions about marijuana. California was the first state to allow the use of medical marijuana, after the passage of Proposition 215 in 1996. Just a few years later, however, in *Gonzales v. Raich* (2005), the Supreme Court ruled that the U.S. government had the authority to criminalize the use of marijuana. In 2009, Attorney General Eric Holder said the federal government would not seek to prosecute patients using marijuana medically, citing limited resources and other priorities. Perhaps emboldened by the national government's stance, Colorado voters approved recreational marijuana use in 2012. Since then, other states have followed. Twenty-three states and the District of Columbia now have laws in place that legalize the use of marijuana to varying degrees. In a number of these cases, the decision was made by voters through initiatives and direct democracy (Figure 7.22).

Figure 7.22   Caption: In 2014, Florida voters considered a proposed amendment to the Florida constitution that would allow doctors to recommend the use of marijuana for patient use. The ballot initiative received 58 percent of the vote, just short of the 60 percent required to pass in Florida.

So where is the problem? First, while citizens of these states believe smoking or consuming marijuana should be legal, the U.S. government does not. The Controlled Substances Act (CSA), passed by Congress in 1970, declares marijuana a dangerous drug and makes its sale a prosecutable act. And despite Holder's statement, a 2013 memo by James Cole, the deputy attorney general, reminded states that marijuana use is still illegal.[116] But the federal government cannot enforce the CSA on its own; it relies on the states' help. And while Congress has decided not to prosecute patients using marijuana for medical reasons, it has not waived the Justice Department's right to prosecute recreational use.[117]

Direct democracy has placed the states and its citizens in an interesting position. States have a legal obligation to enforce state laws and the state constitution, yet they also must follow the laws of the United States. Citizens who use marijuana legally in their state are not using it legally in their country. This leads many to question whether direct democracy gives citizens too much power.

Is it a good idea to give citizens the power to pass laws? Or should this power be subjected to checks and balances, as legislative bills are? Why or why not?

Direct democracy has drawbacks, however. One is that it requires more of voters. Instead of voting based on party, the voter is expected to read and become informed to make smart decisions. Initiatives can fundamentally change a constitution or raise taxes. Recalls remove politicians from office. These are not small decisions. Most citizens, however, do not have the time to perform a lot of research before voting. Given the high number of measures on some ballots, this may explain why many citizens simply skip ballot measures they do not understand. Direct democracy ballot items regularly earn fewer votes than the choice of a governor or president.

When citizens rely on television ads, initiative titles, or advice from others in determining how to vote, they can become confused and make the wrong decisions. In 2008, Californians voted on Proposition 8, titled "Eliminates Rights of Same-Sex Couples to Marry." A yes vote meant a voter wanted to define marriage as only between a woman and man. Even though the information was clear and the law was one of the shortest in memory, many voters were confused. Some thought of the amendment as the same-sex marriage amendment. In short, some people voted *for* the initiative because they thought they were voting *for* same-sex marriage. Others voted against it because they were against same-sex marriage.[118]

Direct democracy also opens the door to special interests funding personal projects. Any group can create an organization to spearhead an initiative or referendum. And because the cost of collecting signatures can be high in many states, signature collection may be backed by interest groups or wealthy individuals wishing to use the initiative to pass pet projects. The 2003 recall of California governor Gray Davis faced difficulties during the signature collection phase, but $2 million in donations by Representative Darrell Issa (R-CA) helped the organization attain nearly one million signatures.[119] Many commentators argued that this example showed direct democracy is not always a process by the people, but rather a process used by the wealthy and business.

Key Terms

ballot fatigue the result when a voter stops voting for offices and initiatives at the bottom of a long ballot

caucus a form of candidate nomination that occurs in a town-hall style format rather than a day-long election; usually reserved for presidential elections

chronic minority voters who belong to political parties that tend not to be competitive in national elections because they are too small to become a majority or because of the Electoral College system distribution in their state

closed primary an election in which only voters registered with a party may vote for that party's candidates

coattail effect the result when a popular presidential candidate helps candidates from his or her party win their own elections

delegates party members who are chosen to represent a particular candidate at the party's state- or national-level nominating convention

district system the means by which electoral votes are divided between candidates based on who wins districts and/or the state

early voting an accommodation that allows voting up to two weeks before Election Day

Electoral College the constitutionally created group of individuals, chosen by the states, with the responsibility of formally selecting the next U.S. president

incumbency advantage the advantage held by officeholders that allows them to often win reelection

incumbent the current holder of a political office

initiative law or constitutional amendment proposed and passed by the voters and subject to review by the state courts; also called a proposition

midterm elections the congressional elections that occur in the even-numbered years between presidential election years, in the middle of the president's term

open primary an election in which any registered voter may vote in any party's primary or caucus

platform the set of issues important to the political party and the party delegates

political action committees (PACs) organizations created to raise money for political campaigns and spend money to influence policy and politics

recall the removal of a politician or government official by the voters

referendum a yes or no vote by citizens on a law or candidate proposed by the state government

residency requirement the stipulation that citizen must live in a state for a determined period of time before a citizen can register to vote as a resident of that state

shadow campaign a campaign run by political action committees and other organizations without the coordination of the candidate

straight-ticket voting the practice of voting only for candidates from the same party

super PACs officially known as Independent Expenditure-Only Committees; organizations that can fundraise and spend as they please to support or attack a candidate but not contribute directly to a candidate or strategize with a candidate's campaign

top-two primary a primary election in which the two candidates with the most votes, regardless of party, become the nominees for the general election

voter fatigue the result when voters grow tired of voting and stay home from the polls

voting-age population the number of citizens over eighteen

voting-eligible population the number of citizens eligible to vote

winner-take-all system all electoral votes for a state are given to the candidate who wins the most votes in that state

Summary

7.1 Voter Registration
Voter registration varies from state to state, depending on local culture and concerns. In an attempt to stop the disenfranchisement of black voters, Congress passed the Voting Rights Act (1965), which prohibited states from denying voting rights based on race, and the Supreme Court determined grandfather clauses and other restrictions were unconstitutional. Some states only require that a citizen be over eighteen and reside in the state. Others include additional requirements. Some states require registration to occur thirty days prior to an election, and some allow voters to register the same day as the election.

Following the passage of the Help America Vote Act (2002), states are required to maintain accurate voter registration rolls and are working harder to register citizens and update records. Registering has become easier over the years; the National Voter Registration Act (1993) requires states to add voter registration to government applications, while an increasing number of states are implementing novel approaches such as online voter registration and automatic registration.

7.2 Voter Turnout
Some believe a healthy democracy needs many participating citizens, while others argue that only informed citizens should vote. When turnout is calculated as a percentage of the voting-age population (VAP), it often appears that just over half of U.S. citizens vote. Using the voting-eligible population (VEP) yields a slightly higher number, and the highest turnout, 87 percent, is calculated as a percentage of registered voters. Citizens older than sixty-five and those with a high income and advanced education are very likely to vote. Those younger than thirty years old, especially if still in school and earning low income, are less likely to vote.

Hurdles in a state's registration system and a high number of yearly elections may also decrease turnout. Some states have turned to early voting and mail-only ballots as ways to combat the limitations of one-day and weekday voting. The Supreme Court's decision in *Shelby v. Holder* led to states' removal from the Voting Rights Act's preclearance list. Many of these states implemented changes to their election laws, including the requirement to show photo identification before voting. Globally, the United States experiences lower turnout than other nations; some counties automatically register citizens or require citizens to vote.

7.3 Elections
The Federal Election Commission was created in an effort to control federal campaign donations and create transparency in campaign finance. Individuals and organizations have contribution limits, and candidates must disclose the source of their funds. However, decisions by the Supreme Court, such as *Citizens United*, have voided sections of the campaign finance law, and businesses and organizations may

now run campaign ads and support candidates for offices. The cases also resulted in the creation of super PACs, which can raise unlimited funds, provided they do not coordinate with candidates' campaigns.

The first stage in the election cycle is nomination, where parties determine who the party nominee will be. State political parties choose to hold either primaries or caucuses, depending on whether they want a fast and private ballot election or an informal, public caucus. Delegates from the local primaries and caucuses will go to state or national conventions to vote on behalf of local and state voters.

During the general election, candidates debate one another and run campaigns. Election Day is in early November, but the Electoral College formally elects the president mid-December. Congressional incumbents often win or lose seats based on the popularity of their party's president or presidential candidate.

7.4 Campaigns and Voting

Campaigns must try to convince undecided voters to vote for a candidate and get the party voters to the polls. Early money allows candidates to start a strong campaign and attract other donations. The election year starts with primary campaigns, in which multiple candidates compete for each party's nomination, and the focus is on name recognition and issue positions. General election campaigns focus on getting party members to the polls. Shadow campaigns and super PACs may run negative ads to influence voters. Modern campaigns use television to create emotions and the Internet to interact with supporters and fundraise.

Most voters will cast a ballot for the candidate from their party. Others will consider the issues a candidate supports. Some voters care about what candidates have done in the past, or what they may do in the future, while others are concerned only about their personal finances. Lastly, some citizens will be concerned with the candidate's physical characteristics. Incumbents have many advantages, including war chests, franking privileges, and gerrymandering.

7.5 Direct Democracy

Direct democracy allows the voters in a state to write laws, amend constitutions, remove politicians from office, and approve decisions made by government. Initiatives are laws or constitutional amendments on the ballot. Referendums ask voters to approve a decision by the government. The process for ballot measures requires the collection of signatures from voters, approval of the measure by state government, and a ballot election. Recalls allow citizens to remove politicians from office. While direct democracy does give citizens a say in the policies and laws of their state, it can also be used by businesses and the wealthy to pass policy goals. Initiatives can also lead to bad policy if voters do not research the measure or misunderstand the law.

Review Questions

1. Which of the following makes it easy for a citizen to register to vote?
    a. grandfather clause
    b. lengthy residency requirement
    c. National Voter Registration Act
    d. competency requirement

2. Which of the following is a reason to make voter registration more difficult?
    a. increase voter turnout
    b. decrease election fraud
    c. decrease the cost of elections
    d. make the registration process faster

3. What unusual step did Oregon take to increase voter registration?
    a. The state automatically registers all citizens over eighteen to vote.
    b. The state ended voter registration.
    c. The state sends every resident a voter registration ballot.
    d. The state allows online voter registration.

4. What effect did the National Voter Registration Act have on voter registration?

5. What challenges do college students face with regard to voter registration?

6. If you wanted to prove the United States is suffering from low voter turnout, a calculation based on which population would yield the lowest voter turnout rate?
a. registered voters
b. voting-eligible population
c. voting-age population
d. voters who voted in the last election

7. What characterizes those most likely to vote in the next election?
a. over forty-five years old
b. income under $30,000
c. high school education or less
d. residency in the South

8. Why do Belgium, Turkey, and Australia have higher voter turnout rates than the United States?
a. compulsory voting laws
b. more elections
c. fewer registration laws
d. more polling locations

9. What recommendations would you make to increase voter turnout in the United States?

10. Why does age affect whether a citizen will vote?

11. If you were going to predict whether your classmates would vote in the next election, what questions would you ask them?

12. A state might hold a primary instead of a caucus because a primary is _____.
a. inexpensive and simple
b. transparent and engages local voters
c. faster and has higher turnout
d. highly active and promotes dialog during voting

13. Which of the following citizens is most likely to run for office?
a. Maria Trejo, a 28-year-old part-time sonogram technician and mother of two
b. Jeffrey Lyons, a 40-year-old lawyer and father of one
c. Linda Tepsett, a 40-year-old full-time orthopedic surgeon
d. Mark Forman, a 70-year-old retired steelworker

14. Where and when do Electoral College electors vote?
a. at their precinct, on Election Day
b. at their state capitol, on Election Day
c. in their state capitol, in December
d. in Washington D.C., in December

15. In which type of election are you most likely to see coattail effects?
a. presidential
b. midterm
c. special
d. caucuses

16. What problems will candidates experience with frontloading?

17. Why have fewer moderates won primaries than they used to?

18. How do political parties influence the state's primary system?

19. Why do parties prefer closed primaries to open primaries?

20. Susan is currently working two part-time jobs and is frustrated about the poor economy. On Election Day, she votes for every challenger on the ballot, because she feels the president and Congress are not doing enough to help her. What type of vote did she cast?
a. retrospective
b. prospective
c. pocketbook
d. straight ticket

21. Which factor is most likely to lead to the incumbency advantage for a candidate?
   a. candidate's socioeconomic status
   b. gerrymandering of the candidate's district
   c. media's support of the candidate
   d. candidate's political party

22. In what ways is voting your party identification an informed choice? In what ways is it lazy?

23. Do physical characteristics matter when voters assess candidates? If so, how?

24. Which of the following is *not* a step in the initiative process?
   a. approval of initiative petition by state or local government
   b. collection of signatures
   c. state-wide vote during a ballot election
   d. signature or veto by state governor

25. A referendum is not purely direct democracy because the _____.
   a. voters propose something but the governor approves it
   b. voters propose and approve something but the legislature also approves it
   c. government proposes something and the voters approve it
   d. government proposes something and the legislature approves it

26. What problems would a voter face when trying to pass an initiative or recall?

27. Why do some argue that direct democracy is simply a way for the wealthy and businesses to get their own policies passed?

Critical Thinking Questions

28. What factors determine whether people turn out to vote in U.S. elections?

29. What can be done to increase voter turnout in the United States?

30. In what ways do primary elections contribute to the rise of partisanship in U.S. politics?

31. How does social media affect elections and campaigns? Is this a positive trend? Why or why not?

32. Should states continue to allow ballot initiatives and other forms of direct democracy? Why or why not?

Suggestions for Further Study

Abrajano, Marisa A., and R. Michael Alvarez. 2012. *New Faces, New Voices: The Hispanic Electorate in America*. Princeton, NJ: Princeton University Press.

Adkins, Randall, ed. 2008. *The Evolution of Political Parties, Campaigns, and Elections: Landmark Documents 1787–2007*. Washington, DC: CQ Press.

Boller, Paul. 2004. *Presidential Campaigns: From George Washington to George W. Bush*. Oxford: Oxford University Press.

The Center for American Women and Politics (cawp.rutgers.edu).

The Center for Responsive Politics (opensecrets.org).

Craig, Stephen C., and David B. Hill, eds. 2011. *The Electoral Challenge: Theory Meets Practice*, 2nd ed. Washington, DC: CQ Press.

Fiorina, Morris. 1981. *Retrospective Voting in American National Elections*. New Haven: Yale University Press.

Frank, Thomas. 2004. *What's the Matter with Kansas? How Conservatives Won the Heart of America*. New York: Henry Holt.

Initiative and Reform Institute (http://www.iandrinstitute.org).

Interactive Electoral College map (270towin.com).

Jacobson, Gary C. 2012. *The Politics of Congressional Elections*, 8th ed. New York: Pearson.

Lewis-Beck, Michael S., William G. Jacoby, Helmut Norpoth, and Herbert F. Weisberg. 2008. *American Vote Revisited*. Ann Arbor: University of Michigan Press.

Lupia, Arthur, and Matthew McCubbins. 1998. *Democratic Dilemma: Can Citizens Learn What They Need to Know?* Cambridge: Cambridge University Press.

Parker, David C. W. 2014. *Battle for the Big Sky: Representation and the Politics of Place in the Race for the U.S. Senate*. Washington, DC: CQ Press.

PolitiFact (www.politifact.com).

Polsby, Nelson, Aaron Wildavsky, Steven Schier, and David Hopkins. 2011. *Presidential Elections: Strategies and Structures of American Politics*. New York: Rowman and Littlefield.

Project Vote Smart (votesmart.org).

Chapter 8

The Media

Figure 8.1 On August 8, 2015, activists for Black Lives Matter in Seattle commandeered presidential candidate Bernie Sanders' campaign rally in an effort to get their message out. (credit: modification of work by Tiffany Von Arnim)

Chapter Outline

Introduction

Democratic primary candidate Bernie Sanders arrived in Seattle on August 8, 2015, to give a speech at a rally to promote his presidential campaign. Instead, the rally was interrupted—and eventually co-opted—by activists for Black Lives Matter (**Figure 8.1**).[1] Why did the group risk alienating Democratic voters by preventing Sanders from speaking? Because Black Lives Matter had been trying to raise awareness of the treatment of black citizens in the United States, and the media has the power to elevate such issues.[2] While some questioned its tactics, the organization's move underscores how important the media are to gaining recognition, and the lengths to which organizations are willing to go to get media attention.[3]

Freedom of the press and an independent media are important dimensions of a liberal society and a necessary part of a healthy democracy. "No government ought to be without censors," said Thomas Jefferson, "and where the press is free, no one ever will."[4] What does it mean to have a free news media? What regulations limit what media can do? How do the media contribute to informing citizens and monitoring politicians and the government, and how do we measure their impact? This chapter explores these and other questions about the role of the media in the United States.

8.1 What Is the Media?

Learning Objectives

By the end of this section, you will be able to:
- Explain what the media are and how they are organized
- Describe the main functions of the media in a free society
- Compare different media formats and their respective audiences

Ours is an exploding media system. What started as print journalism was subsequently supplemented by radio coverage, then network television, followed by cable television. Now, with the addition of the Internet, blogs and social media—a set of applications or web platforms that allow users to immediately communicate with one another—give citizens a wide variety of sources for instant news of all kinds. The Internet also allows citizens to initiate public discussion by uploading images and video for viewing, such as videos documenting interactions between citizens and the police, for example. Provided we are connected digitally, we have a bewildering amount of choices for finding information about the world. In fact, some might say that compared to the tranquil days of the 1970s, when we might read the morning newspaper over breakfast and take in the network news at night, there are now too many choices in today's increasingly complex world of information. This reality may make the news media all the more important to structuring and shaping narratives about U.S. politics. Or the proliferation of competing information sources like blogs and social media may actually weaken the power of the news media relative to the days when news media monopolized our attention.

MEDIA BASICS

The term *media* defines a number of different communication formats from television media, which share information through broadcast airwaves, to print media, which rely on printed documents. The collection of all forms of media that communicate information to the general public is called **mass media**, including television, print, radio, and Internet. One of the primary reasons citizens turn to the media is for news. We expect the media to cover important political and social events and information in a concise and neutral manner.

To accomplish its work, the media employs a number of people in varied positions. Journalists and reporters are responsible for uncovering news stories by keeping an eye on areas of public interest, like politics, business, and sports. Once a journalist has a lead or a possible idea for a story, he or she researches background information and interviews people to create a complete and balanced account. Editors work in the background of the newsroom, assigning stories, approving articles or packages, and editing content for accuracy and clarity. Publishers are people or companies that own and produce print or digital media. They oversee both the content and finances of the publication, ensuring the organization turns a profit and creates a high-quality product to distribute to consumers. Producers oversee the production and finances of visual media, like television, radio, and film.

The work of the news media differs from **public relations**, which is communication carried out to improve the image of companies, organizations, or candidates for office. Public relations is not a neutral information form. While journalists write stories to inform the public, a public relations spokesperson is paid to help an individual or organization get positive press. Public relations materials normally appear as press releases or paid advertisements in newspapers and other media outlets. Some less reputable publications, however, publish paid articles under the news banner, blurring the line between journalism and public relations.

MEDIA TYPES

Each form of media has its own complexities and is used by different demographics. Millennials (currently aged 21–37) are more likely to get news and information from social media, such as YouTube, Twitter, and

Facebook, while Baby Boomers (currently aged 54–72) are most likely to get their news from television, either national broadcasts or local news (Figure 8.2).

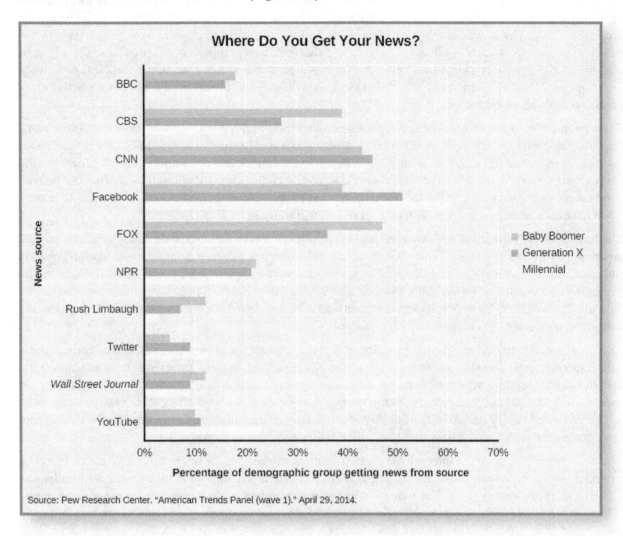

Figure 8.2 Age greatly influences the choice of news sources. Baby Boomers are more likely to get news and information from television, while members of Generation X and Millennials are more likely to use social media.

Television alone offers viewers a variety of formats. Programming may be scripted, like dramas or comedies. It may be unscripted, like game shows or reality programs, or informative, such as news programming. Although most programs are created by a television production company, national networks—like CBS or NBC—purchase the rights to programs they distribute to local stations across the United States. Most local stations are affiliated with a national network corporation, and they broadcast national network programming to their local viewers.

Before the existence of cable and fiber optics, networks needed to own local affiliates to have access to the local station's transmission towers. Towers have a limited radius, so each network needed an affiliate in each major city to reach viewers. While cable technology has lessened networks' dependence on aerial signals, some viewers still use antennas and receivers to view programming broadcast from local towers.

Affiliates, by agreement with the networks, give priority to network news and other programming chosen by the affiliate's national media corporation. Local affiliate stations are told when to air programs or commercials, and they diverge only to inform the public about a local or national emergency. For example, ABC affiliates broadcast the popular television show *Once Upon a Time* at a specific time on a specific day. Should a fire threaten homes and businesses in a local area, the affiliate might preempt it to update citizens on the fire's dangers and return to regularly scheduled programming after the danger has ended.

Most affiliate stations will show local news before and after network programming to inform local viewers of events and issues. Network news has a national focus on politics, international events, the economy, and more. Local news, on the other hand, is likely to focus on matters close to home, such as regional business, crime, sports, and weather.[5] The *NBC Nightly News*, for example, covers presidential campaigns and the White House or skirmishes between North Korea and South Korea, while the NBC affiliate in Los Angeles (KNBC-TV) and the NBC affiliate in Dallas (KXAS-TV) report on the governor's activities or weekend festivals in the region.

Cable programming offers national networks a second method to directly reach local viewers. As the name implies, cable stations transmit programming directly to a local cable company hub, which then sends the signals to homes through coaxial or fiber optic cables. Because cable does not broadcast programming through the airwaves, cable networks can operate across the nation directly without local affiliates. Instead they purchase broadcasting rights for the cable stations they believe their viewers want. For this reason, cable networks often specialize in different types of programming.

The Cable News Network (CNN) was the first news station to take advantage of this specialized format, creating a 24-hour news station with live coverage and interview programs. Other news stations quickly followed, such as MSNBC and FOX News. A viewer might tune in to Nickelodeon and catch family programs and movies or watch ESPN to catch up with the latest baseball or basketball scores. The Cable-Satellite Public Affairs Network, known better as C-SPAN, now has three channels covering Congress, the president, the courts, and matters of public interest.

Cable and satellite providers also offer on-demand programming for most stations. Citizens can purchase cable, satellite, and Internet subscription services (like Netflix) to find programs to watch instantly, without being tied to a schedule. Initially, on-demand programming was limited to rebroadcasting old content and was commercial-free. Yet many networks and programs now allow their new programming to be aired within a day or two of its initial broadcast. In return they often add commercials the user cannot fast-forward or avoid. Thus networks expect advertising revenues to increase.[6]

The on-demand nature of the Internet has created many opportunities for news outlets. While early media providers were those who could pay the high cost of printing or broadcasting, modern media require just a URL and ample server space. The ease of online publication has made it possible for more niche media outlets to form. The websites of the *New York Times* and other newspapers often focus on matters affecting the United States, while channels like BBC America present world news. FOX News presents political commentary and news in a conservative vein, while the Internet site Daily Kos offers a liberal perspective on the news. Politico.com is perhaps the leader in niche journalism.

Unfortunately, the proliferation of online news has also increased the amount of poorly written material with little editorial oversight, and readers must be cautious when reading Internet news sources. Sites like Buzzfeed allow members to post articles without review by an editorial board, leading to articles of varied quality and accuracy. The Internet has also made publication speed a consideration for professional journalists. No news outlet wants to be the last to break a story, and the rush to publication often leads to typographical and factual errors. Even large news outlets, like the Associated Press, have published articles with errors in their haste to get a story out.

The Internet also facilitates the flow of information through social media, which allows users to instantly communicate with one another and share with audiences that can grow exponentially. Facebook and Twitter have millions of daily users. Social media changes more rapidly than the other media formats. While people in many different age groups use sites like Facebook, Twitter, and YouTube, other sites like Snapchat and Yik Yak appeal mostly to younger users. The platforms also serve different functions. Tumblr and Reddit facilitate discussion that is topic-based and controversial, while Instagram is mostly social. A growing number of these sites also allow users to comment anonymously, leading to increases in threats and abuse. The site 4chan, for example, was linked to the 2015 shooting at an Oregon community college.[7]

Regardless of where we get our information, the various media avenues available today, versus years ago, make it much easier for everyone to be engaged. The question is: Who controls the media we rely on? Most media are controlled by a limited number of conglomerates. A conglomerate is a corporation made up of a number of companies, organizations, and media networks. In the 1980s, more than fifty companies owned the majority of television and radio stations and networks. By 2011, six conglomerates controlled most of the broadcast media in the United States: CBS Corporation, Comcast, Time Warner, 21st Century Fox (formerly News Corporation), Viacom, and The Walt Disney Company (Figure 8.3).[8] With the Disney-Fox merger scheduled to close in March 2019, this number will be reduced to five. The Walt Disney Company, for example, owns the ABC Television Network, ESPN, A&E, and Lifetime, in addition to the Disney Channel. Viacom owns BET, Comedy Central, MTV, Nickelodeon, and VH1. Time Warner owns Cartoon Network, CNN, HBO, and TNT, among others. While each of these networks has its own programming, in the end, the conglomerate can make a policy that affects all stations and programming under its control.

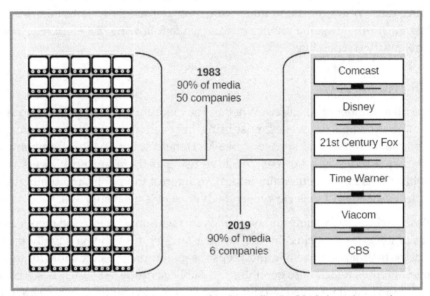

Figure 8.3 In 1983, fifty companies owned 90 percent of U.S. media. By 2012, just six conglomerates controlled the same percentage of U.S. media outlets.

Conglomerates can create a monopoly on information by controlling a sector of a market. When a media conglomerate has policies or restrictions, they will apply to all stations or outlets under its ownership, potentially limiting the information citizens receive. Conglomerate ownership also creates circumstances in which censorship may occur. iHeartMedia (formerly Clear Channel Media) owns music, radio, and billboards throughout the United States, and in 2010, the company refused to run several billboard ads for the St. Pete Pride Festival and Promenade in St. Petersburg, Florida. The festival organizers said the content of two ads, a picture of same-sex couples in close contact with one another, was the reason the ads were not run. Because iHeartMedia owns most of the billboards in the area, this limitation was problematic for the festival and decreased awareness of the event. Those in charge of the festival viewed the refusal as censorship.[9]

Newspapers too have experienced the pattern of concentrated ownership. Gannett Company, while also owning television media, holds a large number of newspapers and news magazines in its control. Many of these were acquired quietly, without public notice or discussion. Gannett's 2013 acquisition of publishing giant A.H. Belo Corporation caused some concern and news coverage, however. The sale would have allowed Gannett to own both an NBC and a CBS affiliate in St. Louis, Missouri, giving it control over programming and advertising rates for two competing stations. The U.S. Department of Justice required Gannett to sell the station owned by Belo to ensure market competition and multi-ownership in St. Louis.[10]

These changes in the format and ownership of media raise the question whether the media still operate as an independent source of information. Is it possible that corporations and CEOs now control the information flow, making profit more important than the impartial delivery of information? The reality is that media outlets, whether newspaper, television, radio, or Internet, are businesses. They have expenses and must raise revenues. Yet at the same time, we expect the media to entertain, inform, and alert us without bias. They must provide some public services, while following laws and regulations. Reconciling these goals may not always be possible.

FUNCTIONS OF THE MEDIA

The media exist to fill a number of functions. Whether the medium is a newspaper, a radio, or a television newscast, a corporation behind the scenes must bring in revenue and pay for the cost of the product. Revenue comes from advertising and sponsors, like McDonald's, Ford Motor Company, and other large corporations. But corporations will not pay for advertising if there are no viewers or readers. So all programs and publications need to entertain, inform, or interest the public and maintain a steady stream of consumers. In the end, what attracts viewers and advertisers is what survives.

The media are also watchdogs of society and of public officials. Some refer to the media as the *fourth estate*, with the branches of government being the first three estates and the media equally participating as the fourth. This role helps maintain democracy and keeps the government accountable for its actions, even if a branch of the government is reluctant to open itself to public scrutiny. As much as social scientists would like citizens to be informed and involved in politics and events, the reality is that we are not. So the media, especially journalists, keep an eye on what is happening and sounds an alarm when the public needs to pay attention.[11]

The media also engages in **agenda setting**, which is the act of choosing which issues or topics deserve public discussion. For example, in the early 1980s, famine in Ethiopia drew worldwide attention, which resulted in increased charitable giving to the country. Yet the famine had been going on for a long time before it was discovered by western media. Even after the discovery, it took video footage to gain the attention of the British and U.S. populations and start the aid flowing.[12] Today, numerous examples of agenda setting show how important the media are when trying to prevent further emergencies or humanitarian crises. In the spring of 2015, when the Dominican Republic was preparing to exile Haitians and undocumented (or under documented) residents, major U.S. news outlets remained silent. However, once the story had been covered several times by Al Jazeera, a state-funded broadcast company based in Qatar, ABC, the *New York Times*, and other network outlets followed.[13] With major network coverage came public pressure for the U.S. government to act on behalf of the Haitians.[14]

Christiane Amanpour on "What Should Be News?"

The media are our connection to the world. Some events are too big to ignore, yet other events, such as the destruction of Middle Eastern monuments or the plight of foreign refugees, are far enough from our shores that they often go unnoticed. What we see is carefully selected, but who decides what should be news?

As the chief international correspondent for CNN, Christiane Amanpour is one media decision maker (Figure 8.4). Over the years, Amanpour has covered events around the world from war to genocide. In an interview with Oprah Winfrey, Amanpour explains that her duty, and that of other journalists, is to make a difference in the world. To do that, "we have to educate people and use the media responsibly."[15] Journalists cannot passively sit by and wait for stories to find them. "Words have consequences: the stories we decide to do, the stories we decide not to do . . . it all matters."[16]

Figure 8.4 Christiane Amanpour accepts the award for the Association for International Broadcasting's Personality of the Year on November 4, 2015. (credit: AIB (Association for International Broadcasting))

As Amanpour points out, journalists are often "on the cutting edge of reform," so if they fail to shed light on events, the results can be tragic. One of her biggest regrets was not covering the genocide in Rwanda in 1994, which cost nearly a million lives. She said the media ignored the event in favor of covering democratic elections in South Africa and a war in Bosnia, and ultimately she believes the media failed the people. "If we don't respect our profession and we see it frittering away into the realm of triviality and sensationalism, we'll lose our standing," she said. "That won't be good for democracy. A thriving society must have a thriving press."

This feeling of responsibility extends to covering moral topics, like genocide. Amanpour feels there shouldn't be equal time given to all sides. "I'm not just a stenographer or someone with a megaphone; when I report, I have to do it in context, to be aware of the moral conundrum. . . . I have to be able to draw a line between victim and aggressor."

Amanpour also believes the media should cover more. When given the full background and details of events, society pays attention to the news. "Individual Americans had an incredible reaction to the [2004 Indian Ocean] tsunami—much faster than their government's reaction," she said. "Americans are a very moral and compassionate people who believe in extending a helping hand, especially when they get the full facts instead of one-minute clips." If the news fulfills its responsibility, as she sees it, the world can show its compassion and help promote freedom.

Why does Amanpour believe the press has a responsibility to report all that they see? Are there situations in which it is acceptable to display partiality in reporting the news? Why or why not?

Before the Internet, traditional media determined whether citizen photographs or video footage would become "news." In 1991, a private citizen's camcorder footage showed four police officers beating an African American motorist named Rodney King in Los Angeles. After appearing on local independent television station, KTLA-TV, and then the national news, the event began a national discussion on police brutality and ignited riots in Los Angeles.[17] The agenda-setting power of traditional media has begun to be appropriated by social media and smartphones, however. Tumbler, Facebook, YouTube, and other Internet sites allow witnesses to instantly upload images and accounts of events and forward the link to friends. Some uploads go viral and attract the attention of the mainstream media, but large network newscasts and major newspapers are still more powerful at initiating or changing a discussion.

The media also promote the public good by offering a platform for public debate and improving citizen awareness. Network news informs the electorate about national issues, elections, and international news. The *New York Times*, *Los Angeles Times*, *NBC Nightly News*, and other outlets make sure voters can easily find out what issues affect the nation. Is terrorism on the rise? Is the dollar weakening? The network news hosts national debates during presidential elections, broadcasts major presidential addresses, and interviews political leaders during times of crisis. Cable news networks now provide coverage of all these topics as well.

Local news has a larger job, despite small budgets and fewer resources (Figure 8.5). Local government and local economic policy have a strong and immediate effect on citizens. Is the city government planning on changing property tax rates? Will the school district change the way Common Core tests are administered? When and where is the next town hall meeting or public forum to be held? Local and social media provide a forum for protest and discussion of issues that matter to the community.

Figure 8.5 Meetings of local governance, such as this meeting of the Independence City Council in Missouri, are rarely attended by more than gadflies and journalists. (credit: "MoBikeFed"/Flickr)

Link to Learning

Want a snapshot of local and state political and policy news? The magazine *Governing (https://openstax.org/l/29governing)* keeps an eye on what is happening in each state, offering articles and analysis on events that occur across the country.

While journalists reporting the news try to present information in an unbiased fashion, sometimes the public seeks opinion and analysis of complicated issues that affect various populations differently, like healthcare reform and the Affordable Care Act. This type of coverage may come in the form of editorials, commentaries, Op-Ed columns, and blogs. These forums allow the editorial staff and informed columnists to express a personal belief and attempt to persuade. If opinion writers are trusted by the public, they have influence.

Walter Cronkite, reporting from Vietnam, had a loyal following. In a broadcast following the Tet Offensive in 1968, Cronkite expressed concern that the United States was mired in a conflict that would end in a stalemate.[18] His coverage was based on opinion after viewing the war from the ground.[19] Although the number of people supporting the war had dwindled by this time, Cronkite's commentary bolstered opposition. Like editorials, commentaries contain opinion and are often written by specialists in a field. Larry Sabato, a prominent political science professor at the University of Virginia, occasionally writes his thoughts for the *New York Times*. These pieces are based on his expertise in politics and elections.[20] Blogs offer more personalized coverage, addressing specific concerns and perspectives for a limited group of readers. Nate Silver's blog, *FiveThirtyEight*, focuses on elections and politics.

8.2 The Evolution of the Media

Learning Objectives

By the end of this section, you will be able to:
- Discuss the history of major media formats
- Compare important changes in media types over time
- Explain how citizens learn political information from the media

The evolution of the media has been fraught with concerns and problems. Accusations of mind control, bias, and poor quality have been thrown at the media on a regular basis. Yet the growth of communications technology allows people today to find more information more easily than any previous generation. Mass media can be print, radio, television, or Internet news. They can be local, national, or international. They can be broad or limited in their focus. The choices are tremendous.

PRINT MEDIA

Early news was presented to local populations through the print press. While several colonies had printers and occasional newspapers, high literacy rates combined with the desire for self-government made Boston a perfect location for the creation of a newspaper, and the first continuous press was started there in 1704.[21] Newspapers spread information about local events and activities. The Stamp Tax of 1765 raised costs for publishers, however, leading several newspapers to fold under the increased cost of paper. The repeal of the Stamp Tax in 1766 quieted concerns for a short while, but editors and writers soon began questioning the right of the British to rule over the colonies. Newspapers took part in the effort to inform citizens of British misdeeds and incite attempts to revolt. Readership across the colonies increased to nearly forty thousand homes (among a total population of two million), and daily papers sprang up in large cities.[22]

Although newspapers united for a common cause during the Revolutionary War, the divisions that occurred during the Constitutional Convention and the United States' early history created a change. The publication of the *Federalist Papers*, as well as the Anti-Federalist Papers, in the 1780s, moved the nation into the **party press era**, in which partisanship and political party loyalty dominated the choice of editorial content. One reason was cost. Subscriptions and advertisements did not fully cover printing costs, and political parties stepped in to support presses that aided the parties and their policies. Papers began printing party propaganda and messages, even publicly attacking political leaders like George Washington. Despite the antagonism of the press, Washington and several other founders felt that freedom of the press was important for creating an informed electorate. Indeed, freedom of the press is enshrined in the Bill of Rights in the first amendment.

Between 1830 and 1860, machines and manufacturing made the production of newspapers faster and less expensive. Benjamin Day's paper, the *New York Sun*, used technology like the linotype machine to mass-produce papers (Figure 8.6). Roads and waterways were expanded, decreasing the costs of distributing printed materials to subscribers. New newspapers popped up. The popular penny press papers and magazines contained more gossip than news, but they were affordable at a penny per issue. Over time, papers expanded their coverage to include racing, weather, and educational materials. By 1841, some news reporters considered themselves responsible for upholding high journalistic standards, and under the editor (and politician) Horace Greeley, the *New-York Tribune* became a nationally respected newspaper. By the end of the Civil War, more journalists and newspapers were aiming to meet professional standards of accuracy and impartiality.[23]

(a)   (b)

Figure 8.6 Benjamin Day (a) founded the first U.S. penny press, *The Sun*, in 1833. *The Sun*, whose front page from November 26, 1834, is shown above (b), was a morning newspaper published in New York from 1833 to 1950.

Yet readers still wanted to be entertained. Joseph Pulitzer and the *New York World* gave them what they wanted. The tabloid-style paper included editorial pages, cartoons, and pictures, while the front-page news was sensational and scandalous. This style of coverage became known as **yellow journalism**. Ads sold quickly thanks to the paper's popularity, and the Sunday edition became a regular feature of the newspaper. As the *New York World's* circulation increased, other papers copied Pulitzer's style in an effort to sell papers. Competition between newspapers led to increasingly sensationalized covers and crude issues.

In 1896, Adolph Ochs purchased the *New York Times* with the goal of creating a dignified newspaper that would provide readers with important news about the economy, politics, and the world rather than gossip and comics. The *New York Times* brought back the informational model, which exhibits impartiality and accuracy and promotes transparency in government and politics. With the arrival of the Progressive Era, the media began **muckraking**: the writing and publishing of news coverage that exposed corrupt business and government practices. Investigative work like Upton Sinclair's serialized novel *The Jungle* led to changes in the way industrial workers were treated and local political machines were run. The Pure Food and Drug Act and other laws were passed to protect consumers and employees from unsafe food processing practices. Local and state government officials who participated in bribery and corruption became the centerpieces of exposés.

Some muckraking journalism still appears today, and the quicker movement of information through the system would seem to suggest an environment for yet more investigative work and the punch of exposés than in the past. However, at the same time there are fewer journalists being hired than there used to be. The scarcity of journalists and the lack of time to dig for details in a 24-hour, profit-oriented news model make investigative stories rare.[24] There are two potential concerns about the decline of investigative journalism in the digital age. First, one potential shortcoming is that the quality of news content will become uneven in depth and quality, which could lead to a less informed citizenry. Second, if investigative journalism in its systematic form declines, then the cases of wrongdoing that are the objects of such investigations would have a greater chance of going on undetected.

In the twenty-first century, newspapers have struggled to stay financially stable. Print media earned $44.9 billion from ads in 2003, but only $16.4 billion from ads in 2014.[25] Given the countless alternate forms of news, many of which are free, newspaper subscriptions have fallen. Advertising and especially classified ad revenue dipped. Many newspapers now maintain both a print and an Internet presence in order to compete for readers. The rise of free news blogs, such as the *Huffington Post*, have made it difficult for newspapers to force readers to purchase online subscriptions to access material they place behind a **digital paywall**. Some local newspapers, in an effort to stay visible and profitable, have turned to social media, like Facebook and Twitter. Stories can be posted and retweeted, allowing readers to comment and forward material.[26] Yet, overall, newspapers have adapted, becoming leaner—though less thorough and investigative—versions of their earlier selves.

RADIO

Radio news made its appearance in the 1920s. The National Broadcasting Company (NBC) and the Columbia Broadcasting System (CBS) began running sponsored news programs and radio dramas. Comedy programs, such as *Amos 'n' Andy*, *The Adventures of Gracie*, and *Easy Aces*, also became popular during the 1930s, as listeners were trying to find humor during the Depression (Figure 8.7). Talk shows, religious shows, and educational programs followed, and by the late 1930s, game shows and quiz shows were added to the airwaves. Almost 83 percent of households had a radio by 1940, and most tuned in regularly.[27]

(a)   (b)

Figure 8.7 The "golden age of radio" included comedy shows like *Easy Aces*, starring Goodman and Jane Ace (a), and *Amos 'n' Andy*, starring Freeman Gosden and Charles Correll, shown here celebrating their program's tenth anniversary in 1938 (b). These programs helped amuse families during the dark years of the Depression.

Not just something to be enjoyed by those in the city, the proliferation of the radio brought communications to rural America as well. News and entertainment programs were also targeted to rural communities. WLS in Chicago provided the *National Farm and Home Hour* and the *WLS Barn Dance*. WSM in Nashville began to broadcast the live music show called the *Grand Ole Opry*, which is still broadcast every week and is the longest live broadcast radio show in U.S. history.[28]

As radio listenership grew, politicians realized that the medium offered a way to reach the public in a personal manner. Warren Harding was the first president to regularly give speeches over the radio. President Herbert Hoover used radio as well, mainly to announce government programs on aid and unemployment relief.[29] Yet it was Franklin D. Roosevelt who became famous for harnessing the political power of radio. On entering office in March 1933, President Roosevelt needed to quiet public fears about the economy and prevent people from removing their money from the banks. He delivered his first radio speech eight days after assuming the presidency:

> "My friends: I want to talk for a few minutes with the people of the United States about banking—to talk with the comparatively few who understand the mechanics of banking, but more particularly with the overwhelming majority of you who use banks for the making of deposits and the drawing of checks. I want to tell you what has been done in the last few days, and why it was done, and what the next steps are going to be."[30]

Roosevelt spoke directly to the people and addressed them as equals. One listener described the chats as soothing, with the president acting like a father, sitting in the room with the family, cutting through the political nonsense and describing what help he needed from each family member.[31] Roosevelt would sit down and explain his ideas and actions directly to the people on a regular basis, confident that he could convince voters of their value.[32] His speeches became known as "fireside chats" and formed an important way for him to promote his New Deal agenda (Figure 8.8). Roosevelt's combination of persuasive rhetoric and the media allowed him to expand both the government and the presidency beyond their traditional roles.[33]

(a)   (b)

Figure 8.8   As radio listenership became widespread in the 1930s (a), President Franklin D. Roosevelt took advantage of this new medium to broadcast his "fireside chats" and bring ordinary Americans into the president's world (b). (credit a: modification of work by George W. Ackerman; credit b: modification of work by the Library of Congress)

During this time, print news still controlled much of the information flowing to the public. Radio news programs were limited in scope and number. But in the 1940s the German annexation of Austria, conflict in Europe, and World War II changed radio news forever. The need and desire for frequent news updates about the constantly evolving war made newspapers, with their once-a-day printing, too slow. People wanted to know what was happening, and they wanted to know immediately. Although initially reluctant to be on the air, reporter Edward R. Murrow of CBS began reporting live about Germany's actions from his posts in Europe. His reporting contained news and some commentary, and even live coverage during Germany's aerial bombing of London. To protect covert military operations during the war, the White House had placed guidelines on the reporting of classified information, making a legal exception to the First Amendment's protection against government involvement in the press. Newscasters voluntarily agreed to suppress information, such as about the development of the atomic bomb and movements of the military, until after the events had occurred.[34]

The number of professional and amateur radio stations grew quickly. Initially, the government exerted little legislative control over the industry. Stations chose their own broadcasting locations, signal strengths, and frequencies, which sometimes overlapped with one another or with the military, leading to tuning problems for listeners. The Radio Act (1927) created the Federal Radio Commission (FRC), which made the first effort to set standards, frequencies, and license stations. The Commission was under heavy pressure from Congress, however, and had little authority. The Communications Act of 1934 ended the FRC and created the Federal Communications Commission (FCC), which continued to work with radio stations to assign frequencies and set national standards, as well as oversee other forms of broadcasting and telephones. The FCC regulates interstate communications to this day. For example, it prohibits the use of certain profane words during certain hours on public airwaves.

Prior to WWII, radio frequencies were broadcast using amplitude modulation (AM). After WWII, frequency modulation (FM) broadcasting, with its wider signal bandwidth, provided clear sound with less static and became popular with stations wanting to broadcast speeches or music with high-quality sound. While radio's importance for distributing news waned with the increase in television usage, it remained popular for listening to music, educational talk shows, and sports broadcasting. Talk stations began to gain ground in the 1980s on both AM and FM frequencies, restoring radio's importance in politics. By the 1990s, talk shows had gone national, showcasing broadcasters like Rush Limbaugh and Don Imus.

In 1990, Sirius Satellite Radio began a campaign for FCC approval of satellite radio. The idea was to broadcast digital programming from satellites in orbit, eliminating the need for local towers. By 2001, two satellite stations had been approved for broadcasting. Satellite radio has greatly increased programming with many specialized offerings, such as channels dedicated to particular artists. It is generally subscription-based and offers a larger area of coverage, even to remote areas such as deserts and oceans. Satellite programming is also exempt from many of the FCC regulations that govern regular radio stations. Howard Stern, for example, was fined more than $2 million while on public airwaves, mainly for his sexually explicit discussions.[35] Stern moved to Sirius Satellite in 2006 and has since been free of oversight and fines.

TELEVISION

Television combined the best attributes of radio and pictures and changed media forever. The first official broadcast in the United States was President Franklin Roosevelt's speech at the opening of the 1939 World's Fair in New York. The public did not immediately begin buying televisions, but coverage of World War II changed their minds. CBS reported on war events and included pictures and maps that enhanced the news for viewers. By the 1950s, the price of television sets had dropped, more televisions stations were being created, and advertisers were buying up spots.

As on the radio, quiz shows and games dominated the television airwaves. But when Edward R. Murrow made the move to television in 1951 with his news show *See It Now*, television journalism gained its foothold (Figure 8.9). As television programming expanded, more channels were added. Networks such as ABC, CBS, and NBC began nightly newscasts, and local stations and affiliates followed suit.

Figure 8.9 Edward R. Murrow's move to television increased the visibility of network news. In *The Challenge of Ideas* (1961) pictured above, Murrow discussed the Cold War between the Soviet Union and the United States alongside films stars such as John Wayne.

Even more than radio, television allows politicians to reach out and connect with citizens and voters in deeper ways. Before television, few voters were able to see a president or candidate speak or answer questions in an interview. Now everyone can decode body language and tone to decide whether candidates or politicians are sincere. Presidents can directly convey their anger, sorrow, or optimism during addresses.

The first television advertisements, run by presidential candidates Dwight D. Eisenhower and Adlai Stevenson in the early 1950s, were mainly radio jingles with animation or short question-and-answer sessions. In 1960, John F. Kennedy's campaign used a Hollywood-style approach to promote his image as young and vibrant. The Kennedy campaign ran interesting and engaging ads, featuring Kennedy, his wife Jacqueline, and everyday citizens who supported him.

Television was also useful to combat scandals and accusations of impropriety. Republican vice presidential candidate Richard Nixon used a televised speech in 1952 to address accusations that he had taken money from a political campaign fund illegally. Nixon laid out his finances, investments, and debts and ended by saying that the only election gift the family had received was a cocker spaniel the children named Checkers.[36] The "Checkers speech" was remembered more for humanizing Nixon than for proving he had not taken money from the campaign account. Yet it was enough to quiet accusations. Democratic vice presidential nominee Geraldine Ferraro similarly used television to answer accusations in 1984, holding a televised press conference to answer questions for over two hours about her husband's business dealings and tax returns.[37]

In addition to television ads, the 1960 election also featured the first televised presidential debate. By that time most households had a television. Kennedy's careful grooming and practiced body language allowed viewers to focus on his presidential demeanor. His opponent, Richard Nixon, was still recovering from a severe case of the flu. While Nixon's substantive answers and debate skills made a favorable impression on radio listeners, viewers' reaction to his sweaty appearance and obvious discomfort demonstrated that live television had the potential to make or break a candidate.[38] In 1964, Lyndon B. Johnson was ahead in the polls, and he let Barry Goldwater's campaign know he did not want to debate.[39] Nixon, who ran for president again in 1968 and 1972, declined to debate. Then in 1976, President Gerald Ford, who was behind in the polls, invited Jimmy Carter to debate, and televised debates became a regular part of future presidential campaigns.[40]

Link to Learning

Visit **American Rhetoric (https://openstax.org/l/29americanrhet)** for free access to speeches, video, and audio of famous presidential and political speeches.

Between the 1960s and the 1990s, presidents often used television to reach citizens and gain support for policies. When they made speeches, the networks and their local affiliates carried them. With few independent local stations available, a viewer had little alternative but to watch. During this "Golden Age of Presidential Television," presidents had a strong command of the media.[41]

Some of the best examples of this power occurred when presidents used television to inspire and comfort the population during a national emergency. These speeches aided in the "rally 'round the flag" phenomenon, which occurs when a population feels threatened and unites around the president.[42] During these periods, presidents may receive heightened approval ratings, in part due to the media's decision about what to cover.[43] In 1995, President Bill Clinton comforted and encouraged the families of the employees and children killed at the bombing of the Oklahoma City Federal Building. Clinton reminded the nation that children learn through action, and so we must speak up against violence and face evil acts with good acts.[44]

Following the terrorist attacks in New York and Washington on September 11, 2001, President George W. Bush's bullhorn speech from the rubble of Ground Zero in New York similarly became a rally. Bush spoke to the workers and first responders and encouraged them, but his short speech became a viral clip demonstrating the resilience of New Yorkers and the anger of a nation.[45] He told New Yorkers, the country, and the world that Americans could hear the frustration and anguish of New York, and that the terrorists would soon hear the United States (**Figure 8.10**).

(a)   (b)

Figure 8.10   Presidents Clinton and Bush were both called upon to calm the people after mass killings. In April 1996, President Bill Clinton and First Lady Hillary Rodham Clinton lay flowers at the site of the former Alfred P. Murrah federal building just before the one-year anniversary of the Oklahoma City bombing (a). Three days after the terrorist attacks of 9/11 brought down the World Trade Center in New York City, George W. Bush declares to the crowd, "I can hear you! The rest of the world hears you! And the people . . . and the people who knocked these buildings down will hear all of us soon!" (b)

Following their speeches, both presidents also received a bump in popularity. Clinton's approval rating rose from 46 to 51 percent, and Bush's from 51 to 90 percent.[46]

NEW MEDIA TRENDS

The invention of cable in the 1980s and the expansion of the Internet in the 2000s opened up more options for media consumers than ever before. Viewers can watch nearly anything at the click of a button, bypass commercials, and record programs of interest. The resulting saturation, or inundation of information, may lead viewers to abandon the news entirely or become more suspicious and fatigued about politics.[47] This effect, in turn, also changes the president's ability to reach out to citizens. For example, viewership of the president's annual State of the Union address has decreased over the years, from sixty-seven million viewers in 1993 to thirty-two million in 2015.[48] Citizens who want to watch reality television and movies can easily avoid the news, leaving presidents with no sure way to communicate with the public.[49] Other voices, such as those of talk show hosts and political pundits, now fill the gap.

Electoral candidates have also lost some media ground. In *horse-race coverage*, modern journalists analyze campaigns and blunders or the overall race, rather than interviewing the candidates or discussing their issue positions. Some argue that this shallow coverage is a result of candidates' trying to control the journalists by limiting interviews and quotes. In an effort to regain control of the story, journalists begin analyzing campaigns without input from the candidates.[50] The use of social media by candidates provides a countervailing trend. President Trump's hundreds of election tweets are the stuff of legend. These tweets kept his press coverage up, although they also were problematic for him at times. The final days of the contest saw no new tweets from Trump as he attempted to stay on message.

Milestone

The First Social Media Candidate

When president-elect Barack Obama admitted an addiction to his Blackberry, the signs were clear: A new generation was assuming the presidency.[51] Obama's use of technology was a part of life, not a campaign pretense. Perhaps for this reason, he was the first candidate to fully embrace social media.

While John McCain, the 2008 Republican presidential candidate, focused on traditional media to run his campaign, Obama did not. One of Obama's campaign advisors was Chris Hughes, a cofounder of Facebook. The campaign allowed Hughes to create a powerful online presence for Obama, with sites on YouTube, Facebook, MySpace, and more. Podcasts and videos were available for anyone looking for information about the candidate. These efforts made it possible for information to be forwarded easily between friends and colleagues. It also allowed Obama to connect with a younger generation that was often left out of politics.

By Election Day, Obama's skill with the web was clear: he had over two million Facebook supporters, while McCain had 600,000. Obama had 112,000 followers on Twitter, and McCain had only 4,600.[52]

Are there any disadvantages to a presidential candidate's use of social media and the Internet for campaign purposes? Why or why not?

The availability of the Internet and social media has moved some control of the message back into the presidents' and candidates' hands. Politicians can now connect to the people directly, bypassing journalists. When Barack Obama's minister, the Reverend Jeremiah Wright, was accused of making inflammatory racial sermons in 2008, Obama used YouTube to respond to charges that he shared Wright's beliefs. The video drew more than seven million views.[53] To reach out to supporters and voters, the White House maintains a YouTube channel and a Facebook site, as did the recent Republican Speaker of the House of Representatives, John Boehner.

Social media, like Facebook, also placed journalism in the hands of citizens: **citizen journalism** occurs when citizens use their personal recording devices and cell phones to capture events and post them on the Internet. In 2012, citizen journalists caught both presidential candidates by surprise. Mitt Romney was taped by a bartender's personal camera saying that 47 percent of Americans would vote for President Obama because they were dependent on the government.[54] Obama was recorded by a *Huffington Post* volunteer saying that some Midwesterners "cling to guns or religion or antipathy to people who aren't like them" due to their frustration with the economy.[55] More recently, as Donald Trump was trying to close out the fall 2016 campaign, his musings about having his way with women were revealed on the infamous Billy Bush Access Hollywood tape. These statements became nightmares for the campaigns. As journalism continues to scale back and hire fewer professional writers in an effort to control costs, citizen journalism may become the new normal.[56]

Another shift in the new media is a change in viewers' preferred programming. Younger viewers, especially members of Generation X and Millennials, like their newscasts to be humorous. The popularity of *The Daily Show* and *The Colbert Report* demonstrate that news, even political news, can win young viewers if delivered well.[57] Such **soft news** presents news in an entertaining and approachable manner, painlessly introducing a variety of topics. While the depth or quality of reporting may be less than ideal, these shows can sound an alarm as needed to raise citizen awareness (Figure 8.11).[58]

Figure 8.11 In June 2009, Stephen Colbert of *The Colbert Report* took his soft news show on the road, heading to Iraq for a week. During the first episode, Colbert interviewed Ray Odierno, commanding general of the coalition forces stationed in Iraq. (credit: The U.S. Army)

Viewers who watch or listen to programs like John Oliver's *Last Week Tonight* are more likely to be aware and observant of political events and foreign policy crises than they would otherwise be.[59] They may view opposing party candidates more favorably because the low-partisan, friendly interview styles allow politicians to relax and be conversational rather than defensive.[60] Because viewers of political comedy shows watch the news frequently, they may, in fact, be more politically knowledgeable than citizens viewing national news. In two studies researchers interviewed respondents and asked knowledge questions about current events and situations. Viewers of *The Daily Show* scored more correct answers than viewers of news programming and news stations.[61] That being said, it is not clear whether the number of viewers is large enough to make a big impact on politics, nor do we know whether the learning is long term or short term.[62]

Get Connected!

Becoming a Citizen Journalist

Local government and politics need visibility. College students need a voice. Why not become a citizen journalist? City and county governments hold meetings on a regular basis and students rarely attend. Yet issues relevant to students are often discussed at these meetings, like increases in street parking fines, zoning for off-campus housing, and tax incentives for new businesses that employ part-time student labor. Attend some meetings, ask questions, and write about the experience on your Facebook page. Create a blog to organize your reports or use Storify to curate a social media debate. If you prefer videography, create a YouTube channel to document your reports on current events, or Tweet your live video using Periscope or Meerkat.

Not interested in government? Other areas of governance that affect students are the university or college's Board of Regents meetings. These cover topics like tuition increases, class cuts, and changes to student conduct policies. If your state requires state institutions to open their meetings to the public, consider attending. You might be the one to notify your peers of changes that affect them.

What local meetings could you cover? What issues are important to you and your peers?

8.3 Regulating the Media

Learning Objectives

By the end of this section, you will be able to:
- Identify circumstances in which the freedom of the press is not absolute
- Compare the ways in which the government oversees and influences media programming

The Constitution gives Congress responsibility for promoting the general welfare. While it is difficult to define what this broad dictate means, Congress has used it to protect citizens from media content it deems inappropriate. Although the media are independent participants in the U.S. political system, their liberties are not absolute and there are rules they must follow.

MEDIA AND THE FIRST AMENDMENT

The U.S. Constitution was written in secrecy. Journalists were neither invited to watch the drafting, nor did the framers talk to the press about their disagreements and decisions. Once it was finished, however, the Constitution was released to the public and almost all newspapers printed it. Newspaper editors also published commentary and opinion about the new document and the form of government it proposed. Early support for the Constitution was strong, and Anti-Federalists (who opposed it) argued that their concerns were not properly covered by the press. The eventual printing of *The Federalist Papers*, and the lesser-known Anti-Federalist Papers, fueled the argument that the press was vital to American democracy. It was also clear the press had the ability to affect public opinion and therefore public policy.[63]

The approval of the First Amendment, as a part of the Bill of Rights, demonstrated the framers' belief that a free and vital press was important enough to protect. It said:

> "Congress shall make no law respecting an establishment of religion, or prohibiting the free exercise thereof; or abridging the freedom of speech, or of the press; or the right of the people peaceably to assemble, and to petition the government for a redress of grievances."

This amendment serves as the basis for the political freedoms of the United States, and freedom of the press plays a strong role in keeping democracy healthy. Without it, the press would not be free to alert citizens to government abuses and corruption. In fact, one of New York's first newspapers, the *New York Weekly Journal*, began under John Peter Zenger in 1733 with the goal of routing corruption in the colonial government. After the colonial governor, William Cosby, had Zenger arrested and charged with seditious libel in 1835, his lawyers successfully defended his case and Zenger was found not guilty, affirming the importance of a free press in the colonies (Figure 8.12).

Figure 8.12 In defending John Peter Zenger against charges of libel against colonial governor William Cosby, Andrew Hamilton argued that a statement is not libelous if it can be proved. (credit: modification of work by the Library of Congress)

The media act as informants and messengers, providing the means for citizens to become informed and serving as a venue for citizens to announce plans to assemble and protest actions by their government. Yet the government must ensure the media are acting in good faith and not abusing their power. Like the other First Amendment liberties, freedom of the press is not absolute. The media have limitations on their freedom to publish and broadcast.

Slander and Libel

First, the media do not have the right to commit **slander**, speak false information with an intent to harm a person or entity, or **libel**, print false information with an intent to harm a person or entity. These acts constitute defamation of character that can cause a loss of reputation and income. The media do not have the right to free speech in cases of libel and slander because the information is known to be false. Yet on a weekly basis, newspapers and magazines print stories that are negative and harmful. How can they do this and not be sued?

First, libel and slander occur only in cases where false information is presented as fact. When editors or columnists write opinions, they are protected from many of the libel and slander provisions because they are not claiming their statements are facts. Second, it is up to the defamed individual or company to bring a lawsuit against the media outlet, and the courts have different standards depending on whether the claimant is a private or public figure. A public figure must show that the publisher or broadcaster acted in "reckless disregard" when submitting information as truth or that the author's intent was malicious. This test goes back to the *New York Times v. Sullivan* (1964) case, in which a police commissioner in Alabama sued over inaccurate statements in a newspaper advertisement.[64] Because the commissioner was a public figure, the U.S. Supreme Court applied a stringent test of malice to determine whether the advertisement was libel; the court deemed it was not.

A private individual must make one of the above arguments or argue that the author was negligent in not making sure the information was accurate before publishing it. For this reason, newspapers and magazines are less likely to stray from hard facts when covering private individuals, yet they can be willing to stretch the facts when writing about politicians, celebrities, or public figures. But even stretching the truth can be costly for a publisher. In 2010, *Star* magazine published a headline, "Addiction Nightmare: Katie

Drug Shocker," leading readers to believe actress Katie Holmes was taking drugs. While the article in the magazine focuses on the addictive quality of Scientology sessions rather than drugs, the implication and the headline were different. Because drugs cause people to act erratically, directors might be less inclined to hire Holmes if she were addicted to drugs. Thus Holmes could argue that she had lost opportunity and income from the headline. While the publisher initially declined to correct the story, Holmes filed a $50 million lawsuit, and *Star's* parent company American Media, Inc. eventually settled. *Star* printed an apology and made a donation to a charity on Holmes' behalf.[65]

Classified Material

The media have only a limited right to publish material the government says is classified. If a newspaper or media outlet obtains classified material, or if a journalist is witness to information that is classified, the government may request certain material be redacted or removed from the article. In many instances, government officials and former employees give journalists classified paperwork in an effort to bring public awareness to a problem. If the journalist calls the White House or Pentagon for quotations on a classified topic, the president may order the newspaper to stop publication in the interest of national security. The courts are then asked to rule on what is censored and what can be printed.

The line between the people's right to know and national security is not always clear. In 1971, the Supreme Court heard the Pentagon Papers case, in which the U.S. government sued the *New York Times* and the *Washington Post* to stop the release of information from a classified study of the Vietnam War. The Supreme Court ruled that while the government can impose **prior restraint** on the media, meaning the government can prevent the publication of information, that right is very limited. The court gave the newspapers the right to publish much of the study, but revelation of troop movements and the names of undercover operatives are some of the few approved reasons for which the government can stop publication or reporting.

During the second Persian Gulf War, FOX News reporter Geraldo Rivera convinced the military to embed him with a U.S. Army unit in Iraq to provide live coverage of its day-to-day activities. During one of the reports he filed while traveling with the 101st Airborne Division, Rivera had his camera operator record him drawing a map in the sand, showing where his unit was and using Baghdad as a reference point. Rivera then discussed where the unit would go next. Rivera was immediately removed from the unit and escorted from Iraq.[66] The military exercised its right to maintain secrecy over troop movements, stating that Rivera's reporting had given away troop locations and compromised the safety of the unit. Rivera's future transmissions and reporting were censored until he was away from the unit.

MEDIA AND FCC REGULATIONS

The liberties enjoyed by newspapers are overseen by the U.S. court system, while television and radio broadcasters are monitored by both the courts and a government regulatory commission.

The Radio Act of 1927 was the first attempt by Congress to regulate broadcast materials. The act was written to organize the rapidly expanding number of radio stations and the overuse of frequencies. But politicians feared that broadcast material would be obscene or biased. The Radio Act thus contained language that gave the government control over the quality of programming sent over public airwaves, and the power to ensure that stations maintained the public's best interest.[67]

The Communications Act of 1934 replaced the Radio Act and created a more powerful entity to monitor the airwaves—a seven-member Federal Communications Commission (FCC) to oversee both radio and telephone communication. The FCC, which now has only five members (Figure 8.13), requires radio stations to apply for licenses, granted only if stations follow rules about limiting advertising, providing a public forum for discussion, and serving local and minority communities. With the advent of television, the FCC was given the same authority to license and monitor television stations. The FCC now also enforces ownership limits to avoid monopolies and censors materials deemed inappropriate. It has no jurisdiction over print media, mainly because print media are purchased and not broadcast.

Figure 8.13 In June 2018, the leadership of the FCC included (from left to right) Jessica Rosenworcel, Michael O'Rielly, Ajit Pai, and Brendan Carr. (credit: Federal Communications Commission)

Link to Learning

Concerned about something you heard or viewed? Would you like to file a complaint about an obscene radio program or place your phone number on the Do Not Call list? The FCC (https://openstax.org/l/29fccgov) oversees each of these.

To maintain a license, stations are required to meet a number of criteria. The **equal-time rule**, for instance, states that registered candidates running for office must be given equal opportunities for airtime and advertisements at non-cable television and radio stations beginning forty-five days before a primary election and sixty days before a general election. Should WBNS in Columbus, Ohio, agree to sell Senator Marco Rubio thirty seconds of airtime for a presidential campaign commercial, the station must also sell all other candidates in that race thirty seconds of airtime at the same price. This rate cannot be more than the station charges favored commercial advertisers that run ads of the same class and during the same time period.[68] More importantly, should Fox5 in Atlanta give Bernie Sanders five minutes of free airtime for an infomercial, the station must honor requests from all other candidates in the race for five minutes of free equal air time or a complaint may be filed with the FCC.[69] In 2015, Donald Trump, when he was running for the Republican presidential nomination, appeared on *Saturday Night Live*. Other Republican candidates made equal time requests, and NBC agreed to give each candidate twelve minutes and five seconds of air time on a Friday and Saturday night, as well as during a later episode of *Saturday Night Live*.[70]

The FCC does waive the equal-time rule if the coverage is purely news. If a newscaster is covering a political rally and is able to secure a short interview with a candidate, equal time does not apply. Likewise, if a news programs creates a short documentary on the problem of immigration reform and chooses to include clips from only one or two candidates, the rule does not apply.[71] But the rule may include shows that are not news. For this reason, some stations will not show a movie or television program if a candidate appears in it. In 2003, Arnold Schwarzenegger and Gary Coleman, both actors, became candidates in California's gubernatorial recall election. Television stations did not run Coleman's sitcom *Diff'rent Strokes* or Schwarzenegger's movies, because they would have been subject to the equal time provision. With 135 candidates on the official ballot, stations would have been hard-pressed to offer thirty-minute and two-hour time slots to all.[72] Even the broadcasting of the president's State of the Union speech can trigger the equal-time provisions. Opposing parties in Congress now use their time immediately following the State of the Union to offer an official rebuttal to the president's proposals.[73]

While the idea behind the equal-time rule is fairness, it may not apply beyond candidates to supporters of that candidate or of a cause. Hence, there potentially may be a loophole in which broadcasters can give free time to just one candidate's supporters. In the 2012 Wisconsin gubernatorial recall election, Scott Walker's supporters were allegedly given free air time to raise funds and ask for volunteers while opponent Tom Barrett's supporters were not.[74] According to someone involved in the case, the FCC declined to intervene after a complaint was filed on the matter, saying the equal-time rule applied only to the actual candidates, and that the case was an instance of the now-dead **fairness doctrine**.[75] The fairness doctrine was instituted in 1949 and required licensed stations to cover controversial issues in a balanced manner by providing listeners with information about all perspectives on any controversial issue. If one candidate, cause, or supporter was given an opportunity to reach the viewers or listeners, the other side was to be given a chance to present its side as well. The fairness doctrine ended in the 1980s, after a succession of court cases led to its repeal by the FCC in 1987, with stations and critics arguing the doctrine limited debate of controversial topics and placed the government in the role of editor.[76]

The FCC also maintains **indecency regulations** over television, radio, and other broadcasters, which limit indecent material and keep the public airwaves free of obscene material.[77] While the Supreme Court has declined to define obscenity, it is identified using a test outlined in *Miller v. California* (1973).[78] Under the Miller test, obscenity is something that appeals to deviants, breaks local or state laws, and lacks value.[79] The Supreme Court determined that the presence of children in the audience trumped the right of broadcasters to air obscene and profane programming. However, broadcasters can show indecent programming or air profane language between the hours of 10 p.m. and 6 a.m.[80]

The Supreme Court has also affirmed that the FCC has the authority to regulate content. When a George Carlin skit was aired on the radio with a warning that material might be offensive, the FCC still censored it. The station appealed the decision and lost.[81] Fines can range from tens of thousands to millions of dollars, and many are levied for sexual jokes on radio talk shows and nudity on television. In 2004, Janet Jackson's wardrobe malfunction during the Super Bowl's half-time show cost the CBS network $550,000.

While some FCC violations are witnessed directly by commission members, like Jackson's exposure at the Super Bowl, the FCC mainly relies on citizens and consumers to file complaints about violations of equal time and indecency rules. Approximately 2 percent of complaints to the FCC are about radio programming and 10 percent about television programming, compared to 71 percent about telephone complaints and 15 percent about Internet complaints.[82] Yet what constitutes a violation is not always clear for citizens wishing to complain, nor is it clear what will lead to a fine or license revocation. In October 2014, parent advocacy groups and consumers filed complaints and called for the FCC to fine ABC for running a sexually charged opening scene in the drama *Scandal* immediately after *It's the Great Pumpkin, Charlie Brown*—without an ad or the cartoon's credits to act as a buffer between the very different types of programming.[83] The FCC did not fine ABC.

The Telecommunications Act of 1996 brought significant changes to the radio and television industries. It dropped the limit on the number of radio stations (forty) and television stations (twelve) a single company could own. It also allowed networks to purchase large numbers of cable stations. In essence, it reduced competition and increased the number of conglomerates. Some critics, such as Common Cause, argue that the act also raised cable prices and made it easier for companies to neglect their public interest obligations.[84] The act also changed the role of the FCC from regulator to monitor. The Commission oversees the purchase of stations to avoid media monopolies and adjudicates consumer complaints against radio, television, and telephone companies.

An important change in government regulation of the press in the name of the fairness of coverage relates to net neutrality. Net neutrality rules were promulgated in 2015 by the Obama administration.

These regulations required internet service providers to give everyone equal access to their services and disallowed biased charging of internet access fees. Early in the Trump Administration, the Federal Communications Commission (FCC) reversed that course by throwing out the policy of net neutrality.[85]

Finding a Middle Ground

Watch Dog or Paparazzi?

We expect the media to keep a close eye on the government. But at what point does the media coverage cross from informational to sensational?

In 2012, former secretary of state Hillary Clinton was questioned about her department's decisions regarding the U.S. consulate in Benghazi, Libya. The consulate had been bombed by militants, leading to the death of an ambassador and a senior service officer. It was clear the United States had some knowledge that there was a threat to the consulate, and officials wondered whether requests to increase security at the consulate had been ignored. Clinton was asked to appear before a House Select Committee to answer questions, and the media began its coverage. While some journalists limited their reporting to Benghazi, others did not. Clinton was hounded about everything from her illness (dubbed the "Benghazi-flu") to her clothing to her facial expressions to her choice of eyeglasses.[86] Even her hospital stay was questioned.[87] Some argued the expanded coverage was due to political attacks on Clinton, who at that time was widely perceived to be the top contender for the Democratic presidential nomination in 2016.[88] Republican majority leader Kevin McCarthy later implied that the hearings were an attempt to make Clinton look untrustworthy.[89] Yet Clinton was again brought before the House Select Committee on Benghazi as late as October 2015 (Figure 8.14).

Figure 8.14 On October 22, 2015, the House Select Committee on Benghazi listened to testimony from former Secretary of State Hillary Clinton for close to eleven hours.

This coverage should lead us to question whether the media gives us the information we need, or the information we want. Were people concerned about an attack on U.S. state officials working abroad, or did they just want to read rumors and attacks on Clinton? Did Republicans use the media's tendency to pursue a target as a way to hurt Clinton in the polls? If the media gives us what we want, the answer seems to be that we wanted the media to act as both watchdog and paparazzi.

How should the press have acted in this case if it were behaving only as the watchdog of democracy?

MEDIA AND TRANSPARENCY

The press has had some assistance in performing its muckraking duty. Laws that mandate federal and many state government proceedings and meeting documents be made available to the public are called **sunshine laws**. Proponents believe that open disagreements allow democracy to flourish and darkness allows corruption to occur. Opponents argue that some documents and policies are sensitive, and that the sunshine laws can inhibit policymaking.

While some documents may be classified due to national or state security, governments are encouraged to limit the over-classification of documents. The primary legal example for sunshine laws is the **Freedom of Information Act (FOIA)**, passed in 1966 and signed by President Lyndon B. Johnson. The act requires the executive branch of the U.S. government to provide information requested by citizens and was intended to increase openness in the executive branch, which had been criticized for hiding information. Citizens wishing to obtain information may request documents from the appropriate agencies, and agencies may charge fees if the collection and copying of the requested documentation requires time and labor.[90] FOIA also identifies data that does not need to be disclosed, such as human resource and medical records, national defense records, and material provided by confidential sources, to name a few.[91] Not all presidents have embraced this openness, however. President Ronald Reagan, in 1981, exempted the CIA and FBI from FOIA requests.[92] Information requests have increased significantly in recent years, with U.S. agencies receiving over 700,000 requests in 2014, many directed to the Departments of State and Defense, thus creating a backlog.[93]

Link to Learning

Want to request a government document but unsure where to start? If the agency is a part of the U.S. government, the Freedom of Information Act (https://openstax.org/l/29foiagov) portal will help you out.

Few people file requests for information because most assume the media will find and report on important problems. And many people, including the press, assume the government, including the White House, sufficiently answers questions and provides information about government actions and policies. This expectation is not new. During the Civil War, journalists expected to have access to those representing the government, including the military. But William Tecumseh Sherman, a Union general, maintained distance between the press and his military. Following the publication of material Sherman believed to be protected by government censorship, a journalist was arrested and nearly put to death. The event spurred the creation of accreditation for journalists, which meant a journalist must be approved to cover the White House and the military before entering a controlled area. All accredited journalists also need approval by military field commanders before coming near a military zone.[94]

To cover war up close, more journalists are asking to travel with troops during armed conflict. In 2003, George W. Bush's administration decided to allow more journalists in the field, hoping the concession would reduce friction between the military and the press. The U.S. Department of Defense placed fifty-eight journalists in a media boot camp to prepare them to be embedded with military regiments in Iraq. Although the increase in embedded journalists resulted in substantial in-depth coverage, many journalists felt their colleagues performed poorly, acting as celebrities rather than reporters.[95]

The line between journalists' expectation of openness and the government's willingness to be open has continued to be a point of contention. Some administrations use the media to increase public support during times of war, as Woodrow Wilson did in World War I. Other presidents limit the media in order to limit dissent. In 1990, during the first Persian Gulf War, journalists received all publication material from the military in a prepackaged and staged manner. Access to Dover, the air force base that receives coffins of U.S. soldiers who die overseas, was closed. Journalists accused George H. W. Bush's administration of limiting access and forcing them to produce bad pieces. The White House believed it controlled the message.[96] The ban was later lifted.

In his 2008 presidential run, Barack Obama promised to run a transparent White House.[97] Yet once in office, he found that transparency makes it difficult to get work done, and so he limited access and questions. In his first year in office, George W. Bush, who was criticized by Obama as having a closed government, gave 147 question-and-answer sessions with journalists, while Obama gave only 46. Even Helen Thomas, a long-time liberal White House press correspondent, said the Obama administration tried to control both information and journalists (Figure 8.15).[98]

Figure 8.15 President Barack Obama and White House correspondent Helen Thomas set aside their differences over transparency to enjoy cupcakes in honor of their shared birthday on August 4, 2009.

Because White House limitations on the press are not unusual, many journalists rely on confidential sources. In 1972, under the cloak of anonymity, the associate director of the Federal Bureau of Investigation, Mark Felt, became a news source for Bob Woodward and Carl Bernstein, political reporters at the *Washington Post*. Felt provided information about a number of potential stories and was Woodward's main source for information about President Richard Nixon's involvement in a series of illegal activities, including the break-in at Democratic Party headquarters in Washington's Watergate office complex. The information eventually led to Nixon's resignation and the indictment of sixty-nine people in his administration. Felt was nicknamed "Deep Throat," and the journalists kept his identity secret until 2005.[99]

The practice of granting anonymity to sources is sometimes referred to as **reporter's privilege**. Fueled by the First Amendment's protection of the press, journalists have long offered to keep sources confidential to protect them from government prosecution. To illustrate, as part of the investigation into the outing of Valerie Plame as a CIA officer, *New York Times* reporter Judith Miller was jailed for refusing to reveal "Scooter" Libby, Vice President Dick Cheney's chief of staff, as her confidential government source.[100] Reporter's privilege has increased the number of instances in which whistleblowers and government employees have given journalists tips or documents to prompt investigation into questionable government practices. Edward Snowden's 2013 leak to the press regarding the U.S. government's massive internal surveillance and tapping program was one such case.

In 1972, however, the Supreme Court determined that journalists are not exempt from subpoenas and that courts could force testimony to name a confidential source. Journalists who conceal a source and thereby protect him or her from being properly tried for a crime may spend time in jail for contempt of court. In the case of *Branzburg v. Hayes* (1972), three journalists were placed in contempt of court for refusing to divulge sources.[101] The journalists appealed to the Supreme Court. In a 5–4 decision, the justices determined that freedom of the press did not extend to the confidentiality of sources. A concurring opinion did state that the case should be seen as a limited ruling, however. If the government needed to know a source due to a criminal trial, it could pursue the name of that source.[102]

More recently, the Supreme Court refused to hear an appeal from *New York Times* journalist James Risen, who was subpoenaed and ordered to name a confidential source who had provided details about a U.S. government mission designed to harm Iran's nuclear arms program. Risen was finally released from the subpoena, but the battle took seven years and the government eventually collected enough other evidence to make his testimony less crucial to the case.[103] Overall, the transparency of the government is affected more by the executive currently holding office than by the First Amendment.

8.4 The Impact of the Media

Learning Objectives

By the end of this section, you will be able to:
- Identify forms of bias that exist in news coverage and ways the media can present biased coverage
- Explain how the media cover politics and issues
- Evaluate the impact of the media on politics and policymaking

In what ways can the media affect society and government? The media's primary duty is to present us with information and alert us when important events occur. This information may affect what we think and the actions we take. The media can also place pressure on government to act by signaling a need for intervention or showing that citizens want change. For these reasons, the quality of the media's coverage matters.

MEDIA EFFECTS AND BIAS

Concerns about the effects of media on consumers and the existence and extent of media bias go back to the 1920s. Reporter and commentator Walter Lippmann noted that citizens have limited personal experience with government and the world and posited that the media, through their stories, place ideas in citizens' minds. These ideas become part of the citizens' frame of reference and affect their decisions. Lippmann's statements led to the **hypodermic theory**, which argues that information is "shot" into the receiver's mind and readily accepted.[104]

Yet studies in the 1930s and 1940s found that information was transmitted in two steps, with one person reading the news and then sharing the information with friends. People listened to their friends, but not to those with whom they disagreed. The newspaper's effect was thus diminished through conversation. This discovery led to the **minimal effects theory**, which argues the media have little effect on citizens and voters.[105] By the 1970s, a new idea, the **cultivation theory**, hypothesized that media develop a person's view of the world by presenting a perceived reality.[106] What we see on a regular basis is our reality. Media can then set norms for readers and viewers by choosing what is covered or discussed.

In the end, the consensus among observers is that media have some effect, even if the effect is subtle. This raises the question of how the media, even general newscasts, can affect citizens. One of the ways is through **framing**: the creation of a narrative, or context, for a news story. The news often uses frames to place a story in a context so the reader understands its importance or relevance. Yet, at the same time, framing affects the way the reader or viewer processes the story.

Episodic framing occurs when a story focuses on isolated details or specifics rather than looking broadly at a whole issue. *Thematic framing* takes a broad look at an issue and skips numbers or details. It looks at how the issue has changed over a long period of time and what has led to it. For example, a large, urban city is dealing with the problem of an increasing homeless population, and the city has suggested ways to improve the situation. If journalists focus on the immediate statistics, report the current percentage of homeless people, interview a few, and look at the city's current investment in a homeless shelter, the coverage is episodic. If they look at homelessness as a problem increasing everywhere, examine the reasons people become homeless, and discuss the trends in cities' attempts to solve the problem, the coverage is thematic. Episodic frames may create more sympathy, while a thematic frame may leave the reader or viewer emotionally disconnected and less sympathetic (Figure 8.16).

Figure 8.16 Civil war in Syria has led many to flee the country, including this woman living in a Syrian refugee camp in Jordan in September 2015. Episodic framing of the stories of Syrian refugees, and their deaths, turned government inaction into action. (credit: Enes Reyhan)

Link to Learning

For a closer look at framing and how it influences voters, read "How the Media Frames Political Issues" (https://openstax.org/l/29scotlondoness) , a review essay by Scott London.

Framing can also affect the way we see race, socioeconomics, or other generalizations. For this reason, it is linked to **priming**: when media coverage predisposes the viewer or reader to a particular perspective on a subject or issue. If a newspaper article focuses on unemployment, struggling industries, and jobs moving overseas, the reader will have a negative opinion about the economy. If then asked whether he or she approves of the president's job performance, the reader is primed to say no. Readers and viewers are able to fight priming effects if they are aware of them or have prior information about the subject.

COVERAGE EFFECTS ON GOVERNANCE AND CAMPAIGNS

When it is spotty, the media's coverage of campaigns and government can sometimes affect the way government operates and the success of candidates. In 1972, for instance, the McGovern-Fraser reforms created a voter-controlled primary system, so party leaders no longer pick the presidential candidates. Now the media are seen as kingmakers and play a strong role in influencing who will become the Democratic and Republican nominees in presidential elections. They can discuss the candidates' messages, vet their credentials, carry sound bites of their speeches, and conduct interviews. The candidates with the most media coverage build momentum and do well in the first few primaries and caucuses. This, in turn, leads to more media coverage, more momentum, and eventually a winning candidate. Thus, candidates need the media.

In the 1980s, campaigns learned that tight control on candidate information created more favorable media coverage. In the presidential election of 1984, candidates Ronald Reagan and George H. W. Bush began using an issue-of-the-day strategy, providing quotes and material on only one topic each day. This strategy limited what journalists could cover because they had only limited quotes and sound bites to use in their reports. In 1992, both Bush's and Bill Clinton's campaigns maintained their carefully drawn candidate images by also limiting photographers and television journalists to photo opportunities at rallies and campaign venues. The constant control of the media became known as the "bubble," and journalists were less effective when they were in the campaign's bubble. Reporters complained this coverage was campaign advertising rather than journalism, and a new model emerged with the 1996 election.[107]

Campaign coverage now focuses on the spectacle of the season, rather than providing information about the candidates. Colorful personalities, strange comments, lapse of memories, and embarrassing revelations are more likely to get air time than the candidates' issue positions. Donald Trump may be the best example of shallower press coverage of a presidential election. Some argue that newspapers and news programs are limiting the space they allot to discussion of the campaigns.[108] Others argue that citizens want to see updates on the race and electoral drama, not boring issue positions or substantive reporting.[109] It may also be that journalists have tired of the information games played by politicians and have taken back control of the news cycles.[110] All these factors have likely led to the shallow press coverage we see today, sometimes dubbed *pack journalism* because journalists follow one another rather than digging for their own stories. Television news discusses the strategies and blunders of the election, with colorful examples. Newspapers focus on polls. In an analysis of the 2012 election, Pew Research found that 64 percent of stories and coverage focused on campaign strategy. Only 9 percent covered domestic issue positions; 6 percent covered the candidates' public records; and, 1 percent covered their foreign policy positions.[111]

For better or worse, coverage of the candidates' statements get less air time on radio and television, and sound bites, or clips, of their speeches have become even shorter. In 1968, the average sound bite from Richard Nixon was 42.3 seconds, while a recent study of television coverage found that sound bites had decreased to only eight seconds in the 2004 election.[112] The clips chosen to air were attacks on opponents 40 percent of the time. Only 30 percent contained information about the candidate's issues or events. The study also found the news showed images of the candidates, but for an average of only twenty-five seconds while the newscaster discussed the stories.[113]

This study supports the argument that shrinking sound bites are a way for journalists to control the story and add their own analysis rather than just report on it.[114] Candidates are given a few minutes to try to argue their side of an issue, but some say television focuses on the argument rather than on information. In 2004, Jon Stewart of Comedy Central's *The Daily Show* began attacking the CNN program *Crossfire* for being theater, saying the hosts engaged in reactionary and partisan arguing rather than true debating.[115] Some of Stewart's criticisms resonated, even with host Paul Begala, and *Crossfire* was later pulled from the air.[116]

The media's discussion of campaigns has also grown negative. Although biased campaign coverage dates back to the period of the partisan press, the increase in the number of cable news stations has made the problem more visible. Stations like FOX News and MSNBC are overt in their use of bias in framing stories. During the 2012 campaign, seventy-one of seventy-four MSNBC stories about Mitt Romney were highly negative, while FOX News' coverage of Obama had forty-six out of fifty-two stories with negative information (Figure 8.17). The major networks—ABC, CBS, and NBC—were somewhat more balanced, yet the overall coverage of both candidates tended to be negative.[117]

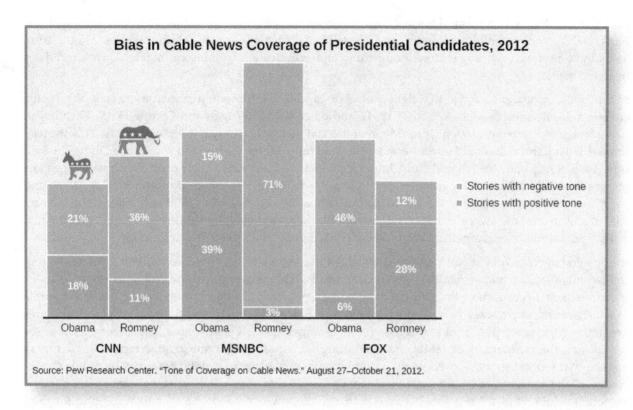

Figure 8.17 Media coverage of campaigns is increasingly negative, with cable news stations demonstrating more bias in their framing of stories during the 2012 campaign.

Due in part to the lack of substantive media coverage, campaigns increasingly use social media to relay their message. Candidates can create their own sites and pages and try to spread news through supporters to the undecided. In 2012, both Romney and Obama maintained Facebook, Twitter, and YouTube accounts to provide information to voters. Yet, on social media, candidates still need to combat negativity, from both the opposition and supporters. Stories about Romney that appeared in the mainstream media were negative 38 percent of the time, while his coverage in Facebook news was negative 62 percent of the time and 58 percent of the time on Twitter.[118] In the 2016 election cycle, both party nominees heavily used social media. Donald Trump's scores of tweets became very prominent as he tweeted during Clinton's convention acceptance speech and sometimes at all hours of the night. Clinton also used Twitter, but less so than Trump, though arguably staying better on message. Trump tended to rail on about topics and at one point was even drawn into a Twitter battle with Senator Elizabeth Warren (D-MA). Hillary Clinton also used Facebook for longer messages and imaging.

Once candidates are in office, the chore of governing begins, with the added weight of media attention. Historically, if presidents were unhappy with their press coverage, they used personal and professional means to change its tone. Franklin D. Roosevelt, for example, was able to keep journalists from printing stories through gentleman's agreements, loyalty, and the provision of additional information, sometimes off the record. The journalists then wrote positive stories, hoping to keep the president as a source. John F. Kennedy hosted press conferences twice a month and opened the floor for questions from journalists, in an effort to keep press coverage positive.[119]

When presidents and other members of the White House are not forthcoming with information, journalists must press for answers. Dan Rather, a journalist for CBS, regularly sparred with presidents in an effort to get information. When Rather interviewed Richard Nixon about Vietnam and Watergate, Nixon was hostile and uncomfortable.[120] In a 1988 interview with then-vice president George H. W. Bush, Bush accused Rather of being argumentative about the possible cover-up of a secret arms sale with Iran:

> Rather: I don't want to be argumentative, Mr. Vice President.

Bush: You do, Dan.

Rather: No—no, sir, I don't.

Bush: This is not a great night, because I want to talk about why I want to be president, why those 41 percent of the people are supporting me. And I don't think it's fair to judge my whole career by a rehash of Iran. How would you like it if I judged your career by those seven minutes when you walked off the set in New York? [121]

One of the more profound changes with President Trump compared to prior presidents revolves around his relationship with the press. Trump rarely holds press conferences, choosing instead to tweet what he is thinking to the world. Whereas previous presidents spent much effort to cultivate relationships with the media in order to court public opinion, Trump has instead criticized the media as untrustworthy and producing "fake news." This approach has led to critical coverage of the president across all but a few press outlets. Moreover, President Trump's attack on the media has led key outlets, like CNN and the Washington Post, to take action. CNN sued in federal court to get one of their news reporters (Jim Acosta) reinstated on the White House beat after he was thrown out of the West Wing. The Washington Post has run the tagline "Democracy Dies in Darkness" on its website regularly since President Trump began his assault on the free press. [122]

Cabinet secretaries and other appointees also talk with the press, sometimes making for conflicting messages. The creation of the position of press secretary and the White House Office of Communications both stemmed from the need to send a cohesive message from the executive branch. Currently, the White House controls the information coming from the executive branch through the Office of Communications and decides who will meet with the press and what information will be given.

But stories about the president often examine personality, or the president's ability to lead the country, deal with Congress, or respond to national and international events. They are less likely to cover the president's policies or agendas without a lot of effort on the president's behalf. [123] When Obama first entered office in 2009, journalists focused on his battles with Congress, critiquing his leadership style and inability to work with Representative Nancy Pelosi, then Speaker of the House. To gain attention for his policies, specifically the American Recovery and Reinvestment Act (ARRA), Obama began traveling the United States to draw the media away from Congress and encourage discussion of his economic stimulus package. Once the ARRA had been passed, Obama began travelling again, speaking locally about why the country needed the Affordable Care Act and guiding media coverage to promote support for the act. [124]

Congressional representatives have a harder time attracting media attention for their policies. House and Senate members who use the media well, either to help their party or to show expertise in an area, may increase their power within Congress, which helps them bargain for fellow legislators' votes. Senators and high-ranking House members may also be invited to appear on cable news programs as guests, where they may gain some media support for their policies. Yet, overall, because there are so many members of Congress, and therefore so many agendas, it is harder for individual representatives to draw media coverage. [125]

It is less clear, however, whether media coverage of an issue leads Congress to make policy, or whether congressional policymaking leads the media to cover policy. In the 1970s, Congress investigated ways to stem the number of drug-induced deaths and crimes. As congressional meetings dramatically increased, the press was slow to cover the topic. The number of hearings was at its highest from 1970 to 1982, yet media coverage did not rise to the same level until 1984. [126] Subsequent hearings and coverage led to national policies like DARE and First Lady Nancy Reagan's "Just Say No" campaign (Figure 8.18).

(a)   (b)

Figure 8.18 First Lady Nancy Reagan speaks at a "Just Say No" rally in Los Angeles on May 13, 1987 (a). The Drug Abuse Resistance Education (D.A.R.E.) is an anti-drug, anti-gang program founded in 1983 by a joint initiative of the Los Angeles Police Department and the Los Angeles Unified School District.

Later studies of the media's effect on both the president and Congress report that the media has a stronger agenda-setting effect on the president than on Congress. What the media choose to cover affects what the president thinks is important to voters, and these issues were often of national importance. The media's effect on Congress was limited, however, and mostly extended to local issues like education or child and elder abuse.[127] If the media are discussing a topic, chances are a member of Congress has already submitted a relevant bill, and it is waiting in committee.

COVERAGE EFFECTS ON SOCIETY

The media choose what they want to discuss. This agenda setting creates a reality for voters and politicians that affects the way people think, act, and vote. Even if the crime rate is going down, for instance, citizens accustomed to reading stories about assault and other offenses still perceive crime to be an issue.[128] Studies have also found that the media's portrayal of race is flawed, especially in coverage of crime and poverty. One study revealed that local news shows were more likely to show pictures of criminals when they were African American, so they overrepresented blacks as perpetrators and whites as victims.[129] A second study found a similar pattern in which Latinos were underrepresented as victims of crime and as police officers, while whites were overrepresented as both.[130] Voters were thus more likely to assume that most criminals are black and most victims and police officers are white, even though the numbers do not support those assumptions.

Network news similarly misrepresents the victims of poverty by using more images of blacks than whites in its segments. Viewers in a study were left believing African Americans were the majority of the unemployed and poor, rather than seeing the problem as one faced by many races.[131] The misrepresentation of race is not limited to news coverage, however. A study of images printed in national magazines, like *Time* and *Newsweek*, found they also misrepresented race and poverty. The magazines were more likely to show images of young African Americans when discussing poverty and excluded the elderly and the young, as well as whites and Latinos, which is the true picture of poverty.[132]

Racial framing, even if unintentional, affects perceptions and policies. If viewers are continually presented with images of African Americans as criminals, there is an increased chance they will perceive members of this group as violent or aggressive.[133] The perception that most recipients of welfare are working-age African Americans may have led some citizens to vote for candidates who promised to reduce welfare benefits.[134] When survey respondents were shown a story of a white unemployed individual, 71 percent listed unemployment as one of the top three problems facing the United States, while only 53 percent did so if the story was about an unemployed African American.[135]

Word choice may also have a priming effect. News organizations like the *Los Angeles Times* and the Associated Press no longer use the phrase "illegal immigrant" to describe undocumented residents. This may be due to the desire to create a "sympathetic" frame for the immigration situation rather than a "threat" frame.[136]

Media coverage of women has been similarly biased. Most journalists in the early 1900s were male, and women's issues were not part of the newsroom discussion. As journalist Kay Mills put it, the women's movement of the 1960s and 1970s was about raising awareness of the problems of equality, but writing about rallies "was like trying to nail Jell-O to the wall."[137] Most politicians, business leaders, and other authority figures were male, and editors' reactions to the stories were lukewarm. The lack of women in the newsroom, politics, and corporate leadership encouraged silence.[138]

In 1976, journalist Barbara Walters became the first female coanchor on a network news show, *The ABC Evening News*. She was met with great hostility from her coanchor Harry Reasoner and received critical coverage from the press.[139] On newspaper staffs, women reported having to fight for assignments to well-published **beats**, or to be assigned areas or topics, such as the economy or politics, that were normally reserved for male journalists. Once female journalists held these assignments, they feared writing about women's issues. Would it make them appear weak? Would they be taken from their coveted beats?[140] This apprehension allowed poor coverage of women and the women's movement to continue until women were better represented as journalists and as editors. Strength of numbers allowed them to be confident when covering issues like health care, childcare, and education.[141]

Link to Learning

The **Center for American Women in Politics (https://openstax.org/l/29cawprutgers)** researches the treatment women receive from both government and the media, and they share the data with the public.

The media's historically uneven coverage of women continues in its treatment of female candidates. Early coverage was sparse. The stories that did appear often discussed the candidate's viability, or ability to win, rather than her stand on the issues.[142] Women were seen as a novelty rather than as serious contenders who needed to be vetted and discussed. Modern media coverage has changed slightly. One study found that female candidates receive more favorable coverage than in prior generations, especially if they are incumbents.[143] Yet a different study found that while there was increased coverage for female candidates, it was often negative.[144] And it did not include Latina candidates.[145] Without coverage, they are less likely to win.

The historically negative media coverage of female candidates has had another concrete effect: Women are less likely than men to run for office. One common reason is the effect negative media coverage has on families.[146] Many women do not wish to expose their children or spouses to criticism.[147] In 2008, the nomination of Sarah Palin as Republican candidate John McCain's running mate validated this concern (**Figure 8.19**). Some articles focused on her qualifications to be a potential future president or her record on the issues. But others questioned whether she had the right to run for office, given she had young children, one of whom has developmental disabilities.[148] Her daughter, Bristol, was criticized for becoming pregnant while unmarried.[149] Her husband was called cheap for failing to buy her a high-priced wedding ring.[150] Even when candidates ask that children and families be off-limits, the press rarely honors the requests. So women with young children may wait until their children are grown before running for office, if they choose to run at all.

Figure 8.19 When Sarah Palin found herself on the national stage at the Republican Convention in September 2008, media coverage about her selection as John McCain's running mate included numerous questions about her ability to serve based on personal family history. Attacks on candidates' families lead many women to postpone or avoid running for office. (credit: Carol Highsmith)

Key Terms

agenda setting the media's ability to choose which issues or topics get attention

beat the coverage area assigned to journalists for news or stories

citizen journalism video and print news posted to the Internet or social media by citizens rather than the news media

cultivation theory the idea that media affect a citizen's worldview through the information presented

digital paywall the need for a paid subscription to access published online material

equal-time rule an FCC policy that all candidates running for office must be given the same radio and television airtime opportunities

fairness doctrine a 1949 Federal Communications Commission (FCC) policy, now defunct, that required holders of broadcast licenses to cover controversial issues in a balanced manner

framing the process of giving a news story a specific context or background

Freedom of Information Act (FOIA) a federal statute that requires public agencies to provide certain types of information requested by citizens

hypodermic theory the idea that information is placed in a citizen's brain and accepted

indecency regulations laws that limit indecent and obscene material on public airwaves

libel printed information about a person or organization that is not true and harms the reputation of the person or organization

mass media the collection of all media forms that communicate information to the general public

minimal effects theory the idea that the media have little effect on citizens

muckraking news coverage focusing on exposing corrupt business and government practices

party press era period during the 1780s in which newspaper content was biased by political partisanship

priming the process of predisposing readers or viewers to think a particular way

prior restraint a government action that stops someone from doing something before they are able to do it (e.g., forbidding someone to publish a book he or she plans to release)

public relations biased communication intended to improve the image of people, companies, or organizations

reporter's privilege the right of a journalist to keep a source confidential

slander spoken information about a person or organization that is not true and harms the reputation of the person or organization

soft news news presented in an entertaining style

sunshine laws laws that require government documents and proceedings to be made public

yellow journalism sensationalized coverage of scandals and human interest stories

Summary

8.1 What Is the Media?
The media encompass all communications that transmit facts or information to citizens and includes the mass media in print and on the radio, television, and Internet. Television takes many forms, such as local, network, cable, or satellite. Historically, programming was transmitted from networks to local stations and broadcast via the airwaves, while fiber-optic cables now allow for national programming to transmit directly. Technological advances allow on-demand and streaming access for programming, leading to changes in advertising and scheduling practices. Conglomerates are large media corporations that own many stations and other companies; therefore, they can create a monopoly and decrease the flow of information to the public. The media serves to entertain the public, watch for corruption, set the national agenda, and promote the public good. In each of these roles, the media informs the public about what is happening and signals when citizens should act.

8.2 The Evolution of the Media
Newspapers were vital during the Revolutionary War. Later, in the party press era, party loyalty governed coverage. At the turn of the twentieth century, investigative journalism and muckraking appeared, and newspapers began presenting more professional, unbiased information. The modern print media have fought to stay relevant and cost-efficient, moving online to do so.

Most families had radios by the 1930s, making it an effective way for politicians, especially presidents, to reach out to citizens. While the increased use of television decreased the popularity of radio, talk radio still provides political information. Modern presidents also use television to rally people in times of crisis, although social media and the Internet now offer a more direct way for them to communicate. While serious newscasts still exist, younger viewers prefer soft news as a way to become informed.

8.3 Regulating the Media
While freedom of the press is an important aspect of the Bill of Rights, this freedom is not absolute and may be regulated by the U.S. government. The press cannot libel or slander individuals or publish information about troop movements or undercover operatives. The Federal Communications Commission can enforce limits on television and radio programming by fining or revoking licenses. Broadcast material cannot be obscene, and indecent programs can be broadcast only between 10 p.m. and 6 a.m. Stations must also give political candidates equal time for advertising and interviews.

The media help governments maintain transparency. Sunshine laws require some governments and government agencies to make meeting documents public. Some presidents have encouraged journalists and allowed questioning while others have avoided the press. Lack of openness by government officials leads journalists to use confidential sources for important or classified information. The Supreme Court does not give the press complete freedom to keep sources confidential, though the government can choose whom it prosecutes for hiding sources.

8.4 The Impact of the Media
Writers began to formally study media bias in the 1920s. Initially, the press was seen as being able to place information in our minds, but later research found that the media have a minimal effect on recipients. A more recent theory is that the media cultivates our reality by presenting information that creates our perceptions of the world. The media does have the ability to frame what it presents, and it can also prime citizens to think a particular way, which changes how they react to new information.

The media's coverage of electoral candidates has increasingly become analysis rather than reporting. Sound bites from candidates are shorter. The press now provides horse-race coverage on the campaigns rather than in-depth coverage on candidates and their positions, forcing voters to look for other sources, like social media, for information. Current coverage of the government focuses more on what the president does than on presidential policies. Congress, on the other hand, is rarely affected by the media. Most topics discussed by the media are already being discussed by members of Congress or its committees.

The media frame discussions and choose pictures, information, and video to support stories, which may affect the way people vote on social policy and in elections.

Review Questions

1. A local station that broadcasts national network programming is called a(an) _____ station.
   a. affiliate
   b. cable
   c. digital
   d. network

2. Cable programming is often _____.
   a. local
   b. national
   c. network
   d. sports

3. A conglomerate is a corporation that _____.
   a. owns all television news stations in a state
   b. owns many businesses and media networks
   c. owns only radio stations
   d. owns only televisions and newspapers

4. When acting as an agenda setter, the media _____.
   a. decides which issues deserve public attention
   b. covers presidential campaigns equally
   c. reports on corruption in government
   d. brings in advertising revenue for the media corporation

5. How can conglomerates censor information?

6. In what ways is media responsible for promoting the public good?

7. Why is social media an effective way to spread news and information?

8. Newspapers during the Revolutionary War period tended to _____.
   a. give fake news and sensationalize stories
   b. unite the colonists and provide information about the British
   c. print party propaganda
   d. attack colonial politicians

9. Muckraking occurs when newspapers _____.
   a. investigate problems in government and business
   b. investigate actions of celebrities
   c. print sensational news on the front page to sell papers
   d. print more editorials and opinion pieces to sell papers

10. Radio quiz shows and comedy shows were most popular in the _____.
    a. 1900s
    b. 1930s
    c. 1970s
    d. 1990s

11. Television news became a regular feature during _____ due to the public's demand for _____ to explain current events.
    a. WWI; images and maps
    b. Great Depression; charts and tables
    c. WWII; images and maps
    d. Vietnam War; charts and tables

12. Why did Franklin D. Roosevelt's fireside chats help the president enact his policies?

13. How have modern presidents used television to reach out to citizens?

14. Why is soft news good at reaching out and educating viewers?

15. In which circumstance would the courts find libel?
    a. A reporter uses a source that incorrectly states a celebrity is using drugs.
    b. A columnist writes his opinion about whether an actor is hiding a drug problem.
    c. A television reporter delivers a story about increased drug use at the local college.
    d. A reporter writes that local college students are drug dealers but has no sources.

16. The Supreme Court determined that the right of the press to print classified material _____.
    a. is obsolete, and the press may never print classified material
    b. is partial, and the press may print classified material only if it does not compromise troops or covert operatives
    c. is complete, and the press may print anything it likes
    d. has not yet been defined

17. The Federal Communications Commission oversees the programming of which entities?
    a. television
    b. television and radio
    c. television, radio, and satellite
    d. television, radio, satellite, and cable

18. Which of the following is a reasonable exception to the Freedom of Information Act?
    a. medical records for government employees
    b. budget for the Department of Labor
    c. minutes from a president's cabinet meeting
    d. transcript of meetings between Department of State negotiators and Russian trade negotiators

19. Why is it a potential problem that the equal-time rule does not apply to candidates' supporters?

20. Under what circumstances might a journalist be compelled to give up a source?

21. Which of the following is an example of episodic framing?
    a. a story on drug abuse that interviews addicts and discusses reasons for addiction and government responses to help addicts
    b. a story on how drug abuse policy has changed since 1984
    c. a story on candidates' answers to a drug question in a debate
    d. a story detailing arguments against needle exchange programs

22. According to research, why might a woman decide not to run for office?
    a. She feels the work is too hard.
    b. She fears her positions will be covered too closely by the press.
    c. She fears the media will criticize her family.
    d. She fears the campaign will be too expensive.

23. Media coverage of a race tends to _____.
    a. accurately portray all races equally
    b. accurately portray whites and blacks as victims
    c. overrepresent whites and the elderly as poor
    d. overrepresent African Americans as poor

24. How might framing or priming affect the way a reader or viewer thinks about an issue?

25. Why would inaccurate coverage of race and gender affect policy or elections?

Critical Thinking Questions

26. In what ways can the media change the way a citizen thinks about government?

27. In what ways do the media protect people from a tyrannical government?

28. Should all activities of the government be open to media coverage? Why or why not? In what circumstances do you think it would be appropriate for the government to operate without transparency?

29. Have changes in media formats created a more accurate, less biased media? Why or why not?

30. How does citizen journalism use social media to increase coverage of world events?

Suggestions for Further Study

Baum, Matthew A. 2003. *Soft News Goes to War: Public Opinion and American Foreign Policy in the New Media Age*. Princeton, NJ: Princeton University Press.

Baum, Matthew A., and Philip B. K. Potter. 2015. *War and Democratic Constraint: How the Public Influences Foreign Policy*. Princeton, NJ: Princeton University Press.

Cohen, Jeffrey. 2008. *The Presidency in the Era of 24-Hour News*. Princeton, NJ: Princeton University Press.

Eshbaugh-Soha, Matthew, and Jeffrey Peake. 2011. *Breaking through the Noise: Presidential Leadership, Public Opinion, and the News*. Stanford, CA: Stanford University Press.

Fellow, Anthony R. 2013. *American Media History*. Boston: Cengage.

Graber, Doris A., and Johanna L. Dunaway. 2014. *Mass Media and American Politics*. Thousand Oaks, CA: CQ Press.

PIyengar, Shanto. 2016. *Media Politics: A Citizen's Guide,* 3rd ed. New York: W. W. Norton.

Iyengar, Shanto, and Donald R. Kinder. 2010. *News That Matters: Television and American Opinion*. Chicago: University Of Chicago Press.

Lawless, Jennifer L., and Richard L. Fox. 2010. *It Still Takes A Candidate: Why Women Don't Run for Office*. Cambridge: Cambridge University Press.

Malecha, Gary, and Daniel J. Reagan. 2011. *The Public Congress: Congressional Deliberation in a New Media Age*. New York: Routledge.

Media Matters (http://mediamatters.org/).

Media Research Center (http://www.mrc.org/).

Patterson, Thomas. 2013. *Informing the News: The Need for Knowledge-Based Journalism*. New York: Vintage.

Politifact (http://www.politifact.com/).

Rozell, Mark, and Jeremy Mayer. 2008. *Media Power, Media Politics*. Lanham, MD: Rowman & Littlefield.

West, Darrell M. 2013. *Air Wars*. Thousand Oaks, CA: CQ Press.

Chapter 9

Political Parties

Figure 9.1 The families of the 2012 presidential candidates joined in the festivities at the Democratic National Convention in Charlotte, North Carolina, (left) and the Republican National Convention in Tampa, Florida (right). (credit right: modification of work by "PBS NewsHour"/Flickr)

Chapter Outline

9.1 What Are Parties and How Did They Form?
9.2 The Two-Party System
9.3 The Shape of Modern Political Parties
9.4 Divided Government and Partisan Polarization

Introduction

In 2012, Barack Obama accepted his second nomination to lead the Democratic Party into the presidential election (Figure 9.1). During his first term, he had been attacked by pundits for his failure to convince congressional Republicans to work with him. Despite that, he was wildly popular in his own party, and voters reelected him by a comfortable margin. His second term seemed to go no better, however, with disagreements between the parties resulting in government shutdowns and the threat of credit defaults. Yet just a few decades ago, then-president Dwight D. Eisenhower was criticized for failing to create a clear vision for his Republican Party, and Congress was lampooned for what was deemed a lack of real conflict over important issues. Political parties, it seems, can never get it right—they are either too polarizing or too noncommittal.

While people love to criticize political parties, the reality is that the modern political system could not exist without them. This chapter will explore why the party system may be the most important component of any true democracy. What are political parties? Why do they form, and why has the United States typically had only two? Why have political parties become so highly structured? Finally, why does it seem that parties today are more polarized than they have been in the past?

9.1 What Are Parties and How Did They Form?

Learning Objectives

By the end of this section, you will be able to:
- Describe political parties and what they do
- Differentiate political parties from interest groups
- Explain how U.S. political parties formed

At some point, most of us have found ourselves part of a group trying to solve a problem, like picking a restaurant or movie to attend, or completing a big project at school or work. Members of the group probably had various opinions about what should be done. Some may have even refused to help make the decision or to follow it once it had been made. Still others may have been willing to follow along but were less interested in contributing to a workable solution. Because of this disagreement, at some point, someone in the group had to find a way to make a decision, negotiate a compromise, and ultimately do the work needed for the group to accomplish its goals.

This kind of collective action problem is very common in societies, as groups and entire societies try to solve problems or distribute scarce resources. In modern U.S. politics, such problems are usually solved by two important types of organizations: interest groups and political parties. There are many interest groups, all with opinions about what should be done and a desire to influence policy. Because they are usually not officially affiliated with any political party, they generally have no trouble working with either of the major parties. But at some point, a society must find a way of taking all these opinions and turning them into solutions to real problems. That is where political parties come in. Essentially, **political parties** are groups of people with similar interests who work together to create and implement policies. They do this by gaining control over the government by winning elections. Party platforms guide members of Congress in drafting legislation. Parties guide proposed laws through Congress and inform party members how they should vote on important issues. Political parties also nominate candidates to run for state government, Congress, and the presidency. Finally, they coordinate political campaigns and mobilize voters.

POLITICAL PARTIES AS UNIQUE ORGANIZATIONS

In *Federalist* No. 10, written in the late eighteenth century, James Madison noted that the formation of self-interested groups, which he called factions, was inevitable in any society, as individuals started to work together to protect themselves from the government. Interest groups and political parties are two of the most easily identified forms of factions in the United States. These groups are similar in that they are both mediating institutions responsible for communicating public preferences to the government. They are not themselves government institutions in a formal sense. Neither is directly mentioned in the U.S. Constitution nor do they have any real, legal authority to influence policy. But whereas interest groups often work indirectly to influence our leaders, political parties are organizations that try to directly influence public policy through its members who seek to win and hold public office. Parties accomplish this by identifying and aligning sets of issues that are important to voters in the hopes of gaining support during elections; their positions on these critical issues are often presented in documents known as a **party platform** (Figure 9.2), which is adopted at each party's presidential nominating convention every four years. If successful, a party can create a large enough electoral coalition to gain control of the government. Once in power, the party is then able to deliver, to its voters and elites, the policy preferences they choose by electing its partisans to the government. In this respect, parties provide choices to the electorate, something they are doing that is in such sharp contrast to their opposition.

Figure 9.2 The party platform adopted at the first national convention of the Progressive Party in 1912. Among other items, this platform called for disclosure requirements for campaign contributions, an eight-hour workday, a federal income tax, and women's suffrage.

Link to Learning

You can read the full platform of the Republican Party (https://openstax.org/l/29gopplatform) and the Democratic Party (https://openstax.org/l/29demplatform) at their respective websites.

Winning elections and implementing policy would be hard enough in simple political systems, but in a country as complex as the United States, political parties must take on great responsibilities to win elections and coordinate behavior across the many local, state, and national governing bodies. Indeed, political differences between states and local areas can contribute much complexity. If a party stakes out issue positions on which few people agree and therefore builds too narrow a coalition of voter support, that party may find itself marginalized. But if the party takes too broad a position on issues, it might find itself in a situation where the members of the party disagree with one another, making it difficult to pass legislation, even if the party can secure victory.

It should come as no surprise that the story of U.S. political parties largely mirrors the story of the United States itself. The United States has seen sweeping changes to its size, its relative power, and its social and demographic composition. These changes have been mirrored by the political parties as they have sought to shift their coalitions to establish and maintain power across the nation and as party leadership has changed. As you will learn later, this also means that the structure and behavior of modern parties largely parallel the social, demographic, and geographic divisions within the United States today. To understand how this has happened, we look at the origins of the U.S. party system.

HOW POLITICAL PARTIES FORMED

National political parties as we understand them today did not really exist in the United States during the early years of the republic. Most politics during the time of the nation's founding were local in nature and based on elite politics, limited suffrage (or the ability to vote in elections), and property ownership. Residents of the various colonies, and later of the various states, were far more interested in events in their state legislatures than in those occurring at the national level or later in the nation's capital. To the extent that national issues did exist, they were largely limited to collective security efforts to deal with external rivals, such as the British or the French, and with perceived internal threats, such as conflicts with Native Americans.

Soon after the United States emerged from the Revolutionary War, however, a rift began to emerge between two groups that had very different views about the future direction of U.S. politics. Thus, from the very beginning of its history, the United States has had a system of government dominated by two different philosophies. Federalists, who were largely responsible for drafting and ratifying the U.S. Constitution, generally favored the idea of a stronger, more centralized republic that had greater control over regulating the economy.[1] Anti-Federalists preferred a more confederate system built on state equality and autonomy.[2] The Federalist faction, led by Alexander Hamilton, largely dominated the government in the years immediately after the Constitution was ratified. Included in the Federalists was President George Washington, who was initially against the existence of parties in the United States. When Washington decided to exit politics and leave office, he warned of the potential negative effects of parties in his farewell address to the nation, including their potentially divisive nature and the fact that they might not always focus on the common good but rather on partisan ends. However, members of each faction quickly realized that they had a vested interest not only in nominating and electing a president who shared their views, but also in winning other elections. Two loosely affiliated party coalitions, known as the Federalists and the Democratic-Republicans, soon emerged. The Federalists succeeded in electing their first leader, John Adams, to the presidency in 1796, only to see the Democratic-Republicans gain victory under Thomas Jefferson four years later in 1800.

Milestone

The "Revolution of 1800": Uniting the Executive Branch under One Party

When the U.S. Constitution was drafted, its authors were certainly aware that political parties existed in other countries (like Great Britain), but they hoped to avoid them in the United States. They felt the importance of states in the U.S. federal structure would make it difficult for national parties to form. They also hoped that having a college of electors vote for the executive branch, with the top two vote-getters becoming president and vice president, would discourage the formation of parties. Their system worked for the first two presidential elections, when essentially all the electors voted for George Washington to serve as president. But by 1796, the Federalist and Anti-Federalist camps had organized into electoral coalitions. The Anti-Federalists joined with many others active in the process to become known as the Democratic-Republicans. The Federalist John Adams won the Electoral College vote, but his authority was undermined when the vice presidency went to Democratic-Republican Thomas Jefferson, who finished second. Four years later, the Democratic-Republicans managed to avoid this outcome by coordinating the electors to vote for their top two candidates. But when the vote ended in a tie, it was ultimately left to Congress to decide who would be the third president of the United States (Figure 9.3).

| Thomas Jefferson
Democratic-Republican
73 Electoral votes | Aaron Burr
Democratic-Republican
73 Electoral votes |

Figure 9.3   Thomas Jefferson almost lost the presidential election of 1800 to his own running mate when a flaw in the design of the Electoral College led to a tie that had to be resolved by Congress.

In an effort to prevent a similar outcome in the future, Congress and the states voted to ratify the Twelfth Amendment, which went into effect in 1804. This amendment changed the rules so that the president and vice president would be selected through separate elections within the Electoral College, and it altered the method that Congress used to fill the offices in the event that no candidate won a majority. The amendment essentially endorsed the new party system and helped prevent future controversies. It also served as an early effort by the two parties to collude to make it harder for an outsider to win the presidency.

Does the process of selecting the executive branch need to be reformed so that the people elect the president and vice president directly, rather than through the Electoral College? Should the people vote separately on each office rather than voting for both at the same time? Explain your reasoning.

Growing regional tensions eroded the Federalist Party's ability to coordinate elites, and it eventually collapsed following its opposition to the War of 1812.[3] The Democratic-Republican Party, on the other hand, eventually divided over whether national resources should be focused on economic and mercantile development, such as tariffs on imported goods and government funding of internal improvements like roads and canals, or on promoting populist issues that would help the "common man," such as reducing or eliminating state property requirements that had prevented many men from voting.[4]

In the election of 1824, numerous candidates contended for the presidency, all members of the Democratic-

Republican Party. Andrew Jackson won more popular votes and more votes in the Electoral College than any other candidate. However, because he did not win the majority (more than half) of the available electoral votes, the election was decided by the House of Representatives, as required by the Twelfth Amendment. The Twelfth Amendment limited the House's choice to the three candidates with the greatest number of electoral votes. Thus, Andrew Jackson, with 99 electoral votes, found himself in competition with only John Quincy Adams, the second place finisher with 84 electoral votes, and William H. Crawford, who had come in third with 41. The fourth-place finisher, Henry Clay, who was no longer in contention, had won 37 electoral votes. Clay strongly disliked Jackson, and his ideas on government support for tariffs and internal improvements were similar to those of Adams. Clay thus gave his support to Adams, who was chosen on the first ballot. Jackson considered the actions of Clay and Adams, the son of the Federalist president John Adams, to be an unjust triumph of supporters of the elite and referred to it as "the corrupt bargain."[5]

This marked the beginning of what historians call the Second Party System (the first parties had been the Federalists and the Jeffersonian Republicans), with the splitting of the Democratic-Republicans and the formation of two new political parties. One half, called simply the Democratic Party, was the party of Jackson; it continued to advocate for the common people by championing westward expansion and opposing a national bank. The branch of the Democratic-Republicans that believed that the national government should encourage economic (primarily industrial) development was briefly known as the National Republicans and later became the Whig Party[6]. In the election of 1828, Democrat Andrew Jackson was triumphant. Three times as many people voted in 1828 as had in 1824, and most cast their ballots for him.[7]

The formation of the Democratic Party marked an important shift in U.S. politics. Rather than being built largely to coordinate elite behavior, the Democratic Party worked to organize the electorate by taking advantage of state-level laws that had extended suffrage from male property owners to nearly all white men.[8] This change marked the birth of what is often considered the first modern political party in any democracy in the world.[9] It also dramatically changed the way party politics was, and still is, conducted. For one thing, this new party organization was built to include structures that focused on organizing and mobilizing voters for elections at all levels of government. The party also perfected an existing spoils system, in which support for the party during elections was rewarded with jobs in the government bureaucracy after victory.[10] Many of these positions were given to party bosses and their friends. These men were the leaders of **political machines**, organizations that secured votes for the party's candidates or supported the party in other ways. Perhaps more importantly, this election-focused organization also sought to maintain power by creating a broader coalition and thereby expanding the range of issues upon which the party was constructed.[11]

Link to Learning

Each of the two main U.S. political parties today—the Democrats (https://openstax.org/l/29demcratsorg) and the Republicans (https://openstax.org/l/29gopwebsite) —maintains an extensive website with links to its affiliated statewide organizations, which in turn often maintain links to the party's country organizations.

By comparison, here are websites for the Green Party (https://openstax.org/l/29greenparty) and the Libertarian Party (https://openstax.org/l/29libertarian) that are two other parties in the United States today.

The Democratic Party emphasized **personal politics**, which focused on building direct relationships with voters rather than on promoting specific issues. This party dominated national politics from Andrew Jackson's presidential victory in 1828 until the mid-1850s, when regional tensions began to threaten the nation's very existence. The growing power of industrialists, who preferred greater national authority, combined with increasing tensions between the northern and southern states over slavery, led to the rise of the Republican Party and its leader Abraham Lincoln in the election of 1860, while the Democratic Party dominated in the South. Like the Democrats, the Republicans also began to utilize a mass approach to party design and organization. Their opposition to the expansion of slavery, and their role in helping to stabilize the Union during Reconstruction, made them the dominant player in national politics for the next several decades.[12]

The Democratic and Republican parties have remained the two dominant players in the U.S. party system since the Civil War (1861–1865). That does not mean, however, that the system has been stagnant. Every political actor and every citizen has the ability to determine for him- or herself whether one of the two parties meets his or her needs and provides an appealing set of policy options, or whether another option is preferable.

At various points in the past 170 years, elites and voters have sought to create alternatives to the existing party system. Political parties that are formed as alternatives to the Republican and Democratic parties are known as **third parties**, or minor parties (Figure 9.4). In 1892, a third party known as the Populist Party formed in reaction to what its constituents perceived as the domination of U.S. society by big business and a decline in the power of farmers and rural communities. The Populist Party called for the regulation of railroads, an income tax, and the popular election of U.S. senators, who at this time were chosen by state legislatures and not by ordinary voters.[13] The party's candidate in the 1892 elections, James B. Weaver, did not perform as well as the two main party candidates, and, in the presidential election of 1896, the Populists supported the Democratic candidate William Jennings Bryan. Bryan lost, and the Populists once again nominated their own presidential candidates in 1900, 1904, and 1908. The party disappeared from the national scene after 1908, but its ideas were similar to those of the Progressive Party, a new political party created in 1912.

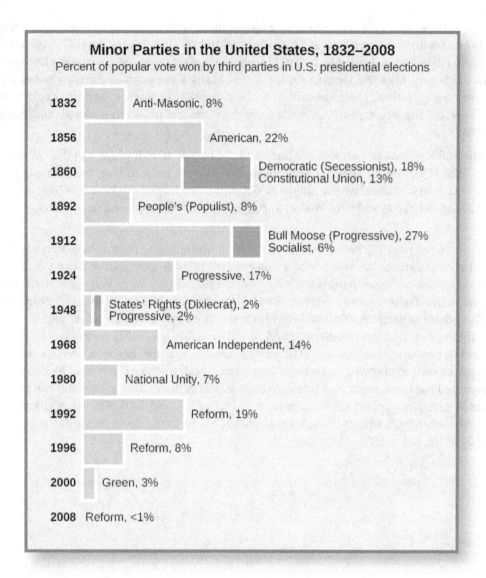

Figure 9.4 Various third parties, also known as minor parties, have appeared in the United States over the years. Some, like the Socialist Party, still exist in one form or another. Others, like the Anti-Masonic Party, which wanted to protect the United States from the influence of the Masonic fraternal order and garnered just under 8 percent of the popular vote in 1832, are gone.

In 1912, former Republican president Theodore Roosevelt attempted to form a third party, known as the Progressive Party, as an alternative to the more business-minded Republicans. The Progressives sought to correct the many problems that had arisen as the United States transformed itself from a rural, agricultural nation into an increasingly urbanized, industrialized country dominated by big business interests. Among the reforms that the Progressive Party called for in its 1912 platform were women's suffrage, an eight-hour workday, and workers' compensation. The party also favored some of the same reforms as the Populist Party, such as the direct election of U.S. senators and an income tax, although Populists tended to be farmers while the Progressives were from the middle class. In general, Progressives sought to make government more responsive to the will of the people and to end political corruption in government. They wished to break the power of party bosses and political machines, and called upon states to pass laws allowing voters to vote directly on proposed legislation, propose new laws, and recall from office incompetent or corrupt elected officials. The Progressive Party largely disappeared after 1916, and most members returned to the Republican Party.[14] The party enjoyed a brief resurgence in 1924, when Robert "Fighting Bob" La Follette ran unsuccessfully for president under the Progressive banner.

In 1948, two new third parties appeared on the political scene. Henry A. Wallace, a vice president under Franklin Roosevelt, formed a new Progressive Party, which had little in common with the earlier Progressive Party. Wallace favored racial desegregation and believed that the United States should have closer ties to the Soviet Union. Wallace's campaign was a failure, largely because most people believed his policies, including national healthcare, were too much like those of communism, and this party also vanished. The other third party, the States' Rights Democrats, also known as the Dixiecrats, were white, southern Democrats who split from the Democratic Party when Harry Truman, who favored civil rights for African Americans, became the party's nominee for president. The Dixiecrats opposed all attempts by the federal government to end segregation, extend voting rights, prohibit discrimination in employment, or otherwise promote social equality among races.[15] They remained a significant party that threatened Democratic unity throughout the 1950s and 1960s. Other examples of third parties in the United States include the American Independent Party, the Libertarian Party, United We Stand America, the Reform Party, and the Green Party.

None of these alternatives to the two major political parties had much success at the national level, and most are no longer viable parties. All faced the same fate. Formed by charismatic leaders, each championed a relatively narrow set of causes and failed to gain broad support among the electorate. Once their leaders had been defeated or discredited, the party structures that were built to contest elections collapsed. And within a few years, most of their supporters were eventually pulled back into one of the existing parties. To be sure, some of these parties had an electoral impact. For example, the Progressive Party pulled enough votes away from the Republicans to hand the 1912 election to the Democrats. Thus, the third-party rival's principal accomplishment was helping its least-preferred major party win, usually at the short-term expense of the very issue it championed. In the long run, however, many third parties have brought important issues to the attention of the major parties, which then incorporated these issues into their platforms. Understanding why this is the case is an important next step in learning about the issues and strategies of the modern Republican and Democratic parties. In the next section, we look at why the United States has historically been dominated by only two political parties.

9.2 The Two-Party System

Learning Objectives

By the end of this section, you will be able to:
- Describe the effects of winner-take-all elections
- Compare plurality and proportional representation
- Describe the institutional, legal, and social forces that limit the number of parties
- Discuss the concepts of party alignment and realignment

One of the cornerstones of a vibrant democracy is citizens' ability to influence government through voting. In order for that influence to be meaningful, citizens must send clear signals to their leaders about what they wish the government to do. It only makes sense, then, that a democracy will benefit if voters have several clearly differentiated options available to them at the polls on Election Day. Having these options means voters can select a candidate who more closely represents their own preferences on the important issues of the day. It also gives individuals who are considering voting a reason to participate. After all, you are more likely to vote if you care about who wins and who loses. The existence of two major parties, especially in our present era of strong parties, leads to sharp distinctions between the candidates and between the party organizations.

Why do we have two parties? The **two-party system** came into being because the structure of U.S. elections, with one seat tied to a geographic district, tends to lead to dominance by two major political parties. Even when there are other options on the ballot, most voters understand that minor parties have no real chance of winning even a single office. Hence, they vote for candidates of the two major parties in order to support a potential winner. Of the 535 members of the House and Senate, only a handful identify as something other than Republican or Democrat. Third parties have fared no better in presidential elections. No third-party candidate has ever won the presidency. Some historians or political scientists might consider Abraham Lincoln to have been such a candidate, but in 1860, the Republicans were a major party that had subsumed members of earlier parties, such as the Whig Party, and they were the only major party other than the Democratic Party.

ELECTION RULES AND THE TWO-PARTY SYSTEM

A number of reasons have been suggested to explain why the structure of U.S. elections has resulted in a two-party system. Most of the blame has been placed on the process used to select its representatives. First, most elections at the state and national levels are winner-take-all: The candidate who receives the greatest overall number of votes wins. Winner-take-all elections with one representative elected for one geographic district allow voters to develop a personal relationship with "their" representative to the government. They know exactly whom to blame, or thank, for the actions of that government. But these elections also tend to limit the number of people who run for office. Otherwise-qualified candidates might not stand for election if they feel the incumbent or another candidate has an early advantage in the race. And since voters do not like to waste votes, third parties must convince voters they have a real chance of winning races before voters will take them seriously. This is a tall order given the vast resources and mobilization tools available to the existing parties, especially if an incumbent is one of the competitors. In turn, the likelihood that third-party challengers will lose an election bid makes it more difficult to raise funds to support later attempts.[16]

Winner-take-all systems of electing candidates to office, which exist in several countries other than the United States, require that the winner receive either the majority of votes or a plurality of the votes. U.S. elections are based on **plurality voting**. Plurality voting, commonly referred to as **first-past-the-post**, is based on the principle that the individual candidate with the most votes wins, whether or not he or she gains a majority (51 percent or greater) of the total votes cast. For instance, Abraham Lincoln won the presidency in 1860 even though he clearly lacked majority support given the number of candidates in the race. In 1860, four candidates competed for the presidency: Lincoln, a Republican; two Democrats, one from the northern wing of the party and one from the southern wing; and a member of the newly formed Constitutional Union Party, a southern party that wished to prevent the nation from dividing over the issue of slavery. Votes were split among all four parties, and Lincoln became president with only 40 percent of the vote, not a majority of votes cast but more than any of the other three candidates had received, and enough to give him a majority in the Electoral College, the body that ultimately decides presidential elections. Plurality voting has been justified as the simplest and most cost-effective method for identifying a victor in a democracy. A single election can be held on a single day, and the victor of the competition is easily selected. On the other hand, systems in which people vote for a single candidate in an individual district often cost more money because drawing district lines and registering voters according to district is often expensive and cumbersome.[17]

In a system in which individual candidates compete for individual seats representing unique geographic districts, a candidate must receive a fairly large number of votes in order to win. A political party that appeals to only a small percentage of voters will always lose to a party that is more popular.[18] Because second-place (or lower) finishers will receive no reward for their efforts, those parties that do not attract enough supporters to finish first at least some of the time will eventually disappear because their supporters realize they have no hope of achieving success at the polls.[19] The failure of third parties to win and the possibility that they will draw votes away from the party the voter had favored before—resulting in a win for the party the voter liked least—makes people hesitant to vote for the third party's candidates a second time. This has been the fate of all U.S. third parties—the Populist Party, the Progressives, the Dixiecrats, the Reform Party, and others.

In a proportional electoral system, however, parties advertise who is on their candidate list and voters pick a party. Then, legislative seats are doled out to the parties based on the proportion of support each party receives. While the Green Party in the United States might not win a single congressional seat in some years thanks to plurality voting, in a proportional system, it stands a chance to get a few seats in the legislature regardless. For example, assume the Green Party gets 7 percent of the vote. In the United States, 7 percent will never be enough to win a single seat, shutting the Green candidates out of Congress entirely, whereas in a proportional system, the Green Party will get 7 percent of the total number of legislative seats available. Hence, it could get a foothold for its issues and perhaps increase its support over time. But with plurality voting, it doesn't stand a chance.

Third parties, often born of frustration with the current system, attract supporters from one or both of the existing parties during an election but fail to attract enough votes to win. After the election is over, supporters experience remorse when their least-favorite candidate wins instead. For example, in the 2000 election, Ralph Nader ran for president as the candidate of the Green Party. Nader, a longtime consumer activist concerned with environmental issues and social justice, attracted many votes from people who usually voted for Democratic candidates. This has caused some to claim that Democratic nominee Al Gore lost the 2000 election to Republican George W. Bush, because Nader won Democratic votes in Florida that might otherwise have gone to Gore (**Figure 9.5**).[20]

(a)   (b)

Figure 9.5 Ralph Nader, a longtime consumer advocate and crusader for social justice and the environment, campaigned as an independent in 2008 (a). However, in 2000, he ran for the presidency as the Green Party candidate. He received votes from many Democrats, and some analysts claim Nader's campaign cost Al Gore the presidency—an ironic twist for a politician who would come to be known primarily for his environmental activism, even winning the Nobel Peace Prize in 2007 (b) for his efforts to inform the public about climate change. (credit a: modification of work by "Mely-o"/Flikr"; credit b: modification of work by "kangotraveler"/Flickr)

Abandoning plurality voting, even if the winner-take-all election were kept, would almost certainly increase the number of parties from which voters could choose. The easiest switch would be to a **majoritarian voting** scheme, in which a candidate wins only if he or she enjoys the support of a majority of voters. If no candidate wins a majority in the first round of voting, a run-off election is held among the top contenders. Some states conduct their primary elections within the two major political parties in this way.

A second way to increase the number of parties in the U.S. system is to abandon the winner-take-all approach. Rather than allowing voters to pick their representatives directly, many democracies have chosen to have voters pick their preferred party and allow the party to select the individuals who serve in government. The argument for this method is that it is ultimately the party and not the individual who will influence policy. Under this model of **proportional representation**, legislative seats are allocated to competing parties based on the total share of votes they receive in the election. As a result, any given election can have multiple winners, and voters who might prefer a smaller party over a major one have a chance to be represented in government (Figure 9.6).

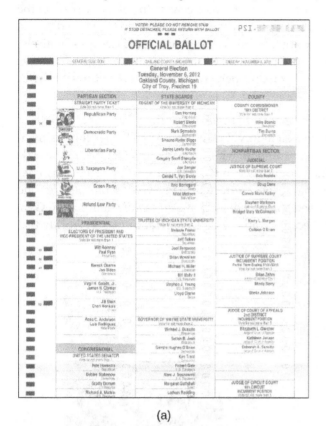 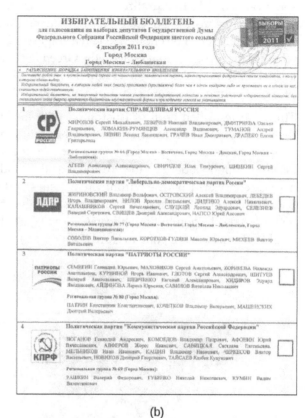

(a)   (b)

Figure 9.6 While a U.S. ballot (a) for first-past-the-post elections features candidates' names, the ballots of proportional representation countries list the parties. On this Russian ballot (b), the voter is offered a choice of Social Democratic, Nationalist, Socialist, and Communist parties, among others.

One possible way to implement proportional representation in the United States is to allocate legislative seats based on the national level of support for each party's presidential candidate, rather than on the results of individual races. If this method had been used in the 1996 elections, 8 percent of the seats in Congress would have gone to Ross Perot's Reform Party because he won 8 percent of the votes cast. Even though Perot himself lost, his supporters would have been rewarded for their efforts with representatives who had a real voice in government. And Perot's party's chances of survival would have greatly increased.

Electoral rules are probably not the only reason the United States has a two-party system. We need only look at the number of parties in the British or Canadian systems, both of which are winner-take-all plurality systems like that in the United States, to see that it is possible to have more than two parties while still directly electing representatives. The two-party system is also rooted in U.S. history. The first parties, the Federalists and the Jeffersonian Republicans, disagreed about how much power should be given to the federal government, and differences over other important issues further strengthened this divide. Over time, these parties evolved into others by inheriting, for the most part, the general ideological positions and constituents of their predecessors, but no more than two major parties ever formed. Instead of parties arising based on region or ethnicity, various regions and ethnic groups sought a place in one of the two major parties.

Scholars of voting behavior have also suggested at least three other characteristics of the U.S. system that are likely to influence party outcomes: the Electoral College, demobilized ethnicity, and campaign and election laws. First, the United States has a presidential system in which the winner is selected not directly by the popular vote but indirectly by a group of electors known collectively as the Electoral College. The winner-take-all system also applies in the Electoral College. In all but two states (Maine and Nebraska), the total of the state's electoral votes go to the candidate who wins the plurality of the popular vote in that state. Even if a new, third party is able to win the support of a lot of voters, it must be able to do so in several states in order to win enough electoral votes to have a chance of winning the presidency.[21]

Besides the existence of the Electoral College, political scientist Gary W. Cox has also suggested that the relative prosperity of the United States and the relative unity of its citizens have prevented the formation of "large dissenting groups" that might give support to third parties.[22] This is similar to the argument that the United States does not have viable third parties, because none of its regions is dominated by mobilized ethnic minorities that have created political parties in order to defend and to address concerns solely of interest to that ethnic group. Such parties are common in other countries.

Finally, party success is strongly influenced by local election laws. Someone has to write the rules that govern elections, and those rules help to determine outcomes. In the United States, such rules have been written to make it easy for existing parties to secure a spot for their candidates in future elections. But some states create significant burdens for candidates who wish to run as independents or who choose to represent new parties. For example, one common practice is to require a candidate who does not have the support of a major party to ask registered voters to sign a petition. Sometimes, thousands of signatures are required before a candidate's name can be placed on the ballot (Figure 9.7), but a small third party that does have large numbers of supporters in some states may not be able to secure enough signatures for this to happen.[23]

Figure 9.7 Costa Constantinides (right), while campaigning in 2013 to represent the 22nd District on the New York City Council, said, "Few things are more important to a campaign than the petition process to get on the ballot. We were so pumped up to get started that we went out at 12:01 a.m. on June 4 to start collecting signatures right away!" Constantinides won the election later that year. (credit: modification of work by Costa Constantinides)

Link to Learning

Visit **Fair Vote (https://openstax.org/l/29fairvoteweb)** for a discussion of ballot access laws across the country.

Given the obstacles to the formation of third parties, it is unlikely that serious challenges to the U.S. two-party system will emerge. But this does not mean that we should view it as entirely stable either. The U.S. party system is technically a loose organization of fifty different state parties and has undergone several considerable changes since its initial consolidation after the Civil War. Third-party movements may have played a role in some of these changes, but all resulted in a shifting of party loyalties among the U.S. electorate.

CRITICAL ELECTIONS AND REALIGNMENT

Political parties exist for the purpose of winning elections in order to influence public policy. This requires them to build coalitions across a wide range of voters who share similar preferences. Since most U.S. voters identify as moderates,[24] the historical tendency has been for the two parties to compete for "the middle" while also trying to mobilize their more loyal bases. If voters' preferences remained stable for long periods of time, and if both parties did a good job of competing for their votes, we could expect Republicans and Democrats to be reasonably competitive in any given election. Election outcomes would probably be based on the way voters compared the parties on the most important events of the day rather than on electoral strategy.

There are many reasons we would be wrong in these expectations, however. First, the electorate isn't entirely stable. Each generation of voters has been a bit different from the last. Over time, the United States has become more socially liberal, especially on topics related to race and gender, and Millennials—those aged 21–37—are more liberal than members of older generations.[25] The electorate's economic preferences have changed, and different social groups are likely to become more engaged in politics now than they did in the past. Surveys conducted in 2016, for example, revealed that candidates' religion is less important to voters than it once was. Also, as young Latinos reach voting age, they seem more inclined to vote than do their parents, which may raise the traditionally low voting rates among this ethnic group.[26] Internal population shifts and displacements have also occurred, as various regions have taken their turn experiencing economic growth or stagnation, and as new waves of immigrants have come to U.S. shores.

Additionally, the major parties have not always been unified in their approach to contesting elections. While we think of both Congress and the presidency as national offices, the reality is that congressional elections are sometimes more like local elections. Voters may reflect on their preferences for national policy when deciding whom to send to the Senate or the House of Representatives, but they are very likely to view national policy in the context of its effects on their area, their family, or themselves, not based on what is happening to the country as a whole. For example, while many voters want to reduce the federal budget, those over sixty-five are particularly concerned that no cuts to the Medicare program be made.[27] One-third of those polled reported that "senior's issues" were most important to them when voting for national officeholders.[28] If they hope to keep their jobs, elected officials must thus be sensitive to preferences in their home constituencies as well as the preferences of their national party.

Finally, it sometimes happens that over a series of elections, parties may be unable or unwilling to adapt their positions to broader socio-demographic or economic forces. Parties need to be aware when society changes. If leaders refuse to recognize that public opinion has changed, the party is unlikely to win in the next election. For example, people who describe themselves as evangelical Christians are an important Republican constituency; they are also strongly opposed to abortion.[29] Thus, even though the majority of U.S. adults believe abortion should be legal in at least some instances, such as when a pregnancy is the result of rape or incest, or threatens the life of the mother, the position of many Republican presidential candidates in 2016 was to oppose abortion in all cases.[30] As a result, many women view the Republican Party as unsympathetic to their interests and are more likely to support Democratic candidates.[31] Similarly (or simultaneously), groups that have felt that the party has served their causes in the past may decide to look elsewhere if they feel their needs are no longer being met. Either way, the party system will be upended as a result of a **party realignment**, or a shifting of party allegiances within the electorate (Table 9.1).[32]

Periods of Party Dominance and Realignment

Era	Party Systems and Realignments
1796–1824	First Party System: Federalists (urban elites, southern planters, New England) oppose Democratic-Republicans (rural, small farmers and artisans, the South and the West).
1828–1856	Second Party System: Democrats (the South, cities, farmers and artisans, immigrants) oppose Whigs (former Federalists, the North, middle class, native-born Americans).
1860–1892	Third Party System: Republicans (former Whigs plus African Americans) control the presidency. Only one Democrat, Grover Cleveland, is elected president (1884, 1892).
1896–1932	Fourth Party System: Republicans control the presidency. Only one Democrat, Woodrow Wilson, is elected president (1912, 1916). Challenges to major parties are raised by Populists and Progressives.
1932–1964	Fifth Party System. Democrats control the presidency. Only one Republican, Dwight Eisenhower, is elected president (1952, 1956). Major party realignment as African Americans become part of the Democratic coalition.
1964–present	Sixth Party System. No one party controls the presidency. Ongoing realignment as southern whites and many northern members of the working class begin to vote for Republicans. Latinos and Asians immigrate, most of whom vote for Democrats.

Table 9.1 There have been six distinctive periods in U.S. history when new political parties have emerged, control of the presidency has shifted from one party to another, or significant changes in a party's makeup have occurred.

One of the best-known party realignments occurred when Democrats moved to include African Americans and other minorities into their national coalition during the Great Depression. After the Civil War, Republicans, the party of Lincoln, were viewed as the party that had freed the slaves. Their efforts to provide blacks with greater legal rights earned them the support of African Americans in both the South, where they were newly enfranchised, and the Northeast. When the Democrats, the party of the Confederacy, lost control of the South after the Civil War, Republicans ruled the region. However, the Democrats regained control of the South after the removal of the Union army in 1877. Democrats had largely supported slavery before the Civil War, and they opposed postwar efforts to integrate African Americans into society after they were liberated. In addition, Democrats in the North and Midwest drew their greatest support from labor union members and immigrants who viewed African Americans as competitors for jobs and government resources, and who thus tended to oppose the extension of rights to African Americans as much as their southern counterparts did.[33]

While the Democrats' opposition to civil rights may have provided regional advantages in southern or urban elections, it was largely disastrous for national politics. From 1868 to 1931, Democratic candidates won just four of sixteen presidential elections. Two of these victories can be explained as a result of the spoiler effect of the Progressive Party in 1912 and then Woodrow Wilson's reelection during World War I in 1916. This rather-dismal success rate suggested that a change in the governing coalition would be needed if the party were to have a chance at once again becoming a player on the national level.

That change began with the 1932 presidential campaign of Franklin Delano Roosevelt. FDR determined that his best path toward victory was to create a new coalition based not on region or ethnicity, but on the suffering of those hurt the most during the Great Depression. This alignment sought to bring African American voters in as a means of shoring up support in major urban areas and the Midwest, where many southern blacks had migrated in the decades after the Civil War in search of jobs and better education for their children, as well as to avoid many of the legal restrictions placed on them in the South. Roosevelt accomplished this realignment by promising assistance to those hurt most by the Depression, including African Americans.

The strategy worked. Roosevelt won the election with almost 58 percent of the popular vote and 472 Electoral College votes, compared to incumbent Herbert Hoover's 59. The 1932 election is considered an example of a **critical election**, one that represents a sudden, clear, and long-term shift in voter allegiances. After this election, the political parties were largely identified as being divided by differences in their members' socio-economic status. Those who favor stability of the current political and economic system tend to vote Republican, whereas those who would most benefit from changing the system usually favor Democratic candidates. Based on this alignment, the Democratic Party won the next five consecutive presidential elections and was able to build a political machine that dominated Congress into the 1990s, including holding an uninterrupted majority in the House of Representatives from 1954 until 1994.

The realignment of the parties did have consequences for Democrats. African Americans became an increasingly important part of the Democratic coalition in the 1940s through the 1960s, as the party took steps to support civil rights.[34] Most changes were limited to the state level at first, but as civil rights reform moved to the national stage, rifts between northern and southern Democrats began to emerge.[35] Southern Democrats became increasingly convinced that national efforts to provide social welfare and encourage racial integration were violating state sovereignty and social norms. By the 1970s, many had begun to shift their allegiance to the Republican Party, whose pro-business wing shared their opposition to the growing encroachment of the national government into what they viewed as state and local matters.[36]

Almost fifty years after it had begun, the realignment of the two political parties resulted in the flipping of post-Civil War allegiances, with urban areas and the Northeast now solidly Democratic, and the South and rural areas overwhelmingly voting Republican. The result today is a political system that provides Republicans with considerable advantages in rural areas and most parts of the Deep South.[37] Democrats dominate urban politics and those parts of the South, known as the Black Belt, where the majority of residents are African American.

9.3 The Shape of Modern Political Parties

Learning Objectives

By the end of this section, you will be able to:
- Differentiate between the party in the electorate and the party organization
- Discuss the importance of voting in a political party organization
- Describe party organization at the county, state, and national levels
- Compare the perspectives of the party in government and the party in the electorate

We have discussed the two major political parties in the United States, how they formed, and some of the smaller parties that have challenged their dominance over time. However, what exactly do political parties do? If the purpose of political parties is to work together to create and implement policies by winning elections, how do they accomplish this task, and who actually participates in the process?

The answer was fairly straightforward in the early days of the republic when parties were little more than electoral coalitions of like-minded, elite politicians. But improvements in strategy and changes in the electorate forced the parties to become far more complex organizations that operate on several levels in the U.S. political arena. Modern political parties consist of three components identified by political scientist V. O. Key: the party in the electorate (the voters); the party organization (which helps to coordinate everything the party does in its quest for office); and the party in office (the office holders). To understand how these various elements work together, we begin by thinking about a key first step in influencing policy in any democracy: winning elections.

THE PARTY-IN-THE-ELECTORATE

A key fact about the U.S. political party system is that it's all about the votes. If voters do not show up to vote for a party's candidates on Election Day, the party has no chance of gaining office and implementing its preferred policies. As we have seen, for much of their history, the two parties have been adapting to changes in the size, composition, and preferences of the U.S. electorate. It only makes sense, then, that parties have found it in their interest to build a permanent and stable presence among the voters. By fostering a sense of loyalty, a party can insulate itself from changes in the system and improve its odds of winning elections. The **party-in-the-electorate** are those members of the voting public who consider themselves to be part of a political party and/or who consistently prefer the candidates of one party over the other.

What it means to be part of a party depends on where a voter lives and how much he or she chooses to participate in politics. At its most basic level, being a member of the party-in-the-electorate simply means a voter is more likely to voice support for a party. These voters are often called **party identifiers**, since they usually represent themselves in public as being members of a party, and they may attend some party events or functions. Party identifiers are also more likely to provide financial support for the candidates of their party during election season. This does not mean self-identified Democrats will support *all* the party's positions or candidates, but it does mean that, on the whole, they feel their wants or needs are more likely to be met if the Democratic Party is successful.

Party identifiers make up the majority of the voting public. Gallup, the polling agency, has been collecting data on voter preferences for the past several decades. Its research suggests that historically, over half of American adults have called themselves "Republican" or "Democrat" when asked how they identify themselves politically (Figure 9.8). Even among self-proclaimed independents, the overwhelming majority claim to lean in the direction of one party or the other, suggesting they behave as if they identified with a party during elections even if they preferred not to publicly pick a side. Partisan support is so strong that, in a poll conducted from August 5 to August 9, 2015, about 88 percent of respondents said they either identified with or, if they were independents, at least leaned toward one of the major political parties.[38] Thus, in a poll conducted in January 2016, even though about 42 percent of respondents said they were independent, this does not mean that they are not, in fact, more likely to favor one party over the other.[39]

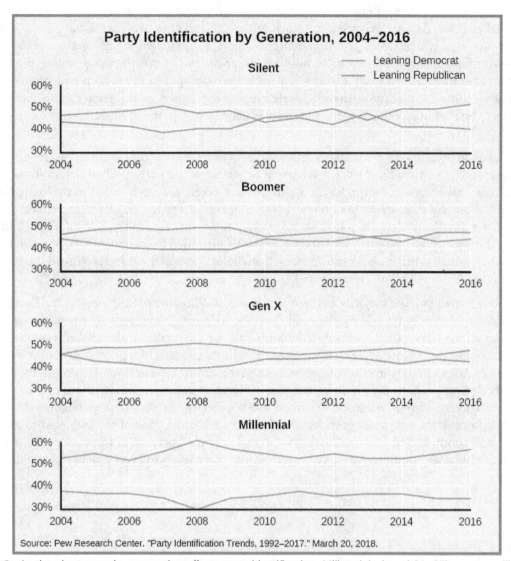

Figure 9.8 As the chart reveals, generation affects party identification. Millennials (aged 21–37) are more likely to identify as or lean towards the Democratic Party and less likely to favor Republicans than are their Baby Boomer parents and grandparents (born between 1946 and 1964).

Strictly speaking, party identification is not quite the same thing as party membership. People may call themselves Republicans or Democrats without being registered as a member of the party, and the Republican and Democratic parties do not require individuals to join their formal organization in the same way that parties in some other countries do. Many states require voters to declare a party affiliation before participating in primaries, but primary participation is irregular and infrequent, and a voter may change his or her identity long before changing party registration. For most voters, party identification is informal at best and often matters only in the weeks before an election. It does matter, however, because party identification guides some voters, who may know little about a particular issue or candidate, in casting their ballots. If, for example, someone thinks of him- or herself as a Republican and always votes Republican, he or she will not be confused when faced with a candidate, perhaps in a local or county election, whose name is unfamiliar. If the candidate is a Republican, the voter will likely cast a ballot for him or her.

Party ties can manifest in other ways as well. The actual act of registering to vote and selecting a party reinforces party loyalty. Moreover, while pundits and scholars often deride voters who blindly vote their party, the selection of a party in the first place can be based on issue positions and ideology. In that regard, voting your party on Election Day is not a blind act—it is a shortcut based on issue positions.

THE PARTY ORGANIZATION

A significant subset of American voters views their party identification as something far beyond simply a shortcut to voting. These individuals get more energized by the political process and have chosen to become more active in the life of political parties. They are part of what is known as the party organization. The **party organization** is the formal structure of the political party, and its active members are responsible for coordinating party behavior and supporting party candidates. It is a vital component of any successful party because it bears most of the responsibility for building and maintaining the party "brand." It also plays a key role in helping select, and elect, candidates for public office.

Local Organizations

Since winning elections is the first goal of the political party, it makes sense that the formal party organization mirrors the local-state-federal structure of the U.S. political system. While the lowest level of party organization is technically the **precinct**, many of the operational responsibilities for local elections fall upon the county-level organization. The county-level organization is in many ways the workhorse of the party system, especially around election time. This level of organization frequently takes on many of the most basic responsibilities of a democratic system, including identifying and mobilizing potential voters and donors, identifying and training potential candidates for public office, and recruiting new members for the party. County organizations are also often responsible for finding rank and file members to serve as volunteers on Election Day, either as officials responsible for operating the polls or as monitors responsible for ensuring that elections are conducted honestly and fairly. They may also hold regular meetings to provide members the opportunity to meet potential candidates and coordinate strategy (Figure 9.9). Of course, all this is voluntary and relies on dedicated party members being willing to pitch in to run the party.

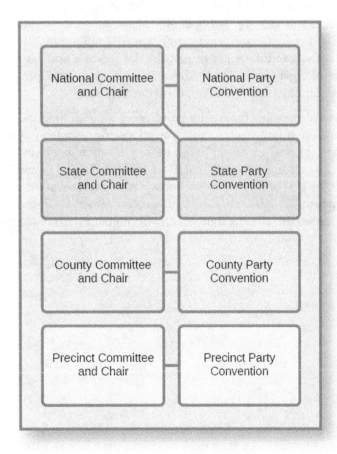

Figure 9.9 Political parties are bottom-up structures, with lower levels often responsible for selecting delegates to higher-level offices or conventions.

State Organizations

Most of the county organizations' formal efforts are devoted to supporting party candidates running for county and city offices. But a fair amount of political power is held by individuals in statewide office or in state-level legislative or judicial bodies. While the county-level offices may be active in these local competitions, most of the coordination for them will take place in the state-level organizations. Like their more local counterparts, state-level organizations are responsible for key party functions, such as statewide candidate recruitment and campaign mobilization. Most of their efforts focus on electing high-ranking officials such as the governor or occupants of other statewide offices (e.g., the state's treasurer or attorney general) as well as candidates to represent the state and its residents in the U.S. Senate and the U.S. House of Representatives. The greater value of state- and national-level offices requires state organizations to take on several key responsibilities in the life of the party.

Link to Learning

Visit the following Republican (https://openstax.org/l/29iowagoporg) and Democratic (https://openstax.org/l/29ridemocrats) sites to see what party organizations look like on the local level. Although these sites are for different parties in different parts of the country, they both inform visitors of local party events, help people volunteer to work for the party, and provide a convenient means of contributing to the party.

First, state-level organizations usually accept greater fundraising responsibilities than do their local counterparts. Statewide races and races for national office have become increasingly expensive in recent years. The average cost of a successful House campaign was $1.2 million in 2014; for Senate races, it was $8.6 million.[40] While individual candidates are responsible for funding and running their own races, it is typically up to the state-level organization to coordinate giving across multiple races and to develop the staffing expertise that these candidates will draw upon at election time.

State organizations are also responsible for creating a sense of unity among members of the state party. Building unity can be very important as the party transitions from sometimes-contentious nomination battles to the all-important general election. The state organization uses several key tools to get its members working together towards a common goal. First, it helps the party's candidates prepare for state primary elections or caucuses that allow voters to choose a nominee to run for public office at either the state or national level. Caucuses are a form of town hall meeting at which voters in a precinct get together to voice their preferences, rather than voting individually throughout the day (Figure 9.10).

Figure 9.10 Caucus-goers gather at a Democratic precinct caucus on January 3, 2008, in Iowa City, Iowa. Caucuses are held every two years in more than 1650 Iowa precincts.

Second, the state organization is also responsible for drafting a state platform that serves as a policy guide for partisans who are eventually selected to public office. These platforms are usually the result of a negotiation between the various coalitions within the party and are designed to ensure that everyone in the party will receive some benefits if their candidates win the election. Finally, state organizations hold a statewide convention at which delegates from the various county organizations come together to discuss the needs of their areas. The state conventions are also responsible for selecting delegates to the national convention.

National Party Organization

The local and state-level party organizations are the workhorses of the political process. They take on most of the responsibility for party activities and are easily the most active participants in the party formation and electoral processes. They are also largely invisible to most voters. The average citizen knows very little of the local party's behavior unless there is a phone call or a knock on the door in the days or weeks before an election. The same is largely true of the activities of the state-level party. Typically, the only people who notice are those who are already actively engaged in politics or are being targeted for donations.

But most people are aware of the presence and activity of the national party organizations for several reasons. First, many Americans, especially young people, are more interested in the topics discussed at the national level than at the state or local level. According to John Green of the Ray C. Bliss Institute of Applied Politics, "Local elections tend to be about things like sewers, and roads and police protection—which are not as dramatic an issue as same-sex marriage or global warming or international affairs."[41] Presidential elections and the behavior of the U.S. Congress are also far more likely to make the news broadcasts than the activities of county commissioners, and the national-level party organization is mostly responsible for coordinating the activities of participants at this level. The national party is a fundraising army for presidential candidates and also serves a key role in trying to coordinate and direct the efforts of the House and Senate. For this reason, its leadership is far more likely to become visible to media consumers, whether they intend to vote or not.

A second reason for the prominence of the national organization is that it usually coordinates the grandest spectacles in the life of a political party. Most voters are never aware of the numerous county-level meetings or coordinating activities. Primary elections, one of the most important events to take place at the state level, have a much lower turnout than the nationwide general election. In 2012, for example, only one-third of the eligible voters in New Hampshire voted in the state's primary, one of the earliest and thus most important in the nation; however, 70 percent of eligible voters in the state voted in the general election in November 2012.[42] People may see or read an occasional story about the meetings of the state committees or convention but pay little attention. But the national conventions, organized and sponsored by the national-level party, can dominate the national discussion for several weeks in late summer, a time when the major media outlets are often searching for news. These conventions are the definition of a media circus at which high-ranking politicians, party elites, and sometimes celebrities, such as actor/director Clint Eastwood (Figure 9.11), along with individuals many consider to be the future leaders of the party are brought before the public so the party can make its best case for being the one to direct the future of the country.[43] National party conventions culminate in the formal nomination of the party nominees for the offices of president and vice president, and they mark the official beginning of the presidential competition between the two parties.

Figure 9.11 In August 2012, Clint Eastwood—actor, director, and former mayor of Carmel-by-the-Sea, California—spoke at the Republican National Convention accompanied by an empty chair representing the Democratic incumbent president Barack Obama.

In the past, national conventions were often the sites of high drama and political intrigue. As late as 1968, the identities of the presidential and/or vice-presidential nominees were still unknown to the general public when the convention opened. It was also common for groups protesting key events and issues of the day to try to raise their profile by using the conventions to gain the media spotlight. National media outlets would provide "gavel to gavel" coverage of the conventions, and the relatively limited number of national broadcast channels meant most viewers were essentially forced to choose between following the conventions or checking out of the media altogether. Much has changed since the 1960s, however, and between 1960 and 2004, viewership of both the Democratic National Convention and the Republican National Convention had declined by half.[44]

National conventions are not the spectacles they once were, and this fact is almost certainly having an impact on the profile of the national party organization. Both parties have come to recognize the value of the convention as a medium through which they can communicate to the average viewer. To ensure that they are viewed in the best possible light, the parties have worked hard to turn the public face of the convention into a highly sanitized, highly orchestrated media event. Speakers are often required to have their speeches prescreened to ensure that they do not deviate from the party line or run the risk of embarrassing the eventual nominee—whose name has often been known by all for several months. And while protests still happen, party organizations have becoming increasingly adept at keeping protesters away from the convention sites, arguing that safety and security are more important than First Amendment rights to speech and peaceable assembly. For example, protestors were kept behind concrete barriers and fences at the Democratic National Convention in 2004.[45]

With the advent of cable TV news and the growth of internet blogging, the major news outlets have found it unnecessary to provide the same level of coverage they once did. Between 1976 and 1996, ABC and

CBS cut their coverage of the nominating conventions from more than fifty hours to only five. NBC cut its coverage to fewer than five hours.[46] One reason may be that the outcome of nominating conventions are also typically known in advance, meaning there is no drama. Today, the nominee's acceptance speech is expected to be no longer than an hour, so it will not take up more than one block of prime-time TV programming.

This is not to say the national conventions are no longer important, or that the national party organizations are becoming less relevant. The conventions, and the organizations that run them, still contribute heavily to a wide range of key decisions in the life of both parties. The national party platform is formally adopted at the convention, as are the key elements of the strategy for contesting the national campaign. And even though the media is paying less attention, key insiders and major donors often use the convention as a way of gauging the strength of the party and its ability to effectively organize and coordinate its members. They are also paying close attention to the rising stars who are given time at the convention's podium, to see which are able to connect with the party faithful. Most observers credit Barack Obama's speech at the 2004 Democratic National Convention with bringing him to national prominence.[47]

Insider Perspective

Conventions and Trial Balloons

While both political parties use conventions to help win the current elections, they also use them as a way of elevating local politicians to the national spotlight. This has been particularly true for the Democratic Party. In 1988, the Democrats tapped Arkansas governor Bill Clinton to introduce their nominee Michael Dukakis at the convention. Clinton's speech was lampooned for its length and lack of focus, but it served to get his name in front of Democratic voters. Four years later, Clinton was able to leverage this national exposure to help his own presidential campaign. The pattern was repeated when Illinois state senator Barack Obama gave the keynote address at the 2004 convention (Figure 9.12). Although he was only a candidate for the U.S. Senate at the time, his address caught the attention of the Democratic establishment and ultimately led to his emergence as a viable presidential candidate just four years later.

Figure 9.12   Barack Obama gives his "Two Americas" speech at the Democratic National Convention in Boston in July 2004. At the time, he was an Illinois state senator running for the U.S. Senate.

Should the media devote more attention to national conventions? Would this help voters choose the candidate they want to vote for?

Link to Learning

Bill Clinton's lengthy nomination speech (https://openstax.org/l/29billclinnomsp) in 1988 was much derided, but served the purpose of providing national exposure to a state governor. Barack Obama's inspirational speech (https://openstax.org/l/29barobanomsp) at the 2004 national convention resulted in immediate speculation as to his wider political aspirations.

THE PARTY-IN-GOVERNMENT

One of the first challenges facing the **party-in-government**, or the party identifiers who have been elected or appointed to hold public office, is to achieve their policy goals. The means to do this is chosen in meetings of the two major parties; Republican meetings are called party conferences and Democrat meetings are called party caucuses. Members of each party meet in these closed sessions and discuss what items to place on the legislative agenda and make decisions about which party members should serve on the committees that draft proposed laws. Party members also elect the leaders of their respective parties in the House and the Senate, and their party whips. Leaders serve as party managers and are the highest-ranking members of the party in each chamber of Congress. The party whip ensures that members are present when a piece of legislation is to be voted on and directs them how to vote. The whip is the second-highest ranking member of the party in each chamber. Thus, both the Republicans and the Democrats have a leader and a whip in the House, and a leader and a whip in the Senate. The leader and whip of the party that holds the majority of seats in each house are known as the majority leader and the majority whip. The leader and whip of the party with fewer seats are called the minority leader and the minority whip. The party that controls the majority of seats in the House of Representatives also elects someone to serve as Speaker of the House. People elected to Congress as independents (that is, not members of either the Republican or Democratic parties) must choose a party to conference or caucus with. For example, Senator Bernie Sanders of Vermont, who originally ran for Senate as an independent candidate, caucuses with the Democrats and ran for the presidency as a Democrat. He returned to the Senate in 2017 as an independent.[48]

Link to Learning

The political parties in government must represent their parties and the entire country at the same time. One way they do this is by creating separate governing and party structures in the legislature, even though these are run by the same people. Check out some of the more important leadership organizations and their partisan counterparts in the House of Representatives (https://openstax.org/l/29hofreporg) and the Senate (https://openstax.org/l/29senateorga) leadership.

Get Connected!

Party Organization from the Inside

Interested in a cool summer job? Want to actually make a difference in your community? Consider an internship at the Democratic National Committee (DNC) or Republican National Committee (RNC). Both organizations offer internship programs for college students who want hands-on experience working in community outreach and grassroots organizing. While many internship opportunities are based at the national headquarters in Washington, DC, openings may exist within state party organizations.

Internship positions can be very competitive; most applicants are juniors or seniors with high grade-point averages and strong recommendations from their faculty. Successful applicants get an inside view of government, build a great professional network, and have the opportunity to make a real difference in the lives of their friends and families.

Visit the DNC or RNC website and find out what it takes to be an intern. While there, also check out the state party organization. Is there a local leader you feel you could work for? Are any upcoming events scheduled in your state?

One problem facing the party-in-government relates to the design of the country's political system. The U.S. government is based on a complex principle of separation of powers, with power divided among the executive, legislative, and judiciary branches. The system is further complicated by federalism, which relegates some powers to the states, which also have separation of powers. This complexity creates a number of problems for maintaining party unity. The biggest is that each level and unit of government has different constituencies that the office holder must satisfy. The person elected to the White House is more beholden to the national party organization than are members of the House or Senate, because members of Congress must be reelected by voters in very different states, each with its own state-level and county-level parties.

Some of this complexity is eased for the party that holds the executive branch of government. Executive offices are typically more visible to the voters than the legislature, in no small part because a single person holds the office. Voters are more likely to show up at the polls and vote if they feel strongly about the candidate running for president or governor, but they are also more likely to hold that person accountable for the government's failures.[49]

Members of the legislature from the executive's party are under a great deal of pressure to make the executive look good, because a popular president or governor may be able to help other party members win office. Even so, partisans in the legislature cannot be expected to simply obey the executive's orders. First, legislators may serve a constituency that disagrees with the executive on key matters of policy. If the issue is important enough to voters, as in the case of gun control or abortion rights, an office holder may feel his or her job will be in jeopardy if he or she too closely follows the party line, even if that means disagreeing with the executive. A good example occurred when the Civil Rights Act of 1964, which desegregated public accommodations and prohibited discrimination in employment on the basis of race, was introduced in Congress. The bill was supported by Presidents John F. Kennedy and Lyndon Johnson, both of whom were Democrats. Nevertheless, many Republicans, such as William McCulloch, a conservative representative from Ohio, voted in its favor while many southern Democrats opposed it.[50]

A second challenge is that each house of the legislature has its own leadership and committee structure, and those leaders may not be in total harmony with the president. Key benefits like committee appointments, leadership positions, and money for important projects in their home district may hinge on legislators following the lead of the party. These pressures are particularly acute for the **majority party**, so named because it controls more than half the seats in one of the two chambers. The Speaker of the House and the Senate majority leader, the majority party's congressional leaders, have significant tools at their disposal to punish party members who defect on a particular vote. Finally, a member of the **minority**

party must occasionally work with the opposition on some issues in order to accomplish any of his or her constituency's goals. This is especially the case in the Senate, which is a super-majority institution. Sixty votes (of the 100 possible) are required to get anything accomplished, because Senate rules allow individual members to block legislation via holds and filibusters. The only way to block the blocking is to invoke *cloture*, a procedure calling for a vote on an issue, which takes 60 votes.

9.4 Divided Government and Partisan Polarization

Learning Objectives

By the end of this section, you will be able to:
- Discuss the problems and benefits of divided government
- Define party polarization
- List the main explanations for partisan polarization
- Explain the implications of partisan polarization

In 1950, the American Political Science Association's Committee on Political Parties (APSA) published an article offering a criticism of the current party system. The parties, it argued, were too similar. Distinct, cohesive political parties were critical for any well-functioning democracy. First, distinct parties offer voters clear policy choices at election time. Second, cohesive parties could deliver on their agenda, even under conditions of lower bipartisanship. The party that lost the election was also important to democracy because it served as the "loyal opposition" that could keep a check on the excesses of the party in power. Finally, the paper suggested that voters could signal whether they preferred the vision of the current leadership or of the opposition. This signaling would keep both parties accountable to the people and lead to a more effective government, better capable of meeting the country's needs.

But, the APSA article continued, U.S. political parties of the day were lacking in this regard. Rarely did they offer clear and distinct visions of the country's future, and, on the rare occasions they did, they were typically unable to enact major reforms once elected. Indeed, there was so much overlap between the parties when in office that it was difficult for voters to know whom they should hold accountable for bad results. The article concluded by advocating a set of reforms that, if implemented, would lead to more distinct parties and better government. While this description of the major parties as being too similar may have been accurate in the 1950s; that is no longer the case.[51]

THE PROBLEM OF DIVIDED GOVERNMENT

The problem of majority versus minority politics is particularly acute under conditions of **divided government**. Divided government occurs when one or more houses of the legislature are controlled by the party in opposition to the executive. Unified government occurs when the same party controls the executive and the legislature entirely. Divided government can pose considerable difficulties for both the operations of the party and the government as a whole. It makes fulfilling campaign promises extremely difficult, for instance, since the cooperation (or at least the agreement) of both Congress and the president is typically needed to pass legislation. Furthermore, one party can hardly claim credit for success when the other side has been a credible partner, or when nothing can be accomplished. Party loyalty may be challenged too, because individual politicians might be forced to oppose their own party agenda if it will help their personal reelection bids.

Divided government can also be a threat to government operations, although its full impact remains unclear.[52] For example, when the divide between the parties is too great, government may shut down. A 1976 dispute between Republican president Gerald Ford and a Democrat-controlled Congress over the issue of funding for certain cabinet departments led to a ten-day shutdown of the government (although the federal government did not cease to function entirely). But beginning in the 1980s, the interpretation that Republican president Ronald Reagan's attorney general gave to a nineteenth-century law required a complete shutdown of federal government operations until a funding issue was resolved (**Figure 9.13**).[53]

Clearly, the parties' willingness to work together and compromise can be a very good thing. However, the past several decades have brought an increased prevalence of divided government. Since 1969, the U.S. electorate has sent the president a Congress of his own party in only seven of twenty-three congressional elections, and during George W. Bush's first administration, the Republican majority was so narrow that a combination of resignations and defections gave the Democrats control before the next election could be held.

Over the short term, however, divided government can make for very contentious politics. A well-functioning government usually requires a certain level of responsiveness on the part of both the executive and the legislative branches. This responsiveness is hard enough if government is unified under one party. During the presidency of Democrat Jimmy Carter (1977–1980), despite the fact that both houses of Congress were controlled by Democratic majorities, the government was shut down on five occasions because of conflict between the executive and legislative branches.[54] Shutdowns are even more likely when the president and at least one house of Congress are of opposite parties. During the presidency of Ronald Reagan, for example, the federal government shut down eight times; on seven of those occasions, the shutdown was caused by disagreements between Reagan and the Republican-controlled Senate on the one hand and the Democrats in the House on the other, over such issues as spending cuts, abortion rights, and civil rights.[55] More such disputes and government shutdowns took place during the administrations of George H. W. Bush, Bill Clinton, and Barack Obama, when different parties controlled Congress and the presidency. The most recent government shutdown, the longest in U.S. history, began in December 2018 under the 115th Congress, when the presidency and both houses were controlled by Republican majorities, but continued into the 116th, which features a Democratically controlled House and a Republican Senate.

For the first few decades of the current pattern of divided government, the threat it posed to the government appears to have been muted by a high degree of **bipartisanship**, or cooperation through compromise. Many pieces of legislation were passed in the 1960s and 1970s with reasonably high levels of support from both parties. Most members of Congress had relatively moderate voting records, with regional differences within parties that made bipartisanship on many issues more likely.

Figure 9.13 In the early 1980s, Republican president Ronald Reagan (left) and Democratic Speaker of the House Tip O'Neil (right) worked together to pass key pieces of legislation, even though they opposed each other on several issues. (credit: Ronald Reagan Presidential Library & Museum)

For example, until the 1980s, northern and midwestern Republicans were often fairly progressive, supporting racial equality, workers' rights, and farm subsidies. Southern Democrats were frequently quite socially and racially conservative and were strong supporters of states' rights. Cross-party cooperation on these issues was fairly frequent. But in the past few decades, the number of moderates in both houses of Congress has declined. This has made it more difficult for party leadership to work together on a range of important issues, and for members of the minority party in Congress to find policy agreement with an opposing party president.

THE IMPLICATIONS OF POLARIZATION

The past thirty years have brought a dramatic change in the relationship between the two parties as fewer conservative Democrats and liberal Republicans have been elected to office. As political **moderates**, or individuals with ideologies in the middle of the ideological spectrum, leave the political parties at all levels, the parties have grown farther apart ideologically, a result called **party polarization**. In other words, at least organizationally and in government, Republicans and Democrats have become increasingly dissimilar from one another (**Figure 9.14**). In the party-in-government, this means fewer members of Congress have mixed voting records; instead they vote far more consistently on issues and are far more likely to side with their party leadership.[56] It also means a growing number of moderate voters aren't participating in party politics. Either they are becoming independents, or they are participating only in the general election and are therefore not helping select party candidates in primaries.

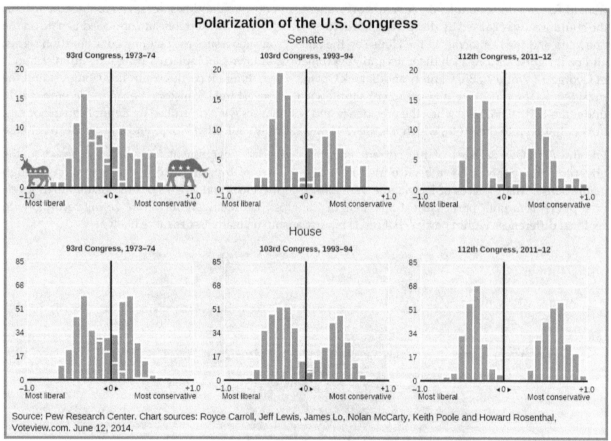

Figure 9.14 The number of moderates has dropped since 1973 as both parties have moved toward ideological extremes.

What is most interesting about this shift to increasingly polarized parties is that it does not appear to have happened as a result of the structural reforms recommended by APSA. Rather, it has happened because moderate politicians have simply found it harder and harder to win elections. There are many conflicting theories about the causes of polarization, some of which we discuss below. But whatever its origin, party polarization in the United States does not appear to have had the net positive effects that the APSA committee was hoping for. With the exception of providing voters with more distinct choices, positives of polarization are hard to find. The negative impacts are many. For one thing, rather than reducing interparty conflict, polarization appears to have only amplified it. For example, the Republican

Party (or the GOP, standing for Grand Old Party) has historically been a coalition of two key and overlapping factions: pro-business rightists and social conservatives. The GOP has held the coalition of these two groups together by opposing programs designed to redistribute wealth (and advocating small government) while at the same time arguing for laws preferred by conservative Christians. But it was also willing to compromise with pro-business Democrats, often at the expense of social issues, if it meant protecting long-term business interests.

Recently, however, a new voice has emerged that has allied itself with the Republican Party. Born in part from an older third-party movement known as the Libertarian Party, the Tea Party is more hostile to government and views government intervention in all forms, and especially taxation and the regulation of business, as a threat to capitalism and democracy. It is less willing to tolerate interventions in the market place, even when they are designed to protect the markets themselves. Although an anti-tax faction within the Republican Party has existed for some time, some factions of the Tea Party movement are also active at the intersection of religious liberty and social issues, especially in opposing such initiatives as same-sex marriage and abortion rights.[57] The Tea Party has argued that government, both directly and by neglect, is threatening the ability of evangelicals to observe their moral obligations, including practices some perceive as endorsing social exclusion.

Although the Tea Party is a movement and not a political party, 86 percent of Tea Party members who voted in 2012 cast their votes for Republicans.[58] Some members of the Republican Party are closely affiliated with the movement, and before the 2012 elections, Tea Party activist Grover Norquist exacted promises from many Republicans in Congress that they would oppose any bill that sought to raise taxes.[59] The inflexibility of Tea Party members has led to tense floor debates and was ultimately responsible for the 2014 primary defeat of Republican majority leader Eric Cantor and the 2015 resignation of the sitting Speaker of the House John Boehner. In 2015, Chris Christie, John Kasich, Ben Carson, Marco Rubio, and Ted Cruz, all of whom were Republican presidential candidates, signed Norquist's pledge as well (Figure 9.15).

(a)   (b)

Figure 9.15 Vying for the Republican nomination, 2016 presidential candidates Ted Cruz (a) and John Kasich (b), like many other Republicans, signed a pledge not to raise taxes if elected.

Movements on the left have also arisen. The Occupy Wall Street movement was born of the government's response to the Great Recession of 2008 and its assistance to endangered financial institutions, provided through the Troubled Asset Relief Program, TARP (Figure 9.16). The Occupy Movement believed the recession was caused by a failure of the government to properly regulate the banking industry. The Occupiers further maintained that the government moved swiftly to protect the banking industry from the worst of the recession but largely failed to protect the average person, thereby worsening the growing economic inequality in the United States.

Figure 9.16   On September 30, 2011, Occupy Wall Street protesters marched to the headquarters of the New York Police Department to protest police brutality that occurred in response to the movement's occupation of Zuccotti Park in Lower Manhattan. (credit: modification of work by David Shankbone)

While the Occupy Movement itself has largely fizzled, the anti-business sentiment to which it gave voice continues within the Democratic Party, and many Democrats have proclaimed their support for the movement and its ideals, if not for its tactics.[60] Champions of the left wing of the Democratic Party, however, such as former presidential candidate Senator Bernie Sanders and Massachusetts senator Elizabeth Warren, have ensured that the Occupy Movement's calls for more social spending and higher taxes on the wealthy remain a prominent part of the national debate. Their popularity, and the growing visibility of race issues in the United States, have helped sustain the left wing of the Democratic Party. Bernie Sanders' presidential run made these topics and causes even more salient, especially among younger voters. This reality led Hillary Clinton to move left during the primaries and attempt to win people over. However, the left never warmed up to Clinton after Sanders exited the race. After Clinton lost to Trump, many on the left blamed Clinton for not going far enough left, and they further claimed that Sanders would have had a better chance at beating Trump.[61]

Unfortunately, party factions haven't been the only result of party polarization. By most measures, the U.S. government in general and Congress in particular have become less effective in recent years. Congress has passed fewer pieces of legislation, confirmed fewer appointees, and been less effective at handling the national purse than in recent memory. If we define effectiveness as legislative productivity, the 106th Congress (1999–2000) passed 463 pieces of substantive legislation (not including commemorative legislation, such as bills proclaiming an official doughnut of the United States). The 107th Congress (2000–2001) passed 294 such pieces of legislation. By 2013–2014, the total had fallen to 212.[62]

Perhaps the clearest sign of Congress' ineffectiveness is that the threat of government shutdown has become a constant. Shutdowns occur when Congress and the president are unable to authorize and appropriate funds before the current budget runs out. This is now an annual problem. Relations between the two parties became so bad that financial markets were sent into turmoil in 2014 when Congress failed to increase the government's line of credit before a key deadline, thus threatening a U.S. government default on its loans. While any particular trend can be the result of multiple factors, the decline of key measures of institutional confidence and trust suggest the negative impact of polarization. Public approval ratings for Congress have been near single digits for several years, and a poll taken in February 2016 revealed that only 11 percent of respondents thought Congress was doing a "good or excellent job."[63] In the wake of the Great Recession, President Obama's average approval rating remained low for several years, despite an overall trend in economic growth since the end of 2008, before he enjoyed an uptick in support during his final year in office.[64] Typically, economic conditions are a significant driver of presidential approval, suggesting the negative effect of partisanship on presidential approval.

THE CAUSES OF POLARIZATION

Scholars agree that some degree of polarization is occurring in the United States, even if some contend it is only at the elite level. But they are less certain about exactly why, or how, polarization has become such a mainstay of American politics. Several conflicting theories have been offered. The first and perhaps best argument is that polarization is a party-in-government phenomenon driven by a decades-long **sorting** of the voting public, or a change in party allegiance in response to shifts in party position.[65] According to the sorting thesis, before the 1950s, voters were mostly concerned with state-level party positions rather than national party concerns. Since parties are bottom-up institutions, this meant local issues dominated elections; it also meant national-level politicians typically paid more attention to local problems than to national party politics.

But over the past several decades, voters have started identifying more with national-level party politics, and they began to demand their elected representatives become more attentive to national party positions. As a result, they have become more likely to pick parties that consistently represent national ideals, are more consistent in their candidate selection, and are more willing to elect office-holders likely to follow their party's national agenda. One example of the way social change led to party sorting revolves around race.

The Democratic Party returned to national power in the 1930s largely as the result of a coalition among low socio-economic status voters in northern and midwestern cities. These new Democratic voters were religiously and ethnically more diverse than the mostly white, mostly Protestant voters who supported Republicans. But the southern United States (often called the "Solid South") had been largely dominated by Democratic politicians since the Civil War. These politicians agreed with other Democrats on most issues, but they were more evangelical in their religious beliefs and less tolerant on racial matters. The federal nature of the United States meant that Democrats in other parts of the country were free to seek alliances with minorities in their states. But in the South, African Americans were still largely disenfranchised well after Franklin Roosevelt had brought other groups into the Democratic tent.

The Democratic alliance worked relatively well through the 1930s and 1940s when post-Depression politics revolved around supporting farmers and helping the unemployed. But in the late 1950s and early 1960s, social issues became increasingly prominent in national politics. Southern Democrats, who had supported giving the federal government authority for economic redistribution, began to resist calls for those powers to be used to restructure society. Many of these Democrats broke away from the party only to find a home among Republicans, who were willing to help promote smaller national government and greater states' rights.[66] This shift was largely completed with the rise of the evangelical movement in politics, when it shepherded its supporters away from Jimmy Carter, an evangelical Christian, to Ronald Reagan in the 1980 presidential election.

At the same time social issues were turning the Solid South towards the Republican Party, they were having the opposite effect in the North and West. Moderate Republicans, who had been champions of racial equality since the time of Lincoln, worked with Democrats to achieve social reform. These Republicans found it increasing difficult to remain in their party as it began to adjust to the growing power of the small government–states' rights movement. A good example was Senator Arlen Specter, a moderate Republican who represented Pennsylvania and ultimately switched to become a Democrat before the end of his political career.

A second possible culprit in increased polarization is the impact of technology on the public square. Before the 1950s, most people got their news from regional newspapers and local radio stations. While some national programming did exist, most editorial control was in the hands of local publishers and editorial boards. These groups served as a filter of sorts as they tried to meet the demands of local markets.

As described in detail in the media chapter, the advent of television changed that. Television was a powerful tool, with national news and editorial content that provided the same message across the country. All viewers saw the same images of the women's rights movement and the war in Vietnam. The expansion of news coverage to cable, and the consolidation of local news providers into big corporate conglomerates, amplified this nationalization. Average citizens were just as likely to learn what it meant to be a Republican from a politician in another state as from one in their own, and national news coverage made it much more difficult for politicians to run away from their votes. The information explosion that followed the heyday of network TV by way of cable, the Internet, and blogs has furthered this nationalization trend.

A final possible cause for polarization is the increasing sophistication of **gerrymandering**, or the manipulation of legislative districts in an attempt to favor a particular candidate (Figure 9.17). According to the gerrymandering thesis, the more moderate or heterogeneous a voting district, the more moderate the politician's behavior once in office. Taking extreme or one-sided positions on a large number of issues would be hazardous for a member who needs to build a diverse electoral coalition. But if the district has been drawn to favor a particular group, it now is necessary for the elected official to serve only the portion of the constituency that dominates.

Figure 9.17 This cartoon, which inspired the term gerrymander, was printed in the *Boston Gazette* on March 26, 1812, after the Massachusetts legislature redistricted the state to favor the party of the sitting governor, Elbridge Gerry.

Gerrymandering is a centuries-old practice. There has always been an incentive for legislative bodies to draw districts in such a way that sitting legislators have the best chance of keeping their jobs. But changes in law and technology have transformed gerrymandering from a crude art into a science. The first advance came with the introduction of the "one-person-one-vote" principle by the U.S. Supreme Court in 1962. Before then, it was common for many states to practice **redistricting**, or redrawing of their electoral maps, *only* if they gained or lost seats in the U.S. House of Representatives. This can happen once every ten years as a result of a constitutionally mandated **reapportionment** process, in which the number of House seats given to each state is adjusted to account for population changes.

But if there was no change in the number of seats, there was little incentive to shift district boundaries. After all, if a legislator had won election based on the current map, any change to the map could make losing seats more likely. Even when reapportionment led to new maps, most legislators were more concerned with protecting their own seats than with increasing the number of seats held by their party. As a result, some districts had gone decades without significant adjustment, even as the U.S. population changed from largely rural to largely urban. By the early 1960s, some electoral districts had populations several times greater than those of their more rural neighbors.

However, in its one-person-one-vote decision in *Reynolds v. Simms* (1964), the Supreme Court argued that everyone's vote should count roughly the same regardless of where they lived.[67] Districts had to be adjusted so they would have roughly equal populations. Several states therefore had to make dramatic changes to their electoral maps during the next two redistricting cycles (1970–1972 and 1980–1982). Map designers, no longer certain how to protect individual party members, changed tactics to try and create **safe seats** so members of their party could be assured of winning by a comfortable margin. The basic rule of thumb was that designers sought to draw districts in which their preferred party had a 55 percent or better chance of winning a given district, regardless of which candidate the party nominated.

Of course, many early efforts at post-*Reynolds* gerrymandering were crude since map designers had no good way of knowing exactly where partisans lived. At best, designers might have a rough idea of voting patterns between precincts, but they lacked the ability to know voting patterns in individual blocks or neighborhoods. They also had to contend with the inherent mobility of the U.S. population, which meant the most carefully drawn maps could be obsolete just a few years later. Designers were often forced to use crude proxies for party, such as race or the socio-economic status of a neighborhood (Figure 9.18). Some maps were so crude they were ruled unconstitutionally discriminatory by the courts.

Gerrymandering in Austin, TX, 2003–2015

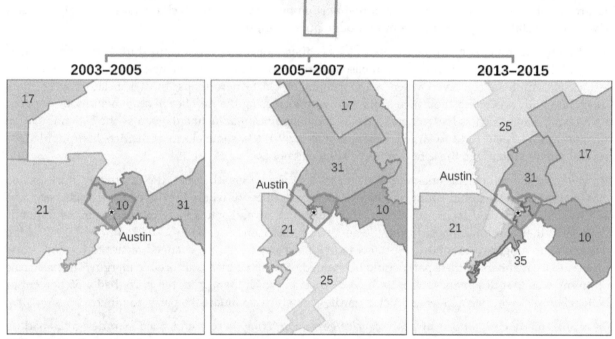

Figure 9.18 Examples of gerrymandering in Texas, where the Republican-controlled legislature redrew House districts to reduce the number of Democratic seats by combining voters in Austin with those near the border, several hundred miles away. Today, Austin is represented by six different congressional representatives.

Proponents of the gerrymandering thesis point out that the decline in the number of moderate voters began during this period of increased redistricting. But it wasn't until later, they argue, that the real effects could be seen. A second advance in redistricting, via computer-aided map making, truly transformed gerrymandering into a science. Refined computing technology, the ability to collect data about potential voters, and the use of advanced algorithms have given map makers a good deal of certainty about where to place district boundaries to best predetermine the outcomes. These factors also provided better predictions about future population shifts, making the effects of gerrymandering more stable over time. Proponents argue that this increased efficiency in map drawing has led to the disappearance of moderates in Congress.

According to political scientist Nolan McCarty, there is little evidence to support the redistricting hypothesis alone. First, he argues, the Senate has become polarized just as the House of Representatives has, but people vote for Senators on a statewide basis. There are no gerrymandered voting districts in elections for senators. Research showing that more partisan candidates first win election to the House before then running successfully for the Senate, however, helps us understand how the Senate can also become partisan.[68] Furthermore, states like Wyoming and Vermont, which have only one Representative and thus elect House members on a statewide basis as well, have consistently elected people at the far ends of the ideological spectrum.[69] Redistricting did contribute to polarization in the House of Representatives, but it took place largely in districts that had undergone significant change.[70]

Furthermore, polarization has been occurring throughout the country, but the use of increasingly polarized district design has not. While some states have seen an increase in these practices, many states were already largely dominated by a single party (such as in the Solid South) but still elected moderate representatives. Some parts of the country have remained closely divided between the two parties, making overt attempts at gerrymandering difficult. But when coupled with the sorting phenomenon discussed above, redistricting probably is contributing to polarization, if only at the margins.

Finding a Middle Ground

The Politics of Redistricting

Voters in a number of states have become so worried about the problem of gerrymandering that they have tried to deny their legislatures the ability to draw district boundaries. The hope is that by taking this power away from whichever party controls the state legislature, voters can ensure more competitive districts and fairer electoral outcomes.

In 2000, voters in Arizona approved a referendum that created an independent state commission responsible for drafting legislative districts. But the Arizona legislature fought back against the creation of the commission, filing a lawsuit that claimed only the legislature had the constitutional right to draw districts. Legislators asked the courts to overturn the popular referendum and end the operation of the redistricting commission. However, the U.S. Supreme Court upheld the authority of the independent commission in a 5–4 decision titled *Arizona State Legislature v. Arizona Independent Redistricting Commission* (2015).[71]

Currently, only five states use fully independent commissions—ones that do not include legislators or other elected officials—to draw the lines for both state legislative and congressional districts. These states are Arizona, California, Idaho, Montana, and Washington. In Florida, the League of Women Voters and Common Cause challenged a new voting districts map supported by state Republicans, because they did not believe it fulfilled the requirements of amendments made to the state constitution in 2010 requiring that voting districts not favor any political party or incumbent.[72]

Do you think redistricting is a partisan issue? Should commissions draw districts instead of legislators? If commissions are given this task, who should serve on them?

Link to Learning

Think you have what it takes to gerrymander a district? Play the redistricting game (https://openstax.org/l/29redistrictgam) and see whether you can find new ways to help out old politicians.

Key Terms

bipartisanship a process of cooperation through compromise

critical election an election that represents a sudden, clear, and long-term shift in voter allegiances

divided government a condition in which one or more houses of the legislature is controlled by the party in opposition to the executive

first-past-the-post a system in which the winner of an election is the candidate who wins the greatest number of votes cast, also known as plurality voting

gerrymandering the manipulation of legislative districts in an attempt to favor a particular candidate

majoritarian voting a type of election in which the winning candidate must receive at least 50 percent of the votes, even if a run-off election is required

majority party the legislative party with over half the seats in a legislative body, and thus significant power to control the agenda

minority party the legislative party with less than half the seats in a legislative body

moderate an individual who falls in the middle of the ideological spectrum

party identifiers individuals who represent themselves in public as being part of a party

party organization the formal structure of the political party and the active members responsible for coordinating party behavior and supporting party candidates

party platform the collection of a party's positions on issues it considers politically important

party polarization the shift of party positions from moderate towards ideological extremes

party realignment a shifting of party alliances within the electorate

party-in-government party identifiers who have been elected to office and are responsible for fulfilling the party's promises

party-in-the-electorate members of the voting public who consider themselves part of a political party or who consistently prefer the candidates of one party over the other

personal politics a political style that focuses on building direct relationships with voters rather than on promoting specific issues

plurality voting the election rule by which the candidate with the most votes wins, regardless of vote share

political machine an organization that secures votes for a party's candidates or supports the party in other ways, usually in exchange for political favors such as a job in government

political parties organizations made up of groups of people with similar interests that try to directly influence public policy through their members who seek and hold public office

precinct the lowest level of party organization, usually organized around neighborhoods

proportional representation a party-based election rule in which the number of seats a party receives is a function of the share of votes it receives in an election

reapportionment the reallocation of House seats between the states to account for population changes

redistricting the redrawing of electoral maps

safe seat a district drawn so members of a party can be assured of winning by a comfortable margin

sorting the process in which voters change party allegiances in response to shifts in party position

third parties political parties formed as an alternative to the Republican and Democratic parties, also known as minor parties

two-party system a system in which two major parties win all or almost all elections

Summary

9.1 What Are Parties and How Did They Form?
Political parties are vital to the operation of any democracy. Early U.S. political parties were formed by national elites who disagreed over how to divide power between the national and state governments. The system we have today, divided between Republicans and Democrats, had consolidated by 1860. A number of minor parties have attempted to challenge the status quo, but they have largely failed to gain traction despite having an occasional impact on the national political scene.

9.2 The Two-Party System
Electoral rules, such as the use of plurality voting, have helped turn the United States into a two-party system dominated by the Republicans and the Democrats. Several minor parties have attempted to challenge the status quo, but usually they have only been spoilers that served to divide party coalitions. But this doesn't mean the party system has always been stable; party coalitions have shifted several times in the past two hundred years.

9.3 The Shape of Modern Political Parties
Political parties exist primarily as a means to help candidates get elected. The United States thus has a relatively loose system of party identification and a bottom-up approach to party organization structure built around elections. Lower levels, such as the precinct or county, take on the primary responsibility for voter registration and mobilization, whereas the higher state and national levels are responsible for electing major candidates and shaping party ideology. The party in government is responsible for implementing the policies on which its candidates run, but elected officials also worry about winning reelection.

9.4 Divided Government and Partisan Polarization
A divided government makes it difficult for elected officials to achieve their policy goals. This problem has gotten worse as U.S. political parties have become increasingly polarized over the past several decades. They are both more likely to fight with each other and more internally divided than just a few decades ago. Some possible causes include sorting and improved gerrymandering, although neither alone offers a completely satisfactory explanation. But whatever the cause, polarization is having negative short-term consequences on American politics.

Review Questions

1. Which supporter of federalism warned people about the dangers of political parties?
 a. John Adams
 b. Alexander Hamilton
 c. James Madison
 d. George Washington

2. Which of the following was not a third-party challenger?
 a. Whig Party
 b. Progressive Party
 c. Dixiecrats
 d. Green Party

3. Why were the early U.S. political parties formed?

4. What techniques led the Democratic Party to national prominence in the 1830s through 1850s?

5. In which type of electoral system do voters select the party of their choice rather than an individual candidate?
 a. proportional representation
 b. first-past-the-post
 c. plurality voting
 d. majoritarian voting

6. Which of the following does *not* represent a major contributing factor in party realignment?
 a. demographic shifts
 b. changes in key issues
 c. changes in party strategies
 d. third parties

7. What impact, if any, do third parties typically have on U.S. elections?

8. In what ways do political parties collude with state and local government to prevent the rise of new parties?

9. Which level of party organization is most responsible for helping the party's nominee win the presidency?
 a. precinct
 b. county
 c. state
 d. national

10. How do members of the party organization differ from party identifiers? What role does each play in the party as a whole?

11. Why is winning votes so important to political parties? How does the need to win elections affect party structures?

12. What are the positives and negatives of partisan polarization?

13. What is the sorting thesis, and what does it suggest as the cause of party polarization?

14. Does gerrymandering lead to increased polarization?

15. How have the Tea Party and Occupy Wall Street Movement affected partisan politics?

Critical Thinking Questions

16. Is it possible for a serious third party to emerge in the United States, positioned ideologically between the Democrats on the left and the Republicans on the right? Why or why not?

17. In what ways are political parties of the people and in what ways might they be more responsive to elites?

18. If you were required to become active in some aspect of a political party, what activity and level of party organization would you choose and why?

19. Is it preferable for the U.S. government to have unified party control or divided government? Why?

20. In general, do parties make the business of government easier or harder to accomplish?

Suggestions for Further Study

Aldrich, John. 1995. *Why Parties?* Chicago: University of Chicago Press.

Brewer, Mark D., and L. Sandy Maisel. 2013. *The Parties Respond: Changes in American Parties and Campaigns*, 5th ed. Boulder, CO: Westview Press.

Brunell, Thomas L. 2008. *Redistricting and Representation: Why Competitive Elections are Bad for America*. New York: Routledge Press.

Cox, Gary W., and Jonathan Katz. 2002. *Elbridge Gerry's Salamander: The Electoral Consequences of the Reapportionment Revolution*. Cambridge, UK: Cambridge University Press.

Fiorina, Morris P. 2006. *Culture War? The Myth of a Polarized America*. 2nd ed. New York: Pearson Longman.

Hershey, Marjorie Randon. 2014. *Party Politics in America*, 16th ed. New York: Pearson Longman.

Hibbing, John R., and Elizabeth Theiss-Morse. 1995. *Congress as Public Enemy: Public Attitudes towards American Political Institutions*. Cambridge: Cambridge University Press.

Keith, Bruce E., et al. 1992. *The Myth of the Independent Voter*. Berkeley, CA. Berkeley University Press.

McCarthy, Nolan, Keith T. Poole and Howard Rosenthal. 2008. *Polarized America: The Dance of Ideology and Unequal Riches*. Cambridge, MA: MIT Press.

Noel, Hans. 2014. *Political Ideologies and Political Parties in America*. Cambridge: Cambridge University Press.

Sinclair, Barbara. 2005. *Party Wars*. Norman, OK: University of Oklahoma Press.

Chapter 10

Interest Groups and Lobbying

Figure 10.1 On April 15 (or "tax day"), 2010, members of the Tea Party movement rallied at the Minnesota State Capitol in St. Paul in favor of smaller government and against the Affordable Care Act (left). Two years later, supporters of the law (right) demonstrated in front of the U.S. Supreme Court during oral arguments in *National Federation of Independent Business v. Sebelius*, in which the Court eventually upheld most provisions of the law. (credit left: modification of work by "Fibonacci Blue"/Flickr; credit right: modification of work by LaDawna Howard)

Chapter Outline

10.1 Interest Groups Defined
10.2 Collective Action and Interest Group Formation
10.3 Interest Groups as Political Participation
10.4 Pathways of Interest Group Influence
10.5 Free Speech and the Regulation of Interest Groups

Introduction

The 2010 Patient Protection and Affordable Care Act (ACA), also known as Obamacare, represented a substantial overhaul of the U.S. healthcare system.[1] Given its potential impact, interest group representatives (lobbyists) from the insurance industry, hospitals, medical device manufacturers, and organizations representing doctors, patients, and employers all tried to influence what the law would look like and the way it would operate. Ordinary people took to the streets to voice their opinion (Figure 10.1). Some state governors sued to prevent a requirement in the law that their states expand Medicaid coverage. A number of interest groups challenged the law in court, where two Supreme Court decisions have left it largely intact.

Interest groups like those for and against the ACA play a fundamental role in representing individuals, corporate interests, and the public before the government. They help inform the public and lawmakers about issues, monitor government actions, and promote policies that benefit their interests, using all three branches of government at the federal, state, and local levels.

In this chapter, we answer several key questions about interest groups. What are they, and why and how do they form? How do they provide avenues for political participation? Why are some groups advantaged by the lobbying of government representatives, while others are disadvantaged? Finally, how do interest groups try to achieve their objectives, and how are they regulated?

10.1 Interest Groups Defined

Learning Objectives

By the end of this section, you will be able to:

- Explain how interest groups differ from political parties
- Evaluate the different types of interests and what they do
- Compare public and private interest groups

While the term *interest group* is not mentioned in the U.S. Constitution, the framers were aware that individuals would band together in an attempt to use government in their favor. In *Federalist* No. 10, James Madison warned of the dangers of "factions," minorities who would organize around issues they felt strongly about, possibly to the detriment of the majority. But Madison believed limiting these factions was worse than facing the evils they might produce, because such limitations would violate individual freedoms. Instead, the natural way to control factions was to let them flourish and compete against each other. The sheer number of interests in the United States suggests that many have, indeed, flourished. They compete with similar groups for membership, and with opponents for access to decision-makers. Some people suggest there may be too many interests in the United States. Others argue that some have gained a disproportionate amount of influence over public policy, whereas many others are underrepresented.

Madison's definition of factions can apply to both interest groups and political parties. But unlike political parties, interest groups do not function primarily to elect candidates under a certain party label or to directly control the operation of the government. Political parties in the United States are generally much broader coalitions that represent a significant proportion of citizens. In the American two-party system, the Democratic and Republican Parties spread relatively wide nets to try to encompass large segments of the population. In contrast, while interest groups may support or oppose political candidates, their goals are usually more issue-specific and narrowly focused on areas like taxes, the environment, and gun rights or gun control, or their membership is limited to specific professions. They may represent interests ranging from well-known organizations, such as the Sierra Club, IBM, or the American Lung Association, to obscure ones, such as the North Carolina Gamefowl Breeders Association. Thus, with some notable exceptions, specific interest groups have much more limited membership than do political parties.

Political parties and interest groups both work together and compete for influence, although in different ways. While interest group activity often transcends party lines, many interests are perceived as being more supportive of one party than the other. The American Conservative Union, Citizens United, the National Rifle Association, and National Right to Life are more likely to have relationships with Republican lawmakers than with Democratic ones. Americans for Democratic Action, Moveon.org, and the Democratic Governors Association all have stronger relationships with the Democratic Party. Parties and interest groups do compete with each other, however, often for influence. At the state level, we typically observe an inverse relationship between them in terms of power. Interest groups tend to have greater influence in states where political parties are comparatively weaker.

WHAT ARE INTEREST GROUPS AND WHAT DO THEY WANT?

Definitions abound when it comes to interest groups, which are sometimes referred to as special interests, interest organizations, pressure groups, or just interests. Most definitions specify that *interest group* indicates any formal association of individuals or organizations that attempt to influence government decision-making and/or the making of public policy. Often, this influence is exercised by a lobbyist or a lobbying firm.

Formally, a **lobbyist** is someone who represents the interest organization before government, is usually compensated for doing so, and is required to register with the government in which he or she lobbies, whether state or federal. The lobbyist's primary goal is usually to influence policy. Most interest organizations engage in lobbying activity to achieve their objectives. As you might expect, the interest hires a lobbyist, employs one internally, or has a member volunteer to lobby on its behalf. For present purposes, we might restrict our definition to the relatively broad one in the Lobbying Disclosure Act.[2] This act requires the registration of lobbyists representing any interest group and devoting more than 20 percent of their time to it.[3] Clients and lobbying firms must also register with the federal government based on similar requirements. Moreover, campaign finance laws require disclosure of campaign contributions given to political candidates by organizations.

Link to Learning

Visit this **site (https://openstax.org/l/29opensecrets)** to research donations and campaign contributions given to political candidates by organizations.

Lobbying is not limited to Washington, DC, however, and many interests lobby there as well as in one or more states. Each state has its own laws describing which individuals and entities must register, so the definitions of lobbyists and interests, and of what lobbying is and who must register to do it, also vary from state to state. Therefore, while a citizen contacting a lawmaker to discuss an issue is generally not viewed as lobbying, an organization that devotes a certain amount of time and resources to contacting lawmakers may be classified as lobbying, depending on local, state, or federal law.

Largely for this reason, there is no comprehensive list of all interest groups to tell us how many there are in the United States. Estimates of the number vary widely, suggesting that if we use a broad definition and include all interests at all levels of government, there may be more than 200,000.[4] Following the passage of the Lobbying Disclosure Act in 1995, we had a much better understanding of the number of interests registered in Washington, DC; however, it was not until several years later that we had a complete count and categorization of the interests registered in each of the fifty states.[5]

Political scientists have categorized interest groups in a number of ways.[6] First, interest groups may take the form of **membership organizations**, which individuals join voluntarily and to which they usually pay dues. Membership groups often consist of people who have common issues or concerns, or who want to be with others who share their views. The National Rifle Association (NRA) is a membership group consisting of members who promote gun rights (Figure 10.2). For those who advocate greater regulation of access to firearms, such as background checks prior to gun purchases, the Brady Campaign to Prevent Gun Violence is a membership organization that weighs in on the other side of the issue.[7]

(a)   (b)

Figure 10.2   A Florida member of the NRA proudly displays his support of gun rights (a). In December 2012, CREDO, a San Francisco telecommunications company that supports progressive causes, called on the NRA to stop blocking Congress from passing gun control legislation (b). (credit a: modification of work by Daniel Oines; credit b: modification of work by Josh Lopez)

Interest groups may also form to represent companies, corporate organizations, and governments. These groups do not have individual members but rather are offshoots of corporate or governmental entities with a compelling interest to be represented in front of one or more branches of government. Verizon and Coca-Cola will register to lobby in order to influence policy in a way that benefits them. These corporations will either have one or more **in-house lobbyists**, who work for one interest group or firm and represent their organization in a lobbying capacity, and/or will hire a **contract lobbyist**, individuals who work for firms that represent a multitude of clients and are often hired because of their resources and their ability to contact and lobby lawmakers, to represent them before the legislature.

Governments such as municipalities and executive departments such as the Department of Education register to lobby in an effort to maximize their share of budgets or increase their level of autonomy. These government institutions are represented by a **legislative liaison**, whose job is to present issues to decision-makers. For example, a state university usually employs a lobbyist, legislative liaison, or government affairs person to represent its interests before the legislature. This includes lobbying for a given university's share of the budget or for its continued autonomy from lawmakers and other state-level officials who may attempt to play a greater oversight role.

In 2015, thirteen states had their higher education budgets cut from the previous year, and nearly all states have seen some cuts to higher education funding since the recession began in 2008.[8] In 2015, as in many states, universities and community colleges in Mississippi lobbied the legislature over pending budget cuts.[9] These examples highlight the need for universities and state university systems to have representation before the legislature. On the federal level, universities may lobby for research funds from government departments. For example, the Departments of Defense and Homeland Security may be willing to fund scientific research that might better enable them to defend the nation.

Interest groups also include **associations**, which are typically groups of institutions that join with others, often within the same trade or industry (trade associations), and have similar concerns. The American Beverage Association[10] includes Coca-Cola, Red Bull North America, ROCKSTAR, and Kraft Foods. Despite the fact that these companies are competitors, they have common interests related to the manufacturing, bottling, and distribution of beverages, as well as the regulation of their business activities. The logic is that there is strength in numbers, and if members can lobby for tax breaks or eased regulations for an entire industry, they may all benefit. These common goals do not, however, prevent individual association members from employing in-house lobbyists or contract lobbying firms to represent their own business or organization as well. Indeed, many members of associations are competitors who also seek representation individually before the legislature.

Link to Learning

Visit the website of an association like the American Beverage Association (https://openstax.org/l/29ambevassoc) or the American Bankers Association (https://openstax.org/l/29amerbankassoc) and look over the key issues it addresses. Do any of the issues it cares about surprise you? What areas do you think members can agree about? Are there issues on which the membership might disagree? Why would competitors join together when they normally compete for business?

Finally, sometimes individuals volunteer to represent an organization. They are called amateur or volunteer lobbyists, and are typically not compensated for their lobbying efforts. In some cases, citizens may lobby for pet projects because they care about some issue or cause. They may or may not be members of an interest group, but if they register to lobby, they are sometimes nicknamed "hobbyists."

Lobbyists representing a variety of organizations employ different techniques to achieve their objectives. One method is **inside lobbying** or direct lobbying, which takes the interest group's message directly to a government official such as a lawmaker.[11] Inside lobbying tactics include testifying in legislative hearings and helping to draft legislation. Numerous surveys of lobbyists have confirmed that the vast majority rely on these inside strategies. For example, nearly all report that they contact lawmakers, testify before the legislature, help draft legislation, and contact executive agencies. Trying to influence government appointments or providing favors to members of government are somewhat less common insider tactics.

Many lobbyists also use **outside lobbying** or indirect lobbying tactics, whereby the interest attempts to get its message out to the public.[12] These tactics include issuing press releases, placing stories and articles in the media, entering coalitions with other groups, and contacting interest group members, hoping that they will individually pressure lawmakers to support or oppose legislation. An environmental interest group like the Sierra Club, for example, might issue a press release or encourage its members to contact their representatives in Congress about legislation of concern to the group. It might also use outside tactics if there is a potential threat to the environment and the group wants to raise awareness among its members and the public (Figure 10.3). Members of Congress are likely to pay attention when many constituents contact them about an issue or proposed bill. Many interest groups, including the Sierra Club, will use a combination of inside and outside tactics in their lobbying efforts, choosing whatever strategy is most likely to help them achieve their goals.

Figure 10.3 In February 2013, members of the Sierra Club joined a march on Los Angeles City Hall to demand action on climate change and protest the development of the Keystone pipeline. (credit: Charlie Kaijo)

The primary goal of most interests, no matter their lobbying approach, is to influence decision-makers and public policies. For example, National Right to Life, an anti-abortion interest group, lobbies to encourage government to enact laws that restrict abortion access, while NARAL Pro-Choice America lobbies to promote the right of women to have safe choices about abortion. Environmental interests like the Sierra Club lobby for laws designed to protect natural resources and minimize the use of pollutants. On the other hand, some interests lobby to reduce regulations that an organization might view as burdensome. Air and water quality regulations designed to improve or protect the environment may be viewed as onerous by industries that pollute as a byproduct of their production or manufacturing process. Other interests lobby for budgetary allocations; the farm lobby, for example, pressures Congress to secure new farm subsidies or maintain existing ones. Farm subsidies are given to some farmers because they grow certain crops and to other farmers so they will *not* grow certain crops.[13] As expected, any bill that might attempt to alter these subsidies raises the antennae of many agricultural interests.

INTEREST GROUP FUNCTIONS

While influencing policy is the primary goal, interest groups also monitor government activity, serve as a means of political participation for members, and provide information to the public and to lawmakers. According to the National Conference of State Legislatures, by November 2015, thirty-six states had laws requiring that voters provide identification at the polls.[14] A civil rights group like the National Association for the Advancement of Colored People (NAACP) will keep track of proposed voter-identification bills in state legislatures that might have an effect on voting rights. This organization will contact lawmakers to voice approval or disapproval of proposed legislation (inside lobbying) and encourage group members to take action by either donating money to it or contacting lawmakers about the proposed bill (outside lobbying). Thus, a member of the organization or a citizen concerned about voting rights need not be an expert on the legislative process or the technical or legal details of a proposed bill to be informed about potential threats to voting rights. Other interest groups function in similar ways. For example, the NRA monitors attempts by state legislatures to tighten gun control laws.

Interest groups facilitate political participation in a number of ways. Some members become active within a group, working on behalf of the organization to promote its agenda. Some interests work to increase membership, inform the public about issues the group deems important, or organize rallies and promote get-out-the-vote efforts. Sometimes groups will utilize events to mobilize existing members or encourage new members to join. For example, following Barack Obama's presidential victory in 2008, the NRA used the election as a rallying cry for its supporters, and it continues to attack the president on the issue of guns, despite the fact that gun rights have in some ways expanded over the course of the Obama presidency. Interest groups also organize letter-writing campaigns, stage protests, and sometimes hold fundraisers for their cause or even for political campaigns.

Some interests are more broadly focused than others. AARP (formerly the American Association of Retired Persons) has approximately thirty-seven million members and advocates for individuals fifty and over on a variety of issues including health care, insurance, employment, financial security, and consumer protection (Figure 10.4).[15] This organization represents both liberals and conservatives, Democrats and Republicans, and many who do not identify with these categorizations. On the other hand, the Association of Black Cardiologists is a much smaller and far-narrower organization. Over the last several decades, some interest groups have sought greater specialization and have even fragmented. As you may imagine, the Association of Black Cardiologists is more specialized than the American Medical Association, which tries to represent all physicians regardless of race or specialty.

Figure 10.4 Health care is an important concern for AARP and its members, so the organization makes sure to maintain connections with key policymakers in this area, such as Katherine Sebelius, secretary of Health and Human Services from 2009 to 2014, shown here with John Rother, director of legislation and public policy for AARP. (credit: modification of work by Chris Smith, HHS)

PUBLIC VS. PRIVATE INTEREST GROUPS

Interest groups and organizations represent both private and public interests in the United States. *Private interests* usually seek **particularized benefits** from government that favor either a single interest or a narrow set of interests. For example, corporations and political institutions may lobby government for tax exemptions, fewer regulations, or favorable laws that benefit individual companies or an industry more generally. Their goal is to promote private goods. Private goods are items individuals can own, including corporate profits. An automobile is a private good; when you purchase it, you receive ownership. Wealthy individuals are more likely to accumulate private goods, and they can sometimes obtain private goods from governments, such as tax benefits, government subsidies, or government contracts.

On the other hand, **public interest groups** attempt to promote public, or collective, goods. Such **collective goods** are benefits—tangible or intangible—that help most or all citizens. These goods are often produced collectively, and because they may not be profitable and everyone may not agree on what public goods are best for society, they are often underfunded and thus will be underproduced unless there is government involvement. The Tennessee Valley Authority, a government corporation, provides electricity in some places where it is not profitable for private firms to do so. Other examples of collective goods are public safety, highway safety, public education, and environmental protection. With some exceptions, if an environmental interest promotes clean air or water, most or all citizens are able to enjoy the result. So if the Sierra Club encourages Congress to pass legislation that improves national air quality, citizens receive the benefit regardless of whether they are members of the organization or even support the legislation. Many environmental groups are public interest groups that lobby for and raise awareness of issues that affect large segments of the population.[16]

As the clean air example above suggests, collective goods are generally nonexcludable, meaning all or most people are entitled to the public good and cannot be prevented from enjoying it. Furthermore, collective goods are generally not subject to crowding, so that even as the population increases, people still have access to the entire public good. Thus, the military does not protect citizens only in Texas and Maryland while neglecting those in New York and Idaho, but instead it provides the collective good of national defense equally to citizens in all states. As another example, even as more cars use a public roadway, under most circumstances, additional drivers still have the option of using the same road. (High-occupancy vehicle lanes may restrict some lanes of a highway for drivers who do not car pool.)

10.2 Collective Action and Interest Group Formation

Learning Objectives

By the end of this section, you will be able to:
- Explain the concept of collective action and its effect on interest group formation
- Describe free riding and the reasons it occurs
- Discuss ways to overcome collective action problems

In any group project in which you have participated, you may have noticed that a small number of students did the bulk of the work while others did very little. Yet everyone received the same grade. Why do some do all the work, while others do little or none? How is it possible to get people to work when there is a disincentive to do so? This situation is an example of a collective action problem, and it exists in government as well as in public and private organizations. Whether it is Congress trying to pass a budget or an interest group trying to motivate members to contact lawmakers, organizations must overcome collective action problems to be productive. This is especially true of interest groups, whose formation and survival depend on members doing the necessary work to keep the group funded and operating.

COLLECTIVE ACTION AND FREE RIDING

Collective action problems exist when people have a disincentive to take action.[17] In his classic work, *The Logic of Collective Action*, economist Mancur Olson discussed the conditions under which collective actions problems would exist, and he noted that they were prevalent among organized interests. People tend not to act when the perceived benefit is insufficient to justify the costs associated with engaging in the action. Many citizens may have concerns about the appropriate level of taxation, gun control, or environmental protection, but these concerns are not necessarily strong enough for them to become politically active. In fact, most people take no action on most issues, either because they do not feel strongly enough or because their action will likely have little bearing on whether a given policy is adopted. Thus, there is a disincentive to call your member of Congress, because rarely will a single phone call sway a politician on an issue.

Why do some students elect to do little on a group project? The answer is that they likely prefer to do something else and realize they can receive the same grade as the rest of the group without contributing to the effort. This result is often termed the **free rider problem**, because some individuals can receive benefits (get a free ride) without helping to bear the cost. When National Public Radio (NPR) engages in a fund-raising effort to help maintain the station, many listeners will not contribute. Since it is unlikely that any one listener's donation will be decisive in whether NPR has adequate funding to continue to operate, most listeners will not contribute to the costs but instead will free ride and continue to receive the benefits of listening.

Collective action problems and free riding occur in many other situations as well. If union membership is optional and all workers will receive a salary increase regardless of whether they make the time and money commitment to join, some workers may free ride. The benefits sought by unions, such as higher wages, collective bargaining rights, and safer working conditions, are often enjoyed by all workers regardless of whether they are members. Therefore, free riders can receive the benefit of the pay increase without helping defray the cost by paying dues, attending meetings or rallies, or joining protests, like that shown in Figure 10.5.

Figure 10.5 In February 2009, in protest over the "union-busting" efforts of the Rite-Aid Corporation, members of the AFL-CIO demonstrated at the drugstore chain's corporate headquarters in Camp Hill, Pennsylvania. (credit: Amy Niehouse)

If free riding is so prevalent, why are there so many interest groups and why is interest group membership so high in the United States? One reason is that free riding can be overcome in a variety of ways. Olson argued, for instance, that some groups are better able than others to surmount collective action problems.[18] They can sometimes maintain themselves by obtaining financial support from patrons outside the group.[19] Groups with financial resources have an advantage in mobilizing in that they can offer incentives or hire a lobbyist. Smaller, well-organized groups also have an advantage. For one thing, opinions within smaller groups may be more similar, making it easier to reach consensus. It is also more difficult for members to free ride in a smaller group. In comparison, larger groups have a greater number of individuals and therefore more viewpoints to consider, making consensus more difficult. It may also be easier to free ride because it is less obvious in a large group when any single person does not contribute. However, if people do not lobby for their own interests, they may find that they are ignored, especially if smaller but more active groups with interests opposed to theirs lobby on behalf of themselves. Even though the United States is a democracy, policy is often made to suit the interests of the few instead of the needs of the many.

Group leaders also play an important role in overcoming collective action problems. For instance, political scientist Robert Salisbury suggests that group leaders will offer incentives to induce activity among individuals.[20] Some offer **material incentives**, which are tangible benefits of joining a group. AARP, for example, offers discounts on hotel accommodations and insurance rates for its members, while dues are very low, so they can actually save money by joining. Group leaders may also offer **solidary incentives**, which provide the benefit of joining with others who have the same concerns or are similar in other ways. Some scholars suggest that people are naturally drawn to others with similar concerns. The NAACP is a civil rights groups concerned with promoting equality and eliminating discrimination based on race, and members may join to associate with others who have dealt with issues of inequality.[21]

Similarly, **purposive incentives** focus on the issues or causes promoted by the group. Someone concerned about protecting individual rights might join a group like the American Civil Liberties Union (ACLU) because it supports the liberties guaranteed in the U.S. Constitution, even the free expression of unpopular views.[22] Members of the ACLU sometimes find the messages of those they defend (including Nazis and the Ku Klux Klan) deplorable, but they argue that the principle of protecting civil liberties is critical to U.S. democracy. In many ways, the organization's stance is analogous to James Madison's defense of factions mentioned earlier in this chapter. A commitment to protecting rights and liberties can serve as an incentive in overcoming collective action problems, because members or potential members care enough about the issues to join or participate. Thus, interest groups and their leadership will use whatever incentives they have at their disposal to overcome collective action problems and mobilize their members.

Finally, sometimes collective action problems are overcome because there is little choice about whether to join an organization. For example, some organizations may require membership in order to participate in a profession. To practice law, individuals may be required to join the American Bar Association or a state bar association. In the past, union membership could be required of workers, particularly in urban areas controlled by political machines consisting of a combination of parties, elected representatives, and interest groups.

Link to Learning

Visit the Free Rider Problem (https://openstax.org/l/29freeridprob) for a closer look at free riding as a philosophical problem. Think of a situation you have been in where a collective action problem existed or someone engaged in free riding behavior. Why did the collective action problem or free riding occur? What could have been done to overcome the problem? How will knowledge of these problems affect the way you act in future group settings?

DISTURBANCE THEORY AND COLLECTIVE ACTION

In addition to the factors discussed above that can help overcome collective action problems, external events can sometimes help mobilize groups and potential members. Some scholars argue that **disturbance theory** can explain why groups mobilize due to an event in the political, economic, or social environment.[23] For example, in 1962, Rachel Carson published *Silent Spring*, a book exposing the dangers posed by pesticides such as DDT.[24] The book served as a catalyst for individuals worried about the environment and the potential dangers of pesticides. The result was an increase in both the number of environmental interest groups, such as Greenpeace and American Rivers, and the number of members within them.

More recently, several shooting deaths of unarmed young African American men have raised awareness of racial issues in the United States and potential problems in policing practices. In 2014, Ferguson, Missouri, erupted in protests and riots following a decision not to indict Darren Wilson, a white police officer, in the fatal shooting of Michael Brown, who had allegedly been involved in a theft at a local convenience store and ended up in a dispute with the officer.[25] The incident mobilized groups representing civil rights, such as the protestors in Figure 10.6, as well as others supporting the interests of police officers.

Figure 10.6 Protestors in Washington, DC, rally against the decision not to indict police officer Darren Wilson in the 2014 shooting death of teenager Michael Brown in Ferguson, Missouri. (credit: modification of work by Neil Cooler)

Both the *Silent Spring* and Ferguson examples demonstrate the idea that people will naturally join groups in response to disturbances. Some mobilization efforts develop more slowly and may require the efforts of group leaders. Sometimes political candidates can push issues to the forefront, which may result in interest group mobilization. The recent focus on immigration, for example, has resulted in the mobilization of those in support of restrictive policies as well as those opposed to them (Figure 10.7). Rather than being a single disturbance, debate about immigration policy has ebbed and flowed in recent years, creating what might best be described as a series of minor disturbances. When, during his presidential candidacy, Donald Trump made controversial statements about immigrants, many rallied both for and against him.[26]

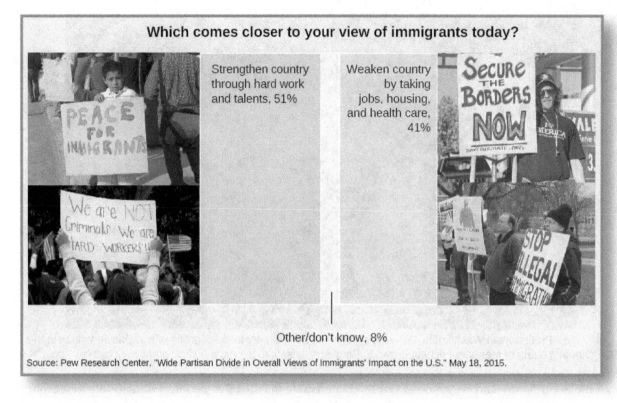

Figure 10.7 Protestors take to the streets on different sides of the immigration issue. Some argue that the United States is a nation of immigrants, whereas others demonstrate in support of greater restrictions on immigration.

Finding a Middle Ground

Student Activism and Apathy

Student behavior is somewhat paradoxical when it comes to political participation. On one hand, students have been very active on college campuses at various times over the past half-century. Many became politically active in the 1960s as part of the civil rights movement, with some joining campus groups that promoted civil rights, while others supported groups that opposed these rights. In the late 1960s and early 1970s, college campuses were very active in opposition to the Vietnam War. More recently, in 2015, students at the University of Missouri protested against the university system president, who was accused of not taking racial issues at the university seriously. The student protests were supported by civil rights groups like the NAACP, and their efforts culminated in the president's resignation.[27]

Yet at the same time, students participate by voting and joining groups at lower rates than members of other age cohorts. Why is it the case that students can play such an important role in facilitating political change in some cases, while at the same time they are typically less active than other demographic groups?

Are there groups on campus that represent issues important to you? If not, find out what you could do to start such a group.

10.3 Interest Groups as Political Participation

Learning Objectives

By the end of this section, you will be able to:

- Analyze how interest groups provide a means for political participation
- Discuss recent changes to interest groups and the way they operate in the United States
- Explain why lower socioeconomic status citizens are not well represented by interest groups
- Identify the barriers to interest group participation in the United States

Interest groups offer individuals an important avenue for political participation. Tea Party protests, for instance, gave individuals all over the country the opportunity to voice their opposition to government actions and control. Likewise, the Occupy Wall Street movement also gave a voice to those individuals frustrated with economic inequality and the influence of large corporations on the public sector. Individually, the protestors would likely have received little notice, but by joining with others, they drew substantial attention in the media and from lawmakers (Figure 10.8). While the Tea Party movement might not meet the definition of interest groups presented earlier, its aims have been promoted by established interest groups. Other opportunities for participation that interest groups offer or encourage include voting, campaigning, contacting lawmakers, and informing the public about causes.

Figure 10.8 In 2011, an Occupy Wall Street protestor highlights that the concerns of individual citizens are not always heard by those in the seats of power. (credit: Timothy Krause)

GROUP PARTICIPATION AS CIVIC ENGAGEMENT

Joining interest groups can help facilitate civic engagement, which allows people to feel more connected to the political and social community. Some interest groups develop as **grassroots movements**, which often begin from the bottom up among a small number of people at the local level. Interest groups can amplify the voices of such individuals through proper organization and allow them to participate in ways that would be less effective or even impossible alone or in small numbers. The Tea Party is an example of a so-called **astroturf movement**, because it is not, strictly speaking, a grassroots movement. Many trace the party's origins to groups that champion the interests of the wealthy such as Americans for Prosperity and Citizens for a Sound Economy. Although many ordinary citizens support the Tea Party because of its opposition to tax increases, it attracts a great deal of support from elite and wealthy sponsors, some of whom are active in lobbying. The FreedomWorks political action committee (PAC), for example, is a conservative advocacy group that has supported the Tea Party movement. FreedomWorks is an offshoot of the interest group Citizens for a Sound Economy, which was founded by billionaire industrialists David H. and Charles G. Koch in 1984.

According to political scientists Jeffrey Berry and Clyde Wilcox, interest groups provide a means of representing people and serve as a link between them and government.[28] Interest groups also allow people to actively work on an issue in an effort to influence public policy. Another function of interest groups is to help educate the public. Someone concerned about the environment may not need to know what an acceptable level of sulfur dioxide is in the air, but by joining an environmental interest group, he or she can remain informed when air quality is poor or threatened by legislative action. A number of education-related interests have been very active following cuts to education spending in many states, including North Carolina, Mississippi, and Wisconsin, to name a few.

Interest groups also help frame issues, usually in a way that best benefits their cause. Abortion rights advocates often use the term "pro-choice" to frame abortion as an individual's private choice to be made free of government interference, while an anti-abortion group might use the term "pro-life" to frame its position as protecting the life of the unborn. "Pro-life" groups often label their opponents as "pro-abortion," rather than "pro-choice," a distinction that can affect the way the public perceives the issue. Similarly, scientists and others who believe that human activity has had a negative effect on the earth's temperature and weather patterns attribute such phenomena as the increasing frequency and severity of storms to "climate change." Industrialists and their supporters refer to alterations in the earth's climate as "global warming." Those who dispute that such a change is taking place can thus point to blizzards and low temperatures as evidence that the earth is not becoming warmer.

Interest groups also try to get issues on the government agenda and to monitor a variety of government programs. Following the passage of the ACA, numerous interest groups have been monitoring the implementation of the law, hoping to use successes and failures to justify their positions for and against the legislation. Those opposed have utilized the court system to try to alter or eliminate the law, or have lobbied executive agencies or departments that have a role in the law's implementation. Similarly, teachers' unions, parent-teacher organizations, and other education-related interests have monitored implementation of the *No Child Left Behind Act* promoted and signed into law by President George W. Bush.

Milestone

Interest Groups as a Response to Riots

The LGBT (lesbian, gay, bisexual, and transgender) movement owes a great deal to the gay rights movement of the 1960s and 1970s, and in particular to the 1969 riots at the Stonewall Inn in New York's Greenwich Village. These were a series of violent responses to a police raid on the bar, a popular gathering place for members of the LGBT community. The riots culminated in a number of arrests but also raised awareness of the struggles faced by members of the gay and lesbian community.[29] The Stonewall Inn has recently been granted landmark status by New York City's Landmarks Preservation Commission (Figure 10.9).

Figure 10.9   The Stonewall Inn in New York City's Greenwich Village was the site of arrests and riots in 1969 that, like the building itself, became an important landmark in the LGBT movement. (credit: Steven Damron)

The Castro district in San Francisco, California, was also home to a significant LGBT community during the same time period. In 1978, the community was shocked when Harvey Milk, a gay local activist and sitting member of San Francisco's Board of Supervisors, was assassinated by a former city supervisor due to political differences.[30] This resulted in protests in San Francisco and other cities across the country and the mobilization of interests concerned about gay and lesbian rights.

Today, advocacy interest organizations like Human Rights Watch and the Human Rights Council are at the forefront in supporting members of the LGBT community and popularizing a number of relevant issues. They played an active role in the effort to legalize same-sex marriage in individual states and later nationwide. Now that same-sex marriage is legal, these organizations and others are dealing with issues related to continuing discrimination against members of this community. One current debate centers around whether an individual's religious freedom allows him or her to deny services to members of the LGBT community.

What do you feel are lingering issues for the LGBT community? What approaches could you take to help increase attention and support for gay and lesbian rights? Do you think someone's religious beliefs should allow them the freedom to discriminate against members of the LGBT community? Why or why not?

TRENDS IN PUBLIC INTEREST GROUP FORMATION AND ACTIVITY

A number of changes in interest groups have taken place over the last three or four decades in the United States. The most significant change is the tremendous increase in both the number and type of groups.[31] Political scientists often examine the diversity of registered groups, in part to determine how well they reflect the variety of interests in society. Some areas may be dominated by certain industries, while others may reflect a multitude of interests. Some interests appear to have increased at greater rates than others. For example, the number of institutions and corporate interests has increased both in Washington and in the states. Telecommunication companies like Verizon and AT&T will lobby Congress for laws beneficial to their businesses, but they also target the states because state legislatures make laws that can benefit or harm their activities. There has also been an increase in the number of public interest groups that represent the public as opposed to economic interests. U.S. PIRG is a public interest group that represents the public on issues including public health, the environment, and consumer protection.[32]

Get Connected!

Public Interest Research Groups

Public interest research groups (PIRGs) have increased in recent years, and many now exist nationally and at the state level. PIRGs represent the public in a multitude of issue areas, ranging from consumer protection to the environment, and like other interests, they provide opportunities for people to make a difference in the political process. PIRGs try to promote the common or public good, and most issues they favor affect many or even all citizens. Student PIRGs focus on issues that are important to students, including tuition costs, textbook costs, new voter registration, sustainable universities, and homelessness. Consider the cost of a college education. You may want to research how education costs have increased over time. Are cost increases similar across universities and colleges? Are they similar across states? What might explain similarities and differences in tuition costs? What solutions might help address the rising costs of higher education?

How can you get involved in the drive for affordable college education? Consider why students might become engaged in it and why they might not do so. A number of countries have made tuition free or nearly free.[33] Is this feasible or desirable in the United States? Why or why not?

Link to Learning

Take a look at the website (https://openstax.org/l/29studPIRGS) for Student PIRGs. What issues does this interest group address? Are these issues important to you? How can you get involved? Visit this section of their site (https://openstax.org/l/29studPIRGSfin) to learn more about their position on financing higher education.

What are the reasons for the increase in the number of interest groups? In some cases, it simply reflects new interests in society. Forty years ago, stem cell research was not an issue on the government agenda, but as science and technology advanced, its techniques and possibilities became known to the media and the public, and a number of interests began lobbying for and against this type of research. Medical research firms and medical associations will lobby in favor of greater spending and increased research on stem cell research, while some religious organizations and anti-abortion groups will oppose it. As societal attitudes change and new issues develop, and as the public becomes aware of them, we can expect to see the rise of interests addressing them.

The devolution of power also explains some of the increase in the number and type of interests, at least at the state level. As power and responsibility shifted to state governments in the 1980s, the states began to handle responsibilities that had been under the jurisdiction of the federal government. A number of federal welfare programs, for example, are generally administered at the state level. This means interests might be better served targeting their lobbying efforts in Albany, Raleigh, Austin, or Sacramento, rather than only in Washington, DC. As the states have become more active in more policy areas, they have become prime targets for interests wanting to influence policy in their favor.[34]

We have also seen increased specialization by some interests and even fragmentation of existing interests. While the American Medical Association may take a stand on stem cell research, the issue is not critical to the everyday activities of many of its members. On the other hand, stem cell research is highly salient to members of the American Neurological Association, an interest organization that represents academic neurologists and neuroscientists. Accordingly, different interests represent the more specialized needs of different specialties within the medical community, but **fragmentation** can occur when a large interest like this has diverging needs. Such was also the case when several unions split from the AFL-CIO (American Federation of Labor-Congress of Industrial Organizations), the nation's largest federation of unions, in 2005.[35] Improved technology and the development of social media have made it easier for smaller groups to form and to attract and communicate with members. The use of the Internet to raise money has also made it possible for even small groups to receive funding.

None of this suggests that an unlimited number of interests can exist in society. The size of the economy has a bearing on the number of interests, but only up to a certain point, after which the number increases at a declining rate. As we will see below, the limit on the number of interests depends on the available resources and levels of competition.

Over the last few decades, we have also witnessed an increase in professionalization in lobbying and in the sophistication of lobbying techniques. This was not always the case, because lobbying was not considered a serious profession in the mid-twentieth century. Over the past three decades, there has been an increase in the number of contract lobbying firms. These firms are often effective because they bring significant resources to the table, their lobbyists are knowledgeable about the issues on which they lobby, and they may have existing relationships with lawmakers. In fact, relationships between lobbyists and legislators are often ongoing, and these are critical if lobbyists want access to lawmakers. However, not every interest can afford to hire high-priced contract lobbyists to represent it. As Table 10.1 suggests, a great deal of money is spent on lobbying activities.

Top Lobbying Firms in 2014

Lobbying Firm	Total Lobbying Annual Income
Akin, Gump et al.	$35,550,000
Squire Patton Boggs	$31,540,000
Podesta Group	$25,070,000
Brownstein, Hyatt et al.	$23,400,000
Van Scoyoc Assoc.	$21,420,000
Holland & Knight	$19,250,000
Capitol Counsel	$17,930,000
K&L Gates	$17,420,000
Williams & Jensen	$16,430,000
BGR Group	$15,470,000
Peck Madigan Jones	$13,395,000
Cornerstone Government Affairs	$13,380,000
Ernst & Young	$12,440,000
Hogan Lovells	$12,410,000
Capitol Tax Partners	$12,390,000
Cassidy & Assoc.	$12,090,000

Table 10.1 This table lists the top twenty U.S. lobbying firms in 2014 as determined by total lobbying income.[36]

Top Lobbying Firms in 2014

Lobbying Firm	Total Lobbying Annual Income
Fierce, Isakowitz & Blalock	$11,970,000
Covington & Burling	$11,537,000
Mehlman, Castagnetti et al.	$11,180,000
Alpine Group	$10,950,00

Table 10.1 This table lists the top twenty U.S. lobbying firms in 2014 as determined by total lobbying income.[36]

We have also seen greater limits on inside lobbying activities. In the past, many lobbyists were described as "good ol' boys" who often provided gifts or other favors in exchange for political access or other considerations. Today, restrictions limit the types of gifts and benefits lobbyists can bestow on lawmakers. There are certainly fewer "good ol' boy" lobbyists, and many lobbyists are now full-time professionals. The regulation of lobbying is addressed in greater detail below.

HOW REPRESENTATIVE IS THE INTEREST GROUP SYSTEM?

Participation in the United States has never been equal; wealth and education, components of socioeconomic status, are strong predictors of political engagement.[37] We already discussed how wealth can help overcome collective action problems, but lack of wealth also serves as a barrier to participation more generally. These types of barriers pose challenges, making it less likely for some groups than others to participate.[38] Some institutions, including large corporations, are more likely to participate in the political process than others, simply because they have tremendous resources. And with these resources, they can write a check to a political campaign or hire a lobbyist to represent their organization. Writing a check and hiring a lobbyist are unlikely options for a disadvantaged group (Figure 10.10).

Figure 10.10   A protestor at an Occupy Times Square rally in October 2011. (credit: Geoff Stearns)

Individually, the poor may not have the same opportunities to join groups.[39] They may work two jobs to make ends meet and lack the free time necessary to participate in politics. Further, there are often financial barriers to participation. For someone who punches a time-clock, spending time with political groups may be costly and paying dues may be a hardship. Certainly, the poor are unable to hire expensive lobbying firms to represent them. Structural barriers like voter identification laws may also disproportionately affect people with low socioeconomic status, although the effects of these laws may not be fully understood for some time.

The poor may also have low levels of **efficacy**, which refers to the conviction that you can make a difference or that government cares about you and your views. People with low levels of efficacy are less likely to participate in politics, including voting and joining interest groups. Therefore, they are often underrepresented in the political arena.

Minorities may also participate less often than the majority population, although when we control for wealth and education levels, we see fewer differences in participation rates. Still, there is a bias in participation and representation, and this bias extends to interest groups as well. For example, when fast food workers across the United States went on strike to demand an increase in their wages, they could do little more than take to the streets bearing signs, like the protestors shown in Figure 10.11. Their opponents, the owners of restaurant chains and others who pay their employees minimum wage, could hire groups such as the Employment Policies Institute, which paid for billboard ads in Times Square in New York City. The billboards implied that raising the minimum wage was an insult to people who worked hard and discouraged people from getting an education to better their lives.[40]

Figure 10.11   Unlike their opponents, these minimum-wage workers in Minnesota have limited ways to make their interests known to government. However, they were able to increase their political efficacy by joining fast food workers in a nationwide strike on April 15, 2015, to call for a $15 per hour minimum wage and improved working conditions. (credit: "Fibonacci Blue"/Flickr)

Finally, people do not often participate because they lack the political skill to do so or believe that it is impossible to influence government actions.[41] They might also lack interest or could be apathetic. Participation usually requires some knowledge of the political system, the candidates, or the issues. Younger people in particular are often cynical about government's response to the needs of non-elites.

How do these observations translate into the way different interests are represented in the political system? Some **pluralist** scholars like David Truman suggest that people naturally join groups and that there will be a great deal of competition for access to decision-makers.[42] Scholars who subscribe to this pluralist view assume this competition among diverse interests is good for democracy. Political theorist Robert Dahl argued that "all active and legitimate groups had the potential to make themselves heard."[43] In many ways, this is an optimistic assessment of representation in the United States.

However, not all scholars accept the premise that mobilization is natural and that all groups have the potential for access to decision-makers. The **elite critique** suggests that certain interests, typically businesses and the wealthy, are advantaged and that policies more often reflect their wishes than anyone else's. Political scientist E. E. Schattschneider noted that "the flaw in the pluralist heaven is that the heavenly chorus sings with a strong upperclass accent."[44] A number of scholars have suggested that businesses and other wealthy interests are often overrepresented before government, and that poorer interests are at a comparative disadvantage.[45] For example, as we've seen, wealthy corporate interests have the means to hire in-house lobbyists or high-priced contract lobbyists to represent them. They can also afford to make financial contributions to politicians, which at least may grant them access. The ability to overcome collective action problems is not equally distributed across groups; as Mancur Olson noted, small groups and those with economic advantages were better off in this regard.[46] Disadvantaged interests face many challenges including shortages of resources, time, and skills.

A study of almost eighteen hundred policy decisions made over a twenty-year period revealed that the interests of the wealthy have much greater influence on the government than those of average citizens. The approval or disapproval of proposed policy changes by average voters had relatively little effect on whether the changes took place. When wealthy voters disapproved of a particular policy, it almost never was enacted. When wealthy voters favored a particular policy, the odds of the policy proposal's passing increased to more than 50 percent.[47] Indeed, the preferences of those in the top 10 percent of the population in terms of income had an impact fifteen times greater than those of average income. In terms of the effect of interest groups on policy, Gilens and Page found that business interest groups had twice the influence of public interest groups.[48]

Figure 10.12 shows contributions by interests from a variety of different sectors. We can draw a few notable observations from the table. First, large sums of money are spent by different interests. Second, many of these interests are business sectors, including the real estate sector, the insurance industry, businesses, and law firms.

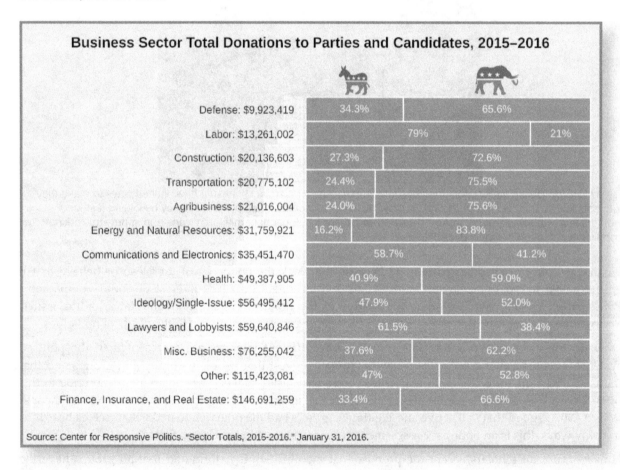

Business Sector Total Donations to Parties and Candidates, 2015–2016

	Democrat	Republican
Defense: $9,923,419	34.3%	65.6%
Labor: $13,261,002	79%	21%
Construction: $20,136,603	27.3%	72.6%
Transportation: $20,775,102	24.4%	75.5%
Agribusiness: $21,016,004	24.0%	75.6%
Energy and Natural Resources: $31,759,921	16.2%	83.8%
Communications and Electronics: $35,451,470	58.7%	41.2%
Health: $49,387,905	40.9%	59.0%
Ideology/Single-Issue: $56,495,412	47.9%	52.0%
Lawyers and Lobbyists: $59,640,846	61.5%	38.4%
Misc. Business: $76,255,042	37.6%	62.2%
Other: $115,423,081	47%	52.8%
Finance, Insurance, and Real Estate: $146,691,259	33.4%	66.6%

Source: Center for Responsive Politics. "Sector Totals, 2015-2016." January 31, 2016.

Figure 10.12 The chart above shows the dollar amounts contributed from PACs, soft money (including directly from corporate and union treasuries), and individual donors to Democratic (blue) and Republican (red) federal candidates and political parties during the 2015–2016 election cycle, as reported to the Federal Election Commission.

Interest group politics are often characterized by whether the groups have access to decision-makers and can participate in the policy-making process. The **iron triangle** is a hypothetical arrangement among three elements (the corners of the triangle): an interest group, a congressional committee member or chair, and an agency within the bureaucracy.[49] Each element has a symbiotic relationship with the other two, and it is difficult for those outside the triangle to break into it. The congressional committee members, including the chair, rely on the interest group for campaign contributions and policy information, while the interest group needs the committee to consider laws favorable to its view. The interest group and the committee need the agency to implement the law, while the agency needs the interest group for information and the committee for funding and autonomy in implementing the law.[50]

An alternate explanation of the arrangement of duties carried out in a given policy area by interest groups, legislators, and agency bureaucrats is that these actors are the experts in that given policy area. Hence, perhaps they are the ones most qualified to process policy in the given area. Some view the iron triangle idea as outdated. Hugh Heclo of George Mason University has sketched a more open pattern he calls an **issue network** that includes a number of different interests and political actors that work together in support of a single issue or policy.[51]

Some interest group scholars have studied the relationship among a multitude of interest groups and political actors, including former elected officials, the way some interests form coalitions with other interests, and the way they compete for access to decision-makers.[52] Some coalitions are long-standing, while others are temporary. Joining coalitions does come with a cost, because it can dilute preferences and split potential benefits that the groups attempt to accrue. Some interest groups will even align themselves with opposing interests if the alliance will achieve their goals. For example, left-leaning groups might oppose a state lottery system because it disproportionately hurts the poor (who participate in this form of gambling at higher rates), while right-leaning groups might oppose it because they view gambling as a sinful activity. These opposing groups might actually join forces in an attempt to defeat the lottery.

While most scholars agree that some interests do have advantages, others have questioned the overwhelming dominance of certain interests. Additionally, **neopluralist** scholars argue that certainly some interests are in a privileged position, but these interests do not always get what they want.[53] Instead, their influence depends on a number of factors in the political environment such as public opinion, political culture, competition for access, and the relevance of the issue. Even wealthy interests do not always win if their position is at odds with the wish of an attentive public. And if the public cares about the issue, politicians may be reluctant to defy their constituents. If a prominent manufacturing firm wants fewer regulations on environmental pollutants, and environmental protection is a salient issue to the public, the manufacturing firm may not win in every exchange, despite its resource advantage. We also know that when interests mobilize, opposing interests often counter-mobilize, which can reduce advantages of some interests. Thus, the conclusion that businesses, the wealthy, and elites win in every situation is overstated.[54]

A good example is the recent dispute between fast food chains and their employees. During the spring of 2015, workers at McDonald's restaurants across the country went on strike and marched in protest of the low wages the fast food giant paid its employees. Despite the opposition of restaurant chains and claims by the National Restaurant Association that increasing the minimum wage would result in the loss of jobs, in September 2015, the state of New York raised the minimum wage for fast food employees to $15 per hour, an amount to be phased in over time. Buoyed by this success, fast food workers in other cities continued to campaign for a pay increase, and many low-paid workers have promised to vote for politicians who plan to boost the federal minimum wage.[55]

10.4 Pathways of Interest Group Influence

Learning Objectives

By the end of this section, you will be able to:
- Describe how interest groups influence the government through elections
- Explain how interest groups influence the government through the governance processes

Many people criticize the huge amounts of money spent in politics. Some argue that interest groups have too much influence on who wins elections, while others suggest influence is also problematic when interests try to sway politicians in office. There is little doubt that interest groups often try to achieve their objectives by influencing elections and politicians, but discovering whether they have succeeded in changing minds is actually challenging because they tend to support those who already agree with them.

INFLUENCE IN ELECTIONS

Interest groups support candidates who are sympathetic to their views in hopes of gaining access to them once they are in office.[56] For example, an organization like the NRA will back candidates who support Second Amendment rights. Both the NRA and the Brady Campaign to Prevent Gun Violence (an interest group that favors background checks for firearm purchases) have grading systems that evaluate candidates and states based on their records of supporting these organizations.[57] To garner the support of the NRA, candidates must receive an A+ rating for the group. In much the same way, Americans for Democratic Action, a liberal interest group, and the American Conservative Union, a conservative interest group, both rate politicians based on their voting records on issues these organizations view as important.[58]

These ratings, and those of many other groups, are useful for interests and the public in deciding which candidates to support and which to oppose. Incumbents have electoral advantages in terms of name recognition, experience, and fundraising abilities, and they often receive support because interest groups want access to the candidate who is likely to win. Some interest groups will offer support to the challenger, particularly if the challenger better aligns with the interest's views or the incumbent is vulnerable. Sometimes, interest groups even hedge their bets and give to both major party candidates for a particular office in the hopes of having access regardless of who wins.

Some interests groups form political action committees (PACs), groups that collect funds from donors and distribute them to candidates who support their issues. As Figure 10.13 makes apparent, many large corporations like Honeywell International, AT&T, and Lockheed Martin form PACs to distribute money to candidates.[59] Other PACs are either politically or ideologically oriented. For example, the MoveOn.org PAC is a progressive group that formed following the impeachment trial of President Bill Clinton, whereas

GOPAC is a Republican PAC that promotes state and local candidates of that party. PACs are limited in the amount of money that they can contribute to individual candidates or to national party organizations; they can contribute no more than $5,000 per candidate per election and no more than $15,000 a year to a national political party. Individual contributions to PACs are also limited to $5,000 a year.

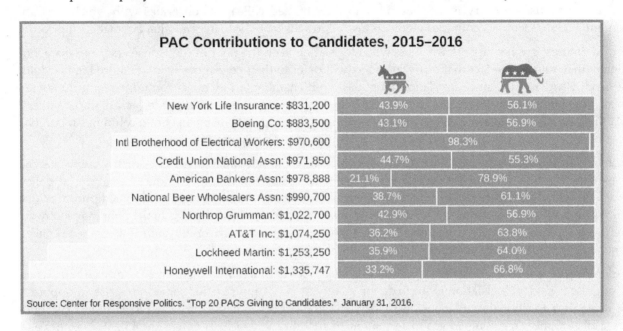

Figure 10.13 Corporations and associations spend large amounts of money on elections via affiliated PACs. This chart reveals the amount donated to Democratic (blue) and Republican (red) candidates by the top ten PACs during the most recent election cycle.

PACs through which corporations and unions can spend virtually unlimited amounts of money on behalf of political candidates are called super PACs.[60] As a result of a 2010 Supreme Court decision, *Citizens United v. Federal Election Commission*, there is no limit to how much money unions or corporations can donate to super PACs. Unlike PACs, however, super PACs cannot contribute money directly to individual candidates. If the 2014 elections were any indication, super PACs will continue to spend large sums of money in an attempt to influence future election results.

INFLUENCING GOVERNMENTAL POLICY

Interest groups support candidates in order to have access to lawmakers once they are in office. Lawmakers, for their part, lack the time and resources to pursue every issue; they are policy generalists. Therefore, they (and their staff members) rely on interest groups and lobbyists to provide them with information about the technical details of policy proposals, as well as about fellow lawmakers' stands and constituents' perceptions. These **voting cues** give lawmakers an indication of how to vote on issues, particularly those with which they are unfamiliar. But lawmakers also rely on lobbyists for information about ideas they can champion and that will benefit them when they run for reelection.[61]

Interest groups likely cannot target all 535 lawmakers in both the House and the Senate, nor would they wish to do so. There is little reason for the Brady Campaign to Prevent Gun Violence to lobby members of Congress who vehemently oppose any restrictions on gun access. Instead, the organization will often contact lawmakers who are amenable to some restrictions on access to firearms. Thus, interest groups first target lawmakers they think will consider introducing or sponsoring legislation.

Second, they target members of relevant committees.[62] If a company that makes weapons systems wants to influence a defense bill, it will lobby members of the Armed Services Committees in the House and the Senate or the House and Senate appropriations committees if the bill requires new funding.

Many members of these committees represent congressional districts with military bases, so they often sponsor or champion bills that allow them to promote policies popular with their districts or state. Interest groups attempt to use this to their advantage. But they also conduct strategic targeting because legislatures function by respectfully considering fellow lawmakers' positions. Since lawmakers cannot possess expertise on every issue, they defer to their trusted colleagues on issues with which they are unfamiliar. So targeting committee members also allows the lobbyist to inform other lawmakers indirectly.

Third, interest groups target lawmakers when legislation is on the floor of the House and/or Senate, but again, they rely on the fact that many members will defer to their colleagues who are more familiar with a given issue. Finally, since legislation must past both chambers in identical form, interest groups may target members of the conference committees whose job it is to iron out differences across the chambers. At this negotiation stage, a 1 percent difference in, say, the corporate income tax rate could mean millions of dollars in increased or decreased revenue or taxation for various interests.

Interest groups also target the budgetary process in order to maximize benefits to their group. In some cases, their aim is to influence the portion of the budget allocated to a given policy, program, or policy area. For example, interests for groups that represent the poor may lobby for additional appropriations for various welfare programs; those interests opposed to government assistance to the poor may lobby for reduced funding to certain programs. It is likely that the legislative liaison for your university or college spends time trying to advocate for budgetary allocations in your state.

Interest groups also try to defeat legislation that may be detrimental to their views. For example, when Congress considers legislation to improve air quality, it is not unusual for some industries to oppose it if it requires additional regulations on factory emissions. In some cases, proposed legislation may serve as a disturbance, resulting in group formation or mobilization to help defeat the bill. For example, a proposed tax increase may result in the formation or mobilization of anti-tax groups that will lobby the legislature and try to encourage the public to oppose the proposed legislation. Prior to the election in 2012, political activist Grover Norquist, the founder of Americans for Tax Reform (ATR), asked all Republican members of Congress to sign a "Taxpayer Protection Pledge" that they would fight efforts to raise taxes or to eliminate any deductions that were not accompanied by tax cuts. Ninety-five percent of the Republicans in Congress signed the pledge.[63] Some interests arise solely to defeat legislation and go dormant after they achieve their immediate objectives.

Once legislation has been passed, interest groups may target the executive branch of government, whose job is to implement the law. The U.S. Department of Veterans Affairs has some leeway in providing care for military veterans, and interests representing veterans' needs may pressure this department to address their concerns or issues. Other entities within the executive branch, like the Securities and Exchange Commission, which maintains and regulates financial markets, are not designed to be responsive to the interests they regulate, because to make such a response would be a conflict of interest. Interest groups may lobby the executive branch on executive, judicial, and other appointments that require Senate confirmation. As a result, interest group members may be appointed to positions in which they can influence proposed regulation of the industry of which they are a part.

In addition to lobbying the legislative and executive branches of government, many interest groups also lobby the judicial branch. Lobbying the judiciary takes two forms, the first of which was mentioned above. This is lobbying the executive branch about judicial appointments the president makes and lobbying the Senate to confirm these appointments. The second form of lobbying consists of filing amicus briefs, which are also known as "friend of the court" briefs. These documents present legal arguments stating why a given court should take a case and/or why a court should rule a certain way. In *Obergefell v. Hodges* (2015), the Supreme Court case that legalized same-sex marriage nationwide, numerous interest groups filed amicus briefs.[64] For example, the Human Rights Campaign, shown demonstrating in Figure 10.14, filed a brief arguing that the Fourteenth Amendment's due process and equal protection clauses required that same-sex couples be afforded the same rights to marry as opposite-sex couples. In a 5–4 decision, the U.S. Supreme Court agreed.

Figure 10.14 Members of the Human Rights Campaign, an interest that supports LGBT rights, march toward the Supreme Court on June 26, 2015, the day that the *Obergefell v. Hodges* decision is announced. (credit: modification of work by Matt Popovich)

Link to Learning

The briefs submitted in *Obergefell v. Hodges* are available on the website (https://openstax.org/l/29scotusobvhod) of the U.S. Supreme Court. What arguments did the authors of these briefs make, other than those mentioned in this chapter, in favor of Obergefell's position?

Measuring the effect of interest groups' influence is somewhat difficult because lobbyists support lawmakers who would likely have supported them in the first place. Thus, National Right to Life, an anti-abortion interest group, does not generally lobby lawmakers who favor abortion rights; instead, it supports lawmakers and candidates who have professed "pro-life" positions. While some scholars note that lobbyists sometimes try to influence those on the fence or even their enemies, most of the time, they support like-minded individuals. Thus, contributions are unlikely to sway lawmakers to change their views; what they do buy is access, including time with lawmakers. The problem for those trying to assess whether interest groups influence lawmakers, then, is that we are uncertain what would happen in the absence of interest group contributions. For example, we can only speculate what the ACA might have looked like had lobbyists from a host of interests not lobbied on the issue.

Link to Learning

Examine websites for the American Conservative Union (https://openstax.org/l/29amerconuni) and Americans for Democratic Action (https://openstax.org/l/29amerdemact) that compile legislative ratings and voting records. On what issues do these organizations choose to take positions? Where do your representatives and senators rank according to these groups? Are these rankings surprising?

10.5 Free Speech and the Regulation of Interest Groups

Learning Objectives

By the end of this section, you will be able to:

- Identify the various court cases, policies, and laws that outline what interest groups can and cannot do
- Evaluate the arguments for and against whether contributions are a form of freedom of speech

How are lobbying and interest group activity regulated? As we noted earlier in the chapter, James Madison viewed factions as a necessary evil and thought preventing people from joining together would be worse than any ills groups might cause. The First Amendment guarantees, among other things, freedom of speech, petition, and assembly. However, people have different views on how far this freedom extends. For example, should freedom of speech as afforded to individuals in the U.S. Constitution also apply to corporations and unions? To what extent can and should government restrict the activities of lobbyists and lawmakers, limiting who may lobby and how they may do it?

INTEREST GROUPS AND FREE SPEECH

Most people would agree that interest groups have a right under the Constitution to promote a particular point of view. What people do not necessarily agree upon, however, is the extent to which certain interest group and lobbying activities are protected under the First Amendment.

In addition to free speech rights, the First Amendment grants people the right to assemble. We saw above that pluralists even argued that assembling in groups is natural and that people will gravitate toward others with similar views. Most people acknowledge the right of others to assemble to voice unpopular positions, but this was not always the case. At various times, groups representing racial and religious minorities, communists, and members of the LGBT community have had their First Amendment rights to speech and assembly curtailed. And as noted above, organizations like the ACLU support free speech rights regardless of whether the speech is popular.

Today, the debate about interest groups often revolves around whether the First Amendment protects the rights of individuals and groups to give money, and whether government can regulate the use of this money. In 1971, the Federal Election Campaign Act was passed, setting limits on how much presidential and vice-presidential candidates and their families could donate to their own campaigns.[65] The law also allowed corporations and unions to form PACs and required public disclosure of campaign contributions and their sources. In 1974, the act was amended in an attempt to limit the amount of money spent on congressional campaigns. The amended law banned the transfer of union, corporate, and trade association money to parties for distribution to campaigns.

In *Buckley v. Valeo* (1976), the Supreme Court upheld Congress's right to regulate elections by restricting contributions to campaigns and candidates. However, at the same time, it overturned restrictions on expenditures by candidates and their families, as well as total expenditures by campaigns.[66] In 1979, an exemption was granted to get-out-the vote and grassroots voter registration drives, creating what has become known as the soft-money loophole; **soft money** was a way in which interests could spend money on behalf of candidates without being restricted by federal law. To close this loophole, Senators John McCain and Russell Feingold sponsored the Bipartisan Campaign Reform Act in 2002 to ban parties from collecting and distributing unregulated money.

Some continued to argue that campaign expenditures are a form of speech, a position with which two recent Supreme Court decisions are consistent. The *Citizens United v. Federal Election Commission*[67] and the *McCutcheon v. Federal Election Commission*[68] cases opened the door for a substantially greater flow of money into elections. **Citizens United** overturned the soft money ban of the Bipartisan Campaign Reform Act and allowed corporations and unions to spend unlimited amounts of money on elections. Essentially, the Supreme Court argued in a 5–4 decision that these entities had free speech rights, much like individuals, and that free speech included campaign spending. The *McCutcheon* decision further extended spending allowances based on the First Amendment by striking down aggregate contribution limits. These limits put caps on the total contributions allowed and some say have contributed to a subsequent increase in groups and lobbying activities (**Figure 10.15**).

Figure 10.15 With his *Harper's Weekly* cartoon of William "Boss" Tweed with a moneybag for a head, Thomas Nast provided an enduring image of the corrupting power of money on politics. Some denounce "fat cat" lobbyists and the effects of large sums of money in lobbying, while others suggest that interests have every right to spend money to achieve their objectives.

Link to Learning

Read about the **rights (https://openstax.org/l/29nprcorprig)** that corporations share with people.

Should corporations have the same rights as people?

The Koch Brothers

Conservative billionaires Charles and David Koch have become increasingly active in U.S. elections in recent years. These brothers run Koch Industries, a multinational corporation that manufactures and produces a number of products including paper, plastics, petroleum-based products, and chemicals. In the 2012 election, the Koch brothers and their affiliates spent nearly $400 million supporting Republican candidates. Many people have suggested that this spending helped put many Republicans in office. The Kochs and their related organizations planned to raise and spend nearly $900 million on the 2016 elections; however network spending in that cycle amounted to approximately $250 million, with plans to increase spending on the 2018 midterms to levels more closely aligned with 2012 spending.[69] Critics have accused them and other wealthy donors of attempting to buy elections. However, others point out that their activities are legal according to current campaign finance laws and recent Supreme Court decisions, and that these individuals, their companies, and their affiliates should be able to spend what they want politically. As you might expect, there are wealthy donors on both the political left and the right who will continue to spend money on U.S. elections. Some critics have called for a constitutional amendment restricting spending that would overturn recent Supreme Court decisions.[70]

Do you agree, as some have argued, that the Constitution protects the ability to donate unlimited amounts of money to political candidates as a First Amendment right? Is spending money a form of exercising free speech? If so, does a PAC have this right? Why or why not?

REGULATING LOBBYING AND INTEREST GROUP ACTIVITY

While the Supreme Court has paved the way for increased spending in politics, lobbying is still regulated in many ways.[71] The 1995 Lobbying Disclosure Act defined who can and cannot lobby, and requires lobbyists and interest groups to register with the federal government.[72] The Honest Leadership and Open Government Act of 2007 further increased restrictions on lobbying. For example, the act prohibited contact between members of Congress and lobbyists who were the spouses of other Congress members. The laws broadened the definition of lobbyist and require detailed disclosure of spending on lobbying activity, including who is lobbied and what bills are of interest. In addition, President Obama's Executive Order 13490 prohibited appointees in the executive branch from accepting gifts from lobbyists and banned them from participating in matters, including the drafting of any contracts or regulations, involving the appointee's former clients or employer for a period of two years. The states also have their own registration requirements, with some defining lobbying broadly and others more narrowly.

Second, the federal and state governments prohibit certain activities like providing gifts to lawmakers and compensating lobbyists with commissions for successful lobbying. Many activities are prohibited to prevent accusations of vote buying or currying favor with lawmakers. Some states, for example, have strict limits on how much money lobbyists can spend on lobbying lawmakers, or on the value of gifts lawmakers can accept from lobbyists. According to the Honest Leadership and Open Government Act, lobbyists must certify that they have not violated the law regarding gift giving, and the penalty for knowingly violating the law increased from a fine of $50,000 to one of $200,000. Also, **revolving door laws** also prevent lawmakers from lobbying government immediately after leaving public office. Members of the House of Representatives cannot register to lobby for a year after they leave office, while senators have a two-year "cooling off" period before they can officially lobby. Former cabinet secretaries must wait the same period of time after leaving their positions before lobbying the department of which they had been the head. These laws are designed to restrict former lawmakers from using their connections in government to give them an advantage when lobbying. Still, many former lawmakers do become lobbyists, including former Senate majority leader Trent Lott and former House minority leader Richard Gephardt.

Third, governments require varying levels of disclosure about the amount of money spent on lobbying efforts. The logic here is that lawmakers will think twice about accepting money from controversial donors. The other advantage to disclosure requirements is that they promote transparency. Many have argued that the public has a right to know where candidates get their money. Candidates may be reluctant to accept contributions from donors affiliated with unpopular interests such as hate groups. This was one of the key purposes of the Lobbying Disclosure Act and comparable laws at the state level.

Finally, there are penalties for violating the law. Lobbyists and, in some cases, government officials can be fined, banned from lobbying, or even sentenced to prison. While state and federal laws spell out what activities are legal and illegal, the attorneys general and prosecutors responsible for enforcing lobbying regulations may be understaffed, have limited budgets, or face backlogs of work, making it difficult for them to investigate or prosecute alleged transgressions. While most lobbyists do comply with the law, exactly how the laws alter behavior is not completely understood. We know the laws prevent lobbyists from engaging in certain behaviors, such as by limiting campaign contributions or preventing the provision of certain gifts to lawmakers, but how they alter lobbyists' strategies and tactics remains unclear.

The need to strictly regulate the actions of lobbyists became especially relevant after the activities of lobbyist Jack Abramoff were brought to light (Figure 10.16). A prominent lobbyist with ties to many of the Republican members of Congress, Abramoff used funds provided by his clients to fund reelection campaigns, pay for trips, and hire the spouses of members of Congress. Between 1994 and 2001, Abramoff, who then worked as a lobbyist for a prominent law firm, paid for eighty-five members of Congress to travel to the Northern Mariana Islands, a U.S. territory in the Pacific. The territory's government was a client of the firm for which he worked. At the time, Abramoff was lobbying Congress to exempt the Northern Mariana Islands from paying the federal minimum wage and to allow the territory to continue to operate sweatshops in which people worked in deplorable conditions. In 2000, while representing Native American casino interests who sought to defeat anti-gambling legislation, Abramoff paid for a trip to Scotland for Tom DeLay, the majority whip in the House of Representatives, and an aide. Shortly thereafter, DeLay helped to defeat anti-gambling legislation in the House. He also hired DeLay's wife Christine to research the favorite charity of each member of Congress and paid her $115,000 for her efforts.[73] In 2008, Jack Abramoff was sentenced to four years in prison for tax evasion, fraud, and corruption of public officials.[74] He was released early, in December 2010.

Figure 10.16 Jack Abramoff (center) began his lifetime engagement in politics with his involvement in the 1980 presidential campaign of Ronald Reagan (left) while an undergraduate at Brandeis University and continued it with his election to chair of the College Republican National Committee in a campaign managed by Grover Norquist (right). Abramoff thus gained unique access to influential politicians, upon which he capitalized in his later work as a DC lobbyist. Since his release from federal prison in 2010 after being convicted for illegal lobbying activity, Abramoff has become an outspoken critic of the lobbying industry.[75]

Key Terms

association groups of companies or institutions that organize around a common set of concerns, often within a given industry or trade

astroturf movement a political movement that resembles a grassroots movement but is often supported or facilitated by wealthy interests and/or elites

Citizens United *Citizens United v. Federal Election Commission* was a 2010 Supreme Court case that granted corporations and unions the right to spend unlimited amounts of money on elections

collective good a good such as public safety or clean air, often produced by government, that is generally available to the population as a whole

contract lobbyist a lobbyist who works for a contract lobbying firm that represents clients before government

disturbance theory the theory that an external event can lead to interest group mobilization

efficacy the belief that you make a difference and that government cares about you and your views

elite critique the proposition that wealthy and elite interests are advantaged over those without resources

fragmentation the result when a large interest group develops diverging needs

free rider problem the situation that occurs when some individuals receive benefits (get a free ride) without helping to bear the cost

grassroots movement a political movement that often begins from the bottom up, inspired by average citizens concerned about a given issue

in-house lobbyist an employee or executive within an organization who works as a lobbyist on behalf of the organization

inside lobbying the act of contacting and taking the organization's message directly to lawmakers in an attempt to influence policy

iron triangle three-way relationship among congressional committees, interests groups, and the bureaucracy

issue network a group of interest groups and people who work together to support a particular issue or policy

legislative liaison a person employed by a governmental entity such as a local government, executive department, or university to represent the organization before the legislature

lobbyist a person who represents an organization before government in an attempt to influence policy

material incentives substantive monetary or physical benefits given to group members to help overcome collective action problems

membership organization an interest group that usually consists of dues-paying members who organize around a particular cause or issue

neopluralist a person who suggests that all groups' access and influence depend on the political environment

outside lobbying the act of lobbying indirectly by taking the organization's message to the public, often through the use of the media and/or by issue press releases, in hopes that the public will then put pressure on lawmakers

particularized benefit a benefit that generally accrues to a narrow segment of society

pluralist a person who believes many groups healthily compete for access to decision-makers

public interest group an interest group that seeks a public good, which is something that accrues to all

purposive incentives benefits to overcome collective action problems that appeal to people's support of the issue or cause

revolving door laws laws that require a cooling-off period before government officials can register to lobby after leaving office

soft money money that interests can spend on behalf of candidates without being restricted by federal law

solidary incentives benefits based on the concept that people like to associate with those who are similar to them

voting cues sources—including fellow lawmakers, constituents, and interest groups—that lawmakers often use to help them decide how to vote, especially on unfamiliar issues

Summary

10.1 Interest Groups Defined

Some interest groups represent a broad set of interests, while others focus on only a single issue. Some interests are organizations, like businesses, corporations, or governments, which register to lobby, typically to obtain some benefit from the legislature. Other interest groups consist of dues-paying members who join a group, usually voluntarily. Some organizations band together, often joining trade associations that represent their industry or field. Interest groups represent either the public interest or private interests. Private interests often lobby government for particularized benefits, which are narrowly distributed. These benefits usually accrue to wealthier members of society. Public interests, on the other hand, try to represent a broad segment of society or even all persons.

10.2 Collective Action and Interest Group Formation

Interest groups often have to contend with disincentives to participate, particularly when individuals realize their participation is not critical to a group's success. People often free ride when they can obtain benefits without contributing to the costs of obtaining these benefits. To overcome these challenges, group leaders may offer incentives to members or potential members to help them mobilize. Groups that are small, wealthy, and/or better organized are sometimes better able to overcome collective action problems. Sometimes external political, social, or economic disturbances result in interest group mobilization.

10.3 Interest Groups as Political Participation

Interest groups afford people the opportunity to become more civically engaged. Socioeconomic status is an important predictor of who will likely join groups. The number and types of groups actively lobbying to get what they want from government have been increasing rapidly. Many business and public interest groups have arisen, and many new interests have developed due to technological advances, increased specialization of industry, and fragmentation of interests. Lobbying has also become more sophisticated in recent years, and many interests now hire lobbying firms to represent them.

Some scholars assume that groups will compete for access to decision-makers and that most groups have the potential to be heard. Critics suggest that some groups are advantaged by their access to economic resources. Yet others acknowledge these resource advantages but suggest that the political environment is equally important in determining who gets heard.

10.4 Pathways of Interest Group Influence

Interest groups support candidates sympathetic to their views in hopes of gaining access to them once they are in office. PACs and super PACs collect money from donors and distribute it to political groups that they support. Lawmakers rely on interest groups and lobbyists to provide them with information about the technical details of policy proposals, as well as about fellow lawmakers' stands and constituents' perceptions, for cues about how to vote on issues, particularly those with which they are unfamiliar. Lobbyists also target the executive and judiciary branches.

10.5 Free Speech and the Regulation of Interest Groups

Some argue that contributing to political candidates is a form of free speech. According to this view, the First Amendment protects the right of interest groups to give money to politicians. However, others argue that monetary contributions should not be protected by the First Amendment and that corporations and unions should not be treated as individuals, although the Supreme Court has disagreed. Currently, lobbyist and interest groups are restricted by laws that require them to register with the federal government and abide by a waiting period when moving between lobbying and lawmaking positions. Interest groups and their lobbyists are also prohibited from undertaking certain activities and are required to disclose their lobbying activities. Violation of the law can, and sometimes does, result in prison sentences for lobbyists and lawmakers alike.

Review Questions

1. Someone who lobbies on behalf of a company that he or she works for as part of his or her job is _____.

   a. an in-house lobbyist
   b. a volunteer lobbyist
   c. a contract lobbyist
   d. a legislative liaison

2. How are collective goods different from private goods?

   a. Collective goods offer particularized benefits, while private goods are broadly distributed.
   b. Collective goods and private goods both offer particularized benefits.
   c. Collective goods and private goods both offer broadly distributed benefits.
   d. Collective goods offer broadly distributed benefits, while private goods offer particularized benefits.

3. Why might several competing corporations join together in an association?

   a. because there is often strength in numbers
   b. because they often have common issues that may affect an entire industry
   c. because they can all benefit from governmental policies
   d. all the above

4. What benefits do private and public interests bring to society? What are some disadvantages of private and public interests?

5. What type of incentives appeal to someone's concern about a cause?

   a. solidary incentives
   b. purposive incentives
   c. material incentives
   d. negative incentives

6. Which of the following is the best example of a solidary benefit?
    a. joining a group to be with others like you
    b. joining a group to obtain a monetary benefit
    c. joining a group because you care about a cause
    d. joining a group because it is a requirement of your job

7. What are some ways to overcome collective action problems?

8. Why do some groups have an easier time overcoming collective action problems?

9. What changes have occurred in the lobbying environment over the past three or four decades?
    a. There is more professional lobbying.
    b. Many interests lobby both the national government and the states.
    c. A fragmentation of interests has taken place.
    d. all the above

10. Which of the following is an aspect of iron triangles?
    a. fluid participation among interests
    b. a great deal of competition for access to decision-makers
    c. a symbiotic relationship among Congressional committees, executive agencies, and interest groups
    d. three interest groups that have formed a coalition

11. What does group participation provide to citizens?

12. Why don't lower-income groups participate more in the interest group system?

13. What are some barriers to participation?

14. Which of the following is true of spending in politics?
    a. The Supreme Court has yet to address the issue of money in politics.
    b. The Supreme Court has restricted spending on politics.
    c. The Supreme Court has opposed restrictions on spending on politics.
    d. The Supreme Court has ruled that corporations may spend unlimited amounts of money but unions may not.

15. What is a difference between a PAC and a super PAC?
    a. PACs can contribute directly to candidates, but super PACs cannot.
    b. Conservative interests favor PACs over super PACs.
    c. Contributions to PACs are unlimited, but restrictions have been placed on how much money can be contributed to super PACs.
    d. Super PACS are much more likely to support incumbent candidates than are PACs.

16. How do interest groups lobby the judicial branch?

17. How do interest groups and their lobbyists decide which lawmakers to lobby? And where do they do so?

18. Revolving door laws are designed to do which of the following?
    a. prevent lawmakers from utilizing their legislative relationships by becoming lobbyists immediately after leaving office
    b. help lawmakers find work after they leave office
    c. restrict lobbyists from running for public office
    d. all the above

19. In what ways are lobbyists regulated?
    a. Certain activities are prohibited.
    b. Contributions must be disclosed.
    c. Lobbying is prohibited immediately after leaving office.
    d. all the above

20. How might disclosure requirements affect lobbying?

Critical Thinking Questions

21. How might we get more people engaged in the interest group system?

22. Are interest groups good or bad for democracy? Defend and explain your answer.

23. Why does it matter how we define interest group?

24. How do collective action problems serve as barriers to group formation, mobilization, and maintenance? If you were a group leader, how might you try to overcome these problems?

25. Is it possible to balance the pursuit of private goods with the need to promote the public good? Is this balance a desired goal? Why or why not?

26. How representative are interest groups in the United States? Do you agree that "all active and legitimate groups have the potential to make themselves heard?" Or is this potential an illusion? Explain your answer.

27. Evaluate the *Citizens United* decision. Why might the Court have considered campaign contributions a form of speech? Would the Founders have agreed with this decision? Why or why not?

28. How do we regulate interest groups and lobbying activity? What are the goals of these regulations? Do you think these regulations achieve their objectives? Why or why not? If you could alter the way we regulate interest group activity and lobbying, how might you do so in a way consistent with the Constitution and recent Supreme Court decisions?

Suggestions for Further Study

Baumgartner, Frank R., and Beth L. Leech. 1998. *Basic Interests: The Importance of Groups in Politics and in Political Science.* Princeton, NJ: Princeton University Press.

Baumgartner, Frank R., et al. 2009. *Lobbying and Policy Change.* Chicago: University of Chicago Press.

Clark, Peter B., and James Q. Wilson, "Incentive Systems: A Theory of Organizations," *Administration Science Quarterly* 6 (1961): 129–166.

Dahl, Robert A. 1956. *A Preface to Democratic Theory.* Chicago: University of Chicago Press.

———. 1961. *Who Governs? Democracy and Power in an American City.* New Haven, CT: Yale University Press.

Lindblom, Charles E. 1977. *Politics and Markets: The World's Political-Economic Systems.* New York: Basic Books.

Olson, Mancur. 1965. *The Logic of Collective Action.* Cambridge: Harvard University Press.

Rosenstone, Steven J. and John Mark Hansen. 1993. *Mobilization, Participation and Democracy in America.* New York: Macmillan.

Salisbury, Robert, "An Exchange Theory of Interest Groups," *Midwest Journal of Political Science* 13 (1969): 1–32.

Schattschneider, E. E. 1960. *The Semisovereign People: A Realist's View of Democracy in America.* New York:

Holt, Rinehart and Winston.

Truman, David. 1951. *The Governmental Process*. New York: Alfred A. Knopf, chapter 4.

Wright, John R. 1996. *Interest Groups and Congress: Lobbying, Contributions, and Influence*. Needham Heights, MA: Allyn and Bacon.

Chapter 11

Congress

Figure 11.1 While the Capitol is the natural focus point of Capitol Hill and the workings of Congress, the Capitol complex includes over a dozen buildings, including the House of Representatives office buildings (left), the Senate office buildings (far right), the Library of Congress buildings (lower left), and the Supreme Court (lower right). (credit: modification of work by the Library of Congress)

Chapter Outline

11.1 The Institutional Design of Congress
11.2 Congressional Elections
11.3 Congressional Representation
11.4 House and Senate Organizations
11.5 The Legislative Process

Introduction

When U.S. citizens think of governmental power, they most likely think of the presidency. The framers of the Constitution, however, clearly intended that Congress would be the cornerstone of the new republic. After years of tyranny under a king, they had little interest in creating another system with an overly powerful single individual at the top. Instead, while recognizing the need for centralization in terms of a stronger national government with an elected executive wielding its own authority, those at the Constitutional Convention wanted a strong representative assembly at the national level that would use careful consideration, deliberate action, and constituent representation to carefully draft legislation to meet the needs of the new republic. Thus, Article I of the Constitution grants several key powers to Congress, which include overseeing the budget and all financial matters, introducing legislation, confirming or rejecting judicial and executive nominations, and even declaring war.

Today, however, Congress is the institution most criticized by the public, and the most misunderstood. How exactly does Capitol Hill operate (Figure 11.1)? What are the different structures and powers of the House of Representatives and the Senate? How are members of Congress elected? How do they reach their decisions about legislation, budgets, and military action? This chapter addresses these aspects and more as it explores "the first branch" of government.

11.1 The Institutional Design of Congress

Learning Objectives

By the end of this section, you will be able to:

- Describe the role of Congress in the U.S. constitutional system
- Define bicameralism
- Explain gerrymandering and the apportionment of seats in the House of Representatives
- Discuss the three kinds of powers granted to Congress

The origins of the U.S. Constitution and the convention that brought it into existence are rooted in failure—the failure of the Articles of Confederation. After only a handful of years, the states of the union decided that the Articles were simply unworkable. In order to save the young republic, a convention was called, and delegates were sent to assemble and revise the Articles. From the discussions and compromises in this convention emerged Congress in the form we recognize today. In this section, we will explore the debates and compromises that brought about the bicameral (two-chamber) Congress, made up of a House of Representatives and Senate. We will also explore the goals of bicameralism and how it functions. Finally, we will look at the different ways seats are apportioned in the two chambers.

THE GREAT COMPROMISE AND THE BASICS OF BICAMERALISM

Only a few years after the adoption of the Articles of Confederation, the republican experiment seemed on the verge of failure. States deep in debt were printing increasingly worthless paper currency, many were mired in interstate trade battles with each other, and in western Massachusetts, a small group of Revolutionary War veterans angry over the prospect of losing their farms broke into armed open revolt against the state, in what came to be known as Shays' Rebellion. The conclusion many reached was that the Articles of Confederation were simply not strong enough to keep the young republic together. In the spring of 1787, a convention was called, and delegates from all the states (except Rhode Island, which boycotted the convention) were sent to Philadelphia to hammer out a solution to this central problem.

The meeting these delegates convened became known as the Constitutional Convention of 1787. Although its prescribed purpose was to revise the Articles of Confederation, a number of delegates charted a path toward disposing of the Articles entirely. Under the Articles, the national legislature had been made up of a single chamber composed of an equal number of delegates from each of the states. Large states, like Virginia, felt it would be unfair to continue with this style of legislative institution. As a result, Virginia's delegates proposed a plan that called for **bicameralism**, or the division of legislators into two separate assemblies. In this proposed two-chamber Congress, states with larger populations would have more representatives in each chamber. Predictably, smaller states like New Jersey were unhappy with this proposal. In response, they issued their own plan, which called for a single-chamber Congress with equal representation and more state authority (Figure 11.2).

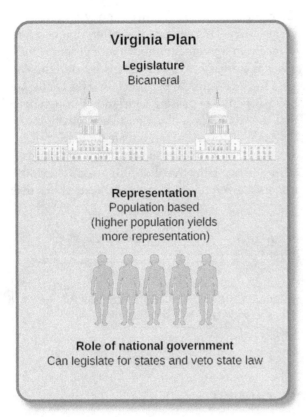
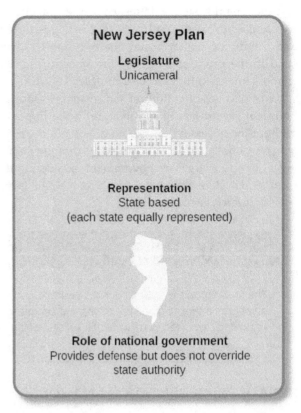

Figure 11.2 The Virginia or "large state" plan called for a two-chamber legislature, with representation by population in each chamber. The plan proposed by smaller states like New Jersey favored maintaining a one-house Congress in which all states were equally represented.

The storm of debate over how to allocate power between large and small states was eventually calmed by a third proposal. The Connecticut Compromise, also called the Great Compromise, proposed a bicameral congress with members apportioned differently in each house. The upper house, the Senate, was to have two members from each state. This soothed the fears of the small states. In the lower house, the House of Representatives, membership would be proportional to the population in each state. This measure protected the interests of the large states.

In the final draft of the U.S. Constitution, the bicameral Congress established by the convention of 1787 was given a number of powers and limitations. These are outlined in Article I (Appendix B). This article describes the minimum age of congresspersons (Section 2), requires that Congress meet at least once a year (Section 4), guarantees members' pay (Section 6), and gives Congress the power to levy taxes, borrow money, and regulate commerce (Section 8). These powers and limitations were the Constitutional Convention's response to the failings of the Articles of Confederation.

Although the basic design of the House and Senate resulted from a political deal between large and small states, the bicameral legislature established by the convention did not emerge from thin air. The concept had existed in Europe as far back as the medieval era. At that time, the two chambers of a legislature were divided based on class and designed to reflect different types of representation. The names of the two houses in the United Kingdom's bicameral parliament still reflect this older distinction today: the House of Lords and the House of Commons. Likewise, those at the Constitutional Convention purposely structured the U.S. Senate differently from the House of Representatives in the hopes of encouraging different representative memberships in the two houses. Initially, for example, the power to elect senators was given to the state legislatures instead of to the voting public as it is now. The minimum age requirement is also lower for the House of Representatives: A person must be at least twenty-five years old to serve in the House, whereas one must be at least thirty to be a senator.

The bicameral system established at the Constitutional Convention and still followed today requires the two houses to pass identical **bills**, or proposed items of legislation. This ensures that after all amending and modifying has occurred, the two houses ultimately reach an agreement about the legislation they send to the president. Passing the same bill in both houses is no easy feat, and this is by design. The framers intended there to be a complex and difficult process for legislation to become law. This challenge serves a number of important and related functions. First, the difficulty of passing legislation through both houses makes it less likely, though hardly impossible, that the Congress will act on fleeting instincts or without the necessary deliberation. Second, the bicameral system ensures that large-scale dramatic reform is exceptionally difficult to pass and that the status quo is more likely to win the day. This maintains a level of conservatism in government, something the landed elite at the convention preferred. Third, the bicameral system makes it difficult for a single faction or interest group to enact laws and restrictions that would unfairly favor it.

Link to Learning

The website of the U.S. Congress Visitor Center (https://openstax.org/l/29VisitCong) contains a number of interesting online exhibits and informational tidbits about the U.S. government's "first branch" (so called because it is described in Article I of the Constitution).

SENATE REPRESENTATION AND HOUSE APPORTIONMENT

The Constitution specifies that every state will have two senators who each serve a six-year term. Therefore, with fifty states in the Union, there are currently one hundred seats in the U.S. Senate. Senators were originally appointed by state legislatures, but in 1913, the Seventeenth Amendment was approved, which allowed for senators to be elected by popular vote in each state. Seats in the House of Representatives are distributed among the states based on each state's population and each member of the House is elected by voters in a specific congressional district. Each state is guaranteed at least one seat in the House (Table 11.1).

The 116th Congress

	House of Representatives	Senate
Total Number of Members	435	100
Number of Members per State	1 or more, based on population	2
Length of Term of Office	2 years	6 years
Minimum Age Requirement	25	30

Table 11.1

Congressional **apportionment** today is achieved through the *equal proportions method*, which uses a mathematical formula to allocate seats based on U.S. Census Bureau population data, gathered every ten years as required by the Constitution. At the close of the first U.S. Congress in 1791, there were sixty-five representatives, each representing approximately thirty thousand citizens. Then, as the territory of the United States expanded, sometimes by leaps and bounds, the population requirement for each new district increased as well. Adjustments were made, but the roster of the House of Representatives continued to grow until it reached 435 members after the 1910 census. Ten years later, following the 1920 census and with urbanization changing populations across the country, Congress failed to reapportion membership because it became deadlocked on the issue. In 1929, an agreement was reached to permanently cap the number of seats in the House at 435.

Redistricting occurs every ten years, after the U.S. Census has established how many persons live in the United States and where. The boundaries of legislative districts are redrawn as needed to maintain similar numbers of voters in each while still maintaining a total number of 435 districts. Because local areas can see their population grow as well as decline over time, these adjustments in district boundaries are typically needed after ten years have passed. Currently, there are seven states with only one representative (Alaska, Delaware, Montana, North Dakota, South Dakota, Vermont, and Wyoming), whereas the most populous state, California, has a total of fifty-three congressional districts (Figure 11.3).

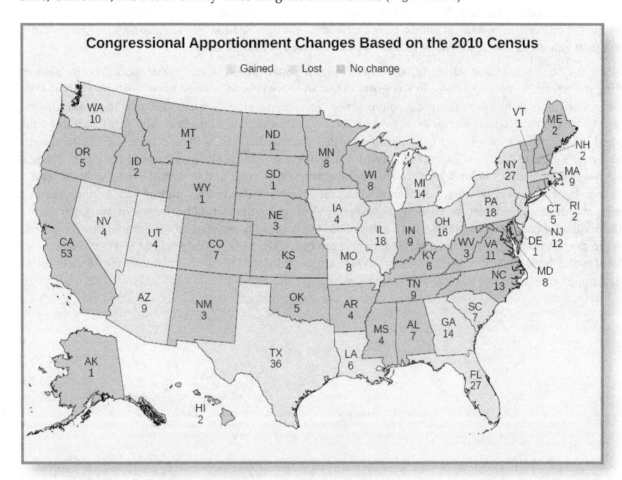

Figure 11.3 Although the total number of seats in the House of Representatives has been capped at 435, the apportionment of seats by state may change each decade following the official census. In this map, we see the changes in seat reapportionment that followed the 2010 Census.

Two remaining problems in the House are the size of each representative's **constituency**—the body of voters who elect him or her—and the challenge of Washington, DC. First, the average number of citizens in a congressional district now tops 700,000. This is arguably too many for House members to remain very close to the people. George Washington advocated for thirty thousand per elected member to retain effective representation in the House. The second problem is that the approximately 675,000 residents of the federal district of Washington (District of Columbia) do not have voting representation. Like those living in the U.S. territories, they merely have a non-voting delegate.[1]

The stalemate in the 1920s wasn't the first time reapportionment in the House resulted in controversy (or the last). The first incident took place before any apportionment had even occurred, while the process was being discussed at the Constitutional Convention. Representatives from large slave-owning states believed their slaves should be counted as part of the total population. States with few or no slaves predictably argued against this. The compromise eventually reached allowed for each slave (who could not vote) to count as three-fifths of a person for purposes of congressional representation. Following the abolition of slavery and the end of Reconstruction, the former slave states in the South took a number of steps to prevent former slaves and their children from voting. Yet because these former slaves were now free persons, they were counted fully toward the states' congressional representation.

Attempts at African American disenfranchisement continued until the civil rights struggle of the 1960s finally brought about the Voting Rights Act of 1965. The act cleared several final hurdles to voter registration and voting for African Americans. Following its adoption, many Democrats led the charge to create congressional districts that would enhance the power of African American voters. The idea was to create *majority-minority districts* within states, districts in which African Americans became the majority and thus gained the electoral power to send representatives to Congress.

While the strangely drawn districts succeeded in their stated goals, nearly quintupling the number of African American representatives in Congress in just over two decades, they have frustrated others who claim they are merely a new form of an old practice, gerrymandering. *Gerrymandering* is the manipulation of legislative district boundaries as a way of favoring a particular candidate. The term combines the word salamander, a reference to the strange shape of these districts, with the name of Massachusetts governor Elbridge Gerry, who in 1812, signed a redistricting plan designed to benefit his party. Despite the questionable ethics behind gerrymandering, the practice is legal, and both major parties have used it to their benefit. It is only when political redistricting appears to dilute the votes of racial minorities that gerrymandering efforts can be challenged under the Voting Rights Act. Other forms of gerrymandering are frequently employed in states where a dominant party seeks to maintain that domination. As we saw in the chapter on political parties, gerrymandering can be a tactic to draw district lines in a way that creates "safe seats" for a particular political party. In states like Maryland, these are safe seats for Democrats. In states like Louisiana, they are safe seats for Republicans (Figure 11.4).

Gerrymandering in Austin, TX, 2003–2015

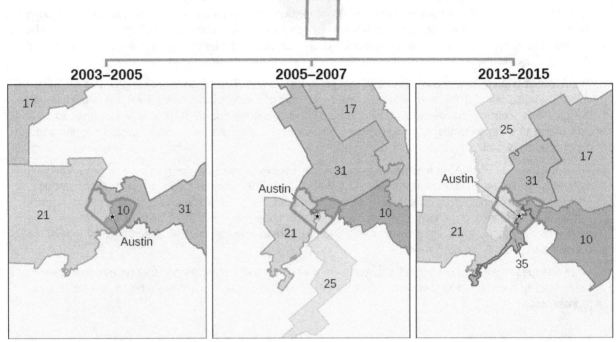

Figure 11.4 These maps show examples of gerrymandering in Texas, where the Republican-controlled legislature has redrawn House districts to reduce the number of Democratic seats by combining voters in Austin with those in surrounding counties, sometimes even several hundred miles away. Today, Austin is represented by six different congressional representatives.

Racial Gerrymandering and the Paradox of Minority Representation

In Ohio, one skirts the shoreline of Lake Erie like a snake. In Louisiana, one meanders across the southern part of the state from the eastern shore of Lake Ponchartrain, through much of New Orleans and north along the Mississippi River to Baton Rouge. And in Illinois, another wraps around the city of Chicago and its suburbs in a wandering line that, when seen on a map, looks like the mouth of a large, bearded alligator attempting to drink from Lake Michigan.

These aren't geographical features or large infrastructure projects. Rather, they are racially gerrymandered congressional districts. Their strange shapes are the product of careful district restructuring organized around the goal of enhancing the votes of minority groups. The alligator-mouth District 4 in Illinois, for example, was drawn to bring a number of geographically autonomous Latino groups in Illinois together in the same congressional district.

While the strategy of creating majority-minority districts has been a success for minorities' representation in Congress, its long-term effect has revealed a disturbing paradox: Congress as a whole has become less enthusiastic about minority-specific issues. How is this possible? The problem is that by creating districts with high percentages of minority constituents, strategists have made the other districts less diverse. The representatives in those districts are under very little pressure to consider the interests of minority groups. As a result, they typically do not.[2]

What changes might help correct this problem? Are majority-minority districts no longer an effective strategy for increasing minority representation in Congress? Are there better ways to achieve a higher level of minority representation?

CONGRESSIONAL POWERS

The authority to introduce and pass legislation is a very strong power. But it is only one of the many that Congress possesses. In general, congressional powers can be divided into three types: enumerated, implied, and inherent. An **enumerated power** is a power explicitly stated in the Constitution. An **implied power** is one not specifically detailed in the Constitution but inferred as necessary to achieve the objectives of the national government. And an **inherent power**, while not enumerated or implied, must be assumed to exist as a direct result of the country's existence. In this section, we will learn about each type of power and the foundations of legitimacy they claim. We will also learn about the way the different branches of government have historically appropriated powers not previously granted to them and the way congressional power has recently suffered in this process.

Article I, Section 8, of the U.S. Constitution details the enumerated powers of the legislature. These include the power to levy and collect taxes, declare war, raise an army and navy, coin money, borrow money, regulate commerce among the states and with foreign nations, establish federal courts and bankruptcy rules, establish rules for immigration and naturalization, and issue patents and copyrights. Other powers, such as the ability of Congress to override a presidential veto with a two-thirds vote of both houses, are found elsewhere in the Constitution (Article II, Section 7, in the case of the veto override). The first of these enumerated powers, to levy taxes, is quite possibly the most important power Congress possesses. Without it, most of the others, whether enumerated, implied, or inherent, would be largely theoretical. The power to levy and collect taxes, along with the appropriations power, gives Congress what is typically referred to as "the power of the purse" (Figure 11.5). This means Congress controls the money.

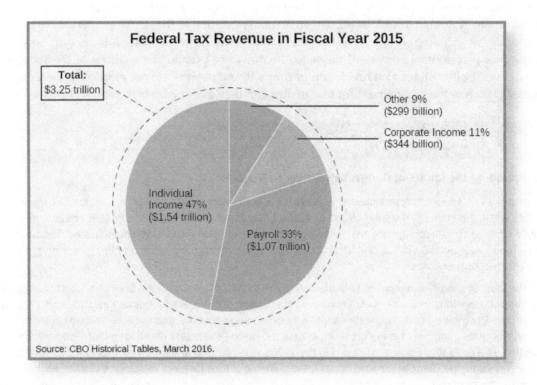

Federal Tax Revenue in Fiscal Year 2015

Total: $3.25 trillion

Other 9% ($299 billion)

Corporate Income 11% ($344 billion)

Individual Income 47% ($1.54 trillion)

Payroll 33% ($1.07 trillion)

Source: CBO Historical Tables, March 2016.

Figure 11.5 The ability to levy and collect taxes is the first, and most important, of Congress's enumerated powers. In 2015, U.S. federal tax revenue totaled $3.25 trillion.

Some enumerated powers invested in the Congress were included specifically to serve as checks on the other powerful branches of government. These include Congress's sole power to introduce legislation, the Senate's final say on many presidential nominations and treaties signed by the president, and the House's ability to impeach or formally accuse the president or other federal officials of wrongdoing (the first step in removing the person from office; the second step, trial and removal, takes place in the U.S. Senate). Each of these powers also grants Congress **oversight** of the actions of the president and his or her administration—that is, the right to review and monitor other bodies such as the executive branch. The fact that Congress has the sole power to introduce legislation effectively limits the power of the president to develop the same laws he or she is empowered to enforce. The Senate's exclusive power to give final approval for many of the president's nominees, including cabinet members and judicial appointments, compels the president to consider the needs and desires of Congress when selecting top government officials. Finally, removing a president from office who has been elected by the entire country should never be done lightly. Giving this responsibility to a large deliberative body of elected officials ensures it will occur only very rarely.

Despite the fact that the Constitution outlines specific enumerated powers, most of the actions Congress takes on a day-to-day basis are not actually included in this list. The reason is that the Constitution not only gives Congress the power to make laws but also gives it some general direction as to what those laws should accomplish. The "necessary and proper clause" directs Congress "to make all Laws which shall be necessary and proper for carrying into Execution the foregoing Powers, and all other Powers vested by this Constitution in the Government of the United States, or in any Department or Officer thereof." Laws that regulate banks, establish a minimum wage, and allow for the construction and maintenance of interstate highways are all possible because of the implied powers granted by the necessary and proper clause. Today, the overwhelming portion of Congress's work is tied to the necessary and proper clause.

Finally, Congress's inherent powers are unlike either the enumerated or the implied powers. Inherent powers are not only not mentioned in the Constitution, but they do not even have a convenient clause in the Constitution to provide for them. Instead, they are powers Congress has determined it must assume if the government is going to work at all. The general assumption is that these powers were deemed so essential to any functioning government that the framers saw no need to spell them out. Such powers include the power to control borders of the state, the power to expand the territory of the state, and the power to defend itself from internal revolution or coups. These powers are not granted to the Congress, or to any other branch of the government for that matter, but they exist because the country exists.

Finding a Middle Ground

Understanding the Limits of Congress's Power to Regulate

One of the most important constitutional anchors for Congress's implicit power to regulate all manner of activities within the states is the short clause in Article I, Section 8, which says Congress is empowered to "to regulate Commerce with foreign Nations, and among the several States, and with Indian Tribes." The Supreme Court's broad interpretation of this so-called commerce clause has greatly expanded the power and reach of Congress over the centuries.

From the earliest days of the republic until the end of the nineteenth century, the Supreme Court consistently handed down decisions that effectively broadened the Congress's power to regulate interstate and intrastate commerce.[3] The growing country, the demands of its expanding economy, and the way changes in technology and transportation contributed to the shrinking of space between the states demanded that Congress be able to function as a regulator. For a short period in the 1930s when federal authority was expanded to combat the Great Depression, the Court began to interpret the commerce clause far more narrowly. But after this interlude, the court's interpretation swung in an even-broader direction. This change proved particularly important in the 1960s, when Congress rolled back racial segregation throughout much of the South and beyond, and in the 1970s, as federal environmental regulations and programs took root.

But in *United States v. Lopez*, a decision issued in 1995, the Court changed course again and, for the first time in half a century, struck down a law as an unconstitutional overstepping of the commerce clause.[4] Five years later, the Court did it again, convincing many that the country may be witnessing the beginning of a rollback in Congress's power to regulate in the states. When the Patient Protection and Affordable Care Act (also known as the ACA, or Obamacare) came before the Supreme Court in 2012, many believed the Court would strike it down. Instead, the justices took the novel approach of upholding the law based on the Congress's enumerated power to tax, rather than the commerce clause. The decision was a shock to many.[5] And, by not upholding the law on the basis of the commerce clause, the Court left open the possibility that it would continue to pursue a narrower interpretation of the clause.

What are the advantages of the Supreme Court's broad interpretation of the commerce clause? How do you think this interpretation affects the balance of power between the branches of government? Why are some people concerned that the Court's view of the clause could change?

In the early days of the republic, Congress's role was rarely if ever disputed. However, with its decision in *Marbury v. Madison* (1803), the Supreme Court asserted its authority over judicial review and assumed the power to declare laws unconstitutional.[6] Yet, even after that decision, the Court was reluctant to use this power and didn't do so for over half a century. Initially, the presidency was also a fairly weak branch of government compared with the legislature. But presidents have sought to increase their power almost from the beginning, typically at the expense of the Congress. By the nature of the enumerated powers provided to the president, it is during wartime that the chief executive is most powerful and Congress least powerful. For example, President Abraham Lincoln, who oversaw the prosecution of the Civil War, stretched the bounds of his legal authority in a number of ways, such as by issuing the Emancipation Proclamation that freed slaves in the confederate states.[7]

In the twentieth century, the modern tussle over power between the Congress and the president really began. There are two primary reasons this struggle emerged. First, as the country grew larger and more complex, the need for the government to assert its regulatory power grew. The executive branch, because of its hierarchical organization with the president at the top, is naturally seen as a more smoothly run governmental machine than the cumbersome Congress. This gives the president advantages in the struggle for power and indeed gives Congress an incentive to delegate authority to the president on processes, such as trade agreements and national monument designations, that would be difficult for the legislature to carry out. The second reason has to do with the president's powers as commander-in-chief in the realm of foreign policy.

The twin disasters of the Great Depression in the 1930s and World War II, which lasted until the mid-1940s, provided President Franklin D. Roosevelt with a powerful platform from which to expand presidential power. His popularity and his ability to be elected four times allowed him to greatly overshadow Congress. As a result, Congress attempted to restrain the power of the presidency by proposing the Twenty-Second Amendment to the Constitution, which limited a president to only two full terms in office.[8] Although this limitation is a significant one, it has not held back the tendency for the presidency to assume increased power.

In the decades following World War II, the United States entered the Cold War, a seemingly endless conflict with the Soviet Union without actual war, and therefore a period that allowed the presidency to assert more authority, especially in foreign affairs. In an exercise of this increased power, in the 1950s, President Harry Truman effectively went around an enumerated power of Congress by sending troops into battle in Korea without a congressional declaration of war (Figure 11.6). By the time of the Kennedy administration in the 1960s, the presidency had assumed nearly all responsibility for creating foreign policy, effectively shutting Congress out.

Following the twin scandals of Vietnam and Watergate in the early 1970s, Congress attempted to assert itself as a coequal branch, even in creating foreign policy, but could not hold back the trend. The War Powers Resolution (covered in the foreign policy chapter) was intended to strengthen congressional war powers but ended up clarifying presidential authority in the first sixty days of a military conflict. The war on terrorism after 9/11 has also strengthened the president's hand. Today, the seemingly endless bickering between the president and the Congress is a reminder of the ongoing struggle for power between the branches, and indeed between the parties, in Washington, DC.

Figure 11.6 President Truman did not think it necessary to go through Congress to prosecute the war in Korea. This action opened the door to an extended era in which Congress has been effectively removed from decisions about whether to go to war, an era that continues today.

11.2 Congressional Elections

Learning Objectives

By the end of this section, you will be able to:

- Explain how fundamental characteristics of the House and Senate shape their elections
- Discuss campaign funding and the effects of incumbency in the House and Senate
- Analyze the way congressional elections can sometimes become nationalized

The House and Senate operate very differently, partly because their members differ in the length of their terms, as well as in their age and other characteristics. In this section, we will explore why constitutional rules affect the elections for the two types of representatives and the reason the two bodies function differently by design. We also look at campaign finance to better understand how legislators get elected and stay elected.

UNDERSTANDING THE HOUSE AND SENATE

The U.S. Constitution is very clear about who can be elected as a member of the House or Senate. A House member must be a U.S. citizen of at least seven years' standing and at least twenty-five years old. Senators are required to have nine years' standing as citizens and be at least thirty years old when sworn in. Representatives serve two-year terms, whereas senators serve six-year terms. Per the Supreme Court decision in *U.S. Term Limits v. Thornton* (1995), there are currently no term limits for either senators or representatives, despite efforts by many states to impose them in the mid-1990s.[9] House members are elected by the voters in their specific congressional districts. There are currently 435 congressional districts in the United States and thus 435 House members, and each state has a number of House districts roughly proportional to its share of the total U.S. population, with states guaranteed at least one House member. Two senators are elected by each state.

The structural and other differences between the House and Senate have practical consequences for the way the two chambers function. The House of Representatives has developed a stronger and more structured leadership than the Senate. Because its members serve short, two-year terms, they must regularly answer to the demands of their constituency when they run for election or reelection. Even House members of the same party in the same state will occasionally disagree on issues because of the different interests of their specific districts. Thus, the House can be highly partisan at times.

In contrast, members of the Senate are furthest from the demands and scrutiny of their constituents. Because of their longer six-year terms, they will see every member of the House face his or her constituents multiple times before they themselves are forced to seek reelection. Originally, when a state's two U.S. senators were appointed by the state legislature, the Senate chamber's distance from the electorate was even greater. Also, unlike members of the House who can seek the narrower interests of their district, senators must maintain a broader appeal in order to earn a majority of the votes across their entire state. In addition, the rules of the Senate allow individual members to slow down or stop legislation they dislike. These structural differences between the two chambers create real differences in the actions of their members. The heat of popular, sometimes fleeting, demands from constituents often glows red hot in the House. The Senate has the flexibility to allow these passions to cool. Dozens of major initiatives were passed by the House and had a willing president, for example, only to be defeated in the Senate. In 2012, the Buffett Rule would have implemented a minimum tax rate of 30 percent on wealthy Americans. Sixty senators had to agree to bring it to a vote, but the bill fell short of that number and died.[10] Similarly, although the ACA became widely known as "Obamacare," the president did not send a piece of legislation to Capitol Hill; he asked Congress to write the bills. Both the House and Senate authored their own versions of the legislation. The House's version was much bolder and larger in terms of establishing a national health care system. However, it did not stand a chance in the Senate, where a more moderate version of the legislation was introduced. In the end, House leaders saw the Senate version as preferable to doing nothing and ultimately supported it.

CONGRESSIONAL CAMPAIGN FUNDING

Modern political campaigns in the United States are expensive, and they have been growing more so. For example, in 1986, the costs of running a successful House and Senate campaign were $776,687 and $6,625,932, respectively, in 2014 dollars. By 2014, those values had shot to $1,466,533 and $9,655,660 (Figure 11.7).[11] Raising this amount of money takes quite a bit of time and effort. Indeed, a presentation for incoming Democratic representatives suggested a daily Washington schedule of five hours reaching out to donors, while only three or four were to be used for actual congressional work. As this advice reveals, raising money for reelection constitutes a large proportion of the work a congressperson does. This has caused many to wonder whether the amount of money in politics has truly become a corrupting influence. However, overall, the lion's share of direct campaign contributions in congressional elections comes from individual donors, who are less influential than the political action committees (PACs) that contribute the remainder.[12]

Figure 11.7   The most expensive House race in 2014 was that of Speaker of the House John Boehner (right), a Republican from Ohio, who spent over $17 million to hold his seat. He later resigned in 2015 and was replaced as Speaker by Paul Ryan (left) of Wisconsin's 1st District.[13]

Nevertheless, the complex problem of funding campaigns has a long history in the United States. For nearly the first hundred years of the republic, there were no federal campaign finance laws. Then, between the late nineteenth century and the start of World War I, Congress pushed through a flurry of reforms intended to bring order to the world of campaign finance. These laws made it illegal for politicians to solicit contributions from civil service workers, made corporate contributions illegal, and required candidates to report their fundraising. As politicians and donors soon discovered, however, these laws were full of loopholes and were easily skirted by those who knew the ins and outs of the system.

Another handful of reform attempts were therefore pushed through in the wake of World War II, but then Congress neglected campaign finance reform for a few decades. That lull ended in the early 1970s when the Federal Election Campaign Act was passed. Among other things, it created the Federal Election Commission (FEC), required candidates to disclose where their money was coming from and where they were spending it, limited individual contributions, and provided for public financing of presidential campaigns.

Another important reform occurred in 2002, when Senators John McCain (R-AZ) and Russell Feingold (D-WI) drafted, and Congress passed, the Bipartisan Campaign Reform Act (BCRA), also referred to as the McCain-Feingold Act. The purpose of this law was to limit the use of "soft money," which is raised for purposes like party-building efforts, get-out-the-vote efforts, and issue-advocacy ads. Unlike "hard money" contributed directly to a candidate, which is heavily regulated and limited, soft money had almost no regulations or limits. It had never been a problem before the mid-1990s, when a number of very imaginative political operatives developed a great many ways to spend this money. After that, soft-money donations skyrocketed. But the McCain-Feingold bill greatly limited this type of fundraising.

McCain-Feingold placed limits on total contributions to political parties, prohibited coordination between candidates and PAC campaigns, and required candidates to include personal endorsements on their political ads. Until 2010, it also limited advertisements run by unions and corporations thirty days before a primary and sixty days before a general election.[14] The FEC's enforcement of the law spurred numerous court cases challenging it. The most controversial decision was handed down by the Supreme Court in 2010, whose ruling on *Citizens United v. Federal Election Commission* led to the removal of spending limits on corporations. Justices in the majority argued that the BCRA violated a corporation's free-speech rights.[15]

The *Citizens United* case began as a lawsuit against the FEC filed by Citizens United, a nonprofit organization that wanted to advertise a documentary critical of former senator and Democratic hopeful Hillary Clinton on the eve of the 2008 Democratic primaries. Advertising or showing the film during this time window was prohibited by the McCain-Feingold Act. But the Court found that this type of restriction violated the organization's First Amendment right to free speech. As critics of the decision predicted at the time, the Court thus opened the floodgates to private soft money flowing into campaigns again.

In the wake of the *Citizens United* decision, a new type of advocacy group emerged, the super PAC. A traditional PAC is an organization designed to raise hard money to elect or defeat candidates. Such PACs tended to be run by businesses and other groups, like the Teamsters Union and the National Rifle Association, to support their special interests. They are highly regulated in regard to the amount of money they can take in and spend, but super PACs aren't bound by these regulations. While they cannot give money directly to a candidate or a candidate's party, they can raise and spend unlimited funds, and they can spend independently of a campaign or party. In the 2012 election cycle, for example, super PACs spent just over $600 million dollars and raised about $200 million more.[16]

At the same time, several limits on campaign contributions have been upheld by the courts and remain in place. Individuals may contribute up to $2700 per candidate per election. Individuals may also give $5000 to PACs and $33,400 to a national party committee. PACs that contribute to more than one candidate are permitted to contribute $5000 per candidate per election, and up to $15,000 to a national party. PACs created to give money to only one candidate are limited to only $2700 per candidate, however (Figure 11.8).[17] The amounts are adjusted every two years, based on inflation. These limits are intended to create a more equal playing field for the candidates, so that candidates must raise their campaign funds from a broad pool of contributors.

CONTRIBUTION LIMITS FOR 2015-2016 FEDERAL ELECTIONS					
DONORS	RECIPIENTS				
	Candidate Committee	PAC[1] (SSF and Nonconnected)	State/District/ Local Party Committee	National Party Committee	Additional National Party Committee Accounts[2]
Individual	$2,700* per election	$5,000 per year	$10,000 per year (combined)	$33,400* per year	$100,200* per account, per year
Candidate Committee	$2,000 per election	$5,000 per year	Unlimited Transfers	Unlimited Transfers	
PAC-Multicandidate	$5,000 per election	$5,000 per year	$5,000 per year (combined)	$15,000 per year	$45,000 per account, per year
PAC-Nonmulticandidate	$2,700 per election	$5,000 per year	$10,000 per year (combined)	$33,400* per year	$100,200* per account, per year
State/District/Local Party Committee	$5,000 per election	$5,000 per year	Unlimited Transfers		
National Party Committee	$5,000 per election[3]	$5,000 per year			

*- Indexed for inflation in odd-numbered years.

[1] "PAC" here refers to a committee that makes contributions to other federal political committees. Independent-expenditure-only political committees (sometimes called "super PACs") may accept unlimited contributions, including from corporations and labor organizations.

[2] The limits in this column apply to a national party committee's accounts for: (i) the presidential nominating convention; (ii) election recounts and contests and other legal proceedings; and (iii) national party headquarters buildings. A party's national committee, Senate campaign committee and House campaign committee are each considered separate national party committees with separate limits. Only a national party committee, not the parties' national congressional campaign committees, may have an account for the presidential nominating convention.

[3] Additionally, a national party committee and its Senatorial campaign committee may contribute up to $46,800 combined per campaign to each Senate candidate.

Source: Federal Election Commission. "Contribution Limits for 2015–2016 Federal Elections." June 25, 2015.

Figure 11.8 The Federal Election Commission has strict federal election guidelines on who can contribute, to whom, and how much.

Link to Learning

The **Center for Responsive Politics (https://openstax.org/l/29OpnSecrt)** reports donation amounts that are required by law to be disclosed to the Federal Elections Commission. One finding is that, counter to conventional wisdom, the vast majority of direct campaign contributions come from individual donors, not from PACs and political parties.

INCUMBENCY EFFECTS

Not surprisingly, the jungle of campaign financing regulations and loopholes is more easily navigated by incumbents in Congress than by newcomers. Incumbents are elected officials who currently hold an office. The amount of money they raise against their challengers demonstrates their advantage. In 2014, for example, the average Senate incumbent raised $12,144,933, whereas the average challenger raised only

$1,223,566.[18] This is one of the many reasons incumbents win a large majority of congressional races each electoral cycle. Incumbents attract more money because people want to give to a winner. In the House, the percentage of incumbents winning reelection has hovered between 85 and 100 percent for the last half century. In the Senate, there is only slightly more variation, given the statewide nature of the race, but it is still a very high majority of incumbents who win reelection (Figure 11.9). As these rates show, even in the worst political environments, incumbents are very difficult to defeat.

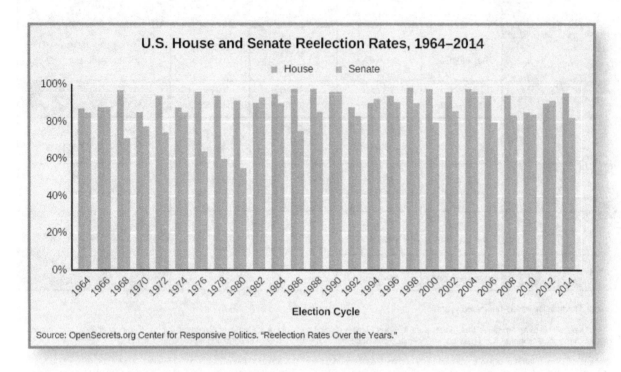

Figure 11.9 Historically, incumbents in both the House and the Senate enjoy high rates of reelection.

The historical difficulty of unseating an incumbent in the House or Senate is often referred to as the *incumbent advantage* or the *incumbency effect*. The advantage in financing is a huge part of this effect, but it is not the only important part. Incumbents often have a much higher level of name recognition. All things being equal, voters are far more likely to select the name of the person they recall seeing on television and hearing on the radio for the last few years than the name of a person they hardly know. And donors are more likely to want to give to a proven winner.

But more important is the way the party system itself privileges incumbents. A large percentage of congressional districts across the country are "safe seats" in uncompetitive districts, meaning candidates from a particular party are highly likely to consistently win the seat. This means the functional decision in these elections occurs during the primary, not in the general election. Political parties in general prefer to support incumbents in elections, because the general consensus is that incumbents are better candidates, and their record of success lends support to this conclusion. That said, while the political parties themselves to a degree control and regulate the primaries, popular individual candidates and challengers sometimes rule the day. This has especially been the case in recent years as conservative incumbents have been "primaried" by challengers more conservative than they.

Insider Perspective

The End of Incumbency Advantage?

At the start of 2014, House majority whip Eric Cantor, a representative from Virginia, was at the top of his game. He was handsome, popular with talk show hosts and powerful insiders, an impressive campaign fundraiser and speaker, and apparently destined to become Speaker of the House when the current speaker stepped down. Four months later, Cantor lost the opportunity to run for his own congressional seat in a shocking primary election upset that shook the Washington political establishment to its core.

What happened? How did such a powerful incumbent lose a game in which the cards had been stacked so heavily in his favor? Analyses of the stunning defeat quickly showed there were more chinks in Cantor's polished armor than most wanted to admit. But his weakness wasn't that he was unable to play the political game. Rather, he may have learned to play it too well. He became seen as too much of a Washington insider.

Cantor's ambition, political skill, deep connections to political insiders, and ability to come out squeaky clean after even the dirtiest political tussling should have given him a clear advantage over any competitor. But in the political environment of 2014, when conservative voices around the country criticized the party for ignoring the people and catering to political insiders, his strengths became weaknesses. Indeed, Cantor was the only highest-level Republican representative sacrificed to conservative populism.

Were the winds of change blowing for incumbents? Between 1946 and 2012, only 5 percent of incumbent senators and 2 percent of House incumbents lost their party primaries.[19] In 2014, Cantor was one of four House incumbents who did so, while no incumbent senators suffered defeat. All evidence suggests the incumbent advantage, especially in the primary system, is alive and well. The story of Eric Cantor may very well be the classic case of an exception proving the rule.

If you are a challenger running against an incumbent, what are some strategies you could use to make the race competitive? Would Congress operate differently if challengers defeated incumbents more often?

Another reason incumbents wield a great advantage over their challengers is the state power they have at their disposal.[20] One of the many responsibilities of a sitting congressperson is *constituent casework*. Constituents routinely reach out to their congressperson for powerful support to solve complex problems, such as applying for and tracking federal benefits or resolving immigration and citizenship challenges.[21] Incumbent members of Congress have paid staff, influence, and access to specialized information that can help their constituents in ways other persons cannot. And congresspersons are hardly reticent about their efforts to support their constituents. Often, they will publicize their casework on their websites or, in some cases, create television advertisements that boast of their helpfulness. Election history has demonstrated that this form of publicity is very effective in garnering the support of voters.

LOCAL AND NATIONAL ELECTIONS

The importance of airing positive constituent casework during campaigns is a testament to the accuracy of saying, "All politics is local." This phrase, attributed to former Speaker of the House Tip O'Neill (D-MA), essentially means that the most important motivations directing voters are rooted in local concerns. In general, this is true. People naturally feel more driven by the things that affect them on a daily basis. These are concerns like the quality of the roads, the availability of good jobs, and the cost and quality of public education. Good senators and representatives understand this and will seek to use their influence and power in office to affect these issues for the better. This is an age-old strategy for success in office and elections.

Political scientists have taken note of some voting patterns that appear to challenge this common assumption, however. In 1960, political scientist Angus Campbell proposed the **surge-and-decline theory** to explain these patterns.[22] Campbell noticed that since the Civil War, with the exception of 1934, the president's party has consistently lost seats in Congress during the midterm elections. He proposed that the reason was a surge in political stimulation during presidential elections, which contributes to greater turnout and brings in voters who are ordinarily less interested in politics. These voters, Campbell argued, tend to favor the party holding the presidency. In contrast, midterm elections witness the opposite effect. They are less stimulating and have lower turnout because less-interested voters stay home. This shift, in Campbell's theory, provides an advantage to the party not currently occupying the presidency.

In the decades since Campbell's influential theory was published, a number of studies have challenged his conclusions. Nevertheless, the pattern of midterm elections benefiting the president's opposition has persisted.[23] Only in exceptional years has this pattern been broken: first in 1998 during President Bill Clinton's second term and the Monica Lewinsky scandal, when exit polls indicated most voters opposed the idea of impeaching the president, and then again in 2002, following the 9/11 terrorist attacks and the ensuing declaration of a "war on terror."

The evidence does suggest that national concerns, rather than local ones, can function as powerful motivators at the polls. Consider, for example, the role of the Iraq War in bringing about a Democratic rout of the Republicans in the House in 2006 and in the Senate in 2008. Unlike previous wars in Europe and Vietnam, the war in Iraq was fought by a very small percentage of the population.[24] The vast majority of citizens were not soldiers, few had relatives fighting in the war, and most did not know anyone who directly suffered from the prolonged conflict. Voters in large numbers were motivated by the political and economic disaster of the war to vote for politicians they believed would end it (Figure 11.10).

Figure 11.10 Wars typically have the power to nationalize local elections. What makes the Iraq War different is that the overwhelming majority of voters had little to no intimate connection with the conflict and were motivated to vote for those who would end it. (credit: "Lipton sale"/Wikimedia Commons)

Congressional elections may be increasingly driven by national issues. Just two decades ago, straight-ticket, party-line voting was still relatively rare across most of the country.[25] In much of the South, which began to vote overwhelmingly Republican in presidential elections during the 1960s and 1970s, Democrats were still commonly elected to the House and Senate. The candidates themselves and the important local issues, apart from party affiliation, were important drivers in congressional elections. This began to change in the 1980s and 1990s, as Democratic representatives across the region began to dwindle. And the South isn't alone; areas in the Northeast and the Northwest have grown increasingly Democratic. Indeed, the 2014 midterm election was the most nationalized election in many decades. Voters who favor a particular party in a presidential election are now much more likely to also support that same party in House and Senate elections than was the case just a few decades ago.

11.3 Congressional Representation

Learning Objectives

By the end of this section, you will be able to:
- Explain the basics of representation
- Describe the extent to which Congress as a body represents the U.S. population
- Explain the concept of collective representation
- Describe the forces that influence congressional approval ratings

The tension between local and national politics described in the previous section is essentially a struggle between interpretations of representation. Representation is a complex concept. It can mean paying careful attention to the concerns of constituents, understanding that representatives must act as they see fit based on what they feel best for the constituency, or relying on the particular ethnic, racial, or gender diversity of those in office. In this section, we will explore three different models of representation and the concept of descriptive representation. We will look at the way members of Congress navigate the challenging terrain of representation as they serve, and all the many predictable and unpredictable consequences of the decisions they make.

TYPES OF REPRESENTATION: LOOKING OUT FOR CONSTITUENTS

By definition and title, senators and House members are representatives. This means they are intended to be drawn from local populations around the country so they can speak for and make decisions for those local populations, their constituents, while serving in their respective legislative houses. That is, **representation** refers to an elected leader's looking out for his or her constituents while carrying out the duties of the office.[26]

Theoretically, the process of constituents voting regularly and reaching out to their representatives helps these congresspersons better represent them. It is considered a given by some in representative democracies that representatives will seldom ignore the wishes of constituents, especially on salient issues that directly affect the district or state. In reality, the job of representing in Congress is often quite complicated, and elected leaders do not always know where their constituents stand. Nor do constituents always agree on everything. Navigating their sometimes contradictory demands and balancing them with the demands of the party, powerful interest groups, ideological concerns, the legislative body, their own personal beliefs, and the country as a whole can be a complicated and frustrating process for representatives.

Traditionally, representatives have seen their role as that of a delegate, a trustee, or someone attempting to balance the two. A representative who sees him- or herself as a delegate believes he or she is empowered merely to enact the wishes of constituents. Delegates must employ some means to identify the views of their constituents and then vote accordingly. They are not permitted the liberty of employing their own reason and judgment while acting as representatives in Congress. This is the **delegate model of representation**.

In contrast, a representative who understands their role to be that of a trustee believes he or she is entrusted by the constituents with the power to use good judgment to make decisions on the constituents' behalf. In the words of the eighteenth-century British philosopher Edmund Burke, who championed the **trustee model of representation**, "Parliament is not a congress of ambassadors from different and hostile interests . . . [it is rather] a deliberative assembly of one nation, with one interest, that of the whole."[27] In the modern setting, trustee representatives will look to party consensus, party leadership, powerful interests, the member's own personal views, and national trends to better identify the voting choices they should make.

Understandably, few if any representatives adhere strictly to one model or the other. Instead, most find themselves attempting to balance the important principles embedded in each. Political scientists call this the **politico model of representation**. In it, members of Congress act as either trustee or delegate based on rational political calculations about who is best served, the constituency or the nation.

For example, every representative, regardless of party or conservative versus liberal leanings, must remain firm in support of some ideologies and resistant to others. On the political right, an issue that demands support might be gun rights; on the left, it might be a woman's right to an abortion. For votes related to such issues, representatives will likely pursue a delegate approach. For other issues, especially complex questions the public at large has little patience for, such as subtle economic reforms, representatives will tend to follow a trustee approach. This is not to say their decisions on these issues run contrary to public opinion. Rather, it merely means they are not acutely aware of or cannot adequately measure the extent to which their constituents support or reject the proposals at hand. It could also mean that the issue is not salient to their constituents. Congress works on hundreds of different issues each year, and constituents are likely not aware of the particulars of most of them.

DESCRIPTIVE REPRESENTATION IN CONGRESS

In some cases, representation can seem to have very little to do with the substantive issues representatives in Congress tend to debate. Instead, proper representation for some is rooted in the racial, ethnic, socioeconomic, gender, and sexual identity of the representatives themselves. This form of representation is called **descriptive representation**.

At one time, there was relatively little concern about descriptive representation in Congress. A major reason is that until well into the twentieth century, white men of European background constituted an overwhelming majority of the voting population. African Americans were routinely deprived of the opportunity to participate in democracy, and Hispanics and other minority groups were fairly insignificant in number and excluded by the states. While women in many western states could vote sooner, all women were not able to exercise their right to vote nationwide until passage of the Nineteenth Amendment in 1920, and they began to make up more than 5 percent of either chamber only in the 1990s.

Many advances in women's rights have been the result of women's greater engagement in politics and representation in the halls of government, especially since the founding of the National Organization for Women in 1966 and the National Women's Political Caucus (NWPC) in 1971. The NWPC was formed by Bella Abzug (Figure 11.11), Gloria Steinem, Shirley Chisholm, and other leading feminists to encourage women's participation in political parties, elect women to office, and raise money for their campaigns. For example, Patsy Mink (D-HI) (Figure 11.11), the first Asian American woman elected to Congress, was the coauthor of the Education Amendments Act of 1972, Title IX of which prohibits sex discrimination in education. Mink had been interested in fighting discrimination in education since her youth, when she opposed racial segregation in campus housing while a student at the University of Nebraska. She went to law school after being denied admission to medical school because of her gender. Like Mink, many other women sought and won political office, many with the help of the NWPC. Today, EMILY's List, a PAC founded in 1985 to help elect pro-choice Democratic women to office, plays a major role in fundraising for female candidates. In the 2012 general election, 80 percent of the candidates endorsed by EMILY's List won a seat.[28]

(a)   (b)

Figure 11.11 Patsy Mink (a), a Japanese American from Hawaii, was the first Asian American woman elected to the House of Representatives. In her successful 1970 congressional campaign, Bella Abzug (b) declared, "This woman's place is in the House... the House of Representatives!"

In the wake of the Civil Rights Movement, African American representatives also began to enter Congress in increasing numbers. In 1971, to better represent their interests, these representatives founded the Congressional Black Caucus (CBC), an organization that grew out of a Democratic select committee formed in 1969. Founding members of the CBC include Ralph Metcalfe (D-IL), a former sprinter from Chicago who had medaled at both the Los Angeles (1932) and Berlin (1936) Olympic Games, and Shirley Chisholm, a founder of the NWPC and the first African American woman to be elected to the House of Representatives (Figure 11.12).

Figure 11.12 This photo shows the founding members of the Congressional Black Caucus, which at the time of its founding in 1971 had only thirteen members. Currently, forty-six African Americans serve in Congress.

In recent decades, Congress has become much more descriptively representative of the United States. The 116th Congress, which began in January 2019, had a historically large percentage of racial and ethnic minorities. African Americans made up the largest percentage, with fifty-seven members, while Latinos accounted for forty-six members, up from thirty just a decade before.[29] Yet, demographically speaking, Congress as a whole is still a long way from where the country is and remains largely white, male, and wealthy. For example, although more than half the U.S. population is female, only 25 percent of Congress is. Congress is also overwhelmingly Christian (Figure 11.13).

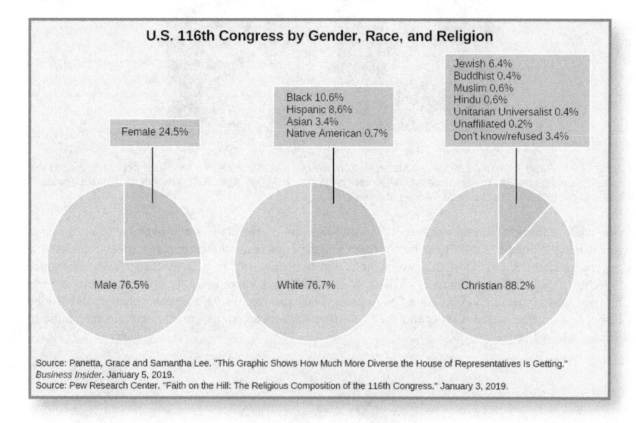

Figure 11.13 The diversity of the country is not reflected in the U.S. Congress, whose current membership is approximately 76 percent male, 77 percent white, and 88 percent Christian.

REPRESENTING CONSTITUENTS

Ethnic, racial, gender, or ideological identity aside, it is a representative's actions in Congress that ultimately reflect his or her understanding of representation. Congress members' most important function as lawmakers is writing, supporting, and passing bills. And as representatives of their constituents, they are charged with addressing those constituents' interests. Historically, this job has included what some have affectionately called "bringing home the bacon" but what many (usually those outside the district in question) call **pork-barrel politics**. As a term and a practice, pork-barrel politics—federal spending on projects designed to benefit a particular district or set of constituents—has been around since the nineteenth century, when barrels of salt pork were both a sign of wealth and a system of reward. While pork-barrel politics are often deplored during election campaigns, and earmarks—funds appropriated for specific projects—are no longer permitted in Congress (see feature box below), legislative control of local appropriations nevertheless still exists. In more formal language, *allocation*, or the influencing of the national budget in ways that help the district or state, can mean securing funds for a specific district's project like an airport, or getting tax breaks for certain types of agriculture or manufacturing.

Get Connected!

Language and Metaphor

The language and metaphors of war and violence are common in politics. Candidates routinely "smell blood in the water," "battle for delegates," go "head-to-head," "cripple" their opponent, and "make heads roll." But references to actual violence aren't the only metaphorical devices commonly used in politics. Another is mentions of food. Powerful speakers frequently "throw red meat to the crowds;" careful politicians prefer to stick to "meat-and-potato issues;" and representatives are frequently encouraged by their constituents to "bring home the bacon." And the way members of Congress typically "bring home the bacon" is often described with another agricultural metaphor, the "earmark."

In ranching, an earmark is a small cut on the ear of a cow or other animal to denote ownership. Similarly, in Congress, an earmark is a mark in a bill that directs some of the bill's funds to be spent on specific projects or for specific tax exemptions. Since the 1980s, the earmark has become a common vehicle for sending money to various projects around the country. Many a road, hospital, and airport can trace its origins back to a few skillfully drafted earmarks.

Relatively few people outside Congress had ever heard of the term before the 2008 presidential election, when Republican nominee Senator John McCain touted his career-long refusal to use the earmark as a testament to his commitment to reforming spending habits in Washington.[30] McCain's criticism of the earmark as a form of corruption cast a shadow over a previously common legislative practice. As the country sank into recession and Congress tried to use spending bills to stimulate the economy, the public grew more acutely aware of its earmarking habits. Congresspersons then were eager to distance themselves from the practice. In fact, the use of earmarks to encourage Republicans to help pass health care reform actually made the bill less popular with the public.

In 2011, after Republicans took over the House, they outlawed earmarks. But with deadlocks and stalemates becoming more common, some quiet voices have begun asking for a return to the practice. They argue that Congress works because representatives can satisfy their responsibilities to their constituents by making deals. The earmarks are those deals. By taking them away, Congress has hampered its own ability to "bring home the bacon."

Are earmarks a vital part of legislating or a corrupt practice that was rightly jettisoned? Pick a cause or industry, and investigate whether any earmarks ever favored it, or research the way earmarks have hurt or helped your state or district, and decide for yourself.

Follow-up activity: Find out where your congressional representative stands on the ban on earmarks and write to support or dissuade him or her.

Such budgetary allocations aren't always looked upon favorably by constituents. Consider, for example, the passage of the ACA in 2010. The desire for comprehensive universal health care had been a driving position of the Democrats since at least the 1960s. During the 2008 campaign, that desire was so great among both Democrats and Republicans that both parties put forth plans. When the Democrats took control of Congress and the presidency in 2009, they quickly began putting together their plan. Soon, however, the politics grew complex, and the proposed plan became very contentious for the Republican Party.

Nevertheless, the desire to make good on a decades-old political promise compelled Democrats to do everything in their power to pass something. They offered sympathetic members of the Republican Party valuable budgetary concessions; they attempted to include allocations they hoped the opposition might feel compelled to support; and they drafted the bill in a purposely complex manner to avoid future challenges. These efforts, however, had the opposite effect. The Republican Party's constituency interpreted the allocations as bribery and the bill as inherently flawed, and felt it should be scrapped entirely. The more Democrats dug in, the more frustrated the Republicans became (**Figure 11.14**).

Figure 11.14 In 2009, the extended debates and legislative maneuvering in Congress over the proposed health care reform bill triggered a firestorm of disapproval from the Republicans and protests from their supporters. In many cases, hyperbole ruled the day. (credit: "dbking"/Flickr)

The Republican opposition, which took control of the House during the 2010 midterm elections, promised constituents they would repeal the law. Their attempts were complicated, however, by the fact that Democrats still held the Senate and the presidency. Yet, the desire to represent the interests of their constituents compelled Republicans to use another tool at their disposal, the symbolic vote. During the 112th and 113th Congresses, Republicans voted more than sixty times to either repeal or severely limit the reach of the law. They understood these efforts had little to no chance of ever making it to the president's desk. And if they did, he would certainly have vetoed them. But it was important for these representatives to demonstrate to their constituents that they understood their wishes and were willing to act on them.

Historically, representatives have been able to balance their role as members of a national legislative body with their role as representatives of a smaller community. The Obamacare fight, however, gave a boost to the growing concern that the power structure in Washington divides representatives from the needs of their constituency.[31] This has exerted pressure on representatives to the extent that some now pursue a more straightforward delegate approach to representation. Indeed, following the 2010 election, a handful of Republicans began living in their offices in Washington, convinced that by not establishing a residence in Washington, they would appear closer to their constituents at home.[32]

COLLECTIVE REPRESENTATION AND CONGRESSIONAL APPROVAL

The concept of **collective representation** describes the relationship between Congress and the United States as a whole. That is, it considers whether the institution itself represents the American people, not just whether a particular member of Congress represents his or her district. Predictably, it is far more difficult for Congress to maintain a level of collective representation than it is for individual members of Congress to represent their own constituents. Not only is Congress a mixture of different ideologies, interests, and party affiliations, but the collective constituency of the United States has an even-greater level of diversity. Nor is it a solution to attempt to match the diversity of opinions and interests in the United States with those in Congress. Indeed, such an attempt would likely make it more difficult for Congress to maintain collective representation. Its rules and procedures require Congress to use flexibility, bargaining, and concessions. Yet, it is this flexibility and these concessions, which many now interpret as corruption, that tend to engender the high public disapproval ratings experienced by Congress.

After many years of deadlocks and bickering on Capitol Hill, the national perception of Congress is near an all-time low. According to Gallup polls, Congress has a stunningly poor approval rating of about 16 percent. This is unusual even for a body that has rarely enjoyed a high approval rating. For example, for nearly two decades following the Watergate scandal in the early 1970s, the national approval rating of Congress hovered between 30 and 40 percent.[33]

Yet, incumbent reelections have remained largely unaffected. The reason has to do with the remarkable ability of many in the United States to separate their distaste for Congress from their appreciation for their own representative. Paradoxically, this tendency to hate the group but love one's own representative actually perpetuates the problem of poor congressional approval ratings. The reason is that it blunts voters' natural desire to replace those in power who are earning such low approval ratings.

As decades of polling indicate, few events push congressional approval ratings above 50 percent. Indeed, when the ratings are graphed, the two noticeable peaks are at 57 percent in 1998 and 84 percent in 2001 (Figure 11.15). In 1998, according to Gallup polling, the rise in approval accompanied a similar rise in other mood measures, including President Bill Clinton's approval ratings and general satisfaction with the state of the country and the economy. In 2001, approval spiked after the September 11 terrorist attacks and the Bush administration launched the "War on Terror," sending troops first to Afghanistan and later to Iraq. War has the power to bring majorities of voters to view their Congress and president in an overwhelmingly positive way.[34]

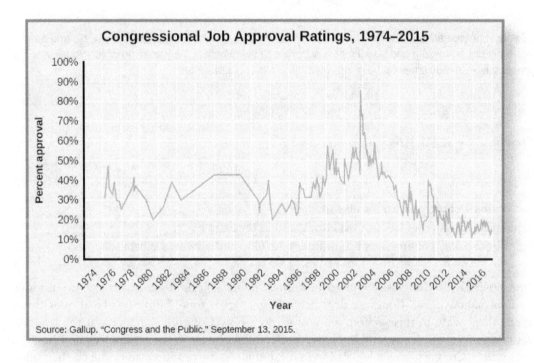

Figure 11.15 Congress's job approval rating reached a high of 84 percent in October 2001 following the 9/11 terrorist attacks. It has declined fairly steadily ever since, reaching a low of 9 percent in November 2013, just after the federal government shutdown in the previous month.

Nevertheless, all things being equal, citizens tend to rate Congress more highly when things get done and more poorly when things do not get done. For example, during the first half of President Obama's first term, Congress's approval rating reached a relative high of about 40 percent. Both houses were dominated by members of the president's own party, and many people were eager for Congress to take action to end the deep recession and begin to repair the economy. Millions were suffering economically, out of work, or losing their jobs, and the idea that Congress was busy passing large stimulus packages, working on finance reform, and grilling unpopular bank CEOs and financial titans appealed to many. Approval began to fade as the Republican Party slowed the wheels of Congress during the tumultuous debates over Obamacare and reached a low of 9 percent following the federal government shutdown in October 2013.

One of the events that began the approval rating's downward trend was Congress's divisive debate over national deficits. A deficit is what results when Congress spends more than it has available. It then conducts additional deficit spending by increasing the national debt. Many modern economists contend that during periods of economic decline, the nation should run deficits, because additional government spending has a stimulative effect that can help restart a sluggish economy. Despite this benefit, voters rarely appreciate deficits. They see Congress as spending wastefully during a time when they themselves are cutting costs to get by.

The disconnect between the common public perception of running a deficit and its legitimate policy goals is frequently exploited for political advantage. For example, while running for the presidency in 2008, Barack Obama slammed the deficit spending of the George W. Bush presidency, saying it was "unpatriotic." This sentiment echoed complaints Democrats had been issuing for years as a weapon against President Bush's policies. Following the election of President Obama and the Democratic takeover of the Senate, the concern over deficit spending shifted parties, with Republicans championing a spendthrift policy as a way of resisting Democratic policies.

Link to Learning

Find your representative at the U.S. House website (https://openstax.org/l/29FndHReps) and then explore his or her website and social media accounts to see whether the issues on which your representative spends time are the ones you think are most appropriate.

11.4 House and Senate Organizations

Learning Objectives

By the end of this section, you will be able to:
- Explain the division of labor in the House and in the Senate
- Describe the way congressional committees develop and advance legislation

Not all the business of Congress involves bickering, political infighting, government shutdowns, and Machiavellian maneuvering. Congress does actually get work done. Traditionally, it does this work in a very methodical way. In this section, we will explore how Congress functions at the leadership and committee levels. We will learn how the party leadership controls their conferences and how the many committees within Congress create legislation that can then be moved forward or die on the floor.

PARTY LEADERSHIP

The party leadership in Congress controls the actions of Congress. Leaders are elected by the two-party conferences in each chamber. In the House of Representatives, these are the House Democratic Conference and the House Republican Conference. These conferences meet regularly and separately not only to elect their leaders but also to discuss important issues and strategies for moving policy forward. Based on the number of members in each conference, one conference becomes the majority conference and the other becomes the minority conference. Independents like Senator Bernie Sanders will typically join one or the other major party conference, as a matter of practicality and often based on ideological affinity. Without the membership to elect their own leadership, independents would have a very difficult time getting things done in Congress unless they had a relationship with the leaders.

Despite the power of the conferences, however, the most important leadership position in the House is actually elected by the entire body of representatives. This position is called the **Speaker of the House** and is the only House officer mentioned in the Constitution. The Constitution does not require the Speaker to be a member of the House, although to date, all fifty-four Speakers have been. The Speaker is the presiding officer, the administrative head of the House, the partisan leader of the majority party in the House, and an elected representative of a single congressional district (**Figure 11.16**). As a testament to the importance of the Speaker, since 1947, the holder of this position has been second in line to succeed the president in an emergency, after the vice president.

(a)   (b)

Figure 11.16   Republican Mitch McConnell of Kentucky (a), the majority leader in the Senate, and Democrat Nancy Pelosi of California (b), the Speaker of the House, are the most powerful congressional leaders in their respective chambers.

The Speaker serves until his or her party loses, or until he or she is voted out of the position or chooses to step down. Republican Speaker John Boehner became the latest Speaker to walk away from the position when it appeared his position was in jeopardy. This event shows how the party conference (or caucus) oversees the leadership as much as, if not more than, the leadership oversees the party membership in the chamber. The Speaker is invested with quite a bit of power, such as the ability to assign bills to committees and decide when a bill will be presented to the floor for a vote. The Speaker also rules on House procedures, often delegating authority for certain duties to other members. He or she appoints members and chairs to committees, creates **select committees** to fulfill a specific purpose and then disband, and can even select a member to be speaker *pro tempore*, who acts as Speaker in the Speaker's absence. Finally, when the Senate joins the House in a joint session, the Speaker presides over these sessions, because they are usually held in the House of Representatives.

Below the Speaker, the majority and minority conferences each elect two leadership positions arranged in hierarchical order. At the top of the hierarchy are the floor leaders of each party. These are generally referred to as the majority and minority leaders. The **minority leader** has a visible if not always a powerful position. As the official leader of the opposition, he or she technically holds the rank closest to that of the Speaker, makes strategy decisions, and attempts to keep order within the minority. However, the majority rules the day in the House, like a cartel. On the majority side, because it holds the speakership, the **majority leader** also has considerable power. Historically, moreover, the majority leader tends to be in the best position to assume the speakership when the current Speaker steps down.

Below these leaders are the two party's respective **whips**. A whip's job, as the name suggests, is to whip up votes and otherwise enforce party discipline. Whips make the rounds in Congress, telling members the position of the leadership and the collective voting strategy, and sometimes they wave various carrots and sticks in front of recalcitrant members to bring them in line. The remainder of the leadership positions in the House include a handful of chairs and assistantships.

Like the House, the Senate also has majority and minority leaders and whips, each with duties very similar to those of their counterparts in the House. Unlike the House, however, the Senate doesn't have a Speaker. The duties and powers held by the Speaker in the House fall to the majority leader in the Senate. Another difference is that, according to the U.S. Constitution, the Senate's president is actually the elected vice president of the United States, but he or she may vote only in case of a tie. Apart from this and very few other exceptions, the president of the Senate does not actually operate in the Senate. Instead, the Constitution allows for the Senate to choose a **president** *pro tempore*—usually the most senior senator of the majority party—who presides over the Senate. Despite the title, the job is largely a formal and powerless role. The real power in the Senate is in the hands of the majority leader (Figure 11.16) and the minority leader. Like the Speaker of the House, the majority leader is the chief spokesperson for the majority party, but unlike in the House he or she does not run the floor alone. Because of the traditions of unlimited debate and the filibuster, the majority and minority leaders often occupy the floor together in an attempt to keep things moving along. At times, their interactions are intense and partisan, but for the Senate to get things done, they must cooperate to get the sixty votes needed to run this super-majority legislative institution.

THE COMMITTEE SYSTEM

With 535 members in Congress and a seemingly infinite number of domestic, international, economic, agricultural, regulatory, criminal, and military issues to deal with at any given moment, the two chambers must divide their work based on specialization. Congress does this through the committee system. Specialized committees (or subcommittees) in both the House and the Senate are where bills originate and most of the work that sets the congressional agenda takes place. Committees are roughly approximate to a bureaucratic department in the executive branch. There are well over two hundred committees, subcommittees, select committees, and joint committees in the Congress. The core committees are called **standing committees**. There are twenty standing committees in the House and sixteen in the Senate (Table 11.2).

Congressional Standing and Permanent Select Committees

House of Representatives	Senate
Agriculture	Agriculture, Nutrition, and Forestry
Appropriations	Appropriations
Armed Services	Armed Services
Budget	Banking, Housing, and Urban Affairs
Education and Labor	Budget
Energy and Commerce	Commerce, Science, and Transportation
Ethics	Energy and Natural Resources
Financial Services	Environment and Public Works
Foreign Affairs	Ethics (select)
Homeland Security	Finance
House Administration	Foreign Relations
Intelligence (select)	Health, Education, Labor and Pensions

Table 11.2

Congressional Standing and Permanent Select Committees

House of Representatives	Senate
Judiciary	Homeland Security and Governmental Affairs
Natural Resources	Indian Affairs
Oversight and Government Reform	Intelligence (select)
Rules	Judiciary
Science, Space, and Technology	Rules and Administration
Small Business	Small Business and Entrepreneurship
Transportation and Infrastructure	Veterans' Affairs
Veterans' Affairs	
Ways and Means	

Table 11.2

Members of both parties compete for positions on various committees. These positions are typically filled by majority and minority members to roughly approximate the ratio of majority to minority members in the respective chambers, although committees are chaired by members of the majority party. Committees and their chairs have a lot of power in the legislative process, including the ability to stop a bill from going to the floor (the full chamber) for a vote. Indeed, most bills die in committee. But when a committee is eager to develop legislation, it takes a number of methodical steps. It will reach out to relevant agencies for comment on resolutions to the problem at hand, such as by holding hearings with experts to collect information. In the Senate, committee hearings are also held to confirm presidential appointments (Figure 11.17). After the information has been collected, the committee meets to discuss amendments and legislative language. Finally, the committee will send the bill to the full chamber along with a committee report. The report provides the majority opinion about why the bill should be passed, a minority view to the contrary, and estimates of the proposed law's cost and impact.

Figure 11.17 On July 13, 2009, Supreme Court justice Sonia Sotomayor began the first day of her confirmation hearings before the U.S. Senate Committee on the Judiciary. The Senate Judiciary Committee is one of the oldest of the sixteen standing committees in the Senate.

Four types of committees exist in the House and the Senate. The first is the standing, or permanent, committee. This committee is the first call for proposed bills, fewer than 10 percent of which are reported out of committee to the floor. The second type is the **joint committee**. Joint committee members are appointed from both the House and the Senate, and are charged with exploring a few key issues, such as the economy and taxation. However, joint committees have no bill-referral authority whatsoever—they are informational only. A **conference committee** is used to reconcile different bills passed in both the House and the Senate. The conference committees are appointed on an ad hoc basis as necessary when a bill passes the House and Senate in different forms. Conference committees are sometimes skipped in the interest of expedience, in which one of the chambers relents to the other chamber. For example, the House demurred to the Senate over the Affordable Care Act instead of going to battle in a conference committee. Still, conference committees are the norm on most major pieces of legislation. A recent example is the Tax Cuts and Jobs Act of 2017, passed in December. Finally, ad hoc, special, or select committees are temporary committees set up to address specific topics. These types of committees often conduct special investigations, such as on aging or ethics.

Committee hearings can become politically driven public spectacles. Consider the House Select Committee on Benghazi, the committee assembled by Republicans to further investigate the 2011 attacks on the U.S. Consulate in Benghazi, Libya. This prolonged investigation became particularly partisan as Republicans trained their guns on then-secretary of state Hillary Clinton, who was running for the presidency at the time. In two multi-hour hearings in which Secretary Clinton was the only witness, Republicans tended to grandstand in the hopes of gaining political advantage or tripping her up, while Democrats tended to use their time to ridicule Republicans (Figure 11.18).[35] In the end, the long hearings uncovered little more than the elevated state of partisanship in the House, which had scarcely been a secret before.

Figure 11.18 On October 22, 2015, former Secretary of State Hillary Clinton testified for the second time before the House Select Committee on Benghazi, answering questions from members for more than eight hours.

Members of Congress bring to their roles a variety of specific experiences, interests, and levels of expertise, and try to match these to committee positions. For example, House members from states with large agricultural interests will typically seek positions on the Agriculture Committee. Senate members with a background in banking or finance may seek positions on the Senate Finance Committee. Members can request these positions from their chambers' respective leadership, and the leadership also selects the committee chairs.

Committee chairs are very powerful. They control the committee's budget and choose when the committee will meet, when it will hold hearings, and even whether it will consider a bill (Figure 11.19). A chair can convene a meeting when members of the minority are absent or adjourn a meeting when things are not progressing as the majority leadership wishes. Chairs can hear a bill even when the rest of the committee objects. They do not remain in these powerful positions indefinitely, however. In the House, rules prevent committee chairs from serving more than six consecutive years and from serving as the chair of a subcommittee at the same time. A senator may serve only six years as chair of a committee but may, in some instances, also serve as a chair or ranking member of another committee.

(a)   (b)

Figure 11.19 In 2016, Republican Chuck Grassley of Iowa (a), the chair of the Senate Judiciary Committee, refused to hold hearings on the nomination of Merrick Garland to the Supreme Court, despite the urging of his committee colleagues. In the meantime, Garland met with numerous senators, such as Republican Susan Collins of Maine (b). As of Election Day, no hearings had been held, and Garland's nomination expired on January 3, 2017. Just ten days after his inauguration, Republican president Donald Trump announced his nomination of Neil Gorsuch to the Court. Gorsuch was confirmed in April 2017, despite a filibuster by the Democrats.

Because the Senate is much smaller than the House, senators hold more committee assignments than House members. There are sixteen standing committees in the Senate, and each position must be filled. In contrast, in the House, with 435 members and only twenty standing committees, committee members have time to pursue a more in-depth review of a policy. House members historically defer to the decisions of committees, while senators tend to view committee decisions as recommendations, often seeking additional discussion that could lead to changes.

Link to Learning

Take a look at the scores of committees (https://openstax.org/l/29SenComms) in the House (https://openstax.org/l/29HosComms) and Senate. The late House Speaker Tip O'Neill once quipped that if you didn't know a new House member's name, you could just call him Mr. Chairperson.

11.5 The Legislative Process

Learning Objectives

By the end of this section, you will be able to:
- Explain the steps in the classic bill-becomes-law diagram
- Describe the modern legislative processes that alter the classic process in some way

A dry description of the function of congressional leadership and the many committees and subcommittees in Congress may suggest that the drafting and amending of legislation is a finely tuned process that has become ever more refined over the course of the last few centuries. In reality, however, committees are more likely to kill legislation than to pass it. And the last few decades have seen a dramatic transformation in the way Congress does business. Creative interpretations of rules and statues have turned small loopholes into the large gateways through which much congressional work now gets done. In this section, we will explore both the traditional legislative route by which a bill becomes a law and the modern incarnation of the process. We will also learn how and why the transformation occurred.

THE CLASSIC LEGISLATIVE PROCESS

The traditional process by which a bill becomes a law is called the *classic legislative process*. First, legislation must be drafted. Theoretically, anyone can do this. Much successful legislation has been initially drafted by someone who is not a member of Congress, such as a think tank or advocacy group, or the president. However, Congress is under no obligation to read or introduce this legislation, and only a bill introduced by a member of Congress can hope to become law. Even the president must rely on legislators to introduce his or her legislative agenda.

Technically, bills that raise revenue, like tax bills, must begin in the House. This exception is encoded within the Constitution in Article I, Section 7, which states, "All Bills for raising Revenue shall originate in the House of Representatives; but the Senate may propose or concur with amendments as on other Bills." Yet, despite the seemingly clear language of the Constitution, Congress has found ways to get around this rule.

Once legislation has been proposed, however, the majority leadership consults with the parliamentarian about which committee to send it to. Each chamber has a *parliamentarian*, an advisor, typically a trained lawyer, who has studied the long and complex rules of the chamber. While Congress typically follows the advice of its parliamentarians, it is not obligated to, and the parliamentarian has no power to enforce his or her interpretation of the rules. Once a committee has been selected, the committee chair is empowered to move the bill through the committee process as he or she sees fit. This occasionally means the chair will refer the bill to one of the committee's subcommittees.

Whether at the full committee level or in one of the subcommittees, the next step is typically to hold a hearing on the bill. If the chair decides to not hold a hearing, this is tantamount to killing the bill in committee. The hearing provides an opportunity for the committee to hear and evaluate expert opinions on the bill or aspects of it. Experts typically include officials from the agency that would be responsible for executing the bill, the bill's sponsors from Congress, and industry lobbyists, interest groups, and academic experts from a variety of relevant fields. Typically, the committee will also accept written statements from the public concerning the bill in question. For many bills, the hearing process can be very routine and straightforward.

Once hearings have been completed, the bill enters the **markup** stage. This is essentially an amending and voting process. In the end, with or without amendments, the committee or subcommittee will vote. If the committee decides not to advance the bill at that time, it is tabled. *Tabling a bill* typically means the bill is dead, but there is still an option to bring it back up for a vote again. If the committee decides to advance the bill, however, it is printed and goes to the chamber, either the House or the Senate. For the sake of example, we will assume that a bill goes first to the House (although the reverse could be true, and, in fact, bills can move simultaneously through both chambers). Before it reaches the House floor, it must first go through the House Committee on Rules. This committee establishes the rules of debate, such as time limits and limits on the number and type of amendments. After these rules have been established, the bill moves through the floor, where it is debated and amendments can be added. Once the limits of debate and amendments have been reached, the House holds a vote. If a simple majority, 50 percent plus 1, votes to advance the bill, it moves out of the House and into the Senate.

Once in the Senate, the bill is placed on the calendar so it can be debated. Or, more typically, the Senate will also consider the bill (or a companion version) in its own committees. Since the Senate is much smaller than the House, it can afford to be much more flexible in its rules for debate. Typically, senators allow each other to talk and debate as long as the speaker wants, though they can agree as a body to create time limits. But without these limits, debate continues until a motion to table has been offered and voted on.

This flexibility about speaking in the Senate gave rise to a unique tactic, the **filibuster**. The word "filibuster" comes from the Dutch word *vrijbuiter*, which means pirate. And the name is appropriate, since a senator who launches a filibuster virtually hijacks the floor of the chamber by speaking for long periods of time, thus preventing the Senate from closing debate and acting on a bill. The tactic was perfected in the 1850s as Congress wrestled with the complicated issue of slavery. After the Civil War, the use of the filibuster became even more common. Eventually, in 1917, the Senate passed Rule 22, which allowed the chamber to hold a **cloture** vote to end debate. To invoke cloture, the Senate had to get a two-thirds majority. This was difficult to do, but it generally did prevent anyone from hijacking the Senate floor, with the salient exception of Senator Strom Thurmond's record twenty-four-hour filibuster of the Civil Rights Act.

In 1975, after the heightened partisanship of the civil rights era, the Senate further weakened the filibuster by reducing the number needed for cloture from two-thirds to three-fifths, or sixty votes, where it remains today (except for judicial nominations for which only fifty-five votes are needed to invoke cloture). Moreover, filibusters are not permitted on the annual budget reconciliation act (the Reconciliation Act of 2010 was the act under which the implementing legislation for Obamacare was passed).

Milestone

The Noble History of the Filibuster?

When most people think of the Senate filibuster, they probably picture actor Jimmy Stewart standing exasperated at a podium and demanding the Senate come to its senses and do the right thing. Even for those not familiar with the classic Frank Capra film *Mr. Smith Goes to Washington*, the image of a heroic single senator sanding up to the power of the entire chamber while armed only with oratorical skill naturally tends to inspire. Unfortunately, the history of the filibuster is less heartwarming.

This is not to say that noble causes haven't been championed by filibustering senators; they most certainly have. But they have largely been overshadowed by the outright ridiculous and sometimes racist filibusters of the twentieth century. In the first category, the fifteen-and-a-half-hour marathon of Senator Huey Long of Louisiana stands out: Hoping to retain the need for Senate confirmation of some jobs he wanted to keep from his political enemies, Long spent much of his filibuster analyzing the Constitution, talking about his favorite recipes, and telling amusing stories, as was his custom.

In a defining moment for the filibuster, Senator Strom Thurmond of South Carolina spoke for twenty-four hours and eighteen minutes against a weak civil rights bill in 1957. A vocal proponent of segregation and white supremacy, Thurmond had made no secret of his views and had earlier run for the presidency on a segregationist platform. Nor was Thurmond the first to use the filibuster to preserve segregation and prevent the expansion of civil rights for African Americans. Groups of dedicated southern senators used the filibuster to prevent the passage of anti-lynching legislation on multiple occasions during the first half of the twentieth century. Later, when faced with the 1964 Civil Rights Act, southern senators staged a fifty-seven-day filibuster to try and kill it. But the momentum of the nation was against them. The bill passed over their obstructionism and helped to reduce segregation.

Is the filibuster the tool of the noble minority attempting to hold back the tide of a powerful minority? Or does its history as a weapon supporting segregation expose it as merely a tactic of obstruction?

Because both the House and the Senate can and often do amend bills, the bills that pass out of each chamber frequently look different. This presents a problem, since the Constitution requires that both chambers pass identical bills. One simple solution is for the first chamber to simply accept the bill that ultimately makes it out of the second chamber. Another solution is for first chamber to further amend the second chamber's bill and send it back to the second chamber. Congress typically takes one of these two options, but about one in every eight bills cannot be resolved in this way. These bills must be sent to a conference committee that negotiates a reconciliation both chambers can accept without amendment.

Only then can the bill progress to the president's desk for signature or veto. If the president does veto the bill, both chambers must muster a two-thirds vote to overcome the veto and make the bill law without presidential approval (Figure 11.20).

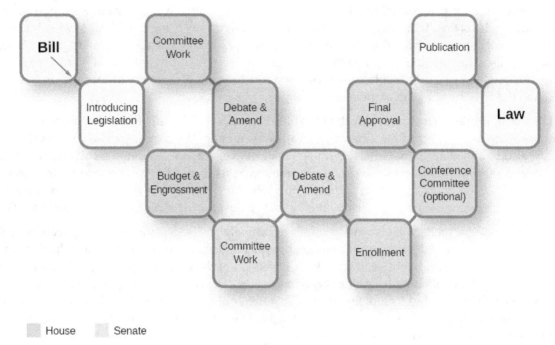

House   Senate

Figure 11.20 The process by which a bill becomes law is long and complicated, but it is designed to ensure that in the end all parties are satisfied with the bill's provisions.

Link to Learning

For one look at the classic legislative process, visit YouTube (https://openstax.org/l/29SRjaBill) to view "I'm Just a Bill" from the ABC *Schoolhouse Rock!* series.

MODERN LEGISLATION IS DIFFERENT

For much of the nation's history, the process described above was the standard method by which a bill became a law. Over the course of the last three and a half decades, however, changes in rules and procedure have created a number of alternate routes. Collectively, these different routes constitute what some political scientists have described as a new but unorthodox legislative process. According to political scientist Barbara Sinclair, the primary trigger for the shift away from the classic legislative route was the budget reforms of the 1970s. The 1974 Budget and Impoundment Control Act gave Congress a mechanism for making large, all-encompassing, budget decisions. In the years that followed, the budget process gradually became the vehicle for creating comprehensive policy changes. One large step in this transformation occurred in 1981 when President Ronald Reagan's administration suggested using the budget to push through his economic reforms.

The benefit of attaching the reforms to the budget resolution was that Congress could force an up or down (yea or nay) vote on the whole package. Such a packaged bill is called an *omnibus bill*.[36] Creating and voting for an omnibus bill allows Congress to quickly accomplish policy changes that would have taken many votes and the expending of great political capital over a long period of time. This and successive similar uses of the budget process convinced many in Congress of the utility of this strategy. During the contentious and ideologically divided 1990s, the budget process became the common problem-solving mechanism in the legislature, thus laying the groundwork for the way legislation works today.

An important characteristic feature of modern legislating is the greatly expanded power and influence of the party leadership over the control of bills. One reason for this change was the heightened partisanship that stretches back to the 1980s and is still with us today. With such high political stakes, the party leadership is reluctant to simply allow the committees to work things out on their own. In the House, the leadership uses special rules to guide bills through the legislative process and toward a particular outcome. Uncommon just a few decades ago, these now widely used rules restrict debate and options, and are designed to focus the attention of members.

The practice of multiple referrals, with which entire bills or portions of those bills are referred to more than one committee, greatly weakened the different specialization monopolies committees held primarily in the House but also to an extent in the Senate. With less control over the bills, committees naturally reached out to the leadership for assistance. Indeed, as a testament to its increasing control, the leadership may sometimes avoid committees altogether, preferring to work things out on the floor. And even when bills move through the committees, the leadership often seeks to adjust the legislation before it reaches the floor.

Another feature of the modern legislative process, exclusively in the Senate, is the application of the modern filibuster. Unlike the traditional filibuster, in which a senator took the floor and held it for as long as possible, the modern filibuster is actually a perversion of the cloture rules adopted to control the filibuster. When partisanship is high, as it has been frequently, the senators can request cloture before any bill can get a vote. This has the effect of increasing the number of votes needed for a bill to advance from a simple majority of fifty-one to a super majority of sixty. The effect is to give the Senate minority great power to obstruct if it is inclined to do so.

Link to Learning

The Library of Congress's Thomas website (https://openstax.org/l/29LibofCong) has provided scholars, citizens, and media with a bounty of readily available data on members and bills for more than two decades.

Key Terms

apportionment the process by which seats in the House of Representatives are distributed among the fifty states

bicameralism the political process that results from dividing a legislature into two separate assemblies

bill proposed legislation under consideration by a legislature

cloture a parliamentary process to end a debate in the Senate, as a measure against the filibuster; invoked when three-fifths of senators vote for the motion

collective representation the relationship between Congress and the United States as a whole, and whether the institution itself represents the American people

conference committee a special type of joint committee that reconciles different bills passed in the House and Senate so a single bill results

constituency the body of voters, or constituents, represented by a particular politician

delegate model of representation a model of representation in which representatives feel compelled to act on the specific stated wishes of their constituents

descriptive representation the extent to which a body of representatives represents the descriptive characteristics of their constituencies, such as class, race, ethnicity, and gender

enumerated powers the powers given explicitly to the federal government by the Constitution to regulate interstate and foreign commerce, raise and support armies, declare war, coin money, and conduct foreign affairs

filibuster a parliamentary maneuver used in the Senate to extend debate on a piece of legislation as long as possible, typically with the intended purpose of obstructing or killing it

implied powers the powers not specifically detailed in the U.S. Constitution but inferred as necessary to achieve the objectives of the national government

inherent powers the powers neither enumerated nor implied but assumed to exist as a direct result of the country's existence

joint committee a legislative committee consisting of members from both chambers that investigates certain topics but lacks bill referral authority

majority leader the leader of the majority party in either the House or Senate; in the House, the majority leader serves under the Speaker of the House, in the Senate, the majority leader is the functional leader and chief spokesperson for the majority party

markup the amending and voting process in a congressional committee

minority leader the party member who directs the activities of the minority party on the floor of either the House or the Senate

oversight the right to review and monitor other bodies such as the executive branch

politico model of representation a model of representation in which members of Congress act as either trustee or delegate, based on rational political calculations about who is best served, the constituency or the nation

pork-barrel politics federal spending intended to benefit a particular district or set of constituents

president *pro tempore* the senator who acts in the absence of the actual president of the Senate, who is also the vice president of the United States; the president *pro tempore* is usually the most senior senator of the majority party

representation an elected leader's looking out for his or her constituents while carrying out the duties of the office

select committee a small legislative committee created to fulfill a specific purpose and then disbanded; also called an ad hoc, or special, committee

Speaker of the House the presiding officer of the House of Representatives and the leader of the majority party; the Speaker is second in the presidential line of succession, after the vice president

standing committee a permanent legislative committee that meets regularly

surge-and-decline theory a theory proposing that the surge of stimulation occurring during presidential elections subsides during midterm elections, accounting for the differences we observe in turnouts and results

trustee model of representation a model of representation in which representatives feel at liberty to act in the way they believe is best for their constituents

whip in the House and in the Senate, a high leadership position whose primary duty is to enforce voting discipline in the chambers and conferences

Summary

11.1 The Institutional Design of Congress

The weaknesses of the Articles of Confederation convinced the member states to send delegates to a new convention to revise them. What emerged from the debates and compromises of the convention was instead a new and stronger constitution. The Constitution established a bicameral legislature, with a Senate composed of two members from each state and a House of Representatives composed of members drawn from each state in proportion to its population. Today's Senate has one hundred members representing fifty states, while membership in the House of Representatives has been capped at 435 since 1929. Apportionment in the House is based on population data collected by the U.S. Census Bureau.

The Constitution empowers Congress with enumerated, implied, and inherent powers. Enumerated powers are specifically addressed in the text of the Constitution. Implied powers are not explicitly called out but are inferred as necessary to achieve the objectives of the national goverment. Inherent powers are assumed to exist by virtue of the fact that the country exists. The power of Congress to regulate interstate and intrastate commerce has generally increased, while its power to control foreign policy has declined over the course of the twentieth century.

11.2 Congressional Elections

Since the House is closest to its constituents because reelection is so frequent a need, it tends to be more easily led by fleeting public desires. In contrast, the Senate's distance from its constituents allows it to act more deliberately. Each type of representative, however, must raise considerable sums of money in order to stay in office. Attempts by Congress to rein in campaign spending have largely failed. Nevertheless, incumbents tend to have the easiest time funding campaigns and retaining their seats. They also benefit from the way parties organize primary elections, which are designed to promote incumbency.

11.3 Congressional Representation

Some representatives follow the delegate model of representation, acting on the expressed wishes of their constituents, whereas others take a trustee model approach, acting on what they believe is in their constituents' best interests. However, most representatives combine the two approaches and apply each as political circumstances demand. The standard method by which representatives have shown their fidelity to their constituents, namely "bringing home the bacon" of favorable budget allocations, has come to be interpreted as a form of corruption, or pork-barrel politics.

Representation can also be considered in other ways. Descriptive representation is the level at which Congress reflects the nation's constituents in terms of race, ethnicity, gender, sexuality, and socioeconomic status. Collective representation is the extent to which the institutional body of Congress represents the population as a whole. Despite the incumbency advantage and high opinion many hold of their own legislators, Congress rarely earns an approval rating above 40 percent, and for a number of years the rating has been well below 20 percent.

11.4 House and Senate Organizations

The leader of the House is the Speaker, who also typically the leader of the majority party. In the Senate, the leader is called the majority leader. The minorities in each chamber also have leaders who help create and act on party strategies. The majority leadership in each chamber controls the important committees where legislature is written, amended, and prepared for the floor.

11.5 The Legislative Process

In the classic legislative process, bills are introduced and sent to the appropriate committee. Within the committees, hearings are held and the bill is debated and ultimately sent to the floor of the chamber. On the floor, the bill is debated and amended until passed or voted down. If passed, it moves to the second chamber where the debating and amending begins anew. Eventually, if the bill makes it that far, the two chambers meet in a joint committee to reconcile what are now two different bills. Over the last few decades, however, Congress has adopted a very different process whereby large pieces of legislation covering many different items are passed through the budgeting process. This method has had the effect of further empowering the leadership, to the detriment of the committees. The modern legislative process has also been affected by the increasing number of filibuster threats in the Senate and the use of cloture to forestall them.

Review Questions

1. The Great Compromise successfully resolved differences between _____.
- a. large and small states
- b. slave and non-slave states
- c. the Articles of Confederation and the Constitution
- d. the House and the Senate

2. While each state has two senators, members of the House are apportioned _____.
- a. according to the state's geographic size
- b. based on the state's economic size
- c. according to the state's population
- d. based on each state's need

3. The process of redistricting can present problems for congressional representation because _____.
- a. districts must include urban and rural areas
- b. states can gain but never lose districts
- c. districts are often drawn to benefit partisan groups
- d. states have been known to create more districts than they have been apportioned

4. Which of the following is an implied power of Congress?
   a. the power to regulate the sale of tobacco in the states
   b. the power to increase taxes on the wealthiest one percent
   c. the power to put the president on trial for high crimes
   d. the power to override a presidential veto

5. Briefly explain the benefits and drawbacks of a bicameral system.

6. What are some examples of the enumerated powers granted to Congress in the Constitution?

7. Why does a strong presidency necessarily sap power from Congress?

8. Senate races tend to inspire _____.
   a. broad discussion of policy issues
   b. narrow discussion of specific policy issues
   c. less money than House races
   d. less media coverage than House races

9. The saying "All politics is local" roughly means _____.
   a. the local candidate will always win
   b. the local constituents want action on national issues
   c. the local constituents tend to care about things that affect them
   d. the act of campaigning always occurs at the local level where constituents are

10. What does Campbell's surge-and-decline theory suggest about the outcome of midterm elections?

11. Explain the factors that make it difficult to oust incumbents.

12. A congressperson who pursued a strict delegate model of representation would seek to _____.
   a. legislate in the way he or she believed constituents wanted, regardless of the anticipated outcome
   b. legislate in a way that carefully considered the circumstances and issue so as to reach a solution that is best for everyone
   c. legislate in a way that is best for the nation regardless of the costs for the constituents
   d. legislate in the way that he or she thinks is best for the constituents

13. The increasing value constituents have placed on descriptive representation in Congress has had the effect of _____.
   a. increasing the sensitivity representatives have to their constituents demands
   b. decreasing the rate at which incumbents are elected
   c. increasing the number of minority members in Congress
   d. decreasing the number of majority minority districts

14. How has the growing interpretation of earmarks and other budget allocations as corruption influenced the way congresspersons work?

15. What does polling data suggest about the events that trigger exceptionally high congressional approval ratings?

16. House leaders are more powerful than Senate leaders because of _____.
   a. the majoritarian nature of the House—a majority can run it like a cartel
   b. the larger size of the House
   c. the constitutional position of the House
   d. the State of the Union address being delivered in the House chamber

17. A select committee is different from a standing committee because _____.
   a. a select committee includes member of both chambers, while a standing committee includes only members of the House
   b. a select committee is used for bill reconciliation, while a standing committee is used for prosecutions
   c. a select committee must stay in session, while a standing committee goes to recess
   d. a select committee is convened for a specific and temporary purpose, while a standing committee is permanent

18. Explain how the committees demonstrate a division of labor in Congress based on specialization.

19. Stopping a filibuster requires that _____.
   a. a majority of senators agree on the bill
   b. the speaker steps away from the podium
   c. the chamber votes for cloture
   d. the Speaker or majority leader intervenes

20. Saying a bill is being marked up is just another way to say it is being _____.
   a. tabled
   b. neglected
   c. vetoed
   d. amended

21. The key means of advancing modern legislation is now _____.
   a. committees
   b. the actions of the leadership
   c. the budget process
   d. the filibuster

22. Briefly explain the difference between the classic model of legislating and the modern process.

Critical Thinking Questions

23. The framers of the Constitution designed the Senate to filter the output of the sometimes hasty House. Do you think this was a wise idea? Why or why not?

24. Congress has consistently expanded its own power to regulate commerce among and between the states. Should Congress have this power or should the Supreme Court reel it in? Why?

25. What does the trend toward descriptive representation suggest about what constituents value in their legislature? How might Congress overcome the fact that such representation does not always best serve constituents' interests?

26. What factors contributed most to the transformation away from the classic legislative process and toward the new style?

Suggestions for Further Study

Books:

Binder, Sarah A. 1997. *Minority Rights, Majority Rule: Partisanship and the Development of Congress.* Cambridge, UK: Cambridge University Press.

Davidson, Roger H. and Walter J. Oleszek. 1981. *Congress and Its Members.* Washington, DC: Congressional Quarterly Press.

Dodd, Lawrence C. and Bruce Ian Oppenheimer. 1981. *Congress Reconsidered.* Washington, DC: Congressional Quarterly Press.

Hofstadter, Richard. 1965. *The Paranoid Style in American Politics, and Other Essays.* New York: Knopf.

Mann, Thomas E. and Norman J. Ornstein. 2012. *It's Even Worse Than It Looks: How the American Constitutional System Collided with the New Politics of Extremism*. New York: Basic Books.

Mayhew, David R. 1974. *Congress: The Electoral Connection*. New Haven, CT: Yale University Press.

Mutch, Robert E. 2014. *Buying the Vote: A History of Campaign Finance Reform*. Oxford: Oxford University Press.

Oleszek, Walter J. 1978. *Congressional Procedures and the Policy Process*. Washington: Congressional Quarterly Press.

Sinclair, Barbara. 1997. *Unorthodox Lawmaking: New Legislative Processes in the U.S. Congress*. Washington, DC: CQ Press.

Films:

1939. *Mr. Smith Goes to Washington*.

1957. *A Face in the Crowd*.

1962. *Advise and Consent*.

1972. *The Candidate*.

Chapter 12

The Presidency

Figure 12.1 On January 20, 2009, crowds of people waited on the National Mall in the cold to see the inauguration of Barack Obama. (credit left: modification of work by Teddy Wade; credit right: modification of work by Cecilio Ricardo)

Chapter Outline

12.1 The Design and Evolution of the Presidency

12.2 The Presidential Election Process

12.3 Organizing to Govern

12.4 The Public Presidency

12.5 Presidential Governance: Direct Presidential Action

Introduction

The presidency is the most visible position in the U.S. government (Figure 12.1). During the Constitutional Convention of 1787, delegates accepted the need to empower a relatively strong and vigorous chief executive. But they also wanted this chief executive to be bound by checks from the other branches of the federal government as well as by the Constitution itself. Over time, the power of the presidency has grown in response to circumstances and challenges. However, to this day, a president must still work with the other branches to be most effective. Unilateral actions, in which the president acts alone on important and consequential matters, such as President Barack Obama's strategy on the Iran nuclear deal, are bound to be controversial and suggest potentially serious problems within the federal government. Effective presidents, especially in peacetime, are those who work with the other branches through persuasion and compromise to achieve policy objectives.

What are the powers, opportunities, and limitations of the presidency? How does the chief executive lead in our contemporary political system? What guides his or her actions, including unilateral actions? If it is most effective to work with others to get things done, how does the president do so? What can get in the way of this goal? This chapter answers these and other questions about the nation's most visible leader.

12.1 The Design and Evolution of the Presidency

Learning Objectives

By the end of this section, you will be able to:

- Explain the reason for the design of the executive branch and its plausible alternatives
- Analyze the way presidents have expanded presidential power and why
- Identify the limitations on a president's power

Since its invention at the Constitutional Convention of 1787, the presidential office has gradually become more powerful, giving its occupants a far-greater chance to exercise leadership at home and abroad. The role of the chief executive has changed over time, as various presidents have confronted challenges in domestic and foreign policy in times of war as well as peace, and as the power of the federal government has grown.

INVENTING THE PRESIDENCY

The Articles of Confederation made no provision for an executive branch, although they did use the term "president" to designate the presiding officer of the Confederation Congress, who also handled other administrative duties.[1] The presidency was proposed early in the Constitutional Convention in Philadelphia by Virginia's Edmund Randolph, as part of James Madison's proposal for a federal government, which became known as the Virginia Plan. Madison offered a rather sketchy outline of the executive branch, leaving open whether what he termed the "national executive" would be an individual or a set of people. He proposed that Congress select the executive, whose powers and authority, and even length of term of service, were left largely undefined. He also proposed a "council of revision" consisting of the national executive and members of the national judiciary, which would review laws passed by the legislature and have the power of veto.[2]

Early deliberations produced agreement that the executive would be a single person, elected for a single term of seven years by the legislature, empowered to veto legislation, and subject to impeachment and removal by the legislature. New Jersey's William Paterson offered an alternate model as part of his proposal, typically referred to as the small-state or New Jersey Plan. This plan called for merely amending the Articles of Confederation to allow for an executive branch made up of a committee elected by a unicameral Congress for a single term. Under this proposal, the executive committee would be particularly weak because it could be removed from power at any point if a majority of state governors so desired. Far more extreme was Alexander Hamilton's suggestion that the executive power be entrusted to a single individual. This individual would be chosen by electors, would serve for life, and would exercise broad powers, including the ability to veto legislation, the power to negotiate treaties and grant pardons in all cases except treason, and the duty to serve as commander-in-chief of the armed forces (Figure 12.2).

(a)   (b)

Figure 12.2   Alexander Hamilton (a), who had served under General George Washington (b) during the Revolutionary War, argued for a strong executive in *Federalist* No. 70. Indeed, ten other *Federalist Papers* discuss the role of the presidency.

Debate and discussion continued throughout the summer. Delegates eventually settled upon a single executive, but they remained at a loss for how to select that person. Pennsylvania's James Wilson, who had triumphed on the issue of a single executive, at first proposed the direct election of the president. When delegates rejected that idea, he responded with the suggestion that electors, chosen throughout the nation, should select the executive. Over time, Wilson's idea gained ground with delegates who were uneasy at the idea of an election by the legislature, which presented the opportunity for intrigue and corruption. The idea of a shorter term of service combined with eligibility for reelection also became more attractive to delegates. The framers of the Constitution struggled to find the proper balance between giving the president the power to perform the job on one hand and opening the way for a president to abuse power and act like a monarch on the other.

By early September, the Electoral College had emerged as the way to select a president for four years who was eligible for reelection. This process is discussed more fully in the chapter on elections. Today, the Electoral College consists of a body of 538 people called electors, each representing one of the fifty states or the District of Columbia, who formally cast votes for the election of the president and vice president (Figure 12.3). In forty-eight states and the District of Columbia, the candidate who wins the popular vote in November receives all the state's electoral votes. In two states, Nebraska and Maine, the electoral votes are divided: The candidate who wins the popular vote in the state gets two electoral votes, but the winner of each congressional district also receives an electoral vote.

Figure 12.3 This map shows the distribution by state of delegate votes available in the 2016 national election. The number of Electoral College votes granted to each state equals the total number of representatives and senators that state has in the U.S. Congress or, in the case of Washington, DC, as many electors as it would have if it were a state. The number of representatives may fluctuate based on state population, which is determined every ten years by the U.S. Census.

In the original design implemented for the first four presidential elections (1788–89, 1792, 1796, and 1800), the electors cast two ballots (but only one could go to a candidate from the elector's state), and the person who received a majority won the election. The second-place finisher became vice president. Should no candidate receive a majority of the votes cast, the House of Representatives would select the president, with each state casting a single vote, while the Senate chose the vice president.

While George Washington was elected president twice with this approach, the design resulted in controversy in both the 1796 and 1800 elections. In 1796, John Adams won the presidency, while his opponent and political rival Thomas Jefferson was elected vice president. In 1800, Thomas Jefferson and his running mate Aaron Burr finished tied in the Electoral College. Jefferson was elected president in the House of Representatives on the thirty-sixth ballot. These controversies led to the proposal and ratification of the Twelfth Amendment, which couples a particular presidential candidate with that candidate's running mate in a unified ticket.[3]

For the last two centuries or so, the Twelfth Amendment has worked fairly well. But this doesn't mean the arrangement is foolproof. For example, the amendment created a separate ballot for the vice president but left the rules for electors largely intact. One of those rules states that the two votes the electors cast cannot both be for "an inhabitant of the same state with themselves."[4] This rule means that an elector from, say, Louisiana, could not cast votes for a presidential candidate and a vice presidential candidate who were both from Louisiana; that elector could vote for only one of these people. The intent of the rule was to encourage electors from powerful states to look for a more diverse pool of candidates. But what would happen in a close election where the members of the winning ticket were both from the same state?

The nation almost found out in 2000. In the presidential election of that year, the Republican ticket won the election by a very narrow electoral margin. To win the presidency or vice presidency, a candidate must get 270 electoral votes (a majority). George W. Bush and Dick Cheney won by the skin of their teeth with just 271. Both, however, were living in Texas. This should have meant that Texas's 32 electoral votes could have gone to only one or the other. Cheney anticipated this problem and had earlier registered to vote in Wyoming, where he was originally from and where he had served as a representative years earlier.[5] It's hard to imagine that the 2000 presidential election could have been even more complicated than it was, but thanks to that seemingly innocuous rule in Article II of the Constitution, that was a real possibility.

Despite provisions for the election of a vice president (to serve in case of the president's death, resignation, or removal through the impeachment process), and apart from the suggestion that the vice president should be responsible for presiding over the Senate, the framers left the vice president's role undeveloped. As a result, the influence of the vice presidency has varied dramatically, depending on how much of a role the vice president is given by the president. Some vice presidents, such as Dan Quayle under President George H. W. Bush, serve a mostly ceremonial function, while others, like Dick Cheney under President George W. Bush, become a partner in governance and rival the White House chief of staff in terms of influence.

Link to Learning

Read about **James Madison's evolving views (https://openstax.org/l/29JMpres)** of the presidency and the Electoral College.

In addition to describing the process of election for the presidency and vice presidency, the delegates to the Constitutional Convention also outlined who was eligible for election and how Congress might remove the president. Article II of the Constitution lays out the agreed-upon requirements—the chief executive must be at least thirty-five years old and a "natural born" citizen of the United States (or a citizen at the time of the Constitution's adoption) who has been an inhabitant of the United States for at least fourteen years.[6] While Article II also states that the term of office is four years and does not expressly limit the number of times a person might be elected president, after Franklin D. Roosevelt was elected four times (from 1932 to 1944), the Twenty-Second Amendment was proposed and ratified, limiting the presidency to two four-year terms.

An important means of ensuring that no president could become tyrannical was to build into the Constitution a clear process for removing the chief executive—**impeachment**. Impeachment is the act of charging a government official with serious wrongdoing; the Constitution calls this wrongdoing high crimes and misdemeanors. The method the framers designed required two steps and both chambers of the Congress. First, the House of Representatives could impeach the president by a simple majority vote. In the second step, the Senate could remove him or her from office by a two-thirds majority, with the chief justice of the Supreme Court presiding over the trial. Upon conviction and removal of the president, if that occurred, the vice president would become president.

Three presidents have faced impeachment proceedings in the House; none has been both impeached by the House and removed by the Senate. In the wake of the Civil War, President Andrew Johnson faced congressional contempt for decisions made during Reconstruction. President Richard Nixon faced an overwhelming likelihood of impeachment in the House for his cover-up of key information relating to the 1972 break-in at the Democratic Party's campaign headquarters at the Watergate hotel and apartment complex. Nixon likely would have also been removed by the Senate, since there was strong bipartisan consensus for his impeachment and removal. Instead, he resigned before the House and Senate could exercise their constitutional prerogatives.

The most recent impeachment was of President Bill Clinton, brought on by his lying about an extramarital affair with a White House intern named Monica Lewinsky. House Republicans felt the affair and Clinton's initial public denial of it rose to a level of wrongdoing worthy of impeachment. House Democrats believed it fell short of an impeachable offense and that a simply censure made better sense. Clinton's trial in the Senate went nowhere because too few Senators wanted to move forward with removing the president.

Thus, impeachment remains a rare event indeed and removal has never occurred. Still, the fact that a president could be impeached and removed is an important reminder of the role of the executive in the broader system of shared powers. The same outcome occurred in the case of Andrew Johnson in the nineteenth century though he came closer to the threshold of votes needed for removal than did Clinton.

The Constitution that emerged from the deliberations in Philadelphia treated the powers of the presidency in concise fashion. The president was to be commander-in-chief of the armed forces of the United States, negotiate treaties with the advice and consent of the Senate, and receive representatives of foreign nations (Figure 12.4). Charged to "take care that the laws be faithfully executed," the president was given broad power to pardon those convicted of federal offenses, except for officials removed through the impeachment process.[7] The chief executive would present to Congress information about the state of the union; call Congress into session when needed; veto legislation if necessary, although a two-thirds supermajority in both houses of Congress could override that veto; and make recommendations for legislation and policy as well as call on the heads of various departments to make reports and offer opinions.

Figure 12.4 During visits from foreign heads of state, the president of the United States is often surrounded by representatives of the military, a symbol of the president's dual role as head of state and commander-in-chief. Here, President Barack Obama delivers remarks during a welcoming ceremony for Angela Merkel, chancellor of the Federal Republic of Germany. (credit: Stephen Hassay)

Finally, the president's job included nominating federal judges, including Supreme Court justices, as well as other federal officials, and making appointments to fill military and diplomatic posts. The number of judicial appointments and nominations of other federal officials is great. In recent decades, two-term presidents have nominated well over three hundred federal judges while in office.[8] Moreover, new presidents nominate close to five hundred top officials to their Executive Office of the President, key agencies (such as the Department of Justice), and regulatory commissions (such as the Federal Reserve Board), whose appointments require Senate majority approval.[9]

THE EVOLVING EXECUTIVE BRANCH

No sooner had the presidency been established than the occupants of the office, starting with George Washington, began acting in ways that expanded both its formal and informal powers. For example, Washington established a **cabinet** or group of advisors to help him administer his duties, consisting of the most senior appointed officers of the executive branch. Today, the heads of the fifteen executive departments serve as the president's advisers.[10] And, in 1793, when it became important for the United States to take a stand in the evolving European conflicts between France and other European powers, especially Great Britain, Washington issued a neutrality proclamation that extended his rights as diplomat-in-chief far more broadly than had at first been conceived.

Later presidents built on the foundation of these powers. Some waged undeclared wars, as John Adams did against the French in the Quasi-War (1798–1800). Others agreed to negotiate for significant territorial gains, as Thomas Jefferson did when he oversaw the purchase of Louisiana from France. Concerned that he might be violating the powers of the office, Jefferson rationalized that his not facing impeachment charges constituted Congress's tacit approval of his actions. James Monroe used his annual message in 1823 to declare that the United States would consider it an intolerable act of aggression for European powers to intervene in the affairs of the nations of the Western Hemisphere. Later dubbed the Monroe Doctrine, this declaration of principles laid the foundation for the growth of American power in the twentieth century. Andrew Jackson employed the veto as a measure of policy to block legislative initiatives with which he did not agree and acted unilaterally when it came to depositing federal funds in several local banks around the country instead of in the Bank of the United States. This move changed the way vetoes would be used in the future. Jackson's twelve vetoes were more than those of all prior presidents combined, and he issued them due to policy disagreements (their basis today) rather than as a legal tool to protect against encroachments by Congress on the president's powers.

Of the many ways in which the chief executive's power grew over the first several decades, the most significant was the expansion of presidential war powers. While Washington, Adams, and Jefferson led the way in waging undeclared wars, it was President James K. Polk who truly set the stage for the broad growth of this authority. In 1846, as the United States and Mexico were bickering over the messy issue of where Texas's southern border lay, Polk purposely raised anxieties and ruffled feathers through his envoy in Mexico. He then responded to the newly heightened state of affairs by sending U.S. troops to the Rio Grande, the border Texan expansionists claimed for Texas. Mexico sent troops in response, and the Mexican-American War began soon afterward.[11]

Abraham Lincoln, a member of Congress at the time, was critical of Polk's actions. Later, however, as president himself, Lincoln used presidential war powers and the concepts of military necessity and national security to undermine the Confederate effort to seek independence for the Southern states. In suspending the privilege of the writ of habeas corpus, Lincoln blurred the boundaries between acceptable dissent and unacceptable disloyalty. He also famously used a unilateral proclamation to issue the Emancipation Proclamation, which cited the military necessity of declaring millions of slaves in Confederate-controlled territory to be free. His successor, Andrew Johnson, became so embroiled with Radical Republicans about ways to implement Reconstruction policies and programs after the Civil War that the House of Representatives impeached him, although the legislators in the Senate were unable to successfully remove him from office.[12]

Over the course of the twentieth century, presidents expanded and elaborated upon these powers. The rather vague wording in Article II, which says that the "executive power shall be vested" in the president, has been subject to broad and sweeping interpretation in order to justify actions beyond those specifically enumerated in the document.[13] As the federal bureaucracy expanded, so too did the president's power to grow agencies like the Secret Service and the Federal Bureau of Investigation. Presidents also further developed the concept of **executive privilege**, the right to withhold information from Congress, the judiciary, or the public. This right, not enumerated in the Constitution, was first asserted by George Washington to curtail inquiry into the actions of the executive branch.[14] The more general defense of its use by White House officials and attorneys ensures that the president can secure candid advice from his or her advisors and staff members.

Increasingly over time, presidents have made more use of their unilateral powers, including **executive orders**, rules that bypass Congress but still have the force of law if the courts do not overturn them. More recently, presidents have offered their own interpretation of legislation as they sign it via signing statements (discussed later in this chapter) directed to the bureaucratic entity charged with implementation. In the realm of foreign policy, Congress permitted the widespread use of **executive agreements** to formalize international relations, so long as important matters still came through the Senate in the form of treaties.[15] Recent presidents have continued to rely upon an ever more expansive definition of war powers to act unilaterally at home and abroad. Finally, presidents, often with Congress's blessing through the formal delegation of authority, have taken the lead in framing budgets, negotiating budget compromises, and at times impounding funds in an effort to prevail in matters of policy.

Milestone

The Budget and Accounting Act of 1921

Developing a budget in the nineteenth century was a chaotic mess. Unlike the case today, in which the budgeting process is centrally controlled, Congresses in the nineteenth century developed a budget in a piecemeal process. Federal agencies independently submitted budget requests to Congress, and these requests were then considered through the congressional committee process. Because the government was relatively small in the first few decades of the republic, this approach was sufficient. However, as the size and complexity of the U.S. economy grew over the course of the nineteenth century, the traditional congressional budgeting process was unable to keep up.[16]

Things finally came to a head following World War I, when federal spending and debt skyrocketed. Reformers proposed the solution of putting the executive branch in charge of developing a budget that could be scrutinized, amended, and approved by Congress. However, President Woodrow Wilson, owing to a provision tacked onto the bill regarding presidential appointments, vetoed the legislation that would have transformed the budgeting process in this way. His successor, Warren Harding, felt differently and signed the Budget and Accounting Act of 1921. The act gave the president first-mover advantage in the budget process via the first "executive budget." It also created the first-ever budget staff at the disposal of a president, at the time called the Bureau of the Budget but decades later renamed the Office of Management and Budget (Figure 12.5). With this act, Congress willingly delegated significant authority to the executive and made the president the chief budget agenda setter.

Figure 12.5 In December 1936, the House Appropriations Committee hears Secretary of Treasury Henry Morgenthau, Jr. (bottom, left) and Acting Director of the Budget Daniel Bell (top, right) on the federal finances. (credit: modification of work by the Library of Congress)

The Budget Act of 1921 effectively shifted some congressional powers to the president. Why might Congress have felt it important to centralize the budgeting process in the executive branch? What advantages could the executive branch have over the legislative branch in this regard?

The growth of presidential power is also attributable to the growth of the United States and the power of the national government. As the nation has grown and developed, so has the office. Whereas most important decisions were once made at the state and local levels, the increasing complexity and size of the domestic economy have led people in the United States to look to the federal government more often for solutions. At the same time, the rising profile of the United States on the international stage has meant that the president is a far more important figure as leader of the nation, as diplomat-in-chief, and as commander-in-chief. Finally, with the rise of electronic mass media, a president who once depended on newspapers and official documents to distribute information beyond an immediate audience can now bring that message directly to the people via radio, television, and social media. Major events and crises, such as the Great Depression, two world wars, the Cold War, and the war on terrorism, have further contributed to presidential stature.

12.2 The Presidential Election Process

Learning Objectives

By the end of this section, you will be able to:
- Describe changes over time in the way the president and vice president are selected
- Identify the stages in the modern presidential selection process
- Assess the advantages and disadvantages of the Electoral College

The process of electing a president every four years has evolved over time. This evolution has resulted from attempts to correct the cumbersome procedures first offered by the framers of the Constitution and as a result of political parties' rising power to act as gatekeepers to the presidency. Over the last several decades, the manner by which parties have chosen candidates has trended away from congressional caucuses and conventions and towards a drawn-out series of state contests, called primaries and caucuses, which begin in the winter prior to the November general election.

SELECTING THE CANDIDATE: THE PARTY PROCESS

The framers of the Constitution made no provision in the document for the establishment of political parties. Indeed, parties were not necessary to select the first president, since George Washington ran unopposed. Following the first election of Washington, the political party system gained steam and power in the electoral process, creating separate nomination and general election stages. Early on, the power to nominate presidents for office bubbled up from the party operatives in the various state legislatures and toward what was known as the **king caucus** or congressional caucus. The *caucus* or large-scale gathering was made up of legislators in the Congress who met informally to decide on nominees from their respective parties. In somewhat of a countervailing trend in the general election stage of the process, by the presidential election of 1824, many states were using popular elections to choose their electors. This became important in that election when Andrew Jackson won the popular vote and the largest number of electors, but the presidency was given to John Quincy Adams instead. Out of the frustration of Jackson's supporters emerged a powerful two-party system that took control of the selection process.[17]

In the decades that followed, party organizations, party leaders, and workers met in national conventions to choose their nominees, sometimes after long struggles that took place over multiple ballots. In this way, the political parties kept a tight control on the selection of a candidate. In the early twentieth century, however, some states began to hold primaries, elections in which candidates vied for the support of state delegations to the party's nominating convention. Over the course of the century, the primaries gradually became a far more important part of the process, though the party leadership still controlled the route to nomination through the convention system. This has changed in recent decades, and now a majority of the delegates are chosen through primary elections, and the party conventions themselves are little more than a widely publicized rubber-stamping event.

The rise of the presidential primary and caucus system as the main means by which presidential candidates are selected has had a number of anticipated and unanticipated consequences. For one, the campaign season has grown longer and more costly. In 1960, John F. Kennedy declared his intention to run for the presidency just eleven months before the general election. Compare this to Hillary Clinton, who announced her intention to run nearly two years before the 2008 general election. Today's long campaign seasons are seasoned with a seemingly ever-increasing number of debates among contenders for the nomination. In 2016, when the number of candidates for the Republican nomination became large and unwieldy, two debates among them were held, in which only those candidates polling greater support were allowed in the more important prime-time debate. The runners-up spoke in the other debate.

Finally, the process of going straight to the people through primaries and caucuses has created some opportunities for party outsiders to rise. Neither Ronald Reagan nor Bill Clinton was especially popular with the party leadership of the Republicans or the Democrats (respectively) at the outset. The outsider phenomenon has been most clearly demonstrated, however, in the 2016 presidential nominating process, as those distrusted by the party establishment, such as Senator Ted Cruz and Donald Trump, who never before held political office, raced ahead of party favorites like Jeb Bush early in the primary process (Figure 12.6).

Figure 12.6 Senator Ted Cruz (R-TX), though disliked by the party establishment, was able to rise to the top in the Iowa caucuses in 2016 because of his ability to reach the conservative base of the party. Ultimately, Cruz bowed out of the race when Donald Trump effectively clinched the Republican nomination in Indiana in early May 2016. (credit: Michael Vadon)

The rise of the primary system during the Progressive Era came at the cost of party regulars' control of the process of candidate selection. Some party primaries even allow registered independents or members of the opposite party to vote. Even so, the process tends to attract the party faithful at the expense of independent voters, who often hold the key to victory in the fall contest. Thus, candidates who want to succeed in the primary contests seek to align themselves with committed partisans, who are often at the ideological extreme. Those who survive the primaries in this way have to moderate their image as they enter the general election if they hope to succeed among the rest of the party adherents and the uncommitted.

Primaries offer tests of candidates' popular appeal, while state caucuses testify to their ability to mobilize and organize grassroots support among committed followers. Primaries also reward candidates in different ways, with some giving the winner all the state's convention delegates, while others distribute delegates proportionately according to the distribution of voter support. Finally, the order in which the primary elections and caucus selections are held shape the overall race.[18] Currently, the Iowa caucuses and the New Hampshire primary occur first. These early contests tend to shrink the field as candidates who perform poorly leave the race. At other times in the campaign process, some states will maximize their impact on the race by holding their primaries on the same day that other states do. The media has dubbed these critical groupings "Super Tuesdays," "Super Saturdays," and so on. They tend to occur later in the nominating process as parties try to force the voters to coalesce around a single nominee.

The rise of the primary has also displaced the convention itself as the place where party regulars choose their standard bearer. Once true contests in which party leaders fought it out to elect a candidate, by the 1970s, party conventions more often than not simply served to rubber-stamp the choice of the primaries.

By the 1980s, the convention drama was gone, replaced by a long, televised commercial designed to extol the party's greatness (Figure 12.7). Without the drama and uncertainty, major news outlets have steadily curtailed their coverage of the conventions, convinced that few people are interested. The 2016 elections seem to support the idea that the primary process produces a nominee rather than party insiders. Outsiders Donald Trump on the Republican side and Senator Bernie Sanders on the Democratic side had much success despite significant concerns about them from party elites. Whether this pattern could be reversed in the case of a closely contested selection process remains to be seen.

Figure 12.7 Traditional party conventions, like the Republican national convention in 1964 pictured here, could be contentious meetings at which the delegates made real decisions about who would run. These days, party conventions are little more than long promotional events. (credit: the Library of Congress)

ELECTING THE PRESIDENT: THE GENERAL ELECTION

Early presidential elections, conducted along the lines of the original process outlined in the Constitution, proved unsatisfactory. So long as George Washington was a candidate, his election was a foregone conclusion. But it took some manipulation of the votes of electors to ensure that the second-place winner (and thus the vice president) did not receive the same number of votes. When Washington declined to run again after two terms, matters worsened. In 1796, political rivals John Adams and Thomas Jefferson were elected president and vice president, respectively. Yet the two men failed to work well together during Adams's administration, much of which Jefferson spent at his Virginia residence at Monticello. As noted earlier in this chapter, the shortcomings of the system became painfully evident in 1800, when Jefferson and his running mate Aaron Burr finished tied, thus leaving it to the House of Representatives to elect Jefferson.[19]

The Twelfth Amendment, ratified in 1804, provided for the separate election of president and vice president as well as setting out ways to choose a winner if no one received a majority of the electoral votes. Only once since the passage of the Twelfth Amendment, during the election of 1824, has the House selected the president under these rules, and only once, in 1836, has the Senate chosen the vice president. In several elections, such as in 1876 and 1888, a candidate who received less than a majority of the popular vote has claimed the presidency, including cases when the losing candidate secured a majority of the popular vote. A recent case was the 2000 election, in which Democratic nominee Al Gore won the popular vote, while Republican nominee George W. Bush won the Electoral College vote and hence the presidency. The 2016 election brought another such irregularity as Donald Trump comfortably won the Electoral College by narrowly winning the popular vote in several states, while Hillary Clinton collected nearly 2.9 million more votes nationwide.

Not everyone is satisfied with how the Electoral College fundamentally shapes the election, especially in cases such as those noted above, when a candidate with a minority of the popular vote claims victory over a candidate who drew more popular support. Yet movements for electoral reform, including proposals for a straightforward nationwide direct election by popular vote, have gained little traction.

Supporters of the current system defend it as a manifestation of federalism, arguing that it also guards against the chaos inherent in a multiparty environment by encouraging the current two-party system. They point out that under a system of direct election, candidates would focus their efforts on more populous regions and ignore others.[20] Critics, on the other hand, charge that the current system negates the one-person, one-vote basis of U.S. elections, subverts majority rule, works against political participation in states deemed safe for one party, and might lead to chaos should an elector desert a candidate, thus thwarting the popular will. Despite all this, the system remains in place. It appears that many people are more comfortable with the problems of a flawed system than with the uncertainty of change.[21]

Get Connected!

Electoral College Reform

Following the 2000 presidential election, when then-governor George W. Bush won by a single electoral vote and with over half a million fewer individual votes than his challenger, astonished voters called for Electoral College reform. Years later, however, nothing of any significance had been done. The absence of reform in the wake of such a problematic election is a testament to the staying power of the Electoral College. The 2016 election results were even more disparate. While in 2000, Al Gore won a narrow victory in the popular vote with Bush prevailing by one vote in the Electoral College, in 2016, Clinton won the popular vote by a margin of almost 3 million votes, while Trump won the Electoral College comfortably.

Those who insist that the Electoral College should be reformed argue that its potential benefits pale in comparison to the way the Electoral College depresses voter turnout and fails to represent the popular will. In addition to favoring small states, since individual votes there count more than in larger states due to the mathematics involved in the distribution of electors, the Electoral College results in a significant number of "safe" states that receive no real electioneering, such that nearly 75 percent of the country is ignored in the general election.

One potential solution to the problems with the Electoral College is to scrap it all together and replace it with the popular vote. The popular vote would be the aggregated totals of the votes in the fifty states and District of Columbia, as certified by the head election official of each state. A second solution often mentioned is to make the Electoral College proportional. That is, as each state assigns it electoral votes, it would do so based on the popular vote percentage in their state, rather with the winner-take-all approach almost all the states use today.

A third alternative for Electoral College reform has been proposed by an organization called National Popular Vote. The National Popular Vote movement is an interstate compact between multiple states that sign onto the compact. Once a combination of states constituting 270 Electoral College votes supports the movement, each state entering the compact pledges all of its Electoral College votes to the national popular vote winner. This reform does not technically change the Electoral College structure, but it results in a mandated process that makes the Electoral College reflect the popular vote. Thus far, eleven states with a total of 165 electoral votes among them have signed onto the compact.

In what ways does the current Electoral College system protect the representative power of small states and less densely populated regions? Why might it be important to preserve these protections?

Follow-up activity: View the National Popular Vote (https://openstax.org/l/29NatPopVo) website to learn more about their position. Consider reaching out to them to learn more, offer your support, or even to argue against their proposal.

Link to Learning

See how the Electoral College and the idea of swing states fundamentally shapes elections by experimenting with the interactive Electoral College map (https://openstax.org/l/29ElecCoMap) at 270 to Win.

The general election usually features a series of debates between the presidential contenders as well as a debate among vice presidential candidates. Because the stakes are high, quite a bit of money and resources are expended on all sides. Attempts to rein in the mounting costs of modern general-election campaigns have proven ineffective. Nor has public funding helped to solve the problem. Indeed, starting with Barack Obama's 2008 decision to forfeit public funding so as to skirt the spending limitations imposed, candidates now regularly opt to raise more money rather than to take public funding.[22] In addition, political action committees (PACs), supposedly focused on issues rather than specific candidates, seek to influence the outcome of the race by supporting or opposing a candidate according to the PAC's own interests. But after all the spending and debating is done, those who have not already voted by other means set out on the first Tuesday following the first Monday in November to cast their votes. Several weeks later, the electoral votes are counted and the president is formally elected (Figure 12.8).

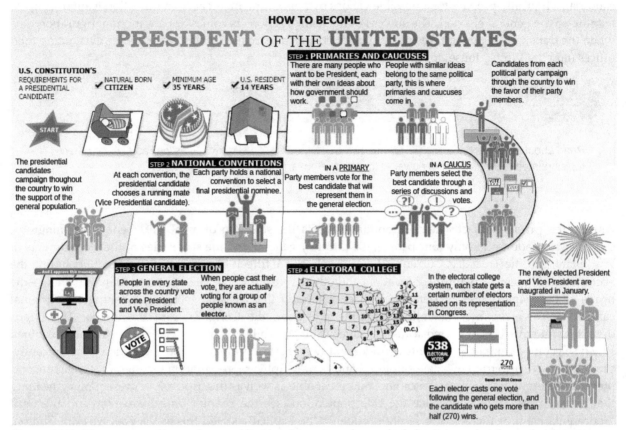

Figure 12.8 The process of becoming president has become an increasingly longer one, but the underlying steps remain largely the same. (credit: modification of work by the U. S. General Services Administration, Federal Citizen Information Center, Ifrah Syed)

12.3 Organizing to Govern

Learning Objectives

By the end of this section, you will be able to:
- Explain how incoming and outgoing presidents peacefully transfer power
- Describe how new presidents fill positions in the executive branch
- Discuss how incoming presidents use their early popularity to advance larger policy solutions

It is one thing to win an election; it is quite another to govern, as many frustrated presidents have discovered. Critical to a president's success in office is the ability to make a deft transition from the previous administration, including naming a cabinet and filling other offices. The new chief executive must also fashion an agenda, which he or she will often preview in general terms in an inaugural address. Presidents usually embark upon their presidency benefitting from their own and the nation's renewed hope and optimism, although often unrealistic expectations set the stage for subsequent disappointment.

TRANSITION AND APPOINTMENTS

In the immediate aftermath of the election, the incoming and outgoing administrations work together to help facilitate the transfer of power. While the General Services Administration oversees the logistics of the process, such as office assignments, information technology, and the assignment of keys, prudent candidates typically prepare for a possible victory by appointing members of a transition team during the lead-up to the general election. The success of the team's actions becomes apparent on inauguration day, when the transition of power takes place in what is often a seamless fashion, with people evacuating their offices (and the White House) for their successors.

Link to Learning

Read about **presidential transitions (https://openstax.org/l/29WHTransP)** as well as explore other topics related to the transfer of power at the White House Transition Project website.

Among the president-elect's more important tasks is the selection of a cabinet. George Washington's cabinet was made up of only four people, the attorney general and the secretaries of the Departments of War, State, and the Treasury. Currently, however, there are fifteen members of the cabinet, including the Secretaries of Labor, Agriculture, Education, and others (Figure 12.9). The most important members—the heads of the Departments of Defense, Justice, State, and the Treasury (echoing Washington's original cabinet)—receive the most attention from the president, the Congress, and the media. These four departments have been referred to as the inner cabinet, while the others are called the outer cabinet. When selecting a cabinet, presidents consider ability, expertise, influence, and reputation. More recently, presidents have also tried to balance political and demographic representation (gender, race, religion, and other considerations) to produce a cabinet that is capable as well as descriptively representative, meaning that those in the cabinet look like the U.S. population (see the chapter on bureaucracy and the term "representative bureaucracy"). A recent president who explicitly stated this as his goal was Bill Clinton, who talked about an "E.G.G. strategy" for senior-level appointments, where the E stands for ethnicity, G for gender, and the second G for geography.

Figure 12.9 The Cabinet Room, shown here during a cabinet meeting on January 31, 2012, adjoins the Oval Office in the West Wing of the White House.

Once the new president has been inaugurated and can officially nominate people to fill cabinet positions, the Senate confirms or rejects these nominations. At times, though rarely, cabinet nominations have failed to be confirmed or have even been withdrawn because of questions raised about the past behavior of the nominee.[23] Prominent examples of such withdrawals were Senator John Tower for defense secretary (George H. W. Bush) and Zoe Baird for attorney general (Bill Clinton): Senator Tower's indiscretions involving alcohol and womanizing led to concerns about his fitness to head the military and his rejection by the Senate,[24] whereas Zoe Baird faced controversy and withdrew her nomination when it was revealed, through what the press dubbed "Nannygate," that house staff of hers were undocumented workers. However, these cases are rare exceptions to the rule, which is to give approval to the nominees that the president wishes to have in the cabinet. Other possible candidates for cabinet posts may decline to be considered for a number of reasons, from the reduction in pay that can accompany entrance into public life to unwillingness to be subjected to the vetting process that accompanies a nomination.

Also subject to Senate approval are a number of non-cabinet subordinate administrators in the various departments of the executive branch, as well as the administrative heads of several agencies and commissions. These include the heads of the Internal Revenue Service, the Central Intelligence Agency, the Office of Management and Budget, the Federal Reserve, the Social Security Administration, the Environmental Protection Agency, the National Labor Relations Board, and the Equal Employment Opportunity Commission. The **Office of Management and Budget** (OMB) is the president's own budget department. In addition to preparing the executive budget proposal and overseeing budgetary implementation during the federal fiscal year, the OMB oversees the actions of the executive bureaucracy.

Not all the non-cabinet positions are open at the beginning of an administration, but presidents move quickly to install their preferred choices in most roles when given the opportunity. Finally, new presidents usually take the opportunity to nominate new ambassadors, whose appointments are subject to Senate confirmation. New presidents make thousands of new appointments in their first two years in office. All the senior cabinet agency positions and nominees for all positions in the Executive Office of the President are made as presidents enter office or when positions become vacant during their presidency. Federal judges serve for life. Therefore, vacancies for the federal courts and the U.S. Supreme Court occur gradually as judges retire.

Throughout much of the history of the republic, the Senate has closely guarded its constitutional duty to consent to the president's nominees, although in the end it nearly always confirms them. Still, the Senate does occasionally hold up a nominee. Benjamin Fishbourn, President George Washington's nomination for a minor naval post, was rejected largely because he had insulted a particular senator.[25] Other rejected nominees included Clement Haynsworth and G. Harrold Carswell, nominated for the U.S. Supreme Court by President Nixon; Theodore Sorensen, nominated by President Carter for director of the Central Intelligence Agency; and John Tower, discussed earlier. At other times, the Senate has used its power to rigorously scrutinize the president's nominees (Figure 12.10). Supreme Court nominee Clarence Thomas, who faced numerous sexual harassment charges from former employees, was forced to sit through repeated questioning of his character and past behavior during Senate hearings, something he referred to as "a high-tech lynching for uppity blacks."[26]

Figure 12.10   In 2013, President Barack Obama nominated former Republican senator Chuck Hagel to run the Department of Defense. The president hoped that by nominating a former senator from the opposition he could ensure the confirmation process would go smoothly. Instead, however, Senator Ted Cruz used the confirmation hearing to question the Vietnam War hero's patriotism. Hagel was eventually confirmed by a 58–41 vote. (credit: Leon E. Panetta)

More recently, the Senate has attempted a new strategy, refusing to hold hearings at all, a strategy of defeat that scholars have referred to as "malign neglect."[27] Despite the fact that one-third of U.S. presidents have appointed a Supreme Court justice in an election year, when Associate Justice Antonin Scalia died unexpectedly in early 2016, Senate majority leader Mitch McConnell declared that the Senate would not hold hearings on a nominee until after the upcoming presidential election.[28] McConnell remained adamant even after President Barack Obama, saying he was acting in fulfillment of his constitutional duty, nominated Merrick Garland, longtime chief judge of the federal Circuit Court of Appeals for the DC Circuit. Garland is highly respected by senators from both parties and won confirmation to his DC circuit position by a 76–23 vote in the Senate. When Republican Donald Trump was elected president in the fall, this strategy appeared to pay off. The Republican Senate and Judiciary Committee confirmed Trump's nominee, Neil Gorsuch, in April 2017, exercising the so-called "nuclear option," which allowed Republicans to break the Democrats' filibuster of the nomination by a simple majority vote.

Other presidential selections are not subject to Senate approval, including the president's personal staff (whose most important member is the White House chief of staff) and various advisers (most notably the national security adviser). The **Executive Office of the President**, created by Franklin D. Roosevelt (FDR), contains a number of advisory bodies, including the Council of Economic Advisers, the National Security Council, the OMB, and the Office of the Vice President. Presidents also choose political advisers, speechwriters, and a press secretary to manage the politics and the message of the administration. In recent years, the president's staff has become identified by the name of the place where many of its members work: the West Wing of the White House. These people serve at the pleasure of the president, and often the president reshuffles or reforms the staff during his or her term. Just as government bureaucracy has expanded over the centuries, so has the White House staff, which under Abraham Lincoln numbered a handful of private secretaries and a few minor functionaries. A recent report pegged the number of employees working within the White House over 450.[29] When the staff in nearby executive buildings of the Executive Office of the President are added in, that number increases four-fold.

Finding a Middle Ground

No Fun at Recess: Dueling Loopholes and the Limits of Presidential Appointments

When Supreme Court justice Antonin Scalia died unexpectedly in early 2016, many in Washington braced for a political sandstorm of obstruction and accusations. Such was the record of Supreme Court nominations during the Obama administration and, indeed, for the last few decades. Nor is this phenomenon restricted to nominations for the highest court in the land. The Senate has been known to occasionally block or slow appointments not because the quality of the nominee was in question but rather as a general protest against the policies of the president and/or as part of the increasing partisan bickering that occurs when the presidency is controlled by one political party and the Senate by the other. This occurred, for example, when the Senate initially refused to nominate anyone to head the Consumer Financial Protection Bureau, established in 2011, because Republicans disliked the existence of the bureau itself.

Such political holdups, however, tend to be the exception rather than the rule. For example, historically, nominees to the presidential cabinet are rarely rejected. And each Congress oversees the approval of around four thousand civilian and sixty-five thousand military appointments from the executive branch.[30] The overwhelming majority of these are confirmed in a routine and systematic fashion, and only rarely do holdups occur. But when they do, the Constitution allows for a small presidential loophole called the recess appointment. The relevant part of Article II, Section 2, of the Constitution reads:

> "The President shall have Power to fill up all Vacancies that may happen during the Recess of the Senate, by granting Commissions which shall expire at the End of their next Session."

The purpose of the provision was to give the president the power to temporarily fill vacancies during times when the Senate was not in session and could not act. But presidents have typically used this loophole to get around a Senate that's inclined to obstruct. Presidents Bill Clinton and George W. Bush made 139 and 171 recess appointments, respectively. President Obama made far fewer recess appointments, with a total of only thirty-two during his presidency.[31] One reason this number is so low is another loophole the Senate began using at the end of George W. Bush's presidency, the pro forma session.

A pro forma session is a short meeting held with the understanding that no work will be done. These sessions have the effect of keeping the Senate officially in session while functionally in recess. In 2012, President Obama decided to ignore the pro forma session and make four recess appointments anyway. The Republicans in the Senate were furious and contested the appointments. Eventually, the Supreme Court had the final say in a 2014 decision that declared unequivocally that "the Senate is in session when it says it is."[32] For now at least, the court's ruling means that the president's loophole and the Senate's loophole cancel each other out. It seems they've found the middle ground whether they like it or not.

What might have been the legitimate original purpose of the recess appointment loophole? Do you believe the Senate is unfairly obstructing by effectively ending recesses altogether so as to prevent the president from making appointments without its approval?

The most visible, though arguably the least powerful, member of a president's cabinet is the vice president. Throughout most of the nineteenth and into the twentieth century, the vast majority of vice presidents took very little action in the office unless fate intervened. Few presidents consulted with their running mates. Indeed, until the twentieth century, many presidents had little to do with the naming of their running mate at the nominating convention. The office was seen as a form of political exile, and that motivated

Republicans to name Theodore Roosevelt as William McKinley's running mate in 1900. The strategy was to get the ambitious politician out of the way while still taking advantage of his popularity. This scheme backfired, however, when McKinley was assassinated and Roosevelt became president (Figure 12.11).

(a)   (b)

Figure 12.11   In September 1901, President William McKinley's assassination, shown here in a sketch by T. Dart Walker (a), made forty-two-year-old vice president Theodore Roosevelt (b) the youngest person to ever assume the office of U.S. president.

Vice presidents were often sent on minor missions or used as mouthpieces for the administration, often with a sharp edge. Richard Nixon's vice president Spiro Agnew is an example. But in the 1970s, starting with Jimmy Carter, presidents made a far more conscious effort to make their vice presidents part of the governing team, placing them in charge of increasingly important issues. Sometimes, as in the case of Bill Clinton and Al Gore, the partnership appeared to be smooth if not always harmonious. In the case of George W. Bush and his very experienced vice president Dick Cheney, observers speculated whether the vice president might have exercised too much influence. Barack Obama's choice for a running mate and subsequent two-term vice president, former Senator Joseph Biden, was picked for his experience, especially in foreign policy. President Obama relied on Vice President Biden for advice throughout his tenure. In any case, the vice presidency is no longer quite as weak as it once was, and a capable vice president can do much to augment the president's capacity to govern across issues if the president so desires.[33]

FORGING AN AGENDA

Having secured election, the incoming president must soon decide how to deliver upon what was promised during the campaign. The chief executive must set priorities, chose what to emphasize, and formulate strategies to get the job done. He or she labors under the shadow of a measure of presidential effectiveness known as the first hundred days in office, a concept popularized during Franklin Roosevelt's first term in the 1930s. While one hundred days is possibly too short a time for any president to boast of any real accomplishments, most presidents do recognize that they must address their major initiatives during their first two years in office. This is the time when the president is most powerful and is given the benefit of the doubt by the public and the media (aptly called the honeymoon period), especially if he or she enters the White House with a politically aligned Congress, as Barack Obama did. However, recent history suggests that even one-party control of Congress and the presidency does not ensure efficient policymaking. This difficulty is due as much to divisions within the governing party as to obstructionist tactics skillfully practiced by the minority party in Congress. Democratic president Jimmy Carter's battles with a Congress controlled by Democratic majorities provide a good case in point.

The incoming president must deal to some extent with the outgoing president's last budget proposal. While some modifications can be made, it is more difficult to pursue new initiatives immediately. Most presidents are well advised to prioritize what they want to achieve during the first year in office and not lose control of their agenda. At times, however, unanticipated events can determine policy, as happened in 2001 when nineteen hijackers perpetrated the worst terrorist attack in U.S. history and transformed U.S. foreign and domestic policy in dramatic ways.

Moreover, a president must be sensitive to what some scholars have termed "political time," meaning the circumstances under which he or she assumes power. Sometimes, the nation is prepared for drastic proposals to solve deep and pressing problems that cry out for immediate solutions, as was the case following the 1932 election of FDR at the height of the Great Depression. Most times, however, the country is far less inclined to accept revolutionary change. Being an effective president means recognizing the difference.[34]

The first act undertaken by the new president—the delivery of an inaugural address—can do much to set the tone for what is intended to follow. While such an address may be an exercise in rhetorical inspiration, it also allows the president to set forth priorities within the overarching vision of what he or she intends to do. Abraham Lincoln used his inaugural addresses to calm rising concerns in the South that he would act to overturn slavery. Unfortunately, this attempt at appeasement fell on deaf ears, and the country descended into civil war. Franklin Roosevelt used his first inaugural address to boldly proclaim that the country need not fear the change that would deliver it from the grip of the Great Depression, and he set to work immediately enlarging the federal government to that end. John F. Kennedy, who entered the White House at the height of the Cold War, made an appeal to talented young people around the country to help him make the world a better place. He followed up with new institutions like the Peace Corps, which sends young citizens around the world to work as secular missionaries for American values like democracy and free enterprise.

Link to Learning

Listen to **clips (https://openstax.org/l/29InaugAd)** of the most famous inaugural address in presidential history at the *Washington Post* website.

12.4 The Public Presidency

Learning Objectives

By the end of this section, you will be able to:
- Explain how technological innovations have empowered presidents
- Identify ways in which presidents appeal to the public for approval
- Explain how the role of first ladies changed over the course of the twentieth century

With the advent of motion picture newsreels and voice recordings in the 1920s, presidents began to broadcast their message to the general public. Franklin Roosevelt, while not the first president to use the radio, adopted this technology to great effect. Over time, as radio gave way to newer and more powerful technologies like television, the Internet, and social media, other presidents have been able magnify their voices to an even-larger degree. Presidents now have far more tools at their disposal to shape public opinion and build support for policies. However, the choice to "go public" does not always lead to political success; it is difficult to convert popularity in public opinion polls into political power. Moreover, the modern era of information and social media empowers opponents at the same time that it provides opportunities for presidents.

THE SHAPING OF THE MODERN PRESIDENCY

From the days of the early republic through the end of the nineteenth century, presidents were limited in the ways they could reach the public to convey their perspective and shape policy. Inaugural addresses and messages to Congress, while circulated in newspapers, proved clumsy devices to attract support, even when a president used plain, blunt language. Some presidents undertook tours of the nation, notably George Washington and Rutherford B. Hayes. Others promoted good relationships with newspaper editors and reporters, sometimes going so far as to sanction a pro-administration newspaper. One president, Ulysses S. Grant, cultivated political cartoonist Thomas Nast to present the president's perspective in the pages of the magazine *Harper's Weekly*.[35] Abraham Lincoln experimented with public meetings recorded by newspaper reporters and public letters that would appear in the press, sometimes after being read at public gatherings (Figure 12.12). Most presidents gave speeches, although few proved to have much immediate impact, including Lincoln's memorable Gettysburg Address.

(a)   (b)

Figure 12.12   While President Abraham Lincoln was not the first president to be photographed, he was the first to use the relatively new power of photography to enhance his power as president and commander-in-chief. Here, Lincoln poses with Union soldiers (a) during his visit to Antietam, Maryland, on October 3, 1862. President Ulysses S. Grant cultivated a relationship with popular cartoonist Thomas Nast, who often depicted the president in the company of "Lady Liberty" (b) in addition to relentlessly attacking his opponent Horace Greeley.

Rather, most presidents exercised the power of patronage (or appointing people who are loyal and help them out politically) and private deal-making to get what they wanted at a time when Congress usually held the upper hand in such transactions. But even that presidential power began to decline with the emergence of civil service reform in the later nineteenth century, which led to most government officials being hired on their merit instead of through patronage. Only when it came to diplomacy and war were presidents able to exercise authority on their own, and even then, institutional as well as political restraints limited their independence of action.

Theodore Roosevelt came to the presidency in 1901, at a time when movie newsreels were becoming popular. Roosevelt, who had always excelled at cultivating good relationships with the print media, eagerly exploited this new opportunity as he took his case to the people with the concept of the presidency as **bully pulpit**, a platform from which to push his agenda to the public. His successors followed suit, and they discovered and employed new ways of transmitting their message to the people in an effort to gain public support for policy initiatives. With the popularization of radio in the early twentieth century, it became possible to broadcast the president's voice into many of the nation's homes. Most famously, FDR used the radio to broadcast his thirty "fireside chats" to the nation between 1933 and 1944.

In the post–World War II era, television began to replace radio as the medium through which presidents reached the public. This technology enhanced the reach of the handsome young president John F. Kennedy and the trained actor Ronald Reagan. At the turn of the twentieth century, the new technology was the Internet. The extent to which this mass media technology can enhance the power and reach of the president has yet to be fully realized.

Other presidents have used advances in transportation to take their case to the people. Woodrow Wilson traveled the country to advocate formation of the League of Nations. However, he fell short of his goal when he suffered a stroke in 1919 and cut his tour short. Both Franklin Roosevelt in the 1930s and 1940s and Harry S. Truman in the 1940s and 1950s used air travel to conduct diplomatic and military business. Under President Dwight D. Eisenhower, a specific plane, commonly called Air Force One, began carrying the president around the country and the world. This gives the president the ability to take his or her message directly to the far corners of the nation at any time.

GOING PUBLIC: PROMISE AND PITFALLS

The concept of **going public** involves the president delivering a major television address in the hope that Americans watching the address will be compelled to contact their House and Senate member and that such public pressure will result in the legislators supporting the president on a major piece of legislation. Technological advances have made it more efficient for presidents to take their messages directly to the people than was the case before mass media (Figure 12.13). Presidential visits can build support for policy initiatives or serve political purposes, helping the president reward supporters, campaign for candidates, and seek reelection. It remains an open question, however, whether choosing to go public actually enhances a president's political position in battles with Congress. Political scientist George C. Edwards goes so far as to argue that taking a president's position public serves to polarize political debate, increase public opposition to the president, and complicate the chances to get something done. It replaces deliberation and compromise with confrontation and campaigning. Edwards believes the best way for presidents to achieve change is to keep issues private and negotiate resolutions that preclude partisan combat. Going public may be more effective in rallying supporters than in gaining additional support or changing minds.[36]

Figure 12.13 With the advent of video technology and cable television, the power of the president to reach huge audiences increased exponentially. President Ronald Reagan, shown here giving one of his most famous speeches in Berlin, was an expert at using technology to help mold and project his presidential image to the public. His training as an actor certainly helped in this regard.

Link to Learning

Today, it is possible for the White House (https://openstax.org/l/29WHLive) to take its case directly to the people via websites like White House Live, where the public can watch live press briefings and speeches.

THE FIRST LADY: A SECRET WEAPON?

The president is not the only member of the First Family who often attempts to advance an agenda by going public. First ladies increasingly exploited the opportunity to gain public support for an issue of deep interest to them. Before 1933, most first ladies served as private political advisers to their husbands. In the 1910s, Edith Bolling Wilson took a more active but still private role assisting her husband, President Woodrow Wilson, afflicted by a stroke, in the last years of his presidency. However, as the niece of one president and the wife of another, it was Eleanor Roosevelt in the 1930s and 1940s who opened the door for first ladies to do something more.

Eleanor Roosevelt took an active role in championing civil rights, becoming in some ways a bridge between her husband and the civil rights movement. She coordinated meetings between FDR and members of the NAACP, championed antilynching legislation, openly defied segregation laws, and pushed the Army Nurse Corps to allow black women in its ranks. She also wrote a newspaper column and had a weekly radio show. Her immediate successors returned to the less visible role held by her predecessors, although in the early 1960s, Jacqueline Kennedy gained attention for her efforts to refurbish the White House along historical lines, and Lady Bird Johnson in the mid- and late 1960s endorsed an effort to beautify public spaces and highways in the United States. She also established the foundations of what came to be known as the Office of the First Lady, complete with a news reporter, Liz Carpenter, as her press secretary.

Betty Ford took over as first lady in 1974 and became an avid advocate of women's rights, proclaiming that she was pro-choice when it came to abortion and lobbying for the ratification of the Equal Rights Amendment (ERA). She shared with the public the news of her breast cancer diagnosis and subsequent mastectomy. Her successor, Rosalynn Carter, attended several cabinet meetings and pushed for the ratification of the ERA as well as for legislation addressing mental health issues (Figure 12.14).

Figure 12.14 On November 19, 1977, Rosalynn Carter (center left) and Betty Ford (center right) attended a rally in favor of the passage of the Equal Rights Amendment.

The increasing public political role of the first lady continued in the 1980s with Nancy Reagan's "Just Say No" antidrug campaign and in the early 1990s with Barbara Bush's efforts on behalf of literacy. The public role of the first lady reach a new level with Hillary Clinton in the 1990s when her husband put her in charge of his efforts to achieve health care reform, a controversial decision that did not meet with political success. Her successors, Laura Bush in the first decade of the twenty-first century and Michelle Obama in the second, returned to the roles played by predecessors in advocating less controversial policies: Laura Bush advocated literacy and education, while Michelle Obama has emphasized physical fitness and healthy diet and exercise. Nevertheless, the public and political profiles of first ladies remain high, and in the future, the president's spouse will have the opportunity to use that unelected position to advance policies that might well be less controversial and more appealing than those pushed by the president.

Insider Perspective

A New Role for the First Lady?

While running for the presidency for the first time in 1992, Bill Clinton frequently touted the experience and capabilities of his wife. There was a lot to brag about. Hillary Rodham Clinton was a graduate of Yale Law School, had worked as a member of the impeachment inquiry staff during the height of the Watergate scandal in Nixon's administration, and had been a staff attorney for the Children's Defense Fund before becoming the first lady of Arkansas. Acknowledging these qualifications, candidate Bill Clinton once suggested that by electing him, voters would get "two for the price of one." The clear implication in this statement was that his wife would take on a far larger role than previous first ladies, and this proved to be the case.[37]

Shortly after taking office, Clinton appointed the first lady to chair the Task Force on National Health Care Reform. This organization was to follow through on his campaign promise to fix the problems in the U.S. healthcare system. Hillary Clinton had privately requested the appointment, but she quickly realized that the complex web of business interests and political aspirations combined to make the topic of health care reform a hornet's nest. This put the Clinton administration's first lady directly into partisan battles few if any previous first ladies had ever faced.

As a testament to both the large role the first lady had taken on and the extent to which she had become the target of political attacks, the recommendations of the task force were soon dubbed "Hillarycare" by opponents. In a particularly contentious hearing in the House, the first lady and Republican representative Dick Armey exchanged pointed jabs with each other. At one point, Armey suggested that the reports of her charm were "overstated" after the first lady likened him to Dr. Jack Kevorkian, a physician known for helping patients commit suicide (Figure 12.15).[38] The following summer, the first lady attempted to use a national bus tour to popularize the health care proposal, although distaste for her and for the program had reached such a fevered pitch that she sometimes was compelled to wear a bulletproof vest. In the end, the efforts came up short and the reform attempts were abandoned as a political failure. Nevertheless, Hillary Clinton remained a political lightning rod for the rest of the Clinton presidency.

Figure 12.15 Hillary Clinton sips from a teacup as she tries to stay calm during a particularly contentious hearing on her health care reform proposals in September 1993. (credit: modification of work by the Library of Congress)

What do the challenges of First Lady Hillary Clinton's foray into national politics suggest about the dangers of a first lady abandoning the traditionally safe nonpartisan goodwill efforts? What do the actions of the first ladies since Clinton suggest about the lessons learned or not learned?

12.5 Presidential Governance: Direct Presidential Action

Learning Objectives

By the end of this section, you will be able to:

- Identify the power presidents have to effect change without congressional cooperation
- Analyze how different circumstances influence the way presidents use unilateral authority
- Explain how presidents persuade others in the political system to support their initiatives
- Describe how historians and political scientists evaluate the effectiveness of a presidency

A president's powers can be divided into two categories: direct actions the chief executive can take by employing the formal institutional powers of the office and informal powers of persuasion and negotiation essential to working with the legislative branch. When a president governs alone through direct action, it may break a policy deadlock or establish new grounds for action, but it may also spark opposition that might have been handled differently through negotiation and discussion. Moreover, such decisions are subject to court challenge, legislative reversal, or revocation by a successor. What may seem to be a sign of strength is often more properly understood as independent action undertaken in the wake of a failure to achieve a solution through the legislative process, or an admission that such an effort would prove futile. When it comes to national security, international negotiations, or war, the president has many more opportunities to act directly and in some cases must do so when circumstances require quick and decisive action.

DOMESTIC POLICY

The president may not be able to appoint key members of his or her administration without Senate confirmation, but he or she can demand the resignation or removal of cabinet officers, high-ranking appointees (such as ambassadors), and members of the presidential staff. During Reconstruction, Congress tried to curtail the president's removal power with the Tenure of Office Act (1867), which required Senate concurrence to remove presidential nominees who took office upon Senate confirmation. Andrew Johnson's violation of that legislation provided the grounds for his impeachment in 1868. Subsequent presidents secured modifications of the legislation before the Supreme Court ruled in 1926 that the Senate had no right to impair the president's removal power.[39] In the case of Senate failure to approve presidential nominations, the president is empowered to issue recess appointments (made while the Senate is in recess) that continue in force until the end of the next session of the Senate (unless the Senate confirms the nominee).

The president also exercises the power of pardon without conditions. Once used fairly sparingly—apart from Andrew Johnson's wholesale pardons of former Confederates during the Reconstruction period—the pardon power has become more visible in recent decades. President Harry S. Truman issued over two thousand pardons and commutations, more than any other post–World War II president.[40] President Gerald Ford has the unenviable reputation of being the only president to pardon another president (his predecessor Richard Nixon, who resigned after the Watergate scandal) (Figure 12.16). While not as generous as Truman, President Jimmy Carter also issued a great number of pardons, including several for draft dodging during the Vietnam War. President Reagan was reluctant to use the pardon as much, as was President George H. W. Bush. President Clinton pardoned few people for much of his presidency, but did make several last-minute pardons, which led to some controversy. By the end of his presidency, Barack Obama had granted 212 pardons, or 6 percent of petitions received, numbers similar to that of his predecessor, George W. Bush.[41] President Trump has used the pardon in a few visible cases. He set aside sentences for controversial former Sheriff Joe Arpaio of Maricopa County, Arizona, and for former Vice President Dick Cheney's confidante, Scooter Libby.[42] It remains to be seen if Trump will pardon the long list of personnel who have been indicted or convicted in the Mueller investigation of Russian meddling in the 2016 election. The list includes his campaign manager Paul Manafort, personal attorney Michael

Cohen, and long-time confidante Roger Stone.[43]

Figure 12.16 In 1974, President Ford became the first and still the only president to pardon a previous president (Richard Nixon). Here he is speaking before the House Judiciary Subcommittee on Criminal Justice meeting explaining his reasons. While the pardon was unpopular with many and may have cost Ford the election two years later, his constitutional power to issue it is indisputable. (credit: modification of work by the Library of Congress)

Presidents may choose to issue executive orders or proclamations to achieve policy goals. Usually, executive orders direct government agencies to pursue a certain course in the absence of congressional action. A more subtle version pioneered by recent presidents is the executive memorandum, which tends to attract less attention. Many of the most famous executive orders have come in times of war or invoke the president's authority as commander-in-chief, including Franklin Roosevelt's order permitting the internment of Japanese Americans in 1942 and Harry Truman's directive desegregating the armed forces (1948). The most famous presidential proclamation was Abraham Lincoln's Emancipation Proclamation (1863), which declared slaves in areas under Confederate control to be free (with a few exceptions).

Executive orders are subject to court rulings or changes in policy enacted by Congress. During the Korean War, the Supreme Court revoked Truman's order seizing the steel industry.[44] These orders are also subject to reversal by presidents who come after, and recent presidents have wasted little time reversing the orders of their predecessors in cases of disagreement. Sustained executive orders, which are those not overturned in courts, typically have some prior authority from Congress that legitimizes them. When there is no prior authority, it is much more likely that an executive order will be overturned by a later president. For this reason, this tool has become less common in recent decades (Figure 12.17).

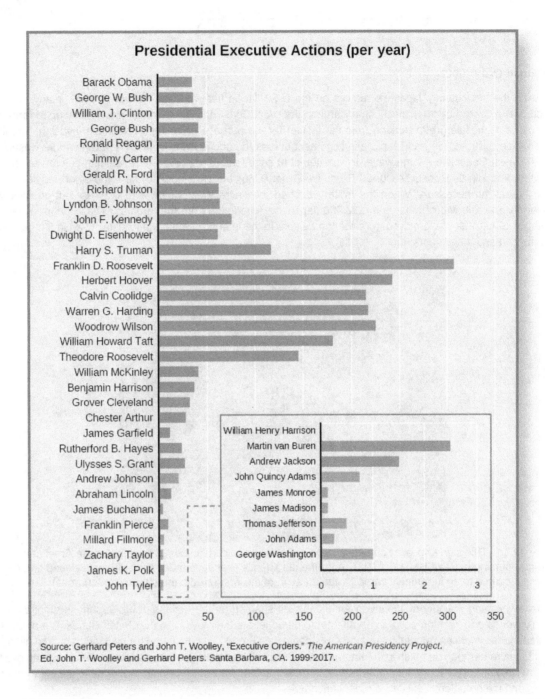

Figure 12.17 Executive actions were unusual until the late nineteenth century. They became common in the first half of the twentieth century but have been growing less popular for the last few decades because they often get overturned in court if the Congress has not given the president prior delegated authority.

Milestone

Executive Order 9066

Following the devastating Japanese attacks on the U.S. Pacific fleet at Pearl Harbor in 1941, many in the United States feared that Japanese Americans on the West Coast had the potential and inclination to form a fifth column (a hostile group working from the inside) for the purpose of aiding a Japanese invasion. These fears mingled with existing anti-Japanese sentiment across the country and created a paranoia that washed over the West Coast like a large wave. In an attempt to calm fears and prevent any real fifth-column actions, President Franklin D. Roosevelt signed Executive Order 9066, which authorized the removal of people from military areas as necessary. When the military dubbed the entire West Coast a military area, it effectively allowed for the removal of more than 110,000 Japanese Americans from their homes. These people, many of them U.S. citizens, were moved to relocation centers in the interior of the country. They lived in the camps there for two and a half years (Figure 12.18).[45]

Figure 12.18 This sign appeared outside a store in Oakland, California, owned by a Japanese American after the bombing of Pearl Harbor in 1941. After the president's executive order, the store was closed and the owner evacuated to an internment camp for the duration of the war. (credit: the Library of Congress)

The overwhelming majority of Japanese Americans felt shamed by the actions of the Japanese empire and willingly went along with the policy in an attempt to demonstrate their loyalty to the United States. But at least one Japanese American refused to go along. His name was Fred Korematsu, and he decided to go into hiding in California rather than be taken to the internment camps with his family. He was soon discovered, turned over to the military, and sent to the internment camp in Utah that held his family. But his challenge to the internment system and the president's executive order continued.

In 1944, Korematsu's case was heard by the Supreme Court. In a 6–3 decision, the Court ruled against him, arguing that the administration had the constitutional power to sign the order because of the need to protect U.S. interests against the threat of espionage.[46] Forty-four years after this decision, President Reagan issued an official apology for the internment and provided some compensation to the survivors. In 2011, the Justice Department went a step further by filing a notice officially recognizing that the solicitor general of the United States acted in error by arguing to uphold the executive order. (The solicitor general is the official who argues cases for the U.S. government before the Supreme Court.) However, despite these actions, in 2014, the late Supreme Court justice Antonin Scalia was documented as saying that while he believed the decision was wrong, it could occur again.[47]

What do the Korematsu case and the internment of over 100,000 Japanese Americans suggest about the extent of the president's war powers? What does this episode in U.S. history suggest about the weaknesses of constitutional checks on executive power during times of war?

Link to Learning

To learn more about the relocation and confinement of Japanese Americans during World War II, visit **Heart Mountain (https://openstax.org/l/29HrtMntn)** online.

Finally, presidents have also used the line-item veto and signing statements to alter or influence the application of the laws they sign. A **line-item veto** is a type of veto that keeps the majority of a spending bill unaltered but nullifies certain lines of spending within it. While a number of states allow their governors the line-item veto (discussed in the chapter on state and local government), the president acquired this power only in 1996 after Congress passed a law permitting it. President Clinton used the tool sparingly. However, those entities that stood to receive the federal funding he lined out brought suit. Two such groups were the City of New York and the Snake River Potato Growers in Idaho.[48] The Supreme Court heard their claims together and just sixteen months later declared unconstitutional the act that permitted the line-item veto.[49] Since then, presidents have asked Congress to draft a line-item veto law that would be constitutional, although none have made it to the president's desk.

On the other hand, **signing statements** are statements issued by a president when agreeing to legislation that indicate how the chief executive will interpret and enforce the legislation in question. Signing statements are less powerful than vetoes, though congressional opponents have complained that they derail legislative intent. Signing statements have been used by presidents since at least James Monroe, but they became far more common in this century.

NATIONAL SECURITY, FOREIGN POLICY, AND WAR

Presidents are more likely to justify the use of executive orders in cases of national security or as part of their war powers. In addition to mandating emancipation and the internment of Japanese Americans, presidents have issued orders to protect the homeland from internal threats. Most notably, Lincoln ordered the suspension of the privilege of the writ of habeas corpus in 1861 and 1862 before seeking congressional legislation to undertake such an act. Presidents hire and fire military commanders; they also use their power as commander-in-chief to aggressively deploy U.S. military force. Congress rarely has taken the lead over the course of history, with the War of 1812 being the lone exception. Pearl Harbor was a salient case where Congress did make a clear and formal declaration when asked by FDR. However, since World War II, it has been the president and not Congress who has taken the lead in engaging the United States in military action outside the nation's boundaries, most notably in Korea, Vietnam, and the Persian Gulf (Figure 12.19).

Figure 12.19 By landing on an aircraft carrier and wearing a flight suit to announce the end of major combat operations in Iraq in 2003, President George W. Bush was carefully emphasizing his presidential power as commander-in-chief. (credit: Tyler J. Clements)

Presidents also issue executive agreements with foreign powers. Executive agreements are formal agreements negotiated between two countries but not ratified by a legislature as a treaty must be. As such, they are not treaties under U.S. law, which require two-thirds of the Senate for ratification. Treaties, presidents have found, are particularly difficult to get ratified. And with the fast pace and complex demands of modern foreign policy, concluding treaties with countries can be a tiresome and burdensome chore. That said, some executive agreements do require some legislative approval, such as those that commit the United States to make payments and thus are restrained by the congressional power of the purse. But for the most part, executive agreements signed by the president require no congressional action and are considered enforceable as long as the provisions of the executive agreement do not conflict with current domestic law.

> ### Link to Learning
>
> The American Presidency Project (https://openstax.org/l/29AmPresProj) has gathered data outlining presidential activity, including measures for executive orders and signing statements.

THE POWER OF PERSUASION

The framers of the Constitution, concerned about the excesses of British monarchial power, made sure to design the presidency within a network of checks and balances controlled by the other branches of the federal government. Such checks and balances encourage consultation, cooperation, and compromise in policymaking. This is most evident at home, where the Constitution makes it difficult for either Congress or the chief executive to prevail unilaterally, at least when it comes to constructing policy. Although much is made of political stalemate and obstructionism in national political deliberations today, the framers did not want to make it too easy to get things done without a great deal of support for such initiatives.

It is left to the president to employ a strategy of negotiation, persuasion, and compromise in order to secure policy achievements in cooperation with Congress. In 1960, political scientist Richard Neustadt put forward the thesis that presidential power is the power to persuade, a process that takes many forms and is expressed in various ways.[50] Yet the successful employment of this technique can lead to significant and durable successes. For example, legislative achievements tend to be of greater duration because they are more difficult to overturn or replace, as the case of health care reform under President Barack Obama suggests. Obamacare has faced court cases and repeated (if largely symbolic) attempts to gut it in Congress. Overturning it will take a new president who opposes it, together with a Congress that can pass the dissolving legislation.

In some cases, cooperation is essential, as when the president nominates and the Senate confirms persons to fill vacancies on the Supreme Court, an increasingly contentious area of friction between branches. While Congress cannot populate the Court on its own, it can frustrate the president's efforts to do so. Presidents who seek to prevail through persuasion, according to Neustadt, target Congress, members of their own party, the public, the bureaucracy, and, when appropriate, the international community and foreign leaders. Of these audiences, perhaps the most obvious and challenging is Congress.

Link to Learning

Read "Power Lessons for Obama" at this **website (https://openstax.org/l/29ObamaPow)** to learn more about applying Richard Neustadt's framework to the leaders of today.

Much depends on the balance of power within Congress: Should the opposition party hold control of both houses, it will be difficult indeed for the president to realize his or her objectives, especially if the opposition is intent on frustrating all initiatives. However, even control of both houses by the president's own party is no guarantee of success or even of productive policymaking. For example, neither Bill Clinton nor Barack Obama achieved all they desired despite having favorable conditions for the first two years of their presidencies. In times of divided government (when one party controls the presidency and the other controls one or both chambers of Congress), it is up to the president to cut deals and make compromises that will attract support from at least some members of the opposition party without excessively alienating members of his or her own party. Both Ronald Reagan and Bill Clinton proved effective in dealing with divided government—indeed, Clinton scored more successes with Republicans in control of Congress than he did with Democrats in charge.

It is more difficult to persuade members of the president's own party or the public to support a president's policy without risking the dangers inherent in going public. There is precious little opportunity for private persuasion while also going public in such instances, at least directly. The way the president and his or her staff handle media coverage of the administration may afford some opportunities for indirect persuasion of these groups. It is not easy to persuade the federal bureaucracy to do the president's bidding unless the chief executive has made careful appointments. When it comes to diplomacy, the president must relay some messages privately while offering incentives, both positive and negative, in order to elicit desired responses, although at times, people heed only the threat of force and coercion.

While presidents may choose to go public in an attempt to put pressure on other groups to cooperate, most of the time they "stay private" as they attempt to make deals and reach agreements out of the public eye. The tools of negotiation have changed over time. Once chief executives played patronage politics, rewarding friends while attacking and punishing critics as they built coalitions of support. But the advent of civil service reform in the 1880s systematically deprived presidents of that option and reduced its scope and effectiveness. Although the president may call upon various agencies for assistance in lobbying for proposals, such as the Office of Legislative Liaison with Congress, it is often left to the chief executive to offer incentives and rewards. Some of these are symbolic, like private meetings in the White House or an appearance on the campaign trail. The president must also find common ground and make compromises acceptable to all parties, thus enabling everyone to claim they secured something they wanted.

Complicating Neustadt's model, however, is that many of the ways he claimed presidents could shape favorable outcomes require going public, which as we have seen can produce mixed results. Political scientist Fred Greenstein, on the other hand, touted the advantages of a "hidden hand presidency," in which the chief executive did most of the work behind the scenes, wielding both the carrot and the stick.[51] Greenstein singled out President Dwight Eisenhower as particularly skillful in such endeavors.

OPPORTUNITY AND LEGACY

What often shapes a president's performance, reputation, and ultimately legacy depends on circumstances that are largely out of his or her control. Did the president prevail in a landslide or was it a closely contested election? Did he or she come to office as the result of death, assassination, or resignation? How much support does the president's party enjoy, and is that support reflected in the composition of both houses of Congress, just one, or neither? Will the president face a Congress ready to embrace proposals or poised to oppose them? Whatever a president's ambitions, it will be hard to realize them in the face of a hostile or divided Congress, and the options to exercise independent leadership are greater in times of crisis and war than when looking at domestic concerns alone.

Then there is what political scientist Stephen Skowronek calls "political time."[52] Some presidents take office at times of great stability with few concerns. Unless there are radical or unexpected changes, a president's options are limited, especially if voters hoped for a simple continuation of what had come before. Other presidents take office at a time of crisis or when the electorate is looking for significant changes. Then there is both pressure and opportunity for responding to those challenges. Some presidents, notably Theodore Roosevelt, openly bemoaned the lack of any such crisis, which Roosevelt deemed essential for him to achieve greatness as a president.

People in the United States claim they want a strong president. What does that mean? At times, scholars point to presidential independence, even defiance, as evidence of strong leadership. Thus, vigorous use of the veto power in key situations can cause observers to judge a president as strong and independent, although far from effective in shaping constructive policies. Nor is such defiance and confrontation always evidence of presidential leadership skill or greatness, as the case of Andrew Johnson should remind us. When is effectiveness a sign of strength, and when are we confusing being headstrong with being strong? Sometimes, historians and political scientists see cooperation with Congress as evidence of weakness, as in the case of Ulysses S. Grant, who was far more effective in garnering support for administration initiatives than scholars have given him credit for.

These questions overlap with those concerning political time and circumstance. While domestic policymaking requires far more give-and-take and a fair share of cajoling and collaboration, national emergencies and war offer presidents far more opportunity to act vigorously and at times independently. This phenomenon often produces the **rally around the flag effect**, in which presidential popularity spikes during international crises. A president must always be aware that politics, according to Otto von Bismarck, is the art of the possible, even as it is his or her duty to increase what might be possible by persuading both members of Congress and the general public of what needs to be done.

Finally, presidents often leave a legacy that lasts far beyond their time in office (Figure 12.20). Sometimes, this is due to the long-term implications of policy decisions. Critical to the notion of legacy is the shaping of the Supreme Court as well as other federal judges. Long after John Adams left the White House in 1801, his appointment of John Marshall as chief justice shaped American jurisprudence for over three decades. No wonder confirmation hearings have grown more contentious in the cases of highly visible nominees. Other legacies are more difficult to define, although they suggest that, at times, presidents cast a long shadow over their successors. It was a tough act to follow George Washington, and in death, Abraham

Lincoln's presidential stature grew to extreme heights. Theodore and Franklin D. Roosevelt offered models of vigorous executive leadership, while the image and style of John F. Kennedy and Ronald Reagan influenced and at times haunted or frustrated successors. Nor is this impact limited to chief executives deemed successful: Lyndon Johnson's Vietnam and Richard Nixon's Watergate offered cautionary tales of presidential power gone wrong, leaving behind legacies that include terms like *Vietnam syndrome* and the tendency to add the suffix "-gate" to scandals and controversies.

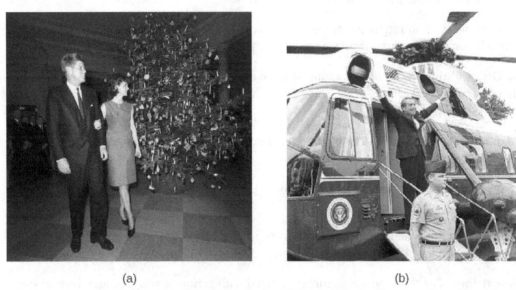

(a) (b)

Figure 12.20 The youth and glamour that John F. Kennedy and first lady Jacqueline brought to the White House in the early 1960s (a) helped give rise to the legend of "one brief shining moment that was Camelot" after Kennedy's presidency was cut short by his assassination on November 22, 1963. Despite a tainted legacy, President Richard Nixon gives his trademark "V for Victory" sign as he leaves the White House on August 9, 1974 (b), after resigning in the wake of the Watergate scandal.

Key Terms

bully pulpit Theodore Roosevelt's notion of the presidency as a platform from which the president could push an agenda

cabinet a group of advisors to the president, consisting of the most senior appointed officers of the executive branch who head the fifteen executive departments

executive agreement an international agreement between the president and another country made by the executive branch and without formal consent by the Senate

Executive Office of the President the administrative organization that reports directly to the president and made up of important offices, units, and staff of the current president and headed by the White House chief of staff

executive order a rule or order issued by the president without the cooperation of Congress and having the force of law

executive privilege the president's right to withhold information from Congress, the judiciary, or the public

going public a term for when the president delivers a major television address in the hope that public pressure will result in legislators supporting the president on a major piece of legislation

impeachment the act of charging a government official with serious wrongdoing, which in some cases may lead to the removal of that official from office

king caucus an informal meeting held in the nineteenth century, sometimes called a congressional caucus, made up of legislators in the Congress who met to decide on presidential nominees for their respective parties

line-item veto a power created through law in 1996 and overturned by the Supreme Court in 1998 that allowed the president to veto specific aspects of bills passed by Congress while signing into law what remained

Office of Management and Budget an office within the Executive Office of the President charged with producing the president's budget, overseeing its implementation, and overseeing the executive bureaucracy

rally around the flag effect a spike in presidential popularity during international crises

signing statement a statement a president issues with the intent to influence the way a specific bill the president signs should be enforced

Summary

12.1 The Design and Evolution of the Presidency

The delegates at the Constitutional Convention proposed creating the office of the president and debated many forms the role might take. The president is elected for a maximum of two four-year terms and can be impeached by Congress for wrongdoing and removed from office. The presidency and presidential power, especially war powers, have expanded greatly over the last two centuries, often with the willing assistance of the legislative branch. Executive privilege and executive orders are two of the presidency's powerful tools. During the last several decades, historical events and new technologies such as radio, television, and the Internet have further enhanced the stature of the presidency.

12.2 The Presidential Election Process

The position of president of the United States was created during the Constitutional Convention. Within a generation of Washington's administration, powerful political parties had overtaken the nominating power of state legislatures and created their own systems for selecting candidates. At first, party leaders kept tight control over the selection of candidates via the convention process. By the start of the twentieth century, however, primary and caucus voting had brought the power to select candidates directly to the people, and the once-important conventions became rubber-stamping events.

12.3 Organizing to Govern

It can be difficult for a new president to come to terms with both the powers of the office and the limitations of those powers. Successful presidents assume their role ready to make a smooth transition and to learn to work within the complex governmental system to fill vacant positions in the cabinet and courts, many of which require Senate confirmation. It also means efficiently laying out a political agenda and reacting appropriately to unexpected events. A new president has limited time to get things done and must take action with the political wind at his or her back.

12.4 The Public Presidency

Despite the obvious fact that the president is the head of state, the U.S. Constitution actually empowers the occupant of the White House with very little authority. Apart from the president's war powers, the office holder's real advantage is the ability to speak to the nation with one voice. Technological changes in the twentieth century have greatly expanded the power of the presidential bully pulpit. The twentieth century also saw a string of more public first ladies. Women like Eleanor Roosevelt and Lady Bird Johnson greatly expanded the power of the first lady's role, although first ladies who have undertaken more nontraditional roles have encountered significant criticism.

12.5 Presidential Governance: Direct Presidential Action

While the power of the presidency is typically checked by the other two branches of government, presidents have the unencumbered power to pardon those convicted of federal crimes and to issue executive orders, which don't require congressional approval but lack the permanence of laws passed by Congress. In matters concerning foreign policy, presidents have at their disposal the executive agreement, which is a much-easier way for two countries to come to terms than a treaty that requires Senate ratification but is also much narrower in scope.

Presidents use various means to attempt to drive public opinion and effect political change. But history has shown that they are limited in their ability to drive public opinion. Favorable conditions can help a president move policies forward. These conditions include party control of Congress and the arrival of crises such as war or economic decline. But as some presidencies have shown, even the most favorable conditions don't guarantee success.

Review Questions

1. Many at the Continental Congress were skeptical of allowing presidents to be directly elected by the legislature because _____.

    a. they were worried about giving the legislature too much power

    b. they feared the opportunities created for corruption

    c. they knew the weaknesses of an electoral college

    d. they worried about subjecting the commander-in-chief to public scrutiny

2. Which of the following is a way George Washington expanded the power of the presidency?

    a. He refused to run again after serving two terms.

    b. He appointed the heads of various federal departments as his own advisors.

    c. He worked with the Senate to draft treaties with foreign countries.

    d. He submitted his neutrality proclamation to the Senate for approval.

3. How did presidents who served in the decades directly after Washington expand the powers of the presidency?

4. What factors contributed to the growth of presidential power in the twentieth century?

5. How did the election of 1824 change the way presidents were selected?

    a. Following this election, presidents were directly elected.

    b. Jackson's supporters decided to create a device for challenging the Electoral College.

    c. The election convinced many that the parties must adopt the king caucus as the primary method for selecting presidents.

    d. The selection of the candidate with fewer electoral votes triggered the rise of party control over nominations.

6. Which of the following is an unintended consequence of the rise of the primary and caucus system?

    a. Sometimes candidates unpopular with the party leadership reach the top.

    b. Campaigns have become shorter and more expensive.

    c. The conventions have become more powerful than the voters.

    d. Often incumbent presidents will fail to be renominated by the party.

7. What problems exist with the Electoral College?

8. The people who make up the modern president's cabinet are the heads of the major federal departments and _____.

    a. must be confirmed by the Senate

    b. once in office are subject to dismissal by the Senate

    c. serve two-year terms

    d. are selected base on the rules of patronage

9. A very challenging job for new presidents is to _____.

    a. move into the White House

    b. prepare and deliver their first State of the Union address

    c. nominate and gain confirmation for their cabinet and hundreds of other officials

    d. prepare their first executive budget

10. How do presidents work to fulfill their campaign promises once in office?

11. President Theodore Roosevelt's concept of the bully pulpit was the office's _____.

    a. authority to use force, especially military force

    b. constitutional power to veto legislation

    c. premier position to pressure through public appeal

    d. ability to use technology to enhance the voice of the president

12. In what ways have first ladies expanded the role of their office over the twentieth century?

13. How were presidents in the eighteenth and nineteenth centuries likely to reach the public? Were these methods effective?

14. The passage of the Tenure of Office Act of 1867 was just one instance in a long line of _____.

    a. struggles for power between the president and the Congress

    b. unconstitutional presidential power grabbing

    c. impeachment trials

    d. arguments over presidential policy

15. Which of the following is an example of an executive agreement?
   a. The president negotiates an agreement with China and submits it to the Senate for ratification.
   b. The president changes a regulation on undocumented immigrant status without congressional approval.
   c. The president signs legally binding nuclear arms terms with Iran without seeking congressional approval.
   d. The president issues recommendations to the Department of Justice on what the meaning of a new criminal statute is.

16. How have the methods presidents use to negotiate with their party and the opposition changed over time?

17. What strategies can presidents employ to win people over to their way of thinking?

Critical Thinking Questions

18. What are the opportunities and limitations for presidential leadership in the contemporary political system?

19. How have presidents used their position to increase the power of the office?

20. What role has technology played increasing the power and reach of presidents?

21. Under what conditions will presidents use direct action? When might they prefer passing a formal policy through Congress as a bill?

22. What do the conditions under which presidents decide to make public pleas suggest about the limits of presidential power?

Suggestions for Further Study

Edwards, George C. 2016. *Predicting the Presidency: The Potential of Persuasive Leadership*. Princeton: Princeton University Press.

Edwards, George C. and Stephen J. Wayne. 2003. *Presidential Leadership: Politics and Policy Making*. Belmont, CA: Wadsworth/Thomson Learning.

Erickson, Robert S. and Christopher Wlezien. 2012. *The Timeline of Presidential Elections: How Campaigns Do (and Do Not) Matter*. Chicago: Chicago University Press.

Greenstein, Fred I. 1982. *The Hidden-Hand Presidency: Eisenhower as Leader*. New York: Basic Books.

Kernell, Samuel. 1986. *Going Public: New Strategies of Presidential Leadership*. Washington, DC: CQ Press.

McGinnis, Joe. 1988. *The Selling of the President*. New York: Penguin Books.

Nelson, Michael. 1984. *The Presidency and the Political System*. Washington, DC: CQ Press.

Neustadt, Richard E. 1990. *Presidential Power and the Modern Presidents: The Politics of Leadership from Roosevelt to Reagan*. New York: Free Press.

Pfiffner, James P. 1994. *The Modern Presidency*. New York: St. Martin's Press.

Pika, Joseph August, John Anthony Maltese, Norman C. Thomas, and Norman C. Thomas. 2002. *The Politics of the Presidency*. Washington, DC: CQ Press.

Porter, Roger B. 1980. *Presidential Decision Making: The Economic Policy Board*. Cambridge: Cambridge University Press.

Skowronek, Stephen. 2011. *Presidential Leadership in Political Time: Reprise and Reappraisal*. Lawrence, KS: University Press of Kansas.

Chapter 13

The Courts

Figure 13.1 The Marriage Equality Act vote in Albany, New York, on July 24, 2011 (left), was just one of a number of cases testing the constitutionality of both federal and state law that ultimately led the Supreme Court to take on the controversial issue of same-sex marriage. In the years leading up to the 2015 ruling that same-sex couples have a right to marry in all fifty states, marriage equality had become a key civil rights issue for the LGBT community, as demonstrated at Seattle's 2012 Pride parade (right). (credit left: modification of work by "Celebration chapel"/Wikimedia; credit right: modification of work by Brett Curtiss)

Chapter Outline

Introduction

If democratic institutions struggle to balance individual freedoms and collective well-being, the judiciary is arguably the branch where the individual has the best chance to be heard. For those seeking protection on the basis of sexual orientation, for example, in recent years, the courts have expanded rights, culminating in 2015 when the Supreme Court ruled that same-sex couples have the right to marry in all fifty states (Figure 13.1).[1]

The U.S. courts pride themselves on two achievements: (1) as part of the system of checks and balances, they protect the sanctity of the U.S. Constitution from breaches by the other branches of government, and (2) they protect individual rights against societal and governmental oppression. At the federal level, nine Supreme Court judges are nominated by the president and confirmed by the Senate for lifetime appointments. This provides them the independence they need to carry out their duties. However, court power is confined to rulings on those cases the courts decide to hear.[2]

How do the courts make decisions, and how do they exercise their power to protect individual rights? How are the courts structured, and what distinguishes the Supreme Court from all others? This chapter answers these and other questions in delineating the power of the judiciary in the United States.

13.1 Guardians of the Constitution and Individual Rights

Learning Objectives

By the end of this section, you will be able to:

- Describe the evolving role of the courts since the ratification of the Constitution
- Explain why courts are uniquely situated to protect individual rights
- Recognize how the courts make public policy

Under the Articles of Confederation, there was no national judiciary. The U.S. Constitution changed that, but its Article III, which addresses "the judicial power of the United States," is the shortest and least detailed of the three articles that created the branches of government. It calls for the creation of "one supreme Court" and establishes the Court's jurisdiction, or its authority to hear cases and make decisions about them, and the types of cases the Court may hear. It distinguishes which are matters of original jurisdiction and which are for appellate jurisdiction. Under **original jurisdiction**, a case is heard for the first time, whereas under **appellate jurisdiction**, a court hears a case on appeal from a lower court and may change the lower court's decision. The Constitution also limits the Supreme Court's original jurisdiction to those rare cases of disputes between states, or between the United States and foreign ambassadors or ministers. So, for the most part, the Supreme Court is an appeals court, operating under appellate jurisdiction and hearing appeals from the lower courts. The rest of the development of the judicial system and the creation of the lower courts were left in the hands of Congress.

To add further explanation to Article III, Alexander Hamilton wrote details about the federal judiciary in *Federalist* No. 78. In explaining the importance of an independent judiciary separated from the other branches of government, he said "interpretation" was a key role of the courts as they seek to protect people from unjust laws. But he also believed "the Judiciary Department" would "always be the least dangerous" because "with no influence over either the sword or the purse," it had "neither force nor will, but merely judgment." The courts would only make decisions, not take action. With no control over how those decisions would be implemented and no power to enforce their choices, they could exercise only judgment, and their power would begin and end there. Hamilton would no doubt be surprised by what the judiciary has become: a key component of the nation's constitutional democracy, finding its place as the chief interpreter of the Constitution and the equal of the other two branches, though still checked and balanced by them.

The first session of the first U.S. Congress laid the framework for today's federal judicial system, established in the Judiciary Act of 1789. Although legislative changes over the years have altered it, the basic structure of the judicial branch remains as it was set early on: At the lowest level are the district courts, where federal cases are tried, witnesses testify, and evidence and arguments are presented. A losing party who is unhappy with a district court decision may appeal to the circuit courts, or U.S. courts of appeals, where the decision of the lower court is reviewed. Still further, appeal to the U.S. Supreme Court is possible, but of the thousands of petitions for appeal, the Supreme Court will typically hear fewer than one hundred a year.[3]

Link to Learning

This public site maintained by the Administrative Office of the U.S. Courts (https://openstax.org/l/29fedcourts) provides detailed information from and about the judicial branch.

HUMBLE BEGINNINGS

Starting in New York in 1790, the early Supreme Court focused on establishing its rules and procedures and perhaps trying to carve its place as the new government's third branch. However, given the difficulty of getting all the justices even to show up, and with no permanent home or building of its own for decades, finding its footing in the early days proved to be a monumental task. Even when the federal government moved to the nation's capital in 1800, the Court had to share space with Congress in the Capitol building. This ultimately meant that "the high bench crept into an undignified committee room in the Capitol beneath the House Chamber."[4]

It was not until the Court's 146th year of operation that Congress, at the urging of Chief Justice—and former president—William Howard Taft, provided the designation and funding for the Supreme Court's own building, "on a scale in keeping with the importance and dignity of the Court and the Judiciary as a coequal, independent branch of the federal government."[5] It was a symbolic move that recognized the Court's growing role as a significant part of the national government (Figure 13.2).

Figure 13.2   The Supreme Court building in Washington, DC, was not completed until 1935. Engraved on its marble front is the motto "Equal Justice Under Law," while its east side says, "Justice, the Guardian of Liberty."

But it took years for the Court to get to that point, and it faced a number of setbacks on the way to such recognition. In their first case of significance, *Chisholm v. Georgia* (1793), the justices ruled that the federal courts could hear cases brought by a citizen of one state against a citizen of another state, and that Article III, Section 2, of the Constitution did not protect the states from facing such an interstate lawsuit.[6] However, their decision was almost immediately overturned by the Eleventh Amendment, passed by Congress in 1794 and ratified by the states in 1795. In protecting the states, the Eleventh Amendment put a prohibition on the courts by stating, "The Judicial power of the United States shall not be construed to extend to any suit in law or equity, commenced or prosecuted against one of the United States by Citizens of another State, or by Citizens or Subjects of any Foreign State." It was an early hint that Congress had the power to change the jurisdiction of the courts as it saw fit and stood ready to use it.

In an atmosphere of perceived weakness, the first chief justice, John Jay, an author of *The Federalist Papers* and appointed by President George Washington, resigned his post to become governor of New York and later declined President John Adams's offer of a subsequent term.[7] In fact, the Court might have remained in a state of what Hamilton called its "natural feebleness" if not for the man who filled the vacancy Jay had refused—the fourth chief justice, John Marshall. Often credited with defining the modern court, clarifying its power, and strengthening its role, Marshall served in the chief's position for thirty-four years. One landmark case during his tenure changed the course of the judicial branch's history (Figure 13.3).[8]

(a)   (b)

Figure 13.3 John Jay (a) was the first chief justice of the Supreme Court but resigned his post to become governor of New York. John Marshall (b), who served as chief justice for thirty-four years, is often credited as the major force in defining the modern court's role in the U.S. governmental system.

In 1803, the Supreme Court declared for itself the power of **judicial review**, a power to which Hamilton had referred but that is not expressly mentioned in the Constitution. Judicial review is the power of the courts, as part of the system of checks and balances, to look at actions taken by the other branches of government and the states and determine whether they are constitutional. If the courts find an action to be unconstitutional, it becomes null and void. Judicial review was established in the Supreme Court case *Marbury v. Madison*, when, for the first time, the Court declared an act of Congress to be unconstitutional.[9] Wielding this power is a role Marshall defined as the "very essence of judicial duty," and it continues today as one of the most significant aspects of judicial power. Judicial review lies at the core of the court's ability to check the other branches of government—and the states.

Since *Marbury*, the power of judicial review has continually expanded, and the Court has not only ruled actions of Congress and the president to be unconstitutional, but it has also extended its power to include the review of state and local actions. The power of judicial review is not confined to the Supreme Court but is also exercised by the lower federal courts and even the state courts. Any legislative or executive action at the federal or state level inconsistent with the U.S. Constitution or a state constitution can be subject to judicial review.[10]

Milestone

Marbury v. Madison (1803)

The Supreme Court found itself in the middle of a dispute between the outgoing presidential administration of John Adams and that of incoming president (and opposition party member) Thomas Jefferson. It was an interesting circumstance at the time, particularly because Jefferson and the man who would decide the case—John Marshall—were themselves political rivals.

President Adams had appointed William Marbury to a position in Washington, DC, but his commission was not delivered before Adams left office. So Marbury petitioned the Supreme Court to use its power under the Judiciary Act of 1789 and issue a writ of mandamus to force the new president's secretary of state, James Madison, to deliver the commission documents. It was a task Madison refused to do. A unanimous Court under the leadership of Chief Justice John Marshall ruled that although Marbury was entitled to the job, the Court did not have the power to issue the writ and order Madison to deliver the documents, because the provision in the Judiciary Act that had given the Court that power was unconstitutional.[11]

Perhaps Marshall feared a confrontation with the Jefferson administration and thought Madison would refuse his directive anyway. In any case, his ruling shows an interesting contrast in the early Court. On one hand, it humbly declined a power—issuing a writ of mandamus—given to it by Congress, but on the other, it laid the foundation for legitimizing a much more important one—judicial review. Marbury never got his commission, but the Court's ruling in the case has become more significant for the precedent it established: As the first time the Court declared an act of Congress unconstitutional, it established the power of judicial review, a key power that enables the judicial branch to remain a powerful check on the other branches of government.

Consider the dual nature of John Marshall's opinion in Marbury v. Madison: *On one hand, it limits the power of the courts, yet on the other it also expanded their power. Explain the different aspects of the decision in terms of these contrasting results.*

THE COURTS AND PUBLIC POLICY

Even with judicial review in place, the courts do not always stand ready just to throw out actions of the other branches of government. More broadly, as Marshall put it, "it is emphatically the province and duty of the judicial department to say what the law is."[12] The United States has a **common law** system in which law is largely developed through binding judicial decisions. With roots in medieval England, the system was inherited by the American colonies along with many other British traditions.[13] It stands in contrast to code law systems, which provide very detailed and comprehensive laws that do not leave room for much interpretation and judicial decision-making. With code law in place, as it is in many nations of the world, it is the job of judges to simply apply the law. But under common law, as in the United States, they interpret it. Often referred to as a system of judge-made law, common law provides the opportunity for the judicial branch to have stronger involvement in the process of law-making itself, largely through its ruling and interpretation on a case-by-case basis.

In their role as policymakers, Congress and the president tend to consider broad questions of public policy and their costs and benefits. But the courts consider specific cases with narrower questions, thus enabling them to focus more closely than other government institutions on the exact context of the individuals, groups, or issues affected by the decision. This means that while the legislature can make policy through statute, and the executive can form policy through regulations and administration, the judicial branch can also influence policy through its rulings and interpretations. As cases are brought to the courts, court decisions can help shape policy.

Consider health care, for example. In 2010, President Barack Obama signed into law the Patient Protection and Affordable Care Act (ACA), a statute that brought significant changes to the nation's healthcare system. With its goal of providing more widely attainable and affordable health insurance and health care, "Obamacare" was hailed by some but soundly denounced by others as bad policy. People who opposed the law and understood that a congressional repeal would not happen any time soon looked to the courts for help. They challenged the constitutionality of the law in *National Federation of Independent Business v. Sebelius*, hoping the Supreme Court would overturn it.[14] The practice of judicial review enabled the law's critics to exercise this opportunity, even though their hopes were ultimately dashed when, by a narrow 5–4 margin, the Supreme Court upheld the health care law as a constitutional extension of Congress's power to tax.

Since this 2012 decision, the ACA has continued to face challenges, the most notable of which have also been decided by court rulings. It faced a setback in 2014, for instance, when the Supreme Court ruled in *Burwell v. Hobby Lobby* that, for religious reasons, some for-profit corporations could be exempt from the requirement that employers provide insurance coverage of contraceptives for their female employees.[15] But the ACA also attained a victory in *King v. Burwell*, when the Court upheld the ability of the federal government to provide tax credits for people who bought their health insurance through an exchange created by the law.[16]

With each ACA case it has decided, the Supreme Court has served as the umpire, upholding the law and some of its provisions on one hand, but ruling some aspects of it unconstitutional on the other. Both supporters and opponents of the law have claimed victory and faced defeat. In each case, the Supreme Court has further defined and fine-tuned the law passed by Congress and the president, determining which parts stay and which parts go, thus having its say in the way the act has manifested itself, the way it operates, and the way it serves its public purpose.

In this same vein, the courts have become the key interpreters of the U.S. Constitution, continuously interpreting it and applying it to modern times and circumstances. For example, it was in 2015 that we learned a man's threat to kill his ex-wife, written in rap lyrics and posted to her Facebook wall, was not a real threat and thus could not be prosecuted as a felony under federal law.[17] Certainly, when the Bill of Rights first declared that government could not abridge freedom of speech, its framers could never have envisioned Facebook—or any other modern technology for that matter.

But freedom of speech, just like many constitutional concepts, has come to mean different things to different generations, and it is the courts that have designed the lens through which we understand the Constitution in modern times. It is often said that the Constitution changes less by amendment and more by the way it is interpreted. Rather than collecting dust on a shelf, the nearly 230-year-old document has come with us into the modern age, and the accepted practice of judicial review has helped carry it along the way.

COURTS AS A LAST RESORT

While the U.S. Supreme Court and state supreme courts exert power over many when reviewing laws or declaring acts of other branches unconstitutional, they become particularly important when an individual or group comes before them believing there has been a wrong. A citizen or group that feels mistreated can approach a variety of institutional venues in the U.S. system for assistance in changing policy or seeking support. Organizing protests, garnering special interest group support, and changing laws through the legislative and executive branches are all possible, but an individual is most likely to find the courts especially well-suited to analyzing the particulars of his or her case.

The adversarial judicial system comes from the common law tradition: In a court case, it is one party versus the other, and it is up to an impartial person or group, such as the judge or jury, to determine which party prevails. The federal court system is most often called upon when a case touches on constitutional rights. For example, when Samantha Elauf, a Muslim woman, was denied a job working for the clothing retailer Abercrombie & Fitch because a headscarf she wears as religious practice violated the company's dress code, the Supreme Court ruled that her First Amendment rights had been violated, making it possible for her to sue the store for monetary damages.

Elauf had applied for an Abercrombie sales job in Oklahoma in 2008. Her interviewer recommended her based on her qualifications, but she was never given the job because the clothing retailer wanted to avoid having to accommodate her religious practice of wearing a headscarf, or hijab. In so doing, the Court ruled, Abercrombie violated Title VII of the Civil Rights Act of 1964, which prohibits employers from discriminating on the basis of race, color, religion, sex, or national origin, and requires them to accommodate religious practices.[18]

Rulings like this have become particularly important for members of religious minority groups, including Muslims, Sikhs, and Jews, who now feel more protected from employment discrimination based on their religious attire, head coverings, or beards.[19] Such decisions illustrate how the expansion of individual rights and liberties for particular persons or groups over the years has come about largely as a result of court rulings made for individuals on a case-by-case basis.

Although the United States prides itself on the Declaration of Independence's statement that "all men are created equal," and "equal protection of the laws" is a written constitutional principle of the Fourteenth Amendment, the reality is less than perfect. But it is evolving. Changing times and technology have and will continue to alter the way fundamental constitutional rights are defined and applied, and the courts have proven themselves to be crucial in that definition and application.

Societal traditions, public opinion, and politics have often stood in the way of the full expansion of rights and liberties to different groups, and not everyone has agreed that these rights should be expanded as they have been by the courts. Schools were long segregated by race until the Court ordered desegregation in *Brown v. Board of Education* (1954), and even then, many stood in opposition and tried to block students at the entrances to all-white schools.[20] Factions have formed on opposite sides of the abortion and handgun debates, because many do not agree that women should have abortion rights or that individuals should have the right to a handgun. People disagree about whether members of the LGBT community should be allowed to marry or whether arrested persons should be read their rights, guaranteed an attorney, and/or have their cell phones protected from police search.

But the Supreme Court has ruled in favor of all these issues and others. Even without unanimous agreement among citizens, Supreme Court decisions have made all these possibilities a reality, a particularly important one for the individuals who become the beneficiaries (Table 13.1). The judicial branch has often made decisions the other branches were either unwilling or unable to make, and Hamilton was right in *Federalist* No. 78 when he said that without the courts exercising their duty to defend the Constitution, "all the reservations of particular rights or privileges would amount to nothing."

Examples of Supreme Court Cases Involving Individuals

Case Name	Year	Court's Decision
Brown v. Board of Education	1954	Public schools must be desegregated.
Gideon v. Wainwright	1963	Poor criminal defendants must be provided an attorney.
Miranda v. Arizona	1966	Criminal suspects must be read their rights.
Roe v. Wade	1973	Women have a constitutional right to abortion.
McDonald v. Chicago	2010	An individual has the right to a handgun in his or her home.
Riley v. California	2014	Police may not search a cell phone without a warrant.
Obergefell v. Hodges	2015	Same-sex couples have the right to marry in all states.

Table 13.1 Over time, the courts have made many decisions that have broadened the rights of individuals. This table is a sampling of some of these Supreme Court cases.

The courts seldom if ever grant rights to a person instantly and upon request. In a number of cases, they have expressed reluctance to expand rights without limit, and they still balance that expansion with the government's need to govern, provide for the common good, and serve a broader societal purpose. For example, the Supreme Court has upheld the constitutionality of the death penalty, ruling that the Eighth Amendment does not prevent a person from being put to death for committing a capital crime and that the government may consider "retribution and the possibility of deterrence" when it seeks capital punishment for a crime that so warrants it.[21] In other words, there is a greater good—more safety and security—that may be more important than sparing the life of an individual who has committed a heinous crime.

Yet the Court has also put limits on the ability to impose the death penalty, ruling, for example, that the government may not execute a person with cognitive disabilities, a person who was under eighteen at the time of the crime, or a child rapist who did not kill his victim.[22] So the job of the courts on any given issue is never quite done, as justices continuously keep their eye on government laws, actions, and policy changes as cases are brought to them and then decide whether those laws, actions, and policies can stand or must go. Even with an issue such as the death penalty, about which the Court has made several rulings, there is always the possibility that further judicial interpretation of what does (or does not) violate the Constitution will be needed.

This happened, for example, as recently as 2015 in a case involving the use of lethal injection as capital punishment in the state of Oklahoma, where death-row inmates are put to death through the use of three drugs—a sedative to bring about unconsciousness (midazolam), followed by two others that cause paralysis and stop the heart. A group of these inmates challenged the use of midazolam as unconstitutional. They argued that since it could not reliably cause unconsciousness, its use constituted an Eighth Amendment violation against cruel and unusual punishment and should be stopped by the courts. The Supreme Court rejected the inmates' claims, ruling that Oklahoma could continue to use midazolam as part of its three-drug protocol.[23] But with four of the nine justices dissenting from that decision, a sharply divided Court leaves open a greater possibility of more death-penalty cases to come. The 2015–2016 session alone includes four such cases, challenging death-sentencing procedures in such states as Florida, Georgia, and Kansas.[24]

Therefore, we should not underestimate the power and significance of the judicial branch in the United States. Today, the courts have become a relevant player, gaining enough clout and trust over the years to take their place as a separate yet coequal branch.

13.2 The Dual Court System

Learning Objectives

By the end of this section, you will be able to:

* Describe the dual court system and its three tiers
* Explain how you are protected and governed by different U.S. court systems
* Compare the positive and negative aspects of a dual court system

Before the writing of the U.S. Constitution and the establishment of the permanent national judiciary under Article III, the states had courts. Each of the thirteen colonies had also had its own courts, based on the British common law model. The judiciary today continues as a **dual court system**, with courts at both the national and state levels. Both levels have three basic tiers consisting of **trial courts**, **appellate courts**, and finally courts of last resort, typically called supreme courts, at the top (Figure 13.4).

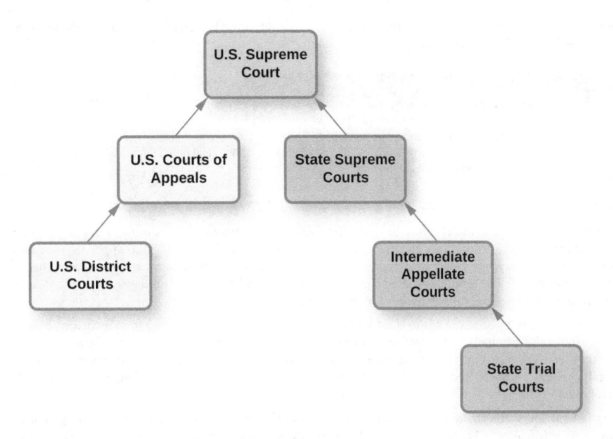

Figure 13.4 The U.S. judiciary features a dual court system comprising a federal court system and the courts in each of the fifty states. On both the federal and state sides, the U.S. Supreme Court is at the top and is the final court of appeal.

To add to the complexity, the state and federal court systems sometimes intersect and overlap each other, and no two states are exactly alike when it comes to the organization of their courts. Since a state's court system is created by the state itself, each one differs in structure, the number of courts, and even name and jurisdiction. Thus, the organization of state courts closely resembles but does not perfectly mirror the more clear-cut system found at the federal level.[25] Still, we can summarize the overall three-tiered structure of the dual court model and consider the relationship that the national and state sides share with the U.S. Supreme Court, as illustrated in Figure 13.4.

Cases heard by the U.S. Supreme Court come from two primary pathways: (1) the circuit courts, or U.S. courts of appeals (after the cases have originated in the federal district courts), and (2) state supreme courts (when there is a substantive federal question in the case). In a later section of the chapter, we discuss the lower courts and the movement of cases through the dual court system to the U.S. Supreme Court. But first, to better understand how the dual court system operates, we consider the types of cases state and local courts handle and the types for which the federal system is better designed.

COURTS AND FEDERALISM

Courts hear two different types of disputes: criminal and civil. Under **criminal law**, governments establish rules and punishments; laws define conduct that is prohibited because it can harm others and impose punishment for committing such an act. Crimes are usually labeled felonies or misdemeanors based on their nature and seriousness; felonies are the more serious crimes. When someone commits a criminal act, the government (state or national, depending on which law has been broken) charges that person with a crime, and the case brought to court contains the name of the charging government, as in *Miranda v. Arizona* discussed below.[26] On the other hand, **civil law** cases involve two or more private (non-government) parties, at least one of whom alleges harm or injury committed by the other. In both criminal and civil matters, the courts decide the remedy and resolution of the case, and in all cases, the U.S. Supreme Court is the final court of appeal.

Although the Supreme Court tends to draw the most public attention, it typically hears fewer than one hundred cases every year. In fact, the entire federal side—both trial and appellate—handles proportionately very few cases, with about 90 percent of all cases in the U.S. court system being heard at the state level.[27] The several hundred thousand cases handled every year on the federal side pale in comparison to the several million handled by the states.

State courts really are the core of the U.S. judicial system, and they are responsible for a huge area of law. Most crimes and criminal activity, such as robbery, rape, and murder, are violations of state laws, and cases are thus heard by state courts. State courts also handle civil matters; personal injury, malpractice, divorce, family, juvenile, probate, and contract disputes and real estate cases, to name just a few, are usually state-level cases.

The federal courts, on the other hand, will hear any case that involves a foreign government, patent or copyright infringement, Native American rights, maritime law, bankruptcy, or a controversy between two or more states. Cases arising from activities across state lines (interstate commerce) are also subject to federal court jurisdiction, as are cases in which the United States is a party. A dispute between two parties not from the same state or nation and in which damages of at least $75,000 are claimed is handled at the federal level. Such a case is known as a diversity of citizenship case.[28]

However, some cases cut across the dual court system and may end up being heard in both state and federal courts. Any case has the potential to make it to the federal courts if it invokes the U.S. Constitution or federal law. It could be a criminal violation of federal law, such as assault with a gun, the illegal sale of drugs, or bank robbery. Or it could be a civil violation of federal law, such as employment discrimination or securities fraud. Also, any perceived violation of a liberty protected by the Bill of Rights, such as freedom of speech or the protection against cruel and unusual punishment, can be argued before the federal courts. A summary of the basic jurisdictions of the state and federal sides is provided in Table 13.2.

Jurisdiction of the Courts: State vs. Federal

State Courts	Federal Courts
Hear most day-to-day cases, covering 90 percent of all cases	Hear cases that involve a "federal question," involving the Constitution, federal laws or treaties, or a "federal party" in which the U.S. government is a party to the case
Hear both civil and criminal matters	Hear both civil and criminal matters, although many criminal cases involving federal law are tried in state courts
Help the states retain their own sovereignty in judicial matters over their state laws, distinct from the national government	Hear cases that involve "interstate" matters, "diversity of citizenship" involving parties of two different states, or between a U.S. citizen and a citizen of another nation (and with a damage claim of at least $75,000)

Table 13.2

While we may certainly distinguish between the two sides of a jurisdiction, looking on a case-by-case basis will sometimes complicate the seemingly clear-cut division between the state and federal sides. It is always possible that issues of federal law may start in the state courts before they make their way over to the federal side. And any case that starts out at the state and/or local level on state matters can make it into the federal system on appeal—but only on points that involve a federal law or question, and usually after all avenues of appeal in the state courts have been exhausted.[29]

Consider the case *Miranda v. Arizona*.[30] Ernesto Miranda, arrested for kidnapping and rape, which are violations of state law, was easily convicted and sentenced to prison after a key piece of evidence—his own signed confession—was presented at trial in the Arizona court. On appeal first to the Arizona Supreme Court and then to the U.S. Supreme Court to exclude the confession on the grounds that its admission was a violation of his constitutional rights, Miranda won the case. By a slim 5–4 margin, the justices ruled that the confession had to be excluded from evidence because in obtaining it, the police had violated Miranda's Fifth Amendment right against self-incrimination and his Sixth Amendment right to an attorney. In the opinion of the Court, because of the coercive nature of police interrogation, no confession can be admissible unless a suspect is made aware of his rights and then in turn waives those rights. For this reason, Miranda's original conviction was overturned.

Yet the Supreme Court considered only the violation of Miranda's constitutional rights, but not whether he was guilty of the crimes with which he was charged. So there were still crimes committed for which Miranda had to face charges. He was therefore retried in state court in 1967, the second time without the confession as evidence, found guilty again based on witness testimony and other evidence, and sent to prison.

Miranda's story is a good example of the tandem operation of the state and federal court systems. His guilt or innocence of the crimes was a matter for the state courts, whereas the constitutional questions raised by his trial were a matter for the federal courts. Although he won his case before the Supreme Court, which established a significant precedent that criminal suspects must be read their so-called Miranda rights before police questioning, the victory did not do much for Miranda himself. After serving prison time, he was stabbed to death in a bar fight in 1976 while out on parole, and due to a lack of evidence, no one was ever convicted in his death.

THE IMPLICATIONS OF A DUAL COURT SYSTEM

From an individual's perspective, the dual court system has both benefits and drawbacks. On the plus side, each person has more than just one court system ready to protect his or her rights. The dual court system provides alternate venues in which to appeal for assistance, as Ernesto Miranda's case illustrates. The U.S. Supreme Court found for Miranda an extension of his Fifth Amendment protections—a constitutional right to remain silent when faced with police questioning. It was a right he could not get solely from the state courts in Arizona, but one those courts had to honor nonetheless.

The fact that a minority voice like Miranda's can be heard in court, and that his or her grievance can be resolved in his or her favor if warranted, says much about the role of the judiciary in a democratic republic. In Miranda's case, a resolution came from the federal courts, but it can also come from the state side. In fact, the many differences among the state courts themselves may enhance an individual's potential to be heard.

State courts vary in the degree to which they take on certain types of cases or issues, give access to particular groups, or promote certain interests. If a particular issue or topic is not taken up in one place, it may be handled in another, giving rise to many different opportunities for an interest to be heard somewhere across the nation. In their research, Paul Brace and Melinda Hall found that state courts are important instruments of democracy because they provide different alternatives and varying arenas for political access. They wrote, "Regarding courts, one size does not fit all, and the republic has survived in part because federalism allows these critical variations."[31]

But the existence of the dual court system and variations across the states and nation also mean that there are different courts in which a person could face charges for a crime or for a violation of another person's rights. Except for the fact that the U.S. Constitution binds judges and justices in all the courts, it is state law that governs the authority of state courts, so judicial rulings about what is legal or illegal may differ from state to state. These differences are particularly pronounced when the laws across the states and the nation are not the same, as we see with marijuana laws today.

Finding a Middle Ground

Marijuana Laws and the Courts

There are so many differences in marijuana laws between states, and between the states and the national government, that uniform application of treatment in courts across the nation is nearly impossible (Figure 13.5). What is legal in one state may be illegal in another, and state laws do not cross state geographic boundary lines—but people do. What's more, a person residing in any of the fifty states is still subject to federal law.

Marijuana Legal Status by State

Legend:
- Illegal
- Decriminalized
- Medicinal only
- Medicinal and decriminalized
- Recreational

Figure 13.5 Marijuana laws vary remarkably across the fifty states. In many states, marijuana use is illegal, as it is under federal law, but some states have decriminalized it, some allow it for medicinal use, and some have done both. Marijuana is currently legal for recreational use in ten states.

For example, a person over the age of twenty-one may legally buy marijuana for recreational use in ten states and for medicinal purpose in more than half the states, but could face charges—and time in court—for possession in a neighboring state where marijuana use is not legal. Under federal law, too, marijuana is still regulated as a Schedule 1 (most dangerous) drug, and federal authorities often find themselves pitted against states that have legalized it. Such differences can lead, somewhat ironically, to arrests and federal criminal charges for people who have marijuana in states where it is legal, or to federal raids on growers and dispensaries that would otherwise be operating legally under their state's law.

Differences among the states have also prompted a number of lawsuits against states with legalized marijuana, as people opposed to those state laws seek relief from (none other than) the courts. They want the courts to resolve the issue, which has left in its wake contradictions and conflicts between states that have legalized marijuana and those that have not, as well as conflicts between states and the national government. These lawsuits include at least one filed by the states of Nebraska and Oklahoma against Colorado. Citing concerns over cross-border trafficking, difficulties with law enforcement, and violations of the Constitution's supremacy clause, Nebraska and Oklahoma have petitioned the U.S. Supreme Court to intervene and rule on the legality of Colorado's marijuana law, hoping to get it overturned.[32] The Supreme Court has yet to take up the case.

How do you think differences among the states and differences between federal and state law regarding marijuana use can affect the way a person is treated in court? What, if anything, should be done to rectify the disparities in application of the law across the nation?

Where you are physically located can affect not only what is allowable and what is not, but also how cases are judged. For decades, political scientists have confirmed that political culture affects the operation of government institutions, and when we add to that the differing political interests and cultures at work within each state, we end up with court systems that vary greatly in their judicial and decision-making processes.[33] Each state court system operates with its own individual set of biases. People with varying interests, ideologies, behaviors, and attitudes run the disparate legal systems, so the results they produce are not always the same. Moreover, the selection method for judges at the state and local level varies. In some states, judges are elected rather than appointed, which can affect their rulings.

Just as the laws vary across the states, so do judicial rulings and interpretations, and the judges who make them. That means there may not be uniform application of the law—even of the same law—nationwide. We are somewhat bound by geography and do not always have the luxury of picking and choosing the venue for our particular case. So, while having such a decentralized and varied set of judicial operations affects the kinds of cases that make it to the courts and gives citizens alternate locations to get their case heard, it may also lead to disparities in the way they are treated once they get there.

13.3 The Federal Court System

Learning Objectives

By the end of this section, you will be able to:
- Describe the differences between the U.S. district courts, circuit courts, and the Supreme Court
- Explain the significance of precedent in the courts' operations
- Describe how judges are selected for their positions

Congress has made numerous changes to the federal judicial system throughout the years, but the three-tiered structure of the system is quite clear-cut today. Federal cases typically begin at the lowest federal level, the district (or trial) court. Losing parties may appeal their case to the higher courts—first to the circuit courts, or U.S. courts of appeals, and then, if chosen by the justices, to the U.S. Supreme Court. Decisions of the higher courts are binding on the lower courts. The **precedent** set by each ruling, particularly by the Supreme Court's decisions, both builds on principles and guidelines set by earlier cases and frames the ongoing operation of the courts, steering the direction of the entire system. Reliance on precedent has enabled the federal courts to operate with logic and consistency that has helped validate their role as the key interpreters of the Constitution and the law—a legitimacy particularly vital in the United States where citizens do not elect federal judges and justices but are still subject to their rulings.

THE THREE TIERS OF FEDERAL COURTS

There are ninety-four U.S. **district courts** in the fifty states and U.S. territories, of which eighty-nine are in the states (at least one in each state). The others are in Washington, DC; Puerto Rico; Guam; the U.S. Virgin Islands; and the Northern Mariana Islands. These are the trial courts of the national system, in which federal cases are tried, witness testimony is heard, and evidence is presented. No district court crosses state lines, and a single judge oversees each one. Some cases are heard by a jury, and some are not.

There are thirteen U.S. **courts of appeals**, or **circuit courts**, eleven across the nation and two in Washington,

DC (the DC circuit and the federal circuit courts), as illustrated in Figure 13.6. Each court is overseen by a rotating panel of three judges who do not hold trials but instead review the rulings of the trial (district) courts within their geographic circuit. As authorized by Congress, there are currently 179 judges. The circuit courts are often referred to as the *intermediate appellate courts* of the federal system, since their rulings can be appealed to the U.S. Supreme Court. Moreover, different circuits can hold legal and cultural views, which can lead to differing outcomes on similar legal questions. In such scenarios, clarification from the U.S. Supreme Court might be needed.

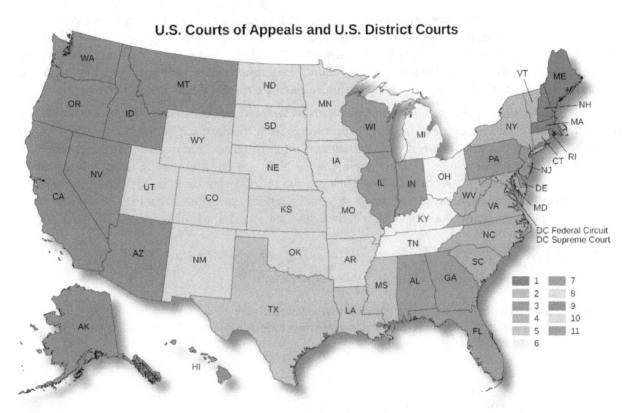

U.S. Courts of Appeals and U.S. District Courts

Figure 13.6 There are thirteen judicial circuits: eleven in the geographical areas marked on the map and two in Washington, DC.

Today's federal court system was not an overnight creation; it has been changing and transitioning for more than two hundred years through various acts of Congress. Since district courts are not called for in Article III of the Constitution, Congress established them and narrowly defined their jurisdiction, at first limiting them to handling only cases that arose within the district. Beginning in 1789 when there were just thirteen, the district courts became the basic organizational units of the federal judicial system. Gradually over the next hundred years, Congress expanded their jurisdiction, in particular over federal questions, which enables them to review constitutional issues and matters of federal law. In the Judicial Code of 1911, Congress made the U.S. district courts the sole general-jurisdiction trial courts of the federal judiciary, a role they had previously shared with the circuit courts.[34]

The circuit courts started out as the trial courts for most federal criminal cases and for some civil suits, including those initiated by the United States and those involving citizens of different states. But early on, they did not have their own judges; the local district judge and two Supreme Court justices formed each circuit court panel. (That is how the name "circuit" arose—judges in the early circuit courts traveled from town to town to hear cases, following prescribed paths or circuits to arrive at destinations where they were needed.[35]) Circuit courts also exercised appellate jurisdiction (meaning they receive appeals on federal district court cases) over most civil suits that originated in the district courts; however, that role ended in 1891, and their appellate jurisdiction was turned over to the newly created circuit courts, or U.S. courts of appeals. The original circuit courts—the ones that did not have "of appeals" added to their name—were abolished in 1911, fully replaced by these new circuit courts of appeals.[36]

While we often focus primarily on the district and circuit courts of the federal system, other federal trial courts exist that have more specialized jurisdictions, such as the Court of International Trade, Court of Federal Claims, and U.S. Tax Court. Specialized federal appeals courts include the Court of Appeals for the Armed Forces and the Court of Appeals for Veterans Claims. Cases from any of these courts may also be appealed to the Supreme Court, although that result is very rare.

On the U.S. Supreme Court, there are nine justices—one chief justice and eight associate justices. Circuit courts each contain three justices, whereas federal district courts have just one judge each. As the national court of last resort for all other courts in the system, the Supreme Court plays a vital role in setting the standards of interpretation that the lower courts follow. The Supreme Court's decisions are binding across the nation and establish the precedent by which future cases are resolved in all the system's tiers.

The U.S. court system operates on the principle of **stare decisis** (Latin for *stand by things decided*), which means that today's decisions are based largely on rulings from the past, and tomorrow's rulings rely on what is decided today. *Stare decisis* is especially important in the U.S. common law system, in which the consistency of precedent ensures greater certainty and stability in law and constitutional interpretation, and it also contributes to the solidity and legitimacy of the court system itself. As former Supreme Court justice Benjamin Cardozo summarized it years ago, "Adherence to precedent must then be the rule rather than the exception if litigants are to have faith in the even-handed administration of justice in the courts."[37]

Link to Learning

With a focus on federal courts and the public, this website reveals the different ways (https://openstax.org/l/29fedcourtpub) the federal courts affect the lives of U.S. citizens and how those citizens interact with the courts.

When the legal facts of one case are the same as the legal facts of another, *stare decisis* dictates that they should be decided the same way, and judges are reluctant to disregard precedent without justification. However, that does not mean there is no flexibility or that new precedents or rulings can never be created. They often are. Certainly, court interpretations can change as times and circumstances change—and as the courts themselves change when new judges are selected and take their place on the bench. For example, the membership of the Supreme Court had changed entirely between *Plessey v. Ferguson* (1896), which brought the doctrine of "separate but equal" and *Brown v. Board of Education* (1954), which required integration.[38]

THE SELECTION OF JUDGES

Judges fulfill a vital role in the U.S. judicial system and are carefully selected. At the federal level, the president nominates a candidate to a judgeship or justice position, and the nominee must be confirmed by a majority vote in the U.S. Senate, a function of the Senate's "advice and consent" role. All judges and justices in the national courts serve lifetime terms of office.

The president sometimes chooses nominees from a list of candidates maintained by the American Bar Association, a national professional organization of lawyers.[39] The president's nominee is then discussed (and sometimes hotly debated) in the Senate Judiciary Committee. After a committee vote, the candidate must be confirmed by a majority vote of the full Senate. He or she is then sworn in, taking an oath of office to uphold the Constitution and the laws of the United States.

When a vacancy occurs in a lower federal court, by custom, the president consults with that state's U.S. senators before making a nomination. Through such **senatorial courtesy**, senators exert considerable influence on the selection of judges in their state, especially those senators who share a party affiliation with the president. In many cases, a senator can block a proposed nominee just by voicing his or her opposition. Thus, a presidential nominee typically does not get far without the support of the senators from the nominee's home state.

Most presidential appointments to the federal judiciary go unnoticed by the public, but when a president has the rarer opportunity to make a Supreme Court appointment, it draws more attention. That is particularly true now, when many people get their news primarily from the Internet and social media. It was not surprising to see not only television news coverage but also blogs and tweets about President Obama's nominees to the high court, Sonia Sotomayor and Elena Kagan, or President Trump's first nominee Neil Gorsuch. (Figure 13.7).

(a)   (b)   (c)

Figure 13.7   President Obama made two appointments to the U.S. Supreme Court, Justices Sonia Sotomayor (a) in 2009 and Elena Kagan (b) in 2010. Since their appointments, both justices have made rulings consistent with a more liberal ideology. The death of Justice Antonin Scalia in February 2016 prompted a third Obama nomination, that of Merrick Garland, in March 2016. However, Senate Judiciary Committee chairman Chuck Grassley (R-IA) refused to schedule a hearing for Obama's nominee and the nomination expired on January 3, 2017. Later that January, the new president, Republican Donald Trump, announced his nomination of Neil Gorsuch (c), who was confirmed in April 2017, despite a filibuster by the Democrats.

Presidential nominees for the courts typically reflect the chief executive's own ideological position. With a confirmed nominee serving a lifetime appointment, a president's ideological legacy has the potential to live on long after the end of his or her term.[40] President Obama surely considered the ideological leanings of his two Supreme Court appointees, and both Sotomayor and Kagan have consistently ruled in a more liberal ideological direction. The timing of the two nominations also dovetailed nicely with the Democratic Party's gaining control of the Senate in the 111th Congress of 2009–2011, which helped guarantee their confirmations.

But some nominees turn out to be surprises or end up ruling in ways that the president who nominated them did not anticipate. Democratic-appointed judges sometimes side with conservatives, just as Republican-appointed judges sometimes side with liberals. Republican Dwight D. Eisenhower reportedly called his nomination of Earl Warren as chief justice—in an era that saw substantial broadening of civil and criminal rights—"the biggest damn fool mistake" he had ever made. Sandra Day O'Connor, nominated by Republican president Ronald Reagan, often became a champion for women's rights. David Souter, nominated by Republican George H. W. Bush, more often than not sided with the Court's liberal wing. Anthony Kennedy, a Reagan appointee who retired in the summer of 2018, was notorious as the Court's swing vote, sometimes siding with the more conservative justices but sometimes not. Current chief justice John Roberts, though most typically an ardent member of the Court's more conservative wing, has twice voted to uphold provisions of the Affordable Care Act.

One of the reasons the framers of the U.S. Constitution included the provision that federal judges would be appointed for life was to provide the judicial branch with enough independence such that it could not easily be influenced by the political winds of the time. The nomination of Brett Kavanaugh tested that notion, as the process became intensely partisan within the Senate and with the nominee himself. (Kavanaugh's previous nomination to the U.S. Court of Appeals for the D.C. Circuit by President George W. Bush in 2003 also stalled for three years over charges of partisanship.) Sharp divisions emerged early in the confirmation process and an upset Kavanaugh called out several Democratic senators in his impassioned testimony in front of the Judiciary Committee. The high partisan drama of the Kavanaugh confirmation compelled Chief Justice Roberts to express concerns about the process and decry the threat of partisanship and conflict of interest on the Court. One analyst suggests that Roberts, not Justice Kavanaugh, will become the new swing vote on the court, replacing the pragmatic Kennedy.[41]

Once a justice has started his or her lifetime tenure on the Court and years begin to pass, many people simply forget which president nominated him or her. For better or worse, sometimes it is only a controversial nominee who leaves a president's legacy behind. For example, the Reagan presidency is often remembered for two controversial nominees to the Supreme Court—Robert Bork and Douglas Ginsburg, the former accused of taking an overly conservative and "extremist view of the Constitution"[42] and the latter of having used marijuana while a student and then a professor at Harvard University (Figure 13.8). President George W. Bush's nomination of Harriet Miers was withdrawn in the face of criticism from both sides of the political spectrum, questioning her ideological leanings and especially her qualifications, suggesting she was not ready for the job.[43] After Miers' withdrawal, the Senate went on to confirm Bush's subsequent nomination of Samuel Alito, who remains on the Court today.

(a)   (b)   (c)

Figure 13.8 Presidential nominations to the Supreme Court sometimes go awry, as illustrated by the failed nominations of Robert Bork (a), Douglas Ginsburg (b), and Harriet Miers (c).

Presidential legacy and controversial nominations notwithstanding, there is one certainty about the overall look of the federal court system: What was once a predominately white, male, Protestant institution is today much more diverse. As a look at Table 13.3 reveals, the membership of the Supreme Court has changed with the passing years.

Supreme Court Justice Firsts

First Catholic	Roger B. Taney (nominated in 1836)
First Jew	Louis J. Brandeis (1916)

Table 13.3

Supreme Court Justice Firsts

First (and only) former U.S. President	William Howard Taft (1921)
First African American	Thurgood Marshall (1967)
First Woman	Sandra Day O'Connor (1981)
First Hispanic American	Sonia Sotomayor (2009)

Table 13.3

The lower courts are also more diverse today. In the past few decades, the U.S. judiciary has expanded to include more women and minorities at both the federal and state levels.[44] However, the number of women and people of color on the courts still lags behind the overall number of white men. As of 2009, the federal judiciary consists of 70 percent white men, 15 percent white women, and between 1 and 8 percent African American, Hispanic American, and Asian American men and women.[45]

13.4 The Supreme Court

Learning Objectives

By the end of this section, you will be able to:
- Analyze the structure and important features of the Supreme Court
- Explain how the Supreme Court selects cases to hear
- Discuss the Supreme Court's processes and procedures

The Supreme Court of the United States, sometimes abbreviated SCOTUS, is a one-of-a-kind institution. While a look at the Supreme Court typically focuses on the nine justices themselves, they represent only the top layer of an entire branch of government that includes many administrators, lawyers, and assistants who contribute to and help run the overall judicial system. The Court has its own set of rules for choosing cases, and it follows a unique set of procedures for hearing them. Its decisions not only affect the outcome of the individual case before the justices, but they also create lasting impacts on legal and constitutional interpretation for the future.

THE STRUCTURE OF THE SUPREME COURT

The original court in 1789 had six justices, but Congress set the number at nine in 1869, and it has remained there ever since. There is one **chief justice**, who is the lead or highest-ranking judge on the Court, and eight **associate justices**. All nine serve lifetime terms, after successful nomination by the president and confirmation by the Senate.

The current court is fairly diverse in terms of gender, religion (Christians and Jews), ethnicity, and ideology, as well as length of tenure. Some justices have served for three decades, whereas others were only recently appointed by President Trump. Figure 13.9 lists the names of the nine justices serving on the Court as of January 2019, along with their year of appointment and the president who nominated them.

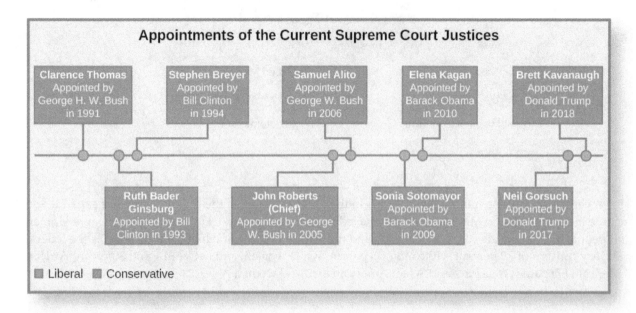

Figure 13.9

Currently, there are five justices who are considered part of the Court's more conservative wing—Chief Justice Roberts and Associate Justices Thomas, Alito, Gorsuch, and Kavanaugh—while four are considered more liberal-leaning—Justices Ginsburg, Breyer, Sotomayor, and Kagan (Figure 13.10). Had the Merrick Garland nomination in March 2016 been allowed to proceed, or had the Democrats retained the presidency in 2016, the replacement for the spots on the court vacated in the wake of the death of Associate Justice Antonin Scalia in February 2016, or the retirement of "swing" vote Anthony Kennedy in July 2018, could have swung many key votes in a moderate or liberal direction. However, with Republican Donald Trump winning the election and the Republicans retaining Senate control, the Court has become more conservative.

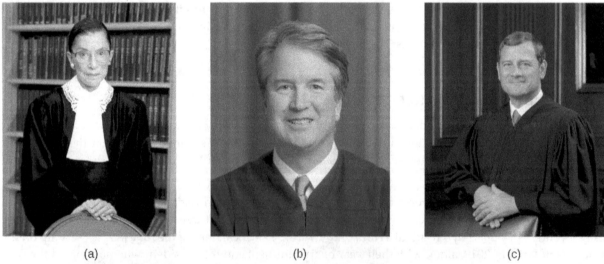

Figure 13.10   Justice Ruth Bader Ginsburg (a) is part of the liberal wing of the current Supreme Court, whereas Justice Brett Kavanaugh (b) represents the conservative wing. Chief Justice John Roberts (c) leads the court as an ardent member of its more conservative wing but has recently expressed concern over partisanship in the wake of the bitter Kavanaugh nomination fight, and may prove to be the new "swing" vote on the court.

Link to Learning

While not formally connected with the public the way elected leaders are, the Supreme Court (https://openstax.org/l/29supremecourt) nonetheless offers visitors a great deal of information at its official website.

For unofficial summaries of recent Supreme Court cases or news about the Court, visit the Oyez website (https://openstax.org/l/29oyez) or SCOTUS (https://openstax.org/l/29scotusblog) blog.

In fact, none of the justices works completely in an ideological bubble. While their numerous opinions have revealed certain ideological tendencies, they still consider each case as it comes to them, and they don't always rule in a consistently predictable or expected way. Furthermore, they don't work exclusively on their own. Each justice has three or four law clerks, recent law school graduates who temporarily work for him or her, do research, help prepare the justice with background information, and assist with the writing of opinions. The law clerks' work and recommendations influence whether the justices will choose to hear a case, as well as how they will rule. As the profile below reveals, the role of the clerks is as significant as it is varied.

Insider Perspective

Profile of a United States Supreme Court Clerk

A Supreme Court clerkship is one of the most sought-after legal positions, giving "thirty-six young lawyers each year a chance to leave their fingerprints all over constitutional law."[46] A number of current and former justices were themselves clerks, including Chief Justice John Roberts, Justices Stephen Breyer and Elena Kagan, and former chief justice William Rehnquist.

Supreme Court clerks are often reluctant to share insider information about their experiences, but it is always fascinating and informative to hear about their jobs. Former clerk Philippa Scarlett, who worked for Justice Stephen Breyer, describes four main responsibilities:[47]

Review the cases: Clerks participate in a "*cert.* pool" (short for writ of *certiorari*, a request that the lower court send up its record of the case for review) and make recommendations about which cases the Court should choose to hear.

Prepare the justices for oral argument: Clerks analyze the filed briefs (short arguments explaining each party's side of the case) and the law at issue in each case waiting to be heard.

Research and draft judicial opinions: Clerks do detailed research to assist justices in writing an opinion, whether it is the majority opinion or a dissenting or concurring opinion.

Help with emergencies: Clerks also assist the justices in deciding on emergency applications to the Court, many of which are applications by prisoners to stay their death sentences and are sometimes submitted within hours of a scheduled execution.

Explain the role of law clerks in the Supreme Court system. What is your opinion about the role they play and the justices' reliance on them?

HOW THE SUPREME COURT SELECTS CASES

The Supreme Court begins its annual session on the first Monday in October and ends late the following June. Every year, there are literally thousands of people who would like to have their case heard before the Supreme Court, but the justices will select only a handful to be placed on the **docket**, which is the list of cases scheduled on the Court's calendar. The Court typically accepts fewer than 2 percent of the as many as ten thousand cases it is asked to review every year.[48]

Case names, written in italics, list the name of a petitioner versus a respondent, as in *Roe v. Wade*, for example.[49] For a case on appeal, you can tell which party lost at the lower level of court by looking at the case name: The party unhappy with the decision of the lower court is the one bringing the appeal and is thus the petitioner, or the first-named party in the case. For example, in *Brown v. Board of Education* (1954), Oliver Brown was one of the thirteen parents who brought suit against the Topeka public schools for discrimination based on racial segregation.

Most often, the petitioner is asking the Supreme Court to grant a **writ of *certiorari***, a request that the lower court send up its record of the case for review. Once a writ of *certiorari* (*cert.* for short) has been granted, the case is scheduled on the Court's docket. The Supreme Court exercises discretion in the cases it chooses to hear, but four of the nine justices must vote to accept a case. This is called the **Rule of Four**.

For decisions about *cert.*, the Court's Rule 10 (Considerations Governing Review on Writ of *Certiorari*) takes precedence.[50] The Court is more likely to grant *certiorari* when there is a conflict on an issue between or among the lower courts. Examples of conflicts include (1) conflicting decisions among different courts of appeals on the same matter, (2) decisions by an appeals court or a state court conflicting with precedent, and (3) state court decisions that conflict with federal decisions. Occasionally, the Court will fast-track a case that has special urgency, such as *Bush v. Gore* in the wake of the 2000 election.[51]

Past research indicated that the amount of interest-group activity surrounding a case before it is granted *cert.* has a significant impact on whether the Supreme Court puts the case on its agenda. The more activity, the more likely the case will be placed on the docket.[52] But more recent research broadens that perspective, suggesting that too much interest-group activity when the Court is considering a case for its docket may actually have diminishing impact and that external actors may have less influence on the work of the Court than they have had in the past.[53] Still, the Court takes into consideration external influences, not just from interest groups but also from the public, from media attention, and from a very key governmental actor—the solicitor general.

The **solicitor general** is the lawyer who represents the federal government before the Supreme Court: He or she decides which cases (in which the United States is a party) should be appealed from the lower courts and personally approves each one presented (Figure 13.11). Most of the cases the solicitor general brings to the Court will be given a place on the docket. About two-thirds of all Supreme Court cases involve the federal government.[54]

The solicitor general determines the position the government will take on a case. The attorneys of his or her office prepare and file the petitions and briefs, and the solicitor general (or an assistant) presents the oral arguments before the Court.

(a)   (b)

Figure 13.11 Thurgood Marshall (a), who later served on the Supreme Court, was appointed solicitor general by Lyndon Johnson and was the first African American to hold the post. Noel Francisco (b) was the forty-seventh solicitor general of the United States, starting his term of office in September 2017.

In other cases in which the United States is not the petitioner or the respondent, the solicitor general may choose to intervene or comment as a third party. Before a case is granted *cert.*, the justices will sometimes ask the solicitor general to comment on or file a brief in the case, indicating their potential interest in getting it on the docket. The solicitor general may also recommend that the justices decline to hear a case. Though research has shown that the solicitor general's special influence on the Court is not unlimited, it remains quite significant. In particular, the Court does not always agree with the solicitor general, and "while justices are not lemmings who will unwittingly fall off legal cliffs for tortured solicitor general recommendations, they nevertheless often go along with them even when we least expect them to."[55]

Some have credited Donald B. Verrilli, the solicitor general under President Obama, with holding special sway over the five-justice majority ruling on same-sex marriage in June 2015. Indeed, his position that denying homosexuals the right to marry would mean "thousands and thousands of people are going to live out their lives and go to their deaths without their states ever recognizing the equal dignity of their relationships" became a foundational point of the Court's opinion, written by then-Justice Anthony Kennedy.[56] With such power over the Court, the solicitor general is sometimes referred to as "the tenth justice."

SUPREME COURT PROCEDURES

Once a case has been placed on the docket, **briefs**, or short arguments explaining each party's view of the case, must be submitted—first by the petitioner putting forth his or her case, then by the respondent. After initial briefs have been filed, both parties may file subsequent briefs in response to the first. Likewise, people and groups that are not party to the case but are interested in its outcome may file an *amicus curiae* ("friend of the court") brief giving their opinion, analysis, and recommendations about how the Court should rule. Interest groups in particular can become heavily involved in trying to influence the judiciary by filing *amicus* briefs—both before and after a case has been granted *cert.* And, as noted earlier, if the United States is not party to a case, the solicitor general may file an *amicus* brief on the government's behalf.

With briefs filed, the Court hears **oral arguments** in cases from October through April. The proceedings are quite ceremonial. When the Court is in session, the robed justices make a formal entrance into the courtroom to a standing audience and the sound of a banging gavel. The Court's marshal presents them with a traditional chant: "The Honorable, the Chief Justice and the Associate Justices of the Supreme Court of the United States. Oyez! Oyez! Oyez! [Hear ye!] All persons having business before the Honorable, the Supreme Court of the United States, are admonished to draw near and give their attention, for the Court is now sitting. God save the United States and this Honorable Court!"[57] It has not gone unnoticed that the Court, which has defended the First Amendment's religious protection and the traditional separation of church and state, opens its every public session with a mention of God.

During oral arguments, each side's lawyers have thirty minutes to make their legal case, though the justices often interrupt the presentations with questions. The justices consider oral arguments not as a forum for a lawyer to restate the merits of his or her case as written in the briefs, but as an opportunity to get answers to any questions they may have.[58] When the United States is party to a case, the solicitor general (or one of his or her assistants) will argue the government's position; even in other cases, the solicitor general may still be given time to express the government's position on the dispute.

When oral arguments have been concluded, the justices have to decide the case, and they do so in **conference**, which is held in private twice a week when the Court is in session and once a week when it is not. The conference is also a time to discuss petitions for *certiorari*, but for those cases already heard, each justice may state his or her views on the case, ask questions, or raise concerns. The chief justice speaks first about a case, then each justice speaks in turn, in descending order of seniority, ending with the most recently appointed justice.[59] The judges take an initial vote in private before the official announcement of their decisions is made public.

Oral arguments are open to the public, but cameras are not allowed in the courtroom, so the only picture we get is one drawn by an artist's hand, an illustration or rendering. Cameras seem to be everywhere today, especially to provide security in places such as schools, public buildings, and retail stores, so the lack of live coverage of Supreme Court proceedings may seem unusual or old-fashioned. Over the years, groups have called for the Court to let go of this tradition and open its operations to more "sunshine" and greater transparency. Nevertheless, the justices have resisted the pressure and remain neither filmed nor photographed during oral arguments.[60]

13.5 Judicial Decision-Making and Implementation by the Supreme Court

Learning Objectives

By the end of this section, you will be able to:
- Describe how the Supreme Court decides cases and issues opinions
- Identify the various influences on the Supreme Court
- Explain how the judiciary is checked by the other branches of government

The courts are the least covered and least publicly known of the three branches of government. The inner workings of the Supreme Court and its day-to-day operations certainly do not get as much public attention as its rulings, and only a very small number of its announced decisions are enthusiastically discussed and debated. The Court's 2015 decision on same-sex marriage was the exception, not the rule, since most court opinions are filed away quietly in the *United States Reports*, sought out mostly by judges, lawyers, researchers, and others with a particular interest in reading or studying them.

Thus, we sometimes envision the justices formally robed and cloistered away in their chambers, unaffected by the world around them, but the reality is that they are not that isolated, and a number of outside factors influence their decisions. Though they lack their own mechanism for enforcement of their rulings and their power remains checked and balanced by the other branches, the effect of the justices' opinions on the workings of government, politics, and society in the United States is much more significant than the attention they attract might indicate.

JUDICIAL OPINIONS

Every Court opinion sets precedent for the future. The Supreme Court's decisions are not always unanimous, however; the published **majority opinion**, or explanation of the justices' decision, is the one with which a majority of the nine justices agree. It can represent a vote as narrow as five in favor to four against. A tied vote is rare but can occur at a time of vacancy, absence, or abstention from a case, perhaps where there is a conflict of interest. In the event of a tied vote, the decision of the lower court stands.

Most typically, though, the Court will put forward a majority opinion. If he or she is in the majority, the chief justice decides who will write the opinion. If not, then the most senior justice ruling with the majority chooses the writer. Likewise, the most senior justice in the dissenting group can assign a member of that group to write the **dissenting opinion**; however, any justice who disagrees with the majority may write a separate dissenting opinion. If a justice agrees with the outcome of the case but not with the majority's reasoning in it, that justice may write a **concurring opinion**.

Court decisions are released at different times throughout the Court's term, but all opinions are announced publicly before the Court adjourns for the summer. Some of the most controversial and hotly debated rulings are released near or on the last day of the term and thus are avidly anticipated (**Figure 13.12**).

Figure 13.12   On June 26, 2015, supporters of marriage equality in front of the U.S. Supreme Court building eagerly await the announcement of a decision in the case of *Obergefell v. Hodges* (2015). (credit: Matt Popovich)

Link to Learning

One of the **most prominent writers (https://openstax.org/l/29fmpubpieces)** on judicial decision-making in the U.S. system is Dr. Forrest Maltzman of George Washington University. Maltzman's articles, chapters, and manuscripts, along with articles by other prominent authors in the field, are downloadable at this site.

INFLUENCES ON THE COURT

Many of the same players who influence whether the Court will grant *cert.* in a case, discussed earlier in this chapter, also play a role in its decision-making, including law clerks, the solicitor general, interest groups, and the mass media. But additional legal, personal, ideological, and political influences weigh on the Supreme Court and its decision-making process. On the legal side, courts, including the Supreme Court, cannot make a ruling unless they have a case before them, and even with a case, courts must rule on its facts. Although the courts' role is interpretive, judges and justices are still constrained by the facts of the case, the Constitution, the relevant laws, and the courts' own precedent.

A justice's decisions are influenced by how he or she defines his role as a jurist, with some justices believing strongly in **judicial activism**, or the need to defend individual rights and liberties, and they aim to stop actions and laws by other branches of government that they see as infringing on these rights. A judge or justice who views the role with an activist lens is more likely to use his or her judicial power to broaden personal liberty, justice, and equality. Still others believe in **judicial restraint**, which leads them to defer decisions (and thus policymaking) to the elected branches of government and stay focused on a narrower interpretation of the Bill of Rights. These justices are less likely to strike down actions or laws as unconstitutional and are less likely to focus on the expansion of individual liberties. While it is typically the case that liberal actions are described as unnecessarily activist, conservative decisions can be activist as well.

Critics of the judiciary often deride activist courts for involving themselves too heavily in matters they believe are better left to the elected legislative and executive branches. However, as Justice Anthony Kennedy has said, "An activist court is a court that makes a decision you don't like."[61]

Justices' personal beliefs and political attitudes also matter in their decision-making. Although we may prefer to believe a justice can leave political ideology or party identification outside the doors of the courtroom, the reality is that a more liberal-thinking judge may tend to make more liberal decisions and a more conservative-leaning judge may tend toward more conservative ones. Although this is not true 100 percent of the time, and an individual's decisions are sometimes a cause for surprise, the influence of ideology is real, and at a minimum, it often guides presidents to aim for nominees who mirror their own political or ideological image. It is likely not possible to find a potential justice who is completely apolitical.

And the courts themselves are affected by another "court"—the court of public opinion. Though somewhat isolated from politics and the volatility of the electorate, justices may still be swayed by special-interest pressure, the leverage of elected or other public officials, the mass media, and the general public. As times change and the opinions of the population change, the court's interpretation is likely to keep up with those changes, lest the courts face the danger of losing their own relevance.

Take, for example, rulings on sodomy laws: In 1986, the Supreme Court upheld the constitutionality of the State of Georgia's ban on sodomy,[62] but it reversed its decision seventeen years later, invalidating sodomy laws in Texas and thirteen other states.[63] No doubt the Court considered what had been happening nationwide: In the 1960s, sodomy was banned in all the states. By 1986, that number had been reduced by about half. By 2002, thirty-six states had repealed their sodomy laws, and most states were only selectively enforcing them. Changes in state laws, along with an emerging LGBT movement, no doubt swayed the Court and led it to the reversal of its earlier ruling with the 2003 decision, *Lawrence v. Texas* (**Figure 13.13**).[64]

Figure 13.13 The Supreme Court's 2003 decision in *Lawrence v. Texas* that overturned an earlier ruling on sodomy made national headlines and shows that Court rulings can change with the times.

Heralded by advocates of gay rights as important progress toward greater equality, the ruling in *Lawrence v. Texas* illustrates that the Court is willing to reflect upon what is going on in the world. Even with their heavy reliance on precedent and reluctance to throw out past decisions, justices are not completely inflexible and do tend to change and evolve with the times.

Get Connected!

The Importance of Jury Duty

Since judges and justices are not elected, we sometimes consider the courts removed from the public; however, this is not always the case, and there are times when average citizens may get involved with the courts firsthand as part of their decision-making process at either the state or federal levels. At some point, if you haven't already been called, you may receive a summons for jury duty from your local court system. You may be asked to serve on federal jury duty, such as U.S. district court duty or federal grand jury duty, but service at the local level, in the state court system, is much more common.

While your first reaction may be to start planning a way to get out of it, participating in jury service is vital to the operation of the judicial system, because it provides individuals in court the chance to be heard and to be tried fairly by a group of their peers. And jury duty has benefits for those who serve as well. You will no doubt come away better informed about how the judicial system works and ready to share your experiences with others. Who knows? You might even get an unexpected surprise, as some citizens in Dallas, Texas did recently when former President George W. Bush showed up to serve jury duty with them.

Have you ever been called to jury duty? Describe your experience. What did you learn about the judicial process? What advice would you give to someone called to jury duty for the first time? If you've never been called to jury duty, what questions do you have for those who have?

THE COURTS AND THE OTHER BRANCHES OF GOVERNMENT

Both the executive and legislative branches check and balance the judiciary in many different ways. The president can leave a lasting imprint on the bench through his or her nominations, even long after leaving office. The president may also influence the Court through the solicitor general's involvement or through the submission of *amicus* briefs in cases in which the United States is not a party.

President Franklin D. Roosevelt even attempted to stack the odds in his favor in 1937, with a "court-packing scheme" in which he tried to get a bill passed through Congress that would have reorganized the judiciary and enabled him to appoint up to six additional judges to the high court (**Figure 13.14**). The bill never passed, but other presidents have also been accused of trying similar moves at different courts in the federal system. Most recently, some members of Congress suggested that President Obama was attempting to "pack" the District of Columbia Circuit Court of Appeals with three nominees. Obama was filling vacancies, not adding judges, but the "packing" term was still bandied about.[65]

Figure 13.14 A 1937 cartoon mocks the court-packing plan of President Franklin D. Roosevelt (depicted on the far right). Roosevelt was not successful in increasing the number of justices on the Supreme Court, and it remains at nine.

Likewise, Congress has checks on the judiciary. It retains the power to modify the federal court structure and its appellate jurisdiction, and the Senate may accept or reject presidential nominees to the federal courts. Faced with a court ruling that overturns one of its laws, Congress may rewrite the law or even begin a constitutional amendment process.

But the most significant check on the Supreme Court is executive and legislative leverage over the implementation and enforcement of its rulings. This process is called judicial implementation. While it is true that courts play a major role in policymaking, they have no mechanism to make their rulings a reality. Remember it was Alexander Hamilton in *Federalist* No. 78 who remarked that the courts had "neither force nor will, but merely judgment." And even years later, when the 1832 Supreme Court ruled the State of Georgia's seizing of Native American lands unconstitutional,[66] President Andrew Jackson is reported to have said, "John Marshall has made his decision, now let him enforce it," and the Court's ruling was basically ignored.[67] Abraham Lincoln, too, famously ignored Chief Justice Roger B. Taney's order finding unconstitutional Lincoln's suspension of habeas corpus rights in 1861, early in the Civil War. Thus, court rulings matter only to the extent they are heeded and followed.

The Court relies on the executive to implement or enforce its decisions and on the legislative branch to fund them. As the Jackson and Lincoln stories indicate, presidents may simply ignore decisions of the Court, and Congress may withhold funding needed for implementation and enforcement. Fortunately for the courts, these situations rarely happen, and the other branches tend to provide support rather than opposition. In general, presidents have tended to see it as their duty to both obey and enforce Court rulings, and Congress seldom takes away the funding needed for the president to do so.

For example, in 1957, President Dwight D. Eisenhower called out the military by executive order to enforce the Supreme Court's order to racially integrate the public schools in Little Rock, Arkansas. Eisenhower told the nation: "Whenever normal agencies prove inadequate to the task and it becomes necessary for the executive branch of the federal government to use its powers and authority to uphold federal courts, the president's responsibility is inescapable."[68] Executive Order 10730 nationalized the Arkansas National Guard to enforce desegregation because the governor refused to use the state National Guard troops to protect the black students trying to enter the school (Figure 13.15).

Figure 13.15 President Eisenhower sent federal troops to escort nine black students (the "Little Rock Nine") into an Arkansas high school in 1957 to enforce the Supreme Court's order outlawing racial segregation in public schools.

So what becomes of court decisions is largely due to their credibility, their viability, and the assistance given by the other branches of government. It is also somewhat a matter of tradition and the way the United States has gone about its judicial business for more than two centuries. Although not everyone agrees with the decisions made by the Court, rulings are generally accepted and followed, and the Court is respected as the key interpreter of the laws and the Constitution. Over time, its rulings have become yet another way policy is legitimately made and justice more adequately served in the United States.

Key Terms

amicus curiae literally a "friend of the court" and used for a brief filed by someone who is interested in but not party to a case

appellate court a court that reviews cases already decided by a lower or trial court and that may change the lower court's decision

appellate jurisdiction the power of a court to hear a case on appeal from a lower court and possibly change the lower court's decision

associate justice a member of the Supreme Court who is not the chief justice

brief a written legal argument presented to a court by one of the parties in a case

chief justice the highest-ranking justice on the Supreme Court

circuit courts the appeals (appellate) courts of the federal court system that review decisions of the lower (district) courts; also called courts of appeals

civil law a non-criminal law defining private rights and remedies

common law the pattern of law developed by judges through case decisions largely based on precedent

concurring opinion an opinion written by a justice who agrees with the Court's majority opinion but has different reasons for doing so

conference closed meeting of the justices to discuss cases on the docket and take an initial vote

courts of appeals the appellate courts of the federal court system that review decisions of the lower (district) courts; also called circuit courts

criminal law a law that prohibits actions that could harm or endanger others, and establishes punishment for those actions

dissenting opinion an opinion written by a justice who disagrees with the majority opinion of the Court

district courts the trial courts of the federal court system where cases are tried, evidence is presented, and witness testimony is heard

docket the list of cases pending on a court's calendar

dual court system the division of the courts into two separate systems, one federal and one state, with each of the fifty states having its own courts

judicial activism a judicial philosophy in which a justice is more likely to overturn decisions or rule actions by the other branches unconstitutional, especially in an attempt to broaden individual rights and liberties

judicial restraint a judicial philosophy in which a justice is more likely to let stand the decisions or actions of the other branches of government

judicial review the power of the courts to review actions taken by the other branches of government and the states and to rule on whether those actions are constitutional

majority opinion an opinion of the Court with which more than half the nine justices agree

Marbury v. Madison the 1803 Supreme Court case that established the courts' power of judicial review and the first time the Supreme Court ruled an act of Congress to be unconstitutional

oral argument words spoken before the Supreme Court (usually by lawyers) explaining the legal reasons behind their position in a case and why it should prevail

original jurisdiction the power of a court to hear a case for the first time

precedent the principles or guidelines established by courts in earlier cases that frame the ongoing operation of the courts, steering the direction of the entire system

Rule of Four a Supreme Court custom in which a case will be heard when four justices decide to do so

senatorial courtesy an unwritten custom by which the president consults the senators in the state before nominating a candidate for a federal vacancy there, particularly for court positions

solicitor general the lawyer who represents the federal government and argues some cases before the Supreme Court

stare decisis the principle by which courts rely on past decisions and their precedents when making decisions in new cases

trial court the level of court in which a case starts or is first tried

writ of *certiorari* an order of the Supreme Court calling up the records of the lower court so a case may be reviewed; sometimes abbreviated *cert.*

Summary

13.1 Guardians of the Constitution and Individual Rights

From humble beginnings, the judicial branch has evolved over the years to a significance that would have been difficult for the Constitution's framers to envision. While they understood and prioritized the value of an independent judiciary in a common law system, they could not have predicted the critical role the courts would play in the interpretation of the Constitution, our understanding of the law, the development of public policy, and the preservation and expansion of individual rights and liberties over time.

13.2 The Dual Court System

The U.S. judicial system features a dual court model, with courts at both the federal and state levels, and the U.S. Supreme Court at the top. While cases may sometimes be eligible for both state and federal review, each level has its own distinct jurisdiction. There are trial and appellate courts at both levels, but there are also remarkable differences among the states in their laws, politics, and culture, meaning that no two state court systems are exactly alike. The diversity of courts across the nation can have both positive and negative effects for citizens, depending on their situation. While it provides for various opportunities for an issue or interest to be heard, it may also lead to case-by-case treatment of individuals, groups, or issues that is not always the same or even-handed across the nation.

13.3 The Federal Court System

The structure of today's three-tiered federal court system, largely established by Congress, is quite clear-cut. The system's reliance on precedent ensures a consistent and stable institution that is still capable of slowly evolving over the years—such as by increasingly reflecting the diverse population it serves. Presidents hope their judicial nominees will make rulings consistent with the chief executive's own ideological leanings. But the lifetime tenure of federal court members gives them the flexibility to act in ways that may or may not reflect what their nominating president intended. Perfect alignment between nominating president and justice is not expected; a judge might be liberal on most issues but conservative on others, or vice versa. However, presidents have sometimes been surprised by the decisions made by their nominees, such as President Eisenhower was by Justice Earl Warren and President Reagan by Justice Anthony Kennedy.

13.4 The Supreme Court

A unique institution, the U.S. Supreme Court today is an interesting mix of the traditional and the modern. On one hand, it still holds to many of the formal traditions, processes, and procedures it has followed for many decades. Its public proceedings remain largely ceremonial and are never filmed or photographed. At the same time, the Court has taken on new cases involving contemporary matters before a nine-justice panel that is more diverse today than ever before. When considering whether to take on a case and then later when ruling on it, the justices rely on a number of internal and external players who assist them with and influence their work, including, but not limited to, their law clerks, the U.S. solicitor general, interest groups, and the mass media.

13.5 Judicial Decision-Making and Implementation by the Supreme Court

Like the executive and legislative branches, the judicial system wields power that is not absolute. There remain many checks on its power and limits to its rulings. Judicial decisions are also affected by various internal and external factors, including legal, personal, ideological, and political influences. To stay relevant, Court decisions have to keep up with the changing times, and the justices' decision-making power is subject to the support afforded by the other branches of government in implementation and enforcement. Nevertheless, the courts have evolved into an indispensable part of our government system—a separate and coequal branch that interprets law, makes policy, guards the Constitution, and protects individual rights.

Review Questions

1. The Supreme Court's power of judicial review _____.
   a. is given to it in the original constitution
   b. enables it to declare acts of the other branches unconstitutional
   c. allows it to hear cases
   d. establishes the three-tiered court system

2. The Supreme Court most typically functions as _____.
   a. a district court
   b. a trial court
   c. a court of original jurisdiction
   d. an appeals court

3. In *Federalist* No. 78, Alexander Hamilton characterized the judiciary as the _____ branch of government.
   a. most unnecessary
   b. strongest
   c. least dangerous
   d. most political

4. Explain one positive and one negative aspect of the lifetime term of office for judges and justices in the federal court system. Why do you believe the constitution's framers chose lifetime terms?

5. What do you find most significant about having a common law system?

6. Of all the court cases in the United States, the majority are handled _____.
   a. by the U.S. Supreme Court
   b. at the state level
   c. by the circuit courts
   d. by the U.S. district courts

7. Both state and federal courts hear matters that involve _____.
   a. civil law only
   b. criminal law only
   c. both civil and criminal law
   d. neither civil nor criminal law

8. A state case is more likely to be heard by the federal courts when _____.
    a. it involves a federal question
    b. a governor requests a federal court hearing
    c. it involves a criminal matter
    d. the state courts are unable to come up with a decision

9. The existence of the dual court system is an unnecessary duplication to some but beneficial to others. Provide at least one positive and one negative characteristic of having overlapping court systems in the United States.

10. Which court would you consider to be closest to the people? Why?

11. Besides the Supreme Court, there are lower courts in the national system called _____.
    a. state and federal courts
    b. district and circuit courts
    c. state and local courts
    d. civil and common courts

12. In standing by precedent, a judge relies on the principle of _____.
    a. *stare decisis*
    b. amicus curiae
    c. judicial activism
    d. laissez-faire

13. The justices of the Supreme Court are _____.
    a. elected by citizens
    b. chosen by the Congress
    c. confirmed by the president
    d. nominated by the president and confirmed by the Senate

14. Do you believe federal judges should be elected rather than appointed? Why or why not?

15. When it comes to filling judicial positions in the federal courts, do you believe race, gender, religion, and ethnicity should matter? Why or why not?

16. The Supreme Court consists of _____.
    a. nine associate justices
    b. one chief justice and eight associate justices
    c. thirteen judges
    d. one chief justice and five associate justices

17. A case will be placed on the Court's docket when _____ justices agree to do so.
    a. four
    b. five
    c. six
    d. all

18. One of the main ways interest groups participate in Supreme Court cases is by _____.

    a. giving monetary contributions to the justices
    b. lobbying the justices
    c. filing *amicus curiae* briefs
    d. protesting in front of the Supreme Court building

19. The lawyer who represents the federal government and argues cases before the Supreme Court is the _____.
    a. solicitor general
    b. attorney general
    c. U.S. attorney
    d. chief justice

20. What do the appointments of the Supreme Court's two newest justices, Neil Gorsuch and Brett Kavanaugh, reveal about the changing selection process for the high court?

21. When using judicial restraint, a judge will usually _____.
    a. refuse to rule on a case
    b. overrule any act of Congress he or she doesn't like
    c. defer to the decisions of the elected branches of government
    d. make mostly liberal rulings

22. When a Supreme Court ruling is made, justices may write a _____ to show they agree with the majority but for different reasons.
   a. brief
   b. dissenting opinion
   c. majority opinion
   d. concurring opinion

23. Which of the following is a check that the legislative branch has over the courts?
   a. Senate approval is needed for the appointment of justices and federal judges.
   b. Congress may rewrite a law the courts have declared unconstitutional.
   c. Congress may withhold funding needed to implement court decisions.
   d. all of the above

24. What are the core factors that determine how judges decide in court cases?

25. Discuss some of the difficulties involved in the implementation and enforcement of judicial decisions.

Critical Thinking Questions

26. In what ways is the court system better suited to protect the individual than are the elected branches of the government?

27. On what types of policy issues do you expect the judicial branch to be especially powerful, and on which do you expect it to exert less power?

28. Discuss the relationship of the judicial branch to the other branches of government. In what ways is the judicial more powerful than other branches? In what ways is SCOTUS less powerful than other branches? Explain.

29. What should be the most important considerations when filling judge and justice positions at the federal level? Why?

30. The shirking of jury duty is a real problem in the United States. Give some reasons for this and suggest what can be done about it.

31. Take a closer look at some of the operational norms of the Supreme Court, such as the Rule of Four or the prohibition on cameras in the courtroom. What is your opinion about them as long-standing traditions, and which (if any), do you believe should be changed? Explain your answer.

Suggestions for Further Study

Books written by current and former justices:

Breyer, Stephen. 2006. *Active Liberty: Interpreting the Democratic Constitution.* New York: Vintage; 2010; Making Democracy Work: A Judge's View. New York: Knopf.

O'Connor, Sandra Day. 2004. *The Majesty of the Law: Reflections of a Supreme Court Justice.* New York: Random House.

Rehnquist, William. 2002. *The Supreme Court.* New York: Vintage.

Scalia, Antonin. 1998. *A Matter of Interpretation: The Federal Courts and the Law.* Princeton, NJ: Princeton

University Press.

Sotomayor, Sonia. 2014. *My Beloved World*. New York: Vintage Books.

Stevens, John Paul. 2011. *Five Chiefs: A Supreme Court Memoir*. New York: Little, Brown.

Thomas, Clarence. 2008. *My Grandfather's Son: A Memoir*. New York: Harper.

Books about the U.S. court system:

Coyle, Marcia. 2013. *The Roberts Court: The Struggle for the Constitution*. New York: Simon and Schuster.

Ferguson, Andrew G. 2013. *Why Jury Duty Matters: A Citizen's Guide to Constitutional Action*. New York: New York University Press.

Millhiser, Ian. 2015. *Injustices: The Supreme Court's History of Comforting the Comfortable and Afflicting the Afflicted*. New York: Nation Books.

Peppers, Todd C., and Artemus Ward. 2012. *In Chambers: Stories of Supreme Court Law Clerks and Their Justices*. Charlottesville: University of Virginia Press.

Tobin, Jeffrey. 2012. *The Oath: The Obama White House and the Supreme Court*. New York: Doubleday.

Vile, John R. 2014. *Essential Supreme Court Decisions: Summaries of Leading Cases in U.S. Constitutional Law*, 16th ed. Lanham: Rowman & Littlefield.

Films:

1981. *The First Monday in October*.

1993. *The Pelican Brief*.

HBO. 2000. *Recount*.

2015. *Confirmation*.

2015. *On the Basis of Sex*.

Chapter 14

State and Local Government

Figure 14.1   In February 2015, parents, students, and teachers rallied against proposed cuts in education funding in the state budget put forth by Arizona governor Doug Ducey. Education policy and administration is primarily a state and local matter. (credit: modification of work by Andy Blackledge)

Chapter Outline

Introduction

Controversial national policy decisions by lawmakers and justices tend to grab headlines and dominate social media, while state and local government matters often evoke less enthusiasm. Yet, if we think about which level of government most directly affects us on a daily basis, it is undoubtedly the level closest to us, including our city, county, school districts, and state government. Whether it is by maintaining roads we drive on each day, supplying clean water with which we brush our teeth, or allocating financial support to higher education, state and local government provides resources that shape our everyday lives, including your final tuition bill (Figure 14.1).

How do state and local governments gain the authority to make these decisions, and how are their actions guided by cultural and other differences between the states? What tensions exist between national and state governments on policy matters, and what unique powers do mayors and governors enjoy? By answering these and other questions, this chapter explores the role of state and local governments in our lives.

14.1 State Power and Delegation

Learning Objectives

By the end of this section, you will be able to:
- Explain how the balance of power between national and state governments shifted with the drafting and ratification of the Constitution
- Identify parts of the Constitution that grant power to the national government and parts that support states' rights
- Identify two fiscal policies by which the federal government exerts control over state policy decisions

When the framers met at the Constitutional Convention in 1787, they had many competing tensions to resolve. For instance, they had to consider how citizens would be represented in the national government, given population differences between the states. In addition, they had to iron out differences of opinion about where to concentrate political power. Would the legislative branch have more authority than the executive branch, and would state governments retain as many rights as they had enjoyed under the Articles of Confederation?

Here we look at the manner in which power was divided between the national and state governments, first under the Articles of Confederation and then under the U.S. Constitution. As you read, observe the shifting power dynamic between the national government and subnational governments at the state and local level.

STATE POWER AT THE FOUNDING

Before the ratification of the Constitution, the state governments' power far exceeded that held by the national government. This distribution of authority was the result of a conscious decision and was reflected in the structure and framework of the Articles of Confederation. The national government was limited, lacking both a president to oversee domestic and foreign policy and a system of federal courts to settle disputes between the states.

Restricting power at the national level gave the states a great deal of authority over and independence from the federal government. Each state legislature appointed its own Congressional representatives, subject to recall by the states, and each state was given the authority to collect taxes from its citizens. But limiting national government power was not the delegates' only priority. They also wanted to prevent any given state from exceeding the authority and independence of the others. The delegates ultimately worked to create a level playing field between the individual states that formed the confederation. For instance, the Articles of Confederation could not be amended without the approval of each state, and each state received one vote in Congress, regardless of population.[1]

It wasn't long after the Articles of Confederation were established that cracks began to appear in their foundation. Congress struggled to conduct business and to ensure the financial credibility of the new country's government. One difficulty was its inability to compel the individual states to cover their portion of Revolutionary War debt. Attempts to recoup these funds through the imposition of tariffs were vetoed by states with a vested financial interest in their failure.[2]

Given the inherent weaknesses in the system set up by the Articles, in 1787 the delegates came together once again to consider amendments to the Articles, but they ended up instead considering a new design for the government (Figure 14.2). To produce more long-term stability, they needed to establish a more effective division of power between the federal and state governments. Ultimately, the framers settled on a system in which power would be shared: The national government had its core duties, the state governments had their duties, and other duties were shared equally between them. Today this structure of power sharing is referred to as federalism.

Figure 14.2 The Articles of Confederation, written in 1777 and adopted in 1781, established the first government of the United States. The Articles were replaced by the Constitution in 1787.

The Constitution allocated more power to the federal government by effectively adding two new branches: a president to head the executive branch and the Supreme Court to head the judicial branch. The specific delegated or **expressed powers** granted to Congress and to the president were clearly spelled out in the body of the Constitution under Article I, Section 8, and Article II, Sections 2 and 3.

In addition to these expressed powers, the national government was given **implied powers** that, while not clearly stated, are inferred. These powers stem from the *elastic clause* in Article I, Section 8, of the Constitution, which provides Congress the authority "to make all Laws which shall be necessary and proper for carrying into Execution the Foregoing powers." This statement has been used to support the federal government's playing a role in controversial policy matters, such as the provision of healthcare, the expansion of power to levy and collect taxes, and regulation of interstate commerce. Finally, Article VI declared that the U.S. Constitution and any laws or treaties made in connection with that document were to supersede constitutions and laws made at the state level. This clause, better known as the *supremacy clause*, makes clear that any conflict in law between the central (or federal) government and the regional (or state) governments is typically resolved in favor of the central government.

Although the U.S. Constitution clearly allocated more power to the federal government than had been the case under the Articles of Confederation, the framers still respected the important role of the states in the new government. The states were given a host of powers independent of those enjoyed by the national government. As one example, they now had the power to establish local governments and to account for the structure, function, and responsibilities of these governments within their state constitutions. This gave states sovereignty, or supreme and independent authority, over county, municipal, school and other special districts.

States were also given the power to ratify amendments to the U.S. Constitution. Throughout U.S. history, all amendments to the Constitution except one have been proposed by Congress and then ratified by either three-fourths of the state legislatures or three-fourths of the state conventions called for ratification purposes. This process ensures that the states have a voice in any changes to the Constitution. The Twenty-First Amendment (repealing the Eighteenth Amendment's prohibition on alcohol) was the only amendment ratified using the state ratifying convention method. Although this path has never been taken, the U.S. Constitution even allows for state legislatures to take a direct and very active role in the amendment proposal process. If at least two-thirds of the state legislatures apply for a national convention, constitutional amendments can be proposed at the convention.

Finding a Middle Ground

Debating the Need for a National Convention

As of 2018, twenty-eight states had passed applications to hold a national convention. These states are pushing for the opportunity to propose a constitutional amendment requiring the national government to balance its budget in the same way most states are mandated to do. For a national convention to be held, at least thirty-four states must submit applications. Thus, only six states currently stand in the way of the first national convention in U.S. history.[3]

Proponents see the convention as an opportunity to propose an amendment they argue is necessary to reduce federal spending and promote fiscal responsibility. The exploding Federal budget deficit adds to these concerns and may create more support for such a process. If not, proponents nevertheless believe the growing roster of states favoring a convention may encourage Congress to take action on its own.

Opponents feel a balanced budget amendment is not realistic given the need for emergency spending in the event of an economic recession. They also worry about the spending cuts and/or tax increases the federal government would have to impose to consistently balance the budget. Some states fear a balanced-budget requirement would limit the federal government's ability to provide them with continued fiscal support. Finally, other opponents argue that states balance only their operating budgets, while themselves assuming massive amounts of debt for capital projects.

But perhaps the greatest fear is of the unknown. A national convention is unprecedented, and there is no limit to the number of amendments delegates to such a convention might propose. However, such changes would still need to be ratified by three-fourths of the state legislatures or state conventions before they could take effect.

What are the potential benefits of a national constitutional convention? What are the risks? Are the benefits worth the risks? Why or why not?

Despite the Constitution's broad grants of state authority, one of the central goals of the Anti-Federalists, a group opposed to several components of the Constitution, was to preserve state government authority, protect the small states, and keep government power concentrated in the hands of the people. For this reason, the Tenth Amendment was included in the Bill of Rights to create a class of powers, known as reserved powers, exclusive to state governments. The amendment specifically reads, "The powers not delegated to the United States by the Constitution, nor prohibited by it to the States, are reserved to the States respectively, or to the people." In essence, if the Constitution does not decree that an activity should be performed by the national government and does not restrict the state government from engaging in it, then the state is seen as having the power to perform the function. In other words, the power is reserved to the states.

Besides reserved powers, the states also retained concurrent powers, or responsibilities shared with the national government. As part of this package of powers, the state and federal governments each have the right to collect income tax from their citizens and corporate tax from businesses. They also share responsibility for building and maintaining the network of interstates and highways and for making and enforcing laws (Figure 14.3). For instance, many state governments have laws regulating motorcycle and bicycle helmet use, banning texting and driving, and prohibiting driving under the influence of drugs or alcohol.

Figure 14.3 State (and sometimes local) governments regulate items having to do with highway safety, such as laws against cellphone use while driving. (credit right: modification of work by "Lord Jim"/Flickr)

THE EVOLUTION OF STATE POWER

Throughout U.S. history, the national and state governments have battled for dominance over the implementation of public policy and the funding of important political programs. Upon taking office in 1933 during the Great Depression (1929–1939), President Franklin D. Roosevelt initiated a series of legislative proposals to boost the economy and put people back to work. The enacted programs allowed the federal government to play a broader role in revitalizing the economy while greatly expanding its power. However, this result was not without its critics. Initially, the Supreme Court overturned several key legislative proposals passed under Roosevelt, reasoning that they represented an overreach of presidential authority and were unconstitutional, such as *Schechter Poultry Corp. v. United States*.[4] Eventually, however, the Supreme Court shifted direction to reflect public opinion, which was decisively behind the president and the need for government intervention in a time of economic turmoil.[5]

Just three decades later, during the 1964 presidential election campaign, incumbent President Lyndon B. Johnson declared a "War on Poverty," instituting a package of Great Society programs designed to improve circumstances for lower-income Americans across the nation. The new programs included Medicare and Medicaid, which are health insurance programs for seniors and low-income citizens respectively, and the food stamp program, which provides food assistance to low-income families. These initiatives greatly expanded the role of the federal government in providing a social safety net.[6] State and local governments became partners in their implementation and also came to rely on the financial support they received from the federal government in the form of program grants.[7]

As the federal government's role in policy creation expanded, so did its level of spending. Spending by the federal government began to surpass that of state and local governments shortly after 1940 (Figure 14.4). It spiked temporarily during the Great Depression and again during World War II, resuming a slow climb with the implementation of Johnson's Great Society programs noted above.

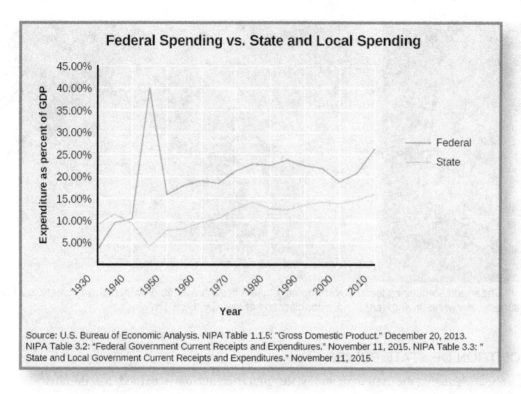

Figure 14.4 After spiking during World War II, spending by the federal government has consistently exceeded that of state and local governments. Between 2000 and 2010, the gap between federal and state spending steadily widened.

Growing financial resources gave the federal government increased power over subnational governments. This increased power was because it could use categorical grants to dictate the terms and conditions state governments had to meet to qualify for financial assistance in a specific policy area. Over time, the federal government even began to require state and local governments to comply with legislative and executive authorizations when funding was not attached. These requests from the federal government are referred to as unfunded mandates and are a source of dissatisfaction to political actors at the state and local level. To provide more transparency to state and local governments and reduce the federal government's use of mandates, the Unfunded Mandates Reform Act was passed in 1995. This act requires the Congressional Budget Office to provide information about the cost of any proposed government mandate that exceeds a specified threshold before the bill can be considered in Congress.[8]

Link to Learning

Explore the latest news on federal mandates at the Congressional Budget Office (https://openstax.org/l/29fedmandates) and the Catalog of Cost Shifts to States (https://openstax.org/l/29catcostshifts) at the National Conference of State Legislatures website.

Despite the national government's power to pass and fund policy that affects lower-level governments, states still have gained considerable headway since the late twentieth century. For instance, with the passage of the Personal Responsibility and Work Opportunity Reconciliation Act in 1996, known as the welfare reform bill, states were given great discretion over the provision of welfare. The federal government reduced its level of monetary support for the program and, in exchange, the states gained more authority over its implementation. States were able to set more restrictive work requirements, to place caps on the number of family members who could receive aid, and to limit the length of time someone could qualify for government assistance.[9]

Since then, states have been granted the flexibility to set policy across a number of controversial policy areas. For instance, a wide array of states require parental consent for abortions performed on minors, set waiting periods before an abortion can be performed, or require patients to undergo an ultrasound before the procedure. As another example, currently, almost half the states allow for the use of medical marijuana and three states have fully legalized it, despite the fact that this practice stands in contradiction to federal law that prohibits the use and distribution of marijuana.

Link to Learning

For more on these two controversial policy areas, explore "An Overview of State Abortion Laws" (https://openstax.org/l/29stateabortlaw) and "State Medical Marijuana Laws." (https://openstax.org/l/29medmarijlaws)

Today, it is not uncommon to see a patchwork of legal decisions granting states more discretion in some policy areas, such as marijuana use, while providing the federal government more authority in others, such as same-sex marriage. Decisions about which level controls policy can reflect the attitudes of government officials and the public, political ideology and the strategic advantage of setting policy on a state-by-state basis, and the necessity of setting uniform policy in the face of an economic downturn or unanticipated national security threat. What has not changed over time is the central role of the U.S. Supreme Court's views in determining how power should be distributed in a federalist system.

POWER AT THE SUBSTATE LEVEL

The U.S. Constitution is silent on the dispersion of power between states and localities within each state. The fact that states are mentioned specifically and local jurisdictions are not has traditionally meant that power independent of the federal government resides first with the state. Through their own constitutions and statutes, states decide what to require of local jurisdictions and what to delegate. This structure represents the legal principle of **Dillon's Rule**, named for Iowa Supreme Court justice John F. Dillon. Dillon argued that state actions trump those of the local government and have supremacy.[10] In this view, cities and towns exist at the pleasure of the state, which means the state can step in and dissolve them or even take them over. Indeed, most states have supremacy clauses over local governments in their constitutions.

However, for practical purposes, state and local governments must work together to ensure that citizens receive adequate services. Given the necessity of cooperation, many states have granted local governments some degree of autonomy and given them discretion to make policy or tax decisions.[11] This added independence is called **home rule**, and the transfer of power is typically spelled out within a **charter**. Charters are similar to state constitutions: they provide a framework and a detailed accounting of local government responsibilities and areas of authority. Potential conflicts can come up over home rule. For example, in 2015, the State of Texas overruled a fracking ban imposed by the City of Denton.[12]

Like state governments, local governments prioritize spending on building and maintaining the transportation infrastructure, supporting educational institutions, promoting community protection, and funding healthcare.[13] As shown in Figure 14.5, local governments, just like state governments, receive a sizeable chunk of their revenue from grants and transfers from other levels of the government. The next biggest source of revenue for local governments is property tax collections.

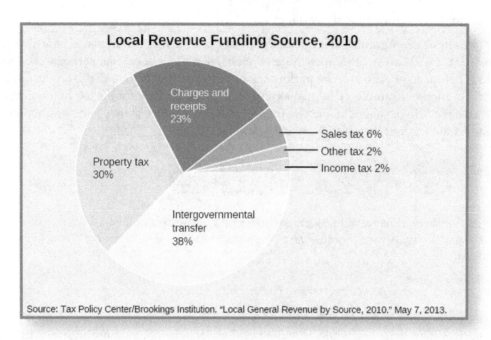

Figure 14.5 The largest source of revenue for local governments is grants and transfers from other levels of the government. The next biggest source is property tax collections.

Property taxes can be assessed on homes, land, and businesses. The local government's reliance on property tax revenue can be problematic for a number of reasons. First, unlike sales tax, the collection of which is spaced out in small increments across multiple transactions, property tax is collected in one or two lump sums and is therefore highly visible and unpopular.[14] In fact, in response to tax rate increases, many states have placed legal or constitutional limits on regional governments' ability to raise property taxes. The trend began in California with the 1978 passage of Proposition 13. This citizen-driven initiative capped the real estate tax at 1 percent of the cash value of property and stopped the practice of reassessing properties for tax purposes whenever a home in the neighborhood was sold.[15] After its passage, a number of other states followed suit, making it more difficult for states to reap the rewards of sharp increases in the market value of property.

Another drawback to local governments' reliance on property tax is that property values vary with the economic health of a given area, the quality of school districts, and the overall desirability of a state, municipality, or county. Significant parcels of land in many cities are also tax-exempt, including property occupied by colleges, churches, and other nonprofit organizations. Boston is a good example as almost 50 percent of the assessed value of property is tax-exempt.[16] College towns face the same challenge.

When the mortgage crisis began in 2007, property values decreased in many areas of the country, and many homeowners defaulted on their mortgages because their homes were now worth less than they had borrowed to buy them. With the decline in property values, local governments faced a loss in tax revenue at the same time states were cutting back on aid; tax collections were also down because of economic conditions and the inability to derive income tax from internet sales. A number of municipalities filed for bankruptcy in the face of fiscal distress during the economic recession. Perhaps the best known municipality was Detroit, Michigan, which filed for Chapter 9 bankruptcy in 2013 (Figure 14.6).

Figure 14.6 This photo shows the wreckage of the ballroom at the Lee Plaza Hotel in Detroit, Michigan. Once a landmark, this building is an example of the city's crumbling infrastructure. (credit: modification of work by Mike Boening)

Detroit filed for bankruptcy due to massive debt obligations and demands for repayment that it could not meet due to a perfect storm of economic and democratic factors. The city owed money to investors who had loaned it money, and it had liabilities resulting from its failure to fulfill its pension and healthcare obligations to city workers. The bankruptcy allowed the city time to develop an exit strategy and negotiate with creditors and union representatives in an effort to restructure its debt load.[17] Indeed, Detroit recently emerged from bankruptcy and has started to rebuild economically.

Detroit's fiscal condition only highlights the unique challenges municipalities face. Local governments have to provide many of the same services as state and national governments, but they are often constrained by the boundaries the state prescribes. They may not have the authority to raise revenue above a certain threshold, and they do not have the ability to pass expenses on to another level of government because they lack sovereignty.

14.2 State Political Culture

Learning Objectives

By the end of this section, you will be able to:
- Compare Daniel Elazar's three forms of political culture
- Describe how cultural differences between the states can shape attitudes about the role of government and citizen participation
- Discuss the main criticisms of Daniel Elazar's theory

Some states, such as Alaska, are endowed with natural resources. They can use their oil or natural gas reserves to their advantage to fund education or reduce taxes. Other states, like Florida, are favored with a climate that attracts tourists and retirees each winter, drawing in revenues to support infrastructure improvements throughout the state. These differences can lead to strategic advantages in the economic fortunes of a state, which can translate into differences in the levels of taxes that must be collected from citizens.

But their economic fortunes are only one component of what makes individual states unique. Theorists have long proposed that states are also unique as a function of their differing political cultures, or their attitudes and beliefs about the functions and expectations of the government. In the book, *American*

Federalism: A View from the States, Daniel Elazar first theorized in 1966 that the United States could be divided into three distinct political cultures: moralistic, individualistic, and traditionalistic (Figure 14.7). The diffusion of these cultures throughout the United States is attributed to the migratory patterns of immigrants who settled in and spread out across the country from the east to the west coast. These settlers had distinct political and religious values that influenced their beliefs about the proper role of government, the need for citizen involvement in the democratic process, and the role of political parties.

Figure 14.7 Daniel Elazar posited that the United States can be divided geographically into three types of political cultures—individualistic, moralistic, and traditionalistic—which spread with the migratory patterns of immigrants across the country.

MORALISTIC POLITICAL CULTURE

In Elazar's framework, states with a **moralistic political culture** see the government as a means to better society and promote the general welfare. They expect political officials to be honest in their dealings with others, put the interests of the people they serve above their own, and commit to improving the area they represent. The political process is seen in a positive light and not as a vehicle tainted by corruption. In fact, citizens in moralistic cultures have little patience for corruption and believe that politicians should be motivated by a desire to benefit the community rather than by a need to profit financially from service.

Moralistic states thus tend to support an expanded role for government. They are more likely to believe government should promote the general welfare by allocating funds to programs that will benefit the poor. In addition, they see it as the duty of public officials to advocate for new programs that will benefit marginal citizens or solve public policy problems, even when public pressure to do so is nonexistent.

The moralistic political culture developed among the Puritans in upper New England. After several generations, these settlers moved westward, and their values diffused across the top of the United States to the upper Great Lakes. In the middle of the 1800s, Scandinavians and Northern Europeans joined this group of settlers and reinforced the Puritans' values. Together, these groups pushed further west through the northern portion of the Midwest and West and then along the West Coast.[18]

States that identify with this culture value citizen engagement and desire citizen participation in all forms of political affairs. In Elazar's model, citizens from moralistic states should be more likely to donate their time and/or resources to political campaigns and to vote. This occurs for two main reasons. First, state law is likely to make it easier for residents to register and to vote because mass participation is valued. Second, citizens who hail from moralistic states should be more likely to vote because elections are truly contested. In other words, candidates will be less likely to run unopposed and more likely to face genuine competition from a qualified opponent. According to Elazar, the heightened competition is a function of individuals' believing that public service is a worthwhile endeavor and an honorable profession.

Milestone

Oregon's Efforts to Expand the Voting Franchise

In 1998, Oregon became the first state to switch to mail-in voting when citizens passed a ballot measure for it to take effect. In March 2015, Governor Kate Brown took another step to expand the voting franchise. She signed a bill into law that makes voter registration automatic for all citizens in the state with a driver's license. These citizens will now be automatically registered to vote in elections and will receive a mail-in ballot before Election Day unless they specifically opt out with the Oregon secretary of state's office.

In the United States, Oregon is the first to institute automatic voter registration, and it anticipates adding several hundred thousand residents to its voter participation list with the passage of this bill.[19] However, the new law lacks the support of Republicans in the state legislature. These party members believe automatic registration makes the voting process too easy for citizens and coerces them into voting.[20] Others argue that Oregon's new law is a positive move. They believe the change is a step in the right direction for democracy and will encourage participation in elections. If Oregon's law were to be adopted across the United States, it would affect about fifty million citizens, the number who are believed to be eligible to vote but who remain unregistered.[21]

What are the benefits of Oregon's automatic voter registration policy? Are there any drawbacks? What advantages and disadvantages might arise if this policy were adopted nationwide?

Finally, in Elazar's view, citizens in moralistic cultures are more likely to support individuals who earn their positions in government on merit rather than as a reward for party loyalty. In theory, there is less incentive to be corrupt if people acquire positions based on their qualifications. In addition, moralistic cultures are more open to third-party participation. Voters want to see political candidates compete who are motivated by the prospect of supporting the broader community, regardless of their party identification.

INDIVIDUALISTIC POLITICAL CULTURE

States that align with Elazar's **individualistic political culture** see the government as a mechanism for addressing issues that matter to individual citizens and for pursuing individual goals. People in this culture interact with the government in the same manner they would interact with a marketplace. They expect the government to provide goods and services they see as essential, and the public officials and bureaucrats who provide them expect to be compensated for their efforts. The focus is on meeting individual needs and private goals rather than on serving the best interests of everyone in the community. New policies will be enacted if politicians can use them to garner support from voters or other interested stakeholders, or if there is great demand for these services on the part of individuals.

According to Elazar, the individualist political culture originated with settlers from non-Puritan England and Germany. The first settlements were in the mid-Atlantic region of New York, Pennsylvania, and New Jersey and diffused into the middle portion of the United States in a fairly straight line from Ohio to Wyoming.

Given their focus on pursuing individual objectives, states with an individualistic mindset will tend to advance tax breaks as a way of trying to boost a state's economy or as a mechanism for promoting individual initiative and entrepreneurship. For instance, New Jersey governor Chris Christie made headlines in 2015 when discussing the incentives he used to attract businesses to the state. Christie encouraged a number of businesses to move to Camden, where unemployment has risen to almost 14 percent, by providing them with hundreds of millions of dollars in tax breaks.[22] The governor hopes these corporate incentives will spur job creation for citizens who need employment in an economically depressed area of the state.

Since this theoretical lens assumes that the objective of politics and the government is to advance individual interests, Elazar argues that individuals are motivated to become engaged in politics only if they have a personal interest in this area or wish to be in charge of the provision of government benefits. They will tend to remain involved if they get enjoyment from their participation or rewards in the form of patronage appointments or financial compensation. As a result of these personal motivations, citizens in individualistic states will tend to be more tolerant of corruption among their political leaders and less likely to see politics as a noble profession in which all citizens should engage.

Finally, Elazar argues that in individualistic states, electoral competition does not seek to identify the candidate with the best ideas. Instead it pits against each other political parties that are well organized and compete directly for votes. Voters are loyal to the candidates who hold the same party affiliation they do. As a result, unlike the case in moralistic cultures, voters do not pay much attention to the personalities of the candidates when deciding how to vote and are less tolerant of third-party candidates.

TRADITIONALISTIC POLITICAL CULTURE

Given the prominence of slavery in its formation, a **traditionalistic political culture**, in Elazar's argument, sees the government as necessary to maintaining the existing social order, the status quo. Only elites belong in the political enterprise, and as a result, new public policies will be advanced only if they reinforce the beliefs and interests of those in power.

Elazar associates traditionalistic political culture with the southern portion of the United States, where it developed in the upper regions of Virginia and Kentucky before spreading to the Deep South and the Southwest. Like the individualistic culture, the traditionalistic culture believes in the importance of the individual. But instead of profiting from corporate ventures, settlers in traditionalistic states tied their economic fortunes to the necessity of slavery on plantations throughout the South.

When elected officials do not prioritize public policies that benefit them, those on the social and economic fringes of society can be plagued by poverty and pervasive health problems. For example, although Figure 14.8 shows that poverty is a problem across the entire United States, the South has the highest incidence. According to the Centers for Disease Control and Prevention, the South also leads the nation in self-reported obesity, closely followed by the Midwest.[23] These statistics present challenges for lawmakers not only in the short term but also in the long term, because they must prioritize fiscal constraints in the face of growing demand for services.

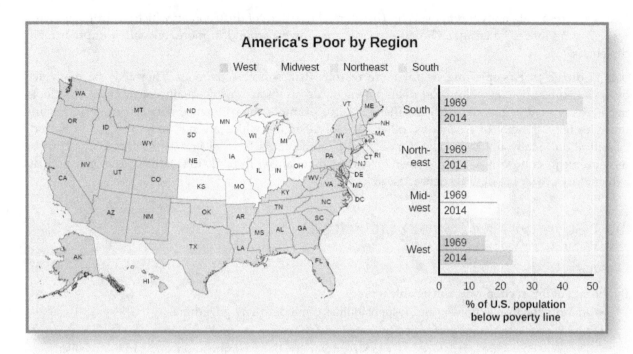

Figure 14.8 While the greatest percentage of those living below the poverty line in the United States is found in the South, migration and immigration patterns over the past fifty years have resulted in a significant increase in the percentage of the nation's poor being located in the West.

While moralistic cultures expect and encourage political participation by all citizens, traditionalistic cultures are more likely to see it as a privilege reserved for only those who meet the qualifications. As a result, voter participation will generally be lower in a traditionalistic culture, and there will be more barriers to participation (e.g., a requirement to produce a photo ID at the voting booth). Conservatives argue that these laws reduce or eliminate fraud on the part of voters, while liberals believe they disproportionally disenfranchise the poor and minorities and constitute a modern-day poll tax.

Link to Learning

Visit the National Conference of State Legislatures for an overview of Voter Identification Requirements (https://openstax.org/l/29voteridreq) by state.

Finally, under a traditionalistic political culture, Elazar argues that party competition will tend to occur between factions within a dominant party. Historically, the Democratic Party dominated the political structure in the South before realignment during the civil rights era. Today, depending on the office being sought, the parties are more likely to compete for voters.

CRITIQUES OF ELAZAR'S THEORY

Several critiques have come to light since Elazar first introduced his theory of state political culture fifty years ago. The original theory rested on the assumption that new cultures could arise with the influx of settlers from different parts of the world; however, since immigration patterns have changed over time, it could be argued that the three cultures no longer match the country's current reality. Today's immigrants are less likely to come from European countries and are more likely to originate in Latin American and Asian countries.[24] In addition, advances in technology and transportation have made it easier for citizens to travel across state lines and to relocate. Therefore, the pattern of diffusion on which the original theory rests may no longer be accurate, because people are moving around in more, and often unpredictable, directions.

It is also true that people migrate for more reasons than simple economics. They may be motivated by social issues such as widespread unemployment, urban decay, or low-quality health care of schools. Such trends may aggravate existing differences, for example the difference between urban and rural lifestyles (e.g., the city of Atlanta vs. other parts of Georgia), which are not accounted for in Elazar's classification. Finally, unlike economic or demographic characteristics that lend themselves to more precise measurement, culture is a comprehensive concept that can be difficult to quantify. This can limit its explanatory power in political science research.

14.3 Governors and State Legislatures

Learning Objectives

By the end of this section, you will be able to:
- Identify the formal powers and responsibilities of modern-day governors
- List the basic functions performed by state legislatures
- Describe how state legislatures vary in size, diversity, party composition, and professionalism

Public opinion regarding Congress has reached a dismal low, with more than 80 percent of those surveyed in 2014 saying they do not feel most members of Congress deserve to be reelected.[25] This attitude stems from partisan rivalry, media coverage that has capitalized on the conflict, fiscal shutdowns, and the general perception that Congress is no longer engaged in lawmaking.

The picture looks quite different at the subnational level, at least where lawmaking is concerned. State representatives and senators have been actively engaged in the lawmaking function, grabbing national attention at times for their controversial and highly partisan policies. Governors have been active in promoting their own policy agendas, either in cooperation with the state legislature or in opposition to it. Among the early 2016 Republican presidential contenders, nine were current or former state governors.[26] Increasingly, governors are using their office and the policies they have signed into law as a platform to gain national attention and to give voters a sense of their priorities should they ascend to the highest office in the country, the presidency.

GOVERNORS IN CHARGE

Anyone elected to the office of governor assumes tremendous responsibility overnight. He or she becomes the spokesperson for the entire state and their political party, accepts blame or praise for handling decision-making in times of crisis, oversees the implementation of public policy, and helps shepherd legislation through the lawmaking process. These tasks require a great deal of skill and demand that governors exhibit different strengths and personality traits. Governors must learn to work well with other lawmakers, bureaucrats, cabinet officials, and with the citizens who elected them to office in the first place. The water crisis in Flint, Michigan, provides a good case in point.

Governors have tremendous power over the legislative branch because they serve year-round and hold office alone. They also command wide press coverage by virtue of being the leading elected official in their state. Finally, while there are variations in degree across the states, most governors have more power relative to their state legislatures than does the U.S. president relative to the U.S. Congress. State executive power flows from factors such as the propensity of state legislatures to meet for only part of the year and their resulting reliance for information on the governor and his/her administration, stronger formal tools (e.g., line-item vetoes), budget-cutting discretion, and the fact that state legislators typically hold down another job besides that of legislator.

Three of the governor's chief functions are to influence the legislative process through an executive budget proposal, a policy agenda, and vetoes. Just as the president gives a State of the Union address once a year, so too do governors give an annual State of the State address before the state legislature (Figure 14.9). In this speech, they discuss economic and political achievements, cite data that supports their accomplishments, and overview the major items on their legislative agenda. This speech signals to members of the state legislature what priorities are high on the governor's list. Those who share the governor's party affiliation will work with him or her to see these goals achieved. Given that governors need the cooperation of state legislators to get their bills introduced and steered through the lawmaking process, they make developing good relationships with lawmakers a priority. This can entail helping lawmakers address the concerns of their constituents, inviting legislators to social events and meals, and scheduling weekly meetings with legislative leaders and committee chairs to discuss policy.[27]

Figure 14.9 Then-governor Nikki Haley delivers her 2015 State of the State address from the State House in Columbia, South Carolina, on January 21, 2015.

In addition to providing a basic list of policy priorities, governors also initiate a budget proposal in most states. Here they indicate funding priorities and spell out the amounts that will be appropriated to various state agencies under their discretion. When the economy is strong, governors may find themselves in the enviable position of having a surplus of tax revenue. That allows them some flexibility to decide whether they want to reduce taxes, direct funds toward a new initiative or program, allocate more funds to current programs, restore funds that were cut during times of fiscal distress, or save surplus revenue in a rainy-day account.[28] Moreover, when cuts must be made, especially when the legislature is not in session, it is typically the governor or his or her finance director who makes the call on what gets cut.

Having introduced his or her priorities, the governor will work on the sidelines to steer favored bills through the legislative process. This may entail holding meetings with committee chairs or other influential lawmakers concerning their legislative priorities, working with the media to try to get favorable coverage of legislative priorities, targeting advocacy organizations to maintain pressure on resistant lawmakers, or testifying in legislative hearings about the possible impacts of the legislation.[29]

Once legislation has made its way through the lawmaking process, it comes to the governor's desk for signature. If a governor signs the bill, it becomes law, and if the governor does not like the terms of the legislation he or she can veto, or reject, the entire bill. The bill can then become law only if a supermajority of legislators overrides the veto by voting in favor of the bill. Since it is difficult for two-thirds or more of state legislators to come together to override a veto (it requires many members of the governor's own party to vote against him or her), the simple act of threatening to veto can be enough to get legislators to make concessions to the governor before he or she will pass the legislation.

The ability to veto legislation is just one of the **formal powers** governors have at their disposal. Formal powers are powers the governor may exercise that are specifically outlined in state constitutions or state law.[30] Unlike U.S. presidents, many governors also have additional veto powers at their disposal, which enhances their ability to check the actions of the legislative branch. For instance, most states provide governors the power of the line-item veto. The **line-item veto** gives governors the ability to strike out a line or individual portions of a bill while letting the remainder pass into law. In addition, approximately 30 percent of governors have the power of an **amendatory veto**, which allows them to send a bill back to the legislature and request a specific amendment to it. Finally, a small number of governors, including the governor of Texas, also have the power of a **reduction veto**, which allows them to reduce the budget proposed in a piece of legislation.[31]

Insider Perspective

The Vanna White and Frankenstein Vetoes in Wisconsin

Although the line-item, reduction, and amendatory vetoes give governors tremendous power to adjust legislation and to check the legislative branch, the most powerful and controversial vetoes, which have allowed governors to make selective deletions from a bill before signing, are dubbed the "Vanna White" veto and the "Frankenstein" veto. (Vanna White hosts the popular game show "Wheel of Fortune," in which contestants guess what a phrase is based on a limited number of letters. As they guess the letters, White indicates the correct letters within the puzzle.) These powers have a colorful history in the state of Wisconsin, where voters have limited their influence on two occasions.

The first occurred in 1990 when voters passed a provision restricting the governor's ability to use the "Vanna White" veto to change a bill by crossing out specific letters within a given word in order to create a new word. After this restriction took effect, the "Frankenstein" veto came into practice, which allowed a governor to remove individual words, numbers, or passages from a bill and string the remaining text together (like the fictional Dr. Frankenstein's monster) in an effort to alter the original intent of the legislation.[32]

As an example of the Frankenstein veto, when an appropriations bill was sent to Wisconsin governor James E. Doyle for signature in 2005, Doyle scrapped over seven hundred words from a passage that would have appropriated millions of dollars to transportation. The words that remained in the bill redirected those funds to education. Lawmakers were outraged, but they were not able to override the veto.[33]

Then, in 2007, Governor Doyle used the veto once again to raise property taxes almost 2 percent.[34] As a result of these controversial moves, the state house and senate passed a referendum to end the ability of governors to create a new sentence by combining words from two or more other sentences. A legislative referendum is a measure passed by the state legislature, such as a constitutional amendment, that goes to the voters for final approval.[35] This referendum went to the voters for approval or rejection in the 2008 election, and the voters banned the practice. Governors in Wisconsin and all the states still have tremendous power to shape legislation, however, through the other types of vetoes discussed in this chapter.

Should any state governor have the powers referred to as the "Vanna White" and "Frankenstein" vetoes? What advantage, if any, might state residents gain from their governor's ability to alter the intent of a bill the legislature has approved and then sign it into law?

Besides the formal power to prepare the budget and veto legislation, legislators also have the power to call special sessions of the legislature for a wide array of reasons. For instance, sessions may be called to address budgetary issues during an economic downturn, to put together a redistricting plan, or to focus intensively on a particular issue the governor wants rectified immediately.[36] In some states, only the governor has the power to call a special session, while in other states this power is shared between the legislative and the executive branches.

Link to Learning

For more details on the calling of legislative Special Sessions (https://openstax.org/l/29legspecsess) visit the National Conference of State Legislatures website.

Although governors have a great deal of power in the legislative arena, this is not their only area of influence. First, as leaders in their political party, governors often work to raise money for other political figures who are up for reelection. A governor who has high public approval ratings may also make campaign appearances on behalf of candidates in tough reelection fights across the state. Governors can draw in supporters, contributions, and media attention that can be beneficial to other political aspirants, and the party will expect them to do their part to ensure the greatest possible number of victories for their candidates. Second, as the spokesperson for their state, governors make every effort to sell the state's virtues and unique characteristics, whether to the media, to other citizens across the United States, to potential business owners, or to legislative leaders in Washington, DC. Governors want to project a positive image of their state that will encourage tourism, relocation, and economic investment within its boundaries. Collectively, governors make a mark through the National Governors Association, which is a powerful lobbying force in the nation's capital.

For example, Texas governor Greg Abbott made headlines in 2015 for writing to the CEO of General Electric (GE), urging the company to relocate its corporate headquarters from Connecticut, which had just raised its corporate tax rate, to Texas.[37] As his state's spokesperson, Abbott promoted Texas's friendly corporate tax structure and investment in transportation and education funding in hopes of enticing GE to relocate there and bring economic opportunities with it. The company has since decided to relocate to Boston, after receiving incentives, worth up to $145 million, from Massachusetts officials.[38] Another example involved Texas governor Rick Perry touring California in 2014 in order to bring prospective businesses from the Golden State to Texas. In what was arguably the biggest round of lobbying by state and local governments toward a big business, Amazon recently conducted a search for a second corporate headquarters. After months of consideration, hundreds of op-eds extolling the virtues of locating in particular communities, Amazon picked two sites—Arlington, Virginia and Long Island City, New York—where it plans to spend over $2 billion at each site.[39]

In March 2015, the governor of Virginia, Terry McAuliffe, and the mayor of Chicago, Rahm Emanuel, both sent letters to corporate heads in Indiana after controversy erupted around the passage of that state's Religious Freedom Restoration Act.[40] This bill is designed to restrict government intrusion into people's religious beliefs unless there is a compelling state interest. It also provides individuals and businesses with the ability to sue if they feel their religious rights have been violated. However, opponents feared the law would be used as a means to discriminate against members of the LGBT community, based on business owners' religious objections to providing services for same-sex couples.[41] In the media firestorm that followed the Indiana law's passage, several prominent companies announced they would consider taking their business elsewhere or cancelling event contracts in the state if the bill were not amended.[42] This led opportunistic leaders in the surrounding area to make appeals to these companies in the hope of luring them out of Indiana. Ultimately, the bill was clarified, likely due in part to corporate pressure on the state to do so.[43] The clarification made it clear that the law could not be used to refuse employment, housing, or service based on an individual's sexual orientation or gender identity.[44]

Controversial legislation like the Religious Freedom Restoration Act is only one of the many environmental factors that can make or break a governor's reputation and popularity. Other challenges and crises that may face governors include severe weather, terrorist attacks, immigration challenges, and budget shortfalls.

New Jersey governor Chris Christie gained national attention in 2012 over his handling of the aftermath of Hurricane Sandy, which caused an estimated $65 billion worth of damage and cost the lives of over 150 individuals along the East Coast of the United States.[45] Christie was famously photographed with President Obama during their joint tour of the damaged areas, and the governor subsequently praised the president for his response (Figure 14.10). Some later criticized Christie for his remarks because of the close proximity between the president's visit and Election Day, along with the fact that the Republican governor and Democratic president were from opposite sides of the political aisle. Critics felt the governor had betrayed his party and that the publicity helped the president win reelection.[46] Others praised the governor for cooperating with the president and reaching across the partisan divide to secure federal support for his state in a time of crisis.[47]

(a)

(b)

Figure 14.10   New Jersey governor Chris Christie (right) hosted President Obama (center) during the president's visit to the state in October 2012 following the destruction brought by Hurricane Sandy (a). After viewing the damage along the coastline of Brigantine, New Jersey, Christie and Obama visited residents at the Brigantine Beach Community Center (b).

If severe winter weather is forecasted or in the event of civil unrest, governors also have the power to call upon the National Guard to assist residents and first responders or aid in storm recovery (Figure 14.11). When governors declare a state of emergency, National Guard troops can be activated to go into local areas and assist with emergency efforts in whatever capacity they are needed.[48] In 2015, many governors in the New England region called press conferences, worked with snow-removal crews and local government officials, set up emergency shelters, and activated travel bans or curfews in the face of crippling snowstorms.[49] When winter storms fail to bring predicted levels of snow, however, politicians can be left to field criticism that they instigated unnecessary panic.[50] Governors feel the weight of their decisions as they try to balance the political risks of overreacting and the human costs of letting the state be caught unprepared for these and other major natural disasters. As the chief spokesperson, they take all the blame or all the credit for their actions. With that said, it is important to note that presidents can enlist the National Guard for federal service as well.

Figure 14.11 Following a massive snowstorm in November 2014, New York governor Andrew Cuomo ordered the mobilization of more than five hundred members of the National Guard to assist with snow removal and traffic control. Here soldiers shovel snow from the roof of the Absolut Care senior center in Orchard Park, New York. (credit: Luke Udell, U.S. Army National Guard)

Governors also have the power to spare or enhance the lives of individuals convicted of crimes in their state. Although they may choose to exercise this formal power only during the closing days of their term, if at all, most governors have the authority to grant pardons just as U.S. presidents do. A **pardon** absolves someone of blame for a crime and can secure his or her release from prison. Governors can also commute sentences, reducing the time an individual must serve,[51] if there are doubts about the person's guilt, concerns about his or her mental health, or reason to feel the punishment was inappropriately harsh. In the past ten years, the governors of New Jersey and Illinois have commuted the sentences of all inmates on death row before repealing the death penalty in their states.[52]

Despite the tremendous formal powers that go with the job, being governor is still personally and professionally challenging. The demands of the job are likely to restrict time with family and require forgoing privacy. In addition, governors will often face circumstances beyond their control. For instance, the state legislature may include a majority of members who do not share the governor's party affiliation. This can make working together more challenging and lead to less cooperation during the legislative session. Another challenge for governors is the plural executive, which refers to the fact that many state officials, such as the lieutenant governor, attorney general, and secretary of state are elected independently from the governor; hence, the governor has no direct control over them the way a president might have sway over U.S. executive officials. Governors can also face spending restrictions due to the economic climate in their state. They may have to make unpopular decisions that weaken their support among voters. The federal government can mandate that states perform some function without giving them any funds to do so. Finally, as we saw above, governors can be swept up in crises or natural disasters they did not anticipate and could not have foreseen. This can drain their energy and hamper their ability to generate good public policy.[53]

THE FUNCTIONS OF STATE LEGISLATURES

State legislatures serve three primary functions. They perform a lawmaking function by researching, writing, and passing legislation. Members represent their districts and work to meet requests for help from citizens within it. Finally, legislatures perform an oversight function for the executive branch.

All state representatives and senators serve on committees that examine, research, investigate, and vote on legislation that relates to the committee's purpose, such as agriculture, transportation, or education. The number of bills introduced in any given session varies. Some state legislatures have more restrictive rules concerning the number of bills any one member can sponsor. Legislators get ideas for bills from lobbyists of various types of interest groups, ranging from corporate groups to labor unions to advocacy organizations. Ideas for bills also come from laws passed in other state legislatures, from policy that diffuses from the federal government, from constituents or citizens in the officeholder's district who approach them with problems they would like to see addressed with new laws, and from their own personal policy agenda, which they brought to office with them. Finally, as we explored previously, legislators also work with the governor's agenda in the course of each legislative session, and they must pass a budget for their state either every year or every two years.

Most bills die in committee and never receive a second or third reading on the floor of the legislature. Lawmaking requires frequent consensus, not just among the legislators in a given house but also between the two chambers. In order for a bill to become law, it must pass through both the state house and the state senate in identical form before going to the governor's desk for final signature.

Besides generating public policy, state legislatures try to represent the interests of their constituents. Edmund Burke was a political philosopher who theorized that representatives are either delegates or trustees.[54] A **delegate legislator** represents the will of those who elected him or her to office and acts in their expressed interest, even when it goes against personal belief about what is ultimately in the constituency's best interest. On the other hand, **trustees** believe they were elected to exercise their own judgment and know best because they have the time and expertise to study and understand an issue. Thus, a trustee will be willing to vote against the desire of the constituency so long as he or she believes it is in the people's best interest. A trustee will also be more likely to vote his or her conscience on issues that are personal to him or her, such as on same-sex marriage or abortion rights.

Regardless of whether representatives adopt a delegate or a trustee mentality, they will all see it as their duty to address the concerns and needs of the people they represent. Typically, this will entail helping members in the district who need assistance or have problems with the government they want addressed. For instance, a constituent may write an elected official asking for help dealing with the bureaucracy such as in a decision made by tax commission, requesting a letter of recommendation for acceptance into a military academy, or proposing a piece of legislation the member can help turn into a law.

Legislators also try to bring particularized benefits back to their district. These benefits might include money that can be spent on infrastructure improvements or grants for research. Finally, members will accept requests from local government officials or other constituents to attend parades, ribbon-cutting ceremonies, or other celebratory events within their district (Figure 14.12). They will also work with teachers and faculty to visit classes or meet with students on field trips to the state capitol.

Figure 14.12 To celebrate the opening of the new Loyola Avenue streetcar line, the mayor of New Orleans, Mitch Landrieu, marched with the St. Augustine "Marching 100" on January 28, 2013. (credit: U.S. Department of Transportation)

The last primary function of state legislators is to oversee the bureaucracy's implementation of public policy, ensuring it occurs in the manner the legislature intended. State legislatures may request that agency heads provide testimony about spending in hearings, or they may investigate particular bureaucratic agencies to ensure that funds are being disbursed as desired.[55] Since legislators have many other responsibilities and some meet for only a few months each year, they may wait to investigate until a constituent or lobbyist brings a problem to their attention.

THE COMPOSITION OF STATE LEGISLATURES

In most states, the legislative function is divided between two bodies: a state house and a state senate. The only exception is Nebraska, which has a unicameral state senate of forty-nine members. State legislatures vary a great deal in terms of the number of legislators in the house and senate, the range of diversity across the membership, the partisan composition of the chamber relative to the governor's affiliation, and the degree of legislative professionalism. This variation can lead to differences in the type of policies passed and the amount of power legislatures wield relative to that of the governor.

According to the National Conference of State Legislatures, at forty members, Alaska's is the smallest state (or lower) house, while New Hampshire's is the largest at four hundred. State senates range in size from twenty members in Alaska to sixty-seven members in Minnesota. The size of the institution can have consequences for the number of citizens each member represents; larger bodies have a smaller legislator-to-constituent ratio (assuming even populations). Larger institutions can also complicate legislative business because reaching consensus is more difficult with more participants.[56]

The term length in the state house is frequently two years, while in the state senate it is more commonly four years. These differences have consequences, too, because representatives in the state house, with the next election always right around the corner, will need to focus on their reelection campaigns more frequently than senators. On the other hand, state senators may have more time to focus on public policy and become policy generalists because they each must serve on multiple committees due to their smaller numbers.

Link to Learning

The **number of legislators and term length (https://openstax.org/l/29legtermleng)** varies by state.

In 2018, according to the National Conference of State Legislatures, women made up 25.4 percent of the nation's state legislators. However, the number varies a great deal across states (Figure 14.13). For instance, in Arizona and Vermont, women account for around 40 percent of the state legislative membership. However, they make up less than 16 percent of the legislatures in Alabama, Louisiana, Oklahoma, South Carolina, West Virginia, and Wyoming.[57]

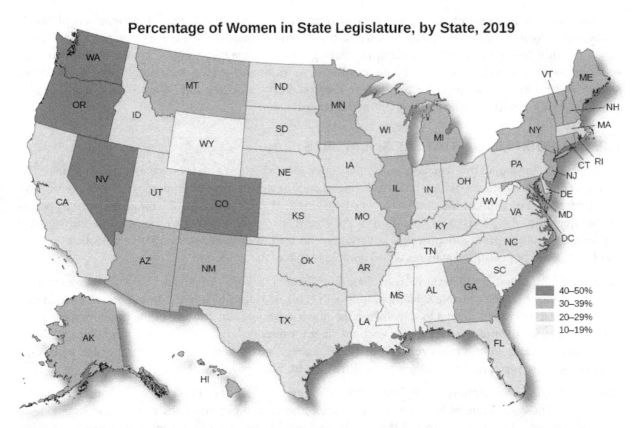

Figure 14.13 In 2019, only one-quarter of state legislators across the United States were women. However, the percentage of women in state legislature varies greatly from state to state.

Data on minority representatives is more difficult to obtain, but 2009 estimates from the National Conference of State Legislatures paired with census estimates from 2010 show that African Americans and Latinos are both underrepresented in state government relative to their percentage of the population. In 2009, African Americans made up approximately 9 percent of state legislators, compared to the 13 percent of the population they constitute nationwide. On the other hand, Latino representatives made up approximately 3 percent of state legislators relative to their 14 percent of the total population in the United States.[58] The proportion of Latinos in the legislature is highest in Arizona, California, New Mexico, and Texas, while the proportion of African Americans is highest in Alabama, Georgia, and Mississippi.

Scholars in political science have spent a great deal of time researching the impact of women and minorities on the legislative process and on voter participation and trust. Some research demonstrates that female and minority representatives are more likely to advocate for policies that are of interest to or will benefit minorities, women, and children.[59] Other research suggests that the presence of African American and Latino representatives increases voter turnout by these groups.[60] Thus, increased diversity in state legislatures can have consequences for voter engagement and for the type of legislation pursued and passed within these bodies.

You can compare the numbers and percentages of women in state legislature (http://www.openstax.org/l/29NCSLwomen) , state by state.

You can also compare the numbers and percentages of African American representatives (https://openstax.org/l/29NCSLafamer) .

Similar information about Latino representation in state legislatures (https://openstax.org/l/29NCSLlatino) is also available.

As of early January 2019, twenty-two states had Republican majorities in the state house and senate, while in fourteen states Democratic majorities were the norm. In thirteen states, party control was split so that the Democratic Party maintained control of one house while the Republican Party maintained control of the other.[61] Figure 14.14 illustrates the partisan composition across the United States. Note that states in New England and the West Coast are more likely to be unified behind the Democratic Party, while Republicans control legislatures throughout the South and in large parts of the Midwest. This alignment largely reflects differing political ideologies, with the more liberal, urban areas of the country leaning Democratic while the more conservative, rural areas are Republican.

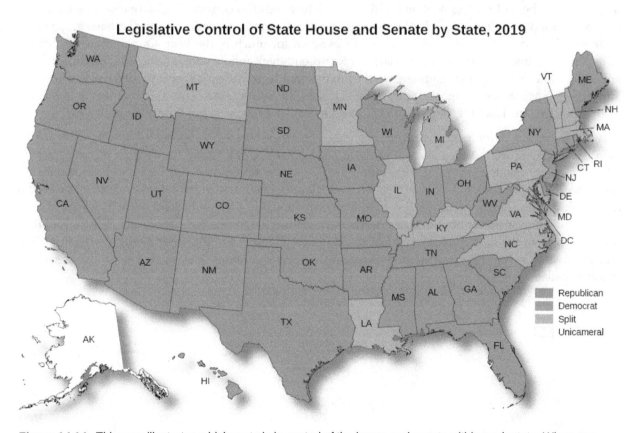

Figure 14.14 This map illustrates which party is in control of the house and senate within each state. When one party controls the senate and another party controls the house, the partisan composition is split. Alaska is white because the lower house allows for ruling by bipartisan coalition.

Like diversity, party composition has consequences for policymaking. Governors who are not from the same party as the one controlling the legislature can find it more difficult to achieve their agenda. This governing circumstance is popularly referred to as *divided government*. In a time of divided government, a governor may have to work harder to build relationships and to broker consensus. In addition, when state party control is divided between the legislative and executive branches, the governor may find that legislators are more likely to muster the numbers to overturn at least some of their vetoes. In contrast, when the governor's own party controls the legislature—a situation known as *unified government*—conventional wisdom suggests that they will have a smoother and more productive relationship with the legislature.

Party composition also matters for the overall legislative agenda. The party in power will elect party members to the top leadership posts in the state house and senate, and it will determine who sits on each of the committees. Committees are chaired by members of the majority party, and the composition of these committees is skewed toward members affiliated with the party in power. This gives the majority party an advantage in meeting its policy objectives and relegates the minority party to the position of obstructionists. In addition, while Republicans and Democrats are both concerned about education, health care, transportation, and other major policy areas, the two parties have different philosophies about what is in the best interest of their citizens and where funds should be allocated to meet those needs. The result is vastly different approaches to handling pressing public policy problems across the states.

As a whole, state legislatures have become progressively more professional. Political scientist Peverill Squire, at several points throughout his career, has measured the degree of state legislative professionalism with a ranking across the fifty states.[62] Legislative professionalism is assessed according to three key factors: state legislators' salary, the length of time they are in session, and the number of staff at their disposal. Members of professional or full-time legislatures tend to consider legislative service their full-time occupation, and they are paid enough not to require a second occupation. They also have larger staffs to assist with their work, and they tend to be in session for much of the year. On the other end of the spectrum are citizen, or part-time, legislatures. Representatives and senators in these legislatures do not enjoy the same perks as their counterparts in professional legislatures. Generally, salary is much lower and so is staff assistance. Members typically need to seek outside employment to supplement their income from legislative work, and the legislature will meet for only a brief period of time during the year.

Between these two extremes are hybrid legislatures. Their members are compensated at a higher rate than in citizen legislatures, but they are still likely to need outside employment to make an income equal to what they were making prior to taking office. These representatives and senators will have some staff assistance but not as much as in a professional legislature. Finally, members in hybrid legislatures will not consider their service to constitute a full-time occupation, but they will spend more than part of their time conducting legislative business. As Figure 14.15 shows, California, New York, and Pennsylvania are home to some of the most professional legislatures in the country. On the other hand, New Hampshire, North Dakota, Wyoming, and South Dakota are among the states that rank lowest on legislative professionalism.[63]

Figure 14.15 This map illustrates the degree of professionalism within state legislatures. States in purple and green tend to meet full-time and have larger staff and salaries, while the opposite conditions exist in states colored in orange and red. States in blue fall somewhere in the middle of these conditions.

Like the other indicators discussed above, legislative professionalism also affects the business of state legislatures. In professional legislatures, elections tend to be more competitive, and the cost of running for a seat is higher because the benefits of being elected are greater. This makes these seats more attractive, and candidates will tend not to run unless they perceive themselves as well qualified. Since the benefits are more generous, elected officials will tend to stay in office longer and develop more policy expertise as a result. This experience can give professional legislatures an edge when dealing with the governor, because they are likely to be in session for about the same amount of time per year as the governor and have the necessary staff to assist them with researching and writing public policy.[64]

Link to Learning

The legislative pay (https://openstax.org/l/29legislapay) varies across states.

Compare the size of legislative staffs (https://openstax.org/l/29legisstaff15) across states for the years 1979, 1988, 1996, 2003, and 2009.

14.4 State Legislative Term Limits

Learning Objectives

By the end of this section, you will be able to:
- Describe the history of state legislative term limits
- Compare the costs and benefits of term limits

Term limits restrict the length of time a member can serve in the state legislature by capping either lifetime service or the number of consecutive terms. The **term limits** movement gained momentum in the 1990s, spreading across a wide array of state legislative institutions. Today, fifteen states have imposed term limits on their state house and state senate members. On the other hand, six states, one as recently as 2004, have repealed the term limits imposed on them by the electorate, through either judicial action in the state Supreme Courts or through legislative action in the state legislature.[65]

THE BASICS OF TERM LIMITS

Under **consecutive term limits**, a member can serve for only a specified period of time in either the state house or the state senate, most commonly eight years. To try to regain a seat in the legislature once the limit has been met, the member will have to wait to run for office again. If the member succeeds, the clock will reset and the legislator may once again serve up to the limit set by the state. In states with a **lifetime ban**, such as Oklahoma, members can serve only one time for the number of years allotted, and they are not permitted to run for office again (Figure 14.16).[66]

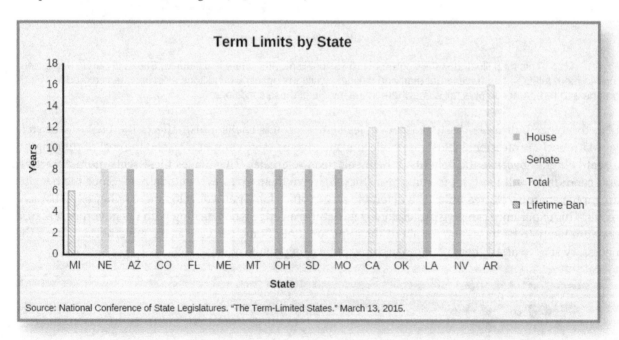

Source: National Conference of State Legislatures. "The Term-Limited States." March 13, 2015.

Figure 14.16 Fifteen states currently have some form of term limits. This chart depicts which states have consecutive term limits or lifetime bans and how long a member can serve under each scenario.

The first term limits were enacted in 1990 in California, Colorado, and Oklahoma. In 1992, eight more states followed suit in one large wave. The last state to enact term limits on legislative members was Nebraska in 2000.[67] However, term limits did not stay in effect in all these states; many state supreme courts repealed them and declared them unconstitutional for a variety of reasons (Figure 14.17). For instance, in Massachusetts and Washington, term limits were deemed unconstitutional because they affected candidate qualifications to compete for a given office. The courts ruled that changes to those qualifications could be made only by amending the state constitution, not by voters changing the state law.[68]

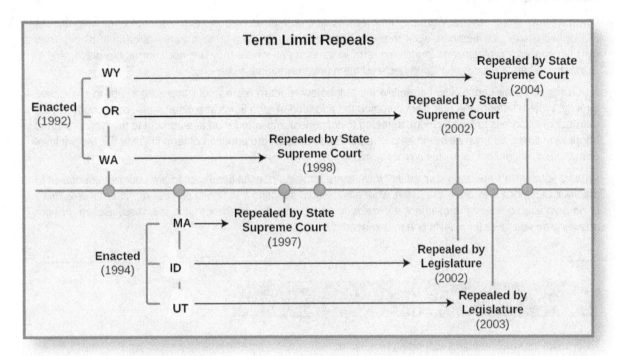

Figure 14.17   A number of states have tried to enact term limits on members of the legislature only to see the laws later repealed by the state legislature or ruled unconstitutional by the state supreme court.

ADVANTAGES OF TERM LIMITS

In many cases, the movement to institute term limits was initiated by voters and passed through citizen initiatives, which allow citizens to place a proposed law or constitutional amendment on the ballot for a popular vote.[69] Proponents of term limits felt new blood was needed in state legislatures to bring fresh ideas and perspectives to lawmaking. In addition, they hoped term limits would compel turnover among members by shortening the time anyone could serve and by reducing the tendency for elected officials to make legislative service their career. In conjunction with this thinking, some supporters hoped term limits would increase the motivation to make good public policy. If members were less focused on reelection and knew they could not serve more than a certain number of years, perhaps they would get right down to the business of making laws and produce innovative policy within a narrow window of time.[70]

For other proponents, the hope was that term limits would increase diversity within the chamber by encouraging more women, members of racial and ethnic minority groups, members of the minority party, and people with unconventional occupations to run for office because seats would be open more frequently. In addition, supporters speculated that increased turnover might prompt higher rates of electoral competition and voter interest. Finally, they believed the loss of long-term legislators due to term limits would allow new members and younger legislators to assume leadership positions within the chamber and committees, creating another way to bring fresh approaches to the lawmaking process. [71]

Get Connected!

Working to Expand Term Limits

One pro–term limits advocacy group, U.S. Term Limits, is dedicated to the expansion of term limits across the United States. Its members work to prevent states from repealing limits that are already in place. They also support efforts by citizens to institute term limits in states where they are not currently in place, and in Congress, where the Supreme Court declared them unconstitutional.[72]

If you support their cause, you can follow the link below to learn more about these efforts or to participate directly. Write a letter to the editor encouraging the adoption of term limits in a given state, or encourage your member of Congress to sign a pledge agreeing to cosponsor and vote for an amendment to the Constitution to adopt term limits. You can also sign an online petition to support the adoption of term limits at the federal level or make a donation to a term-limit advocacy group.

What is your state's policy on term limits? If limits are in place, how have they changed your representation in the state capitol? If they are not in place, what effect would adopting them have on your representation? There is no comparable national movement against term limits, why do you think that is the case? Based on your answers, do you favor term limits or not, and why?

Link to Learning

For more information about supporting term limits, visit U.S. Terms (https://openstax.org/l/29protermadv) an advocacy group for term limits.

DISADVANTAGES OF TERM LIMITS

Although proponents have many reasons for supporting term limits, opponents also have compelling reasons for not supporting their implementation in the state legislature. In addition, research by political scientists has uncovered a number of negative consequences since term limits took effect.

Although proponents argued that term limits would increase legislative diversity, research comparing the rate of female and minority representation in term-limited and non-term-limited states does not bear out this expectation. There is no statistically significant difference in diversity between the two groups of states.[73] Although term limits may have produced more open seats, additional barriers to holding office can still exist and affect the willingness of women and minorities to run for office. In addition, women and minorities are subject to the same term limits as men, and given their low numbers among candidates for office, on balance a legislature can lose more women or minorities than it gains.

Term limits also affect the power structure between the legislative and executive branches and the key sources from whom legislators draw information about bills before the chamber. Research demonstrates that, post-term limits, legislators became more likely to consult with lobbyists to gain information about legislation under consideration than had been the case before term limits.[74] This is likely the result of legislators having less policy expertise and political experience as a function of having fewer years in office, being younger when they first enter legislative service, reducing institutional memory and expertise within the chamber as a whole due to member turnover, or all the above. Interest groups may thus enjoy greater ability to set the agenda and push for policy that favors their organization. This same research also found that under term limits state legislators feel they have lost power relative to the governor and to various bureaucratic agency officials.[75] This presumed loss of power could damage the state legislature's ability to adequately check the actions of the executive branch and to perform legislative functions, such as oversight.

Finally, term limits could affect voter enthusiasm and turnout if voters are disappointed they cannot retain legislators they like or have developed a positive relationship with. Once term limits take effect, all legislators are at the voters' mercy, regardless of the skill or talent they may bring to the office.

14.5 County and City Government

Learning Objectives

By the end of this section, you will be able to:
- Identify the differences between county and municipal governments in terms of their responsibilities and funding sources
- Describe the two primary types of municipal government and the three basic types of county government

County and city governments make up an important component of the overall structure of the government. Not only do they affect citizens directly; it is also easier for citizens to interact with local government officials because their offices and the community's school board or city council meetings are often close by. Despite this fact, voter turnout in local elections tends to be lower than in state and national elections. Municipal and county governments differ in structure and purpose in several ways.

COUNTY GOVERNMENT

County governments serve a larger geographical area than cities and towns, but a smaller area than states. They are created by the state government and typically operate under provisions set out in the state constitution. As such, they are essentially administrative units of the state. Census estimates from 2012 indicate that there are just over three thousand counties in the United States.[76] County systems usually take one of three basic forms: the commission system, the council-administrator system, and the council-elected executive system.

The most common form of county government is the **commission system**. Under this structure, an elected commission, which generally consists of a small number of commissioners, serves as the governing body within the county, performing all legislative and executive functions. These include adopting a budget, passing county resolutions, and hiring and firing county officials.[77]

Under the **council-administrator system**, the voters elect council members to serve for a specified period of time, and the council in turn appoints an administrator to oversee the operation of the government. The administrator serves at the directive of the council and can be terminated by the council. The goal of this arrangement is to divide administrative and policymaking responsibilities between the elected council and the appointed administrator.[78]

Under a **council-elected executive system**, the voters elect both the members of the council and the executive. The executive performs functions similar to those of the state governor. For instance, he or she can veto the actions of the council, draft a budget, and provide suggestions regarding public policy.[79]

Although the tasks they perform can vary from state to state, most counties have a courthouse that houses county officials, such as the sheriff, the county clerk, the assessor, the treasurer, the coroner, and the engineer. These officials carry out a variety of important functions and oversee the responsibilities of running a county government. For instance, the county coroner investigates the cause of death when suspicious circumstances are present. The county clerk oversees the registration of voters and also certifies election results for the county. In addition, this officeholder typically keeps the official birth, death, and marriage records. The county treasurer oversees the collection and distribution of funds within the county, while the county assessor conducts property tax evaluations and informs individual citizens or business owners of their right to contest the appraised value of their property. Finally, a county engineer will oversee the maintenance and construction of county infrastructure.[80] In short, counties help to maintain roads and bridges, courthouses and jails, parks and pools, and public libraries, hospitals, and clinics.[81] To provide these services, county governments typically rely on property tax revenue, a portion of sales tax receipts, and funds from intergovernmental transfers by way of federal or state grants.

CITY GOVERNMENT

Municipal governments oversee the operation and functions of cities and towns. Census estimates for 2012 show just over 19,500 municipal governments and nearly 16,500 township governments in the United States.[82] The vast majority of municipal governments operate on one of two governing models: a mayor-council system or a council-manager system.

Under the **mayor-council system** voters elect both a mayor and members of the city council. The city council performs legislative functions and the mayor the executive functions. Under this system, the mayor may be given a great deal of authority or only limited powers.[83] Under a strong mayor system, the mayor will be able to veto the actions of the council, appoint and fire the heads of city departments, and produce a budget. Under a weak mayor system, the mayor has little authority compared to the council and acts in a ceremonial capacity as a spokesperson for the city.[84]

In a **council-manager system** of government, either the members of the city council are elected by voters along with a mayor who presides over the council, or the voters elect members of the city council and the mayor is chosen from among them. In either case, the city council will then appoint a city manager to carry out the administrative functions of the municipal government. This frees the city council to address political functions such as setting policy and formulating the budget.[85]

Municipal governments are responsible for providing clean water as well as sewage and garbage disposal. They must maintain city facilities, such as parks, streetlights, and stadiums (Figure 14.18). In addition, they address zoning and building regulations, promote the city's economic development, and provide law enforcement, public transportation, and fire protection. Municipal governments typically rely on property tax revenue, user fees from trash collection and the provision of water and sewer services, a portion of sales tax receipts, and taxes on business.

Figure 14.18 The Sporting Park in Kansas City, Kansas, is home to various sporting events. The stadium first opened for business in 2011, and taxpayers financed $146 million of the total cost to build the stadium, an office park, and a youth soccer complex.[86] (credit: Wesley Fryer)

Link to Learning

The International City/County Management Association (ICMA) provides networking opportunities, professional development, and statistical data in order to support local government leaders and other individuals throughout the world. Visit the ICMA Priorities (https://openstax.org/l/29ICMAprior) page to learn what makes a better leader and how you might improve your local community.

Key Terms

amendatory veto a veto that allows a governor to send a bill back to the legislature with a message requesting a specific amendment

charter a document that provides a framework and detailed account of local government responsibilities and areas of authority

commission system an elected commission that serves as the governing body within a given county

consecutive term limits caps allowing a member of the legislature to serve for only a specified period of time in either the state house or senate and forcing a wait before the member can run again

council-administrator system an elected council that appoints an administrator to oversee the operation of the county government

council-elected executive system a county government in which voters elect both the members of the council and the executive

council-manager system a structure of government in which elected members of the city council appoint a city manager to carry out administrative functions

delegate legislator a legislator who represents the will of those who elected him or her to office and acts in their expressed interest, even when it goes against a personal belief about what is ultimately in the constituency's best interest

Dillon's Rule a legal principle that holds state power and actions above those of local governments and declares state governments to be sovereign relative to local governments

expressed powers those powers specifically provided to the Congress and the president in the U.S. Constitution

formal powers those powers a governor may exercise that are specifically outlined in the state constitution or state law

home rule principle that provides local governments some degree of independence from the state government, typically detailed in a charter

implied powers those powers not specifically detailed in the U.S. Constitution but inferred as necessary to achieve the objectives of the national government

individualistic political culture a culture that views the government as a mechanism for addressing issues that matter to individual citizens and for pursuing individual goals

lifetime ban a rule that members can serve only one time in the state legislature for the number of years allotted and may not run again

line-item veto a state governor's ability to strike out a line or individual portions of a bill while letting the remainder pass into law

mayor-council system a structure of government in which both city council members and the mayor are elected by voters

moralistic political culture a culture that views the government as a means to better society and promote the general welfare

pardon a governor's action to absolve someone of blame for a crime and secure his or her release from prison

reduction veto a governor's authority to reduce the amount budgeted in a piece of legislation

term limits rules that restrict the length of time a member can serve in the state legislature

traditionalistic political culture a culture that views the government as necessary to maintaining the existing social order or the status quo

trustee an officeholder who believes he or she was elected to exercise judgment and to know best by virtue of having the time and expertise to study and understand an issue

Summary

14.1 State Power and Delegation
The power structure of government established in the Articles of Confederation was rebalanced in the Constitution to ensure that both the central and the regional governments had some degree of authority and autonomy. Federal and state governments have managed to work out sharing power throughout history, with the federal government often using fiscal policy to encourage compliance from the states. The taxing power of local governments means they face unique pressures during economic downturns.

14.2 State Political Culture
Daniel Elazar's theory argues, based on the cultural values of early immigrants who settled in different regions of the country, the United States is made up of three component cultures: individualistic, moralistic, and traditionalistic. Each culture views aspects of government and politics differently, particularly the nature and purpose of political competition and the role of citizen participation. Critics of the theory say the arrival of recent immigrants from other parts of the globe, the divide between urban and rural lifestyles in a particular state, and new patterns of diffusion and settlement across states and regions mean the theory is no longer an entirely accurate description of reality.

14.3 Governors and State Legislatures
Governors are called upon to work with the state legislature in the lawmaking process, to be the head of their political party, and to be the chief spokespersons and crisis managers for their states. State constitution or state statutes give many governors the power to veto legislation, pardon or commute the sentences of convicted criminals, author a state budget, and call a special session of the state legislature. The three key functions performed by state legislatures are lawmaking, constituency service, and oversight. Legislatures differ in size, diversity, party composition, and level of professionalism across the fifty states.

14.4 State Legislative Term Limits
Whether they cap lifetime service or consecutive terms, term limits have become popular in many states, though some have overturned them as unconstitutional. Proponents believe term limits increase voter participation, encourage more women and minorities to run for office, and help bring diversity and fresh ideas to the legislature. Opponents point to research showing that diversity has not increased in term-limit states, and that younger and less experienced legislators tend to rely more on lobbyists for information about proposed bills. Finally, voters disappointed at losing their favorites may fail to go to the polls.

14.5 County and City Government
County governments can adopt the commission system, the council-administrator system, and the council-elected executive system of government to carry out their functions, which usually include the work of the sheriff, the county clerk, the assessor, the treasurer, the coroner, and the engineer. Municipal governments can use the mayor-council system or the council-manager system and manage services such as the provision of clean water, park maintenance, and local law enforcement. Cities and counties both rely

on tax revenues, especially property taxes, to fund their provision of services.

Review Questions

1. _____ dictate the terms and conditions state governments would have to meet in order to qualify for financial assistance in a specific policy area.
  a. Categorical grants
  b. Block grants
  c. Unfunded mandates
  d. Crossover sanctions

2. The Tenth Amendment created a class of powers exclusive to state governments. These powers are referred to as _____.
  a. enumerated powers
  b. implied powers
  c. reserved powers
  d. none of the above

3. Dillon's Rule gives local governments the freedom and flexibility to make decisions for themselves.
  a. True
  b. False

4. Under the Articles of Confederation, the federal government was quite weak relative to the states. What changes were made to strengthen the role of the federal government under the U.S. Constitution?

5. In a _____ political culture, the government is seen as a mechanism for maintaining the existing social order or status quo.
  a. moralistic
  b. individualistic
  c. traditionalistic
  d. nativistic

6. Under a _____ political culture, citizens will tend to be more tolerant of corruption from their political leaders and less likely to see politics as a noble profession in which all citizens should engage.
  a. moralistic
  b. individualistic
  c. traditionalistic
  d. nativistic

7. _____ was the first state to institute all mail-in voting and automatic voter registration.
  a. California
  b. Oregon
  c. Washington
  d. New York

8. A _____ is an officeholder who represents the will of those who elected him or her and acts in constituents' expressed interest.
  a. delegate
  b. trustee
  c. politico
  d. citizen

9. In a _____ legislature, members tend to have low salaries, shorter sessions, and few staff members to assist them with their legislative functions.
  a. professional
  b. citizen
  c. hybrid
  d. unicameral

10. A(n) _____ veto allows the governor to cross out budget lines in the legislature-approved budget, while signing the remainder of the budget into law.
  a. amendatory
  b. line-item
  c. reduction
  d. Frankenstein

11. Which branch would you consider to be closest to the people? Why?

12. Under consecutive term limits, legislators can serve one time for the number of years allotted and are not permitted to ever compete for the office again.
  a. True
  b. False

13. The most common term limit across the states that have imposed them is _____ years.
a. four
b. six
c. eight
d. twelve

14. When term limits have been overturned, the most common method was _____.
a. a bill passed by the state legislature
b. a decision by the state Supreme Court
c. a voter referendum
d. a governor's decree

15. Term limits have produced a statistically significant increase in the number of women serving in state legislatures.
a. True
b. False

16. Currently, _____ states have term limits in place.
a. five
b. ten
c. fifteen
d. twenty

17. Under the mayor-council system, the _____.
a. legislative and executive responsibilities are separated
b. political and administrative functions are separated
c. mayor chairs the city council
d. city council selects the mayor

18. Which of the following is *not* one of the three forms of county government?
a. the commission system
b. the council-elected executive system
c. the mayor-council system
d. the council-administrator system

19. What are the primary responsibilities of municipal governments?

Critical Thinking Questions

20. What are the advantages and disadvantages of having so many levels of subnational governments in the United States? Explain.

21. In which level of substate government would you be most likely to get involved? Why?

22. Is it preferable for representatives in the state legislature to behave as trustees or as delegates? Why?

23. Do term limits seem to have more advantages or disadvantages? Defend your answer.

Suggestions for Further Study

Council of State Governments. 2014. *The Book of the States*. Lexington, KY: The Council of State Governments.

Elazar, Daniel. 1972. *American Federalism: A View from the States*, 2nd ed. New York: Thomas Y. Crowell Company.

Governing: The State and Localities (http://www.governing.com/).

National Association of Counties (http://www.naco.org/).

National Conference of State Legislatures (http://www.ncsl.org/).

National Governors Association (http://www.nga.org/cms/home.html).

National League of Cities (http://www.nlc.org/).

Rosenthal, Alan. 2013. *The Best Job in Politics; Exploring How Governors Succeed as Policy Leaders*. Thousand Oaks, CA: CQ Press.

———. 2004. *Heavy Lifting: The Job of State Legislatures*. Thousand Oaks, CA: CQ Press.

Wright, Ralph. 2005. *Inside the Statehouse: Lessons from the Speaker*. Washington, DC: CQ Press.

United States Census Bureau, "Quick Facts: United States" (http://quickfacts.census.gov/qfd/index.html).

Chapter 15

The Bureaucracy

Figure 15.1 This 1885 cartoon reflects the disappointment of office seekers who were turned away from bureaucratic positions they believed their political commitments had earned them. It was published just as the U.S. bureaucracy was being transformed from the spoils system to the merit system primarily in use today.

Chapter Outline

15.1 Bureaucracy and the Evolution of Public Administration
15.2 Toward a Merit-Based Civil Service
15.3 Understanding Bureaucracies and their Types
15.4 Controlling the Bureaucracy

Introduction

What does the word "bureaucracy" conjure in your mind? For many, it evokes inefficiency, corruption, red tape, and government overreach (Figure 15.1). For others, it triggers very different images—of professionalism, helpful and responsive service, and government management. Your experience with bureaucrats and the administration of government probably informs your response to the term. The ability of bureaucracy to inspire both revulsion and admiration is one of several features that make it a fascinating object of study.

More than that, the many arms of the federal bureaucracy, often considered the fourth branch of government, are valuable components of the federal system. Without this administrative structure, staffed by nonelected workers who possess particular expertise to carry out their jobs, government could not function the way citizens need it to. That does not mean, however, that bureaucracies are perfect.

What roles do professional government employees carry out? Who are they, and how and why do they acquire their jobs? How do they run the programs of government enacted by elected leaders? Who makes the rules of a bureaucracy? This chapter uncovers the answers to these questions and many more.

15.1 Bureaucracy and the Evolution of Public Administration

Learning Objectives

By the end of this section, you will be able to:

- Define bureaucracy and bureaucrat
- Describe the evolution and growth of public administration in the United States
- Identify the reasons people undertake civil service

Throughout history, both small and large nations have elevated certain types of nonelected workers to positions of relative power within the governmental structure. Collectively, these essential workers are called the bureaucracy. A **bureaucracy** is an administrative group of nonelected officials charged with carrying out functions connected to a series of policies and programs. In the United States, the bureaucracy began as a very small collection of individuals. Over time, however, it grew to be a major force in political affairs. Indeed, it grew so large that politicians in modern times have ridiculed it to great political advantage. However, the country's many **bureaucrats** or **civil servants**, the individuals who work in the bureaucracy, fill necessary and even instrumental roles in every area of government: from high-level positions in foreign affairs and intelligence collection agencies to clerks and staff in the smallest regulatory agencies. They are hired, or sometimes appointed, for their expertise in carrying out the functions and programs of the government.

WHAT DOES A BUREAUCRACY DO?

Modern society relies on the effective functioning of government to provide public goods, enhance quality of life, and stimulate economic growth. The activities by which government achieves these functions include—but are not limited to—taxation, homeland security, immigration, foreign affairs, and education. The more society grows and the need for government services expands, the more challenging bureaucratic management and **public administration** becomes. Public administration is both the implementation of public policy in government bureaucracies and the academic study that prepares civil servants for work in those organizations.

The classic version of a bureaucracy is hierarchical and can be described by an organizational chart that outlines the separation of tasks and worker specialization while also establishing a clear unity of command by assigning each employee to only one boss. Moreover, the classic bureaucracy employs a division of labor under which work is separated into smaller tasks assigned to different people or groups. Given this definition, bureaucracy is not unique to government but is also found in the private and nonprofit sectors. That is, almost all organizations are bureaucratic regardless of their scope and size; although public and private organizations differ in some important ways. For example, while private organizations are responsible to a superior authority such as an owner, board of directors, or shareholders, federal governmental organizations answer equally to the president, Congress, the courts, and ultimately the public. The underlying goals of private and public organizations also differ. While private organizations seek to survive by controlling costs, increasing market share, and realizing a profit, public organizations find it more difficult to measure the elusive goal of operating with efficiency and effectiveness.

Link to Learning

To learn more about the practice of public administration and opportunities to get involved in your local community, explore the American Society for Public Administration (https://openstax.org/l/29AmSoPbAd) website.

Bureaucracy may seem like a modern invention, but bureaucrats have served in governments for nearly as long as governments have existed. Archaeologists and historians point to the sometimes elaborate bureaucratic systems of the ancient world, from the Egyptian scribes who recorded inventories to the biblical tax collectors who kept the wheels of government well greased.[1] In Europe, government bureaucracy and its study emerged before democracies did. In contrast, in the United States, a democracy and the Constitution came first, followed by the development of national governmental organizations as needed, and then finally the study of U.S. government bureaucracies and public administration emerged.[2]

In fact, the long pedigree of bureaucracy is an enduring testament to the necessity of administrative organization. More recently, modern bureaucratic management emerged in the eighteenth century from Scottish economist Adam Smith's support for the efficiency of the division of labor and from Welsh reformer Robert Owen's belief that employees are vital instruments in the functioning of an organization. However, it was not until the mid-1800s that the German scholar Lorenz von Stein argued for public administration as both a theory and a practice since its knowledge is generated and evaluated through the process of gathering evidence. For example, a public administration scholar might gather data to see whether the timing of tax collection during a particular season might lead to higher compliance or returns. Credited with being the father of the science of public administration, von Stein opened the path of administrative enlightenment for other scholars in industrialized nations.

THE ORIGINS OF THE U.S. BUREAUCRACY

In the early U.S. republic, the bureaucracy was quite small. This is understandable since the American Revolution was largely a revolt against executive power and the British imperial administrative order. Nevertheless, while neither the word "bureaucracy" nor its synonyms appear in the text of the Constitution, the document does establish a few broad channels through which the emerging government could develop the necessary bureaucratic administration.

For example, Article II, Section 2, provides the president the power to appoint officers and department heads. In the following section, the president is further empowered to see that the laws are "faithfully executed." More specifically, Article I, Section 8, empowers Congress to establish a post office, build roads, regulate commerce, coin money, and regulate the value of money. Granting the president and Congress such responsibilities appears to anticipate a bureaucracy of some size. Yet the design of the bureaucracy is not described, and it does not occupy its own section of the Constitution as bureaucracy often does in other countries' governing documents; the design and form were left to be established in practice.

Under President George Washington, the bureaucracy remained small enough to accomplish only the necessary tasks at hand.[3] Washington's tenure saw the creation of the Department of State to oversee international issues, the Department of the Treasury to control coinage, and the Department of War to administer the armed forces. The employees within these three departments, in addition to the growing postal service, constituted the major portion of the federal bureaucracy for the first three decades of the republic (Figure 15.2). Two developments, however, contributed to the growth of the bureaucracy well beyond these humble beginnings.

Figure 15.2   The cabinet of President George Washington (far left) consisted of only four individuals: the secretary of war (Henry Knox, left), the secretary of the treasury (Alexander Hamilton, center), the secretary of state (Thomas Jefferson, right), and the attorney general (Edmund Randolph, far right). The small size of this group reflected the small size of the U.S. government in the late eighteenth century. (credit: modification of work by the Library of Congress)

The first development was the rise of centralized party politics in the 1820s. Under President Andrew Jackson, many thousands of party loyalists filled the ranks of the bureaucratic offices around the country. This was the beginning of the **spoils system**, in which political appointments were transformed into political patronage doled out by the president on the basis of party loyalty.[4] Political **patronage** is the use of state resources to reward individuals for their political support. The term "spoils" here refers to paid positions in the U.S. government. As the saying goes, "to the victor," in this case the incoming president, "go the spoils." It was assumed that government would work far more efficiently if the key federal posts were occupied by those already supportive of the president and his policies. This system served to enforce party loyalty by tying the livelihoods of the party faithful to the success or failure of the party. The number of federal posts the president sought to use as appropriate rewards for supporters swelled over the following decades.

The second development was industrialization, which in the late nineteenth century significantly increased both the population and economic size of the United States. These changes in turn brought about urban growth in a number of places across the East and Midwest. Railroads and telegraph lines drew the country together and increased the potential for federal centralization. The government and its bureaucracy were closely involved in creating concessions for and providing land to the western railways stretching across the plains and beyond the Rocky Mountains. These changes set the groundwork for the regulatory framework that emerged in the early twentieth century.

THE FALL OF POLITICAL PATRONAGE

Patronage had the advantage of putting political loyalty to work by making the government quite responsive to the electorate and keeping election turnout robust because so much was at stake. However, the spoils system also had a number of obvious disadvantages. It was a reciprocal system. Clients who wanted positions in the civil service pledged their political loyalty to a particular patron who then provided them with their desired positions. These arrangements directed the power and resources of government toward perpetuating the reward system. They replaced the system that early presidents like Thomas Jefferson had fostered, in which the country's intellectual and economic elite rose to the highest levels of the federal bureaucracy based on their relative merit.[5] Criticism of the spoils system grew, especially in the mid-1870s, after numerous scandals rocked the administration of President Ulysses S. Grant (Figure 15.3).

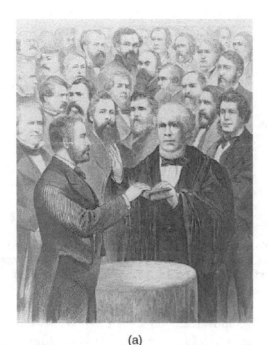

(a)   (b)

Figure 15.3 Caption: It was under President Ulysses S. Grant, shown in this engraving being sworn in by Chief Justice Samuel P. Chase at his inauguration in 1873 (a), that the inefficiencies and opportunities for corruption embedded in the spoils system reached their height. Grant was famously loyal to his supporters, a characteristic that—combined with postwar opportunities for corruption—created scandal in his administration. This political cartoon from 1877 (b), nearly half a century after Andrew Jackson was elected president, ridicules the spoils system that was one of his legacies. In it he is shown riding a pig, which is walking over "fraud," "bribery," and "spoils" and feeding on "plunder." (credit a, b: modification of work by the Library of Congress)

As the negative aspects of political patronage continued to infect bureaucracy in the late nineteenth century, calls for civil service reform grew louder. Those supporting the patronage system held that their positions were well earned; those who condemned it argued that federal legislation was needed to ensure jobs were awarded on the basis of merit. Eventually, after President James Garfield had been assassinated by a disappointed office seeker (Figure 15.4), Congress responded to cries for reform with the Pendleton Act, also called the Civil Service Reform Act of 1883. The act established the Civil Service Commission, a centralized agency charged with ensuring that the federal government's selection, retention, and promotion practices were based on open, competitive examinations in a **merit system**.[6] The passage of this law sparked a period of social activism and political reform that continued well into the twentieth century.

Figure 15.4 In 1881, after the election of James Garfield, a disgruntled former supporter of his, the failed lawyer Charles J. Guiteau, shot him in the back. Guiteau (pictured in this cartoon of the time) had convinced himself he was due an ambassadorship for his work in electing the president. The assassination awakened the nation to the need for civil service reform. (credit: modification of work by the Library of Congress)

As an active member and leader of the Progressive movement, President Woodrow Wilson is often considered the father of U.S. public administration. Born in Virginia and educated in history and political science at Johns Hopkins University, Wilson became a respected intellectual in his fields with an interest in public service and a profound sense of moralism. He was named president of Princeton University, became president of the American Political Science Association, was elected governor of New Jersey, and finally was elected the twenty-eighth president of the United States in 1912.

It was through his educational training and vocational experiences that Wilson began to identify the need for a public administration discipline. He felt it was getting harder to run a constitutional government than to actually frame one. His stance was that "It is the object of administrative study to discover, first, what government can properly and successfully do, and, secondly, how it can do these proper things with the utmost efficiency. . ."[7] Wilson declared that while politics does set tasks for administration, public administration should be built on a science of management, and political science should be concerned with the way governments are administered. Therefore, administrative activities should be devoid of political manipulations.[8]

Wilson advocated separating politics from administration by three key means: making comparative analyses of public and private organizations, improving efficiency with business-like practices, and increasing effectiveness through management and training. Wilson's point was that while politics should be kept separate from administration, administration should not be insensitive to public opinion. Rather, the bureaucracy should act with a sense of vigor to understand and appreciate public opinion. Still, Wilson acknowledged that the separation of politics from administration was an ideal and not necessarily an achievable reality.

THE BUREAUCRACY COMES OF AGE

The late nineteenth and early twentieth centuries were a time of great bureaucratic growth in the United States: The Interstate Commerce Commission was established in 1887, the Federal Reserve Board in 1913, the Federal Trade Commission in 1914, and the Federal Power Commission in 1920.

With the onset of the Great Depression in 1929, the United States faced record levels of unemployment and the associated fall into poverty, food shortages, and general desperation. When the Republican president and Congress were not seen as moving aggressively enough to fix the situation, the Democrats won the 1932 election in overwhelming fashion. President Franklin D. Roosevelt and the U.S. Congress rapidly reorganized the government's problem-solving efforts into a series of programs designed to revive the economy, stimulate economic development, and generate employment opportunities. In the 1930s, the federal bureaucracy grew with the addition of the Federal Deposit Insurance Corporation to protect and regulate U.S. banking, the National Labor Relations Board to regulate the way companies could treat their workers, the Securities and Exchange Commission to regulate the stock market, and the Civil Aeronautics Board to regulate air travel. Additional programs and institutions emerged with the Social Security Administration in 1935 and then, during World War II, various wartime boards and agencies. By 1940, approximately 700,000 U.S. workers were employed in the federal bureaucracy.[9]

Under President Lyndon B. Johnson in the 1960s, that number reached 2.2 million, and the federal budget increased to $332 billion.[10] This growth came as a result of what Johnson called his Great Society program, intended to use the power of government to relieve suffering and accomplish social good. The Economic Opportunity Act of 1964 was designed to help end poverty by creating a Job Corps and a Neighborhood Youth Corps. Volunteers in Service to America was a type of domestic Peace Corps intended to relieve the effects of poverty. Johnson also directed more funding to public education, created Medicare as a national insurance program for the elderly, and raised standards for consumer products.

All of these new programs required bureaucrats to run them, and the national bureaucracy naturally ballooned. Its size became a rallying cry for conservatives, who eventually elected Ronald Reagan president for the express purpose of reducing the bureaucracy. While Reagan was able to work with Congress to reduce some aspects of the federal bureaucracy, he contributed to its expansion in other ways, particularly in his efforts to fight the Cold War.[11] For example, Reagan and Congress increased the defense budget dramatically over the course of the 1980s.[12]

"The Nine Most Terrifying Words in the English Language"

The two periods of increased bureaucratic growth in the United States, the 1930s and the 1960s, accomplished far more than expanding the size of government. They transformed politics in ways that continue to shape political debate today. While the bureaucracies created in these two periods served important purposes, many at that time and even now argue that the expansion came with unacceptable costs, particularly economic costs. The common argument that bureaucratic regulation smothers capitalist innovation was especially powerful in the Cold War environment of the 1960s, 70s, and 80s. But as long as voters felt they were benefiting from the bureaucratic expansion, as they typically did, the political winds supported continued growth.

In the 1970s, however, Germany and Japan were thriving economies in positions to compete with U.S. industry. This competition, combined with technological advances and the beginnings of computerization, began to eat away at American prosperity. Factories began to close, wages began to stagnate, inflation climbed, and the future seemed a little less bright. In this environment, tax-paying workers were less likely to support generous welfare programs designed to end poverty. They felt these bureaucratic programs were adding to their misery in order to support unknown others.

In his first and unsuccessful presidential bid in 1976, Ronald Reagan, a skilled politician and governor of California, stoked working-class anxieties by directing voters' discontent at the bureaucratic dragon he proposed to slay. When he ran again four years later, his criticism of bureaucratic waste in Washington carried him to a landslide victory. While it is debatable whether Reagan actually reduced the size of government, he continued to wield rhetoric about bureaucratic waste to great political advantage. Even as late as 1986, he continued to rail against the Washington bureaucracy (Figure 15.5), once declaring famously that "the nine most terrifying words in the English language are: I'm from the government, and I'm here to help."

Figure 15.5   As seen in this 1976 photograph, President Ronald Reagan frequently and intentionally dressed in casual clothing to symbolize his distance from the government machinery he loved to criticize. (credit: Ronald Reagan Library)

Why might people be more sympathetic to bureaucratic growth during periods of prosperity? In what way do modern politicians continue to stir up popular animosity against bureaucracy to political advantage? Is it effective? Why or why not?

15.2 Toward a Merit-Based Civil Service

Learning Objectives

By the end of this section, you will be able to:

- Explain how the creation of the Civil Service Commission transformed the spoils system of the nineteenth century into a merit-based system of civil service
- Understand how carefully regulated hiring and pay practices helps to maintain a merit-based civil service

While the federal bureaucracy grew by leaps and bounds during the twentieth century, it also underwent a very different evolution. Beginning with the Pendleton Act in the 1880s, the bureaucracy shifted away from the spoils system toward a merit system. The distinction between these two forms of bureaucracy is crucial. The evolution toward a civil service in the United States had important functional consequences. Today the United States has a civil service that carefully regulates hiring practices and pay to create an environment in which, it is hoped, the best people to fulfill each civil service responsibility are the same people hired to fill those positions.

THE CIVIL SERVICE COMMISSION

The Pendleton Act of 1883 was not merely an important piece of reform legislation; it also established the foundations for the merit-based system that emerged in the decades that followed. It accomplished this through a number of important changes, although three elements stand out as especially significant. First, the law attempted to reduce the impact of politics on the civil service sector by making it illegal to fire or otherwise punish government workers for strictly political reasons. Second, the law raised the qualifications for employment in civil service positions by requiring applicants to pass exams designed to test their competence in a number of important skill and knowledge areas. Third, it allowed for the creation of the United States Civil Service Commission (CSC), which was charged with enforcing the elements of the law.[13]

The CSC, as created by the Pendleton Act, was to be made up of three commissioners, only two of whom could be from the same political party. These commissioners were given the responsibility of developing and applying the competitive examinations for civil service positions, ensuring that the civil service appointments were apportioned among the several states based on population, and seeing to it that no person in the public service is obligated to contribute to any political cause. The CSC was also charged with ensuring that all civil servants wait for a probationary period before being appointed and that no appointee uses his or her official authority to affect political changes either through coercion or influence. Both Congress and the president oversaw the CSC by requiring the commission to supply an annual report on its activities first to the president and then to Congress.

In 1883, civil servants under the control of the commission amounted to about 10 percent of the entire government workforce. However, over the next few decades, this percentage increased dramatically. The effects on the government itself of both the law and the increase in the size of the civil service were huge. Presidents and representatives were no longer spending their days doling out or terminating appointments. Consequently, the many members of the civil service could no longer count on their political patrons for job security. Of course, job security was never guaranteed before the Pendleton Act because all positions were subject to the rise and fall of political parties. However, with civil service appointments no longer tied to partisan success, bureaucrats began to look to each other in order to create the job security the previous system had lacked. One of the most important ways they did this was by creating civil service organizations such as the National Association of All Civil Service Employees, formed in 1896. This organization worked to further civil service reform, especially in the area most important to civil service professionals: ensuring greater job security and maintaining the distance between themselves and the political parties that once controlled them.[14]

Over the next few decades, civil servants gravitated to labor unions in much the same way that employees in the private sector did. Through the power of their collective voices amplified by their union representatives, they were able to achieve political influence. The growth of federal labor unions accelerated after the Lloyd–La Follette Act of 1912, which removed many of the penalties civil servants faced when joining a union. As the size of the federal government and its bureaucracy grew following the Great Depression and the Roosevelt reforms, many became increasingly concerned that the Pendleton Act prohibitions on political activities by civil servants were no longer strong enough. As a result of these mounting concerns, Congress passed the Hatch Act of 1939—or the Political Activities Act. The main provision of this legislation prohibits bureaucrats from actively engaging in political campaigns and from using their federal authority via bureaucratic rank to influence the outcomes of nominations and elections.

Despite the efforts throughout the 1930s to build stronger walls of separation between the civil service bureaucrats and the political system that surrounds them, many citizens continued to grow skeptical of the growing bureaucracy. These concerns reached a high point in the late 1970s as the Vietnam War and the Watergate scandal prompted the public to a fever pitch of skepticism about government itself. Congress and the president responded with the Civil Service Reform Act of 1978, which abolished the Civil Service Commission. In its place, the law created two new federal agencies: the Office of Personnel Management (OPM) and the Merit Systems Protection Board (MSPB). The OPM has responsibility for recruiting, interviewing, and testing potential government employees in order to choose those who should be hired. The MSPB is responsible for investigating charges of agency wrongdoing and hearing appeals when corrective actions are ordered. Together these new federal agencies were intended to correct perceived and real problems with the merit system, protect employees from managerial abuse, and generally make the bureaucracy more efficient.[15]

MERIT-BASED SELECTION

The general trend from the 1880s to today has been toward a civil service system that is increasingly based on merit (Figure 15.6). In this system, the large majority of jobs in individual bureaucracies are tied to the needs of the organization rather than to the political needs of the party bosses or political leaders. This purpose is reflected in the way civil service positions are advertised. A general civil service position announcement will describe the government agency or office seeking an employee, an explanation of what the agency or office does, an explanation of what the position requires, and a list of the knowledge, skills, and abilities, commonly referred to as KSAs, deemed especially important for fulfilling the role. A budget analyst position, for example, would include KSAs such as experience with automated financial systems, knowledge of budgetary regulations and policies, the ability to communicate orally, and demonstrated skills in budget administration, planning, and formulation. The merit system requires that a person be evaluated based on his or her ability to demonstrate KSAs that match those described or better. The individual who is hired should have better KSAs than the other applicants.

Figure 15.6 Historically, African Americans have gravitated to the civil service in large numbers, although it was only in 2009 that an African American, Eric Holder (pictured here), rose to the position of U.S. attorney general. In 2014, African Americans represented 18 percent of the civil service, a number disproportionately larger than their share of the population, (about 13 percent). While there are many reasons for this, a prominent one is that the merit-based nature of the civil service offered African Americans far more opportunities for advancement than the private sector, where racial discrimination played a large role.

Many years ago, the merit system would have required all applicants to also test well on a civil service exam, as was stipulated by the Pendleton Act. This mandatory testing has since been abandoned, and now approximately eighty-five percent of all federal government jobs are filled through an examination of the applicant's education, background, knowledge, skills, and abilities.[16] That would suggest that some 20 percent are filled through appointment and patronage. Among the first group, those hired based on merit, a small percentage still require that applicants take one of the several civil service exams. These are sometimes positions that require applicants to demonstrate broad critical thinking skills, such as foreign service jobs. More often these exams are required for positions demanding specific or technical knowledge, such as customs officials, air traffic controllers, and federal law enforcement officers. Additionally, new online tests are increasingly being used to screen the ever-growing pool of applicants.[17]

Civil service exams currently test for skills applicable to clerical workers, postal service workers, military personnel, health and social workers, and accounting and engineering employees among others. Applicants with the highest scores on these tests are most likely to be hired for the desired position. Like all organizations, bureaucracies must make thoughtful investments in human capital. And even after hiring people, they must continue to train and develop them to reap the investment they make during the hiring process.

Get Connected!

A Career in Government: Competitive Service, Excepted Service, Senior Executive Service

One of the significant advantages of the enormous modern U.S. bureaucracy is that many citizens find employment there to be an important source of income and meaning in their lives. Job opportunities exist in a number of different fields, from foreign service with the State Department to information and record clerking at all levels. Each position requires specific background, education, experience, and skills.

There are three general categories of work in the federal government: competitive service, excepted service, and senior executive service. *Competitive service* positions are closely regulated by Congress through the Office of Personnel Management to ensure they are filled in a fair way and the best applicant gets the job (Figure 15.7). Qualifications for these jobs include work history, education, and grades on civil service exams. Federal jobs in the *excepted service* category are exempt from these hiring restrictions. Either these jobs require a far more rigorous hiring process, such as is the case at the Central Intelligence Agency, or they call for very specific skills, such as in the Nuclear Regulatory Commission. Excepted service jobs allow employers to set their own pay rates and requirements. Finally, *senior executive service* positions are filled by men and women who are able to demonstrate their experience in executive positions. These are leadership positions, and applicants must demonstrate certain executive core qualifications (ECQs). These qualifications are leading change, being results-driven, demonstrating business acumen, and building better coalitions.

Figure 15.7   The U.S. Office of Personnel Management regulates hiring practices in the U.S. Civil Service.

What might be the practical consequences of having these different job categories? Can you think of some specific positions you are familiar with and the categories they might be in?

Link to Learning

Where once federal jobs would have been posted in post offices and newspapers, they are now posted online. The most common place aspiring civil servants look for jobs is on USAjobs.gov, a web-based platform offered by the Office of Personnel Management for agencies to find the right employees. Visit their website to see the types of jobs (https://openstax.org/l/29USAjbgov) currently available in the U.S. bureaucracy.

Civil servants receive pay based on the U.S. Federal General Schedule. A **pay schedule** is a chart that shows salary ranges for different levels (grades) of positions vertically and for different ranks (steps) of seniority horizontally. The Pendleton Act of 1883 allowed for this type of pay schedule, but the modern version of the schedule emerged in the 1940s and was refined in the 1990s. The modern General Schedule includes fifteen grades, each with ten steps (Figure 15.8). The grades reflect the different required competencies, education standards, skills, and experiences for the various civil service positions. Grades GS-1 and GS-2 require very little education, experience, and skills and pay little. Grades GS-3 through GS-7 and GS-8 through GS-12 require ascending levels of education and pay increasingly more. Grades GS-13 through GS-15 require specific, specialized experience and education, and these job levels pay the most. When hired into a position at a specific grade, employees are typically paid at the first step of that grade, the lowest allowable pay. Over time, assuming they receive satisfactory assessment ratings, they will progress through the various levels. Many careers allow for the civil servants to ascend through the grades of the specific career as well.[18]

Grade	Pay Range (Steps 1-10)
GS-1	$21,672–$27,114
GS-2	$24,367–$30,671
GS-3	$26,587–$34,561
GS-4	$29,847–$38,798
GS-5	$33,394–$43,414
GS-6	$37,223–$48,385
GS-7	$41,365–$53,773
GS-8	$45,810–$59,557
GS-9	$50,598–$65,778
GS-10	$55,720–$72,437
GS-11	$61,218–$79,586
GS-12	$73,375–$95,388
GS-13	$87,252–$113,428
GS-14	$103,106–$134,038
GS-15	$121,280–$157,663

Figure 15.8 The modern General Schedule is the predominant pay scale within the United States civil service and includes fifteen grades, each with ten steps. Each higher grade typically requires a higher level of education: GS-1 has no qualifying amount, GS-2 requires a high school diploma or equivalent, GS-5 requires four years of education beyond high school or a bachelor's degree, GS-9 requires a master's or equivalent graduate degree, and so on. At GS-13 and above, appropriate specialized experience is required for all positions.

The intention behind these hiring practices and structured pay systems is to create an environment in which those most likely to succeed are in fact those who are ultimately appointed. The systems almost naturally result in organizations composed of experts who dedicate their lives to their work and their agency. Equally important, however, are the drawbacks. The primary one is that permanent employees can become too independent of the elected leaders. While a degree of separation is intentional and desired, too much can result in bureaucracies that are insufficiently responsive to political change. Another downside is that the accepted expertise of individual bureaucrats can sometimes hide their own chauvinistic impulses. The merit system encouraged bureaucrats to turn to each other and their bureaucracies for support and stability. Severing the political ties common in the spoils system creates the potential for bureaucrats to steer actions toward their own preferences even if these contradict the designs of elected leaders.

15.3 Understanding Bureaucracies and their Types

Learning Objectives

By the end of this section, you will be able to:
- Explain the three different models sociologists and others use to understand bureaucracies
- Identify the different types of federal bureaucracies and their functional differences

Turning a spoils system bureaucracy into a merit-based civil service, while desirable, comes with a number of different consequences. The patronage system tied the livelihoods of civil service workers to their party loyalty and discipline. Severing these ties, as has occurred in the United States over the last century and a half, has transformed the way bureaucracies operate. Without the patronage network, bureaucracies form their own motivations. These motivations, sociologists have discovered, are designed to benefit and perpetuate the bureaucracies themselves.

MODELS OF BUREAUCRACY

Bureaucracies are complex institutions designed to accomplish specific tasks. This complexity, and the fact that they are organizations composed of human beings, can make it challenging for us to understand how bureaucracies work. Sociologists, however, have developed a number of models for understanding the process. Each model highlights specific traits that help explain the organizational behavior of governing bodies and associated functions.

The Weberian Model

The classic model of bureaucracy is typically called the ideal Weberian model, and it was developed by Max Weber, an early German sociologist. Weber argued that the increasing complexity of life would simultaneously increase the demands of citizens for government services. Therefore, the ideal type of bureaucracy, the Weberian model, was one in which agencies are apolitical, hierarchically organized, and governed by formal procedures. Furthermore, specialized bureaucrats would be better able to solve problems through logical reasoning. Such efforts would eliminate entrenched patronage, stop problematic decision-making by those in charge, provide a system for managing and performing repetitive tasks that required little or no discretion, impose order and efficiency, create a clear understanding of the service provided, reduce arbitrariness, ensure accountability, and limit discretion.[19]

The Acquisitive Model

For Weber, as his ideal type suggests, the bureaucracy was not only necessary but also a positive human development. Later sociologists have not always looked so favorably upon bureaucracies, and they have developed alternate models to explain how and why bureaucracies function. One such model is called the acquisitive model of bureaucracy. The acquisitive model proposes that bureaucracies are naturally competitive and power-hungry. This means bureaucrats, especially at the highest levels, recognize that limited resources are available to feed bureaucracies, so they will work to enhance the status of their own bureaucracy to the detriment of others.

This effort can sometimes take the form of merely emphasizing to Congress the value of their bureaucratic task, but it also means the bureaucracy will attempt to maximize its budget by depleting all its allotted resources each year. This ploy makes it more difficult for legislators to cut the bureaucracy's future budget, a strategy that succeeds at the expense of thrift. In this way, the bureaucracy will eventually grow far beyond what is necessary and create bureaucratic waste that would otherwise be spent more efficiently among the other bureaucracies.

The Monopolistic Model

Other theorists have come to the conclusion that the extent to which bureaucracies compete for scarce resources is not what provides the greatest insight into how a bureaucracy functions. Rather, it is the absence of competition. The model that emerged from this observation is the *monopolistic model*.

Proponents of the monopolistic model recognize the similarities between a bureaucracy like the Internal Revenue Service (IRS) and a private monopoly like a regional power company or internet service provider that has no competitors. Such organizations are frequently criticized for waste, poor service, and a low level of client responsiveness. Consider, for example, the Bureau of Consular Affairs (BCA), the federal bureaucracy charged with issuing passports to citizens. There is no other organization from which a U.S. citizen can legitimately request and receive a passport, a process that normally takes several weeks. Thus there is no reason for the BCA to become more efficient or more responsive or to issue passports any faster.

There are rare bureaucratic exceptions that typically compete for presidential favor, most notably organizations such as the Central Intelligence Agency, the National Security Agency, and the intelligence agencies in the Department of Defense. Apart from these, bureaucracies have little reason to become more efficient or responsive, nor are they often penalized for chronic inefficiency or ineffectiveness. Therefore, there is little reason for them to adopt cost-saving or performance measurement systems. While some economists argue that the problems of government could be easily solved if certain functions are privatized to reduce this prevailing incompetence, bureaucrats are not as easily swayed.

TYPES OF BUREAUCRATIC ORGANIZATIONS

A bureaucracy is a particular government unit established to accomplish a specific set of goals and objectives as authorized by a legislative body. In the United States, the federal bureaucracy enjoys a great degree of autonomy compared to those of other countries. This is in part due to the sheer size of the federal budget, approximately \$3.5 trillion as of 2015.[20] And because many of its agencies do not have clearly defined lines of authority—roles and responsibilities established by means of a chain of command—they also are able to operate with a high degree of autonomy. However, many agency actions are subject to judicial review. In *Schechter Poultry Corp. v. United States* (1935), the Supreme Court found that agency authority seemed limitless.[21] Yet, not all bureaucracies are alike. In the U.S. government, there are four general types: cabinet departments, independent executive agencies, regulatory agencies, and government corporations.

Cabinet Departments

There are currently fifteen cabinet departments in the federal government. Cabinet departments are major executive offices that are directly accountable to the president. They include the Departments of State, Defense, Education, Treasury, and several others. Occasionally, a department will be eliminated when government officials decide its tasks no longer need direct presidential and congressional oversight, such as happened to the Post Office Department in 1970.

Each cabinet department has a head called a secretary, appointed by the president and confirmed by the Senate. These secretaries report directly to the president, and they oversee a huge network of offices and agencies that make up the department. They also work in different capacities to achieve each department's mission-oriented functions. Within these large bureaucratic networks are a number of undersecretaries, assistant secretaries, deputy secretaries, and many others. The Department of Justice is the one department that is structured somewhat differently. Rather than a secretary and undersecretaries, it has an attorney general, an associate attorney general, and a host of different bureau and division heads (Table 15.1).

Members of the Cabinet

Department	Year Created	Secretary as of January 2019	Purpose
State	1789	Mike Pompeo	Oversees matters related to foreign policy and international issues relevant to the country
Treasury	1789	Steven Mnuchin	Oversees the printing of U.S. currency, collects taxes, and manages government debt
Justice	1870	Matthew Whitaker (acting attorney general)	Oversees the enforcement of U.S. laws, matters related to public safety, and crime prevention
Interior	1849	David Bernhardt (acting)	Oversees the conservation and management of U.S. lands, water, wildlife, and energy resources
Agriculture	1862	Sonny Perdue	Oversees the U.S. farming industry, provides agricultural subsidies, and conducts food inspections
Commerce	1903	Wilbur Ross	Oversees the promotion of economic growth, job creation, and the issuing of patents
Labor	1913	Alex Acosta	Oversees issues related to wages, unemployment insurance, and occupational safety
Defense	1947	Patrick M. Shanahan (acting)	Oversees the many elements of the U.S. armed forces, including the Army, Navy, Marine Corps, and Air Force
Health and Human Services	1953	Alex Azar	Oversees the promotion of public health by providing essential human services and enforcing food and drug laws
Housing and Urban Development	1965	Ben Carson	Oversees matters related to U.S. housing needs, works to increase homeownership, and increases access to affordable housing
Transportation	1966	Elaine Chao	Oversees the country's many networks of national transportation
Energy	1977	Rick Perry	Oversees matters related to the country's energy needs, including energy security and technological innovation
Education	1980	Betsy DeVos	Oversees public education, education policy, and relevant education research
Veterans Affairs	1989	Robert Wilkie	Oversees the services provided to U.S. veterans, including health care services and benefits programs
Homeland Security	2002	Kirstjen Nielsen	Oversees agencies charged with protecting the territory of the United States from natural and human threats

Table 15.1 This table outlines all the current cabinet departments, along with the year they were created, their current top administrator, and other special details related to their purpose and functions.

Individual cabinet departments are composed of numerous levels of bureaucracy. These levels descend from the department head in a mostly hierarchical pattern and consist of essential staff, smaller offices, and bureaus. Their tiered, hierarchical structure allows large bureaucracies to address many different issues by deploying dedicated and specialized officers. For example, below the secretary of state are a number of undersecretaries. These include undersecretaries for political affairs, for management, for economic growth, energy, and the environment, and many others. Each controls a number of bureaus and offices. Each bureau and office in turn oversees a more focused aspect of the undersecretary's field of specialization (Figure 15.9). For example, below the undersecretary for public diplomacy and public affairs are three bureaus: educational and cultural affairs, public affairs, and international information programs. Frequently, these bureaus have even more specialized departments under them. Under the bureau of educational and cultural affairs are the spokesperson for the Department of State and his or her staff, the Office of the Historian, and the United States Diplomacy Center.[22]

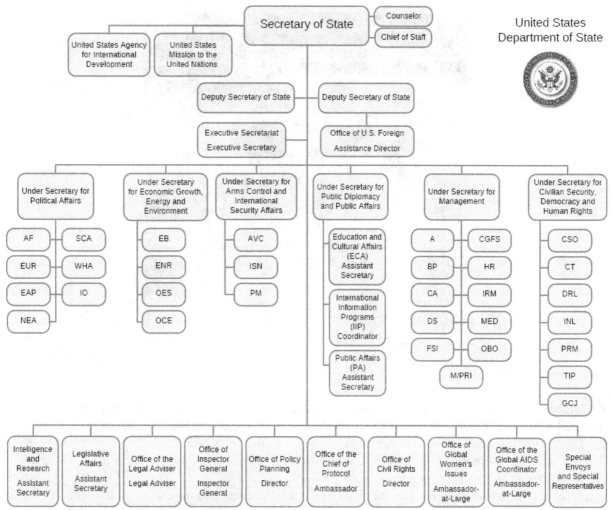

Figure 15.9 The multiple levels of the Department of State each work in a focused capacity to help the entire department fulfill its larger goals. (credit: modification of work by the U. S. Department of State)

Link to Learning

Created in 1939 by President Franklin D. Roosevelt to help manage the growing responsibilities of the White House, the Executive Office of the President (https://openstax.org/l/29ExOfPres) still works today to "provide the President with the support that he or she needs to govern effectively."

Independent Executive Agencies and Regulatory Agencies

Like cabinet departments, independent executive agencies report directly to the president, with heads appointed by the president. Unlike the larger cabinet departments, however, independent agencies are assigned far more focused tasks. These agencies are considered independent because they are not subject to the regulatory authority of any specific department. They perform vital functions and are a major part of the bureaucratic landscape of the United States. Some prominent independent agencies are the Central Intelligence Agency (CIA), which collects and manages intelligence vital to national interests, the National Aeronautics and Space Administration (NASA), charged with developing technological innovation for the purposes of space exploration (Figure 15.10), and the Environmental Protection Agency (EPA), which enforces laws aimed at protecting environmental sustainability.

Figure 15.10   While the category "independent executive agency" may seem very ordinary, the actions of some of these agencies, like NASA, are anything but. (credit: NASA)

An important subset of the independent agency category is the regulatory agency. Regulatory agencies emerged in the late nineteenth century as a product of the progressive push to control the benefits and costs of industrialization. The first regulatory agency was the Interstate Commerce Commission (ICC), charged with regulating that most identifiable and prominent symbol of nineteenth-century industrialism, the railroad. Other regulatory agencies, such as the Commodity Futures Trading Commission, which regulates U.S. financial markets and the Federal Communications Commission, which regulates radio and television, have largely been created in the image of the ICC. These independent regulatory agencies cannot be influenced as readily by partisan politics as typical agencies and can therefore develop a good deal of power and authority. The Securities and Exchange Commission (SEC) illustrates well the potential power of such agencies. The SEC's mission has expanded significantly in the digital era beyond mere regulation of stock floor trading.

Government Corporations

Agencies formed by the federal government to administer a quasi-business enterprise are called **government corporations**. They exist because the services they provide are partly subject to market forces and tend to generate enough profit to be self-sustaining, but they also fulfill a vital service the government has an interest in maintaining. Unlike a private corporation, a government corporation does not have stockholders. Instead, it has a board of directors and managers. This distinction is important because whereas a private corporation's profits are distributed as dividends, a government corporation's profits are dedicated to perpetuating the enterprise. Unlike private businesses, which pay taxes to the federal government on their profits, government corporations are exempt from taxes.

The most widely used government corporation is the U.S. Postal Service. Once a cabinet department, it was transformed into a government corporation in the early 1970s. Another widely used government corporation is the National Railroad Passenger Corporation, which uses the trade name Amtrak (Figure 15.11). Amtrak was the government's response to the decline in passenger rail travel in the 1950s and 1960s as the automobile came to dominate. Recognizing the need to maintain a passenger rail service despite dwindling profits, the government consolidated the remaining lines and created Amtrak.[23]

Figure 15.11 Had the U.S. government not created Amtrak in the 1970s, passenger rail service might have ceased to exist in the United States. (credit: the Library of Congress)

THE FACE OF DEMOCRACY

Those who work for the public bureaucracy are nearly always citizens, much like those they serve. As such they typically seek similar long-term goals from their employment, namely to be able to pay their bills and save for retirement. However, unlike those who seek employment in the private sector, public bureaucrats tend to have an additional motivator, the desire to accomplish something worthwhile on behalf of their country. In general, individuals attracted to public service display higher levels of public service motivation (PSM). This is a desire most people possess in varying degrees that drives us to seek fulfillment through doing good and contributing in an altruistic manner.[24]

Dogs and Fireplugs

In *Caught between the Dog and the Fireplug, or How to Survive Public Service (2001),* author Kenneth Ashworth provides practical advice for individuals pursuing a career in civil service.[25] Through a series of letters, Ashworth shares his personal experience and professional expertise on a variety of issues with a relative named Kim who is about to embark upon an occupation in the public sector. By discussing what life is like in the civil service, Ashworth provides an "in the trenches" vantage point on public affairs. He goes on to discuss hot topics centering on bureaucratic behaviors, such as (1) having sound etiquette, ethics, and risk aversion when working with press, politicians, and unpleasant people; (2) being a subordinate while also delegating; (3) managing relationships, pressures, and influence; (4) becoming a functional leader; and (5) taking a multidimensional approach to addressing or solving complex problems.

Ashworth says that politicians and civil servants differ in their missions, needs, and motivations, which will eventually reveal differences in their respective characters and, consequently, present a variety of challenges. He maintains that a good civil servant must realize he or she will need to be in the thick of things to provide preeminent service without actually being seen as merely a bureaucrat. Put differently, a bureaucrat walks a fine line between standing up for elected officials and their respective policies—the dog—and at the same time acting in the best interest of the public—the fireplug.

In what ways is the problem identified by author Kenneth Ashworth a consequence of the merit-based civil service?

Bureaucrats must implement and administer a wide range of policies and programs as established by congressional acts or presidential orders. Depending upon the agency's mission, a bureaucrat's roles and responsibilities vary greatly, from regulating corporate business and protecting the environment to printing money and purchasing office supplies. Bureaucrats are government officials subject to legislative regulations and procedural guidelines. Because they play a vital role in modern society, they hold managerial and functional positions in government; they form the core of most administrative agencies. Although many top administrators are far removed from the masses, many interact with citizens on a regular basis.

Given the power bureaucrats have to adopt and enforce public policy, they must follow several legislative regulations and procedural guidelines. A *regulation* is a rule that permits government to restrict or prohibit certain behaviors among individuals and corporations. Bureaucratic rulemaking is a complex process that will be covered in more detail in the following section, but the rulemaking process typically creates *procedural guidelines*, or more formally, *standard operating procedures*. These are the rules that lower-level bureaucrats must abide by regardless of the situations they face.

Elected officials are regularly frustrated when bureaucrats seem not follow the path they intended. As a result, the bureaucratic process becomes inundated with **red tape**. This is the name for the procedures and rules that must be followed to get something done. Citizens frequently criticize the seemingly endless networks of red tape they must navigate in order to effectively utilize bureaucratic services, although these devices are really meant to ensure the bureaucracies function as intended.

15.4 Controlling the Bureaucracy

Learning Objectives

By the end of this section, you will be able to:

- Explain the way Congress, the president, bureaucrats, and citizens provide meaningful oversight over the bureaucracies
- Identify the ways in which privatization has made bureaucracies both more and less efficient

As our earlier description of the State Department demonstrates, bureaucracies are incredibly complicated. Understandably, then, the processes of rulemaking and bureaucratic oversight are equally complex. Historically, at least since the end of the spoils system, elected leaders have struggled to maintain control over their bureaucracies. This challenge arises partly due to the fact that elected leaders tend to have partisan motivations, while bureaucracies are designed to avoid partisanship. While that is not the only explanation, elected leaders and citizens have developed laws and institutions to help rein in bureaucracies that become either too independent, corrupt, or both.

BUREAUCRATIC RULEMAKING

Once the particulars of implementation have been spelled out in the legislation authorizing a new program, bureaucracies move to enact it. When they encounter grey areas, many follow the federal **negotiated rulemaking** process to propose a solution, that is, detailing how particular new federal polices, regulations, and/or programs will be implemented in the agencies. Congress cannot possibly legislate on that level of detail, so the experts in the bureaucracy do so.

Negotiated rulemaking is a relatively recently developed bureaucratic device that emerged from the criticisms of bureaucratic inefficiencies in the 1970s, 1980s, and 1990s.[26] Before it was adopted, bureaucracies used a procedure called *notice-and-comment rulemaking*. This practice required that agencies attempting to adopt rules publish their proposal in the *Federal Register*, the official publication for all federal rules and proposed rules. By publishing the proposal, the bureaucracy was fulfilling its obligation to allow the public time to comment. But rather than encouraging the productive interchange of ideas, the comment period had the effect of creating an adversarial environment in which different groups tended to make extreme arguments for rules that would support their interests. As a result, administrative rulemaking became too lengthy, too contentious, and too likely to provoke litigation in the courts.

Link to Learning

The *Federal Register* was once available only in print. Now, however, it is available online and is far easier to navigate and use. Have a look (https://openstax.org/l/29FedRegis) at all the important information the government's journal posts online.

Reformers argued that these inefficiencies needed to be corrected. They proposed the *negotiated rulemaking process*, often referred to as regulatory negotiation, or "reg-neg" for short. This process was codified in the Negotiated Rulemaking Acts of 1990 and 1996, which encouraged agencies to employ negotiated rulemaking procedures. While negotiated rulemaking is required in only a handful of agencies and plenty still use the traditional process, others have recognized the potential of the new process and have adopted it.

In negotiated rulemaking, neutral advisors known as convenors put together a committee of those who have vested interests in the proposed rules. The convenors then set about devising procedures for reaching a consensus on the proposed rules. The committee uses these procedures to govern the process through which the committee members discuss the various merits and demerits of the proposals. With the help of neutral mediators, the committee eventually reaches a general consensus on the rules.

GOVERNMENT BUREAUCRATIC OVERSIGHT

The ability for bureaucracies to develop their own rules and in many ways control their own budgets has often been a matter of great concern for elected leaders. As a result, elected leaders have employed a number of strategies and devices to control public administrators in the bureaucracy.

Congress is particularly empowered to apply oversight of the federal bureaucracy because of its power to control funding and approve presidential appointments. The various bureaucratic agencies submit annual summaries of their activities and budgets for the following year, and committees and subcommittees in both chambers regularly hold hearings to question the leaders of the various bureaucracies. These hearings are often tame, practical, fact-finding missions. Occasionally, however, when a particular bureaucracy has committed or contributed to a blunder of some magnitude, the hearings can become quite animated and testy.

This occurred in 2013 following the realization by Congress that the IRS had selected for extra scrutiny certain groups that had applied for tax-exempt status. While the error could have been a mere mistake or have resulted from any number of reasons, many in Congress became enraged at the thought that the IRS might purposely use its power to inconvenience citizens and their groups.[27] The House directed its Committee on Oversight and Government Reform to launch an investigation into the IRS, during which time it interviewed and publicly scrutinized a number of high-ranking civil servants (Figure 15.12).

Figure 15.12   In this photograph, Lois Lerner, the former director of the Internal Revenue Service's Exempt Organizations Unit, sits before an oversight committee in Congress following a 2013 investigation. On the advice of her attorney, Lerner invoked her Fifth Amendment right not to incriminate herself and refused to answer questions.

Link to Learning

The mission of the U.S. House Oversight Committee is to "ensure the efficiency, effectiveness, and accountability of the federal government and all its agencies." The committee is an important congressional check on the power of the bureaucracy. Visit the **website (https://openstax.org/l/ 29USOvCom)** for more information about the U.S. House Oversight Committee.

Perhaps Congress's most powerful oversight tool is the Government Accountability Office (GAO).[28] The GAO is an agency that provides Congress, its committees, and the heads of the executive agencies with auditing, evaluation, and investigative services. It is designed to operate in a fact-based and nonpartisan manner to deliver important oversight information where and when it is needed. The GAO's role is to produce reports, mostly at the insistence of Congress. In the approximately nine hundred reports it completes per year, the GAO sends Congress information about budgetary issues for everything from education, health care, and housing to defense, homeland security, and natural resource management.[29] Since it is an office within the federal bureaucracy, the GAO also supplies Congress with its own annual performance and accountability report. This report details the achievements and remaining weaknesses in the actions of the GAO for any given year.

Apart from Congress, the president also executes oversight over the extensive federal bureaucracy through a number of different avenues. Most directly, the president controls the bureaucracies by appointing the heads of the fifteen cabinet departments and of many independent executive agencies, such as the CIA, the EPA, and the Federal Bureau of Investigation. These cabinet and agency appointments go through the Senate for confirmation.

The other important channel through which the office of the president conducts oversight over the federal bureaucracy is the Office of Management and Budget (OMB).[30] The primary responsibility of the OMB is to produce the president's annual budget for the country. With this huge responsibility, however, comes a number of other responsibilities. These include reporting to the president on the actions of the various executive departments and agencies in the federal government, overseeing the performance levels of the bureaucracies, coordinating and reviewing federal regulations for the president, and delivering executive orders and presidential directives to the various agency heads.

Finding a Middle Ground

Controversy and the CFPB: Overseeing a Bureau Whose Job Is Oversight

During the 1990s, the two political parties in the United States had largely come together over the issue of the federal bureaucracy. While differences remained, a great number of bipartisan attempts to roll back the size of government took place during the Clinton administration. This shared effort began to fall apart during the presidency of Republican George W. Bush, who made repeated attempts to use contracting and privatization to reduce the size of the federal bureaucracy more than Democrats were willing to accept.

This growing division was further compounded by Great Recession that began in 2007. For many on the left side of the political spectrum, the onset of the recession reflected a failure of weakened federal bureaucracies to properly regulate the financial markets. To those on the right, it merely reinforced the belief that government bureaucracies are inherently inefficient. Over the next few years, as the government attempted to grapple with the consequences of the recession, these divisions only grew.

The debate over one particular bureaucratic response to the recession provides important insight into these divisions. The bureau in question is the Consumer Financial Protection Bureau (CFPB), an agency created in 2011 specifically to oversee certain financial industries that had proven themselves to be especially prone to abusive practices, such as sub-prime mortgage lenders and payday lenders. To many in the Republican Party, this new bureau was merely another instance of growing the federal bureaucracy to take care of problems caused by an inefficient government. To many in the Democratic Party, the new agency was an important cop on a notably chaotic street.

Divisions over this agency were so bitter that Republicans refused for a time to allow the Senate to consider confirming anyone to head the new bureau (Figure 15.13). Many wanted the bureau either scrapped or headed by a committee that would have to generate consensus in order to act. They attempted to cut the bureau's budget and erected mountains of red tape designed to slow the CFPB's achievement of its goals. During the height of the recession, many Democrats saw these tactics as a particularly destructive form of obstruction while the country reeled from the financial collapse.

Figure 15.13 In this photograph, Elizabeth Warren, then a law school professor who proposed the CFPB, stands with President Obama and Richard Cordray, the president's pick to serve as director of the new agency. Warren is currently a U.S. senator from Massachusetts.

As the recession recedes into the past, however, the political heat the CFPB once generated has steadily declined. Republicans still push to reduce the power of the bureau and Democrats in general still support it, but lack of urgency has pushed these differences into the background. Indeed, there may be a growing consensus between the two parties that the bureau should be more tightly controlled. In the spring of 2016, as the agency was announcing new rules to help further restrict the predatory practices of payday lenders, a handful of Democratic members of Congress, including the party chair, joined Republicans to draft legislation to prevent the CFPB from further regulating lenders. This trajectory has continued in the Trump Administration where there have been significant efforts made to slow the agency down dramatically.[31]

What do these divisions suggest about the way Congress exercises oversight over the federal bureaucracy? Do you think this oversight is an effective way to control a bureaucracy as large and complex as the U.S. federal bureaucracy? Why or why not?

CITIZEN BUREAUCRATIC OVERSIGHT

A number of laws passed in the decades between the end of the Second World War and the late 1970s have created a framework through which citizens can exercise their own bureaucratic oversight. The two most important laws are the Freedom of Information Act of 1966 and the Government in Sunshine Act of 1976.[32] Like many of the modern bureaucratic reforms in the United States, both emerged during a period of heightened skepticism about government activities.

The first, the Freedom of Information Act of 1966 (FOIA), emerged in the early years of the Johnson presidency as the United States was conducting secret Cold War missions around the world, the U.S. military was becoming increasingly mired in the conflict in Vietnam, and questions were still swirling around the Kennedy assassination. FOIA provides journalists and the general public the right to request records from various federal agencies. These agencies are required by law to release that information unless it qualifies for one of nine exemptions. These exceptions cite sensitive issues related to national security or foreign policy, internal personnel rules, trade secrets, violations of personnel privacy rights, law enforcement information, and oil well data (Figure 15.14). FOIA also compels agencies to post some types of information for the public regularly without being requested.

Figure 15.14 As this CIA document shows, even information released under FOIA can be greatly restricted by the agencies releasing it. The black marks cover information the CIA deemed particularly sensitive.

In fiscal year 2015, the government received 713,168 FOIA requests, with just three departments—Defense, Homeland Security, and Justice—accounting for more than half those queries.[33] The Center for Effective Government analyzed the fifteen federal agencies that receive the most FOIA requests and concluded that they generally struggle to implement public disclosure rules. In its latest report, published in 2015 and using 2012 and 2013 data (the most recent available), ten of the fifteen did not earn satisfactory overall grades, scoring less than seventy of a possible one hundred points.[34]

The Government in Sunshine Act of 1976 is different from FOIA in that it requires all multi-headed federal agencies to hold their meetings in a public forum on a regular basis. The name "Sunshine Act" is derived from the old adage that "sunlight is the best disinfectant"—the implication being that governmental and bureaucratic corruption thrive in secrecy but shrink when exposed to the light of public scrutiny. The act defines a meeting as any gathering of agency members in person or by phone, whether in a formal or informal manner.

Like FOIA, the Sunshine Act allows for exceptions. These include meetings where classified information is discussed, proprietary data has been submitted for review, employee privacy matters are discussed, criminal matters are brought up, and information would prove financially harmful to companies were it released. Citizens and citizen groups can also follow rulemaking and testify at hearings held around the country on proposed rules. The rulemaking process and the efforts by federal agencies to keep open records and solicit public input on important changes are examples of responsive bureaucracy.

GOVERNMENT PRIVATIZATION

A more extreme, and in many instances, more controversial solution to the perceived and real inefficiencies in the bureaucracy is **privatization**. In the United States, largely because it was born during the Enlightenment and has a long history of championing free-market principles, the urge to privatize government services has never been as strong as it is in many other countries. There are simply far fewer government-run services. Nevertheless, the federal government has used forms of privatization and contracting throughout its history. But following the growth of bureaucracy and government services during President Johnson's Great Society in the mid-1960s, a particularly vocal movement began calling for a rollback of government services.

This movement grew stronger in the 1970s and 1980s as politicians, particularly on the right, declared that air needed to be let out of the bloated federal government. In the 1990s, as President Bill Clinton and especially his vice president, Al Gore, worked to aggressively shrink the federal bureaucracy, privatization came to be embraced across the political spectrum.[35] The rhetoric of privatization—that market competition would stimulate innovation and efficiency—sounded like the proper remedy to many people and still does. But to many others, talk of privatization is worrying. They contend that certain government functions are simply not possible to replicate in a private context.

When those in government speak of privatization, they are often referring to one of a host of different models that incorporate the market forces of the private sector into the function of government to varying degrees.[36] These include using contractors to supply goods and/or services, distributing government vouchers with which citizens can purchase formerly government-controlled services on the private market, supplying government grants to private organizations to administer government programs, collaborating with a private entity to finance a government program, and even fully divesting the government of a function and directly giving it to the private sector (Figure 15.15). We will look at three of these types of privatization shortly.

Figure 15.15 Following his reelection in 2004, President George W. Bush attempted to push a proposal to partially privatize Social Security. The proposal did not make it to either the House or Senate floor for a vote.

Divestiture, or full privatization, occurs when government services are transferred, usually through sale, from government bureaucratic control into an entirely market-based, private environment. At the federal level this form of privatization is very rare, although it does occur. Consider the Student Loan Marketing Association, often referred to by its nickname, Sallie Mae. When it was created in 1973, it was designed to be a government entity for processing federal student education loans. Over time, however, it gradually moved further from its original purpose and became increasingly private. Sallie Mae reached full privatization in 2004.[37] Another example is the U.S. Investigations Services, Inc., which was once the investigative branch of the Office of Personnel Management (OPM) until it was privatized in the 1990s. At the state level, however, the privatization of roads, public utilities, bridges, schools, and even prisons has become increasingly common as state and municipal authorities look for ways to reduce the cost of government.

Possibly the best-known form of privatization is the process of issuing government contracts to private companies in order for them to provide necessary services. This process grew to prominence during President Bill Clinton's National Partnership for Reinventing Government initiative, intended to streamline the government bureaucracy. Under President George W. Bush, the use of contracting out federal services reached new heights. During the Iraq War, for example, large corporations like Kellogg Brown & Root, owned by Haliburton at the time, signed government contracts to perform a number of services once done by the military, such as military base construction, food preparation, and even laundry services. By 2006, reliance on contracting to run the war was so great that contractors outnumbered soldiers. Such contracting has faced quite a bit of criticism for both its high cost and its potential for corruption and inefficiencies.[38] However, it has become so routine that it is unlikely to slow any time soon.

Third-party financing is a far more complex form of privatization than divestiture or contracting. Here the federal government signs an agreement with a private entity so the two can form a *special-purpose vehicle* to take ownership of the object being financed. The special-purpose vehicle is empowered to reach out to private financial markets to borrow money. This type of privatization is typically used to finance government office space, military base housing, and other large infrastructure projects. Departments like the Congressional Budget Office have frequently criticized this form of privatization as particularly inefficient and costly for the government.

One the most the most important forms of bureaucratic oversight comes from inside the bureaucracy itself. Those within are in the best position to recognize and report on misconduct. But bureaucracies tend to jealously guard their reputations and are generally resistant to criticism from without and from within. This can create quite a problem for insiders who recognize and want to report mismanagement and even criminal behavior. The personal cost of doing the right thing can be prohibitive.[39] For a typical bureaucrat faced with the option of reporting corruption and risking possible termination or turning the other way and continuing to earn a living, the choice is sometimes easy.

Under heightened skepticism due to government inefficiency and outright corruption in the 1970s, government officials began looking for solutions. When Congress drafted the Civil Service Reform Act of 1978, it specifically included rights for federal **whistleblowers,** those who publicize misdeeds committed within a bureaucracy or other organization, and set up protection from reprisals. The act's Merit Systems Protection Board is a quasi-juridical institutional board headed by three members appointed by the president and confirmed by the Senate that hears complaints, conducts investigations into possible abuses, and institutes protections for bureaucrats who speak out.[40] Over time, Congress and the president have strengthened these protections with additional acts. These include the Whistleblower Protection Act of 1989 and the Whistleblower Protection Enhancement Act of 2012, which further compelled federal agencies to protect whistleblowers who reasonably perceive that an institution or the people in the institution are acting inappropriately (Figure 15.16).

Figure 15.16 In 2013, Edward Snowden, an unknown computer professional working under contract within the National Security Agency, copied and released to the press classified information that revealed an expansive and largely illegal secret surveillance network the government was operating within the United States. Fearing reprisals, Snowden fled to Hong Kong and then Moscow. Some argue that his actions were irresponsible and he should be prosecuted. Others champion his actions and hold that without them, the illegal spying would have continued. Regardless, the Snowden case reveals important weaknesses in whistleblower protections in the United States. (credit: modification of work by Bruno Sanchez-Andrade Nuño)

Key Terms

bureaucracy an administrative group of nonelected officials charged with carrying out functions connected to a series of policies and programs

bureaucrats the civil servants or political appointees who fill nonelected positions in government and make up the bureaucracy

civil servants the individuals who fill nonelected positions in government and make up the bureaucracy; also known as bureaucrats

government corporation a corporation that fulfills an important public interest and is therefore overseen by government authorities to a much larger degree than private businesses

merit system a system of filling civil service positions by using competitive examinations to value experience and competence over political loyalties

negotiated rulemaking a rulemaking process in which neutral advisors convene a committee of those who have vested interests in the proposed rules and help the committee reach a consensus on them

patronage the use of government positions to reward individuals for their political support

pay schedule a chart that shows salary ranges for different levels of positions vertically and for different ranks of seniority horizontally

privatization measures that incorporate the market forces of the private sector into the function of government to varying degrees

public administration the implementation of public policy as well as the academic study that prepares civil servants to work in government

red tape the mechanisms, procedures, and rules that must be followed to get something done

spoils system a system that rewards political loyalties or party support during elections with bureaucratic appointments after victory

whistleblower a person who publicizes misdeeds committed within a bureaucracy or other organization

Summary

15.1 Bureaucracy and the Evolution of Public Administration
During the post-Jacksonian era of the nineteenth century, the common charge against the bureaucracy was that it was overly political and corrupt. This changed in the 1880s as the United States began to create a modern civil service. The civil service grew once again in Franklin D. Roosevelt's administration as he expanded government programs to combat the effects of the Great Depression. The most recent criticisms of the federal bureaucracy, notably under Ronald Reagan, emerged following the second great expansion of the federal government under Lyndon B Johnson in the 1960s.

15.2 Toward a Merit-Based Civil Service
The merit-based system of filling jobs in the government bureaucracy elevates ability and accountability over political loyalties. Unfortunately, this system also has its downsides. The most common complaint is that the bureaucrats are no longer as responsive to elected public officials as they once had been. This, however, may be a necessary tradeoff for the level of efficiency and specialization necessary in the modern world.

15.3 Understanding Bureaucracies and their Types

To understand why some bureaucracies act the way they do, sociologists have developed a handful of models. With the exception of the ideal bureaucracy described by Max Weber, these models see bureaucracies as self-serving. Harnessing self-serving instincts to make the bureaucracy work the way it was intended is a constant task for elected officials. One of the ways elected officials have tried to grapple with this problem is by designing different types of bureaucracies with different functions. These types include cabinet departments, independent regulatory agencies, independent executive agencies, and government corporations.

15.4 Controlling the Bureaucracy

To reduce the intra-institutional disagreements the traditional rulemaking process seemed to bring, the negotiated rulemaking process was designed to encourage consensus. Both Congress and the president exercise direct oversight over the bureaucracy by holding hearings, making appointments, and setting budget allowances. Citizens exercise their oversight powers through their use of the Freedom of Information Act (FOIA) and by voting. Finally, bureaucrats also exercise oversight over their own institutions by using the channels carved out for whistleblowers to call attention to bureaucratic abuses.

Review Questions

1. During George Washington's administration, there were _____ cabinet positions.
   a. four
   b. five
   c. six
   d. seven

2. The "spoils system" allocated political appointments on the basis of _____.
   a. merit
   b. background
   c. party loyalty
   d. specialized education

3. Two recent periods of large-scale bureaucratic expansion were _____.
   a. the 1930s and the 1960s
   b. the 1920s and the 1980s
   c. the 1910s and the 1990s
   d. the 1930s and the 1950s

4. Briefly explain the underlying reason for the emergence of the spoils system.

5. The Civil Service Commission was created by the _____.
   a. Pendleton Act of 1883
   b. Lloyd–La Follette Act of 1912
   c. Hatch Act of 1939
   d. Political Activities Act of 1939

6. The Civil Service Reform Act of 1978 created the Office of Personnel Management and the

_____.
   a. Civil Service Commission
   b. Merit Systems Protection Board
   c. "spoils system"
   d. General Schedule

7. Briefly explain the benefits and drawbacks of a merit system.

8. Which describes the ideal bureaucracy according to Max Weber?
   a. an apolitical, hierarchically organized agency
   b. an organization that competes with other bureaucracies for funding
   c. a wasteful, poorly organized agency
   d. an agency that shows clear electoral responsiveness

9. Which of the following models of bureaucracy best accounts for the way bureaucracies tend to push Congress for more funding each year?
   a. the Weberian model
   b. the acquisitive model
   c. the monopolistic model
   d. the ideal model

10. An example of a government corporation is
_____.

   a. NASA
   b. the State Department
   c. Amtrak
   d. the CIA

11. Briefly explain why government might create a government corporation.

12. The Freedom of Information Act of 1966 helps citizens exercise oversight over the bureaucracy by
_____.

   a. empowering Congress
   b. opening government records to citizen scrutiny
   c. requiring annual evaluations by the president
   d. forcing agencies to hold public meetings

13. When reformers speak of bureaucratic privatization, they mean all the following processes except _____.

   a. divestiture
   b. government grants
   c. whistleblowing
   d. third-party financing

14. Briefly explain the advantages of negotiated rulemaking.

Critical Thinking Questions

15. What concerns might arise when Congress delegates decision-making authority to unelected leaders, sometimes called the fourth branch of government?

16. In what ways might the patronage system be made more efficient?

17. Does the use of bureaucratic oversight staff by Congress and by the OMB constitute unnecessary duplication? Why or why not?

18. Which model of bureaucracy best explains the way the government currently operates? Why?

19. Do you think Congress and the president have done enough to protect bureaucratic whistleblowers? Why or why not?

Suggestions for Further Study

Frederickson, H. G., K. B. Smith, C. W. Larimer, and M. J. Licari. 2003. *Public Administration Theory Primer*, 2nd ed. Boulder, CO: Westview Press.

Fry, B. R. 1989. *Mastering Public Administration: From Max Weber to Dwight Waldo*. London: Chatham House.

McKinney, J. B. and L. C. Howard. 1998. *Public Administration: Balancing Power and Accountability*, 2nd ed. Westport, CT: Praeger.

Riccucci, N. M. 2010. *Public Administration: Traditions of Inquiry and Philosophies of Knowledge*. Washington, DC: Georgetown University Press.

Shafritz, J. M., A.C. Hyde, and S. J. Parkes. 2003. *Classics of Public Administration*. Boston: Wadsworth.

Wilson, J. Q. 1991. *Bureaucracy: What Government Agencies Do and Why They Do It*. New York: Basic Books.

Chapter 16

Domestic Policy

Figure 16.1 Minnesota Tea Party members protest in 2011, demanding repeal of the recently enacted Patient Protection and Affordable Care Act. Protests against expanding the federal government's role in the economy often use "socialism" as a negative label, even when defending existing examples of government-run programs such as Medicare. (credit: modification of work by "Fibonacci Blue"/Flickr)

Chapter Outline

16.1 What Is Public Policy?
16.2 Categorizing Public Policy
16.3 Policy Arenas
16.4 Policymakers
16.5 Budgeting and Tax Policy

Introduction

On March 25, 2010, both chambers of Congress passed the Health Care and Education Reconciliation Act (HCERA).[1] The story of the HCERA, which expanded and improved some provisions of the Patient Protection and Affordable Care Act (ACA), also known as Obamacare, is a complicated tale of insider politics in which the Democratic Party was able to enact sweeping health care and higher education reforms over fierce Republican opposition (Figure 16.1). Some people laud the HCERA as an example of getting things done in the face of partisan gridlock in Congress; others see it a case of government power run amok. Regardless of your view, the HCERA vividly demonstrates public policymaking in action.

Each of the individual actors and institutions in the U.S. political system, such as the president, Congress, the courts, interest groups, and the media, gives us an idea of the component parts of the system and their functions. But in the study of public policy, we look at the larger picture and see all the parts working together to make laws, like the HCERA, that ultimately affect citizens and their communities.

What is public policy? How do different areas of policy differ, and what roles do policy analysts and advocates play? What programs does the national government currently provide? And how do budgetary policy and politics operate? This chapter answers these questions and more.

16.1 What Is Public Policy?

By the end of this section, you will be able to:
- Explain the concept of public policy
- Discuss examples of public policy in action

It is easy to imagine that when designers engineer a product, like a car, they do so with the intent of satisfying the consumer. But the design of any complicated product must take into account the needs of regulators, transporters, assembly line workers, parts suppliers, and myriad other participants in the manufacture and shipment process. And manufacturers must also be aware that consumer tastes are fickle: A gas-guzzling sports car may appeal to an unmarried twenty-something with no children; but what happens to product satisfaction when gas prices fluctuate, or the individual gets married and has children?

In many ways, the process of designing domestic policy isn't that much different. The government, just like auto companies, needs to ensure that its citizen-consumers have access to an array of goods and services. And just as in auto companies, a wide range of actors is engaged in figuring out how to do it. Sometimes, this process effectively provides policies that benefit citizens. But just as often, the process of policymaking is muddied by the demands of competing interests with different opinions about society's needs or the role that government should play in meeting them. To understand why, we begin by thinking about what we mean by the term "public policy."

PUBLIC POLICY DEFINED

One approach to thinking about **public policy** is to see it as the broad strategy government uses to do its job. More formally, it is the relatively stable set of purposive governmental actions that address matters of concern to some part of society.[2] This description is useful in that it helps to explain both what public policy is and what it isn't. First, public policy is a guide to legislative action that is more or less fixed for long periods of time, not just short-term fixes or single legislative acts. Policy also doesn't happen by accident, and it is rarely formed simply as the result of the campaign promises of a single elected official, even the president. While elected officials are often important in shaping policy, most policy outcomes are the result of considerable debate, compromise, and refinement that happen over years and are finalized only after input from multiple institutions within government as well as from interest groups and the public.

Consider the example of health care expansion. A follower of politics in the news media may come away thinking the reforms implemented in 2010 were as sudden as they were sweeping, having been developed in the final weeks before they were enacted. The reality is that expanding health care access had actually been a priority of the Democratic Party for several decades. What may have seemed like a policy developed over a period of months was in fact formed after years of analysis, reflection upon existing policy, and even trial implementation of similar types of programs at the state level. Even before passage of the ACA (2010), which expanded health care coverage to millions, and of the HCERA (2010), more than 50 percent of all health care expenditures in the United States already came from federal government programs such as Medicare and Medicaid. Several House and Senate members from both parties along with First Lady Hillary Clinton had proposed significant expansions in federal health care policy during the Democratic administration of Bill Clinton, providing a number of different options for any eventual health care overhaul.[3] Much of what became the ACA was drawn from proposals originally developed at the state level, by none other than Obama's 2012 Republican presidential opponent Mitt Romney when he was governor of Massachusetts.[4]

In addition to being thoughtful and generally stable, public policy deals with issues of concern to some large segment of society, as opposed to matters of interest only to individuals or a small group of people.

Governments frequently interact with individual actors like citizens, corporations, or other countries. They may even pass highly specialized pieces of legislation, known as private bills, which confer specific privileges on individual entities. But public policy covers only those issues that are of interest to larger segments of society or that directly or indirectly affect society as a whole. Paying off the loans of a specific individual would not be public policy, but creating a process for loan forgiveness available to certain types of borrowers (such as those who provide a public service by becoming teachers) would certainly rise to the level of public policy.

A final important characteristic of public policy is that it is more than just the actions of government; it also includes the behaviors or outcomes that government action creates. Policy can even be made when government refuses to act in ways that would change the status quo when circumstances or public opinion begin to shift.[5] For example, much of the debate over gun safety policy in the United States has centered on the unwillingness of Congress to act, even in the face of public opinion that supports some changes to gun policy. In fact, one of the last major changes occurred in 2004, when lawmakers' inaction resulted in the expiration of a piece of legislation known as the Federal Assault Weapons Ban (1994).[6]

PUBLIC POLICY AS OUTCOMES

Governments rarely want to keep their policies a secret. Elected officials want to be able to take credit for the things they have done to help their constituents, and their opponents are all too willing to cast blame when policy initiatives fail. We can therefore think of policy as the formal expression of what elected or appointed officials are trying to accomplish. In passing the HCERA (2010), Congress declared its policy through an act that directed how it would appropriate money. The president can also implement or change policy through an executive order, which offers instructions about how to implement law under his or her discretion (Figure 16.2). Finally, policy changes can come as a result of court actions or opinions, such as *Brown v. Board of Education of Topeka* (1954), which formally ended school segregation in the United States.[7]

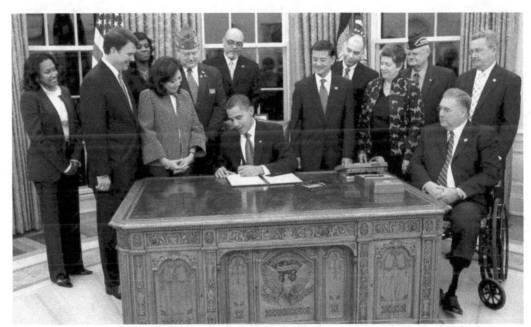

Figure 16.2 President Obama signs a 2009 executive order to accelerate the federal government's recruitment and hiring of returning veterans. Executive orders are an expression of public policy undertaken at the discretion of the president.

Typically, elected and even high-ranking appointed officials lack either the specific expertise or tools needed to successfully create and implement public policy on their own. They turn instead to the vast government bureaucracy to provide policy guidance. For example, when Congress passed the Clean Water Act (1972), it dictated that steps should be taken to improve water quality throughout the country. But it ultimately left it to the bureaucracy to figure out exactly how 'clean' water needed to be. In doing so, Congress provided the Environmental Protection Agency (EPA) with discretion to determine how much pollution is allowed in U.S. waterways.

There is one more way of thinking about policy outcomes: in terms of winners and losers. Almost by definition, public policy promotes certain types of behavior while punishing others. So, the individuals or corporations that a policy favors are most likely to benefit, or win, whereas those the policy ignores or punishes are likely to lose. Even the best-intended policies can have unintended consequences and may even ultimately harm someone, if only those who must pay for the policy through higher taxes. A policy designed to encourage students to go to liberal arts colleges may cause trade school enrollment to decline. Strategies to promote diversity in higher education may make it more difficult for qualified white or male applicants to get accepted into competitive programs. Efforts to clean up drinking water supplies may make companies less competitive and cost employees their livelihood. Even something that seems to help everyone, such as promoting charitable giving through tax incentives, runs the risk of lowering tax revenues from the rich (who contribute a greater share of their income to charity) and shifting tax burdens to the poor (who must spend a higher share of their income to achieve a desired standard of living). And while policy pronouncements and bureaucratic actions are certainly meant to rationalize policy, it is whether a given policy helps or hurts constituents (or is perceived to do so) that ultimately determines how voters will react toward the government in future elections.

Finding a Middle Ground

The Social Safety Net

During the Great Depression of the 1930s, the United States created a set of policies and programs that constituted a social safety net for the millions who had lost their jobs, their homes, and their savings (Figure 16.3). Under President Franklin Delano Roosevelt, the federal government began programs like the Work Progress Administration and Civilian Conservation Corps to combat unemployment and the Home Owners' Loan Corporation to refinance Depression-related mortgage debts. As the effects of the Depression eased, the government phased out many of these programs. Other programs, like Social Security or the minimum wage, remain an important part of the way the government takes care of the vulnerable members of its population. The federal government has also added further social support programs, like Medicaid, Medicare, and the Special Supplemental Nutrition Program for Women, Infants, and Children, to ensure a baseline or minimal standard of living for all, even in the direst of times.

Figure 16.3 In 1937, during the Great Depression, families in Calipatria, California, waited in line for relief checks, part of the federal government's newly introduced social safety net. (credit: modification of work by the Library of Congress)

In recent decades, however, some have criticized these safety net programs for inefficiency and for incentivizing welfare dependence. They deride "government leeches" who use food stamps to buy lobster or other seemingly inappropriate items. Critics deeply resent the use of taxpayer money to relieve social problems like unemployment and poverty; workers who may themselves be struggling to put food on the table or pay the mortgage feel their hard-earned money should not support other families. "If I can get by without government support," the reasoning goes, "those welfare families can do the same. Their poverty is not my problem."

So where should the government draw the line? While there have been some instances of welfare fraud, the welfare reforms of the 1990s have made long-term dependence on the federal government less likely as the welfare safety net was pushed to the states. And with the income gap between the richest and the poorest at its highest level in history, this topic is likely to continue to receive much discussion in the coming years.

Where is the middle ground in the public policy argument over the social safety net? How can the government protect its most vulnerable citizens without placing an undue burden on others?

Link to Learning

Explore **historical data on United States budgets and spending (https://openstax.org/l/29WH1940)** from 1940 to the present from the Office of Management and Budget.

16.2 Categorizing Public Policy

Learning Objectives

By the end of this section, you will be able to:

- Describe the different types of goods in a society
- Identify key public policy domains in the United States
- Compare the different forms of policy and the way they transfer goods within a society

The idea of public policy is by its very nature a politically contentious one. Among the differences between American liberals and conservatives are the policy preferences prevalent in each group. Modern liberals tend to feel very comfortable with the idea of the government shepherding progressive social and economic reforms, believing that these will lead to outcomes more equitable and fair for all members of society. Conservatives, on the other hand, often find government involvement onerous and overreaching. They feel society would function more efficiently if oversight of most "public" matters were returned to the private sphere. Before digging too deeply into a discussion of the nature of public policy in the United States, let us look first at why so many aspects of society come under the umbrella of public policy to begin with.

DIFFERENT TYPES OF GOODS

Think for a minute about what it takes to make people happy and satisfied. As we live our daily lives, we experience a range of physical, psychological, and social needs that must be met in order for us to be happy and productive. At the very least, we require food, water, and shelter. In very basic subsistence societies, people acquire these through farming crops, digging wells, and creating shelter from local materials (see Figure 16.4). People also need social interaction with others and the ability to secure goods they acquire, lest someone else try to take them. As their tastes become more complex, they may find it advantageous to exchange their items for others; this requires not only a mechanism for barter but also a system of transportation. The more complex these systems are, the greater the range of items people can access to keep them alive and make them happy. However, this increase in possessions also creates a stronger need to secure what they have acquired.

Figure 16.4 This Library of Congress photo shows an early nineteenth-century subsistence farm in West Virginia, which once included crops, livestock, and an orchard. (credit: modification of work by the Library of Congress)

Economists use the term *goods* to describe the range of commodities, services, and systems that help us satisfy our wants or needs. This term can certainly apply to the food you eat or the home you live in, but it can also describe the systems of transportation or public safety used to protect them. Most of the goods you interact with in your daily life are *private goods*, which means that they can be owned by a particular person or group of people, and are excluded from use by others, typically by means of a price. For example, your home or apartment is a private good reserved for your own use because you pay rent or make mortgage payments for the privilege of living there. Further, private goods are finite and can run out if overused, even if only in the short term. The fact that private goods are excludable and finite makes them tradable. A farmer who grows corn, for instance, owns that corn, and since only a finite amount of corn exists, others may want to trade their goods for it if their own food supplies begin to dwindle.

Proponents of **free-market economics** believe that the market forces of supply and demand, working without any government involvement, are the most effective way for markets to operate. One of the basic principles of free-market economics is that for just about any good that can be privatized, the most efficient means for exchange is the marketplace. A well-functioning market will allow producers of goods to come together with consumers of goods to negotiate a trade. People facilitate trade by creating a currency—a common unit of exchange—so they do not need to carry around everything they may want to trade at all times. As long as there are several providers or sellers of the same good, consumers can negotiate with them to find a price they are willing to pay. As long as there are several buyers for a seller's goods, providers can negotiate with them to find a price buyers are willing to accept. And, the logic goes, if prices begin to rise too much, other sellers will enter the marketplace, offering lower prices.

A second basic principle of free-market economics is that it is largely unnecessary for the government to protect the value of private goods. Farmers who own land used for growing food have a vested interest in protecting their land to ensure its continued production. Business owners must protect the reputation of their business or no one will buy from them. And, to the degree that producers need to ensure the quality of their product or industry, they can accomplish that by creating a group or association that operates outside government control. In short, industries have an interest in self-regulating to protect their own value. According to free-market economics, as long as everything we could ever want or need is a private good, and so long as every member of society has some ability to provide for themselves and their families, public policy regulating the exchange of goods and services is really unnecessary.

Some people in the United States argue that the self-monitoring and self-regulating incentives provided by the existence of private goods mean that sound public policy requires very little government action.

Known as **libertarians**, these individuals believe government almost always operates less efficiently than the private sector (the segment of the economy run for profit and not under government control), and that government actions should therefore be kept to a minimum.

Even as many in the United States recognize the benefits provided by private goods, we have increasingly come to recognize problems with the idea that all social problems can be solved by exclusively private ownership. First, not all goods can be classified as strictly private. Can you really consider the air you breathe to be private? Air is a difficult good to privatize because it is not excludable—everyone can get access to it at all times—and no matter how much of it you breathe, there is still plenty to go around. Geographic regions like forests have environmental, social, recreational, and aesthetic value that cannot easily be reserved for private ownership. Resources like migrating birds or schools of fish may have value if hunted or fished, but they cannot be owned due to their migratory nature. Finally, national security provided by the armed forces protects all citizens and cannot reasonably be reserved for only a few.

These are all examples of what economists call *public goods*, sometimes referred to as collective goods. Unlike private property, they are not excludable and are essentially infinite. Forests, water, and fisheries, however, are a type of public good called *common goods*, which are not excludable but may be finite. The problem with both public and common goods is that since no one owns them, no one has a financial interest in protecting their long-term or future value. Without government regulation, a factory owner can feel free to pollute the air or water, since he or she will have no responsibility for the pollution once the winds or waves carry it somewhere else (see Figure 16.5). Without government regulation, someone can hunt all the migratory birds or deplete a fishery by taking all the fish, eliminating future breeding stocks that would maintain the population. The situation in which individuals exhaust a common resource by acting in their own immediate self-interest is called the *tragedy of the commons*.

Figure 16.5   Air pollution billows from a power plant before the installation of emission control equipment for the removal of sulfur dioxide and particulate matter. Can you see why uncontrolled pollution is an example of the "tragedy of the commons"?

A second problem with strict adherence to free-market economics is that some goods are too large, or too expensive, for individuals to provide them for themselves. Consider the need for a marketplace: Where does the marketplace come from? How do we get the goods to market? Who provides the roads and bridges? Who patrols the waterways? Who provides security? Who ensures the regulation of the currency? No individual buyer or seller could accomplish this. The very nature of the exchange of private goods requires a system that has some of the openness of public or common goods, but is maintained by either groups of individuals or entire societies.

Economists consider goods like cable TV, cellphone service, and private schools to be toll goods. *Toll goods* are similar to public goods in that they are open to all and theoretically infinite if maintained, but they are paid for or provided by some outside (nongovernment) entity. Many people can make use of them, but only if they can pay the price. The name "toll goods" comes from the fact that, early on, many toll roads were in fact privately owned commodities. Even today, states from Virginia to California have allowed private companies to build public roads in exchange for the right to profit by charging tolls.[8]

So long as land was plentiful, and most people in the United States lived a largely rural subsistence lifestyle, the difference between private, public, common, and toll goods was mostly academic. But as public lands increasingly became private through sale and settlement, and as industrialization and the rise of mass production allowed monopolies and oligopolies to become more influential, support for public policies regulating private entities grew. By the beginning of the twentieth century, led by the Progressives, the United States had begun to search for ways to govern large businesses that had managed to distort market forces by monopolizing the supply of goods. And, largely as a result of the Great Depression, people wanted ways of developing and protecting public goods that were fairer and more equitable than had existed before. These forces and events led to the increased regulation of public and common goods, and a move for the public sector—the government—to take over of the provision of many toll goods.

CLASSIC TYPES OF POLICY

Public policy, then, ultimately boils down to determining the distribution, allocation, and enjoyment of public, common, and toll goods within a society. While the specifics of policy often depend on the circumstances, two broad questions all policymakers must consider are a) who pays the costs of creating and maintaining the goods, and b) who receives the benefits of the goods? When private goods are bought and sold in a market place, the costs and benefits go to the participants in the transaction. Your landlord benefits from receipt of the rent you pay, and you benefit by having a place to live. But non-private goods like roads, waterways, and national parks are controlled and regulated by someone other than the owners, allowing policymakers to make decisions about who pays and who benefits.

In 1964, Theodore Lowi argued that it was possible to categorize policy based upon the degree to which costs and benefits were concentrated on the few or diffused across the many. One policy category, known as **distributive policy**, tends to collect payments or resources from many but concentrates direct benefits on relatively few. Highways are often developed through distributive policy. Distributive policy is also common when society feels there is a social benefit to individuals obtaining private goods such as higher education that offer long-term benefits, but the upfront cost may be too high for the average citizen.

One example of the way distributive policy works is the story of the Transcontinental Railroad. In the 1860s, the U.S. government began to recognize the value of building a robust railroad system to move passengers and freight around the country. A particular goal was connecting California and the other western territories acquired during the 1840s war with Mexico to the rest of the country. The problem was that constructing a nationwide railroad system was a costly and risky proposition. To build and support continuous rail lines, private investors would need to gain access to tens of thousands of miles of land, some of which might be owned by private citizens. The solution was to charter two private corporations—the Central Pacific and Union Pacific Railroads—and provide them with resources and land grants to facilitate the construction of the railroads (see Figure 16.6).[9] Through these grants, publicly owned land was distributed to private citizens, who could then use it for their own gain. However, a broader public gain was simultaneously being provided in the form of a nationwide transportation network.

Figure 16.6 In an example of distributive policy, the Union Pacific Railroad was given land and resources to help build a national railroad system. Here, its workers construct the Devil's Gate Bridge in Utah in 1869.

The same process operates in the agricultural sector, where various federal programs help farmers and food producers through price supports and crop insurance, among other forms of assistance. These programs help individual farmers and agriculture companies stay afloat and realize consistent profits. They also achieve the broader goal of providing plenty of sustenance for the people of the United States, so that few of us have to "live off the land."

Milestone

The Hoover Dam: The Federal Effort to Domesticate the Colorado River

As westward expansion led to development of the American Southwest, settlers increasingly realized that they needed a way to control the frequent floods and droughts that made agriculture difficult in the region. As early as 1890, land speculators had tried diverting the Colorado River for this purpose, but it wasn't until 1922 that the U.S. Bureau of Reclamation (then called the Reclamation Service) chose the Black Canyon as a good location for a dam to divert the river. Since it would affect seven states (as well as Mexico), the federal government took the lead on the project, which eventually cost $49 million and more than one hundred lives. The dam faced significant opposition from members of other states, who felt its massive price tag (almost $670 million in today's dollars[10]) benefitted only a small group, not the whole nation. However, in 1928, Senator Hiram Johnson and Representative Phil Swing, both Republicans from California, won the day. Congress passed the Boulder Canyon Project Act, authorizing the construction of one of the most ambitious engineering feats in U.S. history. The Hoover Dam (Figure 16.7), completed in 1935, served the dual purposed of generating hydroelectric power and irrigating two million acres of land from the resulting reservoir (Lake Mead).

Figure 16.7 Workers construct the Hoover Dam, a distributive policy project, in Nevada in 1932.

Was the construction of the Hoover Dam an effective expression of public policy? Why or why not?

Link to Learning

Visit this **site (https://openstax.org/l/29HoovDam)** to see how the U.S. Bureau of Reclamation (USBR) presented the construction of the Hoover Dam. How would you describe the bureau's perspective?

American Rivers is an advocacy group whose goal is to protect and restore rivers, including the Colorado River. How does this group's view of the **Hoover Dam (https://openstax.org/l/29Amerivs)** differ from that of the USBR?

Other examples of distributive policy support citizens' efforts to achieve "the American Dream." American society recognizes the benefits of having citizens who are financially invested in the country's future.

Among the best ways to encourage this investment are to ensure that citizens are highly educated and have the ability to acquire high-cost private goods such as homes and businesses. However, very few people have the savings necessary to pay upfront for a college education, a first home purchase, or the start-up costs of a business. To help out, the government has created a range of incentives that everyone in the country pays for through taxes but that directly benefit only the recipients. Examples include grants (such as Pell grants), tax credits and deductions, and subsidized or federally guaranteed loans. Each of these programs aims to achieve a policy outcome. Pell grants exist to help students graduate from college, whereas Federal Housing Administration mortgage loans lead to home ownership.

While distributive policy, according to Lowi, has diffuse costs and concentrated benefits, **regulatory policy** features the opposite arrangement, with concentrated costs and diffuse benefits. A relatively small number of groups or individuals bear the costs of regulatory policy, but its benefits are expected to be distributed broadly across society. As you might imagine, regulatory policy is most effective for controlling or protecting public or common resources. Among the best-known examples are policies designed to protect public health and safety, and the environment. These regulatory policies prevent manufacturers or businesses from maximizing their profits by excessively polluting the air or water, selling products they know to be harmful, or compromising the health of their employees during production.

In the United States, nationwide calls for a more robust regulatory policy first grew loud around the turn of the twentieth century and the dawn of the Industrial Age. Investigative journalists—called *muckrakers* by politicians and business leaders who were the focus of their investigations—began to expose many of the ways in which manufacturers were abusing the public trust. Although various forms of corruption topped the list of abuses, among the most famous muckraker exposés was *The Jungle*, a 1906 novel by Upton Sinclair that focused on unsanitary working conditions and unsavory business practices in the meat-packing industry.[11] This work and others like it helped to spur the passage of the Pure Food and Drug Act (1906) and ultimately led to the creation of government agencies such as the U.S. Food and Drug Administration (FDA).[12] The nation's experiences during the depression of 1896 and the Great Depression of the 1930s also led to more robust regulatory policies designed to improve the transparency of financial markets and prevent monopolies from forming.

A final type of policy is **redistributive policy**, so named because it redistributes resources in society from one group to another. That is, according to Lowi, the costs are concentrated and so are the benefits, but different groups bear the costs and enjoy the benefits. Most redistributive policies are intended to have a sort of "Robin Hood" effect; their goal is to transfer income and wealth from one group to another such that everyone enjoys at least a minimal standard of living. Typically, the wealthy and middle class pay into the federal tax base, which then funds need-based programs that support low-income individuals and families. A few examples of redistributive policies are Head Start (education), Medicaid (health care), Temporary Assistance for Needy Families (TANF, income support), and food programs like the Supplementary Nutritional Aid Program (SNAP). The government also uses redistribution to incentivize specific behaviors or aid small groups of people. Pell grants to encourage college attendance and tax credits to encourage home ownership are other examples of redistribution.

16.3 Policy Arenas

Learning Objectives

By the end of this section, you will be able to:
- Identify the key domestic arenas of public policy
- Describe the major social safety net programs
- List the key agencies responsible for promoting and regulating U.S. business and industry

In practice, public policy consists of specific programs that provide resources to members of society, create regulations that protect U.S. citizens, and attempt to equitably fund the government. We can broadly categorize most policies based on their goals or the sector of society they affect, although many, such as food stamps, serve multiple purposes. Implementing these policies costs hundreds of billions of dollars each year, and understanding the goals of this spending and where the money goes is of vital importance to citizens and students of politics alike.

SOCIAL WELFARE POLICY

The U.S. government began developing a social welfare policy during the Great Depression of the 1930s. By the 1960s, social welfare had become a major function of the federal government—one to which most public policy funds are devoted—and had developed to serve several overlapping functions. First, social welfare policy is designed to ensure some level of equity in a democratic political system based on competitive, free-market economics. During the Great Depression, many politicians came to fear that the high unemployment and low-income levels plaguing society could threaten the stability of democracy, as was happening in European countries like Germany and Italy. The assumption in this thinking is that democratic systems work best when poverty is minimized. In societies operating in survival mode, in contrast, people tend to focus more on short-term problem-solving than on long-term planning. Second, social welfare policy creates an automatic stimulus for a society by building a **safety net** that can catch members of society who are suffering economic hardship through no fault of their own. For an individual family, this safety net makes the difference between eating and starving; for an entire economy, it could prevent an economic recession from sliding into a broader and more damaging depression.

One of the oldest and largest pieces of social welfare policy is **Social Security**, which cost the United States about $845 billion in 2014 alone.[13] These costs are offset by a 12.4 percent payroll tax on all wages up to $118,500; employers and workers who are not self-employed split the bill for each worker, whereas the self-employed pay their entire share.[14] Social Security was conceived as a solution to several problems inherent to the Industrial Era economy. First, by the 1920s and 1930s, an increasing number of workers were earning their living through manual or day-wage labor that depended on their ability to engage in physical activity (Figure 16.8). As their bodies weakened with age or if they were injured, their ability to provide for themselves and their families was compromised. Second, and of particular concern, were urban widows. During their working years, most American women stayed home to raise children and maintain the household while their husbands provided income. Should their husbands die or become injured, these women had no wage-earning skills with which to support themselves or their families.

Figure 16.8 In 1930, when this Ford automotive plant opened in Long Beach, California, American workers had few economic protections to rely on if they were injured or could not maintain such physical activity as they aged.

Social Security addresses these concerns with three important tools. First and best known is the retirement benefit. After completing a minimum number of years of work, American workers may claim a form of pension upon reaching retirement age. It is often called an **entitlement** program since it guarantees benefits to a particular group, and virtually everyone will eventually qualify for the plan given the relatively low requirements for enrollment. The amount of money a worker receives is based loosely on his or her lifetime earnings. Full retirement age was originally set at sixty-five, although changes in legislation have increased it to sixty-seven for workers born after 1959.[15] A valuable added benefit is that, under certain circumstances, this income may also be claimed by the survivors of qualifying workers, such as spouses and minor children, even if they themselves did not have a wage income.

A second Social Security benefit is a disability payout, which the government distributes to workers who become unable to work due to physical or mental disability. To qualify, workers must demonstrate that the injury or incapacitation will last at least twelve months. A third and final benefit is Supplemental Security Income, which provides supplemental income to adults or children with considerable disability or to the elderly who fall below an income threshold.

During the George W. Bush administration, Social Security became a highly politicized topic as the Republican Party sought to find a way of preventing what experts predicted would be the impending collapse of the Social Security system (Figure 16.9). In 1950, the ratio of workers paying into the program to beneficiaries receiving payments was 16.5 to 1. By 2013, that number was 2.8 to 1 and falling. Most predictions in fact suggest that, due to continuing demographic changes including slower population growth and an aging population, by 2033, the amount of revenue generated from payroll taxes will no longer be sufficient to cover costs. The Bush administration proposed avoiding this by privatizing the program, in effect, taking it out of the government's hands and making individuals' benefits variable instead of defined. The effort ultimately failed, and Social Security's long-term viability continues to remain uncertain. Numerous other plans for saving the program have been proposed, including raising the retirement age, increasing payroll taxes (especially on the wealthy) by removing the $118,500 income cap, and reducing payouts for wealthier retirees. None of these proposals have been able to gain traction, however.

Figure 16.9   President George W. Bush discusses Social Security in Florida at the outset of his second term in 2005.

While Social Security was designed to provide cash payments to sustain the aged and disabled, Medicare and Medicaid were intended to ensure that vulnerable populations have access to health care. **Medicare**, like Social Security, is an entitlement program funded through payroll taxes. Its purpose is to make sure that senior citizens and retirees have access to low-cost health care they might not otherwise have, because most U.S. citizens get their health insurance through their employers. Medicare provides three major forms of coverage: a guaranteed insurance benefit that helps cover major hospitalization, fee-based supplemental coverage that retirees can use to lower costs for doctor visits and other health expenses, and a prescription drug benefit. Medicare faces many of the same long-term challenges as Social Security, due to the same demographic shifts. Medicare also faces the problem that health care costs are rising significantly faster than inflation. In 2014, Medicare cost the federal government almost $597 billion.[16]

Medicaid is a formula-based, health insurance program, which means beneficiaries must demonstrate they fall within a particular income category. Individuals in the Medicaid program receive a fairly comprehensive set of health benefits, although access to health care may be limited because fewer providers accept payments from the program (it pays them less for services than does Medicare). Medicaid differs dramatically from Medicare in that it is partially funded by states, many of which have reduced access to the program by setting the income threshold so low that few people qualify. The ACA (2010) sought to change that by providing more federal money to the states if they agreed to raise minimum income requirements. Many states have refused, which has helped to keep the overall costs of Medicaid lower, even though it has also left many people without health coverage they might receive if they lived elsewhere. Total costs for Medicaid in 2014 were about $492 billion, about $305 billion of which was paid by the federal government.[17]

Collectively, Social Security, Medicare, and Medicaid make up the lion's share of total federal government spending, almost 50 percent in 2014 and more than 50 percent in 2015. Several other smaller programs also provide income support to families. Most of these are formula-based, or means-tested, requiring citizens to meet certain maximum income requirements in order to qualify. A few examples are TANF, SNAP (also called food stamps), the unemployment insurance program, and various housing assistance programs. Collectively, these programs add up to a little over $480 billion.

SCIENCE, TECHNOLOGY, AND EDUCATION

After World War II ended, the United States quickly realized that it had to address two problems to secure its fiscal and national security future. The first was that more than ten million servicemen and women needed to be reintegrated into the workforce, and many lacked appreciable work skills. The second problem was that the United States' success in its new conflict with the Soviet Union depended on the rapid development of a new, highly technical military-industrial complex. To confront these challenges, the U.S. government passed several important pieces of legislation to provide education assistance to workers and research dollars to industry. As the needs of American workers and industry have changed, many of these programs have evolved from their original purposes, but they still remain important pieces of the public policy debate.

Much of the nation's science and technology policy benefits its military, for instance, in the form of research and development funding for a range of defense projects. The federal government still promotes research for civilian uses, mostly through the National Science Foundation, the National Institutes of Health, the National Aeronautics and Space Administration (NASA), and the National Oceanic and Atmospheric Administration. Recent debate over these agencies has focused on whether government funding is necessary or if private entities would be better suited. For example, although NASA continues to develop a replacement for the now-defunct U.S. space shuttle program (Figure 16.10), much of its workload is currently being performed by private companies working to develop their own space launch, resupply, and tourism programs.

Figure 16.10 NASA launches the space shuttle *Discovery* from the Kennedy Space Center in 2007. Should the private sector fund space exploration programs rather than the government? (credit: NASA)

The problem of trying to direct and fund the education of a modern U.S. workforce is familiar to many students of American government. Historically, education has largely been the job of the states. While they have provided a very robust K–12 public education system, the national government has never moved to create an equivalent system of national higher education academies or universities as many other countries have done. As the need to keep the nation competitive with others became more pressing, however, the U.S. government did step in to direct its education dollars toward creating greater equity and ease of access to the existing public and private systems.

The overwhelming portion of the government's education money is spent on student loans, grants, and work-study programs. Resources are set aside to cover job-retraining programs for individuals who lack private-sector skills or who need to be retrained to meet changes in the economy's demands for the labor force. National policy toward elementary and secondary education programs has typically focused on increasing resources available to school districts for nontraditional programs (such as preschool and special needs), or helping poorer schools stay competitive with wealthier institutions.

BUSINESS STIMULUS AND REGULATION

A final key aspect of domestic policy is the growth and regulation of business. The size and strength of the economy is very important to politicians whose jobs depend on citizens' believing in their own future prosperity. At the same time, people in the United States want to live in a world where they feel safe from unfair or environmentally damaging business practices. These desires have forced the government to perform a delicate balancing act between programs that help grow the economy by providing benefits to the business sector and those that protect consumers, often by curtailing or regulating the business sector.

Two of the largest recipients of government aid to business are agriculture and energy. Both are multi-billion dollar industries concentrated in rural and/or electorally influential states. Because voters are affected by the health of these sectors every time they pay their grocery or utility bill, the U.S. government has chosen to provide significant agriculture and energy subsidies to cover the risks inherent in the unpredictability of the weather and oil exploration. Government subsidies also protect these industries' profitability. These two purposes have even overlapped in the government's controversial decision to subsidize the production of ethanol, a fuel source similar to gasoline but generated from corn.

When it comes to regulation, the federal government has created several agencies responsible for providing for everything from worker safety (OSHA, the Occupational Safety and Health Administration), to food safety (FDA), to consumer protection, where the recently created Bureau of Consumer Protection ensures that businesses do not mislead consumers with deceptive or manipulative practices. Another prominent federal agency, the EPA, is charged with ensuring that businesses do not excessively pollute the nation's air or waterways. A complex array of additional regulatory agencies governs specific industries such as banking and finance, which are detailed later in this chapter.

Link to Learning

The policy areas we've described so far fall far short of forming an exhaustive list. This site (https://openstax.org/l/29PoliAgen) contains the major topic categories of substantive policy in U.S. government, according to the Policy Agendas Project. View subcategories by clicking on the major topic categories.

16.4 Policymakers

Learning Objectives

By the end of this section, you will be able to:

- Identify types of policymakers in different issue areas
- Describe the public policy process

Many Americans were concerned when Congress began debating the ACA. As the program took shape, some people felt the changes it proposed were being debated too hastily, would be implemented too quickly, or would summarily give the government control over an important piece of the U.S. economy—the health care industry. Ironically, the government had been heavily engaged in providing health care for decades. More than 50 percent of all health care dollars spent were being spent by the U.S. government well before the ACA was enacted. As you have already learned, Medicare was created decades earlier. Despite protesters' resistance to government involvement in health care, there is no keeping government out of Medicare; the government IS Medicare.

What many did not realize is that few if any of the proposals that eventually became part of the ACA were original. While the country was worried about problems like terrorism, the economy, and conflicts over gay rights, armies of individuals were debating the best ways to fix the nation's health care delivery. Two important but overlapping groups defended their preferred policy changes: policy advocates and policy analysts.

POLICY ADVOCATES

Take a minute to think of a policy change you believe would improve some condition in the United States. Now ask yourself this: "Why do I want to change this policy?" Are you motivated by a desire for justice? Do you feel the policy change would improve your life or that of members of your community? Is your sense of morality motivating you to change the status quo? Would your profession be helped? Do you feel that changing the policy might raise your status?

Most people have some policy position or issue they would like to see altered (see Figure 16.11). One of the reasons the news media are so enduring is that citizens have a range of opinions on public policy, and they are very interested in debating how a given change would improve their lives or the country's. But despite their interests, most people do little more than vote or occasionally contribute to a political campaign. A few people, however, become **policy advocates** by actively working to propose or maintain public policy.

Figure 16.11 In 2010, members of PETA (People for the Ethical Treatment of Animals) demonstrate against a local zoo. As policy advocates, PETA's members often publicize their position on how animals should be treated.

One way to think about policy advocates is to recognize that they hold a normative position on an issue, that is, they have a conviction about what should or ought to be done. The best public policy, in their view, is one that accomplishes a specific goal or outcome. For this reason, advocates often begin with an objective and then try to shape or create proposals that help them accomplish that goal. Facts, evidence, and analysis are important tools for convincing policymakers or the general public of the benefits of their proposals. Private citizens often find themselves in advocacy positions, particularly if they are required to take on leadership roles in their private lives or in their organizations. The most effective advocates are usually hired professionals who form lobbying groups or think tanks to promote their agenda.

A lobbying group that frequently takes on advocacy roles is AARP (formerly the American Association of Retired Persons) (Figure 16.12). AARP's primary job is to convince the government to provide more public resources and services to senior citizens, often through regulatory or redistributive politics. Chief among its goals are lower health care costs and the safety of Social Security pension payments. These aims put AARP in the Democratic Party's electoral coalition, since Democrats have historically been stronger advocates for Medicare's creation and expansion. In 2002, for instance, Democrats and Republicans were debating a major change to Medicare. The Democratic Party supported expanding Medicare to include free or low-cost prescription drugs, while the Republicans preferred a plan that would require seniors to purchase drug insurance through a private insurer. The government would subsidize costs, but many seniors would still have substantial out-of-pocket expenses. To the surprise of many, AARP supported the Republican proposal.

Figure 16.12 First Lady Michelle Obama shows her AARP membership card on her fiftieth birthday in January 2014. AARP is a major policy advocate for older people and retirees.

While Democrats argued that their position would have provided a better deal for individuals, AARP reasoned that the Republican plan had a much better chance of passing. The Republicans controlled the House and looked likely to reclaim control of the Senate in the upcoming election. Then-president George W. Bush was a Republican and would almost certainly have vetoed the Democratic approach. AARP's support for the legislation helped shore up support for Republicans in the 2002 midterm election and also help convince a number of moderate Democrats to support the bill (with some changes), which passed despite apparent public disapproval. AARP had done its job as an advocate for seniors by creating a new benefit it hoped could later be expanded, rather than fighting for an extreme position that would have left it with nothing.[18]

Not all policy advocates are as willing to compromise their positions. It is much easier for a group like AARP to compromise over the amount of money seniors will receive, for instance, than it is for an evangelical religious group to compromise over issues like abortion, or for civil rights groups to accept something less than equality. Nor are women's rights groups likely to accept pay inequality as it currently exists. It is easier to compromise over financial issues than over our individual views of morality or social justice.

POLICY ANALYSTS

A second approach to creating public policy is a bit more objective. Rather than starting with what ought to happen and seeking ways to make it so, **policy analysts** try to identify all the possible choices available to a decision maker and then gauge their impacts if implemented. The goal of the analyst isn't really to encourage the implementation of any of the options; rather, it is to make sure decision makers are fully informed about the implications of the decisions they do make.

Understanding the financial and other costs and benefits of policy choices requires analysts to make strategic guesses about how the public and governmental actors will respond. For example, when policymakers are considering changes to health care policy, one very important question is how many people will participate. If very few people had chosen to take advantage of the new health care plans available under the ACA marketplace, it would have been significantly cheaper than advocates proposed, but it also would have failed to accomplish the key goal of increasing the number of insured. But if people who currently have insurance had dropped it to take advantage of ACA's subsidies, the program's costs would have skyrocketed with very little real benefit to public health. Similarly, had all states chosen to create their own marketplaces, the cost and complexity of ACA's implementation would have been greatly reduced.

Because advocates have an incentive to understate costs and overstate benefits, policy analysis tends to be a highly politicized aspect of government. It is critical for policymakers and voters that policy analysts provide the most accurate analysis possible. A number of independent or semi-independent think tanks have sprung up in Washington, DC, to provide assessments of policy options. Most businesses or trade organizations also employ their own policy-analysis wings to help them understand proposed changes or even offer some of their own. Some of these try to be as impartial as possible. Most, however, have a known bias toward policy advocacy. The Cato Institute, for example, is well known and highly respected policy analysis group that both liberal and conservative politicians have turned to when considering policy options. But the Cato Institute has a known libertarian bias; most of the problems it selects for analysis have the potential for private sector solutions. This means its analysts tend to include the rosiest assumptions of economic growth when considering tax cuts and to overestimate the costs of public sector proposals.

Link to Learning

The RAND Corporation (https://openstax.org/l/29RANDCorp) has conducted objective policy analysis for corporate, nonprofit, and government clients since the mid-twentieth century. What are some of the policy areas it has explored?

Both the Congress and the president have tried to reduce the bias in policy analysis by creating their own theoretically nonpartisan policy branches. In Congress, the best known of these is the **Congressional Budget Office**, or CBO. Authorized in the 1974 Congressional Budget and Impoundment Control Act, the CBO was formally created in 1975 as a way of increasing Congress's independence from the executive branch. The CBO is responsible for scoring the spending or revenue impact of all proposed legislation to assess its net effect on the budget. In recent years, it has been the CBO's responsibility to provide Congress with guidance on how to best balance the budget (see Figure 16.13). The formulas that the CBO uses in scoring the budget have become an important part of the policy debate, even as the group has tried to maintain its nonpartisan nature.

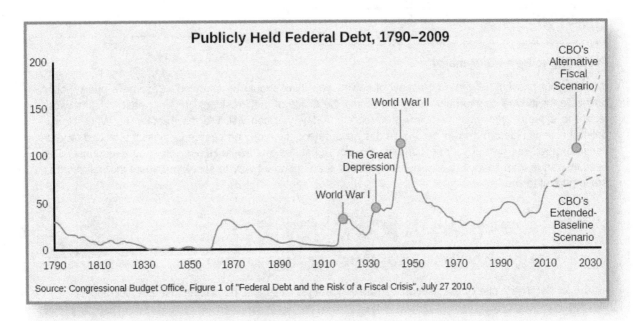

Figure 16.13 The Congressional Budget Office (CBO) is responsible for studying the impact of all proposed legislation to assess its net effect on the budget and tracking federal debt. For example, this 2010 CBO chart shows federal debt held by the public as a percentage of gross domestic product from 1790 through 2010 and projected to 2035.

In the executive branch, each individual department and agency is technically responsible for its own policy analysis. The assumption is that experts in the Federal Communications Commission or the Federal Elections Commission are best equipped to evaluate the impact of various proposals within their policy domain. Law requires that most regulatory changes made by the federal government also include the opportunity for public input so the government can both gauge public opinion and seek outside perspectives.

Executive branch agencies are usually also charged with considering the economic impact of regulatory action, although some agencies have been better at this than others. Critics have frequently singled out the EPA and OSHA for failing to adequately consider the impact of new rules on business. Within the White House itself, the Office of Management and Budget (OMB) was created to "serve the President of the United States in implementing his [or her] vision" of policy. Policy analysis is important to the OMB's function, but as you can imagine, it frequently compromises its objectivity during policy formulation.

Link to Learning

How do the OMB (https://openstax.org/l/29WHgov) and the CBO (https://openstax.org/l/29CBOgov) compare when it comes to impartiality?

Get Connected!

Preparing to Be a Policymaker

What is your passion? Is there an aspect of society you think should be changed? Become a public policy advocate for it! One way to begin is by petitioning the Office of the President. In years past, citizens wrote letters to express grievances or policy preferences. Today, you can visit We the People, the White House online petitions platform (Figure 16.14). At this government site, you can search for petitions related to your cause or post your own. If your petition gets enough signatures, the White House will issue a response. The petitions range from serious to silly, but the process is an important way to speak out about the policies that are important to you.

Figure 16.14   The White House petition website encourages citizens to participate in the democratic process.

Follow-up activity: Choose an issue you are passionate about. Visit We the People (https://openstax.org/l/ 29WHpet) to see if there is already a petition there concerning your chosen issue. If so, join the community promoting your cause. If not, create your own petition and try to gather enough signatures to receive an official response.

THE POLICY PROCESS

The policy process contains four sequential stages: (1) agenda setting, (2) policy enactment, (3) policy implementation, and (4) evaluation. Given the sheer number of issues already processed by the government, called the continuing agenda, and the large number of new proposals being pushed at any one time, it is typically quite difficult to move a new policy all the way through the process.

Agenda setting is the crucial first stage of the public policy process. Agenda setting has two subphases: problem identification and alternative specification. Problem identification identifies the issues that merit discussion. Not all issues make it onto the governmental agenda because there is only so much attention that government can pay. Thus, one of the more important tasks for a policy advocate is to frame his or her issue in a compelling way that raises a persuasive dimension or critical need.[19] For example, health care reform has been attempted on many occasions over the years. One key to making the topic salient has been to frame it in terms of health care access, highlighting the percentage of people who do not have health insurance.

Alternative specification, the second subphase of agenda setting, considers solutions to fix the difficulty raised in problem identification. For example, government officials may agree in the problem subphase that the increase in childhood obesity presents a societal problem worthy of government attention. However, the solution can be complex, and people who otherwise agree might come into conflict over what the best answer is. Alternatives might range from reinvestment in school physical education programs and health education classes, to taking soda and candy machines out of the schools and requiring good nutrition in school lunches. Agenda setting ends when a given problem has been selected, a solution has been paired with that problem, and the solution goes to the decision makers for a vote. Acid rain provides another nice illustration of agenda setting and the problems and solutions subphases. Acid rain is a widely recognized problem that did not make it on to the governmental policy agenda until Congress passed the Air Quality Act of 1967, long after environmental groups started asking for laws to regulate pollution.

In the second policy phase, enactment, the elected branches of government typically consider one specific solution to a problem and decide whether to pass it. This stage is the most visible one and usually garners the most press coverage. And yet it is somewhat anticlimatic. By the time a specific policy proposal (a solution) comes out of agenda setting for a yes/no vote, it can be something of a foregone conclusion that it will pass.

Once the policy has been enacted—usually by the legislative and/or executive branches of the government, like Congress or the president at the national level or the legislature or governor of a state—government agencies do the work of actually implementing it. On a national level, policy implementation can be either top-down or bottom-up. In **top-down implementation**, the federal government dictates the specifics of the policy, and each state implements it the same exact way. In **bottom-up implementation**, the federal government allows local areas some flexibility to meet their specific challenges and needs.[20]

Evaluation, the last stage of the process, should be tied directly to the policy's desired outcomes. Evaluation essentially asks, "How well did this policy do what we designed it to do?" The answers can sometimes be surprising. In one hotly debated case, the United States funded abstinence-only sex education for teens with the goal of reducing teen pregnancy. A 2011 study published in the journal *PLoS One*, however, found that abstinence-only education actually *increased* teen pregnancy rates.[21] The information from the evaluation stage can feed back into the other stages, informing future decisions and creating a public policy cycle.

16.5 Budgeting and Tax Policy

Learning Objectives

By the end of this section, you will be able to:
- Discuss economic theories that shape U.S. economic policy
- Explain how the government uses fiscal policy tools to maintain a healthy economy
- Analyze the taxing and spending decisions made by Congress and the president
- Discuss the role of the Federal Reserve Board in monetary policy

A country spends, raises, and regulates money in accordance with its values. In all, the federal government's budget for 2016 was $3.8 trillion. This chapter has provided a brief overview of some of the budget's key areas of expenditure, and thus some insight into modern American values. But these values are only part of the budgeting story. Policymakers make considerable effort to ensure that long-term priorities are protected from the heat of the election cycle and short-term changes in public opinion. The decision to put some policymaking functions out of the reach of Congress also reflects economic philosophies about the best ways to grow, stimulate, and maintain the economy. The role of politics in drafting the annual budget is indeed large (Figure 16.15), but we should not underestimate the challenges elected officials face as a result of decisions made in the past.

Figure 16.15 Strategists discuss the budget in the Roosevelt Room of the White House in 2009.

APPROACHES TO THE ECONOMY

Until the 1930s, most policy advocates argued that the best way for the government to interact with the economy was through a hands-off approach formally known as *laissez-faire* economics. These policymakers believed the key to economic growth and development was the government's allowing private markets to operate efficiently. Proponents of this school of thought believed private investors were better equipped than governments to figure out which sectors of the economy were most likely to grow and which new products were most likely to be successful. They also tended to oppose government efforts to establish quality controls or health and safety standards, believing consumers themselves would punish bad behavior by not trading with poor corporate citizens. Finally, laissez-faire proponents felt that keeping government out of the business of business would create an automatic cycle of economic growth and contraction. Contraction phases in which there is no economic growth for two consecutive quarters, called **recessions**, would bring business failures and higher unemployment. But this condition, they believed, would correct itself on its own if the government simply allowed the system to operate.

The Great Depression challenged the laissez-faire view, however. When President Franklin Roosevelt came to office in 1933, the United States had already been in the depths of the Great Depression for several years, since the stock market crash of 1929. Roosevelt sought to implement a new approach to economic regulation known as Keynesianism. Named for its developer, the economist John Maynard Keynes, **Keynesian economics** argues that it is possible for a recession to become so deep, and last for so long, that the typical models of economic collapse and recovery may not work. Keynes suggested that economic growth was closely tied to the ability of individuals to consume goods. It didn't matter how or where investors wanted to invest their money if no one could afford to buy the products they wanted to make. And in periods of extremely high unemployment, wages for newly hired labor would be so low that new workers would be unable to afford the products they produced.

Keynesianism counters this problem by increasing government spending in ways that improve consumption. Some of the proposals Keynes suggested were payments or pension for the unemployed and retired, as well as tax incentives to encourage consumption in the middle class. His reasoning was that these individuals would be most likely to spend the money they received by purchasing more goods, which in turn would encourage production and investment. Keynes argued that the wealthy class of producers and employers had sufficient capital to meet the increased demand of consumers that government incentives would stimulate. Once consumption had increased and capital was flowing again, the government would reduce or eliminate its economic stimulus, and any money it had borrowed to create it could be repaid from higher tax revenues.

Keynesianism dominated U.S. fiscal or spending policy from the 1930s to the 1970s. By the 1970s, however, high inflation began to slow economic growth. There were a number of reasons, including higher oil prices and the costs of fighting the Vietnam War. However, some economists, such as Arthur Laffer, began to argue that the social welfare and high tax policies created in the name of Keynesianism were overstimulating the economy, creating a situation in which demand for products had outstripped investors' willingness to increase production.[22] They called for an approach known as **supply-side economics**, which argues that economic growth is largely a function of the productive capacity of a country. Supply-siders have argued that increased regulation and higher taxes reduce the incentive to invest new money into the economy, to the point where little growth can occur. They have advocated reducing taxes and regulations to spur economic growth.

MANDATORY SPENDING VS. DISCRETIONARY SPENDING

The desire of Keynesians to create a minimal level of aggregate demand, coupled with a Depression-era preference to promote social welfare policy, led the president and Congress to develop a federal budget with spending divided into two broad categories: mandatory and discretionary (see Figure 16.16). Of these, **mandatory spending** is the larger, consisting of about $2.5 trillion of the projected 2017 budget, or roughly 59 percent of all federal expenditures.[23]

The overwhelming portion of mandatory spending is earmarked for entitlement programs guaranteed to those who meet certain qualifications, usually based on age, income, or disability. These programs, discussed above, include Medicare and Medicaid, Social Security, and major income security programs such as unemployment insurance and SNAP. The costs of programs tied to age are relatively easy to estimate and grow largely as a function of the aging of the population. Income and disability payments are a bit more difficult to estimate. They tend to go down during periods of economic recovery and rise when the economy begins to slow down, in precisely the way Keynes suggested. A comparatively small piece of the mandatory spending pie, about 14 percent, is devoted to benefits designated for former federal employees, including military retirement and many Veterans Administration programs.

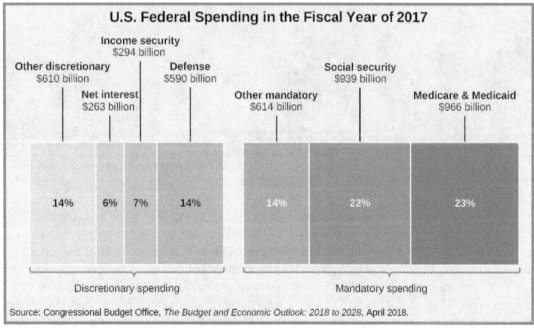

Figure 16.16 This chart of U.S. federal spending for 2015 shows the proportions of mandatory and discretionary spending, about 60 percent and 40 percent, respectively.

Congress is ultimately responsible for setting the formulas for mandatory payouts, but as we saw in the earlier discussion regarding Social Security, major reforms to entitlement formulas are difficult to enact. As a result, the size and growth of mandatory spending in future budgets are largely a function of previous legislation that set the formulas up in the first place. So long as supporters of particular programs can block changes to the formulas, funding will continue almost on autopilot. Keynesians support this mandatory spending, along with other elements of social welfare policy, because they help maintain a minimal level of consumption that should, in theory, prevent recessions from turning into depressions, which are more severe downturns.

Portions of the budget not devoted to mandatory spending are categorized as **discretionary spending** because Congress must pass legislation to authorize money to be spent each year. About 50 percent of the approximately $1.2 trillion set aside for discretionary spending each year pays for most of the operations of government, including employee salaries and the maintenance of federal buildings. It also covers science and technology spending, foreign affairs initiatives, education spending, federally provided transportation costs, and many of the redistributive benefits most people in the United States have come to take for granted.[24] The other half of discretionary spending—and the second-largest component of the total budget—is devoted to the military. (Only Social Security is larger.) Defense spending is used to maintain the U.S. military presence at home and abroad, procure and develop new weapons, and cover the cost of any wars or other military engagements in which the United States is currently engaged (**Figure 16.17**).

Figure 16.17　The war in Afghanistan, ongoing since 2001, has cost the United States billions of dollars in discretionary military spending authorized by Congress every year.

In theory, the amount of revenue raised by the national government should be equal to these expenses, but with the exception of a brief period from 1998 to 2000, that has not been the case. The economic recovery from the 2007–2009 recession, and budget control efforts implemented since then, have managed to cut the annual **deficit**—the amount by which expenditures are greater than revenues—by more than half. However, the amount of money the U.S. government needed to borrow to pay its bills in 2016 was still in excess of $400 billion[25]. This was in addition to the country's almost $19 trillion of total **debt**—the amount of money the government owes its creditors—at the end of 2015, according to the Department of the Treasury.

Balancing the budget has been a major goal of both the Republican and Democratic parties for the past several decades, although the parties tend to disagree on the best way to accomplish the task. One frequently offered solution, particularly among supply-side advocates, is to simply cut spending. This has proven to be much easier said than done. If Congress were to try to balance the budget only through discretionary spending, it would need to cut about one-third of spending on programs like defense, higher education, agriculture, police enforcement, transportation, and general government operations. Given the number and popularity of many of these programs, it is difficult to imagine this would be possible. To use spending cuts alone as a way to control the deficit, Congress will almost certainly be required to cut or control the costs of mandatory spending programs like Social Security and Medicare—a radically unpopular step.

TAX POLICY

The other option available for balancing the budget is to increase revenue. All governments must raise revenue in order to operate. The most common way is by applying some sort of tax on residents (or on their behaviors) in exchange for the benefits the government provides (Figure 16.18). As necessary as taxes are, however, they are not without potential downfalls. First, the more money the government collects to cover its costs, the less residents are left with to spend and invest. Second, attempts to raise revenues through taxation may alter the behavior of residents in ways that are counterproductive to the state and the broader economy. Excessively taxing necessary and desirable behaviors like consumption (with a sales tax) or investment (with a capital gains tax) will discourage citizens from engaging in them, potentially slowing economic growth. The goal of tax policy, then, is to determine the most effective way of meeting the nation's revenue obligations without harming other public policy goals.

Figure 16.18   A U.S. marine fills out an income tax form. Income taxes in the United States are progressive taxes.

As you would expect, Keynesians and supply-siders disagree about which forms of tax policy are best. Keynesians, with their concern about whether consumers can really stimulate demand, prefer **progressive taxes** systems that increase the effective tax rate as the taxpayer's income increases. This policy leaves those most likely to spend their money with more money to spend. For example, in 2015, U.S. taxpayers paid a 10 percent tax rate on the first $18,450 of income, but 15 percent on the next $56,450 (some income is excluded).[26] The rate continues to rise, to up to 39.6 percent on any taxable income over $464,850. These brackets are somewhat distorted by the range of tax credits, deductions, and incentives the government offers, but the net effect is that the top income earners pay a greater portion of the overall income tax burden than do those at the lowest tax brackets. According to the Pew Research Center, based on tax returns in 2014, 2.7 percent of filers made more than $250,000. Those 2.7 percent of filers paid 52 percent of the income tax paid.[27]

Supply-siders, on the other hand, prefer **regressive tax** systems, which lower the overall rate as individuals make more money. This does not automatically mean the wealthy pay less than the poor, simply that the percentage of their income they pay in taxes will be lower. Consider, for example, the use of **excise taxes** on specific goods or services as a source of revenue.[28] Sometimes called "sin taxes" because they tend to be applied to goods like alcohol, tobacco, and gasoline, excise taxes have a regressive quality, since the amount of the good purchased by the consumer, and thus the tax paid, does not increase at the same rate as income. A person who makes $250,000 per year is likely to purchase more gasoline than a person who makes $50,000 per year (Figure 16.19). But the higher earner is not likely to purchase *five times more* gasoline, which means the proportion of his or her income paid out in gasoline taxes is less than the proportion for a lower-earning individual.

Figure 16.19 A gas station shows fuel prices over $3.00 a gallon in 2005, shortly after Hurricane Katrina disrupted gas production in the Gulf of Mexico. Taxes on gasoline that are based on the quantity purchased are regressive taxes.

Another example of a regressive tax paid by most U.S. workers is the payroll tax that funds Social Security. While workers contribute 7.65 percent of their income to pay for Social Security and their employers pay a matching amount, in 2015, the payroll tax was applied to only the first $118,500 of income. Individuals who earned more than that, or who made money from other sources like investments, saw their overall tax rate fall as their income increased.

In 2015, the United States raised about $3.2 trillion in revenue. Income taxes ($1.54 trillion), payroll taxes on Social Security and Medicare ($1.07 trillion), and excise taxes ($98 billion) make up three of the largest sources of revenue for the federal government. When combined with corporate income taxes ($344 billion), these four tax streams make up about 95 percent of total government revenue. The balance of revenue is split nearly evenly between revenues from the Federal Reserve and a mix of revenues from import tariffs, estate and gift taxes, and various fees or fines paid to the government (Figure 16.20). The Tax Cuts and Jobs Act, which was passed in December 2017 by the Republican-controlled Congress and significantly reduced the income tax rate paid by corporations, has led to a widening budget deficit. November 2018 featured the largest single-month deficit in the history of the country, with $411 billion in spending and only $206 billion in receipts, and the annual budget shortfall is approaching $1 trillion.[29]

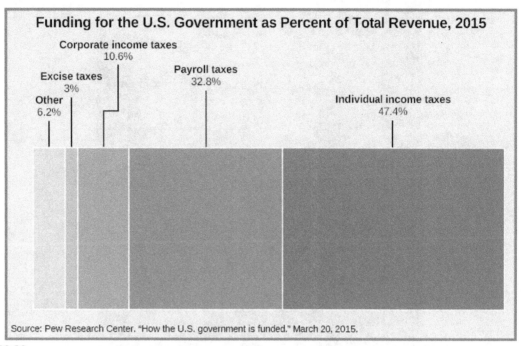

Figure 16.20

THE FEDERAL RESERVE BOARD AND INTEREST RATES

Financial panics arise when too many people, worried about the solvency of their investments, try to withdraw their money at the same time. Such panics plagued U.S. banks until 1913 (Figure 16.21), when Congress enacted the Federal Reserve Act. The act established the Federal Reserve System, also known as the Fed, as the central bank of the United States. The Fed's three original goals to promote were maximum employment, stable prices, and moderate long-term interest rates.[30] All of these goals bring stability. The Fed's role is now broader and includes influencing monetary policy (the means by which the nation controls the size and growth of the money supply), supervising and regulating banks, and providing them with financial services like loans.

Figure 16.21 Investors crowd Wall Street during the Bankers Panic of 1907.

The Federal Reserve System is overseen by a board of governors, known as the Federal Reserve Board. The president of the United States appoints the seven governors, each of whom serves a fourteen-year term (the terms are staggered). A chair and vice chair lead the board for terms of four years each. The most important work of the board is participating in the Federal Open Market Committee to set monetary policy, like interest rate levels and macroeconomic policy. The board also oversees a network of twelve regional Federal Reserve Banks, each of which serves as a "banker's bank" for the country's financial institutions.

Insider Perspective

The Role of the Federal Reserve Chair

If you have read or watched the news for the past several years, perhaps you have heard the names Janet Yellen, Ben Bernanke, or Alan Greenspan. Bernanke, Greenspan, and Yellen are all recent past chairs of the board of governors of the Federal Reserve System; Jerome Powell is the current chair (Figure 16.22). The role of the Fed chair is one of the most important in the country. By raising or lowering banks' interest rates, the chair has the ability reduce inflation or stimulate growth. The Fed's dual mandate is to keep inflation low (under 2 percent) and unemployment low (below 5 percent), but efforts to meet these goals can often lead to contradictory monetary policies.

(a)   (b)

Figure 16.22 Economist Alan Greenspan (a) was chair of the board of governors of the Federal Reserve System from 1987 to 2006, the second-longest tenure of any chair. Janet Yellen (b) succeeded Ben Bernanke as chair in 2014, after serving as vice chair for four years. Prior to serving on the Federal Reserve Board, Yellen was president and CEO of the Federal Reserve Bank of San Francisco. She was succeeded by Jerome Powell in February 2018.

The Fed, and by extension its chair, have a tremendous responsibility. Many of the economic events of the past five decades, both good and bad, are the results of Fed policies. In the 1970s, double-digit inflation brought the economy almost to a halt, but when Paul Volcker became chair in 1979, he raised interest rates and jump-started the economy. After the stock market crash of 1987, then-chair Alan Greenspan declared, "The Federal Reserve, consistent with its responsibilities as the nation's central bank, affirmed today its readiness to...support the economic and financial system."[31] His lowering of interest rates led to an unprecedented decade of economic growth through the 1990s. In the 2000s, consistently low interest rates and readily available credit contributed to the sub-prime mortgage boom and subsequent bust, which led to a global economic recession beginning in 2008.

Should the important tasks of the Fed continue to be pursued by unelected appointees like those profiled in this box, or should elected leaders be given the job? Why?

Link to Learning

Do you think you have what it takes to be chair of the Federal Reserve Board? Play this **game (https://openstax.org/l/29ChrtheFed)** and see how you fare!

Key Terms

bottom-up implementation a strategy in which the federal government allows local areas some flexibility to meet their specific challenges and needs in implementing policy

Congressional Budget Office the congressional office that scores the spending or revenue impact of all proposed legislation to assess its net effect on the budget

debt the total amount the government owes across all years

deficit the annual amount by which expenditures are greater than revenues

discretionary spending government spending that Congress must pass legislation to authorize each year

distributive policy a policy that collect payments or resources broadly but concentrates direct benefits on relatively few

entitlement a program that guarantees benefits to members of a specific group or segment of the population

excise taxes taxes applied to specific goods or services as a source of revenue

free-market economics a school of thought that believes the forces of supply and demand, working without any government intervention, are the most effective way for markets to operate

Keynesian economics an economic policy based on the idea that economic growth is closely tied to the ability of individuals to consume goods

laissez-faire an economic policy that assumes the key to economic growth and development is for the government to allow private markets to operate efficiently without interference

libertarians people who believe that government almost always operates less efficiently than the private sector and that its actions should be kept to a minimum

mandatory spending government spending earmarked for entitlement programs guaranteeing support to those who meet certain qualifications

Medicaid a health insurance program for low-income citizens

Medicare an entitlement health insurance program for older people and retirees who no longer get health insurance through their work

policy advocates people who actively work to propose or maintain public policy

policy analysts people who identify all possible choices available to a decision maker and assess the potential impact of each

progressive tax a tax that tends to increase the effective tax rate as the wealth or income of the tax payer increases

public policy the broad strategy government uses to do its job; the relatively stable set of purposive governmental behaviors that address matters of concern to some part of society

recession a temporary contraction of the economy in which there is no economic growth for two consecutive quarters

redistributive policy a policy in which costs are born by a relatively small number of groups or individuals, but benefits are expected to be enjoyed by a different group in society

regressive tax a tax applied at a lower overall rate as individuals' income rises

regulatory policy a policy that regulates companies and organizations in a way that protects the public

safety net a way to provide for members of society experiencing economic hardship

Social Security a social welfare policy for people who no longer receive an income from employment

supply-side economics an economic policy that assumes economic growth is largely a function of a country's productive capacity

top-down implementation a strategy in which the federal government dictates the specifics of public policy and each state implements it the same exact way

Summary

16.1 What Is Public Policy?
Public policy is the broad strategy government uses to do its job, the relatively stable set of purposive governmental behaviors that address matters of concern to some part of society. Most policy outcomes are the result of considerable debate, compromise, and refinement that happen over years and are finalized only after input from multiple institutions within government. Health care reform, for instance, was developed after years of analysis, reflection on existing policy, and even trial implementation at the state level.

People evaluate public policies based on their outcomes, that is, who benefits and who loses. Even the best-intended policies can have unintended consequences and may even ultimately harm someone, if only those who must pay for the policy through higher taxes.

16.2 Categorizing Public Policy
Goods are the commodities, services, and systems that satisfy people's wants or needs. Private goods can be owned by a particular person or group, and are excluded from use by others, typically by means of a price. Free-market economists believe that the government has no role in regulating the exchange of private goods because the market will regulate itself. Public goods, on the other hand, are goods like air, water, wildlife, and forests that no one owns, so no one has responsibility for them. Most people agree the government has some role to play in regulating public goods.

We categorize policy based upon the degree to which costs and benefits are concentrated on the few or diffused across the many. Distributive policy collects from the many and benefits the few, whereas regulatory policy focuses costs on one group while benefitting larger society. Redistributive policy shares the wealth and income of some groups with others.

16.3 Policy Arenas
The three major domestic policy areas are social welfare; science, technology, and education; and business stimulus and regulation. Social welfare programs like Social Security, Medicaid, and Medicare form a safety net for vulnerable populations. Science, technology, and education policies have the goal of securing the United States' competitive advantages. Business stimulus and regulation policies have to balance business' needs for an economic edge with consumers' need for protection from unfair or unsafe practices. The United States spends billions of dollars on these programs.

16.4 Policymakers
The two groups most engaged in making policy are policy advocates and policy analysts. Policy advocates are people who feel strongly enough about something to work toward changing public policy to fix it. Policy analysts, on the other hand, aim for impartiality. Their role is to assess potential policies and predict

their outcomes. Although they are in theory unbiased, their findings often reflect specific political leanings.

The public policy process has four major phases: identifying the problem, setting the agenda, implementing the policy, and evaluating the results. The process is a cycle, because the evaluation stage should feed back into the earlier stages, informing future decisions about the policy.

16.5 Budgeting and Tax Policy

Until the Great Depression of the 1930s, the U.S. government took a *laissez-faire* or hands-off approach to economic policy, assuming that if left to itself, the economy would go through cycles of boom and bust, but would remain healthy overall. Keynesian economic policies, with their emphasis on government spending to increase consumer consumption, helped raise the country out of the Depression.

The goal of federal fiscal policy is to have a balanced budget, in which expenditures and revenues match up. More frequently, the budget has a deficit, a gap between expenditures and revenues. It is very difficult to reduce the budget, which consists of mandatory and discretionary spending, but no one really wants to raise revenue by raising taxes. One way monetary policies can change the economy is through the level of interest rates. The Federal Reserve Board sets these rates and thus guiding monetary policy in the United States.

Review Questions

1. Which of the following is *not* an example of a public policy outcome?
- a. the creation of a program to combat drug trafficking
- b. the passage of the Affordable Care Act (Obamacare)
- c. the passage of tax cuts during the George W. Bush administration
- d. none of the above; all are public policy outcomes

2. Public policy _____.
- a. is more of a theory than a reality
- b. is typically made by one branch of government acting alone
- c. requires multiple actors and branches to carry out
- d. focuses on only a few special individuals

3. What are some of the challenges to getting a new public policy considered and passed as law?

4. Toll goods differ from public goods in that _____.
- a. they provide special access to some and not all
- b. they require the payment of a fee up front
- c. they provide a service for only the wealthy
- d. they are free and available to all

5. Which type of policy directly benefits the most citizens?
- a. regulatory policy
- b. distributive policy
- c. redistributive policy
- d. self-regulatory policy

6. Of the types of goods introduced in this section, which do you feel is the most important to the public generally and why? Which public policies are most important and why?

7. Social Security and Medicare are notable for their assistance to which group?
- a. the poor
- b. young families starting out
- c. those in urban areas
- d. the elderly

8. Setting aside Social Security and Medicare, other entitlement programs in the U.S. government _____.
- a. constitute over half the budget
- b. constitute well under one-quarter of the budget
- c. are paid for by the states with no cost to the Federal government
- d. none of the above

9. What societal ills are social welfare programs designed to address?

10. Which stage of the public policy process includes identification of problems in need of fixing?

    a. agenda setting

    b. enactment

    c. implementation

    d. evaluation

11. Policy analysts seek _____.

    a. evidence

    b. their chosen outputs

    c. influence

    d. money

12. In the implementation phase of the policy process, is it better to use a top-down approach or a bottom-up approach on Federal policies? Why?

13. A deficit is _____.

    a. the overall amount owed by government for past borrowing

    b. the annual budget shortfall between revenues and expenditures

    c. the cancellation of an entitlement program

    d. all the above

14. Entitlement (or mandatory) spending is _____.

    a. formula-based spending that goes to individual citizens

    b. a program of contracts to aerospace companies

    c. focused on children

    d. concentrated on education

15. When times are tough economically, what can the government do to get the economy moving again?

Critical Thinking Questions

16. What might indicate that a government is passing the policies the country needs?

17. If you had to define the poverty line, what would you expect people to be able to afford just above that line? For those below that line, what programs should the government offer to improve quality of life?

18. What is the proper role of the government in regulating the private sector so people are protected from unfair or dangerous business practices? Why?

19. Is it realistic to expect the U.S. government to balance its budget? Why or why not?

20. What in your view is the most important policy issue facing the United States? Why is it important and which specific problems need to be solved?

21. What are some suggested solutions to the anticipated Social Security shortfall? Why haven't these solutions tended to gain support?

22. Whose role is more important in a democracy, the policy advocate's or the policy analyst's? Why?

23. Which stage of the policy progress is the most important and why?

Suggestions for Further Study

Alesina, Alberto and Howard Rosenthal. 1995. *Partisan Politics, Divided Government and the Economy*. New York: Cambridge University Press.

Baumgartner, Frank R. and Bryan D. Jones. 1993. *Agendas and Instability in American Politics*. Chicago: University of Chicago Press.

Birkland, Thomas A. 1997. *After Disaster: Agenda Setting, Public Policy, and Focusing Events*. Washington, DC: Georgetown University Press.

Glick, Henry R. 1992. *The Right to Die: Policy Innovation and Its Consequences*. New York: Columbia University Press.

Guell, Robert. 2014. Issues in Economics Today, 7th ed. New York: McGraw-Hill Education.

Keech, William R. 1995. *Economic Politics: The Costs of Democracy*. New York: Cambridge University Press.

Kingdon, John W. 1995. *Agendas, Alternatives and Public Policies*, 2nd ed. New York: HarperCollins.

Lowi, Theodore J. 1969. *The End of Liberalism: Ideology, Policy, and the Crisis of Public Authority*. New York: W.W. Norton.

Pierson, Paul. 2004. *Politics in Time: History, Institutions, and Social Analysis*. Princeton, NJ: Princeton University Press.

Riker, William H. 1986. *The Art of Political Manipulation*. New Haven, CT: Yale University Press.

Robertson, David B. and Dennis R. Judd. 1989. *The Development of American Public Policy: The Structure of Policy Restraint*. Glenview, IL: Scott, Foresman.

Rochefort, David A. and Roger W. Cobb. 1994. *The Politics of Problem Definition: Shaping the Policy Agenda*. Lawrence, KS: University Press of Kansas.

Sabatier, Paul A. 1999. *Theories of the Policy Process*. Boulder, CO: Westview Press.

Chapter 17

Foreign Policy

Figure 17.1 U.S. president Donald Trump and Russian president Vladimir Putin shake hands for the cameras during the APEC Summit on November 10, 2017 in Da Nang, Vietnam. (credit: President of the Russian Federation/ www.kremlin.ru)

Chapter Outline

17.1 Defining Foreign Policy

17.2 Foreign Policy Instruments

17.3 Institutional Relations in Foreign Policy

17.4 Approaches to Foreign Policy

Introduction

The U.S. government interacts with a large number of international actors, from other governments to private organizations, to fight global problems like terrorism and human trafficking, and to meet many other national foreign policy goals such as encouraging trade and protecting the environment. Sometimes these goals are conflicting. Perhaps because of these realities, the president is in many ways the leader of the foreign policy domain. When the United States wishes to discuss important issues with other nations, the president (or a representative such as the secretary of state) typically does the talking, as when President Donald Trump visited with Russian president Vladimir Putin in 2017 (Figure 17.1).

But don't let this image mislead you. While the president is the country's foreign policy leader, Congress also has many foreign policy responsibilities, including approving treaties and agreements, allocating funding, making war, and confirming ambassadors. These and various other activities constitute the patchwork quilt that is U.S. foreign policy.

How are foreign and domestic policymaking different, and how are they linked? What are the main foreign policy goals of the United States? How do the president and Congress interact in the foreign policy realm? In what different ways might foreign policy be pursued? This chapter will delve into these and other issues to present an overview U.S. foreign policy.

17.1 Defining Foreign Policy

Learning Objectives

By the end of this section, you will be able to:
- Explain what foreign policy is and how it differs from domestic policy
- Identify the objectives of U.S. foreign policy
- Describe the different types of foreign policy
- Identify the U.S. government's main challenges in the foreign policy realm

When we consider policy as our chapter focus, we are looking broadly at the actions the U.S. government carries out for particular purposes. In the case of foreign policy, that purpose is to manage its relationships with other nations of the world. Another distinction is that policy results from a course of action or a pattern of actions over time, rather than from a single action or decision. For example, U.S. foreign policy with Russia has been forged by several presidents, as well as by cabinet secretaries, House and Senate members, and foreign policy agency bureaucrats. Policy is also purposive, or intended to do something; that is, policymaking is not random. When the United States enters into an international agreement with other countries on aims such as free trade or nuclear disarmament, it does so for specific reasons. With that general definition of policy established, we shall now dig deeper into the specific domain of U.S. foreign policy.

FOREIGN POLICY BASICS

What is **foreign policy**? We can think of it on several levels, as "the goals that a state's officials seek to attain abroad, the values that give rise to those objectives, and the means or instruments used to pursue them."[1] This definition highlights some of the key topics in U.S. foreign policy, such as national goals abroad and the manner in which the United States tries to achieve them. Note too that we distinguish foreign policy, which is externally focused, from domestic policy, which sets strategies internal to the United States, though the two types of policies can become quite intertwined. So, for example, one might talk about Latino politics as a domestic issue when considering educational policies designed to increase the number of Hispanic Americans who attend and graduate from a U.S. college or university.[2] However, as demonstrated in the primary debates leading up to the 2016 election, Latino politics can quickly become a foreign policy matter when considering topics such as immigration from and foreign trade with countries in Central America and South America (Figure 17.2).[3]

Figure 17.2 Domestic issues can sometimes become international ones when it comes to such topics as foreign trade. Here, President George W. Bush shakes hands with legislators and administration officials after signing the Central American Free Trade Agreement (CAFTA) Implementation Act on August 2, 2005.

What are the objectives of U.S. foreign policy? While the goals of a nation's foreign policy are always open to debate and revision, there are nonetheless four main goals to which we can attribute much of what the U.S. government does in the foreign policy realm: (1) the protection of the U.S. and its citizens, (2) the maintenance of access to key resources and markets, (3) the preservation of a balance of power in the world, and (4) the protection of human rights and democracy.

The first goal is the protection of the United States and the lives of it citizens, both while they are in the United States and when they travel abroad. Related to this security goal is the aim of protecting the country's allies, or countries with which the United States is friendly and mutually supportive. In the international sphere, threats and dangers can take several forms, including military threats from other nations or terrorist groups and economic threats from boycotts and high tariffs on trade.

In an economic boycott, the United States ceases trade with another country unless or until it changes a policy to which the United States objects. Ceasing trade means U.S. goods cannot be sold in that country and its goods cannot be sold in the United States. For example, in recent years the United States and other countries implemented an economic boycott of Iran as it escalated the development of its nuclear energy program. The recent Iran nuclear deal is a pact in which Iran agrees to halt nuclear development while the United States and six other countries lift economic sanctions to again allow trade with Iran. Barriers to trade also include tariffs, or fees charged for moving goods from one country to another. Protectionist trade policies raise tariffs so that it becomes difficult for imported goods, now more expensive, to compete on price with domestic goods. Free trade agreements seek to reduce these trade barriers.

The second main goal of U.S. foreign policy is to ensure the nation maintains access to key resources and markets across the world. Resources include natural resources, such as oil, and economic resources, including the infusion of foreign capital investment for U.S. domestic infrastructure projects like buildings, bridges, and weapons systems. Of course, access to the international marketplace also means access to goods that American consumers might want, such as Swiss chocolate and Australian wine. U.S. foreign policy also seeks to advance the interests of U.S. business, to both sell domestic products in the international marketplace and support general economic development around the globe (especially in developing countries).

A third main goal is the preservation of a balance of power in the world. A **balance of power** means no one nation or region is much more powerful militarily than are the countries of the rest of the world. The achievement of a perfect balance of power is probably not possible, but general stability, or predictability in the operation of governments, strong institutions, and the absence of violence within and between nations may be. For much of U.S. history, leaders viewed world stability through the lens of Europe. If the European continent was stable, so too was the world. During the **Cold War** era that followed World War II, stability was achieved by the existence of dual superpowers, the United States and the Soviet Union, and by the real fear of the nuclear annihilation of which both were capable. Until approximately 1989–1990, advanced industrial democracies aligned themselves behind one of these two superpowers.

Today, in the post–Cold War era, many parts of Europe are politically more free than they were during the years of the Soviet bloc, and there is less fear of nuclear war than when the United States and the Soviet Union had missiles pointed at each other for four straight decades. However, despite the mostly stabilizing presence of the European Union (EU), which now has twenty-eight member countries, several wars have been fought in Eastern Europe and the former Soviet Union. Moreover, the EU itself faces some challenges, including a vote in the United Kingdom to leave the EU, the ongoing controversy about how to resolve the national debt of Greece, and the crisis in Europe created by thousands of refugees from the Middle East.

Carefully planned acts of terrorism in the United States, Asia, and Europe have introduced a new type of enemy into the balance of power equation—nonstate or nongovernmental organizations, such as al-Qaeda and ISIS (or ISIL), consisting of various terrorist cells located in many different countries and across all continents (Figure 17.3).

Figure 17.3 President Barack Obama, along with French president François Hollande and Paris mayor Anne Hidalgo, place roses on the makeshift memorial in front of the Bataclan concert hall, one of the sites targeted in the Paris terrorist attacks of November 13, 2015.

The fourth main goal of U.S. foreign policy is the protection of human rights and democracy. The payoff of stability that comes from other U.S. foreign policy goals is peace and tranquility. While certainly looking out for its own strategic interests in considering foreign policy strategy, the United States nonetheless attempts to support international peace through many aspects of its foreign policy, such as foreign aid, and through its support of and participation in international organizations such as the United Nations, the North Atlantic Treaty Organization (NATO), and the Organization of American States.

The **United Nations (UN)** is perhaps the foremost international organization in the world today. The main institutional bodies of the UN are the General Assembly and the Security Council. The General Assembly includes all member nations and admits new members and approves the UN budget by a two-thirds majority. The Security Council includes fifteen countries, five of which are permanent members (including the United States) and ten that are non-permanent and rotate on a five two-year-term basis. The entire membership is bound by decisions of the Security Council, which makes all decisions related to international peace and security. Two other important units of the UN are the International Court of Justice in The Hague (Netherlands) and the UN Secretariat, which includes the Secretary-General of the UN and the UN staff directors and employees.

Milestone

The Creation of the United Nations

One of the unique and challenging aspects of global affairs is the fact that no world-level authority exists to mandate when and how the world's nations interact. After the failed attempt by President Woodrow Wilson and others to formalize a "League of Nations" in the wake of World War I in the 1920s, and on the heels of a worldwide depression that began in 1929, came World War II, history's deadliest military conflict. Now, in the early decades of the twenty-first century, it is common to think of the September 11 terrorist attacks in 2001 as the big game-changer. Yet while 9/11 was hugely significant in the United States and abroad, World War II was even more so. The December 1941 Japanese attack on Pearl Harbor (Hawaii) was a comparable surprise-style attack that plunged the United States into war.

The scope of the conflict, fought in Europe and the Pacific Ocean, and Hitler's nearly successful attempt to take over Europe entirely, struck fear in minds and hearts. The war brought about a sea change in international relations and governance, from the Marshall Plan to rebuild Europe, to NATO that created a cross-national military shield for Western Europe, to the creation of the UN in 1945, when the representatives of fifty countries met and signed the Charter of the United Nations in San Francisco, California (Figure 17.4).

Figure 17.4 On June 26, 2015, then-House minority leader Nancy Pelosi (D-CA) joined UN secretary-general Ban Ki-moon, California governor Jerry Brown, and other dignitaries to commemorate the seventieth anniversary of the adoption of the UN Charter in San Francisco. (credit: modification of work by "Nancy Pelosi"/Flickr)

Today, the United Nations, headquartered in New York City, includes 193 of the 195 nations of the world. It is a voluntary association to which member nations pay dues based on the size of their economy. The UN's main purposes are to maintain peace and security, promote human rights and social progress, and develop friendly relationships among nations.

Follow-up activity: In addition to facilitating collective decision-making on world matters, the UN carries out many different programs. Go to the UN website (https://openstax.org/l/29UNmain) to find information about three different UN programs that are carried out around the world.

An ongoing question for the United States in waging the war against terrorism is to what degree it should work in concert with the UN to carry out anti-terrorism initiatives around the world in a multilateral manner, rather than pursuing a "go it alone" strategy of unilateralism. The fact that the U.S. government has such a choice suggests the voluntary nature of the United States (or another country) accepting world-level governance in foreign policy. If the United States truly felt bound by UN opinion regarding the manner in which it carries out its war on terrorism, it would approach the UN Security Council for approval.

Another cross-national organization to which the United States is tied, and that exists to forcefully represent Western allies and in turn forge the peace, is the **North Atlantic Treaty Organization (NATO)**. NATO was formed after World War II as the Cold War between East and West started to emerge. While more militaristic in approach than the United Nations, NATO has the goal of protecting the interests of Europe and the West and the assurance of support and defense from partner nations. However, while it is a strong military coalition, it has not sought to expand and take over other countries. Rather, the peace and stability of Europe are its main goals. NATO initially included only Western European nations and the United States. However, since the end of the Cold War, additional countries from the East, such as Turkey, have entered into the NATO alliance.

Besides participating in the UN and NATO, the United States also distributes hundreds of millions of dollars each year in foreign aid to improve the quality of life of citizens in developing countries. The United States may also forgive the foreign debts of these countries. By definition, developing countries are not modernized in terms of infrastructure and social services and thus suffer from instability. Helping them modernize and develop stable governments is intended as a benefit to them and a prop to the stability of the world. An alternative view of U.S. assistance is that there are more nefarious goals at work, that perhaps it is intended to buy influence in developing countries, secure a position in the region, obtain access to resources, or foster dependence on the United States.

The United States pursues its four main foreign policy goals through several different foreign policy types, or distinct substantive areas of foreign policy in which the United States is engaged. These types are trade, diplomacy, sanctions, military/defense, intelligence, foreign aid, and global environmental policy.

Trade policy is the way the United States interacts with other countries to ease the flow of commerce and goods and services between countries. A country is said to be engaging in **protectionism** when it does not permit other countries to sell goods and services within its borders, or when it charges them very high tariffs (or import taxes) to do so. At the other end of the spectrum is a **free trade** approach, in which a country allows the unfettered flow of goods and services between itself and other countries. At times the United States has been free trade–oriented, while at other times it has been protectionist. Perhaps its most free trade–oriented move was the 1991 implementation of the North American Free Trade Agreement (NAFTA). This pact removed trade barriers and other transaction costs levied on goods moving between the United States, Mexico, and Canada.

Critics see a free trade approach as problematic and instead advocate for protectionist policies that shield U.S. companies and their products against cheaper foreign products that might be imported here. One of the more prominent recent examples of protectionist policies occurred in the steel industry, as U.S. companies in the international steel marketplace struggled with competition from Chinese factories in particular.

The **balance of trade** is the relationship between a country's inflow and outflow of goods. The United States sells many goods and services around the world, but overall it maintains a trade deficit, in which more goods and services are coming in from other countries than are going out to be sold overseas. The current U.S. trade deficit is $37.4 billion, which means the value of what the United States imports from other countries is much larger than the value of what it exports to other countries.[4] This trade deficit has led some to advocate for protectionist trade policies.

For many, foreign policy is synonymous with diplomacy. **Diplomacy** is the establishment and maintenance of a formal relationship between countries that governs their interactions on matters as diverse as tourism, the taxation of goods they trade, and the landing of planes on each other's runways. While diplomatic relations are not always rosy, when they are operating it does suggest that things are going well between the countries. Diplomatic relations are formalized through the sharing of ambassadors. Ambassadors are country representatives who live and maintain an office (known as an embassy) in the other country. Just as exchanging ambassadors formalizes the bilateral relationship between countries, calling them home signifies the end of the relationship. Diplomacy tends to be the U.S. government's first step when it tries to resolve a conflict with another country.

To illustrate how international relations play out when countries come into conflict, consider what has become known as the Hainan Island incident. In 2001, a U.S. spy plane collided with a Chinese jet fighter near Chinese airspace, where U.S. planes were not authorized to be. The Chinese jet fighter crashed and the pilot died. The U.S. plane made an emergency landing on the island of Hainan. China retrieved the aircraft and captured the U.S. pilots. U.S. ambassadors then attempted to negotiate for their return. These negotiations were slow and ended up involving officials of the president's cabinet, but they ultimately worked. Had they not succeeded, an escalating set of options likely would have included diplomatic sanctions (removal of ambassadors), economic sanctions (such as an embargo on trade and the flow of money between the countries), minor military options (such as establishment of a no-fly zone just outside Chinese airspace), or more significant military options (such as a focused campaign to enter China and get the pilots back). Nonmilitary tools to influence another country, like economic sanctions, are referred to as **soft power**, while the use of military power is termed **hard power**.[5]

At the more serious end of the foreign policy decision-making spectrum, and usually as a last resort when diplomacy fails, the U.S. military and defense establishment exists to provide the United States the ability to wage war against other state and nonstate actors. Such war can be offensive, as were the Iraq War in 2003 and the 1989 removal of Panamanian leader Manuel Noriega. Or it can be defensive, as a means to respond to aggression from others, such as the Persian Gulf War in 1991, also known as Operation Desert Storm (Figure 17.5). The potential for military engagement, and indeed the scattering about the globe of hundreds of U.S. military installations, can also be a potential source of foreign policy strength for the United States. On the other hand, in the world of diplomacy, such an approach can be seen as imperialistic by other world nations.

Figure 17.5 President George H. W. Bush greets U.S. troops stationed in Saudi Arabia on Thanksgiving Day in 1990. The first troops were deployed there in August 1990, as part of Operation Desert Shield, which was intended to build U.S. military strength in the area in preparation for an eventual military operation.

Intelligence policy is related to defense and includes the overt and covert gathering of information from foreign sources that might be of strategic interest to the United States. The intelligence world, perhaps more than any other area of foreign policy, captures the imagination of the general public. Many books, television shows, and movies entertain us (with varying degrees of accuracy) through stories about U.S. intelligence operations and people.

Foreign aid and global environmental policy are the final two foreign policy types. With both, as with the other types, the United States operates as a strategic actor with its own interests in mind, but here it also acts as an international steward trying to serve the common good. With foreign aid, the United States provides material and economic aid to other countries, especially developing countries, in order to improve their stability and their citizens' quality of life. This type of aid is sometimes called humanitarian aid; in 2013 the U.S. contribution totaled $32 billion. Military aid is classified under military/defense or national security policy (and totaled $8 billion in 2013). At $40 billion the total U.S. foreign aid budget for 2013 was sizeable, though it represented less than 1 percent of the entire federal budget.[6]

Global environmental policy addresses world-level environmental matters such as climate change and global warming, the thinning of the ozone layer, rainforest depletion in areas along the Equator, and ocean pollution and species extinction. The United States' commitment to such issues has varied considerably over the years. For example, the United States was the largest country not to sign the 1997 Kyoto Protocol on greenhouse gas emissions. However, few would argue that the U.S. government has not been a leader on global environmental matters.

UNIQUE CHALLENGES IN FOREIGN POLICY

U.S. foreign policy is a massive and complex enterprise. What are its unique challenges for the country?

First, there exists no true world-level authority dictating how the nations of the world should relate to one another. If one nation negotiates in bad faith or lies to another, there is no central world-level government authority to sanction that country. This makes diplomacy and international coordination an ongoing bargain as issues evolve and governmental leaders and nations change. Foreign relations are certainly made smoother by the existence of cross-national voluntary associations like the United Nations, the Organization of American States, and the African Union. However, these associations do not have strict enforcement authority over specific nations, unless a group of member nations takes action in some manner (which is ultimately voluntary).

The European Union is the single supranational entity with some real and significant authority over its member nations. Adoption of its common currency, the euro, brings with it concessions from countries on a variety of matters, and the EU's economic and environmental regulations are the strictest in the world. Yet even the EU has enforcement issues, as evidenced by the battle within its ranks to force member Greece to reduce its national debt or the recurring problem of Spain overfishing in the North Atlantic Ocean. The withdrawal of the United Kingdom from the European Union (commonly referred to as Brexit, short for British exit) also points to the struggles that supra-national institutions like the EU can face.

International relations take place in a relatively open venue in which it is seldom clear how to achieve collective action among countries generally or between the United States and specific other nations in particular. When does it make sense to sign a multinational pact and when doesn't it? Is a particular bilateral economic agreement truly as beneficial to the United States as to the other party, or are we giving away too much in the deal? These are open and complicated questions, which the various schools of thought discussed later in the chapter will help us answer.

A second challenge for the United States is the widely differing views among countries about the role of government in people's lives. The government of hardline communist North Korea regulates everything in its people's lives every day. At the other end of the spectrum are countries with little government activity at all, such as parts of the island of New Guinea. In between is a vast array of diverse approaches to governance. Countries like Sweden provide cradle-to-grave human services programs like health care and education that in some parts of India are minimal at best. In Egypt, the nonprofit sector provides many services rather than the government. The United States relishes its tradition of freedom and the principle of limited government, but practice and reality can be somewhat different. In the end, it falls somewhere in the middle of this continuum because of its focus on law and order, educational and training services, and old-age pensions and health care in the form of Social Security and Medicare.

The challenge of pinpointing the appropriate role of government may sound more like a domestic than a foreign policy matter, and to some degree it is an internal choice about the way government interacts with the people. Yet the internal (or domestic) relationship between a government and its people can often become intertwined with foreign policy. For example, the narrow stance on personal liberty that Iran has taken in recent decades led other countries to impose economic sanctions that crippled the country internally. Some of these sanctions have eased in light of the new nuclear deal with Iran. So the domestic and foreign policy realms are intertwined in terms of what we view as national priorities—whether they consist of nation building abroad or infrastructure building here at home, for example. This latter choice is often described as the "guns versus butter" debate.

A third, and related, unique challenge for the United States in the foreign policy realm is other countries' varying ideas about the appropriate form of government. These forms range from democracies on one side to various authoritarian (or nondemocratic) forms of government on the other. Relations between the United States and democratic states tend to operate more smoothly, proceeding from the shared core assumption that government's authority comes from the people. Monarchies and other nondemocratic forms of government do not share this assumption, which can complicate foreign policy discussions immensely. People in the United States often assume that people who live in a nondemocratic country would prefer to live in a democratic one. However, in some regions of the world, such as the Middle East, this does not seem to be the case—people often prefer having stability within a nondemocratic system over changing to a less predictable democratic form of government. Or they may believe in a theocratic form of government. And the United States does have formal relations with some more totalitarian and monarchical governments, such as Saudi Arabia, when it is in U.S. interests to do so.

A fourth challenge is that many new foreign policy issues transcend borders. That is, there are no longer simply friendly states and enemy states. Problems around the world that might affect the United States, such as terrorism, the international slave trade, and climate change, originate with groups and issues that are not country-specific. They are transnational. So, for example, while we can readily name the enemies of the Allied forces in World War II (Germany, Italy, and Japan), the U.S. war against terrorism has been aimed at terrorist groups that do not fit neatly within the borders of any one country with which the United States could quickly interact to solve the problem. Intelligence-gathering and focused military intervention are needed more than traditional diplomatic relations, and relations can become complicated when the United States wants to pursue terrorists within other countries' borders. An ongoing example is the use of U.S. drone strikes on terrorist targets within the nation of Pakistan, in addition to the 2011 campaign that resulted in the death of Osama bin Laden, the founder of al-Qaeda (Figure 17.6).

Figure 17.6 President Barack Obama (second from left) with Vice President Joe Biden (far left), Secretary of State Hillary Clinton (second from right), Secretary of Defense Robert Gates (far right), and other national security advisers in the Situation Room of the White House, watching the successful raid on Osama bin Laden's compound on May 1, 2011.

The fifth and final unique challenge is the varying conditions of the countries in the world and their effect on what is possible in terms of foreign policy and diplomatic relations. Relations between the United States and a stable industrial democracy are going to be easier than between the United States and an unstable developing country being run by a military junta (a group that has taken control of the government by force). Moreover, an unstable country will be more focused on establishing internal stability than on broader world concerns like environmental policy. In fact, developing countries are temporarily exempt from the requirements of certain treaties while they seek to develop stable industrial and governmental frameworks.

Link to Learning

The **Council on Foreign Relations (https://openstax.org/l/29ConclFrgRel)** is one of the nation's oldest organizations that exist to promote thoughtful discussion on U.S. foreign policy.

17.2 Foreign Policy Instruments

Learning Objectives

By the end of this section, you will be able to:
- Describe the outputs of broadly focused U.S. foreign policy
- Describe the outputs of sharply focused U.S. foreign policy
- Analyze the role of Congress in foreign policy

The decisions or outputs of U.S. foreign policy vary from presidential directives about conducting drone strikes to the size of the overall foreign relations budget passed by Congress, and from presidential summits with other heads of state to U.S. views of new policies considered in the UN Security Council. In this section, we consider the outputs of foreign policy produced by the U.S. government, beginning with broadly focused decisions and then discussing more sharply focused strategies. Drawing this distinction brings some clarity to the array of different policy outcomes in foreign policy. Broadly focused decisions typically take longer to formalize, bring in more actors in the United States and abroad, require more resources to carry out, are harder to reverse, and hence tend to have a lasting impact. Sharply focused outputs tend to be processed quickly, are often unilateral moves by the president, have a shorter time horizon, are easier for subsequent decision-makers to reverse, and hence do not usually have so lasting an impact as broadly focused foreign policy outputs.

BROADLY FOCUSED FOREIGN POLICY OUTPUTS

Broadly focused foreign policy outputs not only span multiple topics and organizations, but they also typically require large-scale spending and take longer to implement than sharply focused outputs. In the realm of broadly focused outputs, we will consider public laws, the periodic reauthorization of the foreign policy agencies, the foreign policy budget, international agreements, and the appointment process for new executive officials and ambassadors.

Public Laws

When we talk about new laws enacted by Congress and the president, we are referring to public laws. *Public laws*, sometimes called statutes, are policies that affect more than a single individual. All policies enacted by Congress and the president are public laws, except for a few dozen each year. They differ from *private laws*, which require some sort of action or payment by a specific individual or individuals named in the law.

Many statutes affect what the government can do in the foreign policy realm, including the National Security Act, the Patriot Act, the Homeland Security Act, and the War Powers Resolution. The National Security Act governs the way the government shares and stores information, while the Patriot Act (passed immediately after 9/11) clarifies what the government may do in collecting information about people in the name of protecting the country. The Homeland Security Act of 2002 authorized the creation of a massive new federal agency, the Department of Homeland Security, consolidating powers that had been under the jurisdiction of several different agencies. Their earlier lack of coordination may have prevented the United States from recognizing warning signs of the 9/11 terrorist attacks.

The War Powers Resolution was passed in 1973 by a congressional override of President Richard Nixon's veto. The bill was Congress's attempt to reassert itself in war-making. Congress has the power to declare war, but it had not formally done so since Japan's 1941 attack on Pearl Harbor brought the United States into World War II. Yet the United States had entered several wars since that time, including in Korea, in Vietnam, and in focused military campaigns such as the failed 1961 Bay of Pigs invasion of Cuba. The War Powers Resolution created a new series of steps to be followed by presidents in waging military conflict with other countries.

Its main feature was a requirement that presidents get approval from Congress to continue any military campaign beyond sixty days. To many, however, the overall effect was actually to strengthen the role of the president in war-making. After all, the law clarified that presidents could act on their own for sixty days before getting authorization from Congress to continue, and many smaller-scale conflicts are over within sixty days. Before the War Powers Resolution, the first approval for war was supposed to come from Congress. In theory, Congress, with its constitutional war powers, could act to reverse the actions of a president once the sixty days have passed. However, a clear disagreement between Congress and the president, especially once an initiative has begun and there is a "rally around the flag" effect, is relatively rare. More likely are tough questions about the campaign to which continuing congressional funding is tied.

Reauthorization

All federal agencies, including those dedicated to foreign policy, face reauthorization every three to five years. If not reauthorized, agencies lose their legal standing and the ability to spend federal funds to carry out programs. Agencies typically are reauthorized, because they coordinate carefully with presidential and congressional staff to get their affairs in order when the time comes. However, the reauthorization requirements do create a regular conversation between the agency and its political principals about how well it is functioning and what could be improved.

The federal budget process is an important annual tradition that affects all areas of foreign policy. The foreign policy and defense budgets are part of the discretionary budget, or the section of the national budget that Congress vets and decides on each year. Foreign policy leaders in the executive and legislative branches must advocate for funding from this budget, and while foreign policy budgets are usually renewed, there are enough proposed changes each year to make things interesting. In addition to new agencies, new cross-national projects are proposed each year to add to infrastructure and increase or improve foreign aid, intelligence, and national security technology.

Agreements

International agreements represent another of the broad-based foreign policy instruments. The United States finds it useful to enter into international agreements with other countries for a variety of reasons and on a variety of different subjects. These agreements run the gamut from bilateral agreements about tariffs to multinational agreements among dozens of countries about the treatment of prisoners of war. One recent multinational pact was the seven-country Iran Nuclear Agreement in 2015, intended to limit nuclear development in Iran in exchange for the lifting of long-standing economic sanctions on that country (Figure 17.7).

Figure 17.7 The ministers of foreign affairs and other officials from China, France, Germany, the European Union, Iran, Russia, and the United Kingdom join Secretary of State John Kerry (far right) in April 2015 to announce the framework that would lead to the multinational Iran Nuclear Agreement. (credit: modification of work by the U.S. Department of State)

The format that an international agreement takes has been the point of considerable discussion in recent years. The U.S. Constitution outlines the **treaty** process in Article II. The president negotiates a treaty, the Senate consents to the treaty by a two-thirds vote, and finally the president ratifies it. Despite that constitutional clarity, today over 90 percent of the international agreements into which the United States enters are not treaties but rather executive agreements.[7] Executive agreements are negotiated by the president, and in the case of **sole executive agreements**, they are simultaneously approved by the president as well. On the other hand, **congressional-executive agreements**, like the North American Free Trade Agreement (NAFTA), are negotiated by the president and then approved by a simple majority of the House and Senate (rather than a two-thirds vote in the Senate as is the case for a treaty). In the key case of *United States v. Pink* (1942), the Supreme Court ruled that executive agreements were legally equivalent to treaties provided they did not alter federal law.[8] Most executive agreements are not of major importance and do not spark controversy, while some, like the Iran Nuclear Agreement, generate considerable debate. Many in the Senate thought the Iran deal should have been completed as a treaty rather than as a sole executive agreement.

Finding a Middle Ground

Treaty or Executive Agreement?

Should new international agreements into which the United States enters be forged through the Article II treaty process of the U.S. Constitution, or through executive agreements? This question arose again in 2015 as the Iran Nuclear Agreement was being completed. That pact required Iran to halt further nuclear development and agree to nuclear inspections, while the United States and five other signatories lifted long-standing economic sanctions on Iran. The debate over whether the United States should have entered the agreement and whether it should have been a treaty rather than an executive agreement was conducted in the news media and on political comedy shows like *The Daily Show*.

Your view on the form of the pact will depend on how you see executive agreements being employed. Do presidents use them to circumvent the Senate (as the "evasion hypothesis" suggests)? Or are they an efficient tool that saves the Senate Committee on Foreign Relations the work of processing hundreds of agreements each year?

Politicians' opinions about the form of the Iran Nuclear Agreement fell along party lines. Democrats accepted the president's decision to use an executive agreement to finalize the pact, which they tended to support. Republicans, who were overwhelmingly against the pact, favored the use of the treaty process, which would have allowed them to vote the deal down. In the end, the president used an executive agreement and the pact was enacted. The downside is that an executive agreement can be reversed by the next president. Treaties are much more difficult to undo because they require a new process to be undertaken in the Senate in order for the president to gain approval.

Which approach do you favor for the Iran Nuclear Agreement, an executive agreement or a treaty? Why?

Link to Learning

Watch **"Under Miner" (https://openstax.org/l/29UnderMin)** and **"Start Wars" (https://openstax.org/l/29StartWars)** to see the take of Jon Stewart and *The Daily Show* on the Iran Nuclear Agreement.

Appointments

The last broad type of foreign policy output consists of the foreign policy appointments made when a new president takes office. Typically, when the party in the White House changes, more new appointments are made than when the party does not change, because the incoming president wants to put in place people who share his or her agenda. This was the case in 2001 when Republican George W. Bush succeeded Democrat Bill Clinton, and again in 2009 when Democrat Barack Obama succeeded Bush.

Most foreign policy–related appointments, such as secretary of state and the various undersecretaries and assistant secretaries, as well as all ambassadors, must be confirmed by a majority vote of the Senate (Figure 17.8). Presidents seek to nominate people who know the area to which they're being appointed and who will be loyal to the president rather than to the bureaucracy in which they might work. They also want their nominees to be readily confirmed. As we will see in more detail later in the chapter, an isolationist group of appointees will run the country's foreign policy agencies very differently than a group that is more internationalist in its outlook. Isolationists might seek to pull back from foreign policy involvement around the globe, while internationalists would go in the other direction, toward more involvement and toward acting in conjunction with other countries.

(a)   (b)   (c)

Figure 17.8   Madeleine Albright (a), the first female secretary of state, was nominated by President Bill Clinton and unanimously confirmed by the Senate 99–0. Colin Powell (b), nominated by George W. Bush, was also unanimously confirmed. Condoleezza Rice (c) had a more difficult road, earning thirteen votes against, at the time the most for any secretary of state nominee since Henry Clay in 1825. According to Senator Barbara Boxer (D-CA), senators wanted "to hold Dr. Rice and the Bush administration accountable for their failures in Iraq and in the war on terrorism." The confirmation of Rex Tillerson, CEO of ExxonMobil, in February 2017, received the most opposition of any secretary of state, with forty-three votes against. His successor, Mike Pompeo, was confirmed 57–42 in April 2018.

SHARPLY FOCUSED FOREIGN POLICY OUTPUTS

In addition to the broad-based foreign policy outputs above, which are president-led with some involvement from Congress, many other decisions need to be made. These sharply focused foreign policy outputs tend to be exclusively the province of the president, including the deployment of troops and/or intelligence agents in a crisis, executive summits between the president and other heads of state on targeted matters of foreign policy, presidential use of military force, and emergency funding measures to deal with foreign policy crises. These measures of foreign policy are more quickly enacted and demonstrate the "energy and dispatch" that Alexander Hamilton, writing in the *Federalist Papers*, saw as inherent in the institution of the presidency. Emergency spending does involve Congress through its power of the purse, but Congress tends to give presidents what they need to deal with emergencies. That said, the framers were consistent in wanting checks and balances sprinkled throughout the Constitution, including in the area of foreign policy and war powers. Hence, Congress has several roles, as discussed at points throughout this chapter.

Perhaps the most famous foreign policy emergency was the Cuban Missile Crisis in 1962. With the Soviet Union placing nuclear missiles in Cuba, just a few hundred miles from Florida, a Cold War standoff with the United States escalated. The Soviets at first denied the existence of the missiles, but U.S. reconnaissance flights proved they were there, gathering photographic evidence that was presented at the UN (Figure 17.9). The Soviets stood firm, and U.S. foreign policy leaders debated their approach. Some in the military were pushing for aggressive action to take out the missiles and the installation in Cuba, while State Department officials favored a diplomatic route. President John F. Kennedy ended up taking the recommendation of a special committee, and the United States implemented a naval blockade of Cuba that subtly forced the Soviets' hands. The Soviets agreed to remove their Cuban missiles and the United States in turn agreed six months later to remove its missiles from Turkey.

(a)   (b)

Figure 17.9 This low-level U.S. Navy photograph of San Cristobal, Cuba, clearly shows one of the sites built to launch intermediate-range missiles at the United States (a). As the date indicates, it was taken on the last day of the Cuban Missile Crisis. Following the crisis, President Kennedy (far right) met with the reconnaissance pilots who flew the Cuban missions (b). (credit a: modification of work by the National Archives and Record Administration)

Link to Learning

Listen to President Kennedy's speech (https://openstax.org/l/29KennSpch) announcing the naval blockade the United States imposed on Cuba, ending the Cuban Missile Crisis of 1962.

Another form of focused foreign policy output is the presidential summit. Often held at the Presidential Retreat at Camp David, Maryland, these meetings bring together the president and one or more other heads of state. Presidents use these types of summits when they and their visitors need to dive deeply into important issues that are not quickly solved. An example is the 1978 summit that led to the Camp David Accords, in which President Jimmy Carter, Egyptian president Anwar El Sadat, and Israeli prime minister Menachem Begin met privately for twelve days at Camp David negotiating a peace process for the two countries, which had been at odds with each other in the Middle East. Another example is the Malta Summit between President George H. W. Bush and Soviet leader Mikhail Gorbachev, which took place on the island of Malta over two days in December 1989 (Figure 17.10). The meetings were an important symbol of the end of the Cold War, the Berlin Wall having come down just a few months earlier.

(a)   (b)

Figure 17.10 President Jimmy Carter meets with Egypt's Anwar El Sadat (left) and Israel's Menachem Begin (right) at Camp David in 1978 (a). President George H. W. Bush (right) dines with Mikhail Gorbachev (left) at the Malta Summit in 1989 (b). (credit b: modification of work by the National Archives and Records Administration)

Another focused foreign policy output is the military use of force. Since the 1941 Pearl Harbor attacks and the immediate declaration of war by Congress that resulted, all such initial uses of force have been authorized by the president. Congress in many cases has subsequently supported additional military action, but the president has been the instigator. While there has sometimes been criticism, Congress has never acted to reverse presidential action. As discussed above, the War Powers Resolution clarified that the first step in the use of force was the president's, for the first sixty days. A recent example of the military use of force was the U.S. role in enforcing a no-fly zone over Libya in 2011, which included kinetic strikes—or active engagement of the enemy—to protect anti-government forces on the ground. U.S. fighter jets flew out of Aviano Air Base in northern Italy (Figure 17.11).

Figure 17.11 One example of a sharply focused foreign policy output is the use of the U.S. military abroad. Here, the Air Force fighter jets used to enforce a 2011 no-fly zone over Libya return to a NATO air base in northeastern Italy. (credit: Tierney P. Wilson)

The final example of a focused foreign policy input is the passage of an emergency funding measure for a specific national security task. Congress tends to pass at least one emergency spending measure per year, which must be signed by the president to take effect, and it often provides funding for domestic disasters. However, at times foreign policy matters drive an emergency spending measure, as was the case right after the 9/11 attacks. In such a case, the president or the administration proposes particular amounts for emergency foreign policy plans.

17.3 Institutional Relations in Foreign Policy

Learning Objectives

By the end of this section, you will be able to:
- Describe the use of shared power in U.S. foreign policymaking
- Explain why presidents lead more in foreign policy than in domestic policy
- Discuss why individual House and Senate members rarely venture into foreign policy
- List the actors who engage in foreign policy

Institutional relationships in foreign policy constitute a paradox. On the one hand, there are aspects of foreign policymaking that necessarily engage multiple branches of government and a multiplicity of actors. Indeed, there is a complexity to foreign policy that is bewildering, in terms of both substance and process. On the other hand, foreign policymaking can sometimes call for nothing more than for the president to make a formal decision, quickly endorsed by the legislative branch. This section will explore the institutional relationships present in U.S. foreign policymaking.

FOREIGN POLICY AND SHARED POWER

While presidents are more empowered by the Constitution in foreign than in domestic policy, they nonetheless must seek approval from Congress on a variety of matters; chief among these is the basic budgetary authority needed to run foreign policy programs. Indeed, most if not all of the foreign policy instruments described earlier in this chapter require interbranch approval to go into effect. Such approval may sometimes be a formality, but it is still important. Even a sole executive agreement often requires subsequent funding from Congress in order to be carried out, and funding calls for majority support from the House and Senate. Presidents lead, to be sure, but they must consult with and engage the Congress on many matters of foreign policy. Presidents must also delegate a great deal in foreign policy to the bureaucratic experts in the foreign policy agencies. Not every operation can be run from the West Wing of the White House.

At bottom, the United States is a separation-of-powers political system with authority divided among executive and legislative branches, including in the foreign policy realm. Table 17.1 shows the formal roles of the president and Congress in conducting foreign policy.

Roles of the President and Congress in Conducting Foreign Policy

Policy Output	Presidential Role	Congressional Role
Public laws	Proposes, signs into law	Proposes, approves for passage
Agency reauthorizations	Proposes, signs into law	Approves for passage
Foreign policy budget	Proposes, signs into law	Authorizes/appropriates for passage
Treaties	Negotiates, ratifies	Senate consents to treaty (two-thirds)
Sole executive agreements	Negotiates, approves	None (unless funding is required)
Congressional-executive agreements	Negotiates	Approves by majority vote
Declaration of war	Proposes	Approves by majority vote
Military use of force	Carries out operations at will (sixty days)	Approves for operations beyond sixty days

Table 17.1

Roles of the President and Congress in Conducting Foreign Policy

Policy Output	Presidential Role	Congressional Role
Presidential appointments	Nominates candidates	Senate approves by majority vote

Table 17.1

The main lesson of Table 17.1 is that nearly all major outputs of foreign policy require a formal congressional role in order to be carried out. Foreign policy might be done by executive say-so in times of crisis and in the handful of sole executive agreements that actually pertain to major issues (like the Iran Nuclear Agreement). In general, however, a consultative relationship between the branches in foreign policy is the usual result of their constitutional sharing of power. A president who ignores Congress on matters of foreign policy and does not keep them briefed may find later interactions on other matters more difficult. Probably the most extreme version of this potential dynamic occurred during the Eisenhower presidency. When President Dwight D. Eisenhower used too many executive agreements instead of sending key ones to the Senate as treaties, Congress reacted by considering a constitutional amendment (the Bricker Amendment) that would have altered the treaty process as we know it. Eisenhower understood the message and began to send more agreements through the process as treaties.[9]

Shared power creates an incentive for the branches to cooperate. Even in the midst of a crisis, such as the Cuban Missile Crisis in 1962, it is common for the president or senior staff to brief congressional leaders in order to keep them up to speed and ensure the country can stand unified on international matters. That said, there are areas of foreign policy where the president has more discretion, such as the operation of intelligence programs, the holding of foreign policy summits, and the mobilization of troops or agents in times of crisis. Moreover, presidents have more power and influence in foreign policymaking than they do in domestic policymaking. It is to that power that we now turn.

THE TWO PRESIDENCIES THESIS

When the media cover a domestic controversy, such as social unrest or police brutality, reporters consult officials at different levels and in branches of government, as well as think tanks and advocacy groups. In contrast, when an international event occurs, such as a terrorist bombing in Paris or Brussels, the media flock predominately to one actor—the president of the United States—to get the official U.S. position.

In the realm of foreign policy and international relations, the president occupies a leadership spot that is much clearer than in the realm of domestic policy. This dual domestic and international role has been described by the **two presidencies thesis**. This theory originated with University of California–Berkeley professor Aaron Wildavsky and suggests that there are two distinct presidencies, one for foreign policy and one for domestic policy, and that presidents are more successful in foreign than domestic policy. Let's look at the reasoning behind this thesis.

The Constitution names the president as the commander-in-chief of the military, the nominating authority for executive officials and ambassadors, and the initial negotiator of foreign agreements and treaties. The president is the agenda-setter for foreign policy and may move unilaterally in some instances. Beyond the Constitution, presidents were also gradually given more authority to enter into international agreements without Senate consent by using the executive agreement. We saw above that the passage of the War Powers Resolution in 1973, though intended as a statute to rein in executive power and reassert Congress as a check on the president, effectively gave presidents two months to wage war however they wish. Given all these powers, we have good reason to expect presidents to have more influence and be more successful in foreign than in domestic policy.

A second reason for the stronger foreign policy presidency has to do with the informal aspects of power.

In some eras, Congress will be more willing to allow the president to be a clear leader and speak for the country. For instance, the Cold War between the Eastern bloc countries (led by the Soviet Union) and the West (led by the United States and Western European allies) prompted many to want a single actor to speak for the United States. A willing Congress allowed the president to take the lead because of urgent circumstances (Figure 17.12). Much of the Cold War also took place when the parties in Congress included more moderates on both sides of the aisle and the environment was less partisan than today. A phrase often heard at that time was, "Partisanship stops at the water's edge." This means that foreign policy matters should not be subject to the bitter disagreements seen in party politics.

(a)

(b)

Figure 17.12 President John F. Kennedy gives a speech about freedom in the shadow of the Berlin Wall (a). The wall was erected in 1963 by East Germany to keep its citizens from defecting to West Berlin. On September 14, 2001, President George W. Bush promises justice at the site of the destroyed World Trade Center in New York City (b). Rescue workers responded by chanting "U.S.A., U.S.A.!" (credit a: modification of work by the John F. Kennedy Library)

Does the thesis's expectation of a more successful foreign policy presidency apply today? While the president still has stronger foreign policy powers than domestic powers, the governing context has changed in two key ways. First, the Cold War ended in 1989 with the demolition of the Berlin Wall, the subsequent disintegration of the Soviet Union, and the eventual opening up of Eastern European territories to independence and democracy. These dramatic changes removed the competitive superpower aspect of the Cold War, in which the United States and the USSR were dueling rivals on the world stage. The absence of the Cold War has led to less of a rally-behind-the-president effect in the area of foreign policy.

Second, beginning in the 1980s and escalating in the 1990s, the Democratic and Republican parties began to become polarized in Congress. The moderate members in each party all but disappeared, while more ideologically motivated candidates began to win election to the House and later the Senate. Hence, the Democrats in Congress became more liberal on average, the Republicans became more conservative, and the moderates from each party, who had been able to work together, were edged out. It became increasingly likely that the party opposite the president in Congress might be more willing to challenge his initiatives, whereas in the past it was rare for the opposition party to publicly stand against the president in foreign policy.

Finally, several analysts have tried applying the two presidencies thesis to contemporary presidential-congressional relationships in foreign policy. Is the two presidencies framework still valid in the more partisan post–Cold War era? The answer is mixed. On the one hand, presidents are more successful on foreign policy votes in the House and Senate, on average, than on domestic policy votes. However, the gap has narrowed. Moreover, analysis has also shown that presidents are opposed more often in Congress, even on the foreign policy votes they win.[10] Democratic leaders regularly challenged Republican George W. Bush on the Iraq War and it became common to see the most senior foreign relations committee members of the Republican Party opposing the foreign policy positions of Democratic president Barack Obama. Such challenging of the president by the opposition party simply didn't happen during the Cold

War.

In the current Trump administration, there has been a distinct shift in foreign policy style. While for some regions, like South America, Trump has been content to let the foreign policy bureaucracies proceed as they always have, in certain areas, the president has become quite pivotal in changing the direction of American foreign policy. For example, he stepped away from two key international agreements—the Iran-Nuclear Deal and the Paris climate change accords. Moreover, his actions in Syria have been quite unilateral, employing bombing raids unilaterally on two occasions. This approach reflects more of a neoconservative foreign policy approach, similar to Obama's widespread use of drone strikes.

Therefore, it seems presidents no longer enjoy unanimous foreign policy support as they did in the early 1960s. They have to work harder to get a consensus and are more likely to face opposition. Still, because of their formal powers in foreign policy, presidents are overall more successful on foreign policy than on domestic policy.

THE PERSPECTIVE OF HOUSE AND SENATE MEMBERS

Congress is a bicameral legislative institution with 100 senators serving in the Senate and 435 representatives serving in the House. How interested in foreign policy are typical House and Senate members?

While key White House, executive, and legislative leaders monitor and regularly weigh in on foreign policy matters, the fact is that individual representatives and senators do so much less often. Unless there is a foreign policy crisis, legislators in Congress tend to focus on domestic matters, mainly because there is not much to be gained with their constituents by pursuing foreign policy matters.[11] Domestic policy matters resonate more strongly with the voters at home. A sluggish economy, increasing health care costs, and crime matter more to them than U.S. policy toward North Korea, for example. In an open-ended Gallup poll question from early 2016 about the "most important problem" in the United States, fewer than 15 percent of respondents named a foreign policy topic (half of those respondents mentioned immigration). These results suggest that foreign policy is not at the top of many voters' minds. In the end, legislators must be responsive to constituents in order to be good representatives and to achieve reelection.[12]

However, some House and Senate members do wade into foreign policy matters. First, congressional party leaders in the majority and minority parties speak on behalf of their institution and their party on all types of issues, including foreign policy. Some House and Senate members ask to serve on the foreign policy committees, such as the Senate Committee on Foreign Relations, the House Foreign Affairs Committee, and the two defense committees (Figure 17.13). These members might have military bases within their districts or states and hence have a constituency reason for being interested in foreign policy. Legislators might also simply have a personal interest in foreign policy matters that drives their engagement in the issue. Finally, they may have ambitions to move into an executive branch position that deals with foreign policy matters, such as secretary of state or defense, CIA director, or even president.

(a)   (b)

Figure 17.13   Senator Cory Booker (D-NJ) (a) serves on the Senate Committee on Foreign Relations, along with Senator Jim Risch (R-ID) (b), who chairs the committee.

Get Connected!

Let People Know What You Think!

Most House and Senate members do not engage in foreign policy because there is no electoral benefit to doing so. Thus, when citizens become involved, House members and senators will take notice. Research by John Kingdon on roll-call voting and by Richard Hall on committee participation found that when constituents are activated, their interest becomes salient to a legislator and he or she will respond.[13]

One way you can become active in the foreign policy realm is by writing a letter or e-mail to your House member and/or your two U.S. senators about what you believe the U.S. foreign policy approach in a particular area ought to be. Perhaps you want the United States to work with other countries to protect dolphins from being accidentally trapped in tuna nets. You can also state your position in a letter to the editor of your local newspaper, or post an opinion on the newspaper's website where a related article or op-ed piece appears. You can share links to news coverage on Facebook or Twitter and consider joining a foreign policy interest group such as Greenpeace.

When you engaged in foreign policy discussion as suggested above, what type of response did you receive?

Link to Learning

For more information on the two key congressional committees on U.S. foreign policy, visit the Senate Committee on Foreign Relations (https://openstax.org/l/29SeCoFrRel) and the House Foreign Affairs Committee (https://openstax.org/l/29HoForAfCom) websites.

THE MANY ACTORS IN FOREIGN POLICY

A variety of actors carry out the various and complex activities of U.S. foreign policy: White House staff, executive branch staff, and congressional leaders.

The White House staff members engaged in foreign policy are likely to have very regular contact with the president about their work. The national security advisor heads the president's National Security Council, a group of senior-level staff from multiple foreign policy agencies, and is generally the president's top foreign policy advisor. Also reporting to the president in the White House is the director of the Central Intelligence Agency (CIA). Even more important on intelligence than the CIA director is the director of national intelligence, a position created in the government reorganizations after 9/11, who oversees the entire intelligence community in the U.S. government. The Joint Chiefs of Staff consist of six members, one each from the Army, Navy, Air Force, and Marines, plus a chair and vice chair. The chair of the Joint Chiefs of Staff is the president's top uniformed military officer. In contrast, the secretary of defense is head of the entire Department of Defense but is a nonmilitary civilian. The U.S. trade representative develops and directs the country's international trade agenda. Finally, within the Executive Office of the President, another important foreign policy official is the director of the president's Office of Management and Budget (OMB). The OMB director develops the president's yearly budget proposal, including funding for the foreign policy agencies and foreign aid.

In addition to those who work directly in the White House or Executive Office of the President, several important officials work in the broader executive branch and report to the president in the area of foreign policy. Chief among these is the secretary of state. The secretary of state is the nation's chief diplomat, serves in the president's cabinet, and oversees the Foreign Service. The secretary of defense, who is the civilian (nonmilitary) head of the armed services housed in the Department of Defense, is also a key cabinet member for foreign policy (as mentioned above). A third cabinet secretary, the secretary of homeland security, is critically important in foreign policy, overseeing the massive Department of Homeland Security (Figure 17.14).

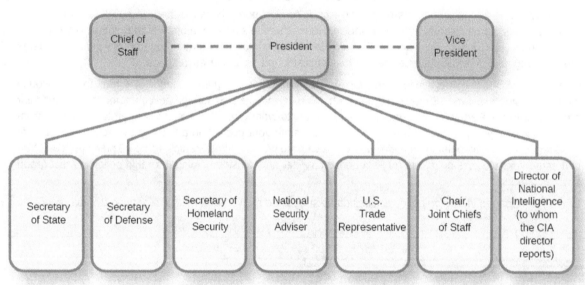

Multiple Foreign Policy Directors

Figure 17.14

Former Secretary of Defense Robert Gates

Former secretary of defense Robert Gates served under both Republican and Democratic presidents. First Gates rose through the ranks of the CIA to become the director during the George H. W. Bush administration. He then left government to serve as an academic administrator at Texas A&M University in College Station, Texas, where he rose to the position of university president. He was able to win over reluctant faculty and advance the university's position, including increasing the faculty at a time when budgets were in decline in Texas. Then, when Secretary of Defense Donald Rumsfeld resigned, President George W. Bush invited Gates to return to government service as Rumsfeld's replacement. Gates agreed, serving in that capacity for the remainder of the Bush years and then for several years in the Obama administration before retiring from government service a second time (Figure 17.15). He has generally been seen as thorough, systematic, and fair.

Figure 17.15   In March 2011, then-secretary of defense Robert Gates (left) held talks with Afghan president Hamid Karzai in Kabul, Afghanistan. (credit: Cherie Cullen)

In his memoir, *Duty: Memoirs of a Secretary at War*,[14] Secretary Gates takes issue with the actions of both the presidents for whom he worked, but ultimately he praises them for their service and for upholding the right principles in protecting the United States and U.S. military troops. In this and earlier books, Gates discusses the need to have an overarching plan but says plans cannot be too tight or they will fail when things change in the external environment. After leaving politics, Gates served as president of the Boy Scouts of America, where he presided over the change in policy that allowed openly gay scouts and leaders, an issue with which he had had experience as secretary of defense under President Obama. In that role Gates oversaw the end of the military's "Don't ask, don't tell" policy.[15]

What do you think about a cabinet secretary serving presidents from two different political parties? Is this is a good idea? Why or why not?

The final group of official key actors in foreign policy are in the U.S. Congress. The Speaker of the House, the House minority leader, and the Senate majority and minority leaders are often given updates on foreign policy matters by the president or the president's staff. They are also consulted when the president needs foreign policy support or funding. However, the experts in Congress who are most often called on for their views are the committee chairs and the highest-ranking minority members of the relevant House and Senate committees. In the House, that means the Foreign Affairs Committee and the Committee on Armed Services. In the Senate, the relevant committees are the Committee on Foreign Relations and the Armed Services Committee. These committees hold regular hearings on key foreign policy topics, consider budget authorizations, and debate the future of U.S. foreign policy.

17.4 Approaches to Foreign Policy

Learning Objectives

By the end of this section, you will be able to:

- Explain classic schools of thought on U.S. foreign policy
- Describe contemporary schools of thought on U.S. foreign policy
- Delineate the U.S. foreign policy approach with Russia and China

Frameworks and theories help us make sense of the environment of governance in a complex area like foreign policy. A variety of schools of thought exist about how to approach foreign policy, each with different ideas about what "should" be done. These approaches also vary in terms of what they assume about human nature, how many other countries ought to be involved in U.S. foreign policy, and what the tenor of foreign policymaking ought to be. They help us situate the current U.S. approach to many foreign policy challenges around the world.

CLASSIC APPROACHES

A variety of traditional concepts of foreign policy remain helpful today as we consider the proper role of the United States in, and its approach to, foreign affairs. These include isolationism, the idealism versus realism debate, liberal internationalism, hard versus soft power, and the grand strategy of U.S. foreign policy.

From the end of the Revolutionary War in the late eighteenth century until the early twentieth century, **isolationism**—whereby a country stays out of foreign entanglements and keeps to itself—was a popular stance in U.S. foreign policy. Among the founders, Thomas Jefferson especially was an advocate of isolationism or non-involvement. He thought that by keeping to itself, the United States stood a better chance of becoming a truly free nation. This fact is full of irony, because Jefferson later served as ambassador to France and president of the United States, both roles that required at least some attention to foreign policy. Still, Jefferson's ideas had broad support. After all, Europe was where volatile changes were occurring. The new nation was tired of war, and there was no reason for it to be entangled militarily with anyone. Indeed, in his farewell address, President George Washington famously warned against the creation of "entangling alliances."[16]

Despite this legacy, the United States was pulled squarely into world affairs with its entry into World War I. But between the Armistice in 1918 that ended that war and U.S. entry into World War II in 1941, isolationist sentiment returned, based on the idea that Europe should learn to govern its own affairs. Then, after World War II, the United States engaged the world stage as one of two superpowers and the military leader of Europe and the Pacific. Isolationism never completely went away, but now it operated in the background. Again, Europe seemed to be the center of the problem, while political life in the United States seemed calmer somehow.

The end of the Cold War opened up old wounds as a variety of smaller European countries sought independence and old ethnic conflicts reappeared. Some in the United States felt the country should again be isolationist as the world settled into a new political arrangement, including a vocal senator, Jesse Helms (R-NC), who was against the United States continuing to be the military "policeman" of the world. Helms was famous for opposing nearly all treaties brought to the Senate during his tenure. Congressman Ron Paul (R-TX) and his son Senator Rand Paul (R-KY) were both isolationist candidates for the presidency (in 2008 and 2016, respectively); both thought the United States should retreat from foreign entanglements, spend far less on military and foreign policy, and focus more on domestic issues.

At the other end of the spectrum is **liberal internationalism**. Liberal internationalism advocates a foreign policy approach in which the United States becomes proactively engaged in world affairs. Its adherents assume that liberal democracies must take the lead in creating a peaceful world by cooperating as a community of nations and creating effective world structures such as the United Nations. To fully understand liberal internationalism, it is helpful to understand the idealist versus realist debate in international relations. Idealists assume the best in others and see it as possible for countries to run the world together, with open diplomacy, freedom of the seas, free trade, and no militaries. Everyone will take care of each other. There is an element of idealism in liberal internationalism, because the United States assumes other countries will also put their best foot forward. A classic example of a liberal internationalist is President Woodrow Wilson, who sought a League of Nations to voluntarily save the world after World War I.

Realists assume that others will act in their own self-interest and hence cannot necessarily be trusted. They want a healthy military and contracts between countries in case others want to wiggle out of their commitments. Realism also has a place in liberal internationalism, because the United States approaches foreign relationships with open eyes and an emphasis on self-preservation.

Soft power, or diplomacy, with which the United States often begins a foreign policy relationship or entanglement, is in line with liberal internationalism and idealism, while hard power, which allows the potential for military force, is the stuff of realism. For example, at first the United States was rather isolationist in its approach to China, assuming it was a developing country of little impact that could safely be ignored. Then President Nixon opened up China as an area for U.S. investment, and an era of open diplomatic relations began in the early 1970s (Figure 17.16). As China modernized and began to dominate the trade relationship with the United States, many came to see it through a realist lens and to consider whether China's behavior really warranted its beneficial most-favored-nation trading status.

Figure 17.16 President Nixon and First Lady Patricia Nixon visited the Great Wall on their 1972 trip to China. The Chinese showed them the sights and hosted a banquet for them in the Great Hall of the People. Nixon was the first U.S. president to visit China following the Communist victory in the civil war in 1949. (credit: National Archives and Records Administration)

The final classic idea of foreign policy is the so-called grand strategy—employing all available diplomatic, economic, and military resources to advance the national interest. The grand strategy invokes the possibility of hard power, because it relies on developing clear strategic directions for U.S. foreign policy and the methods to achieve those goals, often with military capability attached. The U.S. foreign policy plan in Europe and Asia after World War II reflects a grand strategy approach. In order to stabilize the world, the United States built military bases in Italy, Germany, Spain, England, Belgium, Japan, Guam, and Korea. It still operates nearly all these, though often under a multinational arrangement such as NATO.

These bases help preserve stability on the one hand, and U.S. influence on the other.

MORE RECENT SCHOOLS OF THOUGHTS

Two particular events in foreign policy caused many to change their views about the proper approach to U.S. involvement in world affairs. First, the debacle of U.S. involvement in the civil war in Vietnam in the years leading up to 1973 caused many to rethink the country's traditional **containment** approach to the Cold War. Containment was the U.S. foreign policy goal of limiting the spread of communism. In Vietnam the United States supported one governing faction within the country (democratic South Vietnam), whereas the Soviet Union supported the opposing governing faction (communist North Vietnam). The U.S. military approach of battlefield engagement did not translate well to the jungles of Vietnam, where "guerilla warfare" predominated.

Skeptics became particularly pessimistic about liberal internationalism given how poorly the conflict in Vietnam had played out. U.S. military forces withdrew from South Vietnam in 1973, and Saigon, its capital, fell to North Vietnam and the communists eighteen months later. Many of those pessimists then became neoconservatives on foreign policy.

Neoconservatives believe that rather than exercising restraint and always using international organizations as the path to international outcomes, the United States should aggressively use its might to promote its values and ideals around the world. The aggressive use (or threat) of hard power is the core value of **neoconservatism**. Acting unilaterally is acceptable in this view, as is adopting a preemptive strategy in which the United States intervenes militarily before the enemy can make its move. Preemption is a new idea; the United States has tended to be retaliatory in its use of military force, as in the case of Pearl Harbor at the start of World War II. Examples of neoconservativism in action are the 1980s U.S. campaigns in Central American countries to turn back communism under President Ronald Reagan, the Iraq War of 2003 led by President George W. Bush and his vice president Dick Cheney (Figure 17.17), and the use of drones as counterterrorism weapons during the Obama administration.

Figure 17.17 Heading to a going-away party for departing defense secretary Donald Rumsfeld in December 2006, former president George W. Bush (left) walks with then-vice president (and former secretary of defense) Dick Cheney (center), the prototypical twenty-first century foreign policy neoconservative. Rumsfeld is on the right. (credit: modification of work by D. Myles Cullen)

Neo-isolationism, like earlier isolationism, advocates keeping free of foreign entanglements. Yet no advanced industrial democracy completely separates itself from the rest of the world. Foreign markets beckon, tourism helps spur economic development at home and abroad, and global environmental challenges require cross-national conversation. In the twenty-first century, **neo-isolationism** means distancing the United States from the United Nations and other international organizations that get in the way. The strategy of **selective engagement**—retaining a strong military presence and remaining engaged across the world through alliances and formal installations—is used to protect the national security interests of the United States. However, this strategy also seeks to avoid being the world's policeman.

The second factor that changed minds about twenty-first century foreign policy is the rise of elusive new enemies who defy traditional designations. Rather than countries, these enemies are terrorist groups such as al-Qaeda and ISIS (or ISIL) that spread across national boundaries. A hybrid approach to U.S. foreign policy that uses multiple schools of thought as circumstances warrant may thus be the wave of the future. President Obama often took a hybrid approach. In some respects, he was a liberal internationalist seeking to put together broad coalitions to carry out world business. At the same time, his sending teams of troops and drones to take out terrorist targets in other legitimate nation-states without those states' approval fits with a neoconservative approach. Finally, his desire to not be the "world's policeman" led him to follow a practice of selective engagement.

Link to Learning

Several interest groups debate what should happen in U.S. foreign policy, many of which are included in this list (https://votesmart.org/interest-groups/NA/32#.Wg38ykqnGUk) compiled by project Vote Smart.

U.S. FOREIGN POLICY IN THE COLD WAR AND WITH CHINA

The foreign policy environment from the end of World War II until the end of the Cold War in 1990 was dominated by a duel of superpowers between the United States and its Western allies on the one hand and the Soviet Union and the communist bloc of countries in the East on the other. Both superpowers developed thousands of weapons of mass destruction and readied for a potential world war to be fought with nuclear weapons. That period was certainly challenging and ominous at times, but it was simpler than the present era. Nations knew what team they were on, and there was generally an incentive to not go to war because it would lead to the unthinkable—the end of the Earth as we know it, or mutually assured destruction. The result of this logic, essentially a standoff between the two powers, is sometime referred to as nuclear deterrence.

When the Soviet Union imploded and the Cold War ended, it was in many ways a victory for the West and for democracy. However, once the bilateral nature of the Cold War was gone, dozens of countries sought independence and old ethnic conflicts emerged in several regions of the world, including Eastern Europe. This new era holds great promise, but it is in many ways more complex than the Cold War. The rise of cross-national terrorist organizations further complicates the equation because the enemy hides within the borders of potentially dozens of countries around the globe. In summary, the United States pursues a variety of topics and goals in different areas of the world in the twenty-first century.

The Soviet Union dissolved into many component parts after the Cold War, including Russia, various former Soviet republics like Georgia and Ukraine, and smaller nation-states in Eastern Europe, such as the Czech Republic. The general approach of the United States has been to encourage the adoption of democracy and economic reforms in these former Eastern bloc countries. Many of them now align with the EU and even with the West's cross-national military organization, NATO. With freedoms can come conflict, and there has been much of that in these fledgling countries as opposition coalitions debate how the future course should be charted, and by whom. Under President Vladimir Putin, Russia is again trying to strengthen its power on the country's western border, testing expansionism while invoking Russian nationalism. The United States is adopting a defensive position and trying to prevent the spread of Russian influence. The EU and NATO factor in here from the standpoint of an internationalist approach.

In many ways the more visible future threat to the United States is China, the potential rival superpower of the future. A communist state that has also encouraged much economic development, China has been growing and modernizing for more than thirty years. Its nearly 1.4 billion citizens are stepping onto the world economic stage with other advanced industrial nations. In addition to fueling an explosion of industrial domestic development, public and private Chinese investors have spread their resources to every continent and most countries of the world. Indeed, Chinese investors lend money to the United States government on a regular basis, as U.S. domestic borrowing capacity is pushed to the limit in most years.

Many in the United States are worried by the lack of freedom and human rights in China. During the Tiananmen Square massacre in Beijing on June 4, 1989, thousands of pro-democracy protestors were arrested and many were killed as Chinese authorities fired into the crowd and tanks crushed people who attempted to wall them out. Over one thousand more dissidents were arrested in the following weeks as the Chinese government investigated the planning of the protests in the square. The United States instituted minor sanctions for a time, but President George H. W. Bush chose not to remove the most-favored-nation trading status of this long-time economic partner. Most in the U.S. government, including leaders in both political parties, wish to engage China as an economic partner at the same time that they keep a watchful eye on its increasing influence around the world, especially in developing countries. President Trump, on the other hand, has been assertive in Asia, imposing a series of tariffs designed particularly to hit goods imported from China.

Elsewhere in Asia, the United States has good relationships with most other countries, especially South Korea and Japan, which have both followed paths the United States favored after World War II. Both countries embraced democracy, market-oriented economies, and the hosting of U.S. military bases to stabilize the region. North Korea, however, is another matter. A closed, communist, totalitarian regime, North Korea has been testing nuclear bombs in recent decades, to the concern of the rest of the world. Here, again, President Trump has been assertive, challenging the North Koreans to come to the bargaining table. It is an open question how much change this assertiveness will achieve, but it is significant that a dialogue has actually begun. Like China many decades earlier, India is a developing country with a large population that is expanding and modernizing. Unlike China, India has embraced democracy, especially at the local level.

Link to Learning

You can plot U.S. government attention to different types of policy matters (including international affairs and foreign aid and its several dozen more focused subtopics) by using the online trend analysis tool (https://openstax.org/l/29ComAgen) at the Comparative Agendas Project.

Key Terms

balance of power a situation in which no one nation or region is much more powerful militarily than any other in the world

balance of trade the relationship between a country's inflow and outflow of goods

Cold War the period from shortly after World War II until approximately 1989–1990 when advanced industrial democracies divided behind the two superpowers (East: Soviet Union, West: United States) and the fear of nuclear war abounded

congressional executive agreement an international agreement that is not a treaty and that is negotiated by the president and approved by a simple majority of the House and Senate

containment the effort by the United States and Western European allies, begun during the Cold War, to prevent the spread of communism

diplomacy the establishment and maintenance of a formal relationship between countries

foreign policy a government's goals in dealing with other countries or regions and the strategy used to achieve them

free trade a policy in which a country allows the unfettered flow of goods and services between itself and other countries

hard power the use or threat of military power to influence the behavior of another country

isolationism a foreign policy approach that advocates a nation's staying out of foreign entanglements and keeping to itself

liberal internationalism a foreign policy approach of becoming proactively engaged in world affairs by cooperating in a community of nations

neo-isolationism a policy of distancing the United States from the United Nations and other international organizations, while still participating in the world economy

neoconservatism the belief that, rather than exercising restraint, the United States should aggressively use its might to promote its values and ideals around the world

North Atlantic Treaty Organization (NATO) a cross-national military organization with bases in Belgium and Germany formed to maintain stability in Europe

protectionism a policy in which a country does not permit other countries to sell goods and services within its borders or charges them very high tariffs (import taxes) to do so

selective engagement a policy of retaining a strong military presence and remaining engaged across the world

soft power nonmilitary tools used to influence another country, such as economic sanctions

sole executive agreement an international agreement that is not a treaty and that is negotiated and approved by the president acting alone

treaty an international agreement entered by the United States that requires presidential negotiation with other nation(s), consent by two-thirds of the Senate, and final ratification by the president

two presidencies thesis the thesis by Wildavsky that there are two distinct presidencies, one for foreign and one for domestic policy, and that presidents are more successful in foreign than domestic policy

United Nations (UN) an international organization of nation-states that seeks to promote peace, international relations, and economic and environmental programs

Summary

17.1 Defining Foreign Policy

As the president, Congress, and others carry out U.S. foreign policy in the areas of trade, diplomacy, defense, intelligence, foreign aid, and global environmental policy, they pursue a variety of objectives and face a multitude of challenges. The four main objectives of U.S. foreign policy are the protection of the United States and its citizens and allies, the assurance of continuing access to international resources and markets, the preservation of a balance of power in the world, and the protection of human rights and democracy.

The challenges of the massive and complex enterprise of U.S. foreign policy are many. First, there exists no true world-level authority dictating how the nations of the world should relate to one another. A second challenge is the widely differing views among countries about the role of government in people's lives. A third is other countries' varying ideas about the appropriate form of government. A fourth challenge is that many new foreign policy issues transcend borders. Finally, the varying conditions of the countries in the world affect what is possible in foreign policy and diplomatic relations.

17.2 Foreign Policy Instruments

U.S. foreign policy outputs vary considerably. At one end of the continuum are sharply focused outputs such as the presidential use of military force via a specific drone strike on an enemy target, or the forging of a presidential summit with another country's president or head of state. At the other end of the spectrum are broadly focused outputs that typically bring more involvement from the Congress and other world leaders, such as the process to formalize a multilateral treaty on the global environment or the process to finalize the U.S. diplomatic budget each fiscal year. Broadly focused outputs typically take more time to decide, involve more nation-states, are more expensive, and are quite difficult to reverse once in place. Sharply focused outputs are faster, tend to be led by the president, and are easier for future policymakers to undo.

17.3 Institutional Relations in Foreign Policy

Many aspects of foreign policymaking rely on the powers shared between Congress and the president, including foreign policy appointments and the foreign affairs budget. Within the executive branch, an array of foreign policy leaders report directly to the president. Foreign policy can at times seem fragmented and diffuse because of the complexity of actors and topics. However, the president is clearly the leader, having both formal authority and the ability to delegate to Congress, as explained in the two presidencies thesis. With this leadership, presidents at times can make foreign policymaking quick and decisive, especially when it calls for executive agreements and the military use of force.

17.4 Approaches to Foreign Policy

Classic theories of foreign policy divide into the isolationist camp and the internationalist camp. The use of hard versus soft power comes into play in the internationalist route. Neoconservatism, a more recent school of thought in foreign policy, takes the view that the United States should go it alone as a single superpower, retreating from foreign involvement with the exception of trade and economic policy.

In the end, the complexity of international relationships, combined with a multifaceted decision-making process and a multiplicity of actors, leads to a U.S. foreign policy approach that uses a bit of all the schools of thought. The United States is being neoconservative when drone strikes are carried out unilaterally within the boundaries of another sovereign nation. It is being internationalist when building a coalition on the Iran nuclear deal or when participating in NATO initiatives.

Review Questions

1. Why are foreign policy issues more complicated than domestic policy issues?
  a. They are more specific.
  b. They are more complex.
  c. The international environment is unpredictable.
  d. They are more expensive.

2. Which of the following is not a foreign policy type?
  a. trade policy
  b. intelligence policy
  c. war-making
  d. bureaucratic oversight

3. The goals of U.S. foreign policy include _____.
  a. keeping the country safe
  b. securing access to foreign markets
  c. protecting human rights
  d. all the above

4. What are two key differences between domestic policymaking and foreign policymaking?

5. A sole executive agreement is likely to be in effect longer than is a treaty.
  a. true
  b. false

6. All the following are examples of sharply focused foreign policy outputs *except* _____.
  a. presidential summits
  b. military uses of force
  c. emergency spending measures
  d. international agreements

7. The War Powers Resolution _____.
  a. strengthened congressional war powers
  b. strengthened presidential war powers
  c. affected the presidency and congress equally
  d. ultimately had little impact on war-making

8. The federal budget process matters in foreign policy for all the following reasons *except* _____.
  a. Congress has the power of the purse, so the president needs its approval
  b. the budget provides the funding needed to run the foreign policy agencies
  c. the budget for every presidential action has to be approved in advance
  d. the budget allows political institutions to increase funding in key new areas

9. Which types of foreign policy outputs have more impact, broadly conceived ones or sharply focused ones? Why?

10. In terms of formal powers in the realm of foreign policy, _____.
  a. the president is entirely in charge
  b. the president and Congress share power
  c. Congress is entirely in charge
  d. decisions are delegated to experts in the bureaucracy

11. Why do House members and senators tend to be less active on foreign policy matters than domestic ones?
  a. Foreign policy matters are more technical and difficult.
  b. Legislators do not want to offend certain immigrant groups within their constituency.
  c. Constituents are more directly affected by domestic policy topics than foreign ones.
  d. Legislators themselves are not interested in foreign policy matters.

12. Neoconservativism is an isolationist foreign policy approach of a nation keeping to itself and engaging less internationally.
  a. true
  b. false

13. President George W. Bush was a proponent of liberal internationalism in his foreign policy.
  a. true
  b. false

14. The U.S. policy of containment during the Cold War related to keeping _____.
   a. terrorism from spreading
   b. rogue countries like North Korea from developing nuclear weapons
   c. communism from spreading
   d. oil prices from rising

15. The use of drones within other countries' borders is consistent with which school of thought?
   a. liberal internationalism
   b. neoconservativism
   c. neo-isolationism
   d. grand strategy

16. What are the pros and cons of the neoconservative foreign policy approach followed in recent decades?

Critical Thinking Questions

17. In your view, what are the best ways to get the community of nations working together?

18. What are the three most important foreign policy issues facing the United States today? Why?

19. Which is more important as an influencer of foreign policy, the president or a cabinet department like the Department of State or Defense? Why?

20. What do you think is the most advantageous school of thought for the United States to follow in foreign policy in the future? Why?

21. If you were president and wanted to gather support for a new foreign policy initiative, which three U.S. foreign policy actors would you approach and why?

Suggestions for Further Study

Brands, H. William. 1994. *The United States in the World: A History of American Foreign Policy.* Boston: Houghton Mifflin.

Howell, William G. and Jon C. Pevehouse. 2007. *While Dangers Gather: Congressional Checks on Presidential War Powers.* Princeton, NJ: Princeton University Press.

Krutz, Glen S. and Jeffrey S. Peake. 2009. *Treaty Politics and the Rise of Executive Agreements: International Commitments in a System of Shared Powers.* Ann Arbor: University of Michigan Press.

Nye, Joseph S. 2004. *Soft Power: The Means to Success in World Politics.* New York: Public Affairs.

APPENDIX A | Declaration of Independence

When in the Course of human events, it becomes necessary for one people to dissolve the political bands which have connected them with another, and to assume among the powers of the earth, the separate and equal station to which the Laws of Nature and of Nature's God entitle them, a decent respect to the opinions of mankind requires that they should declare the causes which impel them to the separation.

We hold these truths to be self-evident, that all men are created equal, that they are endowed by their Creator with certain unalienable Rights, that among these are Life, Liberty and the pursuit of Happiness. —That to secure these rights, Governments are instituted among Men, deriving their just powers from the consent of the governed, —That whenever any Form of Government becomes destructive of these ends, it is the Right of the People to alter or to abolish it, and to institute new Government, laying its foundation on such principles and organizing its powers in such form, as to them shall seem most likely to effect their Safety and Happiness. Prudence, indeed, will dictate that Governments long established should not be changed for light and transient causes; and accordingly all experience hath shewn, that mankind are more disposed to suffer, while evils are sufferable, than to right themselves by abolishing the forms to which they are accustomed. But when a long train of abuses and usurpations, pursuing invariably the same Object evinces a design to reduce them under absolute Despotism, it is their right, it is their duty, to throw off such Government, and to provide new Guards for their future security. —Such has been the patient sufferance of these Colonies; and such is now the necessity which constrains them to alter their former Systems of Government. The history of the present King of Great Britain is a history of repeated injuries and usurpations, all having in direct object the establishment of an absolute Tyranny over these States. To prove this, let Facts be submitted to a candid world.

He has refused his Assent to Laws, the most wholesome and necessary for the public good.

He has forbidden his Governors to pass Laws of immediate and pressing importance, unless suspended in their operation till his Assent should be obtained; and when so suspended, he has utterly neglected to attend to them.

He has refused to pass other Laws for the accommodation of large districts of people, unless those people would relinquish the right of Representation in the Legislature, a right inestimable to them and formidable to tyrants only.

He has called together legislative bodies at places unusual, uncomfortable, and distant from the depository of their public Records, for the sole purpose of fatiguing them into compliance with his measures.

He has dissolved Representative Houses repeatedly, for opposing with manly firmness his invasions on the rights of the people.

He has refused for a long time, after such dissolutions, to cause others to be elected; whereby the Legislative powers, incapable of Annihilation, have returned to the People at large for their exercise; the State remaining in the mean time exposed to all the dangers of invasion from without, and convulsions within.

He has endeavoured to prevent the population of these States; for that purpose obstructing the Laws for Naturalization of Foreigners; refusing to pass others to encourage their migrations hither, and raising the conditions of new Appropriations of Lands.

He has obstructed the Administration of Justice, by refusing his Assent to Laws for establishing Judiciary powers.

He has made Judges dependent on his Will alone, for the tenure of their offices, and the amount and payment of their salaries.

He has erected a multitude of New Offices, and sent hither swarms of Officers to harrass our people, and eat out their substance.

He has kept among us, in times of peace, Standing Armies without the Consent of our legislatures.

He has affected to render the Military independent of and superior to the Civil power.

He has combined with others to subject us to a jurisdiction foreign to our constitution, and unacknowledged by our laws; giving his Assent to their Acts of pretended Legislation:

For Quartering large bodies of armed troops among us:

For protecting them, by a mock Trial, from punishment for any Murders which they should commit on the Inhabitants of these States:

For cutting off our Trade with all parts of the world:

For imposing Taxes on us without our Consent:

For depriving us in many cases, of the benefits of Trial by Jury:

For transporting us beyond Seas to be tried for pretended offences

For abolishing the free System of English Laws in a neighbouring Province, establishing therein an Arbitrary government, and enlarging its Boundaries so as to render it at once an example and fit instrument for introducing the same absolute rule into these Colonies:

For taking away our Charters, abolishing our most valuable Laws, and altering fundamentally the Forms of our Governments:

For suspending our own Legislatures, and declaring themselves invested with power to legislate for us in all cases whatsoever.

He has abdicated Government here, by declaring us out of his Protection and waging War against us.

He has plundered our seas, ravaged our Coasts, burnt our towns, and destroyed the lives of our people.

He is at this time transporting large Armies of foreign Mercenaries to compleat the works of death, desolation and tyranny, already begun with circumstances of Cruelty & perfidy scarcely paralleled in the most barbarous ages, and totally unworthy the Head of a civilized nation.

He has constrained our fellow Citizens taken Captive on the high Seas to bear Arms against their Country, to become the executioners of their friends and Brethren, or to fall themselves by their Hands.

He has excited domestic insurrections amongst us, and has endeavoured to bring on the inhabitants of our frontiers, the merciless Indian Savages, whose known rule of warfare, is an undistinguished destruction of all ages, sexes and conditions.

In every stage of these Oppressions We have Petitioned for Redress in the most humble terms: Our repeated Petitions have been answered only by repeated injury. A Prince whose character is thus marked by every act which may define a Tyrant, is unfit to be the ruler of a free people.

Nor have We been wanting in attentions to our Brittish brethren. We have warned them from time to time of attempts by their legislature to extend an unwarrantable jurisdiction over us. We have reminded them of the circumstances of our emigration and settlement here. We have appealed to their native justice and magnanimity, and we have conjured them by the ties of our common kindred to disavow these usurpations, which, would inevitably interrupt our connections and correspondence. They too have been deaf to the voice of justice and of consanguinity. We must, therefore, acquiesce in the necessity, which denounces our Separation, and hold them, as we hold the rest of mankind, Enemies in War, in Peace Friends.

We, therefore, the Representatives of the united States of America, in General Congress, Assembled, appealing to the Supreme Judge of the world for the rectitude of our intentions, do, in the Name, and by Authority of the good People of these Colonies, solemnly publish and declare, That these United Colonies are, and of Right ought to be Free and Independent States; that they are Absolved from all Allegiance to the British Crown, and that all political connection between them and the State of Great Britain, is and ought to be totally dissolved; and that as Free and Independent States, they have full Power to levy War, conclude Peace, contract Alliances, establish Commerce, and to do all other Acts and Things which Independent States may of right do. And for the support of this Declaration, with a firm reliance on the protection of divine Providence, we mutually pledge to each other our Lives, our Fortunes and our sacred Honor.

The 56 signatures on the Declaration appear in the positions indicated:

Column 1

Georgia:

Button Gwinnett

Lyman Hall

George Walton

Column 2

North Carolina:

William Hooper

Joseph Hewes

John Penn

South Carolina:

Edward Rutledge

Thomas Heyward, Jr.

Thomas Lynch, Jr.

Arthur Middleton

Column 3

Massachusetts:

John Hancock

Maryland:

Samuel Chase

William Paca

Thomas Stone

Charles Carroll of Carrollton

Virginia:

George Wythe

Richard Henry Lee

Thomas Jefferson

Benjamin Harrison

Thomas Nelson, Jr.

Francis Lightfoot Lee

Carter Braxton

Column 4

Pennsylvania:

Robert Morris

Benjamin Rush

Benjamin Franklin

John Morton

George Clymer

James Smith

George Taylor

James Wilson

George Ross

Delaware:

Caesar Rodney

George Read

Thomas McKean

Column 5

New York:

William Floyd

Philip Livingston

Francis Lewis

Lewis Morris

New Jersey:

Richard Stockton

John Witherspoon

Francis Hopkinson

John Hart

Abraham Clark

Column 6

New Hampshire:

Josiah Bartlett

William Whipple

Massachusetts:

Samuel Adams

John Adams

Robert Treat Paine

Elbridge Gerry

Rhode Island:

Stephen Hopkins

William Ellery

Connecticut:

Roger Sherman

Samuel Huntington

William Williams

Oliver Wolcott

New Hampshire:

Matthew Thornton

APPENDIX B | The Constitution of the United States

We the People of the United States, in Order to form a more perfect Union, establish Justice, insure domestic Tranquility, provide for the common defence, promote the general Welfare, and secure the Blessings of Liberty to ourselves and our Posterity, do ordain and establish this Constitution for the United States of America.

Article. I.

Section. 1.

All legislative Powers herein granted shall be vested in a Congress of the United States, which shall consist of a Senate and House of Representatives.

Section. 2.

The House of Representatives shall be composed of Members chosen every second Year by the People of the several States, and the Electors in each State shall have the Qualifications requisite for Electors of the most numerous Branch of the State Legislature.

No Person shall be a Representative who shall not have attained to the Age of twenty five Years, and been seven Years a Citizen of the United States, and who shall not, when elected, be an Inhabitant of that State in which he shall be chosen.

Representatives and direct Taxes shall be apportioned among the several States which may be included within this Union, according to their respective Numbers, which shall be determined by adding to the whole Number of free Persons, including those bound to Service for a Term of Years, and excluding Indians not taxed, three fifths of all other Persons. The actual Enumeration shall be made within three Years after the first Meeting of the Congress of the United States, and within every subsequent Term of ten Years, in such Manner as they shall by Law direct. The Number of Representatives shall not exceed one for every thirty Thousand, but each State shall have at Least one Representative; and until such enumeration shall be made, the State of New Hampshire shall be entitled to chuse three, Massachusetts eight, Rhode-Island and Providence Plantations one, Connecticut five, New-York six, New Jersey four, Pennsylvania eight, Delaware one, Maryland six, Virginia ten, North Carolina five, South Carolina five, and Georgia three.

When vacancies happen in the Representation from any State, the Executive Authority thereof shall issue Writs of Election to fill such Vacancies.

The House of Representatives shall chuse their Speaker and other Officers; and shall have the sole Power of Impeachment.

Section. 3.

The Senate of the United States shall be composed of two Senators from each State, chosen by the Legislature thereof, for six Years; and each Senator shall have one Vote.

Immediately after they shall be assembled in Consequence of the first Election, they shall be divided as equally as may be into three Classes. The Seats of the Senators of the first Class shall be vacated at the Expiration of the second Year, of the second Class at the Expiration of the fourth Year, and of the third Class at the Expiration of the sixth Year, so that one third may be chosen every second Year; and if Vacancies happen by Resignation, or otherwise, during the Recess of the Legislature of any State, the Executive thereof may make temporary Appointments until the next Meeting of the Legislature, which shall then fill such Vacancies.

No Person shall be a Senator who shall not have attained to the Age of thirty Years, and been nine Years a Citizen of the United States, and who shall not, when elected, be an Inhabitant of that State for which he shall be chosen.

The Vice President of the United States shall be President of the Senate, but shall have no Vote, unless they be equally divided.

The Senate shall chuse their other Officers, and also a President pro tempore, in the Absence of the Vice President, or when he shall exercise the Office of President of the United States.

The Senate shall have the sole Power to try all Impeachments. When sitting for that Purpose, they shall be on Oath or Affirmation. When the President of the United States is tried, the Chief Justice shall preside: And no Person shall be convicted without the Concurrence of two thirds of the Members present.

Judgment in Cases of Impeachment shall not extend further than to removal from Office, and disqualification to hold and enjoy any Office of honor, Trust or Profit under the United States: but the Party convicted shall nevertheless be liable and subject to Indictment, Trial, Judgment and Punishment, according to Law.

Section. 4.

The Times, Places and Manner of holding Elections for Senators and Representatives, shall be prescribed in each State by the Legislature thereof; but the Congress may at any time by Law make or alter such Regulations, except as to the Places of chusing Senators.

The Congress shall assemble at least once in every Year, and such Meeting shall be on the first Monday in December, unless they shall by Law appoint a different Day.

Section. 5.

Each House shall be the Judge of the Elections, Returns and Qualifications of its own Members, and a Majority of each shall constitute a Quorum to do Business; but a smaller Number may adjourn from day to day, and may be authorized to compel the Attendance of absent Members, in such Manner, and under such Penalties as each House may provide.

Each House may determine the Rules of its Proceedings, punish its Members for disorderly Behaviour, and, with the Concurrence of two thirds, expel a Member.

Each House shall keep a Journal of its Proceedings, and from time to time publish the same, excepting such Parts as may in their Judgment require Secrecy; and the Yeas and Nays of the Members of either House on any question shall, at the Desire of one fifth of those Present, be entered on the Journal.

Neither House, during the Session of Congress, shall, without the Consent of the other, adjourn for more than three days, nor to any other Place than that in which the two Houses shall be sitting.

Section. 6.

The Senators and Representatives shall receive a Compensation for their Services, to be ascertained by Law, and paid out of the Treasury of the United States. They shall in all Cases, except Treason, Felony and Breach of the Peace, be privileged from Arrest during their Attendance at the Session of their respective Houses, and in going to and returning from the same; and for any Speech or Debate in either House, they shall not be questioned in any other Place.

No Senator or Representative shall, during the Time for which he was elected, be appointed to any civil Office under the Authority of the United States, which shall have been created, or the Emoluments whereof shall have been encreased during such time; and no Person holding any Office under the United States, shall be a Member of either House during his Continuance in Office.

Section. 7.

All Bills for raising Revenue shall originate in the House of Representatives; but the Senate may propose or concur with Amendments as on other Bills.

Every Bill which shall have passed the House of Representatives and the Senate, shall, before it become a Law, be presented to the President of the United States; If he approve he shall sign it, but if not he shall return it, with his Objections to that House in which it shall have originated, who shall enter the Objections at large on their Journal, and proceed to reconsider it. If after such Reconsideration two thirds of that House shall agree to pass the Bill, it shall be sent, together with the Objections, to the other House, by which it shall likewise be reconsidered, and if approved by two thirds of that House, it shall become a Law. But in all such Cases the Votes of both Houses shall be determined by yeas and Nays, and the Names of the Persons voting for and against the Bill shall be entered on the Journal of each House respectively. If any Bill shall not be returned by the President within ten Days (Sundays excepted) after it shall have been presented to him, the Same shall be a Law, in like Manner as if he had signed it, unless the Congress by their Adjournment prevent its Return, in which Case it shall not be a Law.

Every Order, Resolution, or Vote to which the Concurrence of the Senate and House of Representatives may be necessary (except on a question of Adjournment) shall be presented to the President of the United States; and before the Same shall take Effect, shall be approved by him, or being disapproved by him, shall be repassed by two thirds of the Senate and House of Representatives, according to the Rules and Limitations prescribed in the Case of a Bill.

Section. 8.

The Congress shall have Power To lay and collect Taxes, Duties, Imposts and Excises, to pay the Debts and provide for the common Defence and general Welfare of the United States; but all Duties, Imposts and Excises shall be uniform throughout the United States;

To borrow Money on the credit of the United States;

To regulate Commerce with foreign Nations, and among the several States, and with the Indian Tribes;

To establish an uniform Rule of Naturalization, and uniform Laws on the subject of Bankruptcies throughout the United States;

To coin Money, regulate the Value thereof, and of foreign Coin, and fix the Standard of Weights and Measures;

To provide for the Punishment of counterfeiting the Securities and current Coin of the United States;

To establish Post Offices and post Roads;

To promote the Progress of Science and useful Arts, by securing for limited Times to Authors and Inventors the exclusive Right to their respective Writings and Discoveries;

To constitute Tribunals inferior to the supreme Court;

To define and punish Piracies and Felonies committed on the high Seas, and Offences against the Law of Nations;

To declare War, grant Letters of Marque and Reprisal, and make Rules concerning Captures on Land and Water;

To raise and support Armies, but no Appropriation of Money to that Use shall be for a longer Term than two Years;

To provide and maintain a Navy;

To make Rules for the Government and Regulation of the land and naval Forces;

To provide for calling forth the Militia to execute the Laws of the Union, suppress Insurrections and repel Invasions;

To provide for organizing, arming, and disciplining, the Militia, and for governing such Part of them as may be employed in the Service of the United States, reserving to the States respectively, the Appointment of the Officers, and the Authority of training the Militia according to the discipline prescribed by Congress;

To exercise exclusive Legislation in all Cases whatsoever, over such District (not exceeding ten Miles square) as may, by Cession of particular States, and the Acceptance of Congress, become the Seat of the Government of the United States, and to exercise like Authority over all Places purchased by the Consent of the Legislature of the State in which the Same shall be, for the Erection of Forts, Magazines, Arsenals, dock-Yards, and other needful Buildings;—And

To make all Laws which shall be necessary and proper for carrying into Execution the foregoing Powers, and all other Powers vested by this Constitution in the Government of the United States, or in any Department or Officer thereof.

Section. 9.

The Migration or Importation of such Persons as any of the States now existing shall think proper to admit, shall not be prohibited by the Congress prior to the Year one thousand eight hundred and eight, but a Tax or duty may be imposed on such Importation, not exceeding ten dollars for each Person.

The Privilege of the Writ of Habeas Corpus shall not be suspended, unless when in Cases of Rebellion or Invasion the public Safety may require it.

No Bill of Attainder or ex post facto Law shall be passed.

No Capitation, or other direct, Tax shall be laid, unless in Proportion to the Census or enumeration herein before directed to be taken.

No Tax or Duty shall be laid on Articles exported from any State.

No Preference shall be given by any Regulation of Commerce or Revenue to the Ports of one State over those of another: nor shall Vessels bound to, or from, one State, be obliged to enter, clear, or pay Duties in another.

No Money shall be drawn from the Treasury, but in Consequence of Appropriations made by Law; and a regular Statement and Account of the Receipts and Expenditures of all public Money shall be published from time to time.

No Title of Nobility shall be granted by the United States: And no Person holding any Office of Profit or Trust under them, shall, without the Consent of the Congress, accept of any present, Emolument, Office, or Title, of any kind whatever, from any King, Prince, or foreign State.

Section. 10.

No State shall enter into any Treaty, Alliance, or Confederation; grant Letters of Marque and Reprisal; coin Money; emit Bills of Credit; make any Thing but gold and silver Coin a Tender in Payment of Debts; pass any Bill of Attainder, ex post facto Law, or Law impairing the Obligation of Contracts, or grant any Title of Nobility.

No State shall, without the Consent of the Congress, lay any Imposts or Duties on Imports or Exports, except what may be absolutely necessary for executing it's inspection Laws: and the net Produce of all Duties and Imposts, laid by any State on Imports or Exports, shall be for the Use of the Treasury of the United States; and all such Laws shall be subject to the Revision and Controul of the Congress.

No State shall, without the Consent of Congress, lay any Duty of Tonnage, keep Troops, or Ships of War in time of Peace, enter into any Agreement or Compact with another State, or with a foreign Power, or engage in War, unless actually invaded, or in such imminent Danger as will not admit of delay.

Article. II.

Section. 1.

The executive Power shall be vested in a President of the United States of America. He shall hold his Office during the Term of four Years, and, together with the Vice President, chosen for the same Term, be elected, as follows

Each State shall appoint, in such Manner as the Legislature thereof may direct, a Number of Electors, equal to the whole Number of Senators and Representatives to which the State may be entitled in the Congress: but no Senator or Representative, or Person holding an Office of Trust or Profit under the United States, shall be appointed an Elector.

The Electors shall meet in their respective States, and vote by Ballot for two Persons, of whom one at least shall not be an Inhabitant of the same State with themselves. And they shall make a List of all the Persons voted for, and of the Number of Votes for each; which List they shall sign and certify, and transmit sealed to the Seat of the Government of the United States, directed to the President of the Senate. The President of the Senate shall, in the Presence of the Senate and House of Representatives, open all the Certificates, and the Votes shall then be counted. The Person having the greatest Number of Votes shall be the President, if such Number be a Majority of the whole Number of Electors appointed; and if there be more than one who have such Majority, and have an equal Number of Votes, then the House of Representatives shall immediately chuse by Ballot one of them for President; and if no Person have a Majority, then from the five highest on the List the said House shall in like Manner chuse the President. But in chusing the President, the Votes shall be taken by States, the Representation from each State having one Vote; A quorum for this Purpose shall consist of a Member or Members from two thirds of the States, and a Majority of all the States shall be necessary to a Choice. In every Case, after the Choice of the President, the Person having the greatest Number of Votes of the Electors shall be the Vice President. But if there should remain two or more who have equal Votes, the Senate shall chuse from them by Ballot the Vice President.

The Congress may determine the Time of chusing the Electors, and the Day on which they shall give their Votes; which Day shall be the same throughout the United States.

No Person except a natural born Citizen, or a Citizen of the United States, at the time of the Adoption of this Constitution, shall be eligible to the Office of President; neither shall any Person be eligible to that Office who shall not have attained to the Age of thirty five Years, and been fourteen Years a Resident within the United States.

In Case of the Removal of the President from Office, or of his Death, Resignation, or Inability to discharge the Powers and Duties of the said Office, the Same shall devolve on the Vice President, and the Congress may by Law provide for the Case of Removal, Death, Resignation or Inability, both of the President and Vice President, declaring what Officer shall then act as President, and such Officer shall act accordingly, until the Disability be removed, or a President shall be elected.

The President shall, at stated Times, receive for his Services, a Compensation, which shall neither be increased nor diminished during the Period for which he shall have been elected, and he shall not receive within that Period any other Emolument from the United States, or any of them.

Before he enter on the Execution of his Office, he shall take the following Oath or Affirmation:—"I do solemnly swear (or affirm) that I will faithfully execute the Office of President of the United States, and will to the best of my Ability, preserve, protect and defend the Constitution of the United States."

Section. 2.

The President shall be Commander in Chief of the Army and Navy of the United States, and of the Militia of the several States, when called into the actual Service of the United States; he may require the Opinion, in writing, of the principal Officer in each of the executive Departments, upon any Subject relating to the Duties of their respective Offices, and he shall have Power to grant Reprieves and Pardons for Offences against the United States, except in Cases of Impeachment.

He shall have Power, by and with the Advice and Consent of the Senate, to make Treaties, provided two thirds of the Senators present concur; and he shall nominate, and by and with the Advice and Consent of the Senate, shall appoint Ambassadors, other public Ministers and Consuls, Judges of the supreme Court, and all other Officers of the United States, whose Appointments are not herein otherwise provided for, and which shall be established by Law: but the Congress may by Law vest the Appointment of such inferior Officers, as they think proper, in the President alone, in the Courts of Law, or in the Heads of Departments.

The President shall have Power to fill up all Vacancies that may happen during the Recess of the Senate, by granting Commissions which shall expire at the End of their next Session.

Section. 3.

He shall from time to time give to the Congress Information of the State of the Union, and recommend to their Consideration such Measures as he shall judge necessary and expedient; he may, on extraordinary Occasions, convene both Houses, or either of them, and in Case of Disagreement between them, with Respect to the Time of Adjournment, he may adjourn them to such Time as he shall think proper; he shall receive Ambassadors and other public Ministers; he shall take Care that the Laws be faithfully executed, and shall Commission all the Officers of the United States.

Section. 4.

The President, Vice President and all civil Officers of the United States, shall be removed from Office on Impeachment for, and Conviction of, Treason, Bribery, or other high Crimes and Misdemeanors.

Article III.

Section. 1.

The judicial Power of the United States, shall be vested in one supreme Court, and in such inferior Courts as the Congress may from time to time ordain and establish. The Judges, both of the supreme and inferior Courts, shall hold their Offices during good Behaviour, and shall, at stated Times, receive for their Services, a Compensation, which shall not be diminished during their Continuance in Office.

Section. 2.

The judicial Power shall extend to all Cases, in Law and Equity, arising under this Constitution, the Laws of the United States, and Treaties made, or which shall be made, under their Authority;—to all Cases affecting Ambassadors, other public Ministers and Consuls;—to all Cases of admiralty and maritime Jurisdiction;—to Controversies to which the United States shall be a Party;—to Controversies between two or more States;—between a State and Citizens of another State,—between Citizens of different States,—between Citizens of the same State claiming Lands under Grants of different States, and between a State, or the Citizens thereof, and foreign States, Citizens or Subjects.

In all Cases affecting Ambassadors, other public Ministers and Consuls, and those in which a State shall be Party, the supreme Court shall have original Jurisdiction. In all the other Cases before mentioned, the supreme Court shall have appellate Jurisdiction, both as to Law and Fact, with such Exceptions, and under such Regulations as the Congress shall make.

The Trial of all Crimes, except in Cases of Impeachment, shall be by Jury; and such Trial shall be held in the State where the said Crimes shall have been committed; but when not committed within any State, the Trial shall be at such Place or Places as the Congress may by Law have directed.

Section. 3.

Treason against the United States, shall consist only in levying War against them, or in adhering to their Enemies, giving them Aid and Comfort. No Person shall be convicted of Treason unless on the Testimony of two Witnesses to the same overt Act, or on Confession in open Court.

The Congress shall have Power to declare the Punishment of Treason, but no Attainder of Treason shall work Corruption of Blood, or Forfeiture except during the Life of the Person attainted.

Article. IV.

Section. 1.

Full Faith and Credit shall be given in each State to the public Acts, Records, and judicial Proceedings of every other State. And the Congress may by general Laws prescribe the Manner in which such Acts, Records and Proceedings shall be proved, and the Effect thereof.

Section. 2.

The Citizens of each State shall be entitled to all Privileges and Immunities of Citizens in the several States.

A Person charged in any State with Treason, Felony, or other Crime, who shall flee from Justice, and be found in another State, shall on Demand of the executive Authority of the State from which he fled, be delivered up, to be removed to the State having Jurisdiction of the Crime.

No Person held to Service or Labour in one State, under the Laws thereof, escaping into another, shall, in Consequence of any Law or Regulation therein, be discharged from such Service or Labour, but shall be delivered up on Claim of the Party to whom such Service or Labour may be due.

Section. 3.

New States may be admitted by the Congress into this Union; but no new State shall be formed or erected within the Jurisdiction of any other State; nor any State be formed by the Junction of two or more States, or Parts of States, without the Consent of the Legislatures of the States concerned as well as of the Congress.

The Congress shall have Power to dispose of and make all needful Rules and Regulations respecting the Territory or other Property belonging to the United States; and nothing in this Constitution shall be so construed as to Prejudice any Claims of the United States, or of any particular State.

Section. 4.

The United States shall guarantee to every State in this Union a Republican Form of Government, and shall protect each of them against Invasion; and on Application of the Legislature, or of the Executive (when the Legislature cannot be convened), against domestic Violence.

Article. V.

The Congress, whenever two thirds of both Houses shall deem it necessary, shall propose Amendments to this Constitution, or, on the Application of the Legislatures of two thirds of the several States, shall call a Convention for proposing Amendments, which, in either Case, shall be valid to all Intents and Purposes, as Part of this Constitution, when ratified by the Legislatures of three fourths of the several States, or by Conventions in three fourths thereof, as the one or the other Mode of Ratification may be proposed by the Congress; Provided that no Amendment which may be made prior to the Year One thousand eight hundred and eight shall in any Manner affect the first and fourth Clauses in the Ninth Section of the first Article; and that no State, without its Consent, shall be deprived of its equal Suffrage in the Senate.

Article. VI.

All Debts contracted and Engagements entered into, before the Adoption of this Constitution, shall be as valid against the United States under this Constitution, as under the Confederation.

This Constitution, and the Laws of the United States which shall be made in Pursuance thereof; and all Treaties made, or which shall be made, under the Authority of the United States, shall be the supreme Law of the Land; and the Judges in every State shall be bound thereby, any Thing in the Constitution or Laws of any State to the Contrary notwithstanding.

The Senators and Representatives before mentioned, and the Members of the several State Legislatures, and all executive and judicial Officers, both of the United States and of the several States, shall be bound by Oath or Affirmation, to support this Constitution; but no religious Test shall ever be required as a Qualification to any Office or public Trust under the United States.

Article. VII.

The Ratification of the Conventions of nine States, shall be sufficient for the Establishment of this Constitution between the States so ratifying the Same.

Done in Convention by the Unanimous Consent of the States present the Seventeenth Day of September in the Year of our Lord one thousand seven hundred and Eighty seven and of the Independance of the United States of America the Twelfth In witness whereof We have hereunto subscribed our Names,

G. Washington

Presidt and deputy from Virginia

Delaware

Geo: Read

Gunning Bedford jun

John Dickinson

Richard Bassett

Jaco: Broom

Maryland

James McHenry

Dan of St Thos. Jenifer

Danl. Carroll

Virginia

John Blair

James Madison Jr.

North Carolina

Wm. Blount

Richd. Dobbs Spaight

Hu Williamson

South Carolina

J. Rutledge

Charles Cotesworth Pinckney

Charles Pinckney

Pierce Butler

Georgia

William Few

Abr Baldwin

New Hampshire

John Langdon

Nicholas Gilman

Massachusetts

Nathaniel Gorham

Rufus King

Connecticut

Wm. Saml. Johnson

Roger Sherman

New York

Alexander Hamilton

New Jersey

Wil: Livingston

David Brearley

Wm. Paterson

Jona: Dayton

Pensylvania

B Franklin

Thomas Mifflin

Robt. Morris

Geo. Clymer

Thos. FitzSimons

Jared Ingersoll

James Wilson

Gouv Morris

Constitutional Amendments

The U.S. Bill of Rights (Amendments 1–10)

The Preamble to The Bill of Rights

Congress of the United States begun and held at the City of New-York, on Wednesday the fourth of March, one thousand seven hundred and eighty nine.

The Conventions of a number of the States, having at the time of their adopting the Constitution, expressed a desire, in order to prevent misconstruction or abuse of its powers, that further declaratory and restrictive clauses should be added: And as extending the ground of public confidence in the Government, will best ensure the beneficent ends of its institution.

Resolved by the Senate and House of Representatives of the United States of America, in Congress assembled, two thirds of both Houses concurring, that the following Articles be proposed to the Legislatures of the several States, as amendments to the Constitution of the United States, all, or any of which Articles, when ratified by three fourths of the said Legislatures, to be valid to all intents and purposes, as part of the said Constitution; viz.

Articles in addition to, and Amendment of the Constitution of the United States of America, proposed by Congress, and ratified by the Legislatures of the several States, pursuant to the fifth Article of the original Constitution.

Note: The following text is a transcription of the first ten amendments to the Constitution in their original form. These amendments were ratified December 15, 1791, and form what is known as the "Bill of Rights."

Amendment I

Congress shall make no law respecting an establishment of religion, or prohibiting the free exercise thereof; or abridging the freedom of speech, or of the press; or the right of the people peaceably to assemble, and to petition the Government for a redress of grievances.

Amendment II

A well regulated Militia, being necessary to the security of a free State, the right of the people to keep and bear Arms, shall not be infringed.

Amendment III

No Soldier shall, in time of peace be quartered in any house, without the consent of the Owner, nor in time of war, but in a manner to be prescribed by law.

Amendment IV

The right of the people to be secure in their persons, houses, papers, and effects, against unreasonable searches and seizures, shall not be violated, and no Warrants shall issue, but upon probable cause, supported by Oath or affirmation, and particularly describing the place to be searched, and the persons or things to be seized.

Amendment V

No person shall be held to answer for a capital, or otherwise infamous crime, unless on a presentment or indictment of a Grand Jury, except in cases arising in the land or naval forces, or in the Militia, when in actual service in time of War or public danger; nor shall any person be subject for the same offence to be twice put in jeopardy of life or limb; nor shall be compelled in any criminal case to be a witness against himself, nor be deprived of life, liberty, or property, without due process of law; nor shall private property be taken for public use, without just compensation.

Amendment VI

In all criminal prosecutions, the accused shall enjoy the right to a speedy and public trial, by an impartial jury of the State and district wherein the crime shall have been committed, which district shall have been previously ascertained by law, and to be informed of the nature and cause of the accusation; to be confronted with the witnesses against him; to have compulsory process for obtaining witnesses in his favor, and to have the Assistance of Counsel for his defence.

Amendment VII

In Suits at common law, where the value in controversy shall exceed twenty dollars, the right of trial by jury shall be preserved, and no fact tried by a jury, shall be otherwise re-examined in any Court of the United States, than according to the rules of the common law.

Amendment VIII

Excessive bail shall not be required, nor excessive fines imposed, nor cruel and unusual punishments inflicted.

Amendment IX

The enumeration in the Constitution, of certain rights, shall not be construed to deny or disparage others retained by the people.

Amendment X

The powers not delegated to the United States by the Constitution, nor prohibited by it to the States, are reserved to the States respectively, or to the people.

Amendment XI

The Judicial power of the United States shall not be construed to extend to any suit in law or equity, commenced or prosecuted against one of the United States by Citizens of another State, or by Citizens or Subjects of any Foreign State.

Amendment XII

The Electors shall meet in their respective states and vote by ballot for President and Vice-President, one of whom, at least, shall not be an inhabitant of the same state with themselves; they shall name in their ballots the person voted for as President, and in distinct ballots the person voted for as Vice-President, and they shall make distinct lists of all persons voted for as President, and of all persons voted for as Vice-President, and of the number of votes for each, which lists they shall sign and certify, and transmit sealed to the seat of the government of the United States, directed to the President of the Senate; — the President of the Senate shall, in the presence of the Senate and House of Representatives, open all the certificates and the votes shall then be counted; — The person having the greatest number of votes for President, shall be the President, if such number be a majority of the whole number of Electors appointed; and if no person have such majority, then from the persons having the highest numbers not exceeding three on the list of those voted for as President, the House of Representatives shall choose immediately, by ballot, the President. But in choosing the President, the votes shall be taken by states, the representation from each state having one vote; a quorum for this purpose shall consist of a member or members from two-thirds of the states, and a majority of all the states shall be necessary to a choice. [And if the House of Representatives shall not choose a President whenever the right of choice shall devolve upon them, before the fourth day of March next following, then the Vice-President shall act as President, as in case of the death or other constitutional disability of the President. —]* The person having the greatest number of votes as Vice-President, shall be the Vice-President, if such number be a majority of the whole number of Electors appointed, and if no person have a majority, then from the two highest numbers on the list, the Senate shall choose the Vice-President; a quorum for the purpose shall consist of two-thirds of the whole number of Senators, and a majority of the whole number shall be necessary to a choice. But no person constitutionally ineligible to the office of President shall be eligible to that of Vice-President of the United States.

*Superseded by Section 3 of the 20th amendment.

Amendment XIII

Section 1.

Neither slavery nor involuntary servitude, except as a punishment for crime whereof the party shall have been duly convicted, shall exist within the United States, or any place subject to their jurisdiction.

Section 2.

Congress shall have power to enforce this article by appropriate legislation.

Amendment XIV

Section 1.

All persons born or naturalized in the United States, and subject to the jurisdiction thereof, are citizens of the United States and of the State wherein they reside. No State shall make or enforce any law which shall abridge the privileges or immunities of citizens of the United States; nor shall any State deprive any person of life, liberty, or property, without due process of law; nor deny to any person within its jurisdiction the equal protection of the laws.

Section 2.

Representatives shall be apportioned among the several States according to their respective numbers, counting the whole number of persons in each State, excluding Indians not taxed. But when the right to vote at any election for the choice of electors for President and Vice-President of the United States, Representatives in Congress, the Executive and Judicial officers of a State, or the members of the Legislature thereof, is denied to any of the male inhabitants of such State, being twenty-one years of age,* and citizens of the United States, or in any way abridged, except for participation in rebellion, or other crime, the basis of representation therein shall be reduced in the proportion which the number of such male citizens shall bear to the whole number of male citizens twenty-one years of age in such State.

Section 3.

No person shall be a Senator or Representative in Congress, or elector of President and Vice-President, or hold any office, civil or military, under the United States, or under any State, who, having previously taken an oath, as a member of Congress, or as an officer of the United States, or as a member of any State legislature, or as an executive or judicial officer of any State, to support the Constitution of the United States, shall have engaged in insurrection or rebellion against the same, or given aid or comfort to the enemies thereof. But Congress may by a vote of two-thirds of each House, remove such disability.

Section 4.

The validity of the public debt of the United States, authorized by law, including debts incurred for payment of pensions and bounties for services in suppressing insurrection or rebellion, shall not be questioned. But neither the United States nor any State shall assume or pay any debt or obligation incurred in aid of insurrection or rebellion against the United States, or any claim for the loss or emancipation of any slave; but all such debts, obligations and claims shall be held illegal and void.

Section 5.

The Congress shall have the power to enforce, by appropriate legislation, the provisions of this article.

Changed by Section 1 of the 26th amendment.

Amendment XV

Section 1.

The right of citizens of the United States to vote shall not be denied or abridged by the United States or by any State on account of race, color, or previous condition of servitude—

Section 2.

The Congress shall have the power to enforce this article by appropriate legislation.

Amendment XVI

The Congress shall have power to lay and collect taxes on incomes, from whatever source derived, without apportionment among the several States, and without regard to any census or enumeration.

Amendment XVII

The Senate of the United States shall be composed of two Senators from each State, elected by the people thereof, for six years; and each Senator shall have one vote. The electors in each State shall have the qualifications requisite for electors of the most numerous branch of the State legislatures.

When vacancies happen in the representation of any State in the Senate, the executive authority of such State shall issue writs of election to fill such vacancies: *Provided,* That the legislature of any State may empower the executive thereof to make temporary appointments until the people fill the vacancies by election as the legislature may direct.

This amendment shall not be so construed as to affect the election or term of any Senator chosen before it becomes valid as part of the Constitution.

Amendment XVIII

Section 1.

After one year from the ratification of this article the manufacture, sale, or transportation of intoxicating liquors within, the importation thereof into, or the exportation thereof from the United States and all territory subject to the jurisdiction thereof for beverage purposes is hereby prohibited.

Section 2.

The Congress and the several States shall have concurrent power to enforce this article by appropriate legislation.

Section 3.

This article shall be inoperative unless it shall have been ratified as an amendment to the Constitution by the legislatures of the several States, as provided in the Constitution, within seven years from the date of the submission hereof to the States by the Congress.

Amendment XIX

The right of citizens of the United States to vote shall not be denied or abridged by the United States or by any State on account of sex.

Congress shall have power to enforce this article by appropriate legislation.

Amendment XX

Section 1.

The terms of the President and the Vice President shall end at noon on the 20th day of January, and the terms of Senators and Representatives at noon on the 3d day of January, of the years in which such terms would have ended if this article had not been ratified; and the terms of their successors shall then begin.

Section 2.

The Congress shall assemble at least once in every year, and such meeting shall begin at noon on the 3d day of January, unless they shall by law appoint a different day.

Section 3.

If, at the time fixed for the beginning of the term of the President, the President elect shall have died, the Vice President elect shall become President. If a President shall not have been chosen before the time fixed for the beginning of his term, or if the President elect shall have failed to qualify, then the Vice President elect shall act as President until a President shall have qualified; and the Congress may by law provide for the case wherein neither a President elect nor a Vice President elect shall have qualified, declaring who shall then act as President, or the manner in which one who is to act shall be selected, and such person shall act accordingly until a President or Vice President shall have qualified.

Section 4.

The Congress may by law provide for the case of the death of any of the persons from whom the House of Representatives may choose a President whenever the right of choice shall have devolved upon them, and for the case of the death of any of the persons from whom the Senate may choose a Vice President whenever the right of choice shall have devolved upon them.

Section 5.

Sections 1 and 2 shall take effect on the 15th day of October following the ratification of this article.

Section 6.

This article shall be inoperative unless it shall have been ratified as an amendment to the Constitution by the legislatures of three-fourths of the several States within seven years from the date of its submission.

Amendment XXI

Section 1.

The eighteenth article of amendment to the Constitution of the United States is hereby repealed.

Section 2.

The transportation or importation into any State, Territory, or possession of the United States for delivery or use therein of intoxicating liquors, in violation of the laws thereof, is hereby prohibited.

Section 3.

This article shall be inoperative unless it shall have been ratified as an amendment to the Constitution by conventions in the several States, as provided in the Constitution, within seven years from the date of the submission hereof to the States by the Congress.

Amendment XXII

Section 1.

No person shall be elected to the office of the President more than twice, and no person who has held the office of President, or acted as President, for more than two years of a term to which some other person was elected President shall be elected to the office of the President more than once. But this Article shall not apply to any person holding the office of President when this Article was proposed by the Congress, and shall not prevent any person who may be holding the office of President, or acting as President, during the term within which this Article becomes operative from holding the office of President or acting as

President during the remainder of such term.

Section 2.

This article shall be inoperative unless it shall have been ratified as an amendment to the Constitution by the legislatures of three-fourths of the several States within seven years from the date of its submission to the States by the Congress.

Amendment XXIII

Section 1.

The District constituting the seat of Government of the United States shall appoint in such manner as the Congress may direct:

A number of electors of President and Vice President equal to the whole number of Senators and Representatives in Congress to which the District would be entitled if it were a State, but in no event more than the least populous State; they shall be in addition to those appointed by the States, but they shall be considered, for the purposes of the election of President and Vice President, to be electors appointed by a State; and they shall meet in the District and perform such duties as provided by the twelfth article of amendment.

Section 2.

The Congress shall have power to enforce this article by appropriate legislation.

Amendment XXIV

Section 1.

The right of citizens of the United States to vote in any primary or other election for President or Vice President, for electors for President or Vice President, or for Senator or Representative in Congress, shall not be denied or abridged by the United States or any State by reason of failure to pay any poll tax or other tax.

Section 2.

The Congress shall have power to enforce this article by appropriate legislation.

Amendment XXV

Section 1.

In case of the removal of the President from office or of his death or resignation, the Vice President shall become President.

Section 2.

Whenever there is a vacancy in the office of the Vice President, the President shall nominate a Vice President who shall take office upon confirmation by a majority vote of both Houses of Congress.

Section 3.

Whenever the President transmits to the President pro tempore of the Senate and the Speaker of the House of Representatives his written declaration that he is unable to discharge the powers and duties of his office, and until he transmits to them a written declaration to the contrary, such powers and duties shall be discharged by the Vice President as Acting President.

Section 4.

Whenever the Vice President and a majority of either the principal officers of the executive departments or of such other body as Congress may by law provide, transmit to the President pro tempore of the Senate and the Speaker of the House of Representatives their written declaration that the President is unable to discharge the powers and duties of his office, the Vice President shall immediately assume the powers and duties of the office as Acting President.

Thereafter, when the President transmits to the President pro tempore of the Senate and the Speaker of the House of Representatives his written declaration that no inability exists, he shall resume the powers and duties of his office unless the Vice President and a majority of either the principal officers of the executive department or of such other body as Congress may by law provide, transmit within four days to the President pro tempore of the Senate and the Speaker of the House of Representatives their written declaration that the President is unable to discharge the powers and duties of his office. Thereupon Congress shall decide the issue, assembling within forty-eight hours for that purpose if not in session. If the Congress, within twenty-one days after receipt of the latter written declaration, or, if Congress is not in session, within twenty-one days after Congress is required to assemble, determines by two-thirds vote of both Houses that the President is unable to discharge the powers and duties of his office, the Vice President shall continue to discharge the same as Acting President; otherwise, the President shall resume the powers and duties of his office.

Amendment XXVI

Section 1.

The right of citizens of the United States, who are eighteen years of age or older, to vote shall not be denied or abridged by the United States or by any State on account of age.

Section 2.

The Congress shall have power to enforce this article by appropriate legislation.

Amendment XXVII

No law, varying the compensation for the services of the Senators and Representatives, shall take effect, until an election of Representatives shall have intervened.

APPENDIX C | Federalist Papers #10 and #51

Federalist Paper #10: The Union as a Safeguard Against Domestic Faction and Insurrection

From the New York Packet.

Friday, November 23, 1787.

Author: James Madison

To the People of the State of New York:

AMONG the numerous advantages promised by a well-constructed Union, none deserves to be more accurately developed than its tendency to break and control the violence of faction. The friend of popular governments never finds himself so much alarmed for their character and fate, as when he contemplates their propensity to this dangerous vice. He will not fail, therefore, to set a due value on any plan which, without violating the principles to which he is attached, provides a proper cure for it. The instability, injustice, and confusion introduced into the public councils, have, in truth, been the mortal diseases under which popular governments have everywhere perished; as they continue to be the favorite and fruitful topics from which the adversaries to liberty derive their most specious declamations. The valuable improvements made by the American constitutions on the popular models, both ancient and modern, cannot certainly be too much admired; but it would be an unwarrantable partiality, to contend that they have as effectually obviated the danger on this side, as was wished and expected. Complaints are everywhere heard from our most considerate and virtuous citizens, equally the friends of public and private faith, and of public and personal liberty, that our governments are too unstable, that the public good is disregarded in the conflicts of rival parties, and that measures are too often decided, not according to the rules of justice and the rights of the minor party, but by the superior force of an interested and overbearing majority. However anxiously we may wish that these complaints had no foundation, the evidence, of known facts will not permit us to deny that they are in some degree true. It will be found, indeed, on a candid review of our situation, that some of the distresses under which we labor have been erroneously charged on the operation of our governments; but it will be found, at the same time, that other causes will not alone account for many of our heaviest misfortunes; and, particularly, for that prevailing and increasing distrust of public engagements, and alarm for private rights, which are echoed from one end of the continent to the other. These must be chiefly, if not wholly, effects of the unsteadiness and injustice with which a factious spirit has tainted our public administrations.

By a faction, I understand a number of citizens, whether amounting to a majority or a minority of the whole, who are united and actuated by some common impulse of passion, or of interest, adversed to the rights of other citizens, or to the permanent and aggregate interests of the community.

There are two methods of curing the mischiefs of faction: the one, by removing its causes; the other, by controlling its effects.

There are again two methods of removing the causes of faction: the one, by destroying the liberty which is essential to its existence; the other, by giving to every citizen the same opinions, the same passions, and the same interests.

It could never be more truly said than of the first remedy, that it was worse than the disease. Liberty is to faction what air is to fire, an aliment without which it instantly expires. But it could not be less folly to abolish liberty, which is essential to political life, because it nourishes faction, than it would be to wish the annihilation of air, which is essential to animal life, because it imparts to fire its destructive agency.

The second expedient is as impracticable as the first would be unwise. As long as the reason of man continues fallible, and he is at liberty to exercise it, different opinions will be formed. As long as the connection subsists between his reason and his self-love, his opinions and his passions will have a reciprocal influence on each other; and the former will be objects to which the latter will attach themselves. The diversity in the faculties of men, from which the rights of property originate, is not less an insuperable obstacle to a uniformity of interests. The protection of these faculties is the first object of government. From the protection of different and unequal faculties of acquiring property, the possession of different degrees and kinds of property immediately results; and from the influence of these on the sentiments and views of the respective proprietors, ensues a division of the society into different interests and parties.

The latent causes of faction are thus sown in the nature of man; and we see them everywhere brought into different degrees of activity, according to the different circumstances of civil society. A zeal for different opinions concerning religion, concerning government, and many other points, as well of speculation as of practice; an attachment to different leaders ambitiously contending for pre-eminence and power; or to persons of other descriptions whose fortunes have been interesting to the human passions, have, in turn, divided mankind into parties, inflamed them with mutual animosity, and rendered them much more disposed to vex and oppress each other than to co-operate for their common good. So strong is this propensity of mankind to fall into mutual animosities, that where no substantial occasion presents itself, the most frivolous and fanciful distinctions have been sufficient to kindle their unfriendly passions and excite their most violent conflicts. But the most common and durable source of factions has been the various and unequal distribution of property. Those who hold and those who are without property have ever formed distinct interests in society. Those who are creditors, and those who are debtors, fall under a like discrimination. A landed interest, a manufacturing interest, a mercantile interest, a moneyed interest, with many lesser interests, grow up of necessity in civilized nations, and divide them into different classes, actuated by different sentiments and views. The regulation of these various and interfering interests forms the principal task of modern legislation, and involves the spirit of party and faction in the necessary and ordinary operations of the government.

No man is allowed to be a judge in his own cause, because his interest would certainly bias his judgment, and, not improbably, corrupt his integrity. With equal, nay with greater reason, a body of men are unfit to be both judges and parties at the same time; yet what are many of the most important acts of legislation, but so many judicial determinations, not indeed concerning the rights of single persons, but concerning the rights of large bodies of citizens? And what are the different classes of legislators but advocates and parties to the causes which they determine? Is a law proposed concerning private debts? It is a question to which the creditors are parties on one side and the debtors on the other. Justice ought to hold the balance between them. Yet the parties are, and must be, themselves the judges; and the most numerous party, or, in other words, the most powerful faction must be expected to prevail. Shall domestic manufactures be encouraged, and in what degree, by restrictions on foreign manufactures? are questions which would be differently decided by the landed and the manufacturing classes, and probably by neither with a sole regard to justice and the public good. The apportionment of taxes on the various descriptions of property is an act which seems to require the most exact impartiality; yet there is, perhaps, no legislative act in which greater opportunity and temptation are given to a predominant party to trample on the rules of justice. Every shilling with which they overburden the inferior number, is a shilling saved to their own pockets.

It is in vain to say that enlightened statesmen will be able to adjust these clashing interests, and render them all subservient to the public good. Enlightened statesmen will not always be at the helm. Nor, in many cases, can such an adjustment be made at all without taking into view indirect and remote considerations, which will rarely prevail over the immediate interest which one party may find in disregarding the rights of another or the good of the whole.

The inference to which we are brought is, that the CAUSES of faction cannot be removed, and that relief is only to be sought in the means of controlling its EFFECTS.

If a faction consists of less than a majority, relief is supplied by the republican principle, which enables the majority to defeat its sinister views by regular vote. It may clog the administration, it may convulse the society; but it will be unable to execute and mask its violence under the forms of the Constitution. When a majority is included in a faction, the form of popular government, on the other hand, enables it to sacrifice to its ruling passion or interest both the public good and the rights of other citizens. To secure the public good and private rights against the danger of such a faction, and at the same time to preserve the spirit and the form of popular government, is then the great object to which our inquiries are directed. Let me add that it is the great desideratum by which this form of government can be rescued from the opprobrium under which it has so long labored, and be recommended to the esteem and adoption of mankind.

By what means is this object attainable? Evidently by one of two only. Either the existence of the same passion or interest in a majority at the same time must be prevented, or the majority, having such coexistent passion or interest, must be rendered, by their number and local situation, unable to concert and carry into effect schemes of oppression. If the impulse and the opportunity be suffered to coincide, we well know that neither moral nor religious motives can be relied on as an adequate control. They are not found to be such on the injustice and violence of individuals, and lose their efficacy in proportion to the number combined together, that is, in proportion as their efficacy becomes needful.

From this view of the subject it may be concluded that a pure democracy, by which I mean a society consisting of a small number of citizens, who assemble and administer the government in person, can admit of no cure for the mischiefs of faction. A common passion or interest will, in almost every case, be felt by a majority of the whole; a communication and concert result from the form of government itself; and there is nothing to check the inducements to sacrifice the weaker party or an obnoxious individual. Hence it is that such democracies have ever been spectacles of turbulence and contention; have ever been found incompatible with personal security or the rights of property; and have in general been as short in their lives as they have been violent in their deaths. Theoretic politicians, who have patronized this species of government, have erroneously supposed that by reducing mankind to a perfect equality in their political rights, they would, at the same time, be perfectly equalized and assimilated in their possessions, their opinions, and their passions.

A republic, by which I mean a government in which the scheme of representation takes place, opens a different prospect, and promises the cure for which we are seeking. Let us examine the points in which it varies from pure democracy, and we shall comprehend both the nature of the cure and the efficacy which it must derive from the Union.

The two great points of difference between a democracy and a republic are: first, the delegation of the government, in the latter, to a small number of citizens elected by the rest; secondly, the greater number of citizens, and greater sphere of country, over which the latter may be extended.

The effect of the first difference is, on the one hand, to refine and enlarge the public views, by passing them through the medium of a chosen body of citizens, whose wisdom may best discern the true interest of their country, and whose patriotism and love of justice will be least likely to sacrifice it to temporary or partial considerations. Under such a regulation, it may well happen that the public voice, pronounced by the representatives of the people, will be more consonant to the public good than if pronounced by the people themselves, convened for the purpose. On the other hand, the effect may be inverted. Men of factious tempers, of local prejudices, or of sinister designs, may, by intrigue, by corruption, or by other means, first obtain the suffrages, and then betray the interests, of the people. The question resulting is, whether small or extensive republics are more favorable to the election of proper guardians of the public weal; and it is clearly decided in favor of the latter by two obvious considerations:

In the first place, it is to be remarked that, however small the republic may be, the representatives must be raised to a certain number, in order to guard against the cabals of a few; and that, however large it may be, they must be limited to a certain number, in order to guard against the confusion of a multitude. Hence, the number of representatives in the two cases not being in proportion to that of the two constituents, and being proportionally greater in the small republic, it follows that, if the proportion of fit characters be not less in the large than in the small republic, the former will present a greater option, and consequently a greater probability of a fit choice.

In the next place, as each representative will be chosen by a greater number of citizens in the large than in the small republic, it will be more difficult for unworthy candidates to practice with success the vicious arts by which elections are too often carried; and the suffrages of the people being more free, will be more likely to centre in men who possess the most attractive merit and the most diffusive and established characters.

It must be confessed that in this, as in most other cases, there is a mean, on both sides of which inconveniences will be found to lie. By enlarging too much the number of electors, you render the representatives too little acquainted with all their local circumstances and lesser interests; as by reducing it too much, you render him unduly attached to these, and too little fit to comprehend and pursue great and national objects. The federal Constitution forms a happy combination in this respect; the great and aggregate interests being referred to the national, the local and particular to the State legislatures.

The other point of difference is, the greater number of citizens and extent of territory which may be brought within the compass of republican than of democratic government; and it is this circumstance principally which renders factious combinations less to be dreaded in the former than in the latter. The smaller the society, the fewer probably will be the distinct parties and interests composing it; the fewer the distinct parties and interests, the more frequently will a majority be found of the same party; and the smaller the number of individuals composing a majority, and the smaller the compass within which they are placed, the more easily will they concert and execute their plans of oppression. Extend the sphere, and you take in a greater variety of parties and interests; you make it less probable that a majority of the whole will have a common motive to invade the rights of other citizens; or if such a common motive exists, it will be more difficult for all who feel it to discover their own strength, and to act in unison with each other. Besides other impediments, it may be remarked that, where there is a consciousness of unjust or dishonorable purposes, communication is always checked by distrust in proportion to the number whose concurrence is necessary.

Hence, it clearly appears, that the same advantage which a republic has over a democracy, in controlling the effects of faction, is enjoyed by a large over a small republic,--is enjoyed by the Union over the States composing it. Does the advantage consist in the substitution of representatives whose enlightened views and virtuous sentiments render them superior to local prejudices and schemes of injustice? It will not be denied that the representation of the Union will be most likely to possess these requisite endowments. Does it consist in the greater security afforded by a greater variety of parties, against the event of any one party being able to outnumber and oppress the rest? In an equal degree does the increased variety of parties comprised within the Union, increase this security. Does it, in fine, consist in the greater obstacles opposed to the concert and accomplishment of the secret wishes of an unjust and interested majority? Here, again, the extent of the Union gives it the most palpable advantage.

The influence of factious leaders may kindle a flame within their particular States, but will be unable to spread a general conflagration through the other States. A religious sect may degenerate into a political faction in a part of the Confederacy; but the variety of sects dispersed over the entire face of it must secure the national councils against any danger from that source. A rage for paper money, for an abolition of debts, for an equal division of property, or for any other improper or wicked project, will be less apt to pervade the whole body of the Union than a particular member of it; in the same proportion as such a malady is more likely to taint a particular county or district, than an entire State.

In the extent and proper structure of the Union, therefore, we behold a republican remedy for the diseases most incident to republican government. And according to the degree of pleasure and pride we feel in being republicans, ought to be our zeal in cherishing the spirit and supporting the character of Federalists.

Federalist Paper #51: The Structure of the Government Must Furnish the Proper Checks and Balances Between the Different Departments

From the New York Packet.

Friday, February 8, 1788.

Author: Alexander Hamilton or James Madison

To the People of the State of New York:

TO WHAT expedient, then, shall we finally resort, for maintaining in practice the necessary partition of power among the several departments, as laid down in the Constitution? The only answer that can be given is, that as all these exterior provisions are found to be inadequate, the defect must be supplied, by so contriving the interior structure of the government as that its several constituent parts may, by their mutual relations, be the means of keeping each other in their proper places. Without presuming to undertake a full development of this important idea, I will hazard a few general observations, which may perhaps place it in a clearer light, and enable us to form a more correct judgment of the principles and structure of the government planned by the convention. In order to lay a due foundation for that separate and distinct exercise of the different powers of government, which to a certain extent is admitted on all hands to be essential to the preservation of liberty, it is evident that each department should have a will of its own; and consequently should be so constituted that the members of each should have as little agency as possible in the appointment of the members of the others. Were this principle rigorously adhered to, it would require that all the appointments for the supreme executive, legislative, and judiciary magistracies should be drawn from the same fountain of authority, the people, through channels having no communication whatever with one another. Perhaps such a plan of constructing the several departments would be less difficult in practice than it may in contemplation appear. Some difficulties, however, and some additional expense would attend the execution of it. Some deviations, therefore, from the principle must be admitted. In the constitution of the judiciary department in particular, it might be inexpedient to insist rigorously on the principle: first, because peculiar qualifications being essential in the members, the primary consideration ought to be to select that mode of choice which best secures these qualifications; secondly, because the permanent tenure by which the appointments are held in that department, must soon destroy all sense of dependence on the authority conferring them. It is equally evident, that the members of each department should be as little dependent as possible on those of the others, for the emoluments annexed to their offices. Were the executive magistrate, or the judges, not independent of the legislature in this particular, their independence in every other would be merely nominal. But the great security against a gradual concentration of the several powers in the same department, consists in giving to those who administer each department the necessary constitutional means and personal motives to resist encroachments of the others. The provision for defense must in this, as in all other cases, be made commensurate to the danger of attack. Ambition must be made to counteract ambition. The interest of the man must be connected with the constitutional rights of the place. It may be a reflection on human nature, that such devices should be necessary to control the abuses of government. But what is government itself, but the greatest of all reflections on human nature? If men were angels, no government would be necessary. If angels were to govern men, neither external nor internal controls on government would be necessary. In framing a government which is to be administered by men over men, the great difficulty lies in this: you must first enable the government to control the governed; and in the next place oblige it to control itself. A dependence on the people is, no doubt, the primary control on the government; but experience has taught mankind the necessity of auxiliary precautions. This policy of supplying, by opposite and rival interests, the defect of better motives, might be traced through the whole system of human affairs, private as well as public. We see it particularly displayed in all the subordinate distributions of power, where the constant aim is to divide and arrange the several offices in such a manner as that each may be a check on the other that the private interest of every individual may be a sentinel over the public rights. These inventions of prudence cannot be less requisite in the distribution of the supreme powers of the State. But it is not possible to give to each department an equal power of self-defense. In republican government, the legislative authority necessarily predominates. The remedy for this inconveniency is to divide the legislature into different branches; and to render them, by different modes of election and different principles of action, as little connected with each other as the nature of their common functions and their common dependence on the society will admit. It may even be necessary to guard against dangerous encroachments by still further precautions. As the weight of the legislative authority requires that it should be thus divided, the weakness of the executive may require, on the other hand, that it should be fortified. An absolute negative on the legislature appears, at first view, to be the natural defense with which the executive magistrate should be armed. But perhaps it would be neither altogether safe nor alone sufficient. On ordinary occasions it might not be exerted with the requisite firmness, and on extraordinary occasions it might be perfidiously abused. May not this defect of an absolute negative be supplied by some qualified connection between this weaker department and the weaker branch of the stronger department, by which the latter may be led to support the constitutional rights of the former, without being too much detached from the rights of its own department? If the principles on which these observations are founded be just, as I persuade myself they are, and they be applied as a criterion to the several State constitutions, and to the federal Constitution it will be found that if the latter does not perfectly correspond with them, the former are infinitely less able to bear such a test. There are, moreover, two considerations particularly applicable to the federal system of America, which place that system in a very interesting point of view. First. In a single republic, all the power surrendered by the people is submitted to the administration of a single government; and the usurpations are guarded against by a division of the government into distinct and separate departments. In the compound republic of America, the power surrendered by the people is first divided between two distinct governments, and then the portion allotted to each subdivided among distinct and separate departments. Hence a double security arises to the rights of the people. The different governments will control each other, at the same time that each will be controlled by itself. Second. It is of great importance in a republic not only to guard the society against the oppression of its rulers, but to guard one part of the society against the injustice of the other part. Different interests necessarily exist in different classes of citizens. If a majority be united by a common interest, the rights of the minority will be insecure. There are but two methods of providing against this evil: the one by creating a will in the community independent of the majority that is, of the society itself; the other, by comprehending in the society so many separate descriptions of citizens as will render an unjust combination of a majority of the whole very improbable, if not impracticable. The first method prevails in all governments possessing an hereditary or self-appointed authority. This, at best, is but a precarious security; because a power independent of the society may as well espouse the unjust views of the major, as the rightful interests of the minor party, and may possibly be turned against both parties. The second method will be exemplified in the federal republic of the United States. Whilst all authority in it will be derived from and dependent on the society, the society itself will be broken into so many parts, interests, and classes of citizens, that the rights of individuals, or of the minority, will be in little danger from interested combinations of the majority. In a free government the security for civil rights must be the same as that for religious rights. It consists in the one case in the multiplicity of interests, and in the other in the multiplicity of sects. The degree of security in both cases will depend on the number of interests and sects; and this may be presumed to depend on the extent of country and number of people comprehended under the same government. This view of the subject must particularly recommend a proper federal system to all the sincere and considerate friends of republican government, since it shows that in exact proportion as the territory of the Union may be formed into more circumscribed Confederacies, or States oppressive combinations of a majority will be facilitated: the best security, under the republican forms, for the rights of every class of citizens, will be diminished: and consequently the stability and independence of some member of the government, the only other security, must be proportionately increased. Justice is the end of government. It is the end of civil society. It ever has been and ever will be pursued until it be obtained, or until liberty be lost in the pursuit. In a society under the forms of which the stronger faction can readily unite and oppress the weaker, anarchy may as truly be said to reign as in a state of nature, where the weaker individual is not secured against the violence of the stronger; and as, in the latter state, even the stronger individuals are prompted, by the uncertainty of their condition, to submit to a government which may protect the weak as well as themselves; so, in the former state, will the more powerful factions or parties be gradually induced, by a like motive, to wish for a government which will protect all parties, the weaker as well as the more powerful. It can be little doubted that if the State of Rhode Island was separated from the Confederacy and left to itself, the insecurity of rights under the popular form of government within such narrow limits would be displayed by such reiterated oppressions of factious majorities that some power altogether independent of the people would soon be called for by the voice of the very factions whose misrule had proved the necessity of it. In the extended republic of the United States, and among the great variety of interests, parties, and sects which it embraces, a coalition of a majority of the whole society could seldom take place on any other principles than those of justice and the general good; whilst there being thus less danger to a minor from the will of a major party, there must be less pretext, also, to provide for the security of the former, by introducing into the government a will not dependent on the latter, or, in other words, a will independent of the society itself. It is no less certain than it is important, notwithstanding the contrary opinions which have been entertained, that the larger the society, provided it lie within a practical sphere, the more duly capable it will be of self-government. And happily for the REPUBLICAN CAUSE, the practicable sphere may be carried to a very great extent, by a judicious modification and mixture of the FEDERAL PRINCIPLE.

PUBLIUS.

APPENDIX D | Electoral College Votes by State, 2012–2020

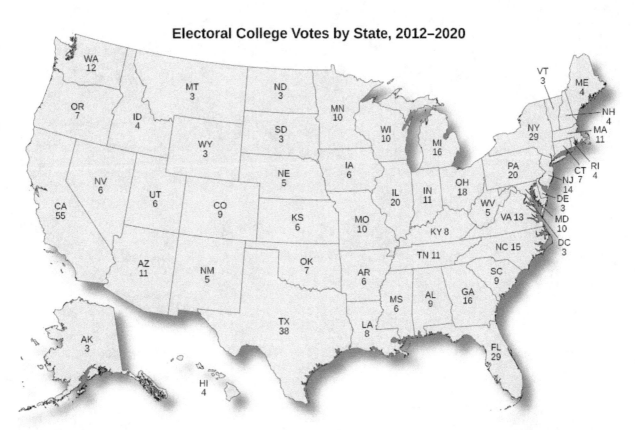

Electoral College Votes by State, 2012–2020

Figure D1   The number of Electoral College votes granted to each state equals the total number of representatives and senators that state has in the U.S. Congress or, in the case of Washington, DC, as many electors as it would have if it were a state. The number of representatives may fluctuate based on state population, which is determined every ten years by the U.S. Census, mandated by Article I, Section 2 of the Constitution. The most recent census was conducted in 2010.

APPENDIX E | Selected Supreme Court Cases

A. L. A. Schechter Poultry Corp. v. United States, **295 U.S. 495 (1935).** This case represented a challenge to the constitutionality of a law called the National Industrial Recovery Act. This law was a major part of President Franklin D. Roosevelt's attempt to rebuild the nation's economy during the Great Depression. Major industries in the United States, however, objected to the way the law empowered the president to regulate aspects of American industry, such as labor conditions and even pay. In the unanimous decision, the court determined that the act was unconstitutional because it shifted the power to regulate commerce from the legislative branch to the executive branch.

Arizona v. United States, **567 U.S. ___ (2012).** This case involved federal attempts to prevent an Arizona state immigration law (S.B. 1070) from being enforced. The United States brought suit, arguing that immigration law is exclusively in the federal domain. Agreeing with the federal government, a federal district court enjoined specific provisions in the law. Arizona appealed to the Supreme Court to overturn the decision. In a 5–3 decision, the court found that specific provisions in the law did conflict with federal law, while others were constitutional.

Brown v. Board of Education of Topeka, **347 U.S. 483 (1954).** This case represented a challenge to the principle of "separate but equal" established by *Plessy v. Ferguson* in 1896. The case was brought by students who were denied admittance to certain public schools based exclusively on race. The unanimous decision in *Brown v. Board* determined that the existence of racially segregated public schools violated the equal protection clause of the Fourteenth Amendment. The court decided that schools segregated by race perpetrated harm by giving legal sanction to the idea that African Americans were inherently inferior. The ruling effectively overturned *Plessy v. Ferguson* and removed the legal supports for segregated schools nationwide.

Buckley v. Valeo, **424 U.S. 1 (1976).** This case concerned the power of the then recently created Federal Election Commission to regulate the financing of political campaigns. These restrictions limited the amount of contributions that could be made to candidates and required political contributions to be disclosed, among other things. In 1975, Senator James Buckley filed suit, arguing that these limits amounted to a violation of First Amendment protections on free speech and free association. In a series of decisions in this complex case, the court determined that these restrictions did not violate the First Amendment.

Burwell v. Hobby Lobby Stores, Inc., **573 U.S. ___ (2014).** This case involved a challenge to the mandate in the Patient Protection and Affordable Care Act that required that all employment-based group health care plans provide coverage for certain types of contraceptives. The law, however, allowed exemptions for religious employers such as churches that held a religious-based opposition to contraception. The plaintiffs in the case argued that Hobby Lobby, a large family-owned chain of arts and crafts stores, was run based on Christian principles and therefore should be exempt as well because of the Religious Freedom Restoration Act of 1993 (RFRA). The 5–4 decision in *Burwell v. Hobby Lobby* agreed with the plaintiffs and declared that RFRA permits for-profit companies like Hobby Lobby to deny coverage for contraception in their health plans when that coverage violates a religious belief.

Bush v. Gore, **531 U.S. 98 (2000).** Following voting in the November 2000 presidential election, observers recognized that the outcome of the very close national election hinged on the outcome of the election in Florida. Because the Florida election was so close, manual recounts were called for by the state's supreme court. Then-governor George W. Bush, who was ahead in the initial count, appealed to the U.S. Supreme Court to halt the manual recount and to declare that the method of manual recount being used violated his rights to equal protection and due process. The court issued a two-part *per curiam* opinion on the case. (In a *per curiam* opinion, the court makes it clear that the decision in the case is not intended to set a legal precedent.) In the first part, the court ruled in a 7–2 decision that the manual recount did violate the plaintiff's right to equal protection. In the second part, decided by a smaller 5–4 margin, the court ruled that there was not sufficient time to adjust the recount procedure and conduct a full recount. The effect of this ruling gave the Florida electoral votes, and thus the presidency, to George W. Bush.

Citizens United v. Federal Election Commission, **558 U.S. 310 (2010).** In 2007, the nonprofit corporation Citizens United was prevented by the Federal Election Commission (FEC) from showing a movie about then-presidential candidate Hillary Clinton. The FEC noted that showing the movie violated the Bipartisan Campaign Reform Act (BCRA). BCRA prohibited campaign communications one month before a primary election and two months before a general election, required donors to be disclosed, and prohibited corporations from using their general funds for campaign communications. The plaintiffs argued that these restrictions constituted a violation of the First Amendment. The 5–4 decision in *Citizens United v. FEC* agreed with the plaintiffs and concluded that the restrictions imposed by BCRA and enforced by the FEC violated the corporation's First Amendment right to free expression.

Dred Scott v. Sandford, **60 U.S. 393 (1856).** This case concerned the constitutionality of the Missouri Compromise, which declared that certain states would be entirely free of slavery. Dred Scott, a slave, was brought by his owner into free territories. When the owner brought him back to Missouri, a slave state, Dred Scott sued claiming that his time living in free territory made him free. After failing in his attempts in Missouri, Scott appealed to the Supreme Court. In a 7–2 decision, the court declared that the relevant parts of the Missouri Compromise were unconstitutional, and that Scott remained a slave as a result.

Gideon v. Wainwright, **372 U.S. 335 (1963).** In 1961, Clarence E. Gideon was arrested and accused of breaking into a poolroom and stealing money from a cigarette machine. Not being able to afford a lawyer, and being denied a public defender by the judge, Gideon defended himself and was subsequently found guilty. Gideon appealed to the Supreme Court declaring that the denial by the trial judge constituted a violation of his constitutional right to representation. The unanimous decision by the court in *Gideon v. Wainwright* agreed that the Sixth Amendment required that those facing felony criminal charges be supplied with legal representation.

King v. Burwell, **576 U.S. ___ (2015).** When Congress wrote and passed the Patient Protection and Affordable Care Act in 2010, lawmakers intended for states to create exchanges through which residents in those states could purchase health care insurance plans. For those residents who could not afford the premiums, the law also allowed for tax credits to help reduce the cost. If states didn't create an exchange, the federal government created the exchange for the state. While the intention of the lawmakers was for the tax credits to apply to the federally created exchanges as well, the language of the law was somewhat unclear on this point. Residents in Virginia brought suit against the law arguing that the law should be interpreted in a way that withholds tax credits from those participating in the federally created exchange. In the 6–3 decision, the court disagreed, stating that viewing the law in its entirety made it clear that the intent of the law was to provide the tax credits to those participating in either exchange.

Lawrence v. Texas, **539 U.S. 558 (2003).** This case concerned two men in Houston who in 1998 were prosecuted and convicted under a Texas law that forbade certain types of intimate sexual relations between two persons of the same sex. The men appealed to the Supreme Court arguing that their Fourteenth Amendment rights to equal protection and privacy were violated when they were prosecuted for consensual sexual intimacy in their own home. In the 6–3 decision in *Lawrence v. Texas*, the court concluded that while so-called anti-sodomy statutes like the law in Texas did not violate one's right to equal protection, they did violate the due process clause of the Fourteenth Amendment. The court stated that the government had no right to infringe on the liberty of persons engaging in such private and personal acts.

Marbury v. Madison, **5 U.S. 137 (1803).** This case involved the nomination of justices of the peace in Washington, DC, by President John Adams at the end of his term. Despite the Senate confirming the nominations, some of the commissions were not delivered before Adams left office. The new president, Thomas Jefferson, decided not to deliver the commissions. William Marbury, one of the offended justices, sued, saying that the Judiciary Act of 1789 empowered the court to force Secretary of State James Madison to deliver the commissions. In the unanimous decision in *Marbury v. Madison*, the court declared that while Marbury's rights were violated when Madison refused to deliver the commission, the court did not have the power to force the secretary to do so despite what the Judiciary Act says. In declaring that the law conflicted with the U.S. Constitution, the case established the principle of judicial review wherein the Supreme Court has the power to declare laws passed by Congress and signed by the president to be unconstitutional.

McDonald v. Chicago, **561 U.S. 742 (2010).** This case developed as a consequence of the decision in *District of Columbia v. Heller*, 554 U.S. 570 (2008), which dismissed a Washington, DC, handgun ban as a violation of the Second Amendment. In *McDonald v. Chicago*, the plaintiffs argued that the Fourteenth Amendment had the effect of applying the Second Amendment to the states, not just to the federal government. In a 5–4 decision, the court agreed with the plaintiffs and concluded that rights like the right to keep and bear arms are important enough for maintaining liberty that the Fourteenth Amendment rightly applies them to the states.

Miranda v. Arizona, **384 U.S. 436 (1966).** When Ernesto Miranda was arrested, interrogated, and confessed to kidnapping in 1963, the arresting officers neglected to inform him of his Fifth Amendment right not to self-incriminate. After being found guilty at trial, Miranda appealed to the Supreme Court, insisting that the officers violated his Fifth Amendment rights. The 5–4 decision in *Miranda v. Arizona* found that the right to not incriminate oneself relies heavily on the suspect's right to be informed of these rights at the time of arrest. The opinion indicated that suspects must be told that they have the right to an attorney and the right to remain silent in order to ensure that any statements they provide are issued voluntarily.

National Federation of Independent Business v. Sebelius, **567 U.S. ___ (2012).** This case represented a challenge to the constitutionality of the Patient Protection and Affordable Care Act. The suing states argued that the Medicare expansion and the individual mandate that required citizens to purchase health insurance or pay a fine were both unconstitutional. The 5–4 decision found that the Medicare expansion was permissible, but that the federal government could not withhold all Medicare funding for states that refused to accept the expansion. More importantly, it found that Congress had the power to apply the mandate to purchase health insurance under its enumerated power to tax.

New York Times Co. v. Sullivan, **376 U.S. 254 (1964).** This case began when the *New York Times* published a full-page advertisement claiming that the arrest of Martin Luther King, Jr. in Alabama was part of a concerted effort to ruin him. Insulted, an Alabama official filed a libel suit against the newspaper. Under Alabama law, which did not require that persons claiming libel have to show harm, the official won a judgment. The *New York Times* appealed to the Supreme Court, arguing that the ruling violated its First Amendment right to free speech. In a unanimous decision, the court declared that the First Amendment protects even false statements by the press, as long as those statements are not made with actual malice.

Obergefell v. Hodges, **576 U.S. ___ (2015).** This case concerned groups of same-sex couples who brought suits against a number of states and relevant agencies that refused to recognize same-sex marriages created in states where such marriages were legal. In the 5–4 decision, the court found that not only did the Fourteenth Amendment provision for equal protection under the law require that states recognize same-sex marriages formed in other states, but that no state could deny marriage licenses to same-sex couples if they also issued them to other types of couples.

Plessy v. Ferguson, **163 U.S. 537 (1896).** When Homer Plessy, a man of mixed racial heritage, sat in a whites-only railroad car in an attempt to challenge a Louisiana law that required railroad cars be segregated, he was arrested and convicted. Appealing his conviction to the Supreme Court, he argued that the segregation law was a violation of the principle of equal protection under the law in the Fourteenth Amendment. In a 7–1 decision, the court disagreed, indicating that the law was not a violation of the equal protection principle because the different train cars were separate but equal. Plessy v. Ferguson's "separate but equal" remained a guiding principle of segregation until *Brown v. Board of Education* (1954).

Roe v. Wade, **410 U.S. 113 (1973).** This case involved a pregnant woman from Texas who desired to terminate her pregnancy. At the time, Texas only allowed abortions in cases where the woman's life was in danger. Using the pseudonym "Jane Roe," the woman appealed to the Supreme Court, arguing that the

Constitution provides women the right to terminate an abortion. The 7–2 decision in *Roe v. Wade* sided with the plaintiff and declared that the right to privacy upheld in the decision in *Griswold v. Connecticut* (1965) included a woman's right to an abortion. In balancing the rights of the woman with the interests of the states to protect human life, the court created a trimester framework. In the first trimester, a pregnant woman could seek an abortion without restriction. In the second and third trimesters, however, the court asserted that states had an interest in regulating abortions, provided that those regulations were based on health needs.

Schechter Poultry Corp. v. United States. See ***A. L. A. Schechter Poultry Corp. v. United States.***

Shelby County v. Holder, **570 U.S. ___ (2013).** After decades in which African Americans encountered obstacles to voting, particularly in southern states, Congress passed the Voting Rights Act of 1965. Among other things, the law prohibited certain congressional districts from changing election laws without federal authorization. In 2010, Shelby County in Alabama brought a suit against the U.S. attorney general, claiming that both section five of the act, which required districts to seek preapproval, and section four, which determined which districts had to seek preapproval, were unconstitutional. In a 5–4 decision, the court found that both sections violated the Tenth Amendment.

United States v. Windsor, **570 U.S. ___ (2013).** When Thea Clara Spyer died in 2009, she left her estate to her wife, Edith Windsor, with whom she had been legally married in Canada years before. Because of a 1996 U.S. law called the Defense of Marriage Act (DOMA), this marriage was not recognized by the federal government. As a result, Windsor was compelled to pay an enormous tax on the inheritance, which she would not have had to pay had the federal government recognized the marriage. Appealing to the Supreme Court, Windsor argued that DOMA was unconstitutional because it deprives same-sex couples of their Fifth Amendment right to equal protection. In the 5–4 decision, the court agreed with Windsor, stating that DOMA was intended to treat certain married couples differently in blatant violation of their Fifth Amendment rights.

Answer Key

Chapter 1

1. B **3.** In a representative democracy, people elect representatives to make political decisions and pass laws for them. In a direct democracy, people make all political decisions and pass laws themselves. **5.** D **7.** A **9.** D **11.** People can pay attention to the news in order to be aware of the most important issues of the day. They can contribute money to a campaign or attend a rally in support of a political candidate whose views they favor. They can write letters to members of Congress and to state and local politicians. They can vote.

Chapter 2

1. C **3.** Americans believed all people (i.e., white males) possessed the rights to life, liberty, and property. The best way to protect these rights was by limiting the power of government and allowing people to govern themselves. **5.** C **7.** C **9.** Separation of powers refers to the process of dividing government into different branches and giving different responsibilities and powers to each branch. In this way, the separate branches must work together to govern the nation. For example, according to the Constitution, Congress has the power to draft legislation. However, the president must sign a piece of proposed legislation before it becomes a law. Thus, the president and Congress must work together to make the nation's laws. **11.** D **13.** B **15.** The Fourteenth Amendment gave citizenship to African Americans and made all Americans equal before the law regardless of race or color. Over the years it has also been used to require states to guarantee their residents the same protections as those granted by the federal government in the Bill of Rights

Chapter 3

1. B **3.** The following parts of the Constitution sketch the powers of the states and the federal government: Article I, Section 8; the supremacy clause of Article VI; and the Tenth Amendment. The following parts of the Constitution detail the limits on their authority: Article I, Sections 9 and 10; Bill of Rights; Fourteenth Amendment; and the civil rights amendments. **5.** C **7.** C **9.** The *McCulloch* decision established the doctrine of implied powers, meaning the federal government can create policy instruments deemed necessary and appropriate to fulfill its constitutional responsibilities. The case also affirmed the principle of national supremacy embodied in Article VI of the Constitution, namely, that the Constitution and legitimate federal laws trump state laws. **11.** D **13.** A **15.** D **17.** B **19.** Federalism can trigger a race to the bottom, leading states to reduce workplace regulations and social benefits for employees; it can obstruct federal efforts to address national problems; and it can deepen economic and social disparities among states.

Chapter 4

1. A **3.** C **5.** Selective incorporation is the process of expanding the application of the Bill of Rights to also include the states. It became necessary in order to guarantee people's civil liberties equally across all states. **7.** C **9.** The two clauses together protect religious liberty but from opposite directions. The establishment clause prevents governments from having an official religion (thus giving all religions a chance to flourish), while the free exercise clause clearly empowers individuals to practice as they wish. **11.** A **13.** D **15.** Someone accused of a crime may take a plea bargain because it reflects a clear path forward rather than the uncertainty of a trial. Typically plea bargains result in weaker punishments than does a court trial. **17.** C **19.** C **21.** A right listed in the Bill of Rights is afforded clearer protection than one developed incrementally through court precedents.

Chapter 5

1. C **3.** D **5.** B **7.** The Civil Rights Act of 1964 outlawed discrimination in employment based on race, color, national origin, religion, and sex and created the Equal Employment Opportunity Commission to investigate discrimination and enforce the provisions of the bill. It also prohibited segregation in public accommodations and encouraged integration in education. **9.** C **11.** D **13.** Both groups lost their ancestral lands to whites who also attempted to destroy their culture. Both groups also suffer high levels of poverty and unemployment today. Most Native American tribes are allowed to govern themselves, but so far Native Hawaiians are not. **15.** A

Chapter 6

1. D **3.** A **5.** Family and/or school are the agents of socialization that have the strongest impact on an individual. **7.** A **9.** If a pollster interviews only a certain type of person, the sample will be biased and the poll will be inaccurate. **11.** B **13.** D **15.** When the issues balance two controversial concerns, such as a limited budget and personal financial needs, or religious liberty and equality. **17.** B **19.** Representatives run for election every two years and must constantly raise campaign money. They abide by public opinion because do not have time to explain their actions or mend fences before each election.

Chapter 7

1. C **3.** A **5.** The main challenge is figuring out where students wish to register, at home or at college. Out-of-state students have an even greater challenge because they have moved across state lines. **7.** A **9.** To increase voter turnout in the United States, I would suggest these options: move to all-mail voting, hold elections on weekends, automatically register voters, and pass federal law that further reduces impediments to voter registration. **11.** I would ask them their age, educational level, interest in politics, income level, and whether they voted in the last election. **13.** B **15.** A **17.** Candidates with extreme viewpoints gain media attention, and primary voters are more ideologically motivated than voters in other elections. **19.** Closed primaries do not allow voters affiliated with other parties to vote, thus keeping the decision inside the party. **21.** B **23.** Voters tend to vote for candidates who look attractive and competent. They may consider race, gender, height, weight, and other physical attributes. **25.** C **27.** People of means can easily form interest groups to propose initiatives/recalls and that have the resources to pay for signature collection.

Chapter 8

1. A **3.** B **5.** Conglomerates set policies that affect all organizations and networks within the corporation. If Disney refuses to air programming with a certain actor, all stations in the Disney conglomerate might be required to forgo programming with that actor. **7.** Social media allow citizens and businesses to quickly forward information and news to large groups of friends and followers. **9.** A **11.** C **13.** The State of the Union address and "rally 'round the flag" speeches help explain policies and offer comfort after crises. **15.** A **17.** D **19.** Supporters can act as advertisements, raise donations, and ask for volunteers to help a campaign. **21.** A **23.** D **25.** If we are presented with a reality, it affects the way we vote and the policies we support.

Chapter 9

1. D **3.** Early parties were electoral coalitions of elites, mostly in the U.S. Congress. They were mostly designed to help win House elections and the presidency, but they quickly expanded activities to the state level. **5.** A **7.** Third parties bring important issues to the attention of the major parties. They also often serve as spoilers in the elections they enter. **9.** D **11.** Parties can't influence and enact policy without winning. They must organize at each level at which elections take place in order to contest elections and develop candidates. **13.** The sorting thesis says that voters change party allegiances in response to shifts in party position. It suggests that polarization is a function of voters' paying more attention to national politics and voting more consistently. **15.** They have pulled their respective parties further to the ideological poles and have changed the issues parties consider. They may also have made compromise more difficult.

Chapter 10

1. A **3.** D **5.** B **7.** Incentives that help overcome collective action problems include material, solidary, and purposive benefits. These are often offered by group leaders. Sometimes, political, economic, or social disturbances help overcome collective action problems by mobilizing groups. **9.** D **11.** By joining interest groups, individuals can participate in ways that go beyond simple voting. They can interact with others with similar views. They can become civically engaged by becoming more connected to their communities, they can participate in protests and letter-writing campaigns, and they can inform others about the issues. **13.** Numerous barriers prevent people from participating in politics. Some people lack time or other resources to participate. Lower-income individuals and groups may lack the necessary civic skills to participate effectively. Institutional barriers like voter identification laws may disproportionately affect some people more than others. **15.** A **17.** Interest groups and lobbyists often attempt to gain access by first supporting candidates when they run for office. Since incumbents have an advantage, lobbyists often contribute to them. Second, once legislative members are in office, interest groups and their lobbyists try to encourage them to sponsor legislation the groups wants. They may target sympathetic lawmakers, legislative leaders, and members of important committees. **19.** D

Chapter 11

1. A **3.** C **5.** A primary benefit of a bicameral system is the way it demands careful consideration and deliberate action on the part of the legislators. A primary drawback is that it is tougher overall to pass legislation and makes it extremely difficult to push through large-scale reforms. **7.** The executive and legislative branches complement and check each other. The purpose of dividing their roles is to prevent either from becoming too powerful. As a result, when one branch assumes more power, it necessarily assumes that power from the other branch. **9.** C **11.** Incumbents chase off would-be challengers because they are able to raise more money given that people want to back a winner and that voters know incumbents by name because they won the office in a previous election. The challengers who do take on incumbents typically lose soundly for the same reasons. **13.** C **15.** The peaks of congressional approval ratings have each occurred when the United States began military involvements overseas. This suggests that the start of a foreign war is one of the few things that triggers a positive reevaluation of Congress. **17.** D **19.** C **21.** C

Chapter 12

1. B **3.** John Adams expanded the war powers by waging undeclared war, Thomas Jefferson negotiated the purchase of Louisiana from France, and James Monroe took direct control of foreign policymaking when he issued the Monroe

Doctrine. **5.** D **7.** There are many problems with the Electoral College. First, small states are over-represented in the Electoral College. Second, the state by state set-up of the college, in the modern era, leads to states that are safe wins for one party, leaving a handful of states that get all the attention. Finally, its outcomes can differ from the outcome of actual citizen voting (also known as the national popular vote. **9.** C **11.** C **13.** Presidents of the eighteenth and nineteenth centuries might make speeches or publish letters in newspapers across the country. These methods may have been effective in their day, but not in comparison to the ability of modern presidents with television, radio, and the Internet at their disposal. **15.** C **17.** Presidents can use road trips across the country, major speeches, and rewards to people in their camp. Historically, however, these techniques have only rarely been successful. What works best is for a president find a popular position to get out in front of.

Chapter 13

1. B **3.** C **5.** The judicial branch is involved in the system of law-making in the United States. Through their interpretation of the law, judges are an important part of the legal system and influence the way law is made and interpreted. They don't just apply the law; they also make it. **7.** C **9.** Overlapping court systems provide each individual with more than just one court to protect his or her rights. A person seeking a wrong to be righted may have alternate places to pursue his or her case. On the other hand, having overlapping court systems opens the door to the possibility of unequal or disparate administration of justice. **11.** B **13.** D **15.** The United States has become much more diverse, and it is only fitting that the judicial branch more accurately reflects the demographic composition of the population. At the same time, judicial positions should be filled by the most competent and qualified candidates. **17.** A **19.** A **21.** C **23.** D **25.** The judicial branch has no power of its own over implementation of enforcement of its rulings and is thus dependent on the other two branches to make this happen, relying on the executive to enforce its decisions and on the legislature to fund it. Hamilton said the judiciary has "no influence over either the sword or the purse" and "neither force nor will, but merely judgment," stressing the court system's reliance on assistance from the other two branches.

Chapter 14

1. A **3.** B **5.** C **7.** B **9.** B **11.** The state legislature, particularly the state house, where members represent fewer people per district. Constituency service is part of the job of a state representative or senator, and house members' need to be frequently reelected means they will have to pay attention to the electorate. **13.** C **15.** B **17.** A **19.** Municipal governments are responsible for providing clean water as well as sewage and garbage disposal. They maintain city facilities, such as parks, streetlights, and stadiums. In addition, they address zoning and building regulations, promote economic development, and provide law enforcement, public transportation, and fire protection.

Chapter 15

1. A **3.** A **5.** A **7.** A benefit of the merit system is that it helps to ensure the most qualified applicants are given the position. A drawback is that the bureaucracy is less responsive to the will of elected leaders than under patronage. **9.** B **11.** Congress tends to create government corporations to perform services that respond to market forces but are too important to the public to be allowed to fail. **13.** C

Chapter 16

1. D **3.** Approval of a new policy requires government to recognize that a problem needs solving, and the approval of the elected branches of government. This process can take a long time. **5.** A **7.** D **9.** Need-based programs exist to provide at least a minimal standard of living for those in dire straits and to provide opportunities to improve their fate in life. In the short term, they allow mere survival, while in the long term, they can help the individual and society. **11.** A **13.** B **15.** A Keynesian approach would recommend deficit spending to stimulate the economy. Supply-side economists would advocate cutting taxes to get more money flowing in the economy.

Chapter 17

1. C **3.** D **5.** B **7.** B **9.** Broadly conceived foreign policy outputs tend to have a longer impact overall because of their permanence, though sharply focused foreign policy outputs can have more impact in the short term. **11.** C **12.** B **14.** C **16.** The pros are that the United States is less bogged down in international process and can move more quickly to squelch conflict. The cons are that the United States, in acting alone, might offend other countries that would prefer everyone act together, and that the country might decide to go directly to military-based solutions rather than using diplomacy.

References

American Government and Civic Engagement

1. Paul A. Samuelson. 1954. "The Pure Theory of Public Expenditure," *Review of Economics and Statistics* 36, No. 4: 387–389.

2. John L. Mikesell. 2014. *Fiscal Administration: Analysis and Applications for the Public Sector*, 9th ed. Boston: Wadsworth.

3. Juliet Elperin, "U.S. Tightens Fishing Policy, Setting 2012 Catch Limits for All Mandated Species," *Washington Post*, 8 January 2012.

4. Michael Lipka. 5 November 2015. "7 Facts about Atheists," http://www.pewresearch.org/fact-tank/2015/11/05/7-facts-about-atheists/.

5. Within this this realm of representative governments, there exists considerable variance in how democratic the systems actually are. The following website contains such information: https://www.eiu.com/topic/democracy-index.

6. C. Wright Mills. 1956. *The Power Elite*. New York: Oxford University Press.

7. Jack L. Walker. 1966. "A Critique of the Elitist Theory of Democracy," *The American Political Science Review* 60, No. 2: 295.

8. The Ivy League is technically an athletic conference in the Northeast comprised of sports teams from eight institutions of higher education—Brown University, Columbia University, Cornell University, Dartmouth College, Harvard University, University of Pennsylvania, Princeton University, and Yale University—however, the term is also used to connote academic excellence or social elitism.

9. "Directory of Representatives." U.S. House of Representatives. https://www.house.gov/representatives. "Senators of the 116th Congress." United States Senate. https://www.senate.gov/general/contact_information/senators_cfm.cfm.

10. Kyla Calvert Mason. 22 April 2014. "Percentage of Americans with College Degrees Rises, Paying for Degrees Tops Financial Challenges," http://www.pbs.org/newshour/rundown/percentage-americans-college-degrees-rises-paying-degrees-tops-financial-challenges/.

11. Jennifer E. Manning. 24 November 2014. "Membership of the 113th Congress: A Profile." *Congressional Research Service*, p. 3 (Table 2).

12. Drew Desilver. 18 December 2018. "A Record Number of Women Will be Serving in the New Congress." FactTank. http://www.pewresearch.org/fact-tank/2018/12/18/record-number-women-in-congress/.

13. Paul V. Fontelo and David Hawkings. February 2018. "Ranking the Net Worth of the 115th." Roll Call. https://www.rollcall.com/wealth-of-congress. Randy Leonard and Paul V. Fontelo. 2 March 2018. "Every Member of Congress' Wealth in One Chart." Roll Call. https://www.rollcall.com/news/politics/every-member-congress-wealth-one-chart.

14. Lindsey Burke. 20 April 2009. "How Members of the 111th Congress Practice Private School Choice." The Heritage Foundation. https://www.heritage.org/education/report/how-members-the-111th-congress-practice-private-school-choice.

15. "The Non-Governmental Order: Will NGOs Democratise, or Merely Disrupt, Global Governance?" *The Economist*, 9 December 1999.

16. Ronald J. Hrebenar. 1997. *Interest Group Politics in America*, 3rd ed. New York: Routledge, 14; Clive S. Thomas. 2004. *Research Guide to U.S. and International Interest Groups*. Westport, CT: Praeger, 106.

17. Dahl, *Who Governs?* 91–93.

18. *McCullen v. Coakley*, 573 U.S. __ (2014); Melissa Jeltsen, "The Reality of Abortion Clinics without Buffer Zones," *The Huffington Post*, 13 July 2014.

19. Gail Bambrick. 11 December 2012. "Fracking: Pro and Con," https://now.tufts.edu/articles/fracking-pro-and-con.

20. "Gun Show Background Checks State Laws," http://www.governing.com/gov-data/safety-justice/gun-show-firearms-bankground-checks-state-laws-map.html (February 18, 2016).

21. Russel Berman. 22 March 2018. "Congress's 'Baby Steps' on Guns." *The Atlantic.* https://www.theatlantic.com/politics/archive/2018/03/congress-guns-fix-nics-baby-steps/556250/

22. Robert D. Putnam. 2001. *Bowling Alone: The Collapse and Revival of American Community*. New York: Simon & Schuster, 75.

23. ———. 1995. "Bowling Alone: America's Declining Social Capital," *Journal of Democracy* 6: 66–67, 69; "About Social Capital," https://www.hks.harvard.edu/programs/saguaro/about-social-capital (May 2, 2016).

24. Everett Ladd. *The Ladd Report*. http://movies2.nytimes.com/books/first/l/ladd-report.html

25. April Clark. "Rethinking the Decline in Social Capital." *American Politics Research*. April 29, 2014. https://journals.sagepub.com/doi/pdf/10.1177/1532673X14531071

26. Emily Badger. "The Terrible Loneliness of Growing Up Poor in Robert Putnam's America." *The Washington Post*. March 6, 2015. https://www.washingtonpost.com/news/wonk/wp/2015/03/06/the-terrible-loneliness-of-growing-up-poor-in-robert-putnams-america/?noredirect=on&utm_term=.32998051b18a

27. Jared Keller. 4 May 2015. "Young Americans are Opting Out of Politics, but Not Because They're Cynical," http://www.psmag.com/politics-and-law/young-people-are-not-so-politically-inclined.

28. Winston Ross, "Ritchie Torres: Gay, Hispanic and Powerful," *Newsweek*, 25 January 2015.

29. Pew Research Center. 26 April 2018. "Political Engagement, Knowledge, and the Midterms." http://www.people-press.org/2018/04/26/10-political-engagement-knowledge-and-the-midterms/.

30. Harvard Kennedy School Institute of Politics. 17 October 2018. *Survey of Young Americans' Attitudes toward Politics and Public Service*. https://iop.harvard.edu/sites/default/files/content/Harvard-IOP-Fall-2018-poll-toplines.pdf.

31. Center for Information and Research on Civic Learning and Engagement (CIRCLE). 7 November 2018. "Young People Dramatically Increase Their Turnout to 31%, Shape 2018 Midterm Elections." CIRCLE. https://civicyouth.org/young-people-dramatically-increase-their-turnout-31-percent-shape-2018-midterm-elections/.

32. Marc Hetherington and Thomas Rudolph, "Why Don't Americans Trust the Government?" *The Washington Post*, 30 January 2014.

33. Keller, "Young Americans are Opting Out."

34. Tami Luhby and Jennifer Agiesta. 8 November 2016. "Exit Polls: Clinton Fails to Energize African-Americans, Latinos and the Young, http://www.cnn.com/2016/11/08/politics/first-exit-polls-2016/.

35. Harvard Institute of Politics, "No Front-Runner among Prospective Republican Candidates," http://iop.harvard.edu/no-front-runner-among-prospective-republican-candidates-hillary-clinton-control-democratic-primary (May 2, 2016).

36. Jocelyn Kiley and Michael Dimock. 25 September 2014. "The GOP's Millennial Problem Runs Deep," http://www.pewresearch.org/fact-tank/2014/09/25/the-gops-millennial-problem-runs-deep/.

37. "Keeping Students from the Polls," *New York Times*, 26 December 2011.

38. 18 October 2006. "Who Votes, Who Doesn't, and Why," http://www.people-press.org/2006/10/18/

who-votes-who-doesnt-and-why/.

39. Jonathan M. Ladd. 11 September 2015. "Don't Worry about Special Interests," https://www.vox.com/mischiefs-of-faction/2015/9/11/9279615/economic-inequality-special-interests.

The Constitution and Its Origins

1. Nathaniel Philbrick. 2006. *Mayflower: A Story of Courage, Community, and War*. New York: Penguin, 41.

2. François Furstenberg. 2008. "The Significance of the Trans-Appalachian Frontier in Atlantic History," *The American Historical Review* 113 (3): 654.

3. Bernhard Knollenberg. 1975. *Growth of the American Revolution: 1766-1775*. New York: Free Press, 95-96.

4. Stuart Bruchey. 1990. Enterprise: *The Dynamic Economy of a Free People*. Cambridge, MA: Harvard University Press, 223.

5. Joseph J. Ellis. 2015. *The Quartet: Orchestrating the Second American Revolution, 1783-1789*. New York: Knopf, 92.

6. David P. Szatmary. 1980. *Shays' Rebellion: The Making of an Agrarian Insurrection*. Amherst, MA: University of Massachusetts Press, 84-86, 102-104.

7. U.S. Department of Commerce. Bureau of the Census. 1790. *Statistical Abstract of the United States*. Washington, DC: Department of Commerce.

8. U.S. Const. art. I, § 9.

9. U.S. Const. art. IV, § 2.

10. R. E. Neustadt. 1960. *Presidential Power and the Politics of Leadership*. New York: Wiley, 33.

11. Pauline Maier. 2010. *Ratification: The People Debate the Constitution*, 1787-1788. New York: Simon & Schuster, 464.

12. Maier, *Ratification*, 431.

13. Letter from Thomas Jefferson to James Madison, March 15, 1789, https://www.gwu.edu/~ffcp/exhibit/p7/p7_1text.html.

14. Isaac Krannick. 1999. "The Great National Discussion: The Discourse of Politics in 1787." In *What Did the Constitution Mean to Early Americans?* ed. Edward Countryman. Boston: Bedford/St. Martins, 52.

15. Krannick, *Great National Discussion*, 42-43.

16. Krannick, *Great National Discussion*, 42.

17. Evelyn C. Fink and William H. Riker. 1989. "The Strategy of Ratification." In *The Federalist Papers and the New Institutionalism*, eds. Bernard Grofman and Donald Wittman. New York: Agathon, 229.

18. Fink and Riker, *Strategy of Ratification*, 221.

American Federalism

1. See John Kincaid. 1975. "Federalism." In *Civitas: A Framework for Civil Education*, eds. Charles Quigley and Charles Bahmueller. Calabasas, CA: Center for Civic Education, 391–392; William S. Riker. 1975. "Federalism." In *Handbook of Political Science*, eds. Fred Greenstein and Nelson Polsby. Reading, MA: Addison-Wesley, 93–172.

2. Garry Willis, ed. 1982. *The Federalist Papers by Alexander Hamilton, James Madison and John Jay*. New York: Bantam Books, 237.

3. *Arizona v. United States*, 567 U.S. __ (2012).

4. *United States v. Wrightwood Dairy Co.*, 315 U.S. 110 (1942).

5. Ronald L. Watts. 1999. *Comparing Federal Systems*, 2nd ed. Kingston, Ontario: McGill-Queen's University, 6–7; Daniel J. Elazar. 1992. *Federal Systems of the World: A Handbook of Federal, Confederal and Autonomy Arrangements*. Harlow, Essex: Longman Current Affairs.

6. Jack Rakove. 2007. *James Madison and the Creation of the American Republic*. New York: Pearson; Samuel H. Beer. 1998. *To Make a Nation: The Rediscovery of American Federalism*. Cambridge, MA: Harvard University Press.

7. Elton E. Richter. 1929. "Exclusive and Concurrent Powers in the Federal Constitution," *Notre Dame Law Review* 4, No. 8: 513–542. http://scholarship.law.nd.edu/cgi/viewcontent.cgi?article=4416&context=ndlr

8. *Baehr v. Lewin*. 1993. 74 Haw. 530.

9. *United States v. Windsor*, 570 U.S. __ (2013).

10. Adam Liptak, "Supreme Court Delivers Tacit Win to Gay Marriage," *New York Times*, 6 October, 2014.

11. *Obergefell v. Hodges*, 576 U.S. ___ (2015).

12. Data reported by http://www.usgovernmentrevenue.com/federal_revenue. State and local government figures are estimated.

13. *Pollock v. Farmers' Loan & Trust Co.*, 158 U.S. 601 (1895).

14. See Robert Jay Dilger, "Federal Grants to State and Local Governments: A Historical Perspective on Contemporary Issues," *Congressional Research Service*, Report 7-5700, 5 March 2015.

15. Jeffrey L. Barnett et al. 2014. *2012 Census of Governments: Finance-State and Local Government Summary Report*, Appendix Table A-1. December 17. Washington, DC: United States Census Bureau, 2.

16. Dilger, "Federal Grants to State and Local Governments," 4.

17. James Feyrer and Bruce Sacerdote. 2011. "Did the Stimulus Stimulate? Real Time Estimates of the Effects of the American Recovery and Reinvestment Act" (Working Paper No. 16759), Cambridge, MA: National Bureau of Economic Research. http://www.nber.org/papers/w16759.pdf

18. Data reported by the Center on Budget and Policy Priorities. 2015. "Policy Basics: Where Do Our Federal Tax Dollars Go?" March 11. http://www.cbpp.org/research/policy-basics-where-do-our-federal-tax-dollars-go

19. The Lehrman Institute. "The Founding Trio: Washington, Hamilton and Jefferson." http://lehrmaninstitute.org/history/FoundingTrio.asp

20. *McCulloch v. Maryland*, 17 U.S. 316 (1819).

21. *Gibbons v. Ogden*, 22 U.S. 1 (1824).

22. *Gibbons v. Ogden*, 22 U.S. 1 (1824).

23. W. Kirk Wood. 2008. *Nullification, A Constitutional History, 1776–1833*. Lanham, MD: University Press of America.

24. *Dred Scott v. Sandford*, 60 U.S. 393 (1857).

25. Joseph R. Marbach, Troy E. Smith, and Ellis Katz. 2005. *Federalism in America: An Encyclopedia*. Westport, CT: Greenwood Publishing.

26. Marc Allen Eisner. 2014. *The American Political Economy: Institutional Evolution of Market and State*. New York: Routledge.

27. Eisner, *The American Political Economy*; Stephen Skowronek. 1982. *Building a New American State: The Expansion of National Administrative Capacities, 1877–1920*. Cambridge, MA: Cambridge University Press.

28. *United States v. E. C. Knight*, 156 U.S. 1 (1895).

29. *Lochner v. New York*, 198 U.S. 45 (1905).

30. *Hammer v. Dagenhart*, 247 U.S. 251 (1918).

31. Nicholas Crafts and Peter Fearon. 2010. "Lessons from the 1930s Great Depression," *Oxford Review of Economic Policy* 26: 286–287; Gene Smiley. "The Concise Encyclopedia of Economics: Great Depression." http://www.econlib.org/library/Enc/GreatDepression.html

32. Marbach et al, *Federalism in America: An Encyclopedia.*

33. Jeff Shesol. 2010. *Supreme Power: Franklin Roosevelt vs. The Supreme Court.* New York: W. W. Norton.

34. *National Labor Relations Board (NLRB) v. Jones & Laughlin Steel*, 301 U.S. 1 (1937).

35. Lawrence R. Jacobs and Theda Skocpol. 2014. "Progressive Federalism and the Contested Implemented of Obama's Health Reform," In *The Politics of Major Policy Reform in Postwar America*, eds. Jeffrey A. Jenkins and Sidney M. Milkis. New York: Cambridge University Press.

36. R. Kent Weaver. 2000. *Ending Welfare as We Know It.* Washington, DC: The Brookings Institution.

37. Allen Schick. 2007. *The Federal Budget*, 3rd ed. Washington, DC: The Brookings Institution.

38. Dilger, "Federal Grants to State and Local Governments," 30–31.

39. *United States v. Lopez*, 514 U.S. 549 (1995).

40. See *Printz v. United States*, 521 U.S. 898 (1997).

41. Morton Grodzins. 2004. "The Federal System." In *American Government Readings and Cases*, ed. P. Woll. New York: Pearson Longman, 74–78.

42. Dilger, "Federal Grants to State and Local Governments."

43. John Mikesell. 2014. *Fiscal Administration*, 9th ed. Boston: Wadsworth Publishing.

44. Dilger, "Federal Grants to State and Local Governments," 5.

45. ——, "Federal Grants to State and Local Governments," Table 4.

46. Schick, *The Federal Budget.*

47. Robert Jay Dilger and Eugene Boyd. 15 July 2014. "Block Grants: Perspectives and Controversies." *Congressional Research Service*, Report R40486, 1–3. Isaac Shapiro, David Reich, Chloe Cho, and Richard Kogan. 28 March 2017. "Trump Budget Would Cut Block Grants Dramatically, Underscoring Danger of Granting Social Programs." Center on Budgets and Policy Priorities. https://www.cbpp.org/research/federal-budget/trump-budget-would-cut-block-grants-dramatically-underscoring-danger-of.

48. Jonathan Weisman, "Ryan's Budget Would Cut $5 trillion in Spending Over a Decade," *New York Times*, 1 April 2014.

49. Kenneth Finegold, Laura Wherry, and Stephanie Schardin. 2014. "Block Grants: Historical Overview and Lessons Learned," *New Federalism: Issues and Options for States* Series A, No A-63: 1–7.

50. Martha Derthick. 1987. "American Federalism: Madison's Middle Ground in the 1980s," *Public Administration Review* 47, No. 1: 66–74.

51. U.S. Congress. 2017–2018. H. R. 50 – *Unfunded Mandates Information and Transparency Act of 2017.* https://www.congress.gov/bill/115th-congress/house-bill/50.

52. National Governors Association, National Conference of State Legislatures, and American Association of Motor Vehicle Administrators. 2006. *The Real ID Act: National Impact Analysis.* http://www.ncsl.org/print/statefed/real_id_impact_report_final_sept19.pdf

53. Department of Homeland Security. 18 December 2018. "Real ID." https://www.dhs.gov/real-id. Homeland Security. "REAL ID Enforcement in Brief." http://www.dhs.gov/real-id-enforcement-brief# (June 12, 2015); National Conference of State Legislatures. "Countdown to REAL ID." http://www.ncsl.org/research/transportation/count-down-to-real-id.aspx (June 12, 2015).

54. Robert Jay Dilger and Richard S. Beth, "Unfunded Mandates Reform Act: History, Impact, and Issues," *Congressional Research Service*, Report 7-5700, 17 November 2014.

55. John Kincaid. 1990. "From Cooperative Federalism to Coercive Federalism," *Annals of the American Academy of Political and Social Science* 509: 139–152.

56. Carol M. Swain and Virgina M. Yetter. (2014). "Federalism and the Politics of Immigration Reform." In *The Politics of Major Policy Reform in Postwar America*, eds. Jeffery A. Jenkins and Sidney M. Milkis. New York: Cambridge University Press.

57. National Conference of State Legislatures. "State Laws Related to Immigration and Immigrants." http://www.ncsl.org/research/immigration/state-laws-related-to-immigration-and-immigrants.aspx (June 23, 2015).

58. Michele Waslin. 2012. "Discrediting 'Self Deportation' as Immigration Policy," February 6. http://www.immigrationpolicy.org/special-reports/discrediting-%E2%80%9Cself-deportation%E2%80%9D-immigration-policy

59. Daniel González. 2010. "SB 1070 Backlash Spurs Hispanics to Join Democrats," June 8. http://archive.azcentral.com/arizonarepublic/news/articles/2010/06/08/20100608arizona-immigration-law-backlash.html

60. *Arizona v. United States*, 567 U.S. __ (2012).

61. *Arizona v. United States*, 567 U.S. __ (2012).

62. Julia Preston, "Arizona Ruling Only a Narrow Opening for Other States," *New York Times*, 25 June 2012.

63. *United States v. Windsor*, 570 U.S. __ (2013).

64. James Esseks. 2014. "Op-ed: In the Wake of Windsor," June 26. http://www.advocate.com/commentary/2014/06/26/op-ed-wake-windsor (June 24, 2015).

65. *South Dakota v. Dole*, 483 U.S. 203 (1987).

66. Frank Baumgartner and Bryan Jones. 1993. *Agendas and Instability in American Politics*. Chicago: University of Chicago Press.

67. *Roe v. Wade*, 410 U.S. 113 (1973).

68. Elizabeth Nash et al. 2013. "Laws Affecting Reproductive Health and Rights: 2013 State Policy Review." http://www.guttmacher.org/statecenter/updates/2013/statetrends42013.html (June 24, 2015).

69. *New State Ice Co. v. Liebmann*, 285 U.S. 262 (1932).

70. Christine Vestal and Michael Ollove, "Why some state-run health exchanges worked," *USA Today*, 10 December 2013.

71. Jennifer Lawless. 2012. *Becoming a Candidate*. New York: Cambridge University Press.

72. Justin McCarthy. 2014. "Americans Still Trust Local Government More Than State," September 22. http://www.gallup.com/poll/176846/americans-trust-local-government-state.aspx (June 24, 2015).

73. United States Census Bureau. 2017. "Median Household Income (in 2017 Inflation-Adjusted Dollars." 2017 American Community Survey 1-Year Estimates. https://factfinder.census.gov/faces/tableservices/jsf/pages/productview.xhtml?pid=ACS_17_1YR_R1901.US01PRF&prodType=table.

74. Governing the States and Localities. 1 June 2018. "Education Spending per Student by State." http://www.governing.com/gov-data/education-data/state-education-spending-per-pupil-data.html.

75. The Commonwealth Fund. "Aiming Higher: Results from a Scorecard on State Health System Performance, 2014." http://www.commonwealthfund.org/publications/fund-reports/2014/apr/2014-state-scorecard (June 24, 2015).

76. Alexander Hertel-Fernandez. 2012. "Why U.S. Unemployment Insurance is in Financial Trouble," February. http://www.scholarsstrategynetwork.org/sites/default/files/ssn_basic_facts_hertel-fernandez_on_unemployment_insurance_financing.pdf

77. Matt Broaddus and January Angeles. 2012. "Federal Government Will Pick Up Nearly All Costs of Health Reform's Medicaid Expansion," March 28. http://www.cbpp.org/research/federal-government-will-pick-up-nearly-all-costs-of-health-reforms-medicaid-expansion. Henry J. Kaiser Family Foundation. 23 January 2019. "Status of State Action on the Medicaid Expansion Decision." https://www.kff.org/health-reform/state-indicator/state-activity-around-expanding-medicaid-under-the-affordable-care-act/?currentTimeframe=0&sortModel=%7B%22colId%22:%22Location%22,%22sort%22:%22asc%22%7D#note-1.

78. *National Federation of Independent Business v. Sebelius*, 567 U.S. __ (2012).

79. *Shelby County v. Holder*, 570 U.S. __ (2013).

Civil Liberties

1. *Green v. County School Board of New Kent County*, 391 U.S. 430 (1968); *Allen v. Wright*, 468 U.S. 737 (1984).

2. *Ex parte Milligan*, 71 U.S. 2 (1866).

3. *Ex parte Quirin*, 317 U.S. 1 (1942); See William H. Rehnquist. 1998. *All the Laws but One: Civil Liberties in Wartime*. New York: William Morrow.

4. American History from Revolution to Reconstruction and Beyond, "Madison Speech Proposing the Bill of Rights June 8 1789," http://www.let.rug.nl/usa/documents/1786-1800/madison-speech-proposing-the-bill-of-rights-june-8-1789.php (March 4, 2016).

5. Constitution Society, "To the Citizens of the State of New-York," http://www.constitution.org/afp/brutus02.htm (March 4, 2016).

6. *Barron v. Baltimore*, 32 U.S. 243 (1833).

7. *Saenz v. Roe*, 526 U.S. 489 (1999).

8. *McDonald v. Chicago*, 561 U.S. 742 (2010).

9. *Sherbert v. Verner*, 374 U.S. 398 (1963).

10. *Near v. Minnesota*, 283 U.S. 697 (1931).

11. *Lemon v. Kurtzman*, 403 U.S. 602 (1971).

12. *Engel v. Vitale*, 370 U.S. 421 (1962).

13. See, in particular, *Santa Fe Independent School District v. Doe*, 530 U.S. 290 (2000), which found that the school district's including a student-led prayer at high school football games was illegal.

14. *Minersville School District v. Gobitis*, 310 U.S. 586 (1940).

15. *West Virginia State Board of Education v. Barnette*, 319 U.S. 624 (1943); *Watchtower Society v. Village of Stratton*, 536 U.S. 150 (2002).

16. *Gillette v. United States*, 401 U.S. 437 (1971).

17. *Sherbert v. Verner*, 374 U.S. 398 (1963); *Wisconsin v. Yoder*, 406 U.S. 205 (1972).

18. *Employment Division, Department of Human Resources of Oregon v. Smith*, 494 U.S. 872 (1990).

19. Juliet Eilperin, "31 states have heightened religious freedom protections," *Washington Post*, 1 March 2014. http://www.washingtonpost.com/blogs/the-fix/wp/2014/03/01/where-in-the-u-s-are-there-heightened-protections-for-religious-freedom/. Three more states passed state RFRAs in the past year.

20. *Burwell v. Hobby Lobby Stores, Inc.*, 573 U.S. __ (2014).

21. *Obergefell v. Hodges*, 576 U.S. ___ (2015).

22. *Schenck v. United States*, 249 U.S. 47 (1919).

23. *Brandenburg v. Ohio*, 395 U.S. 444 (1969).

24. *Texas v. Johnson*, 491 U.S. 397 (1989).

25. *United States v. Eichman*, 496 U.S. 310 (1990).

26. *Near v. Minnesota*, 283 U.S. 697 (1931).

27. *New York Times Co. v. United States*, 403 U.S. 713 (1971).

28. *New York Times v. Sullivan*, 376 U.S. 254 (1964).

29. See, for example, *Virginia v. Black*, 538 U.S. 343 (2003).

30. *Miller v. California*, 413 U.S. 15 (1973).

31. *Tinker v. Des Moines Independent Community School District*, 393 U.S. 503 (1969).

32. *Hazelwood School District et al. v. Kuhlmeier et al.*, 484 U.S. 260 (1988).

33. *National Socialist Party of America v. Village of Skokie*, 432 U.S. 43 (1977); Snyder v. Phelps, 562 U.S. 443 (2011).

34. *United States v. Cruickshank*, 92 U.S. 542 (1876).

35. *United States v. Miller*, 307 U.S. 174 (1939).

36. *District of Columbia et al. v. Heller*, 554 US 570 (2008), p. 3.

37. Richard Gonzales, "Supreme Court Rejects NRA Challenge to San Francisco Gun Rules," *National Public Radio*, 8 June 2015. http://www.npr.org/sections/thetwo-way/2015/06/08/412917394/supreme-court-rejects-nra-challenge-to-s-f-gun-rules (March 4, 2016).

38. Serge F. Kovaleski and Richard A. Oppel, Jr. 28 September 2018. "A Man Stashed Gus in His Las Vegas Hotel Room. 3 Years Later, a Killer Did the Same." *New York Times*. https://www.nytimes.com/2018/09/28/us/las-vegas-shooting-mgm-lawsuits.html. Michelle Cottle. 28 February 2018. "How Parkland Students Changed the Gun Debate." *The Atlantic*. https://www.theatlantic.com/politics/archive/2018/02/parkland-students-power/554399/.

39. See, for example, *Arizona v. Gant*, 556 U.S. 332 (2009).

40. *Mapp v. Ohio*, 367 U.S. 643 (1961); *Weeks v. United States*, 232 U.S. 383 (1914).

41. *Silverthorne Lumber Co. v. United States*, 251 U.S. 385 (1920).

42. *Miranda v. Arizona*, 384 U.S. 436 (1966).

43. *Kelo et al. v. City of New London et al.*, 545 U.S. 469 (2005).

44. John C. Moritz. 27 November 2018. "Catholic Diocese Fights to Keep Historic Site from Being Used in Trump's Border Wall." *Corpus Christi Caller Times*. https://www.usatoday.com/story/news/politics/2018/11/27/texas-la-lomita-mission-center-border-wall-eminent-domain-fight/2132582002/.

45. See, for example, *Barker v. Wingo*, 407 U.S. 514 (1972).

46. See, for example, *Batson v. Kentucky*, 476 U.S. 79 (1986); *J. E. B. v. Alabama ex rel. T. B.*, 511 U.S. 127 (1994).

47. *Gideon v. Wainwright*, 372 U.S. 335 (1963).

48. *Waters-Pierce Oil Co. v. Texas*, 212 U.S. 86 (1909); *United States v. Bajakajian*, 524 U.S. 321 (1998).

49. See, for example, the discussion in *Wilkerson v. Utah*, 99 U.S. 130 (1879).

50. Perhaps the most notorious example, *Harmelin v. Michigan*, 501 U.S. 957 (1991), upheld a life sentence in a case where the defendant was convicted of possessing just over one pound of cocaine (and no other crime).

51. *Atkins v. Virginia*, 536 U.S. 304 (2002).

52. *Roper v. Simmons*, 543 U.S. 551 (2005).

53. *Kennedy v. Louisiana*, 554 U.S. 407 (2008).

54. Elizabeth Lopatto, "How Many Innocent People Are Sentenced To Death?," *Forbes*, 29 April 2014. http://www.forbes.com/sites/elizabethlopatto/2014/04/29/how-many-innocent-people-are-sentenced-to-death/#6e9ae5175cc1 (March 1, 2016).

55. Dave Mann, "DNA Tests Undermine Evidence in Texas Execution: New Results Show Claude Jones was Put to Death on Flawed Evidence," *Texas Observer*, 11 November 2010. http://www.texasobserver.org/texas-observer-exclusive-dna-tests-undermine-evidence-in-texas-execution/ (March 4, 2016).

56. See, for example, "States With and Without the Death Penalty," Death Penalty Information Center, http://www.deathpenaltyinfo.org/states-and-without-death-penalty (March 4, 2016).

57. *United States v. Darby Lumber*, 312 U.S. 100 (1941).

58. *Printz v. United States*, 521 U.S. 898 (1997); *National Federation of Independent Business v. Sebelius*, 567 U.S. __ (2012).

59. See Douglas Shinkle, "State Constitutional Right to Hunt and Fish." National Conference of State Legislatures, November 9, 2015. http://www.ncsl.org/research/environment-and-natural-resources/state-constitutional-right-to-hunt-and-fish.aspx (March 4, 2016).

60. *Pruneyard Shopping Center v. Robins*, 447 U.S. 74 (1980).

61. The Texas Politics Project, "Trying to Rewrite the Texas Constitution," https://texaspolitics.utexas.edu/archive/html/cons/features/0602_01/slide1.html (March 1, 2016).

62. See *Griswold v. Connecticut*, 381 U.S. 479 (1965). This discussion parallels the debate among the members of the Supreme Court in the *Griswold* case.

63. Samuel Warren and Louis D. Brandeis. 1890. "The Right to Privacy," *Harvard Law Review* 4, No. 193.

64. *Griswold v. Connecticut*, 381 U.S. 479 (1965)

65. *Eisenstadt v. Baird*, 405 U.S. 438 (1972).

66. See Rachel Benson Gold. March 2003. "Lessons from Before Roe: Will Past be Prologue?" *The Guttmacher Report on Public Policy* 6, No. 1. https://www.guttmacher.org/pubs/tgr/06/1/gr060108.html (March 4, 2016).

67. *Roe v. Wade*, 410 U.S. 113 (1973).

68. *Planned Parenthood v. Casey*, 505 U.S. 833 (1992).

69. *Whole Woman's Health v. Hellerstedt*, 579 U.S. ___ (2016).

70. *Bowers v. Hardwick*, 478 U.S. 186 (1986).

71. *Lawrence v. Texas*, 539 U.S. 558 (2003).

72. *Carpenter v. United States*, No. 16-402, 585 U.S. ____ (2018). https://www.supremecourt.gov/opinions/17pdf/16-402_h315.pdf. Alfred Ng. 22 June 2018. "Supreme Court Says Warrant Necessary for Phone Location Data in Win for Privacy." cnet.com. https://www.cnet.com/news/supreme-court-says-warrant-necessary-for-phone-location-data/.

Civil Rights

1. Aaron Morrison, "Ground Zero Mosque 2015: Developer to Build Condos Instead of Islamic Center that Sparked Controversy Around 9/11 Attacks," *International Business Times*, 29 September 2015.

2. Constitutional Rights Foundation. "Race and Voting in the Segregated South," http://www.crf-usa.org/black-history-month/race-and-voting-in-the-segregated-south (April 10, 2016).

3. *Bolling v. Sharpe*, 347 U.S. 497 (1954).

4. *Phyler v. Doe*, 457 U.S. 202 (1982); *F. S. Royster Guano v. Virginia*, 253 U.S. 412 (1920).

5. Cornell University Law School: Legal Information Institute. "Rational Basis," https://www.law.cornell.edu/wex/rational_basis (April 10, 2016); *Nebbia v. New York*, 291 U.S. 502 (1934).

6. *United States v. Carolene Products Co.*, 304 U.S. 144 (1938).

7. *Craig v. Boren*, 429 U.S. 190 (1976); *Clark v. Jeter*, 486 U.S. 456 (1988).

8. *Mississippi University for Women v. Hogan*, 458 U.S. 718 (1982); *United States v. Virginia*, 518 U.S. 515 (1996).

9. Matthew Rosenberg and Dave Philipps, "All Combat Roles Open to Women, Defense Secretary Says," *New York Times*, 3 December 2015; *Rostker v. Goldberg*, 453 U.S. 57 (1981).

10. *Johnson v. California*, 543 U.S. 499 (2005).

11. *Korematsu v. United States*, 323 U.S. 214 (1944).

12. "Mississippi Black Code," https://chnm.gmu.edu/courses/122/recon/code.html (April 10, 2016); "Black Codes and Pig Laws," http://www.pbs.org/tpt/slavery-by-another-name/themes/black-codes/ (April 10, 2016).

13. Catherine K. Harbour, and Pallab K. Maulik. 2010. "History of Intellectual Disability." In *International Encyclopedia of Rehabilitation*, eds. J. H. Stone and M. Blouin. http://cirrie.buffalo.edu/encyclopedia/en/article/143/ (April 10, 2016).

14. Lucia Stanton. 2008. "Thomas Jefferson and Slavery," https://www.monticello.org/site/plantation-and-slavery/thomas-jefferson-and-slavery#footnoteref3_srni04n.

15. "How Did Slavery Disappear in the North?" http://www.abolitionseminar.org/how-did-northern-states-gradually-abolish-slavery/ (April 10, 2016); Nicholas Boston and Jennifer Hallam, "The Slave Experience: Freedom and Emancipation," http://www.pbs.org/wnet/slavery/experience/freedom/history.html (April 10, 2016).

16. Eric Foner. 1970. *Free Soil, Free Labor, Free Men: The Ideology of the Republican Party Before the Civil War*. New York: Oxford University Press, 28, 50, 54.

17. *Dred Scott v. Sandford*, 60 U.S. 393 (1857).

18. David M. Potter. 1977. *The Impending Crisis, 1848–1861*. New York: Harper & Row, 45.

19. David Herbert Donald. 1995. *Lincoln*. New York: Simon & Schuster, 407.

20. Erik Foner. 1988. *Reconstruction: America's Unfinished Revolution, 1863–1877*. New York: Harper & Row, 524–527.

21. Ibid., 595; Alexander Keyssar. 2000. *The Right to Vote: The Contested History of Democracy in the United States*. New York: Basic Books, 105–106.

22. Keyssar, 114–115.

23. Keyssar, 111–112.

24. Kimberly Sambol-Tosco, "The Slave Experience: Education, Arts, and Culture," http://www.pbs.org/wnet/slavery/experience/education/history2.html (April 10, 2016).

25. Keyssar, 112.

26. Alan Greenblat, "The Racial History of the 'Grandfather Clause," *NPR Code Switch*, 22 October 2013. http://www.npr.org/sections/codeswitch/2013/10/21/239081586/the-racial-history-of-the-grandfather-clause.

27. Keyssar, 111.

28. Keyssar, 247.

29. *Plessy v. Ferguson*, 163 U.S. 537 (1896).

30. "NAACP: 100 Years of History," https://donate.naacp.org/pages/naacp-history (April 10, 2016).

31. *Missouri ex rel. Gaines v. Canada*, 305 U.S. 337 (1938).

32. *Brown v. Board of Education of Topeka*, 347 U.S. 483 (1954).

33. "Prayer Pilgrimage for Freedom," http://kingencyclopedia.stanford.edu/encyclopedia/encyclopedia/enc_prayer_pilgrimage_for_freedom_1957/ (April 10, 2016).

34. Jason Sokol. 2006. *There Goes My Everything: White Southerners in the Age of Civil Rights*. New York: Alfred A. Knopf, 116–117.

35. Ibid., 118–120.

36. Ibid., 120, 171, 173.

37. Robert M. Fogelson. 2005. *Bourgeois Nightmares: Suburbia, 1870–1930*. New Haven, CT: Yale University Press, 102–103.

38. *Shelley v. Kraemer*, 334 U.S. 1 (1948).

39. *Loving v. Virginia*, 388 U.S. 1 (1967).

40. *Harper v. Virginia Board of Elections*, 383 U.S. 663 (1966).

41. "Gandhi, Mohandas Karamchand (1869–1948)," http://kingencyclopedia.stanford.edu/encyclopedia/encyclopedia/enc_gandhi_mohandas_karamchand_1869_1948/index.html (April 10, 2016); "Nixon, E. D. (1899–1987)," http://www.blackpast.org/aah/nixon-e-d-nixon-1899-1987(April 10, 2016).

42. *Morgan v. Virginia*, 328 U.S. 373 (1946).

43. See Lynne Olson. 2002. *Freedom's Daughters: The Unsung Heroines of the Civil Rights Movement from 1830–1970*. New York: Scribner, 97; D. F. Gore et al. 2009. *Want to Start a Revolution? Radical Women in the Black Freedom Struggle*. New York: New York University Press; Raymond Arsenault. 2007. *Freedom Riders: 1961 and the Struggle for Racial Justice*. New York: Oxford University Press.

44. See *Heart of Atlanta Motel, Inc. v. United States*, 379 U.S. 241 (1964); *Katzenbach v. McClung*, 379 U.S. 294 (1964), which built on *Wickard v. Filburn*, 317 U.S. 111 (1942).

45. See David Garrow. 1978. *Protest at Selma*. New Haven, CT: Yale University Press; David J. Garrow.1988. *Bearing the Cross: Martin Luther King Jr. and the Southern Christian Leadership Conference*. London: Jonathan Cape.

46. Keyssar, 263–264.

47. *Shelby County v. Holder*, 570 U.S. ___ (2013).

48. Adam Liptak, "Supreme Court Invalidates Key Part of Voting Rights Act," *The New York Times*, 25 June 2013. http://www.nytimes.com/2013/06/26/us/supreme-court-ruling.html; Wendy R. Weiser and Erik Opsal, "The State of Voting in 2014," Brennan Center for Justice, 17 June 2014. http://www.brennancenter.org/analysis/state-voting-2014.

49. Louis E. Lomax. 1963. *When the Word is Given: A Report on Elijah Muhammad, Malcolm X, and the Black Muslim World*. Cleveland, OH: World Publishing, 173–174; David Farber. 1994. *The Age of Great Dreams: America in the 1960s*. New York: Hill and Wang, 207.

50. Dan Keating, "Why Whites Don't Understand Black Segregation," *Washington Post*, 21 November

2014. https://www.washingtonpost.com/news/wonk/wp/2014/11/21/why-whites-dont-understand-black-segregation/.

51. Alana Semuels, "White Flight Never Ended," *The Atlantic*, 30 July 2015. http://www.theatlantic.com/business/archive/2015/07/white-flight-alive-and-well/399980/.

52. Lindsey Cook, "U.S. Education: Still Separate and Unequal," *U.S. News and World Report*, 28 January 2015. http://www.usnews.com/news/blogs/data-mine/2015/01/28/us-education-still-separate-and-unequal.

53. Sokol, 175–177.

54. Jacqueline Jones. 1992. *The Dispossessed: America's Underclasses From the Civil War to the Present*. New York: Basic Books, 274, 290–292.

55. James B. Comey. February 12, 2015. "Hard Truths: Law Enforcement and Race" (speech). https://www.fbi.gov/news/speeches/hard-truths-law-enforcement-and-race.

56. Julie Hirschfeld Davis and Binyamin Appelbaum. 8 July 2015. "Obama Unveils Stricter Rules against Segregation in Housing." *New York Times*. http://www.nytimes.com/2015/07/09/us/hud-issuing-newrules-to-fight-segregation.html?_r=0. Tracy Jan. 24 December 2018. "Ben Carson's HUD Dials Back Investigations into Housing Discrimination." *Washington Post*. https://www.washingtonpost.com/business/economy/ben-carsons-hud-dials-back-investigations-into-housing-discrimination/2018/12/21/65510cea-f743-11e8-863c-9e2f864d47e7_story.html?utm_term=.1776fde23f6b. Diane Yentel. 23 August 2018. "Trump Administration Continues to Undermine Fair Housing Act." *The Hill*. https://thehill.com/opinion/civil-rights/403115-trump-administration-continues-to-undermine-fair-housing-act.

57. Politico Magazine. 12 August 2018. "What Charlottesville Changed." *Politico*. https://www.politico.com/magazine/story/2018/08/12/charlottesville-anniversary-supremacists-protests-dc-virginia-219353

58. *Bakke v. California*, 438 U.S. 265 (1978).

59. *Grutter v. Bollinger*, 539 U.S. 306 (2003).

60. *Fisher v. University of Texas*, 570 U.S. ___ (2013); *Fisher v. University of Texas*, 579 U.S. ___ (2016).

61. Mary Beth Norton. 1980. *Liberty's Daughters: The Revolutionary Experience of American Women, 1750–1800*. New York: Little, Brown, and Company, 46.

62. Ibid., 47.

63. Jan Ellen Lewis. 2011. "Rethinking Women's Suffrage in New Jersey, 1776–1807," *Rutgers Law Review* 63, No. 3, http://www.rutgerslawreview.com/wp-content/uploads/archive/vol63/Issue3/Lewis.pdf.

64. Keyssar, 174.

65. Elizabeth Cady Stanton. 1993. *Eighty Years and More: Reminiscences, 1815–1897*. Boston: Northeastern University Press, 148.

66. Elizabeth Cady Stanton et al. 1887. *History of Woman Suffrage*, vol. 1. Cambridge, MA: Harvard University Press, 73.

67. Jean H. Baker. 2005. *Sisters: The Lives of America's Suffragists*. New York: Hill and Wang, 109.

68. Angelina Grimke. October 2, 1837. "Letter XII Human Rights Not Founded on Sex." In *Letters to Catherine E. Beecher: In Reply to an Essay on Slavery and Abolitionism*. Boston: Knapp, 114–121.

69. Keyssar, 178.

70. Keyssar, 184.

71. Keyssar, 175, 186–187.

72. Keyssar, 214.

73. "Alice Paul," https://www.nwhm.org/education-resources/biography/biographies/alice-paul/ (April 10, 2016).

74. Deborah Rhode. 2009. *Justice and Gender: Sex Discrimination and the Law*. Cambridge, MA: Harvard University Press, 66–67.

75. Mark Hugo Lopez and Ana Gonzalez-Barrera. 6 March 2014. "Women's College Enrollment Gains Leave Men Behind," http://www.pewresearch.org/fact-tank/2014/03/06/womens-college-enrollment-gains-leave-men-behind/; Allie Bidwell, "Women More Likely to Graduate College, but Still Earn Less Than Men," *U.S. News & World Report*, 31 October 2014.

76. "A Current Glance at Women in the Law–July 2014," *American Bar Association*, July 2014; "Medical School Applicants, Enrollment Reach All-Time Highs," Association of American Medical Colleges, October 24, 2013.

77. *Roe v. Wade*, 410 U.S. 113 (1973).

78. "Pay Equity and Discrimination," http://www.iwpr.org/initiatives/pay-equity-and-discrimination (April 10, 2016).

79. Gretchen Livingston. 2 July 2013. "The Rise of Single Fathers," http://www.pewsocialtrends.org/2013/07/02/the-rise-of-single-fathers/.

80. "Poverty in the U.S.: A Snapshot," National Center for Law and Economic Justice, http://www.nclej.org/poverty-in-the-us.php.

81. "Current Numbers," http://www.cawp.rutgers.edu/current-numbers (January 10, 2019).

82. "Statistics," http://www.ncadv.org/learn/statistics (April 10, 2016); "Statistics About Sexual Violence," http://www.nsvrc.org/sites/default/files/publications_nsvrc_factsheet_media-packet_statistics-about-sexual-violence_0.pdf (April 10, 2016).

83. Heather D. Boonstra and Elizabeth Nash. 2014. "A Surge of State Abortion Restrictions Puts Providers–and the Women They Serve–in the Crosshairs," *Guttmacher Policy Review* 17, No. 1, https://www.guttmacher.org/about/gpr/2014/03/surge-state-abortion-restrictions-puts-providers-and-women-they-serve-crosshairs.

84. *Whole Woman's Health v. Hellerstedt*, 579 U.S. ___ (2016).

85. Heather D. Boonstra. 2013. "Insurance Coverage of Abortion: Beyond the Exceptions for Life Endangerment, Rape and Incest," *Guttmacher Policy Review* 16, No. 3, https://www.guttmacher.org/about/gpr/2013/09/insurance-coverage-abortion-beyond-exceptions-life-endangerment-rape-and-incest.

86. "Garbage Man Salary (United States)," http://www.payscale.com/research/US/Job=Garbage_Man/Hourly_Rate (April 10, 2016).

87. "Child Care/Day Care Worker Salary (United States)," http://www.payscale.com/research/US/Job=Child_Care_%2F_Day_Care_Worker/Hourly_Rate (April 10, 2016).

88. Theodore Haas. 1957. "The Legal Aspects of Indian Affairs from 1887 to 1957," *American Academy of Political Science* 311, 12–22.

89. *Elk v. Wilkins*, (1884)112 U.S. 94.

90. See Alan Gallay. 2009. *Indian Slavery in Colonial America*. Lincoln: University of Nebraska Press.

91. See James Wilson. 1998. *The Earth Shall Weep: A History of Native America*. New York: Grove Press.

92. Ibid; Gloria Jahoda. 1975. *Trail of Tears: The Story of American Indian Removal, 1813–1855*. New York: Henry Holt.

93. See Wilson. 1998. *The Earth Shall Weep*.

94. See John Ehle. 1988. *Trail of Tears: The Rise and Fall of the Cherokee Nation*. New York: Doubleday; Theda Perdue and Michael Green. 2007. *The Cherokee Nation and the Trail of Tears*. New York: Penguin Books.

95. *Cherokee Nation v. Georgia*, 30 U.S. 1 (1831).

96. Francis Paul Prucha. 1984. *The Great Father: The United States Government and American Indians*, vol. 1. Lincoln: University of Nebraska Press, 212; Robert V. Remini. 2001. *Andrew Jackson and His Indian Wars*. New York: Viking, 257; *Worcester v. Georgia*, 31 U.S. 515 (1832).

97. Prucha, 241; Ehle, 390–392; Russell Thornton. 1991. "Demography of the Trail of Tears," In *Cherokee Removal: Before and After*, ed. William L. Anderson. Athens: University of Georgia Press, 75–93.

98. "Indian Reservations," http://ic.galegroup.com/ic/uhic/ReferenceDetailsPage/ ReferenceDetailsWindow?zid=2a87fa28f20f1e66b5f663e76873fd8c&action=2&catId=&documentId= GALE | CX3401802046&userGroupName=lnoca_hawken&jsid=f44511ddfece4faafab082109e34a539 (April 10, 2016).

99. Ibid.

100. "Curtis Act (1898)," http://www.okhistory.org/publications/enc/entry.php?entry=CU006 (April 10, 2016).

101. See Gae Whitney Canfield. 1988. *Sarah Winnemucca of the Northern Paiutes*. Norman: University of Oklahoma Press.

102. Indian Reorganization Act of 1934 (P.L. 73–383); "Indian Reservations," http://ic.galegroup.com/ ic/uhic/ReferenceDetailsPage/ ReferenceDetailsWindow?zid=2a87fa28f20f1e66b5f663e76873fd8c&action=2&catId=&documentId= GALE | CX3401802046&userGroupName=lnoca_hawken&jsid=f44511ddfece4faafab082109e34a539 (April 10, 2016).

103. Daniel McCool, Susan M. Olson, and Jennifer L. Robinson. 2007. *Native Vote*. Cambridge, MA: Cambridge University Press, 9, 19.

104. "Indian Reservations," http://ic.galegroup.com/ic/uhic/ReferenceDetailsPage/ ReferenceDetailsWindow?zid=2a87fa28f20f1e66b5f663e76873fd8c&action=2&catId=&documentId= GALE | CX3401802046&userGroupName=lnoca_hawken&jsid=f44511ddfece4faafab082109e34a539 (April 10, 2016).

105. See Troy R. Johnson. 1996. *The Occupation of Alcatraz Island: Indian Self-Determination and the Rise of Indian Activism*. Urbana: University of Illinois Press.

106. Emily Chertoff, "Occupy Wounded Knee: A 71-Day Siege and a Forgotten Civil Rights Movement," *The Atlantic*, 23 October 2012. http://www.theatlantic.com/national/archive/2012/10/occupy- wounded-knee-a-71-day-siege-and-a-forgotten-civil-rights-movement/263998/.

107. Ibid.

108. Public Law 93–638: Indian Self-Determination and Education Assistance Act, as Amended.

109. W. Dale Mason. 2000. *Indian Gaming: Tribal Sovereignty and American Politics*. Norman: University of Oklahoma Press, 60–64.

110. Public Law 95–341: American Indian Religious Freedom, Joint Resolution.

111. Winters v. United States, 207 U.S. 564 (1908).

112. Adam Liptak.27 November 2018. "Is Half of Oklahoma an Indian Reservation? The Supreme Court Sifts the Merits." *New York Times*. https://www.nytimes.com/2018/11/27/us/politics/oklahoma- indian-territory-supreme-court.html.

113. U.S. Commission on Civil Rights, "Racism's Frontier: The Untold Story of Discrimination and

Division in Alaska," http://www.usccr.gov/pubs/sac/ak0402/ch1.htm (April 10, 2016).

114. Ryan Mielke, "Hawaiians' Years of Mistreatment," *Chicago Tribune*, 4 September 1999. http://articles.chicagotribune.com/1999-09-04/news/9909040141_1_hawaiians-oha-land-trust.

115. Brittany Lyte, "Historic Election Could Return Sovereignty to Native Hawaiians," *Aljazeera America* 30 Oct. 2015, http://america.aljazeera.com/articles/2015/10/30/historic-election-could-return-sovereignty-to-native-hawaiians.html.

116. Jason Daley. 28 September 2016. "Rule Allows Native Hawaiians to Form Their Own Government." Smithosian.com. https://www.smithsonianmag.com/smart-news/rule-allows-native-hawaiians-form-their-own-government-180960598/. Brittany Lyte. 5 November 2017. "Native Hawaiians Again Seek Political Sovereignty with a New Constitution." *Washington Post*. https://www.washingtonpost.com/national/native-hawaiians-again-seek-political-sovereignty-with-a-new-constitution/2017/11/05/833842d2-b905-11e7-be94-fabb0f1e9ffb_story.html?noredirect=on&utm_term=.b456552351c1.

117. Jens Manuel Krogstad. 13 June 2014. "One-in-Four Native Americans and Alaska Natives Are Living in Poverty," http://www.pewresearch.org/fact-tank/2014/06/13/1-in-4-native-americans-and-alaska-natives-are-living-in-poverty/.

118. Karina L. Walters, Jane M. Simoni, and Teresa Evans-Campbell. 2002. "Substance Use Among American Indians and Alaska Natives: Incorporating Culture in an 'Indigenist' Stess-Coping Paradigm," *Public Health Reports* 117: S105.

119. Kehaulani Lum, "Native Hawaiians' Trail of Tears," *Chicago Tribune*, 24 August 1999. http://articles.chicagotribune.com/1999-08-24/news/9908240280_1_native-hawaiians-hawaiian-people-aleuts.

120. "Hispanic v. Latino," http://www.soaw.org/resources/anti-opp-resources/108-race/830-hispanic-vs-latino (April 10, 2016).

121. David G. Gutierrez. 1995. *Walls and Mirrors: Mexican Americans, Mexican Immigrants, and the Politics of Ethnicity*. Berkeley: University of California Press, chapter 1.

122. See Abraham Hoffman. 1974. *Unwanted Americans in the Great Depression: Repatriation Pressures, 1929–1939*. Tucson: University of Arizona Press.

123. See Michael Snodgrass. 2011. "The Bracero Program,1942–1964" In *Beyond the Border: The History of Mexican–U.S. Migration*, ed. Mark Overmyer-Velásquez. New York: Oxford University Press, 79–102.

124. See Benjamin Marquez. 1993. *LULAC: The Evolution of a Mexican American Political Organization*. Austin: University of Texas Press.

125. *Mendez v. Westminister School District*, 64 F. Supp. 544 (S.D. Cal. 1946).

126. See Avi Astor. 2009. "Unauthorized Immigration, Securitization, and the Making of Operation Wetback," *Latino Studies* 7: 5–29.

127. See John R. Chavez. 1997. "The Chicano Image and the Myth of Aztlan Rediscovered." In *Myth America: A Historical Anthology* (volume II), eds. Patrick Gerster and Nicholas Cords. New York: Brandywine Press; F. Arturo Rosales. 1996. *Chicano! The History of the Mexican American Civil Rights Movement*. Houston, Texas: Arte Público Press.

128. See Rosales, *American Civil Rights Movement*.

129. See Sal Castro. 2011. *Blowout! Sal Castro and the Chicano Struggle for Educational Justice*. Chapel Hill: University of North Carolina Press.

130. See Randy Shaw. 2008. *Beyond the Fields: Cesar Chavez, the UFW, and the Struggle for Justice in the 21st Century*. Berkeley: University of California Press; Susan Ferriss, Ricardo Sandoval, and Diana Hembree. 1998. *The Fight in the Fields: Cesar Chavez and the Farmworkers Movement*. New York: Houghton Mifflin Harcourt.

131. CNN. 19 March 1998. "Most of California's Prop. 187 Ruled Unconstitutional," http://www.cnn.com/ALLPOLITICS/1998/03/19/prop.187/; Patrick J. McDonnell, "Prop. 187 Found Unconstitutional by Federal Judge," *Los Angeles Times*, 15 November 1997. http://articles.latimes.com/1997/nov/15/news/mn-54053.

132. Teresa Watanabe and Hector Becerra, "500,000 Pack Streets to Protest Immigration Bills," *Los Angeles Times*, 26 March 2006.

133. *Arizona v. United States*, 567 U.S. _ (2012).

134. *Arizona*, 567 U.S.

135. Center for Public Affairs Research. 24 November 2015. "UNO Study: Fertility Rate Gap Between Races, Ethnicities is Shrinking," http://www.unomaha.edu/news/2015/01/fertility.php.

136. Rakesh Kochhar and Richard Fry. 12 December 2014. "Wealth Inequality Has Widened Along Racial, Ethnic Lines Since End of Great Recession," http://www.pewresearch.org/fact-tank/2014/12/12/racial-wealth-gaps-great-recession/; "State High School Graduation Rates By Race, Ethnicity," http://www.governing.com/gov-data/education-data/state-high-school-graduation-rates-by-race-ethnicity.html (April 10, 2016); Mark Hugo Lopez and Richard Fry. 4 September 2013. "Among Recent High School Grads, Hispanic College Enrollment Rates Surpasses That of Whites," http://www.pewresearch.org/fact-tank/2013/09/04/hispanic-college-enrollment-rate-surpasses-whites-for-the-first-time/.

137. Perry Bacon Jr. 6 December 2018. "Trump Has Made U.S. Policy Much More Resistant to Immigration — Without the Wall." https://fivethirtyeight.com/features/trump-hasnt-needed-the-wall-to-remake-u-s-immigration-policy/.

138. See Gabriel Chin and Hrishi Kathrikeyan. 2002. "Preserving Racial Identity: Population Patterns and the Application of Anti-Miscegenation Statutes to Asian Americans, 1910–1950," *Asian Law Journal* 9.

139. See Greg Robinson. 2010. *A Tragedy of Democracy: Japanese Confinement in North America.* New York: Columbia University Press.

140. *Korematsu v. United States*, 323 U.S. 214 (1944).

141. Robinson, *Tragedy of Democracy*.

142. See William Wei. 1993. *The Asian American Movement.* Philadelphia: Temple University Press.

143. *Lau v. Nichols*, 414 U.S. 563 (1974).

144. "The Rise of Asian Americans," http://www.pewsocialtrends.org/asianamericans-graphics/ (April 10, 2016).

145. See Jonathan Ned Katz. 1995. *Gay and American History: Lesbians and Gay Men in the United States.* New York: Thomas Crowell.

146. See David K. Johnson. 2004. *The Lavender Scare: The Cold War Persecution of Gays and Lesbians.* Chicago: University of Chicago Press.

147. See Vern L. Bullough. 2002. *Before Stonewall: Activists for Gay and Lesbian Rights in Historical Context.* New York: Harrington Park Press.

148. See David Carter. 2004. *Stonewall: The Riots That Sparked the Gay Revolution.* New York: St. Martin's Press; Martin Duberman.1993. *Stonewall.* New York: Penguin Books.

149. Public Law 103–160: National Defense Authorization Act for Fiscal Year 1994.

150. NBC News. 22 July 2011. "Obama Certifies End of Military's Gay Ban," http://www.nbcnews.com/id/43859711/ns/us_news-life/#.VrAzFlLxh-U.

151. *Lawrence v. Texas*, 539 U.S. 558 (2003).

152. *Obergefell v. Hodges*, 576 U.S. _ (2015).

153. *City of Boerne v. Flores*, 521 U.S. 507 (1997).

154. "Know Your Rights: Transgender People and the Law," https://www.aclu.org/know-your-rights/transgender-people-and-law (April 10, 2016).

155. Lila Shapiro. 2 Apr. 2015. "Record Number of Reported LGBT Homicides in 2015," http://www.huffingtonpost.com/2015/04/02/lgbt-homicides_n_6993484.html.

156. See Edward J. Larson. 1995. *Sex, Race, and Science: Eugenics in The Deep South*. Baltimore, MD: Johns Hopkins University Press; Rebecca M. Kluchin. 2009. *Fit to Be Tied: Sterilization and Reproductive Rights in America 1950–1980*. New Brunswick, NJ: Rutgers University Press.

157. *Buck v. Bell*, 274 U.S. 200 (1927).

158. Kim Severson, "Thousands Sterilized, A State Weighs Restitution," *New York Times*, 9 December 2011. http://www.nytimes.com/2011/12/10/us/redress-weighed-for-forced-sterilizations-in-north-carolina.html?_r=1&hp.

159. See Nancy Lusignan Schultz. 2000. *Fire and Roses: The Burning of the Charlestown Convent*. New York: Free Press.

160. See Richard L. Bushman. 2005. Joseph Smith: Rough Stone Rolling. New York: Alfred A. Knopf.

161. See Frederic Cople Jaher. 1994. *A Scapegoat in the Wilderness: The Origins and Rise of Anti-Semitism in America*. Cambridge, MA: Harvard University Press.

162. "Combatting Religious Discrimination and Protecting Religious Freedom," http://www.justice.gov/crt/combating-religious-discrimination-and-protecting-religious-freedom-16 (April 10, 2016).

163. Eric Lichtblau, "Crimes Against Muslim Americans and Mosques Rise Sharply," *New York Times*, 17 December 2015. http://www.nytimes.com/2015/12/18/us/politics/crimes-against-muslim-americans-and-mosques-rise-sharply.html?_r=0.

164. *Burwell v. Hobby Lobby Stores, Inc.*, 573 U.S. _ (2014).

The Politics of Public Opinion

1. Erik Hayden, "Mitt Romney's Transition Website: Where 'President-Elect' Romney Lives On," *Time*, 8 November 2012. http://newsfeed.time.com/2012/11/08/mitt-romneys-transition-website-where-president-elect-romney (February 17, 2016).

2. John Sides, "The Romney Campaign's Own Polls Showed It Would Lose," *Washington Post*, 8 October 2013; Charlie Mahtesian, "Rasmussen Explains," *Politico*, 1 November 2012. Jan Crawford, "Adviser: Romney 'Shellshocked' by Loss," *CBS News*, 8 November 2012.

3. Crawford, "Adviser: Romney 'Shellshocked' by Loss."

4. Gallup. 2015. "Gallup Daily: Obama Job Approval." *Gallup*. June 6, 2015. http://www.gallup.com/poll/113980/Gallup-Daily-Obama-Job-Approval.aspx (February 17, 2016); Rasmussen Reports. 2015. "Daily Presidential Tracking Poll." *Rasmussen Reports* June 6, 2015. http://www.rasmussenreports.com/public_content/politics/obama_administration/daily_presidential_tracking_poll (February 17, 2016); Roper Center. 2015. "Obama Presidential Approval." *Roper Center*. June 6, 2015. http://www.ropercenter.uconn.edu/polls/presidential-approval/ (February 17, 2016).

5. V. O. Key, Jr. 1966. *The Responsible Electorate*. Harvard University: Belknap Press.

6. John Zaller. 1992. *The Nature and Origins of Mass Opinion*. Cambridge: Cambridge University Press.

7. Eitan Hersh. 2013. "Long-Term Effect of September 11 on the Political Behavior of Victims' Families and Neighbors." *Proceedings of the National Academy of Sciences of the United States of America* 110 (52):

20959–63.

8. M. Kent Jennings. 2002. "Generation Units and the Student Protest Movement in the United States: An Intra- and Intergenerational Analysis." *Political Psychology* 23 (2): 303–324.

9. United States Senate. 2015. "Party Division in the Senate, 1789-Present," *United States Senate.* June 5, 2015. http://www.senate.gov/pagelayout/history/one_item_and_teasers/partydiv.htm (February 17, 2016). History, Art & Archives. 2015. "Party Divisions of the House of Representatives: 1789–Present." *United States House of Representatives.* June 5, 2015. http://history.house.gov/Institution/Party-Divisions/Party-Divisions/ (February 17, 2016).

10. V. O. Key Jr. 1955. "A Theory of Critical Elections." *Journal of Politics* 17 (1): 3–18.

11. Pew Research Center. 2014. "Political Polarization in the American Public." *Pew Research Center.* June 12, 2014. http://www.people-press.org/2014/06/12/political-polarization-in-the-american-public/ (February 17, 2016).

12. Pew Research Center. 2015. "American Values Survey." *Pew Research Center.* http://www.people-press.org/values-questions/ (February 17, 2016).

13. Virginia Chanley. 2002. "Trust in Government in the Aftermath of 9/11: Determinants and Consequences." *Political Psychology* 23 (3): 469–483.

14. Deborah Schildkraut. 2002. "The More Things Change... American Identity and Mass and Elite Responses to 9/11." *Political Psychology* 23 (3): 532.

15. Joseph Bafumi and Robert Shapiro. 2009. "A New Partisan Voter." *The Journal of Politics* 71 (1): 1–24.

16. Liz Marlantes, "After 9/11, the Body Politic Tilts to Conservatism," *Christian Science Monitor*, 16 January 2002.

17. Liping Weng. 2010. "Shanghai Children's Value Socialization and Its Change: A Comparative Analysis of Primary School Textbooks." *China Media Research* 6 (3): 36–43.

18. David Easton. 1965. *A Systems Analysis of Political Life.* New York: John Wiley.

19. Angus Campbell, Philip Converse, Warren Miller, and Donald Stokes. 2008. *The American Voter: Unabridged Edition.* Chicago: University of Chicago Press. Michael S. Lewis-Beck, William G. Jacoby, Helmut Norpoth, and Herbert F. Weisberg. 2008. *American Vote Revisited.* Ann Arbor: University of Michigan Press.

20. Russell Dalton. 1980. "Reassessing Parental Socialization: Indicator Unreliability versus Generational Transfer." *American Political Science Review* 74 (2): 421–431.

21. Michael S. Lewis-Beck, William G. Jacoby, Helmut Norpoth, and Herbert F. Weisberg. 2008. *American Vote Revisited.* Ann Arbor: University of Michigan Press.

22. Michael Lipka. 2013. "What Surveys Say about Workshop Attendance—and Why Some Stay Home." *Pew Research Center.* September 13, 2013. http://www.pewresearch.org/fact-tank/2013/09/13/what-surveys-say-about-worship-attendance-and-why-some-stay-home/ (February 17, 2016).

23. Arthur Lupia and Mathew D. McCubbins. 1998. *The Democratic Dilemma: Can Citizens Learn What They Need to Know?* New York: Cambridge University Press. John Barry Ryan. 2011. "Social Networks as a Shortcut to Correct Voting." *American Journal of Political Science* 55 (4): 753–766.

24. Sarah Bowen. 2015. "A Framing Analysis of Media Coverage of the Rodney King Incident and Ferguson, Missouri, Conflicts." *Elon Journal of Undergraduate Research in Communications* 6 (1): 114–124.

25. Frederick Engels. 1847. *The Principles of Communism.* Trans. Paul Sweezy. https://www.marxists.org/archive/marx/works/1847/11/prin-com.htm (February 17, 2016).

26. Libertarian Party. 2014. "Libertarian Party Platform." June. http://www.lp.org/platform (February 17, 2016).

27. Arthur Evans, "Predict Landon Electoral Vote to be 315 to 350," *Chicago Tribune*, 18 October 1936.

28. United States Census Bureau. 2012. "Age and Sex Composition in the United States: 2012." *United States Census Bureau*. http://www.census.gov/population/age/data/2012comp.html (February 17, 2016).

29. Rasmussen Reports. 2015. "Daily Presidential Tracking Poll." *Rasmussen Reports*. September 27, 2015. http://www.rasmussenreports.com/public_content/politics/obama_administration/daily_presidential_tracking_poll (February 17, 2016); Pew Research Center. 2015. "Sampling." *Pew Research Center*. http://www.pewresearch.org/methodology/u-s-survey-research/sampling/ (February 17, 2016).

30. American National Election Studies Data Center. 2016. http://electionstudies.org/studypages/download/datacenter_all_NoData.php (February 17, 2016).

31. Michael W. Link and Robert W. Oldendick. 1997. "'Good' Polls / 'Bad' Polls—How Can You Tell? Ten Tips for Consumers of Survey Research." *South Carolina Policy Forum*. http://www.ipspr.sc.edu/publication/Link.htm (February 17, 2016); Pew Research Center. 2015. "Sampling." *Pew Research Center*. http://www.pewresearch.org/methodology/u-s-survey-research/sampling/ (February 17, 2016).

32. "Roper Center. 2015. "Polling Fundamentals – Sampling." *Roper*. http://www.ropercenter.uconn.edu/support/polling-fundamentals-sampling/ (February 17, 2016).

33. Gallup. 2015. "How Does the Gallup World Poll Work?" *Gallup*. http://www.gallup.com/178667/gallup-world-poll-work.aspx (February 17, 2016).

34. Gallup. 2015. "Does Gallup Call Cellphones?" *Gallup*. http://www.gallup.com/poll/110383/does-gallup-call-cell-phones.aspx (February 17, 2016).

35. Mark Blumenthal, "The Case for Robo-Pollsters: Automated Interviewers Have Their Drawbacks, But Fewer Than Their Critics Suggest," *National Journal*, 14 September 2009.

36. Mark Blumenthal, "Is Polling As We Know It Doomed?" *National Journal*, 10 August 2009.

37. Frank Luntz. 2007. *Words That Work: It's Not What You Say, It's What People Hear*. New York: Hyperion.

38. Aaron Blake, "This terrible polls shows Elizabeth Warren beating Hillary Clinton," *Washington Post*, 11 February 2015.

39. Nate Silver. 2010. "The Broadus Effect? Social Desirability Bias and California Proposition 19." *FiveThirtyEightPolitics*. July 27, 2010. http://fivethirtyeight.com/features/broadus-effect-social-desirability-bias/ (February 18, 2016).

40. Nate Silver. 2010. "The Broadus Effect? Social Desirability Bias and California Proposition 19." *FiveThirtyEightPolitics*. July 27, 2010. http://fivethirtyeight.com/features/broadus-effect-social-desirability-bias/ (February 18, 2016).

41. D. Davis. 1997. "The Direction of Race of Interviewer Effects among African-Americans: Donning the Black Mask." *American Journal of Political Science* 41 (1): 309–322.

42. Kate Sheppard, "Top Texas Regulator: Could Russia be Behind City's Proposed Fracking Ban?" *Huffington Post*, 16 July 2014. http://www.huffingtonpost.com/2014/07/16/fracking-ban-denton-russia_n_5592661.html (February 18, 2016).

43. Michael S. Lewis-Beck, William G. Jacoby, Helmut Norpoth, and Herbert F. Weisberg. 2008. *American Vote Revisited*. Ann Arbor: University of Michigan Press.

44. Samuel Popkin. 2008. *The Reasoning Voter: Communication and Persuasion in Presidential Campaigns*. Chicago: University Of Chicago Press. Michael S. Lewis-Beck, William G. Jacoby, Helmut Norpoth, and Herbert F. Weisberg. 2008. *American Vote Revisited*. Ann Arbor: University of Michigan Press.

45. Scott Ashworth, and Ethan Bueno De Mesquita. 2014. "Is Voter Competence Good for Voters? Information, Rationality, and Democratic Performance." *American Political Science Review* 108 (3): 565–587.

46. Gallup. 2015. "U.S. Presidential Election Center." *Gallup*. June 6, 2015. http://www.gallup.com/poll/154559/US-Presidential-Election-Center.aspx (February 18, 2016).

47. "How Groups Voted 2016." 10 January 2019. Roper Center for Public Opinion Research at Cornell University. https://ropercenter.cornell.edu/polls/us-elections/how-groups-voted/groups-voted-2016/.

48. Josh Richman, "Field Poll: California Voters Favor Gun Controls Over Protecting Second Amendment Rights," *San Jose Mercury News*, 26 February 2013.

49. UT Austin. 2015. "Agreement with Concealed Carry Laws." *UT Austin Texas Politics Project*. February 2015. http://texaspolitics.utexas.edu/set/agreement-concealed-carry-laws-february-2015#party-id (February 18, 2016).

50. Stephen Battaglio, "Brian Williams Will Leave 'NBC Nightly News' and Join MSNBC," *LA Times*, 18 June 2015.

51. Pew Research Center. 2015. "Party Identification Trends, 1992–2014." *Pew Research Center*. April 7, 2015. http://www.people-press.org/2015/04/07/party-identification-trends-1992-2014/ (February 18, 2016).

52. Jeffrey Jones. 2014. "Americans Continue to Say a Third Political Party is Needed." *Gallup*. September 24, 2014. http://www.gallup.com/poll/177284/americans-continue-say-third-political-party-needed.aspx (February 18, 2016).

53. Pew Research Center. 2015. "A Different Look at Generations and Partisanship." *Pew Research Center*. April 30, 2015. http://www.people-press.org/2015/04/30/a-different-look-at-generations-and-partisanship/ (February 18, 2016).

54. Pew Research Center. 2015. "Multiracial in America." *Pew Research Center*. June 11, 2015. http://www.pewsocialtrends.org/2015/06/11/multiracial-in-america/ (February 18, 2016).

55. Pew Research Center. 2015. "Economic Conditions." *Pew Research Center*. February 22, 2015. http://www.pewresearch.org/data-trend/national-conditions/economic-conditions/ (February 18, 2016).

56. Pew Research Center. 2015. "Personal Finances." *Pew Research Center*. January 11, 2015. http://www.pewresearch.org/data-trend/national-conditions/personal-finances/ (February 18, 2016).

57. Frank Newport. 2011. "Americans Blame Wasteful Government Spending for Deficit." *Gallup*. April 29, 2011. http://www.gallup.com/poll/147338/Americans-Blame-Wasteful-Government-Spending-Deficit.aspx (February 18, 2016).

58. Harris Poll Online. 2012. "Cutting Government Spending May be Popular But Majorities of the Public Oppose Cuts in Many Big Ticket Items in the Budget." *Harris Poll Online*. March 1, 2012. http://www.harrisinteractive.com/NewsRoom/HarrisPolls/tabid/447/mid/1508/articleId/972/ctl/ReadCustom percent20Default/Default.aspx (February 18, 2016); Frank Newport, and Lydia Saad, 2011. "Americans Oppose Cuts in Education, Social Security, Defense." *Gallup*. January 2, 2011. http://www.gallup.com/poll/145790/Americans-Oppose-Cuts-Education-Social-Security-Defense.aspx (February 18, 2016).

59. Pew Research Center. 2011. "Domestic Issues and Social Policy." *Pew Research Center*. May 4, 2011. http://www.people-press.org/2011/05/04/section-8-domestic-issues-and-social-policy/ (February 18, 2016).

60. Pew Research Center. 2015. "Views of Health Care Law, 2010-2015." *Pew Research Center*. March 3, 2015. http://www.pewresearch.org/fact-tank/2015/03/04/opinions-on-obamacare-remain-divided-along-party-lines-as-supreme-court-hears-new-challenge/ft_acaapprove (February 18, 2016).

61. Pew Research Center. 2014. "Gun Control." *Pew Research Center*. December 7, 2014. http://www.pewresearch.org/data-trend/domestic-issues/gun-control (February 18, 2016).

62. *Obergefell v. Hodges*, 576 U.S. ___ (2015).

63. National Conference of State Legislatures. 2015. "Same Sex Marriage Laws." *National Conference of State Legislatures*. June 26, 2015. http://www.ncsl.org/research/human-services/same-sex-marriage-laws.aspx (February 18, 2016).

64. Pew Research Center. 2014. "Gun Control." *Pew Research Center*. December 7, 2014. http://www.pewresearch.org/data-trend/domestic-issues/gun-control (February 18, 2016).

65. Pew Research Center. 2011. "Domestic Issues and Social Policy." May 4, 2011. *Pew Research Center*. http://www.people-press.org/2011/05/04/section-8-domestic-issues-and-social-policy (February 18, 2016).

66. Gallup interactive Presidential Job Approval Center. https://news.gallup.com/interactives/185273/r.aspx?g_source=WWWV7HP&g_medium=topic&g_campaign=tiles.

67. Gallup. 2015. "Presidential Approval Ratings – George W. Bush." *Gallup*. June 20, 2015. http://www.gallup.com/poll/116500/Presidential-Approval-Ratings-George-Bush.aspx (February 18, 2016).

68. 115 STAT. 2001. "224. Public Law 107-40. Joint Resolution." 107th Congress. http://www.gpo.gov/fdsys/pkg/PLAW-107publ40/pdf/PLAW-107publ40.pdf (February 18, 2016).

69. Pew Research Center. 2008. "Public Attitudes Towards the War in Iraq: 2003-2008." *Pew Research Center*. March 19, 2008. http://www.pewresearch.org/2008/03/19/public-attitudes-toward-the-war-in-iraq-20032008/ (February 18, 2016); Pew Research Center. 2014. "More Now See Failure than Success in Iraq, Afghanistan." *Pew Research Center*. January 30, 2014. http://www.people-press.org/2014/01/30/more-now-see-failure-than-success-in-iraq-afghanistan/ (February 18, 2016).

70. Gallup. 2015. "Presidential Job Approval Center." *Gallup*. June 20, 2015. http://www.gallup.com/poll/124922/Presidential-Job-Approval-Center.aspx?utm_source=PRESIDENTIAL_JOB_APPROVAL&utm_medium=topic&utm_campaign=tiles (February 18, 2016).

71. Gallup. 2015. "Congress and the Public." *Gallup*. June 21, 2015. http://www.gallup.com/poll/1600/Congress-Public.aspx (February 18, 2016).

72. Neil Irwin, "The 1995 Shutdown, from a Budget Official's Perspective," *Washington Post*, 27 September 2013.

73. Gallup. 2015. "Congress and the Public." *Gallup*. June 21, 2015. http://www.gallup.com/poll/1600/Congress-Public.aspx (February 18, 2016); Jeffrey Jones. 2007. "Congress Approval Rating Matches Historical Low." *Gallup*. August 21, 2007. http://www.gallup.com/poll/28456/congress-approval-rating-matches-historical-low.aspx (February 18, 2016).

74. Dan Merica. 2013. "1995 and 2013: Three Differences Between the Two Shutdowns." *CNN*. October 4, 2013. http://www.cnn.com/2013/10/01/politics/different-government-shutdowns/ (February 18, 2016).

75. Paul Lewis, "US Shutdown Drags Into Second Day as Republicans Eye Fresh Debt Ceiling Crisis," *Guardian*, 2 October 2013.

76. Gallup. 2015. "Congress and the Public." *Gallup*. June 21, 2015. http://www.gallup.com/poll/1600/Congress-Public.aspx (February 18, 2016).

77. Andrew Dugan. 2014. "Americans' Approval of Supreme Court New All-Time Low." *Gallup*. July 19, 2014. http://www.gallup.com/poll/163586/americans-approval-supreme-court-near-time-low.aspx (February 18, 2016).

78. James L. Gibson, and Gregory A. Caldeira. 2009. "Knowing the Supreme Court? A Reconsideration of Public Ignorance of the High Court." *Journal of Politics* 71 (2): 429–441.

79. *Bush v. Gore*, 531 U.S. 98 (2000).

80. *National Federation of Independent Business v. Sebelius*, 567 U.S. ___ (2012); Andrew Dugan. 2014. "Americans' Approval of Supreme Court New All-Time Low." *Gallup*. July 19, 2014. http://www.gallup.com/poll/163586/americans-approval-supreme-court-near-time-low.aspx (February 18, 2016).

81. *King v. Burwell*, 576 U.S. ___ (2015); Gallup Polling. 2015. "Supreme Court." *Gallup Polling*. http://www.gallup.com/poll/4732/supreme-court.aspx (February 18, 2016).

82. Donald Mccrone, and James Kuklinski. 1979. "The Delegate Theory of Representation." *American Journal of Political Science* 23 (2): 278–300.

83. Norman Ornstein, and Thomas Mann, eds. 2000. *The Permanent Campaign and Its Future*. Washington: American Enterprise Institute for Public Policy Research and the Brookings Institution.

84. Paul Hitlin. 2013. "The 2016 Presidential Media Primary Is Off to a Fast Start." *Pew Research Center*. October 3, 2013. http://www.pewresearch.org/fact-tank/2013/10/03/the-2016-presidential-media-primary-is-off-to-a-fast-start/ (February 18, 2016).

85. Pew Research Center, 2015. "Hillary Clinton's Favorability Ratings over Her Career." *Pew Research Center*. June 6, 2015. http://www.pewresearch.org/wp-content/themes/pewresearch/static/hillary-clintons-favorability-ratings-over-her-career/ (February 18, 2016).

86. Pew Research Center. 2012. "Winning the Media Campaign." *Pew Research Center*. November 2, 2012. http://www.journalism.org/2012/11/02/winning-media-campaign-2012/ (February 18, 2016).

87. Pew Research Center. 2012. "Fewer Horserace Stories-and Fewer Positive Obama Stories-Than in 2008." *Pew Research Center*. November 2, 2012. http://www.journalism.org/2012/11/01/press-release-6/ (February 18, 2016).

88. Zack Nauth, "Networks Won't Use Exit Polls in State Forecasts," *Los Angeles Times*, 18 January 1985.

89. Seymour Sudman. 1986. "Do Exit Polls Influence Voting Behavior? *The Public Opinion Quarterly* 50 (3): 331–339.

90. Patrick O'Connor. 2015. "WSJ/NBC Poll Finds Hillary Clinton in a Strong Position." *Wall Street Journal*. June 23, 2015. http://www.wsj.com/articles/new-poll-finds-hillary-clinton-tops-gop-presidential-rivals-1435012049.

91. Federal Elections Commission. 2015. "Presidential Receipts." http://www.fec.gov/press/summaries/2016/tables/presidential/presreceipts_2015_q2.pdf (February 18, 2016).

92. Susan Page and Paulina Firozi, "Poll: Hillary Clinton Still Leads Sanders and Biden But By Less," *USA Today*, 1 October 2015.

93. Dan Merica, and Jeff Zeleny. 2015. "Bernie Sanders Nearly Outraises Clinton, Each Post More Than $20 Million." *CNN*. October 1, 2015. http://www.cnn.com/2015/09/30/politics/bernie-sanders-hillary-clinton-fundraising/index.html?eref=rss_politics (February 18, 2016).

94. Robert S. Erikson, Michael B. MacKuen, and James A. Stimson. 2000. "Bankers or Peasants Revisited: Economic Expectations and Presidential Approval." *Electoral Studies* 19: 295–312.

95. Erikson et al, "Bankers or Peasants Revisited: Economic Expectations and Presidential Approval."

96. Michael B. MacKuen, Robert S. Erikson, and James A. Stimson. 1989. "Macropartisanship." *American Political Science Review* 83 (4): 1125–1142.

97. James A. Stimson, Michael B. Mackuen, and Robert S. Erikson. 1995. "Dynamic Representation." *American Political Science Review* 89 (3): 543–565.

98. Stimson et al, "Dynamic Representation."

99. Stimson et al, "Dynamic Representation."

100. Dan Wood. 2009. *Myth of Presidential Representation*. New York: Cambridge University Press, 96-97.

101. Wood, *Myth of Presidential Representation*.

102. U.S. Election Atlas. 2015. "United States Presidential Election Results." *U.S. Election Atlas.* June 22, 2015. http://uselectionatlas.org/RESULTS/ (February 18, 2016).

103. Richard Fleisher, and Jon R. Bond. 1996. "The President in a More Partisan Legislative Arena." *Political Research Quarterly* 49 no. 4 (1996): 729–748.

104. George C. Edwards III, and B. Dan Wood. 1999. "Who Influences Whom? The President, Congress, and the Media." *American Political Science Review* 93 (2): 327–344.

105. Pew Research Center. 2013. "Public Opinion Runs Against Syrian Airstrikes." *Pew Research Center.* September 4, 2013. http://www.people-press.org/2013/09/03/public-opinion-runs-against-syrian-airstrikes/ (February 18, 2016).

106. Paul Bedard. 2013. "Poll-Crazed Clinton Even Polled on His Dog's Name." *Washington Examiner.* April 30, 2013. http://www.washingtonexaminer.com/poll-crazed-bill-clinton-even-polled-on-his-dogs-name/article/2528486.

107. Stimson et al, "Dynamic Representation."

108. Suzanna De Boef, and James A. Stimson. 1995. "The Dynamic Structure of Congressional Elections." *Journal of Politics* 57 (3): 630–648.

109. Stimson et al, "Dynamic Representation."

110. Stimson et al, "Dynamic Representation."

111. Benjamin Cardozo. 1921. *The Nature of the Judicial Process*. New Haven: Yale University Press.

112. Jack Knight, and Lee Epstein. 1998. *The Choices Justices Make*. Washington DC: CQ Press.

113. Kevin T. Mcguire, Georg Vanberg, Charles E Smith, and Gregory A. Caldeira. 2009. "Measuring Policy Content on the U.S. Supreme Court." *Journal of Politics* 71 (4): 1305–1321.

114. Kevin T. McGuire, and James A. Stimson. 2004. "The Least Dangerous Branch Revisited: New Evidence on Supreme Court Responsiveness to Public Preferences." *Journal of Politics* 66 (4): 1018–1035.

115. Thomas Marshall. 1989. *Public Opinion and the Supreme Court*. Boston: Unwin Hyman.

116. Christopher J. Casillas, Peter K. Enns, and Patrick C. Wohlfarth. 2011. "How Public Opinion Constrains the U.S. Supreme Court." *American Journal of Political Science* 55 (1): 74–88.

117. *Town of Greece v. Galloway* 572 U.S. ___ (2014).

118. Gallup. 2015. "Religion." *Gallup.* June 18, 2015. http://www.gallup.com/poll/1690/Religion.aspx (February 18, 2016).

119. Rebecca Riffkin. 2015. "In U.S., Support for Daily Prayer in Schools Dips Slightly." *Gallup.* September 25, 2015. http://www.gallup.com/poll/177401/support-daily-prayer-schools-dips-slightly.aspx.

120. Gallup. 2015. "Supreme Court." *Gallup.* http://www.gallup.com/poll/4732/supreme-court.aspx (February 18, 2016).

121. Stimson et al, "Dynamic Representation."

Voting and Elections

1. Margaret Carlson, "In Iowa, Ted Cruz Shoots Ducks in a Barrel," *Bloomberg View*, 29 October 2013; Steve Peoples, "Sen. Ted Cruz of Texas Heading to New Hampshire," *San Jose Mercury News*, 13 July 2013.

2. "Cruz Filibusters with 'Green Eggs and Ham,' 'Redneck Rules,'" 30 July 2015, http://abcnews.go.com/GMA/video/tea-party-senator-ted-cruz-filibusters-attack-obamacare-20366644.

3. Brandie Peterson, "Election 2016: Why Ted Cruz Picked Liberty University," *CNN*, 23 March 2015.

4. "Transcript: Ted Cruz's Speech at Liberty University," *Washington Post*, 23 March 2015.

5. Stephen Medvic. 2014. *Campaigns and Elections: Players and Processes*, 2nd ed. New York: Routledge.

6. *Guinn v. United States*, 238 U.S. 347 (1915).

7. Medvic, *Campaigns and Elections*.

8. *Shelby County v. Holder*, 570 U.S. ___ (2013).

9. Bernard Grofman, Lisa Handley, and Richard G. Niemi. 1992. *Minority Representation and the Quest for Voting Equality*. New York: Cambridge University Press, 25.

10. "The Canvass," April 2014, Issue 48, http://www.ncsl.org/research/elections-and-campaigns/states-and-election-reform-the-canvass-april-2014.aspx.

11. Tova Wang and Maria Peralta. 22 September 2015. "New Report Released by National Commission on Voting Rights: More Work Needed to Improve Registration and Voting in the U.S." http://votingrightstoday.org/ncvr/resources/electionadmin.

12. Ibid.

13. Royce Crocker, "The National Voter Registration Act of 1993: History, Implementation, and Effects," *Congressional Research Service*, CRS Report R40609, September 18, 2013, https://www.fas.org/sgp/crs/misc/R40609.pdf.

14. "National General Election VEP Turnout Rates, 1789–Present," http://www.electproject.org/national-1789-present (November 4, 2015).

15. John B. Holbein, D. Sunshine Hillygus. 2015. "Making Young Voters: The Impact of Preregistration on Youth Turnout." *American Journal of Political Science* (March). doi:10.1111/ajps.12177.

16. Russell Berman, "Should Voter Registration Be Automatic?" *Atlantic*, 20 March 2015; Maria L. La Ganga, "Under New Oregon Law, All Eligible Voters are Registered Unless They Opt Out," *Los Angeles Times*, 17 March 2015.

17. "'Unusable' Voter Rolls," *Wall Street Journal*, 7 November 2000.

18. "One Hundred Seventh Congress of the United States of America at the Second Session," 23 January 2002. http://www.eac.gov/assets/1/workflow_staging/Page/41.PDF.

19. "Voter List Accuracy," 11 February 2014. http://www.ncsl.org/research/elections-and-campaigns/voter-list-accuracy.aspx

20. Brad Bryant and Kay Curtis, eds. December 2013. "Interstate Crosscheck Program Grows," http://www.kssos.org/forms/communication/canvassing_kansas/dec13.pdf.

21. Troy Kinsey, "Proposed Bills Put Greater Scrutiny on Florida's Voter Purges," *Bay News*, 9 November 2015.

22. Pam Fessler, "Study: 1.8 Million Dead People Still Registered to Vote," *National Public Radio*, 14 February 2013; "Report: Inaccurate, Costly, an Inefficient," *The Pew Charitable Trusts*, February 14, 2012.

23. Fessler, "Study: 1.8 Million Dead People Still Registered to Vote."

24. "Felon Voting Rights," 15 July 2014. http://www.ncsl.org/research/elections-and-campaigns/felon-voting-rights.aspx.

25. Wilson Ring, "Vermont, Maine Only States to Let Inmates Vote," *Associated Press*, 22 October 2008.

26. "Voter's Qualifications and Oath," https://votesmart.org/elections/ballot-measure/1583/voters-qualifications-and-oath#.VjQOJH6rS00 (November 12, 2015).

27. Richard Niemi and Michael Hanmer. 2010. "Voter Turnout Among College Students: New Data and

a Rethinking of Traditional Theories," *Social Science Quarterly* 91, No. 2: 301–323.

28. Michael P. McDonald and Samuel Popkin. 2001. "Myth of the Vanishing Voter," *American Political Science Review* 95, No. 4: 963–974; See also, "What is the Voting-Age Population (VAP) and the Voting-Eligible Population (VEP)?" http://www.electproject.org/home/voter-turnout/faq/denominator (November 12, 2015).

29. McDonald and Popkin, "Myth of the Vanishing Voter," 963–974.

30. Michael B. Farrell. September 16, 2009. "What is the ACORN Controversy About?" *Christian Science Monitor*, http://www.csmonitor.com/USA/Politics/2009/0916/what-is-the-acorn-controversy-about.

31. Jennifer Steinhauer, "Opponents of California Ballot Initiative Seek Inquiry," *New York Times*, 21 November 2007.

32. Lori A. Demeter. 2010. "The Reluctant Voter: Is Same Day Registration the Skeleton Key?" *International Journal of Business and Social Science* 1, No. 1: 191–193.

33. Jane Eisner. 2004. *Taking Back the Vote: Getting American Youth Involved in Our Democracy.* Boston: Beacon Press.

34. "Table 2. Reported Voting and Registration, by Race, Hispanic Origin, Sex, and Age, for the United States: November 2012," https://www.census.gov/hhes/www/socdemo/voting/publications/p20/2012/tables.html (November 6, 2015).

35. Jose Antonio Vargas, "Vote or Die? Well, They Did Vote," *Washington Post*, 9 November 2004; Melissa Dahl. 5 November 2008. "Youth Vote May Have Been Key in Obama's Win," http://www.nbcnews.com/id/27525497/ns/politics-decision_08/t/youth-vote-may-have-been-key-obamas-win/.

36. Thom File, "Young-Adult Voting: An Analysis of Presidential Elections 1964-2012," *United States Census Bureau*, P20-573, April 2014, https://www.census.gov/prod/2014pubs/p20-573.pdf.

37. "Table 5. Reported Voting and Registration, by Age, Sex, and Educational Attainment: November 2012," https://www.census.gov/hhes/www/socdemo/voting/publications/p20/2012/tables.html (November 6, 2015).

38. "Table 7. Reported Voting and Registration of Family Members, by Age and Family Income: November 2012," https://www.census.gov/hhes/www/socdemo/voting/publications/p20/2012/tables.html (November 5, 2015).

39. "Table 4b. Reported Voting and Registration, by Sex, Race and Hispanic Origin, for States: November 2012," https://www.census.gov/hhes/www/socdemo/voting/publications/p20/2012/tables.html (November 2, 2015).

40. J. M. Krogstad and M. H. Lopez. 29 November 2016. "Hillary Clinton won Latino vote but fell below 2012 support for Obama," http://www.pewresearch.org/fact-tank/2016/11/29/hillary-clinton-wins-latino-vote-but-falls-below-2012-support-for-obama/ (February 28, 2018).

41. "Table 1. Reported Voting and Registration, by Sex and Single Years of Age: November 2012," https://www.census.gov/hhes/www/socdemo/voting/publications/p20/2012/tables.html (November 2, 2015).

42. Frank Newport. 12 June 2009. "Women More Likely to Be Democrats, Regardless of Age," http://www.gallup.com/poll/120839/women-likely-democrats-regardless-age.aspx.

43. "Figure 1. Proportion of Eligible Adult Population Who Reported Voting," http://www.cawp.rutgers.edu/sites/default/files/resources/genderdiff.pdf (February 28, 2018).

44. "Table 10. Reported Voting and Registration, by Sex and Single Years of Age: November 2012," https://www.census.gov/hhes/www/socdemo/voting/publications/p20/2012/tables.html (November 2, 2015).

45. Table 1. Reported Voting and Registration, by Sex and Single Years of Age: November 2012. Calculated using total number of people voted divided by total population.

46. Drew Desilver. 6 May 2015. "U.S. Voter Turnout trails Most Developed Countries," http://www.pewresearch.org/fact-tank/2015/05/06/u-s-voter-turnout-trails-most-developed-countries.

47. "Photo ID Law," http://www.in.gov/sos/elections/2401.htm (November 1, 2015).

48. "Obtaining a Photo ID," http://www.in.gov/sos/elections/2625.htm (November 1, 2015).

49. "Media Information Guide for Indiana 2014 General Election," http://www.state.in.us/sos/elections/files/2014_General_Election_Media_Guide_with_Attachments_11.03.2014.pdf (November 13, 2015).

50. David Stout, "Supreme Court Upholds Voter Identification Law in Indiana," *New York Times*, 29 April 2008; *Crawford v. Marion County Election Board*, 553 U.S. 181 (2008).

51. "Jurisdictions Previously Covered by Section 5," http://www.justice.gov/crt/jurisdictions-previously-covered-section-5 (November 1, 2015).

52. *Shelby County v. Holder*, 570 U.S. ___ (2013).

53. *Veasey v. Perry*, 574 U. S. ___ (2014).

54. Patricia Zengerle. 26 September 2012. "Young, Hispanics, Poor Hit Most by US Voter ID Laws: Study," http://www.reuters.com/article/2012/09/26/us-usa-campaign-voterid-idUSBRE88P1CW20120926#FzpCFPvhKPXu4fVA.97.

55. BBC News. 1 November 2018. "US Mid-Terms: What Are the Claims of Voter Suppression?" https://www.bbc.com/news/world-us-canada-45986329..

56. Stefan D. Haag, "Early Voting in Texas: What are the Effects?" *Austin Community College CPPPS Report*, http://www.austincc.edu/cppps/earlyvotingfull/report5.pdf (November 1, 2015).

57. Rich Morin. 23 September 2013. "Early Voting Associated with Lower Turnout," http://www.pewresearch.org/fact-tank/2013/09/23/study-early-voting-associated-with-lower-turnout.

58. The Denver Post Editorial Board, "A Vote of Confidence for Mail Elections in Colorado," *Denver Post*, 10 November 2014.

59. Brian Knowlton, "Disclosure of His 1976 Arrest for Drunken Driving Shakes Campaign, but Voter Reaction Is Uncertain: A November Surprise for Bush," *New York Times*, 4 November 2000.

60. "https://www.nytimes.com/2017/05/17/us/politics/robert-mueller-special-counsel-russia-investigation.html" Rebecca R. Ruiz and Mark Landler. 17 May 2017. "Robert Mueller, Former F.B.I. Director, Is Named Special Counsel for Russia Investigation." *New York Times*. https://www.nytimes.com/2017/05/17/us/politics/robert-mueller-special-counsel-russia-investigation.html.

61. "https://www.nytimes.com/2019/01/25/us/politics/roger-stone-trump-mueller.html" Mark Mazzetti, Eileen Sullivan, and Maggie Haberman. 25 January 2019. "Indicting Roger Stone, Mueller Shows Link between Trump Campaign and WikiLeaks." *New York Times*. https://www.nytimes.com/2019/01/25/us/politics/roger-stone-trump-mueller.html.

62. Harvard IOP, "Trump, Carson Lead Republican Primary; Sanders Edging Clinton Among Democrats, Harvard IOP Poll Finds," news release, December 10, 2015, http://www.iop.harvard.edu/harvard-iop-fall-2015-poll.

63. C. Rallings, M. Thrasher, and G. Borisyuk. 2003. "Seasonal Factors, Voter Fatigue and the Costs of Voting," *Electoral Studies* 22, No. 1: 65–79.

64. Jennifer L. Lawless. 2012. *Becoming a Candidate: Political Ambition and the Decision to Run for Office*. Cambridge: Cambridge University Press.

65. "Partisan Composition of State Houses," http://ballotpedia.org/
Partisan_composition_of_state_houses (November 4, 2015); Zach Holden. 20 November 2014. "No
Contest: 36 Percent of 2014 State Legislative Races Offered No Choice,"
https://www.followthemoney.org/research/blog/no-contest-36-percent-of-2014-state-legislative-races-
offer-no-choice-blog/.

66. "Legislators' Occupations in All States," http://www.ncsl.org/research/about-state-legislatures/
legislator-occupations-national-data.aspx (November 3, 2015).

67. Jennifer L. Lawless and Richard L. Fox. 2010. *It Still Takes a Candidate: Why Women Don't Run for Office.*
Revised Edition. Cambridge: Cambridge University Press.

68. "Women in State Legislatures for 2015," 4 September 2015. http://www.ncsl.org/legislators-staff/
legislators/womens-legislative-network/women-in-state-legislatures-for-2015.aspx.

69. Drew Desilver. 18 December 2018. "A Record Number of Women Will Be Serving in the New
Congress." Pew Research Center. http://www.pewresearch.org/fact-tank/2018/12/18/record-number-
women-in-congress/. Seth Millstein. November 2018. "The Average Age of Congress Will Drop
Dramatically Thanks to Newly-Elected Millennials." Bustle. https://www.bustle.com/p/the-average-
age-of-congress-in-2019-will-drop-dramatically-thanks-to-newly-elected-millennials-13124359.

70. "Reelection Rates Over the Years,"https://www.opensecrets.org/bigpicture/reelect.php (November
12, 2015).

71. "2012 Presidential Campaign Finance," http://www.fec.gov/disclosurep/
pnational.do;jsessionid=293EB5D0106C1C18892DC99478B01A46.worker3 (November 10, 2015).

72. "2014 House and Senate Campaign Finance," http://www.fec.gov/disclosurehs/
hsnational.do;jsessionid=E14EDC00736EF23F31DC86C1C0320049.worker4 (November 12, 2015).

73. "Political Action Committees," http://www.opensecrets.org/pacs/ (November 12, 2015).

74. Greg Scott and Gary Mullen, "Thirty Year Report," *Federal Election Commission*, September 2005,
http://www.fec.gov/info/publications/30year.pdf.

75. Jonathan Bernstein, "They Spent What on Presidential Campaigns?," *Washington Post*, 20 February,
2012.

76. Jaime Fuller, "From George Washington to Shaun McCutcheon: A Brief-ish History of Campaign
Finance Reform," *Washington Post*, 3 April 2014.

77. Federal Corrupt Practices Act of 1925; Hatch Act of 1939; Taft-Hartley Act of 1947

78. Scott and Mullen, "Thirty Year Report."

79. *Buckley v. Valeo*, 424 U.S. 1 (1976).

80. "Bipartisan Campaign Reform Act of 2002," http://www.fec.gov/pages/bcra/bcra_update.shtml
(November 11, 2015); Scott and Mullen, "Thirty Year Report."

81. "Court Case Abstracts," http://www.fec.gov/law/litigation_CCA_W.shtml (November 12, 2015);
Davis v. Federal Election Commission, 554 U.S. 724 (2008).

82. *Citizens United v. FEC*, 558 U.S. 310 (2010).

83. "Citizens United v. Federal Election Commission," http://www.opensecrets.org/news/reports/
citizens_united.php (November 11, 2015); "Independent Expenditure-Only Committees,"
http://www.fec.gov/press/press2011/ieoc_alpha.shtml (November 11, 2015).

84. "Super PACs," https://www.opensecrets.org/pacs/superpacs.php?cycle=2014 (November 11, 2015).

85. "Contribution Limits for the 2015–2016 Federal Elections," http://www.fec.gov/info/
contriblimitschart1516.pdf. (November 11, 2015).

86. Harold Meyerson, "Op-Ed: California's Jungle Primary: Tried it. Dump It," *Los Angeles Times*, 21 June 2014.

87. *California Democratic Party v. Jones*, 530 U.S. 567 (2000).

88. "Voter Turnout," http://www.electproject.org/home/voter-turnout/voter-turnout-data. (November 3, 2015).

89. Josh Putnam, "Presidential Primaries and Caucuses by Month (1976)," *Frontloading HQ* (blog), February 3, 2009, http://frontloading.blogspot.com/2009/02/1976-presidential-primary-calendar.html.

90. William G. Mayer and Andrew Busch. 2004. *The Front-loading Problem in Presidential Nominations*. Washington D.C.: Brookings Institution.

91. Joanna Klonsky, "The Role of Delegates in the U.S. Presidential Nominating Process," *Washington Post*, 6 February 2008.

92. "Party Affiliation and Election Polls," *Pew Research Center*, August 3, 2012.

93. Shanto Iyengar. 2016. *Media Politics: A Citizen's Guide*, 3rd ed. New York: W.W. Norton.

94. Paul Begala. 1 October 2008. "Commentary: 10 Rules for Winning a Debate," http://www.cnn.com/2008/POLITICS/10/01/begala.debate/index.html?iref=24hours.

95. 2nd Congress, Session I, "An Act relative to the Election of a President and Vice President of the United States, and Declaring the Office Who Shall Act as President in Case of Vacancies in the Offices both of President and Vice President," Chapter 8, section 1, image 239. http://memory.loc.gov/ammem/index.html (November 1, 2015).

96. 28th Congress, Session II. 23 January 1845. "An Act to Establish a Uniform Time for Holding Elections for Electors of President and Vice President in all the States of the Union," Statute II, chapter 1, image 721. http://memory.loc.gov/ammem/index.html; 42nd Congress, Session II, "An Act for the Apportionment of Representatives to Congress among the Several Sates According to the Ninth Census." Chapter 11, section 3, http://memory.loc.gov/ammem/index.html (November 1, 2015).

97. Donald Ratcliffe. 2013. "The Right to Vote and the Rise of Democracy, 1787–1828," *Journal of the Early Republic* 33: 219–254; Stanley Lebergott. 1966. "Labor Force and Employment, 1800–1960," In *Output, Employment, and Productivity in the United States after 1800*, ed. Dorothy S. Brady. Ann Arbor, Michigan: *National Bureau of Economic Research*, http://www.nber.org/books/brad66-1.

98. "Presidential Popular Vote Summary for All Candidates Listed on at Least One State Ballot," http://www.fec.gov/pubrec/fe2008/tables2008.pdf (November 7, 2015).

99. Drew Babb, "LBJ's 1964 Attack Ad 'Daisy' Leaves a Legacy for Modern Campaigns," *Washington Post*, 5 September 2014; "1964 Johnson vs. Goldwater," http://www.livingroomcandidate.org/commercials/1964 (November 9, 2015).

100. Stephen Ansolabehere, Shanto Iyengar, Adam Simon, and Nicholas Valentino. 1994. "Does Attack Advertising Demobilize the Electorate?" *The American Political Science Review* 88, No. 4: 829–838.

101. "Super PACs," https://www.opensecrets.org/pacs/superpacs.php?cycle=2014 (November 11, 2015).

102. *...So Goes the Nation*. 2006. Directed by Adam Del Deo and James D. Stern. Beverly Hills: Endgame Entertainment.

103. "Public Knowledge of Current Affairs Little Changed by News and Information Revolutions," *Pew Research Center*, April 15, 2007.

104. "Presidential Electors," http://www.sos.state.co.us/pubs/elections/Results/Abstract/2012/general/president.html (July 15, 2015); "Judicial Retention–Supreme Court," http://www.sos.state.co.us/pubs/elections/Results/Abstract/2012/general/retention/supremeCourt.html (July 15, 2015).

105. Lasse Laustsen. 2014. "Decomposing the Relationship Between Candidates' Facial Appearance and Electoral Success," *Political Behavior* 36, No. 4: 777–791.

106. Alan Silverleib. 15 June 2008. "Analysis: Age an Issue in the 2008 Campaign?" http://www.cnn.com/2008/POLITICS/06/15/mccain.age/index.html?iref=newssearch.

107. Laustsen. "Decomposing the Relationship," 777–791.

108. R. Michael Alvarez and Jonathan Nagler. 2000. "A New Approach for Modelling Strategic Voting in Multiparty Elections," *British Journal of Political Science* 30, No. 1: 57–75.

109. Nathan Thornburgh, "Could Third-Party Candidates Be Spoilers?" *Time*, 3 November 2008.

110. Matthew E. Glassman, "Congressional Franking Privilege: Background and Current Legislation," *Congressional Research Service*, CRS Report RS22771, December 11, 2007, http://fas.org/sgp/crs/misc/RS22771.pdf.

111. *League of United Latin American Citizens v. Perry*, 548 U.S. 399 (2006).

112. "Reelection Rates of the Years," https://www.opensecrets.org/bigpicture/reelect.php (November 2, 2015).

113. "Citizen's Guide to Town Meetings," http://www.sec.state.ma.us/cis/cispdf/Guide_to_Town_Meetings.pdf (November 7, 2015).

114. "How to Qualify an Initiative," http://www.sos.ca.gov/elections/ballot-measures/how-qualify-initiative/ (November 13, 2015).

115. David A. Fahrenthold and Rachel Weiner, "Gov. Walker Survives Recall in Wisconsin," *Washington Post*, 5 June 2012.

116. James M. Cole, "Memorandum for All United States Attorneys," *U.S. Department of Justice*, August 29, 2013, http://www.justice.gov/iso/opa/resources/3052013829132756857467.pdf.

117. "State Medical Marijuana Laws," http://www.ncsl.org/research/health/state-medical-marijuana-laws.aspx#2 (July 20, 2015).

118. Jessica Garrison, "Prop. 8 Leaves Some Voters Puzzled," *Los Angeles Times*, 31 October 2008.

119. Mark Barabak, "10 memorable moments from the recall of Gov. Gray Davis, 10 years later," *Los Angeles Times*, http://www.latimes.com/nation/la-me-recall-pictures-20131001-photogallery.html (August 1, 2015).

The Media

1. Dan Merica, "Black Lives Matter Protesters Shut Down Sanders Event in Seattle," *CNN*, 10 August 2015.

2. http://blacklivesmatter.com/about/ (August 29, 2015).

3. Conor Friedersdorf, "A Conversation about Black Lives Matter and Bernie Sanders," *The Atlantic*, 21 August 2015.

4. Anthony R. Fellow. 2013. *American Media History*. Boston: Cengage, page 67.

5. Jeremy Lipschultz and Michael Hilt. 2003. "Race and Local Television News Crime Coverage," *Studies in Media & Information Literacy Education* 3, No. 4: 1–10.

6. Lucas Shaw, "TV Networks Offering More On Demand to Reduce Ad-Skipping," *Bloomberg Technology*, 24 September 2014.

7. Daniel Marans, "Did the Oregon Shooter Warn of His Plans on 4chan?" *Huffington Post*, 1 October 2015.

8. Vanna Le, "Global 2000: The World's Largest Media Companies of 2014," *Forbes*, 7 May 2014.

9. Stephanie Hayes, "Clear Channel Rejects St. Pete Pride Billboards, Organizers Say," *Tampa Bay Times*, 11 June 2010.

10. Meg James, "DOJ Clears Gannett-Belo Deal but Demands Sale of St. Louis TV Station," *Los Angeles Times*, 16 December 2013.

11. John Zaller. 2003. "A New Standard of News Quality: Burglar Alarms for the Monitorial Citizen," *Political Communication* 20, No. 2: 109–130.

12. Suzanne Ranks, "Ethiopian Famine: How Landmark BBC Report Influenced Modern Coverage," *Guardian*, 22 October 2014.

13. Hisham Aidi, "Haitians in the Dominican Republic in Legal Limbo," *Al Jazeera*, 10 April 2015.

14. "Pressure the Government of the Dominican Republic to Stop its Planned 'Cleaning' of 250,000 Black Dominicans," https://petitions.whitehouse.gov/petition/pressure-government-dominican-republic-stop-its-planned-cleaning-250000-black-dominicans (November 26, 2015); Led Black, "Prevent Humanitarian Tragedy in Dominican Republic," *CNN*, 23 June 2015.

15. "Oprah Talks to Christiane Amanpour," *O, Oprah Magazine*, September 2005. Unless otherwise noted, all quotations in this feature box are from this article.

16. "How Christiane Amanpour Stumbled Into a Career in TV News," *TVNewser*, 10 February 2016.

17. Erik Ortiz, "George Holliday, Who Taped Rodney King Beating, Urges Others to Share Videos," *NBC*, 9 June 2015.

18. "Walter Cronkite's 'We Are Mired in Stalemate' Broadcast, February 27, 1968" *Digital History*, http://www.digitalhistory.uh.edu/active_learning/explorations/vietnam/cronkite.cfm (November 29, 2015).

19. Joel Achenbach, "Cronkite and Vietnam," *Washington Post*, 18 May 2012.

20. Larry Sabato, "Our Leaders, Surprise, Have Strong Views," *New York Times*, 23 February 2009.

21. Fellow. *American Media History*.

22. "Population in the Colonial and Continental Periods," http://www2.census.gov/prod2/decennial/documents/00165897ch01.pdf (November 18, 2015); Fellow. *American Media History*.

23. Fellow. *American Media History*.

24. Lars Willnat and David H. Weaver. 2014. *The American Journalist in the Digital Age: Key Findings*. Bloomington, IN: School of Journalism, Indiana University.

25. Michael Barthel. 29 April 2015. "Newspapers: Factsheet," http://www.journalism.org/2015/04/29/newspapers-fact-sheet/.

26. "Facebook and Twitter—New but Limited Parts of the Local News System," *Pew Research Center*, 5 March 2015.

27. "1940 Census," http://www.census.gov/1940census (September 6, 2015).

28. Steve Craig. 2009. *Out of the Dark: A History of Radio and Rural America*. Tuscaloosa, AL: University of Alabama Press.

29. "Herbert Hoover: Radio Address to the Nation on Unemployment Relief," *The American Presidency Project*, 18 October 1931, http://www.presidency.ucsb.edu/ws/?pid=22855.

30. "Franklin Delano Roosevelt: First Fireside Chat," http://www.americanrhetoric.com/speeches/fdrfirstfiresidechat.html (August 20, 2015).

31. "The Fireside Chats," https://www.history.com/topics/fireside-chats (November 20, 2015); Fellow. *American Media History*, 256.

32. "FDR: A Voice of Hope," http://www.history.com/topics/fireside-chats (September 10, 2015).

33. Mary E. Stuckey. 2012. "FDR, the Rhetoric of Vision, and the Creation of a National Synoptic State." *Quarterly Journal of Speech* 98, No. 3: 297–319.

34. Fellow. *American Media History*.

35. Sheila Marikar, "Howard Stern's Five Most Outrageous Offenses," *ABC News*, 14 May 2012.

36. Lee Huebner, "The Checkers Speech after 60 Years," *The Atlantic*, 22 September 2012.

37. Joel K. Goldstein, "Mondale-Ferraro: Changing History," *Huffington Post*, 27 March 2011.

38. Shanto Iyengar. 2016. *Media Politics: A Citizen's Guide*, 3rd ed. New York: W.W. Norton.

39. Bob Greene, "When Candidates said 'No' to Debates," *CNN*, 1 October 2012.

40. "The Ford/Carter Debates," http://www.pbs.org/newshour/spc/debatingourdestiny/doc1976.html (November 21, 2015); Kayla Webley, "How the Nixon-Kennedy Debate Changed the World," *Time*, 23 September 2010.

41. Matthew A. Baum and Samuel Kernell. 1999. "Has Cable Ended the Golden Age of Presidential Television?" *The American Political Science Review* 93, No. 1: 99–114.

42. Alan J. Lambert1, J. P. Schott1, and Laura Scherer. 2011. "Threat, Politics, and Attitudes toward a Greater Understanding of Rally-'Round-the-Flag Effects," *Current Directions in Psychological Science* 20, No. 6: 343–348.

43. Tim Groeling and Matthew A. Baum. 2008. "Crossing the Water's Edge: Elite Rhetoric, Media Coverage, and the Rally-Round-the-Flag Phenomenon," *Journal of Politics* 70, No. 4: 1065–1085.

44. "William Jefferson Clinton: Oklahoma Bombing Memorial Prayer Service Address," 23 April 1995, http://www.americanrhetoric.com/speeches/wjcoklahomabombingspeech.htm.

45. Ian Christopher McCaleb, "Bush tours ground zero in lower Manhattan," *CNN*, 14 September 2001.

46. "Presidential Job Approval Center," http://www.gallup.com/poll/124922/presidential-job-approval-center.aspx (August 28, 2015).

47. Alison Dagnes. 2010. *Politics on Demand: The Effects of 24-hour News on American Politics*. Santa Barbara, CA: Praeger.

48. "Number of Viewers of the State of the Union Addresses from 1993 to 2015 (in millions)," http://www.statista.com/statistics/252425/state-of-the-union-address-viewer-numbers (August 28, 2015).

49. Baum and Kernell, "Has Cable Ended the Golden Age of Presidential Television?"

50. Shanto Iyengar. 2011. "The Media Game: New Moves, Old Strategies," *The Forum: Press Politics and Political Science* 9, No. 1, http://pcl.stanford.edu/research/2011/iyengar-mediagame.pdf.

51. Jeff Zeleny, "Lose the BlackBerry? Yes He Can, Maybe," *New York Times*, 15 November 2008.

52. Matthew Fraser and Soumitra Dutta, "Obama's win means future elections must be fought online," *Guardian*, 7 November 2008.

53. Iyengar, "The Media Game."

54. David Corn. 29 July 2013. "Mitt Romeny's Incredible 47-Percent Denial," http://www.motherjones.com/mojo/2013/07/mitt-romney-47-percent-denial.

55. Ed Pilkington, "Obama Angers Midwest Voters with Guns and Religion Remark," *Guardian*, 14 April 2008.

56. Amy Mitchell, "State of the News Media 2015," *Pew Research Center*, 29 April 2015.

57. Tom Huddleston, Jr., "Jon Stewart Just Punched a $250 Million Hole in Viacom's Value," *Fortune*, 11 February 2015.

58. John Zaller. 2003. "A New Standard of News Quality: Burglar Alarms for the Monitorial Citizen," *Political Communication* 20, No. 2: 109–130.

59. Matthew A. Baum. 2002. "Sex, Lies and War: How Soft News Brings Foreign Policy to the Inattentive Public," *American Political Science Review* 96, no. 1: 91–109.

60. Matthew Baum. 2003. "Soft News and Political Knowledge: Evidence of Absence or Absence of Evidence?" *Political Communication* 20, No. 2: 173–190.

61. "Public Knowledge of Current Affairs Little Changed by News and Information Revolutions," *Pew Research Center*, 15 April 2007; "What You Know Depends on What You Watch: Current Events Knowledge across Popular News Sources," *Fairleigh Dickinson University*, 3 May 2012, http://publicmind.fdu.edu/2012/confirmed/.

62. Markus Prior. 2003. "Any Good News in Soft News? The Impact of Soft News Preference on Political Knowledge," *Political Communication* 20, No. 2: 149–171.

63. Fellow. *American Media History*.

64. *New York Times Co. v. Sullivan*, 376 U.S. 254 (1964).

65. Jill Serjeant, "Katie Holmes Settles Libel Suit on Drugs Claim," *Reuters*, 28 April 2011, http://www.reuters.com/article/2011/04/28/us-katieholmes-idUSTRE73Q7K620110428.

66. Christ Plante, "Military Kicks Geraldo Out of Iraq," *CNN*, 31 March 2003.

67. Chapter 4—Radio Act of 1927, http://uscode.house.gov/view.xhtml?path=/prelim@title47/chapter4&edition=prelim (May 19, 2016).

68. "Statutes and Rules on Candidate Appearances & Advertising," https://transition.fcc.gov/mb/policy/political/candrule.htm. Section 73.1942 [47 CFR §73.1942] Candidate rates. (November 21, 2015).

69. "Statutes and Rules," Section 73.1941 [47 CFR §73.1941] Equal Opportunities.

70. Eric Deggans, "It's Not Hosting SNL, But NBC Will Give 'Equal Time' To 4 GOP Candidates," *National Public Radio*, 24 November 2015.

71. "47 U.S. Code § 315 - Candidates for public office," *Legal Information Institute*, https://www.law.cornell.edu/uscode/text/47/315.

72. Joel Roberts, "Arnold's Movies Face TV Blackout," *CBS News*, 13 August 2003; Gary Susman, "Arnold's Movies Go off the Air until Election," *Entertainment Weekly*, 13 August 2003.

73. David Schultz and John R. Vile. 2015. *The Encyclopedia of Civil Liberties in America*.

74. Sue Wilson, "FCC: No More Equal Time Requirements for Political Campaign Supporters over Our Public Airwaves," *Huffington Post*, 15 May 2014.

75. William Lake, Letter from the FCC Regarding Capstar Texas LLX, 8 May 2014, http://bradblog.com/Docs/FCC_ZappleDoctrineRuling_050814.pdf.

76. *Syracuse Peace Council vs. FCC*, 867 F.2d 654 (1989); Katy Steinmetz, "The Death of the Fairness Doctrine," *Time*, 23 August 2011.

77. "Obscenity, Indecency, and Profanity," *FCC*, https://www.fcc.gov/encyclopedia/obscenity-indecency-and-profanity (September 10, 2015).

78. *Miller v. California*, 413 U.S. 15 (1973).

79. "Obscenity," *Legal Information Institute at Cornell University*, https://www.law.cornell.edu/wex/obscenity (November 29, 2015).

80. "Consumer Help Center: Obscene, Indecent, and Profane Broadcasts," *FCC*, https://consumercomplaints.fcc.gov/hc/en-us/articles/202731600-Obscene-Indecent-and-Profane-Broadcasts (September 10, 2015).

81. *FCC vs. Pacifica Foundation*, 438 U.S. 726 (1978).

82. "Obscenity, Indecency and Profanity," *Federal Communications Commission*, https://consumercomplaints.fcc.gov/hc/en-us/articles/204009760-Consumer-Complaint-Charts-and-Data-Overview.

83. Jason Molinet, "TV Watchdog Slams ABC for Sex-filled 'Scandal' Opening Immediately After 'Charlie Brown' Special," *Daily News*, 4 November 2104.

84. "The Fallout from the Telecommunications Act of 1996: Unintended Consequences and Lessons Learned," *Common Cause*, 9 May 2005; Mark Baumgartner, "Average Cable Rates on the Rise," *ABC News*, February 15, http://abcnews.go.com/Business/story?id=88614&page=1.

85. Keith Collins. 11 June 2018. "Net Neutrality Has Officially Been Repealed. Here's How That Could Affect You." *New York Times*. https://www.nytimes.com/2018/06/11/technology/net-neutrality-repeal.html.

86. Dana Hughes and Dan Childs, "Hillary Clinton's Glasses are for Concussion, Not Fashion," *ABC News*, 25 January 2013.

87. Mary Bruce, "Hillary Clinton Took 6 Months to 'Get Over' Concussion, Bill Says of Timeline," *ABC News*, 14 May 2014.

88. Dan Merica, "Clinton Campaign, Republicans Clash Over Benghazi Testimony," *CNN*, 25 July 2015.

89. Alex Seitz-Wald, "Kevin McCarthy Credits Benghazi Committee for Clinton Damage," *MSNBC*, 30 September 2015.

90. "The Freedom of Information Act, 5 U.S.C.", *The United States Department of Justice*, http://www.justice.gov/oip/blog/foia-update-freedom-information-act-5-usc-sect-552-amended-public-law-no-104-231-110-stat (September 7, 2015).

91. Ibid.

92. Fellow. *American Media History*.

93. "What is FOIA?" *The Department of Justice*, http://www.foia.gov/index.html (September 8, 2015).

94. Fellow. *American Media History*.

95. Ibid.

96. Ibid.

97. Christopher Beam, "The TMI President," *Slate*, 12 November 2008.

98. Fellow. *American Media History*, 388.

99. Bob Woodward, "How Mark Felt Became 'Deep Throat,'" *The Washington Post*, 20 June 2005.

100. Don Van Natta Jr., Adam Liptak, and Clifford J. Levy, "The Miller Case: A Notebook, a Cause, a Jail Cell and a Deal," *The New York Times*, 16 October 2005.

101. *Branzburg v. Hayes*, 408 U.S. 665 (1972).

102. Adam Liptak, "A Justice's Scribbles on Journalists Rights," *New York Times*, 7 October 2007.

103. Matt Apuzzo, "Times Reporter Will Not Be Called to Testify in Leak," *New York Times*, 12 January 2015.

104. Walter Lippmann. 1922. *Public Opinion*. http://xroads.virginia.edu/~hyper/Lippman/contents.html (August 29, 2015).

105. Bernard Berelson, Paul Lazarsfeld, and William McPhee. 1954. *Voting*. Chicago: University of Chicago Press.

106. George Gerbner, Larry Gross, Michael Morgan, Nancy Signorielli, and Marilyn Jackson-Beeck. 1979.

"The Demonstration of Power: Violence Profile," *Journal of Communication 29*, No.10: 177–196.

107. Elizabeth A. Skewes. 2007. *Message Control: How News Is Made on the Presidential Campaign Trail*. Maryland: Rowman & Littlefield, 79.

108. Stephen Farnsworth and S. Robert Lichter. 2012. "Authors' Response: Improving News Coverage in the 2012 Presidential Campaign and Beyond," *Politics & Policy* 40, No. 4: 547–556.

109. "Early Media Coverage Focuses on Horse Race," *PBS News Hour*, 12 June 2007.

110. Stephen Ansolabehere, Roy Behr, and Shanto Iyengar. 1992. *The Media Game: American Politics in the Television Age*. New York: Macmillan.

111. "Frames of Campaign Coverage," *Pew Research Center*, 23 April 2012, http://www.journalism.org/2012/04/23/frames-campaign-coverage.

112. Kiku Adatto. May 28, 1990. "The Incredible Shrinking Sound Bite," *New Republic* 202, No. 22: 20–23.

113. Erik Bucy and Maria Elizabeth Grabe. 2007. "Taking Television Seriously: A Sound and Image Bite Analysis of Presidential Campaign Coverage, 1992–2004," *Journal of Communication* 57, No. 4: 652–675.

114. Craig Fehrman, "The Incredible Shrinking Sound Bite," *Boston Globe*, 2 January 2011, http://www.boston.com/bostonglobe/ideas/articles/2011/01/02/the_incredible_shrinking_sound_bite/.

115. "Crossfire: Jon Stewart's America," *CNN*, 15 October 2004, http://www.cnn.com/TRANSCRIPTS/0410/15/cf.01.html.

116. Paul Begala, "Begala: The day Jon Stewart blew up my show," *CNN*, 12 February 2015.

117. Pew Research Center: Journalism & Media Staff, "Coverage of the Candidates by Media Sector and Cable Outlet," 1 November 2012.

118. "Winning the Media Campaign 2012," *Pew Research* Center, 2 November 2012.

119. Fred Greenstein. 2009. *The Presidential Difference*. Princeton, NJ: Princeton University Press.

120. "Dan Rather versus Richard Nixon, 1974," YouTube video, :46, from the National Association of Broadcasters annual convention in Houston on March 19,1974, posted by "thecelebratedmisterk," https://www.youtube.com/watch?v=ZGBLAKq8xwc (November 30, 2015); "'A Conversation With the President,' Interview With Dan Rather of the Columbia Broadcasting System," *The American Presidency Project*, 2 January 1972, http://www.presidency.ucsb.edu/ws/?pid=3351.

121. Wolf Blitzer, "Dan Rather's Stand," *CNN*, 10 September 2004.

122. Michael M. Grynbaum. 13 November 2018. "CNN Sues Trump Administration for Barring Jim Acosta from White House." *New York Times*. https://www.nytimes.com/2018/11/13/business/media/cnn-jim-acosta-trump-lawsuit.html. Paul Farhi. 24 February 2017. "The Washington Post's New Slogan Turns Out to Be an Old Saying." https://www.washingtonpost.com/lifestyle/style/the-washington-posts-new-slogan-turns-out-to-be-an-old-saying/2017/02/23/cb199cda-fa02-11e6-be05-1a3817ac21a5_story.html?noredirect=on&utm_term=.f8a0e1c5ef97.

123. Matthew Eshbaugh-Soha and Jeffrey Peake. 2011. *Breaking Through the Noise: Presidential Leadership, Public Opinion, and the News Media*. Stanford, CA: Stanford University Press.

124. Ibid.

125. Gary Lee Malecha and Daniel J. Reagan. 2011. *The Public Congress: Congressional Deliberation in a New Media Age*. New York: Routledge.

126. Frank R. Baumgartner, Bryan D. Jones, and Beth L. Leech. 1997. "Media Attention and Congressional Agendas," In *Do The Media Govern? Politicians, Voters, and Reporters in America*, eds. Shanto Iyengar and Richard Reeves. Thousand Oaks, CA: Sage.

127. George Edwards and Dan Wood. 1999. "Who Influences Whom? The President, Congress, and the Media," *American Political Science Review* 93, No 2: 327–344; Yue Tan and David Weaver. 2007. "Agenda-Setting Effects Among the Media, the Public, and Congress, 1946–2004," *Journalism & Mass Communication Quarterly* 84, No. 4: 729–745.

128. Ally Fogg, "Crime Is Falling. Now Let's Reduce Fear of Crime," *Guardian*, 24 April 24 2013.

129. Travis L. Dixon. 2008. "Crime News and Racialized Beliefs: Understanding the Relationship between Local News Viewing and Perceptions of African Americans and Crime," *Journal of Communication* 58, No. 1: 106–125.

130. Travis Dixon. 2015. "Good Guys Are Still Always in White? Positive Change and Continued Misrepresentation of Race and Crime on Local Television News," *Communication Research*, doi:10.1177/0093650215579223.

131. Travis L. Dixon. 2008. "Network News and Racial Beliefs: Exploring the Connection between National Television News Exposure and Stereotypical Perceptions of African Americans," *Journal of Communication* 58, No. 2: 321–337.

132. Martin Gilens. 1996. "Race and Poverty in America: Public Misperceptions and the American News Media," *Public Opinion Quarterly* 60, No. 4: 515–541.

133. Dixon. "Crime News and Racialized Beliefs."

134. Gilens. "Race and Poverty in America."

135. Shanto Iyengar and Donald R. Kinder. 1987. *News That Matters*. Chicago: University of Chicago Press.

136. Daniel C. Hallin. 2015. "The Dynamics of Immigration Coverage in Comparative Perspective," *American Behavioral Scientist* 59, No. 7: 876–885.

137. Kay Mills. 1996. "What Difference Do Women Journalists Make?" In *Women, the Media and Politics*, ed. Pippa Norris. Oxford, UK: Oxford University Press, 43.

138. Kim Fridkin Kahn and Edie N. Goldenberg. 1997. "The Media: Obstacle or Ally of Feminists?" In *Do the Media Govern?* eds. Shanto Iyengar and Richard Reeves. Thousand Oaks, CA: Sage.

139. Barbara Walters, "Ms. Walters Reflects," *Vanity Fair*, 31 May 2008,

140. Mills. "What Difference Do Women Journalists Make?"

141. Mills. "What Difference Do Women Journalists Make?"

142. Kahn and Goldenberg, "The Media: Obstacle or Ally of Feminists?"

143. Kim Fridkin Kahn. 1994. "Does Gender Make a Difference? An Experimental Examination of Sex Stereotypes and Press Patterns in Statewide Campaigns," *American Journal of Political Science* 38, No. 1: 162–195.

144. John David Rausch, Mark Rozell, and Harry L. Wilson. 1999. "When Women Lose: A Study of Media Coverage of Two Gubernatorial Campaigns," *Women & Politics* 20, No. 4: 1–22.

145. Sarah Allen Gershon. 2013. "Media Coverage of Minority Congresswomen and Voter Evaluations: Evidence from an Online Experimental Study," *Political Research Quarterly* 66, No. 3: 702–714.

146. Jennifer Lawless and Richard Logan Fox. 2005. *It Takes a Candidate: Why Women Don't Run for Office*. Cambridge: Cambridge University Press.

147. Brittany L. Stalsburg, "Running with Strollers: The Impact of Family Life on Political Ambition," *Eagleton Institute of Politics*, Spring 2012, Unpublished Paper, http://www.eagleton.rutgers.edu/research/documents/Stalsburg-FamilyLife-Political-Ambition.pdf (August 28, 2015).

148. Christina Walker, "Is Sarah Palin Being Held to an Unfair Standard?" *CNN*, 8 September 2008.

149. Dana Bash, "Palin's Teen Daughter is Pregnant," *CNN*, 1 September 2008.

150. Jimmy Orr, "Palin Wardrobe Controversy Heightens - Todd is a Cheapo!" *Christian Science Monitor*, 26 October 2008.

Political Parties

1. Larry Sabato and Howard R. Ernst. 2007. *Encyclopedia of American Political Parties and Elections.* New York: Checkmark Books, 151.

2. Saul Cornell. 2016. *The Other Founders: Anti-Federalism and the Dissenting Tradition in America.* Chapel Hill, NC: UNC Press, 11.

3. James H. Ellis. 2009. *A Ruinous and Unhappy War: New England and the War of 1812.* New York: Algora Publishing, 80.

4. Alexander Keyssar. 2009. *The Right to Vote: The Contested History of Democracy in the United States.* New York: Basic Books.

5. R. R. Stenberg, "Jackson, Buchanan, and the "Corrupt Bargain" Calumny," *The Pennsylvania Magazine of History and Biography* 58, no. 1 (1934): 61–85.

6. 2009. "Democratic-Republican Party," In *UXL Encyclopedia of U.S. History*, eds. Sonia Benson, Daniel E. Brannen, Jr., and Rebecca Valentine. Detroit: UXL, 435–436; "Jacksonian Democracy and Modern America," http://www.ushistory.org/us/23f.asp (March 6, 2016).

7. Virginia Historical Society. "Elections from 1789–1828." http://www.vahistorical.org/collections-and-resources/virginia-history-explorer/getting-message-out-presidential-campaign-0 (March 11, 2016).

8. William G. Shade. 1983. "The Second Party System." In *Evolution of American Electoral Systems*, eds. Paul Kleppner, et al. Westport, CT: Greenwood Pres, 77–111.

9. Jules Witcover. 2003. *Party of the People: A History of the Democrats.* New York: Random House, 3.

10. Daniel Walker Howe. 2007. *What Hath God Wrought: The Transformation of America, 1815–1848.* New York: Oxford University Press, 330-34.

11. Sean Wilentz. 2006. *The Rise of American Democracy: Jefferson to Lincoln.* New York: Norton.

12. Calvin Jillson. 1994. "Patterns and Periodicity." In *The Dynamics of American Politics: Approaches and Interpretations*, eds. Lawrence C. Dodd and Calvin C. Jillson. Boulder, CO: Westview Press, 38–41.

13. Norman Pollack. 1976. *The Populist Response to Industrial America: Midwestern Populist Thought.* Cambridge, MA: Harvard University Press, 11–12.

14. 1985. *Congressional Quarterly's Guide to U.S. Elections.* Washington, DC: Congressional Quarterly Inc., 75–78, 387–388.

15. "Platform of the States Rights Democratic Party," http://www.presidency.ucsb.edu/ws/?pid=25851 (March 12, 2016).

16. Robert Richie and Steven Hill, "The Case for Proportional Representation," *Boston Review*, February–March 1998, https://bostonreview.net/archives/BR23.1/richie.html (March 15, 2016).

17. International Institute for Democracy and Electoral Assistance. 2005. *Electoral Design System: The New IDEA Handbook.* Stockholm: International IDEA, 153–156, http://www.idea.int/publications/esd/upload/esd_chapter5.pdf (March 15, 2016).

18. Duverger, Maurice. 1972 "Factors in a Two-Party and Multiparty System." In *Party Politics and Pressure Groups.* New York: Thomas Y. Crowell, 23–32.

19. Jeffrey Sachs. 2011. *The Price of Civilization.* New York: Random House, 107.

20. James Dao, "The 2000 Elections: The Green Party; Angry Democrats, Fearing Nader Cost Them

Presidential Race, Threaten to Retaliate," *The New York Times*, 9 November 2000.

21. Bruce Bartlett, "Why Third Parties Can't Compete," *Forbes*, 14 May 2010.

22. George C. Edwards III. 2011. *Why the Electoral College is Bad for America*, 2nd. ed. New Haven and London: Yale University Press, 176–177.

23. Kevin Liptak, "'Fatal Flaw:' Why Third Parties Still Fail Despite Voter Anger," http://www.cnn.com/2012/05/21/politics/third-party-fail/index.html (March 13, 2016).

24. Morris P. Fiorina, "America's Missing Moderates: Hiding in Plain Sight," 2 February 2013, http://www.the-american-interest.com/2013/02/12/americas-missing-moderates-hiding-in-plain-sight/ (March 1, 2016).

25. Jocelyn Kiley and Michael Dimock, "The GOP's Millennial Problem Runs Deep," 28 September 2014, http://www.pewresearch.org/fact-tank/2014/09/25/the-gops-millennial-problem-runs-deep/ (March 15, 2016).

26. Gabrielle Levy, "'Trump Effect' Driving Push for Latino Voter Registration," *U.S. News & World Report*, 27 January 2016, http://www.usnews.com/news/articles/2016-01-27/trump-effect-driving-push-for-latino-voter-registration (March 15, 2016).

27. "Heading into 2016 Election Season, U.S. Voters Overwhelmingly Concerned About Issues Affecting Seniors, New National Poll Reveals," 26 February 2016, http://www.prnewswire.com/news-releases/heading-into-2016-election-season-us-voters-overwhelmingly-concerned-about-issues-affecting-seniors-new-national-poll-reveals-300226953.html (March 15, 2016).

28. "Morning Consult," 25 February 2016, http://www.bringthevotehome.org/wp-content/uploads/2016/02/160209-BTVH-Memo.pdf (March 15, 2016).

29. Aaron Blake, "The Ten Most Loyal Demographic Groups for Republicans and Democrats," *The Washington Post*, 8 April 2015.

30. Irin Carmon, "GOP Candidates: Ban Abortion, No Exceptions," 7 August 2015, http://www.msnbc.com/msnbc/gop-candidates-ban-abortion-no-exceptions (March 14, 2016).

31. Aaron Blake, "The Ten Most Loyal Demographic Groups for Republicans and Democrats."

32. V.O. Key. 1964. *Politics, Parties, and Pressure Groups*. New York: Crowell.

33. Thomas Streissguth. 2003. *Hate Crimes*. New York: Facts on File, 8.

34. Philip Bump, "When Did Black Americans Start Voting So Heavily Democratic?" *The Washington Post*, 7 July 2015.

35. Edward Carmines and James Stimson. 1989. *Issue Evolution: Race and the Transformation of American Politics*. Princeton, NJ: Princeton University Press.

36. Ian Haney-Lopez, "How the GOP Became the 'White Man's Party,'" 22 December 2013, https://www.salon.com/2013/12/22/how_the_gop_became_the_white_mans_party/ (March 16, 2016).

37. Nate Cohn, "Demise of the Southern Democrat is Now Nearly Complete," *The New York Times*, 4 December 2014.

38. "Party Affiliation," http://www.gallup.com/poll/15370/party-affiliation.aspx (March 1, 2016).

39. Jeffrey L. Jones, "Democratic, Republican Identification Near Historical Lows," http://www.gallup.com/poll/188096/democratic-republican-identification-near-historical-lows.aspx (March 14, 2016).

40. Russ Choma, "Money Won on Tuesday, But Rules of the Game Changed," 5 November 2014, http://www.opensecrets.org/news/2014/11/money-won-on-tuesday-but-rules-of-the-game-changed/ (March 1, 2016).

41. Elizabeth Lehman, "Trend Shows Generation Focuses Mostly on Social, National Issues," http://www.thenewsoutlet.org/survey-local-millennials-more-interested-in-big-issues/ (March 15, 2016).

42. "Voter Turnout," http://www.electproject.org/home/voter-turnout/voter-turnout-data (March 14, 2016).

43. Abdullah Halimah, "Eastwood, the Empty Chair, and the Speech Everyone's Talking About," 31 August 2012, http://www.cnn.com/2012/08/31/politics/eastwood-speech/ (March 14, 2016).

44. "Influence of Democratic and Republican Conventions on Opinions of the Presidential Candidates," http://journalistsresource.org/studies/politics/elections/personal-individual-effects-presidential-conventions-candidate-evaluations (March 14, 2016).

45. Timothy Zick, "Speech and Spatial Tactics," *Texas Law Review* February (2006): 581.

46. Thomas E. Patterson, "Is There a Future for On-the-Air Televised Conventions?" http://journalistsresource.org/wp-content/uploads/2012/08/vv_conv_paper1.pdf (March 14, 2016).

47. Todd Leopold, "The Day America Met Barack Obama," http://www.cnn.com/2008/POLITICS/11/05/obama.meeting/index.html?iref=werecommend (March 14, 2016).

48. Peter Nicholas. 26 July 2016. "Bernie Sanders to Return to Senate as an Independent," http://blogs.wsj.com/washwire/2016/07/26/bernie-sanders-to-return-to-senate-as-an-independent/ (November 9, 2016).

49. Sidney R. Waldman. 2007. *America and the Limits of the Politics of Selfishness.* New York: Lexington Books, 27.

50. Alicia W. Stewart and Tricia Escobedo, "What You Might Not Know About the 1964 Civil Rights Act," 10 April 2014, http://www.cnn.com/2014/04/10/politics/civil-rights-act-interesting-facts/ (March 16, 2016).

51. Nolan McCarty, Keith T. Poole and Howard Rosenthal. 2006. *Polarized America.* Cambridge, MA: MIT Press.

52. David R. Mayhew. 1991. *Divided We Govern.* New Haven: Yale University Press; George C. Edwards, Andrew Barrett and Jeffrey S. Peake, "The Legislative Impact of Divided Government," *American Journal of Political Science* 41, no. 2 (1997): 545–563.

53. Dylan Matthews, "Here is Every Previous Government Shutdown, Why They Happened and How They Ended," *The Washington Post*, 25 September 2013.

54. Matthews, "Here is Every Previous Government Shutdown, Why They Happened and How They Ended."

55. Matthews, "Here is Every Previous Government Shutdown, Why They Happened and How They Ended."

56. Drew Desilver, "The Polarized Congress of Today Has Its Roots in the 1970s," 12 June 2014, http://www.pewresearch.org/fact-tank/2014/06/12/polarized-politics-in-congress-began-in-the-1970s-and-has-been-getting-worse-ever-since/ (March 16, 2016).

57. "The Tea Party and Religion," 23 February 2011, http://www.pewforum.org/2011/02/23/tea-party-and-religion/ (March 16, 2016).

58. "The Tea Party and Religion."

59. Paul Waldman, "Nearly All the GOP Candidates Bow Down to Grover Norquist, *The Washington Post*, 13 August 2015, https://www.washingtonpost.com/blogs/plum-line/wp/2015/08/13/nearly-all-the-gop-candidates-bow-down-to-grover-norquist/ (March 1, 2016).

60. Beth Fouhy, "Occupy Wall Street and Democrats Remain Wary of Each Other," *Huffington Post*, 17

November 2011.

61. Andrew Buncombe. 9 November 2016. "Donald Trump would have lost US election if Bernie Sanders had been the candidate," http://www.independent.co.uk/news/people/presidential-election-donald-trump-would-have-lost-if-bernie-sanders-had-been-the-candidate-a7406346.html (November 9, 2016).

62. Drew Desilver, "In Late Spurt of Activity, Congress Avoids 'Least Productive' Title," 29 December 2014, http://www.pewresearch.org/fact-tank/2014/12/29/in-late-spurt-of-activity-congress-avoids-least-productive-title/ (March 16, 2016).

63. "Congressional Performance," http://www.rasmussenreports.com/public_content/politics/mood_of_america/congressional_performance (March 16, 2016).

64. "Presidential Approval Ratings – Barack Obama," http://www.gallup.com/poll/116479/barack-obama-presidential-job-approval.aspx (March 16, 2016).

65. Morris Fiorina, "Americans Have Not Become More Politically Polarized," *The Washington Post*, 23 June 2014.

66. Ian Haney-Lopez, "How the GOP Became the 'White Man's Party,'" 22 December 2013, https://www.salon.com/2013/12/22/how_the_gop_became_the_white_mans_party/ (March 16, 2016).

67. *Reynolds v. Simms*, 379 U.S. 870 (1964).

68. Sean Theriault. 2013. *The Gingrich Senators: The Roots of Partisan Warfare in Congress*. New York: Oxford University Press.

69. Nolan McCarty, "Hate Our Polarized Politics? Why You Can't Blame Gerrymandering," *The Washington Post*, 26 October 2012.

70. Jamie L. Carson et al., "Redistricting and Party Polarization in the U.S. House of Representatives," *American Politics Research* 35, no. 6 (2007): 878–904.

71. *Arizona State Legislature v. Arizona Independent Redistricting Commission*, 135 S. Ct. 2652 (2015).

72. "Editorial: Republicans Should Accept Redistricting Defeat and Drop Talk of Appeals," 10 January 2016, http://www.fairdistrictsnow.org/news/661/ (March 16, 2016).

Interest Groups and Lobbying

1. Lawrence R. Jacobs and Theda Skocpol 2010. *Health Care Reform and American Politics: What Everyone Needs to Know* Oxford: Oxford University Press.

2. Anthony J. Nownes. 2013. *Interest Groups in American Politics*. Routledge: New York.

3. Nownes, *Interest Groups in American Politics*.

4. Nownes, *Interest Groups in American Politics*.

5. Jennifer Wolak, Adam J. Newmark, Todd McNoldy, David Lowery, and Virginia Gray, "Much of Politics is Still Local: Multistate Representation in State Interest Communities," *Legislative Studies Quarterly* 27 (2002): 527–555.

6. Anthony J. Nownes and Adam J. Newmark. 2013. "Interest Groups in the States." In *Politics in the American States*. Washington, DC: CQ Press, 105–131.

7. The Brady Campaign to Prevent Gun Violence was founded by James and Sarah Brady, after James Brady was permanently disabled by a gunshot following an assassination attempt on then-president Ronald Reagan. At the time of the shooting, Brady was Reagan's press secretary. http://www.bradycampaign.org/jim-and-sarah-brady (March 1, 2016).

8. Michael Mitchell and Michael Leachman, "Years of Cuts Threaten to Put College Out of Reach for More Students," Center on Budget and Policy Priorities, 13 May 2015, http://www.cbpp.org/research/state-budget-and-tax/years-of-cuts-threaten-to-put-college-out-of-reach-for-more-students.

9. Robert Davidson, "Higher Ed Lobbies for More Funds," http://www.wcbi.com/local-news/higher-ed-lobbies-for-more-funds/ (November 3, 2015).

10. http://www.ameribev.org/ (March 1, 2016).

11. Nownes and Newmark, "Interest Groups in the States."

12. Ken Kollman. 1998. *Outside Lobbying: Public Opinion and Interest Groups Strategies*. Princeton, NJ: Princeton University Press.

13. "Milking Taxpayers," *The Economist*, 14 February 2015, http://www.economist.com/news/united-states/21643191-crop-prices-fall-farmers-grow-subsidies-instead-milking-taxpayers.

14. http://www.ncsl.org/research/elections-and-campaigns/voter-id.aspx (November 78, 2015).

15. http://www.aarp.org/about-aarp/ (October 3, 2015).

16. Jeffrey M. Berry and Clyde Wilcox. 2009. *The Interest Group Society*. New York: Pearson.

17. Mancur Olson, Jr. 1965. *The Logic of Collective Action*. Cambridge, MA: Harvard University Press; Frank R. Baumgartner and Beth L. Leech. *Basic Interests: The Importance of Groups in Political Science*. Princeton, NJ: Princeton University Press.

18. Olson, Jr., *The Logic of Collective Action*.

19. Jack Walker, "The Origin and Maintenance of Interest Groups in America," *American Political Science Review* 77 (1983): 390–406.

20. Robert Salisbury, "An Exchange Theory of Interest Groups," *Midwest Journal of Political Science* 13 (1969): 1–32; Peter B. Clark and James Q. Wilson, "Incentive Systems: A Theory of Organizations," *Administration Science Quarterly* 6 (1961): 129–166.

21. https://www.naacp.org/ (March 1, 2016).

22. https://www.aclu.org/ (March 1, 2016).

23. David Truman. 1951. *The Governmental Process*. New York: Alfred A. Knopf.

24. Rachel Caron. 1962. *A Silent Spring*. New York: Mariner Books.

25. "Hundreds of Ferguson Protesters March in Downtown D.C.," http://www.nbcwashington.com/news/local/Ferguson-Protests-Planned-for-DC-Baltimore-Tuesday-283807831.html (March 1, 2016).

26. Jenna Johnson, "Immigration continues to be Donald Trump's rallying issue," *Washington Post*, 22 October 2015, https://www.washingtonpost.com/news/post-politics/wp/2015/10/22/immigration-continues-to-be-donald-trumps-rallying-issue/.

27. http://www.news-leader.com/story/news/2015/11/09/springfield-naacp-responds-mu-president-resignation/75473312/ (March 1, 2016).

28. See in general Jeffrey M. Berry and Clyde Wilcox. 2008. *The Interest Group Society*. 5th ed. New York: Routledge.

29. David Carter. 2010. *Stonewall: The Riots that Sparked the Gay Revolution*. New York: St. Martin's Griffin.

30. http://milkfoundation.org/about/harvey-milk-biography/ (November 8, 2015).

31. Clive S. Thomas and Ronald J. Hrebenar. 1990. "Interest Groups in the States." In *Politics in the American States: A Comparative Analysis*, 5th ed., eds. Virginia Gray, Herbert Jacob, and Robert B. Albritton. Glenview, IL: Scott, Foresman, 123–158; Clive S. Thomas and Ronald J. Hrebenar. 1991. "Nationalization of Interest Groups and Lobbying in the States." In *Interest Group Politics*, 3d ed., eds. Allan J. Cigler and Burdett A. Loomis. Washington, DC: CQ Press, 63–80; Clive S. Thomas and Ronald J. Hrebenar. 1996. "Interest Groups in the States." In *Politics in the American States: A Comparative Analysis*, 6th ed., eds. Virginia Gray, and Herbert Jacob. Washington, DC: CQ Press, 122–158; Clive S. Thomas and Ronald J. Hrebenar. 1999. "Interest Groups in the States." In *Politics in the American States: A Comparative*

Analysis, 7th ed., eds. Virginia Gray, Russell L. Hanson, and Herbert Jacob. Washington, DC: CQ Press, 113–143; Clive S. Thomas and Ronald J. Hrebenar. 2004. "Interest Groups in the States." In *Politics in the American States: A Comparative Analysis*, 8th ed., eds. Virginia Gray and Russell L. Hanson. Washington, DC: CQ Press, 100–128.

32. http://www.uspirg.org/ (November 1, 2015).

33. Rick Noack, "7 countries where Americans can study at universities, in English, for free (or almost free)," *Washington Post*, 29 October 2014, https://www.washingtonpost.com/news/worldviews/wp/2014/10/29/7-countries-where-americans-can-study-at-universities-in-english-for-free-or-almost-free/.

34. Thomas and Hrebenar, "Nationalization of Interest Groups and Lobbying in the States;" Nownes and Newmark, "Interest Groups in the States."

35. Thomas and Hrebenar, "Interest Groups in the States," 1991, 1996, 1999, 2004; Thomas and Hrebenar, "Nationalization of Interest Groups and Lobbying in the States."

36. https://www.opensecrets.org/lobby/top.php?showYear=2014&indexType=l (March 1, 2016).

37. Sidney Verba, Kay Lehmnn Schlozman, and Henry Brady. 1995. *Voice and Equality*. Cambridge, MA: Harvard University Press.

38. Steven J. Rosenstone and John Mark Hansen. 2003. *Mobilization, Participation, and Democracy in America*. New York: Longman.

39. Verba et al., *Voice and Equality*; Mark J. Rozell, Clyde Wilcox, and Michael M. Franz. 2012. *Interest Groups in American Campaigns: The New Face of Electioneering*. Oxford University Press: New York.

40. Aaron Smith, "Conservative Group's Times Square Billboard Attacks a $15 Minimum Wage," 31 August 2015, http://money.cnn.com/2015/08/31/news/economy/times-square-minimum-wage/.

41. Robert Putnam. 2000. *Bowling Alone*. New York: Simon and Shuster; Rosenstone and Hansen, *Mobilization, Participation and Democracy in America*.

42. David B. Truman 1951. *The Governmental Process: Political Interests and Public Opinion*. New York: Knopf.

43. Dahl, Robert A. 1956. *A Preface to Democratic Theory*. Chicago: University of Chicago Press; Dahl, Robert A. 1961. *Who Governs? Democracy and Power in an American City*. New Haven, CT: Yale University Press.

44. E. E. Schattschneider. 1960. *The Semisovereign People: A Realist's View of Democracy in America*. New York: Holt, Rinehart and Winston, 35.

45. W. G. Domhoff. 2009. *Who rules America?* Upper Saddle River, NJ: Prentice Hall; K. L. Schlozman, "What Accent the Heavenly choir? Political Equality and the American Pressure System," *Journal of Politics* 46, No. 2 (1984) 1006–1032; K. L. Schlozman, S. Verba, and H. E. Brady. 2012. *The Unheavenly Chorus: Unequal Political Voice and the Broken Promise of American Democracy*. Princeton, NJ: Princeton University Press.

46. Olson, Jr., *The Logic of Collective Action*.

47. Kevin Drum, "Nobody Cares What You Think Unless You're Rich," *Mother Jones*, 8 April 2014, http://www.motherjones.com/kevin-drum/2014/04/nobody-cares-what-you-think-unless-youre-rich.

48. Larry Bartels, "Rich People Rule!" *Washington Post*, 8 April 2014, https://www.washingtonpost.com/news/monkey-cage/wp/2014/04/08/rich-people-rule/.

49. Frank R. Baumgartner and Beth L. Leech. 1998. *Basic Interests: The Importance of Groups in Political Science*. Princeton, NJ: Princeton University Press.

50. Francis E. Rourke. 1984. *Bureaucracy, Politics, and Public Policy*, 3rd ed. NY: Harper Collins.

51. Hugh Heclo. 1984. "Issue Networks and the Executive Establishment." In *The New American Political*

System, ed. Anthony King. Washington DC: The American Enterprise Institute, 87–124.

52. V. Gray and D. Lowery, "To Lobby Alone or in a Flock: Foraging Behavior among Organized Interests," *American Politics Research* 26, No. 1 (1998): 5–34; M. Hojnacki, "Interest Groups' Decisions to Join Alliances or Work Alone," *American Journal of Political Science* 41, No. 1 (1997): 61–87; Kevin W. Hula. 1999. *Lobbying Together: Interest Group Coalitions in Legislative Politics*. Washington DC: Georgetown University Press.

53. Virginia Gray and David Lowery. 1996. *The Population Ecology of Interest Representation: Lobbying Communities in the American States*. Ann Arbor: University of Michigan Press; Andrew S. McFarland. 2004. *Neopluralism*. Lawrence, KS: University Press of Kansas.

54. Mark A. Smith. 2000. *American Business and Political Power: Public Opinion, Elections, and Democracy*. Chicago: University of Chicago Press; F. R. Baumgartner, J. M. Berry, M. Hojnacki, D. C. Kimball, and B. L. Leech. 2009, *Lobbying and Policy Change*. Chicago: University of Chicago Press.

55. Patrick McGeehan, "New York Plans $15-an-Hour Minimum Wage for Fast Food Workers," *New York Times*, 22 July 2015, http://www.nytimes.com/2015/07/23/nyregion/new-york-minimum-wage-fast-food-workers.html; Paul Davidson, "Fast-Food Workers Strike, Seeing $15 Wage, Political Muscle," *USA Today*, 10 November 2015 http://www.usatoday.com/story/money/2015/11/10/fast-food-strikes-begin/75482782/.

56. John R. Wright. 1996. *Interest Groups and Congress: Lobbying, Contributions, and Influence*. Needham Heights, MA: Allyn and Bacon; Mark J. Rozell, Clyde Wilcox, and Michael M. Franz. 2012. *Interest Groups in American Campaigns: The New Face of Electioneering*. New York: Oxford University Press.

57. https://www.nrapvf.org/grades/; http://www.bradycampaign.org/2013-state-scorecard (March 1, 2016).

58. http://www.adaction.org/pages/publications/voting-records.php; http://acuratings.conservative.org/ (March 1, 2016).

59. https://www.opensecrets.org/pacs/ (March 1, 2016).

60. Conor M. Dowling and Michael G. Miller. 2014. *Super PAC! Money, Elections, and Voters after Citizens United*. New York: Routledge.

61. Wright, *Interest Groups and Congress: Lobbying, Contributions, and Influence*.

62. Richard L. Hall and Frank W. Wayman, "Buying Time: Moneyed Interests and the Mobilization of Bias in Congressional Committees," *American Political Science Review* 84.3 (1990): 797-820.

63. Sean Lengell, "Boehner: Grover Norquist Just a 'Random' Guy," *Washington Times*, 3 November 2011, http://www.washingtontimes.com/blog/inside-politics/2011/nov/3/boehner-grover-norquist-just-random-guy/.

64. *Obergefell v. Hodges*, 576 U.S. ___ (2015).

65. Wright, *Interest Groups and Congress: Lobbying, Contributions, and Influence*; Rozell, Wilcox, and Franz, *Interest Groups in American Campaigns: The New Face of Electioneering*.

66. *Buckley v. Valeo*, 75-436, 424 U.S. 1 (1976).

67. *Citizens United v. Federal Election Commission*, 08-205, 558 U.S. 310 (2010).

68. *McCutcheon v. Federal Election Commission*, 12-536, 572 U.S. ___ (2014).

69. The Associated Press. 29 January 2017. "Koch Political Network to Spend $300M to $400M over 2 Years." *Fortune*. http://fortune.com/2017/01/29/koch-political-network-spending/.

70. Nicholas Confessore, "Koch Brothers' Budget of $889 Million for 2016 Is on Par With Both Parties' Spending," *New York Times*, 26 January 2015, http://www.nytimes.com/2015/01/27/us/politics/kochs-plan-to-spend-900-million-on-2016-campaign.html.

71. Adam J. Newmark, "Measuring State Legislative Lobbying Regulation, 1990–2003." *State Politics and Policy Quarterly* 5 (2005): 182–191; Nownes and Newmark, "Interest Groups in the States."

72. Nownes, *Interest Groups in American Politics*.

73. Geov Parrish, "Making Sense of the Abramoff Scandal," 19 December 2005 http://www.alternet.org/story/29827/making_sense_of_the_abramoff_scandal (March 1, 2016).

74. Neil A. Lewis, "Abramoff Gets 4 Years in Prison for Corruption," *New York Times*, 4 September 2008, http://www.nytimes.com/2008/09/05/washington/05abramoff.html?_r=0.

75. http://gawker.com/5856082/corrupt-lobbyist-jack-abramoffs-plan-to-end-corrupt-lobbying (March 1, 2016).

Congress

1. There are six non-voting delegations representing American Samoa, the District of Columbia, Guam, the Northern Mariana Islands, Puerto Rico, and the U.S. Virgin Islands. While these delegates are not able to vote on legislation, they may introduce it and are able to vote in congressional committees and on procedural matters.

2. Steven Hill, "How the Voting Rights Act Hurts Democrats and Minorities," *The Atlantic*, 17 June 2013, http://www.theatlantic.com/politics/archive/2013/06/how-the-voting-rights-act-hurts-democrats-and-minorities/276893/.

3. Lainie Rutkow and Jon S. Vernick. 2011. "The U.S. Constitution's Commerce Clause, the Supreme Court, and Public Health," *Public Health Report* 126, No. 5 (September–October): 750–753.

4. *United States v. Lopez*, 514 U.S. 549 (1995).

5. *National Federation of Independent Businesses v. Sebelius*, 567 U.S. ___ (2012).

6. *Marbury v. Madison*, 5 U.S. 137 (1803).

7. "Abraham Lincoln: Impact and Legacy," http://millercenter.org/president/biography/lincoln-impact-and-legacy (May 24, 2016).

8. David M. Jordan. 2011. *FDR, Dewey, and the Election of 1944*. Bloomington: Indiana University Press, 290; Paul G. Willis and George L. Willis. 1952. "The Politics of the Twenty-Second Amendment," *The Western Political Quarterly* 5, No. 3: 469–82; Paul B. Davis. 1979. "The Results and Implications of the Enactment of the Twenty-Second Amendment," *Presidential Studies Quarterly* 9, No. 3: 289–303.

9. *U.S. Term Limits, Inc. v. Thornton*, 514 U.S. 779 (1995).

10. http://dailysignal.com/2015/11/11/12-bills-that-the-filibuster-stopped-from-becoming-law/ (May 15, 2016).

11. "The Cost of Winning a House and Senate Seat, 1986–2014," http://www.cfinst.org/pdf/vital/VitalStats_t1.pdf (May 15, 2016).

12. http://www.opensecrets.org/overview/wherefrom.php (May 15, 2016).

13. https://www.opensecrets.org/races/summary.php?id=OH08&cycle=2014 (May 15, 2016).

14. "Bipartisan Campaign Reform Act of 2002," http://www.fec.gov/pages/bcra/bcra_update.shtml (May 15, 2016); Greg Scott and Gary Mullen, "Thirty Year Report," September 2005, http://www.fec.gov/info/publications/30year.pdf (May 15, 2016).

15. *Citizens United v. Federal Election Commission*, 558 U.S. 310 (2010).

16. "2012 Outside Spending, by Super PAC," https://www.opensecrets.org/outsidespending/summ.php?cycle=2012&chrt=V&type=S (May 15, 2016).

17. "Contribution Limits for the 2015-2016 Federal Elections," http://www.fec.gov/info/

contriblimitschart1516.pdf (May 15, 2016).

18. "Incumbent Advantage," http://www.opensecrets.org/overview/incumbs.php?cycle=2014 (May 15, 2016).

19. Larry J. Sabato, Kyle Kondik, and Geoffrey Skelley, "Long Odds for Most Senate Primary Challenges," 30 January 2014, http://www.centerforpolitics.org/crystalball/articles/long-odds-for-most-senate-primary-challenges/ (May 1, 2016).

20. David R. Mayhew. 1974. *Congress: The Electoral Connection*. New Haven, CT: Yale University Press.

21. R. Eric Petersen, "Casework in a Congressional Office: Background, Rules, Laws, and Resources," 24 November 2014, https://www.fas.org/sgp/crs/misc/RL33209.pdf (May 1, 2016).

22. Angus Campbell. 1960. "Surge and Decline: A Study of Electoral Change." *The Public Opinion Quarterly* 24, No. 3: 397–418.

23. "Midterm congressional elections explained: Why the president's party typically loses," 1 October 2014, http://journalistsresource.org/studies/politics/elections/voting-patterns-midterm-congressional-elections-why-presidents-party-typically-loses (May 1, 2016).

24. "A Profile of the Modern Military," 5 October 2011, http://www.pewsocialtrends.org/2011/10/05/chapter-6-a-profile-of-the-modern-military/ (May 1, 2016).

25. Dhrumil Mehta and Harry Enten, "The 2014 Senate Elections Were the Most Nationalized In Decades," 2 December 2014, http://fivethirtyeight.com/datalab/the-2014-senate-elections-were-the-most-nationalized-in-decades/ (May 1, 2016); Gregory Giroux, "Straight-Ticket Voting Rises As Parties Polarize," *Bloomberg*, 29 November 2014, http://www.bloomberg.com/politics/articles/2014-11-29/straightticket-voting-rises-as-parties-polarize (May 1, 2016).

26. Steven S. Smith. 1999. *The American Congress*. Boston, MA: Houghton Mifflin.

27. Edmund Burke, "Speech to the Electors of Bristol," 3 November 1774, http://press-pubs.uchicago.edu/founders/documents/v1ch13s7.html (May 1, 2016).

28. "Claire McCaskill, Emily's List Celebrate Women's Wins in 2012," 14 November 2012, http://abcnews.go.com/blogs/politics/2012/11/claire-mccaskill-emilys-list-celebrate-womens-wins-in-2012/ (May 1, 2016).

29. Grace Panetta and Samantha Lee. 12 January 2019. "This Graphic Shows How Much More Diverse the House of Representatives Is Getting." *Business Insider*. https://www.businessinsider.com/changes-in-gender-racial-diversity-between-the-115th-and-116th-house-2018-12.

30. "Statement by John McCain on Banning Earmarks," 13 March 2008, http://www.presidency.ucsb.edu/ws/?pid=90739 (May 15, 2016); "Press Release - John McCain's Economic Plan," 15 April 2008, http://www.presidency.ucsb.edu/ws/?pid=94082 (May 15, 2016).

31. Kathleen Parker, "Health-Care Reform's Sickeningly Sweet Deals," *The Washington Post*, 10 March 2010, http://www.washingtonpost.com/wp-dyn/content/article/2010/03/09/AR2010030903068.html (May 1, 2016); Dana Milbank, "Sweeteners for the South," *The Washington Post*, 22 November 2009, http://www.washingtonpost.com/wp-dyn/content/article/2009/11/21/AR2009112102272.html (May 1, 2016); Jeffry H. Anderson, "Nebraska's Dark-Horse Candidate and the Cornhusker Kickback," *The Weekly Standard*, 4 May 2014.

32. Phil Hirschkorn and Wyatt Andrews, "One-Fifth of House Freshmen Sleep in Offices," CBS News, 22 January 2011, http://www.cbsnews.com/news/one-fifth-of-house-freshmen-sleep-in-offices/ (May 1, 2016).

33. "Congress and the Public," http://www.gallup.com/poll/1600/congress-public.aspx (May 15, 2016).

34. "Congress and the Public," http://www.gallup.com/poll/1600/congress-public.aspx (May 15, 2016).

35. Amy Davidson, "The Hillary Hearing," *The New Yorker*, 2 November 2015; David A. Graham, "What

Conservative Media Say About the Benghazi Hearing," *The Atlantic*, 23 October 2015.

36. Glen S. Krutz. 2001. *Hitching a Ride: Omnibus Legislating in the U.S. Congress*. Columbus, OH: Ohio State University Press.

The Presidency

1. Articles of Confederation, Article XI, 1781.

2. Jack Rakove and Susan Zlomke. 1987. "James Madison and the Independent Executive," *Presidential Studies Quarterly* 17, No. 2: 293–300.

3. Tadahisa Kuroda. 1994. *The Origins of the Twelfth Amendment: The Electoral College in the Early Republic, 1787-1804*. Westport, CT: Greenwood Publishing.

4. U.S. Constitution, Article II, Section 1.

5. Alan Clendenning, "Court: Cheney Is Wyoming Resident," *ABC News*, 7 December 2000, http://abcnews.go.com/Politics/story?id=122289&page=1 (May 1, 2016).

6. U.S. Constitution, Article II, Section 1.

7. U.S. Constitution, Article II, Section 3.

8. "Judgeship Appointments By President," http://www.uscourts.gov/judges-judgeships/authorized-judgeships/judgeship-appointments-president (May 1, 2016).

9. G. Calvin Mackenzie, "The Real Invisible Hand: Presidential Appointees in the Administration of George W. Bush," http://www.whitehousetransitionproject.org/wp-content/uploads/2016/03/PresAppt-GWB.pdf (May 1, 2016).

10. https://www.justice.gov/about (May 1, 2016).

11. Fred Greenstein. 2010. "The Policy-Driven Leadership of James K. Polk: Making the Most of a Weak Presidency," *Presidential Studies Quarterly* 40, No. 4: 725–33.

12. Michael Les Benedict. 1973. "A New Look at the Impeachment of Andrew Johnson," *Political Science Quarterly* 88, No. 3: 349–67.

13. U.S. Constitution, Article II, Section 1.

14. Mark J. Rozel. 1999. "'The Law': Executive Privilege: Definition and Standards of Application," *Presidential Studies Quarterly* 29, No. 4: 918–30.

15. Glen S. Krutz and Jeffrey S. Peake. 2009. *Treaty Politics and the Rise of Executive Agreements: International Commitments in a System of Shared Powers*. Ann Arbor: University of Michigan Press.

16. Charles Stewart. 1989. *Budget Reform Politics: The Design of the Appropriations Process in the House of Representatives, 1865-1921*. New York: Cambridge University Press.

17. Daniel Myron Greene. 1908. "The Evolution of the National Political Convention," *The Sewanee Review* 16, No. 2: 228–32.

18. Marty Cohen. 2008. *The Party Decides: Presidential Nominations before and after Reform*. Chicago: University of Chicago.

19. James Roger Sharp. 2010. *The Deadlocked Election of 1800: Jefferson, Burr, and the Union in the Balance*. Lawrence: University Press of Kansas.

20. John Samples, "In Defense of the Electoral College," 10 November 2000, http://www.cato.org/publications/commentary/defense-electoral-college (May 1, 2016).

21. Clifton B. Parker, "Now We Know Why It's Time to Dump the Electoral College," *The Fiscal Times*, 12 April 2016, http://www.thefiscaltimes.com/2016/04/12/Now-We-Know-Why-It-s-Time-Dump-Electoral-College.

22. Jason Scott-Sheets, "Public financing is available for presidential candidates. So what's not to like about free money?" 14 April 2016, http://www.opensecrets.org/news/2016/04/public-financing-is-available-for-presidential-candidates-so-whats-not-to-like-about-free-money/.

23. Glen S. Krutz, Richard Fleisher, and Jon R. Bond. 1998. "From Abe Fortas to Zoe Baird." *American Political Science Review* 92, No. 4: 871–882.

24. Michael Oreskes. 1989. "Senate Rejects Tower, 53–47; First Cabinet Veto since '59; Bush Confers on New Choice," *New York Times*, 10 March 1989, http://www.nytimes.com/1989/03/10/us/senate-rejects-tower-53-47-first-cabinet-veto-since-59-bush-confers-new-choice.html.

25. Mark J. Rozell, William D. Pederson, Frank J. Williams. 2000. *George Washington and the Origins of the American Presidency*. Portsmouth, NH: Greenwood Publishing Group, 17.

26. "Hearing of the Senate Judiciary Committee on the Nomination of Clarence Thomas to the Supreme Court," Electronic Text Center, University of Virginia Library, 11 October 1991.

27. Jon R. Bond, Richard Fleisher, and Glen S. Krutz. 2009. "Malign Neglect: Evidence That Delay Has Become the Primary Method of Defeating Presidential Appointments" *Congress & the Presidency* 36, No. 3: 226–243.

28. Barbara Perry, "One-third of all U.S. presidents appointed a Supreme Court justice in an election year," *Washington Post*, 29 February 2016, https://www.washingtonpost.com/news/monkey-cage/wp/2016/02/29/one-third-of-all-u-s-presidents-appointed-a-supreme-court-justice-in-an-election-year/.

29. Jennifer Liberto, "It pays to work for the White House," *CNN Money*, 2 July 2014, http://money.cnn.com/2014/07/02/news/economy/white-house-salaries/ (May 1, 2016).

30. Gary P. Gershman. 2008. *The Legislative Branch of Federal Government: People, Process, and Politics*. Santa Barbara, CA: ABC-CLIO.

31. Bruce Drake, "Obama lags his predecessors in recess appointments," 13 January 2014, http://www.pewresearch.org/fact-tank/2014/01/13/obama-lags-his-predecessors-in-recess-appointments/ (May 1, 2016).

32. *National Labor Relations Board v. Canning*, 573 U.S. ___ (2014).

33. Amy C. Gaudion and Douglas Stuart, "More Than Just a Running Mate," *The New York Times*, 19 July 2012, http://campaignstops.blogs.nytimes.com/2012/07/19/more-than-just-a-running-mate/.

34. Stephen Skowronek. 2011. *Presidential Leadership in Political Time: Reprise and Reappraisal*. Lawrence: University Press of Kansas.

35. Wendy Wick Reaves. 1987. "Thomas Nast and the President," *American Art Journal* 19, No. 1: 61–71.

36. George C. Edwards. 2016. *Predicting the Presidency: The Potential of Persuasive Leadership*. Princeton: Princeton University Press; George C. Edwards and Stephen J. Wayne. 2003. *Presidential Leadership: Politics and Policy Making*. Belmont, CA: Wadsworth/Thomson Learning.

37. Rupert Cornwell, "Bill and Hillary's double trouble: Clinton's 'two for the price of one' pledge is returning to haunt him," *Independent*, 8 March 1994, http://www.independent.co.uk/voices/bill-and-hillarys-double-trouble-clintons-two-for-the-price-of-one-pledge-is-returning-to-haunt-him-1427937.html (May 1, 2016).

38. Tamar Lewin, "First Person; A Feminism That Speaks For Itself," *New York Times*, 3 October 1993, http://www.nytimes.com/1993/10/03/weekinreview/first-person-a-feminism-that-speaks-for-itself.html.

39. *Myers v. United States*, 272 U.S. 52 (1925).

40. "Bush Issues Pardons, but to a Relative Few," *New York Times*, 22 December 2006, http://www.nytimes.com/2006/12/22/washington/22pardon.html.

41. U.S. Department of Justice. "Clemency Statistics." https://www.justice.gov/pardon/clemencystatistics (January 10, 2019).

42. Andrea Marks and Tom Dickinson. 31 January 2019. "A Timeline of Controversial Presidential Pardons." *Rolling Stone*. https://www.rollingstone.com/politics/politics-news/presidential-pardons-787452/.

43. Mark Mazzetti, Eileen Sullivan, and Maggie Haberman. 25 January 2019. "Indicting Roger Stone, Mueller Shows Link between Trump Campaign and WikiLeaks." *New York Times*. https://www.nytimes.com/2019/01/25/us/politics/roger-stone-trump-mueller.html.

44. *Youngstown Sheet & Tube Co. v. Sawyer*, 343 U.S. 579 (1952).

45. Julie Des Jardins, "From Citizen to Enemy: The Tragedy of Japanese Internment," http://www.gilderlehrman.org/history-by-era/world-war-ii/essays/from-citizen-enemy-tragedy-japanese-internment (May 1, 2016).

46. *Korematsu v. United States*, 323 U.S. 214 (1944).

47. Ilya Somin, "Justice Scalia on Kelo and Korematsu," *Washington Post*, 8 February 2014, https://www.washingtonpost.com/news/volokh-conspiracy/wp/2014/02/08/justice-scalia-on-kelo-and-korematsu/.

48. Glen S. Krutz. 2001. *Hitching a Ride: Omnibus Legislating in the U.S. Congress*. Columbus, OH: Ohio State University Press.

49. *Clinton v. City of New York*, 524 U.S. 417 (1998).

50. Richard E. Neustadt. 1960. *Presidential Power and the Modern Presidents* New York: Wiley.

51. Fred I. Greenstein. 1982. *The Hidden-Hand Presidency: Eisenhower as Leader*. New York: Basic Books.

52. Stephen Skowronek. 2011. *Presidential Leadership in Political Time: Reprise and Reappraisal*. Lawrence, KS: University Press of Kansas.

The Courts

1. *Obergefell v. Hodges*, 576 U.S. __ (2015).

2. In cases of original jurisdiction the courts cannot decide—the U.S. Constitution mandates that the U.S. Supreme Court must hear cases of original jurisdiction.

3. "The U.S. Supreme Court." *The Judicial Learning Center*. http://judiciallearningcenter.org/the-us-supreme-court/ (March 1, 2016).

4. Bernard Schwartz. 1993. *A History of the Supreme Court*. New York: Oxford University Press, 16.

5. "Washington D.C. A National Register of Historic Places Travel Itinerary." U.S. Department of the Interior, National Park Service. http://www.nps.gov/nr/travel/wash/dc78.htm (March 1, 2016).

6. *Chisholm v. Georgia*, 2 U.S. 419 (1793).

7. Associated Press. "What You Should Know About Forgotten Founding Father John Jay," *PBS Newshour*. July 4, 2015. http://www.pbs.org/newshour/rundown/forgotten-founding-father.

8. "Life and Legacy." *The John Marshall Foundation*. http://www.johnmarshallfoundation.org (March 1, 2016).

9. *Marbury v. Madison*, 5 U.S. 137 (1803).

10. Stephen Hass. "Judicial Review." *National Juris University*. http://juris.nationalparalegal.edu/(X(1)S(wwbvsi5iswopllt1bfpzfkjd))/JudicialReview.aspx (March 1, 2016).

11. *Marbury v. Madison*, 5 U.S. 137 (1803).

12. *Marbury v. Madison,* 5 U.S. 137 (1803).

13. "The Common Law and Civil Law Traditions." *The Robbins Collection.* School of Law (Boalt Hall). University of California at Berkeley. https://www.law.berkeley.edu/library/robbins/ CommonLawCivilLawTraditions.html (March 1, 2016).

14. *National Federation of Independent Business v. Sebelius,* 567 U.S. __ (2012).

15. *Burwell v. Hobby Lobby,* 573 U.S. __ (2014).

16. *King v. Burwell,* 576 U.S. __ (2015).

17. *Elonis v. United States,* 13-983 U.S. __ (2015).

18. *Equal Employment Opportunity Commission v. Abercrombie & Fitch Stores,* 575 U.S. __ (2015).

19. Liptak, Adam. "Muslim Woman Denied Job Over Head Scarf Wins in Supreme Court." *New York Times.* 1 June 2015. http://www.nytimes.com/2015/06/02/us/supreme-court-rules-in-samantha-elauf-abercrombie-fitch-case.html?_r=0.

20. *Brown v. Board of Education of Topeka,* 347 U.S. 483 (1954).

21. *Gregg v. Georgia,* 428 U.S. 153 (1976).

22. *Atkins v. Virginia,* 536 U.S. 304 (2002); *Roper v. Simmons,* 543 U.S. 551 (2005); *Kennedy v. Louisiana,* 554 U.S. 407 (2008).

23. *Glossip v. Gross,* 576 U.S. __ (2015).

24. "October Term 2015." *SCOTUSblog.* http://www.scotusblog.com/case-files/terms/ ot2015/?sort=mname (March 1, 2016).

25. Bureau of International Information Programs, United States Department of State. *Outline of the U.S. Legal System.* 2004.

26. *Miranda v. Arizona,* 384 U.S. 436 (1966).

27. "State Courts vs. Federal Courts." *The Judicial Learning Center.* http://judiciallearningcenter.org/ state-courts-vs-federal-courts/ (March 1, 2016).

28. "State Courts vs. Federal Courts." *The Judicial Learning Center.* http://judiciallearningcenter.org/ state-courts-vs-federal-courts/ (March 1, 2016).

29. "U.S. Court System." *Syracuse University.* http://www2.maxwell.syr.edu/plegal/scales/court.html (March 1, 2016).

30. *Miranda v. Arizona,* 384 U.S. 436 (1966).

31. Paul R. Brace and Melinda Gann Hall. 2005. "Is Judicial Federalism Essential to Democracy? State Courts in the Federal System." In *Institutions of American Democracy, The Judicial Branch,* eds. Kermit L. Hall and Kevin T. McGuire. New York: Oxford University Press.

32. *States of Nebraska and Oklahoma v. State of Colorado.* Motion for Leave to File Complaint, Complaint and Brief in Support. December 2014. http://www.scribd.com/doc/250506006/Nebraska-Oklahoma-Lawsuit.

33. Joel B. Grossman and Austin Sarat. 1971. "Political Culture and Judicial Research." *Washington University Law Review.* 1971 (2) Symposium: Courts, Judges, Politics—Some Political Science Perspectives. http://openscholarship.wustl.edu/cgi/viewcontent.cgi?article=2777&context=law_lawreview.

34. "The U.S. District Courts and the Federal Judiciary." *Federal Judicial Center.* http://www.fjc.gov/ history/home.nsf/page/courts_district.html (March 1, 2016).

35. "Circuit Riding." *Encyclopedia Britannica.* http://www.britannica.com/topic/circuit-riding (March 1, 2016).

36. "The U.S. Circuit Courts and the Federal Judiciary." *Federal Judicial Center*. http://www.fjc.gov/history/home.nsf/page/courts_circuit.html (March 1, 2016).

37. Benjamin N. Cardozo. 1921. *The Nature of the Judicial Process*. New Haven: Yale University Press. http://www.constitution.org/cmt/cardozo/jud_proc.htm.

38. *Plessy v. Ferguson*, 163 U.S. 537 (1896); *Brown v. Board of Education of Topeka*, 347 U.S. 483 (1954).

39. American Bar Association Coalition for Justice. 2008. "Judicial Selection." In *American Bar Association*, eds. American Judicature Society and Malia Reddick. http://www.americanbar.org/content/dam/aba/migrated/JusticeCenter/Justice/PublicDocuments/judicial_selection_roadmap.authcheckdam.pdf.

40. American Bar Association Coalition for Justice. 2008. "Judicial Selection." In *American Bar Association*, eds. American Judicature Society and Malia Reddick. http://www.americanbar.org/content/dam/aba/migrated/JusticeCenter/Justice/PublicDocuments/judicial_selection_roadmap.authcheckdam.pdf.

41. James Delmont. 13 December 2018. "John Roberts Will Be the New Anthony Kennedy." *American Greatness*. https://www.amgreatness.com/2018/12/13/john-roberts-will-be-the-new-anthony-kennedy/.

42. John M. Broder. "Edward M. Kennedy, Senate Stalwart, Is Dead at 77." *New York Times*. 26 August 2009.

43. Michael A. Fletcher and Charles Babington. "Miers, Under Fire From Right, Withdrawn as Court Nominee." *Washington Post*. 28 October 2005. http://www.washingtonpost.com/wp-dyn/content/article/2005/10/27/AR2005102700547.html.

44. Bureau of International Information Programs. United States Department of State. *Outline of the U.S. Legal System*. 2004.

45. Russell Wheeler. "The Changing Face of the Federal Judiciary." *Governance Studies at Brookings*. August 2009. http://www.brookings.edu/~/media/research/files/papers/2009/8/federal-judiciary-wheeler/08_federal_judiciary_wheeler.pdf.

46. Dahlia Lithwick. "Who Feeds the Supreme Court?" *Slate.com*. September 14, 2015. http://www.slate.com/articles/news_and_politics/jurisprudence/2015/09/supreme_court_feeder_judges_men_and_few_women_send_law_clerks_to_scotus.html.

47. "Role of Supreme Court Law Clerk: Interview with Philippa Scarlett." *IIP Digital*. United States of America Embassy. http://iipdigital.usembassy.gov/st/english/publication/2013/02/20130211142365.html#axzz3grjRwiG (March 1, 2016).

48. "Supreme Court Procedures." *United States Courts*. http://www.uscourts.gov/about-federal-courts/educational-resources/about-educational-outreach/activity-resources/supreme-1 (March 1, 2016).

49. *Roe v. Wade*, 410 U.S. 113 (1973).

50. "Rule 10. Considerations Governing Review on *Certiorari*." *Rules of the Supreme Court of the United States*. Adopted April 19, 2013, Effective July 1, 2013. http://www.supremecourt.gov/ctrules/2013RulesoftheCourt.pdf.

51. *Bush v. Gore*, 531 U.S. 98 (2000).

52. Gregory A. Caldeira and John R. Wright. 1988. "Organized Interests and Agenda-Setting in the U.S. Supreme Court," *American Political Science Review* 82: 1109–1128.

53. Gregory A. Caldeira, John R. Wright, and Christopher Zorn. 2012. "Organized Interests and Agenda Setting in the U.S. Supreme Court Revisited." Presentation at the Second Annual Conference on Institutions and Lawmaking, Emory University. http://polisci.emory.edu/home/cslpe/conference-institutions-law-making/2012/papers/caldeira_wright_zorn_cwzpaper.pdf.

54. "About the Office." Office of the Solicitor General. *The United States Department of Justice*. http://www.justice.gov/osg/about-office-1 (March 1, 2016).

55. Ryan C. Black and Ryan J. Owens. "Solicitor General Influence and the United States Supreme Court." Vanderbilt University. http://www.vanderbilt.edu/csdi/archived/working%20papers/Ryan%20Owens.pdf (March 1, 2016).

56. Mark Joseph Stern., "If SCOTUS Decides in Favor of Marriage Equality, Thank Solicitor General Don Verrilli," *Slate.com*. April 29, 2015. http://www.slate.com/blogs/outward/2015/04/29/don_verrilli_solicitor_general_was_the_real_hero_of_scotus_gay_marriage.html.

57. "The Court and its Procedures." *Supreme Court of the United States*. May 26, 2015.

58. "Supreme Court Procedures." *United States Courts*. http://www.uscourts.gov/about-federal-courts/educational-resources/about-educational-outreach/activity-resources/supreme-1 (March 1, 2016).

59. "Supreme Court Procedures." *United States Courts*. http://www.uscourts.gov/about-federal-courts/educational-resources/about-educational-outreach/activity-resources/supreme-1 (March 1, 2016).

60. Jonathan Sherman. "End the Supreme Court's Ban on Cameras." *New York Times*. 24 April 2015. http://www.nytimes.com/2015/04/24/opinion/open-the-supreme-court-to-cameras.html.

61. Matt Sedensky. "Justice questions way court nominees are grilled." *The Associated Press*. May 14, 2010. http://www.boston.com/news/nation/articles/2010/05/14/justice_questions_way_court_nominees_are_grilled/.

62. *Bowers v. Hardwick*, 478 U.S. 186 (1986).

63. *Lawrence v. Texas*, 539 U.S. 558 (2003).

64. *Lawrence v. Texas*, 539 U.S. 558 (2003).

65. Louis Jacobson. "Is Barack Obama trying to 'pack' the D.C. Circuit Court of Appeals?" *Tampa Bay Times, PolitiFact.com*. June 5, 2013. http://www.politifact.com/truth-o-meter/statements/2013/jun/05/chuck-grassley/barack-obama-trying-pack-dc-circuit-court-appeals/.

66. *Worcester v. Georgia*, 31 U.S. (6 Pet.) 515 (1832).

67. "Court History." *Supreme Court History: The First Hundred Years*. http://www.pbs.org/wnet/supremecourt/antebellum/history2.html (March 1, 2016).

68. Dwight D. Eisenhower. "Radio and Television Address to the American People on the Situation in Little Rock." *Public Papers of the Presidents of the United States: Eisenhower, Dwight D., The American Presidency Project*. September 24, 1957. http://www.presidency.ucsb.edu/ws/?pid=10909.

State and Local Government

1. "Articles of Confederation," https://www.gpo.gov/fdsys/pkg/SMAN-107/pdf/SMAN-107-pg935.pdf (March 14, 2016).

2. "Tax History Museum: The Revolutionary War to the War of 1812 (1777–1815)," http://www.taxhistory.org/www/website.nsf/Web/THM1777?OpenDocument (March 14, 2016).

3. Reid Wilson. 4 April 2015. "Conservative Lawmakers Weigh Bid to Call for Constitutional Convention." *Washington Post*. http://www.washingtonpost.com/politics/conservative-lawmakers-weigh-bid-tocall-for-constitutional-convention/2015/04/04/b25d4f1e-db02-11e4-ba28-f2a685dc7f89_story.html. Jamiles Lartey. "Conservatives Call for Constitutional Intervention Last Seen 230 Years Ago." The Guardian. https://www.theguardian.com/us-news/2018/aug/11/conservatives-call-for-constitutional-convention-alec.

4. *A. L. A. Schechter Poultry Corp. v. United States*, 295 U.S. 495 (1935).

5. William E. Leuchtenburg, "When Franklin Roosevelt Clashed with the Supreme Court—and Lost," *Smithsonian Magazine*, May 2005. http://www.smithsonianmag.com/history/when-franklin-roosevelt-clashed-with-the-supreme-court-and-lost-78497994/.

6. Karen Tumulty, "'Great Society' Agenda Led to Great—and Lasting—Philosophical Divide," *Washington Post*, 8 January 2014. http://www.washingtonpost.com/politics/great-society-agenda-led-to-great--and-lasting--philosophical-divide/2014/01/08/b082e5d0-786d-11e3-b1c5-739e63e9c9a7_story.html.

7. Michael Schuyler. 19 February 2014. "A Short History of Government Taxing and Spending in the United States," http://taxfoundation.org/article/short-history-government-taxing-and-spending-united-states.

8. Philip Joyce, "Is the Era of Unfunded Federal Mandates Over?" *Governing*, 16 April 2014. http://www.governing.com/columns/smart-mgmt/col-is-era-unfunded-federal-mandates-over.html.

9. "State Policy Choices under Welfare Reform," http://www.brookings.edu/research/papers/2002/04/welfare-gais (March 14, 2016).

10. "Why Existing Law Won't Stop Corporations from Harming Your Community," August 31, 2015. http://celdf.org/2015/08/why-existing-law-wont-stop-corporations-from-harming-your-community/ (March 14, 2016).

11. Jesse J. Richardson, Jr. 5 August 2011. "Dillon's Rule is from Mars, Home Rule is from Venus: Local Government Autonomy and the Rules of Statutory Construction," *Publius* 41, No. 4: 662–685.

12. Max B. Baker, "Denton City Council Repeals Fracking Ban," *Fort Worth Star-Telegram*, 16 June 2015. http://www.star-telegram.com/news/business/barnett-shale/article24627469.html.

13. Roberton Williams and Yuri Shadunsky. "State and Local Tax Policy: What are the Sources of Revenue for Local Governments?" http://www.taxpolicycenter.org/briefing-book/state-local/revenues/local_revenue.cfm (March 14, 2016).

14. Charles E. Gilliland. November 2013. "Property Taxes: The Bad, the Good, and the Ugly," Texas A&M University - Real Estate Center, TR 2037. https://assets.recenter.tamu.edu/documents/articles/2037.pdf.

15. "What is Proposition 13?" http://www.californiataxdata.com/pdf/Prop13.pdf (March 14, 2016).

16. Yolanda Perez, John Avault, and Jim Vrabel. December 2002. "Tax Exempt Property in Boston," *Boston Redevelopment Authority Policy Development and Research* Report 562, http://www.californiataxdata.com/pdf/Prop13.pdf.

17. Channon Hodge and David Gillen, "What Bankruptcy Means for Detroit," *New York Times*, 4 December 2013. http://www.nytimes.com/video/business/100000002583690/what-bankruptcy-means-for-detroit.html.

18. Daniel Elazar. 1972. *American Federalism: A View from the States*, 2nd ed. New York: Thomas Y. Crowell Company.

19. Maria L. La Ganga, "Under New Oregon law, All Eligible Voters are Registered Unless They Opt Out," *Los Angeles Times*, 17 March 2015. http://www.latimes.com/nation/la-na-oregon-automatic-voter-registration-20150317-story.html.

20. Jeff Guo, "It's Official: New Oregon Law Will Automatically Register People to Vote," *Washington Post*, 17 March 2015. http://www.washingtonpost.com/blogs/govbeat/wp/2015/03/17/its-official-new-oregon-law-will-automatically-register-people-to-vote/.

21. Alec MacGillis. 18 March 2015. "The Oregon Trail: The State's New Governor is Going on the Offensive in the Battle for Voting Rights," http://www.slate.com/articles/news_and_politics/politics/2015/03/kate_brown_and_automatic_voter_registration_oregon_s_new_governor_has_gone.html.

22. Dean DeChiaro, "$830M in Tax Breaks Later, Christie Says His Camden Plan Won't Work for America," *U.S. News and World Report*, 19 August 2015. http://www.usnews.com/news/articles/2015/08/19/830m-in-tax-breaks-later-christie-says-his-camden-plan-wont-work-for-america.

23. "Division of Nutrition, Physical Activity, and Obesity: Data, Trends and Maps," http://www.cdc.gov/obesity/data/prevalence-maps.html (March 14, 2016).

24. Jie Zong and Jeanne Batalova. 26 February 2015. "Frequently Requested Statistics on Immigrants and Immigration in the United States," http://www.migrationpolicy.org/article/frequently-requested-statistics-immigrants-and-immigration-united-states.

25. Lindsey Cook, "Americans Still Hate Congress," *U.S. News and World Report*, 18 August 2014. http://www.usnews.com/news/blogs/data-mine/2014/08/18/americans-still-hate-congress.

26. Wilson Andrews, Alicia Parlapiano, and Karen Yourish, "Who is Running for President?" *New York Times*, 4 March 2016. http://www.nytimes.com/interactive/2016/us/elections/2016-presidential-candidates.html?_r=0.

27. Alan Rosenthal. 2013. *The Best Job in Politics; Exploring How Governors Succeed as Policy Leaders.* Thousand Oaks, CA: CQ Press.

28. Elaine S. Povich, "Many State Governors Have Budget Problems with Their Own Parties," *Governing*, 4 February 2013. http://www.governing.com/news/headlines/many-state-governors-have-budget-problems-with-their-own-parties.html.

29. "Governors' Powers and Authority," http://www.nga.org/cms/home/management-resources/governors-powers-and-authority.html (March 14, 2016).

30. Laura van Assendelft. 1997. *Governors, Agenda Setting, and Divided Government.* Lanham, MD: University Press of America.

31. National Conference of State Legislatures. "The Veto Process." In *General Legislative Procedures.* Washington, DC: National Conference of State Legislatures, 6-29–6-64. http://www.ncsl.org/documents/legismgt/ilp/98tab6pt3.pdf (March 14, 2016).

32. Monica Davey, "Wisconsin Voters Excise Editing from Governor's Veto Powers," *New York Times*, 3 April 2008. http://www.nytimes.com/2008/04/03/us/03wisconsin.html?_r=0.

33. Daniel C. Vock. 24 April 2007. "Govs Enjoy Quirky Veto Power," http://www.pewtrusts.org/en/research-and-analysis/blogs/stateline/2007/04/24/govs-enjoy-quirky-veto-power.

34. Steven Walters, "Voters Drive Stake into 'Frankenstein Veto'," *Milwaukee Journal Sentinel*, 2 April 2008. http://www.jsonline.com/news/wisconsin/29395824.html.

35. National Conference of State Legislatures. 20 September 2012. "Initiative, Referendum and Recall," http://www.ncsl.org/research/elections-and-campaigns/initiative-referendum-and-recall-overview.aspx.

36. National Conference of State Legislatures. 6 May 2009. "Special Sessions," http://www.ncsl.org/research/about-state-legislatures/special-sessions472.aspx.

37. Patrick Svitek, "Abbott Tries Wooing General Electric to Texas," *The Texas Tribune*, 10 June 2015. https://www.texastribune.org/2015/06/10/abbott-looks-woo-general-electric-connecticut/.

38. Ted Mann and Jon Kamp, "General Electric to Move Headquarters to Boston," *The Wall Street Journal*, 13 January 2016. http://www.wsj.com/articles/general-electric-plans-to-move-headquarters-to-boston-1452703676.

39. Abigail Hess.14 November 2018. "Amazon Says It Will Bring 50,000 Jobs to Its Two New Headquarters—Here's How to Land a Job at the Company." CNBC. https://www.cnbc.com/2018/11/14/amazon-has-promise-to-create-50000-new-jobsheres-how-to-land-one.html.

40. "Virginia Governor Tries to Woo Indiana Businesses," http://www.nbcwashington.com/blogs/first-read-dmv/Virginia-Governor-Tries-to-Woo-Indiana-Businesses-298087131.html (March 14, 2016).

41. Stephanie Wang, "What the 'Religious Freedom' Law Really Means for Indiana," *Indy Star*, 3 April 2015. http://www.indystar.com/story/news/politics/2015/03/29/religious-freedom-law-really-means-indiana/70601584/

42. James Gherardi. March 25, 2015. "Indiana Businesses Concerned Over Economic Impact of Religious Freedom Bill," http://cbs4indy.com/2015/03/25/indiana-businesses-concerned-over-economic-impact-of-religious-freedom-bill/.

43. Tony Cook, Tom LoBianco, and Brian Eason, "Gov. Mike Pence signs RFRA Fix," *Indy Star*, 2 April 2015. http://www.indystar.com/story/news/politics/2015/04/01/indiana-rfra-deal-sets-limited-protections-for-lgbt/70766920/.

44. German Lopez. April 2, 2015. "How Indiana's Religious Freedom Law Sparked a Battle Over LGBT Rights," http://www.vox.com/2015/3/31/8319493/indiana-rfra-lgbt.

45. 29 October 2014. "These Images Show Just How Much Some Neighborhoods Were Changed by Hurricane Sandy," http://www.huffingtonpost.com/2014/10/29/hurricane-sandy-second-anniversary-images_n_6054274.html.

46. Michael Barbaro, "After Obama, Christie Wants a G.O.P. Hug," *New York Times*, 19 November 2012. http://www.nytimes.com/2012/11/20/us/politics/after-embrace-of-obama-chris-christie-woos-a-wary-gop.html?_r=0.

47. Teresa Welsh, "Is Chris Christie a GOP Traitor for His Obama Hurricane Praise?" *U.S. News and World Report*, 1 November 2012. http://www.usnews.com/opinion/articles/2012/11/01/is-chris-christie-a-gop-traitor-for-praising-obamas-response-to-hurricane-sandy

48. Susan Gardner, "Baltimore Erupts into Chaos: Governor activates National Guard," 27 April 2015. http://www.dailykos.com/story/2015/04/27/1380756/-Baltimore-erupts-into-chaos-Governor-activates-National-Guard#.

49. Shira Schoenberg. 2 February 2015. "Governor Calls on 500 Massachusetts National Guard Troops to Dig State Out from Snowstorms," http://www.masslive.com/news/boston/index.ssf/2015/02/in_unprecedented_move_500_nati.html.

50. Leslie Larson and Jennifer Fermino, "Cuomo and de Blasio Tell Storm Critics 'Better Safe Than Sorry'," *New York Daily News*, 27 January 2015. http://www.nydailynews.com/news/politics/cuomo-de-blasio-critics-better-safe-article-1.2093306.

51. "Pardons, Reprieves, Commutations and Respites," http://www.sos.wv.gov/public-services/execrecords/Pages/Pardons.aspx (March 14, 2016).

52. "Clemency Process by State," http://www.deathpenaltyinfo.org/clemency?did=126&scid=13#process (March 14, 2016).

53. Rosenthal, *The Best Job in Politics; Exploring How Governors Succeed as Policy Leaders.*

54. Edmund Burke. 1969. "The English Constitutional System." In *Representation*. Hanna Pitkin. New York: Atherton Press.

55. Ohio Legislative Service Commission. 2015–2016. "Legislative Oversight." In *A Guidebook for Ohio Legislators*, 14th ed. Columbus, OH: Ohio Legislative Service Commission.

56. National Conference of State Legislatures. 11 March 2013. "Number of Legislators and Length of Terms in Years," http://www.ncsl.org/research/about-state-legislatures/number-of-legislators-and-length-of-terms.aspx.

57. National Conference of State Legislatures. 8 January 2019. "Legislatures at a Glance." http://www.ncsl.org/research/about-state-legislatures/legislatures-at-a-glance.aspx.

58. National Conference of State Legislatures. 10 January 2008. "African-American Legislators 2009," http://www.ncsl.org/research/about-state-legislatures/african-american-legislators-in-2009.aspx; "2009 Latino Legislators." http://www.ncsl.org/research/about-state-legislatures/latino-legislators-overview.aspx (March 14, 2016).

59. Chris T. Owens. 2005. "Black Substantive Representation in State Legislatures from 1971–1999," *Social Science Quarterly* 84, No. 5: 779–791; Robert R. Preuhs. 2005. "Descriptive Representation, Legislative Leadership, and Direct Democracy: Latino Influence on English Only Laws in the States, 1984–2002," *State Politics and Policy Quarterly* 5, No. 3: 203–224; Sue Thomas. 1991. "The Impact of Women on State Legislative Policies." *The Journal of Politics* 53, No. 4: 958–976.

60. Rene Rocha, Caroline Tolbert, Daniel Bowen, and Christopher Clark. 2010. "Race and Turnout: Does Descriptive Representation in State Legislatures Increase Minority Voting?" *Political Research Quarterly* 63, No. 4: 890–907.

61. "2014 Legislative Partisan Composition," http://www.ncsl.org/portals/1/ImageLibrary/WebImages/Elections/2014_Leg_Party_Control_map.gif (March 14, 2016).

62. Peverill Squire. 2007. "Measuring State Legislative Professionalism: The Squire Index Revisited." *State Politics & Policy Quarterly* 7, No. 2: 211–227.

63. National Conference of State Legislatures. 1 June 2014. "Table 2. Average Job Time, Compensation and Staff Size by Category of Legislature," http://www.ncsl.org/research/about-state-legislatures/full-and-part-time-legislatures.aspx#average.

64. Peverill, "Measuring State Legislative Professionalism: The Squire Index Revisited."

65. National Conference of State Legislatures. 13 March 2015. "The Term-Limited States," http://www.ncsl.org/research/about-state-legislatures/chart-of-term-limits-states.aspx.

66. See note 65.

67. See note 65.

68. National Conference of State Legislatures. "Term Limits and the Courts," http://www.ncsl.org/research/about-state-legislatures/summaries-of-term-limits-cases.aspx (March 14, 2016).

69. National Conference of State Legislatures. 20 September 2012. "Initiative, Referendum and Recall," http://www.ncsl.org/research/elections-and-campaigns/initiative-referendum-and-recall-overview.aspx.

70. John Carey, Richard Niemi, and Lynda Powell. 2000. *Term Limits in State Legislatures*. Ann Arbor: University of Michigan Press.

71. See note 70.

72. "The U.S. Term Limits Pledge," http://ustermlimitsamendment.org/about-us/ (March 14, 2016).

73. Stanley Caress and Todd Kunioka. 2012. *Term Limits and Their Consequences: The Aftermath of Legislative Reform*. New York: State University of New York Press.

74. Lyke Thompson, Charles Elder, and Richard Elling. 2004. *Political and Institutional Effects of Term Limits*. New York: Palgrave Macmillan.

75. See note above.

76. Brian Lavin. 30 August 2012. "Census Bureau Reports There are 89,004 Local Governments in the United States (CB12-161)," https://www.census.gov/newsroom/releases/archives/governments/cb12-161.html.

77. Frank Coppa. 2000. *County Government: A Guide to Efficient and Accountable Government*. Westport, CT: Greenwood Publishing.

78. Coppa, *County Government: A Guide to Efficient and Accountable Government*.

79. Coppa, *County Government: A Guide to Efficient and Accountable Government*.

80. Coppa, *County Government: A Guide to Efficient and Accountable Government*.

81. http://www.naco.org/counties (March 14, 2016).

82. Lavin, "Census Bureau Reports There are 89,004 Local Governments in the United States (CB12-161)."

83. "Forms of Municipal Government," http://www.nlc.org/build-skills-and-networks/resources/cities-101/city-structures/forms-of-municipal-government (March 14, 2016).

84. "Mayoral Powers," http://www.nlc.org/build-skills-and-networks/resources/cities-101/city-officials/mayoral-powers (March 14, 2016).

85. "Forms of Municipal Government."

86. Mark Alesia, "Kansas City has Stadium Success Story—in Major League Soccer," *Indy Star*, 18 March 2015. http://www.indystar.com/story/news/2015/03/17/kansas-city-stadium-success-story-major-league-soccer/24928853/.

The Bureaucracy

1. For general information on ancient bureaucracies see Amanda Summer. 2012. "The Birth of Bureaucracy". *Archaeology* 65, No. 4: 33–39; Clyde Curry Smith. 1977. "The Birth of Bureaucracy". *The Bible Archaeologist* 40, No. 1: 24–28; Ronald J. Williams. 1972. "Scribal Training in Ancient Egypt," *Journal of the American Oriental Society* 92, No. 2: 214–21.

2. Richard Stillman. 2009. *Public Administration: Concepts and Cases.* 9th edition. Boston: Wadsworth Cengage Learning.

3. For the early origins of the U.S. bureaucracy see Michael Nelson. 1982. "A Short, Ironic History of American National Bureaucracy," *The Journal of Politics* 44 No. 3: 747–78.

4. Daniel Walker Howe. 2007. *What Hath God Wrought: The Transformation of America, 1815-1848*. Oxford: Oxford University Press, 334.

5. Jack Ladinsky. 1966. "Review of Status and Kinship in the Higher Civil Service: Standards of Selection in the Administrations of John Adams, Thomas Jefferson, and Andrew Jackson," *American Sociological Review* 31 No. 6: 863–64.

6. For more on the Pendleton Act and its effects see Sean M. Theriault. 2003. "Patronage, the Pendleton Act, and the Power of the People," *The Journal of Politics* 65 No. 1: 50–68; Craig V. D. Thornton. 1983. "Review of Centenary Issues of the Pendleton Act of 1883: The Problematic Legacy of Civil Service Reform," *Journal of Policy Analysis and Management* 2 No. 4: 653–53.

7. Jack Rabin and James S. Bowman. 1984. "Politics and Administration: Woodrow Wilson and American Public Administration," *Public Administration and Public Policy*; 22: 104.

8. For more on President Wilson's efforts at reform see Kendrick A. Clements. 1998. "Woodrow Wilson and Administrative Reform," *Presidential Studies Quarterly* 28 No. 2: 320–36; Larry Walker. 1989. "Woodrow Wilson, Progressive Reform, and Public Administration," *Political Science Quarterly* 104, No. 3: 509–25.

9. https://www.opm.gov/policy-data-oversight/data-analysis-documentation/federal-employment-reports/historical-tables/executive-branch-civilian-employment-since-1940/ (May 15, 2016).

10. https://www.opm.gov/policy-data-oversight/data-analysis-documentation/federal-employment-reports/historical-tables/total-government-employment-since-1962 (May 15, 2016).

11. For more on LBJ and the Great Society see: John A. Andrew. 1998. *Lyndon Johnson and the Great Society*. Chicago: Ivan R Dee; Julian E. Zelizer. 2015. *The Fierce Urgency of Now: Lyndon Johnson, Congress, and the Battle for the Great Society*. New York: Penguin Press.

12. John Mikesell. 2014. *Fiscal Administration*, 9th ed. Boston: Cengage.

13. United States Civil Service Commission. 1974. *Biography of an Ideal: a history of the federal civil service*. Washington, D.C.: Office of Public Affairs, U.S. Civil Service Commission. 40–44.

14. Ronald N. Johnson and Gary D. Libecap. 1994. *The Federal Civil Service System and the Problem of*

Bureaucracy. Chicago: University of Chicago Press.

15. Patricia W. Ingraham and Carolyn Ban. 1984. *Legislating Bureaucratic Change : The Civil Service Reform Act of 1978*. Albany: State University of New York Press.

16. Dennis V. Damp. 2008. *The Book of U.S. Government Jobs: Where They Are, What's Available, & How to Get One*. McKees Rocks, PA: Bookhaven Press, 30.

17. Lisa Rein, "For federal-worker hopefuls, the civil service exam is making a comeback," *Washington Post*, 2 April 2015, https://www.washingtonpost.com/news/federal-eye/wp/2015/04/02/for-federal-worker-hopefuls-the-civil-service-exam-is-making-a-comeback/.

18. https://www.opm.gov/policy-data-oversight/classification-qualifications/general-schedule-qualification-policies/#url=General-Policies (May 16, 2016).

19. Susan J. Hekman. 1983. "Weber's Ideal Type: A Contemporary Reassessment". *Polity* 16 No. 1: 119–37.

20. Congressional Budget Office Report, https://www.cbo.gov/publication/44172 (June 6, 2016).

21. *A. L. A. Schechter Poultry Corp. v. United States*, 295 U.S. 495 (1935).

22. http://www.state.gov/r/pa/ei/rls/dos/436.htm (June 6, 2016).

23. David C. Nice. 1998. *Amtrak: the history and politics of a national railroad*. Boulder, CO: Lynne Rienner.

24. James L. Perry. 1996. "Measuring Public Service Motivation: An Assessment of Construct Reliability and Validity." *Journal of Public Administration Research and Theory* 6, No. 1: 5–22.

25. Kenneth H. Ashworth. 2001. *Caught Between the Dog and the Fireplug, or, How to Survive Public Service*. Washington, DC: Georgetown University Press.

26. Philip J. Harter. 1982. "Negotiating Regulations: A Cure for Malaise," *Georgetown Law Journal*, 71, No. 1.

27. https://www.treasury.gov/tigta/auditreports/2013reports/201310053fr.pdf (May 1, 2016).

28. http://www.gao.gov/ (May 1, 2016).

29. http://www.gao.gov/about/products/about-gao-reports.html (May 1, 2016).

30. https://www.whitehouse.gov/omb (May 1, 2016).

31. Sylvan Lane. 12 December 2018. "Consumer Bureau Morale Plummeted under Mulvaney: Report." *The Hill*. https://thehill.com/policy/finance/421007-consumer-bureau-morale-plummeted-under-mulvaney-analysis.

32. https://www.law.cornell.edu/uscode/text/5/552; https://www.gpo.gov/fdsys/pkg/STATUTE-90/pdf/STATUTE-90-Pg1241.pdf (June 6, 2016).

33. www.foia.gov (May 1, 2016).

34. http://www.foreffectivegov.org/access-to-information-scorecard-2015/ (May 1, 2016).

35. http://govinfo.library.unt.edu/npr/whoweare/history2.html (June 16, 2016).

36. Kevin R. Kosar. "Privatization and the Federal Government: An Introduction," *CRS Report for Congress*, December 28, 2006. https://www.fas.org/sgp/crs/misc/RL33777.pdf (June 16, 2016).

37. https://www.salliemae.com/about/who-we-are/history/ (June 16, 2016).

38. James Risen, "Controversial Contractors Iraq Works is Split Up," *New York Times*, 24 May 2008. http://www.nytimes.com/2008/05/24/world/middleeast/24contract.html (June 16, 2016).

39. Alan K. Campbell. 1978. "Civil Service Reform: A New Commitment." *Public Administration Review* 38 No. 2, 99.

40. Campbell, "Civil Service Reform," 100.

Domestic Policy

1. "H.R. 4872 — Health Care and Education Reconciliation Act of 2010," https://www.congress.gov/bill/111th-congress/house-bill/4872 (March 1, 2016).

2. James E. Anderson. 2000. *Public Policymaking: An Introduction*, 4th ed. Boston: Houghton Mifflin.

3. "National Health Insurance—A Brief History of Reform Efforts in the U.S.," March 2009, https://kaiserfamilyfoundation.files.wordpress.com/2013/01/7871.pdf (March 1, 2016).

4. "Romneycare vs. Obamacare: Key Similarities & Differences," 13 November 2013. http://boston.cbslocal.com/2013/11/13/romneycare-vs-obamacare-key-similarities-differences/ (March 1, 2016).

5. E. E. Schattschneider. 1960. *The Semi-Sovereign People*. New York: Holt, Rinehart & Winston.

6. Brad Plumer, "Everything you need to know about the assault weapons ban, in one post," *The Washington Post*, 17 December 2012. https://www.washingtonpost.com/news/wonk/wp/2012/12/17/everything-you-need-to-know-about-banning-assault-weapons-in-one-post/ (March 1, 2016).

7. *Brown v. Board of Education of Topeka*, 347 U.S. 483 (1954).

8. David Mildenberg, "Private Toll Road Investors Shift Revenue Risk to States," 26 November 2013. http://www.bloomberg.com/news/articles/2013-11-27/private-toll-road-investors-shift-revenue-risk-to-states (March 1, 2016).

9. http://www.history.com/topics/inventions/transcontinental-railroad (March 1, 2016).

10. http://www.dollartimes.com/inflation/inflation.php?amount=49&year=1919 (March 1, 2016).

11. Upton Sinclair. 1906. *The Jungle*. New York: Grosset and Dunlap.

12. http://www.fda.gov/AboutFDA/WhatWeDo/History/ (March 1, 2016).

13. "An Update to the Budget and Economic Outlook: 2014 to 2024," 27 August 2014. https://www.cbo.gov/publication/45653 (March 1, 2016).

14. "Update 2016," https://www.ssa.gov/pubs/EN-05-10003.pdf (March 1, 2016).

15. https://www.ssa.gov/planners/retire/ageincrease.html (March 1, 2016).

16. "The Facts on Medicare Spending and Financing," http://kff.org/medicare/fact-sheet/medicare-spending-and-financing-fact-sheet/ (March 1, 2016); "National Health Expenditure Fact Sheet," https://www.cms.gov/research-statistics-data-and-systems/statistics-trends-and-reports/nationalhealthexpenddata/nhe-fact-sheet.html (March 1, 2016).

17. "National Health Expenditure Fact Sheet," https://www.cms.gov/research-statistics-data-and-systems/statistics-trends-and-reports/nationalhealthexpenddata/nhe-fact-sheet.html (March 1, 2016).

18. Thomas R. Oliver, Philip R. Lee, and Helene L. Lipton. 2004. "A Political History of Medicare and Prescription Drug Coverage," *Milbank Quarterly* 82, No. 2: 283–354, http://www.ncbi.nlm.nih.gov/pmc/articles/PMC2690175/.

19. Bryan D. Jones and Frank R. Baumgartner. 2005. *The Politics of Attention*. Chicago: University of Chicago Press.

20. Daniel Mazmanian and Paul Sabatier. 1989. *Implementation and Public Policy*. Washington, DC: Rowman and Littlefield.

21. Kathrin F. Stanger-Hall and David W. Hall. 2011. "Abstinence-Only Education and Teen Pregnancy Rates: Why We Need Comprehensive Sex Education in the U.S.," *PLoS One* October 14, http://www.ncbi.nlm.nih.gov/pmc/articles/PMC3194801/.

22. Arthur B. Laffer, Stephen Moore and Peter J. Tanous. 2009. *The End of Prosperity: How Higher Taxes Will Doom the Economy*. New York: Simon & Schuster.

23. "Mandatory Spending in 2015: An Infographic," 6 January 2016. www.cbo.gov/publication/51111 (March 1, 2016).

24. "Discretionary Spending in 2015: An Infographic," 6 January 2016. www.cbo.gov/publication/51112 (March 1, 2016).

25. "The Federal Budget in 2015: An Infographic," 6 January 2016. www.cbo.gov/publication/51110 (March 1, 2016).

26. "2015 Federal Tax Rates, Personal Exemptions, and Standard Deductions," http://www.irs.com/articles/2015-federal-tax-rates-personal-exemptions-and-standard-deductions (March 1, 2016).

27. "High income Americans pay most income taxes, but enough to be 'fair'?" http://www.pewresearch.org/fact-tank/2016/04/13/high-income-americans-pay-most-income-taxes-but-enough-to-be-fair/ (March 1, 2016).

28. "Excise tax," https://www.irs.gov/Businesses/Small-Businesses-&-Self-Employed/Excise-Tax (March 1, 2016).

29. "United States Posts Record Budget Deficit in November." *Washington Post.* 13 December 2018. https://www.washingtonpost.com/business/economy/united-states-posts-record-budget-deficit-in-november/2018/12/13/3cdb2310-fef3-11e8-83c0-b06139e540e5_story.html?utm_term=.d4eb59c09004.

30. "U.S. Code § 225a - Maintenance of long run growth of monetary and credit aggregates," https://www.law.cornell.edu/uscode/text/12/225a (March 1, 2016).

31. https://www.federalreserveeducation.org/about-the-fed/history (March 1, 2016).

Foreign Policy

1. Eugene R. Wittkopf, Christopher M. Jones, and Charles W. Kegley, Jr. 2007. *American Foreign Policy: Pattern and Process*, 7th ed. Belmont, CA: Thomson Wadsworth.

2. Michelle Camacho Liu. 2011. *Investing in Higher Education for Latinos: Trends in Latino College Access and Success.* Washington, DC: National Conference of State Legislatures. http://www.ncsl.org/documents/educ/trendsinlatinosuccess.pdf (May 12, 2016).

3. Charlene Barshefsky and James T. Hill. 2008. *U.S.–Latin America Relations: A New Direction for a New Reality.* Washington, DC: Council on Foreign Relations. i.cfr.org/content/publications/attachments/LatinAmerica_TF.pdf (May 12, 2016).

4. U.S. Census Bureau, "Foreign Trade: U.S. International Trade Data" https://www.census.gov/foreign-trade/data/index.html (May 12, 2016).

5. Joseph S. Nye, Jr. 2005. *Soft Power: The Means to Success in World Politics.* Washington, DC: Public Affairs.

6. U.S. Agency for International Development, "U.S. Overseas Loans and Grants (Greenbook)," https://explorer.usaid.gov/reports-greenbook.html (June 18, 2016); C. Eugene Emery Jr., and Amy Sherman. 2016. "Marco Rubio says foreign aid is less than 1 percent of federal budget," *Politifact*, 11 March 2016. www.politifact.com/truth-o-meter/statements/2016/mar/11/marco-rubio/marco-rubio-says-foreign-aid-less-1-percent-federa/.

7. Glen S. Krutz and Jeffrey S. Peake. 2009. *Treaty Politics and the Rise of Executive Agreements: International Commitments in a System of Shared Powers.* Ann Arbor, MI: University of Michigan Press.

8. *United States v. Pink*, 315 U.S. 203 (1942).

9. Krutz and Peake. *Treaty Politics and the Rise of Executive Agreements.*

10. Jon Bond, Richard Fleisher, Stephen Hanna, and Glen S. Krutz. 2000. "The Demise of the. Two Presidencies," American Politics Quarterly 28, No. 1: 3–25.

11. James M. McCormick. 2010. *American Foreign Policy and Process,* 5th ed. Boston: Wadsworth.

12. The Gallup Organization, "Most Important Problem," http://www.gallup.com/poll/1675/most-important-problem.aspx (May 12, 2016).

13. John W. Kingdon. 1973. *Congressmen's Voting Decisions.* New York: Harper & Row; Richard Hall. 1996. *Participation in Congress.* New Haven, CT: University of Yale Press.

14. Robert M. Gates. 2015. *Duty: Memoirs of a Secretary at War.* New York: Alfred A. Knopf.

15. David A. Graham, "Robert Gates, America's Unlikely Gay-Rights Hero," *The Atlantic,* 28 July 2015. http://www.theatlantic.com/politics/archive/2015/07/robert-gates-boy-scouts-gay-leaders/399716/.

16. "George Washington's Farewell Address." 1796. New Haven, CT: School Avalon Project, Yale Law Library. http://avalon.law.yale.edu/18th_century/washing.asp (May 12, 2016).

Index

progressive tax, 615, 621

Project Vote Smart, 249

property tax, 528

proportional representation, 337, 362

Proposition 13, 528

Proposition 187, 187

Proposition 19, 217

Proposition 8, 280

protectionism, 632, 655

public administration, 558, 585

public goods, 11, 32, 597

public interest group, 373, 397

public opinion, 237

public policy, 590, 621

public relations, 288, 321

Pulitzer, 296

Pure Food and Drug Act, 600

purposive incentives, 375, 397

push poll, 218, 238

Putin, 234, 627, 653

Putnam, 22

R

race-to-the-bottom, 102, 103

Radio Act, 307

rally around the flag effect, 478, 480

Randolph, 56, 166

random sample, 213, 238

ratification, 55

rational basis test, 157, 196

Reagan, 88, 226, 233, 468, 469, 501, 563

Real ID Act, 93

reapportionment, 359, 363

recall, 278, 281

recession, 612, 621

Reconciliation Act, 436

Reconstruction, 162, 196

red tape, 576, 585

redistributive policy, 600, 621

redistricting, 359, 363

reduction veto, 536, 553

referendum, 277, 281

regressive tax, 615, 622

regulatory policy, 600, 622

Rehabilitation Act, 193

Religious Freedom Restoration Act, 122, 192, 537

Religious Land Use and Institutionalized Persons Act, 122

reporter's privilege, 312, 321

representation, 421, 440

representative democracy, 15, 32

representative government, 39

representative sample, 213, 238

republic, 44, 65

reserved powers, 54, 65

residency requirement, 246, 281

revolving door laws, 394, 397

Reynolds v. Simms, 359

Rice, 640

right to privacy, 144, 149

Riley v. California, 491

Risch, 647

Rivera, 307

Roberts, 87, 229, 501, 504

Rock the Vote, 249, 252

Roe v. Wade, 99, 145, 177, 491, 506

Romney, 201, 212, 230

Roosevelt, 61, 86, 212, 232, 233, 298, 334, 341, 413, 449, 464, 468, 511, 525, 562, 593

Roosevelt (FDR), 462

Rule of Four, 506, 515

Rule of Naturalization, 96

Rumsfeld, 652

Rustin, 166

Ryan, 92

S

Sadat, 642

Saenz v. Roe, 115

safe seat, 359, 363

safety net, 601, 622

Salisbury, 375

Sanders, 232, 269, 287, 456

Scalia, 462, 463, 501

Scarlett, 505

Schechter Poultry Corp. v. United States, 525, 571

Schenck v. United States, 124

search warrant, 131, 150

Second Amendment, 62, 113, 129, 221, 225

Second Bank of the United States, 83

Second Continental Congress, 42

Second Party System, 332

Sedition Act, 84

select committee, 429, 440

selective engagement, 652, 655

selective incorporation, 116, 150

CPSIA information can be obtained
at www.ICGtesting.com
Printed in the USA
LVHW060749250621
691022LV00005B/8

9 781680 923179